THE NEW
ENGLISH BIBLE

THE OLD TESTAMENT

THE BIBLE

A NEW ENGLISH TRANSLATION

Planned and Directed by Representatives of

THE BAPTIST UNION OF GREAT BRITAIN AND IRELAND

THE CHURCH OF ENGLAND

THE CHURCH OF SCOTLAND

THE CONGREGATIONAL CHURCH IN ENGLAND AND WALES

THE COUNCIL OF CHURCHES FOR WALES

THE IRISH COUNCIL OF CHURCHES

THE LONDON YEARLY MEETING OF
THE SOCIETY OF FRIENDS

THE METHODIST CHURCH OF GREAT BRITAIN

THE PRESBYTERIAN CHURCH OF ENGLAND

THE BRITISH AND FOREIGN BIBLE SOCIETY

THE NATIONAL BIBLE SOCIETY OF SCOTLAND

THE NEW
ENGLISH BIBLE

THE OLD TESTAMENT

OXFORD UNIVERSITY PRESS
CAMBRIDGE UNIVERSITY PRESS
1970

The New English Bible:
The Old Testament first published 1970

Library of Congress Catalogue Card Number
61-16025

Printed in the United States of America

PREFACE TO
THE NEW ENGLISH BIBLE

In May 1946 the General Assembly of the Church of Scotland received an overture from the Presbytery of Stirling and Dunblane, where it had been initiated by the Reverend G. S. Hendry, recommending that a translation of the Bible be made in the language of the present day, inasmuch as the language of the Authorized Version, already archaic when it was made, had now become even more definitely archaic and less generally understood. The General Assembly resolved to make an approach to other Churches, and, as a result, delegates of the Church of England, the Church of Scotland, and the Methodist, Baptist, and Congregational Churches met in conference in October. They recommended that the work should be undertaken; that a completely new translation should be made, rather than a revision, such as had earlier been contemplated by the University Presses of Oxford and Cambridge; and that the translators should be free to employ a contemporary idiom rather than reproduce the traditional 'biblical' English.

In January 1947 a second conference, held like the first in the Central Hall, Westminster, included representatives of the University Presses. At the request of this conference, the Churches named above appointed representatives to form the Joint Committee on the New Translation of the Bible. This Committee met for the first time in July of the same year. By January 1948, when its third meeting was held, invitations to be represented had been sent to the Presbyterian Church of England, the Society of Friends, the Churches in Wales, the Churches in Ireland, the British and Foreign Bible Society, and the National Bible Society of Scotland: these invitations were accepted. At a much later stage the hierarchies of the Roman Catholic Church in England and Scotland accepted an invitation to appoint representatives, and these attended as observers.

The Joint Committee provided for the actual work of translation from the original tongues by appointing three panels, to deal, respectively, with the Old Testament, the Apocrypha, and the New Testament. Their members were scholars drawn from various British universities, whom the Committee believed to be representative of competent biblical scholarship at the present time. Apprehending, however, that sound scholarship does not necessarily carry with it a delicate sense of English style, the Committee appointed a fourth panel, of trusted literary advisers, to whom all the work of the translating panels was to be submitted for scrutiny. It should be said that denominational considerations played no part in the appointment of the panels.

v

The Joint Committee issued general directions to the panels, in pursuance of the aims which the enterprise had in view. The translating panels adopted the following procedure. An individual was invited to submit a draft translation of a particular book, or group of books. Normally he would be a member of the panel concerned. Very occasionally a draft translation was invited from a scholar outside the panel, who was known to have worked specially on the book in question. The draft was circulated in typescript to members of the panel for their consideration. They then met together and discussed the draft round a table, verse by verse, sentence by sentence. Each member brought his view about the meaning of the original to the judgement of his fellows, and discussion went on until they reached a common mind. There are passages where, in the present state of our knowledge, no one could say with certainty which of two (or even more) possible meanings is intended. In such cases, after careful discussion, alternative meanings have been recorded in footnotes, but only where they seemed of sufficient importance. There is probably no member of a panel who has not found himself obliged to give up, perhaps with lingering regret, a cherished view about the meaning of this or that difficult passage, but in the end the panel accepted corporate responsibility for the interpretation set forth in the translation adopted.

The resultant draft was now remitted to the panel of literary advisers. They scrutinized it, once again, verse by verse, sentence by sentence, and took pains to secure, as best they could, the tone and level of language appropriate to the different kinds of writing to be found in the Bible, whether narrative, familiar discourse, argument, law, rhetoric or poetry. The translation thus amended was returned to the translating panel, who examined it to make sure that the meaning intended had not been in any way misunderstood. Passages of peculiar difficulty might on occasion pass repeatedly between the panels. The final form of the version was reached by agreement between the translators concerned and the literary advisers. It was then ready for submission to the Joint Committee.

Since January 1948 the Joint Committee has met regularly twice a year in the Jerusalem Chamber, Westminster Abbey, with four exceptions during 1954–5 when the Langham Room in the precincts of the Abbey was kindly made available. At these meetings the Committee has received reports on the progress of the work from the Conveners of the four panels, and its members have had in their hands typescripts of the books so far translated and revised. They have made such comments and given such advice or decisions as they judged to be necessary, and from time to time they have met members of the panels in conference.

Of the original members of the panels most have happily been able to stay with the work all through, though some have been lost, through death or otherwise, and their places have been filled by fresh appointments.

The Committee has warmly appreciated the courteous hospitality of the Dean of Westminster and of the Trustees of the Central Hall. We owe a great debt to the support and the experienced counsel of the University Presses of Oxford and Cambridge. We recognize gratefully the service rendered to the enterprise by the Reverend Dr G. S. Hendry and the Reverend Professor J. K. S. Reid, who have successively held the office of Secretary to the Committee. To those who have borne special responsibility, as Chairmen of the Joint Committee, we owe more than could readily be told. Dr J. W. Hunkin, Bishop of Truro, our first Chairman, brought to the work an exuberant vigour and initiative without which the formidable project might hardly have got off the ground at all. On his lamented death in 1950 he was succeeded by Dr A. T. P. Williams, then Bishop of Durham and subsequently Bishop of Winchester, who for eighteen years guided our enterprise with judicious wisdom, tact, and benign firmness, but who to our sorrow died when the end of the task was in sight. To both of these we would put on record the gratitude of the Committee and of all engaged in the enterprise.

If we embarked on mentioning the names of those who have served on the various committees and panels, the list would be a long one; and if we mentioned some and not others, the selection would be an invidious one. There are, nevertheless, three names the omission of which would be utterly wrong. As Vice-Chairman and Director, Dr C. H. Dodd has from start to finish given outstanding leadership and guidance to the project, bringing to the work scholarship, sensitivity, and an ever watchful eye. Professor Sir Godfrey Driver, Joint Director since 1965, has also brought to the work a wealth of knowledge and wisdom; to his enthusiasm, tenacity of purpose, and unflagging devotion the whole enterprise is greatly indebted. Professor W. D. McHardy, Deputy Director since 1968, has made an invaluable contribution particularly, but by no means exclusively, in the sphere of the Apocrypha. It is right that the names of these three scholars should always be associated with The New English Bible. Our debt to them is incalculably great.

DONALD EBOR:
Chairman of the Joint Committee

CONTENTS

CONTENTS

INTRODUCTION

The Old Testament consists of a collection of works composed at various times from the twelfth to the second century B.C.; and much of it, e.g. genealogies, poems and stories, must have been handed down by word of mouth for many generations. It contains, however, scattered references to written texts; but how extensive or widely current these may have been cannot be said, as no manuscripts have survived from the period before the destruction of Jerusalem and the deportation of the Jews into exile in 587/6 B.C. The text therefore is not infrequently uncertain and its meaning obscure.

The whole Old Testament is written in classical Hebrew, except some brief portions which are in the Aramaic language (Ezra 4. 8 – 6. 18 and 7. 12–26, Jeremiah 10. 11, Daniel 2. 4 – 7. 28), a sister language which became the *lingua franca* of the Semitic world.

The earliest surviving form of the Hebrew text is perhaps that found in the Samaritan Pentateuch (Genesis–Deuteronomy). This text must date from a period before the secession of the Samaritans from Judaism, but it is preserved only in manuscripts the earliest of which is tentatively assigned to the eleventh century A.D. It differs from the orthodox Jewish text in some six thousand places, in about one third of which it agrees with the Greek translation, the Septuagint; a few of these differences are doctrinal or political in origin (e.g. Deuteronomy 27. 4), a small number are helpful in difficult passages of the traditional Hebrew text, but the majority have little if any importance. The next witness to the Hebrew text is provided by the Scrolls from Qumrân, commonly called the Dead Sea Scrolls, dated *c*. 150 B.C. to A.D. 75 or thereabouts. These include fragments, often minute, of every book in the Old Testament except Esther, one complete scroll of Isaiah and another of which approximately half has been lost, and a commentary on the first two chapters of Habakkuk containing most of their text. All these agree essentially with the 'received text' of the Old Testament except for orthographic variations or occasional variant readings hardly affecting the sense, and so suggest that stabilization of text is already beginning. Fragments, however, of Samuel and one of Jeremiah have a shortened form of the text like that of the Septuagint in these books. The only other fragment of this period is that known as the Nash Papyrus, which cannot be exactly dated, containing two excerpts from the Law (Exodus 20. 2–17 and Deuteronomy 6. 4–5); its chief interest is that the words are more or less clearly spaced.

Very few manuscripts are said to have survived the destruction of Jerusalem in A.D. 70. Soon after that disaster, therefore, the Jewish religious leaders set about defining the canon and finally standardizing the text. This last process went on for many centuries and resulted in the production of an eclectic text based on arbitrary rather than scientific principles. This was the Massoretic (so called from the Hebrew *massōrāh*, 'tradition') or traditional text found in all Hebrew Bibles.

This text was written in a purely consonantal alphabet, although the scribes at Qumrân had already attempted to indicate the vowels by using certain letters for them (for example *w* for *o* and *u*, and *y* for *e* and *i*). This system, however, was soon found inadequate when, except in very restricted circles, the use of the old Hebrew language was dying out. Accordingly, in order to preserve the correct pronunciation in school and synagogue, the Massoretes inserted signs above or below or within the consonantal symbols to indicate this. Several systems are known, but that devised by the Rabbis of Tiberias (hence known as 'Tiberian') in the fifth to sixth centuries A.D. eventually prevailed. What they preserved, however, was not so much the original pronunciation as that current amongst themselves; further, however helpful these vowel-signs may have been, they are demonstrably not always correct. The present translators have therefore held themselves free to disregard the vowels and to re-vocalize the consonantal text wherever that seems desirable.

This text perpetuated not only genuine divergent readings but also numerous slips of the early copyists, made at a time when it was not copied with such meticulous care as in subsequent ages when it had come to be regarded as canonical and sacred; even then, however, many fresh errors found their way into it. The Rabbis soon felt the need to take account of and preserve any divergences that seemed to them important. They therefore listed a number of variant readings, omissions from and additions to the text as known to them, as well as possible corrections, which perhaps were often nothing but the conjectures of individual scribes. The consonants, however, were generally regarded as unalterable, and the usual method of indicating corrections adopted by the Massoretes was to attach the vowels of the word which they wished to be read to the consonants of that written in the text, although it might be an entirely different word.

One such substitution calls for special notice as affecting the divine name. This, written *YHWH*, was normally replaced by 'God' or 'Lord' as too sacred for common use (Exodus 20. 7 and Leviticus 24. 16), being uttered only by the priest in the temple giving the priestly benediction (Numbers 6. 24-27). The true pronunciation was already passing into oblivion before A.D. 70; but Christian writers between A.D. 150 and A.D. 450 have *Yaouai* and *Yabē* (*Yavē*) in Greek characters, and early magical texts have *Yhbyh* (*Yahvêh*) in Aramaic characters, all pointing to *Yahweh* as the original pronunciation. The Massoretes, however, never vocalized the divine name as

Yahweh; instead, to the consonants *YHWH* they added the vowels of *'ădônāy*, 'my Lord' (replacing *ă* by *ĕ* as required by Hebrew phonetic laws), or of *'ĕlōhîm*, 'God', thus warning the reader to use one or other of these words in place of the divine name; and the early translators generally substituted 'Lord' for it. The Massoretes, however, did not intend the vowels of either of these words to be attached to the consonants of the divine name as though it was *Yĕhôwāh* or *Yĕhôwîh*, both grammatically impossible and meaningless forms; this uncouth combination, written *Ieōa* in Greek letters in Hellenistic magical texts, did not become effective until *Yehova* or *Jehova* or *Johova* appeared in two Latin works dated in A.D. 1278 and A.D. 1303; the shortened *Jova* (declined like a Latin noun) came into use in the sixteenth century. The Reformers preferred *Jehovah*, which first appeared as *Iehouah* in A.D. 1530 in Tyndale's translation of the Pentateuch (Exodus 6. 3), from which it passed into other Protestant Bibles. The present translators have retained the incorrect but now customary 'JEHOVAH' in the text of passages where it is explained in a note (Exodus 3.15 and 6. 3; cp. Genesis 4. 26) and in four place-names (Genesis 22. 14, Exodus 17. 15, Judges 6. 24, Ezekiel 48. 35); elsewhere they have put 'LORD' or 'GOD' in capital letters.

The Hebrew text as thus edited by the Massoretes became virtually a single recension probably remaining substantially unaltered from the second century A.D., but this text has not survived in any manuscripts dated before the ninth to eleventh centuries A.D. Unsatisfactory as it may be, however, it is perforce reproduced in all printed Hebrew Bibles. These began to appear late in the fifteenth century, when printed copies of single books or groups of books came from various presses, followed by the first complete Bibles in 1488 and 1491; but the text of Jacob ben Chayyim's Rabbinic Bible (Venice, 1524–5) is that found in most modern Bibles. Collections of various readings were published in the eighteenth and nineteenth centuries, unfortunately taken from late manuscripts and therefore of relatively little value. The most-used modern edition, with selected variations from Hebrew manuscripts and the principal divergences in the ancient versions implying a different Hebrew text, together with emendations proposed by modern scholars, is the third edition of R. Kittel's *Biblia Hebraica* (Stuttgart, 1937). It is the basis of the present translation.

The Hebrew text as thus handed down is full of errors of every kind due to defective archetypes and successive copyists' errors, confusion of letters (of which several in the Hebrew alphabet are singularly alike), omissions and insertions, displacements of words and even of whole sentences or paragraphs; and copyists' unhappy attempts to rectify mistakes have often only increased the confusion.

The order of the books of the Old Testament followed in the present translation, though not entirely the same as that found in Hebrew manuscripts and in the ancient versions, is that of the Authorized and Revised Versions.

In early inscriptions the writing commonly runs on continuously with no division between the words; but already *c.* 1000–700 B.C. some have points or vertical strokes to divide them. By the sixth century B.C. this use of points was becoming rare and words were being separated by spaces; and the reader was further assisted, when the Aramaic script replaced the old Phoenician script, by the peculiar forms of several letters used at the end of a word. The Greek translators of the Hebrew text, however, still divide words wrongly, and errors caused by such false divisions can be traced occasionally in Jerome's Latin translations and linger even in the Massoretic text, although words are properly divided in the Scrolls. The main Scroll of Isaiah, like the Nash Papyrus, occasionally separates verses by a space; but this process was not completed until the Massoretes introduced a vertical stroke, afterwards replaced by two points resembling a colon, to divide the verses. They also devised various systems of breaking up the text into paragraphs. Finally, the present division of the text into chapters, ascribed to Stephen Langton, Archbishop of Canterbury, was adopted into Latin Bibles in the thirteenth century A.D.; their numbering is found in Hebrew manuscripts *c.* A.D. 1330 and in Hebrew Bibles first in the Complutensian Polyglot Bible (A.D. 1514–17).

The present translators have inserted their own headings, which are not found in the Hebrew text, to define longer sections; otherwise they have more or less accepted the paragraphing of the Authorized and Revised Versions without much regard to the Massoretic system; they have often, however, broken up the text into shorter sections than those of these two versions. They have adopted the Massoretic system of verses but have occasionally run two or three verses together in order to bring out the sense or to avoid a cumbrous or awkward sentence.

In the Hebrew text, headings are prefixed to many of the Psalms. Some are historical notices, obviously deduced from the text and often unsuitable; all are of doubtful value. Others are musical directions, which are found also in one other poem (Habakkuk 3. 1, 9, 13, 19); they are now for the most part unintelligible, and even the ancient translators seem to have been ignorant of their meaning. Further, the Syriac version has totally different headings throughout the Psalter. As such headings are almost certainly not original, they have been omitted from the present translation.

The treatment of verse raises special problems. Only three books were regarded by the Massoretes as poetry (Job, Psalms, Proverbs), and they have their own accentuation in the Hebrew text; this however does not always coincide with the obvious metre or rather rhythm of the poem, which is based on parallelism of thought between the two halves of the line and on the number of units of sense, not of metrical feet of so many syllables, in each half. When these clash, the present translators have disregarded the Massoretic system and adapted the English text to rhythmical necessity. Further, the Massoretes have treated all the prophetic books as prose; but since the middle of the eighteenth century much in them has been recognized as verse, or prose mixed with verse, and the editors of these books in Kittel's *Biblia Hebraica* have printed whatever can be regarded as poetry in verse-form. The translators, therefore, have followed this system while using their own judgement in accepting or rejecting it in any given passage.

The verses in a few Psalms and in one or two poems outside the Psalter begin each with a successive letter of the alphabet; but no attempt has been made to reproduce such acrostic arrangements in this translation. They occasionally help to restore the order of the lines (Nahum 1. 2–14) and once to join two Psalms which have been wrongly separated (Psalms 9–10). In Psalm 119, each group of eight verses begins with the same letter, following the order of the alphabet, and Jerome has added the Hebrew names of the letters in Latin characters at the head of each group; but, as they are not in the Hebrew text, though preserved in the Authorized and Revised Versions, they have been here omitted.

Occasionally groups of verses are marked off by a common refrain; and this once or twice enables a displaced fragment of a poem to be restored to its proper position with the others sharing this refrain (Psalms 42–43 and Isaiah 5. 24–25 and 9. 8 – 10. 4).

Lastly, the Hebrew text of the Song of Songs does not differentiate between the speakers. They are distinguished, however, in two manuscripts of the Septuagint, though perhaps not always correctly, and can often be inferred from the gender and number of the persons addressed; they have therefore been added, according as they seem appropriate, in italic type in the present translation. Elsewhere the translators have here and there inserted the speaker's name when it has not been given for some time and have also occasionally added 'he says' or the like when the sense seems to be obscured by the absence of such indications.

Where the problem before the translators was that of correcting errors in the Hebrew text in order to make sense, they had recourse, first of all, to the ancient versions, of which a considerable number has survived.

The earliest version is the Greek translation made in Egypt in the third and second centuries B.C. It was designed to meet the needs of Greek-speaking Jews after the dispersion of the Jews following on the conquests of Alexander the Great (who died in 323 B.C.). According to tradition the Pentateuch was translated by seventy-two elders, six from each of the twelve tribes of Israel, and so the Greek version of the Old Testament came to be called the Septuagint, from the Latin *septuaginta*, 'seventy'. Written in the 'common dialect' of the Greek language current in the Mediterranean world, it is clearly the work of different translators of varying skill; for example, the Pentateuch is reasonably well translated, but the rest of the books, especially the poetical books, are often very poorly done and even contain sheer absurdities. Errors apart, this translation is now literal, now paraphrastic and now interpretative. Further, the underlying Hebrew text differed in many places from the Massoretic text; so, for example, the Septuagint represents a shortened form of the text of 1 and 2 Samuel and has the chapters of Jeremiah in an entirely different order. Yet, even though the Greek text itself is frequently corrupt, it is very often useful for recovering the original Hebrew text, if used with caution and skill. Early in the Christian era, when its defects were becoming increasingly apparent, several scholars attempted to revise it or make new recensions or translations based on it. Such were Aquila, whose renderings were often ludicrously literal, Symmachus, who replaced Hebraisms by idiomatic Greek expressions, and Theodotion, who made a free revision which was thought so good that his rendering of Daniel actually displaced that of the Septuagint. Some considerable time afterwards other scholars produced fresh recensions of the Greek text, amongst which that commonly associated with the name of Lucian may be included. Only fragments of the first three, apart from Theodotion's Daniel, have survived from the Hexaplar (i.e. six-columned) Bible made by Origen (*c.* A.D. 185–254), and Lucian's work is thought to lie behind certain Greek manuscripts. The history of these recensions is buried in obscurity; but most of them have something, however small, to contribute to the translation of the Hebrew Bible.

As Christianity spread westwards, the need of a Latin translation began to make itself felt, and the Old Latin Version, or perhaps rather Versions, came into existence, made from the Septuagint, about the end of the second century A.D. It is known partly from manuscripts, none complete, but mostly from quotations in the Fathers. The defects of this version, however, were so patent that Pope Damasus towards the end of the fourth century A.D. instructed Jerome to revise it. He began with two revisions of the Psalter, the 'Roman Psalter' based on the Old Latin Version, and the Gallican Psalter (so called as finding ready acceptance in Gaul) made from the Septuagint; he then produced Latin revisions of five other books (of which Job alone survives) based on the Septuagint, and finally new translations of the canonical books made from the Hebrew text, including one of the Psalms known as the 'Psalter according to the Hebrews', which failed to displace the Gallican Psalter in the Latin Bible. This version, made with the help of Jewish scholars and commonly called the Vulgate, by its idiomatic and forceful renderings was the best of the ancient translations; but, being based on the Massoretic 'received text', it is not so useful as the Septuagint for the recovery of the original Hebrew.

As the classical language of the Old Testament ceased to be understood by the common people in Palestine, an interpreter followed up every verse of the Law and every three verses of the Prophets when read in the synagogue by an Aramaic translation which was often spun out into a long but edifying paraphrase. Such interpretations, known as Targums (so called from the Aramaic *targûm*, 'translation'), tended to become traditional and had already begun to be written down before the Christian era; for Gamaliel, St Paul's teacher, ordered one of the Book of Job to be buried and his grandson declared such a work heretical. There are Targums to all the Old Testament books except Daniel, Ezra, and Nehemiah; and fourteen or fifteen such Targums are extant. Of these the most important are the so-called Targum of Onkelos on the Pentateuch and that of Jonathan on the Former and Latter Prophets, which are reasonably literal and therefore helpful in recovering the Hebrew text where it is corrupt.

The first Syriac version, called the Peshitta (meaning the 'simple', i.e. literal, version), was made for the Eastern Church between the first and third centuries A.D. Though affected by the Septuagint, it is basically a rendering of the Massoretic text and so occasionally elucidates difficult passages. The Syrohexaplar Version is a Syriac translation, made in the seventh century A.D., of Origen's text of the Septuagint as found in the fifth column of his Hexaplar Bible; its language so slavishly imitates the Greek of the parent text that it is invaluable, where it has been preserved, for restoring that text. Fragments of yet another Syriac version have been preserved, and the names of three others are known.

A number of other versions made between the third and ninth centuries A.D. in different languages are extant but, being made from or influenced by the Greek and Syriac versions, rarely help with problems of the Hebrew text. Several Arabic versions of diverse date, not all complete, exist, notably those of the Pentateuch, of which one lies behind the Samaritan Targum, and of a few books by Saʿadyah (tenth century A.D.) and another of the Pentateuch by 'Abû Saʿid (thirteenth century A.D.), which is the *textus receptus* of the Arabic Pentateuch now used by the Samaritans; the work of these two translators is from time to time helpful as embodying Jewish traditions.

These ancient versions, especially when they agree, contribute in varying degrees to the restoration of the Hebrew text when incapable of translation as it stands; and they also contribute much to the understanding of the Hebrew language. No Hebrew literature contemporary with the Old Testament is available to the Hebraist; only a few inscriptions carved in rock or stone or daubed on potsherds have been preserved, and these throw but little light on the Hebrew language. Further, the range of subjects with which the Old Testament deals is limited, although it is spread over a period of some thousand years. Consequently its surviving vocabulary is small, numbering only about 7,500 different words, of which nearly a quarter occur only once each; and the meaning of many of these is quite unknown or can perhaps only be guessed from the context or learnt from the ancient translators if they have preserved it. The meaning, however, of not a few words is clearly unknown even to them.

Some of these rare words were explained, not always rightly, by medieval Jewish scholars from surviving traditions or by comparing them with cognate Arabic words. This last method was revived by Christian scholars in the seventeenth century and was greatly advanced during the following two centuries, when the Syriac and Ethiopic languages were also used; but the Babylonian and Assyrian languages did not become available till the decipherment of the cuneiform inscriptions in the middle of the nineteenth century. The authors of the Revised Version were able to make some use of these languages; but the huge accumulation of texts, including native glossaries, in them now provides a source on which the present translators have been able to draw for the explanation of many unknown or misunderstood Hebrew words and phrases.

The general understanding of the Hebrew Scriptures has also been greatly helped by archaeological discoveries made during the past century. These serve mostly to illustrate the setting of a particular passage or custom, but they occasionally throw light on a word of unknown meaning.

In the last resort the scholar may be driven to conjectural emendation of the Hebrew text. This is practised as sparingly as possible in the present translation, and attention is always (except where changes only in vocalization are involved) drawn to it in the notes.

Another difficulty in translating the Old Testament is one inherent in the circumstances of time and place. Long ago Erasmus remarked that the student of Scripture ought to be 'tolerably versed in other branches of learning...and especially in knowledge of the natural objects—animals, trees, precious stones —of the countries mentioned in the Scriptures; for, if we are familiar with the country, we can in thought follow the history and picture it in our own minds, so that we seem not only to read it but to see it'. This goal indeed is not always easy to reach. Palestine differs greatly from the western world in its physical features and natural history, and the English language has no words for much that is characteristic of the country. The same problem arises with the arts and crafts, articles of clothing and vessels in daily use, the institutions of the family, administration and army, religion and cult. The translators, in seeking a way round many such problems, have made every effort to avoid the introduction of anachronisms and words reflecting an entirely different social background. They have transliterated technical terms where strict accuracy seemed to be required, but rendered them by some word or phrase approaching or suggesting the original sense where this was not so. Notably the rendering of the terms for each kind of offering or sacrifice has been standardized in the laws, whereas they have been translated more freely, without much regard to consistency, in the Psalms and other poetical passages where no technical problems are involved.

The translators have resorted to a paraphrase when the original Hebrew word or phrase does not lend itself to literal reproduction; but they have generally given that in a note. They have also, on the one hand, here and there expanded a Hebrew idiom to avoid a Hebraism likely to be unintelligible to English readers, especially as Hebrew is able to express in three or four words what may require a dozen or so to make it intelligible in the English language; on the other hand, they have sometimes abbreviated the text when the original Hebrew has seemed by English standards unduly repetitive.

Hebrew writers are fond of playing on words, both common nouns and proper names; but no attempt has been made to reproduce such puns, if only because the result is generally something unnatural and bizarre. This problem is especially tantalizing in regard to proper names such as those of the patriarchs and the family of Naomi, all of whose characters are reflected in their names; such points can rarely be brought out in a foreign language, and the explanation of the names has been relegated to the notes.

Previous official translations of the Bible have been for the most part revisions of those that have preceded them. So the Authorized Version was practically a revision of Coverdale's work, and its language was largely that of the sixteenth rather than of the seventeenth century. The Revisers of the nineteenth century were instructed 'to introduce as few alterations as possible into the Text of the Authorised Version' and 'to limit, as far as possible, the expression of such alterations to the language of the Authorised and earlier English Versions'. The obvious consequence of such instructions was that the language of the Revised Version tended to be several centuries out of date when it appeared; it even contained Latinisms which had come down from the Vulgate through a succession of English translations and which had long gone out of use. The present translators, therefore, were instructed to keep their language as close to current usage as they could, while avoiding expressions likely to be proved ephemeral. This task they have tried to perform to the best of their ability. They are well aware that a precise equivalent for a

Hebrew word can only rarely be found in another language, and that complete success in such an undertaking is unattainable; but they have had in mind not only the importance of making sense, which is not always apparent in previous translations, but also the needs of ordinary readers with no special knowledge of the ancient East; and they trust that such readers may find illumination in the present version.

G. R. D.

GUIDE TO THE NOTES

The footnotes in this edition of the Old Testament serve (*a*) to give cross-references to parallel passages, chiefly in the historical books, (*b*) to indicate where verses or parts of verses have been transposed, (*c*) to give the meaning of proper names where it appears to be reflected in the context, (*d*) to give an alternative interpretation where the Hebrew is capable of such, (*e*) to draw attention to the literal meaning of the Hebrew where English idiom markedly differs, (*f*) to indicate where the reading of other Hebrew manuscripts, or of one or other of the versions, has been followed either in whole (e.g. '*so Sept.*') or in part (e.g. '*cp. Sept.*'), and (*g*) to indicate places where the translators have adopted what seemed to them the most probable correction of the text where the Hebrew and the ancient versions cannot be convincingly translated as they stand.

Unless otherwise indicated by its wording, a note refers to the single word against which the reference is placed.

Abbreviations, etc., are given on pages xxii–xxiii.

ABBREVIATIONS, ETC.

I   *ch(s).*   chapter(s)

      cp.   compare

      lit.   literally

      mng.   meaning

      MS(S).   manuscript(s), i.e. Hebrew manuscript(s), unless otherwise stated

      om.   omit(s)

      or   indicating an alternative interpretation

      poss.   possible

      prob.   probable

      rdg.   reading

II   *Aq.*   Aquila (Greek translator of the Old Testament)

      Aram.   Aramaic (text or word)

      Heb.   Hebrew (text or word)

      Josephus   Flavius Josephus (A.D. 37/8–*c.* 100), author of the *Jewish Archaeology*, commonly called the *Jewish Antiquities*, published in A.D. 93/4.

      Luc. Sept.   Lucian's recension of the Septuagint

      Pesh.   Peshitta or Peshitto (Syriac version of the Old Testament)

      Sam.   Samaritan Pentateuch

      Scroll(s)   Scroll(s), commonly called the Dead Sea Scrolls, found at Qumrân

      Sept.   Septuagint (Greek version of the Old Testament)

      Symm.   Symmachus (Greek translator of the Old Testament)

      Targ.   Targum (Aramaic version of the Old Testament)

      Theod.   Theodotion (author of a revision of the Septuagint)

      Vulg.   Vulgate (Latin version of the Old Testament)

      [...]   In the text itself square brackets are used to indicate words that are probably late additions to the Hebrew text

III *Books of the Old Testament*

Gen.	Genesis	*Eccles.*	Ecclesiastes
Exod.	Exodus	*S. of S.*	Song of Songs
Lev.	Leviticus	*Isa.*	Isaiah
Num.	Numbers	*Jer.*	Jeremiah
Deut.	Deuteronomy	*Lam.*	Lamentations
Josh.	Joshua	*Ezek.*	Ezekiel
Judg.	Judges	*Dan.*	Daniel
Ruth	Ruth	*Hos.*	Hosea
1 Sam.	1 Samuel	*Joel*	Joel
2 Sam.	2 Samuel	*Amos*	Amos
1 Kgs.	1 Kings	*Obad.*	Obadiah
2 Kgs.	2 Kings	*Jonah*	Jonah
1 Chr.	1 Chronicles	*Mic.*	Micah
2 Chr.	2 Chronicles	*Nahum*	Nahum
Ezra	Ezra	*Hab.*	Habakkuk
Neh.	Nehemiah	*Zeph.*	Zephaniah
Esther	Esther	*Hag.*	Haggai
Job	Job	*Zech.*	Zechariah
Ps(s).	Psalm(s)	*Mal.*	Malachi
Prov.	Proverbs		

MARGINAL NUMBERS

The conventional verse divisions in the Old Testament are based on those in Hebrew manuscripts. Nevertheless any system of division into numbered verses is foreign to the spirit of this translation, which is intended to convey the meaning in natural English —the prose in paragraphs, the poetic passages in lines corresponding to the structure of the Hebrew.

For purposes of reference, and of comparison with other translations, verse numbers are placed in the margin opposite the line in which the first word belonging to the verse in question appears. Sometimes, however, successive verses are combined in a continuous translation, so that the precise point where a new verse begins cannot be fixed; in these cases the verse numbers, joined by a hyphen, are placed at the point where the passage begins.

GENESIS

The creation of the world

IN THE BEGINNING of creation, when God made heaven 1
and earth,*ᵃ* the earth was without form and void, with darkness 2
over the face of the abyss, and a mighty wind that swept*ᵇ* over the
surface of the waters. God said, 'Let there be light', and there was 3
light; and God saw that the light was good, and he separated light from 4
darkness. He called the light day, and the darkness night. So evening 5
came, and morning came, the first day.

God said, 'Let there be a vault between the waters, to separate water 6
from water.' So God made the vault, and separated the water under 7
the vault from the water above it, and so it was; and God called the 8
vault heaven. Evening came, and morning came, a second day.

God said, 'Let the waters under heaven be gathered into one place, 9
so that dry land may appear'; and so it was. God called the dry land 10
earth, and the gathering of the waters he called seas; and God saw that
it was good. Then God said, 'Let the earth produce fresh growth, 11
let there be on the earth plants bearing seed, fruit-trees bearing fruit
each with seed according to its kind.' So it was; the earth yielded fresh 12
growth, plants bearing seed according to their kind and trees bearing
fruit each with seed according to its kind; and God saw that it was
good. Evening came, and morning came, a third day. 13

God said, 'Let there be lights in the vault of heaven to separate day 14
from night, and let them serve as signs both for festivals and for seasons
and years. Let them also shine in the vault of heaven to give light on 15
earth.' So it was; God made the two great lights, the greater to govern 16
the day and the lesser to govern the night; and with them he made
the stars. God put these lights in the vault of heaven to give light on 17
earth, to govern day and night, and to separate light from darkness; 18
and God saw that it was good. Evening came, and morning came, a 19
fourth day.

God said, 'Let the waters teem with countless living creatures, and 20
let birds fly above the earth across the vault of heaven.' God then 21
created the great sea-monsters and all living creatures that move and
swarm in the waters, according to their kind, and every kind of bird;

[a] Or In the beginning God created heaven and earth. [b] Or and the spirit of God
hovering.

I

22 and God saw that it was good. So he blessed them and said, 'Be fruitful and increase, fill the waters of the seas; and let the birds increase on
23 land.' Evening came, and morning came, a fifth day.
24 　 God said, 'Let the earth bring forth living creatures, according to their kind: cattle, reptiles, and wild animals, all according to their
25 kind.' So it was; God made wild animals, cattle, and all reptiles, each
26 according to its kind; and he saw that it was good. Then God said, 'Let us make man in our image and likeness to rule the fish in the sea, the birds of heaven, the cattle, all wild animals on earth,*a* and all
27 reptiles that crawl upon the earth.' So God created man in his own image; in the image of God he created him; male and female he
28 created them. God blessed them and said to them, 'Be fruitful and increase, fill the earth and subdue it, rule over the fish in the sea, the birds of heaven, and every living thing that moves upon the earth.'
29 God also said, 'I give you all plants that bear seed everywhere on earth, and every tree bearing fruit which yields seed: they shall be yours for
30 food. All green plants I give for food to the wild animals, to all the birds of heaven, and to all reptiles on earth, every living creature.'
31 So it was; and God saw all that he had made, and it was very good. Evening came, and morning came, a sixth day.
2 　 Thus heaven and earth were completed with all their mighty throng.
2 On the sixth*b* day God completed all the work he had been doing, and
3 on the seventh day he ceased from all his work. God blessed the seventh day and made it holy, because on that day he ceased from all the work he had set himself*c* to do.
4 　 This is the story of the making of heaven and earth when they were created.

The beginnings of history

5 WHEN THE LORD GOD made earth and heaven, there was neither shrub nor plant growing wild upon the earth, because the LORD God had sent no rain on the earth; nor was there any man
6 to till the ground. A flood*d* used to rise out of the earth and water all
7 the surface of the ground. Then the LORD God formed a man*e* from the dust of the ground*f* and breathed into his nostrils the breath of life.
8 Thus the man became a living creature. Then the LORD God planted a garden in Eden away to the east, and there he put the man whom he
9 had formed. The LORD God made trees spring from the ground, all trees pleasant to look at and good for food; and in the middle of the

[a] *So Pesh.; Heb.* all the earth.　[b] *So Sam.; Heb.* seventh.　[c] set himself: *prob. rdg., cp. Sept.; Heb.* created.　[d] *Or* mist.　[e] *Heb.* adam.　[f] *Heb.* adamah.

2

garden he set the tree of life and the tree of the knowledge of good and evil.

There was a river flowing from Eden to water the garden, and when 10 it left the garden it branched into four streams. The name of the first is 11 Pishon; that is the river which encircles all the land of Havilah, where the gold*a* is. The gold*a* of that land is good; bdellium*b* and cornelians 12 are also to be found there. The name of the second river is Gihon; this 13 is the one which encircles all the land of Cush. The name of the third is 14 Tigris; this is the river which runs east of Asshur. The fourth river is the Euphrates.

The LORD God took the man and put him in the garden of Eden to 15 till it and care for it. He told the man, 'You may eat from every tree in 16 the garden, but not from the tree of the knowledge of good and evil; 17 for on the day that you eat from it, you will certainly die.' Then the 18 LORD God said, 'It is not good for the man to be alone. I will provide a partner for him.' So God formed out of the ground all the wild 19 animals and all the birds of heaven. He brought them to the man to see what he would call them, and whatever the man called each living creature, that was its name. Thus the man gave names to all cattle, to 20 the birds of heaven, and to every wild animal; but for the man himself no partner had yet been found. And so the LORD God put the man into 21 a trance, and while he slept, he took one of his ribs and closed the flesh over the place. The LORD God then built up the rib, which he had 22 taken out of the man, into a woman. He brought her to the man, and 23 the man said:

> 'Now this, at last—
> bone from my bones,
> flesh from my flesh!—
> this shall be called woman,*c*
> for from man*d* was this taken.'

That is why a man leaves his father and mother and is united to his 24 wife, and the two become one flesh. Now they were both naked, the 25 man and his wife, but they had no feeling of shame towards one another.

THE SERPENT WAS more crafty than any wild creature that the LORD 3 God had made. He said to the woman, 'Is it true that God has forbidden you to eat from any tree in the garden?' The woman answered 2 the serpent, 'We may eat the fruit of any tree in the garden, except for 3 the tree in the middle of the garden; God has forbidden us either to eat or to touch the fruit of that; if we do, we shall die.' The serpent said, 4 'Of course you will not die. God knows that as soon as you eat it, your 5

[*a*] *Or* frankincense.   [*b*] *Or* gum resin.   [*c*] *Heb.* ishshah.   [*d*] *Heb.* ish.

eyes will be opened and you will be like gods[a] knowing both good and
6 evil.' When the woman saw that the fruit of the tree was good to eat,
and that it was pleasing to the eye and tempting to contemplate, she
took some and ate it. She also gave her husband some and he ate it.
7 Then the eyes of both of them were opened and they discovered that
they were naked; so they stitched fig-leaves together and made themselves loincloths.

8 The man and his wife heard the sound of the LORD God walking in
the garden at the time of the evening breeze and hid from the LORD
9 God among the trees of the garden. But the LORD God called to the
10 man and said to him, 'Where are you?' He replied, 'I heard the sound
as you were walking in the garden, and I was afraid because I was
11 naked, and I hid myself.' God answered, 'Who told you that you
were naked? Have you eaten from the tree which I forbade you?'
12 The man said, 'The woman you gave me for a companion, she gave
13 me fruit from the tree and I ate it.' Then the LORD God said to
the woman, 'What is this that you have done?' The woman said,
14 'The serpent tricked me, and I ate.' Then the LORD God said to the
serpent:

> 'Because you have done this you are accursed
> more than all cattle and all wild creatures.
> On your belly you shall crawl, and dust you shall eat
> all the days of your life.
15   I will put enmity between you and the woman,
> between your brood and hers.
> They shall strike at your head,
> and you shall strike at their heel.'

16 To the woman he said:

> 'I will increase your labour and your groaning,
> and in labour you shall bear children.
> You shall be eager[b] for your husband,
> and he shall be your master.'

17 And to the man he said:

> 'Because you have listened to your wife
> and have eaten from the tree which I forbade you,
> accursed shall be the ground on your account.
> With labour you shall win your food from it
> all the days of your life.
18   It will grow thorns and thistles for you,
> none but wild plants for you to eat.

[a] *Or* God.   [b] *Or* feel an urge.

4

> You shall gain your bread by the sweat of your brow   19
> until you return to the ground;
> for from it you were taken.
> Dust you are, to dust you shall return.'

The man called his wife Eve[a] because she was the mother of all 20
who live. The LORD God made tunics of skins for Adam and his wife 21
and clothed them. He said, 'The man has become like one of us, 22
knowing good and evil; what if he now reaches out his hand and takes
fruit from the tree of life also, eats it and lives for ever?' So the LORD 23
God drove him out of the garden of Eden to till the ground from which
he had been taken. He cast him out, and to the east of the garden of 24
Eden he stationed the cherubim and a sword whirling and flashing to
guard the way to the tree of life.

The man lay with his wife Eve, and she conceived and gave birth to 4
Cain. She said, 'With the help of the LORD I have brought a man into
being.' Afterwards she had another child, his brother Abel. Abel was 2
a shepherd and Cain a tiller of the soil. The day came when Cain 3
brought some of the produce of the soil as a gift to the LORD; and Abel 4
brought some of the first-born of his flock, the fat portions of them.[b]
The LORD received Abel and his gift with favour; but Cain and his 5
gift he did not receive. Cain was very angry and his face fell. Then 6
the LORD said to Cain, 'Why are you so angry and cast down?

> If you do well, you are accepted;[c]   7
> if not, sin is a demon crouching at the door.
> It shall be eager for you, and you will be mastered by it.'[d]

Cain said to his brother Abel, 'Let us go into the open country.'[e] 8
While they were there, Cain attacked his brother Abel and murdered
him. Then the LORD said to Cain, 'Where is your brother Abel?' Cain 9
answered, 'I do not know. Am I my brother's keeper?' The LORD said, 10
'What have you done? Hark! your brother's blood that has been shed
is crying out to me from the ground. Now you are accursed, and 11
banished from[f] the ground which has opened its mouth wide to receive
your brother's blood, which you have shed. When you till the ground, 12
it will no longer yield you its wealth. You shall be a vagrant and a
wanderer on earth.' Cain said to the LORD, 'My punishment is heavier 13
than I can bear; thou hast driven me today from the ground, and 14
I must hide myself from thy presence. I shall be a vagrant and a
wanderer on earth, and anyone who meets me can kill me.' The LORD 15
answered him, 'No: if anyone kills Cain, Cain shall be avenged seven-

[a] *That is* Life.   [b] *Or* some of the first-born, that is the sucklings, of his flock.   [c] *Or* you hold your head up.   [d] *Or* but you must master it.   [e] Let us...country: *so Sam.; Heb. om.*   [f] and banished from: *or* more than (*cp. 3. 17*).

fold.' So the LORD put a mark on Cain, in order that anyone meeting
16 him should not kill him. Then Cain went out from the LORD's presence
and settled in the land of Nod*a b* to the east of Eden.

17 Then Cain lay with his wife; and she conceived and bore Enoch.
Cain was then building a city, which he named Enoch after his son.
18 Enoch begot Irad; Irad begot Mehujael; Mehujael begot Methushael;
Methushael begot Lamech.

19 Lamech married two wives, one named Adah and the other Zillah.
20 Adah bore Jabal who was the ancestor of herdsmen who live in tents;
21 and his brother's name was Jubal; he was the ancestor of those who
22 play the harp and pipe. Zillah, the other wife, bore Tubal-cain, the
master of all coppersmiths and blacksmiths, and Tubal-cain's sister
23 was Naamah. Lamech said to his wives:

> 'Adah and Zillah, listen to me;
> wives of Lamech, mark what I say:
> I kill a man for wounding me,
> a young man for a blow.
24 > Cain may be avenged seven times,
> but Lamech seventy-seven.'

25 Adam lay with his wife again. She bore a son, and named him Seth,*c*
'for', she said, 'God has granted me another son in place of Abel,
26 because Cain killed him.' Seth too had a son, whom he named Enosh.
At that time men began to invoke the LORD*d* by name.

5 THIS IS THE RECORD of the descendants of Adam. On the day when
2 God created man he made him in the likeness of God. He created them
male and female, and on the day when he created them, he blessed
them and called them man.

3 Adam was one hundred and thirty years old when he begot a son in
4 his likeness and image, and named him Seth. After the birth of Seth
5 he lived eight hundred years, and had other sons and daughters. He
lived nine hundred and thirty years, and then he died.

6 Seth was one hundred and five years old when he begot Enosh.
7 After the birth of Enosh he lived eight hundred and seven years, and
8 had other sons and daughters. He lived nine hundred and twelve years,
and then he died.

9,*e* 10 Enosh was ninety years old when he begot Kenan. After the birth
of Kenan he lived eight hundred and fifteen years, and had other sons
11 and daughters. He lived nine hundred and five years, and then he died.

[a] *That is* Wandering. [b] *and settled...Nod: or and he lived as a wanderer in the land.*
[c] *That is* Granted. [d] *This represents the Hebrew consonants* YHWH, *probably
pronounced* Yahweh, *but traditionally read as* Jehovah. [e] *Verses 9–32: cp. 1 Chr. 1. 2–4.*

commanded. Towards the end of seven days the waters of the flood 10 came upon the earth. In the year when Noah was six hundred years old, 11 on the seventeenth day of the second month, on that very day, all the springs of the great abyss broke through, the windows of the sky were opened, and rain fell on the earth for forty days and forty nights. 12 On that very day Noah entered the ark with his sons, Shem, Ham and 13 Japheth, his own wife, and his three sons' wives. *a*Wild animals of 14 every kind, cattle of every kind, reptiles of every kind that move upon the ground, and birds of every kind*b*—all came to Noah in the ark, two 15 by two of all creatures that had life*c* in them. Those which came were 16 one male and one female of all living things; they came in as God had commanded Noah, and the LORD closed the door on him. The flood 17 continued upon the earth for forty days, and the waters swelled and lifted up the ark so that it rose high above the ground. They swelled and 18 increased over the earth, and the ark floated on the surface of the waters. More and more the waters increased over the earth until they covered 19 all the high mountains everywhere under heaven. The waters increased 20 and the mountains were covered to a depth of fifteen cubits. Every 21 living creature that moves on earth perished, birds, cattle, wild animals, all reptiles, and all mankind. Everything died that had the breath of 22 life*d* in its nostrils, everything on dry land. God wiped out every living 23 thing that existed on earth, man and beast, reptile and bird; they were all wiped out over the whole earth, and only Noah and his company in the ark survived.

When the waters had increased over the earth for a hundred and fifty 24 days, God thought of Noah and all the wild animals and the cattle with 8 him in the ark, and he made a wind pass over the earth, and the waters began to subside. The springs of the abyss were stopped up, and so 2 were the windows of the sky; the downpour from the skies was checked. The water gradually receded from the earth, and by the end of a 3 hundred and fifty days it had disappeared. On the seventeenth day of 4 the seventh month the ark grounded on a mountain in Ararat. The 5 water continued to recede until the tenth month, and on the first day of the tenth month the tops of the mountains could be seen.

After forty days Noah opened the trap-door that he had made in the 6 ark, and released a raven to see whether the water had subsided,*e* but 7 the bird continued flying to and fro until the water on the earth had dried up. Noah waited for seven days,*f* and then he released a dove from 8 the ark to see whether the water on the earth had subsided further. But 9 the dove found no place where she could settle, and so she came back

[a] *So Sept.; Heb. prefixes* They. [b] *So Sept.; Heb. adds* every winged bird. [c] *Lit.* spirit of life. [d] *So Sept.; Heb.* breath of the spirit of life. [e] to see...subsided: *so Sept.; Heb. om.* [f] Noah...days: *prob. rdg., cp. verse 10; Heb. om.*

to him in the ark, because there was water over the whole surface of the earth. Noah stretched out his hand, caught her and took her into the
10 ark. He waited another seven days and again released the dove from
11 the ark. She came back to him towards evening with a newly plucked olive leaf in her beak. Then Noah knew for certain that the water
12 on the earth had subsided still further. He waited yet another seven
13 days and released the dove, but she never came back. And so it came about that, on the first day of the first month of his six hundred and first year, the water had dried up on the earth, and Noah removed the hatch and looked out of the ark. The surface of the ground was dry.
14 By the twenty-seventh day of the second month the whole earth was
15, 16 dry. And God said to Noah, 'Come out of the ark, you and your wife,
17 your sons and their wives. Bring out every living creature that is with you, live things of every kind, bird and beast and every reptile that moves on the ground, and let them swarm over the earth and be
18 fruitful and increase there.' So Noah came out with his sons, his wife,
19 and his sons' wives. Every wild animal, all cattle, every bird, and every reptile that moves on the ground,[a] came out of the ark by families.
20 Then Noah built an altar to the LORD. He took ritually clean beasts
21 and birds of every kind, and offered whole-offerings on the altar. When the LORD smelt the soothing odour, he said within himself, 'Never again will I curse the ground because of man, however evil his inclinations may be from his youth upwards. I will never again kill every living creature, as I have just done.

22   While the earth lasts
        seedtime and harvest, cold and heat,
        summer and winter, day and night,
        shall never cease.'

9 GOD BLESSED NOAH and his sons and said to them, 'Be fruitful and
2 increase, and fill the earth. The fear and dread of you shall fall upon all wild animals on earth, on all birds of heaven, on everything that moves upon the ground and all fish in the sea; they are given into your hands.
3 Every creature that lives and moves shall be food for you; I give you
4 them all, as once I gave you all green plants. But you must not eat the
5 flesh with the life, which is the blood, still in it. And further, for your life-blood I will demand satisfaction; from every animal I will require it, and from a man also I will require satisfaction for the death of his fellow-man.

[a] all cattle...ground: *so Sept.; Heb.* every reptile and every bird, everything that moves on the ground.

He that sheds the blood of a man,   6
for that man his blood shall be shed;
for in the image of God
has God made man.

But you must be fruitful and increase, swarm throughout the earth and   7
rule*a* over it.'

God spoke to Noah and to his sons with him: 'I now make my   8,9
covenant with you and with your descendants after you, and with   10
every living creature that is with you, all birds and cattle, all the wild
animals with you on earth, all that have come out of the ark.*b* I will   11
make my covenant with you: never again shall all living creatures be
destroyed by the waters of the flood, never again shall there be a flood
to lay waste the earth.'

God said, 'This is the sign of the covenant which I establish between   12
myself and you and every living creature with you, to endless generations:

My bow I set in the cloud,   13
sign of the covenant
between myself and earth.
When I cloud the sky over the earth,   14
the bow shall be seen in the cloud.

Then will I remember the covenant which I have made between myself   15
and you and living things of every kind. Never again shall the waters
become a flood to destroy all living creatures. The bow shall be in the   16
cloud; when I see it, it will remind me of the everlasting covenant
between God and living things on earth of every kind.' God said to   17
Noah, 'This is the sign of the covenant which I make between myself
and all that lives on earth.'

The sons of Noah who came out of the ark were Shem, Ham and   18
Japheth; Ham was the father of Canaan. These three were the sons of   19
Noah, and their descendants spread over the whole earth.

Noah, a man of the soil, began the planting of vineyards. He drank   20,21
some of the wine, became drunk and lay naked inside his tent. When   22
Ham, father of Canaan, saw his father naked, he told his two brothers
outside. So Shem and Japheth took a cloak, put it on their shoulders   23
and walked backwards, and so covered their father's naked body; their
faces were turned the other way, so that they did not see their father
naked. When Noah woke from his drunken sleep, he learnt what his   24
youngest son had done to him, and said: 25

'Cursed be Canaan,
slave of slaves
shall he be to his brothers.'

[a] *Prob. rdg., cp. 1. 28; Heb.* increase.   [b] *So Sept.; Heb. adds* to all wild animals on earth.

26 And he continued:

> 'Bless, O Lord,
> the tents of Shem;[a]
> may Canaan be his slave.

27   May God extend[b] Japheth's bounds,
> let him dwell in the tents of Shem,
> may Canaan be their slave.'

28, 29 After the flood Noah lived for three hundred and fifty years, and he was nine hundred and fifty years old when he died.

10 These are the descendants of the sons of Noah, Shem, Ham and Japheth, the sons born to them after the flood.

2[c] The sons of Japheth: Gomer, Magog, Madai, Javan,[d] Tubal, 3 Meshech and Tiras. The sons of Gomer: Ashkenaz, Riphath and 4 Togarmah. The sons of Javan: Elishah, Tarshish, Kittim[e] and 5 Rodanim.[f] From these the peoples of the coasts and islands separated into their own countries, each with their own language, family by family, nation by nation.

6,[g]7 The sons of Ham: Cush, Mizraim,[h] Put and Canaan. The sons of Cush: Seba, Havilah, Sabtah, Raamah and Sabtecha. The sons of 8 Raamah: Sheba and Dedan. Cush was the father of Nimrod, who 9 began to show himself a man of might on earth; and he was a mighty hunter before the Lord, as the saying goes, 'Like Nimrod, a mighty 10 hunter before the Lord.' His kingdom in the beginning consisted of 11 Babel, Erech, and Accad, all of them in the land of Shinar. From that 12 land he migrated to Asshur and built Nineveh, Rehoboth-Ir, Calah, and 13[i] Resen, a great city between Nineveh and Calah. From Mizraim sprang 14 the Lydians, Anamites, Lehabites, Naphtuhites, Pathrusites, Casluhites, and the Caphtorites,[j] from whom the Philistines were descended.

15 Canaan was the father of Sidon, who was his eldest son, and Heth,[k] 16, 17 the Jebusites, the Amorites, the Girgashites, the Hivites, the Arkites, 18 the Sinites, the Arvadites, the Zemarites, and the Hamathites. Later the 19 Canaanites spread, and then the Canaanite border ran from Sidon towards Gerar all the way to Gaza; then all the way to Sodom and 20 Gomorrah, Admah and Zeboyim as far as Lasha. These were the sons of Ham, by families and languages with their countries and nations.

21 Sons were born also to Shem, elder brother of Japheth, the ancestor 22[l] of all the sons of Eber. The sons of Shem: Elam, Asshur, Arphaxad, 23 Lud[m] and Aram. The sons of Aram: Uz, Hul, Gether and Mash.

[a] Bless...Shem: *prob. rdg.; Heb.* Blessed is the Lord the God of Shem.   [b] *Heb.* japht. [c] *Verses 2–4: cp. 1 Chr. 1. 5–7.*   [d] *Or* Greece.   [e] *Or* Tarshish of the Kittians.   [f] *So Sam.; Heb.* Dodanim.   [g] *Verses 6–8: cp. 1 Chr. 1. 8–10.*   [h] *Or* Egypt.   [i] *Verses 13–18: cp. 1 Chr. 1. 11–16.*   [j] and the Caphtorites: *transposed from end of verse; cp. Amos 9. 7.* [k] *Or* the Hittites.   [l] *Verses 22–29: cp. 1 Chr. 1. 17–23.*   [m] *Or* the Lydians.

Arphaxad was the father of Shelah, and Shelah the father of Eber. 24
Eber had two sons: one was named Peleg,*a* because in his time the 25
earth was divided; and his brother's name was Joktan. Joktan was 26
the father of Almodad, Sheleph, Hazarmoth, Jerah, Hadoram, Uzal, 27
Diklah, Obal, Abimael, Sheba, Ophir, Havilah and Jobab. All these 28, 29
were sons of Joktan. They lived in the eastern hill-country, from Mesha 30
all the way to Sephar. These were the sons of Shem, by families and 31
languages with their countries and nations.

These were the families of the sons of Noah according to their 32
genealogies, nation by nation; and from them came the separate
nations on earth after the flood.

ONCE UPON A TIME all the world spoke a single language and used 11
the same*b* words. As men journeyed in the east, they came upon a plain 2
in the land of Shinar and settled there. They said to one another, 3
'Come, let us make bricks and bake them hard'; they used bricks for
stone and bitumen for mortar. 'Come,' they said, 'let us build ourselves 4
a city and a tower with its top in the heavens, and make a name for
ourselves; or we shall be dispersed all over the earth.' Then the LORD 5
came down to see the city and tower which mortal men had built, and 6
he said, 'Here they are, one people with a single language, and now
they have started to do this; henceforward nothing they have a mind to
do will be beyond their reach. Come, let us go down there and confuse 7
their speech, so that they will not understand what they say to one
another.' So the LORD dispersed them from there all over the earth, and 8
they left off building the city. That is why it is called Babel,*c* because 9
the LORD there made a babble of the language of all the world; from
that place the LORD scattered men all over the face of the earth.

This is the table of the descendants of Shem. Shem was a hundred 10*d*
years old when he begot Arphaxad, two years after the flood. After the 11
birth of Arphaxad he lived five hundred years, and had other sons and
daughters. Arphaxad was thirty-five years old when he begot Shelah. 12
After the birth of Shelah he lived four hundred and three years, and 13
had other sons and daughters.

Shelah was thirty years old when he begot Eber. After the birth of Eber 14, 15
he lived four hundred and three years, and had other sons and daughters.

Eber was thirty-four years old when he begot Peleg. After the birth 16, 17
of Peleg he lived four hundred and thirty years, and had other sons
and daughters.

Peleg was thirty years old when he begot Reu. After the birth of Reu 18, 19
he lived two hundred and nine years, and had other sons and daughters.

[a] *That is* Division.   [b] *Or* used few.   [c] *That is* Babylon.   [d] *Verses 10–26: cp. 1 Chr.
1. 24–27.*

20, 21   Reu was thirty-two years old when he begot Serug. After the birth of Serug he lived two hundred and seven years, and had other sons and daughters.

22, 23   Serug was thirty years old when he begot Nahor. After the birth of Nahor he lived two hundred years, and had other sons and daughters.

24, 25   Nahor was twenty-nine years old when he begot Terah. After the birth of Terah he lived a hundred and nineteen years, and had other sons and daughters.

26   Terah was seventy years old when he begot Abram, Nahor and Haran.

27   This is the table of the descendants of Terah. Terah was the father
28 of Abram, Nahor and Haran. Haran was the father of Lot. Haran died in the presence of his father in the land of his birth, Ur of the Chaldees.
29 Abram and Nahor married wives; Abram's wife was called Sarai, and Nahor's Milcah. She was Haran's daughter; and he was also the father
30, 31 of Milcah and of Iscah. Sarai was barren; she had no child. Terah took his son Abram, his grandson Lot the son of Haran, and his daughter-in-law Sarai Abram's wife, and they set out from Ur of the Chaldees for the land of Canaan. But when they reached Harran, they settled
32 there. Terah was two hundred and five*a* years old when he died in Harran.

Abraham and Isaac

12 T HE LORD SAID TO ABRAM, 'Leave your own country, your kinsmen, and your father's house, and go to a country that I will
2 show you. I will make you into a great nation, I will bless you and make your name so great that it shall be used in blessings:

3   Those that bless you I will bless,
those that curse you, I will execrate.
All the families on earth
will pray to be blessed as you are blessed.'

4 And so Abram set out as the LORD had bidden him, and Lot went with
5 him. Abram was seventy-five years old when he left Harran. He took his wife Sarai, his nephew Lot, all the property they had collected, and all the dependants they had acquired in Harran, and they started on
6 their journey to Canaan. When they arrived, Abram passed through the country to the sanctuary at Shechem, the terebinth-tree of Moreh. At
7 that time the Canaanites lived in this land. There the LORD appeared to Abram and said, 'I give this land to your descendants.' So Abram built

[a] *Or, with Sam.*, one hundred and forty-five.

an altar there to the Lord who had appeared to him. Thence he went 8
on to the hill-country east of Bethel and pitched his tent between
Bethel on the west and Ai on the east. There he built an altar to the
Lord and invoked the Lord by name. Thus Abram journeyed by 9
stages towards the Negeb.

There came a famine in the land, so severe that Abram went down 10
to Egypt to live there for a while. When he was approaching Egypt, he 11
said to his wife Sarai, 'I know very well that you are a beautiful woman,
and that when the Egyptians see you, they will say, "She is his wife"; 12
then they will kill me but let you live. Tell them that you are my sister, 13
so that all may go well with me because of you and my life may be
spared on your account.' When Abram arrived in Egypt, the Egyptians 14
saw that she was indeed very beautiful. Pharaoh's courtiers saw her and 15
praised her to Pharaoh, and she was taken into Pharaoh's household. He 16
treated Abram well because of her, and Abram came to possess sheep
and cattle and asses, male and female slaves, she-asses, and camels. But 17
the Lord struck Pharaoh and his household with grave diseases on
account of Abram's wife Sarai. Pharaoh summoned Abram and said to 18
him, 'Why have you treated me like this? Why did you not tell me that
she is your wife? Why did you say that she was your sister, so that I took 19
her as a wife? Here she is: take her and be gone.' Then Pharaoh gave 20
his men orders, and they sent Abram away with his wife and all that
he had.

Abram went up from Egypt into the Negeb, he and his wife and all 13
that he had, and Lot went with him. Abram was now very rich in cattle 2
and in silver and gold. From the Negeb he journeyed by stages to 3
Bethel, to the place between Bethel and Ai where he had pitched his
tent in the beginning, where he had set up an altar on the first occasion 4
and had invoked the Lord by name. Now Lot was travelling with 5
Abram, and he too possessed sheep and cattle and tents. The land could 6
not support them both together; for their livestock were so numerous
that they could not settle in the same district, and there were quarrels 7
between Abram's herdsmen and Lot's. The Canaanites and the
Perizzites were then living in the land. So Abram said to Lot, 'Let there 8
be no quarrelling between us, between my herdsmen and yours; for we
are close kinsmen. The whole country is there in front of you; let us 9
part company. If you go left, I will go right; if you go right, I will go
left.' Lot looked up and saw how well-watered the whole Plain of the 10
Jordan was; all the way to Zoar it was like the Garden of the Lord, like
the land of Egypt. This was before the Lord had destroyed Sodom and
Gomorrah. So Lot chose all the Plain of the Jordan and took the 11
road on the east side. Thus they parted company. Abram settled in the 12
land of Canaan; but Lot settled among the cities of the Plain and

13 pitched his tents near Sodom. Now the men of Sodom were wicked, great sinners against the LORD.

14   After Lot and Abram had parted, the LORD said to Abram, 'Raise your eyes and look into the distance from the place where you are,
15 north and south, east and west. All the land you can see I will give to
16 you and to your descendants for ever. I will make your descendants countless as the dust of the earth; if anyone could count the dust upon
17 the ground, then he could count your descendants. Now go through
18 the length and breadth of the land, for I give it to you.' So Abram moved his tent and settled by the terebinths of Mamre at Hebron; and there he built an altar to the LORD.

14 IT WAS IN THE TIME of Amraphel king of Shinar, Arioch king of
2 Ellasar, Kedorlaomer king of Elam, and Tidal king of Goyim. They went to war against Bera king of Sodom, Birsha king of Gomorrah, Shinab king of Admah, Shemeber king of Zeboyim, and the king of
3 Bela, that is Zoar. These kings joined forces in the valley of Siddim,
4 which is now the Dead Sea. They had been subject to Kedorlaomer
5 for twelve years, but in the thirteenth year they rebelled. Then in the fourteenth year Kedorlaomer and his confederate kings came and defeated the Rephaim in Ashteroth-karnaim, the Zuzim in Ham, the
6 Emim in Shaveh-kiriathaim, and the Horites in the hill-country
7 from Seir[a] as far as El-paran on the edge of the wilderness. On their way back they came to En-mishpat, which is now Kadesh, and laid waste all the country of the Amalekites and also that of the Amorites
8 who lived in Hazazon-tamar. Then the kings of Sodom, Gomorrah, Admah, Zeboyim, and Bela, which is now Zoar, marched out and drew
9 up their forces against them in the valley of Siddim, against Kedor-laomer king of Elam, Tidal king of Goyim, Amraphel king of Shinar,
10 and Arioch king of Ellasar, four kings against five. Now the valley of Siddim was full of bitumen pits; and when the kings of Sodom and Gomorrah fled, they fell into them, but the rest escaped to the hill-
11 country. The four kings captured all the flocks and herds of Sodom and
12 Gomorrah and all their provisions, and went away. They also carried off Lot, Abram's nephew, who was living in Sodom, and with him his
13 flocks and herds. But a fugitive came and told Abram the Hebrew, who at that time was dwelling by the terebinths of Mamre the Amorite. This Mamre was the brother of Eshcol and Aner, who were allies of
14 Abram. When Abram heard that his kinsman had been taken prisoner, he mustered[b] his retainers, men born in his household, three hundred
15 and eighteen of them, and pursued as far as Dan. Abram and his followers surrounded the enemy by night, attacked them and pursued

[a] *Prob. rdg.; Heb.* in their hill-country, Seir.   [b] *So Sam.; Heb.* emptied out.

them as far as Hobah, north of Damascus; he then brought back all the 16
flocks and herds and also his kinsman Lot with his flocks and herds,
together with the women and the other captives.*a* On his return from 17
this defeat of Kedorlaomer and his confederate kings, the king of
Sodom came out to meet him in the valley of Shaveh, which is now
the King's Valley.

Then Melchizedek king of Salem brought food and wine. He was 18
priest of God Most High,*b* and he pronounced this blessing on Abram: 19

> 'Blessed be Abram
> by God Most High,
> creator*c* of heaven and earth.
> And blessed be God Most High, 20
> who has delivered your enemies into your power.'

Abram gave him a tithe of all the booty.

The king of Sodom said to Abram, 'Give me the people, and you can 21
take the property'; but Abram said to the king of Sodom, 'I lift my 22
hand and swear by the LORD, God Most High, creator of heaven and
earth: not a thread or a shoe-string will I accept of anything that is 23
yours. You shall never say, "I made Abram rich." I will accept nothing 24
but what the young men have eaten and the share of the men who went
with me. Aner, Eshcol, and Mamre shall have their share.'

AFTER THIS the word of the LORD came to Abram in a vision. He said, 15
'Do not be afraid, Abram, I am giving you a very great reward.'*d* Abram 2
replied, 'Lord GOD, what canst thou give me? I have no standing among
men, for the heir to*e* my household is Eliezer of Damascus.' Abram 3
continued, 'Thou hast given me no children, and so my heir must be
a slave born in my house.' Then came the word of the LORD to him: 4
'This man shall not be your heir; your heir shall be a child of your own
body.' He took Abram outside and said, 'Look up into the sky, and count 5
the stars if you can. So many', he said, 'shall your descendants be.'

Abram put his faith in the LORD, and the LORD counted that faith 6
to him as righteousness; he said to him, 'I am the LORD who brought 7
you out from Ur of the Chaldees to give you this land to occupy.'
Abram said, 'O Lord GOD, how can I be sure that I shall occupy it?' 8
The LORD answered, 'Bring me a heifer three years old, a she-goat 9
three years old, a ram three years old, a turtle-dove, and a fledgling.'
He brought him all these, halved the animals down the middle and 10
placed each piece opposite its corresponding piece, but he did not halve

[a] *Lit.* the people. [b] God Most High: *Heb.* El-Elyon [c] *Or* owner. [d] I am giving
...reward: *or* I am your shield, your very great reward. [e] the heir to: *prob. rdg., cp.*
Pesh.; Heb. obscure.

11 the birds. When the birds of prey swooped down on the carcasses,
12 Abram scared them away. Then, as the sun was going down, a trance
13 came over Abram and great fear*a* came upon him. The LORD said to
Abram, 'Know this for certain, that your descendants will be aliens
living in a land that is not theirs; they will be slaves, and will be held in
14 oppression there for four hundred years. But I will punish that nation
whose slaves they are, and after that they shall come out with great
15 possessions. You yourself shall join your fathers in peace and be buried
16 in a good old age; and the fourth generation shall return here, for the
17 Amorites will not be ripe for punishment till then.' The sun went down
and it was dusk, and there appeared a smoking brazier and a flaming
18 torch passing between the divided pieces. That very day the LORD made
a covenant with Abram, and he said, 'To your descendants I give this
land from the River of Egypt to the Great River, the river Euphrates,
19, 20 the territory of the Kenites, Kenizzites, Kadmonites, Hittites, Periz-
21 zites, Rephaim, Amorites, Canaanites, Girgashites, Hivites,*b* and
Jebusites.'

16 Abram's wife Sarai had borne him no children. Now she had an
2 Egyptian slave-girl whose name was Hagar, and she said to Abram,
'You see that the LORD has not allowed me to bear a child. Take my
slave-girl; perhaps I shall found a family through her.' Abram agreed
3 to what his wife said; so Sarai, Abram's wife, brought her slave-girl,
Hagar the Egyptian, and gave her to her husband Abram as a wife.*c*
4 When this happened Abram had been in Canaan for ten years. He lay
with Hagar and she conceived; and when she knew that she was with
5 child, she despised her mistress. Sarai said to Abram, 'I have been
wronged and you must answer for it. It was I who gave my slave-girl
into your arms, but since she has known that she is with child, she has
despised me. May the LORD see justice done between you and me.'
6 Abram replied to Sarai, 'Your slave-girl is in your hands; deal with her
as you will.' So Sarai ill-treated her and she ran away.

7 The angel of the LORD found her by a spring of water in the wilder-
8 ness on the way to Shur, and he said, 'Hagar, Sarai's slave-girl, where
have you come from and where are you going?' She answered, 'I am
9 running away from Sarai my mistress.' The angel of the LORD said to
10 her, 'Go back to your mistress and submit to her ill-treatment.' The
angel also said, 'I will make your descendants too many to be counted.'
11 And the angel of the LORD said to her:

> 'You are with child and will bear a son.
> You shall name him Ishmael,*d*
> because the LORD has heard of your ill-treatment.

[a] *Lit.* and fear with dense darkness. [b] *So Sam.; Heb. om.* [c] *Or* concubine.
[d] *That is* God heard.

18

He shall be a man like the wild ass,   12
his hand against every man
and every man's hand against him;
and he shall live at odds with*a* all his kinsmen.'

She called the LORD who was speaking to her by the name El-Roi,*b* for   13
she said, 'Have I indeed seen God and still live*c* after that vision?'
That is why men call the well Beer-lahai-roi;*d* it lies between Kadesh   14
and Bered. Hagar bore Abram a son, and he named the child she bore   15
him Ishmael. Abram was eighty-six years old when Hagar bore Ishmael.   16

When Abram was ninety-nine years old, the LORD appeared to him   17
and said, 'I am God Almighty.*e* Live always in my presence and be
perfect, so that I may set my covenant between myself and you and   2
multiply your descendants.' Abram threw himself down on his face,   3
and God spoke with him and said, 'I make this covenant, and I make   4
it with you: you shall be the father of a host of nations. Your name shall   5
no longer be Abram,*f* your name shall be Abraham,*g* for I make you
father of a host of nations. I will make you exceedingly fruitful; I will   6
make nations out of you, and kings shall spring from you. I will fulfil   7
my covenant between myself and you and your descendants after you,
generation after generation, an everlasting covenant, to be your God,
yours and your descendants' after you. As an everlasting possession   8
I will give you and your descendants after you the land in which you
now are aliens, all the land of Canaan, and I will be God to your
descendants.'

God said to Abraham, 'For your part, you must keep my covenant,   9
you and your descendants after you, generation by generation. This is   10
how you shall keep my covenant between myself and you and your
descendants after you: circumcise yourselves, every male among you.
You shall circumcise the flesh of your foreskin, and it shall be the sign   11
of the covenant between us. Every male among you in every generation   12
shall be circumcised on the eighth day, both those born in your house
and any foreigner, not of your blood but bought with your money.
Circumcise both those born in your house and those bought with your   13
money; thus shall my covenant be marked in your flesh as an everlasting covenant. Every uncircumcised male, everyone who has not had   14
the flesh of his foreskin circumcised, shall be cut off from the kin of his
father. He has broken my covenant.'

God said to Abraham, 'As for Sarai your wife; you shall call her not   15
Sarai,*h* but Sarah.*i* I will bless her and give you a son by her. I will   16

[*a*] *Or* live to the east of...   [*b*] *That is* God of a vision.   [*c*] God and still live: *prob. rdg.;*
Heb. hither.   [*d*] *That is* the Well of the Living One of Vision.   [*e*] God Almighty: *Heb.*
El-Shaddai.   [*f*] *That is* High Father.   [*g*] *That is* Father of a Multitude.   [*h*] *That is*
Mockery.   [*i*] *That is* Princess.

bless her and she shall be the mother of nations; the kings of many

17 people shall spring from her.' Abraham threw himself down on his face; he laughed and said to himself, 'Can a son be born to a man who is

18 a hundred years old? Can Sarah bear a son when she is ninety?' He said

19 to God, 'If only Ishmael might live under thy special care!' But God replied, 'No. Your wife Sarah shall bear you a son, and you shall call him Isaac.[a] With him I will fulfil my covenant, an everlasting covenant

20 with his descendants after him. I have heard your prayer for Ishmael. I have blessed him and will make him fruitful. I will multiply his descendants; he shall be father of twelve princes, and I will raise a

21 great nation from him. But my covenant I will fulfil with Isaac, whom

22 Sarah will bear to you at this season next year.' When he had finished talking with Abraham, God ascended and left him.

23 Then Abraham took Ishmael his son, everyone who had been born in his household and everyone bought with money, every male in his household, and he circumcised them that very same day in the flesh of

24 their foreskins as God had told him to do. Abraham was ninety-nine

25 years old when he circumcised the flesh of his foreskin. Ishmael was thirteen years old when he was circumcised in the flesh of his foreskin.

26, 27 Both Abraham and Ishmael were circumcised on the same day, and all the men of his household, born in the house or bought with money from foreigners, were circumcised with him.

18 THE LORD APPEARED to Abraham by the terebinths of Mamre. As Abraham was sitting at the opening of his tent in the heat of the day,

2 he looked up and saw three men standing in front of him. When he saw them, he ran from the opening of his tent to meet them and bowed low

3 to the ground. 'Sirs,' he said, 'if I have deserved your favour, do not

4 pass by my humble self without a visit. Let me send for some water so

5 that you may wash your feet and rest under a tree; and let me fetch a little food so that you may refresh yourselves. Afterwards you may continue the journey which has brought you my way.' They said, 'Do

6 by all means as you say.' So Abraham hurried into the tent to Sarah and said, 'Take three measures of flour quickly, knead it and make some

7 cakes.' Then Abraham ran to the cattle, chose a fine tender calf and

8 gave it to a servant, who hurriedly prepared it. He took curds and milk and the calf he had prepared, set it before them, and waited on them

9 himself under the tree while they ate. They asked him where Sarah his

10 wife was, and he said, 'There, in the tent.' The stranger said, 'About this time next year I will be sure to come back to you, and Sarah your wife shall have a son.' Now Sarah was listening at the opening of the

11 tent, and he was close beside it. Both Abraham and Sarah had grown

[a] *That is* He laughed.

very old, and Sarah was past the age of child-bearing. So Sarah laughed 12
to herself and said, 'I am past bearing children now that I am out of
my time, and my husband is old.' The LORD said to Abraham, 'Why 13
did Sarah laugh and say, "Shall I indeed bear a child when I am old?"
Is anything impossible for the LORD? In due season I will come back 14
to you, about this time next year, and Sarah shall have a son.' Sarah 15
lied because she was frightened, and denied that she had laughed; but
he said, 'Yes, you did laugh.'

The men set out and looked down towards Sodom, and Abraham 16
went with them to start them on their way. The LORD thought to him- 17
self, 'Shall I conceal from Abraham what I intend to do? He will 18
become a great and powerful nation, and all nations on earth will pray
to be blessed as he is blessed. I have taken care of him on purpose that 19
he may charge his sons and family after him to conform to the way of
the LORD and to do what is right and just; thus I shall fulfil all that
I have promised for him.' So the LORD said, 'There is a great outcry 20
over Sodom and Gomorrah; their sin is very grave. I must go down and 21
see whether their deeds warrant the outcry which has reached me. I am
resolved to know the truth.' When the men turned and went towards 22
Sodom, Abraham remained standing before the LORD. Abraham drew 23
near him and said, 'Wilt thou really sweep away good and bad together?
Suppose there are fifty good men in the city; wilt thou really sweep it 24
away, and not pardon the place because of the fifty good men? Far be 25
it from thee to do this—to kill good and bad together; for then the good
would suffer with the bad. Far be it from thee. Shall not the judge of all
the earth do what is just?' The LORD said, 'If I find in the city of 26
Sodom fifty good men, I will pardon the whole place for their sake.'
Abraham replied, 'May I presume to speak to the Lord, dust and ashes 27
that I am: suppose there are five short of the fifty good men? Wilt thou 28
destroy the whole city for a mere five men?' He said, 'If I find forty-
five there I will not destroy it.' Abraham spoke again, 'Suppose forty 29
can be found there?'; and he said, 'For the sake of the forty I will
not do it.' Then Abraham said, 'Please do not be angry, O Lord, if 30
I speak again: suppose thirty can be found there?' He answered, 'If
I find thirty there I will not do it.' Abraham continued, 'May I presume 31
to speak to the Lord: suppose twenty can be found there?' He replied,
'For the sake of the twenty I will not destroy it.' Abraham said, 'I pray 32
thee not to be angry, O Lord, if I speak just once more: suppose ten
can be found there?' He said, 'For the sake of the ten I will not
destroy it.' When the LORD had finished talking with Abraham, he left 33
him, and Abraham returned home.

The two angels came to Sodom in the evening, and Lot was sitting **19**
in the gateway of the city. When he saw them he rose to meet them and

2 bowed low with his face to the ground. He said, 'I pray you, sirs, turn aside to my humble home, spend the night there and wash your feet; you can rise early and continue your journey.' 'No,' they answered, 'we
3 will spend the night in the street.' But Lot was so insistent that they did turn aside and enter his house. He prepared a meal for them, baking
4 unleavened cakes, and they ate them. Before they lay down to sleep, the men of Sodom, both young and old, surrounded the house—every-
5 one without exception. They called to Lot and asked him where the men were who had entered his house that night. 'Bring them out', they shouted, 'so that we can have intercourse with them.'
6   Lot went out into the doorway to them, closed the door behind him
7,8 and said, 'No, my friends, do not be so wicked. Look, I have two daughters, both virgins; let me bring them out to you, and you can do what you like with them; but do not touch these men, because they
9 have come under the shelter of my roof.' They said, 'Out of our way! This man has come and settled here as an alien, and does he now take it upon himself to judge us? We will treat you worse than them.' They
10 crowded in on the man Lot and pressed close to smash in the door. But
11 the two men inside reached out, pulled Lot in, and closed the door. Then they struck the men in the doorway with blindness, both small and great, so that they could not find the door.
12   The two men said to Lot, 'Have you anyone else here, sons-in-law, sons, or daughters, or any who belong to you in the city? Get them out
13 of this place, because we are going to destroy it. The outcry against it
14 has been so great that the LORD has sent us to destroy it.' So Lot went out and spoke to his intended sons-in-law.*a* He said, 'Be quick and leave this place; the LORD is going to destroy the city.' But they did not take him seriously.
15   As soon as it was dawn, the angels urged Lot to go, saying, 'Be quick, take your wife and your two daughters who are here, or you will be
16 swept away when the city is punished.' When he lingered, they took him by the hand, with his wife and his daughters, and, because the
17 LORD had spared him, led him on until he was outside the city. When they had brought them out, they said, 'Flee for your lives; do not look back and do not stop anywhere in the Plain. Flee to the hills or you
18,19 will be swept away.' Lot replied, 'No, sirs. You have shown your servant favour and you have added to your unfailing care for me by saving my life, but I cannot escape to the hills; I shall be overtaken by
20 the disaster, and die. Look, here is a town, only a small place, near enough for me to reach quickly. Let me escape to it—it is very small—
21 and save my life.' He said to him, 'I grant your request: I will not over-
22 throw this town you speak of. But flee there quickly, because I can do

[a] *Or* his sons-in-law, who had married his daughters.

nothing until you are there.' That is why the place was called Zoar.[a]
The sun had risen over the land as Lot entered Zoar; and then the 23, 24
LORD rained down fire and brimstone from the skies on Sodom and
Gomorrah. He overthrew those cities and destroyed all the Plain, with 25
everyone living there and everything growing in the ground. But Lot's 26
wife, behind him, looked back, and she turned into a pillar of salt.

Next morning Abraham rose early and went to the place where he 27
had stood in the presence of the LORD. He looked down towards Sodom 28
and Gomorrah and all the wide extent of the Plain, and there he saw
thick smoke rising high from the earth like the smoke of a lime-kiln.
Thus, when God destroyed the cities of the Plain, he thought of 29
Abraham and rescued Lot from the disaster, the overthrow of the cities
where he had been living.

Lot went up from Zoar and settled in the hill-country with his two 30
daughters, because he was afraid to stay in Zoar; he lived with his
two daughters in a cave. The elder daughter said to the younger, 'Our 31
father is old and there is not a man in the country to come to us in the
usual way. Come now, let us make our father drink wine and then lie 32
with him and in this way keep the family alive through our father.' So 33
that night they gave him wine to drink, and the elder daughter came
and lay with him, and he did not know when she lay down and when
she got up. Next day the elder said to the younger, 'Last night I lay 34
with my father. Let us give him wine to drink again tonight; then you
go in and lie with him. So we shall keep the family alive through our
father.' So they gave their father wine to drink again that night, and the 35
younger daughter went and lay with him, and he did not know when
she lay down and when she got up. In this way both Lot's daughters 36
came to be with child by their father. The elder daughter bore a son 37
and called him Moab; he was the ancestor of the present Moabites. The 38
younger also bore a son, whom she called Ben-ammi; he was the
ancestor of the present Ammonites.

ABRAHAM JOURNEYED by stages from there into the Negeb, and 20
settled between Kadesh and Shur, living as an alien in Gerar. He said 2
that Sarah his wife was his sister, and Abimelech king of Gerar sent and
took her. But God came to Abimelech in a dream by night and said, 3
'You shall die because of this woman whom you have taken. She is
a married woman.' Now Abimelech had not gone near her; and he said, 4
'Lord, wilt thou destroy an innocent people? Did he not tell me himself 5
that she was his sister, and she herself said that he was her brother. It
was with a clear conscience[b] and in all innocence that I did this.'
God said to him in the dream, 'Yes: I know that you acted with a clear 6

[a] *That is* Small. [b] *Lit.* in complete sincerity.

23

conscience. Moreover, it was I who held you back from committing
7 a sin against me: that is why I did not let you touch her. Send back the
man's wife now; he is a prophet, and he will intercede on your behalf,
and you shall live. But if you do not send her back, I tell you that you
8 are doomed to die, you and all that is yours.' So Abimelech rose early
in the morning, summoned all his servants and told them the whole
9 story; the men were terrified. Abimelech then summoned Abraham and
said to him, 'Why have you treated us like this? What harm have I done
to you that you should bring this great sin on me and my kingdom?
10 You have done a thing that ought not to be done.' And he asked
11 Abraham, 'What was your purpose in doing this?' Abraham answered,
'I said to myself, There can be no fear of God in this place, and they
12 will kill me for the sake of my wife. She is in fact my sister, she is my
father's daughter though not by the same mother; and she became my
13 wife. When God set me wandering from my father's house, I said to
her, "There is a duty towards me which you must loyally fulfil:
14 wherever we go, you must say that I am your brother."' Then Abimelech took sheep and cattle, and male and female slaves, gave them to
15 Abraham, and returned his wife Sarah to him. Abimelech said, 'My
16 country lies before you; settle wherever you please.' To Sarah he said,
'I have given your brother a thousand pieces of silver, so that your own
people may turn a blind eye on it all, and you will be completely
17 vindicated.' Then Abraham interceded with God, and God healed
Abimelech, his wife, and his slave-girls, and they bore children;
18 for the LORD had made every woman in Abimelech's household barren
on account of Abraham's wife Sarah.

21 The LORD showed favour to Sarah as he had promised, and made
2 good what he had said about her. She conceived and bore a son to
3 Abraham for his old age, at the time which God had appointed. The
4 son whom Sarah bore to him, Abraham named Isaac.*a* When Isaac was
eight days old Abraham circumcised him, as God had commanded.
5 Abraham was a hundred years old when his son Isaac was born.
6 Sarah said, 'God has given me good reason to laugh, and everybody
7 who hears will laugh with me.' She said, 'Whoever would have told
Abraham that Sarah would suckle children? Yet I have borne him a son
8 for his old age.' The boy grew and was weaned, and on the day of his
9 weaning Abraham gave a feast. Sarah saw the son whom Hagar the
10 Egyptian had borne to Abraham laughing at him, and she said to
Abraham, 'Drive out this slave-girl and her son; I will not have this
11 slave-girl's son sharing the inheritance with my son Isaac.' Abraham
12 was vexed at this on his son Ishmael's account, but God said to him,
'Do not be vexed on account of the boy and the slave-girl. Do what

[a] *That is* He laughed.

24

Sarah says, because you shall have descendants through Isaac. I will 13
make a great*a* nation of the slave-girl's son too, because he is your own
child.'

Abraham rose early in the morning, took some food and a waterskin 14
full of water and gave it to Hagar; he set the child on her shoulder and
sent her away, and she went and wandered in the wilderness of
Beersheba. When the water in the skin was finished, she thrust the 15
child under a bush, and went and sat down some way off, about two 16
bowshots away, for she said, 'How can I watch the child die?' So she
sat some way off, weeping bitterly. God heard the child crying, and the*b* 17
angel of God called from heaven to Hagar, 'What is the matter, Hagar?
Do not be afraid: God has heard the child crying where you laid him.
Get to your feet, lift the child up and hold him in your arms, because 18
I will make of him a great nation.' Then God opened her eyes and she 19
saw a well full of water; she went to it, filled her waterskin and gave the
child a drink. God was with the child, and he grew up and lived in the 20-21
wilderness of Paran. He became an archer, and his mother found him
a wife from Egypt.

Now about that time Abimelech, with Phicol the commander of his 22
army, addressed Abraham in these terms: 'God is with you in all that
you do. Now swear an oath to me in the name of God, that you will 23
not break faith with me, my offspring, or my descendants. As I have
kept faith with you, so shall you keep faith with me and with the
country where you have come to live as an alien.' Abraham said, 'I 24
swear.' It happened that Abraham had a complaint against Abimelech 25
about a well which Abimelech's men had seized. Abimelech said, 'I do 26
not know who did this. You never told me, and I have heard nothing
about it till now.' So Abraham took sheep and cattle and gave them 27
to Abimelech; and the two of them made a pact. Abraham set seven 28
ewe-lambs apart, and when Abimelech asked him why he had set these 29
lambs apart, he said, 'Accept these from me in token that I dug this 30
well.' Therefore that place was called Beersheba,*c* because there the 31
two of them swore an oath. When they had made the pact at Beersheba, 32
Abimelech and Phicol the commander of his army returned at once to
the country of the Philistines, and Abraham planted a strip of ground*d* at 33
Beersheba. There he invoked the LORD, the everlasting God, by name,
and he lived as an alien in the country of the Philistines for many a year. 34

THE TIME CAME when God put Abraham to the test. 'Abraham', he 22
called, and Abraham replied, 'Here I am.' God said, 'Take your son 2
Isaac, your only son, whom you love, and go to the land of Moriah.

[a] *So Sam.; Heb. om.* [b] *Or* an. [c] *That is* Well of Seven *and* Well of an Oath.
[d] *Or* planted a tamarisk.

There you shall offer him as a sacrifice on one of the hills which I will
3 show you.' So Abraham rose early in the morning and saddled his ass,
and he took with him two of his men and his son Isaac; and he split
the firewood for the sacrifice, and set out for the place of which God
4 had spoken. On the third day Abraham looked up and saw the place in
5 the distance. He said to his men, 'Stay here with the ass while I and the
boy go over there; and when we have worshipped we will come back to
6 you.' So Abraham took the wood for the sacrifice and laid it on his
son Isaac's shoulder; he himself carried the fire and the knife, and the
7 two of them went on together. Isaac said to Abraham, 'Father', and
he answered, 'What is it, my son?' Isaac said, 'Here are the fire and the
8 wood, but where is the young beast for the sacrifice?' Abraham
answered, 'God will provide himself with a young beast for a sacrifice,
9 my son.' And the two of them went on together and came to the place
of which God had spoken. There Abraham built an altar and arranged
the wood. He bound his son Isaac and laid him on the altar on top of
10 the wood. Then he stretched out his hand and took the knife to kill his
11 son; but the angel of the Lord called to him from heaven, 'Abraham,
12 Abraham.' He answered, 'Here I am.' The angel of the Lord said,
'Do not raise your hand against the boy; do not touch him. Now I know
that you are a God-fearing man. You have not withheld from me your
13 son, your only son.' Abraham looked up, and there he saw a*a* ram
caught by its horns in a thicket. So he went and took the ram and
14 offered it as a sacrifice instead of his son. Abraham named that place
Jehovah-jireh;*b* and to this day the saying is: 'In the mountain of the
15 Lord it was provided.' Then the angel of the Lord called from heaven
16 a second time to Abraham, 'This is the word of the Lord: By my own
self I swear: inasmuch as you have done this and have not withheld
17 your son, your only son, I will bless you abundantly and greatly
multiply your descendants until they are as numerous as the stars in
the sky and the grains of sand on the sea-shore. Your descendants shall
18 possess the cities*c* of their enemies. All nations on earth shall pray to be
blessed as your descendants are blessed, and this because you have
obeyed me.'

19   Abraham went back to his men, and together they returned to
Beersheba; and there Abraham remained.

20   After this Abraham was told, 'Milcah has borne sons to your brother
21 Nahor: Uz his first-born, then his brother Buz, and Kemuel father of
22,23 Aram, and Kesed, Hazo, Pildash, Jidlaph and Bethuel; and a daughter,
Rebecca, has been born to Bethuel.' These eight Milcah bore to
24 Abraham's brother Nahor. His concubine, whose name was Reumah,
also bore him sons: Tebah, Gaham, Tahash and Maacah.

[a] a: *so many MSS.; others* behind.   [b] *That is* the Lord will provide.   [c] *Lit.* gates.

Sarah lived for a hundred and twenty-seven years,[a] and died in 23 1,2 Kiriath-arba, which is Hebron, in Canaan. Abraham went in to mourn over Sarah and to weep for her. At last he rose and left the presence 3 of the dead. He said to the Hittites,[b] 'I am an alien and a settler among 4 you. Give me land enough for a burial-place, so that I can give my dead proper burial.' The Hittites answered Abraham, 'Do, pray, listen 5,6 to what we have to say, sir. You are a mighty prince among us. Bury your dead in the best grave we have. There is not one of us who will deny you his grave or hinder you from burying your dead.' Abraham stood up and then bowed low to the Hittites, the people of 7 that country. He said to them, 'If you are willing to let me give my dead 8 proper burial, then listen to me and speak for me to Ephron son of Zohar, asking him to give me the cave that belongs to him at Mach- 9 pelah, at the far end of his land. Let him give it to me for the full price, so that I may take possession of it as a burial-place within your territory.' Ephron the Hittite was sitting with the others, and he gave 10 Abraham this answer in the hearing of everyone as they came into the city gate: 'No, sir; hear what I have to say. I will make you a gift of the 11 land and I will also give you the cave which is on it. In the presence of all my kinsmen I give it to you; so bury your dead.' Abraham bowed 12 low before the people of the country and said to Ephron in their 13 hearing, 'If you really mean it—but do listen to me! I give you the price of the land: take it and I will bury my dead there.' And Ephron 14 answered, 'Do listen to me, sir: the land is worth four hundred shekels of 15 silver. But what is that between you and me? There you may bury your dead.' Abraham came to an agreement with him and weighed out the 16 amount that Ephron had named in the hearing of the Hittites, four hundred shekels of the standard recognized by merchants. Thus the 17 plot of land belonging to Ephron at Machpelah to the east of Mamre, the plot, the cave that is on it, every tree on the plot, within the whole area, became the legal possession of Abraham, in the presence of all the 18 Hittites as they came into the city gate. After this Abraham buried his wife 19 Sarah in the cave on the plot of land at Machpelah to the east of Mamre, which is Hebron, in Canaan. Thus the plot and the cave on it became 20 Abraham's possession as a burial-place, by purchase from the Hittites.

BY THIS TIME Abraham had become a very old man, and the LORD 24 had blessed him in all that he did. Abraham said to his servant, who 2 had been long in his service and was in charge of all his possessions, 'Put your hand under my thigh: I want you to swear by the LORD, the 3 God of heaven and earth, that you will not take a wife for my son from the women of the Canaanites in whose land I dwell; you must go to 4

[a] *So Sept.; Heb. adds* the years of the life of Sarah.   [b] *Lit.* the sons of Heth.

my own country and to my own kindred to find a wife for my son
5 Isaac.' The servant said to him, 'What if the woman is unwilling to
come with me to this country? Must I in that event take your son back
6 to the land from which you came?' Abraham said to him, 'On no
7 account are you to take my son back there. The LORD the God of heaven
who took me from my father's house and the land of my birth, the LORD
who swore to me that he would give this land to my descendants—he
will send his angel before you, and from there you shall take a wife for
8 my son. If the woman is unwilling to come with you, then you will be
released from your oath to me; but you must not take my son back
9 there.' So the servant put his hand under his master Abraham's thigh
and swore an oath in those terms.

10   The servant took ten camels from his master's herds, and also all
kinds of gifts from his master; he set out for Aram-naharaim*a* and
11 arrived at the city where Nahor lived. Towards evening, the time when
the women come out to draw water, he made the camels kneel down by
12 the well outside the city. He said, 'O LORD God of my master Abraham,
give me good fortune this day; keep faith with my master Abraham.
13 Here I stand by the spring, and the women of the city are coming out
14 to draw water. Let it be like this: I shall say to a girl, "Please lower your
jar so that I may drink"; and if she answers, "Drink, and I will water
your camels also", that will be the girl whom thou dost intend for thy
servant Isaac. In this way I shall know that thou hast kept faith with
my master.'

15   Before he had finished praying silently,*b* he saw Rebecca coming out
with her water-jug on her shoulder. She was the daughter of Bethuel
16 son of Milcah, the wife of Abraham's brother Nahor. The girl was very
beautiful, a virgin, who had had no intercourse with a man. She went
17 down to the spring, filled her jar and came up again. Abraham's servant
hurried to meet her and said, 'Give me a sip of water from your jar.'
18 'Drink, sir', she answered, and at once lowered her jar on to her hand
19 to let him drink. When she had finished giving him a drink, she said,
'Now I will draw water for your camels until they have had enough.'
20 So she quickly emptied her jar into the water-trough, hurried again to
21 the well to draw water and watered all the camels. The man was
watching quietly to see whether or not the LORD had made his journey
22 successful. When the camels had finished drinking, the man took a gold
nose-ring weighing half a shekel, and two bracelets for her wrists
23 weighing ten shekels, also of gold, and said, 'Tell me, please, whose
daughter you are. Is there room in your father's house for us to spend
24 the night?' She answered, 'I am the daughter of Bethuel, the son of
25 Nahor and Milcah; and we have plenty of straw and fodder and also

[a] *That is* Aram of Two Rivers. [b] *So* Sam., *cp. verse 45; Heb. om.; lit.* in his heart.

room for you to spend the night.' So the man bowed down and 26
prostrated himself to the LORD. He said, 'Blessed be the LORD the God 27
of my master Abraham, who has not failed to keep faith and truth with
my master; for I have been guided by the LORD to the house of my
master's kinsman.'

The girl ran to her mother's house and told them what had happened. 28
Now Rebecca had a brother named Laban; and, when he saw the nose- 29-30
ring, and also the bracelets on his sister's wrists, and heard his sister
Rebecca tell what the man had said to her, he ran out to the man at the
spring. When he came to him and found him still standing there by the
camels, he said, 'Come in, sir, whom the LORD has blessed. Why stay 31
outside? I have prepared the house, and there is room for the camels.'
So he brought the man into the house, unloaded the camels and pro- 32
vided straw and fodder for them, and water for him and all his men to
wash their feet. Food was set before him, but he said, 'I will not eat 33
until I have delivered my message.' Laban said, 'Let us hear it.' He 34
answered, 'I am the servant of Abraham. The LORD has greatly blessed 35
my master, and he has become a man of power. The LORD has given
him flocks and herds, silver and gold, male and female slaves, camels
and asses. My master's wife Sarah in her old age bore him a son, to 36
whom he has given all that he has. So my master made me swear an 37
oath, saying, "You shall not take a wife for my son from the women of
the Canaanites in whose land I dwell; but you shall go to my father's 38
house and to my family to find a wife for him." So I said to my master, 39
"What if the woman will not come with me?" He answered, "The LORD, 40
in whose presence I have lived, will send his angel with you and will
make your journey successful. You shall take a wife for my son from
my family and from my father's house; then you shall be released from 41
the charge I have laid upon you. But if, when you come to my family,
they will not give her to you, you shall still be released from the charge."
So I came to the spring today, and I said, "O LORD God of my master 42
Abraham, if thou wilt make my journey successful, let it be like this. 43
Here I stand by the spring. When a young woman comes out to draw
water, I shall say to her, 'Give me a little water to drink from your jar.'
If she answers, 'Yes, do drink, and I will draw water for your camels 44
as well', she is the woman whom the LORD intends for my master's
son." Before I had finished praying silently, I saw Rebecca coming out 45
with her water-jar on her shoulder. She went down to the spring and
drew some water, and I said to her, "Please give me a drink." She 46
quickly lowered her jar from her shoulder and said, "Drink; and I will
water your camels as well." So I drank, and she also gave my camels
water. I asked her whose daughter she was, and she said, "I am the 47
daughter of Bethuel, the son of Nahor and Milcah." Then I put the

48 ring in her nose and the bracelets on her wrists, and I bowed low and prostrated myself before the LORD. I blessed the LORD the God of my master Abraham, who had led me by the right road to take my master's
49 niece for his son. Now tell me if you will keep faith and truth with my master. If not, say so, and I will turn elsewhere.'*a*
50 Laban and Bethuel answered, 'This is from the LORD; we can say
51 nothing for or against. Here is Rebecca herself; take her and go. She
52 shall be the wife of your master's son, as the LORD has decreed.' When Abraham's servant heard what they said, he prostrated himself on the
53 ground before the LORD. Then he brought out gold and silver ornaments, and robes, and gave them to Rebecca, and he gave costly gifts
54 to her brother and her mother. He and his men then ate and drank and spent the night there. When they rose in the morning, he said, 'Give
55 me leave to go back to my master.' Her brother and her mother said, 'Let the girl stay with us for a few days, say ten days, and then she
56 shall go.' But he said to them, 'Do not detain me, for the LORD has
57 granted me success. Give me leave to return to my master.' They said,
58 'Let us call the girl and see what she says.' They called Rebecca and asked her if she would go with the man, and she said, 'Yes, I will go.'
59 So they let their sister Rebecca and her nurse go with Abraham's
60 servant and his men. They blessed Rebecca and said to her:

'You are our sister, may you be the mother of myriads;
may your sons possess the cities*b* of their enemies.'

61 Then Rebecca and her companions mounted their camels at once and followed the man. So the servant took Rebecca and went his way.
62 Isaac meanwhile had moved on as far as Beer-lahai-roi and was
63 living in the Negeb. One evening when he had gone out into the open country hoping to meet them,*c* he looked up and saw camels approaching.
64 When Rebecca raised her eyes and saw Isaac, she slipped hastily from
65 her camel, saying to the servant, 'Who is that man walking across the open towards us?' The servant answered, 'It is my master.' So she
66 took her veil and covered herself. The servant related to Isaac all that
67 had happened. Isaac conducted her into the tent*d* and took her as his wife. So she became his wife, and he loved her and was consoled for the death of his mother.

25 1*e* ABRAHAM MARRIED another wife, whose name was Keturah.
2 She bore him Zimran, Jokshan, Medan, Midian, Ishbak and Shuah.
3 Jokshan became the father of Sheba and Dedan. The sons of Dedan
4 were Asshurim, Letushim and Leummim, and the sons of Midian

[*a*] *Lit.* to right or to left.   [*b*] *Lit.* gate.   [*c*] hoping...them: *or* to relieve himself.
[*d*] *Prob. rdg.; Heb. adds* Sarah his mother.   [*e*] *Verses 1–4: cp. 1 Chr. 1. 32, 33.*

were Ephah, Epher, Enoch, Abida and Eldaah. All these were
descendants of Keturah.

Abraham had given all that he had to Isaac; and he had already in 5,6
his lifetime given presents to the sons of his concubines, and had sent
them away eastwards, to a land of the east, out of his son Isaac's way.
Abraham had lived for a hundred and seventy-five years when he 7,8
breathed his last. He died at a good old age, after a very long life, and
was gathered to his father's kin. His sons, Isaac and Ishmael, buried 9
him in the cave at Machpelah, on the land of Ephron son of Zohar the
Hittite, east of Mamre, the plot which Abraham had bought from 10
the Hittites. There Abraham was buried with his wife Sarah. After the 11
death of Abraham, God blessed his son Isaac, who settled close by
Beer-lahai-roi.

This is the table of the descendants of Abraham's son Ishmael, 12
whom Hagar the Egyptian, Sarah's slave-girl, bore to him. These are 13[a]
the names of the sons of Ishmael named in order of their birth:
Nebaioth, Ishmael's eldest son, then Kedar, Adbeel, Mibsam, Mishma, 14
Dumah, Massa, Hadad,[b] Teman,[c] Jetur, Naphish and Kedemah. 15
These are the sons of Ishmael, after whom their hamlets and encamp- 16
ments were named, twelve princes according to their tribal groups.
Ishmael had lived for a hundred and thirty-seven years when he 17
breathed his last. So he died and was gathered to his father's kin.
Ishmael's sons inhabited the land from Havilah to Shur, which is east 18
of Egypt on the way to Asshur, having settled to the east of his brothers.

THIS IS THE TABLE of the descendants of Abraham's son Isaac. 19
Isaac's father was Abraham. When Isaac was forty years old he married 20
Rebecca the daughter of Bethuel the Aramaean from Paddan-aram and
the sister of Laban the Aramaean. Isaac appealed to the LORD on behalf 21
of his wife because she was barren; the LORD yielded to his entreaty,
and Rebecca conceived. The children pressed hard on each other in her 22
womb, and she said, 'If this is how it is with me, what does it mean?'
So she went to seek guidance of the LORD. The LORD said to her: 23

'Two nations in your womb,
two peoples, going their own ways from birth!
One shall be stronger than the other;
the older shall be servant to the younger.'

When her time had come, there were indeed twins in her womb. The 24,25
first came out red, hairy all over like a hair-cloak, and they named him
Esau.[d] Immediately afterwards his brother was born with his hand 26

[a] *Verses 13–16: cp. 1 Chr. 1. 29–31.* [b] *Or, with one MS.,* Harar. [c] *So Sept.; Heb.*
Tema. [d] *That is* Covering.

31

grasping Esau's heel, and they called him Jacob.[a] Isaac was sixty years
27 old when they were born. The boys grew up; and Esau became skilful
in hunting, a man of the open plains, but Jacob led a settled life and
28 stayed among the tents. Isaac favoured Esau because he kept him
29 supplied with venison, but Rebecca favoured Jacob. One day Jacob
prepared a broth and when Esau came in from the country, exhausted,
30 he said to Jacob, 'I am exhausted; let me swallow some of that
31 red broth': this is why he was called Edom.[b] Jacob said, 'Not till you
32 sell me your rights as the first-born.' Esau replied, 'I am at death's
33 door; what use is my birthright to me?' Jacob said, 'Not till you
34 swear!'; so he swore an oath and sold his birthright to Jacob. Then
Jacob gave Esau bread and the lentil broth, and he ate and drank and
went away without more ado. Thus Esau showed how little he valued
his birthright.

26   There came a famine in the land—not the earlier famine in Abraham's
time—and Isaac went to Abimelech the Philistine king at Gerar.
2 The LORD appeared to Isaac and said, 'Do not go down to Egypt, but
3 stay in this country as I bid you. Stay in this country and I will be with
you and bless you, for to you and to your descendants I will give all
these lands. Thus shall I fulfil the oath which I swore to your father
4 Abraham. I will make your descendants as many as the stars in the sky;
I will give them all these lands, and all the nations of the earth will pray
5 to be blessed as they are blessed—all because Abraham obeyed me and
6 kept my charge, my commandments, my statutes, and my laws.' So
Isaac lived in Gerar.
7   When the men of the place asked him about his wife, he told them
that she was his sister; he was afraid to say that Rebecca was his wife,
8 in case they killed him because of her; for she was very beautiful. When
they had been there for some considerable time, Abimelech the
Philistine king looked down from his window and saw Isaac and his
9 wife Rebecca laughing together. He summoned Isaac and said, 'So she
is your wife, is she? What made you say she was your sister?' Isaac
10 answered, 'I thought I should be killed because of her.' Abimelech said,
'Why have you treated us like this? One of the people might easily have
gone to bed with your wife, and then you would have made us liable to
11 retribution.' So Abimelech warned all the people, threatening that
whoever touched this man or his wife would be put to death.
12   Isaac sowed seed in that land, and that year he reaped a hundred-
13 fold, and the LORD blessed him. He became more and more powerful,
14 until he was very powerful indeed. He had flocks and herds and
15 many slaves, so that the Philistines were envious of him. They had
stopped up all the wells dug by the slaves in the days of Isaac's father

[a] *That is* He caught by the heel.   [b] *That is* Red.

Abraham, and filled them with earth. Isaac dug them again, all those 18
wells dug in his father Abraham's time, and stopped up by the
Philistines after his death, and he called them by the names which his
father had given them.

Then Abimelech said to him, 'Go away from here; you are too 16
strong for us.' So Isaac left that place and encamped in the valley of 17
Gerar, and stayed there. Then Isaac's slaves dug in the valley and 19*a*
found a spring of running water, but the shepherds of Gerar quarrelled 20
with Isaac's shepherds, claiming the water as theirs. He called the well
Esek,*b* because they made difficulties for him. His men then dug 21
another well, but the others quarrelled with him over that also, so he
called it Sitnah.*c* He moved on from there and dug another well, but 22
there was no quarrel over that one, so he called it Rehoboth,*d* saying,
'Now the LORD has given us plenty of room and we shall be fruitful
in the land.'

Isaac went up country from there to Beersheba. That same night the 23, 24
LORD appeared to him there and said, 'I am the God of your father
Abraham. Fear nothing, for I am with you. I will bless you and give
you many descendants for the sake of Abraham my servant.' So Isaac 25
built an altar there and invoked the LORD by name. Then he pitched his
tent there, and there also his slaves dug a well. Abimelech came to him 26
from Gerar with Ahuzzath his friend and Phicol the commander of his
army. Isaac said to them, 'Why have you come here? You hate me and 27
you sent me away.' They answered, 'We have seen plainly that the 28
LORD is with you, so we thought, "Let the two of us put each other to
the oath and make a treaty that will bind us." We have not attacked 29
you, we have done you nothing but good, and we let you go away
peaceably. Swear that you will do us no harm, now that the LORD has
blessed you.' So Isaac gave a feast and they ate and drank. They rose 30, 31
early in the morning and exchanged oaths. Then Isaac bade them
farewell, and they parted from him in peace. The same day Isaac's slaves 32
came and told him about a well that they had dug: 'We have found
water', they said. He named the well Shibah.*e* This is why the city is 33
called Beersheba*f* to this day.

When Esau was forty years old he married Judith daughter of 34
Beeri the Hittite, and Basemath daughter of Elon the Hittite; this 35
was a bitter grief to Isaac and Rebecca.

[*a*] *Verse 18 transposed to follow 15.*   [*b*] *That is* Difficulty.   [*c*] *That is* Enmity.   [*d*] *That is*
Plenty of room.   [*e*] *That is* Oath.   [*f*] *That is* Well of an Oath.

Jacob and Esau

27 WHEN ISAAC GREW OLD and his eyes became so dim that he
could not see, he called his elder son Esau and said to him, 'My
2 son', and he answered, 'Here I am.' Isaac said, 'Listen now: I am old
3 and I do not know when I may die. Take your hunting gear, your
quiver and your bow, and go out into the country and get me some
4 venison. Then make me a savoury dish of the kind I like, and bring it
5 to me to eat so that I may give you my blessing before I die.' Now
Rebecca was listening as Isaac talked to his son Esau. When Esau went
6 off into the country to find some venison and bring it home, she said
to her son Jacob, 'I heard your father talking to your brother Esau, and
7 he said, "Bring me some venison and make it into a savoury dish so that
I may eat it and bless you in the presence of the LORD before I die."
8,9 Listen to me, my son, and do what I tell you. Go to the flock and
pick me out two fine young kids, and I will make them into a savoury
10 dish for your father, of the kind he likes. Then take them in to your
father, and he will eat them so that he may bless you before he dies.'
11 Jacob said to his mother Rebecca, 'But my brother Esau is a hairy man,
12 and my skin is smooth. Suppose my father feels me, he will know I am
tricking him and I shall bring a curse upon myself instead of a blessing.'
13 His mother answered him, 'Let the curse fall on me, my son, but do as
14 I say; go and bring me the kids.' So Jacob fetched them and brought
them to his mother, who made them into a savoury dish of the kind that
15 his father liked. Then Rebecca took her elder son's clothes, Esau's best
clothes which she kept by her in the house, and put them on her younger
16 son Jacob. She put the goatskins on his hands and on the smooth nape
17 of his neck; and she handed her son Jacob the savoury dish and the
18 bread she had made. He came to his father and said, 'Father.' He
19 answered, 'Yes, my son; who are you?' Jacob answered his father, 'I
am Esau, your elder son. I have done as you told me. Come, sit up and
20 eat some of my venison, so that you may give me your blessing.' Isaac said
to his son, 'What is this that you found so quickly?', and Jacob answered,
21 'It is what the LORD your God put in my way.' Isaac then said to Jacob,
'Come close and let me feel you, my son, to see whether you are really
22 my son Esau.' When Jacob came close to his father, Isaac felt him and
said, 'The voice is Jacob's voice, but the hands are the hands of Esau.'
23 He did not recognize him because his hands were hairy like Esau's,
24 and that is why he blessed him. He said, 'Are you really my son Esau?',
25 and he answered, 'Yes.' Then Isaac said, 'Bring me some of your*a*

[a] *So Sept.; Heb. om.*

venison to eat, my son, so that I may give you my blessing.' Then
Jacob brought it to him, and he ate it; he brought wine also, and he
drank it. Then his father Isaac said to him, 'Come near, my son, and 26
kiss me.' So he came near and kissed him, and when Isaac smelt the 27
smell of his clothes, he blessed him and said:

> 'Ah! The smell of my son is like the smell of open country
>   blessed by the LORD.
> God give you dew from heaven   28
> and the richness of the earth,
> corn and new wine in plenty!
> Peoples shall serve you,   29
> nations bow down to you.
>   Be lord over your brothers;
> may your mother's sons bow down to you.
> A curse upon those who curse you;
> a blessing on those who bless you!'

Isaac finished blessing Jacob; and Jacob had scarcely left his father 30
Isaac's presence, when his brother Esau came in from his hunting. He 31
too made a savoury dish and brought it to his father. He said, 'Come,
father, and eat some of my venison, so that you may give me your
blessing.' His father Isaac said, 'Who are you?' He said, 'I am Esau, 32
your elder son.' Then Isaac became greatly agitated*a* and said, 'Then 33
who was it that hunted and brought me venison? I ate it all before you
came in and I blessed him, and the blessing will stand.' When Esau 34
heard what his father said, he gave a loud and bitter cry and said, 'Bless
me too, father.' But Isaac said, 'Your brother came treacherously and 35
took away your blessing.' Esau said, 'He is rightly called Jacob.*b* This 36
is the second time he has supplanted me. He took away my right as the
first-born and now he has taken away my blessing. Have you kept back
any blessing for me?' Isaac answered, 'I have made him lord over you, 37
and I have given him all his brothers as slaves. I have bestowed upon
him corn and new wine for his sustenance. What is there left that I can
do for you, my son?' Esau asked his father, 'Had you then only one 38
blessing, father? Bless me too, my father.' And Esau cried bitterly.
Then his father Isaac answered: 39

> 'Your dwelling shall be far from the richness of the earth,
>   far from the dew of heaven above.
> By your sword shall you live,   40
> and you shall serve your brother;
> but the time will come when you grow restive
> and break off his yoke from your neck.'

[*a*] *Or* incensed. [*b*] *That is* He supplanted.

35

41 Esau bore a grudge against Jacob because of the blessing which his father had given him, and he said to himself, 'The time of mourning for my father will soon be here; then I will kill my brother Jacob.'

42 When Rebecca was told what her elder son Esau was saying, she called her younger son Jacob, and she said to him, 'Esau your brother is 43 threatening to kill you. Now, my son, listen to me. Slip away at once 44 to my brother Laban in Harran. Stay with him for a while until your 45 brother's anger cools. When it has subsided and he forgets what you have done to him, I will send and fetch you back. Why should I lose you both in one day?'

46 Rebecca said to Isaac, 'I am weary to death of Hittite women! If Jacob marries a Hittite woman like those who live here, my life will not 28 be worth living.' Isaac called Jacob, blessed him and gave him instruc- 2 tions. He said, 'You must not marry one of these women of Canaan. Go at once to the house of Bethuel, your mother's father, in Paddan-aram, and there find a wife, one of the daughters of Laban, your mother's 3 brother. God Almighty bless you, make you fruitful and increase your 4 descendants until they become a host of nations. May he bestow on you and your offspring the blessing of Abraham, and may you thus possess the country where you are now living, the land which God gave to 5 Abraham!' So Isaac sent Jacob away, and he went to Paddan-aram to Laban, son of Bethuel the Aramaean, and brother to Rebecca the mother 6 of Jacob and Esau. Esau discovered that Isaac had given Jacob his blessing and had sent him away to Paddan-aram to find a wife there; and that when he blessed him he had forbidden him to marry a woman of 7 Canaan, and that Jacob had obeyed his father and mother and gone to 8 Paddan-aram. Then Esau, seeing that his father disliked the women of 9 Canaan, went to Ishmael, and, in addition to his other wives, he married Mahalath sister of Nebaioth and daughter of Abraham's son Ishmael.

10 Jacob set out from Beersheba and went on his way towards Harran. 11 He came to a certain place and stopped there for the night, because the sun had set; and, taking one of the stones there, he made it a pillow for 12 his head and lay down to sleep. He dreamt that he saw a ladder, which rested on the ground with its top reaching to heaven, and angels of 13 God were going up and down upon it. The LORD was standing beside him[a] and said, 'I am the LORD, the God of your father Abraham and the God of Isaac. This land on which you are lying I will give to you and 14 your descendants. They shall be countless as the dust upon the earth, and you shall spread far and wide, to north and south, to east and west. All the families of the earth shall pray to be blessed as you and your 15 descendants are blessed. I will be with you, and I will protect you wherever you go and will bring you back to this land; for I will not

[a] *Or* on it *or* by it.

36

leave you until I have done all that I have promised.' Jacob woke from 16
his sleep and said, 'Truly the LORD is in this place, and I did not
know it.' Then he was afraid and said, 'How fearsome is this place! 17
This is no other than the house of God, this is the gate of heaven.'
Jacob rose early in the morning, took the stone on which he had laid 18
his head, set it up as a sacred pillar and poured oil on the top of it.
He named that place Beth-El;[a] but the earlier name of the city was Luz. 19
     Thereupon Jacob made this vow: 'If God will be with me, if he will 20
protect me on my journey and give me food to eat and clothes to wear,
and I come back safely to my father's house, then the LORD shall be 21
my God, and this stone which I have set up as a sacred pillar shall be 22
a house of God. And of all that thou givest me, I will without fail allot
a tenth part to thee.'

JACOB CONTINUED HIS JOURNEY and came to the land of the 29
eastern tribes. There he saw a well in the open country and three flocks 2
of sheep lying beside it, because the flocks were watered from that well.
Over its mouth was a huge stone, and all the herdsmen used to gather 3
there and roll it off the mouth of the well and water the flocks; then
they would put it back in its place over the well. Jacob said to them, 4
'Where are you from, my friends?' 'We are from Harran', they replied.
He asked them if they knew Laban the grandson[b] of Nahor. They 5
answered, 'Yes, we do.' 'Is he well?' Jacob asked; and they answered, 6
'Yes, he is well, and here is his daughter Rachel coming with the flock.'
Jacob said, 'The sun is still high, and the time for folding the sheep has 7
not yet come. Water the flocks and then go and graze them.' But they 8
replied, 'We cannot, until all the herdsmen have gathered together and
the stone is rolled away from the mouth of the well; then we can water
our flocks.' While he was talking to them, Rachel came up with her 9
father's flock, for she was a shepherdess. When Jacob saw Rachel, the 10
daughter of Laban his mother's brother, with Laban's flock, he stepped
forward, rolled the stone off the mouth of the well and watered Laban's
sheep. He kissed Rachel, and was moved to tears. He told her that he 11, 12
was her father's kinsman and Rebecca's son; so she ran and told her
father. When Laban heard the news of his sister's son Jacob, he ran to 13
meet him, embraced him, kissed him warmly and welcomed him to his
home. Jacob told Laban everything, and Laban said, 'Yes, you are my 14
own flesh and blood.' So Jacob stayed with him for a whole month.
     Laban said to Jacob, 'Why should you work for me for nothing 15
simply because you are my kinsman? Tell me what your wages ought
to be.' Now Laban had two daughters: the elder was called Leah, and 16
the younger Rachel. Leah was dull-eyed, but Rachel was graceful and 17

[a] *That is* House of God.   [b] *Lit.* son.

37

18 beautiful. Jacob had fallen in love with Rachel and he said, 'I will work
19 seven years for your younger daughter Rachel.' Laban replied, 'It is
better that I should give her to you than to anyone else; stay with me.'
20 So Jacob worked seven years for Rachel, and they seemed like a few
21 days because he loved her. Then Jacob said to Laban, 'I have served
22 my time. Give me my wife so that we may sleep together.' So Laban
23 gathered all the men of the place together and gave a feast. In the
evening he took his daughter Leah and brought her to Jacob, and
24 Jacob slept with her. At the same time Laban gave his slave-girl Zilpah
25 to his daughter Leah. But when morning came, Jacob saw that it was
Leah and said to Laban, 'What have you done to me? Did I not work
26 for Rachel? Why have you deceived me?' Laban answered, 'In our
country it is not right to give the younger sister in marriage before the
27 elder. Go through with the seven days' feast for the elder, and the
younger shall be given you in return for a further seven years' work.'
28 Jacob agreed, and completed the seven days for Leah.
29   Then Laban gave Jacob his daughter Rachel as wife; and he gave his
30 slave-girl Bilhah to serve his daughter Rachel. Jacob slept with Rachel
also; he loved her rather than Leah, and he worked for Laban for a
31 further seven years. When the LORD saw that Leah was not loved, he
32 granted her a child; but Rachel was childless. Leah conceived and bore
a son; and she called him Reuben,*a* for she said, 'The LORD has seen
33 my humiliation; now my husband will love me.' Again she conceived
and bore a son and said, 'The LORD, hearing that I am not loved, has
34 given me this child also'; and she called him Simeon.*b* She conceived
again and bore a son; and she said, 'Now that I have borne him three
sons my husband and I will surely be united.' So she called him Levi.*c*
35 Once more she conceived and bore a son; and she said, 'Now I will
praise the LORD'; therefore she named him Judah.*d* Then for a while
she bore no more children.

30   When Rachel found that she bore Jacob no children, she became
jealous of her sister and said to Jacob, 'Give me sons, or I shall die.'
2 Jacob said angrily to Rachel, 'Can I take the place of God, who has
3 denied you children?' She said, 'Here is my slave-girl Bilhah. Lie with
her, so that she may bear sons to be laid upon my knees, and through
4 her I too may build up a family.' So she gave him her slave-girl Bilhah
5 as a wife, and Jacob lay with her. Bilhah conceived and bore Jacob a
6 son. Then Rachel said, 'God has given judgement for me; he has
7 indeed heard me and given me a son', so she named him Dan.*e* Rachel's
8 slave-girl Bilhah again conceived and bore Jacob another son. Rachel
said, 'I have played a fine trick on my sister, and it has succeeded'; so

[a] *That is* See, a son. [b] *That is* Hearing. [c] *That is* Union. [d] *That is* Praise.
[e] *That is* He has given judgement.

she named him Naphtali.*a* When Leah found that she was bearing no 9
more children, she took her slave-girl Zilpah and gave her to Jacob as
a wife, and Zilpah bore Jacob a son. Leah said, 'Good fortune has 10, 11
come', and she named him Gad.*b* Zilpah, Leah's slave-girl, bore Jacob 12
another son, and Leah said, 'Happiness has come,*c* for young women 13
will call me happy.' So she named him Asher.*d*

In the time of wheat-harvest Reuben went out and found some 14
mandrakes in the open country and brought them to his mother Leah.
Then Rachel asked Leah for some of her son's mandrakes, but Leah 15
said, 'Is it so small a thing to have taken away my husband, that you
should take my son's mandrakes as well?' But Rachel said, 'Very well,
let him sleep with you tonight in exchange for your son's mandrakes.'
So when Jacob came in from the country in the evening, Leah went 16
out to meet him and said, 'You are to sleep with me tonight; I have
hired you with my son's mandrakes.' That night he slept with her, and 17
God heard Leah's prayer, and she conceived and bore a fifth son. Leah 18
said, 'God has rewarded me, because I gave my slave-girl to my
husband.' So she named him Issachar.*e* Leah again conceived and bore 19
a sixth son. She said, 'God has endowed me with a noble dowry. Now 20
my husband will treat me in princely style, because I have borne him
six sons.' So she named him Zebulun.*f* Later she bore a daughter and 21
named her Dinah. Then God thought of Rachel; he heard her prayer 22
and gave her a child; so she conceived and bore a son and said, 'God 23
has taken away my humiliation.' She named him Joseph,*g* saying, 'May 24
the LORD add another son!'

When Rachel had given birth to Joseph, Jacob said to Laban, 'Let 25
me go, for I wish to return to my own home and country. Give me my 26
wives and my children for whom I have served you, and I will go; for
you know what service I have done for you.' Laban said to him, 'Let 27
me have my say, if you please. I have become prosperous and the LORD
has blessed me for your sake. So now tell me what I owe you in wages, 28
and I will give it you.' Jacob answered, 'You must know how I have 29
served you, and how your herds have prospered under my care. You 30
had only a few when I came, but now they have increased beyond
measure, and the LORD brought blessings to you wherever I went. But
is it not time for me to provide for my family?' Laban said, 'Then what 31
shall I give you?', but Jacob answered, 'Give me nothing; I will mind
your flocks*h* as before, if you will do what I suggest. Today I will go 32
over your flocks and pick out from them*i* every black lamb, and all the

[*a*] *That is* Trickery. [*b*] *That is* Good Fortune. [*c*] *So Targ.; Heb.* By my happiness.
[*d*] *That is* Happy. [*e*] *That is* Reward. [*f*] *That is* Prince. [*g*] *The name may mean
either* He takes away *or* May he add. [*h*] *Prob. rdg.; Heb. adds* I will watch. [*i*] *So Sept.;
Heb. adds* every spotted and brindled sheep and . . .

33 brindled and the spotted goats, and they shall be my wages. This is a
fair offer, and it will be to my own disadvantage later on, when we come
to settling my wages: every goat amongst mine that is not spotted or
brindled and every lamb that is not black will have been stolen.'
34, 35 Laban said, 'Agreed; let it be as you have said.' But that day he
removed the he-goats that were striped and brindled and all the spotted
and brindled she-goats, all that had any white on them, and every ram
36 that was black, and he handed them over to his own sons. Then he put
a distance of three days' journey between himself and Jacob, while
37 Jacob was left tending those of Laban's flocks that remained. Thereupon
Jacob took fresh rods of white poplar, almond, and plane tree, and
38 peeled off strips of bark, exposing the white of the rods. Then he fixed
the peeled rods upright in the troughs at the watering-places where the
flocks came to drink; they faced the she-goats that were on heat when
39 they came to drink. They felt a longing for the rods and they gave birth
40 to young that were striped and spotted and brindled. As for the rams,
Jacob divided them, and let the ewes run only with such of the rams in
Laban's flocks as were striped and black; and thus he bred separate
41 flocks for himself, which he did not add to Laban's sheep. As for the
goats, whenever the more vigorous were on heat, he put the rods in
42 front of them at the troughs so that they would long for the rods; he did
not put them there for the weaker goats. Thus the weaker came to be
43 Laban's and the stronger Jacob's. So Jacob increased in wealth more
and more until he possessed great flocks, male and female slaves,
camels, and asses.

31 JACOB LEARNT that Laban's sons were saying, 'Jacob has taken
everything that was our father's, and all his wealth has come from our
2 father's property.' He also noticed that Laban was not so well disposed
3 to him as he had once been. Then the LORD said to Jacob, 'Go back to
the land of your fathers and to your kindred. I will be with you.'
4 So Jacob sent to fetch Rachel and Leah to his flocks out in the country
5 and said to them, 'I see that your father is not as well disposed to me
6 as once he was; yet the God of my father has been with me. You know
7 how I have served your father to the best of my power, but he has
cheated me and changed my wages ten times over. Yet God did not let
8 him do me any harm. If Laban said, "The spotted ones shall be your
wages", then all the flock bore spotted young; and if he said, "The
striped ones shall be your wages", then all the flock bore striped young.
9, 10 God has taken away your father's property and has given it to me. In the
season when the flocks were on heat, I had a dream: I looked up and
saw that the he-goats mounting the flock were striped and spotted and
11 dappled. The angel of God said to me in my dream, "Jacob", and I

replied, "Here I am", and he said, "Look up and see: all the he-goats 12
mounting the flock are striped and spotted and dappled. I have seen all
that Laban is doing to you. I am the God who appeared to you at*a* 13
Bethel where you anointed a sacred pillar and where you made your
vow. Now leave this country at once and return to the land of your
birth."' Rachel and Leah answered him, 'We no longer have any part 14
or lot in our father's house. Does he not look on us as foreigners, now 15
that he has sold us and spent on himself the whole of the money paid
for us? But all the wealth which God has saved from our father's 16
clutches is ours and our children's. Now do everything that God has
said.' Jacob at once set his sons and his wives on camels, and drove off 17, 18
all the herds and livestock*b* which he had acquired in Paddan-aram, to
go to his father Isaac in Canaan.

When Laban the Aramaean had gone to shear his sheep, Rachel stole 19
her father's household gods,*c* and Jacob deceived Laban, keeping his 20
departure secret. So Jacob ran away with all that he had, crossed the 21
River and made for the hill-country of Gilead. Three days later, when 22
Laban heard that Jacob had run away, he took his kinsmen with him, 23
pursued Jacob for seven days and caught up with him in the hill-
country of Gilead. But God came to Laban in a dream by night and 24
said to him, 'Be careful to say nothing to Jacob, either good or bad.'

When Laban overtook him, Jacob had pitched his tent in the hill- 25
country of Gilead, and Laban pitched his in the company of his
kinsmen in the same hill-country. Laban said to Jacob, 'What have you 26
done? You have deceived me and carried off my daughters as though
they were captives taken in war. Why did you slip away secretly without 27
telling me? I would have set you on your way with songs and the music
of tambourines and harps. You did not even let me kiss my daughters 28
and their children. In this you were at fault. It is in my power to do 29
you an injury, but yesterday the God of your father spoke to me; he
told me to be careful to say nothing to you, either good or bad. I know 30
that you went away because you were homesick and pining for your
father's house, but why did you steal my gods?'

Jacob answered, 'I was afraid; I thought you would take your 31
daughters from me by force. Whoever is found in possession of your 32
gods shall die for it. Let our kinsmen here be witnesses: point out
anything I have that is yours, and take it back.' Jacob did not know
that Rachel had stolen the gods. So Laban went into Jacob's tent and 33
Leah's tent and that of the two slave-girls, but he found nothing. When
he came out of Leah's tent he went into Rachel's. Now she had taken 34
the household gods and put them in the camel-bag and was sitting on

[a] who...at: *so Sept.; Heb. om.* [b] *So Pesh.; Heb. adds* which he had acquired, the
herds he had purchased. [c] *Heb.* teraphim.

them. Laban went through everything in the tent and found nothing.
35 Rachel said to her father, 'Do not take it amiss, sir, that I cannot rise
in your presence: the common lot of woman is upon me.' So for all
his search Laban did not find his household gods.

36   Jacob was angry, and he expostulated with Laban, exclaiming, 'What
have I done wrong? What is my offence, that you have come after me
37 in hot pursuit and gone through all my possessions? Have you found
anything belonging to your household? If so, set it here in front of my
38 kinsmen and yours, and let them judge between the two of us. In all
the twenty years I have been with you, your ewes and she-goats have
39 never miscarried; I have not eaten the rams of your flocks; I have never
brought to you the body of any animal mangled by wild beasts, but
I bore the loss myself; you claimed compensation from me for anything
40 stolen by day or by night. This was the way of it: by day the heat
41 consumed me and the frost by night, and sleep deserted me. For
twenty years I have been in your household. I worked for you fourteen
years to win your two daughters and six years for your flocks, and you
42 changed my wages ten times over. If the God of my father, the God of
Abraham and the Fear of Isaac, had not been with me, you would have
sent me away empty-handed. But God saw my labour and my hardships, and last night he rebuked you.'

43   Laban answered Jacob, 'The daughters are my daughters, the
children are my children, the flocks are my flocks; all that you see is
mine. But as for my daughters, what can I do today about them and the
44 children they have borne? Come now, we will make an agreement, you
45 and I, and let it stand as a witness between us.' So Jacob chose a great
46 stone and set it upright as a sacred pillar. Then he told his kinsmen to
gather stones, and they took them and built a cairn, and there beside
47 the cairn they ate together. Laban called it Jegar-sahadutha,*a* and
48 Jacob called it Gal-ed.*b* Laban said, 'This cairn is witness today
49 between you and me.' For this reason it was named Gal-ed; it was also
named Mizpah,*c* for Laban said, 'May the LORD watch between you
50 and me, when we are parted from each other's sight. If you ill-treat
my daughters or take other wives beside them when no one is there to
51 see, then God be witness between us.' Laban said further to Jacob,
'Here is this cairn, and here the pillar which I have set up between us.
52 This cairn is witness and the pillar is witness: I for my part will not
pass beyond this cairn to your side, and you for your part shall not pass
53 beyond this cairn and this pillar to my side to do an injury, otherwise
the God of Abraham and the God of Nahor will judge between us.'*d*
And Jacob swore this oath in the name of the Fear of Isaac his father.

[a] *Aramaic for* Cairn of Witness. [b] *Hebrew for* Cairn of Witness. [c] *That is* Watch-
tower. [d] *So Sept.; Heb. adds* the God of their father.

He slaughtered an animal for sacrifice, there in the hill-country, and 54 summoned his kinsmen to the feast. So they ate together and spent the night there.

Laban rose early in the morning, kissed his daughters and their 55*a* children, blessed them and went home again. Then Jacob continued his 32 journey and was met by angels of God. When he saw them, Jacob said, 2 'This is the company of God', and he called that place Mahanaim.*b*

Jacob sent messengers on ahead to his brother Esau to the district of 3 Seir in the Edomite country, and this is what he told them to say to 4 Esau, 'My lord, your servant Jacob says, I have been living with Laban and have stayed there till now. I have oxen, asses, and sheep, and male 5 and female slaves, and I have sent to tell you this, my lord, so that I may win your favour.' The messengers returned to Jacob and said, 'We 6 met your brother Esau already on the way to meet you with four hundred men.' Jacob, much afraid and distressed, divided the people 7 with him, as well as the sheep, cattle, and camels, into two companies, thinking that, if Esau should come upon one company and destroy it, 8 the other company would survive. Jacob said, 'O God of my father 9 Abraham, God of my father Isaac, O Lord at whose bidding I came back to my own country and to my kindred, and who didst promise me prosperity, I am not worthy of all the true and steadfast love which 10 thou hast shown to me thy servant. When I crossed the Jordan, I had nothing but the staff in my hand; now I have two companies. Save me, 11 I pray, from my brother Esau, for I am afraid that he may come and destroy me, sparing neither mother nor child. But thou didst say, 12 I will prosper you and will make your descendants like the sand of the sea, which is beyond all counting.'

Jacob spent that night there; and as a present for his brother Esau 13 he chose from the herds he had with him two hundred she-goats, 14 twenty he-goats, two hundred ewes and twenty rams, thirty milch- 15 camels with their young, forty cows and ten young bulls, twenty she-asses and ten he-asses. He put each herd separately into the care of a 16 servant and said to each, 'Go on ahead of me, and leave gaps between the herds.' Then he gave these instructions to the first: 'When my brother 17 Esau meets you and asks you to whom you belong and where you are going and who owns these beasts you are driving, you are to say, "They 18 belong to your servant Jacob; he sends them as a present to my lord Esau, and he is behind us."' He gave the same instructions to the 19 second, to the third, and all the drovers, telling them to say the same thing to Esau when they met him. And they were to add, 'Your servant 20 Jacob is behind us'; for he thought, 'I will appease him with the present that I have sent on ahead, and afterwards, when I come into his

[*a*] *32. 1 in Heb.*   [*b*] *That is* Two Companies.

21 presence, he will perhaps receive me kindly.' So Jacob's present went on ahead of him, but he himself spent that night at Mahaneh.

22 During the night Jacob rose, took his two wives, his two slave-girls,
23 and his eleven sons, and crossed the ford of Jabbok. He took them and
24 sent them across the gorge with all that he had. So Jacob was left alone,
25 and a man wrestled with him there till[a] daybreak. When the man saw that he could not throw Jacob, he struck him in the hollow of his thigh,
26 so that Jacob's hip was dislocated as they wrestled. The man said, 'Let me go, for day is breaking', but Jacob replied, 'I will not let you go
27 unless you bless me.' He said to Jacob, 'What is your name?', and he
28 answered, 'Jacob.' The man said, 'Your name shall no longer be Jacob, but Israel,[b] because you strove with God and with men, and prevailed.'
29 Jacob said, 'Tell me, I pray, your name.' He replied, 'Why do you ask
30 my name?', but he gave him his blessing there. Jacob called the place Peniel,[c] 'because', he said, 'I have seen God face to face and my life
31 is spared.' The sun rose as Jacob passed through Penuel, limping
32 because of his hip. This is why the Israelites to this day do not eat the sinew of the nerve that runs in the hollow of the thigh; for the man had struck Jacob on that nerve in the hollow of the thigh.

33 Jacob raised his eyes and saw Esau coming towards him with four hundred men; so he divided the children between Leah and Rachel and
2 the two slave-girls. He put the slave-girls with their children in front,
3 Leah with her children next, and Rachel with Joseph last. He then went on ahead of them, bowing low to the ground seven times as he ap-
4 proached his brother. Esau ran to meet him and embraced him; he
5 threw his arms round him and kissed him, and they wept. When Esau looked up and saw the women and children, he said, 'Who are these with you?' Jacob replied, 'The children whom God has graciously
6 given to your servant.' The slave-girls came near, each with her
7 children, and they bowed low. Then Leah with her children came near and bowed low, and afterwards Joseph and Rachel came near and
8 bowed low also. Esau said, 'What was all that company of yours that I met?' And he answered, 'It was meant to win favour with you, my
9 lord.' Esau answered, 'I have more than enough. Keep what is yours,
10 my brother.' But Jacob said, 'On no account: if I have won your favour, then, I pray, accept this gift from me; for, you see, I come into your
11 presence as into that of a god, and you receive me favourably. Accept this gift which I bring you; for God has been gracious to me, and I have all I want.' So he urged him, and he accepted it.

12, 13 Then Esau said, 'Let us set out, and I will go at your pace.' But Jacob answered him, 'You must know, my lord, that the children are small; the flocks and herds are suckling their young and I am con-

[a] *Or* at.   [b] *That is* God strove.   [c] *That is* Face of God (*elsewhere* Penuel).

44

cerned for them, and if the men overdrive them for a single day, all my
beasts will die. I beg you, my lord, to go on ahead, and I will go by 14
easy stages at the pace of the children and of the livestock that I am
driving, until I come to my lord in Seir.' Esau said, 'Let me detail 15
some of my own men to escort you', but he replied, 'Why should my
lord be so kind to me?' That day Esau turned back towards Seir, 16
but Jacob set out for Succoth; and there he built himself a house and 17
made shelters for his cattle. Therefore he named that place Succoth.*a*

On his journey from Paddan-aram, Jacob came safely to the city of 18
Shechem in Canaan and pitched his tent to the east of it. The strip 19
of country where he had pitched his tent he bought from the sons of
Hamor father of Shechem for a hundred sheep.*b* There he set up an 20
altar and called it El-Elohey-Israel.*c*

DINAH, THE DAUGHTER whom Leah had borne to Jacob, went out to 34
visit the women of the country, and Shechem, son of Hamor the 2
Hivite the local prince, saw her; he took her, lay with her and dishonoured her. But he remained true to Jacob's daughter Dinah; he 3
loved the girl and comforted her. So Shechem said to his father Hamor, 4
'Get me this girl for a wife.' When Jacob heard that Shechem had 5
violated his daughter Dinah, his sons were with the herds in the open
country, so he said nothing until they came home. Meanwhile Shechem's 6
father Hamor came out to Jacob to discuss it with him. When Jacob's 7
sons came in from the country and heard, they were grieved and angry,
because in lying with Jacob's daughter he had done what the Israelites
held to be an outrage, an intolerable thing. Hamor appealed to them in 8
these terms: 'My son Shechem is in love with this girl; I beg you to let
him have her as his wife. Let us ally ourselves in marriage; you shall 9
give us your daughters, and you shall take ours in exchange. You must 10
settle among us. The country is open to you; make your home in it,
move about freely and acquire land of your own.' And Shechem said to 11
the girl's father and brothers, 'I am eager to win your favour and I will
give whatever you ask. Fix the bride-price and the gift as high as you 12
like, and I will give whatever you ask; but you must give me the girl in
marriage.'

Jacob's sons gave a dishonest reply to Shechem and his father 13
Hamor, laying a trap for them because Shechem had violated their
sister Dinah: 'We cannot do this,' they said; 'we cannot give our sister 14
to a man who is uncircumcised; for we look on that as a disgrace. There 15
is one condition on which we will consent: if you will follow our
example and have every male among you circumcised, we will give you 16

[a] *That is* Shelters.   [b] *Or* pieces of money (*cp. Josh. 24. 32; Job 42. 11*).   [c] *That is*
God the God of Israel.

our daughters and take yours for ourselves. Then we can live among
17 you, and we shall all become one people. But if you refuse to listen to
18 us and be circumcised, we will take the girl and go away.' Their
19 proposal pleased Hamor and his son Shechem; and the young man,
who was held in respect above anyone in his father's house, did not
hesitate to do what they had said, because his heart was taken by Jacob's
daughter.

20   So Hamor and Shechem went back to the city gate and addressed
21 their fellow-citizens: 'These men are friendly to us; let them live in our
country and move freely in it. The land has room enough for them. Let
22 us marry their daughters and give them ours. But these men will agree
to live with us and become one people on this one condition only: every
23 male among us must be circumcised as they have been. Will not their
herds, their livestock, and all their chattels then be ours? We need only
24 consent to their condition, and then they are free to live with us.' All
the able-bodied*a* men agreed with Hamor and Shechem, and every
25 single one of them was circumcised, every able-bodied male. Then two
days later, while they were still in great pain, Jacob's two sons Simeon
and Levi, full brothers to Dinah, armed themselves with swords, boldly
26 entered the city and killed every male. They cut down Hamor and his
son Shechem and took Dinah from Shechem's house and went off with
27 her. Then Jacob's other*b* sons came in over the dead bodies and
28 plundered the city, to avenge their sister's dishonour. They seized
flocks, cattle, asses, and everything, both inside the city and outside in
29 the open country; they also carried off all their possessions, their
dependants, and their women, and plundered everything in the houses.
30   Jacob said to Simeon and Levi, 'You have brought trouble on me,
you have made my name stink among the people of the country, the
Canaanites and the Perizzites. My numbers are few; if they muster
against me and attack me, I shall be destroyed, I and my household
31 with me.' They answered, 'Is our sister to be treated as a common
whore?'

35 GOD SAID TO JACOB, 'Go up to Bethel and settle there; build an
altar there to the God who appeared to you when you were running
2 away from your brother Esau.' So Jacob said to his household and to all
who were with him, 'Rid yourselves of the foreign gods which you have
3 among you, purify yourselves, and see your clothes are mended.*c* We
are going to Bethel, so that I can set up an altar there to the God who
answered me in the day of my distress, and who has been with me all
4 the way that I have come.' So they handed over to Jacob all the foreign
gods in their possession and the rings from their ears, and he buried

[*a*] *Lit.* going out of the city gate. [*b*] *So Vulg.; Heb. om.* [*c*] *Or* change your clothes.

them under the terebinth-tree near Shechem. Then they set out, and 5
the cities round about were panic-stricken, and the inhabitants dared not
pursue the sons of Jacob. Jacob and all the people with him came to 6
Luz, that is Bethel, in Canaan. There he built an altar, and he called 7
the place El-bethel, because it was there that God had revealed himself
to him when he was running away from his brother. Rebecca's nurse 8
Deborah died and was buried under the oak below Bethel, and he
named it Allon-bakuth.*a*

God appeared again to Jacob when he came back from Paddan-aram 9
and blessed him. God said to him: 10

> 'Jacob is your name,
> but your name shall no longer be Jacob:
> Israel shall be your name.'

So he named him Israel. And God said to him: 11

> 'I am God Almighty.
> Be fruitful and increase as a nation;
> a host of nations shall come from you,
> and kings shall spring from your body.
> The land which I gave to Abraham and Isaac I give to you; 12
> and to your descendants after you I give this land.'

God then left him,*b* and Jacob erected a sacred pillar in the place where 13, 14
God had spoken with him, a pillar of stone, and he offered a drink-
offering over it and poured oil on it. Jacob called the place where God 15
had spoken with him Bethel.

They set out from Bethel, and when there was still some distance to 16
go to Ephrathah, Rachel was in labour and her pains were severe.
While her pains were upon her, the midwife said, 'Do not be afraid, 17
this is another son for you.' Then with her last breath, as she was 18
dying, she named him Ben-oni,*c* but his father called him Benjamin.*d*
So Rachel died and was buried by the side of the road to Ephrathah, 19
that is Bethlehem. Jacob set up a sacred pillar over her grave; it is 20
known to this day as the Pillar of Rachel's Grave. Then Israel journeyed 21
on and pitched his tent on the other side of Migdal-eder. While Israel 22
was living in that district, Reuben went and lay with his father's
concubine Bilhah, and Israel came to hear of it.

The sons of Jacob were twelve. The sons of Leah: Jacob's first-born 23
Reuben, then Simeon, Levi, Judah, Issachar and Zebulun. The sons of 24
Rachel: Joseph and Benjamin. The sons of Rachel's slave-girl Bilhah: 25

[a] *That is* Oak of Weeping. [b] *So Vulg.; Heb. adds* in the place where he had spoken
with him. [c] *That is* Son of my ill luck. [d] *That is* Son of good luck *or* Son of the
right hand.

26 Dan and Naphtali. The sons of Leah's slave-girl Zilpah: Gad and
27 Asher. These were Jacob's sons, born to him in Paddan-aram. Jacob
came to his father Isaac at Mamre by Kiriath-arba, that is Hebron,
28 where Abraham and Isaac had dwelt. Isaac had lived for a hundred and
29 eighty years when he breathed his last. He died and was gathered to his
father's kin at a very great age, and his sons Esau and Jacob buried him.

36 THIS IS THE TABLE of the descendants of Esau: that is Edom.
2 Esau took Canaanite women in marriage, Adah daughter of Elon the
Hittite and Oholibamah daughter of Anah son*[a]* of Zibeon the Horite,*[b]*
3 and Basemath, Ishmael's daughter, sister of Nebaioth.
4,*[c]*5   Adah bore Eliphaz to Esau; Basemath bore Reuel, and Oholibamah
bore Jeush, Jalam and Korah. These were Esau's sons, born to him in
6 Canaan. Esau took his wives, his sons and daughters and everyone in
his household, his herds, his cattle, and all the chattels that he had
acquired in Canaan, and went to the district of Seir*[d]* out of the way of
7 his brother Jacob, because they had so much stock that they could not
live together; the land where they were staying could not support them
8 because of their herds. So Esau lived in the hill-country of Seir. Esau
is Edom.
9   This is the table of the descendants of Esau father of the Edomites
in the hill-country of Seir.
10   These are the names of the sons of Esau: Eliphaz was the son of
11 Esau's wife Adah. Reuel was the son of Esau's wife Basemath. The sons
12 of Eliphaz were Teman, Omar, Zepho, Gatam and Kenaz. Timna was
concubine to Esau's son Eliphaz, and she bore Amalek to him. These
13 are the descendants of Esau's wife Adah. These are the sons of Reuel:
Nahath, Zerah, Shammah and Mizzah. These were the descendants of
14 Esau's wife Basemath. These were the sons of Esau's wife Oholibamah
daughter of Anah son*[a]* of Zibeon. She bore him Jeush, Jalam and
Korah.
15   These are the chiefs descended from Esau. The sons of Esau's
eldest son Eliphaz: chief Teman, chief Omar, chief Zepho, chief Kenaz,
16 chief Korah, chief Gatam, chief Amalek. These are the chiefs descended
from Eliphaz in Edom. These are the descendants of Adah.
17   These are the sons of Esau's son Reuel: chief Nahath, chief Zerah,
chief Shammah, chief Mizzah. These are the chiefs descended from
Reuel in Edom. These are the descendants of Esau's wife Basemath.
18   These are the sons of Esau's wife Oholibamah: chief Jeush, chief
Jalam, chief Korah. These are the chiefs born to Oholibamah daughter
of Anah wife of Esau.

[a] *So Sam.; Heb.* daughter.   [b] *Prob. rdg. (cp. verses 20, 21); Heb.* Hivite.   [c] *Verses 4, 5,*
9–13: cp. 1 Chr. 1. 35–37.   [d] Seir: *so Pesh.; Heb. om.*

These are the sons of Esau, that is Edom, and these are their chiefs. 19
These are the sons of Seir the Horite, the original inhabitants of the 20[a]
land: Lotan, Shobal, Zibeon, Anah, Dishon, Ezer and Dishan. These 21
are the chiefs of the Horites, the sons of Seir in Edom. The sons of 22
Lotan were Hori and Hemam, and Lotan had a sister named Timna.
These are the sons of Shobal: Alvan, Manahath, Ebal, Shepho and 23
Onam.
These are the sons of Zibeon: Aiah and Anah. This is the Anah who 24
found some mules[b] in the wilderness while he was tending the asses of
his father Zibeon. These are the children of Anah: Dishon and 25
Oholibamah daughter of Anah.
These are the children of Dishon:[c] Hemdan, Eshban, Ithran and 26
Cheran. These are the sons of Ezer: Bilhan, Zavan and Akan. These 27, 28
are the sons of Dishan: Uz and Aran.
These are the chiefs descended from the Horites: chief Lotan, chief 29
Shobal, chief Zibeon, chief Anah, chief Dishon, chief Ezer, chief 30
Dishan. These are the chiefs that were descended from the Horites
according to their clans in the district of Seir.
These are the kings who ruled over Edom before there were kings in 31[d]
Israel: Bela son of Beor became king in Edom, and his city was named 32
Dinhabah; when he died, he was succeeded by Jobab son of Zerah of 33
Bozrah. When Jobab died, he was succeeded by Husham of Teman. 34
When Husham died, he was succeeded by Hadad son of Bedad, who 35
defeated Midian in Moabite country. His city was named Avith.
When Hadad died, he was succeeded by Samlah of Masrekah. When 36, 37
Samlah died, he was succeeded by Saul of Rehoboth on the River.
When Saul died, he was succeeded by Baal-hanan son of Akbor. When 38, 39
Baal-hanan died, he was succeeded by Hadar.[e] His city was named
Pau; his wife's name was Mehetabel daughter of Matred a woman
of Me-zahab.[f]
These are the names of the chiefs descended from Esau, according to 40
their families, their places, by name: chief Timna, chief Alvah, chief
Jetheth, chief Oholibamah, chief Elah, chief Pinon, chief Kenaz, chief 41, 42
Teman, chief Mibzar, chief Magdiel, and chief Iram: all chiefs of 43
Edom according to their settlements in the land which they possessed.
(Esau is the father of the Edomites.)

[a] *Verses 20–28: cp. 1 Chr. 1. 38–42.* [b] *Heb. word of uncertain mng.* [c] *So verse 21
and 1 Chr. 1. 41; Heb.* Dishan. [d] *Verses 31–43: cp. 1 Chr. 1. 43–54.* [e] *Or* Hadad; *cp.
1 Chr. 1. 50.* [f] *Or* daughter of Mezahab.

Joseph in Egypt

37 SO JACOB LIVED in Canaan, the country in which his father had
2 settled. And this is the story of the descendants of Jacob.
When Joseph was a boy of seventeen, he used to accompany his
brothers, the sons of Bilhah and Zilpah, his father's wives, when they
were in charge of the flock; and he brought their father a bad report of
3 them. Now Israel loved Joseph more than any other of his sons, because
he was a child of his old age, and he made him a long, sleeved robe.
4 When his brothers saw that their father loved him more than any of
them, they hated him and could not say a kind word to him.
5 Joseph had a dream; and when he told it to his brothers, they hated
6 him still more. He said to them, 'Listen to this dream I have had.
7 We were in the field binding sheaves, and my sheaf rose on end and
stood upright, and your sheaves gathered round and bowed low before
8 my sheaf.' His brothers answered him, 'Do you think you will one day
be a king and lord it over us?' and they hated him still more because of
9 his dreams and what he said. He had another dream, which he told to
his father and[a] his brothers. He said, 'Listen: I have had another dream.
10 The sun and moon and eleven stars were bowing down to me.' When he
told it to his father and his brothers, his father took him to task: 'What
is this dream of yours?' he said. 'Must we come and bow low to the
11 ground before you, I and your mother and your brothers?' His
brothers were jealous of him, but his father did not forget.
12 Joseph's brothers went to mind their father's flocks in Shechem.
13 Israel said to him, 'Your brothers are minding the flocks in Shechem;
14 come, I will send you to them', and he said, 'I am ready.' He said to
him, 'Go and see if all is well with your brothers and the sheep, and
bring me back word.' So he sent off Joseph from the vale of Hebron and
15 he came to Shechem. A man met him wandering in the open country
16 and asked him what he was looking for. He replied, 'I am looking for
17 my brothers. Tell me, please, where they are minding the flocks.' The
man said, 'They have gone away from here; I heard them speak of
going to Dothan.' So Joseph followed his brothers and he found them
18 in Dothan. They saw him in the distance, and before he reached them,
19 they plotted to kill him. They said to each other, 'Here comes that
20 dreamer. Now is our chance; let us kill him and throw him into one of
these pits and say that a wild beast has devoured him. Then we shall see
21 what will come of his dreams.' When Reuben heard, he came to his
22 rescue, urging them not to take his life. 'Let us have no bloodshed', he

[a] his father and: so Sept.; Heb. om.

said. 'Throw him into this pit in the wilderness, but do him no bodily harm.' He meant to save him from them so as to restore him to his father. When Joseph came up to his brothers, they stripped him of the 23 long, sleeved robe which he was wearing, took him and threw him into 24 the pit. The pit was empty and had no water in it.

Then they sat down to eat some food and, looking up, they saw an 25 Ishmaelite caravan coming in from Gilead on the way down to Egypt, with camels carrying gum tragacanth and balm and myrrh. Judah said to 26 his brothers, 'What shall we gain by killing our brother and concealing his death? Why not sell him to the Ishmaelites? Let us do him no harm, 27 for he is our brother, our own flesh and blood'; and his brothers agreed with him. Meanwhile some Midianite merchants passed by and drew 28 Joseph up out of the pit. They sold him for twenty pieces of silver to the Ishmaelites, and they brought Joseph to Egypt. When Reuben went 29 back to the pit, Joseph was not there. He rent his clothes and went back 30 to his brothers and said, 'The boy is not there. Where can I go?'

Joseph's brothers took his robe, killed a goat and dipped it in the 31 goat's blood. Then they tore the robe, the long, sleeved robe, brought 32 it to their father and said, 'Look what we have found. Do you recognize it? Is this your son's robe or not?' Jacob did recognize it, and he 33 replied, 'It is my son's robe. A wild beast has devoured him. Joseph has been torn to pieces.' Jacob rent his clothes, put on sackcloth and 34 mourned his son for a long time. His sons and daughters all tried to 35 comfort him, but he refused to be comforted. He said, 'I will go to my grave*a* mourning for my son.' Thus Joseph's father wept for him. Mean- 36 while the Midianites had sold Joseph in Egypt to Potiphar, one of Pharaoh's eunuchs, the captain of the guard.*b*

ABOUT THAT TIME Judah left his brothers and went south and pitched 38 his tent in company with an Adullamite named Hirah. There he saw 2 Bathshua the daughter of a Canaanite*c* and married her. He slept with her, and she conceived and bore a son, whom she*d* called Er. She con- 3, 4 ceived again and bore a son whom she called Onan. Once more she 5 conceived and bore a son whom she called Shelah, and she*e* ceased to bear children*f* when she had given birth to him. Judah found a wife for 6 his eldest son Er; her name was Tamar. But Judah's eldest son Er was 7 wicked in the LORD's sight, and the LORD took his life. Then Judah 8 told Onan to sleep with his brother's wife, to do his duty as the husband's brother and raise up issue for his brother. But Onan knew 9 that the issue would not be his; so whenever he slept with his brother's

[a] my grave: *Heb.* Sheol. [b] *Or* executioner. [c] *Lit.* saw the daughter of a Canaanite whose name was Shua (*cp. verse 12*). [d] *So some MSS.; others* he. [e] *So Sept.; Heb.* and he shall be. [f] ceased...children: *or* was at Kezib.

10 wife, he spilled his seed on the ground so as not to raise up issue for his brother. What he did was wicked in the LORD's sight, and the LORD took
11 his life. Judah said to his daughter-in-law Tamar, 'Remain as a widow in your father's house until my son Shelah grows up'; for he was afraid that he too would die like his brothers. So Tamar went and stayed in her father's house.
12 Time passed, and Judah's wife Bathshua died. When he had finished mourning, he and his friend Hirah the Adullamite went up to
13 Timnath at sheep-shearing. When Tamar was told that her father-in-
14 law was on his way to shear his sheep at Timnath, she took off her widow's weeds, veiled her face, perfumed herself and sat where the road forks in two directions on the way to Timnath. She did this because she knew that Shelah had grown up and she had not been
15 given to him as a wife. When Judah saw her, he thought she was a
16 prostitute, although she had veiled her face. He turned to her where she sat by the roadside and said, 'Let me lie with you', not knowing that she was his daughter-in-law. She said, 'What will you give me to lie
17 with me?' He answered, 'I will send you a kid from my flock', but she
18 said, 'Will you give me a pledge until you send it?' He asked what pledge he should give her, and she replied, 'Your seal and its cord, and the staff which you hold in your hand.' So he gave them to her and lay
19 with her, and she conceived. She then rose and went home, took off her
20 veil and resumed her widow's weeds. Judah sent the kid by his friend the Adullamite in order to recover the pledge from the woman, but he
21 could not find her. He asked the men of that place, 'Where is that temple-prostitute, the one who was sitting where the road forks?', but they
22 answered, 'There is no temple-prostitute here.' So he went back to Judah and told him that he had not found her and that the men of the
23 place had said there was no such prostitute there. Judah said, 'Let her keep my pledge, or we shall get a bad name. I did send a kid, but you
24 could not find her.' About three months later Judah was told that his daughter-in-law Tamar had behaved like a common prostitute and through her wanton conduct was with child. Judah said, 'Bring her out
25 so that she may be burnt.' But when she was brought out, she sent to her father-in-law and said, 'The father of my child is the man to whom these things belong. See if you recognize whose they are, the engraving
26 on the seal, the pattern of the cord, and the staff.' Judah recognized them and said, 'She is more in the right than I am, because I did not give her to my son Shelah.' He did not have intercourse with her again.
27, 28 When her time was come, there were twins in her womb, and while she was in labour one of them put out a hand. The midwife took a scarlet thread and fastened it round the wrist, saying, 'This one appeared
29 first.' No sooner had he drawn back his hand, than his brother came

out and the midwife said, 'What! you have broken out first!' So he was
named Perez.*a* Soon afterwards his brother was born with the scarlet 30
thread on his wrist, and he was named Zerah.*b*

WHEN JOSEPH WAS taken down to Egypt, he was bought by 39
Potiphar, one of Pharaoh's eunuchs, the captain of the guard, an
Egyptian. Potiphar bought him from the Ishmaelites who had brought
him there. The LORD was with Joseph and he prospered. He lived in 2
the house of his Egyptian master, who saw that the LORD was with him 3
and was giving him success in all that he undertook. Thus Joseph found 4
favour with his master, and he became his personal servant. Indeed,
his master put him in charge of his household and entrusted him with
all that he had. From the time that he put him in charge of his house- 5
hold and all his property, the LORD blessed the Egyptian's household
for Joseph's sake. The blessing of the LORD was on all that was his in
house and field. He left everything he possessed in Joseph's care, and 6
concerned himself with nothing but the food he ate.

Now Joseph was handsome and good-looking, and a time came when 7
his master's wife took notice of him and said, 'Come and lie with me.'
But he refused and said to her, 'Think of my master. He does not know 8
as much as I do about his own house, and he has entrusted me with all
he has. He has given me authority in this house second only to his own, 9
and has withheld nothing from me except you, because you are his
wife. How can I do anything so wicked, and sin against God?' She 10
kept asking Joseph day after day, but he refused to lie with her and be in
her company. One day he came into the house as usual to do his work, 11
when none of the men of the household were there indoors. She caught 12
him by his cloak, saying, 'Come and lie with me', but he left the cloak
in her hands and ran out of the house. When she saw that he had left 13
his cloak in her hands and had run out of the house, she called out to the 14
men of the household, 'Look at this! My husband has brought in a
Hebrew to make a mockery of us. He came in here to lie with me, but
I gave a loud scream. When he heard me scream and call out, he left his 15
cloak in my hand and ran off.' She kept his cloak with her until his 16
master came home, and then she repeated her tale. She said, 'That 17
Hebrew slave whom you brought in to make a mockery of me, has been
here with me. But when I screamed for help and called out, he left his 18
cloak in my hands and ran off.' When Joseph's master heard his wife's 19
story of what his slave had done to her, he was furious. He took Joseph 20
and put him in the Round Tower, where the king's prisoners were kept;
and there he stayed in the Round Tower. But the LORD was with 21
Joseph and kept faith with him, so that he won the favour of the

[a] *That is* Breaking out.   [b] *That is* Redness.

53

22 governor of the Round Tower. He put Joseph in charge of all the
23 prisoners in the tower and of all their work.*a* He ceased to concern
himself with anything entrusted to Joseph, because the LORD was with
Joseph and gave him success in everything.

40 It happened later that the king's butler and his baker offended their
2 master the king of Egypt. Pharaoh was angry with these two eunuchs,
3 the chief butler and the chief baker, and he put them in custody in the
house of the captain of the guard, in the Round Tower where Joseph
4 was imprisoned. The captain of the guard appointed Joseph as their
5 attendant, and he waited on them. One night, when they had been in
prison for some time, they both had dreams, each needing its own
interpretation—the king of Egypt's butler and his baker who were
6 imprisoned in the Round Tower. When Joseph came to them in the
7 morning, he saw that they looked dejected. So he asked these eunuchs,
who were in custody with him in his master's house, why they were so
8 downcast that day. They replied, 'We have each had a dream and there
is no one to interpret it for us.' Joseph said to them, 'Does not inter-
9 pretation belong to God? Tell me your dreams.' So the chief butler
told Joseph his dream: 'In my dream', he said, 'there was a vine in
10 front of me. On the vine there were three branches, and as soon as it
11 budded, it blossomed and its clusters ripened into grapes. Now I had
Pharaoh's cup in my hand, and I plucked the grapes, crushed them
12 into Pharaoh's cup and put the cup into Pharaoh's hand.' Joseph said
to him, 'This is the interpretation. The three branches are three days:
13 within three days Pharaoh will raise you*b* and restore you to your post,
and then you will put the cup into Pharaoh's hand as you used to do
14 when you were his butler. But when things go well with you, if you
think of me, keep faith with me and bring my case to Pharaoh's notice
15 and help me to get out of this house. By force I was carried off*c* from
the land of the Hebrews, and I have done nothing here to deserve
being put in this dungeon.'

16 When the chief baker saw that Joseph had given a favourable interpretation, he said to him, 'I too had a dream, and in my dream there
17 were three baskets of white bread on my head. In the top basket there
was every kind of food which the baker prepares for Pharaoh, and the
18 birds were eating out of the top basket on my head.' Joseph answered,
19 'This is the interpretation. The three baskets are three days: within
three days Pharaoh will raise you*d* and hang you up on a tree, and the
birds of the air will eat your flesh.'

20 The third day was Pharaoh's birthday and he gave a feast for all
his servants. He raised*e* the chief butler and the chief baker in the

[a] *So Sept.; Heb. adds* he was doing.   [b] *Lit.* lift up your head.   [c] *Or* stolen.   [d] *Lit.*
lift up your head; *so Vulg.; Heb. adds* from off you.   [e] *Lit.* lifted up the heads of.

presence of his court. He restored the chief butler to his post, and 21
the butler put the cup into Pharaoh's hand; but he hanged the chief 22
baker. All went as Joseph had said in interpreting the dreams for
them. Even so the chief butler did not remember Joseph, but forgot 23
him.

Nearly two years later Pharaoh had a dream: he was standing by the 41
Nile, and there came up from the river seven cows, sleek and fat, and 2
they grazed on the reeds. After them seven other cows came up from 3
the river, gaunt and lean, and stood on the river-bank beside the first
cows. The cows that were gaunt and lean devoured the cows that were 4
sleek and fat. Then Pharaoh woke up. He fell asleep again and had a 5
second dream: he saw seven ears of corn, full and ripe, growing on one
stalk. Growing up after them were seven other ears, thin and shrivelled 6
by the east wind. The thin ears swallowed up the ears that were full and 7
ripe. Then Pharaoh woke up and knew that it was a dream. When 8
morning came, Pharaoh was troubled in mind; so he summoned all the
magicians and sages of Egypt. He told them his dreams,*a* but there was
no one who could interpret them for him. Then Pharaoh's chief butler 9
spoke up and said, 'It is time for me to recall my faults. Once Pharaoh 10
was angry with his servants, and he imprisoned me and the chief baker
in the house of the captain of the guard. One night we both had dreams, 11
each needing its own interpretation. We had with us a young Hebrew, 12
a slave of the captain of the guard, and we told him our dreams and he
interpreted them for us, giving each man's dream its own interpretation. Each dream came true as it had been interpreted to us: I was 13
restored to my position, and he was hanged.'

Pharaoh thereupon sent for Joseph, and they hurriedly brought him 14
out of the dungeon. He shaved and changed his clothes, and came in to
Pharaoh. Pharaoh said to him, 'I have had a dream, and no one can 15
interpret it to me. I have heard it said that you can understand and
interpret dreams.' Joseph answered, 'Not I, but God, will answer for 16
Pharaoh's welfare.' Then Pharaoh said to Joseph, 'In my dream I was 17
standing on the bank of the Nile, and there came up from the river 18
seven cows, fat and sleek, and they grazed on the reeds. After them 19
seven other cows came up that were poor, very gaunt and lean; I have
never seen such gaunt creatures in all Egypt. These lean, gaunt cows 20
devoured the first cows, the fat ones. They were swallowed up, but 21
no one could have guessed that they were in the bellies of the others,
which looked as gaunt as before. Then I woke up. After I had fallen 22
asleep again,*b* I saw in a dream seven ears of corn, full and ripe, growing
on one stalk. Growing up after them were seven other ears, shrivelled, 23
thin, and blighted by the east wind. The thin ears swallowed up the 24

[a] *So Sam.; Heb.* dream.   [b] After...again: *so Sept.; Heb. om.*

seven ripe ears. When I told all this to the magicians, no one could explain it to me.'

25 Joseph said to Pharaoh, 'Pharaoh's dreams are one dream. God has
26 told Pharaoh what he is going to do. The seven good cows are seven years, and the seven good ears of corn are seven years. It is all one
27 dream. The seven lean and gaunt cows that came up after them are seven years, and the empty ears of corn blighted by the east wind will be
28 seven years of famine. It is as I have said to Pharaoh: God has let
29 Pharaoh see what he is going to do. There are to be seven years of great
30 plenty throughout the land. After them will come seven years of famine; all the years of plenty in Egypt will be forgotten, and the famine will
31 ruin the country. The good years will not be remembered in the land
32 because of the famine that follows; for it will be very severe. The doubling of Pharaoh's dream means that God is already resolved to do
33 this, and he will very soon put it into effect. Pharaoh should now look for a shrewd and intelligent man, and put him in charge of the country.
34 This is what Pharaoh should do: appoint controllers over the land, and take one fifth of the produce of Egypt during the seven years of plenty.
35 They should collect all this food produced in the good years that are coming and put the corn under Pharaoh's control in store in the cities,
36 and keep it under guard. This food will be a reserve for the country against the seven years of famine which will come upon Egypt. Thus the country will not be devastated by the famine.'

37, 38 The plan pleased Pharaoh and all his courtiers, and he said to them, 'Can we find a man like this man, one who has the spirit of a god[a] in
39 him?' He said to Joseph, 'Since a god[b] has made all this known to you,
40 there is no one so shrewd and intelligent as you. You shall be in charge of my household, and all my people will depend on your every word.
41 Only my royal throne shall make me greater than you.' Pharaoh said to Joseph, 'I hereby give you authority over the whole land of Egypt.'
42 He took off his signet-ring and put it on Joseph's finger, he had him
43 dressed in fine linen, and hung a gold chain round his neck. He mounted him in his viceroy's chariot and men cried 'Make way!'[c]
44 before him. Thus Pharaoh made him ruler over all Egypt and said to him, 'I am the Pharaoh. Without your consent no man shall lift hand
45 or foot throughout Egypt.' Pharaoh named him Zaphenath-paneah, and he gave him as wife Asenath the daughter of Potiphera priest of On. And Joseph's authority extended over the whole of Egypt.
46 Joseph was thirty years old when he entered the service of Pharaoh king of Egypt. When he took his leave of the king, he made a tour of
47 inspection through the country. During the seven years of plenty there
48 were abundant harvests, and Joseph gathered all the food produced in

[a] *Or* of God.　[b] *Or* God.　[c] *Egyptian word of uncertain mng.*

Egypt during those years and stored it in the cities, putting in each the food from the surrounding country. He stored the grain in huge 49 quantities; it was like the sand of the sea, so much that he stopped measuring: it was beyond all measure.

Before the years of famine came, two sons were born to Joseph by 50 Asenath the daughter of Potiphera priest of On. He named the elder 51 Manasseh,*a* 'for', he said, 'God has caused me to forget all my troubles and my father's family.' He named the second Ephraim,*b* 'for', he said, 52 'God has made me fruitful in the land of my hardships.' When the 53 seven years of plenty in Egypt came to an end, seven years of famine 54 began, as Joseph had foretold. There was famine in every country, but throughout Egypt there was bread. So when the famine spread through 55 all Egypt, the people appealed to Pharaoh for bread, and he ordered them to go to Joseph and do as he told them. In every region there was 56 famine, and Joseph opened all the granaries and sold corn to the Egyptians, for the famine was severe. The whole world came to Egypt 57 to buy corn from Joseph, so severe was the famine everywhere.

WHEN JACOB SAW that there was corn in Egypt, he said to his sons, 42 'Why do you stand staring at each other? I have heard that there is 2 corn in Egypt. Go down and buy some so that we may keep ourselves alive and not starve.' So Joseph's brothers, ten of them, went down to 3 buy grain from Egypt, but Jacob did not let Joseph's brother Benjamin 4 go with them, for fear that he might come to harm.

So the sons of Israel came down with everyone else to buy corn, 5 because of the famine in Canaan. Now Joseph was governor of all 6 Egypt, and it was he who sold the corn to all the people of the land. Joseph's brothers came and bowed to the ground before him, and 7 when he saw his brothers, he recognized them but pretended not to know them and spoke harshly to them. 'Where do you come from?' he asked. 'From Canaan,' they answered, 'to buy food.' Although Joseph 8 had recognized his brothers, they did not recognize him. He remembered 9 also the dreams he had had about them; so he said to them, 'You are spies; you have come to spy out the weak points in our defences.' They answered, 'No, sir: your servants have come to buy food. 10 We are all sons of one man. Your humble servants are honest men, we 11 are not spies.' 'No,' he insisted, 'it is to spy out our weaknesses that 12 you have come.' They answered him, 'Sir, there are twelve of us, all 13 brothers, sons of one man in Canaan. The youngest is still with our father, and one has disappeared.' But Joseph said again to them, 'No, 14 as I said before, you are spies. This is how you shall be put to the proof: 15 unless your youngest brother comes here, by the life of Pharaoh, you

[a] *That is* Causing to forget. [b] *That is* Fruit.

16 shall not leave this place. Send one of your number to bring your brother; the rest will be kept in prison. Thus your story will be tested, and we shall see whether you are telling the truth. If not, then, by the
17 life of Pharaoh, you must be spies.' So he kept them in prison for three days.
18   On the third day Joseph said to the brothers, 'Do what I say and
19 your lives will be spared; for I am a God-fearing man: if you are honest men, your brother there shall be kept in prison, and the rest of you
20 shall take corn for your hungry households and bring your youngest brother to me; thus your words will be proved true, and you will not die.'*a*
21   They said to one another, 'No doubt we deserve to be punished because of our brother, whose suffering we saw; for when he pleaded with us we refused to listen. That is why these sufferings have come
22 upon us.' But Reuben said, 'Did I not tell you not to do the boy a wrong? But you would not listen, and his blood is on our heads, and
23 we must pay.' They did not know that Joseph understood, because he
24 had used an interpreter. Joseph turned away from them and wept. Then, turning back, he played a trick on them. First he took Simeon
25 and bound him before their eyes; then he gave orders to fill their bags with grain, to return each man's silver, putting it in his sack, and to
26 give them supplies for the journey. All this was done; and they loaded
27 the corn on to their asses and went away. When they stopped for the night, one of them opened his sack to give fodder to his ass, and there
28 he saw his silver at the top of the pack. He said to his brothers, 'My silver has been returned to me, and here it is in my pack.' Bewildered and trembling, they said to each other, 'What is this that God has done to us?'
29   When they came to their father Jacob in Canaan, they told him all
30 that had happened to them. They said, 'The man who is lord of the
31 country spoke harshly to us and made out that we were spies. We said
32 to him, "We are honest men, we are not spies. There are twelve of us, all brothers, sons of one father. One has disappeared, and the youngest
33 is with our father in Canaan." This man, the lord of the country, said to us, "This is how I shall find out if you are honest men. Leave one of your brothers with me, take food*b* for your hungry households and go.
34 Bring your youngest brother to me, and I shall know that you are not spies, but honest men. Then I will restore your brother to you, and
35 you can move about the country freely."' But on emptying their sacks, each of them found his silver inside, and when they and their father
36 saw the bundles of silver, they were afraid. Their father Jacob said to them, 'You have robbed me of my children. Joseph has disappeared;

[a] *Prob. rdg.; Heb. adds* and they did so.   [b] *So Sept.; Heb. om.*

Simeon has disappeared; and now you are taking Benjamin. Everything is against me.' Reuben said to his father, 'You may kill both my sons if 37 I do not bring him back to you. Put him in my charge, and I shall bring him back.' But Jacob said, 'My son shall not go with you, for his 38 brother is dead and he alone is left. If he comes to any harm on the journey, you will bring down my grey hairs in sorrow to the grave.'[a]

The famine was still severe in the country. When they had used up 43 1, 2 the corn they had brought from Egypt, their father said to them, 'Go back and buy a little more corn for us to eat.' But Judah replied, 'The 3 man plainly warned us that we must not go into his presence unless our brother was with us. If you let our brother go with us, we will go down 4 and buy food for you. But if you will not let him, we will not go; for 5 the man said to us, "You shall not come into my presence, unless your brother is with you."' Israel said, 'Why have you treated me so badly? 6 Why did you tell the man that you had yet another brother?' They 7 answered, 'He questioned us closely about ourselves and our family: "Is your father still alive?" he asked, "Have you a brother?", and we answered his questions. How could we possibly know that he would tell us to bring our brother to Egypt?' Judah said to his father Israel, 8 'Send the boy with me; then we can start at once. By doing this we shall save our lives, ours, yours, and our dependants', and none of us will starve. I will go surety for him and you may hold me responsible. If I do 9 not bring him back and restore him to you, you shall hold me guilty all my life. If we had not wasted all this time, by now we could have gone 10 back twice over.'

Their father Israel said to them, 'If it must be so, then do this: take 11 in your baggage, as a gift for the man, some of the produce for which our country is famous: a little balsam, a little honey, gum tragacanth, myrrh, pistachio nuts, and almonds. Take double the amount of silver 12 and restore what was returned to you in your packs; perhaps it was a mistake. Take your brother with you and go straight back to the man. 13 May God Almighty make him kindly disposed to you, and may he send 14 back the one[b] whom you left behind, and Benjamin too. As for me, if I am bereaved, then I am bereaved.' So they took the gift and double 15 the amount of silver, and with Benjamin they started at once for Egypt, where they presented themselves to Joseph.

When Joseph saw Benjamin with them, he said to his steward, 16 'Bring these men indoors, kill a beast and make dinner ready, for they will eat with me at noon.' He did as Joseph told him and brought the 17 men into the house. When they came in they were afraid, for they 18 thought, 'We have been brought in here because of that affair of the silver which was replaced in our packs the first time. He means to

[a] *Heb.* Sheol.   [b] *So Sam.; Heb.* other.

trump up some charge against us and victimize us, seize our asses and
19 make us his slaves.' So they approached Joseph's steward and spoke to
20 him at the door of the house. They said, 'Please listen, my lord. After
21 our first visit to buy food, when we reached the place where we were to
spend the night, we opened our packs and each of us found his silver
in full weight at the top of his pack. We have brought it back with us,
22 and have added other silver to buy food. We do not know who put the
23 silver in our packs.' He answered, 'Set your minds at rest; do not be
afraid. It was your God, the God of your father,*[a]* who hid treasure for
you in your packs. I did receive the silver.' Then he brought Simeon
out to them.

24   The steward brought them into Joseph's house and gave them water
25 to wash their feet, and provided fodder for their asses. They had their
gifts ready when Joseph arrived at noon, for they had heard that they
26 were to eat there. When Joseph came into the house, they presented
him with the gifts which they had brought, bowing to the ground
27 before him. He asked them how they were and said, 'Is your father
28 well, the old man of whom you spoke? Is he still alive?' They answered,
'Yes, my lord, our father is still alive and well.' And they bowed low
29 and prostrated themselves. Joseph looked and saw his own mother's
son, his brother Benjamin, and asked, 'Is this your youngest brother,
of whom you told me?', and to Benjamin he said, 'May God be
30 gracious to you, my son!' Joseph was overcome; his feelings for his
brother mastered him, and he was near to tears. So he went into the
31 inner room and wept. Then he washed his face and came out; and,
32 holding back his feelings, he ordered the meal to be served. They
served him by himself, and the brothers by themselves, and the
Egyptians who were at dinner were also served separately; for Egyptians
33 hold it an abomination to eat with Hebrews. The brothers were seated
in his presence, the eldest first according to his age and so on down to
34 the youngest: they looked at one another in astonishment. Joseph sent
them each a portion from what was before him, but Benjamin's was
five times larger than any of the other portions. Thus they drank with
him and all grew merry.

44   Joseph gave his steward this order: 'Fill the men's packs with as
much food as they can carry and put each man's silver at the top of his
2 pack. And put my goblet, my silver goblet, at the top of the youngest
brother's pack with the silver for the corn.' He did as Joseph said.
3 At daybreak the brothers were allowed to take their asses and go on their
4 journey; but before they had gone very far from the city, Joseph said
to his steward, 'Go after those men at once, and when you catch up
5 with them, say, "Why have you repaid good with evil? Why have you

[a] *Or, with Sam.,* fathers.

stolen the silver goblet?^a It is the one from which my lord drinks, and
which he uses for divination. You have done a wicked thing."' When 6
he caught up with them, he repeated all this to them, but they replied, 7
'My lord, how can you say such things? No, sir, God forbid that we
should do any such thing! You remember the silver we found at the 8
top of our packs? We brought it back to you from Canaan. Why should
we steal silver or gold from your master's house? If any one of us is 9
found with the goblet, he shall die; and, what is more, my lord, we will
all become your slaves.' He said, 'Very well, then; I accept what you 10
say. The man in whose possession it is found shall be my slave, but the
rest of you shall go free.' Each man quickly lowered his pack to the 11
ground and opened it. The steward searched them, beginning with the 12
eldest and finishing with the youngest, and the goblet was found in
Benjamin's pack.

At this they rent their clothes; then each man loaded his ass and they 13
returned to the city. Joseph was still in the house when Judah and his 14
brothers came in. They threw themselves on the ground before him,
and Joseph said, 'What have you done? You might have known that 15
a man like myself would practise divination.' Judah said, 'What shall 16
we say, my lord? What can we say to prove our innocence? God has
found out our sin. Here we are, my lord, ready to be made your slaves,
we ourselves as well as the one who was found with the goblet.' Joseph 17
answered, 'God forbid that I should do such a thing! The one who was
found with the goblet shall become my slave, but the rest of you can go
home to your father in peace.'

Then Judah went up to him and said, 'Please listen, my lord. Let me 18
say a word to your lordship, I beg. Do not be angry with me, for you
are as great as Pharaoh. You, my lord, asked us whether we had a father 19
or a brother. We answered, "We have an aged father, and he has a 20
young son born in his old age; this boy's full brother is dead and he
alone is left of his mother's children,^b he alone, and his father loves
him." Your lordship answered, "Bring him down to me so that I may 21
set eyes on him." We told you, my lord, that the boy could not leave his 22
father, and that his father would die if he left him. But you answered, 23
"Unless your youngest brother comes here with you, you shall not
enter my presence again." We went back to your servant our father, and 24
told him what your lordship had said. When our father told us to go and 25
buy food, we answered, "We cannot go down; for without our youngest 26
brother we cannot enter the man's presence; but if our brother is with
us, we will go." Our father, my lord, then said to us, "You know that 27
my wife bore me two sons. One left me, and I said, 'He must have been 28
torn to pieces.' I have not seen him to this day. If you take this one 29

[*a*] Why...goblet?: *so Sept.; Heb. om.*   [*b*] *Or, with one form of Sept.,* to his father.

from me as well, and he comes to any harm, then you will bring down
30 my grey hairs in trouble to the grave."*a* Now, my lord, when I return
to my father without the boy—and remember, his life is bound up
31 with the boy's—what will happen is this: he will see that the boy is not
with us*b* and will die, and your servants will have brought down our
32 father's grey hairs in sorrow to the grave.*a* Indeed, my lord, it was I who
went surety for the boy to my father. I said, "If I do not bring him back
33 to you, then you shall hold me guilty all my life." Now, my lord, let
me remain in place of the boy as your lordship's slave, and let him go
34 with his brothers. How can I return to my father without the boy?
I could not bear to see the misery which my father would suffer.'

45 Joseph could no longer control his feelings in front of his attendants,
and he called out, 'Let everyone leave my presence.' So there was
2 nobody present when Joseph made himself known to his brothers, but
so loudly did he weep that the Egyptians and Pharaoh's household
3 heard him. Joseph said to his brothers, 'I am Joseph; can my father be
still alive?' His brothers were so dumbfounded at finding themselves
4 face to face with Joseph that they could not answer. Then Joseph said
to his brothers, 'Come closer', and so they came close. He said, 'I am
5 your brother Joseph whom you sold into Egypt. Now do not be distressed or take it amiss that you sold me into slavery here; it was God
6 who sent me ahead of you to save men's lives. For there have now been
two years of famine in the country, and there will be another five years
7 with neither ploughing nor harvest. God sent me ahead of you to ensure
that you will have descendants on earth, and to preserve you all, a great
8 band of survivors. So it was not you who sent me here, but God, and he
has made me a father*c* to Pharaoh, and lord over all his household and
9 ruler of all Egypt. Make haste and go back to my father and give him
this message from his son Joseph: "God has made me lord of all
10 Egypt. Come down to me; do not delay. You shall live in the land of
Goshen and be near me, you, your sons and your grandsons, your
11 flocks and herds and all that you have. I will take care of you there, you
and your household and all that you have, and see that you are not
12 reduced to poverty; there are still five years of famine to come." You
can see for yourselves, and so can my brother Benjamin, that it is
13 Joseph himself who is speaking to you. Tell my father of all the honour
which I enjoy in Egypt, tell him all you have seen, and make haste to
14 bring him down here.' Then he threw his arms round his brother
15 Benjamin and wept, and Benjamin too embraced him weeping. He
kissed all his brothers and wept over them, and afterwards his brothers
talked with him.

16 When the report that Joseph's brothers had come reached Pharaoh's

[a] *Heb.* Sheol.   [b] with us: *so Sam.; Heb. om.*   [c] *Or* counsellor.

house, he and all his courtiers were pleased. Pharaoh said to Joseph, 17
'Say to your brothers: "This is what you are to do. Load your beasts and
go to Canaan. Fetch your father and your households and bring them 18
to me. I will give you the best that there is in Egypt, and you shall
enjoy the fat of the land." You shall also tell them:*a* "Take wagons from 19
Egypt for your dependants and your wives and fetch your father and
come. Have no regrets at leaving your possessions, for all the best that 20
there is in Egypt is yours."' The sons of Israel did as they were told, and 21
Joseph gave them wagons, according to Pharaoh's orders, and food for
the journey. He provided each of them with a change of clothing, but 22
to Benjamin he gave three hundred pieces of silver and five changes of
clothing. Moreover he sent his father ten asses carrying the best that 23
there was in Egypt, and ten she-asses loaded with grain, bread, and
provisions for his journey. So he dismissed his brothers, telling them 24
not to quarrel among themselves on the road, and they set out. Thus 25
they went up from Egypt and came to their father Jacob in Canaan.
There they gave him the news that Joseph was still alive and that he 26
was ruler of all Egypt. He was stunned and could not believe it, but they 27
told him all that Joseph had said; and when he saw the wagons which
Joseph had sent to take him away, his spirit revived. Israel said, 'It is 28
enough. Joseph my son is still alive; I will go and see him before I die.'

So ISRAEL SET OUT with all that he had and came to Beersheba 46
where he offered sacrifices to the God of his father Isaac. God said to 2
Israel in a vision by night, 'Jacob, Jacob', and he answered, 'I am here.'
God said, 'I am God, the God of your father. Do not be afraid to go 3
down to Egypt, for there I will make you a great nation. I will go down 4
with you to Egypt, and I myself will bring you back again without fail;
and Joseph shall close your eyes.' So Jacob set out from Beersheba. 5
Israel's sons conveyed their father Jacob, their dependants, and their
wives in the wagons which Pharaoh had sent to carry them. They took 6
the herds and the stock which they had acquired in Canaan and came
to Egypt, Jacob and all his descendants with him, his sons and their 7
sons, his daughters and his sons' daughters: he brought all his
descendants to Egypt.

These are the names of the Israelites who entered Egypt: Jacob and 8*b*
his sons, as follows: Reuben, Jacob's eldest son. The sons of Reuben: 9
Enoch, Pallu, Hezron and Carmi. The sons of Simeon: Jemuel, Jamin, 10
Ohad, Jachin, Zohar, and Saul, who was the son of a Canaanite woman.
The sons of Levi: Gershon, Kohath and Merari. The sons of Judah: 11, 12
Er, Onan, Shelah, Perez and Zerah; of these Er and Onan died in

[a] *So Sept.; Heb.* You are commanded.   [b] *Verses 8–25: cp. Exod. 6. 14–16; Num. 26.*
5–50; 1 Chr. 4. 1, 24; 5. 3; 6. 1; 7. 1, 6, 13, 30; 8. 1–5.

13 Canaan. The sons of Perez were Hezron and Hamul.*a* The sons of
14 Issachar: Tola, Pua, Iob and Shimron. The sons of Zebulun: Sered,
15 Elon and Jahleel. These are the sons of Leah whom she bore to Jacob
in Paddan-aram, and there was also his daughter Dinah. His sons and
daughters numbered thirty-three in all.

16 The sons of Gad: Ziphion, Haggi, Shuni, Ezbon, Eri, Arodi and
17 Areli. The sons of Asher: Imnah, Ishvah, Ishvi, Beriah, and their
18 sister Serah. The sons of Beriah: Heber and Malchiel. These are the
descendants of Zilpah whom Laban gave to his daughter Leah;
sixteen in all, born to Jacob.

19, 20 The sons of Jacob's wife Rachel: Joseph and Benjamin. Manasseh
and Ephraim were born to Joseph in Egypt. Asenath daughter of
21 Potiphera priest of On bore them to him. The sons of Benjamin: Bela,
Becher and Ashbel; and the sons of Bela:*b* Gera, Naaman, Ehi, Rosh,
22 Muppim, Huppim and Ard. These are the descendants of Rachel;
fourteen in all, born to Jacob.

23, 24 The son*c* of Dan: Hushim. The sons of Naphtali: Jahzeel, Guni,
25 Jezer and Shillem. These are the descendants of Bilhah whom Laban
gave to his daughter Rachel; seven in all, born to Jacob.

26 The persons belonging to Jacob who came to Egypt, all his direct
descendants, not counting the wives of his sons, were sixty-six in all.
27 Two sons were born to Joseph in Egypt. Thus the house of Jacob
numbered seventy*d* when it entered Egypt.

28 Judah was sent ahead that he might appear*e* before Joseph in Goshen,
29 and so they entered Goshen. Joseph had his chariot made ready and
went up to meet his father Israel in Goshen. When they met, he threw
his arms round him and wept, and embraced him for a long time,
30 weeping. Israel said to Joseph, 'I have seen your face again, and you are
31 still alive. Now I am ready to die.' Joseph said to his brothers and to his
father's household, 'I will go and tell Pharaoh; I will say to him, "My
brothers and my father's household who were in Canaan have come to
32 me."' Now his brothers were shepherds, men with their own flocks and
herds, and they had brought them with them, their flocks and herds and
33 all that they possessed. So Joseph said, 'When Pharaoh summons you
34 and asks you what your occupation is, you must say, "My lord, we
have been herdsmen all our lives, as our fathers were before us." You
must say this if you are to settle in the land of Goshen, because all
shepherds are an abomination to the Egyptians.'

47 Joseph came and told Pharaoh, 'My father and my brothers have
arrived from Canaan, with their flocks and their cattle and all that they
2 have, and they are now in Goshen.' Then he chose five of his brothers

[a] Or, with Sam., Hamuel. [b] and the sons of Bela: so Sept. (cp. 1 Chr. 8. 3); Heb. om.
[c] Prob. rdg.; Heb. sons. [d] Or, with Sept., seventy-five. [e] So Sam.; Heb. guide.

and presented them to Pharaoh, who asked them what their occupation 3
was, and they answered, 'My lord, we are shepherds, we and our fathers
before us, and we have come to stay in this land; for there is no pasture 4
in Canaan for our sheep, because the famine there is so severe. We beg
you, my lord, to let us settle now in Goshen.' Pharaoh said to Joseph, 5
'So your father and your brothers have come to you. The land of 6
Egypt is yours; settle them in the best part of it. Let them live in
Goshen, and if you know of any capable men among them, make them
chief herdsmen over my cattle.'

Then Joseph brought his father in and presented him to Pharaoh, and 7
Jacob gave Pharaoh his blessing. Pharaoh asked Jacob his age, and he 8,9
answered, 'The years of my earthly sojourn are one hundred and thirty;
hard years they have been and few, not equal to the years that my
fathers lived in their time.' Jacob then blessed Pharaoh and went out 10
from his presence. So Joseph settled his father and his brothers, and 11
gave them lands in Egypt, in the best part of the country, in the district
of Rameses, as Pharaoh had ordered. He supported his father, his 12
brothers, and all his father's household with all the food they needed.[a]

There was no bread in the whole country, so very severe was the 13
famine, and Egypt and Canaan were laid low by it. Joseph collected all 14
the silver in Egypt and Canaan in return for the corn which the people
bought, and deposited it in Pharaoh's treasury. When all the silver in 15
Egypt and Canaan had been used up, the Egyptians came to Joseph
and said, 'Give us bread, or we shall die before your eyes. Our silver is
all spent.' Joseph said, 'If your silver is spent, give me your herds and 16
I will give you bread in return.' So they brought their herds to Joseph, 17
who gave them bread in exchange for their horses, their flocks of sheep
and herds of cattle, and their asses. He maintained them that year with
bread in exchange for their herds. The year came to an end, and the 18
following year they came to him again and said, 'My lord, we cannot
conceal it from you: our silver is all gone and our herds of cattle are
yours. Nothing is left for your lordship but our bodies and our lands.
Why should we perish before your eyes, we and our land as well? Take 19
us and our land in payment for bread, and we and our land alike will be
in bondage to Pharaoh. Give us seed-corn to keep us alive, or we shall
die and our land will become desert.' So Joseph bought all the land in 20
Egypt for Pharaoh, because the Egyptians sold all their fields, so severe
was the famine; the land became Pharaoh's. As for the people, Pharaoh 21
set them to work as slaves[b] from one end of the territory of Egypt to the
other. But Joseph did not buy the land which belonged to the priests; 22
they had a fixed allowance from Pharaoh and lived on this, so that they
had no need to sell their land.

[a] *Lit.* with food to a drop.   [b] *So Sam.; Heb.* gathered them into the cities.

23 Joseph said to the people, 'Listen; I have today bought you and your
24 land for Pharaoh. Here is seed-corn for you. Sow the land, and give one
fifth of the crop to Pharaoh. Four fifths shall be yours to provide seed
for your fields and food for yourselves, your households, and your
25 dependants.' The people said, 'You have saved our lives. If it please
26 your lordship, we will be Pharaoh's slaves.' Joseph established it as a
law in Egypt that one fifth should belong to Pharaoh, and this is still
in force. It was only the priests' land that did not pass into Pharaoh's
hands.

27 Thus Israel settled in Egypt, in Goshen; there they acquired land,
28 and were fruitful and increased greatly. Jacob stayed in Egypt for
seventeen years and lived to be a hundred and forty-seven years old.
29 When the time of his*a* death drew near, he summoned his son Joseph
and said to him, 'If I may now claim this favour from you, put your
hand under my thigh and swear by the LORD*b* that you will deal
30 loyally and truly with me and not bury me in Egypt. When I die like
my forefathers, you shall carry me from Egypt and bury me in their
31 grave.' He answered, 'I will do as you say'; but Jacob said, 'Swear it.'
So he swore the oath, and Israel sank down over the end of the bed.*c*

48 The time came when Joseph was told that his father was ill, so he took
2 with him his two sons, Manasseh and Ephraim. Jacob heard that his
son Joseph was coming to him, and he*d* summoned his strength and
3 sat up on the bed. Jacob said to Joseph, 'God Almighty appeared to me
4 at Luz in Canaan and blessed me. He said to me, "I will make you
fruitful and increase your descendants until they become a host of
nations. I will give this land to your descendants after you as a perpetual
5 possession." Now, your two sons, who were born to you in Egypt
before I came here, shall be counted as my sons; Ephraim and Manasseh
6 shall be mine as Reuben and Simeon are. Any children born to you
after them shall be counted as yours, but in respect of their tribal
territory they shall be reckoned under their elder brothers' names.
7 As I was coming from Paddan-aram*e* I was bereaved of Rachel your
mother*f* on the way, in Canaan, whilst there was still some distance to
go to Ephrath,*g* and I buried her there by the road to Ephrath,*g* that is
Bethlehem.'

8,9 When Israel saw Joseph's sons, he said, 'Who are these?' Joseph
replied to his father, 'They are my sons whom God has given me here.'
Israel said, 'Bring them to me, I beg you, so that I may take them on
10 my knees.'*h* Now Israel's eyes were dim with age, and he could not

---

[a] Heb. Israel's. [b] and...LORD: *prob. rdg., cp. Pesh.*; Heb. om. [c] Or, *with Sept.*, top
of his staff (*cp. Heb. 11. 21*). [d] Heb. Israel. [e] So Sam.; Heb. Paddan. [f] your
mother: *so Sam.*; Heb. om. [g] Or, *with Sam.* (*cp. 35. 16, 19*), Ephrathah. [h] Or *may
bless them.*

see; so Joseph brought the boys close to his father, and he kissed them
and embraced them. He said to Joseph, 'I had not expected to see your 11
face again, and now God has granted me to see your sons also.' Joseph 12
took them from his father's knees and bowed to the ground. Then he 13
took the two of them, Ephraim on his right at Israel's left and Manasseh
on his left at Israel's right, and brought them close to him. Israel 14
stretched out his right hand and laid it on Ephraim's head, although
he was the younger, and, crossing his hands, laid his left hand on
Manasseh's head; but Manasseh was the elder. He blessed Joseph 15
and said:

> 'The God in whose presence my forefathers lived,
>   my forefathers Abraham and Isaac,
>   the God who has been my shepherd all my life until this day,
>   the angel who ransomed me from all misfortune,   16
>   may he bless these boys;
>   they shall be called by my name,
>   and by that of my forefathers, Abraham and Isaac;
>   may they grow into a great people on earth.'

When Joseph saw that his father was laying his right hand on Ephraim's 17
head, he was displeased; so he took hold of his father's hand to move it
from Ephraim's head to Manasseh's. He said, 'That is not right, my 18
father. This is the elder; lay your right hand on his head.' But his father 19
refused; he said, 'I know, my son, I know. He too shall become a
people; he too shall become great, but his younger brother shall be
greater than he, and his descendants shall be a whole nation in themselves.' That day he blessed them and said: 20

> 'When a blessing is pronounced in Israel,
>   men shall use your names*a* and say,
>   God make you like Ephraim and Manasseh',

thus setting Ephraim before Manasseh. Then Israel said to Joseph, 21
'I am dying. God will be with you and will bring you back to the land
of your fathers. I give you one ridge of land*b* more than your brothers: 22
I took it from the Amorites with my sword and my bow.'

JACOB SUMMONED HIS SONS and said, 'Come near, and I will tell 49
you what will happen to you in days to come.

> Gather round me and listen, you sons of Jacob;   2
>   listen to Israel your father.
> Reuben, you are my first-born,   3

[a] *So Sept.; Heb. has the singular.* [b] ridge of land: *Heb.* shechem, *meaning* shoulder.

my strength and the first fruit of my vigour,
excelling in pride, excelling in might,
4   turbulent as a flood, you shall not excel;
because you climbed into your father's bed;
then you defiled his concubine's couch.

5   Simeon and Levi are brothers,
their spades*a* became weapons of violence.

6   My soul shall not enter their council,
my heart shall not join their company;
for in their anger they killed men,
wantonly they hamstrung oxen.

7   A curse be on their anger because it was fierce;
a curse on their wrath because it was ruthless!
I will scatter them in Jacob,
I will disperse them in Israel.

8   Judah, your brothers shall praise you,
your hand is on the neck of your enemies.
Your father's sons shall do you homage.

9   Judah, you lion's whelp,
you have returned from the kill, my son,
and crouch and stretch like a lion;
and, like a lion,*b* who dare rouse you*c*?

10   The sceptre shall not pass from Judah,
nor the staff from his descendants,*d*
so long as tribute is brought to him*e*
and the obedience of the nations is his.

11   To the vine he tethers his ass,
and the colt of his ass to the red vine;
he washes his cloak in wine,
his robes in the blood of grapes.

12   Darker than wine are his eyes,
his teeth whiter than milk.

13   Zebulun dwells by the sea-shore,
his shore is a haven for ships,
and his frontier rests on Sidon.

14   Issachar, a gelded*f* ass
lying down in the cattle-pens,

15   saw that a settled home was good
and that the land was pleasant,
so he bent his back to the burden
and submitted to perpetual forced labour.

[a] *Heb. word of uncertain mng.*   [b] *Or* lioness.   [c] *Heb.* him.   [d] *Lit.* from between his feet.   [e] *so...* him: *or, as otherwise read,* until he comes to Shiloh.   [f] *So Sam.; Heb.* bony.

Dan—how insignificant his people,   16
 lowly as any tribe in Israel!*^a*
Let Dan be a viper on the road,   17
 a horned snake on the path,
 who bites the horse's fetlock
 so that the rider tumbles backwards.

For thy salvation I wait in hope, O LORD.   18

Gad is raided by raiders,   19
 and he raids them from the rear.
Asher shall have rich food as daily fare,   20
 and provide dishes fit for a king.
Naphtali is a spreading terebinth   21
 putting forth lovely boughs.
Joseph is a fruitful tree*^b* by a spring   22
 with branches climbing over the wall.
 The archers savagely attacked him,   23
 they shot at him and pressed him hard,
 but their bow was splintered by the Eternal   24
 and the sinews of their arms were torn apart*^c*
 by the power of the Strong One of Jacob,
 by the name of the Shepherd*^d* of Israel,
 by the God of your father—so may he help you,   25
 by God*^e* Almighty—so may he bless you
 with the blessings of heaven above,
 the blessings of the deep that lurks below.
 The blessings of breast and womb
 and the blessings of your father are stronger   26
 than the blessings of the everlasting pools*^f*
 and the bounty of the eternal hills.
 They shall be on the head of Joseph,
 on the brow of the prince among*^g* his brothers.
Benjamin is a ravening wolf: 27
 in the morning he devours the prey,
 in the evening he snatches a share of the spoil.'

These, then, are the twelve tribes of Israel, and this is what their 28
father Jacob said to them, when he blessed them each in turn. He gave 29
them his last charge and said, 'I shall soon be gathered to my father's
kin; bury me with my forefathers in the cave on the plot of land which

[a] *Or* Dan shall judge his people as one of the tribes of Israel.   [b] *Or* a fruitful ben-tree.
[c] *Prob. rdg., cp. Sept.; Heb.* and the arms of his hands were active.   [d] *Prob. rdg.; Heb.*
adds stone.   [e] *So Sam.; Heb.* with.   [f] *Or* hills.   [g] the prince among: *or* the one
cursed by.

30 belonged to Ephron the Hittite, that is the cave on the plot of land at Machpelah east of Mamre in Canaan, the field which Abraham bought
31 from Ephron the Hittite for a burial-place. There Abraham was buried with his wife Sarah; there Isaac and his wife Rebecca were buried; and
32 there I buried Leah. The land and the cave on it were bought from the
33 Hittites.' When Jacob had finished giving his last charge to his sons, he drew his feet up on to the bed, breathed his last, and was gathered to his father's kin.

50 Then Joseph threw himself upon his father, weeping and kissing his
2 face. He ordered the physicians in his service to embalm his father
3 Israel, and they did so, finishing the task in forty days, which was the usual time for embalming. The Egyptians mourned him for seventy
4 days; and then, when the days of mourning for Israel were over, Joseph approached members of Pharaoh's household and said, 'If I can count on your goodwill, then speak for me to Pharaoh; tell him that
5 my father made me take an oath, saying, "I am dying. Bury me in the grave that I bought*a* for myself in Canaan." Ask him to let me go up and
6 bury my father, and afterwards I will return.' Pharaoh answered, 'Go
7 and bury your father, as he has made you swear to do.' So Joseph went to bury his father, accompanied by all Pharaoh's courtiers, the elders
8 of his household, and all the elders of Egypt, together with all Joseph's own household, his brothers, and his father's household; only their
9 dependants, with the flocks and herds, were left in Goshen. He took
10 with him chariots and horsemen; they were a very great company. When they came to the threshing-floor of Atad beside the river Jordan, they raised a loud and bitter lament; and there Joseph observed seven days'
11 mourning for his father. When the Canaanites who lived there saw this mourning at the threshing-floor of Atad, they said, 'How bitterly the Egyptians are mourning!'; accordingly they named the place beside the Jordan Abel-mizraim.*b*

12, 13 Thus Jacob's sons did what he had told them to do. They took him to Canaan and buried him in the cave on the plot of land at Machpelah, the land which Abraham had bought as a burial-place from Ephron the
14 Hittite, to the east of Mamre. Then, after he had buried his father, Joseph returned to Egypt with his brothers and all who had gone up with him.

15 When their father was dead Joseph's brothers were afraid and said, 'What if Joseph should bear a grudge against us and pay us out for all
16 the harm that we did to him?' They therefore approached*c* Joseph with these words: 'In his last words to us before he died, your father
17 gave us this message for you: "I ask you to forgive your brothers' crime

[a] *Or* dug.   [b] *That is* Mourning (*or* Meadow) of Egypt.   [c] *So some Sept. MSS.; Heb.* commanded.

70

and wickedness; I know they did you harm." So now forgive our crime, we beg; for we are servants of your father's God.' When they said this to him, Joseph wept. His brothers also wept[a] and prostrated themselves 18 before him; they said, 'You see, we are your slaves.' But Joseph said to 19 them, 'Do not be afraid. Am I in the place of God? You meant to do 20 me harm; but God meant to bring good out of it by preserving the lives of many people, as we see today. Do not be afraid. I will provide for you 21 and your dependants.' Thus he comforted them and set their minds at rest.

Joseph remained in Egypt, he and his father's household. He lived 22 there to be a hundred and ten years old and saw Ephraim's children to 23 the third generation; he also recognized as his[b] the children of Manasseh's son Machir. He said to his brothers, 'I am dying; but God will 24 not fail to come to your aid and take you from here to the land which he promised on oath to Abraham, Isaac and Jacob.' He made the sons of 25 Israel take an oath, saying, 'When God thus comes to your aid, you must take my bones with you[c] from here.' So Joseph died at the age of 26 a hundred and ten. He was embalmed and laid in a coffin in Egypt.

[a] *Prob. rdg.; Heb.* came.   [b] he also recognized as his: *lit.* there were born on his knees.
[c] with you: *so many MSS.; others om.*

EXODUS

Israel enslaved in Egypt

1 THESE ARE THE NAMES of the Israelites who entered
2 Egypt with Jacob, each with his household: Reuben, Simeon,
3,4 Levi and Judah; Issachar, Zebulun and Benjamin; Dan and
5 Naphtali, Gad and Asher. There were seventy[a] of them all told, all
direct descendants of Jacob. Joseph was already in Egypt.
6   In course of time Joseph died, he and all his brothers and that whole
7 generation. Now the Israelites were fruitful and prolific; they increased
in numbers and became very powerful,[b] so that the country was over-
8 run by them. Then a new king ascended the throne of Egypt, one who
9 knew nothing of Joseph. He said to his people, 'These Israelites have
10 become too many and too strong for us. We must take precautions to
see that they do not increase any further; or we shall find that, if war
breaks out, they will join the enemy and fight against us, and they will
11 become masters of the country.' So they were made to work in gangs
with officers set over them, to break their spirit with heavy labour. This
12 is how Pharaoh's store-cities, Pithom and Rameses, were built. But the
more harshly they were treated, the more their numbers increased
beyond all bounds, until the Egyptians came to loathe the sight of them.
13,14 So they treated their Israelite slaves with ruthless severity, and made
life bitter for them with cruel servitude, setting them to work on clay
and brick-making, and all sorts of work in the fields. In short they made
ruthless use of them as slaves in every kind of hard labour.
15   Then the king of Egypt spoke to the Hebrew midwives, whose
16 names were Shiphrah and Puah. 'When you are attending the Hebrew
women in childbirth,' he told them, 'watch as the child is delivered[c]
17 and if it is a boy, kill him; if it is a girl, let her live.' But they were God-
fearing women. They did not do what the king of Egypt had told them
18 to do, but let the boys live. So he summoned those Hebrew midwives
19 and asked them why they had done this and let the boys live. They told
Pharaoh that Hebrew women were not like Egyptian women. When
they were in labour they gave birth before the midwife could get to
20 them. So God made the midwives prosper, and the people increased in
21 numbers and in strength. God gave the midwives homes and families of

[a] Or, with Scroll and Sept. (cp. Acts 7. 14), seventy-five. [b] Or numerous. [c] as . . .
delivered: lit. on the birth-stool.

72

their own, because they feared him. Pharaoh then ordered all his people 22
to throw every new-born Hebrew*ᵃ* boy into the Nile, but to let the
girls live.

A descendant of Levi married a Levite woman who conceived and 2 1,2
bore a son. When she saw what a fine child he was, she hid him for
three months, but she could conceal him no longer. So she got a rush 3
basket for him, made it watertight with clay and tar, laid him in it, and
put it among the reeds by the bank of the Nile. The child's sister took 4
her stand at a distance to see what would happen to him. Pharaoh's 5
daughter came down to bathe in the river, while her ladies-in-waiting
walked along the bank. She noticed the basket among the reeds and
sent her slave-girl for it. She took it from her and when she opened it, 6
she saw the child. It was crying, and she was filled with pity for it.
'Why,' she said, 'it is a little Hebrew boy.' Thereupon the sister said 7
to Pharaoh's daughter, 'Shall I go and fetch one of the Hebrew women
as a wet-nurse to suckle the child for you?' Pharaoh's daughter told her 8
to go; so the girl went and called the baby's mother. Then Pharaoh's 9
daughter said to her, 'Here is the child, suckle him for me, and I will
pay you for it myself.' So the woman took the child and suckled him.
When the child was old enough, she brought him to Pharaoh's daughter, 10
who adopted him and called him Moses,*ᵇ* 'because', she said, 'I drew*ᶜ*
him out of the water.'

ONE DAY WHEN Moses was grown up, he went out to his own kinsmen 11
and saw them at their heavy labour. He saw an Egyptian strike one of
his fellow-Hebrews. He looked this way and that, and, seeing there was 12
no one about, he struck the Egyptian down and hid his body in the
sand. When he went out next day, two Hebrews were fighting together. 13
He asked the man who was in the wrong, 'Why are you striking him?'
'Who set you up as an officer and judge over us?' the man replied. 'Do 14
you mean to murder me as you murdered the Egyptian?' Moses was
alarmed. 'The thing must have become known', he said to himself.
When Pharaoh heard of it, he tried to put Moses to death, but Moses 15
made good his escape and settled in the land of Midian.

Now the priest of Midian had seven daughters. One day as Moses sat 16
by a well, they came to draw water and filled the troughs to water their
father's sheep. Some shepherds came and drove them away; but Moses 17
got up, took the girls' part and watered their sheep himself. When the 18
girls came back to their father Reuel, he asked, 'How is it that you are
back so quickly today?' 'An Egyptian rescued us from the shepherds,' 19
they answered; 'and he even drew the water for us and watered the
sheep.' 'But where is he then?' he said to his daughters. 'Why did you 20

[a] *So Sam.; Heb. om.* [b] *Heb.* Mosheh. [c] *Heb. verb* mashah.

21 leave him behind? Go and invite him to eat with us.' So it came about that Moses agreed to live with the man, and he gave Moses his daughter
22 Zipporah in marriage. She bore him a son, and Moses called him Gershom, 'because', he said, 'I have become an alien[a] living in a foreign land.'

23 YEARS PASSED, and the king of Egypt died, but the Israelites still groaned in slavery. They cried out, and their appeal for rescue from
24 their slavery rose up to God. He heard their groaning, and remembered
25 his covenant with Abraham, Isaac and Jacob; he saw the plight of Israel, and he took heed of it.

3 Moses was minding the flock of his father-in-law Jethro, priest of Midian. He led the flock along the side of the wilderness and came to
2 Horeb, the mountain of God. There the angel of the LORD appeared to him in the flame of a burning bush. Moses noticed that, although the
3 bush was on fire, it was not being burnt up; so he said to himself, 'I must go across to see this wonderful sight. Why does not the bush
4 burn away?' When the LORD saw that Moses had turned aside to look, he[b] called to him out of the bush, 'Moses, Moses.' And Moses answered,
5 'Yes, I am here.' God said, 'Come no nearer; take off your sandals; the
6 place where you are standing is holy ground.' Then he said, 'I am the God of your forefathers,[c] the God of Abraham, the God of Isaac, the God of Jacob.' Moses covered his face, for he was afraid to gaze on God.

7 The LORD said, 'I have indeed seen the misery of my people in Egypt. I have heard their outcry against their slave-masters. I have
8 taken heed of their sufferings, and have come down to rescue them from the power of Egypt, and to bring them up out of that country into a fine, broad land; it is a land flowing with milk and honey, the home of Canaanites, Hittites, Amorites, Perizzites, Hivites, and Jebusites.
9 The outcry of the Israelites has now reached me; yes, I have seen the
10 brutality of the Egyptians towards them. Come now; I will send you to
11 Pharaoh and you shall bring my people Israel out of Egypt.' 'But who am I,' Moses said to God, 'that I should go to Pharaoh, and that I
12 should bring the Israelites out of Egypt?' God[d] answered, 'I am[e] with you. This shall be the proof that it is I who have sent you: when you have brought the people out of Egypt, you shall all worship God here on this mountain.'
13 Then Moses said to God, 'If I go to the Israelites and tell them that the God of their forefathers has sent me to them, and they ask me his
14 name, what shall I say?' God answered, 'I AM; that is who I am.[f] Tell

[a] *Heb.* ger. [b] *Heb.* God. [c] *So Sam.; Heb.* father. [d] *So Sept.; Heb. om.* [e] *Or* I will be; *Heb.* ehyeh. [f] I AM...I am: *or* I will be what I will be.

them that I AM has sent you to them.' And God said further, 'You 15
must tell the Israelites this, that it is JEHOVAH[a] the God of their forefathers, the God of Abraham, the God of Isaac, the God of Jacob, who
has sent you to them. This is my name for ever; this is my title in every
generation. Go and assemble the elders of Israel and tell them that 16
JEHOVAH the God of their forefathers, the God of Abraham, Isaac and
Jacob, has appeared to you and has said, "I have indeed turned my
eyes towards you; I have marked all that has been done to you in
Egypt, and I am resolved to bring you up out of your misery in Egypt, 17
into the country of the Canaanites, Hittites, Amorites, Perizzites,
Hivites, and Jebusites, a land flowing with milk and honey." They will 18
listen to you, and then you and the elders of Israel must go to the king
of Egypt. Tell him, "It has happened that the LORD the God of the
Hebrews met us. So now give us leave to go a three days' journey into
the wilderness to offer sacrifice to the LORD our God." I know well 19
that the king of Egypt will not give you leave unless he is compelled.
I shall then stretch out my hand and assail the Egyptians with all the 20
miracles I shall work among them. After that he will send you away.
Further, I will bring this people into such favour with the Egyptians 21
that, when you go, you will not go empty-handed. Every woman shall 22
ask her neighbour or any woman who lives in her house for jewellery
of silver and gold and for clothing. Load your sons and daughters with
them, and plunder Egypt.'

Moses answered, 'But they will never believe me or listen to me; 4
they will say, "The LORD did not appear to you."' The LORD said, 2
'What have you there in your hand?' 'A staff', Moses answered. The 3
LORD said, 'Throw it on the ground.' Moses threw it down and it
turned into a snake. He ran away from it, but the LORD said, 'Put your 4
hand out and seize it by the tail.' He did so and gripped it firmly, and
it turned back into a staff in his hand. 'This is to convince the people 5
that the LORD the God of their forefathers, the God of Abraham, the
God of Isaac, the God of Jacob, has appeared to you.' Then the LORD 6
said, 'Put your hand inside the fold of your cloak.' He did so, and when
he drew it out the skin was diseased, white as snow. The LORD said, 7
'Put it back again', and he did so. When he drew it out this time it was
as healthy as the rest of his body. 'Now,' said the LORD, 'if they do not 8
believe you and do not accept the evidence of the first sign, they may
accept the evidence of the second. But if they are not convinced even 9
by these two signs, and will not accept what you say, then fetch some
water from the Nile and pour it out on the dry ground, and the water
you take from the Nile will turn to blood on the ground.'

[a] *The Hebrew consonants are* YHWH, *probably pronounced* Yahweh, *but traditionally
read* Jehovah.

10 But Moses said, 'O Lord, I have never been a man of ready speech, never in my life, not even now that thou hast spoken to me; I am
11 slow and hesitant of speech.' The Lord said to him, 'Who is it that gives man speech? Who makes him dumb or deaf? Who makes him
12 clear-sighted or blind? Is it not I, the Lord? Go now; I will help your
13 speech and tell you what to say.' But Moses still protested, 'No, Lord,
14 send whom thou wilt.' At this the Lord grew angry with Moses and said, 'Have you not a brother, Aaron the Levite? He, I know, will do all the speaking. He is already on his way out to meet you, and he will
15 be glad indeed to see you. You shall speak to him and put the words in his mouth; I will help both of you to speak and tell you both what to do.
16 He will do all the speaking to the people for you, he will be the mouth-
17 piece, and you will be the god he speaks for. But take this staff, for with it you are to work the signs.'
18 At length Moses went back to Jethro his father-in-law and said, 'Let me return to my kinsfolk in Egypt and see if they are still alive.' Jethro told him to go and wished him well.

19 THE LORD SPOKE to Moses in Midian and said to him, 'Go back to
20 Egypt, for all those who wished to kill you are dead.' So Moses took his wife and children,^a mounted them on an ass and set out for Egypt with
21 the staff of God in his hand. The Lord said to Moses, 'While you are on your way back to Egypt, keep in mind all the portents I have given you power to show. You shall display these before Pharaoh, but I will
22 make him obstinate and he will not let the people go. Then tell Pharaoh
23 that these are the words of the Lord: "Israel is my first-born son. I have told you to let my son go, so that he may worship me. You have refused to let him go, so I will kill your first-born son."'
24 During the journey, while they were encamped for the night, the
25 Lord met Moses, meaning to kill him, but Zipporah picked up a sharp flint, cut off her son's foreskin, and touched him^b with it, saying, 'You
26 are my blood-bridegroom.' So the Lord let Moses alone. Then she said,^c 'Blood-bridegroom by circumcision.'
27 Meanwhile the Lord had ordered Aaron to go and meet Moses in the wilderness. Aaron went and met him at the mountain of God, and he
28 kissed him. Then Moses told Aaron everything, the words the Lord had sent him to say and the signs he had commanded him to perform.
29, 30 Moses and Aaron went and assembled all the elders of Israel. Aaron told them everything that the Lord had said to Moses; he performed
31 the signs before the people, and they were convinced. They heard that the Lord had shown his concern for the Israelites and seen their misery; and they bowed themselves to the ground in worship.

[a] *Or, possibly,* son (*cp. 2. 22; 4. 25*). [b] *Lit.* his feet. [c] *Or* Therefore women say.

After this, Moses and Aaron came to Pharaoh and said, 'These are 5 the words of the LORD the God of Israel: "Let my people go so that they may keep my pilgrim-feast in the wilderness."' 'Who is the 2 LORD,' asked Pharaoh, 'that I should obey him and let Israel go? I care nothing for the LORD: and I tell you I will not let Israel go.' They replied, 'It has happened that the God of the Hebrews met 3 us. So let us go three days' journey into the wilderness to offer sacrifice to the LORD our God, or else he will attack us with pestilence or sword.' But the king of Egypt said, 'Moses and Aaron, what do you 4 mean by distracting the people from their work? Back to your labours! Your people already outnumber the native Egyptians;[a] yet you would 5 have them stop working!'

That very day Pharaoh ordered the people's overseers and their 6 foremen not to supply the people with the straw used in making bricks, 7 as they had done hitherto. 'Let them go and collect their own straw, but see that they produce the same tally of bricks as before. On no 8 account reduce it. They are a lazy people, and that is why they are clamouring to go and offer sacrifice to their god. Keep the men hard 9 at work; let them attend to that and take no notice of a pack of lies.' The overseers and foremen went out and said to the people, 'Pharaoh's 10 orders are that no more straw is to be supplied. Go and get it for your- 11 selves wherever you can find it; but there will be no reduction in your daily task.' So the people scattered all over Egypt to gather stubble for 12 straw, while the overseers kept urging them on, bidding them complete, 13 day after day, the same quantity as when straw was supplied. Then the 14 Israelite foremen were flogged because they were held responsible by Pharaoh's overseers, who asked them, 'Why did you not complete the usual number of bricks yesterday or today?' So the foremen came and 15 appealed to Pharaoh: 'Why do you treat your servants like this?' they said. 'We are given no straw, yet they keep on telling us to make bricks. 16 Here are we being flogged, but it is your people's fault.' But Pharaoh 17 replied, 'You are lazy, you are lazy. That is why you talk about going to offer sacrifice to the LORD. Now go; get on with your work. You will 18 be given no straw, but you must produce the tally of bricks.' When they 19 were told that they must not let the daily tally of bricks fall short, the Israelite foremen saw that they were in trouble. As they came out from 20 Pharaoh's presence they found Moses and Aaron waiting to meet them, and said, 'May this bring the LORD's judgement down upon you: you 21 have made us stink in the nostrils of Pharaoh and his subjects; you have put a sword in their hands to kill us.'

Moses went back to the LORD, and said, 'Why, O Lord, hast thou 22 brought misfortune on this people? And why didst thou ever send me?

[a] *Prob. rdg., cp. Sam.; Heb.* The people of the land are already many.

23 Since I first went to Pharaoh to speak in thy name he has heaped misfortune on thy people, and thou hast done nothing at all to rescue
6 them.' The LORD answered, 'Now you shall see what I will do to Pharaoh. In the end Pharaoh will let them go with a strong hand, nay, will drive them from his country with an outstretched arm.'[a]
2,3 God spoke to Moses and said, 'I am the LORD. I appeared to Abraham, Isaac, and Jacob as God Almighty.[b] But I did not let
4 myself be known to them by my name JEHOVAH.[c] Moreover, I made a covenant with them to give them Canaan, the land where they settled
5 for a time as foreigners. And now I have heard the groaning of the Israelites, enslaved by the Egyptians, and I have called my covenant
6 to mind. Say therefore to the Israelites, "I am the LORD. I will release you from your labours in Egypt. I will rescue you from slavery there. I will redeem you with arm outstretched and with mighty acts of
7 judgement. I will adopt you as my people, and I will become your God. You shall know that I, the LORD, am your God, the God who releases
8 you from your labours in Egypt. I will lead you to the land which I swore with uplifted hand to give to Abraham, to Isaac and to Jacob. I will give it you for your possession. I am the LORD."'
9 Moses repeated these words to the Israelites, but they did not listen to him; they had become impatient because of their cruel slavery.
10,11 Then the LORD spoke to Moses and said, 'Go and tell Pharaoh king
12 of Egypt to set the Israelites free to leave his country.' Moses made answer in the presence of the LORD, 'If the Israelites do not listen to me, how will Pharaoh listen to such a halting speaker as I am[d]?'
13 Thus the LORD spoke to Moses and Aaron and gave them their commission to the Israelites and to Pharaoh, namely that they should bring the Israelites out of Egypt.

14[e] THESE WERE THE HEADS of fathers' families:
Sons of Reuben, Israel's eldest son: Enoch, Pallu, Hezron and Carmi; these were the families of Reuben.
15 Sons of Simeon: Jemuel, Jamin, Ohad, Jachin, Zohar, and Saul, who was the son of a Canaanite woman; these were the families of Simeon.
16 These were the names of the sons of Levi in order of seniority: Gershon, Kohath and Merari. Levi lived to be a hundred and thirty-seven.
17 Sons of Gershon, family by family: Libni and Shimei.
18 Sons of Kohath: Amram, Izhar, Hebron and Uzziel. Kohath lived to be a hundred and thirty-three.

[a] *So Sept.; Heb.* with a strong hand. [b] *Heb.* El-Shaddai. [c] *See note on 3. 15.* [d] to such...I am: *lit.* to me, seeing I am uncircumcised of lips. [e] *Verses 14–16: cp. Gen. 46. 8–11; Num. 26. 5, 6, 12, 13.*

Sons of Merari: Mahli and Mushi.   19

These were the families of Levi in order of seniority. Amram married   20
his father's sister Jochebed, and she bore him Aaron and Moses.
Amram lived to be a hundred and thirty-seven.

Sons of Izhar: Korah, Nepheg and Zichri.   21

Sons of Uzziel: Mishael, Elzaphan and Sithri.   22

Aaron married Elisheba, who was the daughter of Amminadab and   23
the sister of Nahshon, and she bore him Nadab, Abihu, Eleazar and
Ithamar.

Sons of Korah: Assir, Elkanah and Abiasaph; these were the   24
Korahite families.

Eleazar son of Aaron married one of the daughters of Putiel, and she   25
bore him Phinehas. These were the heads of the Levite families,
family by family.

It was this Aaron, together with Moses, to whom the LORD said,   26
'Bring the Israelites out of Egypt, mustered in their tribal hosts.'
These were the men who told Pharaoh king of Egypt to let the Israelites   27
leave Egypt. It was this same Moses and Aaron.

WHEN THE LORD spoke to Moses in Egypt he said, 'I am the LORD.   28, 29
Tell Pharaoh king of Egypt all that I say to you.' Moses made answer   30
in the presence of the LORD, 'I am a halting speaker; how will Pharaoh
listen to me?' The LORD answered Moses, 'See now, I have made you   7
like a god for Pharaoh, with your brother Aaron as your spokesman.[a]
You must tell your brother Aaron all I bid you say, and he will tell   2
Pharaoh, and Pharaoh will let the Israelites go out of his country; but   3
I will make him stubborn. Then will I show sign after sign and portent
after portent in the land of Egypt. But Pharaoh will not listen to you, so   4
I will assert my power in Egypt, and with mighty acts of judgement I
will bring my people, the Israelites, out of Egypt in their tribal hosts.
When I put forth my power against the Egyptians and bring the   5
Israelites out from them, then Egypt will know that I am the LORD.' So   6
Moses and Aaron did exactly as the LORD had commanded. At the   7
time when they spoke to Pharaoh, Moses was eighty years old and
Aaron eighty-three.

The LORD said to Moses and Aaron, 'If Pharaoh demands some   8, 9
portent from you, then you, Moses, must say to Aaron, "Take your
staff and throw it down in front of Pharaoh, and it will turn into a
serpent."' When Moses and Aaron came to Pharaoh, they did as the   10
LORD had told them. Aaron threw down his staff in front of Pharaoh
and his courtiers, and it turned into a serpent. At this, Pharaoh   11
summoned the wise men and the sorcerers, and the Egyptian magicians

[a] *Lit.* prophet.

12 too did the same thing by their spells. Every man threw his staff down, and each staff turned into a serpent; but Aaron's staff swallowed up
13 theirs. Pharaoh, however, was obstinate; as the LORD had foretold, he would not listen to Moses and Aaron.

14 Then the LORD said to Moses, 'Pharaoh is obdurate: he has refused
15 to set the people free. Go to him in the morning on his way out to the river. Stand and wait on the bank of the Nile to meet him, and take
16 with you the staff that turned into a snake. Say this to him: "The LORD the God of the Hebrews sent me to bid you let his people go in order to worship him in the wilderness. So far you have not listened to his
17 words; so now the LORD says, 'By this you shall know that I am the LORD.' With this rod that I have in my hand, I shall now strike the
18 water in the Nile and it will be changed into blood. The fish will die and the river will stink, and the Egyptians will be unable to drink water
19 from the Nile."' The LORD then told Moses to say to Aaron, 'Take your staff and stretch your hand out over the waters of Egypt, its rivers and its streams, and over every pool and cistern, to turn them into blood. There shall be blood throughout the whole of Egypt, blood even in
20 their wooden bowls and jars of stone.' So Moses and Aaron did as the LORD had commanded. He lifted up his staff and struck the water of the Nile in the sight of Pharaoh and his courtiers, and all the water was
21 changed into blood. The fish died and the river stank, and the Egyptians could not drink water from the Nile. There was blood
22 everywhere in Egypt. But the Egyptian magicians did the same thing by their spells; and still Pharaoh remained obstinate, as the LORD had
23 foretold, and did not listen to Moses and Aaron. He turned away, went
24 into his house and dismissed the matter from his mind. Then the Egyptians all dug for drinking water round about the river, because they
25 could not drink from the waters of the Nile itself. This lasted for seven days from the time when the LORD struck the Nile.

8 1*a*   The LORD then told Moses to go into Pharaoh's presence and say to him, 'These are the words of the LORD: "Let my people go in order to
2 worship me. If you refuse to let them go, I will plague the whole of
3 your territory with frogs. The Nile shall swarm with them. They shall come up from the river into your house, into your bedroom and on to your bed, into the houses of your courtiers and your people, into your
4 ovens and your kneading-troughs. The frogs shall clamber over you,
5*b* your people, and your courtiers."' Then the LORD told Moses to say to Aaron, 'Take your staff in your hand and stretch it out over the rivers, streams, and pools, to bring up frogs upon the land of Egypt.'
6 So Aaron stretched out his hand over the waters of Egypt, and the
7 frogs came up and covered all the land. The magicians did the same

[a] 7. 26 *in Heb.*   [b] 8. 1 *in Heb.*

80

thing by their spells: they too brought up frogs upon the land of Egypt. Then Pharaoh summoned Moses and Aaron. 'Pray to the LORD', 8 he said, 'to take the frogs away from me and my people, and I will let the people go to sacrifice to the LORD.' Moses said, 'Of your royal 9 favour, appoint a time when I may intercede for you and your courtiers and people, so that you and your houses may be rid of the frogs, and none be left except in the Nile.' 'Tomorrow', Pharaoh said. 'It shall 10 be as you say,' replied Moses, 'so that you may know there is no one like our God, the LORD. The frogs shall depart from you, from your 11 houses, your courtiers, and your people: none shall be left except in the Nile.' Moses and Aaron left Pharaoh's presence, and Moses appealed 12 to the LORD to remove the frogs which he had brought on Pharaoh. The LORD did as Moses had asked, and in house and courtyard and in 13 the open the frogs all perished. They piled them into countless heaps 14 and the land stank; but when Pharaoh found that he was given relief 15 he became obdurate; as the LORD had foretold, he did not listen to Moses and Aaron.

The LORD then told Moses to say to Aaron, 'Stretch out your staff 16 and strike the dust on the ground, and it will turn into maggots throughout the land of Egypt', and they obeyed. Aaron stretched out his 17 staff and struck the dust, and it turned into maggots on man and beast. All the dust turned into maggots throughout the land of Egypt. The 18 magicians tried to produce maggots in the same way by their spells, but they failed. The maggots were everywhere, on man and beast. 'It is the finger of God', said the magicians to Pharaoh, but Pharaoh 19 remained obstinate; as the LORD had foretold, he did not listen to them.

The LORD told Moses to rise early in the morning and stand in 20 Pharaoh's path as he went out to the river and to say to him, 'These are the words of the LORD: "Let my people go in order to worship me. If you do not let my people go, I will send swarms of flies upon you, 21 your courtiers, your people, and your houses. The houses of the Egyptians shall be filled with the swarms and so shall all the land they live in, but on that day I will make an exception of Goshen, the land 22 where my people live: there shall be no swarms there. Thus you shall know that I, the LORD, am here in the land. I will make a distinction*a* 23 between my people and yours. Tomorrow this sign shall appear."' The 24 LORD did this; dense swarms of flies infested Pharaoh's house and those of his courtiers; throughout Egypt the land was threatened with ruin by the swarms. Pharaoh summoned Moses and Aaron and said to 25 them, 'Go and sacrifice to your God, but in this country.' 'That we 26 cannot do,' replied Moses, 'because the victim we shall sacrifice to the LORD our God is an abomination to the Egyptians. If the Egyptians

[a] So Sept.; Heb. redemption.

27 see us offer such an animal, will they not stone us to death? We must
go a three days' journey into the wilderness to sacrifice to the LORD
28 our God, as he commands us.' 'I will let you go,' said Pharaoh, 'and
you shall sacrifice to your God in the wilderness; only do not go far.
29 Now intercede for me.' Moses answered, 'As soon as I leave you I will
intercede with the LORD. Tomorrow the swarms will depart from
Pharaoh, his courtiers, and his people. Only let not Pharaoh trifle any
more with the people by preventing them from going to sacrifice to the
30, 31 LORD.' Then Moses left Pharaoh and interceded with the LORD. The
LORD did as Moses had said; he removed the swarms from Pharaoh,
32 his courtiers, and his people; not one was left. But once again Pharaoh
became obdurate and did not let the people go.

9   The LORD said to Moses, 'Go into Pharaoh's presence and say to
him, "These are the words of the LORD the God of the Hebrews: 'Let
2 my people go in order to worship me.' If you refuse to let them go and
3 still keep your hold on them, the LORD will strike your grazing herds,
your horses and asses, your camels, cattle, and sheep with a terrible
4 pestilence. But the LORD will make a distinction between Israel's herds
and those of the Egyptians. Of all that belong to Israel not a single one
5 shall die."' The LORD fixed a time and said, 'Tomorrow I will do this
6 throughout the land.' The next day the LORD struck. All the herds of
Egypt died, but from the herds of the Israelites not one single beast
7 died. Pharaoh inquired and was told that not a beast from the herds of
Israel had died; and yet he remained obdurate and did not let the
people go.

8   The LORD said to Moses and Aaron, 'Take handfuls of soot from a
9 kiln. Moses shall toss it into the air in Pharaoh's sight, and it will turn
into a fine dust over the whole of Egypt. All over Egypt it will become
10 festering boils on man and beast.' They took the soot from the kiln and
stood before Pharaoh. Moses tossed it into the air and it produced
11 festering boils on man and beast. The magicians were no match for
Moses because of the boils, which attacked them and all the Egyptians.
12 But the LORD made Pharaoh obstinate; as the LORD had foretold to
Moses, he did not listen to Moses and Aaron.

13   The LORD then told Moses to rise early in the morning, present
himself before Pharaoh, and say to him, 'These are the words of the
LORD the God of the Hebrews: "Let my people go in order to worship
14 me. This time I will strike home with all my plagues against you, your
courtiers, and your people, so that you may know that there is none like
15 me in all the earth. By now I could have stretched out my hand, and
struck you and your people with pestilence, and you would have
16 vanished from the earth. I have let you live only to show you my power
17 and to spread my fame throughout the land. Since you still obstruct my

people and will not let them go, tomorrow at this time I will send a vio- 18
lent hailstorm, such as has never been in Egypt from its first beginnings
until now. Send now and bring your herds under cover, and everything 19
you have out in the open field. If anything, whether man or beast, which
happens to be in the open, is not brought in, the hail will fall on it, and
it will die."' Those of Pharaoh's subjects who feared the word of the 20
LORD hurried their slaves and cattle into their houses. But those who 21
did not take to heart the word of the LORD left their slaves and cattle
in the open.

The LORD said to Moses, 'Stretch out your hand towards the sky to 22
bring down hail on the whole land of Egypt, on man and beast and
every growing thing throughout the land.' Moses stretched out his staff 23
towards the sky, and the LORD sent thunder and hail, with fire flashing
down to the ground. The LORD rained down hail on the land of Egypt,
hail and fiery flashes through the hail, so heavy that there had been 24
nothing like it in all Egypt from the time that Egypt became a nation.
Throughout Egypt the hail struck everything in the fields, both man 25
and beast; it beat down every growing thing and shattered every tree.
Only in the land of Goshen, where the Israelites lived, was there no 26
hail.

Pharaoh sent and summoned Moses and Aaron. 'This time I have 27
sinned,' he said; 'the LORD is in the right; I and my people are in the
wrong. Intercede with the LORD, for we can bear no more of this 28
thunder and hail.[a] I will let you go; you need wait no longer.' Moses 29
said, 'When I leave the city I will spread out my hands in prayer to the
LORD. The thunder shall cease, and there shall be no more hail, so that
you may know that the earth is the LORD's. But you and your subjects— 30
I know that you do not yet fear the LORD God.' (The flax and barley 31
were destroyed because the barley was in the ear and the flax in bud,
but the wheat and spelt were not destroyed because they come later.) 32
Moses left Pharaoh's presence, went out of the city and lifted up his 33
hands to the LORD in prayer: the thunder and hail ceased, and no more
rain fell. When Pharaoh saw that the downpour, the hail, and the 34
thunder had ceased, he sinned again, he and his courtiers, and became
obdurate. So Pharaoh remained obstinate; as the LORD had foretold 35
through Moses, he did not let the people go.

Then the LORD said to Moses, 'Go into Pharaoh's presence. I have 10
made him and his courtiers obdurate, so that I may show these my
signs among them,[b] and so that you can tell your children and grand- 2
children the story: how I made sport of the Egyptians, and what signs
I showed among them. Thus you will know that I am the LORD.' Moses 3
and Aaron went in to Pharaoh and said to him, 'These are the words of

[a] Or, *with Scroll and Sept.*, thunder and hail and fire.   [b] *So Sept.; Heb.* in his midst.

the LORD the God of the Hebrews: "How long will you refuse to humble yourself before me? Let my people go in order to worship me.
4 If you refuse to let my people go, tomorrow I will bring locusts into
5 your country. They shall cover the face of the land so that it cannot be seen. They shall eat up the last remnant left you by the hail. They shall
6 devour every tree that grows in your country-side. Your houses and your courtiers' houses, every house in Egypt, shall be full of them; your fathers never saw the like nor their fathers before them; such a thing has not happened from their time until now."' He turned and
7 left Pharaoh's presence. Pharaoh's courtiers said to him, 'How long must we be caught in this man's toils? Let their menfolk go and worship the LORD their God. Do you not know by now that Egypt is ruined?'
8 So Moses and Aaron were brought back to Pharaoh, and he said to them, 'You may go and worship the LORD your God; but who exactly
9 is to go?' 'All,' said Moses, 'young and old, boys and girls, sheep and
10 cattle; for we have to keep the LORD's pilgrim-feast.' Pharaoh replied, 'Very well then; take your dependants with you when you go; and the LORD be with you. But beware, there is trouble in store for you.
11 No, your menfolk may go and worship the LORD, for that is all you asked.' So they were driven out from Pharaoh's presence.

12 Then the LORD said to Moses, 'Stretch out your hand over Egypt so that the locusts may come*a* and invade the land and devour all the
13 vegetation in it, everything the hail has left.' Moses stretched out his staff over the land of Egypt, and the LORD sent a wind roaring in from the east all that day and all that night. When morning came, the east
14 wind had brought the locusts. They invaded the whole land of Egypt, and settled on all its territory in swarms so dense that the like of them
15 had never been seen before, nor ever will be again. They covered the surface of the whole land till it was black with them. They devoured all the vegetation and all the fruit of the trees that the hail had spared.
16 There was no green left on tree or plant throughout all Egypt. Pharaoh hastily summoned Moses and Aaron. 'I have sinned against the LORD
17 your God and against you', he said. 'Forgive my sin, I pray, just this once. Intercede with the LORD your God and beg him only to remove
18 this deadly plague from me.' Moses left Pharaoh and interceded with the
19 LORD. The LORD changed the wind into a westerly gale, which carried the locusts away and swept them into the Red Sea.*b* There was not a
20 single locust left in all the territory of Egypt. But the LORD made Pharaoh obstinate, and he did not let the Israelites go.

21 Then the LORD said to Moses, 'Stretch out your hand towards the sky so that there may be darkness over the land of Egypt, darkness that
22 can be felt.' Moses stretched out his hand towards the sky, and it

[a] so that...come: *so Sept.*; *Heb.* with the locusts. [b] *Or* the Sea of Reeds.

84

became pitch dark throughout the land of Egypt for three days. Men 23
could not see one another; for three days no one stirred from where he
was. But there was no darkness wherever the Israelites lived. Pharaoh 24
summoned Moses. 'Go', he said, 'and worship the LORD. Your
dependants may go with you; but your flocks and herds must be left
with us.' But Moses said, 'No, you must yourself supply us with 25
animals for sacrifice and whole-offering to the LORD our God; and our 26
own flocks must go with us too—not a hoof must be left behind. We
may need animals from our own flocks to worship the LORD our God;
we ourselves cannot tell until we are there how we are to worship the
LORD.' The LORD made Pharaoh obstinate, and he refused to let them 27
go. 'Out! Pester me no more!' he said to Moses. 'Take care you do not 28
see my face again, for on the day you do, you die.' 'You are right,' said
Moses; 'I shall never see your face again.'

Then the LORD said to Moses, 'One last plague I will bring upon 11
Pharaoh and Egypt. After that he will let you go; he will send you
packing, as a man dismisses a rejected bride. Let the people be told 2
that men and women alike should ask their neighbours for jewellery
of silver and gold.' The LORD made the Egyptians well-disposed 3
towards them, and, moreover, Moses was a very great man in Egypt in
the eyes of Pharaoh's courtiers and of the people.

Moses then said, 'These are the words of the LORD: "At midnight 4
I will go out among the Egyptians. Every first-born creature in the 5
land of Egypt shall die: the first-born of Pharaoh who sits on his
throne, the first-born of the slave-girl at the handmill, and all the
first-born of the cattle. All Egypt will send up a great cry of anguish, a 6
cry the like of which has never been heard before, nor ever will be
again. But among all Israel not a dog's tongue shall be so much as 7
scratched, no man or beast be hurt." Thus you shall know that the
LORD does make a distinction between Egypt and Israel. Then all 8
these courtiers of yours will come down to me, prostrate themselves
and cry, "Go away, you and all the people who follow at your heels."
After that I will go away.' Then Moses left Pharaoh's presence hot
with anger.

The LORD said to Moses, 'Pharaoh will not listen to you; I will 9
therefore show still more portents in the land of Egypt.' All these 10
portents had Moses and Aaron shown in the presence of Pharaoh, and
yet the LORD made him obstinate, and he did not let the Israelites
leave the country.

The institution of the Passover

12 1,2 THE LORD SAID to Moses and Aaron in Egypt: This month is for you the first of months; you shall make it the first month of the 3 year. Speak to the whole community of Israel and say to them: On the tenth day of this month let each man take a lamb or a kid for his family, 4 one for each household, but if a household is too small for one lamb or one kid, then the man and his nearest neighbour may take one between them. They shall share the cost, taking into account both the number of 5 persons and the amount each of them eats. Your lamb or kid must be without blemish, a yearling male. You may take equally a sheep or a 6 goat. You must have it in safe keeping until the fourteenth day of this month, and then all the assembled community of Israel shall slaughter 7 the victim between dusk and dark.*[a]* They must take some of the blood and smear it on the two door-posts and on the lintel of every house in 8 which they eat the lamb. On that night they shall eat the flesh roast on 9 the fire; they shall eat it with unleavened cakes and bitter herbs. You are not to eat any of it raw or even boiled in water, but roasted, head, 10 shins, and entrails. You shall not leave any of it till morning; if anything is left over until morning, it must be destroyed by fire.

11 This is the way in which you must eat it: you shall have your belt fastened,*[b]* your sandals on your feet and your staff in your hand, 12 and you must eat in urgent haste. It is the LORD's Passover. On that night I shall pass through the land of Egypt and kill every first-born of man and beast. Thus will I execute judgement, I the LORD, 13 against all the gods of Egypt. And as for you, the blood will be a sign on the houses in which you are: when I see the blood I will pass over*[c]* you; the mortal blow shall not touch you, when I strike the land of Egypt.

14 You shall keep this day as a day of remembrance, and make it a pilgrim-feast, a festival of the LORD; you shall keep it generation after 15 generation as a rule for all time. For seven days you shall eat un-leavened cakes. On the very first day you shall rid your houses of leaven; from the first day to the seventh anyone who eats leavened 16 bread shall be outlawed*[d]* from Israel. On the first day there shall be a sacred assembly and on the seventh day there shall be a sacred assembly: on these days no work shall be done, except what must be done to 17 provide food for everyone; and that will be allowed. You shall observe these commandments because this was the very day on which I brought

[a] *Lit.* between the two evenings. [b] *Lit.* your loins girt. [c] *Or* stand guard over. [d] *Lit.* cut off.

you out of Egypt in your tribal hosts. You shall observe this day from generation to generation as a rule for all time.

You shall eat unleavened cakes in the first month from the evening 18 which begins the fourteenth day until the evening which begins the twenty-first day. For seven days no leaven may be found in your 19 houses, for anyone who eats anything fermented shall be outlawed from the community of Israel, be he foreigner or native. You must eat 20 nothing fermented. Wherever you live you must eat your cakes unleavened.

Moses summoned all the elders of Israel and said to them, 'Go at 21 once and get sheep for your families and slaughter the Passover. Then take a bunch of marjoram,*a* dip it in the blood in the basin*b* and 22 smear some blood from the basin*c* on the lintel and the two door-posts. Nobody may go out through the door of his house till morning. The 23 LORD will go through Egypt and strike it, but when he sees the blood on the lintel and the two door-posts, he will pass over that door and will not let the destroyer enter your houses to strike you. You shall keep 24 this as a rule for you and your children for all time. When you enter 25 the land which the LORD will give you as he promised, you shall observe this rite. Then, when your children ask you, "What is the 26 meaning of this rite?" you shall say, "It is the LORD's Passover, for he 27 passed over the houses of the Israelites in Egypt when he struck the Egyptians but spared our houses."' The people bowed down and prostrated themselves.

The Israelites went and did all that the LORD had commanded 28 Moses and Aaron; and by midnight the LORD had struck down every 29 first-born in Egypt, from the first-born of Pharaoh on his throne to the first-born of the captive in the dungeon, and the first-born of cattle. Before night was over Pharaoh rose, he and all his courtiers and all the 30 Egyptians, and a great cry of anguish went up, because not a house in Egypt was without its dead. Pharaoh summoned Moses and Aaron 31 while it was still night and said, 'Up with you! Be off, and leave my people, you and your Israelites. Go and worship the LORD, as you ask; take your sheep and cattle, and go; and ask God's blessing on me also.' 32 The Egyptians urged on the people and hurried them out of the 33 country, 'or else', they said, 'we shall all be dead.' The people picked 34 up their dough before it was leavened, wrapped their kneading-troughs in their cloaks, and slung them on their shoulders. Meanwhile the 35 Israelites had done as Moses had told them, asking the Egyptians for jewellery of silver and gold and for clothing. As the LORD had made 36 the Egyptians well-disposed towards them, they let them have what they asked; in this way they plundered the Egyptians.

[*a*] *Or* hyssop.   [*b*] *Or* on the threshold.   [*c*] *Or* from the threshold.

The exodus from Egypt

37 THE ISRAELITES SET OUT from Rameses on the way to Succoth, about six hundred thousand men on foot, not counting dependants.
38 And with them too went a large company of every kind, and cattle in
39 great numbers, both flocks and herds. The dough they had brought from Egypt they baked into unleavened cakes, because there was no leaven; for they had been driven out of Egypt and allowed no time even to get food ready for themselves.

40 The Israelites had been settled in Egypt for four hundred and thirty
41 years. At the end of four hundred and thirty years, on this very day,
42 all the tribes of the LORD came out of Egypt. This was a night of vigil as the LORD waited to bring them out of Egypt. It is the LORD's night; all Israelites keep their vigil generation after generation.

43 The LORD said to Moses and Aaron: These are the rules for the
44 Passover. No foreigner may partake of it; any bought slave may eat it
45 if you have circumcised him; no stranger or hired man may eat it.
46 Each lamb must be eaten inside the one house, and you must not take any of the flesh outside the house. You must not break a single bone
47, 48 of it. The whole community of Israel shall keep this feast. If there are aliens living with you and they are to keep the Passover to the LORD, every male of them must be circumcised, and then he can take part; he shall rank as native-born. No one who is uncircumcised may eat of it.
49 The same law shall apply both to the native-born and to the alien who is living among you.

50 The Israelites did all that the LORD had commanded Moses and
51 Aaron; and on this very day the LORD brought the Israelites out of Egypt mustered in their tribal hosts.

13 1, 2 The LORD spoke to Moses and said, 'Every first-born, the first birth of every womb among the Israelites, you must dedicate to me, both man and beast; it is mine.'

3 Then Moses said to the people, 'Remember this day, the day on which you have come out of Egypt, the land of siavery, because the LORD by the strength of his hand has brought you out. No leaven may
4 be eaten this day, for today, in the month of Abib, is the day of your
5 exodus; and when the LORD has brought you into the country of the Canaanites, Hittites, Amorites, Hivites, and Jebusites, the land which he swore to your forefathers to give you, a land flowing with milk and
6 honey, then you must observe this rite in this same month. For seven days you shall eat unleavened cakes, and on the seventh day there
7 shall be a pilgrim-feast of the LORD. Only unleavened cakes shall be

eaten during the seven days; nothing fermented and no leaven shall be
seen throughout your territory. On that day you shall tell your son, 8
"This commemorates what the LORD did for me when I came out of
Egypt." You shall have the record of it as a sign upon your hand, and 9
upon your forehead as a reminder, to make sure that the law of the
LORD is always on your lips, because the LORD with a strong hand
brought you out of Egypt. This is a rule, and you shall keep it at the 10
appointed time from year to year.

'When the LORD has brought you into the land of the Canaanites as 11
he swore to you and to your forefathers, and given it to you, you shall 12
surrender to the LORD the first birth of every womb; and of all first-
born offspring of your cattle the males belong to the LORD. Every 13
first-born male ass you may redeem with a kid or lamb, but if you do
not redeem it, you must break its neck. Every first-born among your
sons you must redeem. When in time to come your son asks you what 14
this means, you shall say to him, "By the strength of his hand the
LORD brought us out of Egypt, out of the land of slavery. When 15
Pharaoh proved stubborn and refused to let us go, the LORD killed all
the first-born in Egypt both man and beast. That is why I sacrifice to
the LORD the first birth of every womb if it is a male and redeem every
first-born of my sons. You shall have the record of it as a sign upon 16
your hand, and upon your forehead as a phylactery, because by the
strength of his hand the LORD brought us out of Egypt."'

NOW WHEN PHARAOH let the people go, God did not guide them by 17
the road towards the Philistines, although that was the shortest; for he
said, 'The people may change their minds when they see war before
them, and turn back to Egypt.' So God made them go round by way of 18
the wilderness towards the Red Sea; and the fifth generation of
Israelites departed from Egypt.

Moses took the bones of Joseph with him, because Joseph had exacted 19
an oath from the Israelites: 'Some day', he said, 'God will show his
care for you, and then, as you go, you must take my bones with you.'

They set out from Succoth and encamped at Etham on the edge of 20
the wilderness. And all the time the LORD went before them, by day 21
a pillar of cloud to guide them on their journey, by night a pillar of
fire to give them light, so that they could travel night and day. The pillar 22
of cloud never left its place in front of the people by day, nor the pillar
of fire by night.

The LORD spoke to Moses and said, 'Speak to the Israelites: they 14 1,2
are to turn back and encamp before Pi-hahiroth,[a] between Migdol and
the sea to the east of Baal-zephon; your camp shall be opposite, by the

[a] *Or* where the desert tracks begin.

3 sea. Pharaoh will then think that the Israelites are finding themselves in
4 difficult country, and are hemmed in by the wilderness. I will make
Pharaoh obstinate, and he will pursue them, so that I may win glory
for myself at the expense of Pharaoh and all his army; and the
Egyptians shall know that I am the LORD.' The Israelites did as they
were bidden.

5 When the king of Egypt was told that the Israelites had slipped away,
he and his courtiers changed their minds completely, and said, 'What
6 have we done? We have let our Israelite slaves go free!' So Pharaoh
7 put horses to his chariot, and took his troops with him. He took six
hundred picked chariots and all the other chariots of Egypt, with a
8 commander in each. Then Pharaoh king of Egypt, made obstinate by
9 the LORD, pursued the Israelites as they marched defiantly away. The
Egyptians, all Pharaoh's chariots and horses, cavalry and infantry,
pursued them and overtook them encamped beside the sea by Pi-
10 hahiroth to the east of Baal-zephon. Pharaoh was almost upon them
when the Israelites looked up and saw the Egyptians close behind. In
11 their terror they clamoured to the LORD for help and said to Moses,
'Were there no graves in Egypt, that you should have brought us here to
die in the wilderness? See what you have done to us by bringing us out
12 of Egypt! Is not this just what we meant when we said in Egypt, "Leave
us alone; let us be slaves to the Egyptians"? We would rather be slaves
13 to the Egyptians than die here in the wilderness.' 'Have no fear,'
Moses answered; 'stand firm and see the deliverance that the LORD will
bring you this day; for as sure as you see the Egyptians now, you will
14 never see them again. The LORD will fight for you; so hold your peace.'
15 The LORD said to Moses, 'What is the meaning of this clamour? Tell
16 the Israelites to strike camp. And you shall raise high your staff,
stretch out your hand over the sea and cleave it in two, so that the
17 Israelites can pass through the sea on dry ground. For my part I will
make the Egyptians obstinate and they will come after you; thus will
I win glory for myself at the expense of Pharaoh and his army, chariots
18 and cavalry all together. The Egyptians will know that I am the LORD
when I win glory for myself at the expense of their Pharaoh, his
chariots and cavalry.'
19 The angel of God, who had kept in front of the Israelites, moved
away to the rear. The pillar of cloud moved from the front and took its
20 place behind them and so came between the Egyptians and the
Israelites. And the cloud brought on darkness and early nightfall, so
that contact was lost throughout the night.
21 Then Moses stretched out his hand over the sea, and the LORD
drove the sea away all night with a strong east wind and turned the
22 sea-bed into dry land. The waters were torn apart, and the Israelites

went through the sea on the dry ground, while the waters made a wall
for them to right and to left. The Egyptians went in pursuit of them 23
far into the sea, all Pharaoh's horse, his chariots, and his cavalry.
In the morning watch the LORD looked down on the Egyptian army 24
through the pillar of fire and cloud, and he threw them into a panic. He 25
clogged[a] their chariot wheels and made them lumber along heavily, so
that the Egyptians said, 'It is the LORD fighting for Israel against
Egypt; let us flee.' Then the LORD said to Moses, 'Stretch out your 26
hand over the sea, and let the water flow back over the Egyptians, their
chariots and their cavalry.' So Moses stretched out his hand over the 27
sea, and at daybreak the water returned to its accustomed place; but
the Egyptians were in flight as it advanced, and the LORD swept them
out[b] into the sea. The water flowed back and covered all Pharaoh's 28
army, the chariots and the cavalry, which had pressed the pursuit into
the sea. Not one man was left alive. Meanwhile the Israelites had 29
passed along the dry ground through the sea, with the water making
a wall for them to right and to left. That day the LORD saved Israel 30
from the power of Egypt, and the Israelites saw the Egyptians lying
dead on the sea-shore. When Israel saw the great power which the 31
LORD had put forth against Egypt, all the people feared the LORD, and
they put their faith in him and in Moses his servant.

Then Moses and the Israelites sang this song to the LORD: **15**

> I will sing to the LORD, for he has risen up in triumph;
> the horse and his rider he has hurled into the sea.
>> The LORD is my refuge and my defence,   2
>> he has shown himself my deliverer.
>> He is my God, and I will glorify him;
>> he is my father's God, and I will exalt him.
>> The LORD is a warrior: the LORD is his name.   3
>> The chariots of Pharaoh and his army   4
>> he has cast into the sea;
>> the flower of his officers
>> are engulfed in the Red Sea.
>> The watery abyss has covered them,   5
>> they sank into the depths like a stone.
> Thy right hand, O LORD, is majestic in strength: 6
> thy right hand, O LORD, shattered the enemy.
>> In the fullness of thy triumph   7
>> thou didst cast the rebels down:
>> thou didst let loose thy fury;
>> it consumed them like chaff.

[a] *So Sam.; Heb.* took away.   [b] *Lit.* shook them off.

8 At the blast of thy anger the sea piled up:
    the waters stood up like a bank:
    out at sea the great deep congealed.

9 The enemy said, 'I will pursue, I will overtake;
    I will divide the spoil,
    I will glut my appetite upon them;
    I will draw my sword,
    I will rid myself of them.'

10 Thou didst blow with thy blast; the sea covered them.
    They sank like lead in the swelling waves.

11 Who is like thee, O LORD, among the gods[a]?
    Who is like thee, majestic in holiness,
    worthy of awe and praise, who workest wonders?

12 Thou didst stretch out thy right hand,
    earth engulfed them.

13 In thy constant love thou hast led the people
    whom thou didst ransom:
    thou hast guided them by thy strength
    to thy holy dwelling-place.

14 Nations heard and trembled;
    agony seized the dwellers in Philistia.

15 Then the chieftains of Edom were dismayed,
    trembling seized the leaders of Moab,
    all the inhabitants of Canaan were in turmoil;

16 terror and dread fell upon them:
    through the might of thy arm they stayed stone-still,
    while thy people passed, O LORD,
    while the people whom thou madest thy own[b] passed by.

17 Thou broughtest them in and didst plant them
    in the mount that is thy possession,
    the dwelling-place, O LORD, of thy own making,
    the sanctuary, O LORD, which thy own hands prepared.

18 The LORD shall reign for ever and for ever.

19 For Pharaoh's horse, both chariots and cavalry, went into the sea, and the LORD brought back the waters over them, but Israel had 20 passed through the sea on dry ground. And Miriam the prophetess, Aaron's sister, took up her tambourine, and all the women followed her, 21 dancing to the sound of tambourines; and Miriam sang them this refrain:

Sing to the LORD, for he has risen up in triumph;
the horse and his rider he has hurled into the sea.

[a] *Or* in might. [b] madest thy own: *or* didst create.

MOSES LED ISRAEL from the Red Sea out into the wilderness of 22
Shur. For three days they travelled through the wilderness without
finding water. They came to Marah, but could not drink the Marah 23
water because it was bitter; that is why the place was called Marah.
The people complained to Moses and asked, 'What are we to drink?' 24
Moses cried to the LORD, and the LORD showed him a log which he 25
threw into the water, and then the water became sweet.

It was there that the LORD laid down a precept and rule of life; there
he put them to the test. He said, 'If only you will obey the LORD your 26
God, if you will do what is right in his eyes, if you will listen to his
commands and keep all his statutes, then I will never bring upon you
any of the sufferings which I brought on the Egyptians; for I the LORD
am your healer.'

They came to Elim, where there were twelve springs and seventy 27
palm-trees, and there they encamped beside the water.

The whole community of the Israelites set out from Elim and came 16
into the wilderness of Sin, which lies between Elim and Sinai. This was
on the fifteenth day of the second month after they had left Egypt.

The Israelites complained to Moses and Aaron in the wilderness 2
and said, 'If only we had died at the LORD's hand in Egypt, where we 3
sat round the fleshpots and had plenty of bread to eat! But you have
brought us out into this wilderness to let this whole assembly starve to
death.' The LORD said to Moses, 'I will rain down bread from heaven 4
for you. Each day the people shall go out and gather a day's supply, so
that I can put them to the test and see whether they will follow my
instructions or not. But on the sixth day, when they prepare what they 5
bring in, it shall be twice as much as they have gathered on other days.'
Moses and Aaron then said to all the Israelites, 'In the evening you 6
will know that it was the LORD who brought you out of Egypt, and in 7
the morning you will see the glory of the LORD, because he has heeded
your complaints against him; it is not against us that you bring your
complaints; we are nothing.' 'You shall know this', Moses said, 'when 8
the LORD, in answer to your complaints, gives you flesh to eat in the
evening, and in the morning bread in plenty. What are we? It is against
the LORD that you bring your complaints, and not against us.'

Moses told Aaron to say to the whole community of Israel, 'Come 9
into the presence of the LORD, for he has heeded your complaints.'
While Aaron was speaking to the community of the Israelites, they 10
looked towards the wilderness, and there was the glory of the LORD
appearing in the cloud. The LORD spoke to Moses and said, 'I have 11, 12
heard the complaints of the Israelites. Say to them, "Between dusk and
dark you will have flesh to eat and in the morning bread in plenty.
You shall know that I the LORD am your God."'

13   That evening a flock of quails flew in and settled all over the camp,
14 and in the morning a fall of dew lay all around it. When the dew was gone, there in the wilderness, fine flakes appeared, fine as hoar-frost on
15 the ground. When the Israelites saw it, they said to one another, 'What is that?',[a] because they did not know what it was. Moses said to them,
16 'That is the bread which the LORD has given you to eat. This is the command the LORD has given: "Each of you is to gather as much as he can eat: let every man take an omer a head for every person in his
17 tent."' The Israelites did this, and they gathered, some more, some
18 less, but when they measured it by the omer, those who had gathered more had not too much, and those who had gathered less had not too
19 little. Each had just as much as he could eat. Moses said, 'No one may
20 keep any of it till morning.' Some, however, did not listen to Moses; they kept part of it till morning, and it became full of maggots and
21 stank, and Moses was angry with them. Each morning every man gathered as much as he could eat, and when the sun grew hot, it melted
22 away. On the sixth day they gathered twice as much food, two omers
23 each. All the chiefs of the community came and told Moses. 'This', he answered, 'is what the LORD has said: "Tomorrow is a day of sacred rest, a sabbath holy to the LORD." So bake what you want to bake now, and boil what you want to boil; put aside what remains over and keep
24 it safe till morning.' So they put it aside till morning as Moses had
25 commanded, and it did not stink, nor did maggots appear in it. 'Eat it today,' said Moses, 'because today is a sabbath of the LORD. Today you
26 will find none outside. For six days you may gather it, but on the seventh day, the sabbath, there will be none.'
27   Some of the people did go out to gather it on the seventh day, but
28 they found none. The LORD said to Moses, 'How long will you refuse
29 to obey my commands and instructions? The LORD has given you the sabbath, and so he gives you two days' food every sixth day. Let each man stay where he is; no one may stir from his home on the seventh
30 day.' And the people kept the sabbath on the seventh day.
31   Israel called the food manna; it was white, like coriander seed, and it tasted like a wafer made with honey.
32   'This', said Moses, 'is the command which the LORD has given: "Take a full omer of it to be kept for future generations, so that they may see the bread with which I fed you in the wilderness when I brought
33 you out of Egypt."' So Moses said to Aaron, 'Take a jar and fill it with an omer of manna, and store it in the presence of the LORD to be
34 kept for future generations.' Aaron did as the LORD had commanded
35 Moses, and stored it before the Testimony for safe keeping. The Israelites ate the manna for forty years until they came to a land where

[a] *Heb.* man-hu (*cp. verse 31*).

they could settle; they ate it until they came to the border of Canaan. (An omer is one tenth of an ephah.)   36

The whole community of Israel set out from the wilderness of Sin 17 and travelled by stages as the LORD told them. They encamped at Rephidim, where there was no water for the people to drink, and a 2 dispute arose between them and Moses. When they said, 'Give us water to drink', Moses said, 'Why do you dispute with me? Why do you challenge the LORD?' There the people became so thirsty that they 3 raised an outcry against Moses: 'Why have you brought us out of Egypt with our children and our herds to let us all die of thirst?' Moses cried to the LORD, 'What shall I do with these people? In a 4 moment they will be stoning me.' The LORD answered, 'Go forward 5 ahead of the people; take with you some of the elders of Israel and the staff with which you struck the Nile, and go. You will find me waiting 6 for you there, by a rock in Horeb. Strike the rock; water will pour out of it, and the people shall drink.' Moses did this in the sight of the elders of Israel. He named the place Massah*a* and Meribah,*b* because 7 the Israelites had disputed with him and challenged the LORD with their question, 'Is the LORD in our midst or not?'

The Amalekites came and attacked Israel at Rephidim. Moses said 8,9 to Joshua, 'Pick your men, and march out tomorrow to fight for us against Amalek; and I will take my stand on the hill-top with the staff of God in my hand.' Joshua carried out his orders and fought 10 against Amalek while Moses, Aaron and Hur climbed to the top of the hill. Whenever Moses raised his hands Israel had the advantage, and 11 when he lowered his hands Amalek had the advantage. But when his 12 arms grew heavy they took a stone and put it under him and, as he sat, Aaron and Hur held up his hands, one on each side, so that his hands remained steady till sunset. Thus Joshua defeated Amalek and put its 13 people to the sword.

The LORD said to Moses, 'Record this in writing, and tell it to 14 Joshua in these words: "I am resolved to blot out all memory of Amalek from under heaven."' Moses built an altar, and named it Jehovah-nissi 15 and said, 'My oath upon it:*c* the LORD is at war with Amalek generation 16 after generation.'

JETHRO PRIEST OF MIDIAN, father-in-law of Moses, heard all 18 that God had done for Moses and Israel his people, and how the LORD had brought Israel out of Egypt. When Moses had dismissed his wife 2 Zipporah, Jethro his father-in-law had received her and her two sons. 3 The name of the one was Gershom, 'for', said Moses, 'I have become

[*a*] *That is* Challenge.   [*b*] *That is* Dispute.   [*c*] *So Sam.; lit.* Hand upon buttock; *Heb. unintelligible.*

4 an alien*a* living in a foreign land'; the other's name was Eliezer,*b* 'for', he said, 'the God of my father was my help and saved me from Pharaoh's sword.'

5 Jethro, Moses' father-in-law, now came to him with his sons and his wife, to the wilderness where he was encamped at the mountain of God.

6 Moses was told, 'Here*c* is Jethro, your father-in-law, coming to you

7 with your wife and her two sons.' Moses went out to meet his father-in-law, bowed low to him and kissed him, and they greeted one another.

8 When they came into the tent Moses told him all that the LORD had done to Pharaoh and to Egypt for Israel's sake, and about all their

9 hardships on the journey, and how the LORD had saved them. Jethro rejoiced at all the good the LORD had done for Israel in saving them

10-11 from the power of Egypt. He said, 'Blessed be the LORD who has saved you from the power of Egypt and of Pharaoh. Now I know that the LORD is the greatest of all gods, because he has delivered the people from the power of the Egyptians who dealt so arrogantly with

12 them.' Jethro, Moses' father-in-law, brought a whole-offering and sacrifices for God; and Aaron and all the elders of Israel came and shared the meal with Jethro in the presence of God.

13 The next day Moses took his seat to settle disputes among the people, and they were standing round him from morning till evening.

14 When Jethro saw all that he was doing for the people, he said, 'What are you doing for all these people? Why do you sit alone with all of

15 them standing round you from morning till evening?' 'The people

16 come to me', Moses answered, 'to seek God's guidance. Whenever there is a dispute among them, they come to me, and I decide between

17 man and man. I declare the statutes and laws of God.' But his father-

18 in-law said to Moses, 'This is not the best way to do it. You will only wear yourself out and wear out all the people who are here. The task

19 is too heavy for you; you cannot do it by yourself. Now listen to me: take my advice, and God be with you. It is for you to be the people's

20 representative before God, and bring their disputes to him. You must instruct them in the statutes and laws, and teach them how they must

21 behave and what they must do. But you must yourself search for capable, God-fearing men among all the people, honest and incorruptible men, and appoint them over the people as officers over units of

22 a thousand, of a hundred, of fifty or of ten. They shall sit as a permanent court for the people; they must refer difficult cases to you but decide simple cases themselves. In this way your burden will be lightened, and

23 they will share it with you. If you do this, God will give you strength, and you will be able to go on. And, moreover, this whole people will

24 here and now regain peace and harmony.' Moses listened to his

[a] Cp. 2. 22. [b] *That is* God my help. [c] *So Sept.; Heb.* I.

father-in-law and did all he had suggested. He chose capable men from 25
all Israel and appointed them leaders of the people, officers over units
of a thousand, of a hundred, of fifty or of ten. They sat as a permanent 26
court, bringing the difficult cases to Moses but deciding simple cases
themselves. Moses set his father-in-law on his way, and he went back 27
to his own country.

Israel at Mount Sinai

IN THE THIRD MONTH after Israel had left Egypt,*a* they came to the 19
wilderness of Sinai. They set out from Rephidim and entered the 2
wilderness of Sinai, where they encamped, pitching their tents opposite
the mountain. Moses went up the mountain of*b* God, and the LORD 3
called to him from the mountain and said, 'Speak thus to the house of
Jacob, and tell this to the sons of Israel: You have seen with your own 4
eyes what I did to Egypt, and how I have carried you on eagles' wings
and brought you here to me. If only you will now listen to me and keep 5
my covenant, then out of all peoples you shall become my special
possession; for the whole earth is mine. You shall be my kingdom of 6
priests, my holy nation. These are the words you shall speak to the
Israelites.'

Moses came and summoned the elders of the people and set before 7
them all these commands which the LORD had laid upon him. The 8
people all answered together, 'Whatever the LORD has said we will do.'
Moses brought this answer back to the LORD. The LORD said to Moses, 9
'I am now coming to you in a thick cloud, so that I may speak to you
in the hearing of the people, and their faith in you may never fail.'
Moses told the LORD what the people had said, and the LORD said to 10
him, 'Go to the people and hallow them today and tomorrow and
make them wash their clothes. They must be ready by the third day, 11
because on the third day the LORD will descend upon Mount Sinai in
the sight of all the people. You must put barriers round the mountain*c* 12
and say, "Take care not to go up the mountain or even to touch the
edge of it." Any man who touches the mountain must be put to death.
No hand shall touch him;*d* he shall be stoned or shot dead:*e* neither 13
man nor beast may live. But when the ram's horn sounds, they may go
up the mountain.' Moses came down from the mountain to the people. 14
He hallowed them and they washed their clothes. He said to the 15
people, 'Be ready by the third day; do not go near a woman.' On the 16
third day, when morning came, there were peals of thunder and flashes

[a] *Prob. rdg.; Heb. adds* on this day.   [b] the mountain of: *so Sept.; Heb. om.*   [c] *So Sam.;*
Heb. people.   [d] *Or* it.   [e] *Or* hurled to his death.

of lightning, dense cloud on the mountain and a loud trumpet blast; the people in the camp were all terrified.

17 Moses brought the people out from the camp to meet God, and they
18 took their stand at the foot of the mountain. Mount Sinai was all smoking because the LORD had come down upon it in fire; the smoke
19 went up like the smoke of a kiln; all the people were*a* terrified, and the sound of the trumpet grew ever louder. Whenever Moses spoke, God
20 answered him in a peal of thunder.*b* The LORD came down upon the top of Mount Sinai and summoned Moses to the mountain-top, and
21 Moses went up. The LORD said to Moses, 'Go down; warn the people solemnly that they must not force their way through to the LORD to
22 see him, or many of them will perish. Even the priests, who have access to the LORD, must hallow themselves, for fear that the LORD may break
23 out against them.' Moses answered the LORD, 'The people cannot come up Mount Sinai, because thou thyself didst solemnly warn us to set a
24 barrier to the mountain and so to keep it holy.' The LORD therefore said to him, 'Go down; then come up and bring Aaron with you, but let neither priests nor people force their way up to the LORD, for fear that
25 he may break out against them.' So Moses went down to the people and spoke to them.

20 God spoke, and these were his words:
2   I am the LORD your God who brought you out of Egypt, out of the land of slavery.
3   You shall have no other god*c* to set against me.
4   You shall not make a carved image for yourself nor the likeness of anything in the heavens above, or on the earth below, or in the waters under the earth.
5   You shall not bow down to them or worship*d* them; for I, the LORD your God, am a jealous god. I punish the children for the sins of the fathers to the third and fourth generations of those who hate me.
6   But I keep faith with thousands, with*e* those who love me and keep my commandments.
7   You shall not make wrong use of the name of the LORD your God; the LORD will not leave unpunished the man who misuses his name.
8, 9   Remember to keep the sabbath day holy. You have six days to labour
10   and do all your work. But the seventh day is a sabbath of the LORD your God; that day you shall not do any work, you, your son or your daughter, your slave or your slave-girl, your cattle or the alien within
11   your gates; for in six days the LORD made heaven and earth, the sea, and all that is in them, and on the seventh day he rested. Therefore the LORD blessed the sabbath day and declared it holy.

[a] *So some MSS.; others* all the mountain was...   [b] in...thunder: *or* by voice.   [c] *Or* gods.   [d] *Or* or be led to worship.   [e] with...with: *or* for a thousand generations with...

Honour your father and your mother, that you may live long in the 12
land which the LORD your God is giving you.

You shall not commit murder. 13

You shall not commit adultery. 14

You shall not steal. 15

You shall not give false evidence against your neighbour. 16

You shall not covet your neighbour's house; you shall not covet your 17
neighbour's wife, his slave, his slave-girl, his ox, his ass, or anything
that belongs to him.

When all the people saw how it thundered and the lightning flashed, 18
when they heard the trumpet sound and saw the mountain smoking,
they trembled and stood at a distance. 'Speak to us yourself,' they said 19
to Moses, 'and we will listen; but if God speaks to us we shall die.'
Moses answered, 'Do not be afraid. God has come only to test you, so 20
that the fear of him may remain with you and keep you from sin.' So 21
the people stood at a distance, while Moses approached the dark cloud
where God was.

THE LORD SAID to Moses, Say this to the Israelites: You know now 22
that I have spoken to you from heaven. You shall not make gods of 23
silver to be worshipped as well as me, nor shall you make yourselves
gods of gold. You shall make an altar of earth for me, and you shall 24
sacrifice on it both your whole-offerings and your shared*a*-offerings,
your sheep and your cattle. Wherever*b* I cause my name to be invoked,
I will come to you and bless you. If you make an altar of stones for me, 25
you must not build it of hewn stones, for if you use a chisel on it, you
will profane it. You must not mount up to my altar by steps, in case 26
your private parts be exposed on it.

These are the laws you shall set before them: **21**

When you buy a Hebrew slave, he shall be your slave for six years, 2
but in the seventh year he shall go free and pay nothing.

If he comes to you alone, he shall go away alone; but if he is married, 3
his wife shall go away with him.

If his master gives him a wife, and she bears him sons or daughters, 4
the woman and her children shall belong to her master, and the man
shall go away alone. But if the slave should say, 'I love my master, my 5
wife, and my children; I will not go free', then his master shall bring him 6
to God: he shall bring him to the door or the door-post, and his master
shall pierce his ear with an awl, and the man shall be his slave for life.

When a man sells his daughter into slavery, she shall not go free as 7
a male slave may. If her master has not had intercourse with her*c* and 8

[a] *Exact mng. of Heb. uncertain.*   [b] *So Sam.; Heb.* In all the place where.   [c] *So Pesh.;*
Heb. has assigned her to himself.

99

she does not please him, he shall let her be ransomed. He has treated
9 her unfairly and therefore has no right to sell her to strangers. If he
assigns her to his son, he shall allow her the rights of a daughter.
10 If he takes another woman, he shall not deprive the first of meat,
11 clothes, and conjugal rights. If he does not provide her with these
three things, she shall go free without any payment.

12   Whoever strikes another man and kills him shall be put to death.
13 But if he did not act with intent, but they met by act of God, the slayer
14 may flee to a place which I will appoint for you. But if a man has the
presumption to kill another by treachery, you shall take him even from
my altar to be put to death.

15   Whoever strikes his father or mother shall be put to death.

16   Whoever kidnaps a man shall be put to death, whether he has sold
him, or the man is found in his possession.

17   Whoever reviles his father or mother shall be put to death.

18   When men quarrel and one hits another with a stone or with a
19 spade,*a* and the man is not killed but takes to his bed; if he recovers so
as to walk about outside with a stick, then the one who struck him has
no liability, except that he shall pay for loss of time and shall see that
he is cured.

20   When a man strikes his slave or his slave-girl with a stick and the
21 slave dies on the spot, he must be punished. But he shall not be
punished if the slave survives for one day or two, because he is worth
money to his master.

22   When, in the course of a brawl, a man knocks against a pregnant
woman so that she has a miscarriage but suffers no further hurt, then
the offender must pay whatever fine the woman's husband demands
after assessment.

23, 24   Wherever hurt is done, you shall give life for life, eye for eye, tooth
25 for tooth, hand for hand, foot for foot, burn for burn, bruise for bruise,
wound for wound.

26   When a man strikes his slave or slave-girl in the eye and destroys it,
27 he shall let the slave go free in compensation for the eye. When he
knocks out the tooth of a slave or a slave-girl, he shall let the slave go
free in compensation for the tooth.

28   When an ox gores a man or a woman to death, the ox shall be stoned,
and its flesh may not be eaten; the owner of the ox shall be free from
29 liability. If, however, the ox has for some time past been a vicious
animal, and the owner has been duly warned but has not kept it under
control, and the ox kills a man or a woman, then the ox shall be stoned,
30 and the owner shall be put to death as well. If, however, the penalty is
commuted for a money payment, he shall pay in redemption of his life

[a] *Or* fist.

whatever is imposed upon him. If the ox gores a son or a daughter, the 31
same rule shall apply. If the ox gores a slave or slave-girl, its owner shall 32
pay thirty shekels of silver to their master, and the ox shall be stoned.

When a man removes the cover of a well*a* or digs a well*a* and leaves it 33
uncovered, then if an ox or an ass falls into it, the owner of the well 34
shall make good the loss. He shall repay the owner of the beast in
silver, and the dead beast shall be his.

When one man's ox butts another's and kills it, they shall sell the 35
live ox, share the price and also share the dead beast. But if it is known 36
that the ox has for some time past been vicious and the owner has not
kept it under control, he shall make good the loss, ox for ox, but the
dead beast is his.

When a man steals an ox or a sheep and slaughters or sells it, he 22 1*b*
shall repay five beasts for the ox and four sheep for the sheep. He shall 2–4*c*
pay in full; if he has no means, he shall be sold to pay for the theft.
But if the animal is found alive in his possession, be it ox, ass, or
sheep, he shall repay two.

*d*If a burglar is caught in the act and is fatally injured, it is not murder;
but if he breaks in after sunrise and is fatally injured, then it is murder.

When a man burns off a field or a vineyard and lets the fire spread so 5
that it burns another man's field,*e* he shall make restitution from his
own field according to the yield expected; and if the whole field is laid
waste,*f* he shall make restitution from the best part of his own field or
vineyard.

When a fire starts and spreads to a heap of brushwood, so that 6
sheaves, or standing corn, or a whole field is destroyed, he who started
the fire shall make full restitution.

When one man gives another silver or chattels for safe keeping, and 7
they are stolen from that man's house, the thief, if he is found, shall
restore twofold. But if the thief is not found, the owner of the house 8
shall appear before God, to make a declaration that he has not touched
his neighbour's property. In every case of law-breaking involving an 9
ox, an ass, or a sheep, a cloak, or any lost property which may be
claimed, each party shall bring his case before God; he whom God
declares to be in the wrong shall restore twofold to his neighbour.

When a man gives an ass, an ox, a sheep or any beast into his 10
neighbour's keeping, and it dies or is injured or is carried off, there
being no witness, the neighbour shall swear by the LORD that he has 11
not touched the man's property. The owner shall accept this, and no
restitution shall be made. If it has been stolen from him, he shall make 12

[*a*] *Or* cistern.   [*b*] *21. 37 in Heb.*   [*c*] *Verses 2–4 re-arranged thus: 3 B, 4, 2, 3 A.*   [*d*] *22. 1
in Heb.*   [*e*] *Or* When a man uses his field or vineyard for grazing, and lets his beast loose,
and it feeds in another man's field.   [*f*] he shall...waste: *so Sam.; Heb. om.*

13 restitution to the owner. If it has been mauled by a wild beast, he shall bring it in as evidence; he shall not make restitution for what has been mauled.

14 When a man borrows a beast*a* from his neighbour and it is injured or dies while its owner is not with it, the borrower shall make full restitu-
15 tion; but if the owner is with it, the borrower shall not make restitution. If it was hired, only the hire shall be due.

16 When a man seduces a virgin who is not yet betrothed, he shall pay
17 the bride-price for her to be his wife. If her father refuses to give her to him, the seducer shall pay in silver a sum equal to the bride-price for virgins.

18 You shall not allow a witch to live.

19 Whoever has unnatural connection with a beast shall be put to death.

20 Whoever sacrifices to any god but the LORD shall be put to death under solemn ban.

21 You shall not wrong an alien, or be hard upon him; you were your-
22 selves aliens in Egypt. You shall not ill-treat any widow or fatherless
23, 24 child. If you do, be sure that I will listen if they appeal to me; my anger will be roused and I will kill you with the sword; your own wives shall become widows and your children fatherless.

25 If you advance money to any poor man amongst my people, you shall not act like a money-lender: you must not exact interest in advance from him.

26 If you take your neighbour's cloak in pawn, you shall return it to him
27 by sunset, because it is his only covering. It is the cloak in which he wraps his body; in what else can he sleep? If he appeals to me, I will listen, for I am full of compassion.

28 You shall not revile God, nor curse a chief of your own people.

29 You shall not hold back the first of your harvest, whether corn or
30 wine.*b* You shall give me your first-born sons. You shall do the same with your oxen and your sheep. They shall stay with the mother for seven days; on the eighth day you shall give them to me.

31 You shall be holy to me: you shall not eat the flesh of anything in the open country killed by beasts, but you shall throw it to the dogs.

23 You shall not spread a baseless rumour. You shall not make common cause with a wicked man by giving malicious evidence.

2 You shall not be led into wrongdoing by the majority, nor, when you give evidence in a lawsuit, shall you side with the majority to pervert
3 justice;*c* nor shall you favour the poor man in his suit.

4 When you come upon your enemy's ox or ass straying, you shall take
5 it back to him. When you see the ass of someone who hates you lying

[a] a beast: *so Scroll; Heb. om.*   [b] the first...wine: *mng. of Heb. words uncertain.*
[c] justice: *so Sept.; Heb. om.*

helpless under its load, however unwilling you may be to help it, you
must give him a hand with it.

You shall not deprive the poor man of justice in his suit. Avoid all 6,7
lies, and do not cause the death of the innocent and the guiltless; for
I the LORD will never acquit the guilty. You shall not accept a bribe, 8
for bribery makes the discerning man blind and the just man give a
crooked answer.

You shall not oppress the alien, for you know how it feels to be an 9
alien; you were aliens yourselves in Egypt.

For six years you may sow your land and gather its produce; but in 10,11
the seventh year you shall let it lie fallow and leave it alone. It shall
provide food for the poor of your people, and what they leave the wild
animals may eat. You shall do likewise with your vineyard and your
olive-grove.

For six days you may do your work, but on the seventh day you shall 12
abstain from work, so that your ox and your ass may rest, and your
home-born slave and the alien may refresh themselves.

Be attentive to every word of mine. You shall not invoke other gods: 13
your lips shall not speak their names.

Three times a year you shall keep a pilgrim-feast to me. You shall 14,15
celebrate the pilgrim-feast of Unleavened Bread for seven days; you
shall eat unleavened cakes as I have commanded you, at the appointed
time in the month of Abib, for in that month you came out of Egypt.

No one shall come into my presence*a* empty-handed. You shall 16
celebrate the pilgrim-feast of Harvest, with the firstfruits of your work
in sowing the land, and the pilgrim-feast of Ingathering at the end*b* of
the year, when you bring in the fruits of all your work on the land.
These three times a year shall all your males come into the presence of*c* 17
the Lord GOD.

You shall not offer the blood of my sacrifice at the same time as 18
anything leavened.

The fat of my festal offering shall not remain overnight till morning.

You shall bring the choicest firstfruits of your soil to the house of the 19
LORD your God.

You shall not boil a kid in its mother's milk.

And now I send an angel before you to guard you on your way and 20
to bring you to the place I have prepared. Take heed of him and listen 21
to his voice. Do not defy him; he will not pardon your rebelliousness,
for my authority rests in him. If you will only listen to his voice and do 22
all I tell you, then I will be an enemy to your enemies, and I will
harass those who harass you. My angel will go before you and bring 23
you to the Amorites, the Hittites, the Perizzites, the Canaanites, the

[a] *Lit.* see my face... [b] *Or* beginning; *lit.* going out. [c] *Lit.* see the face of...

24 Hivites, and the Jebusites, and I will make an end of them. You are not to bow down to their gods, nor worship them, nor observe their rites, but you shall tear down all their images and smash their sacred pillars.
25 Worship the LORD your God, and he will bless your bread and your
26 water. I will take away all sickness out of your midst. None shall miscarry or be barren in your land. I will grant you a full span of life.
27 I will send my terror before you and throw into confusion all the peoples whom you find in your path. I will make all your enemies turn
28 their backs. I will spread panic before you to drive out in front of you
29 the Hivites, the Canaanites and the Hittites. I will not drive them out all in one year, or the land would become waste and the wild beasts too
30 many for you. I will drive them out little by little until your numbers
31 have grown enough to take possession of the whole country. I will establish your frontiers from the Red Sea to the sea of the Philistines, and from the wilderness to the River. I will give the inhabitants of the country into your power, and you shall drive them out before you.
32, 33 You shall make no covenant with them and their gods. They shall not stay in your land for fear they make you sin against me; for then you would worship their gods, and in this way you would be ensnared.

24 THEN HE SAID to Moses, 'Come up to the LORD, you and Aaron, Nadab and Abihu, and seventy of the elders of Israel. While you are
2 still at a distance, you are to bow down; and then Moses shall approach the LORD by himself, but not the others. The people may not go up with him at all.'
3 Moses came and told the people all the words of the LORD, all his laws. The whole people answered with one voice and said, 'We will do
4 all that the LORD has told us.' Moses wrote down all the words of the LORD. He rose early in the morning and built an altar at the foot of the mountain, and put up twelve sacred pillars, one for each of the twelve
5 tribes of Israel. He then sent the young men of Israel and they sacrificed
6 bulls to the LORD as whole-offerings and shared-offerings. Moses took half the blood and put it in basins and the other half he flung against[a]
7 the altar. Then he took the book of the covenant and read it aloud for all the people to hear. They said, 'We will obey, and do all that the LORD
8 has said.' Moses then took the blood and flung it over the people, saying, 'This is the blood of the covenant which the LORD has made with you on the terms of this book.'
9 Moses went up with Aaron, Nadab and Abihu, and seventy of the
10 elders of Israel, and they saw[b] the God of Israel. Under his feet there was, as it were, a pavement of sapphire,[c] clear blue as the very heavens;
11 but the LORD did not stretch out his hand towards the leaders of Israel.

[a] *Or* upon. [b] *Or* they were afraid of... [c] *Or* lapis lazuli.

They stayed there before God;^a they ate and they drank. The LORD 12
said to Moses, 'Come up to me on the mountain, stay there and let me
give you the tablets of stone, the law and the commandment, which I
have written down that you may teach them.' Moses arose with 13
Joshua his assistant and went up the mountain of God; he said to the 14
elders, 'Wait for us here until we come back to you. You have Aaron
and Hur; if anyone has a dispute, let him go to them.' So Moses went 15
up the mountain and a cloud covered it. The glory of the LORD rested 16
upon Mount Sinai, and the cloud covered the mountain for six days;
on the seventh day he called to Moses out of the cloud. The glory of the 17
LORD looked to the Israelites like a devouring fire on the mountain-top.
Moses entered the cloud and went up the mountain; there he stayed 18
forty days and forty nights.

THE LORD SPOKE to Moses and said: Tell the Israelites to set aside 25 1,2
a contribution for me; you shall accept whatever contribution each
man shall freely offer. This is what you shall accept: gold, silver, 3
copper; violet, purple, and scarlet yarn; fine linen and goats' hair; 4
tanned rams' skins, porpoise^b-hides, and acacia-wood; oil for the lamp, 5,6
balsam for the anointing oil and for the fragrant incense; cornelian and 7
other stones ready for setting in the ephod and the breast-piece.^c
Make me a sanctuary, and I will dwell among them. Make it exactly 8,9
according to the design I show you, the design for the Tabernacle and
for all its furniture. This is how you must make it:
   Make an Ark, a chest of acacia-wood, two and a half cubits long, one 10
cubit and a half wide, and one cubit and a half high. Overlay it with 11
pure gold both inside and out, and put a band of gold all round it.
Cast four gold rings for it, and fasten them to its four feet, two rings on 12
each side. Make poles of acacia-wood and plate them with gold, 13
and insert the poles in the rings at the sides of the Ark to lift it. The 14,15
poles shall remain in the rings of the Ark and never be removed. Put 16
into the Ark the Tokens of the Covenant,^d which I shall give you. Make 17
a cover of pure gold, two and a half cubits long and one cubit and a half
wide. Make two gold cherubim of beaten work at the ends of the cover, 18
one at each end; make each cherub of one piece with the cover. They 19,20
shall be made with wings outspread and pointing upwards, and shall
screen the cover with their wings. They shall be face to face, looking
inwards over the cover. Put the cover above the Ark, and put into 21
the Ark the Tokens that I shall give you. It is there that I shall meet 22
you, and from above the cover, between the two cherubim over the

[a] *Or* They saw God; and... [b] *Strictly* sea-cow. [c] *Or* pouch. [d] Tokens of the
Covenant: *or* Testimony.

Ark of the Tokens, I shall deliver to you all my commands for the Israelites.

23 　　Make a table of acacia-wood, two cubits long, one cubit wide, and
24 one cubit and a half high. Overlay it with pure gold, and put a band of
25 gold all round it. Make a rim round it a hand's breadth wide, and a
26 gold band round the rim. Make four gold rings for the table, and put
27 the rings at the four corners by the legs. The rings, which are to receive
28 the poles for carrying the table, must be adjacent to the rim. Make
the poles of acacia-wood and plate them with gold; they are to be used
29 for carrying the table. Make its dishes and saucers, and its flagons
and bowls from which drink-offerings may be poured: make them of
30 pure gold. Put the Bread of the Presence[a] on the table, to be always
before me.

31 　　Make a lamp-stand of pure gold. The lamp-stand, stem and branches,
shall be of beaten work, its cups, both calyxes and petals, shall be of one
32 piece with it. There are to be six branches springing from its sides;
three branches of the lamp-stand shall spring from the one side and
33 three branches from the other side. There shall be three cups shaped
like almond blossoms, with calyx and petals, on the first branch, three
cups shaped like almond blossoms, with calyx and petals, on the next
branch, and similarly for all six branches springing from the lamp-stand.
34 On the main stem of the lamp-stand there are to be four cups shaped
35 like almond blossoms, with calyx and petals, and there shall be calyxes
of one piece with it under the six branches which spring from the lamp-
36 stand, a single calyx under each pair of branches. The calyxes and the
branches are to be of one piece with it, all a single piece of beaten work
37 of pure gold. Make seven lamps for this and mount them to shed light
38 over the space in front of it. Its tongs and firepans shall be of pure gold.
39 The lamp-stand and all these fittings shall be made from one talent of
40 pure gold. See that you work to the design which you were shown on
the mountain.

26 　　Make the Tabernacle of ten hangings of finely woven linen, and
violet, purple, and scarlet yarn, with cherubim worked on them, all
2 made by a seamster. The length of each hanging shall be twenty-eight
cubits and the breadth four cubits; all are to be of the same size.
3 Five of the hangings shall be joined together, and similarly the other
4 five. Make violet loops along the edge of the last hanging in each set,
5,6 fifty for each set; they must be opposite one another. Make fifty gold
fasteners, join the hangings one to another with them, and the Tabernacle will be a single whole.

7 　　Make hangings of goats' hair, eleven in all, to form a tent over the
8 Tabernacle; each hanging is to be thirty cubits long and four wide; all

[a] *Or* Shewbread.

eleven are to be of the same size. Join five of the hangings together, and 9
similarly the other six; then fold the sixth hanging double at the front
of the tent. Make fifty loops on the edge of the last hanging in the first 10
set and make fifty loops on the joining edge of the second set. Make 11
fifty bronze[a] fasteners, insert them into the loops and join up the tent
to make it a single whole. The additional length of the tent hanging[b] 12
is to fall over the back of the Tabernacle. On each side there will be an 13
additional cubit in the length of the tent hangings; this shall fall over
the two sides of the Tabernacle to cover it. Make for the tent a cover 14
of tanned rams' skins and an outer covering of porpoise-hides.

Make for the Tabernacle planks of acacia-wood as uprights, each 15, 16
plank ten cubits long and a cubit and a half wide, and two tenons for 17
each plank joined to each other. You shall do the same for all the planks
of the Tabernacle. Arrange the planks thus: twenty planks for the 18
south side, facing southwards, with forty silver sockets under them, 19
two sockets under each plank for its two tenons; and for the second or 20
northern side of the Tabernacle, twenty planks, with forty silver 21
sockets, two under each plank. Make six planks for the far end of 22
the Tabernacle on the west. Make two planks for the corners of the 23
Tabernacle at the far end; at the bottom they shall be alike, and at the 24
top, both alike,[c] they shall fit into a single ring. Do the same for both
of them; they shall be for the two corners. There shall be eight planks 25
with their silver sockets, sixteen sockets in all, two sockets under each
plank severally.

Make bars of acacia-wood: five for the planks on the one side of the 26
Tabernacle, five for the planks on the other side and five for the planks 27
on the far end of the Tabernacle on the west. The middle bar is to run 28
along from end to end half-way up the planks. Overlay the planks with 29
gold, make rings of gold on them to hold the bars, and plate the bars
with gold. Set up the Tabernacle according to the design you were 30
shown on the mountain.

Make a Veil of finely woven linen and violet, purple, and scarlet yarn, 31
with cherubim worked on it, all made by a seamster. Fasten it with 32
hooks of gold to four posts of acacia-wood overlaid with gold, standing
in four silver sockets. Hang the Veil below the fasteners and bring the 33
Ark of the Tokens inside the Veil. Thus the Veil will make a clear
separation for you between the Holy Place and the Holy of Holies. Place 34
the cover over the Ark of the Tokens in the Holy of Holies. Put the 35
table outside the Veil and the lamp-stand at the south side of the
Tabernacle, opposite the table which you shall put at the north side.
For the entrance of the tent make a screen of finely woven linen, 36

[a] *Or* copper *and so throughout the description of the Tabernacle.* [b] *Prob. rdg.; Heb. adds*
half the hanging which remains over. [c] *So Sam.; Heb.* perfect.

37 embroidered with violet, purple, and scarlet. Make five posts of acacia-wood for the screen and overlay them with gold; make golden hooks for them and cast five bronze sockets for them.

27 Make the altar of acacia-wood; it shall be square, five cubits long by
2 five cubits broad and three cubits high. Let its horns at the four corners
3 be of one piece with it, and overlay it with bronze. Make for it pots to take away the fat and the ashes, with shovels, tossing bowls, forks, and
4 firepans, all of bronze. Make a grating for it of bronze network, and fit
5 four bronze rings on the network at its four corners. Put it below the ledge of the altar, so that the network comes half-way up the altar.
6 Make poles of acacia-wood for the altar and overlay them with bronze.
7 They shall be inserted in the rings at both sides of the altar to carry it.
8 Leave the altar a hollow shell. As you were shown on the mountain, so shall it be made.

9 Make the court of the Tabernacle. For the one side, the south side facing southwards, the court shall have hangings of finely woven linen
10 a hundred cubits long, with twenty posts and twenty sockets of bronze;
11 the hooks and bands on the posts shall be of silver. Similarly all along the north side there shall be hangings a hundred cubits long, with twenty posts and twenty sockets of bronze; the hooks and bands on the
12 posts shall be of silver. For the breadth of the court, on the west side, there shall be hangings fifty cubits long, with ten posts and ten sockets.
13, 14 On the east side, towards the sunrise, which was fifty cubits, hangings shall extend fifteen cubits from one corner, with three posts and three
15 sockets, and hangings shall extend fifteen cubits from the other corner,
16 with three posts and three sockets. At the gateway of the court, there shall be a screen twenty cubits long of finely woven linen embroidered
17 with violet, purple, and scarlet, with four posts and four sockets. The posts all round the court shall have bands of silver, with hooks of silver,
18 and sockets of bronze. The length of the court shall be a hundred cubits, and the breadth fifty,[a] and the height five cubits, with finely
19 woven linen and bronze sockets throughout. All the equipment needed for serving the Tabernacle, all its pegs and those of the court, shall be of bronze.

20 You yourself are to command the Israelites to bring you pure oil of
21 pounded olives ready for the regular mounting of the lamp. In the Tent of the Presence[b] outside the Veil that hides the Tokens, Aaron and his sons shall keep the lamp in trim from dusk to dawn before the LORD. This is a rule binding on their descendants among the Israelites for all time.

28 You yourself are to summon to your presence your brother Aaron and his sons out of all the Israelites to serve as my priests: Aaron and

[a] *So Sam.; Heb. adds* by fifty.   [b] *Or* Tent of Meeting.

his sons Nadab and Abihu, Eleazar and Ithamar. For your brother ₂
Aaron make sacred vestments, to give him dignity and grandeur. Tell ₃
all the craftsmen whom I have endowed with skill to make the vestments
for the consecration of Aaron as my priest. These are the vestments ₄
they shall make: a breast-piece, an ephod, a mantle, a chequered tunic,
a turban, and a sash. They shall make sacred vestments for Aaron your
brother and his sons to wear when they serve as my priests, using gold; ₅
violet, purple, and scarlet yarn; and fine linen.

The ephod shall be made of gold, and with violet, purple, and ₆
scarlet yarn, and with finely woven linen worked by a seamster.
It shall have two shoulder-pieces joined back and front. The waist- ₇,₈
band on it shall be of the same workmanship and material as the fabric
of the ephod, and shall be of gold, with violet, purple, and scarlet yarn,
and finely woven linen. You shall take two cornelians and engrave on ₉
them the names of the sons of Israel: six of their names on the one ₁₀
stone, and the six other names on the second, all in order of seniority.
With the skill of a craftsman, a seal-cutter, you shall engrave the two ₁₁
stones with the names of the sons of Israel; you shall set them in gold
rosettes, and fasten them on the shoulders of the ephod, as reminders ₁₂
of the sons of Israel. Aaron shall bear their names on his two shoulders
as a reminder before the Lord.

Make gold rosettes and two chains of pure gold worked into the ₁₃,₁₄
form of ropes, and fix them on the rosettes. Make the breast-piece of ₁₅
judgement; it shall be made, like the ephod, by a seamster in gold, with
violet, purple, and scarlet yarn, and finely woven linen. It shall be a ₁₆
square folded, a span long and a span wide. Set in it four rows of ₁₇
precious stones: the first row, sardin, chrysolite and green felspar;
the second row, purple garnet, lapis lazuli and jade; the third row, ₁₈,₁₉
turquoise, agate and jasper; the fourth row, topaz, cornelian and green ₂₀
jasper, all set in gold rosettes. The stones shall correspond to the ₂₁
twelve sons of Israel name by name; each stone shall bear the name of
one of the twelve tribes engraved as on a seal.

Make for the breast-piece chains of pure gold worked into a rope. ₂₂
Make two gold rings, and fix them on the two upper corners of the ₂₃
breast-piece. Fasten the two gold ropes to the two rings at those corners ₂₄
of the breast-piece, and the other ends of the ropes to the two rosettes, ₂₅
thus binding the breast-piece to the shoulder-pieces on the front of the
ephod. Make two gold rings and put them at the two lower corners of ₂₆
the breast-piece on the inner side next to the ephod. Make two gold ₂₇
rings and fix them on the two shoulder-pieces of the ephod, low down
in front, along its seam above the waist-band of the ephod. Then the ₂₈
breast-piece shall be bound by its rings to the rings of the ephod with
violet braid, just above the waist-band of the ephod, so that the breast-

29 piece will not be detached from the ephod. Thus, when Aaron enters the Holy Place, he shall carry over his heart in the breast-piece of judgement the names of the sons of Israel, as a constant reminder before the LORD.

30 Finally, put the Urim and the Thummim into the breast-piece of judgement, and they will be over Aaron's heart when he enters the presence of the LORD. So shall Aaron bear these symbols of judgement upon the sons of Israel over his heart constantly before the LORD.

31, 32 Make the mantle of the ephod a single piece of violet stuff. There shall be a hole for the head in the middle of it. All round the hole there shall be a hem of woven work, with an oversewn edge,[a] so that it
33 cannot be torn. All round its skirts make pomegranates of violet,
34 purple, and scarlet stuff, with golden bells between them, a golden bell and a pomegranate alternately the whole way round the skirts of the
35 mantle. Aaron shall wear it when he ministers, and the sound of it shall be heard when he enters the Holy Place before the LORD and when he comes out; and so he shall not die.

36 Make a rosette of pure gold and engrave on it as on a seal, 'Holy
37 to the LORD'.[b] Fasten it on a violet braid and set it on the very front
38 of the turban. It shall be on Aaron's forehead; he has to bear the blame for shortcomings in the rites with which the Israelites offer their sacred gifts, and the rosette shall be always on his forehead so that they may be acceptable to the LORD.

39 Make the chequered tunic and the turban of fine linen, but the sash
40 of embroidered work. For Aaron's sons make tunics and sashes; and
41 make tall head-dresses to give them dignity and grandeur. With these invest your brother Aaron and his sons, anoint them, install them and
42 consecrate them;[c] so shall they serve me as priests. Make for them
43 linen drawers reaching to the thighs to cover their private parts; and Aaron and his sons shall wear them when they enter the Tent of the Presence or approach the altar to minister in the Holy Place. Thus they will not incur guilt and die. This is a rule binding on him and his descendants for all time.

29 In consecrating them to be my priests this is the rite to be observed.
2 Take a young bull and two rams without blemish. Take unleavened loaves, unleavened cakes mixed with oil, and unleavened wafers
3 smeared with oil, all made of wheaten flour; put them in a single basket and bring them in it. Bring also the bull and the two rams.
4 Bring Aaron and his sons to the entrance of the Tent of the Presence,
5 and wash them with water. Take the vestments and invest Aaron with the tunic, the mantle of the ephod, the ephod itself and the breast-

[a] with an oversewn edge: *lit.* like the opening of a womb. [b] as . . . LORD: *or* 'JEHOVAH' as on a seal in sacred characters. [c] *Lit.* fill their hands.

piece, and fasten the ephod to him with its waist-band. Set the turban 6
on his head, and the symbol of holy dedication on the turban. Take 7
the anointing oil, pour it on his head and anoint him. Then bring his 8
sons forward, invest them with tunics, gird them*ᵃ* with the sashes and 9
tie their tall head-dresses on them. They shall hold the priesthood by
a rule binding for all time.

Next you shall install Aaron and his sons. Bring the bull to the front 10
of the Tent of the Presence, and they shall lay their hands on its head.
Slaughter the bull before the LORD at the entrance to the Tent of the 11
Presence. Take some of its blood, and put it with your finger on the 12
horns of the altar. Pour all the rest*ᵇ* of it at the base of the altar.
Then take the fat covering the entrails, the long lobe of the liver, and 13
the two kidneys with the fat upon them, and burn it on the altar; but 14
the flesh of the bull, and its skin and offal, you shall destroy by fire
outside the camp. It is a sin-offering.

Take one of the rams, and Aaron and his sons shall lay their hands 15
on its head. Then slaughter it, take its blood and fling it against the 16
sides of the altar. Cut the ram up; wash its entrails and its shins, lay 17
them with the pieces and the head, and burn the whole ram on the 18
altar: it is a whole-offering to the LORD; it is a soothing odour, a food-
offering to the LORD.

Take the second ram, and let Aaron and his sons lay their hands on 19
its head. Then slaughter it, take some of its blood, and put it on the 20
lobes of the right ears of Aaron and his sons, and on their right thumbs
and big toes. Fling the rest of the blood against the sides of the altar.
Take some of the blood which is on the altar and some of the anointing 21
oil, and sprinkle it on Aaron and his vestments, and on his sons and
their vestments. So shall he and his vestments, and his sons and their
vestments become holy. Take the fat from the ram, the fat-tail, the fat 22
covering the entrails, the long lobe of the liver, the two kidneys with the
fat upon them, and the right leg: for it is a ram of installation. Take 23
also one round loaf of bread, one cake cooked with oil, and one wafer
from the basket of unleavened bread that is before the LORD. Set all 24
these on the hands of Aaron and of his sons and present them as a
special gift before the LORD. Then take them out of their hands, and 25
burn them on the altar with the whole-offering for a soothing odour to
the LORD: it is a food-offering to the LORD. Take the breast of Aaron's 26
ram of installation, present it as a special gift before the LORD, and it
shall be your perquisite.

Hallow the breast of the special gift and the leg of the contribution, 27
that which is presented and that which is set aside from the ram of
installation, that which is for Aaron and that which is for his sons; and 28

[a] *So Sept.; Heb. adds* Aaron and his sons.   [b] the rest: *so Sept.; Heb. om.*

III

they shall belong to Aaron and his sons, by a rule binding for all time, as a gift from the Israelites, for it is a contribution, set aside from their shared-offerings, their contribution to the LORD.

29,30 Aaron's sacred vestments shall be kept for the anointing and installation of his sons after him. The priest appointed in his stead from among his sons, the one who enters^a the Tent of the Presence to minister in the Holy Place, shall wear them for seven days.

31,32,33,34 Take the ram of installation, and boil its flesh in a sacred place; Aaron and his sons shall eat the ram's flesh and the bread left in the basket, at the entrance to the Tent of the Presence. They shall eat the things with which expiation was made at their installation and their consecration. No unqualified person may eat them, for they are holy. If any of the flesh of the installation, or any of the bread, is left over till morning, you shall destroy it by fire; it shall not be eaten, for it is holy.

35 Do this with Aaron and his sons as I have commanded you, spending seven days over their installation.

36,37 Offer a bull daily, a sin-offering as expiation for sin; offer the sin-offering on the altar when you make expiation for it, and consecrate it by anointing. For seven days you shall make expiation for the altar, and consecrate it, and it shall be most holy. Whatever touches the altar shall be forfeit as sacred.

38,39,40,41,42,43,44,45,46 This is what you shall offer on the altar: two yearling rams regularly every day. You shall offer the one ram at dawn, and the second between dusk and dark, a tenth of an ephah of flour mixed with a quarter of a hin of pure oil of pounded olives, and a drink-offering of a quarter of a hin of wine for the first ram. You shall offer the second ram between dusk and dark, and with it the same grain-offering and drink-offering as at dawn, for a soothing odour: it is a food-offering to the LORD, a regular whole-offering in every generation; you shall make the offering at the entrance to the Tent of the Presence before the LORD, where I meet you and speak to you. I shall meet the Israelites there, and the place will be hallowed by my glory. I shall hallow the Tent of the Presence and the altar; and Aaron and his sons I shall consecrate to serve me as priests. I shall dwell in the midst of the Israelites, I shall become their God, and by my dwelling among them they will know that I am the LORD their God who brought them out of Egypt. I am the LORD their God.

30 Make an altar on which to burn incense; make it of acacia-wood.
2 It shall be square, a cubit long by a cubit broad and two cubits high;
3 the horns of one piece with it. Overlay it with pure gold, the top, the
4 sides all round, and the horns; and put round it a band of gold. Make pairs of gold rings for it; put them under the band at the two corners

[a] *Or* when he enters.

on both sides to receive the poles by which it is to be carried. Make the 5
poles of acacia-wood and overlay them with gold. Put it before the Veil 6
in front of the Ark of the Tokens*a* where I will meet you. On it Aaron 7
shall burn fragrant incense; every morning when he tends the lamps
he shall burn the incense, and when he mounts the lamps between dusk 8
and dark, he shall burn the incense; so there shall be a regular burning
of incense before the LORD for all time. You shall not offer on it any 9
unauthorized incense, nor any whole-offering or grain-offering; and
you shall not pour a drink-offering over it. Aaron shall make expiation 10
with blood on its horns once a year; with blood from the sin-offering of
the yearly Expiation*b* he shall do this for all time. It is most holy to the
LORD.

The LORD spoke to Moses and said: When you number the Israelites 11, 12
for the purpose of registration, each man shall give a ransom for his
life to the LORD,*c* to avert plague among them during the registration.
As each man crosses over to those already counted he shall give half a 13
shekel by the sacred standard (twenty gerahs to the shekel) as a
contribution to the LORD. Everyone from twenty years old and upwards 14
who has crossed over to those already counted shall give a contribution
to the LORD. The rich man shall give no more than the half-shekel, and 15
the poor man shall give no less, when you give the contribution to the
LORD to make expiation for your lives. The money received from the 16
Israelites for expiation you shall apply to the service of the Tent of
the Presence. The expiation for your lives shall be a reminder of the
Israelites to the LORD.

The LORD spoke to Moses and said: Make a bronze basin for 17, 18
ablution with its stand of bronze; put it between the Tent of the
Presence and the altar, and fill it with water with which Aaron and his 19
sons shall wash their hands and feet. When they enter the Tent of the 20
Presence they shall wash with water, lest they die. So also when they
approach the altar to minister, to burn a food-offering to the LORD, they 21
shall wash their hands and feet, lest they die. It shall be a rule for all
time binding on him and his descendants in every generation.

The LORD spoke to Moses and said: You yourself shall take spices 22, 23
as follows: five hundred shekels of sticks of myrrh, half that amount
(two hundred and fifty shekels) of fragrant cinnamon, two hundred and
fifty shekels of aromatic cane, five hundred shekels of cassia by the 24
sacred standard, and a hin of olive oil. From these prepare sacred 25
anointing oil, a perfume compounded by the perfumer's art. This shall
be the sacred anointing oil. Anoint with it the Tent of the Presence and 26
the Ark of the Tokens, the table and all its vessels, the lamp-stand and 27

[a] *So Sam.; Heb. adds* before the cover over the Tokens.   [b] *Or* Atonement.   [c] *So Sept.;*
Heb. adds because of the registration.

28 its fittings, the altar of incense, the altar of whole-offering and all its
29 vessels, the basin and its stand. You shall consecrate them, and they
shall be most holy; whatever touches them shall be forfeit as sacred.
30 Anoint Aaron and his sons, and consecrate them to be my priests.
31 Speak to the Israelites and say: This shall be the holy anointing oil for
32 my service in every generation. It shall not be used for anointing the
human body, and you must not prepare any oil like it after the same
33 prescription. It is holy, and you shall treat it as holy. The man who
compounds perfume like it, or who puts any of it on any unqualified
person, shall be cut off from his father's kin.

34   The LORD said to Moses, Take fragrant spices: gum resin,[a] aromatic
shell, galbanum; add pure frankincense to the spices in equal pro-
35 portions. Make it into incense, perfume made by the perfumer's craft,
36 salted and pure, a holy thing. Pound some of it into fine powder, and
put it in front of the Tokens in the Tent of the Presence, where I shall
37 meet you; you shall treat it as most holy. The incense prepared
according to this prescription you shall not make for your own use.
38 You shall treat it as holy to the LORD. The man who makes any like it
for his own pleasure shall be cut off from his father's kin.

31 1,2 THE LORD SPOKE to Moses and said, Mark this: I have specially
3 chosen Bezalel son of Uri, son of Hur, of the tribe of Judah. I have filled
him with divine spirit, making him skilful and ingenious, expert in
4 every craft, and a master of design, whether in gold, silver, copper,
5 or cutting stones to be set, or carving wood, for workmanship of every
6 kind. Further, I have appointed Aholiab[b] son of Ahisamach of the
tribe of Dan to help him, and I have endowed every skilled craftsman
with the skill which he has. They shall make everything that I have
7 commanded you: the Tent of the Presence, the Ark for the Tokens,
8 the cover over it, and all the furnishings of the tent; the table and its
vessels, the pure lamp-stand and all its fittings, the altar of incense,
9 the altar of whole-offering and all its vessels, the basin and its stand;
10 the stitched vestments, that is the sacred vestments for Aaron the priest
11 and the vestments for his sons when they minister as priests, the
anointing oil and the fragrant incense for the Holy Place. They shall
carry out all I have commanded you.

12,13   The LORD spoke to Moses and said, Speak to the Israelites, you
yourself, and say to them: Above all you shall observe my sabbaths,
for the sabbath is a sign between me and you in every generation that
14 you may know that I am the LORD who hallows you. You shall keep the
sabbath, because it is a holy day for you. If anyone profanes it he must
be put to death. Anyone who does work on it shall be cut off from his

[a] *Or* mastic.   [b] *Or* Oholiab.

father's kin. Work may be done on six days, but on the seventh day 15
there is a sabbath of sacred rest, holy to the LORD. Whoever does work
on the sabbath day must be put to death. The Israelites shall keep the 16
sabbath, they shall keep it in every generation as a covenant for ever.
It is a sign for ever between me and the Israelites, for in six days the 17
LORD made the heavens and the earth, but on the seventh day he ceased
work and refreshed himself.

When he had finished speaking with Moses on Mount Sinai, the 18
LORD gave him the two tablets of the Tokens, tablets of stone written
with the finger of God.

WHEN THE PEOPLE SAW that Moses was so long in coming down 32
from the mountain, they confronted Aaron and said to him, 'Come,
make us gods to go ahead of us. As for this fellow Moses, who brought
us up from Egypt, we do not know what has become of him.' Aaron 2
answered them, 'Strip the gold rings from the ears of your wives[a] and
daughters, and bring them to me.' So all the people stripped them- 3
selves of their gold earrings and brought them to Aaron. He took them 4
out of their hands, cast the metal in a mould, and made it into the
image of a bull-calf. 'These', he[b] said, 'are your gods, O Israel, that
brought you up from Egypt.' Then Aaron was afraid and built an altar 5
in front of it and issued this proclamation, 'Tomorrow there is to be a
pilgrim-feast to the LORD.' Next day the people rose early, offered 6
whole-offerings, and brought shared-offerings. After this they sat down
to eat and drink and then gave themselves up to revelry. But the LORD 7
said to Moses, 'Go down at once, for your people, the people you
brought up from Egypt, have done a disgraceful thing; so quickly have 8
they turned aside from the way I commanded them. They have made
themselves an image of a bull-calf, they have prostrated themselves
before it, sacrificed to it and said, "These are your gods, O Israel, that
brought you up from Egypt."' So the LORD said to Moses, 'I have 9
considered this people, and I see that they are a stubborn people. Now, 10
let me alone to vent my anger upon them, so that I may put an end to
them and make a great nation spring from you.' But Moses set himself 11
to placate the LORD his God: 'O LORD,' he said, 'why shouldst thou
vent thy anger upon thy people, whom thou didst bring out of Egypt
with great power and a strong hand? Why let the Egyptians say, "So 12
he meant evil when he took them out, to kill them in the mountains
and wipe them off the face of the earth"? Turn from thy anger, and
think better of the evil thou dost intend against thy people. Remember 13
Abraham, Isaac and Israel, thy servants, to whom thou didst swear by
thy own self: "I will make your posterity countless as the stars in the

[a] *So Sept.; Heb. adds* and sons.   [b] *So Sept.; Heb.* they.

sky, and all this land, of which I have spoken, I will give to them, and
14 they shall possess it for ever."' So the LORD relented, and spared his
people the evil with which he had threatened them.

15   Moses turned and went down the mountain with the two tablets of
the Tokens in his hands, inscribed on both sides; on the front and on
16 the back they were inscribed. The tablets were the handiwork of God,
17 and the writing was God's writing, engraved on the tablets. Joshua,
hearing the uproar the people were making, said to Moses, 'Listen!
18 There is fighting in the camp.' Moses replied,

> 'This is not the clamour of warriors,
> nor the clamour of a defeated people;
> it is the sound of singing that I hear.'

19 As he approached the camp, Moses saw the bull-calf and the dancing,
and he was angry; he flung the tablets down, and they were shattered
20 to pieces at the foot of the mountain. Then he took the calf they had
made and burnt it; he ground it to powder, sprinkled it on water, and
21 made the Israelites drink it. He demanded of Aaron, 'What did this
people do to you that you should have brought such great guilt upon
22 them?' Aaron replied, 'Do not be angry, sir. The people were deeply
23 troubled; that you well know. And they said to me, "Make us gods to go
ahead of us, because, as for this fellow Moses, who brought us up from
24 Egypt, we do not know what has become of him." So I said to them,
"Those of you who have any gold, strip it off." They gave it me,
25 I threw it in the fire, and out came this bull-calf.' Moses saw that the
people were out of control and that Aaron had laid them open to the
26 secret malice of their enemies. He took his place at the gate of the camp
and said, 'Who is on the LORD's side? Come here to me'; and the
27 Levites all rallied to him. He said to them, 'These are the words of the
LORD the God of Israel: "Arm yourselves, each of you, with his sword.
Go through the camp from gate to gate and back again. Each of you
28 kill his brother, his friend, his neighbour."' The Levites obeyed, and
29 about three thousand of the people died that day. Moses then said,
'Today you have consecrated yourselves to the LORD completely,*a*
because you have turned each against his own son and his own brother
and so have this day brought a blessing upon yourselves.'

30   The next day Moses said to the people, 'You have committed a great
sin. I shall now go up to the LORD; perhaps I may be able to secure
31 pardon for your sin.' So Moses returned to the LORD and said, 'O hear
me! This people has committed a great sin: they have made themselves
32 gods of gold. If thou wilt forgive them, forgive. But if not, blot out my
33 name, I pray, from thy book which thou hast written.' The LORD

[a] *So Sept.; Heb.* Consecrate yourselves to the LORD today.

answered Moses, 'It is the man who has sinned against me that I will blot out from my book. But go now, lead the people to the place which 34 I have told you of. My angel shall go ahead of you, but a day will come when I shall punish them for their sin.' And the LORD smote the people 35 for worshipping the bull-calf which Aaron had made.

THE LORD SPOKE to Moses: 'Come, go up from here, you and the 33 people you have brought up from Egypt, to the land which I swore to Abraham, Isaac, and Jacob that I would give to their posterity. I will 2 send an angel ahead of you, and will drive out the Canaanites, the Amorites and the Hittites and the Perizzites, the Hivites and the Jebusites. I will bring you*a* to a land flowing with milk and honey, but 3 I will not journey in your company, for fear that I annihilate you on the way; for you are a stubborn people.' When the people heard this harsh 4 sentence they went about like mourners, and no man put on his ornaments. The LORD said to Moses, 'Tell the Israelites, "You are a 5 stubborn people: at any moment, if I journey in your company, I may annihilate you. Put away your ornaments now, and I will determine what to do to you."' And so the Israelites stripped off their ornaments, 6 and wore them no more from Mount Horeb onwards.

Moses used to take a*b* tent and pitch it at a distance outside the camp. 7 He called it the Tent of the Presence, and everyone who sought the LORD would go out to the Tent of the Presence outside the camp. When- 8 ever Moses went out to the tent, all the people would rise and stand, each at the entrance to his tent, and follow Moses with their eyes until he entered the tent. When Moses entered it, the pillar of cloud came 9 down, and stayed at the entrance to the tent while the LORD spoke with Moses. As soon as the people saw the pillar of cloud standing at the 10 entrance to the tent, they would all prostrate themselves, every man at the entrance to his tent. The LORD would speak with Moses face to face, 11 as one man speaks to another. Then Moses would return to the camp, but his young assistant, Joshua son of Nun, never moved from inside the tent.

Moses said to the LORD, 'Thou bidst me lead this people up, but thou 12 hast not told me whom thou wilt send with me. Thou hast said to me, "I know you by name, and, further, you have found favour with me." If 13 I have indeed won thy favour, then teach me to know thy way, so that I can know thee and continue in favour with thee, for this nation is thy own people.' The LORD answered, 'I will go with you in person 14 and set your mind at rest.' Moses said to him, 'Indeed if thou dost not 15 go in person, do not send us up from here; for how can it ever be 16 known that I and thy people have found favour with thee, except by

[*a*] I will bring you: *so Sept.; Heb. om.*   [*b*] *Or* the.

thy going with us? So shall we be distinct, I and thy people, from all the
17 peoples*a* on earth.' The LORD said to Moses, 'I will do this thing that
you have asked, because you have found favour with me, and I know
you by name.'

18, 19 And Moses prayed, 'Show me thy glory.' The LORD answered,
'I will make all my goodness*b* pass before you, and I will pronounce in
your hearing the Name JEHOVAH.*c* I will be gracious to whom I will be
gracious, and I will have compassion on whom I will have compassion.'
20 But he added, 'My face you cannot see, for no mortal man may see me
21 and live.' The LORD said, 'Here is a place beside me. Take your stand
22 on the rock and when my glory passes by, I will put you in a crevice of
23 the rock and cover you with my hand until I have passed by. Then
I will take away my hand, and you shall see my back, but my face shall
not be seen.'

34 The LORD said to Moses, 'Cut two stone tablets like the first, and
I will write on the tablets the words which were on the first tablets,
2 which you broke in pieces. Be ready by morning. Then in the morning
3 go up Mount Sinai; stand and wait for me there on the top. No man
shall go up with you, no man shall even be seen anywhere on the
mountain, nor shall flocks or herds graze within sight of that mountain.'
4 So Moses cut two stone tablets like the first, and he rose early in the
morning and went up Mount Sinai as the LORD had commanded him,
5 taking the two stone tablets in his hands. And the LORD came down in
the cloud and took his place beside him and pronounced the Name
6 JEHOVAH. Then the LORD passed in front of him and called aloud,
'JEHOVAH, the LORD, a god compassionate and gracious, long-suffering,
7 ever constant and true, maintaining constancy to thousands, forgiving
iniquity, rebellion, and sin, and not sweeping the guilty clean away;
but one who punishes sons and grandsons to the third and fourth
8 generation for the iniquity of their fathers!' Moses made haste, bowed
9 to the ground and prostrated himself. He said, 'If I have indeed won
thy favour, O Lord, then may the Lord go in our company. However
stubborn a people they are, forgive our iniquity and our sin and take us
as thy own possession.'

10 The LORD said, Here and now I make a covenant. In full view of all
your people I will do such miracles as have never been performed in all
the world or in any nation. All the surrounding peoples shall see the
11 work of the LORD, for fearful is that which I will do for you.*d* Observe
all I command you this day; and I for my part will drive out before you
the Amorites and the Canaanites and the Hittites and the Perizzites and
12 the Hivites and the Jebusites. Be careful not to make a covenant with

[a] *So Sept.; Heb.* people.   [b] *Or* character.   [c] *See note on 3. 15.*   [d] for fearful…for
you: *or* (for he is to be feared) which I will do for you.

the natives of the land against which you are going, or they will prove a snare in your midst. No: you shall demolish their altars, smash their 13 sacred pillars and cut down their sacred poles.*a* You shall not prostrate 14 yourselves to any other god. For the LORD's name is the Jealous God, and a jealous god he is. Be careful not to make a covenant with the 15 natives of the land, or, when they go wantonly after their gods and sacrifice to them, you may be invited, any one of you, to partake of their sacrifices, and marry your sons to their daughters, and when their 16 daughters go wantonly after their gods, they may lead your sons astray too.

You shall not make yourselves gods of cast metal.   17

You shall observe the pilgrim-feast of Unleavened Bread: for seven 18 days, as I have commanded you, you shall eat unleavened cakes at the appointed time, in the month of Abib, because in the month of Abib you went out from Egypt.

Every first birth of the womb belongs to me, and the males*b* of all 19 your herds, both cattle and sheep. You may buy back the first birth of 20 an ass by giving a sheep instead, but if you do not buy it, you must break its neck. You shall buy back all the first-born of your sons, and no one shall come into my presence*c* empty-handed.

For six days you shall work, but on the seventh day you shall cease 21 work; even at ploughing time and harvest you shall cease work.

You shall observe the pilgrim-feast of Weeks, the firstfruits of the 22 wheat harvest, and the pilgrim-feast of Ingathering at the turn of the year. Three times a year all your males shall come into the presence of 23 the Lord, the LORD the God of Israel; for after I have driven out the 24 nations before you and extended your frontiers, there will be no danger from covetous neighbours when you go up these three times to enter the presence of the LORD your God.

You shall not offer the blood of my sacrifice at the same time as any- 25 thing leavened, nor shall any portion of the victim of the pilgrim-feast of Passover remain overnight till morning.

You shall bring the choicest firstfruits of your soil to the house of the 26 LORD your God.

You shall not boil a kid in its mother's milk.

The LORD said to Moses, 'Write these words down, because the 27 covenant I make with you and with Israel is in these words.' So Moses 28 stayed there with the LORD forty days and forty nights, neither eating nor drinking, and wrote down the words of the covenant, the Ten Words,*d* on the tablets. At length Moses came down from Mount Sinai 29 with the two stone tablets of the Tokens in his hands, and when he

[a] sacred poles: *Heb.* asherim.   [b] *So Sept.; Heb. unintelligible.*   [c] *Lit.* see my face.
[d] *Or* Ten Commandments.

descended, he did not know that the skin of his face shone because he
30 had been speaking with the LORD. When Aaron and the Israelites saw
how the skin of Moses' face shone, they were afraid to approach him.
31 He called out to them, and Aaron and all the chiefs in the congregation
32 turned towards him. Moses spoke to them, and afterwards all the
Israelites drew near. He gave them all the commands with which the
33 LORD had charged him on Mount Sinai, and finished what he had to
say.

34   Then Moses put a veil over his face, and whenever he went in before
the LORD to speak with him, he removed the veil until he came out.
Then he would go out and tell the Israelites all the commands he had
35 received. Whenever the skin of Moses' face shone in the sight of the
Israelites, he would put the veil back over his face until he went in
again to speak with the LORD.

35 MOSES CALLED the whole community of Israelites together and
2 thus addressed them: These are the LORD's commands to you: On
six days you may work, but the seventh you are to keep as a sabbath of
sacred rest, holy to the LORD. Whoever works on that day shall be put
3 to death. You are not even to light your fire at home on the sabbath day.
4   These words Moses spoke to all the community of Israelites: This is
5 the command the LORD has given: Each of you set aside a contribution
to the LORD. Let all who wish, bring a contribution to the LORD: gold,
6 silver, copper; violet, purple, and scarlet yarn; fine linen and goats'
7,8 hair; tanned rams' skins, porpoise-hides, and acacia-wood; oil for the
lamp, perfume for the anointing oil and for the fragrant incense;
9 cornelians and other stones ready for setting in the ephod and the
10 breast-piece. Let every craftsman among you come and make everything
11 the LORD has commanded. The Tabernacle, its tent and covering,
12 fasteners, planks, bars, posts, and sockets, the Ark and its poles, the
13 cover and the Veil of the screen, the table, its poles, and all its vessels,
14 and the Bread of the Presence, the lamp-stand for the light, its fittings,
15 lamps and the lamp oil; the altar of incense and its poles, the anointing
oil, the fragrant incense, and the screen for the entrance of the
16 Tabernacle, the altar of whole-offering, its bronze grating, poles, and all
17 appurtenances, the basin and its stand; the hangings of the court, its
18 posts and sockets, and the screen for the gateway of the court; the pegs
19 of the Tabernacle and court and their cords, the stitched vestments for
ministering in the Holy Place, that is the sacred vestments for Aaron
the priest and the vestments for his sons when they minister as priests.
20   The whole community of the Israelites went out from Moses'
21 presence, and everyone who was so minded brought of his own free

will a contribution to the LORD for the making of the Tent of the Presence and all its service, and for the sacred vestments. Men and 22 women alike came and freely brought clasps, earrings, finger-rings, and pendants,[a] gold ornaments of every kind, every one of them presenting a special gift of gold to the LORD. And every man brought what he 23 possessed of violet, purple, and scarlet yarn, fine linen and goats' hair, tanned rams' skins and porpoise-hides. Every man, setting aside a 24 contribution of silver or copper, brought it as a contribution to the LORD, and all who had acacia-wood suitable for any part of the work brought it. Every woman with the skill spun and brought the violet, 25 purple, and scarlet yarn, and fine linen. All the women whose skill 26 moved them spun the goats' hair. The chiefs brought cornelians and 27 other stones ready for setting in the ephod and the breast-piece, the 28 perfume and oil for the light, for the anointing oil, and for the fragrant incense. Every Israelite man and woman who was minded to bring 29 offerings to the LORD for all the work which he had commanded through Moses did so freely.

Moses said to the Israelites, 'Mark this: the LORD has specially 30 chosen Bezalel son of Uri, son of Hur, of the tribe of Judah. He has filled 31 him with divine spirit, making him skilful and ingenious, expert in every craft, and a master of design, whether in gold, silver, and copper, 32 or cutting precious stones for setting, or carving wood, in every kind 33 of design. He has inspired both him and Aholiab son of Ahisamach of 34 the tribe of Dan to instruct workers and designers of every kind, 35 engravers, seamsters, embroiderers in violet, purple, and scarlet yarn and fine linen, and weavers, fully endowing them with skill to execute all kinds of work. Bezalel and Aholiab shall work exactly as the LORD 36 has commanded, and so also shall every craftsman whom the LORD has made skilful and ingenious in these matters, to know how to execute every kind of work for the service of the sanctuary.'

Moses summoned Bezalel, Aholiab, and every craftsman to whom the 2 LORD had given skill and who was willing, to come forward and set to work. They received from Moses every contribution which the 3 Israelites had brought for the work of the service of the sanctuary, but the people still brought freewill offerings morning after morning, so 4 that the craftsmen at work on the sanctuary left what they were doing, every one of them, and came to Moses and said, 'The people are 5 bringing much more than we need for doing the work which the LORD has commanded.' So Moses sent word round the camp that no man or 6 woman should prepare anything more as a contribution for the sanctuary. So the people stopped bringing gifts; what was there already 7 was more than enough for all the work they had to do.

[a] *Heb. word of uncertain mng.*

8 Then all the craftsmen among the workers made the Tabernacle of ten hangings of finely woven linen, and violet, purple, and scarlet
9 yarn, with cherubim worked on them, all made by a seamster. The length of each hanging was twenty-eight cubits and the breadth four
10 cubits, all of the same size. They joined five of the hangings together,
11 and similarly the other five. They made violet loops on the outer edge of the one set of hangings and they did the same for the outer edge of
12 the other set of hangings. They made fifty loops for each hanging; they made also fifty loops for the end hanging in the second set, the
13 loops being opposite each other. They made fifty gold fasteners, with which they joined the hangings one to another, and the Tabernacle became a single whole.

14 They made hangings of goats' hair, eleven in all, to form a tent over
15 the Tabernacle; each hanging was thirty cubits long and four cubits
16 wide, all eleven of the same size. They joined five of the hangings
17 together, and similarly the other six. They made fifty loops on the edge of the outer hanging in the first set and fifty loops on the joining
18 edge of the second set, and fifty bronze fasteners to join up the tent
19 and make it a single whole. They made for the tent a cover of tanned rams' skins and an outer covering of porpoise-hides.

20 They made for the Tabernacle planks of acacia-wood as uprights,
21, 22 each plank ten cubits long and a cubit and a half wide, and two tenons for each plank joined to each other. They did the same for all the
23 planks of the Tabernacle. They arranged the planks thus: twenty planks
24 for the south side, facing southwards, with forty silver sockets under
25 them, two sockets under each plank for its two tenons; and for the
26 second or northern side of the Tabernacle twenty planks with forty
27 silver sockets, two under each plank. They made six planks for the far
28 end of the Tabernacle on the west. They made two planks for the
29 corners of the Tabernacle at the far end; at the bottom they were alike, and at the top, both alike,[a] they fitted into a single ring. They did the
30 same for both of them at the two corners. There were eight planks with their silver sockets, sixteen sockets in all, two sockets under each plank.
31 They made bars of acacia-wood: five for the planks on the one side
32 of the Tabernacle, five bars for the planks on the second side of the Tabernacle, and five bars for the planks on the far end of the Taber-
33 nacle on the west. They made the middle bar to run along from end to
34 end half-way up the frames. They overlaid the frames with gold, made rings of gold on them to hold the bars and plated the bars with gold.
35 They made the Veil of finely woven linen and violet, purple, and
36 scarlet yarn, with cherubim worked on it, all made by a seamster. And they made for it four posts of acacia-wood overlaid with gold, with gold

[a] *So Sam.; Heb.* perfect.

hooks, and cast four silver sockets for them. For the entrance of the 37
tent a screen of finely woven linen was made, embroidered with violet,
purple, and scarlet, and five posts of acacia-wood with their hooks. 38
They overlaid the tops of the posts and the bands round them with
gold; the five sockets for them were of bronze.

Bezalel then made the Ark, a chest of acacia-wood, two and a half 37
cubits long, one cubit and a half wide, and one cubit and a half high.
He overlaid it with pure gold, both inside and out, and put a band of 2
gold all round it. He cast four gold rings to be on its four feet, two rings 3
on each side of it. He made poles of acacia-wood and plated them with 4
gold, and inserted the poles in the rings at the sides of the Ark to lift it. 5
He made a cover of pure gold, two and a half cubits long and one cubit 6
and a half wide. He made two gold cherubim of beaten work at the ends 7
of the cover, one at each end; he made each cherub of one piece with 8
the cover. They had wings outspread and pointing upwards, screening 9
the cover with their wings; they stood face to face, looking inwards
over the cover.

He made the table of acacia-wood, two cubits long, one cubit wide, 10
and one cubit and a half high. He overlaid it with pure gold and put a 11
band of gold all round it. He made a rim round it a hand's breadth 12
wide, and a gold band round the rim. He cast four gold rings for it, 13
and put the rings at the four corners by the four legs. The rings, which 14
were to receive the poles for carrying the table, were close to the rim.
These carrying-poles he made of acacia-wood and plated them with 15
gold. He made the vessels for the table, its dishes and saucers, and its 16
flagons and bowls from which drink-offerings were to be poured; he
made them of pure gold.

He made the lamp-stand of pure gold. The lamp-stand, stem, and 17
branches,[a] were of beaten work, its cups, both calyxes and petals, were
of one piece with it. There were six branches springing from its sides; 18
three branches of the lamp-stand sprang from one side and three
branches from the other side. There were three cups shaped like almond 19
blossoms, with calyx and petals, on the first branch, three cups shaped
like almond blossoms, with calyx and petals, on the next branch, and
similarly for all six branches springing from the lamp-stand. On the 20
main stem of the lamp-stand there were four cups shaped like almond
blossoms, with calyx and petals, and there were calyxes of one piece 21
with it under the six branches which sprang from the lamp-stand, a
single calyx under each pair of branches. The calyxes and the branches 22
were of one piece with it, all a single piece of beaten work of pure gold.
He made its seven lamps, its tongs and firepans of pure gold. The lamp- 23, 24
stand and all these fittings were made from one talent of pure gold.

[a] *So Sam.; Heb.* branch.

25 He made the altar of incense of acacia-wood, square, a cubit long by
26 a cubit broad and two cubits high, the horns of one piece with it. He
overlaid it with pure gold, the top, the sides all round, and the horns,
27 and he put round it a band of gold. He made pairs of gold rings for it;
he put them under the band at the two corners on both sides to receive
28 the poles by which it was to be carried. He made the poles of acacia-
wood and overlaid them with gold.

29 He prepared the sacred anointing oil and the fragrant incense, pure,
compounded by the perfumer's art.

38 He made the altar of whole-offering of acacia-wood, square, five
2 cubits long by five cubits broad and three cubits high. Its horns at the
3 four corners were of one piece with it, and he overlaid it with bronze. He
made all the vessels for the altar, its pots, shovels, tossing bowls, forks,
4 and firepans, all of bronze. He made for the altar a grating of bronze
5 network under the ledge, coming half-way up. He cast four rings for the
6 four corners of the bronze grating to receive the poles, and he made the
7 poles of acacia-wood and overlaid them with bronze. He inserted
the poles in the rings at the sides of the altar to carry it. He left the altar
a hollow shell.

8 The basin and its stand of bronze he made out of the bronze mirrors
of the women who were on duty at the entrance to the Tent of the
Presence.

9 He made the court. For the south side facing southwards the hangings
10 of the court were of finely woven linen a hundred cubits long, with
twenty posts and twenty sockets of bronze; the hooks and bands on the
11 posts were of silver. Along the north side there were hangings of a
hundred cubits, with twenty posts and twenty sockets of bronze; the
12 hooks and bands on the posts were of silver. On the west side there
were hangings fifty cubits long, with ten posts and ten sockets; the
13 hooks and bands on the posts were of silver. On the east side, towards
14-15 the sunrise, fifty cubits, there were hangings on either side of the
gateway of the court; they extended fifteen cubits to one corner, with
their three posts and their three sockets, and fifteen cubits to the second
16 corner, with their three posts and their three sockets. The hangings of
17 the court all round were of finely woven linen. The sockets for the posts
were of bronze, the hooks and bands on the posts of silver, the tops of
them overlaid with silver, and all the posts of the court were bound with
18 silver. The screen at the gateway of the court was of finely woven
linen, embroidered with violet, purple, and scarlet, twenty cubits long
19 and five cubits high to correspond to the hangings of the court, with
four posts and four sockets of bronze, their hooks of silver, and the
20 tops of them and their bands overlaid with silver. All the pegs for the
Tabernacle and those for the court were of bronze.

These were the appointments of the Tabernacle, that is the Tabernacle 21
of the Tokens which was assigned by Moses to the charge of the Levites
under Ithamar son of Aaron the priest. Bezalel son of Uri, son of Hur, 22
of the tribe of Judah made everything the LORD had commanded
Moses. He was assisted by Aholiab son of Ahisamach of the tribe of 23
Dan, an engraver, a seamster, and an embroiderer in fine linen with
violet, purple, and scarlet yarn.

The gold of the special gift used for the work of the sanctuary 24
amounted in all to twenty-nine talents seven hundred and thirty shekels,
by the sacred standard. The silver contributed by the community when 25
registered was one hundred talents one thousand seven hundred and
seventy-five shekels, by the sacred standard.

This amounted to a beka a head, that is half a shekel by the sacred 26
standard, for every man from twenty years old and upwards, who had
been registered, a total of six hundred and three thousand five hundred
and fifty men. The hundred talents of silver were for casting the sockets 27
for the sanctuary and for the Veil, a hundred sockets to a hundred
talents, a talent to a socket. With the one thousand seven hundred and 28
seventy-five shekels he made hooks for the posts, overlaid the tops of the
posts and put bands round them. The bronze of the special gift came to 29
seventy talents two thousand four hundred shekels; with this he made 30
sockets for the entrance to the Tent of the Presence, the bronze altar
and its bronze grating, all the vessels for the altar, the sockets all round 31
the court, the sockets for the posts at the gateway of the court, all the
pegs for the Tabernacle, and the pegs all round the court.

They used violet, purple, and scarlet yarn in making the stitched 39
vestments for ministering in the sanctuary and in making the sacred
vestments for Aaron, as the LORD had commanded Moses.

They made the ephod of gold, with violet, purple, and scarlet yarn, 2
and finely woven linen. The gold was beaten into thin plates, cut and 3
twisted into braid to be worked in by a seamster with the violet,
purple, and scarlet yarn, and fine linen. They made shoulder-pieces for 4
it, joined back and front. The waist-band on it was of the same work- 5
manship and material as the fabric of the ephod; it was gold, with
violet, purple, and scarlet yarn, and finely woven linen, as the LORD
commanded Moses.

They prepared the cornelians, fixed in gold rosettes, engraved by the 6
art of a seal-cutter with the names of the sons of Israel, and fastened 7
them on the shoulders of the ephod as reminders of the sons of Israel,
as the LORD had commanded Moses.

They*a* made the breast-piece; it was worked like the ephod by a 8
seamster, in gold, with violet, purple, and scarlet yarn, and finely

[a] *So Sept.; Heb.* He.

Israel at Mount Sinai

9 woven linen. They made the breast-piece square, folded, a span long
10 and a span wide. They set in it four rows of precious stones: the first
11 row, sardin, chrysolite and green felspar; the second row, purple
12 garnet, lapis lazuli and jade; the third row, turquoise, agate and jasper;
13 the fourth row, topaz, cornelian and green jasper, all set in gold
14 rosettes. The stones corresponded to the twelve sons of Israel, name by
name, each bearing the name of one of the twelve tribes engraved as on
15 a seal. They made for the breast-piece twisted cords of pure gold
16 worked into a rope. They made two gold rosettes and two gold rings,
and they fixed the two rings on the two corners of the breast-piece.
17 They fastened the two gold ropes to the two rings at those corners of
18 the breast-piece, and the other ends of the two ropes to the two
rosettes, thus binding them to the shoulder-pieces on the front of the
19 ephod. They made two gold rings and put them at the two corners of
20 the breast-piece on the inner side next to the ephod. They made two
gold rings and fixed them on the two shoulder-pieces of the ephod, low
down and in front, close to its seam above the waist-band on the ephod.
21 They bound the breast-piece by its rings to the rings of the ephod with
a violet braid, just above the waist-band on the ephod, so that the
breast-piece would not become detached from the ephod; so the LORD
22 had commanded Moses. They made the mantle of the ephod a single
23 piece of woven violet stuff, with a hole in the middle of it which had a
24 hem round it, with an oversewn edge*a* so that it could not be torn. All
round its skirts they made pomegranates of violet, purple, and scarlet
25 stuff, and finely woven linen.*b* They made bells of pure gold and put
26 them all round the skirts of the mantle between the pomegranates, a bell
and a pomegranate alternately the whole way round the skirts of the
mantle, to be worn when ministering, as the LORD commanded Moses.
27 They made the tunics of fine linen, woven work, for Aaron and his
28 sons, the turban of fine linen, the tall head-dresses and their bands all
29 of fine linen, the drawers of finely woven linen, and the sash of finely
woven linen, embroidered in violet, purple, and scarlet, as the LORD
had commanded Moses.
30 They made a rosette of pure gold as the symbol of their holy dedication and inscribed on it as the engraving on a seal, 'Holy to the
31 LORD',*c* and they fastened on it a violet braid to fix it on the turban at
the top, as the LORD had commanded Moses.
32 Thus all the work of the Tabernacle of the Tent of the Presence was
completed, and the Israelites did everything exactly as the LORD had
33 commanded Moses. They brought the Tabernacle to Moses, the tent
34 and all its furnishings, its fasteners, planks, bars, posts and sockets, the

[a] *See 28. 32.* [b] linen: *so Sam.; Heb. om.* [c] on it...LORD: *or* 'JEHOVAH' on it in
sacred characters as engraved on a seal.

covering of tanned rams' skins and the outer covering of porpoise-
hides, the Veil of the screen, the Ark of the Tokens and its poles, the 35
cover, the table and its vessels, and the Bread of the Presence, the pure 36, 37
lamp-stand with its lamps in a row and all its fittings, and the lamp oil,
the gold altar, the anointing oil, the fragrant incense, and the screen at 38
the entrance of the tent, the bronze altar, the bronze grating attached 39
to it, its poles and all its furnishings, the basin and its stand, the 40
hangings of the court, its posts and sockets, the screen for the gateway of
the court, its cords and pegs, and all the equipment for the service
of the Tabernacle for the Tent of the Presence, the stitched vestments 41
for ministering in the sanctuary, that is the sacred vestments for Aaron
the priest and the vestments for his sons when they minister as
priests. As the LORD had commanded Moses, so the Israelites carried 42
out the whole work. Moses inspected all the work, and saw that they 43
had carried it out according to the command of the LORD; and he
blessed them.

THE LORD SPOKE to Moses and said: On the first day of the first 40 1, 2
month you shall set up the Tabernacle, the Tent of the Presence. You 3
shall put the Ark of the Tokens in it and screen the Ark with the Veil.
You shall bring in the table and lay it; then you shall bring in the lamp- 4
stand and mount its lamps. You shall then set the gold altar of incense 5
in front of the Ark of the Tokens and put the screen of the entrance of
the Tabernacle in place. You shall put the altar of whole-offering in 6
front of the entrance of the Tabernacle, the Tent of the Presence.
You shall put the basin between the Tent of the Presence and the altar 7
and put water in it. You shall set up the court all round and put in 8
place the screen of the gateway of the court. You shall take the anointing 9
oil and anoint the Tabernacle and everything in it; thus you shall
consecrate it and all its furnishings, and it shall be holy. You shall 10
anoint the altar of whole-offering and all its vessels; thus shall you
consecrate it, and it shall be most holy. You shall anoint the basin and 11
its stand and consecrate it. You shall bring Aaron and his sons to the 12
entrance of the Tent of the Presence and wash them with the water.
Then you shall clothe Aaron with the sacred vestments, anoint him and 13
consecrate him; so shall he be my priest. You shall then bring forward 14
his sons, clothe them in tunics, anoint them as you anointed their 15
father, and they shall be my priests. Their anointing shall inaugurate a
hereditary priesthood for all time.

Exactly as the LORD had commanded him, so Moses did. In the 16, 17
first month of the second year, on the first day of that month, the
Tabernacle was set up.

Moses set up the Tabernacle. He put the sockets in place, inserted 18

19 the planks, fixed the crossbars and set up the posts. He spread the tent over the Tabernacle and fixed the covering of the tent above it, as the
20 LORD had commanded him. He took the Tokens and put them in the Ark, inserted the poles in the Ark, and put the cover over the top of
21 the Ark. He brought the Ark into the Tabernacle, set up the Veil of the screen and so screened the Ark of the Tokens, as the LORD had com-
22 manded him. He put the table in the Tent of the Presence on the north
23 side of the Tabernacle outside the Veil and arranged bread on it before
24 the LORD, as the LORD had commanded him. He set the lamp-stand in the Tent of the Presence opposite the table at the south side of the
25 Tabernacle and mounted the lamps before the LORD, as the LORD had
26 commanded him. He set up the gold altar in the Tent of the Presence
27 in front of the Veil and burnt fragrant incense on it, as the LORD had
28 commanded him. He set up the screen at the entrance of the Taber-
29 nacle, fixed the altar of whole-offering at the entrance of the Tabernacle, the Tent of the Presence, and offered on it whole-offerings and grain-
30 offerings, as the LORD had commanded him. He set up the basin between the Tent of the Presence and the altar and put water there for
31 washing, and Moses and Aaron and his sons used to wash their hands
32 and feet when they entered the Tent of the Presence or approached the
33 altar, as the LORD had commanded Moses. He set up the court all round the Tabernacle and the altar, and put a screen at the gateway of the court.
34   Thus Moses completed the work, and the cloud covered the Tent of
35 the Presence, and the glory of the LORD filled the Tabernacle. Moses was unable to enter the Tent of the Presence, because the cloud had
36 settled on it and the glory of the LORD filled the Tabernacle. At every stage of their journey, when the cloud lifted from the Tabernacle, the
37 Israelites broke camp; but if the cloud did not lift from the Tabernacle,
38 they did not break camp until the day it lifted. For the cloud of the LORD hovered over the Tabernacle by day, and there was fire in the cloud by night, and the Israelites could see it at every stage of their journey.

LEVITICUS

Laws concerning offerings and sacrifices

THE LORD SUMMONED MOSES and spoke to him 1
from the Tent of the Presence, and said, Say this to the 2
Israelites: When any man among you presents an animal as an
offering to the LORD, the offering may be presented either from the
herd or from the flock.

If his offering is a whole-offering from the cattle, he shall present a 3
male without blemish; he shall present it at the entrance to the Tent of
the Presence before the LORD so as to secure acceptance for himself.
He shall lay his hand on the head of the victim and it will be accepted 4
on his behalf*a* to make expiation for him. He shall slaughter the bull 5
before the LORD, and the Aaronite priests shall present the blood and
fling it against the altar all round at the entrance of the Tent of the
Presence. He shall then flay the victim and cut it up. The sons of 6, 7
Aaron the priest shall kindle a fire on the altar and arrange wood on the
fire. The Aaronite priests shall arrange the pieces, including the head 8
and the suet, on the wood on the altar-fire, the entrails and shins shall 9
be washed in water, and the priest shall burn it all on the altar as a
whole-offering, a food-offering of soothing odour to the LORD.

If the man's whole-offering is from the flock, either from the rams 10
or from the goats, he shall present a male without blemish. He shall 11
slaughter it before the LORD at the north side of the altar, and the
Aaronite priests shall fling the blood against the altar all round. He shall 12
cut it up, and the priest shall arrange the pieces, together with the head
and the suet, on the wood on the altar-fire, the entrails and shins shall 13
be washed in water, and the priest shall present and burn it all on the
altar: it is a whole-offering, a food-offering of soothing odour to the
LORD.

If a man's offering to the LORD is a whole-offering of birds, he shall 14
present turtle-doves or young pigeons as his offering. The priest shall 15
present it at the altar, and shall wrench off the head and burn it on the
altar; and the blood shall be drained out against the side of the altar.
He shall take away the crop and its contents in one piece, and throw it to 16
the east side of the altar where the ashes are. He shall tear it by its wings 17
without severing them completely, and shall burn it on the altar, on

[a] *Or* by him (*the* LORD).

top of the wood of the altar-fire: it is a whole-offering, a food-offering of soothing odour to the LORD.

2   When any person presents a grain-offering to the LORD, his offering shall be of flour. He shall pour oil on it and add frankincense to it.

2   He shall bring it to the Aaronite priests, one of whom shall scoop up a handful of the flour and oil with all the frankincense. The priest shall burn this as a token on the altar, a food-offering of soothing odour to

3   the LORD. The remainder of the grain-offering belongs to Aaron and his sons: it is most sacred, it is taken from the food-offerings of the LORD.

4   When you present as a grain-offering something baked in an oven, it shall consist of unleavened cakes of flour mixed with oil and un-

5   leavened wafers smeared with oil. If your offering is a grain-offering cooked on a griddle, it shall be an unleavened cake of flour mixed with

6   oil. Crumble it in pieces and pour oil on it. This is a grain-offering.

7   If your offering is a grain-offering cooked in a pan, it shall be made

8   of flour with oil. Bring an offering made up in this way to the LORD and

9   present it to the priest, who shall bring it to the altar; then he shall set aside part of the grain-offering as a token and burn it on the altar, a

10   food-offering of soothing odour to the LORD. The remainder of the grain-offering belongs to Aaron and his sons: it is most sacred, it is taken from the food-offerings of the LORD.

11   No grain-offering which you present to the LORD shall be made of anything that ferments; you shall not burn any leaven or any honey as

12   a food-offering to the LORD. As for your offering of firstfruits, you shall present them to the LORD, but they shall not be offered up at the altar

13   as a soothing odour. Every offering of yours which is a grain-offering shall be salted; you shall not fail to put the salt of your covenant with God on your grain-offering. Salt shall accompany all offerings.

14   If you present to the LORD a grain-offering of first-ripe grain, you must present fresh corn roasted, crushed meal from fully ripened corn.

15   You shall add oil to it and put frankincense upon it. This is a grain-

16   offering. The priest shall burn as its token some of the crushed meal, some of the oil, and all the frankincense as a food-offering to the LORD.

3   If a man's offering is a shared-offering from the cattle, male or

2   female, he shall present it without blemish before the LORD. He shall lay his hand on the head of the victim and slaughter it at the entrance to the Tent of the Presence. The Aaronite priests shall fling the blood

3   against the altar all round. One of them shall present part of the shared-offering as a food-offering to the LORD: he shall remove the fat covering

4   the entrails and all the fat upon the entrails, the two kidneys with the fat on them beside the haunches, and the long lobe of the liver with

5   the kidneys. The Aaronites shall burn it on the altar on top of the whole-

offering which is upon the wood on the fire, a food-offering of soothing odour to the LORD.

If a man's offering as a shared-offering to the LORD is from the flock, 6 male or female, he shall present it without blemish. If he is presenting 7 a ram as his offering, he shall present it before the LORD, lay his hand 8 on the head of the victim and slaughter it in front of the Tent of the Presence. The Aaronites shall then fling its blood against the altar all round. He shall present part of the shared-offering as a food-offering to 9 the LORD; he shall remove its fat, the entire fat-tail cut off close by the spine, the fat covering the entrails and all the fat upon the entrails, the two kidneys with the fat on them beside the haunches, and the long 10 lobe of the liver with the kidneys. The priest shall burn it at the altar, 11 as food offered to the LORD.

If the man's offering is a goat, he shall present it before the LORD, 12 lay his hand on its head and slaughter it in front of the Tent of the 13 Presence. The Aaronites shall then fling its blood against the altar all round. He shall present part of the victim as a food-offering to the 14 LORD; he shall remove the fat covering the entrails and all the fat upon the entrails, the two kidneys with the fat on them beside the haunches, 15 and the long lobe of the liver with the kidneys. The priest shall burn 16 this at the altar, as a food-offering of soothing odour. All fat belongs to the LORD. This is a rule for all time from generation to generation 17 wherever you live: you shall not eat any fat or any blood.

THE LORD SPOKE to Moses and said, Say this to the Israelites: These 4 1, 2 are the rules for any man who inadvertently transgresses any of the commandments of the LORD and does anything prohibited by them:

If the anointed priest sins so as to bring guilt on the people, for the 3 sin he has committed he shall present to the LORD a young bull without blemish as a sin-offering. He shall bring the bull to the entrance of the 4 Tent of the Presence before the LORD, lay his hand on its head and slaughter it before the LORD. The anointed priest shall then take some 5 of its blood and bring it to the Tent of the Presence. He shall dip his 6 finger in the blood and sprinkle some of the blood in front of the sacred Veil seven times before the LORD. The priest shall then put some 7 of the blood before the LORD in the Tent of the Presence on the horns of the altar where fragrant incense is burnt, and he shall pour the rest of the bull's blood at the base of the altar of whole-offering at the entrance of the Tent of the Presence. He shall set aside all the fat from 8 the bull of the sin-offering; he shall set aside the fat covering the entrails and all the fat upon the entrails, the two kidneys with the fat on them 9 beside the haunches, and the long lobe of the liver with the kidneys. It 10 shall be set aside as the fat from the ox at the shared-offering is set

aside. The priest shall burn the pieces of fat on the altar of whole-
11 offering. But the skin of the bull and all its flesh, including head and
12 shins, its entrails and offal, the whole of it, he shall take away outside
the camp to a place ritually clean, where the ash-heap is, and destroy it
on a wood-fire on top of the ash-heap.

13   If the whole community of Israel sins inadvertently and the matter is
not known to the assembly, if they do what is forbidden in any com-
14 mandment of the LORD and so incur guilt, then, when the sin they have
committed is notified to them, the assembly shall present a young bull
as a sin-offering and shall bring it in front of the Tent of the Presence.
15 The elders of the community shall lay their hands on the victim's head
16 before the LORD, and it shall be slaughtered before the LORD. The
anointed priest shall then bring some of the blood to the Tent of the
17 Presence, dip his finger in it and sprinkle it in front of the Veil seven
18 times before the LORD. He shall put some of the blood on the horns of
the altar before the LORD in the Tent of the Presence and pour all the
rest at the base of the altar of whole-offering at the entrance of the Tent
19 of the Presence. He shall then set aside all the fat from the bull and
20 burn it on the altar. He shall deal with this bull as he deals with the bull
of the sin-offering, and in this way the priest shall make expiation for
21 their guilt and they shall be forgiven. He shall take the bull outside the
camp and burn it as the other bull was burnt. This is a sin-offering for
the assembly.

22   When a man of standing sins by doing inadvertently what is forbidden in any commandment of the LORD his God, thereby incurring
23 guilt, and the sin he has committed is made known to him, he shall
24 bring as his offering a he-goat without blemish. He shall lay his hand
on the goat's head and shall slaughter it before the LORD in the place
25 where the whole-offering is slaughtered. It is a sin-offering. The priest
shall then take some of the blood of the victim with his finger and put it
on the horns of the altar of whole-offering. He shall pour out the rest
26 of the blood at the base of the altar of whole-offering. He shall burn all
the fat at the altar in the same way as the fat of the shared-offering.
Thus the priest shall make expiation for that man's sin, and it shall be
forgiven him.

27   If any person among the common people sins inadvertently and does
what is forbidden in any commandment of the LORD, thereby incurring
28 guilt, and the sin he has committed is made known to him, he shall
bring as his offering for the sin which he has committed a she-goat
29 without blemish. He shall lay his hand on the head of the victim and
slaughter it in the place where the whole-offering is slaughtered.
30 The priest shall then take some of its blood with his finger and put it
on the horns of the altar of whole-offering. All the rest of the blood he

shall pour at the base of the altar. He shall remove all its fat as the fat 31
of the shared-offering is removed, and the priest shall burn it on the
altar as a soothing odour to the LORD. So the priest shall make expiation
for that person's guilt, and it shall be forgiven him.

If the man brings a sheep as his offering for sin, it shall be a ewe 32
without blemish. He shall lay his hand on the head of the victim and 33
slaughter it as a sin-offering in the place where the whole-offering is
slaughtered. The priest shall then take some of the blood of the victim 34
with his finger and put it on the horns of the altar of whole-offering.
All the rest of the blood he shall pour out at the base of the altar. He 35
shall remove all the fat, as the fat of the sheep is removed from the
shared-offering. The priest shall burn the pieces of fat at the altar on
top of the food-offerings to the LORD, and shall make expiation for the
sin that the man has committed, and it shall be forgiven him.

IF A PERSON HEARS a solemn adjuration to give evidence as a witness 5
to something he has seen or heard and does not declare what he knows,
he commits a sin and must accept responsibility.

If a person touches anything unclean, such as the dead body of an 2
unclean animal, whether wild or domestic, or of an unclean reptile,*a* or 3
if he touches anything unclean in a man, whatever that uncleanness
may be, and it is concealed by him although he is aware of it, he shall
incur guilt. Or if a person rashly utters an oath to do something evil or 4
good, in any matter in which such a man may swear a rash oath, and it
is concealed by him although he is aware of it, he shall in either case
incur guilt. Whenever a man incurs guilt in any of these cases and 5
confesses how he has sinned therein, he shall bring to the LORD, as his 6
penalty for the sin that he has committed, a female of the flock, either
a ewe or a she-goat, as a sin-offering, and the priest shall make expiation
for him on account of his sin which he has committed, and he shall be
pardoned.*b*

But if he cannot afford as much as a young animal, he shall bring to 7
the LORD for the sin*c* he has committed two turtle-doves or two young
pigeons, one for a sin-offering and the other for a whole-offering.
He shall bring them to the priest, and present first the one intended for 8
the sin-offering. He shall wrench its head back without severing it. He 9
shall sprinkle some of the blood of the victim against the side of the
altar, and what is left of the blood shall be drained out at the base of the
altar: it is a sin-offering. He shall deal with the second bird as a whole- 10
offering according to custom, and the priest shall make expiation for the
sin the man has committed, and it shall be forgiven him.

[*a*] *So Sept.; Heb. adds* and it is concealed by him, he will become unclean and incur guilt.
[*b*] which he has...pardoned: *so Sam.; Heb. om.* [*c*] *So Sept.; Heb.* guilt.

11 If the man cannot afford two turtle-doves or two young pigeons, for his sin he shall bring as his offering a tenth of an ephah of flour, as a sin-offering. He shall add no oil to it nor put frankincense on it, because 12 it is a sin-offering. He shall bring it to the priest, who shall scoop up a handful from it as a token and burn it on the altar on the food-offerings 13 to the LORD: it is a sin-offering. The priest shall make expiation for the sin the man has committed in any one of these cases, and it shall be forgiven him. The remainder[a] belongs to the priest, as with the grain-offering.

14, 15 The LORD spoke to Moses and said: When any person commits an offence by inadvertently defaulting in dues sacred to the LORD, he shall bring as his guilt-offering to the LORD a ram without blemish from the flock, the value to be determined by you in silver shekels according to the 16 sacred standard, for a guilt-offering; he shall make good his default in sacred dues, adding one fifth. He shall give it to the priest, who shall make expiation for his sin with the ram of the guilt-offering, and it shall be forgiven him.

17 If and when any person sins unwittingly and does what is forbidden by any commandment of the LORD, thereby incurring guilt, he must 18 accept responsibility. He shall bring to the priest as a guilt-offering a ram without blemish from the flock, valued by you, and the priest shall make expiation for the error into which he has unwittingly fallen, and 19 it shall be forgiven him. It is a guilt-offering; he has been guilty of an offence against the LORD.

6 1,[b] 2 The LORD spoke to Moses and said: When any person sins and commits a grievous fault against the LORD, whether he lies to a fellow-countryman about a deposit or contract, or a theft, or wrongs him by 3 extortion, or finds lost property and then lies about it, and swears a false 4 oath in regard to any sin of this sort that he commits—if he does this, thereby incurring guilt, he shall restore what he has stolen or gained by extortion, or the deposit left with him or the lost property which he 5 found, or anything at all concerning which he swore a false oath. He shall make full restitution, adding one fifth to it, and give it back to 6 the aggrieved party on the day when he offers his guilt-offering. He shall bring to the LORD as his guilt-offering a ram without blemish from the 7 flock, valued by you, as a guilt-offering.[c] The priest shall make expiation for his guilt before the LORD, and he shall be forgiven for any act which has brought guilt upon him.

8,[d] 9 THE LORD SPOKE to Moses and said, Give this command to Aaron and his sons: This is the law of the whole-offering. The whole-offering

[a] The remainder: *so Sept.; Heb. om.* [b] *5. 20 in Heb.* [c] *So Sam.; Heb. adds* to the priest. [d] *6. 1 in Heb.*

shall remain on the altar-hearth all night till morning, and the altar-fire shall be kept burning there. Then the priest, having donned his linen 10 robe and put on linen drawers to cover himself, shall remove the ashes to which the fire reduces the whole-offering on the altar and put them beside the altar. He shall then change into other garments and take the 11 ashes outside the camp to a ritually clean place. The fire shall be kept 12 burning on the altar; it shall never go out. Every morning the priest shall have fresh wood burning thereon, arrange the whole-offering on it, and on top burn the fat from the shared-offerings. Fire shall always be 13 kept burning on the altar; it shall not go out.

This is the law of the grain-offering. The Aaronites shall present it 14 before the LORD in front of the altar. The priest shall set aside a handful 15 of the flour from it, with the oil of the grain-offering, and all the frankincense on it. He shall burn this token of it on the altar as a soothing odour to the LORD. The remainder Aaron and his sons shall 16 eat. It shall be eaten in the form of unleavened cakes and in a holy place. They shall eat it in the court of the Tent of the Presence. It shall 17 not be baked with leaven. I have allotted this to them as their share of my food-offerings. Like the sin-offering and the guilt-offering, it is most sacred. Any male descendant of Aaron may eat it, as a due from 18 the food-offerings to the LORD, for generation after generation for all time. Whatever touches them is to be forfeit as sacred.

The LORD spoke to Moses and said: This is the offering which 19, 20 Aaron and his sons shall present to the LORD:[a] one tenth of an ephah of flour, the usual grain-offering, half of it in the morning and half in the evening. It shall be cooked with oil on a griddle; you shall bring it well- 21 mixed, and so present it crumbled[b] in small pieces as a grain-offering, a soothing odour to the LORD. The anointed priest in the line of Aaron 22 shall offer it. This is a rule binding for all time. It shall be burnt in sacrifice to the LORD as a complete offering. Every grain-offering of a 23 priest shall be a complete offering; it shall not be eaten.

The LORD spoke to Moses and said, Speak to Aaron and his sons in 24, 25 these words: This is the law of the sin-offering. The sin-offering shall be slaughtered before the LORD in the place where the whole-offering is slaughtered; it is most sacred. The priest who officiates shall eat of the 26 flesh; it shall be eaten in a sacred place, in the court of the Tent of the Presence. Whatever touches its flesh is to be forfeit as sacred. If any 27 of the blood is splashed on a garment, that shall be washed[c] in a sacred place. An earthenware vessel in which the sin-offering is boiled shall be 28 smashed. If it has been boiled in a copper vessel, that shall be scoured and rinsed with water. Any male of priestly family may eat of this 29

[a] *Prob. rdg.; Heb. adds* on the day when he is anointed. [b] *Heb. word of uncertain mng.*
[c] *So Sept.; Heb.* you shall wash.

30 offering; it is most sacred. If, however, part of the blood is brought to the Tent of the Presence to make expiation in the holy place, the sin-offering shall not be eaten; it shall be destroyed by fire.

7 1,2 This is the law of the guilt-offering: it is most sacred. The guilt-offering shall be slaughtered in the place where the whole-offering is
3 slaughtered, and its blood shall be flung against the altar all round. The priest shall set aside and present all the fat from it: the fat-tail and the
4 fat covering the entrails, the two kidneys with the fat on them beside
5 the haunches, and the long lobe of the liver with the kidneys. The priest shall burn these pieces on the altar as a food-offering to the Lord; it is
6 a guilt-offering. Any male of priestly family may eat it. It shall be eaten
7 in a sacred place; it is most sacred. There is one law for both sin-offering and guilt-offering: they shall belong to the priest who performs
8 the rite of expiation. The skin of any man's whole-offering shall belong
9 to the priest who presents it. Every grain-offering baked in an oven and everything that is cooked in a pan or on a griddle shall belong to the
10 priest who presents it. Every grain-offering, whether mixed with oil or dry, shall be shared equally among all the Aaronites.

11,12 This is the law of the shared-offering presented to the Lord. If a man presents it as a thank-offering, then, in addition to the thank-offering, he shall present unleavened cakes mixed with oil, wafers of unleavened flour smeared with oil, and well-mixed flour and flat cakes
13 mixed with oil. He shall present flat cakes of leavened bread in addition
14 to his shared thank-offering. One part of every offering he shall present as a contribution for the Lord: it shall belong to the priest who flings the
15 blood of the shared-offering against the altar. The flesh shall be eaten on the day of its presentation; none of it shall be put aside till morning.
16 If a man's sacrifice is a votive offering or a freewill offering, it may be
17 eaten on the day it is presented or on the next day.[a] Any flesh left over
18 on the third day shall be destroyed by fire. If any flesh of his shared-offering is eaten on the third day, the man who has presented it shall not be accepted. It will not be counted to his credit, it shall be reckoned as tainted and the person who eats any of it shall accept responsibility.
19 No flesh which comes into contact with anything unclean shall be eaten; it shall be destroyed by fire.
20 The flesh may be eaten by anyone who is clean, but the person who, while unclean, eats flesh from a shared-offering presented to the Lord
21 shall be cut off from his father's kin. When any person is contaminated by contact with anything unclean, be it man, beast, or reptile,[b] and then eats any of the flesh from the shared-offerings presented to the Lord, that person shall be cut off from his father's kin.

[a] *So Sept.; Heb. adds* and the rest of it shall be eaten.   [b] *So some MSS.; others* noxious thing.

The LORD spoke to Moses and said, Speak to the Israelites in these 22, 23
words: You shall not eat the fat of any ox, sheep, or goat. The fat of an 24
animal that has died a natural death or has been mauled by wild beasts
may be put to any other use, but you shall not eat it. Every man who 25
eats fat from a beast of which he has presented any part as a food-
offering to the LORD shall be cut off from his father's kin.

You shall eat none of the blood, whether of bird or of beast, wherever 26
you may live. Every person who eats any of the blood shall be cut off 27
from his father's kin.

The LORD spoke to Moses and said, Speak to the Israelites in these 28, 29
words: Whoever comes to present a shared-offering shall set aside part
of it as an offering to the LORD. With his own hands he shall bring the 30
food-offerings to the LORD. He shall also bring the fat together with
the breast which is to be presented as a special gift before the LORD; the 31
priest shall burn the fat on the altar, but the breast shall belong to
Aaron and his descendants. You shall give the right hind-leg of your 32
shared-offerings as a contribution for the priest; it shall be the per- 33
quisite of the Aaronite who presents the blood and the fat of the
shared-offering. I have taken from the Israelites the breast of the 34
special gift and the leg of the contribution made out of the shared-
offerings, and have given them as a due from the Israelites to Aaron the
priest and his descendants for all time. This is the portion prescribed 35
for Aaron and his descendants out of the LORD's food-offerings,
appointed on the day when they were presented as priests to the LORD;
and on the day when they were anointed,[a] the LORD commanded that 36
these prescribed portions should be given to them by the Israelites.
This is a rule binding on their descendants for all time.

This, then, is the law of the whole-offering, the grain-offering, the 37
sin-offering, the guilt-offering, the installation-offerings, and the
shared-offerings, with which the LORD charged Moses on Mount Sinai 38
on the day when he commanded the Israelites to present their offerings
to the LORD in the wilderness of Sinai.

The hallowing and installation of the priests

THE LORD SPOKE to Moses and said, 'Take Aaron and his sons 8 1, 2
with him, the vestments, the anointing oil, the ox for a sin-offering,
the two rams, and the basket of unleavened cakes, and assemble all the 3
community at the entrance to the Tent of the Presence.' Moses did as 4
the LORD had commanded him, and the community assembled at the

[a] *Lit.* he anointed him.

5 entrance to the Tent of the Presence. He told the community that this
6 was what the LORD had commanded. He presented Aaron and his sons
7 and washed them in water. He invested Aaron with the tunic, girded him
with the sash, robed him with the mantle, put the ephod on him, tied it
8 with its waist-band and fastened the ephod to him with the band. He
put the breast-piece*a* on him and set the Urim and Thummim in it.
9 He then put the turban upon his head and set the gold rosette as a
symbol of holy dedication on the front of the turban, as the LORD had
10 commanded him. Moses then took the anointing oil, anointed the
11 Tabernacle and all that was within it and consecrated them. He
sprinkled some of the oil seven times on the altar, anointing the altar,
12 all its vessels, the basin and its stand, to consecrate them. He poured
13 some of the anointing oil on Aaron's head and so consecrated him. Moses
then brought the sons of Aaron forward, invested them with tunics,
girded them with sashes*b* and tied their tall head-dresses on them, as the
LORD had commanded him.

14 He then brought up the ox for the sin-offering; Aaron and his sons
15 laid their hands on its head, and he slaughtered it. Moses took some of*c*
the blood and put it with his finger on the horns round the altar. Thus
he purified the altar, and when he had poured out the rest of the blood
at the base of the altar, he consecrated it by making expiation for it.
16 He took all the fat upon the entrails, the long lobe of the liver, and the
17 two kidneys with their fat, and burnt them on the altar, but the ox, its
skin, its flesh, and its offal, he destroyed by fire outside the camp, as
the LORD had commanded him.

18 Moses*d* then brought forward the ram of the whole-offering; Aaron
19 and his sons laid their hands on the ram's head, and he slaughtered it.
20 Moses flung its blood against the altar all round. He cut the ram up and
21 burnt the head, the pieces, and the suet. He washed the entrails and the
shins in water and burnt the whole on the altar. This was a whole-
offering, a food-offering of soothing odour to the LORD, as the LORD
had commanded Moses.

22 Moses then brought forward the second ram, the ram for the installation of priests. Aaron and his sons laid their hands upon its head,
23 and he slaughtered it. Moses took some of its blood and put it on the
lobe of Aaron's right ear, on his right thumb, and on the big toe of his
24 right foot. He then brought forward the sons of Aaron, put some of the
blood on the lobes of their right ears, on their right thumbs, and on the
big toes of their right feet. He flung the rest of the blood against
25 the altar all round; he took the fat, the fat-tail, the fat covering the
entrails, the long lobe of the liver, the two kidneys with their fat, and

[a] Or pouch.　[b] So Sam.; Heb. sash.　[c] some of: so Sept.; Heb. om.　[d] So Sept.; Heb. om.

138

the right leg. Then from the basket of unleavened cakes before the 26
LORD he took one unleavened cake, one cake of bread made with oil,
and one wafer, and laid them on the fatty parts and the right leg. He 27
put the whole on the hands of Aaron and of his sons, and he*a* presented
it as a special gift before the LORD. He took it from their hands and 28
burnt it on the altar on top of the whole-offering. This was an instal-
lation-offering, it was a food-offering of soothing odour to the LORD.

Moses then took the breast and presented it as a special gift before 29
the LORD; it was his portion of the ram of installation, as the LORD had
commanded him. He took some of the anointing oil and some of the 30
blood on the altar and sprinkled it on Aaron and his vestments, and on
his sons and their vestments with him. Thus he consecrated Aaron and
his vestments, and with him his sons and their vestments.

Moses said to Aaron and his sons, 'Boil the flesh of the ram at the 31
entrance to the Tent of the Presence, and eat it there, together with the
bread in the installation-basket, in accordance with the command:
"Aaron and his sons shall eat it." The remainder of the flesh and bread 32
you shall destroy by fire. You shall not leave the entrance to the Tent 33
of the Presence for seven days, until the day which completes the
period of your installation, for it lasts seven days. What was done this 34
day followed the LORD's command to make expiation for you. You shall 35
stay at the entrance to the Tent of the Presence day and night for seven
days, keeping vigil to the LORD, so that you do not die, for so I was
commanded.'

Aaron and his sons did everything that the LORD had commanded 36
through Moses.

On the eighth day Moses summoned Aaron and his sons and the 9
Israelite elders. He said to Aaron, 'Take for yourself a bull-calf for a 2
sin-offering and a ram for a whole-offering, both without blemish, and
present them before the LORD. Then bid the Israelites take a he-goat 3
for a sin-offering, a calf and a lamb, both yearlings without blemish, for
a whole-offering, and a bull and a ram for shared-offerings to be 4
sacrificed before the LORD, together with a grain-offering mixed with
oil. This day the LORD will appear to you.'

They brought what Moses had commanded to the front of the Tent 5
of the Presence, and all the community approached and stood before
the LORD. Moses said, 'This is what the LORD has commanded you 6
to do, so that the glory of the LORD may appear to you. Come near to 7
the altar,' he said to Aaron; 'prepare your sin-offering and your whole-
offering and make expiation for yourself and for your household.*b*
Then prepare the offering of the people and make expiation for them, as
the LORD has commanded.'

[a] *Or, with Vulg.,* they.   [b] *So Sept.; Heb.* for the people.

8 So Aaron came near to the altar and slaughtered the calf, which was
9 his sin-offering. The sons of Aaron presented the blood to him, and he
dipped his finger in the blood and put it on the horns of the altar. The
10 rest of the blood he poured out at the base of the altar. Part of the sin-
offering, the fat, the kidneys, and the long lobe of the liver, he burnt on
11 the altar as the LORD had commanded Moses, but the flesh and the
12 skin he destroyed by fire outside the camp. Then he slaughtered the
whole-offering; his sons handed him the blood, and he flung it against
13 the altar all round. They handed him the pieces of the whole-offering
14 and the head, and he burnt them on the altar. He washed the entrails
and the shins and burnt them on the altar, on top of the whole-offering.
15 He then brought forward the offering of the people. He took the
he-goat, the people's sin-offering, slaughtered it and performed the
16 rite of the sin-offering as he had previously done for himself. He
presented the whole-offering and prepared it in the manner prescribed.
17 He brought forward the grain-offering, took a handful of it and burnt
18 it on the altar, in addition to the morning whole-offering. He slaughtered
the bull and the ram, the shared-offerings of the people. His sons
19 handed him the blood, and he flung it against the altar all round. But
the fatty parts of the bull, the fat-tail of the ram, the fat covering the
entrails, and the two kidneys with the fat upon them,*a* and the long
20 lobe of the liver, all this fat they first put on the breasts of the animals
21 and then burnt it on the altar. Aaron presented the breasts and the right
leg as a special gift before the LORD, as Moses had commanded.
22 Then Aaron lifted up his hands towards the people and pronounced
the blessing over them. He came down from performing the rites of the
23 sin-offering, the whole-offering, and the shared-offerings. Moses and
Aaron entered the Tent of the Presence, and when they came out, they
blessed the people, and the glory of the LORD appeared to all the
24 people. Fire came out from before the LORD and consumed the whole-
offering and the fatty parts on the altar. All the people saw, and they
shouted and fell on their faces.

10 NOW NADAB AND ABIHU, sons of Aaron, took their firepans, put
fire in them, threw incense on the fire and presented before the LORD
2 illicit fire which he had not commanded. Fire came out from before the
LORD and destroyed them; and so they died in the presence of the
3 LORD. Then Moses said to Aaron, 'This is what the LORD meant when
he said: Among those who approach me, I must be treated as holy; in
the presence of all the people I must be given honour.' Aaron was
4 dumbfounded. Moses sent for Mishael and Elzaphan, the sons of
Aaron's uncle Uzziel, and said to them, 'Come and carry your cousins

[a] the fat covering...upon them: *so Sept.; Heb.* and the covering and the kidneys.

outside the camp away from the holy place.' They came and carried 5
them away in their tunics outside the camp, as Moses had told them.
Moses then said to Aaron and to his sons Eleazar and Ithamar, 'You 6
shall not leave your hair dishevelled or tear your clothes in mourning,
lest you die and the LORD be angry with the whole community. Your
kinsmen, all the house of Israel, shall weep for the destruction by fire
which the LORD has kindled. You shall not leave the entrance to the 7
Tent of the Presence lest you die, because the LORD's anointing oil is
on you.' They did as Moses had said.

THE LORD SPOKE to Aaron and said: You and your sons with you 8,9
shall not drink wine or strong drink when you are to enter the Tent of
the Presence, lest you die. This is a rule binding on your descendants
for all time, to make a distinction between sacred and profane, between 10
clean and unclean, and to teach the Israelites all the decrees which the 11
LORD has spoken to them through Moses.
    Moses said to Aaron and his surviving sons Eleazar and Ithamar, 12
'Take what is left over of the grain-offering out of the food-offerings of
the LORD, and eat it without leaven beside the altar; it is most sacred.
You shall eat it in a sacred place; it is your due and that of your sons 13
out of the LORD's food-offerings, for so I was commanded. You shall 14
eat the breast of the special gift and the leg of the contribution in a clean
place, you and your sons and daughters; for they have been given to
you and your children as your due out of the shared-offerings of the
Israelites. The leg of the contribution and the breast of the special gift 15
shall be brought, along with the food-offerings of fat, to be presented as
a special gift before the LORD, and it shall belong to you and your
children together, a due for all time; for so the LORD has commanded.'
    Moses made searching inquiry about the goat of the sin-offering and 16
found that it had been burnt. He was angry with Eleazar and Ithamar,
Aaron's surviving sons, and said, 'Why did you not eat the sin-offering 17
in the sacred place? It is most sacred. It was given to you to take away
the guilt of the community by making expiation for them before the
LORD. If the blood is not brought within the sacred precincts, you shall 18
eat the sin-offering there as I was commanded.' But Aaron replied to 19
Moses, 'See, they have today presented their sin-offering and their
whole-offering before the LORD, and this is what has befallen me; if I
eat a sin-offering today, will it be right in the eyes of the LORD?' When 20
Moses heard this, he deemed it right.

Laws of purification and atonement

11 1,2 THE LORD SPOKE to Moses and Aaron and said, Speak to the
Israelites in these words: Of all animals on land these are the
3 creatures you may eat: you may eat any animal which has a parted
4 foot or a cloven hoof and also chews the cud; those which have only a
cloven hoof or only chew the cud you may not eat. These are: the
camel, because it chews the cud but has not a cloven hoof; you shall
5 regard it as unclean; the rock-badger,*a* because it chews the cud but
6 has not a parted foot; you shall regard it as unclean; the hare, because
it chews the cud but has not a parted foot; you shall regard it as unclean;
7 the pig, because it has a parted foot and a cloven hoof but does not
8 chew the cud; you shall regard it as unclean. You shall not eat
their flesh or even touch their dead bodies; you shall regard them as
unclean.

9 Of creatures that live in water these you may eat: all those that have
10 fins and scales, whether in salt water or fresh; but all that have neither
fins nor scales, whether in salt or fresh water, including both small
creatures in shoals and larger creatures, you shall regard as vermin.
11 They shall be vermin to you; you shall not eat their flesh, and their
12 dead bodies you shall treat as those of vermin. Every creature in
the water that has neither fins nor scales shall be vermin to you.

13 These are the birds you shall regard as vermin, and for this reason
they shall not be eaten: the griffon-vulture,*b* the black vulture, and
14,15 the bearded vulture;*c* the kite and every kind of falcon; every kind of
16 crow,*d* the desert-owl, the short-eared owl, the long-eared owl, and
17 every kind of hawk; the tawny owl, the fisher-owl, and the screech-owl;
18,19 the little owl, the horned owl, the osprey, the stork,*e* every kind of
cormorant, the hoopoe, and the bat.

20 All teeming winged creatures that go on four legs shall be vermin to
21 you, except those which have legs jointed above their feet for leaping
22 on the ground. Of these you may eat every kind of great locust, every
kind of long-headed locust, every kind of green locust, and every kind
23 of desert locust. Every other teeming winged creature that has four
24 legs you shall regard as vermin; you would make yourselves unclean
with them: whoever*f* touches their dead bodies shall be unclean till
25 evening. Whoever picks up their dead bodies shall wash his clothes but
remain unclean till evening.

26 You shall regard as unclean every animal which has a parted foot but

[a] *Or* rock-rabbit. [b] *Or* eagle. [c] *Or* ossifrage. [d] *Or* raven. [e] *Or* heron. [f] *Or* whatever.

has not a cloven hoof and does not chew the cud: whoever^a touches them shall be unclean. You shall regard as unclean all four-footed wild 27 animals that go on flat paws; whoever^a touches their dead bodies shall be unclean till evening. Whoever takes up their dead bodies shall wash 28 his clothes but remain unclean till evening. You shall regard them as unclean.

You shall regard these as unclean among creatures that teem on the 29 ground: the mole-rat,^{b} the jerboa, and every kind of thorn-tailed lizard; the gecko, the sand-gecko, the wall-gecko, the great lizard, and 30 the chameleon. You shall regard these as unclean among teeming 31 creatures; whoever^a touches them when they are dead shall be unclean till evening. Anything on which any of them falls when they are dead 32 shall be unclean, any article of wood or garment or skin or sacking, any article in regular use; it shall be plunged into water but shall remain unclean till evening, when it shall be clean. If any of these falls 33 into an earthenware vessel, its contents shall be unclean and it shall be smashed. Any food on which water from such a vessel is poured shall 34 be unclean, and any drink in such a vessel shall be unclean. Anything 35 on which the dead body of such a creature falls shall be unclean; an oven or a stove shall be broken, for they are unclean and you shall treat them as such; but a spring or a cistern where water collects shall 36 remain clean, though whatever^c touches the dead body shall be unclean. When any of their dead bodies falls on seed intended for sowing, it 37 remains clean; but if the seed has been soaked in water and any dead 38 body falls on it, you shall treat it as unclean.

When any animal allowed as food dies, all that touch the carcass shall 39 be unclean till evening. Whoever eats any of the carcass shall wash his 40 clothes but remain unclean till evening; whoever takes up the carcass shall wash his clothes and be unclean till evening. All creatures that 41 teem on the ground are vermin; they shall not be eaten. All creatures 42 that teem on the ground, crawl on their bellies, go on all fours or have many legs, you shall not eat, because they are vermin which contaminate. You shall not contaminate yourselves through any teeming 43 creature. You shall not defile yourselves with them and make yourselves unclean by them. For I am the LORD your God; you shall make your- 44 selves holy and keep yourselves holy, because I am holy. You shall not defile yourselves with any teeming creature that creeps on the ground. I am the LORD who brought you up from Egypt to become your God. 45 You shall keep yourselves holy, because I am holy.

This, then, is the law concerning beast and bird, every living creature 46 that swims in the water and every living creature that teems on the land. It is to make a distinction between the unclean and the clean, 47

[a] *Or* whatever. [b] *Or* weasel. [c] *Or* whoever.

between living creatures that may be eaten and living creatures that may not be eaten.

12 1,2 The LORD spoke to Moses and said, Speak to the Israelites in these words: When a woman conceives and bears a male child, she shall be unclean for seven days, as in the period of her impurity through 3 menstruation. On the eighth day, the child shall have the flesh of his 4 foreskin circumcised. The woman shall wait for thirty-three days because her blood requires purification; she shall touch nothing that is holy, and shall not enter the sanctuary till her days of purification are 5 completed. If she bears a female child, she shall be unclean for fourteen days as for her menstruation and shall wait for sixty-six days because 6 her blood requires purification. When her days of purification are completed for a son or a daughter, she shall bring a yearling ram for a whole-offering and a young pigeon or a turtle-dove for a sin-offering to 7 the priest at the entrance to the Tent of the Presence. He shall present it before the LORD and make expiation for her, and she shall be clean from the issue of her blood. This is the law for the woman who bears a 8 child, whether male or female. If she cannot afford a ram, she shall bring two turtle-doves or two young pigeons, one for a whole-offering and the other for a sin-offering. The priest shall make expiation for her and she shall be clean.

13 1,2 The LORD spoke to Moses and Aaron and said: When any man has a discoloration on the skin of his body, a pustule or inflammation, and it may develop into the sores of a malignant skin-disease, he shall be 3 brought to the priest, either to Aaron or to one of his sons. The priest shall examine the sore on the skin; if the hairs on the sore have turned white and it appears to be deeper than the skin, it shall be considered the sore of a malignant skin-disease, and the priest, after examination, 4 shall pronounce him ritually unclean. But if the inflammation on his skin is white and seems no deeper than the skin, and the hairs have not 5 turned white, the priest shall isolate the affected person for seven days. If, when he examines him on the seventh day, the sore remains as it was and has not spread in the skin, he shall keep him in isolation for 6 another seven days. When the priest examines him again on the seventh day, if the sore has faded and has not spread in the skin, the priest shall pronounce him ritually clean. It is only a scab; the man shall wash his 7 clothes and so be clean. But if the scab spreads on the skin after he has been to the priest to be pronounced ritually clean, the man shall show 8 himself a second time to the priest. The priest shall examine him again, and if it continues to spread, he shall pronounce him ritually unclean; it is a malignant skin-disease.

9 When anyone has the sores of a malignant skin-disease, he shall be 10 brought to the priest, and the priest shall examine him. If there is a

white mark on the skin, turning the hairs white, and an ulceration appears in the mark, it is a chronic skin-disease on the body, and the 11 priest shall pronounce him ritually unclean; there is no need for isolation because he is unclean already. If the skin-disease breaks out and 12 covers the affected person from head to foot as far as the priest can see, the priest shall examine him, and if he finds the condition spread all 13 over the body, he shall pronounce him ritually clean. It has all gone white; he is clean. But from the moment when raw flesh appears, the 14 man shall be considered unclean. When the priest sees it, he shall 15 pronounce him unclean. Raw flesh is to be considered unclean; it is a malignant skin-disease. On the other hand, when the raw flesh heals 16 and turns white, the man shall go to the priest, who shall examine him, 17 and if the sores have gone white, he shall pronounce him clean. He is ritually clean.

When a fester appears on the skin and heals up, but is followed by a 18, 19 white mark or reddish-white inflammation on the site of the fester, the man shall show himself to the priest. The priest shall examine him; if 20 it seems to be beneath the skin and the hairs have turned white, the priest shall pronounce him ritually unclean. It is a malignant skin-disease which has broken out on the site of the fester. But if the priest on 21 examination finds that it has no white hairs, is not beneath the skin and has faded, he shall isolate him for seven days. If the affection has 22 spread at all in the skin, then the priest shall pronounce him unclean; for it is a malignant skin-disease.[a] But if the inflammation is no worse 23 and has not spread, it is only the scar of the fester, and the priest shall pronounce him ritually clean.

Again, in the case of a burn on the skin, if the raw spot left by the 24 burn becomes a reddish-white or white inflammation, the priest shall 25 examine it. If the hairs on the inflammation have turned white and it is deeper than the skin, it is a malignant skin-disease which has broken out at the site of the burn. The priest shall pronounce the man ritually unclean; it is a malignant skin-disease. But if the priest on examination 26 finds that there is no white hair on the inflammation and it is not beneath the skin and has faded, he shall keep him in isolation for seven days. When the priest examines him on the seventh day, if the inflam- 27 mation has spread at all in the skin, the priest shall pronounce him unclean; it is a malignant skin-disease. But if the inflammation is no 28 worse, has not spread and has faded, it is only a mark from the burn. The priest shall pronounce him ritually clean because it is the scar of the burn.

When a man, or woman, has a sore on the head or chin, the priest 29, 30 shall examine it; and if it seems deeper than the skin and the hair is

[a] malignant skin-disease: *so one MS.; others* sore.

yellow and sparse, the priest shall pronounce him ritually unclean; it
31 is a scurf, a malignant skin-disease of the head or chin. But when the
priest sees the sore, if it appears to be no deeper than the skin and yet
there is no yellow*a* hair on the place, the priest shall isolate the affected
32 person for seven days. He shall examine the sore on the seventh day:
if the scurf has not spread and there are no yellow hairs on it and it
33 seems no deeper than the skin, the man shall get himself shaved except
for the scurfy part, and the priest shall keep him in isolation for
34 another seven days. The priest shall examine it again on the seventh
day, and if the scurf has not spread on the skin and appears to be no
deeper than the skin, the priest shall pronounce him clean. The man
35 shall wash his clothes and so be ritually clean. But if the scurf spreads
36 at all in the skin after the man has been pronounced clean, the priest
shall examine him again. If it has spread in the skin, the priest need not
37 even look for yellow hair; the man is unclean. If, however, the scurf
remains as it was but black hair has begun to grow on it, it has healed.
The man is ritually clean and the priest shall pronounce him so.

38   When a man, or woman, has inflamed patches on the skin and they
39 are white, the priest shall examine them. If they are white and fading,
it is dull-white leprosy that has broken out on the skin. The man is
ritually clean.

40   When a man's hair falls out from his head, he is bald behind but not
41 ritually unclean. If the hair falls out from the front of the scalp, he is
42 bald on the forehead but clean. But if on the bald patch behind or on the
forehead there is a reddish-white sore, it is a malignant skin-disease
43 breaking out on those parts. The priest shall examine him, and if the
discoloured sore on the bald patch behind or on the forehead is reddish-
white, similar in appearance to a malignant skin-disease on the body,
44 the man is suffering from such a disease; he is ritually unclean and the
priest must not fail to pronounce him so. The symptoms are in this
case on his head.

45   One who suffers from a malignant skin-disease shall wear his clothes
torn, leave his hair dishevelled, conceal his upper lip, and cry, 'Un-
46 clean, unclean.' So long as the sore persists, he shall be considered
ritually unclean. The man is unclean: he shall live apart and must stay
outside the settlement.

47   When there is a stain of mould, whether in a garment of wool or
48 linen, or in the warp or weft of linen or wool, or in a skin or anything
49 made of skin; if the stain is greenish or reddish in the garment or skin,
or in the warp or weft, or in anything made of skin, it is a stain of mould
50 which must be shown to the priest. The priest shall examine it and put
51 the stained material aside for seven days. On the seventh day he shall

[a] *So Sept.; Heb.* black.

146

examine it again. If the stain has spread in the garment, warp, weft, or skin, whatever the use of the skin, the stain is a rotting mould: it is ritually unclean. He shall burn the garment or the warp or weft, 52 whether wool or linen, or anything of skin which is stained; because it is a rotting mould, it must be destroyed by fire. But if the priest sees that 53 the stain has not spread in the garment, warp or weft, or anything made of skin, he shall give orders for the stained material to be washed, and 54 then he shall put it aside for another seven days. After it has been 55 washed the priest shall examine the stain; if it has not changed its appearance, although it has not spread, it is unclean and you shall destroy it by fire, whether the rot is on the right side or the wrong. If 56 the priest examines it and finds the stain faded after being washed, he shall tear it out of the garment, skin, warp, or weft. If, however, the 57 stain reappears in the garment, warp or weft, or in anything of skin, it is breaking out afresh and you shall destroy by fire whatever is stained. If you wash the garment, warp, weft, or anything of skin and the stain 58 disappears, it shall be washed a second time and then it shall be ritually clean.

This is the law concerning stain of mould in a garment of wool or 59 linen, in warp or weft, or in anything made of skin; by it they shall be pronounced clean or unclean.

THE LORD SPOKE to Moses and said: This is the law concerning a 14 1, 2 man suffering from a malignant skin-disease. On the day when he is to be cleansed he shall be brought to the priest. The priest shall go out- 3 side the camp and examine him. If the man is healed of his disease, then the priest shall order two clean small birds to be brought alive for 4 the man who is to be cleansed, together with cedar-wood, scarlet thread, and marjoram.[a] He shall order one of the birds to be killed over an 5 earthenware bowl containing fresh water. He shall then take the living 6 bird and the cedar-wood, scarlet thread, and marjoram and dip them and the living bird in the blood of the bird that has been killed over the fresh water. He shall sprinkle the blood seven times on the man who is 7 to be cleansed from his skin-disease and so cleanse him; the living bird he shall release to fly away over the open country. The man to be 8 cleansed shall wash his clothes, shave off all his hair, bathe in water and so be ritually clean. He may then enter the camp but must stay outside his tent for seven days. On the seventh day he shall shave off all the hair on 9 his head, his beard, and his eyebrows, and then shave the rest of his hair, wash his clothes and bathe in water; then he shall be ritually clean.

On the eighth day he shall bring two yearling[b] rams and one yearling 10 ewe, all three without blemish, a grain-offering of three tenths of an

[a] *Or* hyssop.   [b] yearling: *so Sam.; Heb. om.*

147

11 ephah of flour mixed with oil, and one log of oil. The officiating priest shall place the man to be cleansed and his offerings before the LORD at 12 the entrance to the Tent of the Presence. He shall then take one of the rams and offer it with the log of oil as a guilt-offering, presenting them 13 as a special gift before the LORD. The ram shall be slaughtered where the sin-offerings and the whole-offerings are slaughtered, within the sacred precincts, because the guilt-offering, like the sin-offering, 14 belongs to the priest. It is most sacred. The priest shall then take some of the blood of the guilt-offering and put it on the lobe of the right ear of the man to be cleansed, and on his right thumb and the big toe 15 of his right foot. He shall next take the log of oil and pour some of it on 16 the palm of his own left hand, dip his right forefinger into the oil on his left palm and sprinkle some of it with his finger seven times before the 17 LORD. He shall then put some of the oil remaining on his palm on the lobe of the right ear of the man to be cleansed, on his right thumb and on the big toe of his right foot, on top of the blood of the guilt-offering. 18 The remainder of the oil on the priest's palm shall be put upon the head of the man to be cleansed, and thus the priest shall make expiation 19 for him before the LORD. The priest shall then perform the sin-offering and make expiation for the uncleanness of the man who is to be 20 cleansed. After this he shall slaughter the whole-offering and offer it and the grain-offering on the altar. Thus the priest shall make expiation for him, and then he shall be clean.

21 If the man is poor and cannot afford these offerings, he shall bring one young ram as a guilt-offering to be a special gift making expiation for him, and a grain-offering of a tenth of an ephah of flour mixed with 22 oil, and a log of oil, also two turtle-doves or two young pigeons, whichever he can afford, one for a sin-offering and the other for a whole- 23 offering. He shall bring them to the priest for his cleansing on the eighth day, at the entrance to the Tent of the Presence before the LORD. 24 The priest shall take the ram for the guilt-offering and the log of oil, 25 and shall present them as a special gift before the LORD. The ram for the guilt-offering shall then be slaughtered, and the priest shall take some of the blood of the guilt-offering, and put it on the lobe of the right ear of the man to be cleansed and on his right thumb and on the 26 big toe of his right foot. He shall pour some of the oil on the palm of 27 his own left hand and sprinkle some of it with his right forefinger seven 28 times before the LORD. He shall then put some of the oil remaining on his palm on the lobe of the right ear of the man to be cleansed, and on his right thumb and on the big toe of his right foot exactly where the 29 blood of the guilt-offering was put. The remainder of the oil on the priest's palm shall be put upon the head of the man to be cleansed to 30 make expiation for him before the LORD. Of the birds which the man

148

has been able to afford, turtle-doves or young pigeons, whichever it may be, the priest shall deal with one as a sin-offering and with the 31 other as a whole-offering and shall make the grain-offering with them. Thus the priest shall make expiation before the LORD for the man who is to be cleansed. This is the law for the man with a malignant skin- 32 disease who cannot afford the regular offering for his cleansing.

The LORD spoke to Moses and Aaron and said: When you have 33, 34 entered the land of Canaan which I give you to occupy, if I inflict a fungous infection upon a house in the land you have occupied, its 35 owner shall come and report to the priest that there appears to him to be a patch of infection in his house. The priest shall order the house to 36 be cleared before he goes in to examine the infection, or everything in it will become unclean. After this the priest shall go in to inspect the house. If on inspection he finds the patch on the walls consists of 37 greenish or reddish depressions, apparently going deeper than the surface, he shall go out of the house and, standing at the entrance, shall 38 put it in quarantine for seven days. On the seventh day he shall come 39 back and inspect the house, and if the patch has spread in the walls, he shall order the infected stones to be pulled out and thrown away 40 outside the city in an unclean place. He shall then have the house 41 scraped inside throughout, and all the daub*a* they have scraped off*b* shall be tipped outside the city in an unclean place. They shall take 42 fresh stones to replace the others and replaster the house with fresh daub.

If the infection reappears in the house and spreads after the stones 43 have been pulled out and the house scraped*c* and redaubed, the priest 44 shall come and inspect it. If the infection has spread in the house, it is a corrosive growth; the house is unclean. The house shall be demolished, 45 stones, timber, and daub, and it shall all be taken away outside the city to an unclean place. Anyone who has entered the house during the time 46 it has been in quarantine shall be unclean till evening. Anyone who has 47 slept or eaten a meal in the house shall wash his clothes. But if, when 48 the priest goes into the house and inspects it, he finds that the infection has not spread after the redaubing, then he shall pronounce the house ritually clean, because the infection has been cured.

In order to rid the house of impurity, he shall take two small birds, 49 cedar-wood, scarlet thread, and marjoram. He shall kill one of the birds 50 over an earthenware bowl containing fresh water. He shall then take the 51 cedar-wood, marjoram, and scarlet thread, together with the living bird, dip them in the blood of the bird that has been killed and in the fresh water, and sprinkle the house seven times. Thus he shall purify the 52

[a] Or mud.   [b] So Pesh.; Heb. have brought to an end.   [c] So Sept.; Heb. brought to an end.

house, using the blood of the bird, the fresh water, the living bird, the
53 cedar-wood, the marjoram, and the scarlet thread. He shall set the living
bird free outside the city to fly away over the open country, and make
expiation for the house; and then it shall be clean.

54, 55 This is the law for all malignant skin-diseases, and for scurf, for
56 mould in clothes and fungus in houses, for a discoloration of the skin,
57 scab, and inflammation, to declare when these are pronounced unclean
and when clean. This is the law for skin-disease, mould, and fungus.

15 1,2 THE LORD SPOKE to Moses and Aaron and said, Speak to the
Israelites and say to them: When any man has a discharge from his
3 body, the discharge is ritually unclean. This is the law concerning[a] the
uncleanness due to his discharge whether it continues or has been
stopped; in either case he is unclean.

4   Every bed on which the man with a discharge lies down shall be
5 ritually unclean, and everything on which he sits shall be unclean. Any
man who touches the bed shall wash his clothes, bathe in water and
6 remain unclean till evening. Whoever sits on anything on which the
man with a discharge has sat shall wash his clothes, bathe in water and
7 remain unclean till evening. Whoever touches the body of the man with
a discharge shall wash his clothes, bathe in water and remain unclean
8 till evening. If the man spits on one who is ritually clean, the latter
shall wash his clothes, bathe in water and remain unclean till evening.
9, 10 Everything on which the man sits when riding shall be unclean. Whoever touches anything that has been under him shall be unclean till
evening, and whoever handles such things shall wash his clothes, bathe
11 in water and remain unclean till evening. Anyone whom the man with
a discharge touches without having rinsed his hands in water shall
12 wash his clothes, bathe in water and remain unclean till evening. Any
earthenware bowl touched by the man shall be smashed, and every
wooden bowl shall be rinsed with water.

13   When the man is cleansed from his discharge, he shall reckon seven
days to his cleansing, wash his clothes, bathe his body in fresh water
14 and be ritually clean. On the eighth day he shall obtain two turtle-
doves or two young pigeons and, coming before the LORD at the
entrance to the Tent of the Presence, shall give them to the priest.
15 The priest shall deal with one as a sin-offering and the other as a whole-
offering, and shall make for him before the LORD the expiation required
by the discharge.

16   When a man has emitted semen, he shall bathe his whole body in
17 water and be unclean till evening. Every piece of clothing or skin on
which there is any semen shall be washed and remain unclean till

[a] the law concerning: *so Sept.; Heb. om.*

evening. This applies also to the woman with whom a man has had 18
intercourse; they shall both bathe themselves in water and remain
unclean till evening.

When a woman has a discharge of blood, her impurity shall last for 19
seven days; anyone who touches her shall be unclean till evening. Every- 20
thing on which she lies or sits during her impurity shall be unclean.
Anyone who touches her bed shall wash his clothes, bathe in water and 21
remain unclean till evening. Whoever touches anything on which she 22
sits shall wash his clothes, bathe in water and remain unclean till
evening. If he is on the bed or seat where she is sitting, by touching it he 23
shall become unclean till evening. If a man goes so far as to have inter- 24
course with her and any of her discharge gets on to him, then he shall be
unclean for seven days, and every bed on which he lies down shall
be unclean.

When a woman has a prolonged discharge of blood not at the time 25
of her menstruation, or when her discharge continues beyond the
period of menstruation, her impurity shall last all the time of her
discharge; she shall be unclean as during the period of her menstruation. Any bed on which she lies during the time of her discharge shall 26
be like that which she used during menstruation, and everything on
which she sits shall be unclean as in her menstrual uncleanness. Every 27
person who touches them shall be unclean; he shall wash his clothes,
bathe in water and remain unclean till evening. If she is cleansed from 28
her discharge, she shall reckon seven days and after that she shall be
ritually clean. On the eighth day she shall obtain two turtle-doves or 29
two young pigeons and bring them to the priest at the entrance to the
Tent of the Presence. The priest shall deal with one as a sin-offering 30
and with the other as a whole-offering, and make for her before the
LORD the expiation required by her unclean discharge.

In this way you shall warn the Israelites against uncleanness, in 31
order that they may not bring uncleanness upon the Tabernacle where
I dwell among them, and so die.

This is the law for the man who has a discharge, or who has an 32
emission of semen and is thereby unclean, and for the woman who is 33
suffering her menstruation—for everyone, male or female, who has a
discharge, and for the man who has intercourse with a woman who is
unclean.

THE LORD SPOKE to Moses after the death of Aaron's two sons, who 16
died when they offered illicit fire before the LORD.[a] He said to him: 2
Tell your brother Aaron that he must not enter the sanctuary within the
Veil, in front of the cover over the Ark, except at the appointed time,

[a] when...LORD: *so Sept.; Heb.* when they came near before the LORD.

3 on pain of death; for I appear in the cloud above the cover. When Aaron enters the sanctuary, this is what he shall do. He shall bring a
4 young bull for a sin-offering and a ram for a whole-offering. He shall wear a sacred linen tunic and linen drawers to cover himself, and he shall put a linen sash round his waist and wind a linen turban round his head; all these are sacred vestments, and he shall bathe in water before
5 putting them on. He shall take from the community of the Israelites
6 two he-goats for a sin-offering and a ram for a whole-offering. He shall present the bull as a sin-offering and make expiation for himself and
7 his household. Then he shall take the two he-goats and set them before
8 the LORD at the entrance to the Tent of the Presence. He shall cast lots over the two goats, one to be for the LORD and the other for the
9 Precipice.[a] He shall present the goat on which the lot for the LORD has
10 fallen and deal with it as a sin-offering; but the goat on which the lot for the Precipice has fallen shall be made to stand alive before the LORD, for expiation to be made over it before it is driven away into the wilderness to the Precipice.
11 Aaron shall present his bull as a sin-offering, making expiation for himself and his household, and then slaughter the bull as a sin-offering.
12 He shall take a firepan full of glowing embers from the altar before the LORD, and two handfuls of powdered fragrant incense, and bring them
13 within the Veil. He shall put the incense on the fire before the LORD, and the cloud of incense will hide the cover over the Tokens so that
14 he shall not die. He shall take some of the bull's blood and sprinkle it with his finger both on the surface of the cover, eastwards, and seven times in front of the cover.
15 He shall then slaughter the people's goat as a sin-offering, bring its blood within the Veil and do with its blood as he did with the bull's
16 blood, sprinkling it on the cover and in front of it. He shall make for the sanctuary the expiation required by the ritual uncleanness of the Israelites and their acts of rebellion, that is by all their sins; and he shall do the same for the Tent of the Presence, which dwells among
17 them in the midst of all their uncleanness. No other man shall be within the Tent of the Presence from the time when he enters the sanctuary to make expiation until he comes out, and he shall make expiation for himself, his household, and the whole assembly of Israel.
18 He shall then come out to the altar which is before the LORD and make expiation for it. He shall take some of the bull's blood and some of
19 the goat's blood and put it all over the horns of the altar; he shall sprinkle some of the blood on the altar with his finger seven times. So he shall purify it from all the uncleanness of the Israelites and hallow it.
20 When Aaron has finished making expiation for the sanctuary, for

[a] *Or* for Azazel.

the Tent of the Presence, and for the altar, he shall bring forward the live goat. He shall lay both his hands on its head and confess over it all 21 the iniquities of the Israelites and all their acts of rebellion, that is all their sins; he shall lay them on the head of the goat and send it away into the wilderness in charge of a man who is waiting ready. The goat 22 shall carry all their iniquities upon itself into some barren waste and the man shall let it go, there in the wilderness.

Aaron shall then enter the Tent of the Presence, take off the linen 23 clothes which he had put on when he entered the sanctuary, and leave them there. He shall bathe in water in a consecrated place and put on 24 his vestments; then he shall go out and perform his own whole-offering and that of the people, thus making expiation for himself and for the people. He shall burn the fat of the sin-offering upon the altar. The man 25, 26 who drove the goat away to the Precipice shall wash his clothes and bathe in water, and not till then may he enter the camp. The two sin- 27 offerings, the bull and the goat, the blood of which was brought within the Veil to make expiation in the sanctuary, shall be taken outside the camp and destroyed by fire—skin, flesh, and offal. The man who burns 28 them shall wash his clothes and bathe in water, and not till then may he enter the camp.

This[a] shall become a rule binding on you for all time. On the tenth 29 day of the seventh month you shall mortify yourselves; you shall do no work, whether native Israelite or alien settler, because on this day 30 expiation shall be made on your behalf to cleanse you, and so make you clean before the LORD from all your sins. This is a sabbath of sacred 31 rest for you, and you shall mortify yourselves; it is a rule binding for all time. Expiation shall be made by the priest duly anointed and installed 32 to serve in succession to his father; he shall put on the sacred linen clothes and shall make expiation for the holy sanctuary, the Tent of the Presence, 33 and the altar, on behalf of the priests and the whole assembly of the people. This shall become a rule binding on you for all time, to make 34 for the Israelites once a year the expiation required by all their sins.

And Moses carried out the LORD's commands.

The law of holiness

THE LORD SPOKE to Moses and said, Speak to Aaron, his sons, 17 1, 2 and all the Israelites in these words: This is what the LORD has commanded. Any Israelite who slaughters an ox, a sheep, or a goat, 3 either inside or outside the camp, and does not bring it to the entrance 4

[a] *So Sept.; Heb. om.*

of the Tent of the Presence to present it as an offering to the LORD
before the Tabernacle of the LORD shall be held guilty of bloodshed:
5 that man has shed blood and shall be cut off from his people. The
purpose is that the Israelites should bring to the LORD the animals
which they slaughter in the open country; they shall bring them to the
priest at the entrance to the Tent of the Presence and sacrifice them as
6 shared-offerings to the LORD. The priest shall fling the blood against
the altar of the LORD at the entrance to the Tent of the Presence, and
7 burn the fat as a soothing odour to the LORD. They shall no longer
sacrifice their slaughtered beasts to the demons[a] whom they wantonly
follow. This shall be a rule binding on them and their descendants for
all time.
8   You shall say to them: Any Israelite or alien settled in Israel who
9 offers a whole-offering or a sacrifice and does not bring it to the
entrance of the Tent of the Presence to sacrifice it to the LORD shall
be cut off from his father's kin.
10   If any Israelite or alien settled in Israel eats any blood, I will set my
11 face against the eater and cut him off from his people, because the life
of a creature is the blood, and I appoint it to make expiation on the
altar for yourselves: it is the blood, that is the life, that makes expiation.
12 Therefore I have told the Israelites that neither you, nor any alien
settled among you, shall eat blood.
13   Any Israelite or alien settled in Israel who hunts beasts or birds that
may lawfully be eaten shall drain out the blood and cover it with earth,
14 because the life of every living creature is the blood,[b] and I have
forbidden the Israelites to eat the blood of any creature, because the
life of every creature is its blood: every man who eats it shall be cut off.
15   Every person, native or alien, who eats that which has died a natural
death or has been mauled by wild beasts shall wash his clothes and
bathe in water, and remain ritually unclean till evening; then he shall
16 be clean. If he does not wash his clothes and bathe his body, he must
accept responsibility.

18 1,2 THE LORD SPOKE to Moses and said, Speak to the Israelites in these
3 words: I am the LORD your God. You shall not do as they do in Egypt
where you once dwelt, nor shall you do as they do in the land of Canaan
to which I am bringing you; you shall not conform to their institutions.
4 You must keep my laws and conform to my institutions without fail: I
5 am the LORD your God. You shall observe my institutions and my laws:
the man who keeps them shall have life through them. I am the LORD.
6   No man shall approach a blood-relation for intercourse. I am the
7 LORD. You shall not bring shame on your father by intercourse

[a] *Or* satyrs.   [b] *So Sept.; Heb. adds* within it.

154

with your mother: she is your mother; you shall not bring shame upon her. You shall not have intercourse with your father's wife: that is to 8 bring shame upon your father. You shall not have intercourse with 9 your sister, your father's daughter, or your mother's daughter, whether brought up in the family or in another home; you shall not bring shame upon them. You shall not have intercourse with your son's 10 daughter or your daughter's daughter: that is to bring shame upon yourself. You shall not have intercourse with a daughter of your father's 11 wife, begotten by your father: she is your sister, and you shall not bring shame upon her. You shall not have intercourse with your father's 12 sister: she is a blood-relation of your father. You shall not have inter- 13 course with your mother's sister: she is a blood-relation of your mother. You shall not bring shame upon your father's brother by approaching 14 his wife: she is your aunt. You shall not have intercourse with your 15 daughter-in-law: she is your son's wife; you shall not bring shame upon her. You shall not have intercourse with your brother's wife: that is to 16 bring shame upon him. You shall not have intercourse with both a 17 woman and her daughter, nor shall you take her son's daughter or her daughter's daughter to have intercourse with them: they are her blood-relations, and such conduct is lewdness. You shall not take a woman 18 who is your wife's sister to make her a rival-wife, and to have inter-course with her during her sister's lifetime.

You shall not approach a woman to have intercourse with her during 19 her period of menstruation. You shall not have sexual intercourse with 20 the wife of your fellow-countryman and so make yourself unclean with her. You shall not surrender any of your children to Molech and thus 21 profane the name of your God: I am the LORD. You shall not lie with 22 a man as with a woman: that is an abomination. You shall not have 23 sexual intercourse with any beast to make yourself unclean with it, nor shall a woman submit herself to intercourse with a beast: that is a violation of nature. You shall not make yourselves unclean in any of 24 these ways; for in these ways the heathen, whom I am driving out before you, made themselves unclean. This is how the land became 25 unclean, and I punished it for its iniquity so that it spewed out its inhabitants. You, unlike them, shall keep my laws and my rules: none 26 of you, whether natives or aliens settled among you, shall do any of these abominable things. The people who were there before you 27 did these abominable things and the land became unclean. So the land 28 will not spew you out for making it unclean as it spewed them out; for 29 anyone who does any of these abominable things shall be cut off from his people. Observe my charge, therefore, and follow none of the 30 abominable institutions customary before your time; do not make yourselves unclean with them. I am the LORD your God.

19 1,2 THE LORD SPOKE TO MOSES AND SAID, Speak to all the community of the Israelites in these words: You shall be holy, because I, the LORD
3 your God, am holy. You shall revere, every man of you, his mother and his father. You shall keep my sabbaths. I am the LORD your God.
4 Do not resort to idols; you shall not make gods of cast metal for yourselves. I am the LORD your God.

5 When you sacrifice a shared-offering to the LORD, you shall slaughter
6 it so as to win acceptance for yourselves. It must be eaten on the day of your sacrifice or the next day. Whatever is left over till the third day
7 shall be destroyed by fire; it is tainted, and if any of it is eaten on the
8 third day, it will not be acceptable. He who eats it must accept responsibility, because he has profaned the holy-gift to the LORD: that person shall be cut off from his father's kin.

9 When you reap the harvest of your land, you shall not reap right into the edges of your field; neither shall you glean the loose ears of
10 your crop; you shall not completely strip your vineyard nor glean the fallen grapes. You shall leave them for the poor and the alien. I am the LORD your God.

11 You shall not steal; you shall not cheat or deceive a fellow-country-
12 man. You shall not swear in my name with intent to deceive and thus
13 profane the name of your God. I am the LORD. You shall not oppress your neighbour, nor rob him. You shall not keep back a hired man's
14 wages till next morning. You shall not treat the deaf with contempt, nor put an obstruction in the way of the blind. You shall fear your God. I am the LORD.

15 You shall not pervert justice, either by favouring the poor or by subservience to the great. You shall judge your fellow-countryman
16 with strict justice. You shall not go about spreading slander among your father's kin, nor take sides against your neighbour on a capital
17 charge. I am the LORD. You shall not nurse hatred against your brother. You shall reprove your fellow-countryman frankly and so you will have
18 no share in his guilt.*a* You shall not seek revenge, or cherish anger towards your kinsfolk; you shall love your neighbour as a man like yourself. I am the LORD.

19 You shall keep my rules. You shall not allow two different kinds of beast to mate together. You shall not plant your field with two kinds of seed. You shall not put on a garment woven with two kinds of yarn.
20 When a man has intercourse with a slave-girl who has been assigned to another man and neither ransomed nor given her freedom, inquiry shall be made. They shall not be put to death, because she has not been
21 freed. The man shall bring his guilt-offering, a ram, to the LORD to the
22 entrance of the Tent of the Presence, and with it the priest shall make

[a] *Or* and for that you will incur no blame.

expiation for him before the LORD for his sin, and he shall be forgiven the sin he has committed.

When you enter the land, and plant any kind of tree for food, you 23 shall treat it as bearing forbidden*ᵃ* fruit. For three years it shall be forbidden and may not be eaten. In the fourth year all its fruit shall 24 be a holy-gift to the LORD, and this releases it for use.*ᵇ* In the fifth 25 year you may eat its fruit, and thus the yield it gives you shall be increased. I am the LORD your God.

You shall not eat meat with the blood in it. You shall not practise 26 divination or soothsaying. You shall not round off your hair from side 27 to side, and you shall not shave the edge of your beards. You shall not 28 gash yourselves in mourning for the dead; you shall not tattoo yourselves. I am the LORD.

Do not prostitute your daughter and so make her a whore; thus the 29 land shall not play the prostitute and be full of lewdness. You shall keep 30 my sabbaths, and revere my sanctuary. I am the LORD.

Do not resort to ghosts and spirits, nor make yourselves unclean by 31 seeking them out. I am the LORD your God.

You shall rise in the presence of grey hairs, give honour to the aged, 32 and fear your God. I am the LORD.

When an alien settles with you in your land, you shall not oppress 33 him. He shall be treated as a native born among you, and you shall love 34 him as a man like yourself, because you were aliens in Egypt. I am the LORD your God.

You shall not pervert justice in measurement of length, weight, or 35 quantity. You shall have true scales, true weights, true measures dry 36 and liquid. I am the LORD your God who brought you out of Egypt. You shall observe all my rules and laws and carry them out. I am the 37 LORD.

The LORD spoke to Moses and said, Say to the Israelites: Any 20 1,2 Israelite or alien settled in Israel who gives any of his children to Molech shall be put to death: the common people shall stone him. I, for my part, set my face against that man and cut him off from his 3 people, because he has given a child of his to Molech, thus making my sanctuary unclean and profaning my holy name. If the common people 4 connive at it when a man has given a child of his to Molech and do not put him to death, I will set my face against man and family, and both 5 him and all who follow him in his wanton following after Molech,*ᶜ* I will cut off from their people.

I will set my face against the man who wantonly resorts to ghosts 6 and spirits, and I will cut that person off from his people. Hallow 7

[a] *Lit.* uncircumcised. [b] and this...use: *so Sam.; Heb.* a festal jubilation. [c] *Or* in his lusting after human sacrifice.

8 yourselves and be holy, because I the LORD your God am holy.*a* You shall keep my rules and obey them: I am the LORD who hallows you.

9 When any man reviles his father and his mother, he shall be put to death. He has reviled his father and his mother; his blood shall be on

10 his own head. If a man commits adultery with his neighbour's wife,*b*

11 both adulterer and adulteress shall be put to death. The man who has intercourse with his father's wife has brought shame on his father. They shall both be put to death; their blood shall be on their own

12 heads. If a man has intercourse with his daughter-in-law, they shall both be put to death. Their deed is a violation of nature; their blood

13 shall be on their own heads. If a man has intercourse with a man as with a woman, they both commit an abomination. They shall be put

14 to death; their blood shall be on their own heads. If a man takes both a woman and her mother, that is lewdness. Both he and they shall be

15 burnt; thus there shall be no lewdness in your midst. A man who has sexual intercourse with any beast shall be put to death, and you shall

16 kill the beast. If a woman approaches any animal to have intercourse with it, you shall kill both woman and beast. They shall be put to death;

17 their blood shall be on their own heads. If a man takes his sister, his father's daughter or his mother's daughter, and they see one another naked, it is a scandalous disgrace. They shall be cut off in the presence of their people. The man has had intercourse with his sister and he shall

18 accept responsibility. If a man lies with a woman during her monthly period and brings shame upon her, he has exposed her discharge and she has uncovered the source of her discharge; they shall both be cut

19 off from their people. You shall not have intercourse with your mother's sister or your father's sister: it is the exposure of a blood-relation. They

20 shall accept responsibility. A man who has intercourse with his uncle's wife has brought shame upon his uncle. They shall accept responsibility

21 for their sin and shall be proscribed and put to death. If a man takes his brother's wife, it is impurity. He has brought shame upon his brother; they shall be proscribed.

22 You shall keep all my rules and my laws and carry them out, that the

23 land into which I am bringing you to live may not spew you out. You shall not conform to the institutions of the nations whom I am driving

24 out before you: they did all these things and I abhorred them, and I told you that you should occupy their land, and I would give you possession of it, a land flowing with milk and honey. I am the LORD your God:

25 I have made a clear separation between you and the nations, and you shall make a clear separation between clean beasts and unclean beasts and between unclean and clean birds. You shall not make yourselves

[a] *So Sept.; Heb.* because I am the LORD your God. [b] *So Luc. Sept.; Heb. adds* a man commits adultery with the wife of...

vile through beast or bird or anything that creeps on the ground, for I have made a clear separation between them and you, declaring them unclean. You shall be holy to me, because I the LORD am holy. I have made a clear separation between you and the heathen, that you may belong to me. Any may or woman among you who calls up ghosts or spirits shall be put to death. The people shall stone them; their blood shall be on their own heads.

THE LORD SAID to Moses, Say to the priests, the sons of Aaron: 21 A priest shall not render himself unclean for the death of any of his kin except for a near blood-relation, that is for mother, father, son, 2 daughter, brother, or full sister who is unmarried and a virgin; nor 3, 4 shall he make himself unclean for any married woman^a among his father's kin, and so profane himself.

Priests shall not make bald patches on their heads as a sign of 5 mourning, nor cut the edges of their beards, nor gash their bodies. They shall be holy to their God, and they shall not profane the name 6 of their God, because they present the food-offerings of the LORD, the food of their God, and they shall be holy. A priest shall not marry a 7 prostitute or a girl who has lost her virginity, nor shall he marry a woman divorced from her husband; for he is holy to his God. You shall 8 keep him holy because he presents the food of your God; you shall regard him as holy because I the LORD, I who hallow them,^b am holy. When a priest's daughter profanes herself by becoming a prostitute, she 9 profanes her father. She shall be burnt to death.

The high priest, the one among his fellows who has had the anointing 10 oil poured on his head and has been consecrated to wear the vestments, shall neither leave his hair dishevelled nor tear his clothes. He shall not 11 enter the place where any man's dead body lies; not even for his father or his mother shall he render himself unclean. He shall not go out of 12 the sanctuary for fear that he dishonour the sanctuary of his God, because the consecration of the anointing oil of his God is upon him. I am the LORD. He shall marry a woman who is still a virgin. He shall 13, 14 not marry a widow, a divorced woman, a woman who has lost her virginity, or a prostitute, but only a virgin from his father's kin; he shall not dishonour his descendants among his father's kin, for I am 15 the LORD who hallows him.

The LORD spoke to Moses and said, Speak to Aaron in these words: 16, 17 No man among your descendants for all time who has any physical defect shall come and present the food of his God. No man with a 18 defect shall come, whether a blind man, a lame man, a man stunted or overgrown, a man deformed in foot or hand, or with mis-shapen 19, 20

[a] for any married woman: *prob. rdg.; Heb.* husband.   [b] *So Sam.* (*cp. verse 23*); *Heb.* you.

brows or a film over his eye or a discharge*a* from it, a man who has a
21 scab or eruption or has had a testicle ruptured. No descendant of
Aaron the priest who has any defect in his body shall approach to
present the food-offerings of the LORD; because he has a defect he shall
22 not approach to present the food of his God. He may eat the bread of
God both from the holy-gifts and from the holiest of holy-gifts,
23 but he shall not come up to the Veil nor approach the altar, because he
has a defect in his body. Thus he shall not profane my sanctuaries,
because I am the LORD who hallows them.
24   Thus did Moses speak to Aaron and his sons and to all the Israelites.
22 1,2 The LORD spoke to Moses and said, Tell Aaron and his sons that they
must be careful in the handling of the holy-gifts of the Israelites which
they hallow to me, lest they profane my holy name. I am the LORD.
3 Say to them: Any man of your descent for all time who while unclean
approaches the holy-gifts which the Israelites hallow to the LORD shall
4 be cut off from my presence. I am the LORD. No man descended from
Aaron who suffers from a malignant skin-disease, or has a discharge,
shall eat of the holy-gifts until he is cleansed. A man who touches
anything which makes him unclean or who has an emission of semen,
5 a man who touches any vermin which makes him unclean or any
6 human being who makes him unclean: any person who touches such
a thing shall be unclean till sunset and unless he washes his body shall
7 not eat of the holy-gifts. When the sun goes down, he shall be clean,
and after that he may eat from the holy-gifts, because they are his food.
8 He shall not eat an animal that has died a natural death or has been
mauled by wild beasts, thereby making himself unclean. I am the LORD.
9 The priests shall observe my charge, lest they make themselves guilty
10 and die for profaning my name. I am the LORD who hallows them. No
unqualified person may eat any holy-gift; nor may a stranger lodging
11 with a priest or a hired man eat a holy-gift. A slave bought by a priest
with his own money may do so, and slaves born in his household may
12 also share his food. When a priest's daughter marries an unqualified
13 person, she shall not eat any of the contributions of holy-gifts; but if
she is widowed or divorced and is childless and comes back to her father's
house as in her childhood, she shall share her father's food. No unqualified person may eat any of it.
14   When a man inadvertently eats a holy-gift, he shall make good the
15 holy-gift to the priest, adding a fifth to its value. The priests shall not
profane the holy-gifts of the Israelites which they set aside for the
16 LORD; they shall not let men eat their holy-gifts and so incur guilt and
its penalty, because I am the LORD who hallows them.
17,18   The LORD spoke to Moses and said, Speak to Aaron and his sons

[*a*] film...discharge: *the Heb. words are of uncertain mng.*

and to all the Israelites in these words: When any man of the house of
Israel or any alien in Israel presents, whether in fulfilment of a vow or
for a freewill offering, such an offering as is presented to the LORD for
a whole-offering so as to win acceptance for yourselves, it shall be a 19
male without defect, of cattle, sheep, or goats. You shall not present 20
anything which is defective, because it will not be acceptable on your
behalf. When a man presents a shared-offering to the LORD, whether 21
cattle or sheep, to fulfil a special*a* vow or as a freewill offering, if it is
to be acceptable it must be perfect; there shall be no defect in it.
You shall present to the LORD nothing blind, disabled, mutilated, with 22
running sore, scab, or eruption, nor set any such creature on the altar
as a food-offering to the LORD. If a bull or a sheep is overgrown or 23
stunted, you may make of it a freewill offering, but it will not be
acceptable in fulfilment of a vow. If its testicles have been crushed or 24
bruised, torn or cut, you shall not present it to the LORD; this is
forbidden in your land.

You shall not procure any such creature from a foreigner and present 25
it as food for your God. Their deformity is inherent in them, a permanent defect, and they will not be acceptable on your behalf.

The LORD spoke to Moses and said: When a calf, a lamb, or a kid 26,27
is born, it must not be taken from its mother for seven days. From the
eighth day onwards it will be acceptable when offered as a food-
offering to the LORD. You shall not slaughter a cow or sheep at the 28
same time as its young. When you make a thank-offering to the LORD, 29
you shall sacrifice it so as to win acceptance for yourselves; it shall be 30
eaten that same day, and none be left till morning. I am the LORD.

You shall observe my commandments and perform them. I am the 31
LORD. You shall not profane my holy name; I will be hallowed among 32
the Israelites. I am the LORD who hallows you, who brought you out of 33
Egypt to become your God. I am the LORD.

THE LORD SPOKE to Moses and said, Speak to the Israelites in these 23 1,2
words: These are the appointed seasons of the LORD, and you shall
proclaim them as sacred assemblies; these are my appointed seasons.
On six days work may be done, but every seventh day is a sabbath of 3
sacred rest, a day of sacred assembly, on which you shall do no work.
Wherever you live, it is the LORD's sabbath.

These are the appointed seasons of the LORD, the sacred assemblies 4
which you shall proclaim in their appointed order. In the first month 5
on the fourteenth day between dusk and dark is the LORD's Passover.
On the fifteenth day of this month begins the LORD's pilgrim-feast of 6
Unleavened Bread; for seven days you shall eat unleavened cakes.

[a] fulfil a special: *or* discharge a...

7 On the first day there shall be a sacred assembly; you shall not do your
8 daily work. For seven days you shall present your food-offerings to the
Lord. On the seventh day also there shall be a sacred assembly; you
shall not do your daily work.

9, 10   The Lord spoke to Moses and said, Speak to the Israelites in these
words: When you enter the land which I give you, and you reap its
harvest, you shall bring the first sheaf of your harvest to the priest.
11 He shall present the sheaf as a special gift before the Lord on*a* the day
12 after the sabbath, so as to gain acceptance for yourselves. On the day
you present the sheaf, you shall prepare a perfect yearling ram for a
13 whole-offering to the Lord, with the proper grain-offering, two tenths
of an ephah of flour mixed with oil, as a food-offering to the Lord, of
soothing odour, and also with the proper drink-offering, a quarter of a
14 hin of wine. You shall eat neither bread, nor grain, parched or fully
ripened, during that day, the day on which you bring your God his
offering; this is a rule binding on your descendants for all time wherever
you live.

15   From the day after the sabbath, the day on which you bring your
16 sheaf as a special gift, you shall count seven full weeks. The day after
the seventh sabbath will make fifty days, and then you shall present to
17 the Lord a grain-offering from the new crop. You shall bring from
your homes two loaves as a special gift; they shall contain two tenths of
an ephah of flour and shall be baked with leaven. They are the Lord's
18 firstfruits. In addition to the bread you shall present seven perfect
yearling sheep, one young bull, and two rams. They shall be a whole-
offering to the Lord with the proper grain-offering and the proper
19 drink-offering, a food-offering of soothing odour to the Lord. You shall
also prepare one he-goat for a sin-offering and two yearling sheep for
20 a shared-offering, and the priest shall present them in addition to the
bread of the firstfruits as a special gift before the Lord.*b* They shall be
21 a holy-gift to the Lord for the priest. On that same day you shall
proclaim a sacred assembly for yourselves; you shall not do your daily
work. This is a rule binding on your descendants for all time wherever
you live.

22   When you reap the harvest in your land, you shall not reap right into
the edges of your field, neither shall you glean the fallen ears. You shall
leave them for the poor and for the alien. I am the Lord your God.

23, 24   The Lord spoke to Moses and said, Speak to the Israelites in these
words: In the seventh month you shall keep the first day as a sacred
rest, a day of remembrance and acclamation, a day of sacred assembly.
25 You shall not do your daily work; you shall present a food-offering to
the Lord.

[a] *Or* from.   [b] *So Vulg.; Heb. adds* in addition to the two sheep.

The LORD spoke to Moses and said: Further, the tenth day of this 26, 27
seventh month is the Day of Atonement. There shall be a sacred
assembly; you shall mortify yourselves and present a food-offering to
the LORD. On that same day you shall do no work because it is a day of 28
expiation, to make expiation for you before the LORD your God. There- 29
fore every person who does not mortify himself on that day shall be cut
off from his father's kin. I will extirpate any person who does any work 30
on that day. You shall do no work; it is a rule binding on your descend- 31
ants for all time wherever you live. It is for you a sabbath of sacred rest, 32
and you shall mortify yourselves. From the evening of the ninth day
to the following evening you shall keep your sabbath-rest.

The LORD spoke to Moses and said, Speak to the Israelites in these 33, 34
words: On the fifteenth day of this seventh month the LORD's pilgrim-
feast of Tabernacles*a* begins, and it lasts for seven days. On the first day 35
there shall be a sacred assembly; you shall not do your daily work.
For seven days you shall present a food-offering to the LORD; and on 36
the eighth day there shall be a sacred assembly, and you shall present
a food-offering to the LORD. It is the closing ceremony; you shall not
do your daily work.

These are the appointed seasons of the LORD which you shall pro- 37
claim as sacred assemblies for presenting food-offerings to the LORD,
whole-offerings and grain-offerings, shared-offerings and drink-
offerings, each on its day, besides the LORD's sabbaths and all your 38
gifts, your vows, and your freewill offerings to the LORD.

Further, from the fifteenth day of the seventh month, when the 39
harvest has been gathered, you shall keep the LORD's pilgrim-feast for
seven days. The first day is a sacred rest and so is the eighth day. On 40
the first day you shall take the fruit of citrus-trees, palm fronds, and
leafy branches, and willows*b* from the riverside, and you shall rejoice
before the LORD your God for seven days. You shall keep this as a 41
pilgrim-feast in the LORD's honour for seven days every year. It is
a rule binding for all time on your descendants; in the seventh month
you shall hold this pilgrim-feast. You shall live in arbours for seven 42
days, all who are native Israelites, so that your descendants may be 43
reminded how I made the Israelites live in arbours when I brought
them out of Egypt. I am the LORD your God.

Thus Moses announced to the Israelites the appointed seasons of the 44
LORD.

THE LORD SPOKE to Moses and said: Command the Israelites to 24 1, 2
take pure oil of pounded olives ready for the regular mounting of the
lamp outside the Veil of the Tokens in the Tent of the Presence. Aaron 3

[a] *Or* Booths *or* Arbours.   [b] *Or* poplars.

shall keep the lamp in trim regularly from dusk to dawn before the
4 LORD: this is a rule binding on your descendants for all time. The lamps
on the lamp-stand, ritually clean, shall be regularly kept in trim by him
before the LORD.

5 You shall take flour and bake it into twelve loaves, two tenths of an
6 ephah to each. You shall arrange them in two rows, six to a row on the
7 table, ritually clean, before the LORD. You shall sprinkle pure frankincense on the rows,[a] and this shall be a token of the bread, offered to
8 the LORD as a food-offering. Sabbath after sabbath he shall arrange it
regularly before the LORD as a gift from the Israelites. This is a
9 covenant for ever; it is the privilege of Aaron and his sons, and they
shall eat the bread in a holy place, because it is the holiest of holy-gifts.
It is his due out of the food-offerings of the LORD for all time.

10-11   Now there was in the Israelite camp a man whose mother was an
Israelite and his father an Egyptian; his mother's name was Shelomith
daughter of Dibri of the tribe of Dan; and he went out and became
involved in a brawl with an Israelite of pure descent. He uttered the
12 Holy Name in blasphemy, so they brought him to Moses; and they
kept him in custody until the LORD's will should be clearly made
known to them.

13, 14   The LORD spoke to Moses and said, Take the man who blasphemed
out of the camp. Everyone who heard him shall put a hand[b] on his
15 head, and then all the community shall stone him to death. You shall
say to the Israelites: When any man whatever blasphemes his God, he
16 shall accept responsibility for his sin. Whoever utters the Name of the
LORD shall be put to death: all the community shall stone him; alien
or native, if he utters the Name, he shall be put to death.

17   When one man strikes another and kills him, he shall be put to
18 death. Whoever strikes a beast and kills it shall make restitution, life
19 for life. When one man injures and disfigures his fellow-countryman,
20 it shall be done to him as he has done; fracture for fracture, eye for eye,
tooth for tooth; the injury and disfigurement that he has inflicted upon
another shall in turn be inflicted upon him.

21   Whoever strikes a beast and kills it shall make restitution, but who-
22 ever strikes a man and kills him shall be put to death. You shall have
one penalty for alien and native alike. For I am the LORD your God.

23   Thus did Moses speak to the Israelites, and they took the man who
blasphemed out of the camp and stoned him to death. The Israelites
did as the LORD had commanded Moses.

25 1,2 THE LORD SPOKE to Moses on Mount Sinai and said, Speak to the
Israelites in these words: When you enter the land which I give you,

[a] *So Pesh.; Heb.* row.   [b] *Or* their hands.

the land shall keep sabbaths to the LORD. For six years you may sow 3
your fields and for six years prune your vineyards and gather the
harvest, but in the seventh year the land shall keep a sabbath of sacred 4
rest, a sabbath to the LORD. You shall not sow your field nor prune
your vineyard. You shall not harvest the crop that grows from fallen 5
grain, nor gather in the grapes from the unpruned vines. It shall be a
year of sacred rest for the land. Yet what the land itself produces in the 6
sabbath year shall be food for you, for your male and female slaves, for
your hired man, and for the stranger lodging under your roof, for your 7
cattle and for the wild animals in your country. Everything it produces
may be used for food.

You shall count seven sabbaths of years, that is seven times seven 8
years, forty-nine years, and in the seventh month on the tenth day of 9
the month, on the Day of Atonement, you shall send the ram's horn
round. You shall send it through all your land to sound a blast, and 10
so you shall hallow the fiftieth year and proclaim liberation in the land
for all its inhabitants. You shall make this your year of jubilee. Every
man of you shall return to his patrimony, every man to his family.
The fiftieth year shall be your jubilee. You shall not sow, and you shall 11
not harvest the self-sown crop, nor shall you gather in the grapes from
the unpruned vines, because it is a jubilee, to be kept holy by you. You 12
shall eat the produce direct from the land.

In this year of jubilee you shall return, every one of you, to his 13
patrimony. When you sell or buy land amongst yourselves, neither party 14
shall drive a hard bargain. You shall pay your fellow-countryman 15
according to the number of years since the jubilee, and he shall sell to
you according to the number of annual crops. The more years there 16
are to run, the higher the price, the fewer the years, the lower, because
he is selling you a series of crops. You must not victimize one another, 17
but you shall fear your God, because I am the LORD your God. Observe 18
my statutes, keep my judgements and carry them out; and you shall
live in the land in security. The land shall yield its harvest; you shall 19
eat your fill and live there secure. If you ask what you are to eat during 20
the seventh year, seeing that you will neither sow nor gather the harvest,
I will ordain my blessing for you in the sixth year and the land shall 21
produce a crop to carry over three years. When you sow in the eighth 22
year, you will still be eating from the earlier crop; you shall eat the old
until the new crop is gathered in the ninth year.

No land shall be sold outright, because the land is mine, and you 23
are coming into it as aliens and settlers. Throughout the whole land 24
of your patrimony, you shall allow land which has been sold to be
redeemed.

When one of you is reduced to poverty and sells part of his 25

patrimony, his next-of-kin who has the duty of redemption shall come
26 and redeem what his kinsman has sold. When a man has no such next-
27 of-kin and himself becomes able to afford its redemption, he shall take
into account the years since the sale and pay the purchaser the balance
28 up to the jubilee. Then he may return to his patrimony. But if the man
cannot afford to buy back the property, it shall remain in the hands of
the purchaser till the year of jubilee. It shall then revert to the original
owner, and he shall return to his patrimony.

29 When a man sells a dwelling-house in a walled town, he shall retain
the right of redemption till the end of the year of the sale; for a time
30 he shall have the right of redemption. If it is not redeemed before a full
year is out, the house in the walled*a* town shall vest in perpetuity in the
31 buyer and his descendants; it shall not revert at the jubilee. Houses in
unwalled hamlets shall be treated as property in the open country: the
right of redemption shall hold good, and in any case the house shall
32 revert at the jubilee. Levites shall have the perpetual right to redeem
33 houses of their own patrimony in towns belonging to them. If one of the
Levites does not redeem*b* his house in*c* such a town, then it shall still
revert to him at the jubilee, because the houses in Levite towns are their
34 patrimony in Israel. The common land surrounding their towns shall
not be sold, because it is their property in perpetuity.

35 When your brother-Israelite is reduced to poverty and cannot
support himself in the community, you shall assist him as*d* you would an
36 alien or a stranger, and he shall live with you. You shall not charge him
interest on a loan, either by deducting it in advance from the capital
sum, or by adding it on repayment. You shall fear your God, and your
37 brother shall live with you; you shall not deduct interest when advancing him money nor add interest to the payment due for food supplied
38 on credit. I am the LORD your God who brought you out of Egypt to
give you the land of Canaan and to become your God.

39 When your brother is reduced to poverty and sells himself to you, you
40 shall not use him to work for you as a slave. His status shall be that
of a hired man or a stranger lodging with you; he shall work for you
41 until the year of jubilee. He shall then leave your service, with his
children, and go back to his family and to his ancestral property:
42 because they are my slaves whom I brought out of Egypt, they shall
43 not be sold as slaves are sold. You shall not drive him with ruthless
44 severity, but you shall fear your God. Such slaves as you have, male or
female, shall come from the nations round about you; from them you
45 may buy slaves. You may also buy the children of those who have
settled and lodge with you and such of their family as are born in the

[a] So Sept.; Heb. unwalled.   [b] does not redeem: so Vulg.; Heb. redeems.   [c] So Sept.;
Heb. and.   [d] as: so Sept.; Heb. om.

land. These may become your property, and you may leave them to 46
your sons after you; you may use them as slaves permanently. But your
fellow-Israelites you shall not drive with ruthless severity.

When an alien or a stranger living with you becomes rich, and your 47
brother becomes poor and sells himself to the alien or stranger or
to a member of some alien family, he shall have the right of redemption 48
after he has sold himself. One of his brothers may redeem him, or his 49
uncle, his cousin, or any blood-relation of his family, or, if he can
afford it, he may redeem himself. He and his purchaser together shall 50
reckon from the year when he sold himself to the year of jubilee, and
the price shall be adjusted to the number of years. His period of
service with his owner shall be reckoned at the rate of a hired man.
If there are still many years to run to the year of jubilee, he must repay 51
for his redemption a proportionate amount of the sum for which he
sold himself; if there are few, he shall reckon and repay accord- 52
ingly. He shall have the status of a labourer hired from year to year, 53
and you shall not let him be driven with ruthless severity by his
owner. If the man is not redeemed in the intervening years, he and his 54
children shall be released in the year of jubilee; for it is to me that the 55
Israelites are slaves, my slaves whom I brought out of Egypt. I am
the LORD your God.

YOU SHALL NOT MAKE idols for yourselves; you shall not erect a 26
carved image or a sacred pillar; you shall not put a figured stone on
your land to prostrate yourselves upon, because I am the LORD your
God. You shall keep my sabbaths and revere my sanctuary. I am the 2
LORD.

If you conform to my statutes, if you observe my commandments 3
and carry them out, I will give you rain at the proper time; the land 4
shall yield its produce and the trees of the country-side their fruit.
Threshing shall last till vintage and vintage till sowing; you shall eat 5
your fill and live secure in your land. I will give peace in the land, and 6
you shall lie down to sleep with no one to terrify you. I will rid your
land of dangerous beasts and it shall not be ravaged by war. You shall 7
put your enemies to flight and they shall fall in battle before you.
Five of you shall pursue a hundred and a hundred of you ten thousand; 8
so shall your enemies fall in battle before you. I will look upon you 9
with favour, I will make you fruitful and increase your numbers: I will
give my covenant with you its full effect. Your old harvest shall last 10
you in store until you have to clear out the old to make room for the
new. I will establish my Tabernacle among you and will not spurn you. 11
I will walk to and fro among you; I will become your God and you shall 12
become my people. I am the LORD your God who brought you out of 13

Egypt and let you be their slaves no longer; I broke the bars of your
yoke and enabled you to walk upright.

14 But if you do not listen to me, if you fail to keep all these command-
15 ments of mine, if you reject my statutes, if you spurn my judgements,
16 and do not obey all my commandments, but break my covenant, then
be sure that this is what I will do: I will bring upon you sudden terror,
wasting disease, recurrent fever, and plagues that dim the sight and
cause the appetite to fail. You shall sow your seed to no purpose, for
17 your enemies shall eat the crop. I will set my face against you, and you
shall be routed by your enemies. Those that hate you shall hound you
on until you run when there is no pursuit.

18 If after all this you do not listen to me, I will go on to punish you
19 seven times over for your sins. I will break down your stubborn pride.
I will make the sky above you like iron and the earth beneath you like
20 bronze. Your strength shall be spent in vain; your land shall not yield
its produce nor the trees of the land their fruit.

21 If you still defy me and refuse to listen, I will multiply your calamities
22 seven times, as your sins deserve. I will send wild beasts among you;
they shall tear your children from you, destroy your cattle and bring
23 your numbers low; and your roads shall be deserted. If after all this
24 you have not learnt discipline but still defy me, I in turn will defy you
25 and scourge you seven times over for your sins. I will bring war in
vengeance upon you, vengeance irrevocable under covenant; you shall
be herded into your cities, I will send pestilence among you, and you
26 shall be given over to the enemy. I will cut short your daily bread*a* until
ten women can bake your bread in a single oven; they shall dole it out
by weight, and though you eat, you shall not be satisfied.

27, 28 If in spite of this you do not listen to me and still defy me, I will
defy you in anger, and I myself will punish you seven times over for
29 your sins. Instead of meat you shall eat your sons and your daughters.
30 I will destroy your hill-shrines and demolish your incense-altars.
I will pile your rotting carcasses on the rotting logs*b* that were your
31 idols, and I will spurn you. I will make your cities desolate and destroy
your sanctuaries; the soothing odour of your offerings I will not accept.
32 I will destroy your land, and the enemies who occupy it shall be
33 appalled. I will scatter you among the heathen, and I will pursue you
with the naked sword; your land shall be desolate and your cities heaps
34 of rubble. Then, all the time that it lies desolate, while you are in exile
in the land of your enemies, your land shall enjoy its sabbaths to the
35 full. All the time of its desolation it shall have the sabbath rest which it
36 did not have when you lived there. And I will make those of you who
are left in the land of your enemies so ridden with fear that, when a leaf

[a] *Lit.* I will break your stick of bread.   [b] rotting logs: *or* effigies.

flutters behind them in the wind, they shall run as if it were the sword
behind them; they shall fall with no one in pursuit. Though no one 37
pursues them they shall stumble over one another, as if the sword were
behind them, and there shall be no stand made against the enemy. You 38
shall meet your end among the heathen, and your enemies' land shall
swallow you up. Those who are left shall pine away in an enemy 39
land under their own iniquities; and with their fathers' iniquities upon
them too, they shall pine away as they did.

But though they confess their iniquity, their own and their fathers', 40
their treachery, and even their defiance of me, I will defy them in my 41
turn and carry them off into their enemies' land. Yet if then their
stubborn[a] spirit is broken and they accept their punishment in full,
I will remember my covenant with Jacob and my covenant with Isaac, 42
yes, and my covenant with Abraham, and I will remember the land. The 43
land shall be rid of its people and enjoy in full its sabbaths while it lies
desolate, and they shall pay in full the penalty because they rejected my
judgements and spurned my statutes. Yet even then, in their enemies' 44
land, I shall not have rejected nor spurned them, bringing them to an
end and so breaking my covenant with them, because I am the LORD
their God. I will remember on their behalf the covenant with the men 45
of former times whom I brought out of Egypt in full sight of all the
nations, that I might be their God. I am the LORD.

These are the statutes, the judgements, and the laws which the LORD 46
established between himself and the Israelites on Mount Sinai through
Moses.

THE LORD SPOKE to Moses and said, Speak to the Israelites in these 27 1, 2
words: When a man makes a special[b] vow to the LORD which requires
your valuation of living persons, a male between twenty and sixty years 3
old shall be valued at fifty silver shekels, that is shekels by the sacred
standard. If it is a female, she shall be valued at thirty shekels. If the 4, 5
person is between five years old and twenty, the valuation shall be
twenty shekels for a male and ten for a female. If the person is between 6
a month and five years old, the valuation shall be five shekels for a
male and three for a female. If the person is over sixty and a male, the 7
valuation shall be fifteen shekels, but if a female, ten shekels. If the 8
man is too poor to pay the amount of your valuation, the person shall be
set before the priest, and the priest shall value him according to the
sum which the man who makes the vow can afford: the priest shall make
the valuation.

If the vow concerns a beast such as may be offered as an offering to 9
the LORD, then every gift shall be holy to the LORD. He shall not change 10

[a] *Lit.* uncircumcised.   [b] makes a special: *or* discharges a...

169

it for another, or substitute good for bad or bad for good. But if a substitution is in fact made of one beast for another, then both the
11 original beast and its substitute shall be holy to the LORD. If the vow concerns any unclean beast such as may not be offered as an offering to
12 the LORD, then the animal shall be brought before the priest, and he shall value it whether good or bad. The priest's valuation shall be
13 decisive; in case of redemption the payment shall be increased by one fifth.

14 When a man dedicates his house as holy to the LORD, the priest shall value it whether good or bad, and the priest's valuation shall be
15 decisive. If the donor redeems his house, he shall pay the amount of the valuation increased by one fifth, and the house shall be his.

16 If a man dedicates to the LORD part of his ancestral land, you shall value it according to the amount of seed-corn it can carry, at the rate
17 of fifty shekels of silver for a homer of barley seed. If he dedicates his
18 land from the year of jubilee, it shall stand at your valuation; but if he dedicates it after the year of jubilee, the priest shall estimate the price in silver according to the number of years remaining till the next year
19 of jubilee, and this shall be deducted from your valuation. If the man who dedicates his field should redeem it, he shall pay the amount of
20 your valuation in silver, increased by one fifth, and it shall be his. If he does not redeem it but sells the land to another man, it shall no longer
21 be redeemable; when the land reverts at the year of jubilee, it shall be like land that has been devoted, holy to the LORD. It shall belong to the priest as his patrimony.

22 If a man dedicates to the LORD land which he has bought, land
23 which is not part of his ancestral land, the priest shall estimate the amount of the value for the period until the year of jubilee, and the
24 man shall give the amount fixed as at that day; it is holy to the LORD. At the year of jubilee the land shall revert to the man from whom he
25 bought it, whose patrimony it is. Every valuation you make shall be made by the sacred standard (twenty gerahs to the shekel).

26 Notwithstanding, no man may dedicate to the LORD the first-born of a beast which in any case has to be offered as a first-born, whether an
27 ox or a sheep. It is the LORD's. If it is any unclean beast, he may redeem it at your valuation and shall add one fifth; but if it is not redeemed, it
28 shall be sold at your valuation. Notwithstanding, nothing which a man devotes to the LORD irredeemably from his own property, whether man or beast or ancestral land, may be sold or redeemed. Everything so
29 devoted is most holy to the LORD. No human being thus devoted may be redeemed, but he shall be put to death.

30 Every tithe on land, whether from grain or from the fruit of a tree,
31 belongs to the LORD; it is holy to the LORD. If a man wishes to redeem

any of his tithe, he shall pay its value increased by one fifth. Every 32
tenth creature that passes under the counting rod shall be holy to the
LORD; this applies to all tithes of cattle and sheep. There shall be no 33
inquiry whether it is good or bad, and no substitution. If any substitution is made, then both the tithe-animal and its substitute shall be
forfeit as holy; it shall not be redeemed.

These are the commandments which the LORD gave Moses for the 34
Israelites on Mount Sinai.

NUMBERS

Israel in the wilderness of Sinai

1 ON THE FIRST DAY of the second month in the second
year after the Israelites came out of Egypt, the LORD spoke to
Moses at the Tent of the Presence in the wilderness of Sinai
2 in these words: 'Number the whole community of Israel by families in
3 the father's line, recording the name of every male person aged twenty
years and upwards fit for military service. You and Aaron are to make
4 a detailed list of them by their tribal hosts, and you shall have to assist
5 you one head of family from each tribe. These are their names:

of Reuben, Elizur son of Shedeur;
6 of Simeon, Shelumiel son of Zurishaddai;
7 of Judah, Nahshon son of Amminadab;
8 of Issachar, Nethaneel son of Zuar;
9 of Zebulun, Eliab son of Helon;
10 of Joseph: of Ephraim, Elishama son of Ammihud;
of Manasseh, Gamaliel son of Pedahzur;
11 of Benjamin, Abidan son of Gideoni;
12 of Dan, Ahiezer son of Ammishaddai;
13 of Asher, Pagiel son of Ocran;
14 of Gad, Eliasaph son of Reuel;[a]
15 of Naphtali, Ahira son of Enan.'

16 These were the conveners of the whole community, chiefs of their
17 fathers' tribes and heads of Israelite clans. So Moses and Aaron took
18 these men who had been indicated by name. They summoned the
whole community on the first day of the second month, and they
registered their descent by families in the father's line, recording every
19 male person aged twenty years and upwards, as the LORD had told
Moses to do. Thus it was that he drew up the detailed lists in the
wilderness of Sinai:
20 The tribal list of Reuben, Israel's eldest son, by families in the
father's line, with the name of every male person aged twenty years and
21 upwards fit for service, the number in the list of the tribe of Reuben
being forty-six thousand five hundred.
22 The tribal list of Simeon, by families in the father's line, with the

[a] So Sept. (cp. 2. 14); Heb. Deuel.

172

name of every male person aged twenty years and upwards fit for service, the number in the list of the tribe of Simeon being fifty-nine 23 thousand three hundred.

The tribal list of Gad, by families in the father's line, with the names 24 of all men aged twenty years and upwards fit for service, the number in 25 the list of the tribe of Gad being forty-five thousand six hundred and fifty.

The tribal list of Judah, by families in the father's line, with the 26 names of all men aged twenty years and upwards fit for service, the 27 number in the list of the tribe of Judah being seventy-four thousand six hundred.

The tribal list of Issachar, by families in the father's line, with the 28 names of all men aged twenty years and upwards fit for service, the 29 number in the list of the tribe of Issachar being fifty-four thousand four hundred.

The tribal list of Zebulun, by families in the father's line, with the 30 names of all men aged twenty years and upwards fit for service, the 31 number in the list of the tribe of Zebulun being fifty-seven thousand four hundred.

The tribal lists of Joseph: that of Ephraim, by families in the father's 32 line, with the names of all men aged twenty years and upwards fit for service, the number in the list of the tribe of Ephraim being forty 33 thousand five hundred; that of Manasseh, by families in the father's 34 line, with the names of all men aged twenty years and upwards fit for service, the number in the list of the tribe of Manasseh being thirty-two 35 thousand two hundred.

The tribal list of Benjamin, by families in the father's line, with the 36 names of all men aged twenty years and upwards fit for service, the 37 number in the list of the tribe of Benjamin being thirty-five thousand four hundred.

The tribal list of Dan, by families in the father's line, with the names 38 of all men aged twenty years and upwards fit for service, the number in 39 the list of the tribe of Dan being sixty-two thousand seven hundred.

The tribal list of Asher, by families in the father's line, with the 40 names of all men aged twenty years and upwards fit for service, the 41 number in the list of the tribe of Asher being forty-one thousand five hundred.

The tribal list of Naphtali, by families in the father's line, with the 42 names of all men aged twenty years and upwards fit for service, the 43 number in the list of the tribe of Naphtali being fifty-three thousand four hundred.

These were the numbers recorded in the detailed lists by Moses and 44 Aaron and the twelve chiefs of Israel, each representing one tribe and

45 being the head of a family.[a] The total number of Israelites aged twenty years and upwards fit for service, recorded in the lists of fathers'
46 families, was six hundred and three thousand five hundred and fifty.
47 A list of the Levites by their fathers' families was not made.
48,49   The LORD spoke to Moses and said, 'You shall not record the total number of the Levites or make a detailed list of them among the
50 Israelites. You shall put the Levites in charge of the Tabernacle of the Tokens, with its equipment and everything in it. They shall carry the Tabernacle and all its equipment; they alone shall be its attendants and
51 shall pitch their tents round it. The Levites shall take the Tabernacle down when it is due to move and shall put it up when it halts; any
52 unqualified person who comes near it shall be put to death. All other Israelites shall pitch their tents, each tribal host in its proper camp and
53 under its own standard. But the Levites shall encamp round the Tabernacle of the Tokens, so that divine wrath may not follow the whole community of Israel; the Tabernacle of the Tokens shall be in their keeping.'
54   The Israelites did exactly as the LORD had told Moses to do.
2 1,2   The LORD spoke to Moses and Aaron and said, 'The Israelites shall encamp each under his own standard by the emblems of his father's family; they shall pitch their tents round the Tent of the Presence, facing it.
3   'In front of it, on the east, the division of Judah shall be stationed under the standard of its camp by tribal hosts. The chief of Judah shall
4 be Nahshon son of Amminadab. His host, with its members as
5 detailed, numbers seventy-four thousand six hundred men. Next to Judah the tribe of Issachar shall be stationed. Its chief shall be Nethaneel
6 son of Zuar; his host, with its members as detailed, numbers fifty-four
7 thousand four hundred. Then the tribe of Zebulun: its chief shall be
8 Eliab son of Helon; his host, with its members as detailed, numbers
9 fifty-seven thousand four hundred. The number listed in the camp of Judah, by hosts, is one hundred and eighty-six thousand four hundred. They shall be the first to march.
10   'To the south the division of Reuben shall be stationed under the standard of its camp by tribal hosts. The chief of Reuben shall be
11 Elizur son of Shedeur; his host, with its members as detailed, numbers
12 forty-six thousand five hundred. Next to him the tribe of Simeon shall
13 be stationed. Its chief shall be Shelumiel son of Zurishaddai; his host, with its members as detailed, numbers fifty-nine thousand three
14 hundred. Then the tribe of Gad: its chief shall be Eliasaph son of
15 Reuel; his host, with its members as detailed, numbers forty-five
16 thousand six hundred and fifty. The number listed in the camp of

[a] each...family: *prob. rdg.* (*cp. Sam. and Sept.*); *Heb.* each representing a family.

Reuben, by hosts, is one hundred and fifty-one thousand four hundred and fifty. They shall be the second to march.

'When the Tent of the Presence moves, the camp of the Levites shall 17 keep its station in the centre of the other camps; they shall all move in the order of their encamping, each man in his proper place under his standard.

'To the west the division of Ephraim shall be stationed under the 18 standard of its camp by tribal hosts. The chief of Ephraim shall be Elishama son of Ammihud; his host, with its members as detailed, 19 numbers forty thousand five hundred. Next to him the tribe of 20 Manasseh shall be stationed. Its chief shall be Gamaliel son of Pedahzur; his host, with its members as detailed, numbers thirty-two 21 thousand two hundred. Then the tribe of Benjamin: its chief shall be 22 Abidan son of Gideoni; his host, with its members as detailed, numbers 23 thirty-five thousand four hundred. The number listed in the camp of 24 Ephraim, by hosts, is one hundred and eight thousand one hundred. They shall be the third to march.

'To the north the division of Dan shall be stationed under the 25 standard of its camp by tribal hosts. The chief of Dan shall be Ahiezer son of Ammishaddai; his host, with its members as detailed, numbers 26 sixty-two thousand seven hundred. Next to him the tribe of Asher shall 27 be stationed. Its chief shall be Pagiel son of Ocran; his host, with its 28 members as detailed, numbers forty-one thousand five hundred. Then 29 the tribe of Naphtali: its chief shall be Ahira son of Enan; his host, 30 with its members as detailed, numbers fifty-three thousand four hundred. The number listed in the camp of Dan is a hundred and 31 fifty-seven thousand six hundred. They shall march, under their standards, last.'

These were the Israelites listed by their fathers' families. The total 32 number in the camp, recorded by tribal hosts, was six hundred and three thousand five hundred and fifty.

The Levites were not included in the detailed lists with their fellow- 33 Israelites, for so the LORD had commanded Moses. The Israelites did 34 exactly as the LORD had commanded Moses, pitching and breaking camp standard by standard, each man according to his family in his father's line.

THESE WERE the descendants of Aaron and Moses at the time when 3 the LORD spoke to Moses on Mount Sinai. The names of the sons of 2 Aaron were Nadab the eldest, Abihu, Eleazar and Ithamar. These were 3 the names of Aaron's sons, the anointed priests who had been installed in the priestly office. Nadab and Abihu fell dead before the LORD 4 because they had presented illicit fire before the LORD in the wilderness of Sinai. They left no sons; Eleazar and Ithamar continued to perform the priestly office in their father's presence.

5,6 The LORD spoke to Moses and said, 'Bring forward the tribe of Levi
7 and appoint them to serve Aaron the priest and to minister to him. They shall be in attendance on him and on the whole community before the
8 Tent of the Presence, undertaking the service of the Tabernacle. They shall be in charge of all the equipment in the Tent of the Presence, and be in attendance on the Israelites, undertaking the service of the
9 Tabernacle. You shall assign the Levites to Aaron and his sons as
10 especially dedicated to him out of all the Israelites. To Aaron and his line you shall commit the priestly office and they shall perform its duties; any unqualified person who intrudes upon it shall be put to death.'

11,12 The LORD spoke to Moses and said, 'I take the Levites for myself out of all the Israelites as a substitute for the eldest male child of every
13 woman; the Levites shall be mine. For every eldest child, if a boy, became mine when I destroyed all the eldest sons in Egypt. So I have consecrated to myself all the first-born in Israel, both man and beast. They shall be mine. I am the LORD.'

14 The LORD spoke to Moses in the wilderness of Sinai and said,
15 'Make a detailed list of all the Levites by their families in the father's line, every male from the age of one month and upwards.'
16 Moses made a detailed list of them in accordance with the command
17 given him by the LORD. Now these were the names of the sons of Levi:

Gershon, Kohath and Merari.
18 Descendants of Gershon, by families: Libni and Shimei.
19 Descendants of Kohath, by families: Amram, Izhar, Hebron and Uzziel.
20 Descendants of Merari, by families: Mahli and Mushi.

These were the families of Levi, by fathers' families:
21 Gershon: the family of Libni and the family of Shimei. These were
22 the families of Gershon, and the number of males in their list as detailed, from the age of one month and upwards, was seven thousand
23 five hundred. The families of Gershon were stationed on the west,
24,25 behind the Tabernacle. Their chief was Eliasaph son of Lael, and in the service of the Tent of the Presence they were in charge of the Tabernacle and[a] its coverings, of the screen at the entrance to the Tent
26 of the Presence, the hangings of the court, the screen at the entrance to the court all round the Tabernacle and the altar, and of all else needed for its maintenance.
27 Kohath: the family of Amram, the family of Izhar, the family of

[a] *So Sept.; Heb. adds* the tent.

Hebron, the family of Uzziel. These were the families of Kohath, and the number of males, from the age of one month and upwards, was 28 eight thousand six hundred. They were the guardians of the holy things. The families of Kohath were stationed on the south, at the side 29 of the Tabernacle. Their chief was Elizaphan son of Uzziel; they were 30, 31 in charge of the Ark, the table, the lamp-stands and the altars, together with the sacred vessels used in their service, and the screen with every-thing needed for its maintenance. The chief over all the chiefs of the 32 Levites was Eleazar son of Aaron the priest, who was appointed overseer of those in charge of the sanctuary.

Merari: the family of Mahli, the family of Mushi. These were the 33 families of Merari, and the number of males in their list as detailed 34 from the age of one month and upwards was six thousand two hundred. Their chief was Zuriel son of Abihail; they were stationed on the north, 35 at the side of the Tabernacle. The Merarites were in charge of the 36 planks, bars, posts, and sockets of the Tabernacle, together with its vessels and all the equipment needed for its maintenance, the posts, 37 sockets, pegs, and cords of the surrounding court.

In front of the Tabernacle on the east, Moses was stationed, with 38 Aaron and his sons, in front of the Tent of the Presence eastwards. They were in charge of the sanctuary on behalf of the Israelites; any unqualified person who came near would be put to death.

The number of Levites recorded by Moses[a] on the detailed list by 39 families at the command of the LORD was twenty-two thousand males aged one month and upwards.

The LORD said to Moses, 'Make a detailed list of all the male first- 40 born in Israel aged one month and upwards, and count the number of persons. You shall reserve the Levites for me—I am the LORD—in 41 substitution for the eldest sons of the Israelites, and in the same way the Levites' cattle in substitution for the first-born cattle of the Israelites.' As the LORD had told him to do, Moses made a list of all the 42 eldest sons of the Israelites, and the total number of first-born males 43 recorded by name in the register, aged one month and upwards, was twenty-two thousand two hundred and seventy-three.

The LORD spoke to Moses and said, 'Take the Levites as a substitute 44, 45 for all the eldest sons in Israel and the cattle of the Levites as a substi-tute for their cattle. The Levites shall be mine. I am the LORD. The eldest sons in Israel will outnumber the Levites by two hundred 46 and seventy-three. This remainder must be ransomed, and you shall 47 accept five shekels for each of them, taking the sacred shekel and reckoning twenty gerahs to the shekel; you shall give the money with 48 which they are ransomed to Aaron and his sons.'

[a] *So some MSS.; others add* and Aaron.

49   Moses took the money paid as ransom for those who remained over
50 when the substitution of Levites was complete. The amount received
was one thousand three hundred and sixty-five shekels of silver by the
51 sacred standard. In accordance with what the LORD had said, he gave
the money to Aaron and his sons, doing what the LORD had told him
to do.

4 1, 2   The LORD spoke to Moses and Aaron and said, 'Among the Levites,
3 make a count of the descendants of Kohath between the ages of thirty
and fifty, by families in the father's line, comprising everyone who
comes to take duty in the service of the Tent of the Presence.

4   'This is the service to be rendered by the Kohathites in the Tent of
5 the Presence; it is most sacred. When the camp is due to move, Aaron
and his sons shall come and take down the Veil of the screen and cover
6 the Ark of the Tokens with it; over this they shall put a covering of
porpoise-hide[a] and over that again a violet cloth all of one piece; they
7 shall then put its poles in place. Over the Table of the Presence they
shall spread a violet cloth and lay on it the dishes, saucers, and flagons,
and the bowls for drink-offerings; the Bread regularly presented shall
8 also lie upon it; then they shall spread over them a scarlet cloth and
9 over that a covering of porpoise-hide, and put the poles in place. They
shall take a violet cloth and cover the lamp-stand, its lamps, tongs, fire-
10 pans, and all the containers for the oil used in its service; they shall
put it with all its equipment in a sheet of porpoise-hide slung from a
11 pole. Over the gold altar they shall spread a violet cloth, cover it with
12 a porpoise-hide covering, and put its poles in place. They shall take
all the articles used for the service of the sanctuary, put them on a
violet cloth, cover them with a porpoise-hide covering, and sling them
13 from a pole. They shall clear the altar of the fat and ashes, spread a
14 purple cloth over it, and then lay on it all the equipment used in its
service, the firepans, forks, shovels, tossing-bowls, and all the equipment of the altar, spread a covering of porpoise-hide over it and put the
15 poles in place. Once Aaron and his sons have finished covering the
sanctuary and all the sacred equipment, when the camp is due to move,
the Kohathites shall come to carry it; they must not touch it on pain
of death. All these things are the load to be carried by the Kohathites,
16 the things connected with the Tent of the Presence. Eleazar son of
Aaron the priest shall have charge of the lamp-oil, the fragrant incense,
the regular grain-offering, and the anointing oil, with the general oversight of the whole Tabernacle and its contents, the sanctuary and its
equipment.'

17, 18   The LORD spoke to Moses and Aaron and said, 'You must not let
the families of Kohath be extirpated, and lost to the tribe of Levi.

[a] *Strictly* hide of sea-cow.

If they are to live and not die when they approach the most holy things, 19 this is what you must do: Aaron and his sons shall come and set each man to his appointed task and to his load, and the Kohathites them- 20 selves shall not enter to cast even a passing glance[a] on the sanctuary, on pain of death.'

The LORD spoke to Moses and said, 'Number the Gershonites by 21,22 families in the father's line. Make a detailed list of all those between 23 the ages of thirty and fifty who come on duty to perform service in the Tent of the Presence.

'This is the service to be rendered by the Gershonite families, com- 24 prising their general duty and their loads. They shall carry the hangings 25 of the Tabernacle, the Tent of the Presence, its covering, that is the covering of porpoise-hide which is over it, the screen at the entrance to the Tent of the Presence, the hangings of the court, the screen at the 26 entrance to the court surrounding the Tabernacle and the altar, their cords and all the equipment for their service; and they shall perform all the tasks connected with them. These are the acts of service they shall render. All the service of the Gershonites, their loads and their 27 other duties, shall be directed by Aaron and his sons; you shall assign them the loads for which they shall be responsible. This is the service 28 assigned to the Gershonite families in connection with the Tent of the Presence; Ithamar son of Aaron shall be in charge of them.

'You shall make a detailed list of the Merarites by families in the 29 father's line, all those between the ages of thirty and fifty, who come 30 on duty to perform service in the Tent of the Presence.

'These are the loads for which they shall be responsible in virtue of 31 their service in the Tent of the Presence: the planks of the Tabernacle with its bars, posts, and sockets, the posts of the surrounding court 32 with their sockets, pegs, and cords, and all that is needed for the maintenance of them; you shall assign to each man by name the load for which he is responsible. These are the duties of the Merarite 33 families in virtue of their service in the Tent of the Presence. Ithamar son of Aaron the priest shall be in charge of them.'

Moses and Aaron and the chiefs of the community made a detailed 34 list of the Kohathites by families in the father's line, taking all between 35 the ages of thirty and fifty who came on duty to perform service in the Tent of the Presence. The number recorded by families in the detailed 36 lists was two thousand seven hundred and fifty. This was the total 37 number in the detailed lists of the Kohathite families who did duty in the Tent of the Presence; they were recorded by Moses and Aaron as the LORD had told them to do through Moses.

The Gershonites between the ages of thirty and fifty, who came on 38-39

[a] to cast...glance: *lit.* to look as they swallow.

duty for service in the Tent of the Presence, were recorded in detailed
40 lists by families in the father's line. Their number, by families in the
41 father's line, was two thousand six hundred and thirty. This was the
total recorded in the lists of the Gershonite families who came on duty
in the Tent of the Presence, and were recorded by Moses and Aaron
as the LORD had told them to do.

42-43   The families of Merari, between the ages of thirty and fifty, who
came on duty to perform service in the Tent of the Presence, were
44 recorded in detailed lists by families in the father's line. Their number
45 by families was three thousand two hundred. These were recorded in
the Merarite families by Moses and Aaron as the LORD had told them
to do through Moses.

46   Thus Moses and Aaron and the chiefs of Israel made a detailed list
47 of all the Levites by families in the father's line, between the ages of
thirty and fifty years; these were all who came to perform their various
duties and carry their loads in the service of the Tent of the Presence.
48,49 Their number was eight thousand five hundred and eighty. They were
recorded one by one by Moses at the command of the LORD, according
to their general duty and the loads they carried.[a] For so the LORD had
told Moses to do.

5 1,2   THE LORD SPOKE to Moses and said: Command the Israelites to
expel from the camp everyone who suffers from a malignant skin-
disease or a discharge, and everyone ritually unclean from contact with
3 a corpse. You shall put them outside the camp, both male and female,
4 so that they will not defile your camps in which I dwell among you.[b] The
Israelites did this: they put them outside the camp. As the LORD had
said when he spoke to Moses, so the Israelites did.

5,6   The LORD spoke to Moses and said, Say to the Israelites: When
anyone, man or woman, wrongs another and thereby breaks faith with
7 the LORD, that person has incurred guilt which demands reparation. He
shall confess the sin he has committed, make restitution in full with the
addition of one fifth, and give it to the man to whom compensation is
8 due. If there is no next-of-kin to whom compensation can be paid, the
compensation payable in that case shall be the LORD's, for the use of
the priest, in addition to the ram of expiation with which the priest
makes expiation for him.

9   Every contribution made by way of holy-gift which the Israelites
10 bring to the priest shall be the priest's. The priest shall have the holy-
gifts which a man gives; whatever is given to him shall be his.

11,12   The LORD spoke to Moses and said, Speak to the Israelites in these

[a] *Prob. rdg.; Heb. adds* and his registered ones.   [b] *So Pesh.; Heb.* their camps...among
them.

words: When a married woman goes astray, is unfaithful to her
husband, and has sexual intercourse with another man, and this 13
happens without the husband's knowledge, and the crime is undetected,
because, though she has been defiled, there is no direct evidence
against her and she was not caught in the act, but when in such a case 14
a fit of jealousy comes over the husband which causes him to suspect
his wife, she being in fact defiled; or when, on the other hand, a fit of
jealousyᵇ comes over a husband which causes him to suspect his wife,
when she is not in fact defiled; then in either case, the husband shall 15
bring his wife to the priest together with the prescribed offering for
her, a tenth of an ephah of barley meal. He shall not pour oil on it nor
put frankincense on it, because it is a grain-offering for jealousy, a
grain-offering of protestation conveying an imputation of guilt. The 16
priest shall bring her forward and set her before the LORD. He shall 17
take clean*ᵃ* water in an earthenware vessel, and shall take dust from the
floor of the Tabernacle and add it to the water. He shall set the woman 18
before the LORD, uncover her head, and place the grain-offering of
protestation in her hands; it is a grain-offering for jealousy. The priest
shall hold in his own hand the water of contention which brings out the
truth. He shall then put the woman on oath and say to her, 'If no man 19
has had intercourse with you, if you have not gone astray and let
yourself become defiled while owing obedience to your husband, then
may your innocence be established by the water of contention which
brings out the truth. But if, while owing him obedience, you have gone 20
astray and let yourself become defiled, if any man other than your
husband has had intercourse with you' (the priest shall here put the 21
woman on oath with an adjuration, and shall continue), 'may the LORD
make an example of you among your people in adjurations and in
swearing of oaths by bringing upon you miscarriage and untimely
birth;*ᵇ* and this water that brings out the truth shall enter your body, 22
bringing upon you miscarriage and untimely birth.' The woman shall
respond, 'Amen, Amen.' The priest shall write these curses on a scroll 23
and wash them off into the water of contention; he shall make the 24
woman drink the water that brings out the truth, and the water shall
enter her body. The priest shall take the grain-offering for jealousy 25
from the woman's hand, present it as a special gift before the LORD,
and offer it at the altar. He shall take a handful from the grain-offering 26
by way of token, and burn it at the altar; after this he shall make the
woman drink the water. If she has let herself become defiled and has 27
been unfaithful to her husband, then when the priest makes her drink
the water that brings out the truth and the water has entered her body,

[a] *Or* holy.   [b] *Lit.* by making your thigh to fall and your belly to melt away; *similarly*
in verses 22 and 27.

she will suffer a miscarriage or untimely birth, and her name will be-
28 come an example in adjuration among her kin. But if the woman has
not let herself become defiled and is pure, then her innocence is
established and she will bear her child.

29   Such is the law for cases of jealousy, where a woman, owing obedience
30 to her husband, goes astray and lets herself become defiled, or where
a fit of jealousy comes over a man which causes him to suspect his wife.
He shall set her before the Lord, and the priest shall deal with her as
31 this law prescribes. No guilt will attach to the husband, but the woman
shall bear the penalty of her guilt.

6 1,2   The Lord spoke to Moses and said, Speak to the Israelites in these
words: When anyone, man or woman, makes a special[a] vow dedicating
3 himself to the Lord as a Nazirite,[b] he shall abstain from wine and
strong drink. These he shall not drink, nor anything made from the
4 juice of grapes; nor shall he eat grapes, fresh or dried. During the whole
term of his vow he shall eat nothing that comes from the vine, nothing
5 whatever, shoot or berry.[c] During the whole term of his vow no razor
shall touch his head; he shall let his hair grow long and plait it until he
has completed the term of his dedication: he shall keep himself holy
6 to the Lord. During the whole term of his vow he shall not go near
7 a corpse, not even when his father or mother, brother or sister, dies;
he shall not make himself ritually unclean for them, because the
8 Nazirite vow to his God is on his head. He shall keep himself holy to
the Lord during the whole term of his Nazirite vow.

9   If someone suddenly falls dead by his side touching him and thereby
making his hair, which has been dedicated, ritually unclean, he shall
shave his head seven days later, on the day appointed for his ritual
10 cleansing. On the eighth day he shall bring two turtle-doves or two
young pigeons to the priest at the entrance to the Tent of the Presence.
11 The priest shall offer one as a sin-offering and the other as a whole-
offering and shall make expiation for him for the sin he has incurred
through contact with the dead body; and he shall consecrate his head
12 afresh on that day. The man shall re-dedicate himself to the Lord for
the term of his vow and bring a yearling ram as a guilt-offering. The
previous period shall not be reckoned, because the hair which he
dedicated became unclean.

13   The law for the Nazirite, when the term of his dedication is completed, shall be this. He shall be brought to the entrance to the Tent of
14 the Presence and shall present his offering to the Lord: one yearling
ram without blemish as a whole-offering, one yearling ewe without
blemish as a sin-offering, one ram without blemish as a shared-offering,

[a] makes a special: *or* performs a... [b] *That is* separated one *or* dedicated one. [c] *The two Hebrew words are of uncertain meaning.*

and a basket of cakes made of flour mixed with oil, and of wafers smeared 15
with oil, both unleavened, together with the proper grain-offerings and
drink-offerings. The priest shall present all these before the LORD and 16
offer the man's sin-offering and whole-offering; the ram he shall offer 17
as a shared-offering to the LORD, together with the basket of unleavened cakes and the proper grain-offering and drink-offering.
The Nazirite shall shave his head at the entrance to the Tent of the 18
Presence, take the hair which had been dedicated and put it on the fire
where the shared-offering is burning. The priest shall take the shoulder 19
of the ram, after boiling it, and take also one unleavened cake from the
basket and one unleavened wafer, and put them on the palms of the
Nazirite's hands, his hair which had been dedicated having been
shaved. The priest shall then present them as a special gift before the 20
LORD; these, together with the breast of the special gift and the leg of
the contribution, are holy and belong to the priest. When this has been
done, the Nazirite is again free to drink wine.

Such is the law for the Nazirite who has made his vow. Such is the 21
offering he must make to the LORD for his dedication, apart from anything else that he can afford. He must carry out his vow in full according
to the law governing his dedication.

The LORD spoke to Moses and said, Speak to Aaron and his sons in 22, 23
these words: These are the words with which you shall bless the
Israelites:

> The LORD bless you and watch over you; 24
> the LORD make his face shine upon*a* you 25
> and be gracious to you;
> the LORD look kindly on you and give you peace. 26

They shall pronounce my name over the Israelites, and I will bless 27
them.

ON THE DAY THAT Moses completed the setting up of the Taber- 7
nacle, he anointed and consecrated it; he also anointed and consecrated
its equipment, and the altar and its vessels. The chief men of Israel, 2
heads of families—that is the chiefs of the tribes, who had assisted in
preparing the detailed lists—came forward and brought their offering 3
before the LORD, six covered wagons and twelve oxen, one wagon from
every two chiefs and from each one an ox.*b* These they brought forward
before the Tabernacle; and the LORD spoke to Moses and said, 'Accept 4, 5
these from them: they shall be used for the service of the Tent of the
Presence. Assign them to the Levites as their several duties require.'

So Moses accepted the wagons and oxen and assigned them to the 6
Levites. He gave two wagons and four oxen to the Gershonites as 7

[*a*] *Or* to. [*b*] *Or* a bull.

8 required for their service; four wagons and eight oxen to the Merarites as required for their service, in charge of Ithamar the son of Aaron the 9 priest. He gave none to the Kohathites because the service laid upon them was that of the holy things: these they had to carry themselves on their shoulders.

10 When the altar was anointed, the chiefs brought their gift for its 11 dedication and presented their offering before it. The LORD said to Moses, 'Let the chiefs present their offering for the dedication of the altar one by one, on consecutive days.'

12 The chief who presented his offering on the first day was Nahshon 13 son of Amminadab of the tribe of Judah. His offering was one silver dish weighing a hundred and thirty shekels by the sacred standard and one silver tossing-bowl weighing seventy, both full of flour mixed 14 with oil as a grain-offering; one saucer weighing ten gold shekels, full 15 of incense; one young bull, one full-grown ram, and one yearling ram, 16, 17 as a whole-offering; one he-goat as a sin-offering; and two bulls, five full-grown rams, five he-goats, and five yearling rams, as a shared-offering. This was the offering of Nahshon son of Amminadab.

18 On the second day Nethaneel son of Zuar, chief of Issachar, brought 19 his offering. He brought one silver dish weighing a hundred and thirty shekels by the sacred standard and one silver tossing-bowl weighing 20 seventy, both full of flour mixed with oil as a grain-offering; one saucer 21 weighing ten gold shekels, full of incense; one young bull, one full- 22 grown ram, and one yearling ram, as a whole-offering; one he-goat as 23 a sin-offering; and two bulls, five full-grown rams, five he-goats, and five yearling rams, as a shared-offering. This was the offering of Nethaneel son of Zuar.

24 On the third day the chief of the Zebulunites, Eliab son of Helon, 25 came. His offering was one silver dish weighing a hundred and thirty shekels by the sacred standard and one silver tossing-bowl weighing 26 seventy, both full of flour mixed with oil as a grain-offering; one saucer 27 weighing ten gold shekels, full of incense; one young bull, one full- 28 grown ram, and one yearling ram, as a whole-offering; one he-goat as 29 a sin-offering; and two bulls, five full-grown rams, five he-goats, and five yearling rams, as a shared-offering. This was the offering of Eliab son of Helon.

30 On the fourth day the chief of the Reubenites, Elizur son of Shedeur, 31 came. His offering was one silver dish weighing a hundred and thirty shekels by the sacred standard and one silver tossing-bowl weighing 32 seventy, both full of flour mixed with oil as a grain-offering; one saucer 33 weighing ten gold shekels, full of incense; one young bull, one full- 34 grown ram, and one yearling ram, as a whole-offering; one he-goat as 35 a sin-offering; and two bulls, five full-grown rams, five he-goats, and

five yearling rams, as a shared-offering. This was the offering of Elizur son of Shedeur.

On the fifth day the chief of the Simeonites, Shelumiel son of Zurishaddai, came. His offering was one silver dish weighing a hundred and thirty shekels by the sacred standard and one silver tossing-bowl weighing seventy, both full of flour mixed with oil as a grain-offering; one saucer weighing ten gold shekels, full of incense; one young bull, one full-grown ram, and one yearling ram, as a whole-offering; one he-goat as a sin-offering; and two bulls, five full-grown rams, five he-goats, and five yearling rams, as a shared-offering. This was the offering of Shelumiel son of Zurishaddai. 36 37 38,39 40 41

On the sixth day the chief of the Gadites, Eliasaph son of Reuel,[a] came. His offering was one silver dish weighing a hundred and thirty shekels by the sacred standard and one silver tossing-bowl weighing seventy, both full of flour mixed with oil as a grain-offering; one saucer weighing ten gold shekels, full of incense; one young bull, one full-grown ram, and one yearling ram, as a whole-offering; one he-goat as a sin-offering; and two bulls, five full-grown rams, five he-goats, and five yearling rams, as a shared-offering. This was the offering of Eliasaph son of Reuel.[a] 42 43 44 45 46 47

On the seventh day the chief of the Ephraimites, Elishama son of Ammihud, came. His offering was one silver dish weighing a hundred and thirty shekels by the sacred standard and one silver tossing-bowl weighing seventy, both full of flour mixed with oil as a grain-offering; one saucer weighing ten gold shekels, full of incense; one young bull, one full-grown ram, and one yearling ram, as a whole-offering; one he-goat as a sin-offering; and two bulls, five full-grown rams, five he-goats, and five yearling rams, as a shared-offering. This was the offering of Elishama son of Ammihud. 48 49 50,51 52 53

On the eighth day the chief of the Manassites, Gamaliel son of Pedahzur, came. His offering was one silver dish weighing a hundred and thirty shekels by the sacred standard and one silver tossing-bowl weighing seventy, both full of flour mixed with oil as a grain-offering; one saucer weighing ten gold shekels, full of incense; one young bull, one full-grown ram, and one yearling ram, as a whole-offering; one he-goat as a sin-offering; and two bulls, five full-grown rams, five he-goats, and five yearling rams, as a shared-offering. This was the offering of Gamaliel son of Pedahzur. 54 55 56,57 58 59

On the ninth day the chief of the Benjamites, Abidan son of Gideoni, came. His offering was one silver dish weighing a hundred and thirty shekels by the sacred standard and one silver tossing-bowl weighing seventy, both full of flour mixed with oil as a grain-offering; 60 61

[a] *So Sept. (cp. 1. 14; 2. 14); Heb.* Deuel.

62,63 one saucer weighing ten gold shekels, full of incense; one young bull,
64 one full-grown ram, and one yearling ram, as a whole-offering; one he-
65 goat as a sin-offering; and two bulls, five full-grown rams, five he-goats, and five yearling rams, as a shared-offering. This was the offering of Abidan son of Gideoni.

66 On the tenth day the chief of the Danites, Ahiezer son of Ammi-
67 shaddai, came. His offering was one silver dish weighing a hundred and thirty shekels by the sacred standard and one silver tossing-bowl weighing seventy, both full of flour mixed with oil as a grain-offering;
68,69 one saucer weighing ten gold shekels, full of incense; one young bull,
70 one full-grown ram, and one yearling ram, as a whole-offering; one he-
71 goat as a sin-offering; and two bulls, five full-grown rams, five he-goats, and five yearling rams, as a shared-offering. This was the offering of Ahiezer son of Ammishaddai.

72 On the eleventh day the chief of the Asherites, Pagiel son of Ocran,
73 came. His offering was one silver dish weighing a hundred and thirty shekels by the sacred standard and one silver tossing-bowl weighing
74 seventy, both full of flour mixed with oil as a grain-offering; one saucer
75 weighing ten gold shekels, full of incense; one young bull, one full-
76 grown ram, and one yearling ram, as a whole-offering; one he-goat as a
77 sin-offering; and two bulls, five full-grown rams, five he-goats, and five yearling rams, as a shared-offering. This was the offering of Pagiel son of Ocran.

78 On the twelfth day the chief of the Naphtalites, Ahira son of Enan,
79 came. His offering was one silver dish weighing a hundred and thirty shekels by the sacred standard and one silver tossing-bowl weighing
80 seventy, both full of flour mixed with oil as a grain-offering; one saucer
81 weighing ten gold shekels, full of incense; one young bull, one full-
82 grown ram, and one yearling ram, as a whole-offering; one he-goat as
83 a sin-offering; and two bulls, five full-grown rams, five he-goats, and five yearling rams, as a shared-offering. This was the offering of Ahira son of Enan.

84 This was the gift from the chiefs of Israel for the dedication of the altar when it was anointed: twelve silver dishes, twelve silver tossing-
85 bowls, and twelve golden saucers; each silver dish weighed a hundred and thirty shekels, each silver tossing-bowl seventy shekels. The total weight of the silver vessels was two thousand four hundred shekels by
86 the sacred standard. There were twelve golden saucers full of incense, ten shekels each by the sacred standard: the total weight of the gold of
87 the saucers was a hundred and twenty shekels. The number of beasts for the whole-offering was twelve bulls, twelve full-grown rams, and twelve yearling rams, with the prescribed grain-offerings, and twelve
88 he-goats for the sin-offering. The number of beasts for the shared-

offering was twenty-four bulls, sixty full-grown rams, sixty he-goats, and sixty yearling rams. This was the gift for the dedication of the altar when it was anointed. And when Moses entered the Tent of the 89 Presence to speak with God, he heard the Voice speaking from above the cover over the Ark of the Tokens from between the two cherubim: the Voice spoke to him.

The LORD spoke to Moses and said, 'Speak to Aaron in these words: 8 1,2 "When you mount the seven lamps, see that they shed their light forwards in front of the lamp-stand."' Aaron did this: he mounted the 3 lamps, so as to shed light forwards in front of the lamp-stand, as the LORD had instructed Moses. The lamp-stand was made of beaten-work 4 in gold, as well as the stem and the petals. Moses made it to match the pattern which the LORD had shown him.

The LORD spoke to Moses and said: Take the Levites apart from the 5,6 rest of the Israelites and cleanse them ritually. This is what you shall 7 do to cleanse them. Sprinkle lustral water over them; they shall then shave their whole bodies, wash their clothes, and so be cleansed. Next, 8 they shall take a young bull as a whole-offering[a] with its prescribed grain-offering, flour mixed with oil; and you shall take a second young bull as a sin-offering. Bring the Levites before the Tent of the 9 Presence and call the whole community of Israelites together. Bring the 10 Levites before the LORD, and let the Israelites lay their hands on their heads. Aaron shall present the Levites before the LORD as a special gift 11 from the Israelites, and they shall be dedicated to the service of the LORD. The Levites shall lay their hands on the heads of the bulls; one 12 bull shall be offered as a sin-offering and the other as a whole-offering to the LORD, to make expiation for the Levites. Then you shall set the 13 Levites before Aaron and his sons, presenting them to the LORD as a special gift. You shall thus separate the Levites from the rest of the 14 Israelites, and they shall be mine.

After this, the Levites shall enter the Tent of the Presence to serve 15 in it, ritually cleansed and presented as a special gift; for they are given 16 and dedicated to me, out of all the Israelites. I have accepted them as mine in place of all that comes first from the womb, every first child among the Israelites; for every first-born male creature, man or beast, 17 among the Israelites is mine. On the day when I struck down every first-born creature in Egypt, I hallowed all the first-born of the Israelites to myself, and I have accepted the Levites in their place. 18 I have given the Levites to Aaron and his sons, dedicated among the 19 Israelites to perform the service of the Israelites in the Tent of the Presence and to make expiation for them, and then no calamity will befall them when they come close to the sanctuary.

[a] as a whole-offering: *prob. rdg.; Heb. om.*

187

20   Moses and Aaron and the whole community of Israelites carried out all the commands the LORD had given to Moses for the dedication of
21   the Levites. The Levites purified themselves of sin and washed their clothes, and Aaron presented them as a special gift before the LORD
22   and made expiation for them, to cleanse them. Then at last they went in to perform their service in the Tent of the Presence, before Aaron and his sons. Thus the commands the LORD had given to Moses concerning the Levites were all carried out.

23, 24   The LORD spoke to Moses and said: Touching the Levites: they shall begin their active work in the service of the Tent of the Presence at
25   the age of twenty-five. At the age of fifty a Levite shall retire from regular
26   service and shall serve no longer. He may continue to assist his colleagues in attendance in the Tent of the Presence but shall perform no regular service. This is how you shall arrange the attendance of the Levites.

9   In the first month of the second year after they came out of Egypt,
2   the LORD spoke to Moses in the wilderness of Sinai and said, 'Let the
3   Israelites prepare the Passover at the time appointed for it. This shall be between dusk and dark on the fourteenth day of this month, and you shall keep it at this appointed time, observing every rule and custom
4   proper to it.' So Moses told the Israelites to prepare the Passover,
5   and they prepared it on the fourteenth day of the first month, between dusk and dark, in the wilderness of Sinai. The Israelites did exactly as the LORD had instructed Moses.

6   It happened that some men were ritually unclean through contact with a corpse and so could not keep the Passover on the right day. They
7   came before Moses and Aaron that same day and said, 'We are unclean through contact with a corpse. Must we therefore be debarred from presenting the LORD's offering at its appointed time with the rest of the
8   Israelites?' Moses answered, 'Wait, and let me hear what commands the LORD has for you.'

9, 10   The LORD spoke to Moses and said, Tell the Israelites: If any one of you or of your descendants is ritually unclean through contact with a corpse, or if he is away on a long journey, he shall keep a Passover to
11   the LORD none the less. But in that case he shall prepare the victim in the second month, between dusk and dark on the fourteenth day. It
12   shall be eaten with unleavened cakes and bitter herbs; nothing shall be left over till morning, and no bone of it shall be broken. The Passover
13   shall be kept exactly as the law prescribes. The man who, being ritually clean and not absent on a journey, neglects to keep the Passover, shall be cut off from his father's kin, because he has not presented the LORD's offering at its appointed time. That man shall accept responsibility for his sin.

When an alien is settled among you, he also shall keep the Passover 14
to the LORD, observing every rule and custom proper to it. The same
law is binding on you all, alien and native alike.

The journey from Sinai to Edom

ON THE DAY WHEN they set up the Tabernacle, that is the Tent 15
of the Tokens, cloud covered it, and in the evening a brightness
like fire appeared over it till morning. So it continued: the cloud 16
covered it by day[a] and a brightness like fire by night. Whenever the 17
cloud lifted from the tent, the Israelites struck camp, and at the place
where the cloud settled, there they pitched their camp. At the command 18
of the LORD they struck camp, and at the command of the LORD they
encamped again, and continued in camp as long as the cloud rested
over the Tabernacle. When the cloud stayed long over the Tabernacle, 19
the Israelites remained in attendance on the LORD and did not move
on; and it was the same when the cloud continued over the Tabernacle 20
only a few days: at the command of the LORD they remained in camp,
and at the command of the LORD they struck camp. There were also 21
times when the cloud continued only from evening till morning, and in
the morning, when the cloud lifted, they moved on. Whether by day
or by night, they moved as soon as the cloud lifted. Whether it was for 22
a day or two, for a month or a year, whenever the cloud stayed long
over the Tabernacle, the Israelites remained where they were and did
not move on; they did so only when the cloud lifted. At the command 23
of the LORD they encamped, and at his command they struck camp. At
the LORD's command, given through Moses, they remained in attendance on the LORD.

The LORD spoke to Moses and said: Make two trumpets of beaten 10 1,2
silver and use them for summoning the community and for breaking
camp. When both are sounded, the whole community shall muster 3
before you at the entrance to the Tent of the Presence. If a single 4
trumpet is sounded, the chiefs who are heads of the Israelite clans shall
muster. When you give the signal for a shout, those encamped on the 5
east side are to move off. When the signal is given for a second shout 6
those encamped to the south are to move off. A signal to shout is the
signal to move off. When you convene the assembly, you shall sound a 7
trumpet but not raise a shout. This sounding of the trumpets is the 8
duty of the Aaronite priests and shall be a rule binding for all time on
your descendants.

[a] by day: *so Sept.; Heb. om.*

9   When you go into battle against an invader and you are hard pressed by him, you shall raise a cheer when the trumpets sound, and this will serve as a reminder of you before the LORD your God and you will be
10 delivered from your enemies. On your festal days and at your appointed seasons and on the first day of every month, you shall sound the trumpets over your whole-offerings and your shared-offerings, and the trumpets shall be a reminder on your behalf before the LORD^a your God. I am the LORD your God.

11   In the second year, on the twentieth day of the second month, the
12 cloud lifted from the Tabernacle of the Tokens, and the Israelites moved by stages from the wilderness of Sinai, until the cloud came to rest in
13 the wilderness of Paran. The first time that they broke camp at the
14 command of the LORD given through Moses, the standard of the division of Judah moved off first with its tribal hosts: the host of Judah
15 under Nahshon son of Amminadab, the host of Issachar under
16 Nethaneel son of Zuar, and the host of Zebulun under Eliab son of
17 Helon. Then the Tabernacle was taken down, and its bearers, the sons of Gershon and Merari, moved off.

18   Secondly, the standard of the division of Reuben moved off with its
19 tribal hosts: the host of Reuben under Elizur son of Shedeur, the host
20 of Simeon under Shelumiel son of Zurishaddai, and the host of Gad
21 under Eliasaph son of Reuel.^b The Kohathites, the bearers of the holy things,^c moved off next, and on their arrival found the Tabernacle set up.

22   Thirdly, the standard of the division of Ephraim moved off with its
23 tribal hosts: the host of Ephraim under Elishama son of Ammihud, the
24 host of Manasseh under Gamaliel son of Pedahzur, and the host of Benjamin under Abidan son of Gideoni.

25   Lastly, the standard of the division of Dan, the rearguard of all the divisions, moved off with its tribal hosts: the host of Dan under
26 Ahiezer son of Ammishaddai, the host of Asher under Pagiel son of
27 Ocran, and the host of Naphtali under Ahira son of Enan.

28   This was the order of march for the Israelites, mustered in their hosts, and in this order they broke camp.

29   And Moses said to Hobab son of Reuel the Midianite, his brother-in-law, 'We are setting out for the place which the LORD promised to give us. Come with us, and we will deal generously with you, for the LORD
30 has given an assurance of good fortune for Israel.' But he replied, 'No, I will not; I would rather go to my own country and my own
31 people.' Moses said, 'Do not desert us, I beg you; for you know where
32 we ought to camp in the wilderness, and you will be our guide. If you

[a] the LORD: *so some MSS.; others om.*   [b] *So Sept. (cp. 2. 14);* Heb. Deuel.   [c] holy things: *so Sept.;* Heb. sanctuary.

will go with us, then all the good fortune with which the LORD favours us we will share with you.'

Then they moved off from the mountain of the LORD and journeyed 33 for three days, and the Ark of the Covenant of the LORD kept a day's journey*a* ahead of them to find them a place to rest. The cloud of the 34 LORD hung over them by day when they moved camp. Whenever the 35 Ark began to move, Moses said,

'Up, LORD, and may thy enemies be scattered
and those that hate thee flee before thee.'

When it halted, he said,   36

'Rest, LORD of the countless thousands of Israel.'

There came a time when the people complained to the LORD of their 11 hardships. When he heard, he became angry and fire from the LORD broke out among them, and was raging at one end of the camp, when 2 the people appealed to Moses. He interceded with the LORD, and the fire died down. Then they named that place Taberah,*b* because the 3 fire of the LORD had burned among them there.

Now there was a mixed company of strangers who had joined the 4 Israelites. These people began to be greedy for better things, and the Israelites themselves wept once again and cried, 'Will no one give us meat? Think of it! In Egypt we had fish for the asking, cucumbers and 5 water-melons, leeks and onions and garlic. Now our throats are 6 parched; there is nothing wherever we look except this manna.' (The 7 manna looked like coriander seed, the colour of gum resin. The people 8 went about collecting it, ground it up in hand-mills or pounded it in mortars, then boiled it in the pot and made it into cakes. It tasted like butter-cakes. When dew fell on the camp at night, the manna fell 9 with it.) Moses heard the people wailing, all of them in their families 10 at the opening of their tents. Then the LORD became very angry, and Moses was troubled. He said to the LORD, 'Why hast thou brought 11 trouble on thy servant? How have I displeased the LORD that I am burdened with the care of this whole people? Am I their mother? 12 Have I brought them into the world, and am I called upon to carry them in my bosom, like a nurse with her babies, to the land promised by thee on oath to their fathers? Where am I to find meat to give them 13 all? They pester me with their wailing and their "Give us meat to eat." This whole people is a burden too heavy for me; I cannot carry it alone. 14 If that is thy purpose for me, then kill me outright. But if I have won 15 thy favour, let me suffer this trouble at thy hands*c* no longer.'

[a] *So Pesh.; Heb.* a three days' journey.   [b] *That is* Burning.   [c] this trouble...hands:
prob. original rdg., altered in Heb. to my trouble.

16   The LORD answered Moses, 'Assemble seventy elders from Israel,
men known to you as elders and officers in the community; bring them
to me at the Tent of the Presence, and there let them take their stand
17 with you. I will come down and speak with you there. I will take back
part of that same spirit which has been conferred on you and confer it
on them, and they will share with you the burden of taking care for
18 the people; then you will not have to bear it alone. And to the people
you shall say this: "Hallow yourselves in readiness for tomorrow; you
shall have meat to eat. You wailed in the LORD's hearing; you said,
'Will no one give us meat? In Egypt we lived well.' The LORD will
19 give you meat and you shall eat it. Not for one day only, nor for two
20 days, nor five, nor ten, nor twenty, but for a whole month you shall
eat it until it comes out at your nostrils and makes you sick; because you
have rejected the LORD who dwells in your midst, wailing in his presence
and saying, 'Why did we ever come out of Egypt?'"'

21   Moses replied, 'Here am I with six hundred thousand men on the
march around me, and thou dost promise them meat to eat for a whole
22 month. How can the sheep and oxen be slaughtered that would be
enough for them? If all the fish in the sea could be caught, would they
23 be enough?' The LORD said to Moses, 'Is there a limit to the power of
the LORD? You will see this very day whether or not my words come
true.'

24   Moses came out and told the people what the LORD had said. He
assembled seventy men from the elders of the people and stationed them
25 round the Tent. Then the LORD descended in the cloud and spoke to
him. He took back part of that same spirit which he had conferred on
Moses and conferred it on the seventy elders; as the spirit alighted on
them, they fell into a prophetic ecstasy, for the first and only time.

26   Now two men named Eldad and Medad, who had been enrolled
with the seventy, were left behind in the camp. But, though they had
not gone out to the Tent, the spirit alighted on them none the less, and
27 they fell into an ecstasy there in the camp. A young man ran and told
28 Moses that Eldad and Medad were in an ecstasy in the camp, whereupon Joshua son of Nun, who had served with Moses since he was a
29 boy, broke in, 'My lord Moses, stop them!' But Moses said to him,
'Are you jealous on my account? I wish that all the LORD's people
were prophets and that the LORD would confer his spirit on them all!'
30 And Moses rejoined the camp with the elders of Israel.

31   Then a wind from the LORD sprang up; it drove quails in from the
west, and they were flying all round the camp for the distance of a day's
32 journey, three feet[a] above the ground. The people were busy gathering
quails all that day, all night, and all next day, and even the man who got

[a] *Lit.* two cubits.

least gathered ten homers. They spread them out to dry all about the camp. But the meat was scarcely between their teeth, and they had not 33 so much as bitten it, when the LORD's anger broke out against the people and he struck them with a deadly plague. That place was called 34 Kibroth-hattaavah*a* because there they buried the people who had been greedy for meat.

From Kibroth-hattaavah the Israelites went on to Hazeroth, and 35 while they were at Hazeroth, Miriam and Aaron began to speak against 12 Moses. They blamed him for his Cushite wife (for he had married a Cushite woman), and they said, 'Is Moses the only one with*b* whom the 2 LORD has spoken? Has he not spoken with*b* us as well?' Moses was in 3 fact a man of great humility, the most humble man on earth. But the LORD heard them and suddenly he said to Moses, Aaron and Miriam, 4 'Go out all three of you to the Tent of the Presence.' So the three went out, and the LORD descended in a pillar of cloud; he stood at the 5 entrance to the tent and summoned Aaron and Miriam. The two of them went forward, and he said, 6

> 'Listen to my words.
> If he*c* were your prophet and nothing more,
> I would make myself known to him in a vision,
> I would speak with him in a dream.
> But my servant Moses is not such a prophet; 7
> he alone is faithful*d* of all my household.
> With him I speak face to face, 8
> openly and not in riddles.
> He shall see the very form of the LORD.
> How do you dare speak against my servant Moses?'

Thus the anger of the LORD was roused against them, and he left 9 them; and as the cloud moved from the tent, there was Miriam, her 10 skin diseased and white as snow. Aaron turned towards her and saw her skin diseased. Then he said to Moses, 'Pray, my lord, do not make us 11 pay the penalty of sin, foolish and wicked though we have been. Let her not be like something still-born, whose flesh is half eaten away 12 when it comes from the womb.' So Moses cried, 'Not this, O LORD! 13 Heal her, I pray.' The LORD replied, 'Suppose her father had spat in 14 her face, would she not have to remain in disgrace for seven days? Let her be kept for seven days in confinement outside the camp and then be brought back.' So Miriam was kept outside for seven days, and the 15 people did not strike camp until she was brought back. After this they 16 set out from Hazeroth and pitched camp in the wilderness of Paran.

[*a*] *That is* the Graves of Greed. [*b*] *Or* by. [*c*] *Prob. rdg.; Heb.* the LORD. [*d*] *Or to* be trusted.

13 1,2 THE LORD SPOKE TO MOSES AND SAID, 'Send men out to explore the land of Canaan which I am giving to the Israelites; from each of their
3 fathers' tribes send one man, and let him be a man of high rank.' So Moses sent them from the wilderness of Paran at the command of the
4 LORD, all of them leading men among the Israelites. These were their names:

5 from the tribe of Reuben, Shammua son of Zaccur;
5 from the tribe of Simeon, Shaphat son of Hori;
6 from the tribe of Judah, Caleb son of Jephunneh;
7 from the tribe of Issachar, Igal son of Joseph;
8 from the tribe of Ephraim, Hoshea son of Nun;
9 from the tribe of Benjamin, Palti son of Raphu;
10 from the tribe of Zebulun, Gaddiel son of Sodi;
11 from the tribe of Joseph (that is from the tribe of Manasseh), Gaddi son of Susi;
12 from the tribe of Dan, Ammiel son of Gemalli;
13 from the tribe of Asher, Sethur son of Michael;
14 from the tribe of Naphtali, Nahbi son of Vophsi;
15 from the tribe of Gad, Geuel son of Machi.

16 These are the names of the men whom Moses sent to explore the land. But Moses called the son of Nun Joshua, not Hoshea.
17 When Moses sent them to explore the land of Canaan, he said to them, 'Make your way up by the Negeb, and go on into the hill-country.
18 See what the land is like, and whether the people who live there are
19 strong or weak, few or many. See whether it is easy or difficult country in which they live, and whether the cities in which they live are weakly
20 defended or well fortified;[a] is the land fertile or barren, and does it grow trees or not? Go boldly in and take some of its fruit.' It was the season when the first grapes were ripe.
21 They went up and explored the country from the wilderness of Zin
22 as far as Rehob by Lebo-hamath. They went up by the Negeb and came to Hebron, where Ahiman, Sheshai and Talmai, the descendants of Anak,[b] were living. (Hebron was built seven years before Zoan in
23 Egypt.) They came to the gorge of Eshcol,[c] and there they cut a branch with a single bunch of grapes, and they carried it on a pole two at a
24 time; they also picked pomegranates and figs. It was from the bunch of grapes which the Israelites cut there that that place was named the
25 gorge of Eshcol. After forty days they returned from exploring the
26 country, and came back to Moses and Aaron and the whole community of Israelites at Kadesh in the wilderness of Paran. They made their

[a] *Prob. rdg., cp. Sam. MSS.;* Heb. are in camps or in walled cities.   [b] descendants of Anak: *or* tall men.   [c] Eshcol: *that is* Bunch of Grapes.

report to them and to the whole community, and showed them the
fruit of the country. And this was the story they told Moses: 'We made 27
our way into the land to which you sent us. It is flowing with milk and
honey, and here is the fruit it grows; but its inhabitants are sturdy, 28
and the cities are very strongly fortified; indeed, we saw there the
descendants of Anak. We also saw the Amalekites who live in the 29
Negeb, Hittites,*ª* Jebusites, and Amorites who live in the hill-country,
and the Canaanites who live by the sea and along the Jordan.'
　　Then Caleb called for silence before Moses and said, 'Let us go up 30
at once and occupy the country; we are well able to conquer it.' But the 31
men who had gone with him said, 'No, we cannot attack these people;
they are stronger than we are.' Thus their report to the Israelites about 32
the land which they had explored was discouraging: 'The country we
explored', they said, 'will swallow up any who go to live in it. All the
people we saw there are men of gigantic size. When we set eyes on the 33
Nephilim*ᵇ* (the sons of Anak*ᶜ* belong to the Nephilim) we felt no bigger
than grasshoppers; and that is how we looked to them.'
　　Then the whole Israelite community cried out in dismay; all night **14**
long they wept. One and all they made complaints against Moses and 2
Aaron: 'If only we had died in Egypt or in the wilderness!' they said.
'Far happier if we had! Why should the LORD bring us to this land, to 3
die in battle and leave our wives and our dependants to become the
spoils of war? To go back to Egypt would be better than this.' And they 4
began to talk of choosing someone to lead them back.
　　Then Moses and Aaron flung themselves on the ground before the 5
assembled community of the Israelites, and two of those who had explored 6
the land, Joshua son of Nun and Caleb son of Jephunneh, rent their
clothes and addressed the whole community: 'The country we pene- 7
trated and explored', they said, 'is very good land indeed. If the LORD 8
is pleased with us, he will bring us into this land which flows with milk
and honey, and give it to us. But you must not rebel against the LORD. 9
You need not fear the people of the land; for there we shall find food.*ᵈ*
They have lost the protection that they had: the LORD is with us. You
have nothing to fear from them.' But by way of answer the assembled 10
Israelites threatened to stone them, when suddenly the glory of the
LORD appeared to them all in the Tent of the Presence.
　　Then the LORD said to Moses, 'How much longer will this people 11
treat me with contempt? How much longer will they refuse to trust me
in spite of all the signs I have shown among them? I will strike them 12
with pestilence. I will deny them their heritage, and you and your
descendants I will make into a nation greater and more numerous than

[a] *Or, with Sam.*, Hivites.　[b] *Or* giants.　[c] sons of Anak: *or* tall men.　[d] *Lit.* for they
are our food.

13 they.' But Moses answered the LORD, 'What if the Egyptians hear of it? It was thou who didst bring this people out of Egypt by thy strength.
14 What if they tell the inhabitants of this land? They too have heard of thee, LORD, that thou art with this people, and art seen face to face, that thy cloud stays over them, and thou goest before them in a pillar of
15 cloud by day and in a pillar of fire by night. If then thou dost put them all to death at one blow, the nations who have heard these tales
16 of thee will say, "The LORD could not bring this people into the land which he promised them by oath; and so he destroyed them in the wilderness."

17 'Now let the LORD's might be shown in its greatness, true to thy
18 proclamation of thyself—"The LORD, long-suffering, ever constant, who forgives iniquity and rebellion, and punishes sons to the third and fourth generation for the iniquity of their fathers, though he does not
19 sweep them clean away." Thou hast borne with this people from Egypt all the way here; forgive their iniquity, I beseech thee, as befits thy great and constant love.'

20, 21 The LORD said, 'Your prayer is answered; I pardon them. But as
22-23 I live, in very truth the glory of the LORD shall fill the earth. Not one of all those who have seen my glory and the signs which I wrought in Egypt and in the wilderness shall see the country which I promised on oath to their fathers. Ten times they have challenged me and not obeyed my voice. None of those who have flouted me shall see this
24-25 land. But my servant Caleb showed a different spirit: he followed me with his whole heart. Because of this, I will bring him into the land in which he has already set foot, the territory of the Amalekites and the Canaanites who dwell in the Vale, and put his descendants in possession of it. Tomorrow you must turn back and set out for the wilderness by way of the Red Sea.'[a]

26, 27 The LORD spoke to Moses and Aaron and said, 'How long must I tolerate[b] the complaints of this wicked community? I have heard the
28 Israelites making complaints against me. Tell them that this is the very word of the LORD: As I live, I will bring home to you the words I have
29 heard you utter. Here in this wilderness your bones shall lie, every man of you on the register from twenty years old and upwards, because you have
30 made these complaints against me. Not one of you shall enter the land which I swore with uplifted hand should be your home, except only
31 Caleb son of Jephunneh and Joshua son of Nun. As for your dependants, those dependants who, you said, would become the spoils of war, I will bring them in to the land you have rejected, and they shall enjoy
32 it. But as for the rest of you, your bones shall lie in this wilderness;
33 your sons shall be wanderers in the wilderness forty years, paying the

[a] *Or* the Sea of Reeds. [b] must I tolerate: *prob. rdg.; Heb.* for.

penalty of your wanton disloyalty till the last man of you dies there.
Forty days you spent exploring the country, and forty years you shall 34
spend—a year for each day—paying the penalty of your iniquities. You
shall know what it means to have me against you.[a] I, the LORD, have 35
spoken. This I swear to do to all this wicked community who have
combined against me. There shall be an end of them here in this
wilderness; here they shall die.' But the men whom Moses had sent to 36
explore the land, and who came back and by their report set all the
community complaining against him, died of the plague before the 37
LORD; they died of the plague because they had made a bad report.
Of those who went to explore the land, Joshua son of Nun and Caleb 38
son of Jephunneh alone remained alive.

When Moses reported the LORD's words to all the Israelites, the 39
people were plunged in grief. They set out early next morning and 40
made for the heights of the hill-country, saying, 'Look, we are on our
way up to the place the LORD spoke of. We admit that we have been
wrong.' But Moses replied, 'Must you persist in disobeying the LORD's 41
command? No good will come of this. Go no further; you will not 42
have the LORD with you, and your enemies will defeat you. For in front 43
of you are the Amalekites and Canaanites, and you will die by the sword,
because you have ceased to follow the LORD, and he will no longer
be with you.' But they went recklessly on their way towards the heights 44
of the hill-country, though neither the Ark of the Covenant of the LORD
nor Moses moved with them out of the camp; and the Amalekites and 45
Canaanites from those hills came down and fell upon them, and crushed
them at Hormah.

THE LORD SPOKE to Moses and said, Speak to the Israelites in these 15 1, 2
words: When you enter the land where you are to live, the land I am
giving you, you will make food-offerings to the LORD; they may be 3
whole-offerings or any sacrifice made in fulfilment of a special[b] vow or
by way of freewill offering or at one of the appointed seasons. When you
thus make an offering of soothing odour from herd or flock to the
LORD, the man who offers, in presenting it, shall add a grain-offering 4
of a tenth of an ephah of flour mixed with a quarter of a hin of oil.
You shall also add to the whole-offering or shared-offering a quarter 5
of a hin of wine as a drink-offering with each lamb sacrificed.

If the animal is a ram, the grain-offering shall be two tenths of an 6
ephah of flour mixed with a third of a hin of oil, and the wine for the 7
drink-offering shall be a third of a hin; in this way you will make an
offering of soothing odour to the LORD.

When you offer to the LORD a young bull, whether as a whole- 8

[a] *Or* to thwart me.　[b] in fulfilment of a special: *or* to discharge a...

offering or as a sacrifice to fulfil a special[a] vow, or as a shared-offering,
9 you shall add a grain-offering of three tenths of an ephah of flour mixed
10 with half a hin of oil, and for the drink-offering, half a hin of wine; the
whole will thus be a food-offering of soothing odour to the LORD.
11 This is what must be done in each case, for every bull or ram, lamb or
12, 13 kid, whatever the number of each that you offer. Every native Israelite
shall observe these rules in each case when he offers a food-offering of
soothing odour to the LORD.
14 When an alien residing with you or permanently settled among you
offers a food-offering of soothing odour to the LORD, he shall do as you
15 do.[b] There is one and the same rule for you and for the resident alien,
a rule binding for all time on your descendants; you and the alien are
16 alike before the LORD. There shall be one law and one custom for you
and for the alien residing with you.
17, 18 The LORD spoke to Moses and said, Speak to the Israelites in
these words: After you have entered the land into which I am
19 bringing you, whenever you eat the bread of the country, you shall
20 set aside a contribution for the LORD. You shall set aside a cake
made of your first kneading of dough, as you set aside the contribution
21 from the threshing-floor. You must give a contribution to the LORD
from your first kneading of dough; this rule is binding on your
descendants.
22 When through inadvertence you omit to carry out any of these
23 commands which the LORD gave to Moses—any command whatever
that the LORD gave you through Moses on that first day and thereafter
24 and made binding on your descendants—if it be done inadvertently,
unnoticed by the community, then the whole community shall offer
one young bull as a whole-offering, a soothing odour to the LORD, with
its proper grain-offering and drink-offering according to custom; and
25 they shall add one he-goat as a sin-offering. The priest shall make
expiation for the whole community of Israelites, and they shall be
forgiven. The omission was inadvertent; and they have brought their
offering, a food-offering to the LORD; they have made their sin-offering
26 before the LORD for their inadvertence; the whole community of
Israelites and the aliens residing among you shall be forgiven. The
inadvertence was shared by the whole people.
27 If any individual sins inadvertently, he shall present a yearling she-
28 goat as a sin-offering, and the priest shall make expiation before the
29 LORD for the said individual, and he shall be forgiven. For anyone who
sins inadvertently, there shall be one law for all, whether native
30 Israelite or resident alien. But the person who sins presumptuously,
native or alien, insults the LORD. He shall be cut off from his people,

[a] fulfil a special: *or* discharge a... [b] *So Pesh.; Heb. adds* the assembly.

because he has brought the word of the LORD into contempt and 31
violated his command. That person shall be wholly cut off; the guilt
shall be on his head alone.

During the time that the Israelites were in the wilderness, a man was 32
found gathering sticks on the sabbath day. Those who had caught him 33
in the act brought him to Moses and Aaron and all the community, and 34
they kept him in custody, because it was not clearly known what was to
be done with him. The LORD said to Moses, 'The man must be put to 35
death; he must be stoned by all the community outside the camp.' So 36
they took him outside the camp and all stoned him to death, as the
LORD had commanded Moses.

The LORD spoke to Moses and said, Speak to the Israelites in these 37, 38
words: You must make tassels like flowers on the corners of your
garments, you and your children's children. Into this tassel you shall
work a violet thread, and whenever you see this in the tassel, you shall 39
remember all the LORD's commands and obey them, and not go your
own wanton ways, led astray by your own eyes and hearts. This token 40
is to ensure that you remember all my commands and obey them, and
keep yourselves holy, consecrated to your God.

I am the LORD your God who brought you out of Egypt to become 41
your God. I am the LORD your God.

NOW KORAH son of Izhar, son of Kohath, son of Levi, with the 16
Reubenites Dathan and Abiram sons of Eliab and On son of Peleth,
challenged the authority of Moses. With them in their revolt were two 2
hundred and fifty Israelites, all men of rank in the community, conveners of assembly and men of good standing. They confronted Moses 3
and Aaron and said to them, 'You take too much upon yourselves.
Every member of the community is holy and the LORD is among them
all. Why do you set yourselves up above the assembly of the LORD?'
When Moses heard this, he prostrated himself, and he said to Korah 4, 5
and all his company, 'Tomorrow morning the LORD shall declare who
is his, who is holy and may present offerings to him. The man whom the
LORD chooses shall present them. This is what you must do, you, 6
Korah, and all your company: you must take censers and put fire in 7
them, and then place incense on them before the LORD tomorrow. The
man whom the LORD then chooses is the man who is holy. You take too
much upon yourselves, you sons of Levi.'

Moses said to Korah, 'Now listen, you sons of Levi. Is it not enough 8, 9
for you that the God of Israel has set you apart from the community of
Israel, bringing you near him to maintain the service of the Tabernacle
of the LORD and to stand before the community as their ministers? He 10
has brought you near him and your brother Levites with you; now

11 you seek the priesthood as well. That is why you and all your company have combined together against the LORD. What is Aaron that you should make these complaints against him?'

12 Moses sent to fetch Dathan and Abiram sons of Eliab, but they
13 answered, 'We are not coming. Is it a small thing that you have brought us away from a land flowing with milk and honey to let us die in the
14 wilderness? Must you also set yourself up as prince over us? What is more, you have not brought us into a land flowing with milk and honey, nor have you given us fields and vineyards to inherit. Do you think you
15 can hoodwink*a* men like us? We are not coming.' This answer made Moses very angry, and he said to the LORD, 'Take no notice of their murmuring. I have not taken from them so much as a single ass; I have done no wrong to any of them.'

16 Moses said to Korah, 'Present yourselves before the LORD tomorrow,
17 you and all your company, you and they and Aaron. Each man of you is to take his censer and put incense on it. Then you shall present them before the LORD with their two hundred and fifty censers, and you and
18 Aaron shall also bring your censers.' So each man took his censer and put fire in it and placed incense on it; Moses and Aaron took their
19 stand at the entrance to the Tent of the Presence,*b* and Korah gathered his*c* whole company together and faced them at the entrance to the Tent of the Presence.

20 Then the glory of the LORD appeared to the whole community. And
21 the LORD spoke to Moses and Aaron and said, 'Stand apart from this
22 company, so that I may make an end of them in a single instant.' But they prostrated themselves and said, 'O God, God of the spirits of all mankind, if one man sins, wilt thou be angry with the whole com-
23, 24 munity?' But the LORD said to Moses, 'Tell them to stand back from the dwellings of Korah, Dathan and Abiram.'

25 So Moses rose and went to Dathan and Abiram, and the elders of
26 Israel followed him. He said to the whole community, 'Stand well away from the tents of these wicked men; touch nothing of theirs, or you
27 will be swept away because of all their sins.' So they moved away from the places occupied by Korah, Dathan and Abiram. Now Dathan and Abiram, holding themselves erect, had come out to the entrance of
28 their tents with their wives, their sons, and their dependants. Then Moses said, 'This shall prove to you that it is the LORD who sent me to do all these things, and it was not my own heart that prompted me.
29 If these men die a natural death and share the common fate of man, then
30 the LORD has not sent me; but if the LORD makes a great chasm, and the ground opens its mouth and swallows them and all that is theirs, and

[a] *Lit.* gouge out the eyes of... [b] *So some MSS.; others* they stood at the entrance to the Tent of the Presence, and Moses and Aaron... [c] *So Sept.; Heb.* the.

they go down alive to Sheol, then you will know that these men have
held the LORD in contempt.'

Hardly had Moses spoken when the ground beneath them split; the   31, 32
earth opened its mouth and swallowed them and their homes—all the
followers of Korah and all their property. They went down alive into   33
Sheol with all that they had; the earth closed over them, and they
vanished from the assembly. At their cries all the Israelites round them   34
fled, shouting, 'Look to yourselves! the earth will swallow us up.'
Meanwhile fire had come out from the LORD and burnt up the two   35
hundred and fifty men who were presenting the incense.

Then the LORD spoke to Moses and said, 'Bid Eleazar son of Aaron   36,[a] 37
the priest set aside the censers from the burnt remains, and scatter the
fire from them far and wide, because they are holy. And the censers of   38
these men who sinned at the cost of their lives you shall make into
beaten plates to cover the altar; they are holy, because they have been
presented before the LORD. Let them be a sign to the Israelites.'
So Eleazar the priest took the bronze[b] censers which the victims of the   39
fire had presented, and they were beaten into plates to make a covering
for the altar, as a reminder to the Israelites that no person unqualified,   40
not descended from Aaron, should come forward to burn incense before
the LORD, or his fate would be that of Korah and his company. All this
was done as the LORD commanded Eleazar through Moses.

Next day all the community of the Israelites raised complaints   41
against Moses and Aaron and taxed them with causing the death of some
of the LORD's people. As they gathered against Moses and Aaron, they   42
turned towards the Tent of the Presence and saw that the cloud
covered it, and the glory of the LORD appeared. Moses and Aaron came   43
to the front of the Tent of the Presence, and the LORD spoke to Moses   44
and Aaron[c] and said, 'Stand well clear of this community, so that in a   45
single instant I may make an end of them.' Then they prostrated
themselves, and Moses said to Aaron, 'Take your censer, put fire from   46
the altar in it, set incense on it, and go with it quickly to the assembled
community to make expiation for them. Wrath has gone forth already
from the presence of the LORD. The plague has begun.' So Aaron took   47
his censer, as Moses had said, ran into the midst of the assembly and
found that the plague had begun among the people. He put incense on
the censer and made expiation for the people, standing between the   48
dead and the living, and the plague stopped. Fourteen thousand seven   49
hundred died of it, in addition to those who had died for the offence of
Korah. When Aaron came back to Moses at the entrance to the Tent of   50
the Presence, the plague had stopped.

The LORD spoke to Moses and said, 'Speak to the Israelites and tell   17 1,[d] 2

[a] *17. 1 in Heb.*   [b] *Or copper.*   [c] *and Aaron: so Sept.; Heb. om.*   [d] *17. 16 in Heb.*

them to give you a staff for each tribe, one from every tribal chief, twelve
3 in all, and write each man's name on his staff. On Levi's staff write the
name of Aaron, for there shall be one staff for each head of a tribe.
4 You shall put them all in the Tent of the Presence before the Tokens,
5 where I meet you, and the staff of the man I choose shall sprout. I will
rid myself of the complaints of these Israelites, who keep on complaining against you.'
6 Moses thereupon spoke to the Israelites, and each of their chiefs
handed him a staff, each of them one for his tribe, twelve in all, and
7 Aaron's staff among them. Moses put them before the LORD in the
8 Tent of the Tokens, and next day when he entered the tent, he found
that Aaron's staff, the staff for the tribe of Levi, had sprouted. Indeed,
9 it had sprouted, blossomed, and produced ripe almonds. Moses then
brought out the staffs from before the LORD and showed them to all the
Israelites; they saw for themselves, and each man took his own staff.
10 The LORD said to Moses, 'Put back Aaron's staff in front of the Tokens
to be kept as a warning to all rebels, so that you may rid me once and
11 for all of their complaints, and then they shall not die.' Moses did
this; as the LORD had commanded him, so he did.
12 The Israelites said to Moses, 'This is the end of us! We perish, one
13 and all! Every single person who goes near the Tabernacle of the LORD
dies. Is this to be our final end?'

18 THE LORD SAID to Aaron: You and your sons, together with the
members of your father's tribe, shall be fully answerable for the
sanctuary. You and your sons alone shall be answerable for your
2 priestly office; but you shall admit your kinsmen of Levi, your father's
tribe, to be attached to you and assist you while you and your sons are
3 before the Tent of the Tokens. They shall be in attendance on you and
fulfil all the duties of the Tent, but shall not go near the holy vessels
4 and the altar, or they will die and you with them. They shall be attached
to you and be responsible for the maintenance of the Tent of the
Presence in every detail; no unqualified person shall come near you.
5 You yourselves shall be responsible for the sanctuary and the altar, so
6 that wrath may no more fall on the Israelites. I have myself taken the
Levites your kinsmen out of all the Israelites as a gift for you, given to
7 the LORD for the maintenance of the Tent of the Presence. But only
you and your sons may fulfil the duties of your priestly office that
concern the altar or lie within the Veil. This duty is yours; I bestow
on you this gift of priestly service. The unqualified person who
intrudes on it shall be put to death.
8 The LORD said to Aaron: I, the LORD, commit to your control the
contributions made to me, that is all the holy-gifts of the Israelites.

I give them to you and to your sons for your allotted portion due to you in perpetuity. Out of the most holy gifts kept back from the altar-fire 9 this part shall belong to you: every offering, whether grain-offering, sin-offering, or guilt-offering, rendered to me as a most holy gift, belongs to you and to your sons. You shall eat it as befits most holy gifts; every 10 male may eat it. You shall regard it as holy.

This also is yours: the contribution from all such of their gifts as are 11 presented as special gifts by the Israelites. I give them to you and to your sons and daughters with you as a due in perpetuity. Every person in your household who is ritually clean may eat them.

I give you all the choicest of the oil, the choicest of the new wine and 12 the corn, the firstfruits which are given to the LORD. The first-ripe 13 fruits of all produce in the land which are brought to the LORD shall be yours. Everyone in your household who is clean may eat them.

Everything in Israel which has been devoted to God shall be yours. 14

All the first-born of man or beast which are brought to the LORD 15 shall be yours. Notwithstanding, you must accept payment in redemption of any first-born of man and of unclean beasts: at the end of one 16 month you shall redeem it at the fixed price of five shekels of silver by the sacred standard (twenty gerahs to the shekel). You must not, how- 17 ever, allow the redemption of the first-born of a cow, sheep, or goat; they are holy. You shall fling their blood against the altar and burn their fat in sacrifice as a food-offering of soothing odour to the LORD; their 18 flesh shall be yours, as are the breast of the special gift and the right leg.

All the contributions from holy-gifts, which the Israelites set aside 19 for the LORD, I give to you and to your sons and daughters with you as a due in perpetuity. This is a perpetual covenant of salt before the LORD with you and your descendants also.

The LORD said to Aaron: You shall have no patrimony in the land of 20 Israel, no holding among them; I am your holding in Israel, I am your patrimony.

To the Levites I give every tithe in Israel to be their patrimony, in 21 return for the service they render in maintaining the Tent of the Presence. In order that the Israelites may not henceforth approach the 22 Tent and thus incur the penalty of death, the Levites alone shall 23 perform the service of the Tent, and they shall accept the full responsibility for it. This rule is binding on your descendants for all time. They shall have no patrimony among the Israelites, because I give them as 24 their patrimony the tithe which the Israelites set aside as a contribution to the LORD. Therefore I say to them: You shall have no patrimony among the Israelites.

The LORD spoke to Moses and said, Speak to the Levites in these 25, 26 words: When you receive from the Israelites the tithe which I give you

from them as your patrimony, you shall set aside from it the contribu-
27 tion to the LORD, a tithe of the tithe. Your contribution shall count for
you as if it were corn from the threshing-floor and juice from the vat.
28 In this way you too shall set aside the contribution due to the LORD
out of all tithes which you receive from the Israelites and shall give the
29 LORD's contribution to Aaron the priest. Out of all the gifts you receive
you shall set aside the contribution due to the LORD; and the gift which
you hallow[a] must be taken from the choicest of them.
30   You shall say to the Levites: When you have set aside the choicest
part of your portion, the remainder shall count for you as the produce
31 of the threshing-floor and the winepress, and you may eat it anywhere,
you and your households. It is your payment for service in the Tent of
32 the Presence. When you have set aside its choicest part, you will incur
no penalty in respect of it, and you will not be profaning the holy-gifts
of the Israelites; so you will not die.

19 1,2 THE LORD SPOKE to Moses and Aaron and said: This is a law and a
statute which the LORD has ordained. Tell the Israelites to bring you
a red cow without blemish or defect, which has never borne the yoke.
3 You shall give it to Eleazar the priest, and it shall be taken outside the
4 camp and slaughtered[b] to the east of it. Eleazar the priest shall take
some of the blood on his finger and sprinkle it seven times towards the
5 front of the Tent of the Presence. The cow shall be burnt in his sight,
6 skin, flesh, and blood, together with the offal. The priest shall then take
cedar-wood, marjoram, and scarlet thread, and throw them into the
7 heart of the fire in which the cow is burning. He shall wash his clothes
and bathe his body in water; after which he may enter the camp, but
8 he remains ritually unclean till sunset. The man who burnt the cow
shall wash his clothes and bathe his body in water, but he also remains
9 unclean till sunset. Then a man who is clean shall collect the ashes
of the cow and deposit them outside the camp in a clean place. They
shall be reserved for use by the Israelite community in the water of
10 ritual purification; for the cow is a sin-offering. The man who collected
the ashes of the cow shall wash his clothes, but he remains unclean till
sunset. This rule shall be binding for all time on the Israelites and
on the alien who is living with them.
11   Whoever touches a corpse shall be ritually unclean for seven days.
12 He shall get himself purified with the water of ritual purification on the
third day and on the seventh day, and then he shall be clean. If he is not
purified both on the third day and on the seventh, he shall not be clean.
13 Everyone who touches a corpse, that is the body of a man who has died,
and does not purify himself, defiles the Tabernacle of the LORD. That

[a] you hallow: *prob. rdg.; Heb. obscure.* [b] *Or* he shall take it outside the camp and
slaughter it...

person shall be cut off from Israel. The water of purification has not been flung over him; he remains unclean, and his impurity is still upon him.

When a man dies in a tent, this is the law: everyone who goes into the 14 tent and everyone who was inside the tent shall be ritually unclean for seven days, and every open vessel which has no covering tied over it 15 shall also be unclean. In the open, anyone who touches a man killed 16 with a weapon or one who has died naturally, or who touches a human bone or a grave, shall be unclean for seven days. For such uncleanness, 17 they shall take some of the ash from the burnt mass of the sin-offering and add fresh water to it in a vessel. Then a man who is clean shall take 18 marjoram, dip it in the water, and sprinkle the tent with all the vessels in it and all the people who were there, or the man who has touched a human bone, a corpse (whether the man was killed or died naturally), or a grave. The man who is clean shall sprinkle the unclean man on the 19 third day and on the seventh; on the seventh day he shall purify him; then the man shall wash his clothes and bathe in water, and at sunset he shall be clean. If a man who is unclean does not get himself purified, 20 that person shall be cut off from the assembly, because he has defiled the sanctuary of the LORD. The water of purification has not been flung over him: he is unclean. This rule shall be binding on you*a* for all time. 21 The man who sprinkles the water of purification shall also wash his clothes, and whoever touches the water shall be unclean till sunset. Whatever the unclean man touches shall be unclean, and any person 22 who touches that shall be unclean till sunset.

IN THE FIRST MONTH the whole community of Israel reached the 20 wilderness of Zin and stayed some time at Kadesh; there Miriam died and was buried.

There was no water for the community; so they gathered against 2 Moses and Aaron. The people disputed with Moses and said, 'If only 3 we had perished when our brothers perished in the presence of the LORD! Why have you brought the assembly of the LORD into this 4 wilderness for us and our beasts to die here? Why did you fetch us up 5 from Egypt to bring us to this vile place, where nothing will grow, neither corn nor figs, vines nor pomegranates? There is not even any water to drink.' Moses and Aaron came forward in front of the assembly 6 to the entrance of the Tent of the Presence. There they fell prostrate, and the glory of the LORD appeared to them.

The LORD spoke to Moses and said, 'Take a*b* staff, and then with 7, 8 Aaron your brother assemble all the community, and, in front of them all, speak to the rock and it will yield its water. Thus you will produce

[*a*] *So some MSS.; others* them. [*b*] *Or* the.

water for the community out of the rock, for them and their beasts to
9 drink.' Moses left the presence of the LORD with the staff, as he had
10 commanded him. Then he and Aaron gathered the assembly together in
front of the rock, and he said to them, 'Listen to me, you rebels. Must
11 we get water out of this rock for you?' Moses raised his hand and struck
the rock twice with his staff. Water gushed out in abundance and they
12 all drank, men and beasts. But the LORD said to Moses and Aaron,
'You did not trust me so far as to uphold my holiness in the sight of the
Israelites; therefore you shall not lead this assembly into the land which
13 I promised to give them.' Such were the waters of Meribah,^{a} where the
people disputed with the LORD and through which his holiness was
upheld.

The approach to the promised land

14 FROM KADESH MOSES sent envoys to the king of Edom: 'This is
a message from your brother Israel. You know all the hardships we
15 have encountered, how our fathers went down to Egypt, and we lived
there for many years. The Egyptians ill-treated us and our fathers before
16 us, and we cried to the LORD for help. He listened to us and sent an
angel, and he brought us out of Egypt; and now we are here at Kadesh,
17 a town on your frontier. Grant us passage through your country. We
will not trespass on field or vineyard, or drink from your wells. We will
keep to the king's highway; we will not turn off to right or left until
18 we have crossed your territory.' But the Edomites answered, 'You shall
not cross our land. If you do, we will march out and attack you in
19 force.' The Israelites said, 'But we will keep to the main road. If we
and our flocks drink your water, we will pay you for it; we will simply
20 cross your land on foot.' But the Edomites said, 'No, you shall not',
and took the field against them with a large army in full strength.
21 Thus the Edomites refused to allow Israel to cross their frontier, and
Israel went a different way to avoid a conflict.
22   The whole community of Israel set out from Kadesh and came to
23 Mount Hor. At Mount Hor, near the frontier of Edom, the LORD said
24 to Moses and Aaron, 'Aaron shall be gathered to his father's kin. He
shall not enter the land which I promised to give the Israelites, because
25 over the waters of Meribah you rebelled against my command. Take
26 Aaron and his son Eleazar, and go up Mount Hor. Strip Aaron of his
robes and invest Eleazar his son with them, for Aaron shall be taken
27 from you: he shall die there.' Moses did as the LORD had commanded
28 him: they went up Mount Hor in sight of the whole community, and

[a] *That is* Dispute.

Moses stripped Aaron of his robes and invested his son Eleazar with them. There Aaron died on the mountain-top, and Moses and Eleazar came down from the mountain. So the whole community saw that 29 Aaron had died, and all Israel mourned him for thirty days.

When the Canaanite king of Arad who lived in the Negeb heard that 21 the Israelites were coming by way of Atharim, he attacked them and took some of them prisoners. Israel thereupon made a vow to the 2 LORD and said, 'If thou wilt deliver this people into my power, I will destroy their cities.' The LORD listened to Israel and delivered the 3 Canaanites into their power.*a* Israel destroyed them and their cities and called the place Hormah.*b*

Then they left Mount Hor by way of the Red Sea to march round 4 the flank of Edom. But on the way they grew impatient and spoke 5 against God and Moses. 'Why have you brought us up from Egypt', they said, 'to die in the desert where there is neither food nor water? We are heartily sick of this miserable fare.' Then the LORD sent 6 poisonous snakes among the people, and they bit the Israelites so that many of them died. The people came to Moses and said, 'We sinned 7 when we spoke against the LORD and you. Plead with the LORD to rid us of the snakes.' Moses therefore pleaded with the LORD for the people; and the LORD told Moses to make a serpent*c* of bronze*d* and erect it as 8 a standard, so that anyone who had been bitten could look at it and recover. So Moses made a bronze serpent and erected it as a standard, 9 so that when a snake had bitten a man, he could look at the bronze serpent and recover.

The Israelites went on and encamped at Oboth. They moved on from 10, 11 Oboth and encamped at Iye-abarim in the wilderness on the eastern frontier of Moab. From there they moved and encamped by the gorge 12 of the Zared. They moved on from the Zared and encamped by the 13 farther side of the Arnon in the wilderness which extends into Amorite territory, for the Arnon was the Moabite frontier; it lies between Moab and the Amorites. That is why the Book of the Wars of the LORD 14 speaks of Vaheb*e* in Suphah and the gorges:

> Arnon and the watershed of the gorges 15
> that falls away towards the dwellings at Ar
> and slopes towards the frontier of Moab.

From there they moved on to Beer:*f* this is the water-hole where the 16 LORD said to Moses, 'Gather the people together and I will give them water.' It was then that Israel sang this song: 17

[*a*] into their power: *so Sam.; Heb. om.* [*b*] *That is* Destruction. [*c*] *Or* snake. [*d*] a serpent of bronze: *so some Sept. MSS.; Heb.* a poisonous thing. [*e*] *Name meaning* Watershed. [*f*] *Name meaning* Water-hole.

Well up, spring water! Greet it with song,
18   the spring unearthed by the princes,
        laid open by the leaders of the people
          with sceptre and with mace,
        a gift from*a* the wilderness.

19 And they proceeded from Beer*b* to Nahaliel, and from Nahaliel to
20 Bamoth; then from Bamoth to the valley in the Moabite country
   below the summit of Pisgah overlooking the desert.
21, 22   Then Israel sent envoys to the Amorite king Sihon and said, 'Grant
   us passage through your country. We will not trespass on field or
   vineyard, nor will we drink from your wells. We will travel by the
23 king's highway till we have crossed your territory.' But Sihon would
   not grant Israel passage through his territory; he mustered all his
   people and came out against Israel in the wilderness. He advanced as
24 far as Jahaz and attacked Israel, but Israel put them to the sword,
   giving no quarter, and occupied their land from the Arnon to the
   Jabbok, the territory of the Ammonites, where the country became
25 difficult. So Israel took all these Amorite cities and settled in them, that
26 is in Heshbon and all its dependent villages. Heshbon was the capital
   of the Amorite king Sihon, who had fought against the former king of
27 Moab and taken from him all his territory as far as the Arnon. Therefore the bards say:

        Come to Heshbon, come!
      Let us see the city of Sihon rebuilt and restored!
28   For fire blazed out from Heshbon,
        and flames from Sihon's city.
        It devoured Ar of Moab,
        and swept the high ground at Arnon head.

29   Woe to you, Moab;
        it is the end of you, you people of Kemosh.
        He has made his sons fugitives
        and his daughters the prisoners of Sihon the Amorite king.
30   From Heshbon to Dibon their very embers are burnt out
          and they are extinct,
        while the fire*c* spreads onward to Medeba.

31 Thus Israel occupied the territory of the Amorites.
32   Moses then sent men to explore Jazer; the Israelites captured it
   together with its dependent villages*d* and drove out the Amorites living
33 there. Then they turned and advanced along the road to Bashan. Og

[a] *So Sam.; Heb.* and from.   [b] *Prob. rdg.; Heb.* from a gift.   [c] *So Sam.; Heb.* which.
[d] *So Sept.; Heb.* captured its dependent villages.

king of Bashan, with all his people, took the field against them at Edrei. The LORD said to Moses, 'Do not be afraid of him. I have delivered him 34 into your hands, with all his people and his land. Deal with him as you dealt with Sihon the Amorite king who lived in Heshbon.' So they put 35 him to the sword with his sons and all his people, until there was no survivor left, and they occupied his land.

Israel in the plains of Moab

THE ISRAELITES went forward and encamped in the lowlands of 22 Moab on the farther side of the Jordan from Jericho.

Balak son of Zippor saw what Israel had done to the Amorites, and 2, 3 Moab was in terror of the people because there were so many of them. The Moabites were sick with fear at the sight of them; and they said 4 to the elders of Midian, 'This horde will soon lick up everything round us as a bull crops the spring grass.' Balak son of Zippor was at that time king of Moab. He sent a deputation to summon Balaam son of Beor, 5 who was at Pethor by the Euphrates in the land of the Amavites, with this message, 'Look, an entire nation has come out of Egypt; they cover the face of the country and are settling at my very door. Come at 6 once and lay a curse on them, because they are too many for me; then I may be able to defeat them and drive them from the country. I know that those whom you bless are blessed, and those whom you curse are cursed.'

The elders of Moab and Midian took the fees for augury with them, 7 and they came to Balaam and told him what Balak had said. 'Spend this 8 night here,' he said, 'and I will give you whatever answer the LORD gives to me.' So the Moabite chiefs stayed with Balaam. God came to 9 Balaam and asked him, 'Who are these men with you?' Balaam replied, 10 'Balak son of Zippor king of Moab has sent them to me and he says, "Look, a people newly come out of Egypt is covering the face of the 11 country. Come at once and denounce them for me; then I may be able to fight them and drive them away." God said to Balaam, 'You are not 12 to go with them or curse the people, because they are to be blessed.'[a] So Balaam rose in the morning and said to Balak's chiefs, 'Go back to 13 your own country; the LORD has refused to let me go with you.' Then 14 the Moabite chiefs took their leave and went back to Balak, and told him that Balaam had refused to come with them; whereupon Balak sent a 15 second and larger embassy of higher rank than the first. They came to 16 Balaam and told him, 'This is the message from Balak son of Zippor:

[a] *Or* are blessed.

209

17 "Let nothing stand in the way of your coming. I will confer great honour upon you; I will do whatever you ask me. But you must come
18 and denounce this people for me."' Balaam gave this answer to Balak's messengers: 'Even if Balak were to give me all the silver and gold in his house, I could not disobey the command of the LORD my God in any-
19 thing, small or great. But stay here for this night, as the others did, that
20 I may learn what more the LORD has to say to me.' During the night God came to Balaam and said to him, 'If these men have come to summon you, then rise and go with them, but do only what I tell you.'
21 So in the morning Balaam rose, saddled his ass and went with the Moabite chiefs.

22 But God was angry because Balaam was going, and as he came riding on his ass, accompanied by his two servants, the angel of the LORD
23 took his stand in the road to bar his way. When the ass saw the angel standing in the road with his sword drawn, she turned off the road into the fields, and Balaam beat the ass to bring her back on to the road.
24 Then the angel of the LORD stood where the road ran through a
25 hollow, with fenced vineyards on either side. The ass saw the angel and, crushing herself against the wall, crushed Balaam's foot against it, and
26 he beat her again. The angel of the LORD moved on further and stood in a narrow place where there was no room to turn either to right or
27 left. When the ass saw the angel, she lay down under Balaam. At that
28 Balaam lost his temper and beat the ass with his stick. The LORD then made the ass speak, and she said to Balaam, 'What have I done? This
29 is the third time you have beaten me.' Balaam answered the ass, 'You have been making a fool of me. If I had had a sword here, I should have
30 killed you on the spot.' But the ass answered, 'Am I not still the ass which you have ridden all your life? Have I ever taken such a liberty
31 with you before?' He said, 'No.' Then the LORD opened Balaam's eyes: he saw the angel of the LORD standing in the road with his sword drawn,
32 and he bowed down and fell flat on his face before him. The angel said to him, 'What do you mean by beating your ass three times like this?
33 I came out to bar your way but you made straight for me, and three times your ass saw me and turned aside. If she had not*a* turned aside,
34 I should by now have killed you and spared her.' Balaam replied to the angel of the LORD, 'I have done wrong. I did not know that you stood in the road confronting me. But now, if my journey displeases you, I am
35 ready to go back.' The angel of the LORD said to Balaam, 'Go on with these men; but say only what I tell you.' So Balaam went on with Balak's chiefs.

36 When Balak heard that Balaam was coming, he came out to meet him
37 as far as Ar of Moab by the Arnon on his frontier. Balak said to Balaam,

[a] *So Sept.; Heb.* Perhaps she had...

'Did I not send time and again to summon you? Why did you not come? Did you think that I could not do you honour?' Balaam replied, 38 'I have come, as you see. But now that I am here, what power have I of myself to say anything? Whatever the word God puts into my mouth, that is what I will say.' So Balaam went with Balak till they came to 39 Kiriath-huzoth, and Balak slaughtered cattle and sheep and sent them 40 to Balaam and to the chiefs who were with him.

In the morning Balak took Balaam and led him up to the Heights of 41 Baal,*a* from where he could see the full extent of the Israelite host. Then Balaam said to Balak, 'Build me here seven altars and prepare for 23 me seven bulls and seven rams.' Balak did as he asked and offered*b* 2 a bull and a ram on each altar. Then he said to him, 'I have prepared 3-4 the seven altars, and I have offered the bull and the ram on each altar.' Balaam said to Balak, 'Take your stand beside your sacrifice, and let me go off by myself. It may happen that the LORD will meet me. Whatever he reveals to me, I will tell you.' So he went forthwith, and God met him. The LORD put words into Balaam's mouth and said, 'Go back to 5 Balak, and speak as I tell you.' So he went back, and found Balak 6 standing by his sacrifice, and with him all the Moabite chiefs. And 7 Balaam uttered his oracle:

> From Aram,*c* from the mountains of the east,
> Balak king of Moab has brought me:
> 'Come, lay a curse for me on Jacob,
> come, execrate Israel.'
> How can I denounce whom God has not denounced?   8
> How can I execrate whom the LORD has not execrated?
> From the rocky heights I see them,   9
> I watch them from the rounded hills.
> I see a people that dwells alone,
> that has not made itself one with the nations.
> Who can count the host*d* of Jacob   10
> or number the hordes*e* of Israel?
> Let me die as men die who are righteous,
> grant that my end may be as theirs!

Then Balak said to Balaam, 'What is this you have done? I sent for you 11 to denounce my enemies, and what you have done is to bless them.' But 12 he replied, 'Must I not keep to the words that the LORD puts into my mouth?'

Balak then said to him, 'Come with me now to another place from 13 which you will see them, though not the full extent of them; you will

[a] Heights of Baal: *Heb.* Bamoth-baal. [b] *So some MSS.; others* and Balak and Balaam offered. [c] *Or* Syria. [d] *Or* dust. [e] *Or* quarter *or* sands.

14 not see them all. Denounce them for me from there.' So he took him
to the Field of the Watchers*a* on the summit of Pisgah, where he built
15 seven altars and offered a bull and a ram on each altar. Balaam said
to Balak, 'Take your stand beside your sacrifice, and I will meet
16 God over there.' The LORD met Balaam and put words into his
17 mouth, and said, 'Go back to Balak, and speak as I tell you.' So he
went back, and found him standing beside his sacrifice, with the
18 Moabite chiefs. Balak asked what the LORD had said, and Balaam
uttered his oracle:

> Up, Balak, and listen:
> hear what I am charged to say, son of Zippor.
19   God is not a mortal that he should lie,
> not a man that he should change his mind.*b*
> Has he not spoken, and will he not make it good?
> What he has proclaimed, he will surely fulfil.
20   I have received command to bless;
> I will bless*c* and I cannot gainsay it.
21   He has discovered no iniquity in Jacob
> and has seen no mischief in Israel.*d*
> The LORD their God is with them,
> acclaimed among them as king.*e*
22   What its curving horns are to the wild ox,
> God is to them, who brought them out of Egypt.
23   Surely there is no divination in*f* Jacob,
> and no augury in*f* Israel;
> now is the time to say of Jacob
> and of Israel, 'See what God has wrought!'
24   Behold a people rearing up like a lioness,
> rampant like a lion;
> he will not couch till he devours the prey
> and drinks the blood of the slain.

25 Then Balak said to Balaam, 'You will not denounce them; then at least
26 do not bless them'; and he answered, 'Did I not warn you that I must
27 do all the LORD tells me?' Balak replied, 'Come, let me take you to
another place; perhaps God will be pleased to let you denounce them
28 for me from there.' So he took Balaam to the summit of Peor over-
29 looking Jeshimon, and Balaam told him to build seven altars for him
30 there and prepare seven bulls and seven rams. Balak did as Balaam had
said, and he offered a bull and a ram on each altar.

[*a*] Or Field of Zophim. [*b*] Or feel regret. [*c*] So Sam.; Heb. he blessed. [*d*] Or None
can discover calamity in Jacob nor see trouble in Israel. [*e*] Or royal care is bestowed on
them. [*f*] Or against.

But now that Balaam knew that the LORD wished him to bless Israel, 24
he did not go and resort to divination as before. He turned towards the
desert; and as he looked, he saw Israel encamped tribe by tribe. The 2
spirit of God came upon him, and he uttered his oracle: 3

> The very word of Balaam son of Beor,
> the very word of the man whose sight is clear,
> the very word of him who hears the words of God, 4
> who with staring eyes sees in a trance
> the vision from the Almighty:
>> how goodly are your tents, O Jacob, 5
> your dwelling-places, Israel,
> like long rows of palms, 6
> like gardens by a river,
> like lign-aloes planted by the LORD,
> like cedars beside the water!
> The water in his vessels shall overflow, 7
> and his seed shall be like great waters
> so that his king may be taller than Agag,
> and his kingdom lifted high.
> What its curving horns are to the wild ox, 8
> God is to him, who brought him out of Egypt;
> he shall devour his adversaries the nations,
> crunch their bones, and smash their limbs in pieces.
> When he reclines he couches like a lion, 9
> like a lioness, and no one dares rouse him.
> Blessed be they that bless you,
> and they that curse you be accursed!

At that Balak was very angry with Balaam, beat his hands together and 10
said, 'I summoned you to denounce my enemies, and three times you
have persisted in blessing them. Off with you to your own place! 11
I promised to confer great honour upon you, but now the LORD has
kept this honour from you.' Balaam answered, 'But I told your own 12
messengers whom you sent: "If Balak gives me all the silver and gold in 13
his house, I cannot disobey the command of the LORD by doing anything of my own will, good or bad. What the LORD speaks to me, that is
what I will say." Now I am going to my own people; but first, I will 14
warn you what this people will do to yours in the days to come.' So he 15
uttered his oracle:

> The very word of Balaam son of Beor,
> the very word of the man whose sight is clear,
> the very word of him who hears the words of God, 16
> who shares the knowledge of the Most High,

who with staring eyes sees in a trance
the vision from the Almighty:

17   I see him, but not now;
I behold him, but not near:
a star shall come forth out of Jacob,
a comet arise from Israel.
He shall smite the squadrons[a] of Moab,
and beat down all the sons of strife.

18   Edom shall be his by conquest
and Seir, his enemy, shall be his.
Israel shall do valiant deeds;

19   Jacob shall trample them down,
the last survivor from Ar shall he destroy.

20 He saw Amalek and uttered his oracle:

First of all the nations was Amalek,
but his end shall be utter destruction.

21 He saw the Kenites and uttered his oracle:

Your refuge, though it seems secure,
your nest, though set on the mountain crag,

22   is doomed to burning, O Cain.
How long must you dwell there in my sight?

23 He uttered his oracle:

Ah, who are these assembling in the north,

24   invaders[b] from the region of Kittim?
They will lay waste Assyria; they will lay Eber waste:
he too shall perish utterly.

25 Then Balaam arose and returned home, and Balak also went on his
way.

25 WHEN THE ISRAELITES were in Shittim, the people began to have
2 intercourse with Moabite women, who invited them to the sacrifices
offered to their gods; and they ate the sacrificial food and prostrated
3 themselves before the gods of Moab. The Israelites joined in the worship
4 of the Baal of Peor, and the LORD was angry with them. He said to
Moses, 'Take all the leaders of the people and hurl them down to their
death before the LORD in the full light of day, that the fury of his anger
5 may turn away from Israel.' So Moses said to the judges of Israel, 'Put
to death, each one of you, those of his tribe who have joined in the
worship of the Baal of Peor.'

[a] *Or* heads. [b] *So Sept.; Heb. obscure.*

214

One of the Israelites brought a Midianite woman into his family in 6
open defiance of Moses and all the community of Israel, while they
were weeping by the entrance of the Tent of the Presence. Phinehas son 7
of Eleazar, son of Aaron the priest, saw him. He stepped out from the
crowd and took up a spear, and he went into the inner room*a* after the 8
Israelite and transfixed the two of them, the Israelite and the woman,
pinning them together.*b* Thus the plague which had attacked the
Israelites was brought to a stop; but twenty-four thousand had already 9
died.

The LORD spoke to Moses and said, 'Phinehas son of Eleazar, son of 10, 11
Aaron the priest, has turned my wrath away from the Israelites; he
displayed among them the same jealous anger that moved me, and
therefore in my jealousy I did not exterminate the Israelites. Tell him 12
that I hereby grant him my covenant of security of tenure. He and his 13
descendants after him shall enjoy the priesthood under a covenant for all
time, because he showed his zeal for his God and made expiation for the
Israelites.' The name of the Israelite struck down with the Midianite 14
woman was Zimri son of Salu, a chief in a Simeonite family, and the 15
Midianite woman's name was Cozbi daughter of Zur, who was the
head of a group of fathers' families in Midian.

The LORD spoke to Moses and said, 'Make the Midianites suffer as 16, 17–18
they made you suffer with their crafty tricks, and strike them down;
their craftiness was your undoing at Peor and in the affair of Cozbi
their sister, the daughter of a Midianite chief, who was struck down at
the time of the plague that followed Peor.'

AFTER THE PLAGUE the LORD said to Moses and Eleazar the priest, 19; 26 1
son of Aaron, 'Number the whole community of Israel by fathers' 2
families, recording everyone in Israel aged twenty years and upwards
fit for military service.' Moses and Eleazar collected them in the low- 3
lands of Moab by the Jordan near Jericho,*c* all who were twenty years 4
of age and upwards, as the LORD had commanded Moses.

These were the Israelites who came out of Egypt:

Reubenites (Reuben was Israel's eldest son): Enoch, the Enochite 5*d*
family; Pallu, the Palluite family; Hezron, the Hezronite family; 6
Carmi, the Carmite family. These were the Reubenite families; the 7
number in their detailed list was forty-three thousand seven hundred
and thirty. Son of Pallu: Eliab. Sons of Eliab: Nemuel, Dathan and 8, 9
Abiram. These were the same Dathan and Abiram, conveners of the
community, who defied Moses and Aaron and joined the company of
Korah in defying the LORD. Then the earth opened its mouth and 10

[a] *Lit.* alcove. [b] *Lit.* into her belly. [c] *Prob. rdg.; Heb. adds* saying. [d] *Verses
5–50: cp. Gen. 46. 8–25; Exod. 6. 14, 15; 1 Chr. chs. 4–8.*

swallowed them up with Korah, and so their company died, while fire burnt up the two hundred and fifty men, and they became a warning
11 sign. The Korahites, however, did not die.

12 Simeonites, by their families: Nemuel, the Nemuelite family; Jamin,
13 the Jaminite family; Jachin, the Jachinite family; Zerah, the Zarhite
14 family; Saul, the Saulite family. These were the Simeonite families; the number in their detailed list*a* was twenty-two thousand two hundred.

15 Gadites, by their families: Zephon, the Zephonite family; Haggi, the
16 Haggite family; Shuni, the Shunite family; Ozni, the Oznite family;
17 Eri, the Erite family; Arod, the Arodite family; Areli, the Arelite
18 family. These were the Gadite families; the number in their detailed list was forty thousand five hundred.

19 The sons of Judah were Er, Onan, Shelah, Perez and Zerah;*b* Er and
20 Onan died in Canaan. Judahites, by their families: Shelah, the Shelanite family; Perez, the Perezite family; Zerah, the Zarhite family.
21 Perezites: Hezron, the Hezronite family; Hamul, the Hamulite family.
22 These were the families of Judah; the number in their detailed list was seventy-six thousand five hundred.

23 Issacharites, by their families: Tola, the Tolaite family; Pua, the
24 Puite*c* family; Jashub, the Jashubite family; Shimron, the Shimronite
25 family. These were the families of Issachar; the number in their detailed list was sixty-four thousand three hundred.

26 Zebulunites, by their families: Sered, the Sardite family; Elon, the
27 Elonite family; Jahleel, the Jahleelite family. These were the Zebulunite families; the number in their detailed list was sixty thousand five hundred.

28, 29 Josephites, by their families: Manasseh and Ephraim. Manassites: Machir, the Machirite family. Machir was the father of Gilead: Gilead,
30 the Gileadite family. Gileadites: Jeezer, the Jeezerite family; Helek, the
31 Helekite family; Asriel, the Asrielite family; Shechem, the Shechemite
32 family; Shemida, the Shemidaite family; Hepher, the Hepherite
33 family. Zelophehad son of Hepher had no sons, only daughters; their
34 names were Mahlah, Noah, Hoglah, Milcah and Tirzah. These were the families of Manasseh; the number in their detailed list was fifty-two thousand seven hundred.

35 Ephraimites, by their families: Shuthelah, the Shuthalhite family;
36 Becher, the Bachrite family; Tahan, the Tahanite family. Shuthalhites:
37 Eran, the Eranite family. These were the Ephraimite families; the number in their detailed list was thirty-two thousand five hundred. These were the Josephites, by families.

[a] in their detailed list: *so Sept.; Heb. om.* [b] Er...Zerah: *so some Sept. MSS. (cp. Gen. 46. 12); Heb.* Er and Onan. [c] *So Sam.; Heb.* Punite.

Benjamites, by their families: Bela, the Belaite family; Ashbel, the 38
Ashbelite family; Ahiram, the Ahiramite family; Shupham,^a the 39
Shuphamite family; Hupham, the Huphamite family. Belaites: Ard 40
and Naaman. Ard,^b the Ardite family; Naaman, the Naamite family.
These were the Benjamite families; the number in their detailed list 41
was forty-five thousand six hundred.

Danites, by their families: Shuham, the Shuhamite family. These 42
were the families of Dan by their families; the number in the de- 43
tailed list of the Shuhamite family was sixty-four thousand four
hundred.

Asherites, by their families: Imna, the Imnite family; Ishvi, the 44
Ishvite family; Beriah, the Beriite family. Beriite families: Heber, the 45
Heberite family; Malchiel, the Malchielite family. The daughter of 46
Asher was named Serah. These were the Asherite families; the number 47
in their detailed list was fifty-three thousand four hundred.

Naphtalites, by their families: Jahzeel, the Jahzeelite family; Guni, 48
the Gunite family; Jezer, the Jezerite family; Shillem, the Shillemite 49
family. These were the Naphtalite families by their families; the 50
number in their detailed list was forty-five thousand four hundred.

The total in the Israelite lists was six hundred and one thousand 51
seven hundred and thirty.

The LORD spoke to Moses and said, 'The land shall be apportioned 52, 53
among these tribes according to the number of names recorded. To the 54
larger group you shall give a larger property and to the smaller a
smaller; a property shall be given to each in proportion to its size as
shown in the detailed lists. The land, however, shall be apportioned by 55
lot; the lots shall be cast for the properties by families in the father's
line. Properties shall be apportioned by lot between the larger families 56
and the smaller.'

The detailed lists of Levi, by families: Gershon, the Gershonite 57
family; Kohath, the Kohathite family; Merari, the Merarite family.

These were the families of Levi: the Libnite, Hebronite, Mahlite, 58
Mushite, and Korahite families.

Kohath was the father of Amram; Amram's wife was named 59
Jochebed daughter of Levi, born to him in Egypt. She bore to Amram
Aaron, Moses, and their sister Miriam. Aaron's sons were Nadab, 60
Abihu, Eleazar and Ithamar. Nadab and Abihu died because they 61
presented illicit fire before the LORD.

In the detailed lists of Levi the number of males, aged one month and 62
upwards, was twenty-three thousand. They were recorded separately
from the other Israelites because no property was allotted to them
among the Israelites.

[a] *So some MSS.; others* Shephupham. [b] *So Sam.; Heb. om.*

63 These were the detailed lists prepared by Moses and Eleazar the priest when they numbered the Israelites in the lowlands of Moab by
64 the Jordan near Jericho. Among them there was not a single one of the Israelites whom Moses and Aaron the priest had recorded in the
65 wilderness of Sinai; for the LORD had said they should all die in the wilderness. None of them was still living except Caleb son of Jephunneh and Joshua son of Nun.

27 A claim was presented by the daughters of Zelophehad son of Hepher, son of Gilead, son of Machir, son of Manasseh,*a* son of Joseph.
2 Their names were Mahlah, Noah, Hoglah, Milcah and Tirzah. They appeared at the entrance of the Tent of the Presence before Moses, Eleazar the priest, the chiefs, and all the community, and spoke as
3 follows: 'Our father died in the wilderness. He was not among the company of Korah which combined together against the LORD; he died
4 for his own sin and left no sons. Is it right that, because he had no son, our father's name should disappear from his family? Give us our property on the same footing as our father's brothers.'

5,6 So Moses brought their case before the LORD, and the LORD spoke
7 to Moses and said, 'The claim of the daughters of Zelophehad is good. You must allow them to inherit on the same footing as their father's
8 brothers. Let their father's patrimony pass to them. Then say this to the Israelites: "When a man dies leaving no son, his patrimony shall
9 pass to his daughter. If he has no daughter, you shall give it to his
10 brothers. If he has no brothers, you shall give it to his father's brothers.
11 If his father had no brothers, then you shall give possession to the nearest survivor in his family, and he shall inherit. This shall be a legal precedent for the Israelites, as the LORD has commanded Moses."'

12 The LORD said to Moses, 'Go up this mountain, Mount Abarim, and
13 look out over the land which I have given to the Israelites. Then, when you have looked out over it, you shall be gathered to your father's kin
14 like your brother Aaron; for you and Aaron disobeyed my command when the community disputed with me in the wilderness of Zin: you did not uphold my holiness before them at the waters.' These were the waters of Meribah-by-Kadesh in the wilderness of Zin.

15,16 Then Moses said, 'Let the LORD, the God of the spirits of all
17 mankind, appoint a man over the community to go out and come in at their head, to lead them out and bring them home, so that the com-
18 munity of the LORD may not be like sheep without a shepherd.' The LORD answered Moses, 'Take Joshua son of Nun, a man endowed with
19 spirit; lay your hand on him and set him before Eleazar the priest and
20 all the community. Give him his commission in their presence, and delegate some of your authority to him, so that all the community of

[a] *So Vulg.; Heb. adds* of the families of Manasseh.

the Israelites may obey him. He must appear before Eleazar the priest, 21
who will obtain a decision for him by consulting the Urim before the
LORD; at his word they shall go out and shall come home, both Joshua
and the whole community of the Israelites.'

Moses did as the LORD had commanded him. He took Joshua, 22
presented him to Eleazar the priest and the whole community, laid his 23
hands on him and gave him his commission, as the LORD had instructed
him.[a]

THE LORD SPOKE to Moses and said, Give this command to the 28 1, 2
Israelites: See that you present my offerings, the food for the food-
offering of soothing odour, to me at the appointed time.

Tell them: This is the food-offering which you shall present to the 3
LORD: the regular daily whole-offering of two yearling rams without
blemish. One you shall sacrifice in the morning and the second between 4
dusk and dark. The grain-offering shall be a tenth of an ephah of flour 5
mixed with a quarter of a hin of oil of pounded olives. (This was the 6
regular whole-offering made at Mount Sinai, a soothing odour, a food-
offering to the LORD.) The wine[b] for the proper drink-offering shall be 7
a quarter of a hin to each ram; you are to pour out this strong drink in
the holy place as an offering to the LORD. You shall sacrifice the second 8
ram between dusk and dark, with the same grain-offering as at the
morning sacrifice and with the proper drink-offering; it is a food-
offering of soothing odour to the LORD.

For the sabbath day: two yearling rams without blemish, a grain- 9
offering of two tenths of an ephah of flour mixed with oil, and the
proper drink-offering. This whole-offering, presented every sabbath, is 10
in addition to the regular whole-offering and the proper drink-offering.

On the first day of every month you shall present a whole-offering to 11
the LORD, consisting of two young bulls, one ram and seven yearling
rams without blemish. The grain-offering shall be three tenths of flour 12
mixed with oil for each bull, two tenths of flour mixed with oil for the
full-grown ram, and one tenth of flour mixed with oil for each young 13
ram. This is a whole-offering, a food-offering of soothing odour to the
LORD. The proper drink-offering shall be half a hin of wine for each 14
bull, a third for the full-grown ram and a quarter for each young ram.
This is the whole-offering to be made, month by month, throughout the
year. Further, one he-goat shall be sacrificed as a sin-offering to the 15
LORD, in addition to the regular whole-offering and the proper drink-
offering.

The Passover of the LORD shall be held on the fourteenth day of the 16
first month, and on the fifteenth day there shall be a pilgrim-feast; for 17

[a] *So Vulg.; Heb. adds* through Moses. [b] *So Sept.; Heb. om.*

18 seven days you must eat only unleavened cakes. On the first day there
19 shall be a sacred assembly; you shall not do your daily work. As a food-
offering, a whole-offering to the LORD, you shall present two young
20 bulls, one ram, and seven yearling rams, all without blemish. You shall
offer the proper grain-offerings of flour mixed with oil, three tenths for
21 each bull, two tenths for the ram, and one tenth for each of the seven
22 young rams; and as a sin-offering, one he-goat to make expiation for you.
23 All these you shall offer in addition to the morning whole-offering, which
24 is the regular sacrifice. You shall repeat this daily till the seventh day,
presenting food as a food-offering of soothing odour to the LORD, in
addition to the regular whole-offering and the proper drink-offering.
25 On the seventh day there shall be a sacred assembly; you shall not do
your daily work.

26   On the day of Firstfruits, when you bring to the LORD your grain-
offering from the new crop at your Feast of Weeks, there shall be a
27 sacred assembly; you shall not do your daily work. You shall bring
a whole-offering as a soothing odour to the LORD: two young bulls, one
28 full-grown ram, and seven yearling rams. The proper grain-offering
shall be of flour mixed with oil, three tenths for each bull, two tenths
29, 30 for the one ram, and a tenth for each of the seven young rams, and there
31 shall be one he-goat as a sin-offering[a] to make expiation for you; they
shall all be without blemish. All these you shall offer in addition to the
regular whole-offering with the proper grain-offering and drink-offering.

29   On the first day of the seventh month there shall be a sacred
assembly; you shall not do your daily work. It shall be a day of accla-
2 mation. You shall sacrifice a whole-offering as a soothing odour to the
LORD: one young bull, one full-grown ram, and seven yearling rams,
3 without blemish. Their proper grain-offering shall be of flour mixed
4 with oil, three tenths for the bull, two tenths for the one ram, and one
5 tenth for each of the seven young rams, and there shall be one he-goat
6 as a sin-offering to make expiation for you. This is in addition to the
monthly whole-offering and the regular whole-offering with their
proper grain-offerings and drink-offerings according to custom; it is
a food-offering of soothing odour to the LORD.

7   On the tenth day of this seventh month there shall be a sacred
assembly, and you shall mortify yourselves; you shall not do any work.
8 You shall bring a whole-offering to the LORD as a soothing odour: one
young bull, one full-grown ram, and seven yearling rams; they shall
9 all be without blemish. The proper grain-offering shall be of flour
mixed with oil, three tenths for the bull, two tenths for the one ram,
10, 11 and one tenth for each of the seven young rams, and there shall be one
he-goat as a sin-offering, in addition to the expiatory sin-offering and

[a] as a sin-offering: *so Sam.; Heb. om.*

the regular whole-offering, with the proper grain-offering and drink-offering.[a]

On the fifteenth day of the seventh month there shall be a sacred 12 assembly. You shall not do your daily work, but shall keep a pilgrim-feast to the LORD for seven days. As a whole-offering, a food-offering 13 of soothing odour to the LORD, you shall bring thirteen young bulls, two full-grown rams, and fourteen yearling rams; they shall all be without blemish. The proper grain-offering shall be of flour mixed with 14 oil, three tenths for each of the thirteen bulls, two tenths for each of the two rams, and one tenth for each of the fourteen young rams, and 15, 16 there shall be one he-goat as a sin-offering, in addition to the regular whole-offering with the proper grain-offering and drink-offering.

On the second day: twelve young bulls, two full-grown rams, and 17 fourteen yearling rams, without blemish, together with the proper 18 grain-offerings and drink-offerings for bulls, full-grown rams, and young rams, as prescribed according to their number, and there shall 19 be one he-goat as a sin-offering, in addition to the regular whole-offering with the proper grain-offering and drink-offering.[b]

On the third day: eleven bulls, two full-grown rams, and fourteen 20 yearling rams, without blemish, together with the proper grain-21 offerings and drink-offerings for bulls, full-grown rams, and young rams, as prescribed according to their number, and there shall be one 22 he-goat as a sin-offering, in addition to the regular whole-offering, with the proper grain-offering and drink-offering.

On the fourth day: ten bulls, two full-grown rams, and fourteen 23 yearling rams, without blemish, together with the proper grain-offerings 24 and drink-offerings for bulls, full-grown rams, and young rams, as prescribed according to their number, and there shall be one he-goat 25 as a sin-offering, in addition to the regular whole-offering with the proper grain-offering and drink-offering.

On the fifth day: nine bulls, two full-grown rams, and fourteen 26 yearling rams, without blemish, together with the proper grain-27 offerings and drink-offerings for bulls, full-grown rams, and young rams, as prescribed according to their number, and there shall be one 28 he-goat as a sin-offering, in addition to the regular whole-offering with the proper grain-offering and drink-offering.

On the sixth day: eight bulls, two full-grown rams, and fourteen 29 yearling rams, without blemish, together with the proper grain-30 offerings and drink-offerings for bulls, full-grown rams, and young rams, as prescribed according to their number, and there shall be one 31 he-goat as a sin-offering, in addition to the regular whole-offering with the proper grain-offering and drink-offering.[b]

[a] *So Sept.; Heb.* drink-offerings.   [b] *So some MSS.; others* drink-offerings.

32 On the seventh day: seven bulls, two full-grown rams, and fourteen
33 yearling rams, without blemish, together with the proper grain-
offerings and drink-offerings for bulls, full-grown rams, and young
34 rams, as prescribed according to their number, and there shall be one
he-goat as a sin-offering, in addition to the regular whole-offering with
the proper grain-offering and drink-offering.
35 The eighth day you shall keep as a closing ceremony; you shall not
36 do your daily work. As a whole-offering, a food-offering of soothing
odour to the LORD, you shall bring one bull, one full-grown ram, and
37 seven yearling rams, without blemish, together with the proper grain-
offerings and drink-offerings for bulls, full-grown rams, and young
38 rams, as prescribed according to their number, and there shall be one
he-goat as a sin-offering, in addition to the regular whole-offering with
the proper grain-offering and drink-offering.
39 These are the sacrifices which you shall offer to the LORD at the
appointed seasons, in addition to the votive offerings, the freewill
offerings, the whole-offerings, the grain-offerings, the drink-offerings,
and the shared-offerings.
40[a] Moses told the Israelites exactly what the LORD had commanded him.

30 THEN MOSES SPOKE to the heads of the Israelite tribes and said,
2 This is the LORD's command: When a man makes a vow to the LORD
or swears an oath and so puts himself under a binding obligation, he
must not break his word. Every word he has spoken, he must make good.
3 When a woman, still young and living in her father's house, makes a
4 vow to the LORD or puts herself under a binding obligation, if her
father hears of it and keeps silence, then any such vow or obligation
5 shall be valid. But if her father disallows it when he hears of it, none of
her vows or obligations shall be valid; the LORD will absolve her,
6 because her father has disallowed it. If the woman is married when she
7 is under a vow or a binding obligation rashly uttered, then if her
husband hears of it and keeps silence when he hears, her vow or
8 obligation by which she has bound herself shall be valid. If, however,
her husband disallows it when he hears of it and repudiates the vow
which she has taken upon herself or the rash utterance with which she
9 has bound herself, then the LORD will absolve her. Every vow by which
10 a widow or a divorced woman has bound herself shall be valid. But if
it is in her husband's house that a woman makes a vow or puts herself
11 under a binding obligation by an oath, and her husband, hearing of it,
keeps silence and does not disallow it, then every vow and obligation
12 under which she has put herself shall be valid; but if her husband
clearly repudiates them when he hears of them, then nothing that she

[a] *30. 1 in Heb.*

has uttered, whether vow or obligation, shall be valid. Her husband has repudiated them, and the LORD will absolve her.

The husband can confirm or repudiate any vow or oath by which a 13 woman binds herself to mortification. If he maintains silence day after 14 day, he thereby confirms every vow or obligation under which she has put herself: he confirms them, because he kept silence at the time when he heard them. If he repudiates them some time after he has heard 15 them, he shall be responsible for her default.

Such are the decrees which the LORD gave to Moses concerning a 16 husband and his wife and a father and his daughter, still young and living in her father's house.

THE LORD SPOKE to Moses and said, 'You are to exact vengeance 31 1, 2 for Israel on the Midianites and then you will be gathered to your father's kin.'

Then Moses spoke to the people in these words: 'Let some men 3 among you be drafted for active service. They shall fall upon Midian and exact vengeance in the LORD's name. You shall send out a thousand 4 men from each of the tribes of Israel.' So the men were called up from 5 the clans of Israel, a thousand from each tribe, twelve thousand in all, drafted for active service. Moses sent out this force, a thousand from 6 each tribe, with Phinehas son of Eleazar the priest, who was in charge of the holy vessels and of the trumpets to give the signal for the battle-cry. They made war on Midian as the LORD had commanded Moses, and 7 slew all the men. In addition to those slain in battle they killed the 8 kings of Midian—Evi, Rekem, Zur, Hur, and Reba, the five kings of Midian—and they put to death also Balaam son of Beor. The Israelites 9 took captive the Midianite women and their dependants, and carried off all their beasts, their flocks, and their property. They burnt all their 10 cities, in which they had settled, and all their encampments. They took 11 all the spoil and plunder, both man and beast, and brought them— 12 captives, plunder, and spoil—to Moses and Eleazar the priest and to all the community of the Israelites, to the camp in the lowlands of Moab by the Jordan at Jericho.

Moses and Eleazar the priest and all the leaders of the community 13 went to meet them outside the camp. Moses spoke angrily to the officers 14 of the army, the commanders of units of a thousand and of a hundred, who were returning from the campaign: 'Have you spared all the 15 women?' he said. 'Remember, it was they who, on Balaam's departure, 16 set about seducing the Israelites into disloyalty to the LORD that day at Peor, so that the plague struck the community of the LORD. Now kill 17 every male dependant, and kill every woman who has had intercourse with a man, but spare for yourselves every woman among them who has 18

19 not had intercourse. You yourselves, every one of you who has taken life and every one who has touched the dead, must remain outside the camp for seven days. Purify yourselves and your captives on the third
20 day and on the seventh day, and purify also every piece of clothing, every article made of skin, everything woven of goat's hair, and everything made of wood.'

21 Eleazar the priest said to the soldiers returning from battle, 'This is
22-23 a law and statute which the LORD has ordained through Moses. Anything which will stand fire, whether gold, silver, copper, iron, tin, or lead, you shall pass through fire and then it will be clean. Other things shall be purified by the water of ritual purification; whatever cannot
24 stand fire shall be passed through the water. On the seventh day you shall wash your clothes, and then be clean; after this you may re-enter the camp.'

25, 26 The LORD spoke to Moses and said, 'Count all that has been captured, man or beast, you and Eleazar the priest and the heads of
27 families in the community, and divide it equally between the fighting
28 men who went on the campaign and the whole community. You shall levy a tax for the LORD: from the combatants it shall be one out of
29 every five hundred, whether men, cattle, asses, or sheep, to be taken out of their share and given to Eleazar the priest as a contribution for the
30 LORD. Out of the share of the Israelites it shall be one out of every fifty taken, whether man or beast, cattle, asses, or sheep, to be given to the Levites who are in charge of the LORD's Tabernacle.'

31 Moses and Eleazar the priest did as the LORD had commanded
32 Moses. These were the spoils, over and above the plunder taken by the
33 fighting men: six hundred and seventy-five thousand sheep, seventy-
34, 35 two thousand cattle, sixty-one thousand asses; and of persons, thirty-two thousand girls who had had no intercourse with a man.

36 The half-share of those who took part in the campaign was thus
37 three hundred and thirty-seven thousand five hundred sheep, the tax
38 for the LORD from these being six hundred and seventy-five; thirty-six
39 thousand cattle, the tax being seventy-two; thirty thousand five
40 hundred asses, the tax being sixty-one; and sixteen thousand persons,
41 the tax being thirty-two. Moses gave Eleazar the priest the tax levied for the LORD, as the LORD had commanded him.

42-43 The share of the community, being the half-share for the Israelites which Moses divided off from that of the combatants, was three hundred
44 and thirty-seven thousand five hundred sheep, thirty-six thousand
45, 46 cattle, thirty thousand five hundred asses, and sixteen thousand
47 persons. Moses took one out of every fifty, whether man or beast, from the half-share of the Israelites, and gave it to the Levites who were in charge of the LORD's Tabernacle, as the LORD had commanded him.

Then the officers who had commanded the forces on the campaign, 48
the commanders of units of a thousand and of a hundred, came to
Moses and said to him, 'Sir, we have checked the roll of the fighting 49
men who were under our command, and not one of them is missing. So 50
we have brought the gold ornaments, the armlets, bracelets, finger-
rings, earrings, and pendants*a* that each man has found, to offer them
before the LORD as a ransom for our lives.'

Moses and Eleazar the priest received this gold from the commanders 51
of units of a thousand and of a hundred, all of it craftsman's work, and 52
the gold thus levied as a contribution to the LORD weighed sixteen
thousand seven hundred and fifty shekels; for every man in the army 53
had taken plunder. So Moses and Eleazar the priest received the gold 54
from the commanders of units of a thousand and of a hundred, and
brought it to the Tent of the Presence that the LORD might remember
Israel.

Now the Reubenites and the Gadites had large and very numerous 32
flocks, and when they saw that the land of Jazer and Gilead was good
grazing country, they came and said to Moses and Eleazar the priest 2
and to the leaders of the community, 'Ataroth, Dibon, Jazer, Nimrah, 3
Heshbon, Elealeh, Sebam,*b* Nebo, and Beon, the region which the 4
LORD has subdued before the advance of the Israelite community, is
grazing country, and our flocks are our livelihood. If', they said, 'we 5
have found favour with you, sir, then let this country be given to us as
our possession, and do not make us cross the Jordan.' Moses replied 6
to the Gadites and the Reubenites, 'Are your kinsmen to go into battle
while you stay here? How dare you discourage the Israelites from 7
crossing over to the land which the LORD has given them? This is 8
what your fathers did when I sent them out from Kadesh-barnea to
view the land. They went up as far as the gorge of Eshcol and viewed 9
the land, and on their return so discouraged the Israelites that they
would not enter the land which the LORD had given them. The LORD 10
became angry that day, and he solemnly swore: "Because they have not 11
followed me with their whole heart, none of the men who came out of
Egypt, from twenty years old and upwards, shall see the land which
I promised on oath to Abraham, Isaac and Jacob." This meant all 12
except Caleb son of Jephunneh the Kenizzite and Joshua son of Nun,
who followed the LORD with their whole heart. The LORD became 13
angry with Israel, and he made them wander in the wilderness for
forty years until that whole generation was dead which had done what
was wrong in his eyes. And now you are following in your fathers' 14
footsteps, a fresh brood of sinful men to fire the LORD's anger once
more against Israel; for if you refuse to follow him, he will again 15

[a] Heb. *word of uncertain mng.*   [b] Sibmah *in verse 38.*

225

abandon this whole people in the wilderness and you will be the cause of their destruction.'

16 Presently they came forward with this offer: 'We will build folds for
17 our sheep here and towns for our dependants. Then we can be drafted as a fighting force[a] to go at the head of the Israelites until we have brought them to the lands that will be theirs. Meanwhile our dependants can live in the walled towns, safe from the people of the
18 country. We will not return until every Israelite is settled in possession
19 of his patrimony; we will claim no share of the land with them over the Jordan and beyond, because our patrimony has already been allotted
20 to us east of the Jordan.' Moses answered, 'If you stand by your promise, if in the presence of the LORD you are drafted for battle,
21 and the whole draft crosses the Jordan in front of the LORD and remains
22 there until the LORD has driven out his enemies, and the land falls before him, then you may come back and be quit of your obligation to the LORD and to Israel; and this land shall be your possession in the
23 sight of the LORD. But I warn you, if you fail to do all this, you will have
24 sinned against the LORD, and your sin will find you out. So build towns for your dependants and folds for your sheep; but carry out your promise.'

25 The Gadites and Reubenites answered Moses, 'Sir, we are your
26 servants and will do as you command. Our dependants and wives, our
27 flocks and all our beasts shall remain here in the cities of Gilead; but we, all who have been drafted for active service with the LORD, will cross the river and fight, according to your command.'

28 Accordingly Moses gave these instructions to Eleazar the priest and Joshua son of Nun and to the heads of the families in the Israelite
29 tribes: 'If the Gadites and Reubenites, all who have been drafted for battle before the LORD, cross the Jordan with you, and if the land falls into your hands, then you shall give them Gilead for their possession.
30 But if, thus drafted, they fail to cross with you, then they shall acquire
31 land alongside you in Canaan.' The Gadites and Reubenites said in
32 response, 'Sir, the LORD has spoken, and we will obey. Once we have been drafted, we will cross over before the LORD into Canaan; then we shall have our patrimony here beyond the Jordan.'

33 So to the Gadites, the Reubenites, and half the tribe of Manasseh son of Joseph, Moses gave the kingdoms of Sihon king of the Amorites and Og king of Bashan, the whole land with its towns and the country
34, 35 round them. The Gadites built Dibon, Ataroth, Aroer, Atroth-
36 shophan, Jazer, Jogbehah, Beth-nimrah, and Beth-haran, all of them
37[b] walled towns with folds for their sheep. The Reubenites built Heshbon,
38 Elealeh, Kiriathaim, Nebo, Baal-meon (whose name was changed), and

[a] as...force: *so Sept.; Heb. obscure.* [b] *Verses 37, 38: cp. verse 3.*

Sibmah; these were the names they gave to the towns they built. The 39
sons of Machir son of Manasseh invaded Gilead, took it and drove out
the Amorite inhabitants; Moses then assigned Gilead to Machir son of 40
Manasseh, and he made his home there. Jair son of Manasseh attacked 41
and took the tent-villages of Ham*a* and called them Havvoth-jair.*b*
Nobah attacked and took Kenath and its villages and gave it his own 42
name, Nobah.

THESE ARE THE STAGES in the journey of the Israelites, when they 33
were led by Moses and Aaron in their tribal hosts out of Egypt. Moses 2
recorded their starting-points stage by stage as the LORD commanded
him. These are their stages from one starting-point to the next:
   The Israelites left Rameses on the fifteenth day of the first month, 3
the day after the Passover; they marched out defiantly in full view of
all the Egyptians, while the Egyptians were burying all the first-born 4
struck down by the LORD as a judgement on their gods.
   The Israelites left Rameses and encamped at Succoth.   5
   They left Succoth and encamped at Etham on the edge of the 6
wilderness.
   They left Etham, turned back near Pi-hahiroth*c* on the east of 7
Baal-zephon, and encamped before Migdol.
   They left Pi-hahiroth,*d* passed through the Sea into the wilderness, 8
marched for three days through the wilderness of Etham, and en-
camped at Marah.
   They left Marah and came to Elim, where there were twelve springs 9
of water and seventy palm-trees, and encamped there.
   They left Elim and encamped by the Red Sea.   10
   They left the Red Sea and encamped in the wilderness of Sin.   11
   They left the wilderness of Sin and encamped at Dophkah.*e*   12
   They left Dophkah and encamped at Alush.   13
   They left Alush and encamped at Rephidim, where there was no 14
water for the people to drink.
   They left Rephidim and encamped in the wilderness of Sinai.   15
   They left the wilderness of Sinai and encamped at Kibroth-hattaavah. 16
   They left Kibroth-hattaavah and encamped at Hazeroth.   17
   They left Hazeroth and encamped at Rithmah.   18
   They left Rithmah and encamped at Rimmon-parez.   19
   They left Rimmon-parez and encamped at Libnah.   20
   They left Libnah and encamped at Rissah.   21
   They left Rissah and encamped at Kehelathah.   22
   They left Kehelathah and encamped at Mount Shapher.   23

[a] *Prob. rdg.; Heb.* their tent-villages.   [b] *That is* Tent-villages of Jair.   [c] *See Exod.*
14. 2.   [d] *So Sam.; Heb.* They left from before Hahiroth.   [e] *Or, with Sept.,* Rophkah.

24 They left Mount Shapher and encamped at Haradah.
25 They left Haradah and encamped at Makheloth.
26 They left Makheloth and encamped at Tahath.
27 They left Tahath and encamped at Tarah.
28 They left Tarah and encamped at Mithcah.
29 They left Mithcah and encamped at Hashmonah.
30 They left Hashmonah and encamped at Moseroth.
31 They left Moseroth and encamped at Bene-jaakan.
32 They left Bene-jaakan and encamped at Hor-haggidgad.
33 They left Hor-haggidgad and encamped at Jotbathah.
34 They left Jotbathah and encamped at Ebronah.[a]
35 They left Ebronah and encamped at Ezion-geber.
36 They left Ezion-geber and encamped in the wilderness of Zin, that is of Kadesh.
37 They left Kadesh and encamped on Mount Hor on the frontier of Edom.
38 Aaron the priest went up Mount Hor at the command of the LORD and there he died, on the first day of the fifth month in the fortieth year
39 after the Israelites came out of Egypt; he was a hundred and twenty-three years old when he died there.
40 The Canaanite king of Arad, who lived in the Canaanite Negeb, heard that the Israelites were coming.
41 They left Mount Hor and encamped at Zalmonah.
42 They left Zalmonah and encamped at Punon.
43 They left Punon and encamped at Oboth.
44 They left Oboth and encamped at Iye-abarim on the frontier of Moab.
45 They left Iyim and encamped at Dibon-gad.
46 They left Dibon-gad and encamped at Almon-diblathaim.
47 They left Almon-diblathaim and encamped in the mountains of Abarim east of Nebo.
48 They left the mountains of Abarim and encamped in the lowlands of
49 Moab by the Jordan near Jericho. Their camp beside the Jordan extended from Beth-jeshimoth to Abel-shittim in the lowlands of
50 Moab. In the lowlands of Moab by the Jordan near Jericho the LORD
51 spoke to Moses and said, Speak to the Israelites in these words: You
52 will soon be crossing the Jordan to enter Canaan. You must drive out all its inhabitants as you advance, destroy all their carved figures and
53 their images of cast metal, and lay their hill-shrines in ruins. You must take possession of the land and settle there, for to you I have given the
54 land to occupy. You must divide it by lot among your families, each taking its own territory, the large family a large territory and the small

[a] *Or* Abronah.

family a small. It shall be assigned to them according to the fall of the lot, each tribe and family taking its own territory. If you do not drive 55 out the inhabitants of the land as you advance, any whom you leave in possession will become like a barbed hook in your eye and a thorn in your side. They shall continually dispute your possession of the land, and what I meant to do to them I will do to you. 56

The LORD spoke to Moses and said, Give these instructions to the 34 1, 2 Israelites: Soon you will be entering Canaan. This is the land assigned to you as a perpetual patrimony, the land of Canaan thus defined by its frontiers. Your southern border shall start from the wilderness of Zin, 3 where it marches with Edom, and run southwards from the end of the Dead Sea on its eastern side. It shall then turn from the south up the 4 ascent of Akrabbim and pass by Zin, and its southern limit shall be Kadesh-barnea. It shall proceed by Hazar-addar to Azmon and 5 from Azmon turn towards the Torrent of Egypt, and its limit shall be the sea. Your western frontier shall be the Great Sea and the seaboard; 6 this shall be your frontier to the west. This shall be your northern 7 frontier: you shall draw a line from the Great Sea to Mount Hor and 8 from Mount Hor to Lebo-hamath, and the limit of the frontier shall be Zedad. From there it shall run to Ziphron, and its limit shall be 9 Hazar-enan; this shall be your frontier to the north. To the east you 10 shall draw a line from Hazar-enan to Shepham; it shall run down from 11 Shepham to Riblah east of Ain, continuing until it strikes the ridge east of the sea of Kinnereth. The frontier shall then run down to the 12 Jordan and its limit shall be the Dead Sea. The land defined by these frontiers shall be your land.

Moses gave these instructions to the Israelites: This is the land which 13 you shall assign by lot, each taking your own territory; it is the land which the LORD has ordered to be given to nine tribes and a half tribe. For the Reubenites, the Gadites, and the half tribe of Manasseh have 14 already occupied their territories, family by family. These two and a 15 half tribes have received their territory here beyond the Jordan, east of Jericho, towards the sunrise.

The LORD spoke to Moses and said, These are the men who shall 16, 17 assign the land for you: Eleazar the priest and Joshua son of Nun. You shall also take one chief from each tribe to assign the land. 18 These are their names: 19

from the tribe of Judah: Caleb son of Jephunneh;
from the tribe of Simeon: Samuel son of Ammihud; 20
from the tribe of Benjamin: Elidad son of Kislon; 21
from the tribe of Dan: the chief Bukki son of Jogli; 22
from the Josephites: from Manasseh, the chief Hanniel son of 23
Ephod; and from Ephraim, the chief Kemuel son of Shiphtan; 24

25 from Zebulun: the chief Elizaphan son of Parnach;
26 from Issachar: the chief Paltiel son of Azzan;
27 from Asher: the chief Ahihud son of Shelomi;
28 from Naphtali: the chief Pedahel son of Ammihud.
29 These were the men whom the LORD appointed to assign the territories in the land of Canaan.

35 THE LORD SPOKE to Moses in the lowlands of Moab by the Jordan
2 near Jericho and said: Tell the Israelites to set aside towns in their patrimony as homes for the Levites, and give them also the common
3 land surrounding the towns. They shall live in the towns, and keep
4 their beasts, their herds, and all their livestock on the common land. The land of the towns which you give the Levites shall extend from the centre[a] of the town outwards for a thousand cubits in each direction.
5 Starting from the town the eastern boundary shall measure two thousand cubits, the southern two thousand, the western two thousand, and the northern two thousand, with the town in the centre. They shall have this as the common land adjoining their towns.
6 When you give the Levites their towns, six of them shall be cities of refuge, in which the homicide may take sanctuary; and you shall give
7 them forty-two other towns. The total number of towns to be given to
8 the Levites, each with its common land, is forty-eight. When you set aside these towns out of the territory of the Israelites, you shall allot more from the larger tribe and less from the smaller; each tribe shall give towns to the Levites in proportion to the patrimony assigned to it.
9, 10 The LORD spoke to Moses and said, Speak to the Israelites in these
11 words: You are crossing the Jordan to the land of Canaan. You shall designate certain cities to be places of refuge, in which the homicide
12 who has killed a man by accident may take sanctuary. These cities shall be places of refuge from the vengeance of the dead man's next-of-kin, so that the homicide shall not be put to death without standing his trial
13 before the community. The cities appointed as places of refuge shall be
14, 15 six in number, three east of the Jordan and three in Canaan. These six cities shall be places of refuge, so that any man who has taken life inadvertently, whether he be Israelite, resident alien, or temporary settler, may take sanctuary in one of them.
16 If the man strikes his victim with anything made of iron and he dies,
17 then he is a murderer: the murderer must be put to death. If a man has a stone in his hand capable of causing death and strikes another man
18 and he dies, he is a murderer: the murderer must be put to death. If a man has a wooden thing in his hand capable of causing death, and strikes another man and he dies, he is a murderer: the murderer must be put

[a] *Mng. of Heb. uncertain in context.*

to death. The dead man's next-of-kin shall put the murderer to death; 19
he shall put him to death because he had attacked his victim. If the 20
homicide sets upon a man openly of malice aforethought or aims a
missile at him of set purpose and he dies, or if in enmity he falls upon 21
him with his bare hands and he dies, then the assailant must be put to
death; he is a murderer. His next-of-kin shall put the murderer to
death because he had attacked his victim.

If he attacks a man on the spur of the moment, not being his enemy, 22
or hurls a missile at him not of set purpose, or if without looking he 23
throws a stone capable of causing death and it hits a man, then if the
man dies, provided he was not the man's enemy and was not harming
him of set purpose, the community shall judge between the striker and 24
the next-of-kin according to these rules. The community shall protect 25
the homicide from the vengeance of the kinsman and take him back to
the city of refuge where he had taken sanctuary. He must stay there
till the death of the duly anointed high priest. If the homicide ever goes 26
beyond the boundaries of the city where he has taken sanctuary, and the 27
next-of-kin finds him outside and kills him, then the next-of-kin shall
not be guilty of murder. The homicide must remain in the city of 28
refuge till the death of the high priest; after the death of the high priest
he may go back to his property. These shall be legal precedents for you 29
for all time wherever you live.

The homicide shall be put to death as a murderer only on the 30
testimony of witnesses; the testimony of a single witness shall not be
enough to bring him to his death. You shall not accept payment for the 31
life of a homicide guilty of a capital offence; he must be put to death.
You shall not accept a payment from a man who has taken sanctuary in 32
a city of refuge, allowing him to go back before the death of the high
priest and live at large. You shall not defile your land by bloodshed. 33
Blood defiles the land, and expiation cannot be made on behalf of the
land for blood shed on it except by the blood of the man that shed it.
You shall not make the land which you inhabit unclean, the land in 34
which I dwell; for I, the LORD, dwell among the Israelites.

THE HEADS of the fathers' families of Gilead son of Machir, son of 36
Manasseh, one of the families of the sons of Joseph, approached Moses
and the chiefs, heads of families in Israel, and addressed them. 'Sir,' 2
they said, 'the LORD commanded you to distribute the land by lot to
the Israelites, and you were also commanded to give the patrimony of
our brother Zelophehad to his daughters. Now if any of them shall be 3
married to a husband from another Israelite tribe, her patrimony will
be lost to the patrimony of our fathers and be added to that of the tribe
into which she is married, and so part of our allotted patrimony will be

4 lost. Then, when the jubilee year comes round in Israel, her patrimony would be added to the patrimony of the tribe into which she is married, and it would be permanently lost to the patrimony of our fathers' tribe.'

5 So Moses, instructed by the LORD, gave the Israelites this ruling:

6 'The tribe of the sons of Joseph is right. This is the LORD's command for the daughters of Zelophehad: They may marry whom they please,

7 but only within a family of their father's tribe. No patrimony in Israel shall pass from tribe to tribe, but every Israelite shall retain his father's

8 patrimony. Any woman of an Israelite tribe who is an heiress may marry a man from any family in her father's tribe. Thus the Israelites

9 shall retain each one the patrimony of his forefathers. No patrimony shall pass from one tribe to another, but every tribe in Israel shall retain its own patrimony.'

10 The daughters of Zelophehad acted in accordance with the LORD's

11 command to Moses; Mahlah, Tirzah, Hoglah, Milcah and Noah, the daughters of Zelophehad, married sons of their father's brothers.

12 They married within the families of the sons of Manasseh son of Joseph, and their patrimony remained with the tribe of their father's family.

13 These are the commandments and the decrees which the LORD issued to the Israelites through Moses in the lowlands of Moab by the Jordan near Jericho.

DEUTERONOMY

Primary charge of Moses to the people

THESE ARE THE WORDS that Moses spoke to all Israel 1
in Transjordan, in the wilderness, that is to say in the Arabah
opposite Suph, between Paran on the one side and Tophel,
Laban, Hazeroth, and Dizahab on the other. (The journey from Horeb 2
through the hill-country of Seir to Kadesh-barnea takes eleven days.)
On the first day of the eleventh month of the fortieth year, after the 3-4
defeat of Sihon king of the Amorites who ruled in Heshbon, and the
defeat at Edrei of Og king of Bashan who ruled in Ashtaroth, Moses
repeated to the Israelites all the commands that the LORD had given
him for them. It was in Transjordan, in Moab, that Moses resolved to 5
promulgate this law. These were his words: The LORD our God spoke 6
to us at Horeb and said, 'You have stayed on this mountain long
enough; go now, make for the hill-country of the Amorites, and pass on 7
to all their neighbours in the Arabah, in the hill-country, in the Shephelah, in the Negeb, and on the coast, in short, all Canaan and the
Lebanon as far as the great river, the Euphrates. I have laid the land 8
open before you; go in and occupy it, the land which the LORD swore
to give to your forefathers Abraham, Isaac and Jacob, and to their
descendants after them.'
At that time I said to you, 'You are a burden too heavy for me to 9
carry unaided. The LORD your God has increased you so that today you 10
are as numerous as the stars in the sky. May the LORD the God of your 11
fathers increase your number a thousand times and may he bless you as
he promised. How can I bear unaided the heavy burden you are to me, 12
and put up with your complaints? Choose men of wisdom, under- 13
standing, and repute for each of your tribes, and I will set them in
authority over you.' Your answer was, 'What you have told us to do is 14
right.' So I took*a* men of wisdom and repute and set them in authority 15
over you, some as commanders over units of a thousand, of a hundred,
of fifty or of ten, and others as officers, for each of your tribes. And at 16
that time I gave your judges this command: 'You are to hear the cases
that arise among your kinsmen and judge fairly between man and man,
whether fellow-countryman or resident alien. You must be impartial 17
and listen to high and low alike: have no fear of man, for judgement

[a] *So Sept.; Heb. adds* the heads of your tribes.

belongs to God. If any case is too difficult for you, bring it before me
18 and I will hear it.' At the same time I instructed you in all these duties.
19   Then we set out from Horeb, in obedience to the orders of the LORD
our God, and marched through that vast and terrible wilderness, as you
found it to be, on the way to the hill-country of the Amorites; and so
20 we came to Kadesh-barnea. Then I said to you, 'You have reached the
21 hill-country of the Amorites which the LORD our God is giving us. The
LORD your God has indeed now laid the land open before you. Go
forward and occupy it in fulfilment of the promise which the LORD the
22 God of your fathers made you; do not be discouraged or afraid.' But
you all came to me and said, 'Let us send men ahead to spy out the
country and report back to us about the route we should take and the
23 cities we shall find.' I approved this plan and picked twelve of you, one
24 from each tribe. They set out and made their way up into the hill-
25 country as far as the gorge of Eshcol, which they explored. They took
samples of the fruit of the country and brought them back to us, and
made their report: 'It is a rich land that the LORD our God is giving us.'
26   But you refused to go up and rebelled against the command of the
27 LORD your God. You muttered treason in your tents and said, 'It was
because the LORD hated us that he brought us out of Egypt to hand us
28 over to the Amorites to be wiped out. What shall we find up there?
Our kinsmen have discouraged us by their report of a people bigger
and taller than we are, and of great cities with fortifications towering to
the sky. And they told us they saw there the descendants of the
Anakim.'[a]
29   Then I said to you, 'You must not dread them nor be afraid of them.
30 The LORD your God who goes at your head will fight for you and he
31 will do again what you saw him do for you in Egypt and in the wilderness. You saw there how the LORD your God carried you all the way
32 to this place, as a father carries his son.' In spite of this you did not
33 trust the LORD your God, who went ahead on the journey to find a
place for your camp. He went in fire by night to show you the way you
should take, and in a cloud by day.
34   When the LORD heard your complaints, he was indignant and
35 solemnly swore: 'Not one of these men, this wicked generation, shall
36 see the rich land which I swore to give your forefathers, except Caleb
son of Jephunneh. He shall see it, and to him and his descendants I will
give the land on which he has set foot, because he followed the LORD
37 with his whole heart.' On your account the LORD was angry with me
38 also and said, 'You yourself shall never enter it, but Joshua son of
Nun, who is in attendance on you, shall enter it. Encourage him, for he
39 shall put Israel in possession of that land. Your dependants who, you

[a] the descendants...Anakim: *or* the tall men.

234

thought, would become spoils of war, and your children who do not yet know good and evil, they shall enter; I will give it to them, and they shall occupy it. You must turn back and set out for the wilderness by 40 way of the Red Sea.'*a*

You answered me, 'We have sinned against the LORD; we will now 41 go up and attack just as the LORD our God commanded us.' And each of you fastened on his weapons, thinking it an easy thing to invade the hill-country. But the LORD said to me, 'Tell them not to go up and not 42 to fight; for I will not be with them, and their enemies will defeat them.' And I told you this, but you did not listen; you rebelled against the 43 LORD's command and defiantly went up to the hill-country. The 44 Amorites living in the hills came out against you and like bees they chased you; they crushed you at Hormah in Seir. Then you came back 45 and wept before the LORD, but he would not hear you or listen to you. That is why you remained in Kadesh as long as you did.   46

So we turned and set out for the wilderness by way of the Red Sea 2 as the LORD had told me we must do, and we spent many days marching round the hill-country of Seir. Then the LORD said to me, 'You have 2, 3 been long enough marching round these hills; turn towards the north. And give the people this charge: "You are about to go through the 4 territory of your kinsmen the descendants of Esau who live in Seir. Although they are afraid of you, be on your guard and do not provoke 5 them; for I shall not give you any of their land, not so much as a foot's-breadth: I have given the hill-country of Seir to Esau as a possession. You may purchase food from them for silver, and eat it, and you may 6 buy*b* water to drink."' The LORD your God has blessed you in every- 7 thing you have undertaken; he has watched your journey through this great wilderness; these forty years the LORD your God has been with you and you have gone short of nothing. So we went on past our kins- 8 men, the descendants of Esau who live in Seir, and along*c* the road of the Arabah which comes from Elath and Ezion-geber, and we turned and followed the road to the wilderness of Moab. There the LORD said 9 to me, 'Do not harass the Moabites nor provoke them to battle, for I will not give you any of their land as a possession. I have given Ar to the descendants of Lot as a possession.' (The Emim once lived there— 10 a great and numerous people, as tall as the Anakim. The Rephaim also 11 were reckoned as Anakim; but the Moabites called them Emim. The 12 Horites lived in Seir at one time, but the descendants of Esau occupied their territory: they destroyed them as they advanced and then settled in the land instead of them, just as Israel did in their own territory which the LORD gave them.) 'Come now, cross the gorge of the Zared.' 13 So we went across. The journey from Kadesh-barnea to the crossing 14

[a] *Or* the Sea of Reeds. [b] *Or* dig for. [c] *So Sept.; Heb.* past.

of the Zared took us thirty-eight years, until the whole generation of
fighting men had passed away as the LORD had sworn that they would.
15 The LORD's hand was raised against them, and he rooted them out of
the camp to the last man.

16, 17 When the last of the fighting men among the people had died, the
18 LORD spoke to me, 'Today', he said, 'you are to cross by Ar*a* which
19 lies on the frontier of Moab, and when you reach the territory of the
Ammonites, you must not harass them or provoke them to battle, for
I will not give you any Ammonite land as a possession; I have assigned
20 it to the descendants of Lot.' (This also is reckoned as the territory of
the Rephaim, who lived there at one time; but the Ammonites called
21 them Zamzummim. They were a great and numerous people, as tall as
the Anakim, but the LORD destroyed them as the Ammonites advanced
22 and occupied their territory instead of them, just as he had done for the
descendants of Esau who lived in Seir. As they advanced, he destroyed
the Horites so that they occupied their territory and took possession
23 instead of them: so it is to this day. It was Caphtorites from Caphtor
who destroyed the Avvim who lived in the hamlets near Gaza, and
24 settled in the land instead of them.) 'Come, set out on your journey
and cross the gorge of the Arnon, for I have put Sihon the Amorite,
king of Heshbon, and his territory into your hands. Begin to occupy it
25 and provoke him to battle. Today I will begin to put the fear and dread
of you upon all the peoples under heaven; if they so much as hear a
rumour of you, they will quake and tremble before you.'

26 Then I sent messengers from the wilderness of Kedemoth to Sihon
27 king of Heshbon with these peaceful overtures: 'Grant us passage
through your country by the highway: we will keep to the highway,
28 trespassing neither to right nor to left, and we will pay you the full
29 price for the food we eat and the water we drink. The descendants of
Esau who live in Seir granted us passage, and so did the Moabites who
live in Ar. We will simply pass through your land on foot, until we cross
30 the Jordan to the land which the LORD our God is giving us.' But Sihon
king of Heshbon refused to grant us passage; for the LORD your God
had made him stubborn and obstinate, in order that he and his land
31 might become subject to you, as it still is. So the LORD said to me,
'Come, I have begun to deliver Sihon and his territory into your hands.
32 Begin now to occupy his land.' Then Sihon with all his people came
33 out to meet us in battle at Jahaz, and the LORD our God delivered him
34 into our hands; we killed him with his sons and all his people. We
captured all his cities at that time and put to death everyone in the cities,
35 men, women, and dependants; we left no survivor. We took the cattle as
36 booty and plundered the cities we captured. From Aroer on the edge

[a] by Ar: *or* the gully.

of the gorge of the Arnon and the level land of the gorge, as far as Gilead, no city walls were too lofty for us; the LORD our God laid them all open to us. But you avoided the territory of the Ammonites, both the 37 parts along the gorge of the Jabbok and their cities in the hills, thus fulfilling all*a* that the LORD our God had commanded.

Next we turned and advanced along the road to Bashan. Og king of 3 Bashan, with all his people, came out against us at Edrei. The LORD 2 said to me, 'Do not be afraid of him, for I have delivered him into your hands, with all his people and his land. Deal with him as you dealt with Sihon the king of the Amorites who lived in Heshbon.' So the LORD our 3 God also delivered Og king of Bashan into our hands, with all his people. We slaughtered them and left no survivor, and at the same time 4 we captured all his cities; there was not a single town that we did not take from them. In all we took sixty cities, the whole region of Argob, the kingdom of Og in Bashan; all these were fortified cities with high 5 walls, gates, and bars, apart from a great many open settlements. Thus 6 we put to death all the men, women, and dependants in every city, as we did to Sihon king of Heshbon. All the cattle and the spoil from the cities 7 we took as booty for ourselves.

At that time we took from these two Amorite kings in Transjordan 8 the territory that runs from the gorge of the Arnon to Mount Hermon (the mountain that the Sidonians call Sirion and the Amorites Senir), 9 all the cities of the tableland, and the whole of Gilead and Bashan as far 10 as Salcah and Edrei, cities in the kingdom of Og in Bashan. (Only Og 11 king of Bashan remained as the sole survivor of the Rephaim. His sarcophagus of basalt*b* was nearly fourteen feet long and six feet wide,*c* and it may still be seen in the Ammonite city of Rabbah.)

At that time, when we occupied this territory, I assigned to the 12 Reubenites and Gadites the land beyond Aroer on the gorge of the Arnon and half the hill-country of Gilead with its towns. The rest of 13 Gilead and the whole of Bashan the kingdom of Og, all the region of Argob, I assigned to half the tribe of Manasseh. (All Bashan used to be called the land of the Rephaim. Jair son of Manasseh took all the region 14 of Argob as far as the Geshurite and Maacathite border. There are tent-villages in Bashan still called by his name, Havvoth-jair.*d*) To Machir 15 I assigned Gilead, and to the Reubenites and the Gadites I assigned 16 land from Gilead to the gorge of the Arnon, that is to the middle of the gorge; and its territory ran*e f* to the gorge of the Jabbok, the Ammonite frontier, and included the Arabah, with the Jordan and adjacent land, 17

[*a*] *So Sept.; Heb.* and all.   [*b*] *Or* iron.   [*c*] *Lit.* nine cubits long and four cubits wide by the common standard.   [*d*] *That is* Tent-villages of Jair.   [*e*] that is...ran: *or* including the bed of the gorge and the adjacent strip of land...   [*f*] and its territory ran: *prob. rdg.; Heb.* and territory and...

from Kinnereth to the Sea of the Arabah, that is the Dead Sea, below
18 the watershed of Pisgah on the east. At that time I gave you this
command: 'The LORD your God has given you this land to occupy;
let all your fighting men be drafted and cross at the head of their fellow-
19 Israelites. Only your wives and dependants and your livestock—I know
you have much livestock—shall stay in the towns I have given you.
20 This you shall do until the LORD gives your kinsmen security as he has
given it to you, and until they too occupy the land which the LORD your
God is giving them on the other side of the Jordan; then you may
return to the possession which I have given you, every man to his own.'
21 At that time also I gave Joshua this charge: 'You have seen with your
own eyes all that the LORD your God has done to these two kings; he will
22 do the same to all the kingdoms into which you will cross over. Do not
be afraid of them, for the LORD your God himself will fight for you.'
23, 24 At that same time I pleaded with the LORD, 'O Lord GOD, thou hast
begun to show to thy servant thy greatness and thy strong hand: what
god is there in heaven or on earth who can match thy works and mighty
25 deeds? Let me cross over and see that rich land which lies beyond the
26 Jordan, and the fine hill-country and the Lebanon.' But because of you
the LORD brushed me aside and would not listen. 'Enough!' he
27 answered. 'Say no more about this. Go to the top of Pisgah and look
west and north, south and east; look well at what you see, for you shall
28 not cross this river Jordan. Give Joshua his commission, encourage him
and strengthen him; for he will lead this people across, and he will put
them in possession of the land you see before you.'
29 So we remained in the valley opposite Beth-peor.

4 NOW, ISRAEL, LISTEN to the statutes and laws which I am teaching
you, and obey them; then you will live, and go in and occupy the land
2 which the LORD the God of your fathers is giving you. You must not
add anything to my charge, nor take anything away from it. You must
carry out all the commandments of the LORD your God which I lay
upon you.
3 You saw with your own eyes what the LORD did at Baal-peor; the
LORD your God destroyed among you every man who went over to the
4 Baal of Peor, but you who held fast to the LORD your God are all alive
5 today. I have taught you statutes and laws, as the LORD my God
commanded me; these you must duly keep when you enter the land
6 and occupy it. You must observe them carefully, and thereby you will
display your wisdom and understanding to other peoples. When they
hear about these statutes, they will say, 'What a wise and understanding
7 people this great nation is!' What great nation has a god*a* close at hand

[a] Or gods.

as the LORD our God is close to us whenever we call to him? What great 8
nation is there whose statutes and laws are just, as is all this law which
I am setting before you today? But take good care: be on the watch not 9
to forget the things that you have seen with your own eyes, and do not
let them pass from your minds as long as you live, but teach them to
your sons and to your sons' sons. You must never forget that day when 10
you stood before the LORD your God at Horeb, and the LORD said to
me, 'Assemble the people before me; I will make them hear my words
and they shall learn to fear me all their lives on earth, and they shall
teach their sons to do so.' Then you came near and stood at the foot of 11
the mountain. The mountain was ablaze with fire to the very skies:
there was darkness, cloud, and thick mist. When the LORD spoke to you 12
from the fire you heard a voice speaking, but you saw no figure; there
was only a voice. He announced the terms of his covenant to you, 13
bidding you observe the Ten Words,^a and he wrote them on two
tablets of stone. At that time the LORD charged me to teach you statutes 14
and laws which you should observe in the land into which you are
passing to occupy it.

On the day when the LORD spoke to you out of the fire on Horeb, you 15
saw no figure of any kind; so take good care not to fall into the 16
degrading practice of making figures carved in relief, in the form of
a man or a woman, or of any animal on earth or bird that flies in the air, 17
or of any reptile on the ground or fish in the waters under the earth. 18
Nor must you raise your eyes to the heavens and look up to the sun, the 19
moon, and the stars, all the host of heaven, and be led on to bow down
to them and worship them; the LORD your God assigned these for the
worship of^b the various peoples under heaven. But you are the people 20
whom the LORD brought out of Egypt, from the smelting-furnace, and
took for his own possession, as you are to this day. The LORD was angry 21
with me on your account and swore that I should not cross the Jordan
nor enter the rich land which the LORD your God is giving you for
your possession. I shall die in this country; I shall not cross the Jordan, 22
but you are about to cross and occupy that rich land. Be careful not to 23
forget the covenant which the LORD your God made with you, and do
not make yourselves a carved figure of anything which the LORD your
God has forbidden. For the LORD your God is a devouring fire, a 24
jealous god.

When you have children and grandchildren and grow old in the land, 25
if you then fall into the degrading practice of making any kind of
carved figure, doing what is wrong in the eyes of the LORD your God
and provoking him to anger, I summon heaven and earth to witness 26
against you this day: you will soon vanish from the land which you are

[a] Or Ten Commandments. [b] assigned...worship of: or created these for.

to occupy after crossing the Jordan. You will not live long in it; you
27 will be swept away. The LORD will disperse you among the peoples,
and you will be left few in number among the nations to which the
28 LORD will lead you. There you will worship gods made by human hands
out of wood and stone, gods that can neither see nor hear, neither eat
29 nor smell. But if from there you seek the LORD your God, you will find
30 him, if indeed you search with all your heart and soul. When you are in
distress and all these things come upon you, you will in days to come
31 turn back to the LORD your God and obey him. The LORD your God is
a merciful god; he will never fail you nor destroy you, nor will he
forget the covenant guaranteed by oath with your forefathers.

32   Search into days gone by, long before your time, beginning at the
day when God created man on earth; search from one end of heaven to
the other, and ask if any deed as mighty as this has been seen or
33 heard. Did any people ever hear the voice of God speaking out of the
34 fire, as you heard it, and remain alive? Or did ever a god attempt to
come and take a nation for himself away from another nation, with a
challenge, and with signs, portents, and wars, with a strong hand and
an outstretched arm, and with great deeds of terror, as the LORD your
35 God did for you in Egypt in the sight of you all? You have had sure
36 proof that the LORD is God; there is no other. From heaven he let you
hear his voice for your instruction, and on earth he let you see his great
37 fire, and out of the fire you heard his words. Because he loved your
fathers and chose their children after them,[a] he in his own person
38 brought you out of Egypt by his great strength, so that he might drive
out before you nations greater and more powerful than you and bring
39 you in to give you their land in possession as it is today. This day, then,
be sure and take to heart that the LORD is God in heaven above and on
40 earth below; there is no other. You shall keep his statutes and his
commandments which I give you today; then all will be well with you
and with your children after you, and you will live long in the land
which the LORD your God is giving you for all time.

41,42   Then Moses set apart three cities in the east, in Transjordan, to be
places of refuge for the homicide who kills a man without intent, with
no previous enmity between them. If he takes sanctuary in one of these
43 cities his life shall be safe. The cities were: Bezer-in-the-Wilderness
on the tableland for the Reubenites, Ramoth in Gilead for the Gadites,
and Golan in Bashan for the Manassites.

44,45   This is the law which Moses laid down for the Israelites. These are
the precepts, the statutes, and the laws which Moses proclaimed to the
46 Israelites, when they came out of Egypt and were in Transjordan in
the valley opposite Beth-peor in the land of Sihon king of the Amorites

[a] *So Sept.; Heb.* his children after him.

who lived in Heshbon. Moses and the Israelites had defeated him when they came out of Egypt and had occupied his territory and the territory 47 of Og king of Bashan, the two Amorite kings in the east, in Transjordan. The territory ran from Aroer on the gorge of the Arnon to Mount 48 Sirion,[a] that is Hermon; and all the Arabah on the east, in Trans- 49 jordan, as far as the Sea of the Arabah below the watershed of Pisgah.

Moses summoned all Israel and said to them: Listen, O Israel, to 5 the statutes and the laws which I proclaim in your hearing today. Learn them and be careful to observe them. The LORD our God made a 2 covenant with us at Horeb. It was not with our forefathers that the LORD 3 made this covenant, but with us, all of us who are alive and are here this day. The LORD spoke with you face to face on the mountain out of 4 the fire. I stood between the LORD and you at that time to report the 5 words[b] of the LORD; for you were afraid of the fire and did not go up the mountain. And the LORD said:

I am the LORD your God who brought you out of Egypt, out of the 6 land of slavery.

You shall have no other god[c] to set against me. 7

You shall not make a carved image for yourself nor[d] the likeness of 8 anything in the heavens above, or on the earth below, or in the waters under the earth.

You shall not bow down to them or worship[e] them; for I, the LORD 9 your God, am a jealous god. I punish the children for the sins of the fathers to the third and fourth generations of those who hate me. But 10 I keep faith with thousands, with[f] those who love me and keep my commandments.

You shall not make wrong use of the name of the LORD your God; 11 the LORD will not leave unpunished the man who misuses his name.

Keep the sabbath day holy as the LORD your God commanded you. 12 You have six days to labour and do all your work. But the seventh day 13, 14 is a sabbath of the LORD your God; that day you shall not do any work, neither you, your son or your daughter, your slave or your slave-girl, your ox, your ass, or any of your cattle, nor the alien within your gates, so that your slaves and slave-girls may rest as you do. Remember that 15 you were slaves in Egypt and the LORD your God brought you out with a strong hand and an outstretched arm, and for that reason the LORD your God commanded you to keep the sabbath day.

Honour your father and your mother, as the LORD your God 16 commanded you, so that you may live long, and that it may be well with you in the land which the LORD your God is giving you.

[a] *So Pesh., cp. 3. 9; Heb.* Sion. [b] *So Sam.; Heb.* word. [c] *Or* gods. [d] nor: *so many MSS.; others om.* [e] *Or* or be led to worship... [f] with...with: *or* for a thousand generations with...

17 You shall not commit murder.

18 You shall not commit adultery.

19 You shall not steal.

20 You shall not give false evidence against your neighbour.

21 You shall not covet your neighbour's wife; you shall not set your heart on your neighbour's house, his land, his slave, his slave-girl, his ox, his ass, or on anything that belongs to him.

22 These Commandments the LORD spoke in a great voice to your whole assembly on the mountain out of the fire, the cloud, and the thick mist; then he said no more. He wrote them on two tablets of

23 stone and gave them to me. When you heard the voice out of the darkness, while the mountain was ablaze with fire, all the heads of your

24 tribes and the elders came to me and said, 'The LORD our God has shown us his glory and his greatness, and we have heard his voice out of the fire: today we have seen that God may speak with men and they

25 may still live. Why should we now risk death? for this great fire will devour us. If we hear the voice of the LORD our God again, we shall die.

26 Is there any mortal man who has heard the voice of the living God

27 speaking out of the fire, as we have, and has lived? You shall go near and listen to all that the LORD our God says, and report to us all that the LORD our God has said to you; we will listen and obey.'

28 When the LORD heard these words which you spoke to me, he said, 'I have heard what this people has said to you; every word they have

29 spoken is right. Would that they always had such a heart to fear me and to observe all my commandments, so that all might be well with

30 them and their children for ever! Go, and tell them to return to their

31 tents, but you yourself stand here beside me, and I will set forth to you all the commandments, the statutes and laws which you shall teach them to observe in the land which I am giving them to occupy.'

32 You shall be careful to do as the LORD your God has commanded

33 you; do not turn from it to right or to left. You must conform to all the LORD your God commands you, if you would live and prosper and remain long in the land you are to occupy.

6 These are the commandments, statutes, and laws which the LORD your God commanded me to teach you to observe in the land into which

2 you are passing to occupy it, a land flowing with milk and honey,*a* so that you may fear the LORD your God and keep all his statutes and commandments which I am giving you, both you, your sons, and your

3 descendants all your lives, and so that you may live long. If you listen, O Israel, and are careful to observe them, you will prosper and increase greatly as the LORD the God of your fathers promised you.

4, 5 Hear, O Israel, the LORD*b* is our God, one LORD, and you must love

[a] a land...honey: *transposed from verse 3.*   [b] *See note on Exod. 3. 15.*

the LORD your God with all your heart and soul and strength. These 6
commandments which I give you this day are to be kept in your heart;
you shall repeat them to your sons, and speak of them indoors and out 7
of doors, when you lie down and when you rise. Bind them as a sign on 8
the hand and wear them as a phylactery on the forehead; write them 9
up on the door-posts of your houses and on your gates.

The LORD your God will bring you into the land which he swore to 10
your forefathers Abraham, Isaac and Jacob that he would give you, a
land of great and fine cities which you did not build, houses full of good 11
things which you did not provide, rock-hewn cisterns which you did
not hew, and vineyards and olive-groves which you did not plant. When
you eat your fill there, be careful not to forget the LORD who brought 12
you out of Egypt, out of the land of slavery. You shall fear the LORD 13
your God, serve him alone and take your oaths in his name. You must 14
not follow other gods, gods of the nations that are around you; if you 15
do, the LORD your God who is in your midst will be angry with you,
and he will sweep you away off the face of the earth, for the LORD your
God is a jealous god.

You must not challenge the LORD your God as you challenged him 16
at Massah.[a] You must diligently keep the commandments of the LORD 17
your God as well as the precepts and statutes which he gave you. You 18
must do what is right and good in the LORD's eyes so that all may go
well with you, and you may enter and occupy the rich land which the
LORD promised by oath to your forefathers; then you shall drive out all 19
your enemies before you, as the LORD promised.

When your son asks you in time to come, 'What is the meaning of 20
the precepts, statutes, and laws which the LORD our God gave you?', you 21
shall say to him, 'We were Pharaoh's slaves in Egypt, and the LORD
brought us out of Egypt with his strong hand, sending great disasters, 22
signs, and portents against the Egyptians and against Pharaoh and all
his family, as we saw for ourselves. But he led us out from there to 23
bring us into the land and give it to us as he had promised to our forefathers. The LORD commanded us to observe all these statutes and to 24
fear the LORD our God; it will be for our own good at all times, and he
will continue to preserve our lives. It will be counted to our credit if 25
we keep all these commandments in the sight of the LORD our God, as
he has bidden us.'

WHEN THE LORD YOUR GOD brings you into the land which you 7
are entering to occupy and drives out many nations before you—
Hittites, Girgashites, Amorites, Canaanites, Perizzites, Hivites, and

[a] *That is* Challenge.

2 Jebusites, seven nations more numerous and powerful than you—when the LORD your God delivers them into your power and you defeat them, you must put them to death. You must not make a treaty with
3 them or spare them. You must not intermarry with them, neither giving your daughters to their sons nor taking their daughters for your sons;
4 if you do, they will draw your sons away from the LORD*a* and make them worship other gods. Then the LORD will be angry with you and
5 will quickly destroy you. But this is what you must do to them: pull down their altars, break their sacred pillars, hack down their sacred
6 poles*b* and destroy their idols by fire, for you are a people holy to the LORD your God; the LORD your God chose you out of all nations on earth to be his special possession.

7 It was not because you were more numerous than any other nation that the LORD cared for you and chose you, for you were the smallest of
8 all nations; it was because the LORD loved you and stood by his oath to your forefathers, that he brought you out with his strong hand and redeemed you from the land of slavery, from the power of Pharaoh king
9 of Egypt. Know then that the LORD your God is God, the faithful God; with those who love him and keep his commandments he keeps covenant
10 and faith for a thousand generations, but those who defy him and show their hatred for him he repays with destruction: he will not be slow to requite any who so hate him.

11 You are to observe these commandments, statutes, and laws which I give you this day, and keep them.

12 If you listen to these laws and are careful to observe them, then the LORD your God will observe the sworn covenant he made with your
13 forefathers and will keep faith with you. He will love you, bless you and cause you to increase. He will bless the fruit of your body and the fruit of your land, your corn and new wine and oil, the offspring of your herds, and of your lambing flocks, in the land which he swore to your
14 forefathers to give you. You shall be blessed above every other nation; neither among your people nor among your cattle shall there be
15 impotent male or barren female. The LORD will take away all sickness from you; he will not bring upon you any of the foul diseases of Egypt
16 which you know so well, but will bring them upon all your enemies. You shall devour all the nations which the LORD your God is giving over to you. Spare none of them, and do not worship their gods; that is the snare which awaits you.

17 You may say to yourselves, 'These nations outnumber us, how can
18 we drive them out?' But you need have no fear of them; only remember
19 what the LORD your God did to Pharaoh and to the whole of Egypt, the great challenge which you yourselves witnessed, the signs and portents,

[a] *Prob. rdg.; Heb.* me. [b] sacred poles: *Heb.* asherim.

244

the strong hand and the outstretched arm by which the LORD your God brought you out. He will deal thus with all the nations of whom you are afraid. He will also spread panic among them until all who are left or 20 have gone into hiding perish before you. Be in no dread of them, for 21 the LORD your God is in your midst, a great and terrible god. He will 22 drive out these nations before you little by little. You will not be able to exterminate them quickly, for fear the wild beasts become too numerous for you. The LORD your God will deliver these nations over to you and 23 will throw them into great panic in the hour of their destruction. He 24 will put their kings into your hands, and you shall wipe out their name from under heaven. When you destroy them, no man will be able to withstand you. Their idols you shall destroy by fire; you must not covet 25 the silver and gold on them and take it for yourselves, or you will be ensnared by it; for these things are abominable to the LORD your God. You must not introduce any abominable idol into your houses and thus 26 bring yourselves under solemn ban along with it. You shall hold it loathsome and abominable, for it is forbidden under the ban.

You must carefully observe everything that I command you this day 8 so that you may live and increase and may enter and occupy the land which the LORD promised to your forefathers upon oath. You must 2 remember all that road by which the LORD your God has led you these forty years in the wilderness to humble you, to test you and to discover whether or no it was in your heart to keep his commandments. He 3 humbled you and made you hungry; then he fed you on manna which neither you nor your fathers had known before, to teach you that man cannot live on bread alone but lives by every word that comes from the mouth of the LORD. The clothes on your backs did not wear out nor did 4 your feet swell all these forty years. Take this lesson to heart: that the 5 LORD your God was disciplining you as a father disciplines his son; and 6 keep the commandments of the LORD your God, conforming to his ways and fearing him. For the LORD your God is bringing you to a rich land, 7 a land of streams, of springs and underground waters gushing out in hill and valley, a land of wheat and barley, of vines, fig-trees, and pome- 8 granates, a land of olives, oil, and honey. It is a land where you will never 9 live in poverty nor want for anything, a land whose stones are iron-ore and from whose hills you will dig copper. You will have plenty to eat and 10 will bless the LORD your God for the rich land that he has given you.

Take care not to forget the LORD your God and do not fail to keep 11 his commandments, laws, and statutes which I give you this day. When 12 you have plenty to eat and live in fine houses of your own building, when your herds and flocks increase, and your silver and gold and all 13 your possessions increase too, do not become proud and forget the 14 LORD your God who brought you out of Egypt, out of the land of

15 slavery; he led you through the vast and terrible wilderness infested
with poisonous snakes and scorpions, a thirsty, waterless land, where
16 he caused water to flow from the hard rock; he fed you in the wilderness
on manna which your fathers did not know, to humble you and test
17 you, and in the end to make you prosper. Nor must you say to yourselves, 'My own strength and energy have gained me this wealth',
18 but remember the LORD your God; it is he that gives you strength to
become prosperous, so fulfilling the covenant guaranteed by oath with
your forefathers, as he is doing now.

19 If you forget the LORD your God and adhere to other gods, worshipping them and bowing down to them, I give you a solemn warning
20 this day that you will certainly be destroyed. You will be destroyed
because of your disobedience to the LORD your God, as surely as were
the nations whom the LORD destroyed at your coming.

9 Listen, O Israel; this day you will cross the Jordan to occupy the
territory of nations greater and more powerful than you, and great
2 cities with walls towering to the sky. They are great and tall people,
the descendants of the Anakim, of whom you know, for you have
3 heard it said, 'Who can withstand the sons of Anak?' Know then this
day that it is the LORD your God himself who goes at your head as a
devouring fire; he will subdue them and destroy them at your approach;
you shall drive them out and overwhelm them, as he promised you.

4 When the LORD your God drives them out before you, do not say
to yourselves, 'It is because of my own merit that the LORD has brought
5 me in to occupy this land.'[a] It is not because of your merit or your
integrity that you are entering their land to occupy it; it is because of
the wickedness of these nations that the LORD your God is driving them
out before you, and to fulfil the promise which the LORD made to your
forefathers, Abraham, Isaac and Jacob.

6 Know then that it is not because of any merit of yours that the LORD
your God is giving you this rich land to occupy; indeed, you are a
7 stubborn people. Remember and never forget, how you angered the
LORD your God in the wilderness: from the day when you left Egypt
8 until you came to this place you have defied the LORD. In Horeb you
roused the LORD's anger, and the LORD in his wrath was on the point of
9 destroying you. When I went up the mountain to receive the tablets of
stone, the tablets of the covenant which the LORD made with you,
I remained on the mountain forty days and forty nights without food or
10 drink. Then the LORD gave me the two tablets of stone written with
the finger of God, and upon them were all the words the LORD spoke to
you out of the fire, upon the mountain on the day of the assembly.

[a] *So Sept.; Heb. adds* and because of the wickedness of these nations the LORD is driving
them out before you.

At the end of forty days and forty nights the LORD gave me the two 11
tablets of stone, the tablets of the covenant, and said to me, 'Make haste 12
down from the mountain because your people whom you brought out
of Egypt have done a disgraceful thing. They have already turned aside
from the way which I told them to follow and have cast for themselves
an image of metal.'

Then the LORD said to me, 'I have considered this people and I find 13
them a stubborn people. Let me be, and I will destroy them and blot 14
out their name from under heaven; and of you alone I will make a
nation more powerful and numerous than they.' So I turned and went 15
down the mountain, and it was ablaze; and I had the two tablets of the
covenant in my hands. When I saw that you had sinned against the 16
LORD your God and had cast for yourselves an image of a bull-calf,
and had already turned aside from the way the LORD had told you to
follow, I took the two tablets and flung them down and shattered them 17
in the sight of you all. Then once again I lay prostrate before the LORD, 18
forty days and forty nights without food or drink, on account of all the
sins that you had committed, and because you had done what was
wrong in the eyes of the LORD and provoked him to anger. I dreaded 19
the LORD's anger and his wrath which threatened to destroy you; and
once again the LORD listened to me. The LORD was greatly incensed 20
with Aaron also and would have killed him; so I prayed for him as well
at that same time. I took the calf, that sinful thing that you had made, 21
and burnt it and pounded it, grinding it until it was as fine as dust;
then I flung its dust into the torrent that flowed down the mountain.
You also roused the LORD's anger at Taberah, and at Massah, and at 22
Kibroth-hattaavah. Again, when the LORD sent you from Kadesh- 23
barnea with orders to advance and occupy the land which he was
giving you, you defied the LORD your God and did not trust him or
obey him. You were defiant from the day that the LORD*a* first knew you. 24
Forty days and forty nights I lay prostrate before the LORD because he 25
had threatened to destroy you, and I prayed to the LORD and said, 26
'O Lord GOD, do not destroy thy people, thy own possession, whom
thou didst redeem by thy great power and bring out of Egypt by thy
strong hand. Remember thy servants, Abraham, Isaac and Jacob, and 27
overlook the stubbornness of this people, their wickedness and their
sin; otherwise the people in*b* the land out of which thou didst lead us 28
will say, "It is because the LORD was not able to bring them into the
land which he promised them and because he hated them, that he has
led them out to kill them in the wilderness." But they are thy people, 29
thy own possession, whom thou didst bring out by thy great strength
and by thy outstretched arm.'

[*a*] *So Sam.; Heb.* I.   [*b*] the people in: *so Sam.; Heb. om.*

10 AT THAT TIME THE LORD said to me, 'Cut two tablets of stone like the first, and make also a wooden chest, an Ark. Come to me on the
2 mountain, and I will write on the tablets the words that were on the first tablets which you broke in pieces, and you shall put them into the
3 Ark.' So I made the Ark of acacia-wood and cut two tablets of stone like
4 the first, and went up the mountain taking the tablets with me. Then in the same writing as before, the LORD wrote down the Ten Words*a* which he had spoken to you out of the fire, upon the mountain on the
5 day of the assembly, and the LORD gave them to me. I turned and came down the mountain, and I put the tablets in the Ark that I had made, as the LORD had commanded me, and there they have remained ever since.

6*b* (The Israelites journeyed by stages from Beeroth-bene-jaakan to Moserah. There Aaron died and was buried; and his son Eleazar
7 succeeded him in the priesthood. From there they came to Gudgodah
8 and from Gudgodah to Jotbathah, a land of many ravines. At that time the LORD set apart the tribe of Levi to carry the Ark of the Covenant of the LORD, to attend on the LORD and minister to him, and to give the
9 blessing in his name, as they have done to this day. That is why the Levites have no holding or patrimony with their kinsmen; the LORD is their patrimony, as he promised them.)

10 I stayed on the mountain forty days and forty nights, as I did before, and once again the LORD listened to me; he consented not to destroy
11 you. The LORD said to me, 'Set out now at the head of the people so that they may enter and occupy the land which I swore to give to their forefathers.'

12 What then, O Israel, does the LORD your God ask of you? Only to fear the LORD your God, to conform to all his ways, to love him and to
13 serve him with all your heart and soul. This you will do by keeping the commandments of the LORD and his statutes which I give you this day
14 for your good. To the LORD your God belong heaven itself, the highest
15 heaven, the earth and everything in it; yet the LORD cared for your forefathers in his love for them and chose their descendants after them.
16 Out of all nations you were his chosen people as you are this day. So now you must circumcise the foreskin of your hearts and not be
17 stubborn any more, for the LORD your God is God of gods and Lord of lords, the great, mighty, and terrible God. He is no respecter of
18 persons and is not to be bribed; he secures justice for widows and orphans, and loves the alien who lives among you, giving him food and
19 clothing. You too must love the alien, for you once lived as aliens in
20 Egypt. You must fear the LORD your God, serve him, hold fast to him
21 and take your oaths in his name. He is your praise, your God who

[*a*] *Or* Ten Commandments. [*b*] *Verses 6, 7: cp. Num. 33. 31, 32.*

has done for you these great and terrible things which you have seen with your own eyes. When your forefathers went down into Egypt they 22 were only seventy strong, but now the LORD your God has made you countless as the stars in the sky.

You shall love the LORD your God and keep for all time the charge he 11 laid upon you, the statutes, the laws, and the commandments. This day 2 you know the discipline of the LORD, though your children who have neither known nor experienced it do not; you know his greatness, his strong hand and outstretched arm, the signs he worked and his acts in 3 Egypt against Pharaoh the king and his country, and all that he did 4 to the Egyptian army, its horses and chariots, when he caused the waters of the Red Sea to flow over them as they pursued you. In this way the LORD destroyed them, and so things remain to this day. You 5 know what he did for you in the wilderness as you journeyed to this place, and what he did to Dathan and Abiram sons of Eliab, son of 6 Reuben, when the earth opened its mouth and swallowed them in the sight of all Israel, together with their households and their tents and every living thing in their company. With your own eyes you have seen 7 the mighty work that the LORD did.

You shall observe all that I command you this day, so that you may 8 have strength to enter and occupy the land into which you are crossing, and so that you may live long in the land which the LORD swore to your 9 forefathers to give them and their descendants, a land flowing with milk and honey. The land which you are entering to occupy is not like 10 the land of Egypt from which you have come, where, after sowing your seed, you irrigated it by foot like a vegetable garden. But the land into 11 which you are crossing to occupy is a land of mountains and valleys watered by the rain of heaven. It is a land which the LORD your God 12 tends*a* and on which his eye rests from year's end to year's end. If you 13 pay heed to the commandments which I give you this day, and love the LORD your God and serve him with all your heart and soul, then I will 14 send rain for your land in season, both autumn and spring rains, and you will gather your corn and new wine and oil, and I will provide 15 pasture in the fields for your cattle: you shall eat your fill. Take good 16 care not to be led astray in your hearts nor to turn aside and serve other gods and prostrate yourselves to them, or the LORD will become angry 17 with you: he will shut up the skies and there will be no rain, your ground will not yield its harvest, and you will soon vanish from the rich land which the LORD is giving you. You shall take these words of 18 mine to heart and keep them in mind; you shall bind them as a sign on the hand and wear them as a phylactery on the forehead. Teach 19 them to your children, and speak of them indoors and out of doors,

[a] which...tends: *or* whose soil the LORD your God has made firm.

20 when you lie down and when you rise. Write them up on the door-
21 posts of your houses and on your gates. Then you will live long, you
and your children, in the land which the LORD swore to your forefathers
to give them, for as long as the heavens are above the earth.

22 If you diligently keep all these commandments that I now charge
you to observe, by loving the LORD your God, by conforming to his
23 ways and by holding fast to him, the LORD will drive out all these
nations before you and you shall occupy the territory of nations greater
24 and more powerful than you. Every place where you set the soles of
your feet shall be yours. Your borders shall run from the wilderness
to^a the Lebanon and from the River, the river Euphrates, to the
25 western sea. No man will be able to withstand you; the LORD your God
will put the fear and dread of you upon the whole land on which you
26 set foot, as he promised you. Understand that this day I offer you the
27 choice of a blessing and a curse. The blessing will come if you listen
to the commandments of the LORD your God which I give you this day,
28 and the curse if you do not listen to the commandments of the LORD
your God but turn aside from the way that I command you this day
and follow other gods whom you do not know.

29 When the LORD your God brings you into the land which you are
entering to occupy, there on Mount Gerizim you shall pronounce the
30 blessing and on Mount Ebal the curse. (These mountains are on the
other side of the Jordan, close to Gilgal beside the terebinth^b of Moreh,
beyond the road to the west which lies in the territory of the Canaanites
31 of the Arabah.) You are about to cross the Jordan to enter and occupy
the land which the LORD your God is giving you; you shall occupy it
32 and settle in it, and you shall be careful to observe all the statutes and
laws which I set before you this day.

God's laws delivered by Moses

12 THESE ARE THE STATUTES and laws that you shall be careful to
observe in the land which the LORD the God of your fathers is
2 giving you to occupy as long as you live on earth. You shall demolish all
the sanctuaries where the nations whose place you are taking worship
their gods, on mountain-tops and hills and under every spreading tree.
3 You shall pull down their altars and break their sacred pillars, burn their
sacred poles and hack down the idols of their gods and thus blot out
the name of them from that place.
4 You shall not follow such practices in the worship of the LORD your

[a] *Prob. rdg.; Heb.* and.   [b] *So Sept.; Heb.* terebinths.

God, but you shall resort to the place which the LORD your God will 5
choose out of all your tribes to receive his Name that it may dwell
there. There you shall come and bring your whole-offerings and 6
sacrifices, your tithes and contributions, your vows and freewill
offerings, and the first-born of your herds and flocks. There you shall 7
eat before the LORD your God; so you shall find joy in whatever you
undertake, you and your families, because the LORD your God has
blessed you.

You shall not act as we act here today, each of us doing what he 8
pleases, for till now you have not reached the place of rest, the patri- 9
mony which the LORD your God is giving you. You shall cross the 10
Jordan and settle in the land which the LORD your God allots you as
your patrimony; he will grant you peace from all your enemies on
every side, and you will live in security. Then you shall bring every- 11
thing that I command you to the place which the LORD your God will
choose as a dwelling for his Name—your whole-offerings and sacrifices,
your tithes and contributions, and all the choice gifts that you have
vowed to the LORD. You shall rejoice before the LORD your God with 12
your sons and daughters, your male and female slaves, and the Levites
who live in your settlements*a* because they have no holding or patrimony among you.

See that you do not offer your whole-offerings in any place at 13
random, but offer them only at the place which the LORD will choose in 14
one of your tribes, and there you must do all I command you. On the 15
other hand, you may freely kill for food in all your settlements, as the
LORD your God blesses you. Clean and unclean alike may eat it, as they
would eat the meat of gazelle or buck. But on no account must you eat 16
the blood; pour it out on the ground like water. In all your settlements 17
you may not eat any of the tithe of your corn and new wine and oil, or
any of the first-born of your cattle and sheep, or any of the gifts that
you vow, or any of your freewill offerings and contributions; but you 18
shall eat it before the LORD your God in the place that the LORD your
God will choose—you, your sons and daughters, your male and female
slaves, and the Levites in your settlements; so you shall find joy before
the LORD your God in all that you undertake. Be careful not to neglect 19
the Levites in your land as long as you live.

When the LORD your God extends your boundaries, as he has 20
promised you, and you say to yourselves, 'I would like to eat meat',
because you have a craving for it, then you may freely eat it. If the place 21
that the LORD your God will choose to receive his Name is far away,
then you may slaughter a beast from the herds or flocks which the LORD
has given you and freely eat it in your own settlements as I command

[a] *Lit.* gates.

22 you. You may eat it as you would the meat of gazelle or buck; both
23 clean and unclean alike may eat it. But you must strictly refrain from
eating the blood, because the blood is the life; you must not eat the life
24 with the flesh. You must not eat it, you must pour it out on the ground
25 like water. If you do not eat it, all will be well with you and your
children after you; for you will be doing what is right in the eyes of the
26 LORD. But such holy-gifts as you may have and the gifts you have
27 vowed, you must bring to the place which the LORD will choose. You
must present your whole-offerings, both the flesh and the blood, on the
altar of the LORD your God; but of your shared-offerings you shall eat
the flesh, while the blood is to be poured on the altar of the LORD your
28 God. See that you listen and do*a* all that I command you, and then it
will go well with you and your children after you for ever; for you will
be doing what is good and right in the eyes of the LORD your God.
29   When the LORD your God exterminates, as you advance, the nations
whose country you are entering to occupy, you shall take their place
30 and settle in their land. After they have been destroyed, take care that
you are not ensnared into their ways. Do not inquire about their gods
and say, 'How do these nations worship their gods? I too will do the
31 same.' You must not do for the LORD your God what they do, for all
that they do for their gods is hateful and abominable to the LORD. As
sacrifices for their gods they even burn their sons and their daughters.
32*b*   See that you observe everything I command you: you must not add
anything to it, nor take anything away from it.
13   When a prophet or dreamer appears among you and offers you a sign
2 or a portent and calls on you to follow other gods whom you have not
known and worship them, even if the sign or portent should come true,
3 do not listen to the words of that prophet or that dreamer. God is
testing you through him to discover whether you love the LORD your
4 God with all your heart and soul. You must follow the LORD your God
and fear him; you must keep his commandments and obey him, serve
5 him and hold fast to him. That prophet or that dreamer shall be put
to death, for he has preached rebellion against the LORD your God who
brought you out of Egypt and redeemed you from that land of slavery;
he has tried to lead you astray from the path which the LORD your God
commanded you to take. You must rid yourselves of this wickedness.
6   If your brother, your father's son or*c* your mother's son, or your son
or daughter, or the wife of your bosom or your dearest friend should
entice you secretly to go and worship other gods—gods whom neither
7 you nor your fathers have known, gods of the people round about you,
8 near or far, at one end of the land or the other—then you shall not

[*a*] and do: *so Sam.; Heb. om.*   [*b*] *13. 1 in Heb.*   [*c*] your father's son or: *so Sam.; Heb. om.*

consent or listen. You shall have no pity on him, you shall not spare him nor shield him, you shall put him to death; your own hand shall be 9 the first to be raised against him and then all the people shall follow. You shall stone him to death, because he tried to lead you astray from 10 the LORD your God who brought you out of Egypt, out of the land of slavery. All Israel shall hear of it and be afraid; never again will 11 anything as wicked as this be done among you.

When you hear that miscreants*a* have appeared in any of the cities 12–13 which the LORD your God is giving you to occupy, and have led its inhabitants astray by calling on them to serve other gods whom you have not known, then you shall investigate the matter carefully. If, after 14 diligent examination, the report proves to be true and it is shown that this abominable thing has been done among you, you shall put the 15 inhabitants of that city to the sword; you shall lay the city under solemn ban together with everything in it.*b* You shall gather all its 16 goods into the square and burn both city and goods as a complete offering to the LORD your God; and it shall remain a mound of ruins, never to be rebuilt. Let nothing out of all that has been laid under the 17 ban be found in your possession, so that the LORD may turn from his anger and show you compassion; and in his compassion he will increase you as he swore to your forefathers, provided that you obey 18 the LORD your God and keep all his commandments which I give you this day, doing only what is right in the eyes of the LORD your God.

YOU ARE THE SONS of the LORD your God: you shall not gash your- 14 selves nor shave your forelocks*c* in mourning for the dead. You are 2 a people holy to the LORD your God, and the LORD has chosen you out of all peoples on earth to be his special possession.

You shall not eat any abominable thing. These are the animals you 3,4 may eat: ox, sheep, goat, buck, gazelle, roebuck, wild-goat, white- 5 rumped deer, long-horned antelope, and rock-goat. You may eat any 6 animal which has a parted foot or a cloven hoof and also chews the cud; those which only chew the cud or only have a parted or cloven hoof you 7 may not eat. These are: the camel, the hare, and the rock-badger,*d* because they chew the cud but do not have cloven hoofs; you shall regard them as unclean; and the pig, because it has a cloven hoof but 8 does not chew the cud, you shall regard as unclean. You shall not eat their flesh or even touch their dead carcasses. Of creatures that live in 9 water you may eat all those that have fins and scales, but you may not 10 eat any that have neither fins nor scales; you shall regard them as unclean. You may eat all clean birds. These are the birds you may not 11,12

[a] *Lit.* sons of Belial. [b] *So Sept.; Heb. adds* and the cattle to the sword. [c] *Lit.* between your eyes. [d] *Or* rock-rabbit.

13 eat: the griffon-vulture,*ᵃ* the black vulture, the bearded vulture,*ᵇ* the
14, 15 kite,*ᶜ* every kind of falcon,*ᵈ* every kind of crow,*ᵉ* the desert-owl, the
16 short-eared owl, the long-eared owl, every kind of hawk, the tawny
17 owl, the screech-owl, the little owl, the horned owl, the osprey, the
18 fisher-owl, the stork,*ᶠ* every kind of cormorant, the hoopoe, and the bat.
19 All teeming winged creatures you shall regard as unclean; they may
20 not be eaten. You may eat every clean insect.

21 You shall not eat anything that has died a natural death. You shall
give it to the aliens who live in your settlements, and they may eat it,
or you may sell it to a foreigner; for you are a people holy to the LORD
your God.

You shall not boil a kid in its mother's milk.

22 Year by year you shall set aside a tithe of all the produce of your seed,
23 of everything that grows on the land. You shall eat it in the presence of
the LORD your God in the place which he will choose as a dwelling for
his Name—the tithe of your corn and new wine and oil, and the first-
born of your cattle and sheep, so that for all time you may learn to fear
24 the LORD your God. When the LORD your God has blessed you with
prosperity, and the place which he will choose to receive his Name is
far from you and the journey too great for you to be able to carry your
25 tithe, then you may exchange it for silver. You shall tie up the silver
and take it with you to the place which the LORD your God will choose.
26 There you shall spend it as you will on cattle or sheep, wine or strong
drink, or whatever you desire; you shall consume it there with rejoicing,
27 both you and your family, in the presence of the LORD your God. You
must not neglect the Levites who live in your settlements; for they have
no holding or patrimony among you.

28 At the end of every third year you shall bring out all the tithe of your
29 produce for that year and leave it in your settlements so that the
Levites, who have no holding or patrimony among you, and the aliens,
orphans, and widows in your settlements may come and eat their fill.
If you do this the LORD your God will bless you in everything to which
you set your hand.

15 At the end of every seventh year you shall make a remission of debts.
2 This is how the remission shall be made: everyone who holds a pledge
shall remit the pledge of anyone indebted to him. He shall not press a
fellow-countryman for repayment, for the LORD's year of remission has
3 been declared.*ᵍ* You may press foreigners; but if it is a fellow-countryman that holds anything of yours, you must remit all claim upon it.
4-5 There will never be any poor among you if only you obey the LORD your
God by carefully keeping these commandments which I lay upon you

[a] *Or* eagle. [b] *Or* ossifrage. [c] *So Sam., cp. Lev. 11. 14; Heb. has an unknown word.*
[d] *So some MSS.; others add* kite. [e] *Or* raven. [f] *Or* heron. [g] *Or* has come.

this day; for the LORD your God will bless you with great prosperity in the land which he is giving you to occupy as your patrimony. When the 6 LORD your God blesses you, as he promised, you will lend to men of many nations, but you yourselves will not borrow; you will rule many nations, but they will not rule you.

When one of your fellow-countrymen in any of your settlements in 7 the land which the LORD your God is giving you becomes poor, do not be hard-hearted or close-fisted with your countryman in his need. Be open-handed towards him and lend him on pledge as much as he 8 needs. See that you do not harbour iniquitous thoughts[a] when you find 9 that the seventh year, the year of remission, is near, and look askance at your needy countryman and give him nothing. If you do, he will appeal to the LORD against you, and you will be found guilty of sin. Give freely to him and do not begrudge him your bounty, because it is 10 for this very bounty that the LORD your God will bless you in everything that you do or undertake. The poor will always be with you in the 11 land, and for that reason I command you to be open-handed with your countrymen, both poor and distressed, in your own land.

When a fellow-Hebrew, man or woman, sells himself to you as a 12 slave, he shall serve you for six years and in the seventh year you shall set him free. But when you set him free, do not let him go empty- 13 handed. Give to him lavishly from your flock, from your threshing-floor 14 and your winepress. Be generous to him, because the LORD your God has blessed you. Do not take it amiss when you have to set him free, 18 for his six years' service to you has been worth twice[b] the wage of a hired man. Then the LORD your God will bless you in everything you do. Remember that you were slaves in Egypt and the LORD your God 15 redeemed you; that is why I am giving you this command today.

If, however, a slave is content to be with you and says, 'I will not 16 leave you, I love you and your family', then you shall take an awl and 17 pierce through his ear to the door, and he will be your slave for life. You shall treat a slave-girl in the same way.

You shall dedicate to the LORD your God every male first-born of 19[c] your herds and flocks. You shall not plough with the first-born of your cattle, nor shall you shear the first-born of your sheep. Year by year 20 you and your family shall eat them in the presence of the LORD your God, in the place which the LORD will choose. If any animal is defec- 21 tive, if it is lame or blind, or has any other serious defect, you must not sacrifice it to the LORD your God. Eat it in your settlements; both clean 22 and unclean alike may eat it as they would the meat of gazelle or buck. But you must not eat the blood; pour it out on the ground like water. 23

[a] *Lit.* thoughts of Belial.   [b] worth twice: *or* equivalent to.   [c] *Verse 18 transposed to follow verse 14.*

16 OBSERVE THE MONTH OF ABIB and keep the Passover to the LORD
your God, for it was in that month that the LORD your God brought you
2 out of Egypt by night. You shall slaughter a lamb, a kid, or a calf as a
Passover victim to the LORD your God in the place which he will
3 choose as a dwelling for his Name. You shall eat nothing leavened with
it. For seven days you shall eat unleavened cakes, the bread of affliction.
In urgent haste you came out of Egypt, and thus as long as you live
4 you shall commemorate the day of your coming out of Egypt. No leaven
shall be seen in all your territory for seven days, nor shall any of the
flesh which you have slaughtered in the evening of the first day remain
5 overnight till morning. You may not slaughter the Passover victim in
6 any of the settlements which the LORD your God is giving you, but
only in the place which he will choose as a dwelling for his Name;
you shall slaughter the Passover victim in the evening as the sun goes
7 down, the time of your coming out of Egypt. You shall boil it and
eat it in the place which the LORD your God will choose, and then
8 next morning you shall turn and go to your tents. For six days you
shall eat unleavened cakes, and on the seventh day there shall be a
closing ceremony in honour of the LORD your God; you shall do
no work.

9 Seven weeks shall be counted: start counting the seven weeks from
10 the time when the sickle is put to the standing corn; then you shall
keep the pilgrim-feast of Weeks to the LORD your God and offer a
freewill offering in proportion to the blessing that the LORD your God
11 has given you. You shall rejoice before the LORD your God, with your
sons and daughters, your male and female slaves, the Levites who live
in your settlements, and the aliens, orphans, and widows among you.
You shall rejoice in the place which the LORD your God will choose as
12 a dwelling for his Name and remember that you were slaves in Egypt.
You shall keep and observe all these statutes.

13 You shall keep the pilgrim-feast of Tabernacles*a* for seven days,
when you bring in the produce from your threshing-floor and wine-
14 press. You shall rejoice in your feast, with your sons and daughters,
your male and female slaves, the Levites, aliens, orphans, and widows
15 who live in your settlements. For seven days you shall keep this feast
to the LORD your God in the place which he will choose, when the
LORD your God gives you his blessing in all your harvest and in all your
work; you shall keep the feast with joy.

16 Three times a year all your males shall come into the presence of*b*
the LORD your God in the place which he will choose: at the pilgrim-
feasts of Unleavened Bread, of Weeks, and of Tabernacles. No one
17 shall come into the presence of the LORD empty-handed. Each of you

[a] *Or* Booths *or* Arbours.   [b] *Lit.* see the face of.

shall bring such a gift as he can in proportion to the blessing which the LORD your God has given you.

You shall appoint for yourselves judges and officers, tribe by tribe, 18 in every settlement which the LORD your God is giving you, and they shall dispense true justice to the people. You shall not pervert the 19 course of justice or show favour, nor shall you accept a bribe; for bribery makes the wise man blind and the just man give a crooked answer. Justice, and justice alone, you shall pursue, so that you may 20 live and occupy the land which the LORD your God is giving you.

You shall not plant any kind of tree as a sacred pole*a* beside the altar 21 of the LORD your God which you shall build. You shall not set up a 22 sacred pillar, for the LORD your God hates them.

You shall not sacrifice to the LORD your God a bull or sheep that has 17 any defect or serious blemish, for that would be abominable to the LORD your God.

If so be that, in any one of the settlements which the LORD your God 2 is giving you, a man or woman is found among you who does what is wrong in the eyes of the LORD your God, by breaking his covenant and 3 going to worship other gods and prostrating himself before them or before the sun and moon and all the host of heaven—a thing that I have forbidden—then, if it is reported to you or you hear of it, make 4 thorough inquiry. If the report proves to be true, and it is shown that this abominable thing has been done in Israel, then bring the man or 5 woman who has done this wicked deed to the city gate*b* and stone him to death. Sentence of death shall be carried out on the testimony of 6 two or of three witnesses: no one shall be put to death on the testimony of a single witness. The first stones shall be thrown by the witnesses 7 and then all the people shall follow; thus you shall rid yourselves of this wickedness.

When the issue in any lawsuit is beyond your competence, whether it 8 be a case of blood against blood, plea against plea, or blow against blow, that is disputed in your courts,*c* then go up without delay to the place which the LORD your God will choose. There you must go to the 9 levitical priests or to the judge then in office; seek their guidance, and they will pronounce the sentence. You shall act on the pronouncement 10 which they make from the place which the LORD will choose. See that you carry out all their instructions. Act on the instruction which they 11 give you, or on the precedent that they cite; do not swerve from what they tell you, either to right or to left. Anyone who presumes to reject 12 the decision either of the priest who ministers there to the LORD your God, or of the judge, shall die; thus you will rid Israel of wickedness.

[a] sacred pole: *Heb.* asherah. [b] *So Sept.; Heb. adds* the man or the woman. [c] *Lit.* in your gates.

13 Then all the people will hear of it and be afraid, and will never again show such presumption.

14 When you come into the land which the LORD your God is giving you, and occupy it and settle in it, and you then say, 'Let us appoint
15 over us a king, as all the surrounding nations do', you shall appoint as king the man whom the LORD your God will choose. You shall appoint over you a man of your own race; you must not appoint a foreigner,
16 one who is not of your own race. He shall not acquire many horses, nor, to add to his horses, shall he cause the people to go back to Egypt, for this is what the LORD said to you, 'You shall never go back that way.'
17 He shall not acquire many wives and so be led astray; nor shall he
18 acquire great quantities of silver and gold for himself. When he has ascended the throne of the kingdom, he shall make a copy of this law
19 in a book at the dictation of the levitical priests. He shall keep it by him and read from it all his life, so that he may learn to fear the LORD his God and keep all the words of this law and observe these statutes.
20 In this way he shall not become prouder than his fellow-countrymen, nor shall he turn from these commandments to right or to left; then he and his sons will reign long over his kingdom in Israel.

18 The levitical priests, the whole tribe of Levi, shall have no holding or patrimony in Israel; they shall eat the food-offerings of the LORD,
2 their patrimony. They shall have no patrimony among their fellow-countrymen; the LORD is their patrimony, as he promised them.
3 This shall be the customary due of the priests from those of the people who offer sacrifice, whether a bull or a sheep: the shoulders, the
4 cheeks, and the stomach shall be given to the priest. You shall give him also the firstfruits of your corn and new wine and oil, and the first
5 fleeces at the shearing of your flocks. For it was he whom the LORD your God chose from all your tribes to attend on the LORD*ᵃ* and to minister in the name of the LORD, both he and his sons for all time.
6 When a Levite comes from any settlement in Israel where he may be lodging to the place which the LORD will choose, if he comes in the
7 eagerness of his heart and ministers in the name of the LORD his God,
8 like all his fellow-Levites who attend on the LORD there, he shall have an equal share of food with them, besides what he may inherit from his father's family.
9 When you come into the land which the LORD your God is giving you, do not learn to imitate the abominable customs of those other
10 nations. Let no one be found among you who makes his son or daughter pass through fire, no augur or soothsayer or diviner or sorcerer,
11 no one who casts spells or traffics with ghosts and spirits, and no
12 necromancer. Those who do these things are abominable to the LORD,

[a] on the LORD: *so Sam.; Heb. om.*

258

and it is because of these abominable practices that the LORD your God
is driving them out before you. You shall be whole-hearted in your 13
service of the LORD your God.

These nations whose place you are taking listen to soothsayers and 14
augurs, but the LORD your God does not permit you to do this. The 15
LORD your God will raise up a prophet from among you like myself,
and you shall listen to him. All this follows from your request to the 16
LORD your God on Horeb on the day of the assembly. There you said,
'Let us not hear again the voice of the LORD our God, nor see this
great fire again, or we shall die.' Then the LORD said to me, 'What they 17
have said is right. I will raise up for them a prophet like you, one of 18
their own race, and I will put my words into his mouth. He shall
convey all my commands to them, and if anyone does not listen to the 19
words which he will speak in my name I will require satisfaction from
him. But the prophet who presumes to utter in my name what I have 20
not commanded him or who speaks in the name of other gods—that
prophet shall die.' If you ask yourselves, 'How shall we recognize a 21
word that the LORD has not uttered?', this is the answer: When the 22
word spoken by the prophet in the name of the LORD is not fulfilled
and does not come true, it is not a word spoken by the LORD. The
prophet has spoken presumptuously; do not hold him[a] in awe.

WHEN THE LORD your God exterminates the nations whose land he 19
is giving you, and you take their place and settle in their cities and
houses, you shall set apart three cities in the land which he is giving you 2
to occupy. Divide into three districts the territory which the LORD 3
your God is giving you as patrimony, and determine where each city
shall lie. These shall be places in which homicides may take sanctuary.

This is the kind of homicide who may take sanctuary there and save 4
his life: the man who strikes another without intent and with no
previous enmity between them; for instance, the man who goes into 5
a wood with his mate to fell trees, and, when cutting a tree, he relaxes
his grip on the axe,[b] the head glances off the tree, hits the other man
and kills him. The homicide may take sanctuary in any one of these
cities, and his life shall be safe. Otherwise, when the dead man's next- 6
of-kin who had the duty of vengeance pursued him in the heat of
passion, he might overtake him if the distance were great, and take his
life, although the homicide was not liable to the death-penalty because
there had been no previous enmity on his part. That is why I command 7
you to set apart three cities.

If the LORD your God extends your boundaries, as he swore to your 8
forefathers, and gives you the whole land which he promised to them,

[a] Or it. [b] when...axe: or as he swings the axe to cut a tree.

259

9 because you keep all the commandments that I am laying down today and carry them out by loving the LORD your God and by conforming to his ways for all time, then you shall add three more cities of refuge to
10 these three. Let no innocent blood be shed in the land which the LORD your God is giving you as your patrimony, or blood-guilt will fall on you.

11 When one man is the enemy of another, and he lies in wait for him, attacks him and strikes him a blow so that he dies, and then takes
12 sanctuary in one of these cities, the elders of his own city shall send to fetch him; they shall hand him over to the next-of-kin, and he shall die.
13 You shall show him no mercy, but shall rid Israel of the guilt of innocent blood; then all will be well with you.

14 Do not move your neighbour's boundary stone, fixed by the men of former times in the patrimony which you shall occupy in the land the LORD your God gives you for your possession.

15 A single witness may not give evidence against a man in the matter of any crime or sin which he commits: a charge must be established on the evidence of two or of three witnesses.

16 When a malicious witness comes forward to give false evidence against
17 a man, and the two disputants stand before the LORD, before the priests
18 and the judges then in office, if, after careful examination by the judges, he be proved to be a false witness giving false evidence against
19 his fellow, you shall treat him as he intended to treat his fellow, and
20 thus rid yourselves of this wickedness. The rest of the people when they hear of it will be afraid: never again will anything as wicked as this be
21 done among you. You shall show no mercy: life for life, eye for eye, tooth for tooth, hand for hand, foot for foot.

20 WHEN YOU TAKE the field against an enemy and are faced by horses and chariots and an army greater than yours, do not be afraid of them; for the LORD your God, who brought you out of Egypt, will be with
2 you. When you are about to join battle, the priest shall come forward
3 and address the army in these words: 'Hear, O Israel, this day you are joining battle with the enemy; do not lose heart, or be afraid, or give
4 way to panic in face of them; for the LORD your God will go with you
5 to fight your enemy for you and give you the victory.' Then the officers shall address the army in these words: 'Any man who has built a new house and has not dedicated it shall go back to his house; or he may die
6 in battle and another man dedicate it. Any man who has planted a vineyard and has not begun to use it shall go back home; or he may die
7 in battle and another man use it. Any man who has pledged himself to take a woman in marriage and has not taken her shall go back home; or
8 he may die in battle and another man take her.' The officers shall

further address the army: 'Any man who is afraid and has lost heart shall go back home; or his comrades will be discouraged as he is.' When 9 these officers have finished addressing the army, commanders shall be appointed to lead it.

When you advance on a city to attack it, make an offer of peace. If the 10, 11 city accepts the offer and opens its gates to you, then all the people in it shall be put to forced labour and shall serve you. If it does not make 12 peace with you but offers battle, you shall besiege it, and the LORD your 13 God will deliver it into your hands. You shall put all its males to the sword, but you may take the women, the dependants, and the cattle for 14 yourselves, and plunder everything else in the city. You may enjoy the use of the spoil of your enemies which the LORD your God gives you. That is what you shall do to cities at a great distance, as opposed to 15 those which belong to nations near at hand. In the cities of these nations 16 whose land the LORD your God is giving you as a patrimony, you shall not leave any creature alive. You shall annihilate them—Hittites, 17 Amorites, Canaanites, Perizzites, Hivites, Jebusites—as the LORD your God commanded you, so that they may not teach you to imitate all the 18 abominable things that they have done for their gods and so cause you to sin against the LORD your God.

When you are at war, and lay siege to a city for a long time in order 19 to take it, do not destroy its trees by taking the axe to them, for they provide you with food; you shall not cut them down. The trees of the field are not men that you should besiege them. But you may destroy 20 or cut down any trees that you know do not yield food, and use them in siege-works against the city that is at war with you, until it falls.

When a dead body is found lying in open country, in the land which 21 the LORD your God is giving you to occupy, and it is not known who struck the blow, your elders and your judges shall come out and 2 measure the distance to the surrounding towns to find which is nearest. The elders of that town shall take a heifer that has never been mated*a* 3 or worn a yoke, and bring it down to a ravine where there is a stream 4 that never runs dry and the ground is never tilled or sown, and there in the ravine they shall break its neck. The priests, the sons of Levi, shall 5 then come forward; for the LORD your God has chosen them to minister to him and to bless in the name of the LORD, and their voice shall be decisive in all cases of dispute and assault. Then all the elders of the 6 town nearest to the dead body shall wash their hands over the heifer whose neck has been broken in the ravine. They shall solemnly declare: 7 'Our hands did not shed this blood, nor did we witness the bloodshed. Accept expiation, O LORD, for thy people Israel whom thou hast 8 redeemed, and do not let the guilt of innocent blood rest upon thy

[a] *Prob. rdg.; Heb.* put to work.

9 people Israel: let this bloodshed be expiated on their behalf.' Thus, by doing what is right in the eyes of the LORD, you shall rid yourselves of the guilt of innocent blood.

10 When you wage war against your enemy and the LORD your God
11 delivers them into your hands and you take some of them captive, then if you see a comely woman among the captives and take a liking to her,
12 you may marry her. You shall bring her into your house, where she
13 shall shave her head, pare her nails, and discard the clothes which she had when captured. Then she shall stay in your house and mourn for her father and mother for a full month. After that you may have inter-
14 course with her; you shall be her husband and she your wife. But if you no longer find her pleasing, let her go free. You must not sell her, nor treat her harshly, since you have had your will with her.

15 When a man has two wives, one loved and the other unloved, if they
16 both bear him sons, and the son of the unloved wife is the elder, then, when the day comes for him to divide his property among his sons, he shall not treat the son of the loved wife as his first-born in contempt of
17 his true first-born, the son of the unloved wife. He shall recognize the rights of his first-born, the son of the unloved wife, and give him a double share of all that he possesses; for he was the firstfruits of his manhood, and the right of the first-born is his.

18 When a man has a son who is disobedient and out of control, and will not obey his father or his mother, or pay attention when they
19 punish him, then his father and mother shall take hold of him and
20 bring him out to the elders of the town, at the town gate. They shall say to the elders of the town, 'This son of ours is disobedient and out
21 of control; he will not obey us, he is a wastrel and a drunkard.' Then all the men of the town shall stone him to death, and you will thereby rid yourselves of this wickedness. All Israel will hear of it and be afraid.

22 When a man is convicted of a capital offence and is put to death,
23 you shall hang him on a gibbet; but his body shall not remain on the gibbet overnight; you shall bury it on the same day, for a hanged man is offensive[a] in the sight of God. You shall not pollute the land which the LORD your God is giving you as your patrimony.

22 WHEN YOU SEE a fellow-countryman's ox or sheep straying, do not
2 ignore it but take it back to him. If the owner is not a near neighbour and you do not know who he is, take the animal into your own house
3 and keep it with you until he claims it, and then give it back to him. Do the same with his ass or his cloak or anything else that your fellow-countryman has lost, if you find it. You may not ignore it.

[a] *Or* accursed.

When you see your fellow-countryman's ass or ox lying on the road, 4 do not ignore it; you must help him to lift it to its feet again.

No woman shall wear an article of man's clothing, nor shall a man 5 put on woman's dress; for those who do these things are abominable to the LORD your God.

When you come across a bird's nest by the road, in a tree or on the 6 ground, with fledglings or eggs in it and the mother-bird on the nest, do not take both mother and young. Let the mother-bird go free, and 7 take only the young; then you will prosper and live long.

When you build a new house, put a parapet along the roof, or you 8 will bring the guilt of bloodshed on your house if anyone should fall from it.

You shall not sow your vineyard with a second crop, or the full yield 9 will be forfeit, both the yield of the seed you sow and the fruit of the vineyard.

You shall not plough with an ox and an ass yoked together. 10

You shall not wear clothes woven with two kinds of yarn, wool and 11 flax together.

You shall make twisted tassels on the four corners of your cloaks 12 which you wrap round you.

When a man takes a wife and after having intercourse with her turns 13 against her and brings trumped-up charges against her, giving her a 14 bad name and saying, 'I took this woman and slept with her and did not find proof of virginity in her', then the girl's father and mother 15 shall take the proof of her virginity to the elders of the town, at the town gate. The girl's father shall say to the elders, 'I gave my daughter 16 in marriage to this man, and he has turned against her. He has trumped 17 up a charge and said, "I have not found proofs of virginity in your daughter." Here are the proofs.' They shall then spread the garment before the elders of the town. The elders shall take the man and punish 18 him: they shall fine him a hundred pieces of silver because he has 19 given a bad name to a virgin of Israel, and hand them to the girl's father. She shall be his wife: he is not free to divorce her all his life long. If, on the other hand, the accusation is true and no proof of the 20 girl's virginity is found, then they shall bring her out to the door of her 21 father's house and the men of her town shall stone her to death. She has committed an outrage in Israel by playing the prostitute in her father's house: you shall rid yourselves of this wickedness.

When a man is discovered lying with a married woman, they shall 22 both die, the woman as well as the man who lay with her: you shall rid Israel of this wickedness.

When a virgin is pledged in marriage to a man and another man comes 23 upon her in the town and lies with her, you shall bring both of them out 24 to the gate of that town and stone them to death; the girl because, although in the town, she did not cry for help, and the man because he dishonoured another man's wife: you shall rid yourselves of this

25 wickedness. If the man comes upon such a girl in the country and rapes

26 her, then the man alone shall die because he lay with her. You shall do nothing to the girl, she has done nothing worthy of death: this deed is

27 like that of a man who attacks another and murders him, for the man came upon her in the country and, though the girl cried for help, there was no one to rescue her.

28 When a man comes upon a virgin who is not pledged in marriage

29 and forces her to lie with him, and they are discovered, then the man who lies with her shall give the girl's father fifty pieces of silver, and she shall be his wife because he has dishonoured her. He is not free to divorce her all his life long.

30*a* A man shall not take his father's wife: he shall not bring shame on his father.

23 No man whose testicles have been crushed or whose organ has been severed shall become a member of the assembly of the LORD.

2 No descendant of an irregular union, even down to the tenth generation, shall become a member of the assembly of the LORD.

3 No Ammonite or Moabite, even down to the tenth generation, shall become a member of the assembly of the LORD. They shall never

4 become members of the assembly of the LORD, because they did not meet you with food and water on your way out of Egypt, and because they hired Balaam son of Beor from Pethor in Aram-naharaim*b* to

5 revile you. The LORD your God refused to listen to Balaam and turned his denunciation into a blessing, because the LORD your God

6 loved you. You shall never seek their welfare or their good all your life long.

7 You shall not regard an Edomite as an abomination, for he is your

8 own kin; nor an Egyptian, for you were aliens in his land. The third generation of children born to them may become members of the assembly of the LORD.

9 When you are encamped against an enemy, you shall be careful to

10 avoid any foulness. When one of your number is unclean because of an emission of seed at night, he must go outside the camp; he may not

11 come within it. Towards evening he shall wash himself in water, and at

12 sunset he may come back into the camp. You shall have a sign outside

13 the camp showing where you can withdraw. With your equipment you will have a trowel,*c* and when you squat outside, you shall scrape a hole

14 with it and then turn and cover your excrement. For the LORD your God goes about in your camp, to keep you safe and to hand over your

[a] 23. *1 in Heb.* [b] *That is* Aram of Two Rivers. [c] *Lit.* peg.

enemies as you advance, and your camp must be kept holy for fear that he should see something indecent and go with you no further.

You shall not surrender to his master a slave who has taken refuge 15 with you. Let him stay with you anywhere he chooses in any one of 16 your settlements, wherever suits him best; you shall not force him.

No Israelite woman shall become a temple-prostitute, and no 17 Israelite man shall prostitute himself in this way.

You shall not allow a common prostitute's fee, or the pay of a male 18 prostitute, to be brought into the house of the LORD your God in fulfilment of any vow, for both of them are abominable to the LORD your God.

You shall not charge interest on anything you lend to a fellow- 19 countryman, money or food or anything else on which interest can be charged. You may charge interest on a loan to a foreigner but not on a 20 loan to a fellow-countryman, for then the LORD your God will bless you in all you undertake in the land which you are entering to occupy.

When you make a vow to the LORD your God, do not put off its 21 fulfilment; otherwise the LORD your God will require satisfaction of you and you will be guilty of sin. If you choose not to make a vow, you will 22 not be guilty of sin; but if you voluntarily make a vow to the LORD your 23 God, mind what you say and do what you have promised.

When you go into another man's vineyard, you may eat as many 24 grapes as you wish to satisfy your hunger, but you may not put any into your basket.

When you go into another man's standing corn, you may pluck ears 25 to rub in your hands, but you may not put a sickle to his standing corn.

When a man has married a wife, but she does not win his favour 24 because he finds something shameful in her, and he writes her a note of divorce, gives it to her and dismisses her; and suppose after leaving his 2 house she goes off to become the wife of another man, and this next 3 husband turns against her and writes her a note of divorce which he gives her and dismisses her, or dies after making her his wife—then in 4 that case her first husband who dismissed her is not free to take her back to be his wife again after she has become for him unclean. This is abominable to the LORD; you must not bring sin upon the land which the LORD your God is giving you as your patrimony.

When a man is newly married, he shall not be liable for military 5 service or any other public duty. He shall remain at home exempt from service for one year and enjoy the wife he has taken.

No man shall take millstones, or even the upper one alone, in pledge; 6 that would be taking a life in pledge.

When a man is found to have kidnapped a fellow-countryman, an 7

Israelite, and to have treated him harshly and sold him, he shall die: you shall rid yourselves of this wickedness.

8 Be careful how you act in all cases of malignant skin-disease; be careful to observe all that the levitical priests tell you; I gave them my
9 commands which you must obey. Remember what the LORD your God did to Miriam, on your way out of Egypt.

10 When you make a loan to another man, do not enter his house to take
11 a pledge from him. Wait outside, and the man whose creditor you are
12 shall bring the pledge out to you. If he is a poor man, you shall not
13 sleep in the cloak he has pledged. Give it back to him at sunset so that he may sleep in it and bless you; then it will be counted to your credit in the sight of the LORD your God.

14 You shall not keep back the wages of a man*a* who is poor and needy, whether a fellow-countryman or an alien living in your country in one
15 of your settlements. Pay him his wages on the same day before sunset, for he is poor and his heart is set on them: he may appeal to the LORD against you, and you will be guilty of sin.

16 Fathers shall not be put to death for their children, nor children for their fathers; a man shall be put to death only for his own sin.

17 You shall not deprive aliens and*b* orphans of justice nor take a
18 widow's cloak in pledge. Remember that you were slaves in Egypt and the LORD your God redeemed you from there; that is why I command you to do this.

19 When you reap the harvest in your field and forget a swathe, do not go back to pick it up; it shall be left for the alien, the orphan, and the widow, in order that the LORD your God may bless you in all that you undertake.

20 When you beat your olive-trees, do not strip them afterwards; what is left shall be for the alien, the orphan, and the widow.

21 When you gather the grapes from your vineyard, do not glean afterwards; what is left shall be for the alien, the orphan, and the widow.

22 Remember that you were slaves in Egypt; that is why I command you to do this.

25 When two men go to law and present themselves for judgement, the judges shall try the case; they shall acquit the innocent and condemn
2 the guilty. If the guilty man is sentenced to be flogged, the judge shall cause him to lie down and be beaten in his presence; the number of
3 strokes shall correspond to the gravity of the offence. They may give him forty strokes, but not more; otherwise, if they go further and exceed this number, your fellow-countryman will have been publicly degraded.

4 You shall not muzzle an ox while it is treading out the corn.

[a] keep...man: *so Scroll; Heb* oppress a hired man. [b] *So Sept.; Heb. om.*

When brothers live together and one of them dies without leaving a 5
son, his widow shall not marry outside the family. Her husband's
brother shall have intercourse with her; he shall take her in marriage
and do his duty by her as her husband's brother. The first son she bears 6
shall perpetuate the dead brother's name so that it may not be blotted
out from Israel. But if the man is unwilling to take his brother's wife, 7
she shall go to the elders at the town gate and say, 'My husband's
brother refuses to perpetuate his brother's name in Israel; he will not
do his duty by me.' At this the elders of the town shall summon him 8
and reason with him. If he still stands his ground and says, 'I will not
take her', his brother's widow shall go up to him in the presence of the 9
elders; she shall pull his sandal off his foot and spit in his face and
declare: 'Thus we requite the man who will not build up his brother's
family.' His family shall be known in Israel as the House of the 10
Unsandalled Man.

When two men are fighting and the wife of one of them comes near 11
to drag her husband clear of his opponent, if she puts out her hand
and catches hold of the man's genitals, you shall cut off her hand and 12
show her no mercy.

You shall not have unequal weights in your bag, one heavy, the other 13
light. You shall not have unequal measures*a* in your house, one large, 14
the other small. You shall have true and correct weights and true and 15
correct measures, so that you may live long in the land which the LORD
your God is giving you. All who commit these offences, all who deal 16
dishonestly, are abominable to the LORD.

Remember what the Amalekites did to you on your way out of 17
Egypt, how they met you on the road when you were faint and weary 18
and cut off your rear, which was lagging behind exhausted: they
showed no fear of God. When the LORD your God gives you peace 19
from your enemies on every side, in the land which he is giving you to
occupy as your patrimony, you shall not fail to blot out the memory of
the Amalekites from under heaven.

WHEN YOU COME into the land which the LORD your God is giving 26
you to occupy as your patrimony and settle in it, you shall take the 2
firstfruits of all the produce of the soil, which you gather in from the
land which the LORD your God is giving you, and put them in a basket.
Then you shall go to the place which the LORD your God will choose
as a dwelling for his Name and come to the priest, whoever he shall be 3
in those days. You shall say to him, 'I declare this day to the LORD
your God that I have entered the land which the LORD swore to our
forefathers to give us.' The priest shall take the basket from your hand 4

[*a*] *Heb.* ephah.

5 and set it down before the altar of the LORD your God. Then you shall solemnly recite before the LORD your God: 'My father was a homeless[a] Aramaean who went down to Egypt with a small company and lived
6 there until they became a great, powerful, and numerous nation. But the Egyptians ill-treated us, humiliated us and imposed cruel slavery
7 upon us. Then we cried to the LORD the God of our fathers for help, and he listened to us and saw our humiliation, our hardship and
8 distress; and so the LORD brought us out of Egypt with a strong hand and outstretched arm, with terrifying deeds, and with signs and portents.
9 He brought us to this place and gave us this land, a land flowing with
10 milk and honey. And now I have brought the firstfruits of the soil which thou, O LORD, hast given me.' You shall then set the basket
11 before the LORD your God and bow down in worship before him. You shall all rejoice, you and the Levites and the aliens living among you, for all the good things which the LORD your God has given to you and to your family.

12 When you have finished taking a tithe of your produce in the third year, the tithe-year, you shall give it to the Levites and to the aliens, the orphans, and the widows. They shall eat it in your settlements and
13 be well fed. Then you shall declare before the LORD your God: 'I have rid my house of the tithe that was holy to thee and given it to the Levites, to the aliens, the orphans, and the widows, according to all the commandments which thou didst lay upon me. I have not broken or
14 forgotten any of thy commandments. I have not eaten any of the tithe while in mourning, nor have I rid myself of it for unclean purposes,[b] nor offered any of it to[c] the dead. I have obeyed the LORD my God:
15 I have done all that thou didst command me. Look down from heaven, thy holy dwelling-place, and bless thy people Israel and the ground which thou hast given to us as thou didst swear to our forefathers, a land flowing with milk and honey.'

16 This day the LORD your God commands you to keep these statutes and laws: be careful to observe them with all your heart and soul.
17 You have recognized the LORD this day as your God; you are to conform to his ways, to keep his statutes, his commandments, and his
18 laws, and to obey him. The LORD has recognized you this day as his special possession, as he promised you, and to keep his commandments;
19 he will raise you high above all the nations which he has made, to bring him praise and fame and glory, and to be a people holy to the LORD your God, according to his promise.

[a] *Or* wandering. [b] nor have I...purposes: *mng. of Heb. obscure.* [c] *Or* for.

Concluding charge of Moses to the people

M OSES, WITH THE ELDERS of Israel, gave the people this charge: 27 'Keep all the commandments that I lay upon you this day. On 2 the day that you cross the Jordan to the land which the LORD your God is giving you, you shall set up great stones and plaster them over. You shall inscribe on them all the words of this law, when you have 3 crossed over to enter the land which the LORD your God is giving you, a land flowing with milk and honey, as the LORD the God of your fathers promised you. When you have crossed the Jordan you 4 shall set up these stones on Mount Ebal,^{a} as I command you this day, and cover them with plaster. You shall build an altar there to the 5 LORD your God: it shall be an altar of stones on which you shall use no tool of iron. You shall build the altar of the LORD your God 6 with blocks of undressed stone, and you shall offer whole-offerings upon it to the LORD your God. You shall slaughter shared-offerings 7 and eat them there, and rejoice before the LORD your God. You shall 8 inscribe on the stones all the words of this law, engraving them with care.'

Moses and the levitical priests spoke to all Israel, 'Be silent, Israel, 9 and listen; this day you have become a people belonging to the LORD your God. Obey the LORD your God, and observe his commandments 10 and statutes which I lay upon you this day.'

That day Moses gave the people this command: 'Those who shall 11,12 stand for the blessing of the people on Mount Gerizim when you have crossed the Jordan are these: Simeon, Levi, Judah, Issachar, Joseph, and Benjamin. Those who shall stand on Mount Ebal for the curse are 13 these: Reuben, Gad, Asher, Zebulun, Dan, and Naphtali.'

The Levites, in the hearing of all Israel, shall intone^b these words: 14

'A curse upon the man who carves an idol or casts an image, any- 15 thing abominable to the LORD that craftsmen make, and sets it up in secret': the people shall all respond and say, 'Amen.'

'A curse upon him who slights his father or his mother': the people 16 shall all say, 'Amen.'

'A curse upon him who moves his neighbour's boundary stone': the 17 people shall all say, 'Amen.'

'A curse upon him who misdirects a blind man': the people shall all 18 say, 'Amen.'

'A curse upon him who withholds justice from the alien, the orphan, 19 and the widow': the people shall all say, 'Amen.'

[a] Gerizim in Sam. [b] Lit. recite in a high-pitched voice.

269

20   'A curse upon him who lies with his father's wife, for he brings shame upon his father': the people shall all say, 'Amen.'

21   'A curse upon him who lies with any animal': the people shall all say, 'Amen.'

22   'A curse upon him who lies with his sister, his father's daughter or his mother's daughter': the people shall all say, 'Amen.'

23   'A curse upon him who lies with his wife's mother': the people shall all say, 'Amen.'

24   'A curse upon him who strikes another man in secret': the people shall all say, 'Amen.'

25   'A curse upon him who takes reward to kill a man with whom he has no feud': the people shall all say, 'Amen.'

26   'A curse upon any man who does not fulfil this law by doing all that it prescribes': the people shall all say, 'Amen.'

28   IF YOU WILL OBEY the LORD your God by diligently observing all his commandments which I lay upon you this day, then the LORD your

2   God will raise you high above all nations of the earth, and all these blessings shall come to you and light upon you, because you obey the LORD your God:

3   A blessing on you in the city; a blessing on you in the country.

4   A blessing on the fruit of your body, the fruit of your land and of your cattle, the offspring of your herds and of your lambing flocks.

5   A blessing on your basket and your kneading-trough.

6   A blessing on you as you come in; and a blessing on you as you go out.

7   May the LORD deliver up the enemies who attack you and let them be put to rout before you. Though they come out against you by one way, they shall flee before you by seven ways.

8   May the LORD grant you a blessing in your granaries and in all your labours; may the LORD your God bless you in the land which he is giving you.

9   The LORD will set you up as his own holy people, as he swore to you, if you keep the commandments of the LORD your God and conform to

10   his ways. Then all people on earth shall see that the LORD has named

11   you as his very own, and they shall go in fear of you. The LORD will make you prosper greatly in the fruit of your body and of your cattle, and in the fruit of the ground in the land which he swore to your fore-

12   fathers to give you. May the LORD open the heavens for you, his rich treasure house, to give rain upon your land at the proper time and bless everything to which you turn your hand. You shall lend to many

13   nations, but you shall not borrow; the LORD will make you the head and not the tail: you shall be always at the top and never at the bottom, when you listen to the commandments of the LORD your God, which

I give you this day to keep and to fulfil. You shall turn neither to the 14
right nor to the left from all the things which I command you this day
nor shall you follow after and worship other gods.

BUT IF YOU DO NOT OBEY the LORD your God by diligently 15
observing all his commandments and statutes which I lay upon you this
day, then all these maledictions shall come to you and light upon you:
   A curse upon you in the city; a curse upon you in the country. 16
   A curse upon your basket and your kneading-trough. 17
   A curse upon the fruit of your body, the fruit of your land, the off- 18
spring of your herds and of your lambing flocks.
   A curse upon you as you come in; and a curse upon you as you go 19
out.
   May the LORD send upon you starvation, burning thirst, and 20
dysentery,*a* whatever you are about, until you are destroyed and
quickly perish for your evil doings, because you have forsaken me.
   May the LORD cause pestilence to haunt you until he has extermi- 21
nated you out of the land which you are entering to occupy; may the 22
LORD afflict you with wasting disease and recurrent fever, ague and
eruptions; with drought, black blight and red; and may these plague
you until you perish. May the skies above you be bronze, and the earth 23
beneath you iron. May the LORD turn the rain upon your country into 24
fine sand, and may dust come down upon you from the sky until you
are blotted out.
   May the LORD put you to rout before the enemy. Though you go out 25
against them by one way, you shall flee before them by seven ways.
May you be repugnant to all the kingdoms on earth. May your bodies 26
become food for the birds of the air and the wild beasts, with no man
to scare them away.
   May the LORD strike you with Egyptian boils and with tumours,*b* 27
scabs, and itches, for which you will find no cure. May the LORD strike 28
you with madness, blindness, and bewilderment; so that you will grope 29
about in broad daylight, just as a blind man gropes in darkness, and
you will fail to find your way. You will also be oppressed and robbed,
day in, day out, with no one to save you. A woman will be pledged to 30
you, but another shall ravish her; you will build a house but not live
in it; you will plant a vineyard but not enjoy its fruit. Your ox will be 31
slaughtered before your eyes, but you will not eat any of it; and before
your eyes your ass will be stolen and will not come back to you; your
sheep will be given to the enemy, and there will be no one to recover
them. Your sons and daughters will be given to another people while 32
you look on; your eyes will strain after them all day long, and you will

[a] *Or* cursing, confusion, and rebuke.   [b] *Or, as otherwise read,* haemorrhoids.

33 be powerless. A nation whom you do not know shall eat the fruit of your land and all your toil, and your lot will be nothing but brutal

34, 35 oppression. The sights you see will drive you mad. May the LORD strike you on knee and leg with malignant boils for which you will find no cure; they will spread from the sole of your foot to the crown of your

36 head. May the LORD give you up, you and the king whom you have appointed, to a nation whom neither you nor your fathers have known,

37 and there you will worship other gods, gods of wood and stone. You will become a horror, a byword, and an object-lesson to all the peoples amongst whom the LORD disperses you.

38 You will carry out seed for your fields in plenty, but you will harvest

39 little; for the locusts will devour it. You will plant vineyards and cultivate them, but you will not drink the wine or gather the grapes;

40 for the grub will eat them. You will have olive-trees all over your territory, but you will not anoint yourselves with their oil; for your

41 olives will drop off. You will bear sons and daughters, but they will

42 not remain yours because they will be taken into captivity. All your trees and the fruit of the ground will be infested with the mole-cricket.

43 The alien who lives with you will raise himself higher and higher, and

44 you will sink lower and lower. He will lend to you but you will not lend to him: he will be the head and you the tail.

45 All these maledictions will come upon you; they will pursue you and overtake you until you are destroyed because you did not obey the LORD your God by keeping the commandments and statutes which he

46 gave you. They shall be a sign and a portent to you and your descen-

47 dants for ever, because you did not serve the LORD your God with joy

48 and with a glad heart for all your blessings. Then in hunger and thirst, in nakedness and extreme want, you shall serve your enemies whom the LORD will send against you, and they will put a yoke of iron on your

49 neck when they have subdued you. May the LORD raise against you a nation from afar, from the other end of the earth, who will swoop upon you like a vulture, a nation whose language you will not understand,

50 a nation of grim aspect with no reverence for age and no pity for the

51 young. They will devour the young of your cattle and the fruit of your land, when you have been subdued. They will leave you neither corn, nor new wine nor oil, neither the offspring of your herds nor of your

52 lambing flocks, until you are annihilated. They will besiege you in all your cities*a* until they bring down your lofty impregnable walls, those city walls throughout your land in which you trust. They will besiege you within all your cities, throughout the land which the LORD your

53 God has given you. Then you will eat your own children,*b* the flesh of your sons and daughters whom the LORD your God has given you,

[a] *Lit.* gates.   [b] *Lit.* the fruit of your body.

because of the dire straits to which you will be reduced when your enemy besieges you. The pampered, delicate man will not share with 54 his brother, or the wife of his bosom, or his own remaining children, any of the meat which he is eating, the flesh of his own children. He is 55 left with nothing else because of the dire straits to which you will be reduced when your enemy besieges you within your cities. The pam- 56 pered, delicate woman, the woman who has never even tried to put a foot to the ground, so delicate and pampered she is, will not share with her own husband or her son or her daughter the afterbirth which 57 she expels, or any boy or girl that she may bear. She will herself eat them secretly in her extreme want, because of the dire straits to which you will be reduced when your enemy besieges you within your cities.

If you do not observe and fulfil all the law written down in this book, 58 if you do not revere this honoured and dreaded name, this name 'the LORD*a* your God', then the LORD will strike you and your descendants 59 with unimaginable plagues, malignant and persistent, and with sickness, persistent and severe. He will bring upon you once again all the 60 diseases of Egypt which you dread, and they will cling to you. The 61 LORD will bring upon you sickness and plague of every kind not written down in this book of the law, until you are destroyed. Then 62 you who were countless as the stars in the sky will be left few in number, because you did not obey the LORD your God. Just as the 63 LORD took delight in you, prospering and increasing you, so now it will be his delight to destroy and exterminate you, and you will be up-rooted from the land which you are entering to occupy. The LORD will 64 scatter you among all peoples from one end of the earth to the other, and there you will worship other gods whom neither you have known nor your forefathers, gods of wood and stone. Among those nations you 65 will find no peace, no rest for the sole of your foot. Then the LORD will give you an unquiet mind, dim eyes, and failing appetite. Your life 66 will hang continually in suspense, fear will beset you night and day, and you will find no security all your life long. Every morning you will 67 say, 'Would God it were evening!', and every evening, 'Would God it were morning!', for the fear that lives in your heart and the sights that you see. The LORD will bring you sorrowing back to Egypt by that 68 very road of which I said to you, 'You shall not see that road again'; and there you will offer to sell yourselves to your enemies as slaves and slave-girls, but there will be no buyer.

These are the words of the covenant which the LORD commanded 29 1*b* Moses to make with the Israelites in Moab, in addition to the covenant which he made with them on Horeb.

[*a*] *See note on Exod. 3. 15.*   [*b*] *28. 69 in Heb.*

2[a] MOSES SUMMONED ALL THE ISRAELITES and said to them: 'You
have seen with your own eyes all that the LORD did in Egypt to Pharaoh,
3 to all his servants, and to the whole land, the great challenge which you
4 yourselves witnessed, those great signs and portents, but to this day the
LORD has not given you a mind to learn, or eyes to see, or ears to hear.
5 I led you for forty years in the wilderness; your clothes did not wear
6 out on you, nor did your sandals wear out and fall off your feet; you
ate no bread and drank no wine or strong drink, in order that you
7 might learn that I am the LORD your God. You came to this place
where Sihon king of Heshbon and Og king of Bashan came to attack
8 us, and we defeated them. We took their land and gave it as patrimony
9 to the Reubenites, the Gadites, and half the tribe of Manasseh. You
shall observe the provisions of this covenant and keep them so that
you may be successful in all you do.

10   'You all stand here today before the LORD your God, tribal chiefs,[b]
11 elders, and officers, all the men of Israel, with your dependants, your
wives, the aliens who live in your camp—all of them, from those who
12 chop wood to those who draw water—and you are ready to accept the
oath and enter into the covenant which the LORD your God is making
13 with you today. The covenant is to constitute you his people this day,
and he will be your God, as he promised you and as he swore to your
14 forefathers, Abraham, Isaac and Jacob. It is not with you alone that
15 I am making this covenant and this oath, but with all those who stand
here with us today before the LORD our God and also with those who
16 are not here with us today. For you know how we lived in Egypt and
17 how we and you, as we passed through the nations, saw their loathsome
idols and the false gods they had, the gods of wood and stone, of silver
18 and gold. If there should be among you a man or woman, family or
tribe, who is moved today to turn from the LORD our God and to go
worshipping the gods of those nations—if there is among you such a
19 root from which springs gall and wormwood, then when he hears the
terms of this oath, he may inwardly flatter himself and think, "All will
be well with me even if I follow the promptings of my stubborn heart";
20 but this will bring everything to ruin.[c] The LORD will not be willing to
forgive him; for then his anger and resentment will overwhelm this
man, and the denunciations prescribed in this book will fall heavily on
21 him, and the LORD will blot out his name from under heaven. The
LORD will single him out from all the tribes of Israel for disaster to fall
upon him, according to the oath required by the covenant and
prescribed in this book of the law.

22   'The next generation, your sons who follow you and the foreigners

[a] 29. 1 in Heb.   [b] So Pesh.; Heb. your chiefs, your tribes.   [c] but this...ruin: lit. to
the sweeping away of moist and dry.

who come from distant countries, will see the plagues of this land and the ulcers which the LORD has brought upon its people, the whole 23 land burnt up with brimstone and salt, so that it cannot be sown, or yield herb or green plant. It will be as desolate as were Sodom and Gomorrah, Admah and Zeboyim, when the LORD overthrew them in his anger and rage. Then they, and all the nations with them, will ask, 24 "Why has the LORD so afflicted this land? Why has there been this great outburst of wrath?" The answer will be: "Because they forsook 25 the covenant of the LORD the God of their fathers which he made with them when he brought them out of Egypt. They began to worship other 26 gods and to bow down to them, gods whom they had not known and whom the LORD had not assigned to them. The anger of the LORD 27 was roused against that land, so that he brought upon it all the maledictions written in this book. The LORD uprooted them from their soil 28 in anger, in wrath and great fury, and banished them to another land, where they are to this day."

'There are things hidden, and they belong to the LORD our God, but 29 what is revealed belongs to us and our children for ever; it is for us to observe all that is prescribed in this law.

'When these things have befallen you, the blessing and the curse of 30 which I have offered you the choice, if you and your sons take them to heart there in all the countries to which the LORD your God has banished you, if you turn back to him and obey him heart and soul in 2 all that I command you this day, then the LORD your God will show 3 you compassion and restore your fortunes. He will gather you again from all the countries to which he has scattered you. Even though he 4 were to banish you to the four corners of the world,[a] the LORD your God will gather you from there, from there he will fetch you home. The 5 LORD your God will bring you into the land which your forefathers occupied, and you will occupy it again; then he will bring you prosperity and make you more numerous than your forefathers were. The LORD 6 your God will circumcise[b] your hearts and the hearts of your descendants, so that you will love him with all your heart and soul and you will live. Then the LORD your God will turn all these denunciations against 7 your enemies and the foes who persecute you. You will then again obey 8 the LORD and keep all his commandments which I give you this day. The 9-10 LORD your God will make you more than prosperous in all that you do, in the fruit of your body and of your cattle and in the fruits of the earth; for, when you obey the LORD your God by keeping his commandments and statutes, as they are written in this book of the law, and when you turn back to the LORD your God with all your heart and soul, he will again rejoice over you and be good to you, as he rejoiced over your forefathers.

[a] *Lit.* to the end of the heavens.   [b] *Or* incline.

11 'The commandment that I lay on you this day is not too difficult for
12 you, it is not too remote. It is not in heaven, that you should say,
"Who will go up to heaven for us to fetch it and tell it to us, so that we
13 can keep it?" Nor is it beyond the sea, that you should say, "Who will
cross the sea for us to fetch it and tell it to us, so that we can keep it?"
14 It is a thing very near to you, upon your lips[a] and in your heart ready
to be kept.

15 'Today I offer you the choice of life and good, or death and evil.
16 If you obey the commandments of the LORD your God[b] which I give
you this day, by loving the LORD your God, by conforming to his ways
and by keeping his commandments, statutes, and laws, then you will
live and increase, and the LORD your God will bless you in the land
17 which you are entering to occupy. But if your heart turns away and you
do not listen and you are led on to bow down to other gods and worship
18 them, I tell you this day that you will perish; you will not live long in
the land which you will enter to occupy after crossing the Jordan.
19 I summon heaven and earth to witness against you this day: I offer you
the choice of life or death, blessing or curse. Choose life and then you
20 and your descendants will live; love the LORD your God, obey him and
hold fast to him: that is life for you and length of days in the land which
the LORD swore to give to your forefathers, Abraham, Isaac and Jacob.'

31 1,2 Moses finished speaking[c] these words to all Israel, and then he said,
'I am now a hundred and twenty years old, and I can no longer move
about as I please; and the LORD has told me that I may not cross the
3 Jordan. The LORD your God will cross over at your head and destroy
these nations before your advance, and you shall occupy their lands;
4 and, as he directed, Joshua will lead you across. The LORD will do to
these nations as he did to Sihon and Og, kings of the Amorites, and to
5 their lands; he will destroy them. The LORD will deliver them into your
6 power, and you shall do to them as[d] I commanded you. Be strong, be
resolute; you must not dread them or be afraid, for the LORD your
God himself goes with you; he will not fail you or forsake you.'
7 Moses summoned Joshua and said to him in the presence of all
Israel, 'Be strong, be resolute; for it is you who are to lead this people
into the land which the LORD swore to give their forefathers, and you
8 are to bring them into possession of it. The LORD himself goes at your
head; he will be with you; he will not fail you or forsake you. Do not
be discouraged or afraid.'
9 Moses wrote down this law and gave it to the priests, the sons of
Levi, who carried the Ark of the Covenant of the LORD, and to all the
10 elders of Israel. Moses gave them this command: 'At the end of every

[a] *Lit.* in your mouth. [b] If you...your God: *so Sept.; Heb. om.* [c] *So Scroll; Heb.*
Moses went and spoke... [d] *So Sept.; Heb.* according to all the commandment which...

seven years, at the appointed time for the year of remission, at the pilgrim-feast of Tabernacles, when all Israel comes to enter the 11 presence of*a* the LORD your God in the place which he will choose, you shall read this law publicly in the hearing of all Israel. Assemble 12 the people, men, women, and dependants, together with the aliens who live in your settlements, so that they may listen, and learn to fear the LORD your God and observe all these laws with care. Their 13 children, too, who do not know them, shall hear them, and learn to fear the LORD your God all their*b* lives in the land which you will occupy after crossing the Jordan.'

Joshua appointed successor to Moses

THE LORD SAID to Moses, 'The time of your death is drawing 14 near; call Joshua, and then come and stand in the Tent of the Presence so that I may give him his commission.' So Moses and Joshua went and took their stand in the Tent of the Presence; and the LORD 15 appeared in the tent in a pillar of cloud, and the pillar of cloud stood at the entrance of the tent.

The LORD said to Moses, 'You are about to die like your forefathers, 16 and this people, when they come into the land and live among foreigners, will go wantonly after their gods; they will abandon me and break the covenant which I have made with them. Then my anger will be roused 17 against them, and I will abandon them and hide my face from them. They will be an easy prey, and many terrible disasters will come upon them. They will say on that day, "These disasters have come because our God is not among us." On that day I will hide my face because of 18 all the evil they have done in turning to other gods.

'Now write down this rule of life*c* and teach it to the Israelites; make 19 them repeat it, so that it may be on record against them. When I have 20 brought them into the land which I swore to give to their forefathers, a land flowing with milk and honey, and they have plenty to eat and grow fat, they will turn to other gods and worship them, they will spurn me and break my covenant; and many calamities and disasters 21 will follow. Then this rule of life will confront them as a record, for it will not be forgotten by their descendants. For even before I bring them into the land which I swore to give them, I know which way their thoughts incline already.'

That day Moses wrote down this rule of life and taught it to the 22 Israelites. The LORD*d* gave Joshua son of Nun his commission in these 23

[a] *Lit.* see the face of. [b] *So Sam.; Heb.* your. [c] rule of life: *or* song. [d] *Prob. rdg.; Heb.* He.

277

words: 'Be strong, be resolute; for you shall bring the Israelites into the land which I swore to give them, and I will be with you.'

24 When Moses had finished writing down these laws in a book, from
25 beginning to end, he gave this command to the Levites who carried
26 the Ark of the Covenant of the LORD: 'Take this book of the law and put it beside the Ark of the Covenant of the LORD your God to be
27 a witness against you. For I know how defiant and stubborn you are; even during my lifetime you have defied the LORD; how much more,
28 then, will you do so when I am dead? Assemble all the elders of your tribes and your officers; I will say all these things in their hearing and
29 will summon heaven and earth to witness against them. For I know that after my death you will take to degrading practices and turn aside from the way which I told you to follow, and in days to come disaster will come upon you, because you are doing what is wrong in the eyes of the LORD and so provoking him to anger.'

Two historical poems

30 MOSES RECITED this song from beginning to end in the hearing of the whole assembly of Israel:

32   Give ear to what I say, O heavens,
               earth, listen to my words;
2   my teaching shall fall like drops of rain,
               my words shall distil like dew,
               like fine rain upon the grass
               and like the showers on young plants.

3   When I call aloud the name of the LORD,[a]
               you shall respond, 'Great is our God,
4   the creator[b] whose work is perfect,
               and all his ways are just,
               a faithful god, who does no wrong,
               righteous and true is He!'

5   Perverse and crooked generation
               whose faults have proved you no children of his,
6   is this how you repay the LORD,
               you brutish and stupid people?
               Is he not your father who formed you?
               Did he not make you and establish you?
7   Remember the days of old,

[a] *Or* the name JEHOVAH.   [b] *Or* rock.

278

think of the generations long ago;
ask your father to recount it
and your elders to tell you the tale.

When the Most High parcelled out the nations,   8
when he dispersed all mankind,
he laid down the boundaries of every people
according to the number of the sons of God;*a*
but the LORD's share was his own people,   9
Jacob was his allotted portion.
He found him in a desert land,   10
in a waste and howling void.
He protected and trained him,
he guarded him as the apple of his eye,
as an eagle watches over its nest,   11
hovers above its young,
spreads its pinions and takes them up,
and carries them upon its wings.
The LORD alone led him,   12
no alien god at his side.
He made him ride on the heights of the earth   13
and fed him on the harvest of the fields;
he satisfied him with honey from the crags
and oil from the flinty rock,
curds from the cattle, milk from the ewes,   14
the fat of lambs' kidneys,*b*
of rams, the breed of Bashan, and of goats,
with the finest flour of wheat;
and he*c* drank wine from the blood of the grape.
Jacob ate and was well fed,*d*   15
Jeshurun grew fat and unruly,*e*
he*c* grew fat, he*c* grew bloated and sleek.
He forsook God who made him
and dishonoured the Rock of his salvation.
They roused his jealousy with foreign gods   16
and provoked him with abominable practices.
They sacrificed to foreign demons that are no gods,   17
gods who were strangers to them;
they took up with new gods from their neighbours,
gods whom your fathers did not acknowledge.
You forsook the creator*f* who begot you   18

[a] *So Scroll; Heb.* sons of Israel.   [b] kidneys: *transposed from fourth line.*   [c] *So Sept.;*
Heb. you.   [d] Jacob...fed: *so Sam.; Heb. om.*   [e] *Or* and kicked.   [f] *Or* rock.

and cared nothing for God who brought you to birth.

19 The LORD saw and spurned them;
his own sons and daughters provoked him.

20 'I will hide my face from them,' he said;
'let me see what their end will be,
for they are a mutinous generation,
sons who are not to be trusted.

21 They roused my jealousy with a god of no account,
with their false gods they provoked me;
so I will rouse their jealousy with a people of no account,
with a brutish nation I will provoke them.

22 For fire is kindled by my anger,
it burns to the depths of Sheol;
it devours earth and its harvest
and sets fire to the very roots of the mountains.

23 I will heap on them one disaster after another,
I will use up all my arrows on them:

24 pangs of hunger, ravages of plague,
and bitter pestilence.
I will harry them with the fangs of wild beasts
and the poison of creatures that crawl in the dust.

25 The sword will make orphans in the streets
and widows in their own homes;
it will take toll of young man and maid,
of babes in arms and old men.

26 I had resolved to strike them down
and to destroy all memory of them,

27 but I feared that I should be provoked by their foes,
that their enemies would take the credit
and say, "It was not the LORD,
it was we who raised the hand that did this."'

28 They are a nation that lacks good counsel,
devoid of understanding.

29 If only they had the wisdom to understand this
and give thought to their end!

30 How could one man pursue a thousand of them,
how could two put ten thousand to flight,
if their Rock had not sold them to their enemies,
if the LORD had not handed them over?

31 For the enemy have no Rock like ours,
in themselves they are mere fools.

32 Their vines are vines of Sodom,

grown on the terraces of Gomorrah;
their grapes are poisonous,
the clusters bitter to the taste.
Their wine is the venom of serpents,   33
the cruel poison of asps;
all this I have in reserve,   34
sealed up in my storehouses
till the day of[a] punishment and vengeance,   35
till the moment when they slip and fall;
for the day of their downfall is near,
their doom is fast approaching.
The LORD will give his people justice   36
and have compassion on his servants;
for he will see that their strength is gone:
alone, or defended by his clan, no one is left.

He will say, 'Where are your gods,   37
the rock in which you sought shelter,
the gods who ate the fat of your sacrifices   38
and drank the wine of your drink-offerings?
Let them rise to help you!
Let them give you shelter!
See now that I, I am He,   39
and there is no god beside me:
I put to death and I keep alive,
I wound and I heal;
there is no rescue from my grasp.
I lift my hand to heaven   40
and swear: As I live for ever,
when I have whetted my flashing sword,   41
when I have set my hand to judgement,
then I will punish my adversaries
and take vengeance on my enemies.
I will make my arrows drunk with blood,   42
my sword shall devour flesh,
blood of slain and captives,
the heads of the enemy princes.'
Rejoice with him, you heavens,   43
bow down, all you gods, before him;[b]
for he will avenge the blood of his sons[c]
and take vengeance on his adversaries;

[a] till the day of: *so Sam.; Heb.* for me. [b] Rejoice...before him: *so Scroll, cp. Sept.; Heb.* Cause his people to rejoice, O nations. [c] *So Scroll; Heb.* servants.

    he will punish those who hate him
    and make expiation for his people's land.[a]

44   This is the song that Moses came and recited in the hearing of the people, he and Joshua[b] son of Nun.

45,46   Moses finished speaking to all Israel, and then he said, 'Take to heart all these warnings which I solemnly give you this day: command 47 your children to be careful to observe all the words of this law. For you they are no empty words; they are your very life, and by them you shall live long in the land which you are to occupy after crossing the Jordan.'

48,49   That same day the LORD spoke to Moses and said, 'Go up this mount Abarim, Mount Nebo in Moab, to the east of Jericho, and look out over the land of Canaan that I am giving to the Israelites for their 50 possession. On this mountain you shall die and be gathered to your father's kin, just as Aaron your brother died on Mount Hor and was 51 gathered to his father's kin. This is because both of you were unfaithful to me at the waters of Meribah-by-Kadesh in the wilderness of Zin, 52 when you did not uphold my holiness among the Israelites. You shall see the land from a distance but you may not enter the land I am giving to the Israelites.'

33   THIS IS THE BLESSING that Moses the man of God pronounced upon the Israelites before his death:

2
        The LORD came from Sinai
        and shone forth from Seir.
        He showed himself from Mount Paran,
        and with him were myriads of holy ones[c]
        streaming along at his right hand.

3
        Truly he loves his people[d]
        and blesses[e] his saints.[f]
        They sit at his[g] feet
        and receive his[g] instruction,

4
        the law which Moses laid upon us,
        as a possession for the assembly of Jacob.

5
        Then a king arose[h] in Jeshurun,
        when the chiefs of the people were assembled
        together with all the tribes of Israel.

---

[a] he will punish...land: *so Scroll; Heb.* and make expiation for his land, his people.
[b] *Heb.* Hoshea (*cp. Num. 13. 16*). [c] and with...holy ones: *prob. rdg.; Heb.* and he came from myriads of holiness. [d] his people: *so Sept.; Heb.* peoples. [e] *So Pesh.; Heb.* in thy hand. [f] *Or* holy ones. [g] *So Vulg.; Heb.* thy. [h] *Or* Then there was a king...

Of Reuben he said:[a]   6

> May Reuben live and not die out,
> but may he be few in number.

And of Judah he said this: 7

> Hear, O LORD, the cry of Judah
> and join him to his people,
> thou whose hands fight for him,
> who art his helper against his foes.

Of Levi he said: 8

> Thou didst give thy Thummim to Levi,
> thy Urim to thy loyal servant[b]
> whom thou didst prove at Massah,
> for whom thou didst plead at the waters of Meribah,
> who said of his parents, I do not know them,   9
> who did not acknowledge his brothers,
> nor recognize his children.
> They observe thy word
> and keep thy covenant;
> they teach thy precepts to Jacob,   10
> thy law to Israel.
> They offer thee the smoke of sacrifice
> and offerings on thy altar.
> Bless all his powers,[c] O LORD,   11
> and accept the work of his hands.
> Strike his adversaries hip and thigh,
> and may his enemies rise no more.

Of Benjamin he said: 12

> The LORD's beloved dwells in security,
> the High God[d] shields him all the day long,
> and he dwells under his protection.[e]

Of Joseph he said: 13

> The LORD's blessing is on his land
> with precious fruit watered from heaven above[f]
> and from the deep that lurks below,
> with precious fruit ripened by the sun,   14

[a] Of Reuben he said: *prob. rdg.; Heb. om.* [b] Thou didst...servant: *so Sept.; Heb.* Thy Thummim and Urim belong to thy loyal servant. [c] *Or* skill. [d] the High God: *prob. rdg.; Heb.* upon him. [e] under his protection: *lit.* between his shoulders. [f] above: *so some MSS.; others* with dew.

precious fruit, the produce of the months,
15   with all good things from the ancient mountains,
the precious fruit of the everlasting hills,
16   the precious fruits of earth and all its store,
by the favour of him who dwells in the burning bush.
This shall rest*a* upon the head of Joseph,
on the brow of him who was prince among*b* his brothers.
17   In majesty he shall be like a first-born ox,
his horns those of a wild ox
with which he will gore nations
and drive*c* them to the ends of earth.
Such will be the myriads of Ephraim,
and such the thousands of Manasseh.

18 Of Zebulun he said:

Rejoice, Zebulun, when you sally forth,
rejoice in your tents, Issachar.
19   They shall summon nations to the mountain,
there they will offer true sacrifices,
for they shall suck the abundance of the seas
and draw out*d* the hidden wealth of the sand.

20 Of Gad he said:

Blessed be Gad, in his wide domain;
he couches like a lion*e*
tearing an arm or a scalp.
21   He chose the best for himself,
for to him was allotted a ruler's portion,
when the chiefs of the people were assembled together.*f*
He did what the LORD deemed right,
observing his ordinances for Israel.

22 Of Dan he said:

Dan is a lion's cub
springing out from Bashan.

23 Of Naphtali he said:

Naphtali is richly favoured
and full of the blessings of the LORD;
his patrimony stretches to the sea and southward.

[a] *Prob. rdg., cp. Gen. 49. 26; Heb. has an unintelligible form.*   [b] him...among: *or the one cursed by.*   [c] and drive: *prob. rdg.; Heb.* together.   [d] draw out: *prob. rdg.; Heb. obscure.* [e] *Lit.* lioness.   [f] were assembled together: *so Sept.; Heb. obscure.*

Of Asher he said: 24

> Asher is most blest of sons,
> may he be the favourite among[a] his brothers
> and bathe his feet in oil.
> May your bolts be of iron and bronze,   25
> and your strength last as long as you live.
> There is none like the God of Jeshurun   26
> who rides the heavens to your help,
> riding the clouds in his glory,
> who humbled the gods of old   27
> and subdued[b] the ancient powers;
> who drove out the enemy before you
> and gave the word to destroy.
> Israel lives in security,   28
> the tribes of Jacob by themselves,
> in a land of corn and wine[c]
> where the skies drip with dew.
> Happy are you, people of Israel, peerless, set free;   29
> the LORD is the shield that guards you,
> the Blessed One[d] is your glorious sword.
> Your enemies come cringing to you,
> and you shall trample their bodies under foot.

The death of Moses

THEN MOSES WENT UP from the lowlands of Moab to Mount 34 Nebo, to the top of Pisgah, eastwards from Jericho, and the LORD showed him the whole land: Gilead as far as Dan; the whole of 2 Naphtali; the territory of Ephraim and Manasseh, and all Judah as far as the western sea; the Negeb and the Plain; the valley of Jericho, the 3 Vale of Palm Trees, as far as Zoar. The LORD said to him, 'This is the 4 land which I swore to Abraham, Isaac and Jacob that I would give to their descendants. I have let you see it with your own eyes, but you shall not cross over into it.'

There in the land of Moab Moses the servant of the LORD died, as 5 the LORD had said. He was buried in a valley in Moab opposite Beth- 6 peor, but to this day no one knows his burial-place. Moses was a 7 hundred and twenty years old when he died; his sight was not dimmed nor had his vigour failed.[e] The Israelites wept for Moses in the 8

[a] *Or* of.   [b] *Prob. rdg.; Heb.* under.   [c] *Or* new wine.   [d] the Blessed One: *Heb.* Asher.
[e] nor...failed: *or, with Pesh.,* and his cheeks were not sunken.

lowlands of Moab for thirty days; then the time of mourning for
9 Moses was ended. And Joshua son of Nun was filled with the spirit of
wisdom, for Moses had laid his hands on him, and the Israelites listened
to him and did what the LORD had commanded Moses.

10 There has never yet risen in Israel a prophet like Moses, whom the
11 LORD knew face to face: remember all the signs and portents which
the LORD sent him to show in Egypt to Pharaoh and all his servants and
12 the whole land; remember the strong hand of Moses and the terrible
deeds which he did in the sight of all Israel.

THE BOOK OF
JOSHUA

Israel's entry into the promised land

AFTER THE DEATH of Moses the servant of the LORD, 1
the LORD said to Joshua son of Nun, his assistant, 'My servant 2
Moses is dead; now it is for you to cross the Jordan, you and
this whole people of Israel, to the land which I am giving them.
Every place where you set foot is yours: I have given it to you, as 3
I promised Moses. From the desert and the Lebanon to the great river, 4
the river Euphrates, and across all the Hittite country westwards to the
Great Sea,*a* all this shall be your land. No one will ever be able to 5
stand against you: as I was with Moses, so will I be with you; I will
not fail you or forsake you. Be strong, be resolute; it is you who are to 6
put this people in possession of the land which I swore to give to their
fathers. Only be strong and resolute; observe diligently all the law 7
which my servant Moses has given you. You must not turn from it to
right or left, if you would prosper wherever you go. This book of the 8
law must ever be on your lips; you must keep it in mind day and night
so that you may diligently observe all that is written in it. Then you will
prosper and be successful in all that you do. This is my command: be 9
strong, be resolute; do not be fearful or dismayed, for the LORD your
God is with you wherever you go.' Then Joshua told the officers 10
to pass through the camp and give this order to the people: 'Get food 11
ready to take with you; for within three days you will be crossing the
Jordan to occupy the country which the LORD your God is giving you
to possess.' To the Reubenites, the Gadites, and the half tribe of 12
Manasseh, Joshua said, 'Remember the command which Moses the 13
servant of the LORD gave you when he said, "The LORD your God will
grant you security here and will give you this territory." Your wives 14
and dependants and your herds may stay east of the Jordan in the
territory which Moses has given you, but for yourselves, all the
warriors among you must cross over as a fighting force at the head of
your kinsmen. You must help them, until the LORD grants them security 15
like you and they too take possession of the land which the LORD your
God is giving them. You may then return to the land which is your own
possession,*b* the territory which Moses the servant of the LORD has
given you east of the Jordan.' They answered Joshua, 'Whatever you 16

[a] *Or* the Mediterranean Sea. [b] *So Sept.; Heb. adds* and occupy it.

17 tell us, we will do; wherever you send us, we will go. As we obeyed
Moses, so will we obey you; and may the Lord your God be with you
18 as he was with Moses! Whoever rebels against your authority, and fails
to carry out all your orders, shall be put to death. Only be strong and
resolute.'

2   Joshua son of Nun sent two spies out from Shittim secretly with
orders to reconnoitre the country. The two men came to Jericho and
went to the house of a prostitute named Rahab, and spent the night
2 there. It was reported to the king of Jericho that some Israelites had
3 arrived that night to explore the country. So the king sent to Rahab
and said, 'Bring out the men who have come to you and are now in your
4 house; they are here to explore the whole country.' The woman, who
had taken the two men and hidden them,[a] replied, 'Yes, the men did
5 come to me, but I did not know where they came from; and when it
was time to shut the gate at nightfall, they had gone. I do not know
where they were going, but if you hurry after them, you will catch
6 them up.' In fact, she had taken them up on to the roof and concealed
them among the stalks of flax which she had laid out there in rows.
7 The messengers went in pursuit of them down the road to the fords of
the Jordan, and the gate was closed as soon as they had gone out.
8 The men had not yet settled down, when Rahab came up to them on the
9 roof and said to them, 'I know that the Lord has given this land to you,
that terror of you has descended upon us all, and that because of you
10 the whole country is panic-stricken. For we have heard how the Lord
dried up the water of the Red Sea[b] before you when you came out of
Egypt, and what you did to Sihon and Og, the two Amorite kings
11 beyond the Jordan, whom you put to death. When we heard this, our
courage failed us; your coming has left no spirit in any of us; for the
12 Lord your God is God in heaven above and on earth below. Swear to
me now by the Lord that you will keep faith with my family, as I have
13 kept faith with you. Give me a token of good faith; promise that you
will spare the lives of my father and mother, my brothers and sisters
14 and all who belong to them, and save us from death.' The men replied,
'Our lives for yours, so long as you do not betray our business. When
the Lord gives us the country, we will deal honestly and faithfully by
15 you.' She then let them down through an opening by a rope; for the
16 house where she lived was on an angle of the wall. 'Take to the hills,'
she said, 'or the pursuers will come upon you. Hide yourselves there
17 for three days until they come back, and then go on your way.' The
men warned her that they would be released from the oath she had
18 made them take unless she did what they told her. 'When we enter the
land,' they said, 'you must fasten this strand of scarlet cord in the

[a] *Prob. rdg.; Heb.* him.   [b] *Or* the Sea of Reeds.

288

opening through which you have lowered us, and get everybody together here in the house, your father and mother, your brothers and all your family. If anybody goes out of doors into the street, his blood 19 shall be on his own head; we shall be quit of the oath. But if a hand is laid on anyone who stays indoors with you, his blood shall be on our heads. Remember too that, if you betray our business, then we shall be 20 quit of the oath you have made us take.' She replied, 'It shall be as you 21 say', and sent them away. They set off, and she fastened the strand of scarlet cord in the opening. The men made their way into the hills 22 and stayed there three days until the pursuers returned. They had searched all along the road, but had not found them.*a* The two men 23 then turned and came down from the hills, crossed the river and returned to Joshua son of Nun. They told him all that had happened to them and said to him, 'The LORD has put the whole country into 24 our hands, and now all its people are panic-stricken at our approach.'

Joshua rose early in the morning, and he and all the Israelites set out 3 from Shittim and came to the Jordan, where they encamped before crossing the river. At the end of three days the officers passed through 2 the camp, and gave this order to the people: 'When you see the Ark 3 of the Covenant of the LORD your God being carried forward by the levitical priests, then you too shall leave your positions and set out. Follow it, but do not go close to it; keep some distance behind, about 4 a thousand yards.*b* This will show you the way you are to go, for you have not travelled this way before.' Joshua then said to the people, 5 'Hallow yourselves, for tomorrow the LORD will do a great miracle among you.' To the priests he said, 'Lift up the Ark of the Covenant 6 and pass in front of the people.' So they lifted up the Ark of the Covenant and went in front of the people. Then the LORD said to 7 Joshua, 'Today I will begin to make you stand high in the eyes of all Israel, and they shall know that I will be with you as I was with Moses. Give orders to the priests who carry the Ark of the Covenant, and tell 8 them that when they come to the edge of the waters of the Jordan, they are to take their stand in the river.'

Then Joshua said to the Israelites, 'Come here and listen to the 9 words of the LORD your God. By this you shall know that the living God 10 is among you and that he will drive out before you the Canaanites, the Hittites, the Hivites, the Perizzites, the Girgashites, the Amorites, and the Jebusites: the Ark of the Covenant of the LORD,*c* the lord of all the 11 earth, is to cross the Jordan at your head. Choose twelve men from the 12 tribes of Israel, one man from each tribe. When the priests carrying the 13

[*a*] three days...found them: *or* three days while the pursuers scoured the land and searched all along the road, but did not find them.   [*b*] *Lit.* two thousand cubits.   [*c*] of the LORD: *prob. rdg., cp. verse 17; Heb. om.*

Ark of the LORD, the lord of all the earth, set foot in the waters of the Jordan, then the waters of the Jordan will be cut off; the water coming
14 down from upstream will stand piled up like a bank.' So the people set out from their tents to cross the Jordan, with the priests in front of
15 them carrying the Ark of the Covenant. Now the Jordan is in full flood in all its reaches throughout the time of harvest. When the priests
16 reached the Jordan and dipped their feet in the water at the edge, the water coming down from upstream was brought to a standstill; it piled up like a bank for a long way back, as far as Adam, a town near Zarethan. The waters coming down to the Sea of the Arabah, the Dead Sea, were completely cut off, and the people crossed over opposite
17 Jericho. The priests carrying the Ark of the Covenant of the LORD stood firm on the dry bed in the middle of the Jordan; and all Israel passed over on dry ground until the whole nation had crossed the river.

4 WHEN THE WHOLE NATION had finished crossing the Jordan, the
2 LORD said to Joshua, 'Take twelve men from the people, one from each
3 tribe, and order them to lift up twelve stones from this place, out of the middle of the Jordan, where the feet of the priests stood firm. They are to carry them across and set them down in the camp where you spend
4 the night.' Joshua summoned the twelve men whom he had chosen out
5 of the Israelites, one man from each tribe, and said to them, 'Cross over in front of the Ark of the LORD your God as far as the middle of the Jordan, and let each of you take a stone and hoist it on his shoulder,
6 one for each of the tribes of Israel. These stones are to stand as a memorial among you; and in days to come, when your children ask you
7 what these stones mean, you shall tell them how the waters of the Jordan were cut off before the Ark of the Covenant of the LORD when it crossed the Jordan.[a] Thus these stones will always be a reminder to
8 the Israelites.' The Israelites did as Joshua had commanded: they lifted up twelve stones from the middle of the Jordan, as the LORD had instructed Joshua, one for each of the tribes of Israel, carried them across to the camp and set them down there.
9   Joshua set up twelve stones in the middle of the Jordan at the place where the priests stood who carried the Ark of the Covenant, and there
10 they are to this day. The priests carrying the Ark remained standing in the middle of the Jordan until every command which the LORD had told Joshua to give to the people was fulfilled,[b] and the people had made
11 good speed across. When all the people had finished crossing, then the
12 Ark of the LORD crossed, and the priests with it.[c] At the head of the Israelites, there crossed over the Reubenites, the Gadites, and the half

[a] *So Sept.; Heb. adds* the waters of the Jordan were cut off. [b] *So Sept.; Heb. adds* according to all that Moses commanded Joshua. [c] *Prob. rdg.; Heb. adds* before the people.

tribe of Manasseh, as a fighting force, as Moses had told them to do; about forty thousand strong, drafted for active service, they crossed 13 over to the lowlands of Jericho in the presence of the LORD to do battle.

That day the LORD made Joshua stand very high in the eyes of all 14 Israel, and the people revered him, as they had revered Moses all his life.

The LORD said to Joshua, 'Command the priests carrying the Ark 15, 16 of the Tokens to come up from the Jordan.' So Joshua commanded the 17 priests to come up from the Jordan; and when the priests carrying the 18 Ark of the Covenant of the LORD came up from the river-bed, they had no sooner set foot on dry land than the waters of the Jordan came back to their place and filled up all its reaches as before. On the tenth 19 day of the first month the people came up out of the Jordan and camped in Gilgal in the district east of Jericho, and there Joshua set up the 20 twelve stones which they had taken from the Jordan. He said to the 21 Israelites, 'In days to come, when your descendants ask their fathers what these stones mean, you shall explain that the Jordan was dry when 22 Israel crossed over, and that the LORD your God dried up the waters of 23 the Jordan in front of you until you had gone across, just as the LORD your God did at the Red Sea when he dried it up for us until we had crossed. Thus all people on earth will know how strong is the hand of 24 the LORD; and thus they will stand in awe of the LORD your God for ever.'

When all the Amorite kings to the west of the Jordan and all the 5 Canaanite kings by the sea-coast heard that the LORD had dried up the waters before the advance of the Israelites until they had crossed, their courage melted away and there was no more spirit left in them for fear of the Israelites.

At that time the LORD said to Joshua, 'Make knives of flint, seat 2 yourself, and make Israel a circumcised people again.' Joshua there- 3 upon made knives of flint and circumcised the Israelites at Gibeath-haaraloth.[a] This is why Joshua circumcised them: all the males who 4 came out of Egypt, all the fighting men, had died in the wilderness on the journey from Egypt. The people who came out of Egypt had all been 5 circumcised, but not those who had been born in the wilderness during the journey. For the Israelites travelled in the wilderness for forty years, 6 until the whole nation, all the fighting men among them, had passed away, all who came out of Egypt and had disobeyed the voice of the LORD. The LORD swore that he would not allow any of these to see the land which he had sworn to their fathers to give us, a land flowing with milk and honey. So it was their sons, whom he had raised up in their 7 place, that Joshua circumcised; they were uncircumcised because they

[a] *That is* the Hill of Foreskins.

8 had not been circumcised on the journey. When the circumcision of the whole nation was complete, they stayed where they were in camp until
9 they had recovered. The LORD then said to Joshua, 'Today I have rolled away from you the reproaches of the Egyptians.' Therefore the place is called Gilgal[a] to this very day.

10   The Israelites encamped in Gilgal, and at sunset on the fourteenth
11 day of the month they kept the Passover in the lowlands of Jericho. On the day after the Passover, they ate their unleavened cakes and parched
12 grain, and that day it was the produce of the country. It was from that day, when they first ate the produce of the country, that the manna ceased. The Israelites received no more manna; and that year they ate what had grown in the land of Canaan.

13   When Joshua came near Jericho he looked up and saw a man standing in front of him with a drawn sword in his hand. Joshua went up to him
14 and said, 'Are you for us or for our enemies?' And the man said to him, 'I[b] am here as captain of the army of the LORD.' Joshua fell down before him, face to the ground, and said, 'What have you to say to your
15 servant, my lord?' The captain of the LORD's army said to him, 'Take off your sandals; the place where you are standing is holy'; and Joshua did so.

6 JERICHO WAS BOLTED and barred against the Israelites; no one went
2 out, no one came in. The LORD said to Joshua, 'Look, I have delivered
3 Jericho and her king[c] into your hands. You shall march round the city with all your fighting men, making the circuit of it once, for six days
4 running. Seven priests shall go in front of the Ark carrying seven trumpets made from rams' horns. On the seventh day you shall march
5 round the city seven times and the priests shall blow their trumpets. At the blast of the rams' horns, when you hear the trumpet sound, the whole army shall raise a great shout; the wall of the city will collapse
6 and the army shall advance, every man straight ahead.' So Joshua son of Nun summoned the priests and gave them their orders: 'Take up the Ark of the Covenant; let seven priests with seven trumpets of ram's
7 horn go in front of the Ark of the LORD.' Then he said to the army, 'March on and make the circuit of the city, and let the men drafted from the two and a half tribes go in front of the Ark of the LORD.'
8 When Joshua had spoken to the army, the seven priests carrying the seven trumpets of ram's horn before the LORD passed on and blew the
9 trumpets, with the Ark of the Covenant of the LORD following them. The drafted men marched in front of the priests who blew the trumpets, and the rearguard followed the Ark, the trumpets sounding as they

[a] *That is* Rolling Stones.   [b] *So some MSS.; others* And the man said, 'No, I...
[c] *Prob. rdg.; Heb. adds* the fighting men.

marched. But Joshua ordered the army not to shout, or to raise their 10 voices or utter a word, till the day came when he would tell them to shout; then they were to give a loud shout. Thus he caused the Ark of 11 the LORD to go round the city, making the circuit of it once, and then they went back to the camp and spent the night there. Joshua rose early 12 in the morning and the priests took up the Ark of the LORD. The seven 13 priests carrying the seven trumpets of ram's horn went marching in front of the Ark of the LORD, blowing the trumpets as they went, with the drafted men in front of them and the rearguard following the Ark of the LORD, the trumpets sounding as they marched. They marched 14 round the city once on the second day and returned to the camp; this they did for six days. But on the seventh day they rose at dawn and 15 marched seven times round the city in the same way; that was the only day on which they marched round seven times. The seventh time the 16 priests blew the trumpets and Joshua said to the army, 'Shout! The LORD has given you the city. The city shall be under solemn ban: 17 everything in it belongs to the LORD. No one is to be spared except the prostitute Rahab and everyone who is with her in the house, because she hid the men whom we sent. And you must beware of coveting[a] 18 anything that is forbidden under the ban; you must take none of it for yourselves; this would put the Israelite camp itself under the ban and bring trouble on it. All the silver and gold, all the vessels of copper and 19 iron, shall be holy; they belong to the LORD and they must go into the LORD's treasury.' So[b] they blew the trumpets, and when the army 20 heard the trumpet sound, they raised a great shout, and down fell the walls. The army advanced on the city, every man straight ahead, and took it. Under the ban they destroyed everything in the city; they put 21 everyone to the sword, men and women, young and old, and also cattle, sheep, and asses.

But the two men who had been sent out as spies were told by Joshua 22 to go into the prostitute's house and bring out her and all who belonged to her, as they had sworn to do. So the young men went and brought 23 out Rahab, her father and mother, her brothers and all who belonged to her. They brought out the whole family and left them outside the Israelite camp. They then set fire to the city and everything in it, 24 except that they deposited the silver and gold and the vessels of copper and iron in the treasury of the LORD's house. Thus Joshua spared the 25 lives of Rahab the prostitute, her household and all who belonged to her, because she had hidden the men whom Joshua had sent to Jericho as spies; she and her family settled permanently among the Israelites. It 26 was then that Joshua laid this curse on Jericho:

[a] *So Sept.; Heb.* putting under the ban.   [b] *So Sept.; Heb. adds* the people shouted and...

May the LORD's curse light on the man who comes forward
   to rebuild this city of Jericho:
   the laying of its foundations shall cost him his eldest son,
   the setting up of its gates shall cost him his youngest.

27   Thus the LORD was with Joshua, and his fame spread throughout the country.

7   But the Israelites defied the ban: Achan son of Carmi, son of Zabdi, son of Zerah, of the tribe of Judah, took some of the forbidden things, and the LORD was angry with the Israelites.

2   Joshua sent men from Jericho with orders to go up to Ai, near Beth-aven, east of Bethel, and see how the land lay; so the men went up and
3   explored Ai. They returned to Joshua and reported that there was no need for the whole army to move: 'Let some two or three thousand men go forward to attack Ai. Do not make the whole army toil up there; the
4   population is small.' And so about three thousand men went up, but
5   they turned tail before the men of Ai, who killed some thirty-six of them; they chased them all the way from the gate to the Quarries[a] and killed them on the pass. At this the courage of the people melted
6   and flowed away like water. Joshua and the elders of Israel rent their clothes and flung themselves face downwards to the ground; they lay before the Ark of the LORD till evening and threw dust on their heads.
7   Joshua said, 'Alas, O Lord GOD, why didst thou bring this people across the Jordan only to hand us over to the Amorites to be destroyed? If only we had been content to settle on the other side of the Jordan!
8   I beseech thee, O Lord; what can I say, now that Israel has been
9   routed by the enemy? When the Canaanites and all the natives of the country hear of this, they will come swarming around us and wipe us off the face of the earth. What wilt thou do then for the honour of thy great name?'

10   The LORD said to Joshua, 'Stand up; why lie prostrate on your face?
11   Israel has sinned: they have broken the covenant which I laid upon them, by taking forbidden things for themselves. They have stolen them, and concealed it by mingling them with their own possessions.
12   That is why the Israelites cannot stand against their enemies: they are put to flight because they have brought themselves under the ban. Unless they destroy every single thing among them that is forbidden
13   under the ban, I will be with them no longer. Stand up; you must hallow the people; tell them they must hallow themselves for tomorrow. Tell them, These are the words of the LORD the God of Israel: You have forbidden things among you, Israel; you cannot stand against your
14   enemies until you have rid yourselves of them. In the morning come forward tribe by tribe, and the tribe which the LORD chooses shall

[a] *Or* to Shebarim.

come forward clan by clan; the clan which the LORD chooses shall come forward family by family; and the family which the LORD chooses shall come forward man by man. The man who is chosen as the har- 15 bourer of forbidden things shall be burnt, he and all that is his, because he has broken the covenant of the LORD and committed outrage in Israel.' Early in the morning Joshua rose and brought Israel forward 16 tribe by tribe, and the tribe of Judah was chosen. He brought forward 17 the clans of Judah, and the clan of Zerah was chosen; then the clan of Zerah family by family,[a] and the family of[b] Zabdi was chosen. He 18 brought that family forward man by man, and Achan son of Carmi, son of Zabdi, son of Zerah, of the tribe of Judah, was chosen. Then Joshua 19 said to Achan, 'My son, give honour to the LORD the God of Israel and make your confession to him: tell me what you have done, hide nothing from me.' Achan answered Joshua, 'I confess, I have sinned against the 20 LORD the God of Israel. This is what I did: among the booty I caught 21 sight of a fine mantle from Shinar, two hundred shekels of silver, and a bar of gold weighing fifty shekels. I coveted them and I took them. You will find them hidden in the ground inside my tent, with the silver underneath.' So Joshua sent messengers, who ran to the tent, and there 22 was the stuff[c] hidden in the tent with the silver underneath. They took 23 the things from the tent, brought them to Joshua and all the Israelites, and spread them out before the LORD. Then Joshua took Achan son of 24 Zerah, with the silver, the mantle, and the bar of gold, together with his sons and daughters, his oxen, his asses, and his sheep, his tent, and everything he had, and he and all Israel brought them up to the Vale of Achor.[d] Joshua said, 'What trouble you have brought on us! Now 25 the LORD will bring trouble on you.' Then all the Israelites stoned him to death;[e] and they raised a great pile of stones over him, which remains 26 to this day. So the LORD's anger was abated. That is why to this day that place is called the Vale of Achor.

THE LORD SAID to Joshua, 'Do not be fearful or dismayed; take the 8 whole army and attack Ai. I deliver the king of Ai into your hands, him and his people, his city and his country. Deal with Ai and her king as 2 you dealt with Jericho and her king; but you may keep for yourselves the cattle and any other spoil that you may take. Set an ambush for the city to the west of it.' So Joshua and all the army prepared for the 3 assault on Ai. He chose thirty thousand fighting men and dispatched them by night, with these orders: 'Lie in ambush to the west of the 4 city, not far from it, and all of you hold yourselves in readiness. I myself 5

[a] *So some MSS.; others* man by man.   [b] the family of: *so Sept.; Heb. om.*   [c] *Or* the mantle.   [d] *That is* Trouble.   [e] *So Sept.; Heb. adds* and they burnt them with fire and pelted them with stones.

will approach the city with the rest of the army, and when the enemy
come out to meet us as they did last time, we shall take to flight before

6 them. Then they will come out and pursue us until we have drawn them
away from the city, thinking that we have taken to flight as we did last

7 time. While we are in flight, come out from your ambush and occupy

8 the city; the LORD your God will deliver it into your hands. When you
have taken it, set it on fire. Thus you will do what the LORD commands.

9 These are your orders.' So Joshua sent them off, and they went to the
place of ambush and waited between Bethel and Ai to the west of Ai,
while Joshua spent the night with the army.

10   Early in the morning Joshua rose, mustered the army and marched

11 against Ai, he himself and the elders of Israel at its head. All the armed
forces with him marched on until they came within sight of the city.
They encamped north of Ai, with the valley between them and the city;

12 but Joshua took some five thousand men and set them in ambush

14 between Bethel and Ai to the west of the city.*a* When the king of Ai
saw them, he and the citizens rose with all speed that morning and
marched out to do battle against Israel;*b* he did not know that there

15 was an ambush set for him to the west of the city. Joshua and all the
Israelites made as if they were routed by them and fled towards the

16 wilderness, and all the people in the city were called out in pursuit. So

17 they pursued Joshua and were drawn away from the city. Not a man was
left in Ai;*c* they had all gone out in pursuit of the Israelites and during
the pursuit had left the city undefended.

18   Then the LORD said to Joshua, 'Point towards Ai with the dagger you
are holding, for I will deliver the city into your hands.' So Joshua

19 pointed with his dagger towards Ai. At his signal, the men in ambush
rose quickly from their places and, entering the city at a run, took it and

20 promptly set fire to it. The men of Ai looked back and saw the smoke
from the city already going up to the sky; they were powerless to make
their escape in any direction, and the Israelites who had feigned flight

21 towards the wilderness turned on their pursuers. For when Joshua and
all the Israelites saw that the ambush had seized the city and that smoke
was already going up from it, they turned and fell upon the men of Ai.

22 Those who had come out to meet the Israelites were now hemmed in
with Israelites on both sides of them, and the Israelites cut them down

23 until there was not a single survivor, nor had any escaped. The king of

24 Ai was taken alive and brought to Joshua. When the Israelites had cut
down to the last man all the citizens of Ai who were in the open country
or in the wilderness to which they had pursued them, and the massacre

[a] *So Sept.; Heb. adds* (13) So the army pitched camp to the north of the city, and the
rearguard to the west, while Joshua went that night into the valley. [b] *So Sept.; Heb. adds*
for the appointed time, before the Arabah. [c] *So Sept.; Heb. adds* or Bethel.

was complete, they all turned back to Ai and put it to the sword. The 25 number who were killed that day, men and women, was twelve thousand, the whole population of Ai. Joshua held out his dagger and 26 did not draw back his hand until he had put to death all who lived in Ai; but the Israelites kept for themselves the cattle and any other spoil that 27 they took, following the word of the LORD spoken to Joshua. So Joshua 28 burnt Ai to the ground, and left it the desolate ruined mound it remains to this day. He hanged the king of Ai on a tree and left him there 29 till sunset; and when the sun had set, he gave the order and they cut him down and flung down his body at the entrance of the city gate. Over the body they raised a great pile of stones, which is there to this day.

At that time Joshua built an altar to the LORD the God of Israel on 30 Mount Ebal. The altar was of blocks of undressed stone on which no 31 tool of iron had been used, following the commands given to the Israelites by Moses the servant of the LORD, as is described in the book of the law of Moses. At the altar they offered whole-offerings to the LORD, and slaughtered shared-offerings. There in the presence of the 32 Israelites he engraved on blocks*a* of stone a copy of the law of Moses.*b* And all Israel, elders, officers, and judges, took their stand on either 33 side of the Ark, facing the levitical priests who carried the Ark of the Covenant of the LORD—all Israel, native and alien alike. Half of them stood facing Mount Gerizim and half facing Mount Ebal, to fulfil the command of Moses the servant of the LORD that the blessing should be pronounced first. Then Joshua recited the whole of the blessing and 34 the cursing word by word, as they are written in the book of the law. There was not a single word of all that Moses had commanded which 35 he did not read aloud before the whole congregation of Israel, including the women and dependants and the aliens resident in their company.

When the news of these happenings reached all the kings west of the 9 Jordan, in the hill-country, the Shephelah, and all the coast of the Great Sea running up to the Lebanon, the kings of the Hittites, Amorites, Canaanites, Perizzites, Hivites, and Jebusites agreed to join forces and 2 fight against Joshua and Israel.

When the inhabitants of Gibeon heard how Joshua had dealt with 3 Jericho and Ai, they adopted a ruse of their own. They went and 4 disguised themselves, with old sacking for their asses, old wine-skins split and mended, old and patched sandals for their feet, old clothing 5 to wear, and by way of provisions nothing but dry and mouldy bread. They came to Joshua in the camp at Gilgal and said to him and the 6 Israelites, 'We have come from a distant country to ask you now to grant us a treaty.' The Israelites said to the Hivites, 'But maybe you 7

[*a*] *Or* on the blocks.   [*b*] *So Sept.; Heb. adds* which he had engraved.

8 live in our neighbourhood: if so, how can we grant you a treaty?' They said to Joshua, 'We are your slaves.' Joshua asked them who they were
9 and where they came from. 'Sir,' they replied, 'our country is very far away, and we have come because of the renown of the LORD your
10 God. We have heard of his fame, of all that he did to Egypt, and to the two Amorite kings east of the Jordan, Sihon king of Heshbon and Og
11 king of Bashan who lived at Ashtaroth. Our elders and all the people of our country told us to take provisions for the journey and come to meet
12 you, and say, "We are your slaves; please grant us a treaty." Look at our bread; it was hot from the oven when we packed it at home on the
13 day we came away. Now it is dry and mouldy. Look at the wine-skins; they were new when we filled them, and now they are all split; look at
14 our clothes and our sandals, worn out by the long journey.' The chief men*a* of the community accepted some of their provisions, and did not
15 at first seek guidance from the LORD. So Joshua received them peaceably and granted them a treaty, promising to spare their lives, and the chiefs pledged their faith to them on oath.

16 Within three days of granting them the treaty, the Israelites learnt
17 that they were in fact neighbours and lived near by. So the Israelites set out and on the third day they reached their cities; these were
18 Gibeon, Kephirah, Beeroth, and Kiriath-jearim. The Israelites did not slaughter them, because of the oath which the chief men of the community had sworn to them by the LORD the God of Israel, but the
19 people were all indignant with their chiefs. The chiefs all replied to the assembled people, 'But we swore an oath to them by the LORD the
20 God of Israel; we cannot touch them now. What we will do is this: we will spare their lives so that the oath which we swore to them may
21 bring no harm upon us. *b*But though their lives must be spared, they shall be*c* set to chop wood and draw water for the community.' The
22 people agreed to do*d* as their chiefs had said. Joshua summoned the Gibeonites and said, 'Why did you play this trick on us? You told us
23 that you live a long way off, when you are near neighbours. There is a curse upon you for this: for all time you shall provide us with slaves,
24 to chop wood and draw water for the house of my God.' They answered Joshua, 'We were told, sir, that the LORD your God had commanded Moses his servant to give you the whole country and to exterminate all its inhabitants; so because of you we were in terror of our lives, and
25 that is why we did this. We are in your power: do with us whatever
26 you think right and proper.' What he did was this: he saved them from
27 death at the hands of the Israelites, and they did not kill them; but thenceforward he set them to chop wood and draw water for the

[*a*] *So Sept.; Heb.* The men.   [*b*] *So Sept.; Heb. prefixes* And the chiefs said to them.
[*c*] *So Sept.; Heb.* they were.   [*d*] The people...do: *so some Sept. MSS.; Heb. om.*

community and for the altar of the LORD. And to this day they do it at the place which the LORD chose.

When Adoni-zedek king of Jerusalem heard that Joshua had captured 10 Ai and destroyed it (for Joshua had dealt with Ai and her king as he had dealt with Jericho and her king), and that the inhabitants of Gibeon had made their peace with Israel and were living among them, he was[a] 2 greatly alarmed; for Gibeon was a large place, like a royal city: it was larger than Ai, and its men were all good fighters. So Adoni-zedek king 3 of Jerusalem sent to Hoham king of Hebron, Piram king of Jarmuth, Japhia king of Lachish, and Debir king of Eglon, and said, 'Come up 4 and help me, and we will attack the Gibeonites, because they have made their peace with Joshua and the Israelites.' So the five Amorite kings, 5 the kings of Jerusalem, Hebron, Jarmuth, Lachish, and Eglon, joined forces and advanced to take up their positions for the attack on Gibeon. But the men of Gibeon sent this message to Joshua in the camp at 6 Gilgal: 'We are your slaves, do not abandon us, come quickly to our relief. All the Amorite kings in the hill-country have joined forces against us; come and help us.' So Joshua went up from Gilgal with 7 all his forces and all his fighting men. The LORD said to Joshua, 'Do not 8 be afraid of them; I have delivered them into your hands, and not a man will be able to stand against you.' Joshua came upon them 9 suddenly, after marching all night from Gilgal. The LORD threw them 10 into confusion before the Israelites, and Joshua defeated them utterly in Gibeon; he pursued them down the pass of Beth-horon and kept up the slaughter as far as Azekah and Makkedah. As they were fleeing 11 from Israel down the pass, the LORD hurled great hailstones at them out of the sky all the way to Azekah: more died from the hailstones than the Israelites slew by the sword.

On that day when the LORD delivered the Amorites into the hands of 12 Israel, Joshua spoke with the LORD, and he said in the presence of Israel:

Stand still, O Sun, in Gibeon;
stand, Moon, in the Vale of Aijalon.

So the sun stood still and the moon halted until a nation had taken 13 vengeance on its enemies, as indeed is written in the Book of Jashar.[b] The sun stayed in mid heaven and made no haste to set for almost a whole day. Never before or since has there been such a day as this day 14 on which the LORD listened to the voice of a man; for the LORD fought for Israel. So Joshua and all the Israelites returned to the camp at 15 Gilgal.

The five kings fled and hid themselves in a cave at Makkedah, 16 and Joshua was told that they had been found hidden in this cave. 17

[a] *So Pesh.; Heb.* they were.　[b] *Or* the Book of the Upright.

18 Joshua replied, 'Roll some great stones to the mouth of the cave and
19 post men there to keep watch over the kings. But you must not stay;
keep up the pursuit, attack your enemies from the rear and do not let
them reach their cities; the LORD your God has delivered them into
20 your hands.' When Joshua and the Israelites had finished the work of
slaughter and all had been put to the sword—except a few survivors
21 who escaped and entered the fortified cities—the whole army rejoined[a]
Joshua at Makkedah in peace; not a man[b] of the Israelites suffered so
22 much as a scratch on his tongue. Then Joshua said, 'Open the mouth
23 of the cave, and bring me out those five kings.' They did so; they
brought the five kings out of the cave, the kings of Jerusalem, Hebron,
24 Jarmuth, Lachish, and Eglon. When they had brought them to
Joshua, he summoned all the Israelites and said to the commanders
of the troops who had served with him, 'Come forward and put your
feet on the necks of these kings.' So they came forward and put their
25 feet on their necks. Joshua said to them, 'Do not be fearful or dismayed;
be strong and resolute; for the LORD will do this to every enemy you
26 fight against.' And he struck down the kings and slew them; then he
hung their bodies on five trees, where they remained hanging till
27 evening. At sunset, on Joshua's orders they took them down from the
trees and threw them into the cave in which they had hidden; they
piled great stones against its mouth, and there the stones are to this
day.[c]

28 On that same day, Joshua captured Makkedah and put both king
and people to the sword, destroying both them and every living thing
in the city. He left no survivor, and he dealt with the king of Makkedah
29 as he had dealt with the king of Jericho. Then Joshua and all the
30 Israelites marched on from Makkedah to Libnah and attacked it. The
LORD delivered the city and its king to the Israelites, and they put its
people and every living thing in it to the sword; they left no survivor
there, and dealt with its king as they had dealt with the king of Jericho.
31 From Libnah Joshua and all the Israelites marched on to Lachish, took
32 up their positions and attacked it. The LORD delivered Lachish into
their hands; they took it on the second day and put every living thing
in it to the sword, as they had done at Libnah.

33 Meanwhile Horam king of Gezer had advanced to the relief of
Lachish; but Joshua struck them down, both king and people, and not
34 a man of them survived. Then Joshua and all the Israelites marched on
35 from Lachish to Eglon, took up their positions and attacked it; that
same day they captured it and put its inhabitants to the sword,
destroying every living thing in it as they had done at Lachish.

[a] *So Sept.; Heb. adds* at the camp.   [b] *So Sept.; Heb.* not for a man.   [c] and there...
day: *or* on this very day.

From Eglon Joshua and all the Israelites advanced to Hebron and 36
attacked it. They captured it and put its king to the sword together 37
with every living thing in it and in all its villages; as at Eglon, he left
no survivor, destroying it and every living thing in it. Then Joshua 38
and all the Israelites wheeled round towards Debir and attacked it.
They captured the city with its king, and all its villages, put them to the 39
sword and destroyed every living thing; they left no survivor. They
dealt with Debir and its king as they had dealt with Hebron and with
Libnah and its king.

So Joshua massacred the population of the whole region—the hill- 40
country, the Negeb, the Shephelah, the watersheds—and all their kings.
He left no survivor, destroying everything that drew breath, as the
LORD the God of Israel had commanded. Joshua carried the slaughter 41
from Kadesh-barnea to Gaza, over the whole land of Goshen and as far
as Gibeon. All these kings he captured at the same time, and their 42
country with them, for the LORD the God of Israel fought for Israel.
And Joshua returned with all the Israelites to the camp at Gilgal. 43

When Jabin king of Hazor heard of all this, he sent to Jobab king of 11
Madon, to the kings of Shimron and Akshaph, to the northern kings 2
in the hill-country, in the Arabah opposite*a* Kinnereth, in the Shephelah, and in the district of Dor on the west, the Canaanites to the 3
east and the west, the Amorites, Hittites, Perizzites, and Jebusites in the
hill-country, and the Hivites below Hermon in the land of Mizpah.
They took the field with all their forces, a great horde countless as the 4
grains of sand on the sea-shore, among them a great number of horses
and chariots. All these kings made common cause, and came and 5
encamped at the waters of Merom to fight against Israel. The LORD 6
said to Joshua, 'Do not be afraid of them, for at this time tomorrow
I shall deliver them to Israel all dead men; you shall hamstring their
horses and burn their chariots.' So Joshua and his army surprised them 7
by the waters of Merom and fell upon them. The LORD delivered them 8
into the hands of Israel; they struck them down and pursued them as
far as Greater Sidon, Misrephoth on the west, and the Vale of Mizpah
on the east. They struck them down until not a man was left alive.
Joshua dealt with them as the LORD had commanded: he hamstrung 9
their horses and burnt their chariots.

At this point Joshua turned his forces against Hazor, formerly the 10
head of all these kingdoms. He captured the city and put its king to
death with the sword. They killed every living thing in it and wiped 11
them all out; they spared nothing that drew breath, and Hazor itself
they destroyed by fire. So Joshua captured these kings and their cities 12
and put them to the sword, destroying them all, as Moses the servant

[a] *So Sept.; Heb.* south of.

13 of the LORD had commanded. The cities whose ruined mounds are still standing were not burnt by the Israelites; it was Hazor alone that

14 Joshua burnt. The Israelites plundered all these cities and kept for themselves the cattle and any other spoil they took; but they put every living soul to the sword until they had destroyed every one; they did

15 not leave alive any one that drew breath. The LORD laid his commands on his servant Moses, and Moses laid these same commands on Joshua, and Joshua carried them out. Not one of the commands laid on Moses by the LORD did he leave unfulfilled.

16 And so Joshua took the whole country, the hill-country, all the Negeb, all the land of Goshen, the Shephelah, the Arabah, and the Israelite

17 hill-country with the adjoining lowlands. His conquests extended from the bare mountain which leads up to Seir as far as Baal-gad in the Vale of Lebanon under Mount Hermon. He took prisoner all their kings,

18 struck them down and put them to death. It was a long war that he

19 fought against all these kingdoms. Except for the Hivites who lived in Gibeon, not one of their cities came to terms with the Israelites; all

20 were taken by storm. It was the LORD's purpose that they should offer an obstinate resistance to the Israelites in battle, and that thus they should be annihilated without mercy and utterly destroyed,[a] as the LORD had commanded Moses.

21 It was then that Joshua proceeded to wipe out the Anakim from the hill-country, from Hebron, Debir, Anab, all the hill-country of Judah and all the hill-country of Israel, destroying both them and their cities.

22 No Anakim were left in the land taken by the Israelites; they survived only in Gaza, Gath, and Ashdod.

23 Thus Joshua took the whole country, fulfilling all the commands that the LORD had laid on Moses; he assigned it as Israel's patrimony, allotting to each tribe its share; and the land was at peace.

12 These are the names of the kings of the land whom the Israelites slew, and whose territory they occupied beyond the Jordan towards the sunrise from the gorge of the Arnon as far as Mount Hermon and all

2 the Arabah on the east. Sihon the Amorite king who lived in Heshbon: his rule extended from Aroer, which is on the edge of the gorge of the Arnon, along the middle of the gorge and over half Gilead as far as the

3 gorge of the Jabbok, the Ammonite frontier; along the Arabah as far as the eastern side of the Sea of Kinnereth and as far as the eastern side of the Sea of the Arabah, the Dead Sea, by the road to Beth-jeshimoth

4 and from Teman under the watershed of Pisgah. Og[b] king of Bashan, one of the survivors of the Rephaim, who lived in Ashtaroth and Edrei:

---

[a] offer...destroyed: *or* obstinately engage the Israelites in battle so that they should annihilate them without mercy, only that he might destroy them...   [b] *So Sept.; Heb.* the boundary of Og.

he ruled over Mount Hermon, Salcah, all Bashan as far as the Geshurite 5
and Maacathite borders, and half Gilead as far as[a] the boundary of
Sihon king of Heshbon. Moses the servant of the LORD put them to 6
death, he and the Israelites, and he gave their land to the Reubenites,
the Gadites, and half the tribe of Manasseh, as their possession.

These are the names of the kings whom Joshua and the Israelites put 7
to death beyond the Jordan to the west, from Baal-gad in the Vale of
Lebanon as far as the bare mountain that leads up to Seir. Joshua gave
their land to the Israelite tribes to be their possession according to their
allotted shares, in the hill-country, the Shephelah, the Arabah, the 8
watersheds, the wilderness, and the Negeb; lands of the Hittites,
Amorites, Canaanites, Perizzites, Hivites, and Jebusites. The king of 9
Jericho; the king of Ai which is beside Bethel; the king of Jerusalem; 10
the king of Hebron; the king of Jarmuth; the king of Lachish; the 11, 12
king of Eglon; the king of Gezer; the king of Debir; the king of Geder; 13
the king of Hormah; the king of Arad; the king of Libnah; the king of 14, 15
Adullam; the king of Makkedah; the king of Bethel; the king of 16, 17
Tappuah; the king of Hepher; the king of Aphek; the king of Aphek[b]-in- 18
Sharon; the king of Madon; the king of Hazor; the king of Shimron- 19, 20
meron;[c] the king of Akshaph; the king of Taanach; the king of 21
Megiddo; the king of Kedesh; the king of Jokneam-in-Carmel; 22
the king of Dor in the district of Dor; the king of Gaiam-in-Galilee;[d] 23
the king of Tirzah: thirty-one kings in all, one of each town. 24

The division of the land among the tribes

B Y THIS TIME Joshua had become very old, and the LORD said to 13
him, 'You are now a very old man, and much of the country
remains to be occupied. The country which remains is this: all the 2
districts of the Philistines and all the Geshurite country (this is 3
reckoned as Canaanite territory from Shihor to the east of Egypt as far
north as Ekron; and it belongs to the five lords of the Philistines, those
of Gaza, Ashdod, Ashkelon, Gath, and Ekron); all the districts of the
Avvim on the south; all the Canaanite country from the low-lying land 4
which belongs to the Sidonians as far as Aphek, the Amorite frontier;
the land of the Gebalites and all the Lebanon to the east from Baal-gad 5
under Mount Hermon as far as Lebo-hamath. I will drive out in favour 6
of the Israelites all the inhabitants of the hill-country from the Lebanon
as far as Misrephoth on the west, and all the Sidonians. In the mean

[a] as far as: *so Luc. Sept.; Heb. om.*   [b] of Aphek: *prob. rdg.; Heb. om.*   [c] *In 11. 1*
Shimron.   [d] Gaiam-in-Galilee: *prob. rdg., cp. Sept.; Heb.* nations to Gilgal.

time you are to allot all this to the Israelites for their patrimony, as
7 I have commanded you. Distribute this land now to the nine tribes and
8 half the tribe of Manasseh for their patrimony.' For half the tribe of
Manasseh and[a] with them the Reubenites and the Gadites had each
taken their patrimony which Moses gave them east of the Jordan, as
9 Moses the servant of the LORD had ordained. It started from Aroer
which is by the edge of the gorge of the Arnon, and the level land half-
way along the gorge, and included all the tableland from Medeba as
10 far as Dibon; all the cities of Sihon, the Amorite king who ruled in
11 Heshbon, as far as the Ammonite frontier; and it also included Gilead
and the Geshurite and Maacathite territory, and all Mount Hermon
12 and the whole of Bashan as far as Salcah, all the kingdom of Og which
he ruled from both Ashtaroth and Edrei in Bashan. He was a survivor
of the remnant of the Rephaim, but Moses put them both to death and
13 occupied their lands. But the Israelites did not drive out the Geshurites
and the Maacathites; the Geshurites and the Maacathites live among the
14 Israelites to this day. The tribe of Levi, however, received no patrimony;[b]
the LORD the God of Israel is their patrimony, as he promised them.

15 So Moses allotted territory to the tribe of the Reubenites family by
16 family. Their territory started from Aroer which is by the edge of the
gorge of the Arnon, and the level land half-way along the gorge, and
17 included all the tableland as far as Medeba; Heshbon and all its cities
18 on the tableland, Dibon, Bamoth-baal, Beth-baal-meon, Jahaz,
19 Kedemoth, Mephaath, Kiriathaim, Sibmah, Zereth-shahar on the
20 hill in the Vale, Beth-peor, the watershed of Pisgah, and Beth-
21 jeshimoth, all the cities of the tableland, all the kingdom of Sihon the
Amorite king who ruled in Heshbon, whom Moses put to death
together with the princes of Midian, Evi, Rekem, Zur, Hur, and Reba,
22 the vassals of Sihon who dwelt in the country. Balaam son of Beor,
who practised augury, was among those whom the Israelites put to the
23 sword. The boundary of the Reubenites was the Jordan and the
adjacent land: this is the patrimony of the Reubenites family by
family, both the cities and their hamlets.

24, 25   Moses allotted[c] territory to the Gadites family by family. Their
territory was Jazer, all the cities of Gilead and half the Ammonite
26 country as far as Aroer which is east of Rabbah. It reached from
Heshbon as far as Ramoth-mizpeh and Betonim, and from Mahanaim as
27 far as the boundary of Lo-debar; it included in the valley Beth-haram,
Beth-nimrah, Succoth, and Zaphon, the rest of the kingdom of Sihon
king of Heshbon. The boundary was the Jordan and the adjacent land
28 as far as the end of the Sea of Kinnereth east of the Jordan. This is the

[a] For half. . .Manasseh and: *prob. rdg.; Heb. om.*   [b] *So Sept.; Heb. adds* the food-offerings of. . .   [c] *So Sept.; Heb. adds* to the tribe of Gad.

patrimony of the Gadites family by family, both the cities and their hamlets.

Moses allotted territory to the half tribe of Manasseh: it was for half 29 the tribe of the Manassites family by family. Their territory ran from 30 Mahanaim and included all Bashan, all the kingdom of Og king of Bashan and all Havvoth-jair in Bashan—sixty cities. Half Gilead, and 31 Ashtaroth and Edrei the royal cities of Og in Bashan, belong to the sons of Machir son of Manasseh on behalf of half the Machirites family by family.

These are the territories which Moses allotted to the tribes as their 32 patrimonies in the lowlands of Moab east of the Jordan.*a* But to the 33 tribe of Levi he gave no patrimony: the LORD the God of Israel is their patrimony, as he promised them.

Now follow the possessions which the Israelites acquired in the land 14 of Canaan, as Eleazar the priest, Joshua son of Nun, and the heads of the families of the Israelite tribes allotted them. They were assigned 2 by lot, following the LORD's command given through Moses, to the nine and a half tribes. To two and a half tribes Moses had given 3 patrimonies beyond the Jordan; but he gave none to the Levites as he did to the others. The tribe of Joseph formed the two tribes of Manasseh 4 and Ephraim. The Levites were given no share in the land, only cities to dwell in, with their common land for flocks and herds. So the 5 Israelites, following the LORD's command given to Moses, assigned the land.

Now the tribe of Judah had come to Joshua in Gilgal, and Caleb son 6 of Jephunneh the Kenizzite said to him, 'You remember what the LORD said to Moses the man of God concerning you and me at Kadesh-barnea. I was forty years old when Moses the servant of the LORD sent 7 me from there to explore the land, and I brought back an honest report. The others who went with me discouraged the people, but I 8 loyally carried out the purpose of the LORD my God. Moses swore an 9 oath that day and said, "The land on which you have set foot shall be your patrimony and your sons' after you as a possession for ever; for you have loyally carried out the purpose of the LORD my God." Well, 10 the LORD has spared my life as he promised; it is now forty-five years since he made this promise to Moses, at the time when Israel was journeying in the wilderness. Today I am eighty-five years old. I am 11 still as strong as I was on the day when Moses sent me out; I am as fit now for war as I was then and am ready to take the field again. Give 12 me today this hill-country which the LORD then promised me. You heard on that day that the Anakim were there and their cities were large and well fortified. Perhaps the LORD will be with me and I shall

[a] *So Pesh.; Heb. adds* Jericho.

13 dispossess them as he promised.' Joshua blessed Caleb and gave him
14 Hebron for his patrimony, and that is why Hebron remains to this day
in the patrimony of Caleb son of Jephunneh the Kenizzite. It is
because he loyally carried out the purpose of the LORD the God of
15 Israel. Formerly the name of Hebron was Kiriath-arba. This Arba was
the chief man of the Anakim. And the land was at peace.

15   This is the territory allotted to the tribe of the sons of Judah family
by family. It started from the Edomite frontier at the wilderness of
2 Zin and ran as far as the Negeb at its southern end, and it had a
common border with the Negeb at the end of the Dead Sea, where an
3 inlet of water bends towards the Negeb. It continued from the south
by the ascent of Akrabbim, passed by Zin, went up from the south of
Kadesh-barnea, passed by Hezron, went on to Addar and turned round
4 to Karka. It then passed along to Azmon, reached the Torrent of
Egypt, and its limit was the sea. This was their*a* southern boundary.
5   The eastern boundary is the Dead Sea as far as the mouth of the
Jordan and the adjacent land northwards from the inlet of the sea, at
6 the mouth of the Jordan. The boundary goes up to Beth-hoglah; it
passes north of Beth-arabah and thence to the stone of Bohan son of
7 Reuben, thence to Debir from the Vale of Achor, and then turns north
to the districts*b* in front of the ascent of Adummim south of the
gorge. The boundary then passes the waters of En-shemesh and the
8 limit there is En-rogel. It then goes up by the Valley of Ben-hinnom to
the southern slope of the Jebusites (that is Jerusalem). Thence it goes
up to the top of the hill which faces the Valley of Hinnom on the west;
9 this is at the northern end of the Vale of Rephaim. The boundary then
bends round from the top of the hill to the spring of the waters of
Nephtoah, runs round to the cities of Mount Ephron and round to
10 Baalah, that is Kiriath-jearim. It then continues westwards from Baalah
to Mount Seir, passes on to the north side of the slope of Mount
Jearim, that is Kesalon, down to Beth-shemesh and on to Timnah.
11 The boundary then goes north to the slope of Ekron, bends round to
Shikkeron, crosses to Mount Baalah and reaches Jabneel; its limit is
12 the sea. The western boundary is the Great Sea and the land adjacent.
This is the whole circuit of the boundary of the tribe of Judah family
by family.
13   Caleb son of Jephunneh received his share of the land within the
tribe of Judah as the LORD had said to Joshua. It was Kiriath-arba,
14 that is Hebron. This Arba was the ancestor of the Anakim. Caleb
drove out the three Anakim: these were Sheshai, Ahiman and Talmai,
15 descendants of Anak. From there he attacked the inhabitants of Debir;
16 the name of Debir was formerly Kiriath-sepher. Caleb announced that

[a] *So Sept.; Heb.* your.   [b] *Prob. rdg., cp. 18. 17; Heb.* to Gilgal.

whoever should attack Kiriath-sepher and capture it would receive his
daughter Achsah in marriage. Othniel, son of Caleb's brother Kenaz, 17
captured it, and Caleb gave him his daughter Achsah. When she came 18
to him, he incited her[a] to ask her father for a piece of land. As she sat
on the ass, she broke wind, and Caleb asked her, 'What did you mean
by that?' She replied, 'I want a favour from you. You have put me in 19
this dry Negeb; you must give me pools of water as well.' So Caleb
gave her the upper pool and the lower pool.

This is the patrimony of the tribe of the sons of Judah family by 20
family. These are the cities belonging to the tribe of Judah, the full 21
count. By the Edomite frontier in the Negeb: Kabzeel, Eder, Jagur,
Kinah, Dimonah, Ararah,[b] Kedesh, Hazor,[c] Ithnan, Ziph,[c] Telem, 22, 23, 24
Bealoth, Hazor-hadattah,[c] Kerioth-hezron,[d] Amam, Shema, Moladah, 25, 26
Hazar-gaddah, Heshmon,[c] Beth-pelet, Hazar-shual, Beersheba and its 27, 28
villages,[e] Baalah, Iyim,[f] Ezem, Eltolad, Kesil, Hormah, Ziklag, 29, 30, 31
Madmannah, Sansannah, Lebaoth, Shilhim, Ain, and Rimmon: in all, 32
twenty-nine cities with their hamlets.

In the Shephelah: Eshtaol, Zorah, Ashnah, Zanoah, En-gannim, 33, 34
Tappuah, Enam, Jarmuth, Adullam, Socoh, Azekah, Shaaraim, 35, 36
Adithaim, Gederah, namely both parts of Gederah: fourteen cities
with their hamlets. Zenan, Hadashah, Migdal-gad, Dilan, Mizpeh, 37, 38
Joktheel, Lachish, Bozkath, Eglon, Cabbon, Lahmas,[g] Kithlish, 39, 40
Gederoth, Beth-dagon, Naamah, and Makkedah: sixteen cities with 41
their hamlets. Libnah, Ether,[h] Ashan, Jiphtah, Ashnah, Nezib, 42, 43
Keilah, Achzib, and Mareshah: nine cities with their hamlets. Ekron, 44, 45
with its villages and hamlets, and from Ekron westwards, all the cities 46
near Ashdod and their hamlets. Ashdod with its villages and hamlets, 47
Gaza with its villages and hamlets as far as the Torrent of Egypt and
the Great Sea and the land adjacent.

In the hill-country: Shamir, Jattir, Socoh, Dannah, Kiriath-sannah, 48, 49
that is Debir, Anab, Eshtemoh, Anim, Goshen, Holon, and Giloh: 50, 51
eleven cities in all with their hamlets. Arab, Dumah, Eshan, Janim, 52, 53
Beth-tappuah, Aphek,[i] Humtah, Kiriath-arba, that is Hebron, and 54
Zior: nine cities in all with their hamlets. Maon, Carmel, Ziph, Juttah, 55
Jezreel, Jokdeam, Zanoah, Cain, Gibeah, and Timnah: ten cities in all 56, 57
with their hamlets. Halhul, Beth-zur, Gedor, Maarath, Beth-anoth, 58, 59
and Eltekon: six cities in all with their hamlets. Tekoa, Ephrathah,
that is Bethlehem, Peor, Etam, Culom, Tatam, Sores, Carem, Gallim,
Baither, and Manach: eleven cities in all with their hamlets.[j] Kiriath- 60

[a] *So some Sept. MSS.; Heb.* she incited him.   [b] *Prob. rdg.; Heb.* Adadah.   [c] *Omitted
by Sept.*   [d] *So Pesh.; Heb. adds* that is Hazor.   [e] its villages: *so Sept.; Heb.* Biziothiah.
[f] *Omitted in 19. 3 (cp. 1 Chr. 4. 29).*   [g] *Or, with some MSS.,* Lahman.   [h] *Or, with 1
Sam. 30. 30,* Athak.   [i] *Or* Aphekah.   [j] Tekoa...hamlets: *so Sept.; Heb. om.*

baal, that is Kiriath-jearim, and Rabbah: two cities with their hamlets.

61, 62   In the wilderness: Beth-arabah, Middin, Secacah, Nibshan, Irmelach, and En-gedi: six cities with their hamlets.

63   At Jerusalem, the men of Judah were unable to drive out the Jebusites who lived there, and to this day Jebusites and men of Judah live together in Jerusalem.

16   This is the lot that fell to the sons of Joseph: the boundary runs from the Jordan at Jericho, east of the waters of Jericho by the wilderness,
2   and goes up from Jericho into the hill-country to Bethel. It runs on
3   from Bethel to Luz and crosses the Archite border at Ataroth.[a] Westwards it descends to the boundary of the Japhletites as far as the
4   boundary of Lower Beth-horon and Gezer; its limit is the sea. Here Manasseh and Ephraim the sons of Joseph received their patrimony.

5   This was the boundary of the Ephraimites family by family: their
6   eastern boundary ran from Ataroth-addar up to Upper Beth-horon. It continued westwards to Michmethath on the north, going round by the
7   east of Taanath-shiloh and passing by it on the east of Janoah. It descends from Janoah to Ataroth and Naarath, touches Jericho and
8   continues to the Jordan, and from Tappuah it goes westwards by the gorge of Kanah; and its limit is the sea. This is the patrimony of the
9   tribe of Ephraim family by family. There were also cities reserved for the Ephraimites within the patrimony of the Manassites, each of these
10   cities with its hamlets. They did not however drive out the Canaanites who dwelt in Gezer; the Canaanites have lived among the Ephraimites to the present day but have been subject to forced labour in perpetuity.

17   This is the territory allotted to the tribe of Manasseh, Joseph's eldest son. Machir was Manasseh's eldest son and father of Gilead, a fighting man; Gilead and Bashan were allotted to him.

2   The rest of the Manassites family by family were the sons of Abiezer, the sons of Helek, the sons of Asriel, the sons of Shechem, the sons of Hepher, and the sons of Shemida; these were the male offspring of Manasseh son of Joseph family by family.

3   Zelophehad son of Hepher, son of Gilead, son of Machir, son of Manasseh, had no sons but only daughters: their names were Mahlah,
4   Noah, Hoglah, Milcah and Tirzah. They presented themselves before Eleazar the priest and Joshua son of Nun, and before the chiefs, and they said, 'The LORD commanded Moses to allow us to inherit on the same footing as our kinsmen.' They were therefore given a patrimony on the same footing as their father's brothers according to the commandment of the LORD.

5   There fell to Manasseh's lot ten shares, apart from the country of
6   Gilead and Bashan beyond the Jordan, because Manasseh's daughters

[a] Ataroth-addar *in 16. 5; 18. 13.*

had received a patrimony on the same footing as his sons. The country
of Gilead belonged to the rest of Manasseh's sons. The boundary of 7
Manasseh reached from Asher as far as Michmethath, which is to the
east of Shechem, and thence southwards towards Jashub by*a* En-
tappuah. The territory of Tappuah belonged to Manasseh, but Tap- 8
puah itself was on the border of Manasseh and belonged to Ephraim.
The boundary then followed the gorge of Kanah to the south of the 9
gorge (these cities*b* belong to Ephraim, although they lie among the
cities of Manasseh), the boundary of Manasseh being on the north of
the gorge; its limit was the sea. The southern side belonged to Ephraim 10
and the northern to Manasseh, and their*c* boundary was the sea. They
marched with Asher on the north and Issachar on the east. But in 11
Issachar and Asher, Manasseh possessed Beth-shean and its villages,
Ibleam and its villages, the inhabitants of Dor and its villages, the
inhabitants of En-dor and its villages, the inhabitants of Taanach and
its villages, and the inhabitants of Megiddo and its villages. (The third is
the district of Dor.*d*) The Manassites were unable to occupy these 12
cities; the Canaanites maintained their hold on that part of the country.
When the Israelites grew stronger, they put the Canaanites to forced 13
labour, but they did not drive them out.

The sons of Joseph appealed to Joshua and said, 'Why have you 14
given us only one lot and one share as our patrimony? We are a numerous
people; so far the LORD has blessed us.' Joshua replied, 'If you are so 15
numerous, go up into the forest in the territory of the Perizzites and the
Rephaim and clear it for yourselves. You are their near neighbours*e* in
the hill-country of Ephraim.' The sons of Joseph said, 'The hill- 16
country is not enough for us; besides, all the Canaanites have chariots
of iron, those who inhabit the valley beside Beth-shean and its villages
and also those in the Vale of Jezreel.' Joshua replied to the tribes*f* of 17
Joseph, that is Ephraim and Manasseh: 'You are a numerous people
with great resources. You shall not have one lot only. The hill-country 18
is yours. It is forest land; clear it and it shall be yours to its furthest
limits. The Canaanites may be powerful and equipped with chariots of
iron, but you will be able to drive them out.'

THE WHOLE COMMUNITY of the Israelites met together at Shiloh 18
and established the Tent of the Presence there. The country now lay
subdued at their feet, but there remained seven tribes among the 2
Israelites who had not yet taken possession of the patrimonies which
would fall to them. Joshua therefore said to them, 'How much longer 3

[*a*] Jashub by: *prob. rdg.; Heb.* the inhabitants of.   [*b*] these cities: *prob. rdg.; Heb. obscure.*
[*c*] *So Sept.; Heb.* his.   [*d*] The third...Dor: *prob. rdg.; Heb.* The three districts.
[*e*] You are...neighbours: *prob. rdg.; Heb. obscure.*   [*f*] *Lit.* house.

will you neglect to take possession of the land which the LORD the God
4 of your fathers has given you? Appoint three men from each tribe
whom I may send out to travel through the whole country. They shall
make a register showing the patrimony suitable for each tribe, and come
5 back to me, and then it can be shared out among you in seven portions.
Judah shall retain his boundary in the south, and the house of Joseph
6 their boundary in the north. You shall register the land in seven
portions, bring the lists here, and I will cast lots for you in the presence
7 of the LORD our God. Levi has no share among you, because his share
is the priesthood of the LORD; and Gad, Reuben, and the half tribe of
Manasseh have each taken possession of their patrimony east of the
8 Jordan, which Moses the servant of the LORD gave them.' So the men
set out on their journeys. Joshua ordered the emissaries to survey the
country: 'Go through the whole country,' he said, 'survey it and
return to me, and I will cast lots for you here before the LORD in
9 Shiloh.' So the men went and passed through the country; they
registered it on a scroll, city by city, in seven portions, and came to
10 Joshua in the camp at Shiloh. Joshua cast lots for them in Shiloh before
the LORD, and distributed the land there to the Israelites in their
proper shares.
11 This is the lot which fell to the tribe of the Benjamites family by
family. The territory allotted to them lay between the territory of
12 Judah and Joseph. Their boundary at its northern corner starts from
the Jordan; it goes up the slope on the north side of Jericho, continuing westwards into the hill-country, and its limit there is the
13 wilderness of Beth-aven. From there it runs on to Luz, to the southern
slope of Luz, that is Bethel, and down to Ataroth-addar over the hill-
14 country south of Lower Beth-horon. The boundary then bends round
at the west corner southwards from the hill-country above Beth-horon,
and its limit is Kiriath-baal, that is Kiriath-jearim, a city of Judah. This
15 is the western side. The southern side starts from the edge of Kiriath-
16 jearim and ends*a* at the spring of the waters of Nephtoah. It goes down
to the edge of the hill to the east of the Valley of Ben-hinnom, north
of the Vale of Rephaim, down the Valley of Hinnom, to the southern
17 slope of the Jebusites and so to En-rogel. It then bends round north
and comes out at En-shemesh, goes on to the districts in front of
the ascent of Adummim and thence down to the Stone of Bohan son
18 of Reuben. It passes to the northern side of the slope facing the Arabah
19 and goes down to the Arabah, passing the northern slope of Beth-
hoglah, and its limit is the northern inlet of the Dead Sea, at the
southern mouth of the Jordan. This forms the southern boundary.
20 The Jordan is the boundary on the east side. This is the patrimony of

[a] *Prob. rdg.; Heb. adds* westwards and ends...

the Benjamites, the complete circuit of their boundaries family by family.

The cities belonging to the tribe of the Benjamites family by family 21 are: Jericho, Beth-hoglah, Emek-keziz, Beth-arabah, Zemaraim, 22 Bethel, Avvim, Parah, Ophrah, Kephar-ammoni, Ophni, and Geba: 23, 24 twelve cities in all with their hamlets. Gibeon, Ramah, Beeroth, Mizpah, 25, 26 Kephirah, Mozah, Rekem, Irpeel, Taralah, Zela, Eleph, Jebus,[a] that 27, 28 is Jerusalem, Gibeah, and Kiriath-jearim:[b] fourteen cities in all with their hamlets. This is the patrimony of the Benjamites family by family.

The second lot cast was for Simeon, the tribe of the Simeonites 19 family by family. Their patrimony was included in that of Judah. For their patrimony they had Beersheba,[c] Moladah, Hazar-shual, 2, 3 Balah, Ezem, Eltolad, Bethul, Hormah, Ziklag, Beth-marcaboth, Hazar- 4, 5 susah, Beth-lebaoth, and Sharuhen: in all, thirteen cities and their 6 hamlets. They had Ain, Rimmon, Ether, and Ashan: four cities and 7 their hamlets, all the hamlets round these cities as far as Baalath-beer, 8 Ramath-negeb. This was the patrimony of the tribe of Simeon family by family. The patrimony of the Simeonites was part of the land 9 allotted to the men of Judah, because their share was larger than they needed. The Simeonites therefore had their patrimony within the territory of Judah.

The third lot fell to the Zebulunites family by family. The boundary 10 of their patrimony extended to Shadud.[d] Their boundary went up 11 westwards as far as Maralah and touched Dabbesheth and the gorge east of Jokneam. It turned back from Shadud eastwards towards the 12 sunrise up to the border of Kisloth-tabor, on to Daberath and up to Japhia. From there it crossed eastwards towards the sunrise to Gath- 13 hepher, to Ittah-kazin, out to Rimmon, and bent round[e] to Neah. The 14 northern boundary went round to Hannathon, and its limits were the Valley of Jiphtah-el, Kattath, Nahalal, Shimron, Idalah, and Bethlehem: 15 twelve cities in all with their hamlets. These cities and their hamlets 16 were the patrimony of Zebulun family by family.

The fourth lot cast was for the sons of Issachar family by family. 17 Their boundary included Jezreel, Kesulloth, Shunem, Hapharaim, 18, 19 Shion, Anaharath, Rabbith, Kishion, Ebez, Remeth, En-gannim, En- 20, 21 haddah, and Beth-pazzez. The boundary touched Tabor, Shahazumah, 22 and Beth-shemesh, and its limit was the Jordan: sixteen cities with their hamlets. This was the patrimony of the tribe of the sons of Issachar 23 family by family, both cities and hamlets.

[a] *So Sept.; Heb.* the Jebusite. [b] *So Sept.; Heb.* Kiriath. [c] *Prob. rdg., cp. 1 Chr. 4. 28; Heb. adds* and Sheba. [d] *Prob. rdg.; Heb.* Sarid (*similarly in verse 12*). [e] and bent round: *prob. rdg.; Heb.* which stretched.

24   The fifth lot cast was for the tribe of the Asherites family by family.
25, 26   Their boundary included Helkath, Hali, Beten, Akshaph, Alammelech,
Amad, and Mishal; it touched Carmel on the west and the swamp of
27   Libnath. It then turned back towards the east to Beth-dagon, touched
Zebulun and the Valley of Jiphtah-el on the north at Beth-emek and
28   Neiel, and reached Cabul on its northern side, and Abdon,[a] Rehob,
29   Hammon, and Kanah as far as Greater Sidon. The boundary turned
at Ramah, going as far as the fortress city of Tyre, and then back again
30   to Hosah, and its limits to the west were Mehalbeh,[b] Achzib, Acco,[c]
31   Aphek, and Rehob: twenty-two cities in all with their hamlets. This
was the patrimony of the tribe of Asher family by family, these cities
and their hamlets.

32   The sixth lot cast was for the sons of Naphtali family by family.
33   Their boundary started from Heleph and[d] from Elon-bezaanannim and
ran past Adami-nekeb and Jabneel as far as Lakkum, and its limit was
34   the Jordan. The boundary turned back westwards to Aznoth-tabor and
from there on to Hukok. It touched Zebulun on the south, Asher on
35   the west, and the low-lying land by the Jordan on the east. Their
fortified cities were Ziddim, Zer, Hammath, Rakkath, Kinnereth,
36, 37, 38   Adamah, Ramah, Hazor, Kedesh, Edrei, En-hazor, Iron, Migdal-el,
Horem, Beth-anath, and Beth-shemesh: nineteen cities with their
39   hamlets. This was the patrimony of the tribe of Naphtali family by
family, both cities and hamlets.

40   The seventh lot cast was for the tribe of the sons of Dan family by
41   family. The boundary of their patrimony was Zorah, Eshtaol, Ir-
42, 43, 44   shemesh, Shaalabbin, Aijalon, Jithlah, Elon, Timnah, Ekron, Eltekeh,
45, 46   Gibbethon, Baalath, Jehud, Bene-berak, Gath-rimmon; and on the
47   west Jarkon was the boundary[e] opposite Joppa. But the Danites, when
they lost this territory, marched against Leshem, attacked it and
captured it. They put its people to the sword, occupied it and settled in
48   it; and they renamed the place Dan after their ancestor Dan. This was
the patrimony of the tribe of the sons of Dan family by family, these
cities and their hamlets.

49   So the Israelites finished allocating the land and marking out its
frontiers; and they gave Joshua son of Nun a patrimony within their
50   territory. They followed the commands of the LORD and gave him the
city for which he asked, Timnath-serah[f] in the hill-country of Ephraim,
and he rebuilt the city and settled in it.

51   These are the patrimonies which Eleazar the priest and Joshua son

[a] *So some MSS.*, cp. *21. 30; 1 Chr. 6. 74; others* Ebron.   [b] *In Judg. 1. 31* Ahlab.
[c] Mehalbeh...Acco: *prob. rdg.; Heb.* from the district of Achzib and Ummah.   [d] *So
Sept.; Heb. om.*   [e] and on...boundary: *so Sept.; Heb.* Me-jarkon and Rakkon were
on the boundary.   [f] *In Judg. 2. 9* Timnath-heres.

of Nun and the heads of families assigned by lot to the Israelite tribes at Shiloh before the LORD at the entrance of the Tent of the Presence. Thus they completed the distribution of the land.

THE LORD SPOKE TO JOSHUA and commanded him to say this to 20 1, 2 the Israelites: 'You must now appoint your cities of refuge, of which I spoke to you through Moses. They are to be places where the homi- 3 cide, the man who kills another inadvertently without intent, may take sanctuary. You shall single them out as cities of refuge from the vengeance of the dead man's next-of-kin. When a man takes sanctuary 4 in one of these cities, he shall halt at the entrance of the city gate and state his case in the hearing of the elders of that city; if they admit him into the city, they shall grant him a place where he may live as one of themselves. When the next-of-kin comes in pursuit, they shall not 5 surrender him: he struck down his fellow without intent and had not previously been at enmity with him. The homicide may stay in that 6 city until he stands trial before the community. On the death of the ruling high priest, he may return to the city and home from which he has fled.' They dedicated Kedesh in Galilee in the hill-country of 7 Naphtali, Shechem in the hill-country of Ephraim, and Kiriath-arba, that is Hebron, in the hill-country of Judah. Across the Jordan east- 8 wards from Jericho they appointed these cities: from the tribe of Reuben, Bezer-in-the-wilderness on the tableland, from the tribe of Gad, Ramoth in Gilead, and from the tribe of Manasseh, Golan in Bashan. These were the appointed cities where any Israelite or any 9 alien residing among them might take sanctuary. They were intended for any man who killed another inadvertently, to ensure that no one should die at the hand of the next-of-kin until he had stood his trial before the community.

The heads of the Levite families approached Eleazar the priest and 21 Joshua son of Nun and the heads of the families of the tribes of Israel. They came before them at Shiloh in the land of Canaan and said, 'The 2 LORD gave his command through Moses that we were to receive cities to live in, together with the common land belonging to them for our cattle.' The Israelites therefore gave part of their patrimony to the 3 Levites, the following cities with their common land, according to the command of the LORD.

This is the territory allotted to the Kohathite family: those Levites 4 who were descended from Aaron the priest received thirteen cities chosen by lot from the tribes of Judah, Simeon, and Benjamin; the 5 rest of the Kohathites were allotted family by family[a] ten cities from the tribes of Ephraim, Dan, and half Manasseh.

[a] family by family: *prob. rdg.; Heb.* from the families (*similarly in verse 6*).

6   The Gershonites were allotted family by family thirteen cities from the tribes of Issachar, Asher, Naphtali, and the half tribe of Manasseh in Bashan.

7   The Merarites were allotted[a] family by family twelve cities from the tribes of Reuben, Gad, and Zebulun.

8   So the Israelites gave the Levites these cities with their common land, allocating them by lot as the LORD had commanded through Moses.

9   The Israelites designated the following cities out of the tribes of
10 Judah and Simeon for those sons of Aaron who were of the Kohathite
11 families of the Levites, because their lot came out first. They gave them Kiriath-arba (Arba was the father of Anak), that is Hebron, in the hill-
12 country of Judah, and the common land round it, but they gave the open country near the city, and its hamlets, to Caleb son of Jephunneh as his patrimony.

13[b]   To the sons of Aaron the priest they gave Hebron, a city of refuge
14, 15, 16 for the homicide, Libnah, Jattir, Eshtemoa, Holon, Debir, Ashan,[c] Juttah, and Beth-shemesh, each with its common land: nine cities from
17 these two tribes. They also gave cities from the tribe of Benjamin,
18 Gibeon, Geba, Anathoth, and Almon, each with its common land: four
19 cities. The number of the cities with their common land given to the sons of Aaron the priest was thirteen.

20   The cities which the rest of the Kohathite families of the Levites
21 received by lot were from the tribe of Ephraim. They gave them Shechem, a city of refuge for the homicide, in the hill-country of
22 Ephraim, Gezer, Kibzaim, and Beth-horon, each with its common
23 land: four cities. From the tribe of Dan, they gave them Eltekeh,
24 Gibbethon, Aijalon, and Gath-rimmon, each with its common land:
25 four cities. From the half tribe of Manasseh, they gave them Taanach
26 and Gath-rimmon, each with its common land: two cities. The number of the cities belonging to the rest of the Kohathite families with their common land was ten.

27   The Gershonite families of the Levites received, out of the share of the half tribe of Manasseh, Golan in Bashan, a city of refuge for the homicide, and Be-ashtaroth,[d] each with its common land: two cities.
28, 29 From the tribe of Issachar they received Kishon, Daberah, Jarmuth,[e]
30 and En-gannim, each with its common land: four cities. From the tribe
31 of Asher they received Mishal, Abdon, Helkath, and Rehob, each with
32 its common land: four cities. From the tribe of Naphtali they received Kedesh in Galilee, a city of refuge for the homicide, Hammoth-dor,
33 and Kartan, each with its common land: three cities. The number of

---

[a] were allotted: *so Sept.; Heb. om.*   [b] *Verses 13–39: cp. 1 Chr. 6. 57–81.*   [c] *Prob. rdg., cp. 1 Chr. 6. 59; Heb. Ain.*   [d] *Prob. rdg.; Heb. Be-ashtarah.*   [e] *Or, with Sept., Remeth, cp. 19. 21.*

the cities of the Gershonite families with their common land was thirteen.

From the tribe of Zebulun the rest of the Merarite families of the 34 Levites received Jokneam, Kartah, Rimmon,*a* and Nahalal, each with 35 its common land: four cities. East of the Jordan at Jericho,*b* from the 36 tribe of Reuben they were given Bezer-in-the-wilderness on the table-land,*c* a city of refuge for the homicide, Jahaz, Kedemoth, and Mephaath, 37 each with its common land: four cities. From the tribe of Gad they 38 received Ramoth in Gilead, a city of refuge for the homicide, Mahanaim, Heshbon, and Jazer, each with its common land: four cities in all. 39 Twelve cities in all fell by lot to the rest of the Merarite families of the 40 Levites.

The cities of the Levites within the Israelite patrimonies numbered 41 forty-eight in all, with their common land. Each city had its common 42 land round it, and it was the same for all of them.

Thus the LORD gave Israel all the land which he had sworn to give 43 to their forefathers; they occupied it and settled in it. The LORD gave 44 them security on every side as he had sworn to their forefathers. Of all their enemies not a man could withstand them; the LORD delivered all their enemies into their hands. Not a word of the LORD's promises 45 to the house of Israel went unfulfilled; they all came true.

AT THAT TIME JOSHUA summoned the Reubenites, the Gadites, 22 and the half tribe of Manasseh, and said to them, 'You have observed 2 all the commands of Moses the servant of the LORD, and you have obeyed me in all the commands that I too have laid upon you. All this 3 time you have not deserted your brothers; up to this day you have diligently observed the charge laid on you by the LORD your God. And 4 now that the LORD your God has given your brothers security as he promised them, you may turn now and go to your homes in your own land, the land which Moses the servant of the LORD gave you east of the Jordan. But take good care to keep the commands and the law which 5 Moses the servant of the LORD gave you: to love the LORD your God; to conform to his ways; to observe his commandments; to hold fast to him; to serve him with your whole heart and soul.' Joshua blessed 6 them and dismissed them; and they went to their homes. He sent them 7–8 home with his blessing, and with these words: 'Go to your homes richly laden, with great herds, with silver and gold, copper and iron, and with large stores of clothing. See that you share with your kinsmen the spoil you have taken from your enemies.'

Moses had given territory to one half of the tribe of Manasseh in

[a] *Prob. rdg., cp. 19. 13; 1 Chr. 6. 77;* Heb. Dimnah.   [b] East...Jericho: *so Sept.;* Heb. *om.*   [c] Bezer...tableland: *so Sept.;* Heb. Bezer.

Bashan, and Joshua gave territory to the other half west of the Jordan among their kinsmen.

9 So the Reubenites, the Gadites, and the half tribe of Manasseh left the rest of the Israelites and went from Shiloh in Canaan on their way into Gilead, the land which belonged to them according to the decree

10 of the LORD given through Moses. When these tribes came to Geliloth by the Jordan,*a* they built a great altar there by the river for all to see.

11 The Israelites heard that the Reubenites, the Gadites, and the half tribe of Manasseh had built the altar facing the land of Canaan, at

12 Geliloth by the Jordan opposite the Israelite side. When the news reached them, all the community of the Israelites assembled at Shiloh to

13 advance against them with a display of force. At the same time the Israelites sent Phinehas son of Eleazar the priest into the land of Gilead, to the Reubenites, the Gadites, and the half tribe of Manasseh,

14 and ten leading men*b* with him, one from each of the tribes of Israel,

15 each of them the head of a household among the clans of Israel. They came to the Reubenites, the Gadites, and the half tribe of Manasseh

16 in the land of Gilead, and remonstrated with them in these words: 'We speak for the whole community of the LORD. What is this treachery you have committed against the God of Israel? Are you ceasing to follow the LORD and building your own altar this day in defiance of the LORD?

17 Remember our offence at Peor, for which a plague fell upon the community of the LORD; to this day we have not been purified from it.

18 Was that offence so slight that you dare cease to follow the LORD today? If you defy the LORD today, then tomorrow he will be angry with the

19 whole community of Israel. If the land you have taken is unclean, then cross over to the LORD's own land, where the Tabernacle of the LORD now rests, and take a share of it with us; but do not defy the LORD and involve us in your defiance by building an altar of your own apart

20 from the altar of the LORD our God. Remember the treachery of Achan son of Zerah, who defied the ban and the whole community of Israel suffered for it. He was not the only one who paid for that sin with his life.'

21 Then the Reubenites, the Gadites, and the half tribe of Manasseh

22 remonstrated with the heads of the clans of Israel: 'The LORD the God of gods, the LORD the God of gods, he knows, and Israel must know: if this had been an act of defiance or treachery against the LORD, you

23 could not save us today. If we had built ourselves an altar meaning to forsake the LORD, or had offered whole-offerings and grain-offerings upon it, or had presented shared-offerings, the LORD himself would

24 exact punishment. The truth is that we have done this for fear*c* that

[a] *Prob. rdg.; Heb. adds* which was in Canaan.   [b] *So Pesh.; Heb. adds* by households.
[c] *So Pesh.; Heb. adds* from a word.

the day may come when your sons will say to ours, "What have you to do with the LORD, the God of Israel? The LORD put the Jordan as a 25 boundary between our sons and your sons. You have no share in the LORD, you men of Reuben and Gad." Thus your sons will prevent our sons from going in awe of the LORD. So we resolved to set ourselves to 26 build an altar, not for whole-offerings and sacrifices, but as a witness 27 between us and you, and between our descendants after us. Thus we shall be able to do service before the LORD, as we do now, with our whole-offerings, our sacrifices, and our shared-offerings; and your sons will never be able to say to our sons that they have no share in the LORD. And we thought, if ever they do say this to us and our descen- 28 dants, we will point to this copy of the altar of the LORD which we have made, not for whole-offerings and not for sacrifices, but as a witness between us and you. God forbid that we should defy the LORD and 29 forsake him this day by building another altar for whole-offerings, grain-offerings, and sacrifices, in addition to the altar of the LORD our God which stands in front of his Tabernacle.'

When Phinehas the priest and the leaders of the community, the 30 heads of the Israelite clans, who were with him, heard what the Reubenites, the Gadites, and the Manassites said, they were satisfied. Phinehas son of Eleazar the priest said to the Reubenites, Gadites, and 31 Manassites, 'We know now that the LORD is in our midst today; you have not acted treacherously against the LORD, and thus you have preserved all Israel from punishment at his hand.' Then Phinehas son 32 of Eleazar the priest and the leaders left the Reubenites and the Gadites in Gilead and reported to the Israelites in Canaan. The Israelites were 33 satisfied, and they blessed God and thought no more of attacking Reuben and Gad and ravaging their land. The Reubenites and Gadites 34 said, 'The altar is a witness between us that the LORD is God', and they named it 'Witness'.[a]

Joshua's farewell and death

A LONG TIME HAD PASSED since the LORD had given Israel 23 security from all the enemies who surrounded them, and Joshua was now a very old man. He summoned all Israel, their elders and heads 2 of families, their judges and officers, and said to them, 'I have become a very old man. You have seen for yourselves all that the LORD our God 3 has done to these peoples for your sake; it was the LORD God himself who fought for you. I have allotted you your patrimony tribe by tribe, 4

[a] Witness: *so some MSS.; others om.*

the land of all the peoples that I have wiped out and of all these that
remain between the Jordan and the Great Sea which lies towards the
5 setting sun. The LORD your God himself drove them out for your sake;
he drove them out to make room for you, and you occupied their land,
6 as the LORD your God had promised you. Be resolute therefore: observe
and perform everything written in the book of the law of Moses,
7 without swerving to right or to left. You must not associate with the
peoples that are left among you; you must not call upon their gods by
name, nor*a* swear by them nor prostrate yourselves in worship before
8 them. You must hold fast to the LORD your God as you have done
9 down to this day. For your sake the LORD has driven out great and
mighty nations; to this day not a man of them has withstood you.
10 One of you can put to flight a thousand, because the LORD your God
11 fights for you, as he promised. Be on your guard then, love the LORD
12 your God, for*b* if you do turn away and attach yourselves to the peoples
that still remain among you, and intermarry with them and associate
13 with them and they with you, then be sure that the LORD will not
continue to drive those peoples out to make room for you. They will
be snares to entrap you, whips for your backs and barbed hooks in
your eyes, until you vanish from the good land which the LORD your
14 God has given you. And now I am going the way of all mankind. You
know in your heart of hearts that nothing that the LORD your God has
15 promised you has failed to come true, every word of it. But the same
LORD God who has kept his word to you to such good effect can equally
bring every kind of evil on you, until he has rooted you out from this
16 good land which he has given you. If you break the covenant which
the LORD your God has prescribed and prostrate yourselves in worship
before other gods, then the LORD will be angry with you and you will
quickly vanish from the good land he has given you.'

24 Joshua assembled all the tribes of Israel at Shechem. He summoned
the elders of Israel, the heads of families, the judges and officers; and
2 they presented themselves before God. Joshua then said this to all the
people: 'This is the word of the LORD the God of Israel: "Long ago
your forefathers, Terah and his sons Abraham and Nahor, lived beside
3 the Euphrates, and they worshipped other gods. I took your father
Abraham from beside the Euphrates and led him through the length
and breadth of Canaan. I gave him many descendants: I gave him
4 Isaac, and to Isaac I gave Jacob and Esau. I put Esau in possession of
5 the hill-country of Seir, but Jacob and his sons went down to Egypt. I
sent Moses and Aaron, and I struck the Egyptians with plagues—you
know well what I did among them—and after that I brought you out;

[*a*] you must not call...nor: *or* the name of their gods shall not be your boast, nor must
you... [*b*] Be on...for: *or* Take very good care to love the LORD your God, but...

I brought your fathers out of Egypt and you came to the Red Sea. The 6
Egyptians sent their chariots and cavalry to pursue your fathers to the
sea. But when they appealed to the LORD, he put a screen of darkness 7
between you and the Egyptians, and brought the sea down on them and
it covered them; you saw for yourselves what I did to Egypt. For a long
time you lived in the wilderness. Then I brought you into the land of 8
the Amorites who lived east of the Jordan; they fought against you, but
I delivered them into your hands; you took possession of their country
and I destroyed them for your sake. The king of Moab, Balak son of 9
Zippor, took the field against Israel. He sent for Balaam son of Beor to
lay a curse on you, but I would not listen to him. Instead of that he blessed 10
you; and so I saved you from the power of Balak. Then you crossed the 11
Jordan and came to Jericho. The citizens of Jericho fought against you,*a*
but I delivered them into your hands. I spread panic before you, and it 12
was this, not your sword or your bow, that drove out the two kings of
the Amorites. I gave you land on which you had not laboured, cities 13
which you had never built; you have lived in those cities and you eat
the produce of vineyards and olive-groves which you did not plant."

'Hold the LORD in awe then, and worship him in loyalty and truth. 14
Banish the gods whom your fathers worshipped beside the Euphrates
and in Egypt, and worship the LORD. But if it does not please you to 15
worship the LORD, choose here and now whom you will worship: the
gods whom your forefathers worshipped beside the Euphrates, or the
gods of the Amorites in whose land you are living. But I and my
family, we will worship the LORD.' The people answered, 'God forbid 16
that we should forsake the LORD to worship other gods, for it was the 17
LORD our God who brought us and our fathers up from Egypt, that
land of slavery; it was he who displayed those great signs before our
eyes and guarded us on all our wanderings among the many peoples
through whose lands we passed. The LORD drove out before us the 18
Amorites and all the peoples who lived in that country. We too will
worship the LORD; he is our God.' Joshua answered the people, 'You 19
cannot worship the LORD. He is a holy god, a jealous god, and he will
not forgive your rebellion and your sins. If you forsake the LORD and 20
worship foreign gods, he will turn and bring adversity upon you and,
although he once brought you prosperity, he will make an end of you.'
The people said to Joshua, 'No; we will worship the LORD.' He said to 21, 22
them, 'You are witnesses against yourselves that you have chosen the
LORD and will worship him.' 'Yes,' they answered, 'we are witnesses.'
He said to them, 'Then here and now banish the foreign gods that are 23
among you, and turn your hearts to the LORD the God of Israel.' The 24

[a] *Prob. rdg.; Heb. adds* Amorites, Perizzites, Canaanites, Hittites, Girgashites, Hivites,
and Jebusites.

people said to Joshua, 'The LORD our God we will worship and his
25 voice we will obey.' So Joshua made a covenant that day with[a] the
26 people; he drew up a statute and an ordinance for them in Shechem and
wrote its terms in the book of the law of God. He took a great stone
and set it up there under the terebinth[b] in the sanctuary of the LORD,
27 and said to all the people, 'This stone is a witness against us; for it has
heard all the words which the LORD has spoken to us. If you renounce
28 your God, it shall be a witness against you.' Then Joshua dismissed the
people, each man to his patrimony.

29   After these things, Joshua son of Nun the servant of the LORD died;
30 he was a hundred and ten years old. They buried him within the
border of his own patrimony in Timnath-serah in the hill-country of
31 Ephraim to the north of Mount Gaash. Israel served the LORD during
the lifetime of Joshua and of the elders who outlived him and who well
knew all that the LORD had done for Israel.

32   The bones of Joseph, which the Israelites had brought up from
Egypt, were buried in Shechem, in the plot of land which Jacob had
bought from the sons of Hamor father of Shechem for a hundred sheep;[c]
33 and they passed into the patrimony of the house of Joseph. Eleazar son
of Aaron died and was buried in the hill which had been given to
Phinehas his son in the hill-country of Ephraim.

[a] *Or* for.   [b] *Or* pole.   [c] *Or* pieces of money (*cp. Gen. 33. 19; Job 42. 11*).

THE BOOK OF

JUDGES

The conquest of Canaan completed

AFTER THE DEATH of Joshua the Israelites inquired of 1
the LORD which tribe should attack the Canaanites first. The 2
LORD answered, 'Judah shall attack. I hereby deliver the
country into his power.' Judah said to his brother Simeon, 'Go forward 3
with me into my allotted territory, and let us do battle with the
Canaanites; then I in turn will go with you into your territory.' So
Simeon went with him; then Judah advanced to the attack, and the 4
LORD delivered the Canaanites and Perizzites into their hands. They
slaughtered ten thousand of them at Bezek. There they came upon 5
Adoni-bezek, engaged him in battle and defeated the Canaanites and
Perizzites. Adoni-bezek fled, but they pursued him, took him prisoner 6
and cut off his thumbs and his great toes. Adoni-bezek said, 'I once 7
had seventy kings whose thumbs and great toes were cut off picking
up the scraps from under my table. What I have done God has done
to me.' He was brought to Jerusalem and died there.

The men of Judah made an assault on Jerusalem and captured it, 8
put its people to the sword and set fire to the city. Then they turned 9
south to fight the Canaanites of the hill-country, the Negeb, and the
Shephelah. Judah attacked the Canaanites in Hebron, formerly called 10
Kiriath-arba, and defeated Sheshai, Ahiman and Talmai. From there 11
they marched against the inhabitants of Debir, formerly called Kiriath-
sepher. Caleb said, 'Whoever attacks Kiriath-sepher and captures it, 12
to him I will give my daughter Achsah in marriage.' Othniel, son of 13
Caleb's younger brother Kenaz, captured it, and Caleb gave him his
daughter Achsah. When she came to him, he incited her[a] to ask her father 14
for a piece of land. As she sat on the ass, she broke wind, and Caleb
said, 'What did you mean by that?' She replied, 'I want to ask a favour 15
of you. You have put me in this dry Negeb; you must give me pools of
water as well.' So Caleb gave her the upper pool and the lower pool.

The descendants of Moses' father-in-law, the Kenite, went up with 16
the men of Judah from the Vale of Palm Trees to the wilderness of
Judah which is in the Negeb of Arad and settled among the Amalekites.[b]
Judah then accompanied his brother Simeon, attacked the Canaanites 17
in Zephath and destroyed it; hence the city was called Hormah.[c] Judah 18

[a] So Sept.; Heb. she incited him. [b] So one MS. of Sept.; Heb. among the people.
[c] That is Destruction.

321

19 took Gaza, Ashkelon, and Ekron, and the territory of each. The LORD was with Judah and they occupied the hill-country, but they could not drive out the inhabitants of the Vale because they had chariots of iron.

20 Hebron was given to Caleb as Moses had directed, and he drove out the
21 three sons of Anak. But the Benjamites did not drive out the Jebusites of Jerusalem; and the Jebusites have lived on in Jerusalem with the Benjamites till the present day.

22 The tribes*a* of Joseph attacked Bethel, and the LORD was with them.
23, 24 They sent spies to Bethel, formerly called Luz. These spies saw a man coming out of the city and said to him, 'Show us how to enter the city,
25 and we will see that you come to no harm.' So he showed them how to enter, and they put the city to the sword, but let the man and his
26 family go free. He went into Hittite country, built a city and named it Luz, which is still its name today.

27 Manasseh did not drive out the inhabitants of Beth-shean with its villages, nor of Taanach, Dor, Ibleam, and Megiddo, with the villages
28 of each of them; the Canaanites held their ground in that region. Later, when Israel became strong, they put them to forced labour, but they never completely drove them out.

29 Ephraim did not drive out the Canaanites who lived in Gezer, but the Canaanites lived among them there.

30 Zebulun did not drive out the inhabitants of Kitron and Nahalol, but the Canaanites lived among them and were put to forced labour.

31 Asher did not drive out the inhabitants of Acco and Sidon, of Ahlab,*b*
32 Achzib, Helbah, Aphik and Rehob. Thus the Asherites lived among the Canaanite inhabitants and did not drive them out.

33 Naphtali did not drive out the inhabitants of Beth-shemesh and of Beth-anath, but lived among the Canaanite inhabitants and put the inhabitants of Beth-shemesh and Beth-anath to forced labour.

34 The Amorites pressed the Danites back into the hill-country and
35 did not allow them to come down into the Vale. The Amorites held their ground in Mount Heres and in Aijalon and Shaalbim, but the tribes of Joseph increased their pressure on them until they reduced them to forced labour.

36 The boundary of the Edomites*c* ran from the ascent of Akrabbim, upwards from Sela.

2 The angel of the LORD came up from Gilgal to Bokim, and said, 'I brought*d* you up out of Egypt and into the country which I vowed I would give to your forefathers. I said, I will never break my covenant
2 with you, and you in turn must make no covenant with the inhabitants of the country; you must pull down their altars. But you did not obey

[a] *Lit.* house.   [b] Mehalbeh *in Josh. 19. 29.*   [c] *So one form of Sept.; Heb.* Amorites.
[d] *Prob. rdg.; Heb.* I will bring.

me, and look what you have done! So I said, I will not drive them out 3
before you; they will decoy you, and their gods will shut you fast in
the trap.' When the angel of the LORD said this to the Israelites, they 4
all wept and wailed, and so the place was called Bokim;*a* and they 5
offered sacrifices there to the LORD.

Israel under the judges

JOSHUA DISMISSED the people, and the Israelites went off to occupy 6
the country, each man to his allotted portion. As long as Joshua was 7
alive and the elders who survived him—everyone, that is, who had
witnessed the whole great work which the LORD had done for Israel—
the people worshipped the LORD. At the age of a hundred and ten 8
Joshua son of Nun, the servant of the LORD, died, and they buried him 9
within the border of his own property in Timnath-heres north of
Mount Gaash in the hill-country of Ephraim. Of that whole generation, 10
all were gathered to their forefathers, and another generation followed
who did not acknowledge the LORD and did not know what he had done
for Israel. Then the Israelites did what was wrong in the eyes of the 11
LORD, and worshipped the Baalim.*b* They forsook the LORD, their 12
fathers' God who had brought them out of Egypt, and went after other
gods, gods of the races among whom they lived; they bowed down before
them and provoked the LORD to anger; they forsook the LORD and 13
worshipped the Baal and the Ashtaroth.*c* The LORD in his anger made 14
them the prey of bands of raiders and plunderers; he sold them to their
enemies all around them, and they could no longer make a stand.
Every time they went out to battle the LORD brought disaster upon 15
them, as he had said when he gave them his solemn warning, and they
were in dire straits.

The LORD set judges over them, who rescued them from the 16
marauding bands. Yet they did not listen even to these judges, but 17
turned wantonly to worship other gods and bowed down before them;
all too soon they abandoned the path of obedience to the LORD's
commands which their forefathers had followed. They did not obey
the LORD. Whenever the LORD set up a judge over them, he was with 18
that judge, and kept them safe from their enemies so long as he lived.
The LORD would relent as often as he heard them groaning under
oppression and ill-treatment. But as soon as the judge was dead, they 19
would relapse into deeper corruption than their forefathers and give

[a] *That is* Weepers.   [b] The Baalim *were Canaanite deities.*   [c] The Ashtaroth *were Canaanite deities.*

their allegiance to other gods, worshipping them and bowing down
before them. They gave up none of their evil practices and their wilful
20 ways. And the LORD was angry with Israel and said, 'This nation has
broken the covenant which I laid upon their forefathers and has not
21 obeyed me, and now, of all the nations which Joshua left at his death,
22 I will not drive out to make room for them one single man. By their
means I will test Israel, to see whether or not they will keep strictly to
23 the way of the LORD as their forefathers did.' So the LORD left those
nations alone and made no haste to drive them out or give them into
Joshua's hands.

3   These are the nations which the LORD left as a means of testing all
2 the Israelites who had not taken part in the battles for Canaan, his
purpose being to teach succeeding generations of Israel, or those at
3 least who had not learnt in former times, how to make war. These
were: the five lords of the Philistines, all the Canaanites, the Sidonians,
and the Hivites who lived in Mount Lebanon from Mount Baal-
4 hermon as far as Lebo-hamath. His purpose also was to test whether
the Israelites would obey the commands which the LORD had given to
5 their forefathers through Moses. Thus the Israelites lived among the
Canaanites, the Hittites, the Amorites, the Perizzites, the Hivites, and
6 the Jebusites. They took their daughters in marriage and gave their
own daughters to their sons; and they worshipped their gods.
7   The Israelites did what was wrong in the eyes of the LORD; they
forgot the LORD their God and worshipped the Baalim and the
8 Asheroth.[a] The LORD was angry with Israel and he sold them to
Cushan-rishathaim, king of Aram-naharaim,[b] who kept them in
9 subjection for eight years. Then the Israelites cried to the LORD for
help and he raised up a man to deliver them, Othniel son of Caleb's
10 younger brother Kenaz, and he set them free. The spirit of the LORD
came upon him and he became judge over Israel. He took the field,
and the LORD delivered Cushan-rishathaim king of Aram into his
11 hands; Othniel was too strong for him. Thus the land was at peace for
forty years until Othniel son of Kenaz died.
12   Once again the Israelites did what was wrong in the eyes of the LORD,
13 and because of this he roused Eglon king of Moab against Israel. Eglon
mustered the Ammonites and the Amalekites, advanced to attack Israel
14 and took possession of the Vale of Palm Trees. The Israelites were
15 subject to Eglon king of Moab for eighteen years. When they cried to
the LORD for help, he raised up a man to deliver them, Ehud son of
Gera the Benjamite, who was left-handed. The Israelites sent him to
16 pay their tribute to Eglon king of Moab. Ehud made himself a two-

[a] *Plural of* Asherah, *the name of a Canaanite goddess.* [b] *That is* Aram of Two
Rivers.

edged sword, only fifteen inches long,[a] which he fastened on his right side under his clothes, and he brought the tribute to Eglon king of 17 Moab. Eglon was a very fat man. When Ehud had finished presenting 18 the tribute, he sent on the men who had carried it, and he himself 19 turned back from the Carved Stones at Gilgal. 'My lord king,' he said, 'I have a word for you in private.' Eglon called for silence and dismissed all his attendants.[b] Ehud then came up to him as he sat in the 20 roof-chamber of his summer palace and said, 'I have a word from God for you.' So Eglon rose from his seat, and Ehud reached with his left 21 hand, drew the sword from his right side and drove it into his belly. The hilt went in after the blade and the fat closed over the blade; he 22 did not draw the sword out but left it protruding behind.[c] Ehud went 23 out to the porch,[d] shut the doors on him and fastened them. When he 24 had gone away, Eglon's servants came and, finding the doors fastened, they said, 'He must be relieving himself in the closet of his summer palace.' They waited until they were ashamed to delay any longer, and 25 still he did not open the doors of the roof-chamber. So they took the key and opened the doors; and there was their master lying on the floor dead. While they had been waiting, Ehud made his escape; he passed 26 the Carved Stones and escaped to Seirah. When he arrived there, he 27 sounded the trumpet in the hill-country of Ephraim, and the Israelites came down from the hills with him at their head. He said to them, 28 'Follow me, for the LORD has delivered your enemy the Moabites into your hands.' Down they came after him, and they seized the fords of the Jordan against the Moabites and allowed no man to cross. They killed 29 that day some ten thousand Moabites, all of them men of substance and all fighting men; not one escaped. Thus Moab on that day became 30 subject to Israel, and the land was at peace for eighty years.

After Ehud there was Shamgar of Beth-anath.[e] He killed six hundred 31 Philistines with an ox-goad, and he too delivered Israel.

After Ehud's death the Israelites once again did what was wrong in 4 the eyes of the LORD, so he sold them to Jabin the Canaanite king, who 2 ruled in Hazor. The commander of his forces was Sisera, who lived in Harosheth-of-the-Gentiles. The Israelites cried to the LORD for help, 3 because Sisera had nine hundred chariots of iron and had oppressed Israel harshly for twenty years. At that time Deborah wife of Lappi- 4 doth,[f] a prophetess, was judge in Israel. It was her custom to sit 5 beneath the Palm-tree of Deborah between Ramah and Bethel in the hill-country of Ephraim, and the Israelites went up to her for justice.

[a] only...long: *lit.* a short cubit in length. [b] and...attendants: *so Sept.; Heb.* and all his attendants went out. [c] behind: *Heb. word of uncertain mng.* [d] porch: *Heb. word of uncertain mng.* [e] of Beth-anath: *or* son of Anath. [f] wife of Lappidoth: *or* a spirited woman.

6 She sent for Barak son of Abinoam from Kedesh in Naphtali and said to him, 'These are the commands of the LORD the God of Israel: "Go and draw ten thousand men from Naphtali and Zebulun and bring

7 them with you to Mount Tabor, and I will draw Sisera, Jabin's commander, to the Torrent of Kishon with his chariots and all his

8 rabble, and there I will deliver them into your hands."' Barak answered her, 'If you go with me, I will go; but if you will not go, neither will I.'

9 'Certainly I will go with you,' she said, 'but this venture will bring you no glory, because the LORD will leave Sisera to fall into the hands of a

10 woman.' So Deborah rose and went with Barak to Kedesh. Barak summoned Zebulun and Naphtali to Kedesh and marched up with ten thousand men, and Deborah went with him.

11 Now Heber the Kenite had parted company with the Kenites, the descendants of Hobab, Moses' brother-in-law, and he had pitched his tent at Elon-bezaanannim near Kedesh.

12 Word was brought to Sisera that Barak son of Abinoam had gone

13 up to Mount Tabor; so he summoned all his chariots, nine hundred chariots of iron, and his troops, from Harosheth-of-the-Gentiles to the

14 Torrent of Kishon. Then Deborah said to Barak, 'Up! This day the LORD gives Sisera into your hands. Already the LORD has gone out to battle before you.' So Barak came charging down from Mount Tabor

15 with ten thousand men at his back. The LORD put Sisera to rout with all his chariots and his army before Barak's onslaught; but Sisera

16 himself dismounted from his chariot and fled on foot. Barak pursued the chariots and the army as far as Harosheth, and the whole army was

17 put to the sword and perished; not a man was left alive. Meanwhile Sisera fled on foot to the tent of Jael wife of Heber the Kenite, because Jabin king of Hazor and the household of Heber the Kenite were at

18 peace. Jael came out to meet Sisera and said to him, 'Come in here, my lord, come in; do not be afraid.' So he went into the tent, and she

19 covered him with a rug. He said to her, 'Give me some water to drink; I am thirsty.' She opened a skin full of milk, gave him a drink and

20 covered him up again. He said to her, 'Stand at the tent door, and if

21 anybody comes and asks if someone is here, say No.' But Jael, Heber's wife, took a tent-peg, picked up a hammer, crept up to him, and drove the peg into his skull as he lay sound asleep. His brains oozed out on the

22 ground, his limbs twitched, and he died. When Barak came up in pursuit of Sisera, Jael went out to meet him and said to him, 'Come, I will show you the man you are looking for.' He went in with her, and

23 there was Sisera lying dead with the tent-peg in his skull. That day God

24 gave victory to the Israelites over Jabin king of Canaan, and they pressed home their attacks upon that king of Canaan until they had made an end of him.

That day Deborah and Barak son of Abinoam sang this song: 5

For the leaders, the leaders*a* in Israel,   2
for the people who answered the call,
bless ye the LORD.
Hear me, you kings; princes, give ear;   3
I will sing, I will sing to the LORD.
I will raise a psalm to the LORD the God of Israel.
O LORD, at thy setting forth from Seir,   4
when thou camest marching out of the plains of Edom,
earth trembled; heaven quaked;
the clouds streamed down in torrents.
Mountains shook in fear before the LORD, the lord of Sinai, 5
before the LORD, the God of Israel.
In the days of Shamgar of Beth-anath,*b*   6
in the days of Jael, caravans plied no longer;
men who had followed the high roads
went round by devious paths.
Champions there were none,   7
none left in Israel,
until I,*c* Deborah, arose,
arose, a mother in Israel.
They chose new gods,   8
they consorted with demons.*d*
Not a shield, not a lance was to be seen
in the forty thousand of Israel.
Be proud at heart, you marshals of Israel;   9
you among the people that answered the call,
bless ye the LORD.
You that ride your tawny she-asses,   10
that sit on saddle-cloths,
and you that take the road afoot,
      ponder this well.
Hark, the sound of the players striking up   11
in the places where the women draw water!
It is the victories of the LORD that they commemorate there,
his triumphs as the champion of Israel.

Down to the gates came the LORD's people:
      'Rouse, rouse yourself, Deborah,   12
      rouse yourself, lead out the host.
      Up, Barak! Take prisoners in plenty,
      son of Abinoam.'

[a] *Or* For those who had flowing locks. [b] of Beth-anath: *or* son of Anath. [c] *Or* you.
[d] *Or* satyrs.

13   Then down marched the column*a* and its chieftains,
      the people of the LORD marched down*b* like warriors.

14   The men of Ephraim showed a brave front in the vale,*c*
      crying, 'With you, Benjamin! Your clansmen are here!'
      From Machir down came the marshals,
      from Zebulun the bearers of the musterer's staff.

15   Issachar joined with Deborah in the uprising,*d*
      Issachar stood by Barak;
      down into the valley they rushed.
      But Reuben, he was split into factions,
      great were their heart-searchings.*e*

16   What made you linger by the cattle-pens
      to listen to the shrill calling of the shepherds?*f*

17   Gilead stayed beyond Jordan;
      and Dan, why did he tarry by the ships?
      Asher lingered by the sea-shore,
      by its creeks he stayed.

18   The people of Zebulun risked their very lives,
      so did Naphtali on the heights of the battlefield.

19   Kings came, they fought;
      then fought the kings of Canaan
      at Taanach by the waters of Megiddo;
      no plunder of silver did they take.

20   The stars fought from heaven,
      the stars in their courses fought against Sisera.

21   The Torrent of Kishon swept him away,
      the Torrent barred his flight, the Torrent of Kishon;
         march on in might, my soul!

22   Then hammered the hooves of his horses,
      his chargers galloped, galloped away.

23   A curse on Meroz, said the angel of the LORD;
      a curse, a curse on its inhabitants,
      because they brought no help to the LORD,
      no help to the LORD and the fighting men.

24   Blest above women be Jael,
      the wife of Heber the Kenite;
      blest above all women in the tents.

25   He asked for water: she gave him milk,
      she offered him curds in a bowl fit for a chieftain.

---

[a] *Prob. rdg.; Heb.* survivor.   [b] *Prob. rdg.; Heb. adds* to me.   [c] *So Sept.; Heb.* in Amalek.   [d] in the uprising: *prob. rdg.; Heb.* my officers.   [e] *So some MSS.; others have an unknown word.*   [f] *Prob. rdg.; Heb. adds* Reuben was split into factions, great were their heart-searchings.

She stretched out her hand for the tent-peg,   26
her right hand to hammer the weary.
With the hammer she struck Sisera, she crushed his head;
she struck and his brains ebbed out.
At her feet he sank down, he fell, he lay;   27
at her feet he sank down and fell.
Where he sank down, there he fell, done to death.

The mother of Sisera peered through the lattice,   28
through the window she peered and shrilly cried,
'Why are his chariots so long coming?
Why is the clatter of his chariots so long delayed?'
The wisest of her princesses answered her,   29
yes, she found her own answer:
'They must be finding spoil, taking their shares,   30
a wench to each man, two wenches,
booty of dyed stuffs for Sisera,
booty of dyed stuffs,
dyed stuff, and striped, two lengths of striped stuff—
to grace the victor's neck.'

So perish all thine enemies, O LORD;   31
but let all who love thee*a* be like the sun rising in strength.

The land was at peace for forty years.

THE ISRAELITES DID what was wrong in the eyes of the LORD and 6
he delivered them into the hands of Midian for seven years. The 2
Midianites were too strong for Israel, and the Israelites were forced to
find themselves hollow places in the mountains, and caves and strongholds. If the Israelites had sown their seed, the Midianites and the 3
Amalekites and other eastern tribes would come up and attack Israel.
They then pitched their camps in the country and destroyed the crops 4
as far as the outskirts of Gaza, leaving nothing to support life in Israel,
sheep or ox or ass. They came up with their herds and their tents, like 5
a swarm of locusts; they and their camels were past counting. They had
come into the land for its growing crop,*b* and so the Israelites were 6
brought to destitution by the Midianites, and they cried to the LORD
for help. When the Israelites cried to the LORD because of what they 7
had suffered from the Midianites, he sent them a prophet who said to 8
them, 'These are the words of the LORD the God of Israel: I brought
you up from Egypt, that land of slavery. I delivered you from the 9
Egyptians and from all your oppressors. I drove them out before you
and gave you their lands. I said to you, "I am the LORD your God: do 10

[a] *So Pesh.; Heb.* him.   [b] for its growing crop: *or* and laid it waste.

not stand in awe of the gods of the Amorites in whose country you are settling." But you did not listen to me.'

11 Now the angel of the LORD came and sat under the terebinth at Ophrah which belonged to Joash the Abiezrite. His son Gideon was threshing wheat in the winepress, so that he might get it away 12 quickly from the Midianites. The angel of the LORD showed himself to Gideon and said, 'You are a brave man, and the LORD is with you.' 13 Gideon said, 'But pray, my lord, if the LORD really is with us, why has all this happened to us? What has become of all those wonderful deeds of his, of which we have heard from our fathers, when they told us how the LORD brought us out of Egypt? But now the LORD has cast us off 14 and delivered us into the power of the Midianites.' The LORD turned to him and said, 'Go and use this strength of yours to free Israel from 15 the power of the Midianites. It is I that send you.' Gideon said, 'Pray, my lord, how can I save Israel? Look at my clan: it is the weakest in 16 Manasseh, and I am the least in my father's family.' The LORD answered, 'I will be with you, and you shall lay low all Midian as one 17 man.' He replied, 'If I stand so well with you, give me a sign that it is 18 you who speak to me. Please do not leave this place until I come with my gift and lay it before you.' He answered, 'I will stay until you come 19 back.' So Gideon went in, prepared a kid and made an ephah of flour into unleavened cakes. He put the meat in a basket, poured the broth into a pot and brought it out to him under the terebinth. As he 20 approached, the angel of God said to him, 'Take the meat and the cakes, and put them here on the rock and pour out the broth', and he 21 did so. Then the angel of the LORD reached out the staff in his hand and touched the meat and the cakes with the tip of it. Fire sprang up from the rock and consumed the meat and the cakes; and the angel of 22 the LORD was no more to be seen. Then Gideon knew that it was the angel of the LORD and said, 'Alas, Lord GOD! Then it is true: I have 23 seen the angel of the LORD face to face.' But the LORD said to him, 24 'Peace be with you; do not be afraid, you shall not die.' So Gideon built an altar there to the LORD and named it Jehovah-shalom.[a] It stands to this day at Ophrah-of-the-Abiezrites.

25 That night the LORD said to Gideon, 'Take a young bull of your father's, the yearling bull,[b] tear down the altar of Baal which belongs to your father and cut down the sacred pole[c] which stands beside[d] it. 26 Then build an altar of the proper pattern[e] to the LORD your God on the top of this earthwork;[f] take the yearling bull and offer it as a whole-27 offering with the wood of the sacred pole that you cut down.' So

[a] *That is* the LORD is peace. [b] the yearling bull: *prob. rdg.; Heb.* the second bull, seven years old. [c] sacred pole: *Heb.* asherah. [d] *Or* on. [e] of...pattern: *or* with the stones in rows. [f] *Or* stronghold *or* refuge.

Gideon took ten of his servants and did as the LORD had told him. He
was afraid of his father's family and his fellow-citizens, and so he did
it by night, and not by day. When the citizens rose early in the morning, 28
they found the altar of Baal overturned and the sacred pole which had
stood beside it cut down and the yearling bull offered up as a whole-
offering on the altar which he had built. They asked each other who had 29
done it, and, after searching inquiries, were told that it was Gideon
son of Joash. So the citizens said to Joash, 'Bring out your son. He has 30
overturned the altar of Baal and cut down the sacred pole beside it,
and he must die.' But as they crowded round him Joash retorted, 'Are 31
you pleading Baal's cause then? Do you think that it is for you to save
him? Whoever pleads his cause shall be put to death at dawn. If Baal is
a god, and someone has torn down his altar, let him take up his own
cause.' That day Joash named Gideon Jerubbaal,*a* saying, 'Let Baal 32
plead his cause against this man, for he has torn down his altar.'

　All the Midianites, the Amalekites, and the eastern tribes joined 33
forces, crossed the river and camped in the Vale of Jezreel. Then the 34
spirit of the LORD took possession of*b* Gideon; he sounded the trumpet
and the Abiezrites were called out to follow him. He sent messengers 35
all through Manasseh; and they too were called out. He sent messengers to Asher, Zebulun, and Naphtali, and they came up to meet the
others. Gideon said to God, 'If thou wilt deliver Israel through me as 36
thou hast promised—now, look, I am putting a fleece of wool on the 37
threshing-floor. If there is dew only on the fleece and all the ground is
dry, then I shall be sure that thou wilt deliver Israel through me, as
thou hast promised.' And that is what happened. He rose early next 38
day and wrung out the fleece, and he squeezed enough dew from it to
fill a bowl with water. Gideon then said to God, 'Do not be angry with 39
me, but give me leave to speak once again. Let me, I pray thee, make
one more test with the fleece. This time let the fleece alone be dry, and
all the ground be covered with dew.' God let it be so that night: the fleece 40
alone was dry, and on all the ground there was dew.

　Jerubbaal, that is Gideon, and all the people with him rose early and 7
pitched camp at En-harod;*c* the Midianite camp was in the vale to the
north of the hill of Moreh. The LORD said to Gideon, 'The people 2
with you are more than I need to deliver Midian into their hands: Israel
will claim the glory for themselves and say that it is their own strength
that has given them the victory. Now make a proclamation for all the 3
people to hear, that anyone who is scared or frightened is to leave
Mount Galud*d* at once and go back home.' Twenty-two thousand of
them went, and ten thousand were left. The LORD then said to Gideon, 4

[a] *That is* Let Baal plead. [b] took possession of: *lit.* clothed itself with... [c] *That is*
Spring of Fright. [d] *Prob. rdg.; Heb.* Mount Gilead.

'There are still too many. Bring them down to the water, and I will separate them for you there. When I say to you, "This man shall go with you", he shall go; and if I say, "This man shall not go with you",

5 he shall not go.' So Gideon brought the people down to the water and the LORD said to him, 'Make every man who laps the water with his tongue like a dog stand on one side, and on the other[a] every man who

6 goes down on his knees and drinks.' The number of those who lapped was three hundred, and all the rest went down on their knees to drink,

7 putting their hands to their mouths.[b] The LORD said to Gideon, 'With the three hundred men who lapped I will save you and deliver Midian

8 into your hands, and all the rest may go home.' So Gideon sent all these Israelites home, but he kept the three hundred, and they took with them the jars[c] and the trumpets which the people had. The Midianite camp was below him in the vale.

9 That night the LORD said to him, 'Go down at once and attack the

10 camp, for I have delivered it into your hands. If you are afraid to do so,

11 then go down first with your servant Purah and listen to what they are saying. That will give you courage to go down and attack the camp.' So he and his servant Purah went down to the part of the camp where

12 the fighting men lay. Now the Midianites, the Amalekites, and the eastern tribes were so many that they lay there in the valley like a swarm of locusts; there was no counting their camels; in number they were

13 like grains of sand on the sea-shore. When Gideon came close, there was a man telling his companion a dream. He said, 'I dreamt that I saw a hard, stale barley-cake rolling over and over through the Midianite camp; it came to a tent, hit it[d] and turned it upside down, and

14 the tent collapsed.' The other answered, 'Depend upon it, this is the sword of Gideon son of Joash the Israelite. God has delivered Midian

15 and the whole army into his hands.' When Gideon heard the story of the dream and its interpretation, he prostrated himself. Then he went back to the Israelite camp and said, 'Up! The LORD has delivered the

16 camp of the Midianites into your hands.' He divided the three hundred men into three companies, and gave every man a trumpet and an empty

17 jar with a torch inside it. Then he said to them, 'Watch me: when

18 I come to the edge of the camp, do exactly as I do. When I and my men blow our trumpets, you too all round the camp will blow your trumpets, and shout, "For the LORD and for Gideon!"'

19 Gideon and the hundred men who were with him reached the outskirts of the camp at the beginning of the middle watch; the sentries had just been posted. They blew their trumpets and smashed their jars.

[a] on the other: *so Sept.; Heb. om.* [b] putting...mouths: *prob. rdg.; Heb. has this phrase after those who lapped.* [c] *Prob. rdg.; Heb. provisions.* [d] *Prob. rdg.; Heb. adds and it fell.*

The three companies all blew their trumpets and smashed their jars, 20
then grasped the torches in their left hands and the trumpets in their
right, and shouted, 'A sword for the LORD and for Gideon!' Every man 21
stood where he was, all round the camp, and the whole camp leapt up
in a panic and fled. The three hundred blew their trumpets, and 22
throughout the camp the LORD set every man against his neighbour. The
army fled as far as Beth-shittah in Zererah, as far as the ridge of
Abel-meholah by Tabbath. The Israelites from Naphtali and Asher 23
and all Manasseh were called out and they pursued the Midianites.
Gideon sent men through all the hill-country of Ephraim with this 24
message: 'Come down and cut off the Midianites. Hold the fords of the
Jordan against them as far as Beth-barah.' So all the Ephraimites were
called out and they held the fords of the Jordan as far as Beth-barah.
They captured the two Midianite princes, Oreb and Zeeb. Oreb they 25
killed at the Rock of Oreb, and Zeeb by the Winepress of Zeeb, and
they kept up the pursuit of[a] the Midianites; afterwards they brought
the heads of Oreb and Zeeb across the Jordan to Gideon.

The men of Ephraim said to Gideon, 'Why have you treated us like 8
this? Why did you not summon us when you went to fight Midian?';
and they reproached him violently. But he said to them, 'What have I 2
done compared with you? Are not Ephraim's gleanings better than the
whole vintage of Abiezer? God has delivered Oreb and Zeeb, the 3
princes of Midian, into your hands. What have I done compared with
you?' At these words of his, their anger died down.

Gideon came to the Jordan, and he and his three hundred men 4
crossed over to continue the pursuit, weary though they were. He said 5
to the men of Succoth, 'Will you give these men of mine some bread,
for they are weary, and I am pursuing Zebah and Zalmunna, the kings
of Midian?' But the chief men of Succoth replied, 'Are Zebah and 6
Zalmunna already in your hands, that we should give your army
bread?' Gideon said, 'For that, when the LORD delivers Zebah and 7
Zalmunna into my hands, I will thresh your bodies with desert thorns
and briars.' He went on from there to Penuel and made the same 8
request; the men of Penuel answered like the men of Succoth. He said 9
to the men of Penuel, 'When I return safely, I will pull down your
castle.'

Zebah and Zalmunna were in Karkor with their army of fifteen 10
thousand men. These were all that remained of the whole host of the
eastern tribes; a hundred and twenty thousand armed men had fallen
in battle. Gideon advanced along the track used by the tent-dwellers 11
east of Nobah and Jogbehah, and his attack caught the army when they
were off their guard. Zebah and Zalmunna fled; but he went in 12

[a] *So Sept.; Heb.* to.

pursuit of these Midianite kings and captured them both; and their whole army melted away.

13 As Gideon son of Joash was returning from the battle by the Ascent
14 of Heres, he caught a young man from Succoth. He questioned him, and one by one he numbered off the names of the rulers of Succoth
15 and its elders, seventy-seven in all. Gideon then came to the men of Succoth and said, 'Here are Zebah and Zalmunna, about whom you taunted me. "Are Zebah and Zalmunna", you said, "already in your
16 hands, that we should give your weary men bread?"' Then he took the elders of the city and he disciplined those men of Succoth with desert
17 thorns and briars. He also pulled down the castle of Penuel and put the
18 men of the city to death. Then he said to Zebah and Zalmunna, 'What of the men you killed in Tabor?' They answered, 'They were like you,
19 every one had the look of a king's son.' 'They were my brothers,' he said, 'my mother's sons. I swear by the LORD, if you had let them live
20 I would not have killed you'; and he said to his eldest son Jether, 'Up with you, and kill them.' But he was still only a lad, and did not draw
21 his sword, because he was afraid. So Zebah and Zalmunna said, 'Rise up yourself and dispatch us, for you have*a* a man's strength.' So Gideon rose and killed them both, and he took the crescents from the necks of their camels.

22 After this the Israelites said to Gideon, 'You have saved us from the Midianites; now you be our ruler, you and your son and your grand-
23 son.' Gideon replied, 'I will not rule over you, nor shall my son; the
24 LORD will rule over you.' Then he said, 'I have a request to make: will every one of you give me the earrings from his booty?'—for the enemy
25 wore golden earrings, being Ishmaelites. They said, 'Of course, we will give them.' So a cloak was spread out and every man threw on to it the
26 golden earrings from his booty. The earrings for which he asked weighed seventeen hundred shekels of gold; this was in addition to the crescents and pendants and the purple cloaks worn by the Midianite
27 kings, not counting the chains on the necks of their camels. Gideon made it into an ephod and he set it up in his own city of Ophrah. All the Israelites turned wantonly to its worship, and it became a trap to catch Gideon and his household.

28 Thus the Midianites were subdued by the Israelites; they could no longer hold up their heads. For forty years the land was at peace, all
29 the lifetime of Gideon, that is Jerubbaal son of Joash; and he retired to
30 his own home. Gideon had seventy sons, his own offspring, for he had
31 many wives. He had a concubine who lived in Shechem, and she also
32 bore him a son, whom he named Abimelech. Gideon son of Joash died at a ripe old age and was buried in his father's grave at Ophrah-of-the-

[a] *So Sept.; Heb.* he has.

Abiezrites. After his death, the Israelites again went wantonly to the 33
worship of the Baalim and made Baal-berith their god. They forgot the 34
LORD their God who had delivered them from their enemies on every
side, and did not show to the family of Jerubbaal, that is Gideon, the 35
loyalty that was due to them for all the good he had done for Israel.

ABIMELECH SON OF JERUBBAAL went to Shechem to his mother's 9
brothers, and spoke with them and with all the clan of his mother's
family. 'I beg you,' he said, 'whisper a word in the ears of the chief 2
citizens of Shechem. Ask them which is better for them: that seventy
men, all the sons of Jerubbaal, should rule over them, or one man. Tell
them to remember that I am their own flesh and blood.' So his mother's 3
brothers repeated all this to each of them on his behalf; and they were
moved to come over to Abimelech's side, because, as they said, he was
their brother. They gave him seventy pieces of silver from the temple 4
of Baal-berith, and with these he hired idle and reckless men, who
followed him. He came to his father's house in Ophrah and butchered 5
his seventy brothers, the sons of Jerubbaal, on a single stone block, all
but Jotham the youngest, who survived because he had hidden himself.
Then all the citizens of Shechem and all Beth-millo came together and 6
made Abimelech king beside the old propped-up terebinth at Shechem.

When this was reported to Jotham, he went and stood on the summit 7
of Mount Gerizim. He cried at the top of his voice: 'Listen to me, you
citizens of Shechem, and may God listen to you:

'Once upon a time the trees came to anoint a king, and they said to 8
the olive-tree: Be king over us. But the olive-tree answered: What, 9
leave my rich oil by which gods and men are honoured, to come and
hold sway over the trees?

'So the trees said to the fig-tree: Then will you come and be king 10
over us? But the fig-tree answered: What, leave my good fruit and all 11
its sweetness, to come and hold sway over the trees?

'So the trees said to the vine: Then will you come and be king over 12
us? But the vine answered: What, leave my new wine which gladdens 13
gods and men, to come and hold sway over the trees?

'Then all the trees said to the thorn-bush: Will you then be king 14
over us? And the thorn said to the trees: If you really mean to anoint 15
me as your king, then come under the protection of my shadow; if not,
fire shall come out of the thorn and burn up the cedars of Lebanon.'

Then Jotham said, 'Now, have you acted fairly and honestly in 16
making Abimelech king? Have you done the right thing by Jerubbaal
and his household? Have you given my father his due—who fought for 17
you, and threw himself into the forefront of the battle and delivered
you from the Midianites? Today you have risen against my father's 18

family, butchered his seventy sons on a single stone block, and made Abimelech, the son of his slave-girl, king over the citizens of Shechem

19 because he is your brother. In this day's work have you acted fairly and honestly by Jerubbaal and his family? If so, I wish you joy in Abi-

20 melech and wish him joy in you! If not, may fire come out of Abimelech and burn up the citizens of Shechem and all Beth-millo; may fire also come out from the citizens of Shechem and Beth-millo and burn up

21 Abimelech.' After which Jotham slipped away and made his escape; he came to Beer, and there he settled out of reach of his brother Abimelech.

22, 23   After Abimelech had been prince over Israel for three years, God sent an evil spirit to make a breach between Abimelech and the citizens

24 of Shechem, and they played him false. This was done on purpose, so that the violent murder of the seventy sons of Jerubbaal might recoil on their brother Abimelech who did the murder and on the citizens of

25 Shechem who encouraged him to do it. The citizens of Shechem set men to lie in wait for him on the hill-tops, but they robbed all who passed that way, and so the news reached Abimelech.

26   Now Gaal son of Ebed came with his kinsmen to Shechem, and the

27 citizens of Shechem transferred their allegiance to him. They went out into the country-side, picked the early grapes in their vineyards, trod them in the winepress and held festival. They went into the temple of

28 their god, where they ate and drank and reviled Abimelech. 'Who is Abimelech,' said Gaal son of Ebed, 'and who are the Shechemites, that we should be his subjects? Have not this son of Jerubbaal and his lieutenant Zebul been subjects of the men of Hamor the father of

29 Shechem? Why indeed should we be subject to him? If only this people were in my charge I should know how to get rid of Abimelech! I would say[a] to him, "Get your men together, and come out and fight."'

30 When Zebul the governor of the city heard what Gaal son of Ebed said,

31 he was very angry. He resorted to a ruse and sent messengers to Abimelech to say, 'Gaal son of Ebed and his kinsmen have come to

32 Shechem and are turning the city against you. Get up now in the night,

33 you and the people with you, and lie in wait in the open country. Then be up in the morning at sunrise, and advance rapidly against the city. When he and his people come out, do to him what the situation

34 demands.' So Abimelech and his people rose in the night, and lay in

35 wait to attack Shechem, in four companies. Gaal son of Ebed came out and stood in the entrance of the city gate, and Abimelech and his

36 people rose from their hiding-place. Gaal saw them and said to Zebul, 'There are people coming down from the tops of the hills', but Zebul replied, 'What you see is the shadow of the hills, looking like men.'

37 Once more Gaal said, 'There are people coming down from the central

[a] *So Sept.; Heb.* And he said.

ridge[a] of the hills, and one company is coming along the road of the
Soothsayers' Terebinth.' Then Zebul said to him, 'Where are your 38
brave words now? You said, "Who is Abimelech that we should be
subject to him?" Are not these the people you despised? Go out and
fight him.' Gaal led the citizens of Shechem out and attacked Abi- 39
melech, but Abimelech routed him and he fled. The ground was strewn 40
with corpses all the way to the entrance of the gate. Abimelech 41
established himself in Arumah, and Zebul drove away Gaal and his
kinsmen and allowed them no place in Shechem.

Next day the people came out into the open, and this was reported 42
to Abimelech. He on his side took his supporters, divided them into 43
three companies and lay in wait in the open country; and when he saw
the people coming out of the city, he rose and attacked them. Abi- 44
melech and the company[b] with him advanced rapidly and took up
position at the entrance of the city gate, while the other two companies
advanced against all those who were in the open and struck them down.
Abimelech kept up the attack on the city all that day and captured it; 45
he killed the people in it, pulled the city down and sowed the site with
salt. When the occupants of the castle of Shechem heard of this, they 46
went into the great hall[c] of the temple of El-berith. It was reported to 47
Abimelech that all the occupants of the castle of Shechem had collected
together. So he and his people went up Mount Zalmon carrying axes; 48
there he cut brushwood, and took it and hoisted it on his shoulder. He
said to his men, 'You see what I am doing; be quick and do the same.'
So each man cut brushwood; then they followed Abimelech and laid 49
the brushwood against the hall, and burnt it over their heads. Thus all
the occupants of the castle of Shechem died, about a thousand men and
women.

Abimelech then went to Thebez, besieged it and took it. There was 50, 51
a strong castle in the middle of the city, and all the citizens, men and
women, took refuge there. They shut themselves in and went on to the
roof. Abimelech came up to the castle and attacked it. As he approached 52
the entrance to the castle to set fire to it, a woman threw a millstone 53
down on his head and fractured his skull. He called hurriedly to his 54
young armour-bearer and said, 'Draw your sword and dispatch me, or
men will say of me: A woman killed him.' So the young man ran him
through and he died. When the Israelites saw that Abimelech was 55
dead, they all went back to their homes. It was thus that God requited 56
the crime which Abimelech had committed against his father by the
murder of his seventy brothers, and brought all the wickedness of the 57
men of Shechem on their own heads. The curse of Jotham son of
Jerubbaal came home to them.

[a] central ridge: *lit.* navel.   [b] *So Vulg.; Heb.* companies.   [c] *Or* vault.

10   After Abimelech, Tola son of Pua, son of Dodo, a man of Issachar
who lived in Shamir in the hill-country of Ephraim, came in his turn
2 to deliver Israel. He was judge over Israel for twenty-three years, and
when he died he was buried in Shamir.

3   After him came Jair the Gileadite; he was judge over Israel for
4 twenty-two years. He had thirty sons, who rode thirty asses; they had
thirty towns in the land of Gilead, which to this day are called
5 Havvoth-jair.[a] When Jair died, he was buried in Kamon.

6   Once more the Israelites did what was wrong in the eyes of the LORD,
worshipping the Baalim and the Ashtaroth, the deities of Aram and of
Sidon and of Moab, of the Ammonites and of the Philistines. They
7 forsook the LORD and did not worship him. The LORD was angry with
8 Israel, and he sold them to the Philistines and the Ammonites, who[b]
for eighteen years harassed and oppressed the Israelites who lived
9 beyond the Jordan in the Amorite country in Gilead. Then the
Ammonites crossed the Jordan to attack Judah, Benjamin, and
10 Ephraim, so that Israel was in great distress. The Israelites cried to the
LORD for help and said, 'We have sinned against thee; we have for-
11 saken our God and worshipped the Baalim.' And the LORD said to the
Israelites, 'The Egyptians, the Amorites, the Ammonites, the Philis-
12 tines; the Sidonians too and the Amalekites and the Midianites[c]—all
these oppressed you and you cried to me for help; and did not I deliver
13 you? But you forsook me and worshipped other gods; therefore I will
14 deliver you no more. Go and cry for help to the gods you have chosen,
15 and let them save you in the day of your distress.' But the Israelites
said to the LORD, 'We have sinned. Deal with us as thou wilt; only
16 save us this day, we implore thee.' They banished the foreign gods and
worshipped the LORD; and he could endure no longer to see the plight
of Israel.

17   Then the Ammonites were called to arms, and they encamped in
Gilead, while the Israelites assembled and encamped in Mizpah.
18 The people of Gilead and their chief men said to one another, 'If any
man will strike the first blow at the Ammonites, he shall be lord over the
inhabitants of Gilead.'

11   Jephthah the Gileadite was a great warrior; he was the son of Gilead
2 by a prostitute. But Gilead had a wife who bore him several sons, and
when they grew up they drove Jephthah away; they said to him, 'You
have no inheritance in our father's house; you are another woman's
3 son.' So Jephthah, to escape his brothers, went away and settled in the
land of Tob, and swept up a number of idle men who followed him.
4, 5   The time came when the Ammonites made war on Israel, and when

[a] *That is* Tent-villages of Jair.   [b] *Prob. rdg.; Heb. adds* in that year.   [c] *So Sept.;
Heb.* Maon.

the fighting began, the elders of Gilead went to fetch Jephthah from the
land of Tob. They said to him, 'Come and be our commander so that 6
we can fight the Ammonites.' But Jephthah said to the elders of Gilead, 7
'You drove me from my father's house in hatred. Why come to me
now when you are in trouble?' 'It is because of that', they replied, 'that 8
we have turned to you now. Come with us and fight the Ammonites,
and become lord over all the inhabitants of Gilead.' Jephthah said to 9
them, 'If you ask me back to fight the Ammonites and if the LORD
delivers them into my hands, then I will be your lord.' The elders of 10
Gilead said again to Jephthah, 'We swear by the LORD, who shall be
witness between us, that we will do what you say.' Jephthah then went 11
with the elders of Gilead, and the people made him their lord and
commander. And at Mizpah, in the presence of the LORD, Jephthah
repeated all that he had said.

Jephthah sent a mission to the king of Ammon to ask what quarrel 12
he had with them that made him invade their country. The king gave 13
Jephthah's men this answer: 'When the Israelites came up from Egypt,
they took our land from the Arnon as far as the Jabbok and the Jordan.
Give us back these lands in peace.' Jephthah sent a second mission to 14
the king of Ammon, and they said, 'This is Jephthah's answer: Israel 15
did not take either the Moabite country or the Ammonite country.
When they came up from Egypt, the Israelites passed through the 16
wilderness to the Red Sea[a] and came to Kadesh. They then sent 17
envoys to the king of Edom asking him to grant them passage through
his country, but the king of Edom would not hear of it. They sent also
to the king of Moab, but he was not willing; so Israel remained in
Kadesh. They then passed through the wilderness, skirting Edom and 18
Moab, and kept to the east of Moab. They encamped beside the
Arnon, but they did not enter Moabite territory, because the Arnon is
the frontier of Moab. Israel then sent envoys to the king of the 19
Amorites, Sihon king of Heshbon, asking him to give them free
passage through his country to their destination. But Sihon would not 20
grant Israel free passage through his territory; he mustered all his
people, encamped in Jahaz and fought Israel. But the LORD the God of 21
Israel delivered Sihon and all his people into the hands of Israel; they
defeated them and occupied all the territory of the Amorites in that
region. They took all the Amorite territory from the Arnon to the 22
Jabbok and from the wilderness to the Jordan. The LORD the God of 23
Israel drove out the Amorites for the benefit of his people Israel. And
do you now propose to take their place? It is for you to possess what- 24
ever Kemosh your god gives you; and all that the LORD our God gave
us as we advanced is ours. For that matter, are you any better than 25

[a] *Or* the Sea of Reeds.

339

Balak son of Zippor, king of Moab? Did he ever quarrel with Israel or
26 attack them? For three hundred years Israelites have lived in Heshbon
and its dependent villages, in Aroer and its villages, and in all the towns
27 by the Arnon. Why did you not oust*ᵃ* them during all that time? We
have done you no wrong; it is you who are doing us wrong by attacking
us. The LORD who is judge will judge this day between the Israelites
28 and the Ammonites.' But the king of the Ammonites would not listen
to the message which Jephthah had sent him.

29   Then the spirit of the LORD came upon Jephthah and he passed
through Gilead and Manasseh, by Mizpeh of Gilead, and from Mizpeh
30 over to the Ammonites. Jephthah made this vow to the LORD: 'If thou
31 wilt deliver the Ammonites into my hands, then the first creature that
comes out of the door of my house to meet me when I return from them
in peace shall be the LORD's; I will offer that as a whole-offering.'
32 So Jephthah crossed over to attack the Ammonites, and the LORD
33 delivered them into his hands. He routed them with great slaughter all
the way from Aroer to Minnith, taking twenty towns, and as far as
34 Abel-keramim. Thus Israel crushed Ammon. But when Jephthah came
to his house in Mizpah, who should come out to meet him with
tambourines and dances but his daughter, and she his only child; he
35 had no other, neither son nor daughter. When he saw her, he rent his
clothes and said, 'Alas, my daughter, you have broken my heart, such
trouble you have brought upon me. I have made a vow to the LORD
36 and I cannot go back.' She replied, 'Father, you have made a vow to the
LORD; do to me what you have solemnly vowed, since the LORD has
37 avenged you on the Ammonites, your enemies. But, father, grant me
this one favour. For two months let me be, that I may roam*ᵇ* the hills
38 with my companions and mourn that I must die a virgin.' 'Go', he
said, and he let her depart for two months. She went with her com-
39 panions and mourned her virginity on the hills. At the end of two months
she came back to her father, and he fulfilled the vow he had made; she
40 died a virgin. It became a tradition that the daughters of Israel should
go year by year and commemorate the fate of Jephthah's daughter,
four days in every year.

12   The Ephraimites mustered their forces and crossed over to Zaphon.
They said to Jephthah, 'Why did you march against the Ammonites
and not summon us to go with you? We will burn your house over
2 your head.' Jephthah answered, 'I and my people had a feud with the
Ammonites, and had I appealed to you for help, you would not have
3 saved us*ᶜ* from them. When I saw that we were not to look for help from
you, I took my life in my hands and marched against the Ammonites,

[*a*] *Or* recover.   [*b*] *Or* that I may go down country to...   [*c*] and had I...saved us: *or*
I did appeal to you for help, but you would not save us...

and the LORD delivered them into my power. Why then do you attack
me today?' Jephthah then mustered all the men of Gilead and fought 4
Ephraim, and the Gileadites defeated them.[a] The Gileadites seized the 5
fords of the Jordan and held them against Ephraim. When any
Ephraimite who had escaped begged leave to cross, the men of Gilead
asked him, 'Are you an Ephraimite?', and if he said, 'No', they would 6
retort, 'Say Shibboleth.' He would say 'Sibboleth', and because he
could not pronounce the word properly, they seized him and killed
him at the fords of the Jordan. At that time forty-two thousand men of
Ephraim lost their lives.

Jephthah was judge over Israel for six years; when he died he was 7
buried in his own city in[b] Gilead. After him Ibzan of Bethlehem was 8
judge over Israel. He had thirty sons and thirty daughters. He gave 9
away the thirty daughters in marriage and brought in thirty girls for his
sons. He was judge over Israel for seven years, and when he died he 10
was buried in Bethlehem.

After him Elon the Zebulunite was judge over Israel for ten years. 11
When he died, he was buried in Aijalon in the land of Zebulun. Next 12, 13
Abdon son of Hillel the Pirathonite was judge over Israel. He had 14
forty sons and thirty grandsons, who rode each on his own ass. He was
judge over Israel for eight years; and when he died he was buried in 15
Pirathon in the land of Ephraim on the hill of the Amalekite.

Israel oppressed by the Philistines

ONCE MORE THE ISRAELITES did what was wrong in the eyes of 13
the LORD, and he delivered them into the hands of the Philistines
for forty years.

There was a man from Zorah of the tribe of Dan whose name was 2
Manoah and whose wife was barren and childless. The angel of the 3
LORD appeared to her and said, 'You are barren and have no child, but
you shall conceive and give birth to a son. Now you must do as I say: 4
be careful to drink no wine or strong drink, and to eat no forbidden[c]
food; you will conceive and give birth to a son, and no razor shall 5
touch his head, for the boy is to be a Nazirite consecrated to God from
the day of his birth. He will strike the first blow to deliver Israel from
the power of the Philistines.' The woman went and told her husband; 6
she said to him, 'A man of God came to me; his appearance was that

[a] *So some MSS. of Sept.; Heb. adds* for they said, 'You are fugitives from Ephraim, Gilead,
in the midst of Ephraim, in the midst of Manasseh.' [b] in his own city in: *so Sept.; Heb.*
in the cities of... [c] *Lit.* unclean.

of an[a] angel of God, most terrible to see. I did not ask him where he
7 came from nor did he tell me his name. He said to me, "You shall
conceive and give birth to a son. From this time onwards drink no
wine or strong drink and eat no forbidden food, for the boy is to be a
Nazirite consecrated to God from his birth to the day of his death."'
8 Manoah prayed to the LORD, 'If it please thee, O LORD, let the man of
God whom thou didst send come again to tell us what we are to do
9 with the boy who is to be born.' God heard Manoah's prayer, and the
angel of God came again to the woman, who was sitting in the fields;
10 her husband was not with her. The woman ran quickly and said to
him, 'The man who came to me the other day has appeared to me
11 again.' Manoah went with her at once and approached the man and
said, 'Was it you who talked with my wife?' He said, 'Yes, it was I.'
12 'Now when your words come true,' Manoah said, 'what kind of boy
13 will he be and what will he do?' The angel of the LORD answered him,
14 'Your wife must be careful to do all that I told her: she[b] must not taste
anything that comes from the vine. She[b] must drink no wine or strong
drink, and she[b] must eat no forbidden food. She[b] must do what I say.'
15 Manoah said to the angel of the LORD, 'May we urge you to stay? Let
16 us prepare a kid for you.' The angel of the LORD replied, 'Though you
urge me to stay, I will not eat your food; but prepare a whole-offering if
you will, and offer that to the LORD.' Manoah did not perceive that he
17 was the angel of the LORD and said to him, 'What is your name?
18 For we shall want to honour you when your words come true.' The
angel of the LORD said to him, 'How can you ask my name? It is a
19 name of wonder.' Manoah took a kid with the proper grain-offering,
and offered it on the rock to the LORD, to him whose works are full of
20 wonder. And while Manoah and his wife were watching, the flame went
up from the altar towards heaven, and the angel of the LORD went up
in the flame; and seeing this, Manoah and his wife fell on their faces.
21 The angel of the LORD did not appear again to Manoah and his wife;
22 and Manoah knew that he was the angel of the LORD. He said to his
23 wife, 'We are doomed to die, we have seen God',[c] but she replied,
'If the LORD had wanted to kill us, he would not have accepted a
whole-offering and a grain-offering at our hands; he would not now
24-25 have let us see and hear all this.' The woman gave birth to a son and
named him Samson. The boy grew up in Mahaneh-dan between Zorah
and Eshtaol, and the LORD blessed him, and the spirit of the LORD
began to drive him hard.

14   Samson went down to Timnath, and there he saw a woman, one of
2 the Philistines. When he came back, he told his father and mother that
he had seen a Philistine woman in Timnath and asked them to get her

[a] *Or* the.   [b] *Sept. has* he.   [c] *Or* a god.

for him as his wife. His father and mother said to him, 'Is there no ³
woman among your cousins or in all our own people? Must you go and
marry one of the uncircumcised Philistines?' But Samson said to his
father, 'Get her for me, because she pleases me.' His father and mother ⁴
did not know that the LORD was at work in this, seeking an opportunity
against the Philistines, who at that time were masters of Israel.

Samson[a] went down to Timnath and, when he[b] reached the vine- ⁵
yards there, a young lion came at him growling. The spirit of the LORD ⁶
suddenly seized him and, having no weapon in his hand, he tore the
lion in pieces as if it were a kid. He did not tell his parents what he had
done. Then he went down and spoke to the woman, and she pleased ⁷
him. After a time he went down again to take her to wife; he turned ⁸
aside to look at the carcass of the lion, and he saw a swarm of bees in it,
and honey. He scraped the honey into his hands and went on, eating as ⁹
he went. When he came to his father and mother, he gave them some
and they ate it; but he did not tell them that he had scraped the honey
out of the lion's carcass. His father went down to see the woman, and ¹⁰
Samson gave a feast there as the custom of young men was. When the ¹¹
people saw him, they brought thirty young men to be his escort. Samson ¹²
said to them, 'Let me ask you a riddle. If you can guess it during the
seven days of the feast, I will give you thirty lengths of linen and thirty
changes of clothing; but if you cannot guess the answer, then you shall ¹³
give me thirty lengths of linen and thirty changes of clothing.' 'Tell
us your riddle,' they said; 'let us hear it.' So he said to them: ¹⁴

> Out of the eater came something to eat;
> out of the strong came something sweet.

At the end of three days they had failed to guess the riddle. On the ¹⁵
fourth[c] day they said to Samson's wife, 'Coax your husband and make
him tell you[d] the riddle, or we shall burn you and your father's house.
Did you invite us here[e] to beggar us?' So Samson's wife wept over him ¹⁶
and said, 'You do not love me, you only hate me. You have asked my
kinsfolk a riddle and you have not told it to me.' He said to her, 'I have
not told it even to my father and mother; and am I to tell you?' But ¹⁷
she wept over him every day until the seven feast days were ended, and
on the seventh day, because she pestered him, he told her, and she told
the riddle to her kinsfolk. So that same day the men of the city said to ¹⁸
Samson before he entered the bridal chamber:[f]

> What is sweeter than honey?
> What is stronger than a lion?

[a] *Prob. rdg.; Heb. adds* and his father and mother.　[b] *So Sept.; Heb.* they.　[c] *So Sept.;
Heb.* seventh.　[d] *So Sept.; Heb.* us.　[e] *here: so some MSS.; others* or not.　[f] he
entered...chamber: *prob. rdg.; Heb.* the sun went down.

and he replied, 'If you had not ploughed with my heifer, you would not
19 have found out my riddle.' Then the spirit of the LORD suddenly
seized him. He went down to Ashkelon and there he killed thirty men,
took their belts and gave their clothes to the men who had answered his
20 riddle; but he was very angry and went off to his father's house. And
Samson's wife was given in marriage to the friend who had been his
groomsman.

15   After a while, during the time of wheat harvest, Samson went to
visit his wife, taking a kid as a present for her. He said, 'I am going to
my wife in our bridal chamber', but her father would not let him in.
2 He said, 'I was sure that you hated her, so I gave her in marriage to
your groomsman. Her young sister is better than she—take her instead.'
3 But Samson said, 'This time I will settle my score with the Philistines;
4 I will do them some real harm.' So he went and caught three hundred
jackals and got some torches; he tied the jackals tail to tail and fastened
5 a torch between each pair of tails. He then set the torches alight and
turned the jackals loose in the standing corn of the Philistines. He burnt
6 up standing corn and stooks as well, vineyards and*a* olive groves. The
Philistines said, 'Who has done this?' They were told that it was
Samson, because the Timnite, his father-in-law, had taken his wife and
given her to his groomsman. So the Philistines came and burnt her and
7 her father. Samson said, 'If you do things like this, I swear I will be
8 revenged upon you before I have done.' He smote them hip and thigh
with great slaughter; and after that he went down to live in a cave in
the Rock of Etam.

9   The Philistines came up and pitched camp in Judah, and overran
10 Lehi. The men of Judah said, 'Why have you attacked us?' They
answered, 'We have come to take Samson prisoner and serve him as he
11 served us.' So three thousand men from Judah went down to the cave
in the Rock of Etam. They said to Samson, 'Surely you know that the
Philistines are our masters? Now see what you have brought upon us.'
12 He answered, 'I only served them as they had served me.' They said
to him, 'We have come down to bind you and hand you over to the
Philistines.' 'Then you must swear to me', he said, 'that you will not
13 set upon me yourselves.' They answered, 'No; we will only bind you
and hand you over to them, we will not kill you.' So they bound him
14 with two new ropes and brought him up from the cave in the Rock. He
came to Lehi, and when they met him, the Philistines shouted in
triumph; but the spirit of the LORD suddenly seized him, the ropes on
15 his arms became like burnt tow and his bonds melted away. He found
the jaw-bone of an ass, all raw, and picked it up and slew a thousand
16 men. He made this saying:

[*a*] and: *so Sept.; Heb. om.*

With the jaw-bone of an ass*a* I have flayed them like asses;*b*
with the jaw-bone of an ass I have slain a thousand men.

When he had said his say, he threw away the jaw-bone; and he called 17
that place Ramath-lehi.*c* He began to feel very thirsty and cried aloud 18
to the LORD, 'Thou hast let me, thy servant, win this great victory,
and must I now die of thirst and fall into the hands of the uncircumcised?' God split open the Hollow*d* of Lehi and water came out of it. 19
Samson drank, his strength returned and he revived. This is why the
spring in Lehi is called En-hakkore*e* to this day.

Samson was judge over Israel for twenty years in the days of the 20
Philistines.

Samson went to Gaza, and there he saw a prostitute and went in to 16
spend the night with her. The people of Gaza heard*f* that Samson had 2
come, and they surrounded him and lay in wait for him all that night
at the city gate. During the night, however, they took no action, saying
to themselves, 'When day breaks we shall kill him.' Samson lay in bed 3
till midnight; and when midnight came he rose, seized hold of the doors
of the city gate and the two posts, pulled them out, bar and all, hoisted
them on to his shoulders and carried them to the top of the hill east of
Hebron.

After this Samson fell in love with a woman named Delilah, who lived 4
in the valley of Sorek. The lords of the Philistines went up country to 5
see her and said, 'Coax him and find out what gives him his great
strength, and how we can master him, bind him and so hold him
captive; then we will each give you eleven hundred pieces of silver.'
So Delilah said to Samson, 'Tell me what gives you your great strength, 6
and how you can be bound and held captive.' Samson replied, 'If they 7
bind me with seven fresh bowstrings not yet dry, then I shall become
as weak as any other man.' So the lords of the Philistines brought her 8
seven fresh bowstrings not yet dry, and she bound him with them. She 9
had men already hidden in the inner room, and she cried, 'The
Philistines are upon you, Samson!' But he snapped the bowstrings as
a strand of tow snaps when it feels the fire, and his strength was not
tamed. Delilah said to Samson, 'I see you have made a fool of me and 10
told me lies. Tell me this time how you can be bound.' He said to her, 11
'If you bind me tightly with new ropes that have never been used, then
I shall become as weak as any other man.' So Delilah took new ropes 12
and bound him with them. Then she cried, 'The Philistines are upon
you, Samson!', while the men waited hidden in the inner room. He
snapped the ropes off his arms like pack-thread. Delilah said to him, 13

[a] ass: *Heb.* hamor.   [b] I have...asses: *or* I have reddened them blood-red, *or* I have
heaped them in heaps; *Heb.* hamor himmartim.   [c] *That is* Jaw-bone Hill.   [d] *Lit.* Mortar.
[e] *That is* the Crier's Spring.   [f] The...heard: *so Sept.; Heb.* To the people of Gaza.

'You are still making a fool of me and have told me lies. Tell me: how can you be bound?' He said, 'Take the seven loose locks of my hair and weave them into the warp, and then drive them tight with the beater; and I shall become as weak as any other man.' So she lulled him

14 to sleep, wove the seven loose locks of his hair into the warp,*a* and drove them tight with the beater, and cried, 'The Philistines are upon you, Samson!' He woke from sleep and pulled away the warp and the loom

15 with it.*b* She said to him, 'How can you say you love me when you do not confide in me? This is the third time you have made a fool of me and

16 have not told me what gives you your great strength.' She so pestered him with these words day after day, pressing him hard and wearying

17 him to death, that he told her his secret. 'No razor has touched my head,' he said, 'because I am a Nazirite, consecrated to God from the day of my birth. If my head were shaved, then my strength would

18 leave me, and I should become as weak as any other man.' Delilah saw that he had told her his secret; so she sent to the lords of the Philistines and said, 'Come up at once, he has told me his secret.' So the lords of

19 the Philistines came up and brought the money with them. She lulled him to sleep on her knees, summoned a man and he shaved the seven locks of his hair for her. She began to take him captive and his strength

20 left him. Then she cried, 'The Philistines are upon you, Samson!' He woke from his sleep and said, 'I will go out as usual and shake myself';

21 he did not know that the LORD had left him. The Philistines seized him, gouged out his eyes and brought him down to Gaza. There they bound him with fetters of bronze, and he was set to grinding corn in the prison.

22 But his hair, after it had been shaved, began to grow again.

23 The lords of the Philistines assembled together to offer a great sacrifice to their god Dagon and to rejoice before him. They said,

24 'Our god has delivered Samson our enemy into our hands.' The people, when they saw him, praised their god, chanting:

> Our god has delivered our enemy into our hands,
> the scourge of our land who piled it with our dead.

25 When they grew merry, they said, 'Call Samson, and let him fight to make sport for us.' So they summoned Samson from prison and he

26 made sport before them all. They stood him between the pillars, and Samson said to the boy who held his hand, 'Put me where I can feel the

27 pillars which support the temple, so that I may lean against them.' The temple was full of men and women, and all the lords of the Philistines were there, and there were about three thousand men and women on the

28 roof watching Samson as he fought. Samson called on the LORD and

[a] and then drive...warp: *so Sept.; Heb. om.*   [b] the warp...with it: *prob. rdg.; Heb. adds an unintelligible word.*

said, 'Remember me, O Lord GOD, remember me: give me strength only this once, O God, and let me at one stroke be avenged on the Philistines for my two eyes.' He put his arms round the two central 29 pillars which supported the temple, his right arm round one and his left round the other, and braced himself and said, 'Let me die with the 30 Philistines.' Then Samson leaned forward with all his might, and the temple fell on the lords and on all the people who were in it. So the dead whom he killed at his death were more than those he had killed in his life. His brothers and all his father's family came down, carried 31 him up to the grave of his father Manoah between Zorah and Eshtaol and buried him there. He had been judge over Israel for twenty years.

Years of lawlessness

THERE WAS ONCE A MAN named Micah from the hill-country of 17 Ephraim. He said to his mother, 'You remember the eleven 2 hundred pieces of silver which were taken from you, and how you called down a curse on the thief in my hearing? I have the money; I took it and now I will give it back to you.'*a* His mother said, 'May the LORD bless you, my son.' So he gave the eleven hundred pieces of 3 silver back to his mother, and she said, 'I now solemnly dedicate this money of mine to the LORD for the benefit of my son, to make a carved idol and a cast image.' He returned the money to his mother, 4 and she took two hundred pieces of silver and handed them to a silver-smith, who made them into an idol and an image, which stood in Micah's house.

This man Micah had a shrine, and he made an ephod and teraphim*b* 5 and installed one of his sons to be his priest. In those days there was no 6 king in Israel and every man did what was right in his own eyes. Now 7 there was a young man from Bethlehem in Judah, from the clan of Judah, a Levite named Ben-gershom.*c* He had left the city of Bethlehem 8 to go and find somewhere to live. On his way he came to Micah's house in the hill-country of Ephraim. Micah said to him, 'Where have you 9 come from?' He replied, 'I am a Levite from Bethlehem in Judah, and I am looking for somewhere to live.' Micah said to him, 'Stay with me 10 and be priest and father to me. I will give you ten pieces of silver a year, and provide you with food and clothes.'*d* The Levite agreed to stay 11 with the man and was treated as one of his own sons. Micah installed 12

[*a*] and now...you: *transposed from verse 3.* [*b*] *Or* household gods. [*c*] named Ben-gershom: *prob. rdg., cp. 18. 30; Heb.* he lodged there. [*d*] *So Vulg.; Heb. adds* and the Levite went.

the Levite, and the young man became his priest and a member of his
13 household. Micah said, 'Now I know that the LORD will make me
prosper, because I have a Levite for my priest.'

18   In those days there was no king in Israel and the tribe of the Danites
was looking for territory to occupy, because they had not so far come
into possession of the territory*a* allotted to them among the tribes of
2 Israel. The Danites therefore sent out five fighting men of their clan
from Zorah and Eshtaol to prospect, with instructions to go and explore
the land. They came to Micah's house in the hill-country of Ephraim
3 and spent the night there. While they were there, they recognized the
speech of the young Levite; they turned there and then and said to
him, 'Who brought you here? What are you doing? What is your
4 business here?' He said, 'This is all Micah's doing: he has hired me and
5 I have become his priest.' They said to him, 'Then inquire of God on
6 our behalf whether our mission will be successful.' The priest replied,
7 'Go in peace. Your mission is in the LORD's hands.' The five men went
on their way and came to Laish. There they found the inhabitants
living a carefree life, in the same way as the Sidonians, a quiet, carefree
folk, with no hereditary king to keep the country under his thumb.*b*
They were a long way from the Sidonians, and had no contact with the
8 Aramaeans.*c* So the five men went back to Zorah and Eshtaol, and
9 when their kinsmen asked their news, they said, 'Come and attack
them. It is an excellent country that we have seen. Will you hang back
and do nothing about it? Start off now and take possession of the land.
10 When you get there, you will find a people living a carefree life in a
wide expanse of open country. God has delivered it into your hands,
a place where there is no lack of anything on earth.'

11   And so six hundred armed men from the clan of the Danites set out
12 from Zorah and Eshtaol. They went up country and encamped in
Kiriath-jearim in Judah: this is why that place to this day is called
13 Mahaneh-dan;*d* it lies west of Kiriath-jearim. From there they passed
14 on to the hill-country of Ephraim and came to Micah's house. The five
men who had been to explore the country round Laish spoke up and
said to their kinsmen, 'Do you know that in one of these houses there
are now an ephod and teraphim, an idol and an image? Now consider
15 what you had best do.' So they turned aside to*e* Micah's house and
16 greeted him. The six hundred armed Danites took their stand at the
17 entrance of the gate, and the five men who had gone to explore the
country went indoors to take the idol and the image, ephod and

[a] they had...territory: *so Sept.; Heb. obscure.*   [b] with no...thumb: *prob. rdg.; Heb.
and none humiliating anything in the land with inherited authority.*   [c] *So some MSS. of
Sept.; Heb.* men.   [d] *That is* the Camp of Dan.   [e] *So Luc. Sept.; Heb. adds* the house
of the young Levite.

teraphim, while the priest was standing at the entrance with the six
hundred armed men. The five men entered Micah's house and took the 18
idol and the image, ephod and teraphim.*a* The priest asked them what
they were doing, but they said to him, 'Be quiet; not a word. Come with 19
us and be our priest and father. Which is better, to be priest in the
household of one man or to be priest to a whole tribe and clan in
Israel?' This pleased the priest; so he took the ephod and teraphim, 20
the idol and the image,*b* and joined the company. They turned and 21
went off, putting the dependants, the herds, and the valuables in front.
The Danites had gone some distance from Micah's house, when his 22
neighbours were called out in pursuit and caught up with them. They 23
shouted after them, and the Danites turned round and said to Micah,
'What is the matter with you? Why have you come after us?' He said, 24
'You have taken my gods which I made for myself, you have taken the
priest, and you have gone off and left me nothing. How dare you say,
"What is the matter with you?"' The Danites said to him, 'Do not 25
shout at us. We are desperate men and if we fall upon you it will be the
death of yourself and your family.' With that the Danites went on their 26
way and Micah, seeing that they were too strong for him, turned and
went home.

Thus they carried off the priest and the things Micah had made for 27
himself, and attacked Laish, whose people were quiet and carefree.
They put them to the sword and set fire to their city. There was no 28
one to save them, for the city was a long way from Sidon and they had
no contact with the Aramaeans,*c* although the city was in the vale near
Beth-rehob. They rebuilt the city and settled in it, naming it Dan 29
after the name of their forefather Dan, a son of Israel; but its original
name was Laish. The Danites set up the idol, and Jonathan son of 30
Gershom, son of Moses,*d* and his sons were priests to the tribe of Dan
until the people went into exile. (They set up for themselves the idol 31
which Micah had made, and it was there as long as the house of God
was at Shiloh.)

IN THOSE DAYS when no king ruled in Israel, a Levite was living in **19**
the heart of the hill-country of Ephraim. He had taken himself a
concubine from Bethlehem in Judah. In a fit of anger she had left him 2
and had gone to her father's house in Bethlehem in Judah. When she
had been there four months, her husband set out after her with his 3
servant and two asses to appeal to her and bring her back. She brought
him in to the house of her father, who welcomed him when he saw him.

[a] *Prob. rdg.; Heb.* the idol of the ephod, and teraphim and image. [b] *and the image:
so Sept.; Heb. om.* [c] *Prob. rdg., cp. verse 7; Heb.* men. [d] *So some MSS.; others*
Manasseh (*altered from* Moses).

4 His father-in-law, the girl's father, pressed him and he stayed with him
5 three days, and they were well entertained during their visit. On the
fourth day, they rose early in the morning, and he prepared to leave,
but the girl's father said to his son-in-law, 'Have something to eat
6 first, before you go.' So the two of them sat down and ate and drank
together. The girl's father said to the man, 'Why not spend the night
7 and enjoy yourself?' When he rose to go, his father-in-law urged him
8 to stay, and again he stayed for the night. He rose early in the morning
on the fifth day to depart, but the girl's father said, 'Have something
to eat first.' So they lingered till late afternoon, eating and drinking*[a]*
9 together. Then the man stood up to go with his concubine and servant,
but his father-in-law said, 'See how the day wears on towards sunset.*[b]*
Spend the night here and enjoy yourself, and then rise early tomorrow
10 and set out for home.' But the man would not stay the night; he rose
and left. He had reached a point opposite Jebus, that is Jerusalem, with
11 his two laden asses and his concubine, and when they were close to
Jebus, the weather grew wild and stormy, and the young man said to
his master, 'Come now, let us turn into this Jebusite town and spend
12 the night there.' But his master said to him, 'No, not into a strange
town where the people are not Israelites; let us go on to Gibeah.
13 Come, we will go and find some other place, and spend the night in
14 Gibeah or Ramah.' So they went on until sunset overtook them; they
15 were then near Gibeah which belongs to Benjamin. They turned in to
spend the night there, and went and sat down in the open street of the
town; but nobody took them into his house for the night.
16 Meanwhile an old man was coming home in the evening from his work
in the fields. He was from the hill-country of Ephraim, but he lived in
17 Gibeah, where the people were Benjamites. He looked up, saw the
traveller in the open street of the town, and asked him where he was
18 going and where he came from. He answered, 'We are travelling from
Bethlehem in Judah to the heart of the hill-country of Ephraim. I come
from there; I have been to Bethlehem in Judah and I am going home,*[c]*
19 but nobody has taken me into his house. I have straw and provender for
the asses, food and wine for myself, the girl, and the young man; we
20 have all we need, sir.' The old man said, 'You are welcome, I will
21 supply all your wants; you must not spend the night in the street.' So
he took him inside and provided fodder for the asses; they washed their
22 feet, and ate and drank. While they were enjoying themselves, some of
the worst scoundrels in the town surrounded the house, hurling
themselves against the door and shouting to the old man who owned
the house, 'Bring out the man who has gone into your house, for us

[a] and drinking: *so some MSS. of Sept.; Heb. om.* [b] *So Sept.; Heb. adds* Spend the
night: behold the camping of the day. [c] home: *so Sept.; Heb.* to the house of the Lord.

to have intercourse with him.' The owner of the house went outside to ₂₃
them and said, 'No, my friends, do nothing so wicked. This man is my
guest; do not commit this outrage. Here is my daughter, a virgin;*ᵃ* let ₂₄
me bring her*ᵇ* out to you. Rape her*ᵇ* and do to her*ᵇ* what you please;
but you shall not commit such an outrage against this man.' But the ₂₅
men refused to listen to him, so the Levite took hold of his concubine
and thrust her outside for them. They assaulted her and abused her all
night till the morning, and when dawn broke, they let her go. The girl ₂₆
came at daybreak and fell down at the entrance of the man's house
where her master was, and lay there until it was light. Her master rose ₂₇
in the morning and opened the door of the house to set out on his
journey, and there was his concubine lying at the door with her hands
on the threshold. He said to her, 'Get up and let us be off'; but there ₂₈
was no answer. So he lifted her on to his ass and set off for home.
When he arrived there, he picked up a knife, and he took hold of his ₂₉
concubine and cut her up limb by limb into twelve pieces; and he sent
them through the length and breadth of Israel. He told the men he sent ₃₀
with them to say to every Israelite, 'Has the like of this happened or been
seen*ᶜ* from the time the Israelites came up from Egypt till today? Consider this among yourselves and speak your minds.' So everyone who saw
them said, 'No such thing has ever happened or been seen before.'

All the Israelites, the whole community from Dan to Beersheba and **20**
out of Gilead also, left their homes as one man and assembled before
the LORD at Mizpah. The leaders of the people and*ᵈ* all the tribes of ₂
Israel presented themselves in the general assembly of the people of
God, four hundred thousand foot-soldiers armed with swords; and the ₃
Benjamites heard that the Israelites had gone up to Mizpah. The
Israelites asked how this wicked thing had come about, and the Levite, ₄
to whom the murdered woman belonged, answered, 'I and my concubine came to Gibeah in Benjamin to spend the night there. The ₅
citizens of Gibeah rose against me that night and surrounded the house
where I was, intending to kill me; and they raped my concubine and
she died. I took her and cut her in pieces, and sent them through the ₆
length and breadth of Israel, because of the filthy outrage they had
committed in Israel. Now it is for you, the whole of Israel, to say here ₇
and now what you think ought to be done.' All the people rose to their ₈
feet as one man and said, 'Not one of us shall go back to his tent, not
one shall return home. This is what we will now do to Gibeah. We will ₉
draw lots for the attack:*ᵉ* and we will take ten men out of every hundred ₁₀
in all the tribes of Israel, a hundred out of every thousand, and a

[a] *Prob. rdg.; Heb. adds* and his concubine. [b] *Prob. rdg.; Heb.* them. [c] He told...
been seen: *prob. rdg., cp. Sept.; Heb. om.* [d] and: *so Sept.; Heb. om.* [e] We will...
attack: *so Sept.; Heb.* Against it by lot.

thousand out of every ten thousand, to collect provisions from the
people for those who have taken the field against Gibeah in Benjamin
11 to avenge[a] the outrage committed in Israel.' Thus all the Israelites to
a man were massed against the town.
12 The tribes of Israel sent men all through the tribe of Benjamin
saying, 'What is this wicked thing which has happened in your midst?
13 Hand over to us those scoundrels in Gibeah, and we will put them to
death and purge Israel of this wickedness.' But the Benjamites refused
14 to listen to their fellow-Israelites. They flocked from their cities to
15 Gibeah to go to war with the Israelites, and that day they mustered out
of their cities twenty-six thousand men armed with swords. There
16 were also seven hundred picked men from Gibeah,[b] left-handed men,
17 who could sling a stone and not miss by a hair's breadth. The Israelites,
without Benjamin, numbered four hundred thousand men armed with
18 swords, every one a fighting man. The Israelites at once moved on to
Bethel, and there they sought an oracle from God, asking, 'Which of
us shall attack Benjamin first?', and the LORD's answer was, 'Judah
19 shall attack first.' So the Israelites set out at dawn and encamped
20 opposite Gibeah. They advanced to do battle with Benjamin and drew
21 up their forces before the town. The Benjamites made a sally from
Gibeah and left twenty-two thousand of Israel dead on the field that
23[c] day. The Israelites went up to Bethel,[d] lamented before the LORD
until evening and inquired whether they should again attack their
22 brother Benjamin. The LORD said, 'Yes, attack him.' Then the Israelites
took fresh courage and again formed up on the same ground as the
24 first day. So the second day they advanced against the Benjamites,
25 who sallied out from Gibeah to meet them and laid another eighteen
26 thousand armed men low. The Israelites, the whole people, went back
to Bethel, where they sat before the LORD lamenting and fasting until
evening, and they offered whole-offerings and shared-offerings before
27 the LORD. In those days the Ark of the Covenant of God was there,
28 and Phinehas son of Eleazar, son of Aaron, served before the LORD.[e]
The Israelites inquired of the LORD and said, 'Shall we again march
out to battle against Benjamin our brother or shall we desist?' The
LORD answered, 'Attack him: tomorrow I will deliver him into your
29 hands.' Israel then posted men in ambush all round Gibeah.
30 On the third day the Israelites advanced against the Benjamites and
31 drew up their forces at Gibeah as they had before; and the Benjamites
sallied out to meet the army. They were drawn away from the town and

[a] who have...to avenge: *prob. rdg.*, *cp. Sept.*; *Heb.* to do when they come to Geba in
Benjamin.　[b] *So Sept.*; *Heb. adds* out of all this army there were seven hundred picked
men.　[c] *Verses 22 and 23 transposed.*　[d] to Bethel: *prob. rdg.*, *cp. verses 18, 26*; *Heb. om.*
[e] *Or* before the Ark.

began the attack as before by killing a few Israelites, about thirty,[a] on
the highways which led across open country, one to Bethel and the
other to Gibeah. They thought they were defeating them once again, 32
but the Israelites had planned a retreat to draw them away from the
town out on to the highways. Meanwhile the main body of Israelites 33
left their positions and re-formed in Baal-tamar, while those in
ambush, ten thousand picked men all told, burst out from their
position in the neighbourhood of Gibeah[b] and came in on the east of the 34
town. There was soon heavy fighting; yet the Benjamites did not suspect
the disaster that was threatening them. So the LORD put Benjamin to 35
flight before Israel, and on that day the Israelites killed twenty-five
thousand one hundred Benjamites, all armed men.

The men of Benjamin now saw that they had been defeated, for all 36
that the Israelites, trusting in the ambush which they had set by
Gibeah, had given way before them. The men in ambush made a sudden 37
dash on Gibeah, fell on the town from all sides and put all the
inhabitants to the sword. The agreed signal between the Israelites and 38
those in ambush[c] was to be a column of smoke sent up from the town.
The Israelites then faced about in the battle; and Benjamin began to 39
cut down the Israelites, killing about thirty of them,[d] in the belief that
they were defeating them as they had done in the first encounter.
As the column of smoke began to go up from the town, the Benjamites 40
looked back and thought the whole town was going up in flames. When 41
the Israelites faced about, the Benjamites saw that disaster had overtaken them and were seized with panic. They turned and fled before 42
the Israelites in the direction of the wilderness, but the fighting caught
up with them and soon those from the town[e] were among them, cutting
them down. They hemmed in the Benjamites, pursuing them without 43
respite,[f] and overtook them at a point to the east of Gibeah. Eighteen 44
thousand of the Benjamites fell, all of them fighting men. The survivors 45
turned and fled into the wilderness towards the Rock of Rimmon. The
Israelites picked off the stragglers on the roads, five thousand of them,
and chased them until they had cut down and killed two thousand more.
Twenty-five thousand armed men of Benjamin fell in battle that day, 46
all fighting men. The six hundred who survived turned and fled into 47
the wilderness as far as the Rock of Rimmon, and there they remained
for four months. The Israelites then turned back to deal with the 48
Benjamites, and put to the sword the people in the towns and the cattle,
every creature that they found; they also set fire to every town within
their reach.

[a] *Or* about thirty wounded men.   [b] *Prob. rdg., cp. Sept.; Heb.* Geba.   [c] *Prob. rdg.;*
Heb. adds an unintelligible word.   [d] to cut...them: *or* to kill about thirty wounded men
among the Israelites.   [e] *So Vulg.; Heb.* towns.   [f] without respite: *or* from Nohah.

21 In Mizpah the Israelites had bound themselves by oath that none of
² them would marry his daughter to a Benjamite. The people now came
to Bethel and remained there in God's presence till sunset, raising
³ their voices in loud lamentation. They said, 'O LORD God of Israel,
why has it happened in Israel that one tribe should this day be lost to
⁴ Israel?' Next day the people rose early, built an altar there and offered
⁵ whole-offerings and shared-offerings. At that the Israelites asked
themselves whether among all the tribes of Israel there was anyone who
did not go up to the assembly before the LORD; for under the terms of
the great oath anyone who had not gone up to the LORD at Mizpah
⁶ was to be put to death. And the Israelites felt remorse over their brother
Benjamin, because, as they said, 'This day Israel has lost one whole
⁷ tribe.' So they asked, 'What shall we do for wives for those who are
left? We have sworn to the LORD not to give any of our daughters to
⁸ them in marriage. Is there anyone in all the tribes of Israel who did not
go up to the LORD at Mizpah?' Now it happened that no one from
⁹ Jabesh-gilead had come to the camp for the assembly; so when they
held a roll-call of the people, they found that no inhabitant of Jabesh-
¹⁰ gilead was present. Thereupon the community sent off twelve thousand
fighting men with orders to go and put the inhabitants of Jabesh-gilead
¹¹ to the sword, men, women, and dependants. 'This is what you shall do,'
they said: 'put to death every male person, and every woman who has
had intercourse with a man, but spare any who are virgins.' This they
¹² did.ᵃ Among the inhabitants of Jabesh-gilead they found four hundred
young women who were virgins and had not had intercourse with
¹³ a man, and they brought them to the camp at Shiloh in Canaan. Then
the whole community sent messengers to the Benjamites at the Rock of
¹⁴ Rimmon to parley with them, and peace was proclaimed. At this the
Benjamites came back, and were given those of the women of Jabesh-
gilead who had been spared; but these were not enough.

¹⁵ The people were still full of remorse over Benjamin because the
¹⁶ LORD had made this gap in the tribes of Israel, and the elders of the
community said, 'What shall we do for wives for the rest? All the
¹⁷ women in Benjamin have been massacred.' They said, 'Heirs there
must be for the remnant of Benjamin who have escaped! Then Israel
¹⁸ will not see one of its tribes blotted out. We cannot give them our own
daughters in marriage because we have sworn that there shall be a curse
¹⁹ on the man who gives a wife to a Benjamite.' Then they bethought
themselves of the pilgrimage in honour of the LORD, made every year to
Shiloh, the place which lies to the north of Bethel, on the east side of
²⁰ the highway from Bethel to Shechem and to the south of Lebonah. They
²¹ said to the Benjamites, 'Go and hide in the vineyards and keep watch.

[a] but spare...they did: *so Sept.; Heb. om.*

When the girls of Shiloh come out to dance, sally out of the vineyards, and each of you seize one of them for his wife; then make your way home to the land of Benjamin. Then, if their fathers or brothers come 22 and complain to you, say*ᵃ* to them, "Let us keep them with your approval, for none of us has captured a wife in battle. Had you offered them to us, the guilt would be yours."'

All this the Benjamites did. They carried off as many wives as they 23 needed, snatching them as they danced; then they went their way and returned to their patrimony, rebuilt their cities and settled in them. The 24 Israelites also dispersed by tribes and families, and every man went back to his own patrimony.

In those days there was no king in Israel and every man did what was 25 right in his own eyes.

[a] you, say: *lit.* us, we will say.

RUTH

Naomi and Ruth

1 ONG AGO, in the time of the judges, there was a famine in
the land, and a man from Bethlehem in Judah went to live in
2 the Moabite country with his wife and his two sons. The man's
name was Elimelech, his wife's name was Naomi, and the names of
his two sons Mahlon and Chilion. They were Ephrathites from
Bethlehem in Judah. They arrived in the Moabite country and there
they stayed.
3   Elimelech Naomi's husband died, so that she was left with her two
4 sons. These sons married Moabite women, one of whom was called
Orpah and the other Ruth. They had lived there about ten years,
5 when both Mahlon and Chilion died, so that the woman was bereaved
6 of her two sons as well as of her husband. Thereupon she set out with
her two daughters-in-law to return home, because she had heard while
still in the Moabite country that the LORD had cared for his people
7 and given them food. So with her two daughters-in-law she left the
place where she had been living, and took the road home to Judah.
8 Then Naomi said to her two daughters-in-law, 'Go back, both of you,
to your mothers' homes. May the LORD keep faith with you, as you
9 have kept faith with the dead and with me; and may he grant each of
you security in the home of a new husband.' She kissed them and they
10 wept aloud. Then they said to her, 'We will return with you to your
11 own people.' But Naomi said, 'Go back, my daughters. Why should you
go with me? Am I likely to bear any more sons to be husbands for you?
12 Go back, my daughters, go. I am too old to marry again. But even if
I could say that I had hope of a child, if I were to marry this night and
13 if I were to bear sons, would you then wait until they grew up? Would
you then refrain from marrying? No, no, my daughters, my lot is more
14 bitter than yours, because the LORD has been against me.' At this they
wept again. Then Orpah kissed her mother-in-law and returned to
her people,[a] but Ruth clung to her.
15   'You see,' said Naomi, 'your sister-in-law has gone back to her
16 people and her gods;[b] go back with her.' 'Do not urge me to go back
and desert you', Ruth answered. 'Where you go, I will go, and where
you stay, I will stay. Your people shall be my people, and your God

[a] and...people: so Sept.; Heb. om.   [b] Or god.

my God. Where you die, I will die, and there I will be buried. I swear 17
a solemn oath before the LORD your God: nothing but*a* death shall
divide us.' When Naomi saw that Ruth was determined to go with her, 18
she said no more, and the two of them went on until they came to 19
Bethlehem. When they arrived in Bethlehem, the whole town was in
great excitement about them, and the women said, 'Can this be
Naomi?' 'Do not call me Naomi,'*b* she said, 'call me Mara,*c* for it is 20
a bitter lot that the Almighty has sent me. I went away full, and the 21
LORD has brought me back empty. Why do you call me Naomi? The
LORD has pronounced against me; the Almighty has brought disaster
on me.' This is how Naomi's daughter-in-law, Ruth the Moabitess, 22
returned with her from the Moabite country. The barley harvest was
beginning when they arrived in Bethlehem.

Ruth and Boaz

N OW NAOMI HAD a kinsman on her husband's side, a well-to-do 2
man of the family of Elimelech; his name was Boaz. Ruth the 2
Moabitess said to Naomi, 'May I go out to the cornfields and glean
behind anyone who will grant me that favour?' 'Yes, go, my daughter',
she replied. So Ruth went gleaning in the fields behind the reapers. As 3
it happened, she was in that strip of the fields which belonged to Boaz
of Elimelech's family, and there was Boaz coming out from Bethlehem. 4
He greeted the reapers, saying, 'The LORD be with you'; and they
replied, 'The LORD bless you.' Then he asked his servant in charge of 5
the reapers, 'Whose girl is this?' 'She is a Moabite girl', the servant 6
answered, 'who has just come back with Naomi from the Moabite
country. She asked if she might glean and gather among the swathes 7
behind the reapers. She came and has been on her feet with hardly a
moment's rest*d* from daybreak till now.' Then Boaz said to Ruth, 8
'Listen to me, my daughter: do not go and glean in any other field, and
do not look any further, but keep close to my girls. Watch where the 9
men reap, and follow the gleaners; I have given them orders not to
molest you. If you are thirsty, go and drink from the jars the men have
filled.' She fell prostrate before him and said, 'Why are you so kind 10
as to take notice of me when I am only a foreigner?' Boaz answered, 11
'They have told me all that you have done for your mother-in-law
since your husband's death, how you left your father and mother and
the land of your birth, and came to a people you did not know before.
The LORD reward your deed; may the LORD the God of Israel, under 12

[*a*] I swear...nothing but: *or* The LORD your God do so to me and more if... [*b*] *That is*
Pleasure. [*c*] *That is* Bitter. [*d*] *Prob. rdg.; Heb. adds* in the house.

whose wings you have come to take refuge, give you all that you

13 deserve.' 'Indeed, sir,' she said, 'you have eased my mind and spoken kindly to me; may I ask you as a favour not to treat me only as one of

14 your slave-girls?'[a] When meal-time came round, Boaz said to her, 'Come here and have something to eat, and dip your bread into the sour wine.' So she sat beside the reapers, and he passed her some roasted

15 grain. She ate all she wanted and still had some left over. When she got up to glean, Boaz gave the men orders. 'She', he said, 'may glean

16 even among the sheaves; do not scold her. Or you may even pull out some corn from the bundles and leave it for her to glean, without reproving her.'

17 So Ruth gleaned in the field till evening, and when she beat out

18 what she had gleaned, it came to about a bushel[b] of barley. She took it up and went into the town, and her mother-in-law saw how much she had gleaned. Then Ruth brought out what she had saved from her

19 meal and gave it to her. Her mother-in-law asked her, 'Where did you glean today? Which way did you go? Blessings on the man who kindly took notice of you.' So she told her mother-in-law whom she had been working with. 'The man with whom I worked today', she said, 'is

20 called Boaz.' 'Blessings on him from the LORD', said Naomi. 'The LORD has kept faith with the living and the dead. For this man is related

21 to us and is our next-of-kin.' 'And what is more,' said Ruth the Moabitess, 'he told me to stay close to his men until they had finished

22 all his harvest.' 'It is best for you, my daughter,' Naomi answered,

23 'to go out with his girls; let no one catch you in another field.' So she kept close to his girls, gleaning with them till the end of both barley and wheat harvests; but she lived with her mother-in-law.

3 One day Ruth's mother-in-law Naomi said to her, 'My daughter,

2 I want to see you happily settled. Now there is our kinsman Boaz; you were with his girls. Tonight he is winnowing barley at his

3 threshing-floor. Wash and anoint yourself, put on your cloak and go down to the threshing-floor, but do not make yourself known to the

4 man until he has finished eating and drinking. But when he lies down, take note of the place where he lies. Then go in, turn back the covering

5 at his feet and lie down. He will tell you what to do.' 'I will do whatever

6 you tell me', Ruth answered. So she went down to the threshing-floor

7 and did exactly as her mother-in-law had told her. When Boaz had eaten and drunk, he felt at peace with the world and went to lie down at the far end of the heap of grain. She came in quietly, turned back the

8 covering at his feet and lay down. About midnight something disturbed the man as he slept; he turned over and, lo and behold, there was a

[a] may I...slave-girls?: *or* if you please, treat me as one of your slave-girls. [b] *Heb.* ephah.

woman lying at his feet. 'Who are you?' he asked. 'I am your servant, 9
Ruth', she replied.'Now spread your skirt over your servant, because you
are my next-of-kin.' He said, 'The LORD has blessed you, my daughter. 10
This last proof of your loyalty is greater than the first; you have not
sought after any young man, rich or poor. Set your mind at rest, my 11
daughter. I will do whatever you ask; for, as the whole neighbourhood
knows, you are a capable woman. Are you sure that I am the next-of- 12
kin? There is a kinsman even closer than I. Spend the night here and 13
then in the morning, if he is willing to act as your next-of-kin, well and
good; but if he is not willing, I will do so; I swear it by the LORD. Now
lie down till morning.' So she lay at his feet till morning, but rose 14
before one man could recognize another; and he said, 'It must not be
known that a woman has been to the threshing-floor.' Then he said, 15
'Bring me the cloak you have on, and hold it out.' So she held it out,
and he put in six measures of barley and lifted it on her back, and she*a*
went to the town. When she came to her mother-in-law, Naomi asked, 16
'How did things go with you, my daughter?' Ruth told her all that
the man had done for her. 'He gave me these six measures of barley,' 17
she said; 'he would not let me come home to my mother-in-law empty-
handed.' Naomi answered, 'Wait, my daughter, until you see what will 18
come of it. He will not rest until he has settled the matter today.'

Now Boaz had gone up to the city gate, and was sitting there; and, 4
after a time, the next-of-kin of whom he had spoken passed by. 'Here,'
he cried, calling him by name, 'come and sit down.' He came and sat
down. Then Boaz stopped ten elders of the town, and asked them to 2
sit there, and they did so. Then he said to the next-of-kin, 'You will 3
remember the strip of field that belonged to our brother Elimelech.
Naomi has returned from the Moabite country and is selling it.
I promised to open the matter with you, to ask you to acquire it in the 4
presence of those who sit here, in the presence of the elders of my
people. If you are going to do your duty as next-of-kin, then do so,
but if not, someone must do it. So tell me, and then I shall know;
for I come after you as next-of-kin.' He answered, 'I will act as next-
of-kin.' Then Boaz said, 'On the day when you acquire the field from 5
Naomi, you also acquire Ruth*b* the Moabitess, the dead man's wife, so
as to perpetuate the name of the dead man with his patrimony.' There- 6
upon the next-of-kin said, 'I cannot act myself, for I should risk losing
my own patrimony. You must therefore do my duty as next-of-kin.
I cannot act.'

Now in those old days, when property was redeemed or exchanged, 7
it was the custom for a man to pull off his sandal and give it to the
other party. This was the form of attestation in Israel. So the next-of- 8

[a] *So many MSS.; others* he.   [b] *So Vulg.; Heb.* from Ruth.

kin said to Boaz, 'Acquire it for yourself', and pulled off his sandal.
9 Then Boaz declared to the elders and all the people, 'You are witnesses today that I have acquired from Naomi all that belonged to Elimelech
10 and all that belonged to Mahlon and Chilion; and, further, that I have myself acquired Ruth the Moabitess, wife of Mahlon, to be my wife, to perpetuate the name of the deceased with his patrimony, so that his name may not be missing among his kindred and at the gate of his
11 native place. You are witnesses this day.' Then the elders and all who were at the gate said, 'We are witnesses. May the LORD make this woman, who has come to your home, like Rachel and Leah, the two who built up the house of Israel. May you do great things in Ephrathah
12 and keep a name alive in Bethlehem. May your house be like the house of Perez, whom Tamar bore to Judah, through the offspring the LORD will give you by this girl.'

13 So Boaz took Ruth and made her his wife. When they came together,
14 the LORD caused her to conceive and she bore Boaz a son. Then the women said to Naomi, 'Blessed be the LORD today, for he has not left you without a next-of-kin. May the dead man's name*a* be kept alive in
15 Israel. The child*b* will give you new life and cherish you in your old age; for your daughter-in-law who loves you, who has proved better to
16 you than seven sons, has borne him.' Naomi took the child and laid
17 him in her lap and became his nurse. Her neighbours gave him a name: 'Naomi has a son,' they said; 'we will call him Obed.' He was the father of Jesse, the father of David.

18 THIS IS THE GENEALOGY of Perez: Perez was the father of Hezron,
19, 20 Hezron of Ram, Ram of Amminadab, Amminadab of Nahshon,
21, 22 Nahshon of Salmon,*c* Salmon of Boaz, Boaz of Obed, Obed of Jesse, and Jesse of David.

[*a*] *Lit.* May his name. [*b*] *Lit.* He. [*c*] *So some MSS.; others* Salmah.

THE FIRST BOOK OF
SAMUEL

The birth and call of Samuel

THERE WAS A MAN from Ramathaim, a Zuphite[a] from 1
the hill-country of Ephraim, named Elkanah son of Jeroham,
son of Elihu, son of Tohu, son of Zuph an Ephraimite; and he 2
had two wives named Hannah and Peninnah. Peninnah had children,
but Hannah was childless. This man used to go up from his own town 3
every year to worship and to offer sacrifice to the LORD of Hosts in
Shiloh. There Eli's two sons, Hophni and Phinehas, were priests of the
LORD. On the day when Elkanah sacrificed, he gave several shares of 4
the meat to his wife Peninnah with all her sons and daughters; but, 5
although[b] he loved Hannah, he gave her only one share, because the
LORD had not granted her children. Further, Hannah's rival used to 6
torment her and humiliate her because she had no children. Year after 7
year this happened when they[c] went up to the house of the LORD; her
rival used to torment her. Once when she was in tears and would not
eat, her husband Elkanah said to her, 'Hannah, why are you crying and 8
eating nothing? Why are you so miserable? Am I not more to you than
ten sons?' After they had finished eating and drinking at the sacrifice 9-10
at Shiloh, Hannah rose in deep distress, and stood before the LORD[d]
and prayed to him, weeping bitterly. Meanwhile Eli the priest was
sitting on his seat beside the door of the temple of the LORD. Hannah 11
made a vow in these words: 'O LORD of Hosts, if thou wilt deign to
take notice of my trouble and remember me, if thou wilt not forget me
but grant me offspring, then I will give the child to the LORD for his
whole life, and no razor shall ever touch his head.' For a long time she 12
went on praying before the LORD, while Eli watched her lips. Hannah 13
was praying silently; but, although her voice could not be heard, her
lips were moving and Eli took her for a drunken woman. He said to her, 14
'Enough of this drunken behaviour! Go away till the wine has worn
off.' 'No, sir,' she answered, 'I am a sober person, I have drunk no 15
wine or strong drink, and I have been pouring out my heart before the
LORD. Do not think me so degraded, sir; all this time I have been 16
speaking out of the fullness of my grief and misery.' 'Go in peace,' said 17
Eli, 'and may the God of Israel answer the prayer you have made to

[a] a Zuphite: *so Sept.; Heb.* Zophim.   [b] *So Sept.; Heb. unintelligible.*   [c] *So Vulg.;
Heb.* she.   [d] and stood...LORD: *so Sept.; Heb. om.*

18 him.' Hannah said, 'May I be worthy of your kindness.' And she went
19 away and took something to eat, no longer downcast. Next morning
they were up early and, after prostrating themselves before the LORD,
returned to their own home at Ramah. Elkanah had intercourse with
20 his wife Hannah, and the LORD remembered her. She conceived, and
in due time bore a son, whom she named Samuel, 'because', she said,
'I asked the LORD for him.'

21 Elkanah, with his whole household, went up to make the annual
22 sacrifice to the LORD and to redeem his vow. Hannah did not go with
them, but said to her husband, 'When the child is weaned I will come
up with him to enter the presence of the LORD, and he shall[a] stay
23 there always.' Her husband Elkanah said to her, 'Do what you think
best; stay at home until you have weaned him. Only, may the LORD
indeed see your[b] vow fulfilled.' So the woman stayed and nursed her
24 son until she had weaned him; and when she had weaned him, she
took him up with her. She took also a bull three years old,[c] an ephah of
meal, and a flagon of wine, and she brought him, child as he was, into
25 the house of the LORD at Shiloh. They slaughtered the bull, and brought
26 the boy to Eli. Hannah said to him, 'Sir, as sure as you live, I am the
27 woman who stood near you here praying to the LORD. It was this boy
that I prayed for and the LORD has given me what I asked. What
28 I asked I have received; and now I lend him to the LORD; for his
whole life he is lent to the LORD.' And they[d] prostrated themselves there
before the LORD.

2 Then Hannah offered this prayer:

> My heart rejoices in the LORD,
> in the LORD I now hold my head high;
> my mouth is full of derision of my foes,
> exultant because thou hast saved me.

2
> There is none except thee,
> none so holy as the LORD,
> no rock like our God.

3
> Cease your proud boasting,
> let no word of arrogance pass your lips;
> for the LORD is a god of all knowledge:
> he governs all that men do.

4
> Strong men stand in mute[e] dismay
> but those who faltered put on new strength.

5
> Those who had plenty sell themselves for a crust,

[a] come up...he shall: *or* bring him up, and he shall come into the presence of the LORD
and... [b] *So Sept.; Heb.* his. [c] a bull...old: *so Sept.; Heb.* three bulls. [d] *So Pesh.;
Heb.* he. [e] in mute: *prob. rdg.; Heb. obscure.*

362

and the hungry grow strong again.
The barren woman has seven children,
and the mother of many sons is left to languish.

The LORD kills and he gives life,   6
he sends down to Sheol, he can bring the dead up again.
The LORD makes a man poor, he makes him rich,   7
he brings down and he raises up.
He lifts the weak out of the dust   8
and raises the poor from the dunghill;
to give them a place among the great,
to set them in seats of honour.

For the foundations of the earth are the LORD's,
he has built the world upon them.
He will guard the footsteps of his saints,   9
while the wicked sink into silence and gloom;
not by mere strength shall a man prevail.

Those that stand against the LORD will be terrified   10
when the High God*a* thunders out of heaven.
The LORD is judge even to the ends of the earth,
he will give strength to his king
and raise high the head of his anointed prince.

Then Elkanah went to Ramah with his household, but the boy   11
remained behind in the service of the LORD under Eli the priest.
Now Eli's sons were scoundrels and had no regard for the LORD.   12
The custom of the priests in their dealings with the people was this: 13
when a man offered a sacrifice, the priest's servant would come while
the flesh was stewing and would thrust a three-pronged fork into the   14
cauldron or pan or kettle or pot; and the priest would take whatever
the fork brought out. This should have been their practice whenever
Israelites came to sacrifice at Shiloh; but now under Eli's sons,*b* even 15
before the fat was burnt, the priest's servant came and said to the man
who was sacrificing, 'Give me meat to roast for the priest; he will not
accept what has been already stewed, only raw meat.' And if the man   16
answered, 'Let them burn the fat first, and then take what you want',
he said, 'No, give it to me now, or I will take it by force.' The young 17
men's sin was very great in the LORD's sight; for they brought the
LORD's sacrifice into general contempt.
Samuel continued in the service of the LORD, a mere boy with a linen   18
ephod fastened round him. Every year his mother made him a little   19
cloak and took it to him when she went up with her husband to offer

[*a*] the High God: *prob. rdg.; Heb.* upon him.   [*b*] under Eli's sons: *added to help meaning.*

20 the annual sacrifice. Eli would give his blessing to Elkanah and his wife and say, 'The LORD grant you children by this woman in place of the one for which you asked him.'*a* Then they went home again.

21 The LORD showed his care for Hannah, and she conceived and gave birth to three sons and two daughters; meanwhile the boy Samuel grew up in the presence of the LORD.

22 Eli, now a very old man, had heard how his sons were treating all the Israelites, and how they lay with the women who were serving at the

23 entrance to the Tent of the Presence. So he said to them, 'Why do you do such things? I hear from all the people how wickedly you behave.

24 Have done with it, my sons; for it is no good report that I hear spreading

25 among the LORD's people. If a man sins against another man, God will intervene; but if a man sins against the LORD, who can intercede for him?' For all this, they did not listen to their father's rebuke, for the

26 LORD meant that they should die. But the young Samuel, as he grew up, commended himself to the LORD and to men.

27 Now a man of God came to Eli and said, 'This is the word of the LORD: You know that I revealed myself to your forefather when he and

28 his family were in Egypt in slavery*b* in the house of Pharaoh. You know that I chose him from all the tribes of Israel to be my priest, to mount the steps of my altar, to burn sacrifices and to carry*c* the ephod before me; and that I assigned all the food-offerings of the Israelites to your

29 family. Why then do you show disrespect for my sacrifices and the offerings which I have ordained? What makes you resent them?*d* Why do you honour your sons more than me by letting them batten on the

30 choicest offerings of*e* my people Israel? The LORD's word was, "I promise that your house and your father's house shall serve before me for all time"; but now his word is, "I will have no such thing: I will honour those who honour me, and those who despise me shall meet

31 with contempt. The time is coming when I will lop off every limb of your own and of your father's family, so that no man in your house

32 shall come to old age. You will even resent*f* the prosperity I give*g* to

33 Israel; never again shall there be an old man in your house. If I allow any to survive to serve my altar, his*h* eyes will grow dim and his*h*

34 appetite fail, his*h* issue will be weaklings and die off. The fate of your two sons shall be a sign to you: Hophni and Phinehas shall both die

35 on the same day. I will appoint for myself a priest who will be faithful, who will do what I have in my mind and in my heart. I will establish

36 his family to serve in perpetual succession before my anointed king. Any

[a] for which...him: or which you lent him. [b] in slavery: so Sept.; Heb. om. [c] Or wear. [d] What...them?: so Sept.; Heb. a dwelling-place. [e] So Targ.; Heb. to. [f] You...resent: prob. rdg.; Heb. obscure. [g] So Targ.; Heb. he gives. [h] So Sept.; Heb. your.

of your family that still live will come and bow humbly before him to beg a fee, a piece of silver and a loaf, and will ask for a turn of priestly duty to earn a crust of bread."'

So the child Samuel was in the LORD's service under his master Eli. 3 Now in those days the word of the LORD was seldom heard, and no vision was granted. But one night Eli, whose eyes were dim and his 2 sight failing, was lying down in his usual place, while Samuel slept in 3 the temple of the LORD where the Ark of God was. Before the lamp of God had gone out, the LORD called him, and Samuel answered, 'Here 4 I am', and ran to Eli saying, 'You called me: here I am.' 'No, I did not 5 call you,' said Eli; 'lie down again.' So he went and lay down. The LORD 6 called Samuel again, and he got up and went to Eli. 'Here I am,' he said; 'surely you called me.' 'I did not call, my son,' he answered; 'lie down again.' Now Samuel had not yet come to know the LORD, and 7 the word of the LORD had not been disclosed to him. When the LORD 8 called him for the third time, he again went to Eli and said, 'Here I am; you did call me.' Then Eli understood that it was the LORD calling the child; he told Samuel to go and lie down and said, 'If he calls again, 9 say, "Speak, LORD; thy servant hears thee."' So Samuel went and lay down in his place.

The LORD came and stood there, and called, 'Samuel, Samuel', as 10 before. Samuel answered, 'Speak; thy servant hears thee.' The LORD 11 said, 'Soon I shall do something in Israel which will ring in the ears of all who hear it. When that day comes I will make good every word 12 I have spoken against Eli and his family from beginning to end. You 13 are to*a* tell him that my judgement on his house shall stand for ever because*b* he knew of his sons' blasphemies against God*c* and did not rebuke them. Therefore I have sworn to the family of Eli that their 14 abuse of sacrifices and offerings shall never be expiated.'

Samuel lay down till morning and then opened the doors of the house 15 of the LORD, but he was afraid to tell Eli about the vision. Eli called 16 Samuel: 'Samuel, my son', he said; and he answered, 'Here I am.' Eli 17 asked, 'What did the LORD say to you? Do not hide it from me. God forgive you if you hide one word of all that he said to you.' Then 18 Samuel told him everything and hid nothing. Eli said, 'The LORD must do what is good in his eyes.'

As Samuel grew up, the LORD was with him, and none of his words 19 went unfulfilled. From Dan to Beersheba, all Israel recognized that 20 Samuel was confirmed as a prophet of the LORD. So the LORD continued 21 to appear in Shiloh, because he had revealed himself there to Samuel.*d*

[a] *Prob. rdg.; Heb.* I will.   [b] because: *prob. rdg.; Heb.* in guilt.   [c] against God: *prob. original reading, altered in Heb. to* to them.   [d] *Prob. rdg.; Heb. adds* according to the word of the LORD.

The struggle with the Philistines

4 So Samuel's word had authority throughout Israel. And the time came when the Philistines mustered for battle against Israel,[a] and the Israelites went out to meet them. The Israelites encamped at
2 Eben-ezer and the Philistines at Aphek. The Philistines drew up their lines facing the Israelites, and when they joined battle the Israelites were routed by the Philistines, who killed about four thousand men on
3 the field. When the army got back to the camp, the elders of Israel asked, 'Why did the LORD let us be routed today by the Philistines? Let us fetch the Ark of the Covenant of the LORD from Shiloh to go
4 with us and deliver us from the power of our enemies.' So the people sent to Shiloh and fetched the Ark of the Covenant of the LORD of Hosts, who is enthroned upon the cherubim; Eli's two sons, Hophni
5 and Phinehas, were there with the Ark. When the Ark came into the camp all the Israelites greeted it with a great shout, and the earth rang
6 with the shouting. The Philistines heard the noise and asked, 'What is this great shouting in the camp of the Hebrews?' When they knew that
7 the Ark of the LORD had come into the camp, they were afraid and cried, 'A god has come into the camp. We are lost! No such thing has
8 ever happened before. We are utterly lost! Who can deliver us from the power of these mighty gods? These are the very gods who broke the
9 Egyptians and crushed them in the wilderness. Courage, Philistines, and act like men, or you will become slaves to the Hebrews as they
10 were yours. Be men, and fight!' The Philistines then gave battle, and the Israelites were defeated and fled to their homes. It was a great
11 defeat, and thirty thousand Israelite foot-soldiers perished. The Ark of God was taken, and Eli's two sons, Hophni and Phinehas, were killed.
12 A Benjamite ran from the battlefield and reached Shiloh on the same
13 day, his clothes rent and dust on his head. When he arrived Eli was sitting on a seat by the road to Mizpah, for he was deeply troubled about the Ark of God. The man entered the city with his news, and all
14 the people cried out in horror. When Eli heard it, he asked, 'What does
15 this uproar mean?' The man hurried to Eli and told him. Eli was
16 ninety-eight years old and sat staring with sightless eyes; so the man said to him, 'I am the man who has just arrived from the battle; this very day I have escaped from the field.' Eli asked, 'What is the news,
17 my son?' The runner answered, 'The Israelites have fled from the Philistines; utter panic has struck the army; your two sons, Hophni
18 and Phinehas, are killed, and the Ark of God is taken.' At the mention

[a] And...Israel: *so Sept.; Heb. om.*

of the Ark of God, Eli fell backwards from his seat by the gate and broke his neck, for he was old and heavy. So he died; he had been judge over Israel for forty years. His daughter-in-law, the wife of 19 Phinehas, was with child and near her time, and when she heard of the capture of the Ark and the deaths of her father-in-law and her husband, her labour suddenly began and she crouched down and was delivered. As she lay dying, the women who attended her said, 'Do not be afraid; 20 you have a son.' But she did not answer or heed what they said. Then 21 they named the boy Ichabod,[a] saying, 'Glory has departed from Israel' (in allusion to the capture of the Ark of God and the death of her father-in-law and her husband); 'Glory has departed from Israel,' they 22 said, 'because the Ark of God is taken.'

After the Philistines had captured the Ark of God, they brought it 5 from Eben-ezer to Ashdod; and there they carried it into the temple of 2 Dagon and set it beside Dagon himself. When the people of Ashdod 3 rose next morning, there was Dagon fallen face downwards before the Ark of the Lord; so they took him and put him back in his place. Next morning when they rose, Dagon had again fallen face downwards 4 before the Ark of the Lord, with his head and his two hands lying broken off beside his platform; only Dagon's body[b] remained on it. This 5 is why from that day to this the priests of Dagon and all who enter the temple of Dagon at Ashdod do not set foot upon Dagon's platform.

Then the Lord laid a heavy hand upon the people of Ashdod; he 6 threw them into distress and plagued them with tumours,[c] and their territory swarmed with rats.[d] There was death and destruction all through the city.[e] When the men of Ashdod saw this, they said, 'The 7 Ark of the God of Israel shall not stay here, for he has laid a heavy hand upon us and upon Dagon our god.' So they sent and called all the 8 Philistine princes together to ask what should be done with the Ark. They said, 'Let the Ark of the God of Israel be taken across to Gath.' They took it there, and after its arrival the hand of the Lord caused 9 great havoc in the city; he plagued everybody, high and low alike, with the tumours which broke out. Then they sent the Ark of God on to 10 Ekron. When the Ark reached Ekron, the people cried, 'They have brought the Ark of the God of Israel over to us, to kill us and our families.' So they summoned all the Philistine princes and said, 'Send 11 the Ark of the God of Israel away; let it go back to its own place, or it will be the death of us all.' There was death and destruction all through the city; for the hand of God lay heavy upon it. Even those who did 12 not die were plagued with tumours; the cry of the city went up to heaven.

[a] *That is* No-glory.   [b] *Prob. rdg., cp. Sept.; Heb.* only Dagon.   [c] *Or, as otherwise read,* haemorrhoids.   [d] *Or* mice.   [e] and their territory...city: *so Sept.; Heb.* Ashdod and its territory.

6   When the Ark of the LORD had been in their territory for seven
2 months, the Philistines summoned the priests and soothsayers and
asked, 'What shall we do with the Ark of the LORD? Tell us how we
3 ought to send it back to its own place.' They answered, 'If you send
the Ark of the God of Israel back, do not let it go without a gift, but
send it back with a gift for him by way of indemnity; then you will be
healed and restored to favour; there is no reason why his hand should
4 not be lifted from you.' When they were asked, 'What gift shall we
send back to him?', they answered, 'Send five tumours modelled in
gold and five gold rats, one for each of the Philistine princes, for the
5 same plague afflicted all of you[a] and your princes. Make models of
your tumours and of the rats which are ravaging the land, and give
honour to the God of Israel; perhaps he will relax the pressure of his
6 hand on you, on your god, and on your land. Why should you be
stubborn like Pharaoh and the Egyptians? Remember how this god
7 made sport of them until they let Israel go. Now make a new wagon
ready with two milch-cows which have never been yoked; harness the
cows to the wagon, and take their calves from them and drive them back
8 to their stalls. Then take the Ark of the LORD and put it on the wagon,
place in a casket, beside it, the gold offerings that you are sending to
9 him as an indemnity, and let it go where it will. Watch it: if it goes up
towards its own territory to Beth-shemesh, then it is the LORD who has
done us this great injury; but if not, then we shall know that his hand
has not touched us, but we have been the victims of chance.'
10   The men did this. They took two milch-cows and harnessed them
11 to a wagon, shutting up their calves in the stall, and they placed the
Ark of the LORD on the wagon together with the casket, the gold rats,
12 and the models of their haemorrhoids. Then the cows went straight in
the direction of Beth-shemesh; they kept to the same road, lowing as
they went and turning neither right nor left, while the Philistine
13 princes followed them as far as the territory of Beth-shemesh. Now the
people of Beth-shemesh were harvesting their wheat in the Vale, and
14 when they looked up and saw the Ark they rejoiced at the sight of it. The
wagon came to the farm of Joshua of Beth-shemesh and halted there.
Close by stood a great stone; so they chopped up the wood of the wagon
15 and offered the cows as a whole-offering to the LORD. Then the Levites
lifted down the Ark of the LORD and the casket containing the gold
offerings, and laid them on the great stone; and the men of Beth-
shemesh offered whole-offerings and shared-offerings that day to the
16 LORD. The five princes of the Philistines watched all this, and returned
to Ekron the same day.
17   These golden haemorrhoids which the Philistines sent back as a gift

[a] *So some MSS.; others* them.

of indemnity to the LORD were for Ashdod, Gaza, Ashkelon, Gath, and
Ekron, one for each city. The gold rats were for all the towns of the 18
Philistines governed by the five princes, both fortified towns and open
settlements. The great stone*a* where they deposited the Ark of the
LORD stands witness on the farm of Joshua of Beth-shemesh to this
very day.

But the sons of Jeconiah did not rejoice with the rest of the men of 19
Beth-shemesh when they welcomed the Ark of the LORD, and he
struck down seventy of them.*b* The people mourned because the LORD
had struck them so heavy a blow, and the men of Beth-shemesh said, 20
'No one is safe in the presence of the LORD, this holy God. To whom
can we send it, to be rid of him?' So they sent this message to the 21
inhabitants of Kiriath-jearim: 'The Philistines have returned the Ark
of the LORD; come down and take charge of it.' Then the men of 7
Kiriath-jearim came and took the Ark of the LORD away; they brought
it into the house of Abinadab on the hill and consecrated his son
Eleazar as its custodian.

Samuel judge over Israel

SO FOR A LONG WHILE the Ark was housed in Kiriath-jearim; and 2
after some time, twenty years later, there was a movement throughout Israel to follow the LORD. So Samuel addressed these words to the 3
whole nation: 'If your return to the LORD is whole-hearted, banish the
foreign gods and the Ashtaroth from your shrines; turn to the LORD
with heart and mind, and worship him alone, and he will deliver you
from the Philistines.' The Israelites then banished the Baalim and the 4
Ashtaroth, and worshipped the LORD alone.

Samuel summoned all Israel to an assembly at Mizpah, so that he 5
might intercede with the LORD for them. When they had assembled 6
there, they drew water and poured it out before the LORD and fasted
all day, confessing that they had sinned against the LORD. It was at
Mizpah that Samuel acted as judge over Israel.

When the Philistines heard that the Israelites had assembled at 7
Mizpah, their princes marched against them. The Israelites heard that
the Philistines were advancing, and they were afraid. They said to 8
Samuel, 'Do not cease to pray for us to the LORD our God to save us

---

[*a*] The great stone: *so Sept.; Heb.* Abel-haggedolah.　[*b*] But...seventy of them: *prob.
rdg., cp. Sept.; Heb.* And he struck down some of the men of Beth-shemesh because they
had welcomed the Ark of the LORD; he struck down seventy men among the people, fifty
thousand men.

9 from the power of the Philistines.' Thereupon Samuel took a sucking lamb, offered it up complete as a whole-offering and prayed aloud to the LORD on behalf of Israel; and the LORD answered his prayer.
10 As Samuel was offering the sacrifice and the Philistines were advancing to battle with the Israelites, the LORD thundered loud and long over the Philistines and threw them into confusion. They fled in panic before
11 the Israelites, who set out from Mizpah in pursuit and kept up the slaughter of the Philistines till they reached a point below Beth-car.
12 There Samuel took a stone and set it up as a monument between Mizpah and Jeshanah,*a* naming it Eben-ezer,*b* 'for to this point', he
13 said, 'the LORD has helped us.' Thus the Philistines were subdued and no longer encroached on the territory of Israel; and the hand of the
14 LORD was against them as long as Samuel lived. The cities they had captured were restored to Israel, and from Ekron to Gath the border-land was freed from their control. Between Israel and the Amorites
15 peace was maintained. Samuel acted as judge in Israel as long as he
16 lived, and every year went on circuit to Bethel and Gilgal and Mizpah;
17 he dispensed justice at all these places, returning always to Ramah. That was his home and the place from which he governed Israel, and there he built an altar to the LORD.

Saul anointed king

8 WHEN SAMUEL grew old, he appointed his sons to be judges in
2 Israel. The eldest son was named Joel and the second Abiah;
3 they acted as judges in Beersheba. His sons did not follow in their father's footsteps but were intent on their own profit, taking bribes and
4 perverting the course of justice. So all the elders of Israel met, and
5 came to Samuel at Ramah and said to him, 'You are now old and your sons do not follow in your footsteps; appoint us a king to govern us,
6 like other nations.' But their request for a king to govern them dis-
7 pleased Samuel, and he prayed to the LORD. The LORD answered Samuel, 'Listen to the people and all that they are saying; they have not rejected you, it is I whom they have rejected, I whom they will not
8 have to be their king. They are now doing to you just what they have done to me*c* since I brought them up from Egypt: they have forsaken
9 me and worshipped other gods. Hear what they have to say now, but give them a solemn warning and tell them what sort of king will govern
10 them.' Samuel told the people who were asking him for a king all that

[a] *Prob. rdg.* (*cp. 2 Chr. 13. 19*); *Heb.* the tooth. [b] *That is* Stone of Help. [c] *to me: so Sept.; Heb. om.*

the LORD had said to him. 'This will be the sort of king who will 11
govern you', he said. 'He will take your sons and make them serve in
his chariots and with his cavalry, and will make them run before his
chariot. Some he will appoint officers over units of a thousand and units 12
of fifty. Others will plough his fields and reap his harvest; others again
will make weapons of war and equipment for mounted troops. He will 13
take your daughters for perfumers, cooks, and confectioners, and will 14
seize the best of your cornfields, vineyards, and olive-yards, and give
them to his lackeys. He will take a tenth of your grain and your vintage 15
to give to his eunuchs and lackeys. Your slaves, both men and women, 16
and the best of your cattle*a* and your asses he will seize and put to his own
use. He will take a tenth of your flocks, and you yourselves will become 17
his slaves. When that day comes, you will cry out against the king 18
whom you have chosen; but it will be too late, the LORD will not
answer you.' The people refused to listen to Samuel; 'No,' they said, 19
'we will have a king over us; then we shall be like other nations, with 20
a king to govern us, to lead us out to war and fight our battles.' So 21
Samuel, when he had heard what the people said, told the LORD; and 22
he answered, 'Take them at their word and appoint them a king.'
Samuel then dismissed all the men of Israel to their homes.

There was a man from the district of Benjamin, whose name was 9
Kish son of Abiel, son of Zeror, son of Bechorath, son of Aphiah a
Benjamite. He was a man of substance, and had a son named Saul, 2
a young man in his prime; there was no better man among the Israelites
than he. He was a head taller than any of his fellows.

One day some asses belonging to Saul's father Kish had strayed, so 3
he said to his son Saul, 'Take one of the servants with you, and go and
look for the asses.' They crossed the hill-country of Ephraim and went 4
through the district of Shalisha but did not find them; they passed
through the district of Shaalim but they were not there; they passed
through the district of Benjamin but again did not find them. When 5
they had entered the district of Zuph, Saul said to the servant with him,
'Come, we ought to turn back, or my father will stop thinking about the
asses and begin to worry about us.' The servant answered, 'There is 6
a man of God in the city here, who has a great reputation, because
everything he says comes true. Suppose we go there; he may tell us
something about this errand of ours.' Saul said, 'If we do go, what shall 7
we offer him? There is no food left in our packs and we have no
present for the man of God, nothing at all.' The servant answered him 8
again, 'Wait! I have here a quarter-shekel of silver. I can give that to
the man, to tell us what we should do.' Saul said, 'Good! let us go to 10*b*
him.' So they went to the city where the man of God was. (In days 9

[*a*] your cattle: *so Sept.; Heb.* your picked men.   [*b*] *Verses 9 and 10 transposed.*

371

gone by in Israel, when a man wished to consult God, he would say,
'Let us go to the seer.' For what is nowadays called a prophet used to
11 be called a seer.) As they were going up the hill to the city they met
some girls coming out to draw water and asked, 'Shall we find the seer
12 there?' 'Yes,' they said, 'the seer is ahead of you now; he has just*a*
arrived in the city because there is a feast at the hill-shrine today.
13 As you enter the city you will meet him before he goes up to the shrine
to eat; the people will not start until he comes, for he has to bless the
sacrifice before the company can eat. Go up now, and you will find him
14 at once.' So they went up to the city, and just as they were going in,
there was Samuel coming towards them on his way up to the shrine.
15   Now the day before Saul came, the LORD had disclosed his intention
16 to Samuel in these words: 'At this same time tomorrow I will send you
a man from the land of Benjamin. Anoint him prince over my people
Israel, and then he shall deliver my people from the Philistines. I have
seen the sufferings of*b* my people and their cry has reached my ears.'
17 The moment Saul appeared the LORD said to Samuel, 'Here is the man
18 of whom I spoke to you. This man shall rule my people.' Saul came up
to Samuel in the gateway and said, 'Would you tell me where the seer
19 lives?' Samuel replied, 'I am the seer. Go on ahead of me to the hill-
shrine and you shall eat with me today; in the morning I will set you
20 on your way, after telling you what you have on your mind. Trouble
yourself no more about the asses lost three days ago, for they have been
found. But what is it that all Israel is wanting? It is you and your
21 ancestral house.' 'But I am a Benjamite,' said Saul, 'from the smallest
of the tribes of Israel, and my family is the least important of all the
22 families of the tribe of Benjamin. Why do you say this to me?' Samuel
then brought Saul and his servant into the dining-hall and gave them
23 a place at the head of the company, which numbered about thirty. Then
he said to the cook, 'Bring the portion that I gave you and told you to
24 put on one side.' So the cook took up the whole haunch and leg and put
it before Saul; and Samuel said, 'Here is the portion of meat*c* kept for
you. Eat it: it has been reserved for you at this feast to which*d* I have
25 invited the people.' So Saul dined with Samuel that day, and when they
came down from the hill-shrine to the city a bed was spread on the roof
26 for Saul, and he*e* stayed there that night. At dawn Samuel called to
Saul on the roof, 'Get up, and I will set you on your way.' When Saul
27 rose, he and Samuel went out together into the street. As they came to
the end of the town, Samuel said to Saul, 'Tell the boy to go on.' He

[a] the seer...just: *prob. rdg.; Heb.* he is ahead of you, hurry now, for he has today...
[b] the sufferings of: *so Sept.; Heb. om.* [c] the portion of meat: *prob. rdg.; Heb.* what is
left over. [d] to which: *so Vulg.; Heb.* saying. [e] a bed...and he: *so Sept.; Heb.* he
spoke with Saul on the roof and they...

did so, and then Samuel said, 'Stay here a moment, and I will tell you the word of God.'

Samuel took a flask of oil and poured it over Saul's head, and he 10 kissed him and said, 'The LORD anoints you prince over his people Israel; you shall rule the people of the LORD and deliver them from the enemies round about them. You shall have a sign*a* that the LORD has anointed you prince to govern his inheritance: when you leave me today, 2 you will meet two men by the tomb of Rachel at Zelzah in the territory of Benjamin. They will tell you that the asses you are looking for have been found and that your father is concerned for them no longer; he is anxious about you and says again and again, "What shall I do about my son?" From there go across country as far as the terebinth of Tabor, 3 where three men going up to Bethel to worship God will meet you. One of them will be carrying three kids, the second three loaves, and the third a flagon of wine. They will greet you and will offer you two 4 loaves, which you will accept from them. Then when you reach the 5 Hill of God, where the Philistine governor*b c* resides, you will meet a company of prophets coming down from the hill-shrine, led by lute, harp, fife, and drum, and filled with prophetic rapture. Then the spirit 6 of the LORD will suddenly take possession of you, and you too will be rapt like a prophet and become another man. When these signs happen, 7 do whatever the occasion demands; God will be with you. You shall go 8 down to Gilgal ahead of me, and I will come to you to sacrifice whole-offerings and shared-offerings. Wait seven days until I join you; then I will tell you what to do.' As Saul turned to leave Samuel, God gave 9 him a new heart. On that same day all these signs happened. When 10 they reached the Hill there was a company of prophets coming to meet him, and the spirit of God suddenly took possession of him, so that he too was filled with prophetic rapture. When people who had known him 11 previously saw that he was rapt like the prophets, they said to one another, 'What can have happened to the son of Kish? Is Saul also among the prophets?' One of the men of that place said, 'And whose 12 sons are they?' Hence the proverb, 'Is Saul also among the prophets?' When the prophetic rapture had passed, he went home.*d* Saul's uncle 13, 14 said to him and the boy, 'Where have you been?' Saul answered, 'To look for the asses, and when we could not find them, we went to Samuel.' His uncle said, 'Tell me what Samuel said.' 'He told us that the asses 15, 16 had been found', said Saul; but he did not repeat what Samuel had said about his being king.

Meanwhile Samuel summoned the Israelites to the LORD at Mizpah 17 and said to the people, 'This is the word of the LORD the God of Israel: 18

---

[a] The LORD anoints...sign: *so Sept.; Heb. om.* [b] *Or* garrison. [c] *So Sept.; Heb.* governors, *or* garrisons. [d] *Prob. rdg.; Heb.* to the hill-shrine.

I brought Israel up from Egypt; I delivered you from the Egyptians
19 and from all the kingdoms that oppressed you; but today you have
rejected your God who saved you from all your misery and distress;
you have said, "No,[a] set up a king over us." Now therefore take up your
20 positions before the LORD tribe by tribe and clan by clan.' Samuel then
21 presented all the tribes of Israel, and Benjamin was picked by lot. Then
he presented the tribe of Benjamin, family by family, and the family of
Matri was picked. Then he presented the family of Matri, man by
man,[b] and Saul son of Kish was picked; but when they looked for him
22 he could not be found. They went on to ask the LORD, 'Will the man[c]
be coming back?' The LORD answered, 'There he is, hiding among the
23 baggage.' So someone ran and fetched him out, and as he took his
24 stand among the people, he was a head taller than anyone else. Samuel
said to the people, 'Look at the man whom the LORD has chosen; there
is no one like him in this whole nation.' They all acclaimed him,
25 shouting, 'Long live the king!' Samuel then explained to the people
the nature of a king, and made a written record of it on a scroll which he
26 deposited before the LORD; he then dismissed them to their homes. Saul
too went home to Gibeah, and with him went some fighting men[d]
27 whose hearts God had moved. But there were scoundrels who said,
'How can this fellow deliver us?' They thought nothing of him and
brought him no gifts.

11 About a month later[e] Nahash the Ammonite attacked and besieged
Jabesh-gilead. The men of Jabesh said to Nahash, 'Come to terms
2 with us and we will be your subjects.' Nahash answered them, 'On
one condition only will I come to terms with you: that I gouge out your
3 right eyes and bring disgrace on Israel.' The elders of Jabesh-gilead
then said, 'Give us seven days' respite to send messengers throughout
4 Israel and then, if no one relieves us, we will surrender to you.' When
the messengers came to Gibeah, where Saul lived, and delivered their
5 message, all the people broke into lamentation. Saul was just coming
from the field driving in the oxen, and asked why the people were
6 lamenting; and they repeated what the men of Jabesh had said. When
Saul heard this, the spirit of God suddenly seized him. In his anger
7 he took a pair of oxen and cut them in pieces, and sent messengers
with the pieces all through Israel to proclaim that the same would be
done to the oxen of any man who did not follow Saul and Samuel into
battle. The fear of the LORD fell upon the people and they came out,
8 to a man. Saul mustered them in Bezek; there were three hundred
9 thousand men from Israel and thirty thousand from Judah. He[f] said

[a] said, "No: *so many MSS.; others* said to him. [b] Then...by man: *so Sept.; Heb.*
om. [c] *So Sept.; Heb.* a man. [d] *So Sept.; Heb.* with him went the army. [e] *So
Sept.; Heb.* But he was silent. [f] *So Sept.; Heb.* They.

to the men who brought the message, 'Tell the men of Jabesh-gilead,
"Victory will be yours tomorrow by the time the sun is hot."' The men
of Jabesh heard what the messengers reported and took heart; and 10
they said to Nahash, 'Tomorrow we will surrender to you, and then
you may deal with us as you think fit.' Next day Saul drew up his men 11
in three columns; they forced their way right into the enemy camp
during the morning watch and massacred the Ammonites while the
day grew hot, after which the survivors scattered until no two men
were left together.

Then the people said to Samuel, 'Who said that Saul should not 12
reign over us? Hand the men over to us to be put to death.' But Saul 13
said, 'No man shall be put to death on a day when the LORD has won
such a victory in Israel.' Samuel said to the people, 'Let us now go to 14
Gilgal and there renew our allegiance to the kingdom.' So they all went 15
to Gilgal and invested Saul there as king in the presence of the LORD,
sacrificing shared-offerings before the LORD; and Saul and all the
Israelites celebrated the occasion with great joy.

THEN SAMUEL thus addressed the assembled Israelites: 'I have 12
listened to your request and installed a king to rule over you. And the 2
king is now your leader, while I am old and white-haired and my sons
are with you; but I have been your leader ever since I was a child. Here 3
I am. Lay your complaints against me in the presence of the LORD and
of his anointed king. Whose ox have I taken, whose ass have I taken?
Whom have I wronged, whom have I oppressed? From whom have
I taken a bribe, to turn a blind eye? Tell me, and I will make restitution.' They answered, 'You have not wronged us, you have not 4
oppressed us; you have not taken anything from any man.' Samuel 5
then said to them, 'This day the LORD is witness among you, his
anointed king is witness, that you have found my hands empty.' They
said, 'He is witness.' Samuel said to the people, 'Yes, the LORD is 6
witness,*a* the LORD who gave you Moses and Aaron and brought your
fathers out of Egypt. Now stand up, and here in the presence of the 7
LORD I will put the case against you and recite*b* all the victories which
he has won for you and for your fathers. After Jacob and his sons*c* had 8
come down to Egypt and the Egyptians had made them suffer,*d* your
fathers cried to the LORD for help, and he sent Moses and Aaron, who
brought them out of Egypt and settled them in this place. But they 9
forgot the LORD their God, and he abandoned them to Sisera, commander-in-chief of Jabin king of*e* Hazor, to the Philistines, and to the

[*a*] is witness: *so Sept.; Heb. om.*   [*b*] and recite: *so Sept.; Heb. om.*   [*c*] and his sons:
so Sept.; Heb. om.   [*d*] and the Egyptians...suffer: *so Sept.; Heb. om.*   [*e*] Jabin king of:
so Sept.; Heb. om.

10 king of Moab, and they had to fight against them. Then your fathers cried to the LORD for help: "We have sinned, we have forsaken the LORD and we have worshipped the Baalim and the Ashtaroth. But now,
11 if thou wilt deliver us from our enemies, we will worship thee." So the LORD sent Jerubbaal and Barak,*a* Jephthah and Samson,*b* and delivered you from your enemies on every side; and you lived in peace and quiet.

12 'Then, when you saw Nahash king of the Ammonites coming against you, although the LORD your God was your king, you said to me,
13 "No, let us have a king to rule over us." Now, here is the king you
14 asked for; you chose him, and the LORD has set a king over you. If you will revere the LORD and give true and loyal service, if you do not rebel against his commands, and if you and the king who reigns over you are
15 faithful to the LORD your God, well and good; but if you do not obey the LORD, and if you rebel against his commands, then he will set his face against you and against your king.*c*

16 'Stand still, and see the great wonder which the LORD will do before
17 your eyes. It is now wheat harvest; when I call upon the LORD and he sends thunder and rain, you will see and know how wicked it was in
18 the LORD's eyes for you to ask for a king.' So Samuel called upon the LORD and he sent thunder and rain that day; and all the people were in
19 great fear of the LORD and of Samuel. They said to Samuel, 'Pray for us your servants to the LORD your God, to save us from death; for we have added to all our other sins the great wickedness of asking for a
20 king.' Samuel said to the people, 'Do not be afraid; although you have been so wicked, do not give up the worship of the LORD, but serve
21 him with all your heart. Give up*d* the worship of false gods which can
22 neither help nor save, because they are false. For his name's sake the LORD will not cast you off, because he has resolved to make you his own
23 people. As for me, God forbid that I should sin against the LORD and
24 cease to pray for you. I will show you what is right and good: to revere the LORD and worship him faithfully with all your heart. Consider
25 what great things he has done for you; but if you persist in wickedness, you shall be swept away, you and your king.'

13 Saul was fifty years*e* old when he became king, and he reigned over
2 Israel for twenty-two*f* years. He picked three thousand men from Israel, two thousand to be with him in Michmash and the hill-country of Bethel and a thousand to be with Jonathan in Gibeah*g* of Benjamin; and he sent the rest of the people home.
3 Jonathan killed the Philistine governor*h* in Geba, and the news spread

[a] *So Sept.; Heb.* Bedan.   [b] *So Luc. Sept.; Heb.* Samuel.   [c] *So Sept.; Heb.* your fathers.
[d] Give up: *so Targ.; Heb. obscure.*   [e] fifty years: *prob. rdg.; Heb.* a year.   [f] *Prob. rdg.;*
Heb. two.   [g] Geba *in verse 3.*   [h] *Or* garrison.

among the Philistines that the Hebrews were in revolt.[a] Saul sounded
the trumpet all through the land; and when the Israelites all heard that 4
Saul had killed a Philistine governor and that the name of Israel stank
among the Philistines, they answered the call to arms and came to join
Saul at Gilgal.[b] The Philistines mustered to attack Israel; they had 5
thirty thousand chariots and six thousand horse, with infantry as
countless as sand on the sea-shore. They went up and camped at
Michmash, to the east of Beth-aven. The Israelites found themselves in 6
sore straits, for the army was hard pressed, so they hid themselves in
caves and holes and among the rocks, in pits and cisterns. Some of them 7
crossed the Jordan into the district of Gad and Gilead, but Saul
remained at Gilgal, and all the people at his back were in alarm.[c] He 8
waited seven days for his meeting with Samuel, but Samuel did not
come to Gilgal; so the people began to drift away from Saul. He said 9
therefore, 'Bring me the whole-offering and the shared-offerings', and
he offered up the whole-offering. Saul had just finished the sacrifice, 10
when Samuel arrived, and he went out to greet him. Samuel said, 11
'What have you done?', and Saul answered, 'I saw that the people
were drifting away from me, and you yourself had not come as you had
promised, and the Philistines were assembling at Michmash; and 12
I thought, "The Philistines will now move against me at Gilgal, and
I have not placated the LORD"; so I felt compelled to make the whole-
offering myself.' Samuel said to Saul, 'You have behaved foolishly. 13
You have not kept the command laid on you by the LORD your God;
if you had, he would have established your dynasty over Israel for all
time. But now your line will not endure; the LORD will seek a man 14
after his own heart, and will appoint him prince over his people,
because you have not kept the LORD's command.'

Samuel left Gilgal without more ado and went on his way. The rest 15
of the people followed Saul, as he moved from Gilgal towards the
enemy.[d] At Gibeah of Benjamin he mustered the people who were with
him; they were about six hundred men. Saul and his son Jonathan and 16
the men they had with them took up their quarters in Gibeah[e] of
Benjamin, while the Philistines were encamped in Michmash. Raiding 17
parties went out from the Philistine camp in three directions. One
party turned towards Ophrah in the district of Shual, another towards 18
Beth-horon, and the third towards the range of hills overlooking the
valley of Zeboim and the wilderness beyond.

No blacksmith was to be found in the whole of Israel, for the 19

[a] that...revolt: *prob. rdg.; Heb. has* saying, Let the Hebrews hear *after* through the
land. [b] they answered...Gilgal: *or* they were summoned to follow Saul to Gilgal.
[c] but Saul...in alarm: *or* but Saul was still at Gilgal, and all the army joined him there.
[d] and went on...enemy: *prob. rdg., cp. Sept.; Heb. om.* [e] *So Targ.; Heb.* Geba.

Philistines were determined to prevent the Hebrews from making
20 swords and spears. The Israelites had to go down to the Philistines
for their ploughshares, mattocks, axes, and sickles*ᵃ* to be sharpened.
21 The charge was two-thirds of a shekel for ploughshares and mattocks,
and one-third of a shekel for sharpening the axes and setting the
22 goads.*ᵇ* So when war broke out none of the followers of Saul and
Jonathan had either sword or spear; only Saul and Jonathan carried
arms.

23   Now the Philistines had posted a force to hold the pass of Michmash;
14 and one day Saul's son Jonathan said to his armour-bearer, 'Come, let
us go over to the Philistine post beyond that ridge'; but he did not tell
2 his father. Saul, at the time, had his tent under the pomegranate-tree at
Migron on the outskirts of Gibeah; and he had about six hundred men
3 with him. The ephod was carried by Ahijah son of Ahitub, Ichabod's
brother, son of Phinehas son of Eli, the priest of the LORD at Shiloh.
4 Nobody knew that Jonathan had gone. On either side of the pass
through which Jonathan tried to make his way over to the Philistine post
5 stood two sharp columns of rock, called Bozez*ᶜ* and Seneh,*ᵈ* one of
them was on the north towards Michmash, and the other on the south
6 towards Geba. Jonathan said to his armour-bearer, 'Now we will visit
the post of those uncircumcised rascals. Perhaps the LORD will take
a hand in it, and if he will, nothing can stop him. He can bring us safe
7 through, whether we are few or many.' The young man answered, 'Do
8 what you will, go forward; I am with you whatever you do.' 'Good!'
9 said Jonathan, 'we will cross over and let them see us. If they say,
"Stay where you are till we come to you", then we will stay where we
10 are and not go up to them. But if they say, "Come up to us", we will go
up; this will be the sign that the LORD has put them into our power.'
11 So they showed themselves to the Philistines, and the Philistines said,
'Look! Hebrews coming out of the holes where they have been hiding!'
12 And they called across to Jonathan and the young man, 'Come up to
us; we have something to show you.' Jonathan said to the young man,
13 'Come on, the LORD has put them into the power of Israel.' Jonathan
climbed up on hands and feet, and the young man followed him. The
Philistines fell in front of Jonathan, and the young man, coming
14 behind him, dispatched them. In that first attack Jonathan and his
armour-bearer killed about twenty of them, like men cutting*ᵉ* a furrow
15 across a half-acre field. Terror spread through the army in the field and
through the whole people; the men at the post and the raiding parties
were terrified; the very earth quaked, and there was panic.

[*a*] and sickles: *so Sept.; Heb.* and ploughshares. [*b*] one-third...the goads: *prob. rdg.;*
Heb. obscure. [*c*] *That is* Shining. [*d*] *That is* Bramble-bush. [*e*] like men cutting: *so*
Pesh.; Heb. as in half of.

Saul's men on the watch in Gibeah of Benjamin saw the mob of 16
Philistines surging to and fro*a* in confusion; so he ordered the people 17
to call the roll and find out who was missing; and they called the roll
and found that Jonathan and his armour-bearer were absent. Saul said 18
to Ahijah, 'Bring forward the ephod', for it was he who carried the
ephod at that time before Israel.*b* But while Saul was still speaking, the 19
confusion in the Philistine camp was increasing more and more, and he
said to the priest, 'Hold your hand.' Then Saul and all his men with 20
shouting made for the battlefield, where they found the enemy fighting
one another in complete disorder. The Hebrews who up to now had 21
been under the Philistines, and had been with them in camp, changed
sides*c* and joined the Israelites under Saul and Jonathan. All the 22
Israelites in hiding in the hill-country of Ephraim heard that the
Philistines were in flight, and they also joined in and set off in hot
pursuit. The LORD delivered Israel that day, and the fighting passed on 23
beyond Beth-aven.

Now the Israelites on that day had been driven to exhaustion. Saul 24
had adjured the people in these words: 'A curse be on the man who
eats any food before nightfall until I have taken vengeance on my
enemies.' So no one ate any food. Now there was honeycomb*d* in the 25
country-side; but when his men came upon it, dripping with honey 26
though it was, not one of them put his hand to his mouth for fear of
the oath. But Jonathan had not heard his father lay this solemn prohibi- 27
tion on the people, and he stretched out the stick that was in his hand,
dipped the end of it in the honeycomb, put it to his mouth and was
refreshed. One of the people said to him, 'Your father solemnly forbade 28
this; he said, "A curse on the man who eats food today!"' Now the men
were faint with hunger. Jonathan said, 'My father has done the people 29
nothing but harm; see how I am refreshed by this mere taste of honey.
How much better if the people had eaten today whatever they took from 30
their enemies by way of spoil! Then there would indeed have been a
great slaughter of Philistines.'

They defeated the Philistines that day, and pursued them from 31
Michmash to Aijalon. But the people were so faint with hunger that 32
they turned to plunder and seized sheep, cattle, and bullocks; they
slaughtered them on the bare ground, and ate the meat with the blood
in it. Someone told Saul that the people were sinning against the LORD 33
by eating their meat with the blood in it. 'This is treason!' cried Saul.
'Roll a great stone here at once.' He then said, 'Go about among the 34

[*a*] to and fro: *so Sept.; Heb.* and he went thither.   [*b*] 'Bring forward...Israel: *so Sept.;*
Heb. 'Bring forward the Ark of God', for the Ark of God was on that day and the sons of
Israel.   [*c*] changed sides: *so Sept.; Heb.* round and also.   [*d*] Now...honeycomb: *prob.*
rdg.; Heb. All the land went into the forest, and there was honey.

people and tell them to bring their oxen and sheep, and let each man
slaughter his here and eat it; and so they will not sin against the LORD
by eating meat with the blood in it.' So as night fell each man came,
35 driving his own ox, and slaughtered it there. Thus Saul came to build an
altar to the LORD, and this was the first altar to the LORD that Saul built.
36   Saul said, 'Let us go down and make a night attack on the Philistines
and harry them till daylight; we will not spare a man of them.' The
people answered, 'Do what you think best', but the priest said, 'Let us
37 first consult God.' So Saul inquired of God, 'Shall I pursue the
Philistines? Wilt thou put them into Israel's power?'; but this time
38 he received no answer. So he said, 'Let all the leaders of the people
39 come forward and let us find out where the sin lies this day. As the
LORD lives, the deliverer of Israel, even if it lies in my son Jonathan, he
40 shall die.' Not a soul answered him. Then he said to the Israelites, 'All
of you stand on one side, and I and my son Jonathan will stand on the
41 other.' The people answered, 'Do what you think best.' Saul said to
the LORD the God of Israel, 'Why hast thou not answered thy servant
today? If this guilt lie in me or in my son Jonathan, O LORD God of
Israel, let the lot be Urim; if it lie in thy people Israel,*a* let it be
Thummim.' Jonathan and Saul were taken, and the people were
42 cleared. Then Saul said, 'Cast lots between me and my son Jonathan';
43 and Jonathan was taken. Saul said to Jonathan, 'Tell me what you have
done.' Jonathan told him, 'True, I did taste a little honey on the tip
44 of my stick. Here I am; I am ready to die.' Then Saul swore a great
45 oath that Jonathan should die. But the people said to Saul, 'Shall
Jonathan die, Jonathan who has won this great victory in Israel? God
forbid! As the LORD lives, not a hair of his head shall fall to the ground,
for he has been at work with God today.' So the people ransomed
46 Jonathan and he did not die. Saul broke off the pursuit of the Philistines
because they had made their way home.
47   When Saul had made his throne secure in Israel, he fought against
his enemies on every side, the Moabites, the Ammonites, the Edomites,
the king*b* of Zobah, and the Philistines; and wherever he turned he was
48 successful.*c* He displayed his strength by defeating the Amalekites and
freeing Israel from hostile raids.
49   Saul's sons were: Jonathan, Ishyo*d* and Malchishua. These were the
names of his two daughters: Merab the elder and Michal the younger.
50 His wife was Ahinoam daughter of Ahimaaz, and his commander-in-
51 chief was Abner son of his uncle Ner; Kish, Saul's father, and Ner,
Abner's father, were sons*e* of Abiel.

[*a*] Why hast . . . thy people Israel: *so Sept.; Heb. om.* [*b*] *So Sept.; Heb.* kings. [*c*] *Or* he
found ample provision. [*d*] *So Luc. Sept.; Heb.* Ishvo (Ishbosheth *in 2 Sam. 2. 8;* Eshbaal
in 1 Chr. 8. 33). [*e*] *Prob. rdg.; Heb.* son.

There was bitter warfare with the Philistines throughout Saul's life- 52
time; any strong man and any brave man that he found he took into
his own service.

Samuel said to Saul, 'The LORD sent me to anoint you king over his 15
people Israel. Now listen to the voice of the LORD. This is the very 2
word of the LORD of Hosts: "I am resolved to punish the Amalekites
for what they did to Israel, how they attacked them on their way up
from Egypt." Go now and fall upon the Amalekites and destroy them, 3
and put their property under ban. Spare no one; put them all to death,
men and women, children and babes in arms, herds and flocks, camels
and asses.' Thereupon Saul called out the levy and mustered them in 4
Telaim. There were two hundred thousand foot-soldiers and another
ten thousand from Judah.[a] He came to the Amalekite city and halted 5
for a time in the gorge. Meanwhile he sent word to the Kenites to leave 6
the Amalekites and come down, 'or', he said, 'I shall destroy you as
well as them; but you were friendly to Israel when they came up from
Egypt.' So the Kenites left the Amalekites. Then Saul cut the Amale- 7
kites to pieces, all the way from Havilah to Shur on the borders of
Egypt. Agag the king of the Amalekites he took alive, but he destroyed 8
all the people, putting them to the sword. Saul and his army spared 9
Agag and the best of the sheep and cattle, the fat beasts and the lambs[b]
and everything worth keeping; they were unwilling to destroy them,
but anything that was useless and of no value they destroyed.

Then the word of the LORD came to Samuel: 'I repent of having 10, 11
made Saul king, for he has turned his back on me and has not obeyed
my commands.' Samuel was angry; all night he cried aloud to the
LORD. Early next morning he went to meet Saul, but was told that he 12
had gone to Carmel; Saul had set up a monument for himself there,
and had then turned and gone down to Gilgal. There Samuel found 13
him, and Saul greeted him with the words, 'The LORD's blessing
upon you! I have obeyed the LORD's commands.' But Samuel said, 14
'What then is this bleating of sheep in my ears? Why do I hear the
lowing of cattle?' Saul answered, 'The people have taken them from the 15
Amalekites. These are what they spared, the best of the sheep and
cattle, to sacrifice to the LORD your God. The rest we completely
destroyed.' Samuel said to Saul, 'Let be, and I will tell you what the 16
LORD said to me last night.' 'Tell me', said Saul. So Samuel went on, 17
'Time was when you thought little of yourself, but now you are head
of the tribes of Israel, and the LORD has anointed you king over Israel.
The LORD sent you with strict instructions to destroy that wicked 18
nation, the Amalekites; you were to fight against them until you had

[a] *Prob. rdg.; Heb.* ten thousand with the men of Judah.   [b] the fat beasts and the lambs:
so Targ.; Heb. obscure.

19 wiped them out. Why then did you not obey the LORD? Why did you pounce upon the spoil and do what was wrong in the eyes of the LORD?'

20 Saul answered Samuel, 'But I did obey the LORD; I went where the LORD sent me, and I have brought back Agag king of the Amalekites.

21 The rest of them I destroyed. Out of the spoil the people took sheep and oxen, the choicest of the animals laid under ban, to sacrifice to the

22 LORD your God at Gilgal.' Samuel then said:

> Does the LORD desire offerings and sacrifices
>   as he desires obedience?
> Obedience is better than sacrifice,
>   and to listen to him than the fat of rams.

23
> Defiance of him is sinful as witchcraft,
>   yielding to men[a] as evil as[b] idolatry.[c]
> Because you have rejected the word of the LORD,
>   the LORD has rejected you as king.

24   Saul said to Samuel, 'I have sinned. I have ignored the LORD's command and your orders: I was afraid of the people and deferred to

25 them. But now forgive my sin, I implore you, and come back with me,

26 and I will make my submission before the LORD.' Samuel answered, 'I will not come back with you; you have rejected the word of the

27 LORD and therefore the LORD has rejected you as king over Israel.' He

28 turned to go, but Saul caught the edge of his cloak and it tore. And Samuel said to him, 'The LORD has torn the kingdom of Israel from your hand today and will give it to another, a better man than you.

29 God who is the Splendour of Israel does not deceive or change his

30 mind; he is not a man that he should change his mind.' Saul said, 'I have sinned; but honour me this once before the elders of my people and before Israel and come back with me, and I will make my sub-

31 mission to the LORD your God.' So Samuel went back with Saul, and

32 Saul made his submission to the LORD. Then Samuel said, 'Bring Agag king of the Amalekites.' So Agag came to him with faltering step[d]

33 and said, 'Surely the bitterness of death has passed.' Samuel said, 'Your sword has made women childless, and your mother of all women shall be childless too.' Then Samuel hewed Agag in pieces before the LORD at Gilgal.

34   Saul went to his own home at Gibeah, and Samuel went to Ramah;

35 and he never saw Saul again to his dying day, but he mourned for him, because the LORD had repented of having made him king over Israel.

[a] yielding to men: *or* arrogance *or* obstinacy.   [b] as evil as: *prob. rdg.; Heb.* evil and...
[c] *Or* household gods; *Heb.* teraphim.   [d] with faltering step: *prob. rdg., cp. Sept.; Heb.* delicately.

Saul and David

THE LORD SAID to Samuel, 'How long will you mourn for Saul 16
because I have rejected him as king over Israel? Fill your horn
with oil and take it with you; I am sending you to Jesse of Bethlehem;
for I have chosen myself a king among his sons.' Samuel answered, 2
'How can I go? Saul will hear of it and kill me.' 'Take a heifer with
you,' said the LORD; 'say you have come to offer a sacrifice to the LORD,
and invite Jesse to*a* the sacrifice; then I will let you know what you 3
must do. You shall anoint for me the man whom I show you.' Samuel 4
did as the LORD had told him, and went to Bethlehem. The elders of
the city came in haste to meet him, saying, 'Why have you come?
Is all well?' 'All is well,' said Samuel; 'I have come to sacrifice to the 5
LORD. Hallow yourselves and come with me to*b* the sacrifice.' He
himself hallowed Jesse and his sons and invited them to the sacrifice
also. They came, and when Samuel saw Eliab he thought, 'Here, 6
before the LORD, is his anointed king.' But the LORD said to him, 'Take 7
no account of it if he is handsome and tall; I reject him. The LORD
does not see as man sees;*c* men judge by appearances but the LORD
judges by the heart.' Then Jesse called Abinadab and made him 8
pass before Samuel, but he said, 'No, the LORD has not chosen this
one.' Then he presented Shammah, and Samuel said, 'Nor has the 9
LORD chosen him.' Seven of his sons Jesse presented to Samuel, but 10
he said, 'The LORD has not chosen any of these.' Then Samuel asked, 11
'Are these all?' Jesse answered, 'There is still the youngest, but he is
looking after the sheep.' Samuel said to Jesse, 'Send and fetch him;
we will not sit down until he comes.' So he sent and fetched him. He 12
was handsome, with ruddy cheeks and bright eyes.*d* The LORD said,
'Rise and anoint him: this is the man.' Samuel took the horn of oil 13
and anointed him in the presence of his brothers. Then the spirit of the
LORD came upon David and was with him from that day onwards. And
Samuel set out on his way back to Ramah.

The spirit of the LORD had forsaken Saul, and at times an evil spirit 14
from the LORD would seize him suddenly. His servants said to him, 15
'You see, sir, how an evil spirit from God seizes you; why do you not 16
command your servants here to go and find some man who can play the
harp?—then, when an evil spirit from God comes on you, he can play
and you will recover.' Saul said to his servants, 'Find me a man who 17
can play well and bring him to me.' One of his attendants said, 'I have 18

[a] *So Sept.; Heb.* with.   [b] *So Vulg.; Heb.* with.   [c] The LORD...sees: *so Sept.; Heb.*
For not what a man sees.   [d] and bright eyes: *prob. rdg.; Heb. obscure.*

seen a son of Jesse of Bethlehem who can play; he is a brave man and
a good fighter, wise in speech and handsome, and the LORD is with
19 him.' Saul therefore sent messengers to Jesse and asked him to send
20 him his son David, who was with the sheep. Jesse took a homer of
bread, a skin of wine, and a kid, and sent them to Saul by his son David.
21 David came to Saul and entered his service; and Saul loved him dearly,
22 and he became his armour-bearer. So Saul sent word to Jesse: 'Let
23 David stay in my service, for I am pleased with him.' And whenever
a spirit from God came upon Saul, David would take his harp and
play on it, so that Saul found relief; he recovered and the evil spirit
left him alone.

17   The Philistines collected their forces for war and massed at Socoh
in Judah; they camped between Socoh and Azekah at Ephes-dammim.
2 Saul and the Israelites also massed, and camped in the Vale of Elah.
3 They drew up their lines facing the Philistines, the Philistines occupying
a position on one hill and the Israelites on another, with a valley
4 between them. A champion came out from the Philistine camp, a man
5 named Goliath, from Gath; he was over nine feet[a] in height. He had
a bronze helmet on his head, and he wore plate-armour of bronze,
6 weighing five thousand shekels. On his legs were bronze greaves, and
7 one of his weapons was a dagger of bronze. The shaft of his spear was
like a weaver's beam, and its head, which was of iron, weighed six
8 hundred shekels; and his shield-bearer marched ahead of him. The
champion stood and shouted to the ranks of Israel, 'Why do you come
out to do battle, you slaves of Saul? I am the Philistine champion;
9 choose your man to meet me. If he can kill me in fair fight, we will
become your slaves; but if I prove too strong for him and kill him,
10 you shall be our slaves and serve us. Here and now I defy the ranks of
Israel. Give me a man,' said the Philistine, 'and we will fight it out.'
11 When Saul and the Israelites heard what the Philistine said, they were
shaken and dismayed.

12   David was the son of an Ephrathite[b] called Jesse, who had eight
13 sons. By Saul's time he had become a feeble old man, and his three
eldest sons had followed Saul to the war. The eldest was called Eliab,
14 the next Abinadab, and the third Shammah; David was the youngest.
15 The three eldest followed Saul, while David used to go to Saul's camp
and back to Bethlehem to mind his father's flocks.

16   Morning and evening for forty days the Philistine came forward and
17 took up his position. Then one day Jesse said to his son David, 'Take
your brothers an ephah of this parched grain and these ten loaves of
18 bread, and run with them to the camp. These ten cream-cheeses are

[a] over nine feet: *lit.* six cubits and a span. [b] *Prob. rdg.; Heb. adds* Is this the man from
Bethlehem in Judah?

for you to take to the commanding officer. See if your brothers are well
and bring back some token from them.' Saul and the brothers and all 19
the Israelites were in the Vale of Elah, fighting the Philistines. Early 20
next morning David left someone in charge of the sheep, set out on his
errand and went as Jesse had told him. He reached the lines just as the
army was going out to take up position and was raising the war-cry. The 21
Israelites and the Philistines drew up their ranks opposite each other.
David left his things in charge of the quartermaster, ran to the line and 22
went up to his brothers to greet them. While he was talking to them 23
the Philistine champion, Goliath, came out from the Philistine ranks
and issued his challenge in the same words as before; and David heard
him. When the Israelites saw the man they ran from him in fear. 24
'Look at this man who comes out day after day to defy Israel', they 25
said. 'The king is to give a rich reward to the man who kills him; he will
give him his daughter in marriage too and will exempt his family from
service due in Israel.' Then David turned to his neighbours and said, 26
'What is to be done for the man who kills this Philistine and wipes out
our disgrace? And who is he, an uncircumcised Philistine, to defy the
army of the living God?' The people told him how the matter stood 27
and what was to be done for the man who killed him. His elder brother 28
Eliab overheard David talking with the men and grew angry. 'What
are you doing here?' he asked. 'And who have you left to look after
those few sheep in the wilderness? I know you, you impudent young
rascal; you have only come to see the fighting.' David answered, 'What 29
have I done now? I only asked a question.' And he turned away from 30
him to someone else and repeated his question, but everybody gave
him the same answer.

What David had said was overheard and reported to Saul, who sent 31
for him. David said to him, 'Do not lose heart, sir.*a* I will go and fight 32
this Philistine.' Saul answered, 'You cannot go and fight with this 33
Philistine; you are only a lad, and he has been a fighting man all his
life.' David said to Saul, 'Sir, I am my father's shepherd; when a lion 34
or bear comes and carries off a sheep from the flock, I go after it and 35
attack it and rescue the victim from its jaws. Then if it turns on me,
I seize it by the beard and batter it to death. Lions I have killed and 36
bears, and this uncircumcised Philistine will fare no better than they;
he has defied the army of the living God. The Lord who saved me 37
from the lion and the bear will save me from this Philistine.' 'Go then,'
said Saul; 'and the Lord will be with you.' He put his own tunic on 38
David, placed a bronze helmet on his head and gave him a coat of mail
to wear; he then fastened his sword on David*b* over his tunic. But 39

[*a*] Do not...sir: *so Sept.; Heb.* Let no one lose heart.   [*b*] he then...on David: *so Sept.;*
Heb. David fastened on his sword.

David hesitated, because he had not tried them, and said to Saul, 'I cannot go with these, because I have not tried them.' So he took them
40 off. Then he picked up his stick, chose five smooth stones from the brook and put them in a shepherd's bag which served as his pouch.[a] He walked out to meet the Philistine with his sling in his hand.

41 The Philistine came on towards David, with his shield-bearer
42 marching ahead; and he looked David up and down and had nothing but contempt for this handsome lad with his ruddy cheeks and bright
43 eyes.[b] He said to David, 'Am I a dog that you come out against me with
44 sticks?' And he swore at him in the name of his god. 'Come on,' he
45 said, 'and I will give your flesh to the birds and the beasts.' David answered, 'You have come against me with sword and spear and dagger, but I have come against you in the name of the LORD of Hosts,
46 the God of the army of Israel which you have defied. The LORD will put you into my power this day; I will kill you and cut your head off and leave your carcass and the carcasses of the Philistines[c] to the birds and the wild beasts; all the world shall know that there is a God in
47 Israel. All those who are gathered here shall see that the LORD saves neither by sword nor spear; the battle is the LORD's, and he will put you all into our power.'

48 When the Philistine began moving towards him again, David ran
49 quickly to engage him. He put his hand into his bag, took out a stone, slung it, and struck the Philistine on the forehead. The stone sank
50 into his forehead, and he fell flat on his face on the ground. So David proved the victor with his sling and stone; he struck Goliath down and
51 gave him a mortal wound, though he had no sword. Then he ran to the Philistine and stood over him, and grasping his sword, he drew it out of the scabbard, dispatched him and cut off his head. The Philistines,
52 when they saw that their hero was dead, turned and ran. The men of Israel and Judah at once raised the war-cry and hotly pursued them all the way to Gath[d] and even to the gates of Ekron. The road that runs
53 to Shaarim, Gath, and Ekron was strewn with their dead. On their return from the pursuit of the Philistines, the Israelites plundered their
54 camp. David took Goliath's head and carried it to Jerusalem, leaving his weapons in his tent.

55 Saul had said to Abner his commander-in-chief, when he saw David going out against the Philistine, 'That boy there, Abner, whose son is he?' 'By your life, your majesty,' said Abner, 'I do not know.'
56, 57 The king said to Abner, 'Go and find out whose son the lad is.' When David came back after killing the Philistine, Abner took him and

[a] which...pouch: *so Sept.; Heb.* which was his and in the pouch.   [b] handsome...bright eyes: *prob. rdg.; Heb.* obscure.   [c] leave...Philistines: *so Sept.; Heb.* leave the carcass of the Philistines.   [d] *So Sept.; Heb.* a valley.

presented him to Saul with the Philistine's head still in his hand. Saul 58
asked him, 'Whose son are you, young man?', and David answered,
'I am the son of your servant Jesse of Bethlehem.'

That same day, when Saul had finished talking with David, he kept 18 1-2
him and would not let him return any more to his father's house, for
he saw that Jonathan had given his heart to David and had grown to
love him as himself. So Jonathan and David made a solemn compact 3
because each loved the other as dearly as himself. And Jonathan stripped 4
off the cloak he was wearing and his tunic, and gave them to David,
together with his sword, his bow, and his belt. David succeeded so well 5
in every venture on which Saul sent him that he was given a command
in the army, and his promotion pleased the ordinary people, and even
pleased Saul's officers.

At the home-coming of the army when David returned from the 6
slaughter of the Philistines, the women came out from all the cities of
Israel to look on, and the dancers*a* came out to meet King Saul with
tambourines, singing, and dancing. The women as they made merry 7
sang to one another:

> Saul made havoc among thousands
> but David among tens of thousands.

Saul was furious, and the words rankled. He said, 'They have given 8
David tens of thousands and me only thousands; what more can they
do but make him king?' From that day forward Saul kept a jealous eye 9
on David.

Next day an evil spirit from God seized upon Saul; he fell into a 10
frenzy*b* in the house, and David played the harp to him as he had
before. Saul had his spear in his hand, and he hurled it at David, 11
meaning to pin him to the wall; but twice David swerved aside. After 12
this Saul was afraid of David, because he saw that the LORD had forsaken him and was with David. He therefore removed David from his 13
household and appointed him to the command of a thousand men.
David led his men into action, and succeeded in everything that he 14
undertook, because the LORD was with him. When Saul saw how 15
successful he was, he was more afraid of him than ever; all Israel and 16
Judah loved him because he took the field at their head.

Saul said to David, 'Here is my elder daughter Merab; I will give 17
her to you in marriage, but in return you must serve me valiantly and
fight the LORD's battles.' For Saul meant David to meet his end at the
hands of the Philistines and not himself. David answered Saul, 'Who 18
am I and what are my father's people, my kinsfolk, in Israel, that
I should become the king's son-in-law?' However, when the time came 19

[a] *So Sept.; Heb.* and the dances.   [b] *Or* fell into prophetic rapture.

for Saul's daughter Merab to be married to David, she had already
20 been given to Adriel of Meholah. But Michal, Saul's other daughter,
fell in love with David, and when Saul was told of this, he saw that it
21 suited his plans. He said to himself, 'I will give her to him; let her be
the bait that lures him to his death at the hands of the Philistines.' So
22 Saul proposed a second time to make David his son-in-law, and ordered
his courtiers to say to David privately, 'The king is well disposed to
you and you are dear to us all; now is the time for you to marry into the
23 king's family.' When Saul's people spoke in this way to David, he said
to them, 'Do you think that marrying the king's daughter is a matter of
so little consequence that a poor man of no consequence, like myself,
24, 25 can do it?' Saul's courtiers reported what David had said, and he
replied, 'Tell David this: all the king wants as the bride-price is the
foreskins of a hundred Philistines, by way of vengeance on his enemies.'
Saul was counting on David's death at the hands of the Philistines.
26 The courtiers told David what Saul had said, and marriage with the
king's daughter on these terms pleased him well. Before the appointed
27 time, David went out with his men and slew two hundred Philistines;
he brought their foreskins and counted them out to the king in order
to be accepted as his son-in-law. So Saul married his daughter Michal
28 to David. He saw clearly that the LORD was with David, and knew that
29 Michal his daughter had fallen in love with him; and so he grew more
and more afraid of David and was his enemy for the rest of his life.
30   The Philistine officers used to come out to offer single combat; and
whenever they did, David had more success against them than all the
rest of Saul's men, and he won a great name for himself.

19 SAUL SPOKE TO JONATHAN his son and all his household about
2 killing David. But Jonathan was devoted to David and told him that his
father Saul was looking for an opportunity to kill him. 'Be on your
guard tomorrow morning,' he said; 'conceal yourself, and remain in
3 hiding. Then I will come out and join my father in the open country
where you are and speak to him about you, and if I discover anything
4 I will tell you.' Jonathan spoke up for David to his father Saul and said
to him, 'Sir, do not wrong your servant David; he has not wronged you;
5 his conduct towards you has been beyond reproach. Did he not take
his life in his hands when he killed the Philistine, and the LORD won
a great victory for Israel? You saw it, you shared in the rejoicing; why
should you wrong an innocent man and put David to death without
6 cause?' Saul listened to Jonathan and swore solemnly by the LORD that
7 David should not be put to death. So Jonathan called David and told
him all this; then he brought him to Saul, and he was in attendance
on the king as before.

War broke out again, and David attacked the Philistines and dealt 8 them such a blow that they ran before him.

An evil spirit from the LORD came upon Saul as he was sitting in the 9 house with his spear in his hand; and David was playing the harp. Saul 10 tried to pin David to the wall with the spear, but he avoided the king's thrust so that Saul drove the spear into the wall. David escaped and got safely away. That night Saul sent servants to keep watch on David's 11 house, intending to kill him in the morning, but David's wife Michal warned him to get away that night, 'or tomorrow', she said, 'you will be a dead man.' She let David down through a window and he slipped 12 away and escaped. Michal took their household gods*a* and put them on 13 the bed; at its head she laid a goat's-hair rug and covered it all with a cloak. When the men arrived to arrest David she told them he was ill. 14 Saul sent them back to see David for themselves. 'Bring him to me, 15 bed and all,' he said, 'and I will kill him.' When they came, there were 16 the household gods on the bed and the goat's-hair rug at its head. Then 17 Saul said to Michal, 'Why have you played this trick on me and let my enemy get safe away?' And Michal answered, 'He said to me, "Help me to escape or I will kill you."'

Meanwhile David made good his escape and came to Samuel at 18 Ramah, and told him how Saul had treated him. Then he and Samuel went to Naioth and stayed there. Saul was told that David was there, 19 and he sent a party of men to seize him. When they saw the company 20 of prophets in rapture, with Samuel standing at their head, the spirit of God came upon them and they fell into prophetic rapture. When this 21 was reported to Saul he sent another party. These also fell into a rapture, and when he sent more men a third time, they did the same. Saul himself then set out for Ramah and came to the great cistern in 22 Secu. He asked where Samuel and David were and was told that they were at Naioth in Ramah. On his way there the spirit of God came upon 23 him too and he went on, in a rapture as he went, till he came to Naioth in Ramah. There he too stripped off his clothes and like the rest fell 24 into a rapture before Samuel and lay down naked all that day and all that night. That is why men say, 'Is Saul also among the prophets?'

Then David made his escape from Naioth in Ramah and came to 20 Jonathan. 'What have I done?' he asked. 'What is my offence? What does your father think I have done wrong, that he seeks my life?' Jonathan answered him, 'God forbid! There is no thought of putting 2 you to death. I am sure my father will not do anything whatever without telling me. Why should my father hide such a thing from me? I cannot believe it!' David said, 'I am ready to swear to it: your father 3 has said to himself, "Jonathan must not know this or he will resent it",

[a] *Heb.* teraphim.

because he knows that you have a high regard for me. As the LORD lives, your life upon it, there is only a step between me and death.'

4,5 Jonathan said to David, 'What do you want me to do for you?' David answered, 'It is new moon tomorrow, and I ought to dine with the king. Let me go and lie hidden in the fields until the third evening.

6 If your father happens to miss me, then say, "David asked me for leave to pay a rapid visit to his home in Bethlehem, for it is the annual

7 sacrifice there for the whole family." If he says, "Well and good", that will be a good sign for me; but if he flies into a rage, you will know that

8 he is set on doing me wrong. My lord, keep faith with me; for you and I have entered into a solemn compact before the LORD. Kill me yourself

9 if I am guilty. Why let me fall into your father's hands?' 'God forbid!' cried Jonathan. 'If I find my father set on doing you wrong I will tell

10 you.' David answered Jonathan, 'How will you let me know if he

11 answers harshly?' Jonathan said, 'Come with me into the fields.' So

12 they went together into the fields, and Jonathan said to David, 'I promise you, David, in the sight of the LORD*a* the God of Israel, this time tomorrow I will sound my father for the third time and, if he is

13 well disposed to you, I will send and let you know. If my father means mischief, the LORD do the same to me and more, if I do not let you know and get you safely away. The LORD be with you as he has been

14 with my father! I know that as long as I live you will show me faithful

15 friendship, as the LORD requires; and if I should die, you will continue loyal to my family for ever. When the LORD rids the earth of all David's

16 enemies, may the LORD call him*b* to account if he and his house are no

17 longer my friends.'*c* Jonathan pledged himself afresh to David*d*

18 because of his love for him, for he loved him as himself. Then he said to him, 'Tomorrow is the new moon, and you will be missed when your

19 place is empty. So go down at nightfall for the third time to the place where you hid on the evening of the feast and stay by the mound there.*e*

20 Then I will shoot three arrows towards it, as though I were aiming at

21 a mark. Then I will send my boy to find the arrows. If I say to him, "Look, the arrows are on this side of you, pick them up", then you can come out of hiding. You will be quite safe, I swear it; for there will be

22 nothing amiss. But if I say to the lad, "Look, the arrows are on the other side of you, further on", then the LORD has said that you must go;

23 the LORD stand witness between us for ever to the pledges we have exchanged.'

24 So David hid in the fields. The new moon came, the dinner was

25 prepared, and the king sat down to eat. Saul took his customary seat by

---

[a] David, 'I promise...of the LORD: so Pesh.; Heb. David, the LORD... [b] So Luc. Sept.; Heb. David's enemies. [c] he and...friends: so Sept.; Heb. obscure. [d] pledged...to David: so Sept.; Heb. made David swear. [e] Prob. rdg., cp. Sept.; Heb. by the Azel stone.

the wall, and Abner sat beside him; Jonathan too was present, but
David's place was empty. That day Saul said nothing, for he thought 26
that David was absent by some chance, perhaps because he was
ritually unclean. But on the second day,*a* the day after the new moon, 27
David's place was still empty, and Saul said to his son Jonathan, 'Why
has not the son of Jesse come to the feast, either yesterday or today?'
Jonathan answered Saul, 'David asked permission to go to Bethlehem. 28
He asked my leave and said, "Our family is holding a sacrifice in the 29
town and my brother himself has ordered me to be there. Now, if you
have any regard for me, let me slip away to see my brothers." That is
why he has not come to dine with the king.' Saul was angry with 30
Jonathan, 'You son of a crooked and unfaithful mother! You have made
friends with*b* the son of Jesse only to bring shame on yourself and
dishonour on your mother; I see how it will be. As long as Jesse's son 31
remains alive on earth, neither you nor your crown will be safe. Send
at once and fetch him; he deserves to die.' Jonathan answered his father, 32
'Deserves to die! Why? What has he done?' At that, Saul picked up 33
his spear and threatened to kill him; and he knew that his father was
bent on David's death. Jonathan left the table in a rage and ate nothing 34
on the second day of the festival; for he was indignant on David's
behalf because his father had humiliated him.

Next morning, Jonathan went out into the fields to meet David at 35
the appointed time, taking a young boy with him. He said to the boy, 36
'Run and find the arrows; I am going to shoot.' The boy ran on, and he
shot the arrows over his head. When the boy reached the place where 37
Jonathan's arrows had fallen, Jonathan called out after him, 'Look,
the arrows are beyond you. Hurry! No time to lose! Make haste!' The 38
boy gathered up the arrows and brought them to his master; but only 39
Jonathan and David knew what this meant; the boy knew nothing.
Jonathan handed his weapons to the boy and told him to take them back 40
to the city. When the boy had gone, David got up from behind the 41
mound*c* and bowed humbly three times. Then they kissed one another
and shed tears together, until David's grief was even greater than
Jonathan's. Jonathan said to David, 'Go in safety; we have pledged 42
each other in the name of the LORD who is witness for ever between you
and me and between your descendants and mine.'

*d*David went off at once, while Jonathan returned to the city.
David made his way to the priest Ahimelech at Nob, who hurried out 21 1*e*
to meet him and said, 'Why have you come alone and no one with you?'
David answered Ahimelech, 'I am under orders from the king: I was 2
to let no one know about the mission on which he was sending me or

[*a*] on the second day: *so Sept.; Heb.* the second. [*b*] *So Sept.; Heb.* You are choosing.
[*c*] *Prob. rdg., cp. Sept.; Heb.* the Negeb. [*d*] *21. 1 in Heb.* [*e*] *21. 2 in Heb.*

what these orders were. When I took leave of my men I told them to
3 meet me in such and such a place. Now, what have you got by you?
4 Let me have five loaves, or as many as you can find.' The priest
answered David, 'I have no ordinary bread available. There is only the
sacred bread; but have the young men kept themselves from women?'
5 David answered the priest, 'Women have been denied us hitherto,
when I have been on campaign, even an ordinary campaign, and the
young men's bodies have remained holy; and how much more will they
6 be holy today?' So, as there was no other bread there, the priest gave
him the sacred bread, the Bread of the Presence, which had just been
taken from the presence of the LORD to be replaced by freshly baked
7 bread on the day that the old was removed. One of Saul's servants
happened to be there that day, detained before the LORD; his name was
Doeg the Edomite, and he was the strongest of all Saul's herdsmen.
8 David said to Ahimelech, 'Have you a spear or sword here at hand?
I have no sword or other weapon with me, because the king's business
9 was urgent.' The priest answered, 'There is the sword of Goliath the
Philistine whom you slew in the Vale of Elah; it is wrapped up in a
cloak behind the ephod. If you wish to take that, take it; there is no
other weapon here.' David said, 'There is no sword like it; give it
to me.'
10   That day, David went on his way, eluding Saul, and came to Achish
11 king of Gath. The servants of Achish said to him, 'Surely this is David,
the king of his country, the man of whom they sang as they danced:

> Saul made havoc among thousands
> but David among tens of thousands.'

12 These words were not lost on David, and he became very much afraid
13 of Achish king of Gath. So he altered his behaviour in public and acted
like a lunatic in front of them all, scrabbling on the double doors of the
14 city gate and dribbling down his beard. Achish said to his servants,
15 'The man is mad! Why bring him to me? Am I short of madmen that
you bring this one to plague me? Must I have this fellow in my house?'

22 DAVID MADE HIS ESCAPE and went from there to the cave of
Adullam. When his brothers and all his family heard that he was
2 there, they joined him. Men in any kind of distress or in debt or with
a grievance gathered round him, about four hundred in number, and
3 he became their chief. From there David went to Mizpeh in Moab and
said to the king of Moab, 'Let my father and mother come and take
4 shelter with you until I know what God will do for me.' So he left
them at the court of the king of Moab, and they stayed there as long
as David was in his stronghold.

The prophet Gad said to David, 'You must not stay in your strong- 5
hold; go at once into Judah.' So David went as far as the forest of Hareth.
News that David and his men had been seen reached Saul while he was 6
in Gibeah, sitting under the tamarisk-tree on the hill-top with his
spear in his hand and all his retainers standing about him. He said to 7
them, 'Listen to me, you Benjamites: do you expect the son of Jesse
to give you all fields and vineyards, or make you all officers over units
of a thousand and a hundred? Is that why you have all conspired 8
against me? Not one of you told me when my son made a compact
with the son of Jesse; none of you spared a thought for me or told me
that my son had set my own servant against me, who is lying in wait
for me now.'

Then Doeg the Edomite, who was standing with the servants of 9
Saul, spoke: 'I saw the son of Jesse coming to Nob, to Ahimelech son
of Ahitub. Ahimelech consulted the LORD on his behalf, then gave him 10
food and handed over to him the sword of Goliath the Philistine.' The 11
king sent for Ahimelech the priest and his family, who were priests at
Nob, and they all came into his presence. Saul said, 'Now listen, you 12
son of Ahitub', and the man answered, 'Yes, my lord?' Then Saul 13
said to him, 'Why have you and the son of Jesse plotted against me?
You gave him food and the sword too, and consulted God on his
behalf; and now he has risen against me and is at this moment lying
in wait for me.' 'And who among all your servants', answered Ahi- 14
melech, 'is like David, a man to be trusted, the king's son-in-law,
appointed to your staff and holding an honourable place in your household? Have I on this occasion done something profane in consulting 15
God on his behalf? God forbid! I trust that my lord the king will not
accuse me or my family; for I know nothing whatever about it.' But 16
the king said, 'Ahimelech, you must die, you and all your family.' He 17
then turned to the bodyguard attending him and said, 'Go and kill the
priests of the LORD; for they are in league with David, and, though
they knew that he was a fugitive, they did not tell me.' The king's men,
however, were unwilling to raise a hand against the priests of the LORD.
The king therefore said to Doeg the Edomite, 'You, Doeg, go and fall 18
upon the priests'; so Doeg went and fell upon the priests, killing that
day with his own hand eighty-five men who could carry the ephod.[a] He 19
put to the sword every living thing in Nob, the city of priests: men and
women, children and babes in arms, oxen, asses, and sheep. One son 20
of Ahimelech named Abiathar made his escape and joined David. He 21
told David how Saul had killed the priests of the LORD. Then David 22
said to him, 'When Doeg the Edomite was there that day, I knew that
he would inform Saul. I have gambled with the lives of all your father's

[a] *So Sept.; Heb.* the linen ephod.

23 family. Stay here with me, have no fear; he who seeks your life seeks mine, and you will be safe with me.'

23 The Philistines were fighting against Keilah and plundering the
2 threshing-floors; and when David heard this, he consulted the LORD and asked whether he should go and attack the Philistines. The LORD
3 answered, 'Go, attack them, and relieve Keilah.' But David's men said to him, 'As we are now, we have enough to fear from Judah. How
4 much worse if we challenge the Philistine forces at Keilah!' David consulted the LORD once again and the LORD answered him, 'Go to
5 Keilah; I will give the Philistines into your hands.' So David and his men went to Keilah and fought the Philistines; they carried off their cattle, inflicted a heavy defeat on them and relieved the inhabitants.
6 Abiathar son of Ahimelech made good his escape and joined David at
7 Keilah, bringing the ephod with him. Saul was told that David had entered Keilah, and he said, 'God has put him into my hands; for he has walked into a trap by entering a walled town with gates and bars.'
8 He called out the levy to march on Keilah and besiege David and his
9 men. When David learnt how Saul planned his undoing, he told
10 Abiathar the priest to bring the ephod, and then he prayed, 'O LORD God of Israel, I thy servant have heard news that Saul intends to come
11 to Keilah and destroy the city because of me. Will the citizens of Keilah surrender me to him? Will Saul come as I have heard? O LORD God of Israel, I pray thee, tell thy servant.' The LORD answered, 'He will
12 come.' Then David asked, 'Will the citizens of Keilah surrender me
13 and my men to Saul?', and the LORD answered, 'They will.' Then David left Keilah at once with his men, who numbered about six hundred, and moved about from place to place. When the news reached Saul that David had escaped from Keilah, he made no further move.

14 While David was living in the fastnesses of the wilderness of Ziph, in the hill-country, Saul searched for him day after day, but God did
15 not put him into his power. David well knew that Saul had come out to seek his life; and while he was at Horesh in the wilderness of Ziph,
16 Saul's son Jonathan came to him there and gave him fresh courage in
17 God's name: 'Do not be afraid,' he said; 'my father's hand shall not touch you. You will become king of Israel and I shall hold rank after
18 you; and my father knows it.' The two of them made a solemn compact before the LORD; then David remained in Horesh and Jonathan went
19 home. While Saul was at Gibeah the Ziphites brought him this news: 'David, we hear, is in hiding among us in the fastnesses of Horesh on
20 the hill of Hachilah, south of Jeshimon. Come down, your majesty,
21 come whenever you will, and we are able to surrender him to you.' Saul said, 'The LORD has indeed blessed you; you have saved me a world
22 of trouble. Go now and make further inquiry, and find out exactly

where he is and who saw him there. They tell me that he by himself is crafty enough to outwit me. Find out which of his hiding-places he is 23 using; then come back to me at such and such a place, and I will go along with you. So long as he stays in this country, I will hunt him down, if I have to go through all the clans of Judah one by one.' They set out for Ziph without delay, ahead of Saul; David and his 24 men were in the wilderness of Maon in the Arabah to the south of Jeshimon. Saul set off with his men to look for him; but David got wind 25 of it and went down to a refuge in the rocks, and there he stayed in the wilderness of Maon. Hearing of this, Saul went into the wilderness after him; he was on one side of the hill, David and his men on the 26 other. While David and his men were trying desperately to get away and Saul and his followers were closing in for the capture, a runner 27 brought a message to Saul: 'Come at once! the Philistines are harrying the land.' So Saul called off the pursuit and turned back to face the 28 Philistines. This is why that place is called the Dividing Rock. David 29*ᵃ* went up from there and lived in the fastnesses of En-gedi.

When Saul returned from the pursuit of the Philistines, he learnt **24** that David was in the wilderness of En-gedi. So he took three thousand 2 men picked from the whole of Israel and went in search of David and his men to the east of the Rocks of the Wild Goats. There beside the 3 road were some sheepfolds, and near by was a cave, at the far end of which David and his men were sitting concealed. Saul came to the cave and went in to relieve himself. His men said to David, 'The day has 4–7*ᵇ* come: the LORD has put your enemy into your hands, as he promised he would, and you may do what you please with him.' David said to his men, 'God forbid that I should harm my master, the LORD's anointed, or lift a finger against him; he is the LORD's anointed.' So David reproved his men severely and would not let them attack Saul. He himself got up stealthily and cut off a piece of Saul's cloak; but when he had cut it off, his conscience*ᶜ* smote him. Saul rose, left the cave and went on his way; whereupon David also came out of the cave and called 8 after Saul, 'My lord the king!' When Saul looked round, David prostrated himself in obeisance and said to him, 'Why do you listen 9 when they say that David is out to do you harm? Today you can see 10 for yourself that the LORD put you into my power in the cave; I had a mind to kill you, but no, I spared your life and said, "I cannot lift a finger against my master, for he is the LORD's anointed." Look, my 11 dear lord, look at this piece of your cloak in my hand. I cut it off, but I did not kill you; this will show you that I have no thought of violence or treachery against you, and that I have done you no wrong; yet you are resolved to take my life. May the LORD judge between us! but 12

[a] 24. *1 in Heb.* [b] *Verses 4–7 are re-arranged thus: 4a, 6, 7a, 4b, 5, 7b.* [c] *Lit.* heart.

395

though he may take vengeance on you for my sake, I will never lift my
13 hand against you; "One wrong begets another", as the old saying goes,
14 yet I will never lift my hand against you. Who has the king of Israel
come out against? What are you pursuing? A dead dog, a mere flea.
15 The LORD will be judge and decide between us; let him look into my
cause, he will plead for me and will acquit me.'

16   When David had finished speaking, Saul said, 'Is that you, David
17 my son?', and he wept. Then he said, 'The right is on your side, not
mine; you have treated me so well, I have treated you so badly.
18 Your goodness to me this day has passed all bounds: the LORD put me
19 at your mercy but you did not kill me. Not often does a man find his
enemy and let him go safely on his way; so may the LORD reward you
well for what you have done for me today! I know now for certain that
20 you will become king, and that the kingdom of Israel will flourish
21 under your rule. Swear to me by the LORD then that you will not
exterminate my descendants and blot out my name from my father's
22 house.' David swore an oath to Saul; and Saul went back to his home,
while David and his men went up to their fastness.

25 SAMUEL DIED, and all Israel came together to mourn for him, and he
was buried in his house in Ramah. Afterwards David went down to the
wilderness of Paran.

2   There was a man at Carmel in Maon, who had great influence and
owned three thousand sheep and a thousand goats; and he was shearing
3 his flocks in Carmel. His name was Nabal and his wife's name Abigail;
she was a beautiful and intelligent woman, but her husband, a Calebite,
4 was surly and mean. David heard in the wilderness that Nabal was
5 shearing his flocks, and sent ten of his men, saying to them, 'Go up to
6 Carmel, find Nabal and give him my greetings. You are to say, "All
good wishes for the year ahead! Prosperity to yourself, your household,
7 and all that is yours! I hear that you are shearing. Your shepherds have
been with us lately and we did not molest them; nothing of theirs was
8 missing all the time they were in Carmel. Ask your own people and they
will tell you. Receive my men kindly, for this is an auspicious day with
9 us, and give what you can to David your son and your servant."' David's
servants came and delivered this message to Nabal in David's name.
10 When they paused, Nabal answered, 'Who is David? Who is this son
of Jesse? In these days every slave who breaks away from his master
11 sets himself up as a chief.[a] Am I to take my food and my wine[b] and
the meat I have provided for my shearers and give it to men who come
12 from I know not where?' David's men turned and made their way back

[a] *Or* In these days there are many slaves who break away from their master.   [b] *So Sept.;*
Heb. water.

to him and told him all this. He said to his men, 'Buckle on your swords, 13
all of you.' So they buckled on their swords and followed David, four
hundred of them, while two hundred stayed behind with the baggage.

One of the young men said to Abigail, Nabal's wife, 'David sent 14
messengers from the wilderness to ask our master politely for a present,
and he flew out*ᵃ* at them. The men have been very good to us and have 15
not molested us, nor did we miss anything all the time we were going
about with them in the open country. They were as good as a wall 16
round us, night and day, while we were minding the flocks. Think 17
carefully what you had better do, for it is certain ruin for our master
and his whole family; he is such a good-for-nothing*ᵇ* that it is no good
talking to him.' So Abigail hastily collected two hundred loaves and 18
two skins of wine, five sheep ready dressed, five measures*ᶜ* of parched
grain, a hundred bunches of raisins, and two hundred cakes of dried figs,
and loaded them on asses, but told her husband nothing about it. Then 19
she said to her servants, 'Go on ahead, I will follow you.' As she made 20
her way on her ass, hidden by the hill, there were David and his men
coming down towards her, and she met them. David had said, 'It was 21
a waste of time to protect this fellow's property in the wilderness so
well that nothing of his was missing. He has repaid me evil for good.'
David*ᵈ* swore a great oath: 'God do the same to me and more if I leave 22
him a single mother's son alive by morning!'

When Abigail saw David she dismounted in haste and prostrated 23
herself before him, bowing low to the ground at his feet, and said, 'Let 24
me take the blame, my lord, but allow me, your humble servant, to
speak out and let my lord give me a hearing. How can you take any 25
notice of this good-for-nothing? He is just what his name Nabal
means: "Churl" is his name, and churlish his behaviour. I did not
myself, sir, see the men you sent. And now, sir, the Lord has restrained 26
you from bloodshed and from giving vent to your anger. As the Lord
lives, your life upon it, your enemies and all who want to see you
ruined will be like Nabal. Here is the present which I, your humble 27
servant, have brought; give it to the young men under your command.
Forgive me, my lord, if I am presuming; for the Lord will establish your 28
family for ever, because you have fought his wars. No calamity shall
overtake you as long as you live. If any man sets out to pursue you and 29
take your life, the Lord your God will wrap your life up and put it
with his own treasure, but the lives of your enemies he will hurl away
like stones from a sling. When the Lord has made good all his promises 30
to you, and has made you ruler of Israel, there will be no reason why 31
you should stumble or your courage falter because you have shed*ᵉ*

[*a*] flew out: *or* screamed.   [*b*] *Lit.* such a son of Belial.   [*c*] *Heb.* seahs.   [*d*] *So Sept.;*
Heb. David's enemies.   [*e*] because...shed: *so some MSS.; others* or you should shed.

innocent blood or given way to your anger.[a] Then when the LORD
32 makes all you do prosper, you will remember me, your servant.' David
said to Abigail, 'Blessed is the LORD the God of Israel who has sent
33 you today to meet me. A blessing on your good sense, a blessing on you
because you have saved me today from the guilt of bloodshed and from
34 giving way to my anger. For I swear by the life of the LORD the God of
Israel who has kept me from doing you wrong: if you had not come at
once to meet me, not a man of Nabal's household, not a single mother's
35 son, would have been left alive by morning.' Then David took from her
what she had brought him and said, 'Go home in peace, I have listened
to you and I grant your request.'

36 On her return she found Nabal holding a banquet in his house,
a banquet fit for a king. He grew merry and became very drunk, so
drunk that his wife said nothing to him, trivial or serious, till daybreak.
37 In the morning, when the wine had worn off, she told him everything,
38 and he had a seizure and lay there like a stone. Ten days later the LORD
39 struck him again and he died. When David heard that Nabal was dead
he said, 'Blessed be the LORD, who has himself punished Nabal for his
insult, and has kept me his servant from doing wrong. The LORD has
made Nabal's wrongdoing recoil on his own head.' David then sent to
40 make proposals that Abigail should become his wife. And his servants
came to Abigail at Carmel and said to her, 'David has sent us to fetch
41 you to be his wife.' She rose and prostrated herself with her face to the
ground, and said, 'I am his slave to command, I would wash the feet
42 of my lord's servants.' So Abigail made her preparations with all speed
and, with her five maids in attendance, accompanied by David's
43 messengers, rode away on an ass; and she became David's wife. David
had also married Ahinoam of Jezreel; both these women became his
44 wives. Saul meanwhile had given his daughter Michal, David's wife,
to Palti son of Laish from Gallim.

26 THE ZIPHITES CAME to Saul at Gibeah to report that David was in
2 hiding on the hill of Hachilah overlooking Jeshimon. Saul went down
at once to the wilderness of Ziph, taking with him three thousand picked
3 men, to search for David there. He encamped beside the road on the
hill of Hachilah overlooking Jeshimon, while David was still in the
wilderness. As soon as David knew that Saul had come to the wilderness
4 in pursuit of him, he sent out scouts and found that Saul had reached
5 such and such a place. Without delay, he went to the place where Saul
had pitched his camp and observed where Saul and Abner son of Ner,
the commander-in-chief, were lying. Saul lay within the lines with his
6 troops encamped in a circle round him. David turned to Ahimelech

[a] or given...anger: *so Sept.; Heb.* or deliver yourself.

the Hittite and Abishai son of Zeruiah, Joab's brother, and said, 'Who
will venture with me into the camp, to go to Saul?' Abishai answered,
'I will.' David and Abishai entered the camp at night and found Saul 7
lying asleep within the lines with his spear thrust into the ground by
his head. Abner and the army were lying all round him. Abishai said 8
to David, 'God has put your enemy into your power today; let me
strike him and pin him to the ground with one thrust of the spear;
I shall not have to strike twice.' David said to him, 'Do him no harm; 9
who has ever lifted a finger against the LORD's anointed and gone unpunished? As the LORD lives,' went on David, 'the LORD will strike 10
him down; either his time will come and he will die, or he will go down
to battle and meet his end. God forbid that I should lift a finger against 11
the LORD's anointed! But now let us take the spear which is by his
head, and the water-jar, and go.' So David took the spear and the 12
water-jar from beside Saul's head and they went. The whole camp was
asleep; no one saw him, no one knew anything, no one even woke up.
A heavy sleep sent by the LORD had fallen on them.

Then David crossed over to the other side and stood on the top of a 13
hill a long way off; there was no little distance between them. David 14
shouted across to the army and hailed Abner, 'Answer me, Abner!'
He answered, 'Who are you to shout to the king?' David said to 15
Abner, 'Do you call yourself a man? Is there anyone like you in Israel?
Why, then, did you not keep watch over your lord the king, when
someone came to harm your lord the king? This was not well done. 16
As the LORD lives, you deserve to die, all of you, because you have not
kept watch over your master the LORD's anointed. Look! Where are the
king's spear and the water-jar that were by his head?'

Saul recognized David's voice and said, 'Is that you, David my 17
son?' 'Yes, sir, it is', said David. 'Why must your majesty pursue me? 18
What have I done? What mischief am I plotting? Listen, my lord, to 19
what I have to say. If it is the LORD who has set you against me, may an
offering be acceptable to him; but if it is men, a curse on them in the
LORD's name; for they have ousted me today from my share in the
LORD's inheritance and have banished me to serve other gods! Do not 20
let my blood be shed on foreign soil, far from the presence of the LORD,
just because the king of Israel came out to look for a flea, as one might
hunt a partridge over the hills.' Saul answered, 'I have done wrong; 21
come back, David my son. You have held my life precious this day, and
I will never harm you again. I have been a fool, I have been sadly in the
wrong.' David answered, 'Here is the king's spear; let one of your men 22
come across and fetch it. The LORD who rewards uprightness and 23
loyalty will reward the man into whose power he put you today, when
I refused to lift a finger against the LORD's anointed. As I held your 24

life precious today, so may the LORD hold mine precious and deliver
25 me from every distress.' Then Saul said to David, 'A blessing is on
you, David my son. You will do great things and be victorious.' So
David went on his way and Saul returned home.

27 David thought, 'One of these days I shall be killed by Saul. The
best thing for me to do will be to escape into Philistine territory; then
Saul will lose all further hope of finding me anywhere in Israel, search
2 as he may, and I shall escape his clutches.' So David and his six
hundred men crossed the frontier forthwith to Achish son of Maoch
3 king of Gath. David settled in Gath with Achish, taking with him his
men and their families and his two wives, Ahinoam of Jezreel and
4 Abigail of Carmel, Nabal's widow. Saul was told that David had
5 escaped to Gath, and he gave up the search. David said to Achish, 'If
I stand well in your opinion, grant me a place in one of your country
towns where I may settle. Why should I remain in the royal city with
6 your majesty?' Achish granted him Ziklag on that day: that is why
Ziklag still belongs to the kings of Judah.

7,8 David spent a year and four months in Philistine country. He and
his men would sally out and raid the Geshurites, the Gizrites, and the
Amalekites, for it was they who inhabited the country from Telaim[a]
9 all the way to Shur and Egypt. When David raided the country he left
no one alive, man or woman; he took flocks and herds, asses and camels,
10 and clothes too, and then came back again to Achish. When Achish
asked, 'Where was your raid today?', David would answer, 'The
Negeb of Judah' or 'The Negeb of the Jerahmeelites' or 'The Negeb
11 of the Kenites'. Neither man nor woman did David bring back alive
to Gath, for fear that they should denounce him and his men for what
they had done. This was his practice as long as he remained with the
12 Philistines. Achish trusted David, thinking that he had won such a bad
name among his own people the Israelites that he would remain his
subject all his life.

Saul and his sons killed

28 IN THOSE DAYS the Philistines mustered their army for an attack on
Israel. Achish said to David, 'You know that you and your men must
2 take the field with me.' David answered Achish, 'Good, you will learn
what your servant can do.' And Achish said to David, 'I will make you
my bodyguard for life.'
3 By this time Samuel was dead, and all Israel had mourned for him
and buried him in Ramah, his own city; and Saul had banished from

[a] from Telaim: *prob. rdg.; Heb.* from of old.

the land all who trafficked with ghosts and spirits. The Philistines 4
mustered and encamped at Shunem, and Saul gathered all the Israelites
and encamped on Gilboa; and when Saul saw the Philistine force, fear 5
struck him to the heart. He inquired of the LORD, but the LORD did not 6
answer him, whether by dreams or by Urim or by prophets. So he said 7
to his servants, 'Find me a woman who has a familiar spirit, and I will
go and inquire through her.' His servants told him that there was such
a woman at En-dor. Saul put on different clothes and went in disguise 8
with two of his men. He came to the woman by night and said, 'Tell
me my fortunes by consulting the dead, and call up the man I name
to you.' But the woman answered, 'Surely you know what Saul has 9
done, how he has made away with those who call up ghosts and spirits;
why do you press me to do what will lead to my death?' Saul swore 10
her an oath: 'As the LORD lives, no harm shall come to you for this.' The 11
woman asked whom she should call up, and Saul answered, 'Samuel.'
When the woman saw Samuel appear, she shrieked and said to Saul, 12
'Why have you deceived me? You are Saul!' The king said to her, 13
'Do not be afraid. What do you see?' The woman answered, 'I see
a ghostly form coming up from the earth.' 'What is it like?' he asked; 14
she answered, 'Like an old man coming up, wrapped in a cloak.' Then
Saul knew it was Samuel, and he bowed low with his face to the ground,
and prostrated himself. Samuel said to Saul, 'Why have you disturbed 15
me and brought me up?' Saul answered, 'I am in great trouble; the
Philistines are pressing me and God has turned away; he no longer
answers me through prophets or through dreams, and I have summoned
you to tell me what I should do.' Samuel said, 'Why do you ask me, now 16
that the LORD has turned from you and become your adversary? He 17
has done what he foretold through me. He has torn the kingdom from
your hand and given it to another man, to David. You have not obeyed 18
the LORD, or executed the judgement of his fury against the Amalekites;
that is why he has done this to you today. For the same reason the LORD 19
will let your people Israel fall into the hands of the Philistines and, what
is more, tomorrow you and your sons shall be with me. Yes, indeed,
the LORD will give the Israelite army into the hands of the Philistines.'
Saul was overcome and fell his full length to the ground, terrified by 20
Samuel's words. He had no strength left, for he had eaten nothing all
day and all night.

The woman went to Saul and saw that he was much disturbed, and 21
she said to him, 'I listened to what you said and I risked my life to
obey you. Now listen to me: let me set before you a little food to give 22
you strength for your journey.' But he refused to eat anything. When 23
his servants joined the woman in pressing*a* him, he yielded, rose from

[a] *Prob. rdg., cp. Sept.; Heb.* in breaking out on...

24 the ground and sat on the couch. The woman had a fatted calf at home,
which she quickly slaughtered. She took some meal, kneaded it and
25 baked unleavened cakes, which she set before Saul and his servants.
They ate the food and departed that same night.

29 The Philistines mustered all their troops at Aphek, while the
2 Israelites encamped at En-harod*a* in Jezreel. The Philistine princes
were advancing with their troops in units of a hundred and a thousand;
3 David and his men were in the rear of the column with Achish. The
Philistine commanders asked, 'Why are those Hebrews there?' Achish
answered, 'This is David, the servant of Saul king of Israel who has
been with me now for a year or more. I have had no fault to find in
4 him ever since he came over to me.' The Philistine commanders were
indignant and said to Achish, 'Send the man back to the town which
you allotted to him. He shall not fight side by side with us, or he may
turn traitor in the battle. What better way to buy his master's favour,
5 than at the price of our lives? This is that David of whom they sang,
as they danced:

> Saul made havoc among thousands
> but David among tens of thousands.'

6 Achish summoned David and said to him, 'As the LORD lives, you
are an upright man and your service with my troops has well satisfied
me. I have had no fault to find with you ever since you joined me, but
7 the other princes are not willing to accept you. Now go home in peace,
and you will then be doing nothing that they can regard as wrong.'
8 David protested, 'What have I done, or what fault have you found in
me from the day I first entered your service till now, that I should not
9 come and fight against the enemies of my lord the king?' Achish
answered David, 'I agree that you have been as true to me as an angel
of God, but the Philistine commanders insist that you shall not fight
10 alongside them. Now rise early in the morning with those of your
lord's subjects who have followed you, and go to the town which
I allotted to you; harbour no evil thoughts, for I am well satisfied with
11 you.*b* Rise early and start as soon as it is light.' So David and his men
rose early to start that morning on their way back to the land of the
Philistines, while the Philistines went on to Jezreel.

30 On the third day David and his men reached Ziklag. Now the
Amalekites had made a raid into the Negeb, attacked Ziklag and set
2 fire to it; they had carried off all the women, high and low, without
putting one of them to death. These they drove with them and con-
3 tinued their march. When David and his men approached the town,
they found it destroyed by fire, and their wives, their sons, and their

[a] *Prob. rdg.; Heb.* at the spring. [b] *and go...with you: so Sept.; Heb. om.*

daughters carried off. David and the people with him wept aloud until 4
they could weep no more. David's two wives, Ahinoam of Jezreel and 5
Abigail widow of Nabal of Carmel, were among the captives. David 6
was in a desperate position because the people, embittered by the loss
of their sons and daughters, threatened to stone him. So David sought
strength in the LORD his God. He told Abiathar the priest, son of 7
Ahimelech, to bring the ephod. When Abiathar had brought the
ephod, David inquired of the LORD, 'Shall I pursue these raiders? and 8
shall I overtake them?' The answer came, 'Pursue them: you will
overtake them and rescue everyone.' So David and his six hundred 9
men set out and reached the ravine of Besor.*a* Two hundred of them 10
who were too weary to cross the ravine stayed behind, and David with
four hundred pressed on in pursuit.

In the open country they came across an Egyptian and took him to 11
David. They gave him food to eat and water to drink, also a lump of 12
dried figs and two bunches of raisins. When he had eaten these he
revived; for he had had nothing to eat or drink for three days and
nights. David asked him, 'Whose slave are you? and where have you 13
come from?' 'I am an Egyptian boy,' he answered, 'the slave of an
Amalekite, but my master left me behind because I fell ill three days
ago. We had raided the Negeb of the Kerethites, part of Judah, and 14
the Negeb of Caleb; we also set fire to Ziklag.' David asked, 'Can you 15
guide me to this band?' 'Swear to me by God', he answered, 'that
you will not put me to death or hand me back to my master, and I will
guide you to them.' So he led him down, and there they were scattered 16
everywhere, eating and drinking and celebrating the capture of the
great mass of spoil taken from Philistine and Judaean territory.

David attacked from dawn till dusk and continued till next day; only 17
four hundred young men mounted on camels made good their escape.
David rescued all those whom the Amalekites had taken, including his 18
two wives. No one was missing, high or low, sons or daughters, and 19
none of the spoil, nor anything they had taken for themselves: David
recovered everything. They took all the flocks and herds, drove the 20
cattle before him*b* and said, 'This is David's spoil.' When David 21
returned to the two hundred men who had been too weak to follow
him and whom he had left behind at the ravine of Besor, they came
forward to meet him and his men. David greeted them all, inquiring
how things were with them. But some of those who had gone with 22
David, worthless men and scoundrels, broke in and said, 'These men
did not go with us;*c* we will not allot them any of the spoil that we have
retrieved, except that each of them may take his own wife and children

[a] *Prob. rdg.; Heb. adds* those who were left over remained. [b] They took...before
him: *prob. rdg.; Heb.* David took all the flocks and herds; they drove before that cattle.
[c] *So some MSS.; others* me.

23 and then go.' 'That you shall never do,' said David, 'considering[a] what the LORD has given us, and how he has kept us safe and given the 24 raiding party into our hands. Who could agree with what you propose? Those who stayed with the stores shall have the same share as those 25 who went into battle. They shall share and share alike.' From that time onwards, this has been the established custom in Israel down to this day.

26 When David reached Ziklag, he sent some of the spoil to the elders of Judah and[b] to his friends, with this message: 'This is a present for 27 you out of the spoil taken from the LORD's enemies.' He sent to those 28 in Bethuel, in Ramoth-negeb, in Jattir, in Ararah,[c] in Siphmoth, in 29 Eshtemoa, in Rachal, in the cities of the Jerahmeelites, in the cities of 30,31 the Kenites, in Hormah, in Borashan, in Athak, in Hebron, and in all the places over which he and his men had ranged.

31 1[d] The Philistines fought a battle against Israel, and the men of Israel 2 were routed, leaving their dead on Mount Gilboa. The Philistines hotly pursued Saul and his sons and killed the three sons, Jonathan, 3 Abinadab and Malchishua. The battle went hard for Saul, for some archers came upon him and he was wounded in the belly by the archers. 4 So he said to his armour-bearer, 'Draw your sword and run me through, so that these uncircumcised brutes may not come and taunt me and make sport of me.' But the armour-bearer refused, he dared not; 5 whereupon Saul took his own sword and fell on it. When the armour-bearer saw that Saul was dead, he too fell on his sword and died with 6 him. Thus they all died together on that day, Saul, his three sons, and his 7 armour-bearer, as well as his men. And all the Israelites in the district of the Vale and of the Jordan, when they saw that the other Israelites had fled and that Saul and his sons had perished, fled likewise, abandoning their cities, and the Philistines went in and occupied them.

8 Next day, when the Philistines came to strip the slain, they found 9 Saul and his three sons lying dead on Mount Gilboa. They cut off his head and stripped him of his weapons; then they sent messengers through the length and breadth of their land to take the good news to[e] 10 idols and people alike. They deposited his armour in the temple of 11 Ashtoreth and nailed his body on the wall of Beth-shan. When the inhabitants of Jabesh-gilead heard[f] what the Philistines had done to 12 Saul, the bravest of them journeyed together all night long and recovered the bodies of Saul and his sons from the wall of Beth-shan; they brought them[g] back to Jabesh and anointed them there with 13 spices. Then they took their bones and buried them under the tamarisk-tree in Jabesh, and fasted for seven days.

[a] considering: *prob. rdg., cp. Sept.; Heb.* my brothers.   [b] *So Sept.; Heb. om.*   [c] *Prob. rdg.; Heb.* Aroer.   [d] *Verses 1–13: cp. 1 Chr. 10. 1–12.*   [e] to: *so Sept.; Heb.* house of. [f] *So Sept.; Heb. adds* to him.   [g] *So Sept., cp. 1 Chr. 10. 12; Heb.* they came.

THE SECOND BOOK OF
SAMUEL

David's rule at Hebron

W HEN DAVID RETURNED from his victory over 1
the Amalekites, he spent two days in Ziklag. And on the 2
third day after Saul's death a man came from the army
with his clothes rent and dust on his head. When he came into David's
presence he fell to the ground in obeisance, and David asked him 3
where he had come from. He answered, 'I have escaped from the army
of Israel.' And David said to him, 'What news? Tell me.' 'The army 4
has been driven from the field,' he answered, 'and many have fallen
in battle. Saul and Jonathan his son are dead.' David said to the young 5
man who brought the news, 'How do you know that Saul and Jonathan
are dead?' The man answered, 'It so happened that I was on Mount 6
Gilboa and saw Saul leaning on his spear with the chariots and horsemen closing in upon him. He turned round and, seeing me, called to 7
me. I said, "What is it, sir?" He asked who I was, and I said, "An 8
Amalekite." Then he said to me, "Come and stand over me and dis- 9
patch me. I still live, but the throes of death have seized me." So 10
I stood over him and gave him the death-blow; for I knew that, broken
as he was, he could not live. Then I took the crown from his head and
the armlet from his arm, and I have brought them here to you, sir.'
At that David caught at his clothes and rent them, and so did all the 11
men with him. They beat their breasts and wept, because Saul and 12
Jonathan his son and the people of the LORD, the house of Israel, had
fallen in battle; and they fasted till evening. David said to the young 13
man who brought the news, 'Where do you come from?', and he
answered, 'I am the son of an alien, an Amalekite.' 'How is it', said 14
David, 'that you were not afraid to raise your hand to slay the LORD's
anointed?' And he summoned one of his own young men and ordered 15
him to fall upon the man. So the young man struck him down and killed
him; and David said, 'Your blood be on your own head; for out of 16
your own mouth you condemned yourself when you said, "I killed the
LORD's anointed."'

David made this lament over Saul and Jonathan his son; and he 17, 18
ordered that this dirge over them should be taught to the people of
Judah. It was written down and may be found in the Book of Jashar:[a]

[a] *Or* the Book of the Upright.

19   O prince^a of Israel, laid low^b in death!
          How are the men of war fallen!

20   Tell it not in Gath,
          proclaim it not in the streets of Ashkelon,
              lest the Philistine women rejoice,
              lest the daughters of the uncircumcised exult.

21   Hills of Gilboa, let no dew or rain fall on you,
              no showers on the uplands^c!
          For there the shields of the warriors lie tarnished,
              and the shield of Saul, no longer bright with oil.

22   The bow of Jonathan never held back
          from the breast of the foeman, from the blood of the slain;
          the sword of Saul never returned
              empty to the scabbard.

23   Delightful and dearly loved were Saul and Jonathan;
              in life, in death, they were not parted.
          They were swifter than eagles,
              stronger than lions.

24   Weep for Saul, O daughters of Israel!
              who clothed you in scarlet and rich embroideries,
              who spangled your dress with jewels of gold.

25   How are the men of war fallen, fallen on the field!
          O Jonathan, laid low^b in death!

26   I grieve for you, Jonathan my brother;
              dear and delightful you were to me;
          your love for me was wonderful,
              surpassing the love of women.

27   Fallen, fallen are the men of war;
              and their armour left on the field.

2   After this David inquired of the LORD, 'Shall I go up into one of the
cities of Judah?' The LORD answered, 'Go.' David asked, 'To which
2 city?', and the answer came, 'To Hebron.' So David went to Hebron
with his two wives, Ahinoam of Jezreel and Abigail widow of
3 Nabal of Carmel. David also brought the men who had joined him,
4 with their families, and they settled in the city^d of Hebron. The men
of Judah came, and there they anointed David king over the house of
Judah.
    Word came to David that the men of Jabesh-gilead had buried Saul,
5 and he sent them this message: 'The LORD bless you because you kept

[a] *Lit.* gazelle.   [b] *Lit.* on your back.   [c] showers on the uplands: *prob. rdg.; Heb.* fields
of offerings.   [d] *Prob. rdg.; Heb.* cities.

faith with Saul your lord and buried him. For this may the LORD keep 6
faith and truth with you, and I for my part will show you favour too,
because you have done this. Be strong, be valiant, now that Saul your 7
lord is dead, and the people of Judah have anointed me to be king
over them.'

Meanwhile Saul's commander-in-chief, Abner son of Ner, had taken 8
Saul's son Ishbosheth,[a] brought him across the Jordan to Mahanaim,
and made him king over Gilead, the Asherites, Jezreel, Ephraim, and 9
Benjamin, and all Israel. Ishbosheth was forty years old when he 10
became king over Israel, and he reigned two years. The tribe of Judah,
however, followed David. David's rule over Judah in Hebron lasted 11
seven years and a half.

Abner son of Ner, with the troops of Saul's son Ishbosheth, marched 12
out from Mahanaim to Gibeon, and Joab son of Zeruiah marched out 13
with David's troops from Hebron.[b] They met at the pool of Gibeon
and took up their positions one on one side of the pool and the other
on the other side. Abner said to Joab, 'Let the young men come 14
forward and join in single combat before us.' Joab answered, 'Yes,
let them.' So they came up, one by one, and took their places, twelve 15
for Benjamin and for Ishbosheth and twelve from David's men.
Each man seized his opponent by the head and thrust his sword into his 16
side; and thus they fell together. That is why that place, which lies in
Gibeon, was called the Field of Blades.

There ensued a fierce battle that day, and Abner and the men of 17
Israel were defeated by David's troops. All three sons of Zeruiah were 18
there, Joab, Abishai and Asahel. Asahel, who was swift as a gazelle on
the plains, ran straight after Abner, swerving neither to right nor left in 19
his pursuit. Abner turned and asked, 'Is it you, Asahel?' Asahel 20
answered, 'It is.' Abner said, 'Turn aside to right or left, tackle one of 21
the young men and win his belt for yourself.' But Asahel would not
abandon the pursuit. Abner again urged him to give it up. 'Why should 22
I kill you?' he said. 'How could I look Joab your brother in the face?'
When he still refused to turn aside, Abner struck him in the belly with 23
a back-thrust of his spear[c] so that the spear came out behind him, and
he fell dead in his tracks. All who came to the place where Asahel lay
dead stopped there. But Joab and Abishai kept up the pursuit of 24
Abner, until, at sunset, they reached the hill of Ammah, opposite Giah
on the road leading to the pastures of Gibeon.

The Benjamites rallied to Abner and, forming themselves into a 25
single company, took up their stand on the top of the hill of Ammah.[d]

[a] Ishyo *in 1 Sam. 14. 49;* Eshbaal *in 1 Chr. 8. 33.*   [b] from Hebron: *so Sept.; Heb. om.*
[c] a back-thrust of his spear: *prob. rdg.; Heb. obscure.*   [d] the hill of Ammah: *prob. rdg.,*
cp. verse 24; Heb. a single hill.

26 Abner called to Joab, 'Must the slaughter go on for ever? Can you not see that it will be all the more bitter in the end? Will you never recall
27 the people from the pursuit of their kinsmen?' Joab answered, 'As God lives, if you had not spoken, the people would not have given up
28 the pursuit till morning.' Then Joab sounded the trumpet, and all the people abandoned the pursuit of the men of Israel and the fighting
29 ceased. Abner and his men moved along the Arabah all that night, crossed the Jordan and went on all the morning till they reached
30 Mahanaim. When Joab returned from the pursuit of Abner, he assembled his troops and found that, besides Asahel, nineteen of
31 David's men were missing. David's forces had routed the Benjamites and the followers of Abner, killing three hundred and sixty of them.
32 They took up Asahel and buried him in his father's tomb at Bethlehem. Joab and his men marched all night, and as day broke they reached Hebron.

3 THE WAR BETWEEN the houses of Saul and David was long drawn out, David growing steadily stronger while the house of Saul became weaker and weaker.
2*a* Sons were born to David at Hebron. His eldest was Amnon, whose
3 mother was Ahinoam of Jezreel; his second Chileab, whose mother was Abigail widow of Nabal of Carmel; the third Absalom, whose mother
4 was Maacah daughter of Talmai king of Geshur; the fourth Adonijah, whose mother was Haggith; the fifth Shephatiah, whose mother was
5 Abital; and the sixth Ithream, whose mother was David's wife Eglah. These were all born to David at Hebron.
6 As the war between the houses of Saul and David went on, Abner
7 made his position gradually stronger in the house of Saul. Now Saul had had a concubine named Rizpah daughter of Aiah. Ishbosheth asked
8 Abner, 'Why have you slept with my father's concubine?' Abner was very angry at this and exclaimed, 'Am I a baboon in the pay of Judah?*b* Up to now I have been loyal to the house of your father Saul, to his brothers and friends, and I have not betrayed you into David's hands; yet you choose this moment to charge me with disloyalty over this
9 woman. But now, so help me God, I will do all I can to bring about
10 what the LORD swore to do for David: I will set to work to bring down the house of Saul and to put David on the throne over Israel and Judah
11 from Dan to Beersheba.' Ishbosheth could not say another word; he
12 was too much afraid of Abner. Then Abner, seeking to make friends where he could, instead of going to David himself sent envoys with this message: 'Let us come to terms, and I will do all I can to bring the
13 whole of Israel over to you.' David sent answer: 'Good, I will come to

[a] *Verses 2–5: cp. 1 Chr. 3. 1–4.* [b] *Lit.* Am I a dog's head which belongs to Judah?

terms with you, but on this one condition, that you do not come into my presence without bringing Saul's daughter Michal to me.' David 14 also sent messengers to Saul's son Ishbosheth with the demand: 'Hand over to me my wife Michal to whom I was betrothed at the price of a hundred Philistine foreskins.' Thereupon Ishbosheth sent and took her 15 away from her husband, Paltiel son of Laish. Paltiel followed her as far 16 as Bahurim, weeping all the way, until Abner ordered him to go back home, and he went.

Abner now approached the elders of Israel and said, 'For some time 17 past you have wanted David for your king; now is the time to act, for 18 this is the word of the LORD about David: "By the hand of my servant David I will deliver my people Israel from the Philistines and from all their enemies."' Abner spoke also to the Benjamites and then went on to 19 report to David at Hebron all that the Israelites and the Benjamites had agreed. When Abner was admitted to David's presence, there were 20 twenty men with him and David gave a feast for them all. Then Abner 21 said to David, 'I shall now go and bring the whole of Israel over to your majesty, and they shall make a covenant with you. Then you will be king over a realm after your own heart.' David dismissed Abner, granting him safe conduct.

David's men and Joab returned from a raid bringing a great deal of 22 plunder with them, and by this time Abner, after his dismissal, was no longer with David in Hebron. So when Joab and his raiding party 23 arrived, they were greeted with the news that Abner son of Ner had been with the king and had departed under safe conduct. Joab went in 24 to the king and said, 'What have you done? Here you have had Abner with you. How could you let him go? He has got clean away! You know 25 Abner son of Ner: he came meaning to deceive you, to learn all about your movements and to find out what you are doing.' When he left 26 David's presence, Joab sent messengers after Abner and they brought him back from the Pool of Sirah; but David knew nothing of all this. On Abner's return to Hebron, Joab drew him aside in the gateway, as 27 though to speak privately with him, and there, in revenge for his brother Asahel, he stabbed him in the belly, and he died. When 28 David heard the news he said, 'I and my realm are for ever innocent in the sight of the LORD of the blood of Abner son of Ner. May it recoil 29 upon the head of Joab and upon all his family! May the house of Joab never be free from running sore or foul disease, nor lack a son fit only to ply the distaff or doomed to die by the sword or beg his bread!' So 30 Joab and Abishai his brother slew Abner because he had killed their brother Asahel in battle at Gibeon. Then David ordered Joab and all the 31 people with him to rend their clothes, put on sackcloth and beat their breasts for Abner, and the king himself walked behind the bier. They 32

buried Abner in Hebron and the king wept aloud at the tomb, while all
33 the people wept with him. The king made this lament for Abner:

> Must Abner die so base a death?
34 > Your hands were not bound,
> your feet not thrust into fetters;
> you fell as one who falls at a ruffian's hands.

And the people wept for him again.

35   They came to persuade David to eat something; but it was still day
and he swore, 'So help me God! I will not touch food of any kind
36 before sunset.' The people took note of this and approved; indeed,
37 everything the king did pleased them. Everyone throughout Israel
knew on that day that the king had had no hand in the murder of
38 Abner son of Ner. The king said to his servants, 'Do you not know
39 that a warrior, a great man, has fallen this day in Israel? King though
I am, I feel weak and powerless in face of these ruthless sons of
Zeruiah; they are too much for me; the LORD will requite the wrongdoer as he deserves.'

4   When Saul's son Ishbosheth[a] heard that Abner had been killed in
2 Hebron, his courage failed him and all Israel was dismayed. Now
Ishbosheth had[b] two officers, who were captains of raiding parties, and
whose names were Baanah and Rechab; they were Benjamites, sons of
3 Rimmon of Beeroth, Beeroth being reckoned part of Benjamin; but the
Beerothites had fled to Gittaim, where they have lived ever since.
4   (Saul's son Jonathan had a son lame in both feet. He was five years
old when word of the death of Saul and Jonathan came from Jezreel.
His nurse had picked him up and fled, but in her hurry to get away he
fell and was crippled. His name was Mephibosheth.)
5   Rechab and Baanah, the sons of Rimmon of Beeroth, came to the
house of Ishbosheth in the heat of the day and went in, while he was
6 taking his midday rest. Now the door-keeper had been sifting wheat,
but she had grown drowsy and fallen asleep, so Rechab and his brother
7 Baanah crept in,[c] found their way to the room where he was asleep on
the bed, and struck him dead. They cut off his head and took it with
them, and, making their way along the Arabah all night, came to
8 Hebron. They brought Ishbosheth's head to David at Hebron and said
to the king, 'Here is the head of Ishbosheth son of Saul, your enemy,
who sought your life. The LORD has avenged your majesty today on
9 Saul and on his family.' David answered Rechab and his brother

---

[a] *So some MSS.; others om.*   [b] had: *prob. rdg.; Heb. om.*   [c] Now the door-keeper...
crept in: *prob. rdg., cp. Sept.; Heb.* They came right into the house carrying wheat, and
they struck him in the belly; Rechab and his brother Baanah were acting stealthily.
They...

Baanah, the sons of Rimmon of Beeroth, with an oath: 'As the LORD lives, who has rescued me from all my troubles! I seized the man who 10 brought me word that Saul was dead and thought it good news; I killed him in Ziklag, and that was how I rewarded him for his news. How much more when ruffians have killed an innocent man on his 11 bed in his own house? Am I not to take vengeance on you now for the blood you have shed, and rid the earth of you?' David gave the word, 12 and the young men killed them; they cut off their hands and feet and hung them up beside the pool in Hebron, but the head of Ishbosheth they took and buried in Abner's tomb at Hebron.

David king in Jerusalem

NOW ALL THE TRIBES of Israel came to David at Hebron and 5 1*a* said to him, 'We are your own flesh and blood. In the past, while 2 Saul was still king over us, you led the forces of Israel to war and you brought them home again. And the LORD said to you, "You shall be shepherd of my people Israel; you shall be their prince."' All the 3 elders of Israel came to the king at Hebron; there David made a covenant with them before the LORD, and they anointed David king over Israel. David came to the throne at the age of thirty and reigned 4 for forty years. In Hebron he had ruled over Judah for seven years 5 and a half, and for thirty-three years he reigned in Jerusalem over Israel and Judah together.

The king and his men went to Jerusalem to attack the Jebusites, 6 whose land it was. The Jebusites said to David, 'Never shall you come in here; not till you have disposed of the blind and the lame', meaning that David should never come in. None the less David did 7 capture the stronghold of Zion, and it is now known as the City of David. David said on that day, 'Everyone who would kill a Jebusite, 8 let him use his grappling-iron to reach the lame and the blind, David's bitter enemies.' That is why they say, 'No blind or lame man shall come into the LORD's house.'*b*

David took up his residence in the stronghold and called it the City 9 of David. He built the city*c* round it, starting at the Millo and working inwards. So David steadily grew stronger, for the LORD the God of 10 Hosts was with him.

Hiram king of Tyre sent an embassy to David; he sent cedar logs, 11*d* and with them carpenters and stonemasons, who built David a house.

[a] *Verses 1–3, 6–10: cp. 1 Chr. 11. 1–9.* [b] the LORD's house: *lit.* the house. [c] the city: *prob. rdg., cp. 1 Chr. 11. 8; Heb. om.* [d] *Verses 11–25: cp. 1 Chr. 14. 1–16.*

12 David knew by now that the LORD had confirmed him as king over Israel and had made his royal power stand higher for the sake of his people Israel.

13   After he had moved from Hebron he took more concubines and wives from Jerusalem; and more sons and daughters were born to him.

14[a] These are the names of the children born to him in Jerusalem:
15 Shammua, Shobab, Nathan, Solomon, Ibhar, Elishua, Nepheg,
16 Japhia, Elishama, Eliada and Eliphelet.

17   When the Philistines learnt that David had been anointed king over Israel, they came up in force to seek him out. David, hearing of this,
18 took refuge in the stronghold. The Philistines had come and overrun
19 the Vale of Rephaim. So David inquired of the LORD, 'If I attack the Philistines, wilt thou deliver them into my hands?' And the LORD
20 answered, 'Go, I will deliver the Philistines into your hands.' So he went up and attacked them at Baal-perazim and defeated them there. 'The LORD has broken through my enemies' lines,' David said, 'as a river breaks its banks.' That is why the place was named Baal-perazim.[b]
21 The Philistines left their idols behind them there, and David and his men carried them off.

22   The Philistines made another attack and overran the Vale of
23 Rephaim. David inquired of the LORD, who said, 'Do not attack now
24 but wheel round and take them in the rear opposite the aspens. As soon as you hear a rustling sound in the tree-tops, then act at once; for the LORD will have gone out before you to defeat the Philistine army.'
25 David did as the LORD had commanded, and drove the Philistines in flight all the way from Geba[c] to Gezer.

6   After that David again summoned the picked men of Israel, thirty
2[d] thousand in all, and went with the whole army to Baalath-judah[e] to fetch the Ark of God which bears the name of the LORD of Hosts,
3 who is enthroned upon the cherubim. They mounted the Ark of God on a new cart and conveyed it from the house of Abinadab on the hill,
4 with Uzzah and Ahio, sons of Abinadab, guiding the cart. They took it with the Ark of God upon it from Abinadab's house on the hill,
5 with Ahio walking in front. David and all Israel danced for joy before the LORD without restraint to the sound of singing,[f] of harps and lutes,
6 of tambourines and castanets and cymbals. But when they came to a certain threshing-floor, the oxen stumbled, and Uzzah reached out to
7 the Ark of God and took hold of it. The LORD was angry with Uzzah and struck him down there for his rash act. So he died there beside the

---

[a] *Verses 14–16: cp. 1 Chr. 3. 5–8; 14. 4–7.*   [b] *That is* Baal of Break-through.   [c] *Or, with 1 Chr. 14. 16 and Sept.,* Gibeon.   [d] *Verses 2–11: cp. 1 Chr. 13. 6–14.*   [e] to Baalath-judah: *prob. rdg., cp. 1 Chr. 13. 6; Heb.* from the lords of Judah.   [f] without...singing: *prob. rdg., cp. 1 Chr. 13. 8; Heb.* to the beating of batons.

Ark of God. David was vexed because the LORD's anger had broken 8
out upon Uzzah, and he called the place Perez-uzzah,[a] the name it
still bears. David was afraid of the LORD that day and said, 'How can 9
I harbour the Ark of the LORD after this?' He felt he could not take 10
the Ark of the LORD with him to the City of David, but turned aside
and carried it to the house of Obed-edom the Gittite. Thus the Ark of 11
the LORD remained at Obed-edom's house for three months, and the
LORD blessed Obed-edom and all his family.

When they told David that the LORD had blessed Obed-edom's 12[b]
family and all that was his because of the Ark of God, he went and
brought up the Ark of God from the house of Obed-edom to the City
of David with much rejoicing. When the bearers of the Ark of the LORD 13
had gone six steps he sacrificed an ox and a buffalo. David, wearing a 14
linen ephod, danced without restraint before the LORD. He and all the 15
Israelites brought up the Ark of the LORD with shouting and blowing of
trumpets. But as the Ark of the LORD was entering the City of David, 16
Saul's daughter Michal looked down through a window and saw King
David leaping and capering before the LORD, and she despised him in
her heart. When they had brought in the Ark of the LORD, they put it 17
in its place inside the tent that David had pitched for it, and David
offered whole-offerings and shared-offerings before the LORD. After 18
David had completed these sacrifices, he blessed the people in the name
of the LORD of Hosts and gave food to all the people, a flat loaf of 19
bread, a portion of meat,[c] and a cake of raisins, to every man and woman
in the whole gathering of the Israelites. Then all the people went home.
When David returned to greet his household, Michal, Saul's daughter, 20
came out to meet him and said, 'What a glorious day for the king of
Israel, when he exposed his person in the sight of his servants' slave-
girls like any empty-headed fool!' David answered Michal, 'But it was 21
done in the presence of the LORD, who chose me instead of your father
and his family and appointed me prince over Israel, the people of the
LORD. Before the LORD I will dance for joy, yes, and I will earn yet 22
more disgrace and lower myself still more in your[d] eyes. But those girls
of whom you speak, they will honour me for it.' Michal, Saul's 23
daughter, had no child to her dying day.

As soon as the king was established in his house and the LORD had 7 1[e]
given him security from his enemies on all sides, he said to Nathan the 2
prophet, 'Here I live in a house of cedar, while the Ark of God is
housed in curtains.' Nathan answered the king, 'Very well, do what- 3
ever you have in mind, for the LORD is with you.' But that night the 4

---

[a] *That is* Outbreak on Uzzah.   [b] *Verses 12–19: cp. 1 Chr. 15. 25 – 16. 3.*   [c] portion of
meat: *mng. of Heb. word uncertain.*   [d] *So Sept.; Heb.* my.   [e] *Verses 1–29: cp. 1 Chr. 17.
1–27.*

5 word of the LORD came to Nathan: 'Go and say to David my servant,
"This is the word of the LORD: Are you the man to build me a house to
6 dwell in? Down to this day I have never dwelt in a house since I
brought Israel up from Egypt; I made my journey in a tent and a
7 tabernacle. Wherever I journeyed with Israel, did I ever ask any of the
judges*a* whom I appointed shepherds of my people Israel why they had
8 not built me a house of cedar?" Then say this to my servant David:
"This is the word of the LORD of Hosts: I took you from the pastures,
9 and from following the sheep, to be prince over my people Israel. I have
been with you wherever you have gone, and have destroyed all the
enemies in your path. I will make you a great name among the great
10 ones of the earth. I will assign a place for my people Israel; there
I will plant them, and they shall dwell in their own land. They shall be
disturbed no more, never again shall wicked men oppress them as they
11 did in the past, ever since the time when I appointed judges over Israel
my people; and I will give you peace from all your enemies. The LORD
12 has told you that he would build up your royal house. When your life
ends and you rest with your forefathers, I will set up one of your family,
one of your own children, to succeed you and I will establish his
13 kingdom. It is he shall build a house in honour of my name, and I will
14 establish his royal throne for ever. I will be his father, and he shall be
my son. When he does wrong, I will punish him as any father might,
15 and not spare the rod. My love will never be withdrawn from him as
16 I withdrew it from Saul, whom I removed from your path. Your family
shall be established and your kingdom shall stand for all time in my*b*
sight, and your throne shall be established for ever."'
17 Nathan recounted to David all that had been said to him and all
18 that had been revealed. Then King David went into the presence of the
LORD and took his place there and said, 'What am I, Lord GOD, and
19 what is my family, that thou hast brought me thus far? It was a small
thing in thy sight to have planned for thy servant's house in days long
past. But such, O Lord GOD, is the lot of a man embarked on a high
20 career.*c* And now what more can I say? for well thou knowest thy
21 servant David, O Lord GOD. Thou hast made good thy word; it was
thy purpose to spread thy servant's fame, and so thou hast raised me to
22 this greatness. Great indeed art thou, O Lord GOD; we have never
23 heard of one like thee; there is no god but thee. And thy people Israel,
to whom can they be compared? Is there any other*d* nation on earth
whom thou, O God, hast set out to redeem from slavery to be thy
people? Any other for whom thou hast done great and terrible things

[a] *Prob. rdg., cp. 1 Chr. 17. 6; Heb.* tribes. [b] *So some MSS.; others* your. [c] embarked
on a high career: *prob. rdg., cp. 1 Chr. 17. 17; Heb. om.* [d] any other: *so Sept.; Heb.*
one.

to win fame for thyself? Any other whom thou hast redeemed for
thyself from Egypt by driving out other nations and their gods to make
way for them[a]? Thou hast established thy people Israel as thy own for 24
ever, and thou, O LORD, hast become their God. But now, LORD God, 25
perform what thou hast promised for thy servant and his house, and
for all time; make good what thou hast said. May thy fame be great for 26
evermore and let men say, "The LORD of Hosts is God over Israel."
So shall the house of thy servant David be established before thee.
O LORD of Hosts, God of Israel, thou hast shown me thy purpose, in 27
saying to thy servant, "I will build up your house"; and therefore I have
made bold to offer this prayer to thee. Thou, O Lord GOD, art God; 28
thou hast made these noble promises to thy servant, and thy promises
come true; be pleased now to bless thy servant's house that it may 29
continue always before thee; thou, O Lord GOD, hast promised, and
thy blessing shall rest upon thy servant's house for evermore.'

After this David defeated the Philistines and conquered them, and 8 1[b]
took from them Metheg-ha-ammah. He defeated the Moabites, and he 2
made them lie along the ground and measured them off with a length
of cord; for every two lengths that were to be put to death one full
length was spared. The Moabites became subject to him and paid him
tribute. David also defeated Hadadezer the Rehobite, king of Zobah, 3
who was on his way to re-erect his monument of victory by[c] the river
Euphrates. From him David captured seventeen hundred horse and 4
twenty thousand foot; he hamstrung all the chariot-horses, except a
hundred which he retained. When the Aramaeans of Damascus came 5
to the help of Hadadezer king of Zobah, David destroyed twenty-two
thousand of them, and established garrisons among these Aramaeans; 6
they became subject to him and paid him tribute. Thus the LORD gave
David victory wherever he went. David took the gold quivers borne by 7
Hadadezer's servants and brought them to Jerusalem; and he also took 8
a great quantity of bronze[d] from Hadadezer's cities, Betah and Berothai.

When Toi king of Hamath heard that David had defeated the entire 9
army of Hadadezer, he sent his son Joram to King David to greet him 10
and to congratulate him on defeating Hadadezer in battle (for Hadadezer
had been at war with Toi); and he brought with him vessels of silver,
gold, and copper, which King David dedicated to the LORD. He dedi- 11
cated also the silver and gold taken from all the nations he had subdued,
from Edom[e] and Moab, from the Ammonites, the Philistines, and 12
Amalek, as well as part of the spoil taken from Hadadezer the Rehobite,
king of Zobah.

[a] by driving...for them: *so Sept., cp. 1 Chr. 17. 21; Heb. unintelligible.*   [b] *Verses 1–14:
cp. 1 Chr. 18. 1–13.*   [c] re-erect...victory by: *or recover control of the crossings of...*
[d] *Or copper.*   [e] *So some MSS.; others* Aram.

13 David made a great name for himself by the slaughter of eighteen
14 thousand Edomites[a] in the Valley of Salt, and on returning he stationed
garrisons throughout Edom, and all the Edomites were subject to him.
Thus the LORD gave victory to David wherever he went.

15[b] David ruled over the whole of Israel and maintained law and justice
16 among all his people. Joab son of Zeruiah was in command of the army;
17 Jehoshaphat son of Ahilud was secretary of state; Zadok and Abiathar
son of Ahimelech, son of Ahitub,[c] were priests; Seraiah was adjutant-
18 general; Benaiah son of Jehoiada commanded[d] the Kerethite and
Pelethite guards. David's sons were priests.

9 David asked, 'Is any member of Saul's family left, to whom I can
2 show true kindness for Jonathan's sake?' There was a servant of Saul's
family named Ziba; and he was summoned to David. The king asked,
3 'Are you Ziba?', and he answered, 'Your servant, sir.' So the king said,
'Is no member of Saul's family still alive to whom I may show the
kindness that God requires?' 'Yes,' said Ziba, 'there is a son of
4 Jonathan still alive; he is a cripple, lame in both feet.' 'Where is he?'
said the king, and Ziba answered, 'He is staying with Machir son of
Ammiel in Lo-debar.'

5 So the king sent and fetched him from Lo-debar, from the house of
6 Machir son of Ammiel, and when Mephibosheth, son of Jonathan and
Saul's grandson, entered David's presence, he prostrated himself and
did obeisance. David said to him, 'Mephibosheth', and he answered,
7 'Your servant, sir.' Then David said, 'Do not be afraid; I mean to show
you kindness for your father Jonathan's sake, and I will give you back
the whole estate of your grandfather[e] Saul; you shall have a place for
8 yourself at my table.' So Mephibosheth prostrated himself again and
said, 'Who am I that you should spare a thought for a dead dog like
9 me?' Then David summoned Saul's servant Ziba to his presence and
said to him, 'I assign to your master's grandson[f] all the property that
10 belonged to Saul and his family. You and your sons and your slaves
must cultivate the land and bring in the harvest to provide for your
master's household,[g] but Mephibosheth your master's grandson[f] shall
have a place at my table.' This man Ziba had fifteen sons and twenty
11 slaves. Then Ziba answered the king, 'I will do all that your majesty
commands.' So Mephibosheth took his place in the royal[h] household
12 like one of the king's sons. He had a young son, named Mica; and the
13 members of Ziba's household were all Mephibosheth's servants, while

[a] *So some MSS.; others* Aramaeans. [b] *Verses 15–18: cp. 20. 23–26; 1 Kgs. 4. 2–6;
1 Chr. 18. 14–17.* [c] *and Abiathar...Ahitub: prob. rdg., cp. 1 Sam. 22. 11, 20; 2 Sam.
20. 25; Heb.* son of Ahitub and Ahimelech son of Abiathar. [d] *commanded: so Vulg.,
cp. 2 Sam. 20. 23; 1 Chr. 18. 17; Heb.* and. [e] *Lit.* father. [f] *Lit.* son. [g] *So some
Sept. MSS.; Heb.* son. [h] *So Luc. Sept.; Heb.* my.

Mephibosheth lived in Jerusalem and had his regular place at the king's table, crippled as he was in both feet.

Some time afterwards the king of the Ammonites died and was 10 1[a] succeeded by his son Hanun. David said, 'I must keep up the same 2 loyal friendship with Hanun son of Nahash as his father showed me', and he sent a mission to condole with him on the death of his father. But when David's envoys entered the country of the Ammonites, the 3 Ammonite princes said to Hanun their lord, 'Do you suppose David means to do honour to your father when he sends you his condolences? These men of his are spies whom he has sent to find out how to overthrow the city.' So Hanun took David's servants, and he shaved off 4 half their beards, cut off half their garments up to the buttocks, and dismissed them. When David heard how they had been treated, he sent 5 to meet them, for they were deeply humiliated, and ordered them to wait in Jericho and not to return until their beards had grown again. The Ammonites knew that they had fallen into bad odour with David, 6 so they hired the Aramaeans of Beth-rehob and of Zobah to come to their help with twenty thousand infantry; they also hired the king of Maacah with a thousand men, and twelve thousand men from Tob. When David heard of it, he sent out Joab and all the fighting men. 7 The Ammonites came and took up their position at the entrance to the 8 city, while the Aramaeans of Zobah and of Rehob and the men of Tob and Maacah took up theirs in the open country. When Joab saw that 9 he was threatened both front and rear, he detailed some picked Israelite troops and drew them up facing the Aramaeans. The rest of 10 his forces he put under his brother Abishai, who took up a position facing the Ammonites. 'If the Aramaeans prove too strong for me,' he 11 said, 'you must come to my relief; and if the Ammonites prove too strong for you, I will come to yours. Courage! Let us fight bravely for 12 our people and for the cities[b] of our God. And the LORD's will be done.' But when Joab and his men came to close quarters with the Aramaeans, 13 they put them to flight; and when the Ammonites saw them in flight, 14 they too fled before Abishai and entered the city. Then Joab returned from the battle against the Ammonites and came to Jerusalem. The 15 Aramaeans saw that they had been worsted by Israel; but they rallied their forces, and Hadadezer sent to summon other Aramaeans from the 16 Great Bend of the Euphrates, and they advanced to Helam under Shobach, commander of Hadadezer's army. Their movement was 17 reported to David, who immediately mustered all the forces of Israel, crossed the Jordan and advanced to meet them at Helam. There the Aramaeans took up positions facing David and engaged him, but were 18 put to flight by Israel. David slew seven hundred Aramaeans in chariots

[a] *Verses 1–19: cp. 1 Chr. 19. 1–19.* [b] *Or* altars.

and forty thousand horsemen, mortally wounding Shobach, who died
19 on the field. When all the vassal kings of Hadadezer saw that they had
been worsted by Israel, they sued for peace and submitted to the
Israelites. The Aramaeans never dared help the Ammonites again.

11 AT THE TURN of the year, when kings take the field,[a] David sent Joab
out with his other officers and all the Israelite forces, and they ravaged
Ammon and laid siege to Rabbah, while David remained in Jerusalem.
2 One evening David got up from his couch and, as he walked about on
the roof of the palace, he saw from there a woman bathing, and she was
3 very beautiful. He sent to inquire who she was, and the answer came,
'It must be Bathsheba daughter of Eliam and wife of Uriah the
4 Hittite.' So he sent messengers to fetch her, and when she came to him,
he had intercourse with her, though she was still being purified after
5 her period, and then she went home. She conceived, and sent word to
6 David that she was pregnant. David ordered Joab to send Uriah the
7 Hittite to him. So Joab sent him to David, and when he arrived, David
asked him for news of Joab and the troops and how the campaign was
8 going; and then said to him, 'Go down to your house and wash your
feet after your journey.' As he left the palace, a present from the king
9 followed him. But Uriah did not return to his house; he lay down by the
10 palace gate with the king's slaves. David heard that Uriah had not gone
home, and said to him, 'You have had a long journey, why did you
11 not go home?' Uriah answered David, 'Israel and Judah are under
canvas,[b] and so is the Ark, and my lord Joab and your majesty's officers
are camping in the open; how can I go home to eat and drink and to
12 sleep with my wife? By your life, I cannot do this!' David then said to
Uriah, 'Stay here another day, and tomorrow I will let you go.' So
13 Uriah stayed in Jerusalem that day. The next day David invited him
to eat and drink with him and made him drunk. But in the evening
Uriah went out to lie down in his blanket[c] among the king's slaves and
did not go home.
14 The following morning David wrote a letter to Joab and sent Uriah
15 with it. He wrote in the letter, 'Put Uriah opposite the enemy where
the fighting is fiercest and then fall back, and leave him to meet his
16 death.' Joab had been watching the city, and he stationed Uriah at a
17 point where he knew they would put up a stout fight. The men of the
city sallied out and engaged Joab, and some of David's guards fell;
18 Uriah the Hittite was also killed. Joab sent David a dispatch with all
19 the news of the battle and gave the messenger these instructions: 'When
20 you have finished your report to the king, if he is angry and asks, "Why

[a] when...field: *so some MSS.*, *cp. 1 Chr. 20. 1; others* when messengers set out.   [b] under
canvas: *or* at Succoth.   [c] in his blanket: *or* on his pallet.

did you go so near the city during the fight? You must have known there would be shooting from the wall. Remember who killed Abimelech son of Jerubbesheth.[a] It was a woman who threw down an upper millstone on to him from the wall of Thebez and killed him! Why did you go so near the wall?"—if he asks this, then tell him, "Your servant Uriah the Hittite also is dead."'

So the messenger set out and, when he came to David, he made his report as Joab had instructed. David was angry with Joab and said to the messenger, 'Why did you go so near the city during the fight? You must have known you would be struck down from the wall. Remember who killed Abimelech son of Jerubbesheth. Was it not a woman who threw down an upper millstone on to him from the wall of Thebez and killed him? Why did you go near the wall?'[b] He answered, 'The enemy massed against us and sallied out into the open; we pressed them back as far as the gateway. There the archers shot down at us from the wall and some of your majesty's men fell; and your servant Uriah the Hittite is dead.' David said to the man, 'Give Joab this message: "Do not let this distress you—there is no knowing where the sword will strike; press home your attack on the city, and you will take it and raze it to the ground"; and tell him to take heart.'

When Uriah's wife heard that her husband was dead, she mourned for him; and when the period of mourning was over, David sent for her and brought her into his house. She became his wife and bore him a son. But what David had done was wrong in the eyes of the LORD.

The LORD sent Nathan the prophet[c] to David, and when he entered his presence, he said to him, 'There were once two men in the same city, one rich and the other poor. The rich man had large flocks and herds, but the poor man had nothing of his own except one little ewe lamb. He reared it himself, and it grew up in his home with his own sons. It ate from his dish, drank from his cup and nestled in his arms; it was like a daughter to him. One day a traveller came to the rich man's house, and he, too mean to take something from his own flocks and herds to serve to his guest, took the poor man's lamb and served up that.' David was very angry, and burst out, 'As the LORD lives, the man who did this deserves to die! He shall pay for the lamb four times over, because he has done this and shown no pity.' Then Nathan said to David, 'You are the man. This is the word of the LORD the God of Israel to you: "I anointed you king over Israel, I rescued you from the power of Saul, I gave you your master's daughter[d] and his wives to be your own, I gave you the daughters[e] of Israel and Judah; and, had this not been

21

22

23

24

25

26

27

12

2

3

4

5

6

7

8

---

[a] Jerubbaal *in Judg. 9. 1.* [b] David was angry...near the wall?': *so Sept.; Heb. om.* [c] the prophet: *so some MSS.; others om.* [d] *Prob. rdg.; Heb.* house. [e] *So Pesh.; Heb.* house.

9 enough, I would have added other favours as great. Why then have you flouted the word of the LORD by doing what is wrong in my eyes? You have struck down Uriah the Hittite with the sword; the man himself you murdered by the sword of the Ammonites, and you have stolen his
10 wife. Now, therefore, since you have despised me and taken the wife of Uriah the Hittite to be your own wife, your family shall never again
11 have rest from the sword." This is the word of the LORD: "I will bring trouble upon you from within your own family; I will take your wives and give them to another man before your eyes, and he will lie with
12 them in broad daylight. What you did was done in secret; but I will do
13 this in the light of day for all Israel to see."' David said to Nathan, 'I have sinned against the LORD.' Nathan answered him, 'The LORD
14 has laid on another the consequences of your sin: you shall not die, but, because in this you have shown your contempt for the LORD,*a* the boy that will be born to you shall die.'

15   When Nathan had gone home, the LORD struck the boy whom
16 Uriah's wife had borne to David, and he was very ill. David prayed to God for the child; he fasted and went in and spent the night fasting,
17 lying on the ground. The older men of his household tried to get him to rise from the ground, but he refused and would eat no food with
18 them. On the seventh day the boy died, and David's servants were afraid to tell him. 'While the boy was alive,' they said, 'we spoke to him, and he did not listen to us; how can we now tell him that the boy
19 is dead? He may do something desperate.' But David saw his servants whispering among themselves and guessed that the boy was dead. He
20 asked, 'Is the boy dead?', and they answered, 'He is dead.' Then David rose from the ground, washed and anointed himself, and put on fresh clothes; he entered the house of the LORD and prostrated himself there. Then he went home, asked for food to be brought, and when it
21 was ready, he ate it. His servants asked him, 'What is this? While the boy lived you fasted and wept for him, but now that he is dead you rise
22 up and eat.' He answered, 'While the boy was still alive I fasted and wept, thinking, "It may be that the LORD will be gracious to me, and
23 the boy may live." But now that he is dead, why should I fast? Can I bring him back again? I shall go to him; he will not come back to me.'
24 David consoled Bathsheba his wife; he went to her and had intercourse with her, and she gave birth to a son and called*b* him Solomon. And
25 because the LORD loved him, he sent word through Nathan the prophet that for the LORD's sake he should be given the name Jedidiah.*c*
26*d*   Joab attacked the Ammonite city of Rabbah and took the King's Pool.
27 He sent messengers to David with this report: 'I have attacked Rabbah

---

[a] the LORD: *prob. rdg.; Heb.* the enemies of the LORD.   [b] and called: *or, as otherwise read,* and he called.   [c] *That is* Beloved of the LORD.   [d] *Verses 26–31: cp. 1 Chr. 20. 1–3.*

and have taken the pool. You had better muster the rest of the army 28
yourself, besiege the city and take it; otherwise I shall take the city and
the name to be proclaimed over it will be mine.' David accordingly 29
mustered his whole forces, marched to Rabbah, attacked it and took it.
He took the crown from the head of Milcom, which weighed a talent of 30
gold and was set with*a* a precious stone, and this he placed on his own
head. He also removed a great quantity of booty from the city; he took 31
its inhabitants and set them to work with saws and other iron tools,
sharp and toothed, and made them work in the brick-kilns. David did
this to all the cities of the Ammonites; then he and all his people
returned to Jerusalem.

Absalom's rebellion and other conflicts

NOW DAVID'S SON ABSALOM had a beautiful sister named 13
Tamar, and Amnon, another of David's sons, fell in love with her.
Amnon was so distressed that he fell sick with love for his half-sister; 2
for he thought it an impossible thing to approach her since she was a
virgin. But he had a friend named Jonadab, son of David's brother 3
Shimeah, who was a very shrewd man. He said to Amnon, 'Why are 4
you so low-spirited morning after morning, my lord? Will you not tell
me?' So Amnon told him that he was in love with Tamar, his brother
Absalom's sister. Jonadab said to him, 'Take to your bed and pretend 5
to be ill. When your father comes to visit you, say to him, "Please let
my sister Tamar come and give me my food. Let her prepare it in
front of me, so that I may watch her and then take it from her own
hands."' So Amnon lay down and pretended to be ill. When the king 6
came to visit him, he said, 'Sir, let my sister Tamar come and make a
few cakes in front of me, and serve them to me with her own hands.'
So David sent a message to Tamar in the palace: 'Go to your brother 7
Amnon's quarters and prepare a meal for him.' Tamar came to her 8
brother and found him lying down; she took some dough and kneaded
it, made the cakes in front of him and baked them. Then she took the 9
pan and turned them out before him. But Amnon refused to eat and
ordered everyone out of the room. When they had all left, he said to 10
Tamar, 'Bring the food over to the recess so that I may eat from your
own hands.' Tamar took the cakes she had made and brought them to
Amnon in the recess. But when she offered them to him, he caught hold 11
of her and said, 'Come to bed with me, sister.' But she answered, 'No, 12
brother, do not dishonour me, we do not do such things in Israel; do

[a] was set with: *so Pesh.; Heb. om.*

13 not behave like a beast. Where could I go and hide my disgrace?—
and you would sink as low as any beast in Israel. Why not speak
14 to the king for me? He will not refuse you leave to marry me.' He
would not listen, but overpowered her, dishonoured her and raped
her.

15 Then Amnon was filled with utter hatred for her; his hatred was
stronger than the love he had felt, and he said to her, 'Get up and go.'
16 She answered, 'No. It is wicked to send me away. This is harder to
17 bear than all you have done to me.' He would not listen to her, but
summoned the boy who attended him and said, 'Get rid of this woman,
18 put her out and bolt the door after her.' She had on a long, sleeved
robe, the usual dress of unmarried princesses; and the boy turned her
19 out and bolted the door. Tamar threw ashes over her head, rent the
long, sleeved robe that she was wearing, put her hands on her head and
20 went away, sobbing as she went. Her brother Absalom asked her, 'Has
your brother Amnon been with you? Keep this to yourself, he is your
brother; do not take it to heart.' So Tamar remained in her brother
21 Absalom's house, desolate. When King David heard the whole story
he was very angry; but he would not hurt Amnon because he was his
22 eldest son and he loved him.[a] Absalom did not speak a single word to
Amnon, friendly or unfriendly; he hated him for having dishonoured his
sister Tamar.

23 Two years later Absalom invited all the king's sons to his sheep-
24 shearing at Baal-hazor, near Ephron.[b] He approached the king and
said, 'Sir, I am shearing; will your majesty and your servants come?'
25 The king answered, 'No, my son, we must not all come and be a
burden to you.' Absalom pressed[c] him, but David was still unwilling
26 to go and dismissed him with his blessing. But Absalom said, 'If you
cannot, may my brother Amnon come with us?' 'Why should he go
27 with you?' the king asked; but Absalom pressed[c] him again, so he let
Amnon and all the other princes go with him.

28 Then Absalom prepared a feast fit for a king.[d] He gave his servants
these orders: 'Bide your time, and when Amnon is merry with wine
I shall say to you, "Strike." Then kill Amnon. You have nothing to
29 fear, these are my orders; be bold and resolute.' Absalom's servants did
as he had told them, whereupon all the king's sons mounted their mules
in haste and set off for home.

30 While they were on their way, a rumour reached David that Absalom
had murdered all the royal princes and that not one was left alive.
31 The king stood up and rent his clothes and then threw himself on the
ground; all his servants were standing round him with their clothes

[a] but he...loved him: *so Sept.; Heb. om.*   [b] *Prob. rdg.; Heb.* Ephraim.   [c] *So Sept.;
Heb.* broke out on...   [d] Then Absalom...king: *so Sept.; Heb. om.*

rent. Then Jonadab, son of David's brother Shimeah, said, 'Your 32
majesty must not think that they have killed all the young princes; only
Amnon is dead; Absalom has looked black ever since Amnon ravished
his sister Tamar. Your majesty must not pay attention to a mere 33
rumour that all the princes are dead; only Amnon is dead.'

Absalom made good his escape. Meanwhile the sentry looked up and 34
saw a crowd of people coming down the hill from the direction of
Horonaim.*a* He came and reported to the king, 'I see men coming
down the hill from Horonaim.'*b* Then Jonadab said to the king, 'Here 35
come the royal princes, just as I said they would.' As he finished 36
speaking, the princes came in and broke into loud lamentations; the
king and all his servants also wept bitterly.

But Absalom went to take refuge with Talmai son of Ammihur king 37
of Geshur; and for a long while the king mourned for Amnon. Absalom, 38
having escaped to Geshur, stayed there for three years; and David's 39
heart*c* went out to him with longing, for he became reconciled to the
death of Amnon.

Joab son of Zeruiah saw that the king's heart was set on Absalom, 14
so he sent to Tekoah and fetched a wise woman. He said to her, 2
'Pretend to be a mourner; put on mourning, go without anointing
yourself, and behave like a bereaved woman who has been long in
mourning. Then go to the king and repeat what I tell you.' He then 3
told her exactly what she was to say.

When the woman from Tekoah came into the king's presence,*d* she 4
threw herself, face downwards, on the ground and did obeisance, and
cried, 'Help, your majesty!' The king asked, 'What is it?' She answered, 5
'O sir, I am a widow; my husband is dead. I had two sons; they came 6
to blows out in the country where there was no one to part them, and
one of them struck the other and killed him. Now, sir, the kinsmen have 7
risen against me and they all cry, "Hand over the man who has killed
his brother, so that we can put him to death for taking his brother's life,
and so cut off the succession." If they do this, they will stamp out my
last live ember and leave my husband no name and no descendant upon
earth.'*e* 'Go home,' said the king to the woman, 'and I will settle your 8
case.' But the woman continued, 'The guilt be on me, your majesty, 9
and on my father's house; let the king and his throne be blameless.'
The king said, 'If anyone says anything more to you, bring him to me 10
and he shall never molest you again.' Then the woman went on, 'Let 11
your majesty call upon the LORD your God, to prevent his kinsmen
bound to vengeance from doing their worst and destroying my son.'

[a] *Prob. rdg.; Heb.* from a road behind him.   [b] He came...from Horonaim': *so Sept.;*
Heb. om.   [c] David's heart: *so Targ.; Heb.* David.   [d] came...presence: *so some MSS.;*
others said to the king.   [e] *See note on verse 15.*

The king swore, 'As the LORD lives, not a hair of your son's head shall fall to the ground.'

12 The woman then said, 'May I add one word more, your majesty?'
13 'Say on', said the king. So she continued, 'How then could it enter your head to do this same wrong to God's people? Out of your own mouth, your majesty, you condemn yourself: you have refused to bring back
14 the man you have banished. We shall all die; we shall be like water that is spilt on the ground and lost; but God will spare the man who does
15[a] not set himself to keep the outlaw in banishment. I came to say this to your majesty because the people have threatened me. I thought, "If
16 I can only speak to the king, perhaps he will attend to my case; for he will listen, and he will save me from the man who is seeking[b] to cut off
17 me and my son together from Israel, God's own possession." I thought too that the words of my lord the king would be a comfort to me; for your majesty is like the angel of God and can decide between right and
18 wrong. The LORD your God be with you!' Then the king said to the woman, 'Tell me no lies: I shall now ask you a question.' 'Speak on,
19 your majesty', she said. So he asked, 'Is the hand of Joab behind you in all this?' 'Your life upon it, sir!' she answered; 'when your majesty asks a question, there is no way round it, right or left. Yes, your servant Joab did prompt me; it was he who put the whole story into my mouth.
20 He did it to give a new turn to this affair. Your majesty is as wise as the angel of God and knows all that goes on in the land.'

21 The king said to Joab, 'You have my consent; go and fetch back the
22 young man Absalom.' Then Joab humbly prostrated himself, took leave of the king with a blessing and said, 'Now I know that I have found favour with your majesty, because you have granted my humble
23 petition.' Joab went at once to Geshur and brought Absalom to Jeru-
24 salem, but the king said, 'Let him go to his own quarters; he shall not come into my presence.' So Absalom went to his own quarters and did not enter the king's presence.

25 No one in all Israel was so greatly admired for his beauty as Absalom; he was without flaw from the crown of his head to the sole
26 of his foot. His hair, when he cut his hair (as he had to do every year, for he found it heavy), weighed two hundred shekels by the royal standard.
27 Three sons were born to Absalom, and a daughter named Tamar, who was a very beautiful woman.

28 Absalom remained in Jerusalem for two whole years without entering
29 the king's presence. He summoned Joab to send a message by him to the king, but Joab refused to come; he sent for him a second time, but he
30 still refused. Then Absalom said to his servants, 'You know that Joab

[a] *Probably verses 15–17 are misplaced and should follow verse 7.* [b] who is seeking: *so Sept.; Heb. om.*

has a field next to mine with barley growing in it; go and set fire to it.'
So Absalom's servants set fire to the field. Joab promptly came to ₃₁
Absalom in his own quarters and said to him, 'Why have your servants
set fire to my field?' Absalom answered Joab, 'I had sent for you to ₃₂
come here, so that I could ask you to give the king this message from
me: "Why did I leave Geshur? It would be better for me if I were still
there. Let me now come into your majesty's presence and, if I have
done any wrong, put me to death."' When Joab went to the king and ₃₃
told him, he summoned Absalom, who came and prostrated himself
humbly before the king; and he greeted Absalom with a kiss.

AFTER THIS, Absalom provided himself with a chariot and horses and ₁₅
an escort of fifty men. He made it a practice to rise early and stand ₂
beside the road which runs through the city gate. He would hail every
man who had a case to bring before the king for judgement and would
ask him what city he came from. When he answered, 'I come, sir, from
such and such a tribe of Israel', Absalom would say to him, 'I can see ₃
that you have a very good case, but you will get no hearing from the
king.' And he would add, 'If only I were appointed judge in the land, ₄
it would be my business to see that everyone who brought a suit or
a claim got justice from me.' Whenever a man approached to prostrate ₅
himself, Absalom would stretch out his hand, take hold of him and
kiss him. By behaving like this to every Israelite who sought the king's ₆
justice, Absalom stole the affections of the Israelites.

At the end of four*ᵃ* years, Absalom said to the king, 'May I have ₇
leave now to go to Hebron to fulfil a vow there that I made to the
LORD? For when I lived in Geshur, in Aram, I made this vow: "If ₈
the LORD brings me back to Jerusalem, I will become a worshipper of
the LORD in Hebron."'*ᵇ* The king answered, 'Certainly you may go'; so ₉
he set off for Hebron at once. Absalom sent runners through all the ₁₀
tribes of Israel with this message: 'As soon as you hear the sound of the
trumpet, then say, "Absalom is king in Hebron."' Two hundred men ₁₁
accompanied Absalom from Jerusalem; they were invited and went
in all innocence, knowing nothing of the affair. Absalom also sent to ₁₂
summon Ahithophel the Gilonite, David's counsellor, from Giloh his
city, where he was offering the customary sacrifices. The conspiracy
gathered strength, and Absalom's supporters increased in number.

When news reached David that the men of Israel had transferred ₁₃
their allegiance to Absalom, he said to those who were with him in ₁₄
Jerusalem, 'We must get away at once; or there will be no escape from
Absalom for any of us. Make haste, or else he will soon be upon us and
bring disaster on us, showing no mercy to anyone in the city.' The ₁₅

[a] *So Luc. Sept.; Heb.* forty.   [b] in Hebron: *so Luc. Sept.; Heb. om.*

king's servants said to him, 'As your majesty thinks best; we are ready.'

16 When the king departed, all his household followed him except ten
17 concubines, whom he left in charge of the palace. At the Far House the
18 king and all the people who were with him halted. His own servants then stood[a] beside him, while the Kerethite and Pelethite guards and Ittai[b] with the six hundred Gittites under him marched past the king.
19 The king said to Ittai the Gittite, 'Are you here too? Why are you coming with us? Go back and stay with the new king, for you are a
20 foreigner and, what is more, an exile from your own country. You came only yesterday, and today must you be compelled to share my wanderings? I do not know where I am going. Go back home and take your countrymen with you; and may the LORD ever be your steadfast
21 friend.'[c] Ittai swore to the king, 'As the LORD lives, your life upon it, wherever you may be, in life or in death, I, your servant, will be there.'
22 David said to Ittai, 'It is well, march on!' So Ittai the Gittite marched on with his whole company and all the dependants who were with him.
23 The whole country-side re-echoed with their weeping. And the king remained standing[d] while all the people crossed the gorge of the Kidron before him, by way of the olive-tree in the wilderness.[e]
24 Zadok also was there with all the Levites; they were carrying the Ark of the Covenant of God, which they set down beside Abiathar[f] until
25 all the people had passed out of the city. But the king said to Zadok, 'Take the Ark of God back to the city. If I find favour with the LORD, he will bring me back and will let me see the Ark and its dwelling-place
26 again. But if he says he does not want me, then here I am; let him do
27 what he pleases with me.' The king went on to say to Zadok the priest, 'Can you make good use of your eyes? You may safely go back to the city, you and Abiathar,[g] and take with you the two young men, Ahimaaz
28 your son and Abiathar's son Jonathan. Do not forget: I will linger at
29 the Fords of the Wilderness until you can send word to me.' Then Zadok and Abiathar took the Ark of God back to Jerusalem and stayed there.
30 David wept as he went up the slope of the Mount of Olives; he was bare-headed and went bare-foot. The people with him all had their
31 heads uncovered and wept as they went. David had been told[h] that Ahithophel was among the conspirators with Absalom, and he prayed, 'Frustrate, O LORD, the counsel of Ahithophel.'
32 As David was approaching the top of the ridge where it was the

[a] *Prob. rdg.; Heb.* passed. [b] and Ittai: *prob. rdg.; Heb. om.* [c] and may...friend: *so Sept.; Heb.* constant love and truth. [d] *Prob. rdg.; Heb.* passing. [e] by way... wilderness: *prob. rdg.; Heb. obscure.* [f] beside Abiathar: *prob. rdg.; Heb.* and Abiathar went up. [g] you and Abiathar: *prob. rdg., cp. verse* 29; *Heb. om.* [h] *So Sept.; Heb.* David told.

custom to prostrate oneself to God, Hushai the Archite was there to
meet him with his tunic rent and earth on his head. David said to him, 33
'If you come with me you will only be a hindrance; but you can help 34
me to frustrate Ahithophel's plans if you go back to the city and say to
Absalom, "I will be your majesty's servant; up to now I have been your
father's servant, and now I will be yours." You will have with you, as you 35
know, the priests Zadok and Abiathar; tell them everything that you
hear in the king's household. They have with them Zadok's son Ahimaaz 36
and Abiathar's son Jonathan, and through them you may pass on to me
everything you hear.' So Hushai, David's friend, came to the city as 37
Absalom was entering Jerusalem.

When David had moved on a little from the top of the ridge, he was 16
met by Ziba the servant of Mephibosheth, who had with him a pair of
asses saddled and loaded with two hundred loaves, a hundred clusters
of raisins, a hundred bunches of summer fruit, and a flagon of wine.
The king said to him, 'What are you doing with these?' Ziba answered, 2
'The asses are for the king's family to ride on, the bread and the
summer fruit are for the servants to eat, and the wine for anyone who
becomes exhausted in the wilderness.' The king asked, 'Where is your 3
master's grandson?' 'He is staying in Jerusalem,' said Ziba, 'for he
thought that the Israelites might now restore to him his grandfather's
throne.' The king said to Ziba, 'You shall have everything that belongs 4
to Mephibosheth.' Ziba said, 'I am your humble servant, sir; may
I continue to stand well with you.'

As King David approached Bahurim, a man of Saul's family, whose 5
name was Shimei son of Gera, came out, cursing as he came. He 6
showered stones right and left on David and on all the king's servants
and on everyone, soldiers and people alike. This is what Shimei said 7
as he cursed him: 'Get out, get out, you scoundrel! you man of blood!
The LORD has taken vengeance on you for the blood of the house of 8
Saul whose throne you stole, and he has given the kingdom to your son
Absalom. You murderer, see how your crimes have overtaken you!'

Then Abishai son of Zeruiah said to the king, 'Why let this dead dog 9
curse your majesty? I will go across and knock off his head.' But the 10
king said, 'What has this to do with you, you sons of Zeruiah? If he
curses and if the LORD has told him to curse David, who can question
it?' David said to Abishai and to all his servants, 'If my son, my own 11
son, is out to kill me, who can wonder at this Benjamite? Let him be,
let him curse; for the LORD has told him to do it. But perhaps the LORD 12
will mark my sufferings*a* and bestow a blessing on me in place of the
curse laid on me this day.' David and his men continued on their way, 13
and Shimei moved along the ridge of the hill parallel to David's path,

[a] *So Sept.; Heb.* my wickedness.

cursing as he went and hurling stones across the valley at him and
14 kicking up the dust. When the king and all the people with him reached
the Jordan,*a* they were worn out; and they refreshed themselves there.
15 By now Absalom and all his Israelites had reached Jerusalem, and
16 Ahithophel with him. When Hushai the Archite, David's friend, met
17 Absalom he said to him, 'Long live the king! Long live the king!' But
Absalom retorted, 'Is this your loyalty to your friend? Why did you
18 not go with him?' Hushai answered Absalom, 'Because I mean to
attach myself to the man chosen by the LORD, by this people, and by all
19 the men of Israel, and with him I will remain. After all, whom ought
I to serve? Should I not serve the son? I will serve you as I have served
20 your father.' Then Absalom said to Ahithophel, 'Give us your advice:
21 how shall we act?' Ahithophel answered, 'Have intercourse with your
father's concubines whom he left in charge of the palace. Then all
Israel will come to hear that you have given great cause of offence to
your father, and this will confirm the resolution of your followers.'
22 So they set up a tent for Absalom on the roof, and he lay with his
23 father's concubines in the sight of all Israel. In those days a man would
seek counsel of Ahithophel as readily as he might make an inquiry of
the word of God; that was how Ahithophel's counsel was esteemed by
David and Absalom.

17 Ahithophel said to Absalom, 'Let me pick twelve thousand men, and
2 I will pursue David tonight. I shall overtake him when he is tired and
dispirited; I will cut him off from his people and they will all scatter;
3 and I shall kill no one but the king. I will bring all the people over to
you as a bride is brought to her husband. It is only one man's life that
4 you are seeking;*b* the rest of the people will be unharmed.' Absalom
5 and all the elders of Israel approved of Ahithophel's advice; but
Absalom said, 'Summon Hushai the Archite and let us hear what he too
6 has to say.' Hushai came, and Absalom told him all that Ahithophel had
said and asked him, 'Shall we do what he says? If not, say what you
think.'

7 Hushai said to Absalom, 'For once the counsel that Ahithophel has
8 given is not good. You know', he went on, 'that your father and the
men with him are hardened warriors and savage as a bear in the wilds
robbed of her cubs. Your father is an old campaigner and will not spend
9 the night with the main body; even now he will be lying hidden in a pit
or in some such place. Then if any of your men are killed at the outset,
anyone who hears the news will say, "Disaster has overtaken the
10 followers of Absalom." The courage of the most resolute and lion-
hearted will melt away, for all Israel knows that your father is a man of

[a] the Jordan: *so Luc. Sept.; Heb. om.*   [b] as a bride...seeking: *so Sept.; Heb.* as the whole
returns, so is the man you are seeking.

war and has determined men with him. My advice is this. Wait until the 11
whole of Israel, from Dan to Beersheba, is gathered about you, countless as grains of sand on the sea-shore, and then you shall march with
them in person.*a* Then we shall come upon him somewhere, wherever 12
he may be, and descend on him like dew falling on the ground, and not
a man of his family or of his followers will be left alive. If he retreats 13
into a city, all Israel will bring ropes to that city, and we will drag it
into a ravine until not a stone can be found on the site.' Absalom and 14
all the men of Israel said, 'Hushai the Archite gives us better advice
than Ahithophel.' It was the LORD's purpose to frustrate Ahithophel's
good advice and so bring disaster upon Absalom.

Hushai told Zadok and Abiathar the priests all the advice that 15
Ahithophel had given to Absalom and the elders of Israel, and also his
own. 'Now send quickly to David,' he said, 'and warn him not to 16
spend the night at the Fords of the Wilderness but to cross the river at
once, before a blow can be struck at the king and his followers.'
Jonathan and Ahimaaz were waiting at En-rogel, and a servant girl 17
would go and tell them what happened and they would pass it on to
King David; for they could not risk being seen entering the city.
But this time a lad saw them and told Absalom; so the two of them 18
hurried to the house of a man in Bahurim. He had a pit in his courtyard, and they climbed down into it. The man's wife took a covering, 19
spread it over the mouth of the pit and strewed grain over it, and no
one was any the wiser. Absalom's servants came to the house and asked 20
the woman, 'Where are Ahimaaz and Jonathan?' She answered, 'They
went beyond the pool.'*b* The men searched but could not find them;
so they went back to Jerusalem. When they had gone the two climbed 21
out of the pit and went off to report to King David and said, 'Over the
water at once, make haste!', and they told him Ahithophel's plan
against him. So David and all his company began at once to cross the 22
Jordan; by daybreak there was not one who had not reached the other
bank.

When Ahithophel saw that his advice had not been taken he saddled 23
his ass, went straight home to his own city, gave his last instructions to
his household, and hanged himself. So he died and was buried in his
father's grave.

By the time that Absalom had crossed the Jordan with the Israelites, 24
David was already at Mahanaim. Absalom had appointed Amasa as 25
commander-in-chief instead of Joab; he was the son of a man named
Ithra, an Ishmaelite,*c* by Abigal daughter of Nahash and sister to
Joab's mother Zeruiah. The Israelites and Absalom camped in the 26

[a] with them in person: *so Sept.; Heb.* in person in the battle.   [b] *Heb. word of uncertain
mng.*   [c] *So one form of Sept., cp. 1 Chr. 2. 17; Heb.* an Israelite.

27 district of Gilead. When David came to Mahanaim, he was met by Shobi son of Nahash from the Ammonite town Rabbah, Machir son of Ammiel from Lo-debar, and Barzillai the Gileadite from Rogelim,
28 bringing mattresses and blankets, bowls and jugs.*^a* They brought also
29 wheat and barley, meal and parched grain, beans and lentils,*^b* honey and curds, sheep and fat cattle, and offered them to David and his people to eat, knowing that the people must be hungry and thirsty and weary in the wilderness.

18 David mustered the people who were with him, and appointed
2 officers over units of a thousand and a hundred. Then he divided the army in three, one division under the command of Joab, one under Joab's brother Abishai son of Zeruiah, and the third under Ittai the Gittite. The king announced to the army that he was coming out himself
3 with them to battle. But they said, 'No, you must not come out; if we turn and run, no one will take any notice, nor will they, even if half of us are killed; but you*^c* are worth ten thousand of us, and it would be
4 better now for you to remain in the city*^d* in support.' 'I will do what you think best', answered the king; and he then stood beside the gate, and
5 the army marched past in their units of a thousand and a hundred. The king gave orders to Joab, Abishai, and Ittai: 'Deal gently with the young man Absalom for my sake.' The whole army heard the king giving all his officers this order to spare Absalom.

6 The army took the field against the Israelites and the battle was fought
7 in the forest of Ephron.*^e* There the Israelites were routed before the onslaught of David's men; so great was the rout that twenty thousand
8 men fell that day. The fighting spread over the whole country-side, and the forest took toll of more people that day than the sword.

9 Now some of David's men caught sight of Absalom. He was riding a mule and, as it passed beneath a great oak,*^f* his head was caught in its boughs; he found himself in mid air and the mule went on from
10 under him. One of the men who saw it went and told Joab, 'I saw
11 Absalom hanging from an oak.' While the man was telling him, Joab broke in, 'You saw him? Why did you not strike him to the ground then and there? I would have given you ten pieces of silver and a belt.'
12 The man answered, 'If you were to put in my hands a thousand pieces of silver, I would not lift a finger against the king's son; for we all heard the king giving orders to you and Abishai and Ittai that whoever finds
13 himself near the young man Absalom must take great care of him. If I had dealt him a treacherous blow, the king would soon have known,
14 and you would have kept well out of it.' 'That is a lie!' said Joab.

[a] bringing...jugs: *prob. rdg.; Heb.* a couch, bowls and a potter's vessel. [b] *So Sept.; Heb. adds* and parched grain. [c] you: *so Sept.; Heb.* now. [d] in the city: *so Sept.; Heb.* from a city. [e] *Prob. rdg.; Heb.* Ephraim. [f] *Or* terebinth.

'I will make a start and show you.'^a So he picked up three stout sticks and drove them against Absalom's chest while he was held fast in the tree and still alive. Then ten young men who were Joab's armour-bearers closed in on Absalom, struck at him and killed him. Joab sounded the trumpet, and the army came back from the pursuit of Israel because he had called it off. They took Absalom's body and flung it into a great pit in the forest, and raised over it a huge pile of stones. The Israelites all fled to their homes.

The pillar in the King's Vale had been set up by Absalom in his lifetime, for he said, 'I have no son to carry on my name.' He had named the pillar after himself; and to this day it is called Absalom's Monument.

Ahimaaz son of Zadok said, 'Let me run and take the news to the king that the LORD has avenged him and delivered him from his enemies.' But Joab replied, 'This is no day for you to be the bearer of news. Another day you may have news to carry, but not today, because the king's son is dead.' Joab told a Cushite to go and report to the king what he had seen. The Cushite bowed low before Joab and set off running. Ahimaaz pleaded again with Joab, 'Come what may,' he said, 'let me run after the Cushite.' 'Why should you, my son?' asked Joab. 'You will get no reward for your news.' 'Come what may,' he said, 'I will run.' 'Go, then', said Joab. So Ahimaaz ran by the road through the Plain of the Jordan and outstripped the Cushite.

David was sitting between the two gates when the watchman went up to the roof of the gatehouse by the wall and, looking out, saw a man running alone. The watchman called to the king and told him. 'If he is alone,' said the king, 'then he has news.' The man came nearer and nearer. Then the watchman saw another man running. He called down to the gate-keeper and said, 'Look, there is another man running alone.' The king said, 'He too brings news.' The watchman said, 'I see by the way he runs that the first runner is Ahimaaz son of Zadok.' The king said, 'He is a good fellow and shall earn the reward for good news.' Ahimaaz called out to the king, 'All is well!' He bowed low before him and said, 'Blessed be the LORD your God who has given into your hands the men who rebelled against your majesty.' The king asked, 'Is all well with the young man Absalom?' Ahimaaz answered, 'Sir, your servant Joab sent me,^b I saw a great commotion, but I did not know what had happened.' The king told him to stand on one side; so he turned aside and stood there. Then the Cushite came in and said, 'Good news, your majesty! The LORD has avenged you this day on all those who rebelled against you.' The king said to the Cushite, 'Is all

---

[a] I will...show you: *or* I can waste no more time on you like this. [b] Sir...sent me: *prob. rdg.;* Heb. At the sending of Joab the king's servant and your servant.

well with the young man Absalom?' The Cushite answered, 'May all the king's enemies and all rebels who would do you harm be as that 33ᵃ young man is.' The king was deeply moved and went up to the roof-chamber over the gate and wept, crying out as he went, 'O, my son! Absalom my son, my son Absalom! If only I had died instead of you! O Absalom, my son, my son.'

19 Joab was told that the king was weeping and mourning for Absalom;
2 and that day victory was turned to mourning for the whole army,
3 because they heard how the king grieved for his son; they stole into the city like men ashamed to show their faces after a defeat in battle.
4 The king hid his face and cried aloud, 'My son Absalom; O Absalom,
5 my son, my son.' But Joab came into the king's quarters and said to him, 'You have put to shame this day all your servants, who have saved
6 you and your sons and daughters, your wives and your concubines. You love those that hate you and hate those that love you; you have made us feel, officers and men alike, that we are nothing to you; for it is plain that if Absalom were still alive and all of us dead, you would be content.
7 Now go at once and give your servants some encouragement; if you refuse, I swear by the LORD that not a man will stay with you tonight, and that would be a worse disaster than any you have suffered since
8 your earliest days.' Then the king rose and took his seat in the gate; and when the army was told that the king was sitting in the gate, they all appeared before him.

Various events of David's reign

MEANWHILE THE ISRAELITES had all scattered to their homes.
9 Throughout all the tribes of Israel people were discussing it among themselves and saying, 'The king has saved us from our enemies and freed us from the power of the Philistines, and now he has
10 fled the country because of Absalom. But Absalom, whom we anointed king, has fallen in battle; so now why have we no plans for bringing the king back?'
11 What all Israel was saying came to the king's ears.ᵇ So he sent word to Zadok and Abiathar the priests: 'Ask the elders of Judah why they
12 should be the last to bring the king back to his palace. Tell them, "You are my brothers, my flesh and my blood; why are you last to bring me
13 back?" And tell Amasa, "You are my own flesh and blood. You shall be my commander-in-chief, so help me God, for the rest of your life in

[a] *19. 1 in Heb.* [b] What...ears: *prob. rdg.; Heb. has these words after* back to his palace *and adds* to his palace.

432

place of Joab."' David's message won all hearts in Judah, and they sent 14
to the king, urging him to return with all his men.

So the king came back to the Jordan; and the men of Judah came to 15
Gilgal to meet him and escort him across the river. Shimei son of Gera 16
the Benjamite from Bahurim hastened down among the men of Judah
to meet King David with a thousand men from Benjamin; Ziba was 17
there too, the servant of Saul's family, with his fifteen sons and twenty
servants. They rushed into the Jordan under the king's eyes and crossed 18
to and fro conveying his household in order to win his favour.
Shimei son of Gera, when he had crossed the river, fell down before the
king and said to him, 'I beg your majesty not to remember how 19
disgracefully your servant behaved when your majesty left Jerusalem;
do not hold it against me or take it to heart. For I humbly acknowledge 20
that I did wrong, and today I am the first of all the house of Joseph to
come down to meet your majesty.' But Abishai son of Zeruiah objected, 21
'Ought not Shimei to be put to death because he cursed the LORD's
anointed prince?' David answered, 'What right have you, you sons of 22
Zeruiah, to oppose me today? Why should any man be put to death this
day in Israel? I know now that I am king of Israel.' Then the king said 23
to Shimei, 'You shall not die', and confirmed it with an oath.

Saul's grandson Mephibosheth also went down to meet the king. He 24
had not dressed his feet,*a* combed his beard or washed his clothes, from
the day the king went out until he returned victorious. When he came 25
from*b* Jerusalem to meet the king, David said to him, 'Why did you
not go with me, Mephibosheth?' He answered, 'Sir, my servant 26
deceived me; I did intend to harness my ass and ride with the king
(for I am lame), but his stories set your majesty against me. Your 27
majesty is like the angel of God; you must do what you think right.
My father's whole family, one and all, deserved to die at your majesty's 28
hands, but you gave me, your servant, my place at your table. What
further favour can I expect of the king?' The king answered, 'You 29
have said enough. My decision is that you and Ziba are to share the
estate.' Mephibosheth said, 'Let him have it all, now that your 30
majesty has come home victorious.'

Barzillai the Gileadite too had come down from Rogelim, and he 31
went as far as the Jordan with the king to send him on his way. Now 32
Barzillai was very old, eighty years of age; it was he who had provided
for the king while he was at Mahanaim, for he was a man of high
standing. The king said to Barzillai, 'Cross over with me and I will 33
provide for your old age*c* in my household in Jerusalem.' Barzillai 34
answered, 'Your servant is far too old to go up with your majesty to

---

[a] *Josephus has* head. [b] *So some Sept. MSS.; Heb.* to. [c] your old age: *so Sept.; Heb.*
for you.

35 Jerusalem. I am already eighty; and I cannot tell good from bad. I cannot taste what I eat or drink; I cannot hear the voices of men and women singing. Why should I be a burden any longer on your majesty?
36 Your servant will attend the king for a short way across the Jordan; and
37 why should the king reward me so handsomely? Let me go back and end my days in my own city near the grave of my father and mother. Here is my son^a Kimham; let him cross over with your majesty, and do
38 for him what you think best.' The king answered, 'Kimham shall cross with me and I will do for him whatever you think best; and I will do for you whatever you ask.'

39 All the people crossed the Jordan while the king waited.^b The king then kissed Barzillai and gave him his blessing. Barzillai went back to
40 his own home; the king crossed over to Gilgal, Kimham with him. All the people of Judah escorted the king over the river, and so did half the people of Israel.

41 The men of Israel came to the king in a body and said, 'Why should our brothers of Judah have got possession of the king's person by joining King David's own men and then escorting him and his house-
42 hold across the Jordan?' The men of Judah replied, 'Because his majesty is our near kinsman. Why should you resent it? Have we eaten
43 at the king's expense? Have we received any gifts?' The men of Israel answered, 'We have ten times your interest in the king and, what is more, we are senior^c to you; why do you disparage us? Were we not the first to speak of bringing the king back?' The men of Judah used language even fiercer than the men of Israel.

20 There happened to be a man there, a scoundrel named Sheba son of Bichri, a man of Benjamin. He blew the trumpet and cried out:

> What share have we in David?
> We have no lot in the son of Jesse.
> Away to your homes, O Israel.

2 The men of Israel all left David, to follow Sheba son of Bichri, but the men of Judah stood by their king and followed him from the Jordan to Jerusalem.

3 When David came home to Jerusalem he took the ten concubines whom he had left in charge of the palace and put them under guard; he maintained them but did not have intercourse with them. They were kept in confinement to the day of their death, widowed in the prime of life.

4 The king said to Amasa, 'Call up the men of Judah and appear
5 before me again in three days' time.' So Amasa went to call up the men

[a] my son: *so Sept.; Heb.* om. [b] *So Luc. Sept.; Heb.* crossed. [c] senior: *so Sept.; Heb.* in David.

434

of Judah, but it took longer than the time fixed by the king. David said 6
to Abishai, 'Sheba son of Bichri will give us more trouble than
Absalom; take the royal bodyguard and follow him closely. If he has
occupied some fortified cities, he may escape us.' Abishai was followed 7
by Joab^a with the Kerethite and Pelethite guards and all the fighting
men; they left Jerusalem in pursuit of Sheba son of Bichri. When they 8
reached the great stone in Gibeon, Amasa came towards them. Joab
was wearing his tunic and over it a belt supporting a sword in its
scabbard. He came forward, concealing his treachery, and said to 9
Amasa, 'I hope you are well, my brother', and with his right hand he
grasped Amasa's beard to kiss him. Amasa was not on his guard against 10
the sword in Joab's hand. Joab struck him with it in the belly and
his entrails poured out to the ground; he did not strike a second blow,
for Amasa was dead. Joab and his brother Abishai went on in pursuit of
Sheba son of Bichri. One of Joab's young men stood over Amasa and 11
called out, 'Follow Joab, all who are for Joab and for David!' Amasa's 12
body lay soaked in blood in the middle of the road, and when the man
saw how all the people stopped, he rolled him off the road into the field
and threw a cloak over him; for everyone who came by saw the body
and stopped. When he had been dragged from the road, they all went 13
on after Joab in pursuit of Sheba son of Bichri.

Sheba passed through all the tribes of Israel until he came to Abel- 14
beth-maacah,^b and all the clan of Bichri^c rallied to him and followed him
into the city. Joab's forces came up and besieged him in Abel-beth- 15
maacah, raised a siege-ramp against it and began undermining the wall
to bring it down. Then a wise woman stood on the rampart^d and called 16
from the city, 'Listen, listen! Tell Joab to step forward and let me
speak with him.' So he came forward and the woman said, 'Are you 17
Joab?' He answered, 'I am.' 'Listen to what I have to say, sir', she
went on, to which he replied, 'I am listening.' 'In the old days', she 18
said, 'there was a saying, "Go to Abel for the answer", and that settled
the matter. My city is known to be one of the most peaceable and loyal^e 19
in Israel; she is like a watchful mother in Israel, and you are seeking to
kill her. Would you destroy the LORD's own possession?' Joab answered, 20
'God forbid, far be it from me to ruin or destroy! That is not our aim; 21
but a man from the hill-country of Ephraim named Sheba son of Bichri
has raised a revolt against King David; surrender this one man, and
I will retire from the city.' The woman said to Joab, 'His head shall be
thrown to you over the wall.' Then the woman withdrew, and her 22

[a] Abishai...Joab: *prob. rdg.; Heb.* Some men of Joab followed him. [b] *Prob. rdg., cp.*
verse 15; Heb. Abel and Beth-maacah. [c] *Prob. rdg.; Heb.* Beri. [d] stood...rampart:
transposed from verse 15. [e] My city...loyal: *prob. rdg.; Heb.* I am the requited ones of
the loyal ones.

wisdom won over the assembled people; they cut off Sheba's head and threw it to Joab. Then he sounded the trumpet and the whole army left the city and dispersed to their homes, while Joab went back to the king in Jerusalem.

23[a]   Joab was in command of the army,[b] and Benaiah son of Jehoiada
24   commanded the Kerethite and Pelethite guards. Adoram was in charge of the forced levy, and Jehoshaphat son of Ahilud was secretary of state.
25   Sheva was adjutant-general, and Zadok and Abiathar were priests;
26   Ira the Jairite was David's priest.

21 IN DAVID'S REIGN there was a famine that lasted year after year for three years. So David consulted the LORD, and he answered, 'Blood-guilt rests on Saul and on his family because he put the Gibeonites to
2   death.' (The Gibeonites were not of Israelite descent; they were a remnant of Amorite stock whom the Israelites had sworn that they would spare. Saul, however, had sought to exterminate them in his zeal for Israel and Judah.) King David summoned the Gibeonites,
3   therefore, and said to them, 'What can be done for you? How can I make expiation, so that you may have cause to bless the LORD's own
4   people?' The Gibeonites answered, 'Our feud with Saul and his family cannot be settled in silver and gold, and there is no one man in Israel whose death would content us.' 'Then what do you want me to do for
5   you?' asked David. They answered, 'Let us make an end of the man who caused our undoing and ruined us, so that he shall never again
6   have his place within the borders of Israel. Hand over to us seven of that man's sons, and we will hurl them down to their death before[c] the LORD in Gibeah of Saul, the LORD's chosen king.' The king agreed to
7   hand them over, but he spared Mephibosheth son of Jonathan, son of Saul, because of the oath that had been taken in the LORD's name by
8   David and Saul's son Jonathan. The king then took the two sons whom Rizpah daughter of Aiah had borne to Saul, Armoni and Mephi-bosheth, and the five sons whom Merab,[d] Saul's daughter, had borne to
9   Adriel son of Barzillai of Meholah. He handed them over to the Gibeonites, and they flung them down from the mountain before the LORD; the seven of them fell together. They were put to death in the
10 first days of harvest at the beginning of the barley harvest. Rizpah daughter of Aiah took sackcloth and spread it out as a bed for herself on the rock, from the beginning of harvest until the rains came and fell from heaven upon the bodies. She allowed no bird to set upon them by
11 day nor any wild beast by night. When David was told what Rizpah
12 daughter of Aiah the concubine of Saul had done, he went and took the

[a] *Verses 23–26: cp. 8. 16–18; 1 Kgs. 4. 2–6; 1 Chr. 18. 15–17.*   [b] *Prob. rdg., cp. 8. 16; Heb. adds* Israel.   [c] *Or* for.   [d] *So some MSS.; others* Michal.

bones of Saul and his son Jonathan from the citizens of Jabesh-gilead, who had stolen them from the public square at Beth-shan, where the Philistines had hung them on the day they defeated Saul at Gilboa. He removed the bones of Saul and Jonathan from there and gathered 13 up the bones of the men who had been hurled to death. They buried 14 the bones of Saul and his son Jonathan in the territory of Benjamin at Zela, in the grave of his father Kish. Everything was done as the king ordered, and thereafter the LORD was willing to accept prayers offered for the country.

Once again war broke out between the Philistines and Israel. David 15 and his men went down to the battle, but as he fought with the Philistines he fell exhausted. Then Benob, one of the race of the 16 Rephaim, whose bronze spear weighed three hundred shekels*a* and who wore a belt of honour,*b* took David prisoner and was about to kill him. But Abishai son of Zeruiah came to David's help, struck the Philistine 17 down and killed him. Then David's officers took an oath that he should never again go out with them to war, for fear that the lamp of Israel might be extinguished.

Some time later war with the Philistines broke out again in Gob: it 18*c* was then that Sibbechai of Hushah killed Saph, a descendant of the Rephaim. In another war with the Philistines in Gob, Elhanan son of 19 Jair*d* of Bethlehem killed Goliath of Gath, whose spear had a shaft like a weaver's beam. In yet another war in Gath there appeared a giant 20 with six fingers on each hand and six toes on each foot, twenty-four in all. He too was descended from the Rephaim; and, when he defied 21 Israel, Jonathan son of David's brother Shimeai killed him. These four 22 giants were the descendants of the Rephaim in Gath, and they all fell at the hands of David and his men.

THESE ARE THE WORDS of the song David sang to the LORD on the 22 day when the LORD delivered him from the power of all his enemies and from the power of Saul:

> The LORD is my stronghold, my fortress and my champion,   2*e*
> my God, my rock where I find safety;   3
> my shield, my mountain fastness, my strong tower,
> my refuge, my deliverer, who saves me from violence.
> I will call on the LORD to whom all praise is due,   4
> and I shall be delivered from my enemies.
> When the waves of death swept round me,   5
> and torrents of destruction overtook me,

[a] shekels: *prob. rdg.; Heb.* weight.   [b] *Lit.* a new belt.   [c] *Verses 18–22: cp. 1 Chr. 20. 4–7.*   [d] Jair: *prob. rdg., cp. 1 Chr. 20. 5; Heb.* Jaare-oregim.   [e] *Verses 2–51: cp. Ps. 18. 2–50.*

6   the bonds of Sheol tightened about me,
    the snares of death were set to catch me;

7   then in anguish of heart I cried to the LORD,
    I called for help to my God;
    he heard me from his temple,
    and my cry rang in his ears.

8   The earth heaved and quaked,
    heaven's foundations shook;
    they heaved, because he was angry.

9   Smoke rose from his nostrils,
    devouring fire came out of his mouth,
    glowing coals and searing heat.

10   He swept the skies aside as he descended,
    thick darkness lay under his feet.

11   He rode on a cherub, he flew through the air;
    he swooped[a] on the wings of the wind.

12   He curtained himself in darkness
    and made dense vapour his canopy.

13   Thick clouds came out of the radiance before him;
    glowing coals burned brightly.

14   The LORD thundered from the heavens
    and the voice of the Most High spoke out.

15   He loosed his arrows, he sped them far and wide,
    his lightning shafts, and sent them echoing.

16   The channels of the sea-bed were revealed,
    the foundations of earth laid bare
    at the LORD's rebuke,
    at the blast of the breath of his nostrils.

17   He reached down from the height and took me,
    he drew me out of mighty waters,

18   he rescued me from my enemies, strong as they were,
    from my foes when they grew too powerful for me.

19   They confronted me in the hour of my peril,
    but the LORD was my buttress.

20   He brought me out into an open place,
    he rescued me because he delighted in me.

21   The LORD rewarded me as my righteousness deserved;
    my hands were clean, and he requited me.

22   For I have followed the ways of the LORD
    and have not turned wickedly from my God;

23   all his laws are before my eyes,
    I have not failed to follow his decrees.

[a] *Prob. rdg., cp. Ps. 18. 10; Heb.* was seen.

In his sight I was blameless   24
and kept myself from wilful sin;
the LORD requited me as my righteousness deserved   25
and my purity in his eyes.

With the loyal thou showest thyself loyal   26
and with the blameless man blameless.
With the savage man thou showest thyself savage,   27
and*a* tortuous with the perverse.
Thou deliverest humble folk,   28
thou lookest with contempt upon the proud.
Thou, LORD, art my lamp,   29
and the LORD will lighten my darkness.
With thy help I leap over a bank,   30
by God's aid I spring over a wall.

The way of God is perfect,   31
the LORD's word has stood the test;
he is the shield of all who take refuge in him.
What god is there but the LORD?   32
What rock but our God?—
the God who girds me*b* with strength   33
and makes my way blameless,*c*
who makes me swift as a hind   34
and sets me secure on the*d* mountains;
who trains my hands for battle,   35
and my arms aim an arrow tipped with bronze.

Thou hast given me the shield of thy salvation,   36
in thy providence thou makest me great.
Thou givest me room for my steps,   37
my feet have not faltered.
I pursue my enemies and destroy them,   38
I do not return until I have made an end of them.
I make an end of them, I strike them down;   39
they rise no more, they fall beneath my feet.
Thou dost arm me with strength for the battle   40
and dost subdue my foes before me.
Thou settest*e* my foot on my enemies' necks,   41
and I bring to nothing those that hate me.
They cry out*f* and there is no one to help them,   42
they cry to the LORD and he does not answer.

[a] With the savage...savage, and: *or* With the pure thou showest thyself pure, but...
[b] who girds me: *prob. rdg., cp. Ps. 18.32; Heb.* my refuge *or* my strength. [c] and makes...
blameless: *prob. rdg., cp. Ps. 18. 32; Heb. unintelligible.* [d] *So Sept.; Heb.* my. [e] *Prob.
rdg., cp. Ps. 18. 40; Heb. unintelligible.* [f] cry out: *prob. rdg., cp. Ps. 18. 41; Heb.* look.

43   I will pound them fine as dust on the ground,
    like mud in the streets will I trample them.*a*

44   Thou dost deliver me from the clamour of the people,*b*
    and makest*c* me master of the nations.
    A people I never knew shall be my subjects.

45   Foreigners shall come cringing to me;
    as soon as they hear tell of me, they shall obey me.

46   Foreigners shall be brought captive to me,
    and come limping from their strongholds.

47   The LORD lives, blessed is my rock,
    high above all is God my rock and safe refuge.

48   O God, who grantest me vengeance,
    who dost subdue peoples under me,

49   who dost snatch me from my foes and set me over my enemies,
    thou dost deliver me from violent men.

50   Therefore, LORD, I will praise thee among the nations
    and sing psalms to thy name,

51   to one who gives his king great victories
    and in all his acts keeps faith with his anointed king,
    with David and his descendants for ever.

23 These are the last words of David:

    The very word of David son of Jesse,
    the very word of the man whom the High God raised up,
    the anointed prince of the God of Jacob,
    and the singer of Israel's psalms:

2   the spirit of the LORD has spoken through me,
    and his word is on my lips.

3   The God of Israel spoke,
    the Rock of Israel spoke of me:
    'He who rules men in justice,
    who rules in the fear of God,

4   is like the light of morning at sunrise,
    a morning that is cloudless after rain
    and makes the grass sparkle from the earth.'

5   Surely, surely my house is true to God;
    for he has made a pact with me for all time,
    its terms spelled out and faithfully kept,
    my whole salvation, all my*d* delight.

---

[a] *Prob. rdg., cp. Ps. 18. 42;* Heb. adds will I stamp them down. [b] the clamour of the people: *so Sept. and Ps. 18. 43;* Heb. obscure. [c] *So Luc. Sept. and Ps. 18. 43;* Heb. keepest. [d] *Prob. rdg.;* Heb. om.

But the ungodly put forth no shoots,   6
they are all like briars tossed aside;
none dare put out his hand to pick them up,
none touch them but[a] with tool of iron or of wood;   7
they are fit only for burning in the fire.[b]

THESE ARE THE NAMES of David's heroes. First came Ishbosheth [8c]
the Hachmonite,[d] chief of the three;[e] it was he who brandished his
spear[f] over eight hundred dead, all slain at one time. Next to him was 9
Eleazar son of Dodo the Ahohite,[g] one of the heroic three. He was with
David at Pas-dammim where the Philistines[h] had gathered for battle.
When the Israelites fell back, he stood his ground and rained blows on 10
the Philistines until, from sheer weariness, his hand stuck fast to his
sword; and so the LORD brought about a great victory that day. Afterwards the people rallied behind him, but it was only to strip the dead.
Next to him was Shammah son of Agee a Hararite. The Philistines had 11
gathered at Lehi, where there was a field with a fine crop of lentils;
and, when the Philistines put the people to flight, he stood his ground 12
in the field, saved it[i] and defeated them. So the LORD again brought
about a great victory.

Three of the thirty went down towards the beginning of harvest to 13
join David at the cave of Adullam, while a band of Philistines was
encamped in the Vale of Rephaim. At that time David was in the 14
stronghold and a Philistine garrison held Bethlehem. One day a 15
longing came over David, and he exclaimed, 'If only I could have a
drink of water from the well[j] by the gate of Bethlehem!' At this the 16
heroic three made their way through the Philistine lines and drew water
from the well by the gate of Bethlehem and brought it to David. But
David refused to drink it; he poured it out to the LORD and said, 'God 17
forbid that I should do such a thing! Can I drink[k] the blood of these
men who risked their lives for it?' So he would not drink it. Such were
the exploits of the heroic three.

Abishai the brother of Joab son of Zeruiah was chief of the thirty.[l] 18
He once brandished his spear over three hundred dead, and he was
famous among the thirty.[l] Some think he even surpassed the rest of the 19
thirty[m] in reputation, and he became their captain, but he did not rival
the three. Benaiah son of Jehoiada, from Kabzeel, was a hero of many 20

[a] but: *prob. rdg.*; *Heb.* he shall be filled. [b] *Prob. rdg.*; *Heb. adds* in sitting. [c] *Verses
8–39: cp. 1 Chr. 11. 10–41.* [d] *Prob. rdg.*; *Heb.* Josheb-basshebeth a Tahchemonite.
[e] *So Luc. Sept.*; *Heb.* third. [f] who...spear: *prob. rdg., cp. 1 Chr. 11. 11*; *Heb. unintelligible.* [g] the Ahohite: *prob. rdg., cp. 1 Chr. 11. 12*; *Heb.* son of Ahohi. [h] He was
...Philistines: *prob. rdg., cp. 1 Chr. 11. 13*; *Heb.* With David when they taunted them among
the Philistines. [i] saved it: *or* cleared it of the Philistines. [j] *Or* cistern. [k] I drink:
prob. rdg., cp. 1 Chr. 11. 19; *Heb. om.* [l] *So Pesh.*; *Heb.* three. [m] *Prob. rdg.*; *Heb.* three.

exploits. It was he who smote the two champions of Moab, and who
21 went down into a pit and killed a lion on a snowy day. It was he who
also killed the Egyptian, a man of striking appearance armed with a
spear: he went to meet him with a club, snatched the spear out of the
22 Egyptian's hand and killed him with his own weapon. Such were the
23 exploits of Benaiah son of Jehoiada, famous among the heroic thirty.[a] He
was more famous than the rest of the thirty, but he did not rival the
three. David appointed him to his household.

24   Asahel the brother of Joab was one of the thirty, and Elhanan son of
25 Dodo from[b] Bethlehem; Shammah from Harod, and Elika from Harod;
26, 27 Helez from Beth-pelet,[c] and Ira son of Ikkesh from Tekoa; Abiezer
28 from Anathoth, and Mebunnai from Hushah; Zalmon the Ahohite, and
29 Maharai from Netophah; Heled[d] son of Baanah from Netophah, and
30 Ittai son of Ribai from Gibeah of Benjamin; Benaiah from Pirathon,
31 and Hiddai from the ravines of Gaash; Abi-albon from Beth-arabah,[e]
32 and Azmoth from Bahurim;[f] Eliahba from Shaalbon, and Hashem the
33 Gizonite; Jonathan son of[g] Shammah the Hararite, and Ahiam son of
34 Sharar the Hararite;[h] Eliphelet son of Ahasbai son of the Maacathite,
35 and Eliam son of Ahithophel the Gilonite; Hezrai from Carmel, and
36 Paarai the Arbite; Igal son of Nathan from Zobah, and Bani the
37 Gadite; Zelek the Ammonite, and Naharai from Beeroth, armour-
38 bearer to Joab son of Zeruiah; Ira the Ithrite, Gareb the Ithrite,
39 and Uriah the Hittite: there were thirty-seven in all.

24 1[i] ONCE AGAIN THE ISRAELITES felt the LORD's anger, when he
incited David against them and gave him orders that Israel and Judah
2 should be counted. So he instructed Joab and the officers of the army[j]
with him to go round all the tribes of Israel, from Dan to Beersheba,
3 and make a record of the people and report the number to him. Joab
answered, 'Even if the LORD your God should increase the people a
hundredfold and your majesty should live to see it, what pleasure would
4 that give your majesty?' But Joab and the officers were overruled by the
5 king and they left his presence in order to count the people. They
crossed the Jordan and began at Aroer and the level land of the gorge,
6 proceeding towards Gad[k] and Jazer. They came to Gilead and to the
land of the Hittites, to Kadesh,[l] and then to Dan and Iyyon[m] and so

[a] *Prob. rdg.; Heb.* three. [b] *from: so some MSS.; others om.* [c] *Prob. rdg., cp. Josh. 15. 27; Heb.* from Pelet. [d] *So many MSS.; others* Heleb. [e] *Prob. rdg., cp. Josh. 18. 22; Heb.* from Arabah. [f] *Prob. rdg., cp. 1 Chr. 11.33; Heb.* from Barhum. [g] Hashem ...*son of: prob. rdg., cp. 1 Chr. 11. 34; Heb.* the sons of Jashen, Jonathan. [h] *Prob. rdg., cp. 1 Chr. 11. 35; Heb.* Ararite. [i] *Verses 1–25: cp. 1 Chr. 21. 1–27.* [j] Joab...army: *prob. rdg., cp. 1 Chr. 21. 2; Heb.* Joab the officer of the army. [k] began at...Gad: *prob. rdg.; Heb.* encamped in Aroer on the right of the level land of the gorge Gad. [l] of the Hittites, to Kadesh: *so Luc. Sept.; Heb.* of Tahtim, Hodshi. [m] *Prob. rdg., cp. 1 Kgs. 15. 20; Heb.* Yaan.

round[a] towards Sidon. They went as far as the walled city of Tyre and 7 all the towns of the Hivites and Canaanites, and then went on to the Negeb of Judah at Beersheba. They covered the whole country and 8 arrived back at Jerusalem after nine months and twenty days. Joab 9 reported to the king the total number of people: the number of able-bodied men, capable of bearing arms, was eight hundred thousand in Israel and five hundred thousand in Judah.

After he had counted the people David's conscience[b] smote him, and 10 he said to the LORD, 'I have done a very wicked thing: I pray thee, LORD, remove thy servant's guilt, for I have been very foolish.' He rose 11 next morning, and meanwhile the command of the LORD had come to the prophet Gad, David's seer, to go and speak to David: 'This is the 12 word of the LORD: I have three things in store for you; choose one and I will bring it upon you.' So Gad came to David and repeated this to 13 him and said, 'Is it to be three[c] years of famine in your land, or three months of flight with the enemy at your heels, or three days of pestilence in your land? Consider carefully what answer I am to take back to him who sent me.' Thereupon David said to Gad, 'I am in a desperate 14 plight; let us fall into the hands of the LORD, for his mercy is great; and let me not fall into the hands of men.' So the LORD sent a pestilence 15 throughout Israel from morning till the hour of dinner, and from Dan to Beersheba seventy thousand of the people died. Then the angel 16 stretched out his arm towards Jerusalem to destroy it; but the LORD repented of the evil and said to the angel who was destroying the people, 'Enough! Stay your hand.' At that moment the angel of the LORD was standing by the threshing-floor of Araunah the Jebusite.

When David saw the angel who was striking down the people, he 17 said to the LORD, 'It is I who have done wrong, the sin is mine; but these poor sheep, what have they done? Let thy hand fall upon me and upon my family.' That same day Gad came to David and said to him, 18 'Go and set up an altar to the LORD on the threshing-floor of Araunah the Jebusite.' David did what Gad told him to do, and went up as the 19 LORD had commanded. When Araunah looked down and saw the king 20 and his servants coming over towards him, he went out, prostrated himself low before the king and said, 'Why has your majesty come to 21 visit his servant?' David answered, 'To buy the threshing-floor from you to build an altar to the LORD, so that the plague which has attacked the people may be stopped.' Araunah answered David, 'I beg your 22 majesty to take it and sacrifice what you think fit. I have here the oxen for a whole-offering, and their harness and the threshing-sledges for the fuel.' Araunah[d] gave it all to the king for his own use and said to 23

[a] *So Sept.; Heb. obscure.*   [b] *Lit.* heart.   [c] *So Sept., cp. 1 Chr. 21. 12; Heb.* seven.
[d] *Prob. rdg.; Heb. adds* the king.

24 him, 'May the LORD your God accept you.' But the king said to Araunah, 'No, I will buy it from you; I will not offer to the LORD my God whole-offerings that have cost me nothing.' So David bought the
25 threshing-floor and the oxen for fifty shekels of silver. He built an altar to the LORD there and offered whole-offerings and shared-offerings. Then the LORD yielded to his prayer for the land; and the plague in Israel stopped.

THE FIRST BOOK OF
KINGS

The death of David and accession of Solomon

KING DAVID WAS NOW a very old man and, though 1
they wrapped clothes round him, he could not keep warm. So 2
his household said to him, 'Let us find a young virgin for your
majesty, to attend you and take care of you; and let her lie in your
bosom, sir, and make you warm.' So they searched all over Israel for a 3
beautiful maiden and found Abishag, a Shunammite, and brought her
to the king. She was a very beautiful girl, and she took care of the king 4
and waited on him, but he had no intercourse with her.

Now Adonijah, whose mother was Haggith, was boasting that he 5
was to be king; and he had already provided himself with chariots and
horsemen[a] and fifty outrunners. Never in his life had his father 6
corrected him or asked why he behaved as he did. He was a very
handsome man, too, and was next in age to Absalom. He talked with 7
Joab son of Zeruiah and with Abiathar the priest, and they gave him
their strong support; but Zadok the priest, Benaiah son of Jehoiada, 8
Nathan the prophet, Shimei, Rei, and David's bodyguard of heroes,
did not take his side. Adonijah then held a sacrifice of sheep, oxen, and 9
buffaloes at the stone Zoheleth beside En-rogel, and he invited all his
royal brothers and all those officers of the household who were of the
tribe of Judah. But he did not invite Nathan the prophet, Benaiah and 10
the bodyguard, or Solomon his brother.

Then Nathan said to Bathsheba, the mother of Solomon, 'Have you 11
not heard that Adonijah son of Haggith has become king, all unknown
to our lord David? Now come, let me advise you what to do for your 12
own safety and for the safety of your son Solomon. Go in and see King 13
David and say to him, "Did not your majesty swear to me, your servant,
that my son Solomon should succeed you as king; that it was he who
should sit on your throne? Why then has Adonijah become king?" Then 14
while you are still speaking there with the king, I will follow you in and
tell the whole story.'

So Bathsheba went to the king in his private chamber; he was now 15
very old, and Abishag the Shunammite was waiting on him. Bathsheba 16
bowed before the king and prostrated herself. 'What do you want?'
said the king. She answered, 'My lord, you swore to me your servant, by 17

[a] Or a chariot and horses.

445

the LORD your God, that my son Solomon should succeed you as king,
18 and that he should sit on your throne. But now, here is Adonijah
19 become king, all unknown to your majesty. He has sacrificed great
numbers of oxen, buffaloes, and sheep, and has invited to the feast all
the king's sons, and Abiathar the priest, and Joab the commander-in-
20 chief, but he has not invited your servant Solomon. And now,^a your
majesty, all Israel is looking to you to announce who is to succeed you
21 on the throne. Otherwise, when you, sir, rest with your forefathers, my
22 son Solomon and I shall be treated as criminals.' She was still speaking
23 to the king when Nathan the prophet arrived. The king was told that
Nathan was there; he came into the king's presence and prostrated
24 himself with his face to the ground. 'My lord,' he said, 'your majesty
must, I suppose, have declared that Adonijah should succeed you and
25 that he should sit on your throne. He has today gone down and sacrificed
great numbers of oxen, buffaloes, and sheep, and has invited to the
feast all the king's sons, Joab the commander-in-chief,^b and Abiathar
the priest; and at this very moment they are eating and drinking in his
26 presence and shouting, "Long live King Adonijah!" But he has not
invited me your servant, Zadok the priest, Benaiah son of Jehoiada, or
27 your servant Solomon. Has this been done by your majesty's authority,
while we^c your servants have not been told who should succeed you on
28 the throne?' Thereupon King David said, 'Call Bathsheba', and she
29 came into the king's presence and stood before him. Then the king
swore an oath to her: 'As the LORD lives, who has delivered me from all
30 my troubles: I swore by the LORD the God of Israel that Solomon your
son should succeed me and that he should sit on my throne, and this day
31 I give effect to my oath.' Bathsheba bowed low to the king and prostrated herself; and she said, 'May my lord King David live for ever!'
32 Then King David said, 'Call Zadok the priest, Nathan the prophet,
33 and Benaiah son of Jehoiada.' They came into the king's presence and
he gave them these orders: 'Take the officers of the household with you;
mount my son Solomon on the king's mule and escort him down to
34 Gihon. There Zadok the priest and Nathan the prophet shall anoint
him king over Israel. Sound the trumpet and shout, "Long live King
35 Solomon!" Then escort him home again, and he shall come and sit on
my throne and reign in my place; for he is the man that I have appointed
36 prince over Israel and Judah.' Benaiah son of Jehoiada answered the
king, 'It shall be done. And may the LORD, the God of my lord the
37 king, confirm it! As the LORD has been with your majesty, so may he be
with Solomon; may he make his throne even greater than the throne of

[a] And now: *so many MSS.; others* And you.   [b] Joab the commander-in-chief: *so Luc.*
Sept.; Heb. the commanders of the army.   [c] Has this...while we: *or* If this has been
done by your majesty's authority, then we...

my lord King David.' So Zadok the priest, Nathan the prophet, and 38
Benaiah son of Jehoiada, together with the Kerethite and Pelethite
guards, went down and mounted Solomon on King David's mule and
escorted him to Gihon. Zadok the priest took the horn of oil from the 39
Tent of the Lord*a* and anointed Solomon; they sounded the trumpet and
all the people shouted, 'Long live King Solomon!' Then all the people 40
escorted him home in procession, with great rejoicing and playing of
pipes, so that the very earth split with the noise.

Adonijah and his guests had finished their banquet when the noise 41
reached their ears. Joab, hearing the sound of the trumpet, exclaimed,
'What is all this uproar in the city? What has happened?' While he 42
was still speaking, Jonathan son of Abiathar the priest arrived. 'Come
in', said Adonijah. 'You are an honourable man and bring good news.'
'Far otherwise,' Jonathan replied; 'our lord King David has made 43
Solomon king and has sent with him Zadok the priest, Nathan the 44
prophet, and Benaiah son of Jehoiada, together with the Kerethite and
Pelethite guards; they have mounted him on the king's mule, and 45
Zadok the priest and Nathan the prophet have anointed him king at
Gihon, and they have now escorted him home rejoicing, and the city is
in an uproar. That was the noise you heard. More than that, Solomon 46
has taken his seat on the royal throne. Yes, and the officers of the 47
household have been to greet our lord King David with these words:
"May your God make the name of Solomon your son more famous than
your own and his throne even greater than yours", and the king bowed
upon his couch. What is more, he said this: "Blessed be the Lord the 48
God of Israel who has set a successor*b* on my throne this day while
I am still alive to see it."' Then Adonijah's guests all rose in panic and 49
scattered. Adonijah himself, in fear of Solomon, sprang up and went to 50
the altar and caught hold of its horns. Then a message was sent to 51
Solomon: 'Adonijah is afraid of King Solomon; he has taken hold of
the horns of the altar and has said, "Let King Solomon first swear to me
that he will not put his servant to the sword."' Solomon said, 'If he 52
proves himself a man of worth, not a hair of his head shall fall to the
ground; but if he is found to be troublesome, he shall die.' Then King 53
Solomon sent and had him brought down from the altar; he came in
and prostrated himself before the king, and Solomon ordered him home.

When the time of David's death drew near, he gave this last charge 2
to his son Solomon: 'I am going the way of all the earth. Be strong and 2
show yourself a man. Fulfil your duty to the Lord your God; conform 3
to his ways, observe his statutes and his commandments, his judgements
and his solemn precepts, as they are written in the law of Moses, so that
you may prosper in whatever you do and whichever way you turn, and 4

[*a*] *Lit.* the tent, *cp. 2. 28.*   [*b*] *Sept. adds* of my seed.

447

that the LORD may fulfil this promise that he made about me: "If your descendants take care to walk faithfully in my sight with all their heart and with all their soul, you shall never lack a successor on the throne of
5 Israel." You know how Joab son of Zeruiah treated me and what he did to two commanders-in-chief in Israel, Abner son of Ner and Amasa son of Jether. He killed them both, breaking the peace by bloody acts of war; and with that blood he stained the belt about my*a* waist
6 and the sandals on my*a* feet. Do as your wisdom prompts you, and do
7 not let his grey hairs go down to the grave*b* in peace. Show constant friendship to the family of Barzillai of Gilead; let them have their place at your table; they befriended me when I was a fugitive from your
8 brother Absalom. Do not forget Shimei son of Gera, the Benjamite from Bahurim, who cursed me bitterly the day I went to Mahanaim. True, he came down to meet me at the Jordan, and I swore by the
9 LORD that I would not put him to death. But you do not need to let him go unpunished now; you are a wise man and will know how to deal with him; bring down his grey hairs in blood to the grave.'*b*
10   So David rested with his forefathers and was buried in the city of
11 David, having reigned over Israel for forty years, seven in Hebron and
12 thirty-three in Jerusalem; and Solomon succeeded his father David as king and was firmly established on the throne.

The reign of Solomon

13 THEN ADONIJAH son of Haggith came to Bathsheba, the mother of Solomon. 'Do you come as a friend?' she asked. 'As a friend,'
14 he answered; 'I have something to say to you.' 'Tell me', she said.
15 'You know', he went on, 'that the throne was mine and that all Israel was looking to me to be king; but I was passed over and the throne has
16 gone to my brother; it was his by the LORD's will. And now I have one request to make of you; do not refuse me.' 'What is it?' she said.
17 He answered, 'Will you ask King Solomon (he will never refuse you)
18 to give me Abishag the Shunammite in marriage?' 'Very well,' said
19 Bathsheba, 'I will speak for you to the king.' So Bathsheba went in to King Solomon to speak for Adonijah. The king rose to meet her and kissed*c* her, and seated himself on his throne. A throne was set for the
20 king's mother and she sat at his right hand. Then she said, 'I have one small request to make of you; do not refuse me.' 'What is it, mother?'
21 he replied; 'I will not refuse you.' 'It is this, that Abishag the Shunam-
22 mite should be given to your brother Adonijah in marriage.' At that

[a] *So Luc. Sept.; Heb.* his.   [b] *Heb.* Sheol.   [c] *So Sept.; Heb.* prostrated himself to...

Solomon answered his mother, 'Why do you ask for Abishag the Shunammite as wife for Adonijah? you might as well ask for the throne, for he is my elder brother and has both Abiathar the priest and Joab son of Zeruiah on his side.' Then King Solomon swore by the LORD: 'So help me God, Adonijah shall pay for this with his life. As the LORD lives, who has established me and set me on the throne of David my father and has founded a house for me as he promised, this very day Adonijah shall be put to death!' Thereupon King Solomon gave Benaiah son of Jehoiada his orders, and he struck him down and he died.

Abiathar the priest was told by the king to go off to Anathoth to his own estate. 'You deserve to die,' he said, 'but in spite of this day's work I shall not put you to death, for you carried the Ark of the Lord GOD*a* before my father David, and you shared in all the hardships that he endured.' So Solomon dismissed Abiathar from his office as priest of the LORD, and so fulfilled the sentence that the LORD had pronounced against the house of Eli in Shiloh.

News of all this reached Joab, and he fled to the Tent of the LORD and caught hold of the horns of the altar; for he had sided with Adonijah, though not with Absalom. When King Solomon learnt that Joab had fled to the Tent of the LORD and that he was by the altar, he sent*b* Benaiah son of Jehoiada with orders to strike him down. Benaiah came to the Tent of the LORD and ordered Joab in the king's name to come away; but he said, 'No; I will die here.' Benaiah reported Joab's answer to the king, and the king said, 'Let him have his way; strike him down and bury him, and so rid me and my father's house of the guilt for the blood that he wantonly shed. The LORD will hold him responsible for his own death, because he struck down two innocent men who were better men than he, Abner son of Ner, commander of the army of Israel, and Amasa son of Jether, commander of the army of Judah, and ran them through with the sword, without my father David's knowledge. The guilt of their blood shall recoil on Joab and his descendants for all time; but David and his descendants, his house and his throne, will enjoy perpetual prosperity from the LORD.' So Benaiah son of Jehoiada went up to the altar and struck Joab down and killed him, and he was buried in his house on the edge of the wilderness. Thereafter the king appointed Benaiah son of Jehoiada to command the army in his place, and installed Zadok the priest in place of Abiathar.

Next the king sent for Shimei and said to him, 'Build yourself a

[a] the Ark...GOD: *so Heb.; but probably read* the ephod. [b] *Sept. adds* to Joab, saying, 'What has come upon you that you fled to the altar?' And Joab said, 'I was afraid of you; so I fled to the LORD.' So King Solomon sent...

house in Jerusalem and stay there; you are not to leave the city for any
37 other place. If ever you leave it and cross the gorge of the Kidron, you
shall die; make no mistake about that. Your blood will be on your own
38 head.' And Shimei said to the king, 'I accept your sentence; I will do
as your majesty commands.' So for a long time Shimei remained in
39 Jerusalem; but three years later two of his slaves ran away to Achish
son of Maacah, king of Gath. When Shimei heard that his slaves were
40 in Gath, he immediately saddled his ass and went there to Achish in
41 search of his slaves; he came to Gath and returned with them. When
King Solomon was told that Shimei had gone from Jerusalem to Gath
42 and back, he sent for him and said, 'Did I not require you to swear by
the LORD? Did I not give you this solemn warning: "If ever you leave
this city for any other place, you shall die; make no mistake about it"?
43 And you said, "I accept your sentence; I obey." Why then have you
not kept the oath which you swore by the LORD, and the order which
44 I gave you? Shimei, you know in your own heart all the mischief you
did to my father David; the LORD is now making that mischief recoil on
45 your own head. But King Solomon is blessed and the throne of David
46 will be secure before the LORD for all time.' The king then gave orders
to Benaiah son of Jehoiada, and he went out and struck Shimei down;
and he died. Thus Solomon's royal power was securely established.

3 Solomon allied himself to Pharaoh king of Egypt by marrying his
daughter. He brought her to the City of David, until he had finished
building his own house and the house of the LORD and the wall round
2 Jerusalem. The people however continued to sacrifice at the hill-shrines,
for till then no house had been built in honour of the name of the LORD.
3 Solomon himself loved the LORD, conforming to the precepts laid down
by his father David; but he too slaughtered and burnt sacrifices at the
hill-shrines.

4 Now King Solomon went to Gibeon to offer a sacrifice, for that was
the chief hill-shrine, and he used to offer a thousand whole-offerings on
5[a] its altar. There that night the LORD God appeared to him in a dream
6 and said, 'What shall I give you? Tell me.' And Solomon answered,
'Thou didst show great and constant love to thy servant David my
father, because he walked before thee in loyalty, righteousness, and
integrity of heart; and thou hast maintained this great and constant love
towards him and hast now given him a son to succeed him on the
7 throne. Now, O LORD my God, thou hast made thy servant king in
place of my father David, though I am a mere child, unskilled in
8 leadership. And I am here in the midst of thy people, the people of thy
9 choice, too many to be numbered or counted. Give thy servant,
therefore, a heart with skill to listen, so that he may govern thy people

[a] *Verses 5–14: cp. 2 Chr. 1. 7–12.*

justly and distinguish good from evil. For who is equal to the task of
governing this great people of thine?' The Lord was well pleased that 10
Solomon had asked for this, and he said to him, 'Because you have 11
asked for this, and not for long life for yourself, or for wealth, or for the
lives of your enemies, but have asked for discernment in administering
justice, I grant your request; I give you a heart so wise and so under- 12
standing that there has been none like you before your time nor will
be after you. I give you furthermore those things for which you did 13
not ask, such wealth and honour*a* as no king of your time can match.
And if you conform to my ways and observe my ordinances and 14
commandments, as your father David did, I will give you long life.'
Then he awoke, and knew it was a dream.   15

Solomon came to Jerusalem and stood before the Ark of the Covenant
of the Lord; there he sacrificed whole-offerings and brought shared-
offerings, and gave a feast to all his household.

Then there came into the king's presence two women who were 16
prostitutes and stood before him. The first said, 'My lord, this woman 17
and I share the same house, and I gave birth to a child when she was
there with me. On the third day after my baby was born she too gave 18
birth to a child. We were quite alone; no one else was with us in the
house; only the two of us were there. During the night this woman's 19
child died because she overlaid it, and she got up in the middle of the 20
night, took my baby from my side while I, your servant, was asleep,
and laid it in her bosom, putting her dead child in mine. When I got 21
up in the morning to feed my baby, I found him dead; but when
I looked at him closely, I found that it was not the child that I had
borne.' The other woman broke in, 'No; the living child is mine; 22
yours is the dead one', while the first retorted, 'No; the dead child is
yours; mine is the living one.' So they went on arguing in the king's
presence. The king thought to himself, 'One of them says, "This is my 23
child, the living one; yours is the dead one." The other says, "No; it
is your child that is dead and mine that is alive."' Then he said, 'Fetch 24
me a sword.' They brought in a sword and the king gave the order: 25
'Cut the living child in two and give half to one and half to the other.'
At this the woman who was the mother of the living child, moved 26
with love for her child, said to the king, 'Oh! sir, let her have the baby;
whatever you do, do not kill it.' The other said, 'Let neither of us have
it; cut it in two.' Thereupon the king gave judgement: 'Give the living 27
baby to the first woman; do not kill it. She is its mother.' When Israel 28
heard the judgement which the king had given, they all stood in awe of
him; for they saw that he had the wisdom of God within him to
administer justice.

[a] *Or* riches.

4 1, 2[a] KING SOLOMON REIGNED over Israel. His officers were as follows:

In charge of the calendar:[b] Azariah son of Zadok the priest.

3   Adjutant-general:[c] Ahijah son[d] of Shisha.

Secretary of state: Jehoshaphat son of Ahilud.

4   Commander of the army: Benaiah son of Jehoiada.

Priests: Zadok and Abiathar.

5   Superintendent of the regional governors: Azariah son of Nathan.

King's Friend: Zabud son of Nathan.[e]

6   Comptroller of the household: Ahishar.

Superintendent of the forced levy: Adoniram son of Abda.

7   Solomon had twelve regional governors over Israel and they supplied the food for the king and the royal household, each being responsible

8   for one month's provision in the year. These were their names:

Ben-hur in the hill-country of Ephraim.

9   Ben-dekar in Makaz, Shaalbim, Beth-shemesh, Elon, and Beth-hanan.[f]

10   Ben-hesed in Aruboth; he had charge also of Socoh and all the land of Hepher.

11   Ben-abinadab, who had married Solomon's daughter Taphath, in all the district of Dor.

12   Baana son of Ahilud in Taanach and Megiddo, all Beth-shean as far as Abel-meholah beside Zartanah, and from Beth-shean below Jezreel as far as Jokmeam.

13   Ben-geber in Ramoth-gilead, including the tent-villages of Jair son of Manasseh in Gilead and the region of Argob in Bashan, sixty large walled cities with gate-bars of bronze.

14   Ahinadab son of Iddo in Mahanaim.

15   Ahimaaz in Naphtali; he also had married a daughter of Solomon, Basmath.

16   Baanah son of Hushai in Asher and Aloth.

17   Jehoshaphat son of Paruah in Issachar.

18   Shimei son of Elah in Benjamin.

19   Geber son of Uri in Gilead, the land of Sihon king of the Amorites and of Og king of Bashan.

In addition, one governor over all the governors[g] in the land.

20   The people of Judah and Israel were countless as the sands of the sea;

21[h] they ate and they drank, and enjoyed life. Solomon ruled over all the kingdoms from the river Euphrates to Philistia and as far as

---

[a] *Verses 2–6: cp.* 2 Sam. 8. 16–18; 20. 23–26; 1 Chr. 18. 15–17. [b] *In...calendar: prob. rdg.; Heb.* Elihoreph. [c] *Prob. rdg., cp.* 1 Chr. 18. 16; *Heb.* Adjutants-general. [d] *Prob. rdg.; Heb.* sons. [e] *So Sept.; Heb. adds* priest. [f] Elon, and Beth-hanan: *so some MSS.; others* Elon-beth-hanan. [g] over...governors: *prob. rdg.; Heb. om.* [h] 5. 1 *in Heb.*

the frontier of Egypt; they paid tribute and were subject to him all his life.

Solomon's provision for one day was thirty kor of flour and sixty kor 22 of meal, ten fat oxen and twenty oxen from the pastures and a hundred 23 sheep, as well as stags, gazelles, roebucks, and fattened fowl. For he 24 was paramount over all the land west of the Euphrates from Tiphsah to Gaza, ruling all the kings west of the river; and he enjoyed peace on all sides. All through his reign Judah and Israel continued at peace, 25 every man under his own vine and fig-tree, from Dan to Beersheba.

Solomon had forty thousand chariot-horses in his stables and twelve 26 thousand cavalry horses.

The regional governors, each for a month in turn, supplied pro- 27 visions for King Solomon and for all who came to his table; they never fell short in their deliveries. They provided also barley and straw, each 28 according to his duty, for the horses and chariot-horses where it was required.

And God gave Solomon depth of wisdom and insight, and under- 29 standing as wide as the sand on the sea-shore, so that Solomon's 30 wisdom surpassed that of all the men of the east and of all Egypt. For he was wiser than any man, wiser than Ethan the Ezrahite, and 31 Heman, Kalcol, and Darda, the sons of Mahol; his fame spread among all the surrounding nations. He uttered three thousand proverbs, and 32 his songs numbered a thousand and five. He discoursed of trees, from 33 the cedar of Lebanon down to the marjoram that grows out of the wall, of beasts and birds, of reptiles and fishes. Men of all races came to 34 listen to the wisdom of Solomon, and from all the kings of the earth who had heard of his wisdom he received gifts.[a]

WHEN HIRAM KING OF TYRE heard that Solomon had been 5 1[b] anointed king in his father's place, he sent envoys to him, because he had always been a friend of David. Solomon sent this answer to 2[c] Hiram: 'You know that my father David could not build a house in 3 honour of the name of the LORD his God, because he was surrounded by armed nations until the LORD made them subject to him. But now 4 on every side the LORD my God has given me peace; there is no one to oppose me, I fear no attack. So I propose to build a house in honour 5 of the name of the LORD my God, following the promise given by the LORD to my father David: "Your son whom I shall set on the throne in your place will build the house in honour of my name." If therefore 6 you will now give orders that cedars be felled and brought from Lebanon, my men will work with yours, and I will pay you for your

[a] he received gifts: *so Luc. Sept.; Heb. om.* [b] *5. 15 in Heb.* [c] *Verses 2–11: cp. 2 Chr. 2. 3–16.*

men whatever sum you fix; for, as you know, we have none so skilled at felling timber as your Sidonians.'

7 When Hiram received Solomon's message, he was greatly pleased and said, 'Blessed be the LORD today who has given David a wise son
8 to rule over this great people.' And he sent this reply to Solomon: 'I have received your message. In this matter of timber, both cedar
9 and pine, I will do all you wish. My men shall bring down the logs from Lebanon to the sea and I will make them up into rafts to be floated to the place you appoint; I will have them broken up there and you can remove them. You, on your part, will meet my wishes if you
10 provide the food for my household.' So Hiram kept Solomon supplied
11 with all the cedar and pine that he wanted, and Solomon supplied Hiram with twenty thousand kor of wheat as food for his household and twenty kor of oil of pounded olives; Solomon gave this yearly to
12 Hiram. (The LORD had given Solomon wisdom as he had promised him; there was peace between Hiram and Solomon and they concluded
13 an alliance.) King Solomon raised a forced levy from the whole of
14 Israel amounting to thirty thousand men. He sent them to Lebanon in monthly relays of ten thousand, so that the men spent one month in Lebanon and two at home; Adoniram was superintendent of the whole
15 levy. Solomon had also seventy thousand hauliers and eighty thousand
16 quarrymen, apart from the three thousand three hundred foremen in
17 charge of the work who superintended the labourers. By the king's orders they quarried huge, massive blocks for laying the foundation of
18 the LORD's house[a] in hewn stone. Solomon's and Hiram's builders and the Gebalites shaped the blocks and prepared both timber and stone for the building of the house.

6 1[b][c] It was in the four hundred and eightieth year after the Israelites had come out of Egypt, in the fourth year of Solomon's reign over Israel, in the second month of that year, the month of Ziv, that he began to build the house of the LORD.

2 The house which King Solomon built for the LORD was sixty cubits
3 long by twenty cubits broad, and its height was thirty[d] cubits. The vestibule in front of the sanctuary was twenty cubits long, spanning the whole breadth of the house, while it projected ten cubits in front of the
4,5 house; and he furnished the house with embrasures. Then he built a terrace against its wall[e] round both the sanctuary and the inner
6 shrine. He made arcades all round: the lowest arcade[f] was five cubits in depth, the middle six, and the highest seven; for he made rebates all

---

[a] the LORD's house: *lit.* the house. [b] *In chs. 6 and 7 there are several Hebrew technical terms whose meaning is not certain and has to be determined, as well as may be, from the context.* [c] *Verses 1–3: cp. 2 Chr. 3. 2–4.* [d] *Or, with Sept.,* twenty-five. [e] *So Sept.; Heb. adds* round the walls of the house. [f] *So Sept.; Heb.* platform.

round the outside of the main wall so that the bearer beams^a might not
be set into the walls. In the building of the house, only blocks of un- 7
dressed stone direct from the quarry were used; no hammer or axe or
any iron tool whatever was heard in the house while it was being built.

The entrance to the lowest^b arcade was in the right-hand corner of 8
the house; there was access by a spiral stairway from that to the middle
arcade, and from the middle arcade to the highest. So he built the house 9–10
and finished it, having constructed the terrace five cubits high against
the whole building, braced the house with struts of cedar and roofed
it with beams and coffering of cedar.

Then the word of the LORD came to Solomon, saying, 'As for this 11, 12
house which you are building, if you are obedient to my ordinances
and conform to my precepts and loyally observe all my commands,
then I will fulfil my promise to you, the promise I gave to your father
David, and I will dwell among the Israelites and never forsake my 13
people Israel.'

So Solomon built the LORD's house and finished it. He lined the inner 14, 15
walls of the house with cedar boards, covering the interior from floor to
rafters^c with wood; the floor he laid with boards of pine. In the inner- 16
most part of the house he partitioned off a space of twenty cubits with
cedar boards from floor to rafters^c and made of it an inner shrine, to be
the Most Holy Place. The sanctuary in front of this^d was forty cubits 17
long. The cedar inside the house was carved with open flowers and 18
gourds; all was cedar, no stone was left visible.

He prepared an inner shrine in the furthest recesses of the house to 19
receive the Ark of the Covenant of the LORD. ^eThis inner shrine was 20
twenty cubits square and it stood twenty cubits high; he overlaid it
with red gold and made^f an altar of cedar. And Solomon overlaid the 21
inside of the house with red gold and drew a Veil^g with golden chains
across in front of the inner shrine.^h The whole house he overlaid with 22
gold until it was all covered; and the whole of the altar by the inner
shrine he overlaid with gold.

In the inner shrine he made two cherubim of wild olive, each ten 23ⁱ
cubits high. Each wing of the cherubim was five cubits long, and from 24
wing-tip to wing-tip was ten cubits. Similarly the second cherub 25
measured ten cubits; the two cherubim were alike in size and shape, and 26
each ten cubits high. He put the cherubim within the shrine at the 27
furthest recesses and their wings were outspread, so that a wing of the
one cherub touched the wall on one side and a wing of the other

[a] the bearer beams: *so Targ.; Heb. om.* [b] *So Sept.; Heb.* middle. [c] rafters: *so Sept.;
Heb.* walls. [d] The sanctuary in front of this: *so Sept.; Heb.* The house, that is the
sanctuary, before me. [e] *So Vulg.; Heb. prefixes* Before. [f] *So Sept.; Heb.* overlaid.
[g] a Veil: *prob. rdg.; Heb. om.* [h] *Prob. rdg.; Heb. adds* and overlaid it with gold.
[i] *Verses 23–28: cp. 2 Chr. 3. 10–13.*

touched the wall on the other side, and their other wings met in the
28 middle; and he overlaid the cherubim with gold.

29   Round all the walls of the house he carved figures of cherubim,
palm-trees, and open flowers, both in the inner chamber[a] and in the
30 outer. The floor of the house he overlaid with gold, both in the inner
31 chamber[a] and in the outer. At the entrance to the inner shrine he made
a double door of wild olive; the pilasters and the[b] door-posts were
32 pentagonal.[c] The doors were of wild olive, and he carved cherubim,
palms, and open flowers on them, overlaying them with gold and ham-
33 mering the gold upon the cherubim and the palms. Similarly for the
34 doorway of the sanctuary he made a square[d] frame of wild olive and a
35 double door of pine, each leaf having two swivel-pins. On them he carved
cherubim, palms, and open flowers, overlaying them evenly with gold
over the carving.

36   He built the inner court with three courses of dressed stone and one
course of lengths of cedar.

37   In the fourth year of Solomon's reign the foundation of the house of
38 the LORD was laid, in the month of Ziv; and in the eleventh year, in the
month of Bul, which is the eighth month, the house was finished in all
its details according to the specification. It had taken seven years to
build.

7   Solomon had been engaged on his building for thirteen years by the
2 time he had finished it. He built the House of the Forest of Lebanon,
a hundred cubits long, fifty broad, and thirty high, constructed of four
3 rows of cedar columns, over which were laid lengths of cedar. It had
a cedar roof, extending over the beams, which rested on the columns,
4 fifteen in each row; and the number of the beams was forty-five. There
were three rows of window-frames, and the windows corresponded
5 to each other at three levels. All the doorways and the windows[e]
had square frames, and window corresponded to window at three
levels.

6   He made also the colonnade, fifty cubits long and thirty broad,[f]
with a cornice above.

7   He built the Hall of Judgement, the hall containing the throne where
he was to give judgement; this was panelled in cedar from floor to
rafters.[g]

8   His own house where he was to reside, in[h] a court set back from the
colonnade, and the house he made for Pharaoh's daughter whom he had
married, were constructed like the hall.

[a] inner chamber: *so Sept.; Heb.* inwards.   [b] and the: *prob. rdg.; Heb. om.*   [c] *So Sept.;*
Heb. fifth.   [d] *So Sept.; Heb.* from with a fourth...   [e] *So Sept.; Heb.* door-posts.
[f] *Prob. rdg.; Heb. adds* and a colonnade and pillars in front of them.   [g] rafters: *so*
Vulg.; Heb. floor.   [h] *So Arabic version; Heb. om.*

All these were made of heavy blocks of stone, hewn to measure and 9
trimmed with the saw on the inner and outer sides, from foundation
to coping and from the court of the house*a* as far as the great court.
At the base were heavy stones, massive blocks, some ten and some 10
eight cubits in size, and above were heavy stones dressed to measure, 11
and cedar. The great court had three courses of dressed stone all 12
around and a course of lengths of cedar; so had the inner court of the
house of the LORD, and so had the vestibule of the house.

King Solomon fetched from Tyre Hiram, the son of a widow of the 13, 14
tribe of Naphtali. His father, a native of Tyre, had been a worker in
bronze, and he himself was a man of great skill and ingenuity, versed
in every kind of craftsmanship in bronze. Hiram came to King
Solomon and executed all his works.

He cast in a mould the two bronze pillars. One stood eighteen 15*b*
cubits high and it took a cord twelve cubits long to go round it; it was
hollow, and the metal was four fingers thick.*c* The second pillar was the
same.*d* He made two capitals of solid copper to set on the tops of the 16
pillars, each capital five cubits high. He made two*e* bands of orna- 17
mental network, in festoons of chain-work, for the capitals on the tops
of the pillars, a band of network*f* for each capital. Then he made 18
pomegranates*g* in two rows all round on top of the ornamental network
of the one pillar;*h* he did the same with the other capital. (The capitals 19
at the tops of the pillars in the vestibule were shaped like lilies and were
four cubits high.) Upon the capitals at the tops of the two pillars, 20
immediately above the cushion, which was beyond the network upwards, were two hundred pomegranates in rows all round on the two
capitals.*i* Then he erected the pillars at the vestibule of the sanctuary. 21
When he had erected the pillar on the right side, he named it Jachin;*j*
and when he had erected the one on the left side, he named it Boaz.*k*
On the tops of the pillars was lily-work. Thus the work of the pillars 22
was finished.

He then made the Sea of cast metal; it was round in shape, the 23*l*
diameter from rim to rim being ten cubits; it stood five cubits high, and
it took a line thirty cubits long to go round it. All round the Sea on the 24
outside under its rim, completely surrounding the thirty*m* cubits of its
circumference, were two rows of gourds, cast in one piece with the Sea
itself. It was mounted on twelve oxen, three facing north, three west, 25

[a] *Prob. rdg., cp. verse 12; Heb.* from outside. [b] *Verses 15–21: cp. 2 Chr. 3. 15–17.* [c] it
was...thick: *prob. rdg., cp. Jer. 52. 21; Heb. om.* [d] the same: *so Sept.; Heb. om.* [e] He
made two: *so Sept.; Heb. om.* [f] a band of network: *so Sept.; Heb.* seven. [g] *So some
MSS.; others* pillars. [h] *So Sept.; Heb. adds* to cover the capitals on the top of the
pomegranates. [i] the two capitals: *prob. rdg.; Heb.* the second capital. [j] *Or* Jachun,
meaning It shall stand. [k] *Or* Booz, *meaning* In strength. [l] *Verses 23–26: cp. 2 Chr. 4.
2–5.* [m] *Prob. rdg.; Heb.* ten.

three south, and three east, their hind quarters turned inwards; the Sea
26 rested on top of them. Its thickness was a hand-breadth; its rim was
made like that of a cup, shaped like the calyx of a lily; it held two
thousand bath of water.

27 He also made the ten trolleys of bronze; each trolley was four cubits
28 long, four wide, and three high. This was the construction of the trolleys.
29 They had panels set in frames; on these panels were portrayed lions,
oxen, and cherubim, and similarly on the frames. Above and below the
lions, oxen, and cherubim*a* were fillets of hammered work of spiral
30 design. Each trolley had four bronze wheels with axles of bronze; it
also had four flanges and handles beneath the laver, and these handles
31 were of cast metal with a spiral design on their sides. The opening for
the basin was set within a crown which projected one cubit; the
opening was round with a level edge,*b* and it had decorations in relief.
32 (The panels of the trolleys were square, not round.) The four wheels
were beneath the panels, and the wheel-forks were made in one piece
with the trolleys; the height of each wheel was a cubit and a half.
33 The wheels were constructed like those of a chariot, their axles, hubs,
34 spokes, and felloes being all of cast metal. The four handles were at the
35 four corners of each trolley, of one piece with the trolley. At the top of
the trolley there was a circular band half a cubit high; the struts and
36 panels on*c* the trolley were of one piece with it. On the plates, that is
on the panels,*d* he carved cherubim, lions, and palm-trees, wherever
37 there was a blank space, with spiral work all round it. This is how the
ten trolleys were made; all of them were cast alike, having the same size
and the same shape.

38 He then made ten bronze basins, each holding forty bath and
measuring four cubits; there was a basin for each of the ten trolleys.
39 He put five trolleys on the right side of the house and five on the left
side; and he put the Sea in the south-east corner of it.
40*e* Hiram made also the pots,*f* the shovels, and the tossing-bowls. So he
finished all the work which he had undertaken for King Solomon on the
41 house of the LORD: the two pillars; the two bowl-shaped capitals on the
tops of the pillars; the two ornamental networks to cover the two bowl-
42 shaped capitals on the tops of the pillars; the four hundred pomegranates
for the two networks, two rows of pomegranates for each network, to
43 cover the bowl-shaped capitals on the two*g* pillars; the ten trolleys and
44 the ten basins on the trolleys; the one Sea and the twelve oxen which
45 supported it; the pots, the shovels, and the tossing-bowls—all these

[*a*] and cherubim: *prob. rdg.; Heb. om.* [*b*] *Prob. rdg.; Heb. adds* a cubit and a half (*cp.*
verse 32). [*c*] *Prob. rdg.; Heb. adds* the head of. [*d*] *Prob. rdg.; Heb. adds* its struts.
[*e*] *Verses 40–51: cp.* 2 *Chr.* 4. 11–5. 1. [*f*] *So many MSS.; others* basins. [*g*] two: *so
Sept.; Heb.* surface of.

objects in the house of the LORD which Hiram made for King Solomon being of bronze, burnished work. In the Plain of the Jordan the king 46 cast them, in the foundry between Succoth and Zarethan.

Solomon put all these objects in their places; so great was the 47 quantity of bronze used in their making that the weight of it was beyond all reckoning. He made also all the furnishings for the house 48 of the LORD: the golden altar and the golden table upon which was set the Bread of the Presence; the lamp-stands of red gold, five on the 49 right side and five on the left side of the inner shrine; the flowers, lamps, and tongs, of gold; the cups, snuffers, tossing-bowls, saucers, 50 and firepans, of red gold; and the panels for the doors of the inner sanctuary, the Most Holy Place, and for the doors of the house,*ᵃ* of gold.

When all the work which King Solomon did for the house of the 51 LORD was completed, he brought in the sacred treasures of his father David, the silver, the gold, and the vessels, and deposited them in the storehouses of the house of the LORD.

THEN SOLOMON SUMMONED the elders of Israel, all the heads of **8** 1*ᵇ* the tribes who were chiefs of families in Israel, to assemble in Jerusalem, in order to bring up the Ark of the Covenant of the LORD from the City of David, which is called Zion. All the men of Israel assembled in King 2 Solomon's presence at the pilgrim-feast in the month Ethanim, the seventh month. When the elders of Israel had all come, the priests took 3 the Ark of the LORD and carried it up with the Tent of the Presence 4 and all the sacred furnishings of the Tent: it was the priests and the Levites together who carried them up. King Solomon and the whole 5 congregation of Israel, assembled with him before the Ark, sacrificed sheep and oxen in numbers past counting or reckoning. Then the 6 priests brought in the Ark of the Covenant of the LORD to its place, the inner shrine of the house, the Most Holy Place, beneath the wings of the cherubim. The cherubim spread their wings over the place of the 7 Ark; they formed a screen above the Ark and its poles. The poles 8 projected, and their ends could be seen from the Holy Place immediately in front of the inner shrine, but from nowhere else outside; they are there to this day. There was nothing inside the Ark but the two tablets 9 of stone which Moses had deposited there at Horeb, the tablets of the covenant*ᶜ* which the LORD made with the Israelites when they left Egypt.

Then the priests came out of the Holy Place, since the cloud was 10 filling the house of the LORD, and they could not continue to minister 11

[*a*] *Prob. rdg.; Heb. adds* for the temple.   [*b*] *Verses 1–9: cp. 2 Chr. 5. 2–10.*   [*c*] the tablets of the covenant: *so Sept.; Heb. om.*

12[a] because of it, for the glory of the LORD filled his house. And Solomon
said:

> O LORD who hast set the sun in heaven,[b]
> but hast chosen to dwell in thick darkness,
13 > here have I built thee a lofty house,
> a habitation for thee to occupy for ever.

14 And as they stood waiting, the king turned round and blessed all the
15 assembly of Israel in these words: 'Blessed be the LORD the God of
Israel who spoke directly to my father David and has himself fulfilled
16 his promise. For he said, "From the day when I brought my people
Israel out of Egypt, I chose no city out of all the tribes of Israel where
I should build a house for my Name to be there, but[c] I chose David to
17 be over my people Israel." My father David had in mind to build a
18 house in honour of the name of the LORD the God of Israel, but the
LORD said to him, "You purposed to build a house in honour of my
19 name; and your purpose was good. Nevertheless, you shall not build it;
but the son who is to be born to you, he shall build the house in honour
20 of my name." The LORD has now fulfilled his promise: I have succeeded
my father David and taken his place on the throne of Israel, as the
LORD promised; and I have built the house in honour of the name of
21 the LORD the God of Israel. I have assigned therein a place for the Ark
containing the Covenant of the LORD, which he made with our forefathers when he brought them out of Egypt.'

22 Then Solomon, standing in front of the altar of the LORD in the
presence of the whole assembly of Israel, spread out his hands towards
23 heaven and said, 'O LORD God of Israel, there is no god like thee in
heaven above or on earth beneath, keeping covenant with thy servants
and showing them constant love while they continue faithful to thee in
24 heart and soul. Thou hast kept thy promise to thy servant David my
father; by thy deeds this day thou hast fulfilled what thou didst say to
25 him in words. Now therefore, O LORD God of Israel, keep this promise
of thine to thy servant David my father: "You shall never want for a
man appointed by me to sit on the throne of Israel, if only your sons
look to their ways and walk before me as you have walked before me."
26 And now, O God of Israel, let the words which thou didst speak to thy
servant David my father be confirmed.

27 'But can God indeed dwell on earth? Heaven itself, the highest
heaven, cannot contain thee; how much less this house that I have
28 built! Yet attend to the prayer and the supplication of thy servant,
O LORD my God, listen to the cry and the prayer which thy servant
29 utters this day, that thine eyes may ever be upon this house night and

---

[a] *Verses 12–50: cp. 2 Chr. 6. 1–39.* [b] O LORD...heaven: *so Sept.; Heb. om.* [c] *2 Chr.
6. 6 and Sept. add* I chose Jerusalem for my Name to be there, and...

day, this place of which thou didst say, "My Name shall be there"; so
mayest thou hear thy servant when he prays towards this place. Hear 30
the supplication of thy servant and of thy people Israel when they pray
towards this place. Hear thou in heaven thy dwelling and, when thou
hearest, forgive.

'When a man wrongs his neighbour and he is adjured to take an oath, 31
and the adjuration is made before thy altar in this house, then do thou 32
hear in heaven and act: be thou thy servants' judge, condemning the
guilty man and bringing his deeds upon his own head, acquitting the
innocent and rewarding him as his innocence may deserve.

'When thy people Israel are defeated by an enemy because they have 33
sinned against thee, and they turn back to thee, confessing thy name
and making their prayer and supplication to thee in this house, do thou 34
hear in heaven; forgive the sin of thy people Israel and restore them to
the land which thou gavest to their forefathers.

'When the heavens are shut up and there is no rain because thy 35
servant*a* and thy people Israel have sinned against thee, and when they
pray towards this place, confessing thy name and forsaking their sin
when they feel thy punishment, do thou hear in heaven and forgive 36
their sin; so mayest thou teach them the good way which they should
follow; and grant rain to thy land which thou hast given to thy people
as their own possession.

'If there is famine in the land, or pestilence, or black blight or red, or 37
locusts new-sloughed or fully grown; or if their enemies besiege them
in any*b* of their cities; or if plague or sickness befall them, then hear 38
the prayer or supplication of every man among thy people Israel, as
each one, prompted by the remorse of his own heart, spreads out his
hands towards this house: hear it in heaven thy dwelling and forgive, 39
and act. And, as thou knowest a man's heart, reward him according to
his deeds, for thou alone knowest the hearts of all men; and so they 40
will fear thee all their lives in the land thou gavest to our forefathers.

'The foreigner too, the man who does not belong to thy people 41
Israel, but has come from a distant land because of thy fame (for men 42
shall hear of thy great fame and thy strong hand and arm outstretched), when he comes and prays towards this house, hear in heaven 43
thy dwelling and respond to the call which the foreigner makes to thee,
so that like thy people Israel all peoples of the earth may know thy fame
and fear thee, and learn that this house which I have built bears thy
name.

'When thy people go to war with an enemy, wherever thou dost send 44
them, when they pray to the LORD, turning towards this city which
thou hast chosen and towards this house which I have built in honour

[*a*] *So Sept.; Heb.* servants.   [*b*] in any: *so Sept.; Heb.* in the land.

45 of thy name, do thou in heaven hear their prayer and supplication, and grant them justice.

46 'Should they sin against thee (and what man is free from sin?) and shouldst thou in thy anger give them over to an enemy, who carries

47 them captive to his own land, far or near; if in the land of their captivity they learn their lesson and make supplication again to thee in that land

48 and say, "We have sinned and acted perversely and wickedly", if they turn back to thee with heart and soul in the land of their captors, and pray to thee, turning towards their land which thou gavest to their forefathers and towards this city which thou didst choose and this

49 house which I have built in honour of thy name; then in heaven thy dwelling do thou hear their prayer and supplication, and grant them

50 justice. Forgive thy people their sins and transgressions against thee;

51 put pity for them in their captors' hearts. For they are thy possession, thy people whom thou didst bring out of Egypt, from the smelting-

52 furnace, and so thine eyes are ever open to the entreaty of thy servant and of thy people Israel, and thou dost hear whenever they call to thee.

53 Thou thyself hast singled them out from all the peoples of the earth to be thy possession; so thou didst promise through thy servant Moses when thou didst bring our forefathers from Egypt, O Lord God.'

54 When Solomon had finished this prayer and supplication to the LORD, he rose from before the altar of the LORD, where he had been

55 kneeling with his hands spread out to heaven, stood up and in a loud

56 voice blessed the whole assembly of Israel: 'Blessed be the LORD who has given his people Israel rest, as he promised: not one of the promises

57 he made through his servant Moses has failed. The LORD our God be with us as he was with our forefathers; may he never leave us nor

58 forsake us. May he turn our hearts towards him, that we may conform to all his ways, observing his commandments, statutes, and judgements,

59 as he commanded our forefathers. And may the words of my supplication to the LORD be with the LORD our God day and night, that, as the need arises day by day, he may grant justice to his servant and

60 justice to his people Israel. So all the peoples of the earth will know

61 that the LORD is God, he and no other, and you will be perfect in loyalty to the LORD our God as you are this day, conforming to his statutes and observing his commandments.'

62 When the king and all Israel came to offer sacrifices before the LORD,

63 Solomon offered as shared-offerings to the LORD twenty-two thousand oxen and a hundred and twenty thousand sheep; thus it was that the

64ª king and the Israelites dedicated the house of the LORD. On that day also the king consecrated the centre of the court which lay in front[b] of the house of the LORD; there he offered the whole-offering, the grain-

[a] *Verses 64–66: cp. 2 Chr. 7. 7–10.*   [b] *Or to the east.*

offering, and the fat portions of the shared-offerings, because the
bronze altar which stood before the LORD was too small to take them
all, the whole-offering, the grain-offering, and the fat portions of the
shared-offerings.

So Solomon and all Israel with him, a great assembly from Lebo- 65
hamath to the Torrent of Egypt, celebrated the pilgrim-feast at that
time before the LORD our God for seven days.*ᵃ* On the eighth day he 66
dismissed the people; and they blessed the king, and went home happy
and glad at heart for all the prosperity granted by the LORD to his
servant David and to his people Israel.

WHEN SOLOMON had finished the house of the LORD and the royal 9 1*ᵇ*
palace and all the plans for building on which he had set his heart,
the LORD appeared to him a second time, as he had appeared to him at 2
Gibeon. The LORD said to him, 'I have heard the prayer and suppli- 3
cation which you have offered me; I have consecrated this house which
you have built, to receive my Name for all time, and my eyes and my
heart shall be fixed on it for ever. And if you, on your part, live in my 4
sight as your father David lived, in integrity and uprightness, doing all
I command you and observing my statutes and my judgements, then 5
I will establish your royal throne over Israel for ever, as I promised
your father David when I said, "You shall never want for a man upon
the throne of Israel." But if you or your sons turn back from 6
following me and do not observe my commandments and my statutes
which I have set before you, and if you go and serve other gods and
prostrate yourselves before them, then I will cut off Israel from the 7
land which I gave them; I will renounce this house which I have
consecrated in honour of my name, and Israel shall become a byword
and an object lesson among all peoples. And this house will become a 8
ruin;*ᶜ* every passer-by will be appalled and gasp*ᵈ* at the sight of it; and
they will ask, "Why has the LORD so treated this land and this house?"
The answer will be, "Because they forsook the LORD their God, who 9
brought their forefathers out of Egypt, and clung to other gods,
prostrating themselves before them and serving them; that is why the
LORD has brought this great evil on them."'

Solomon had taken twenty years to build the two houses, the house 10*ᵉ*
of the LORD and the royal palace. Hiram king of Tyre had supplied 11
him with all the timber, both cedar and pine, and all the gold, that he
desired, and King Solomon gave Hiram twenty cities in the land of
Galilee. But when Hiram went from Tyre to inspect the cities which 12
Solomon had given him, they did not satisfy him, and he said, 'What 13

[a] *So Sept.; Heb. adds* and seven days, fourteen days.   [b] *Verses 1–9: cp.* 2 Chr. 7. 11–22.
[c] become a ruin: *so Pesh.; Heb.* be high.   [d] *Lit.* hiss.   [e] *Verses 10–28: cp.* 2 Chr. 8. 1–18.

kind of cities are these you have given me, my brother?' And so he

14 called them the Land of Cabul,*a* the name they still bear. Hiram sent a hundred and twenty talents of gold to the king.

15   This is the record of the forced labour which King Solomon conscripted to build the house of the LORD, his own palace, the Millo, the

16 wall of Jerusalem, and Hazor, Megiddo, and Gezer. Gezer had been attacked and captured by Pharaoh king of Egypt, who had burnt it to the ground, put its Canaanite inhabitants to death, and given it as a

17 marriage gift to his daughter, Solomon's wife; and Solomon rebuilt it.

18 He also built Lower Beth-horon, Baalath, and Tamar*b* in the wilder-

19 ness,*c* as well as all his store-cities, and the towns where he quartered his chariots and horses; and he carried out all his cherished plans for building in Jerusalem, in the Lebanon, and throughout his whole

20 dominion. All the survivors of the Amorites, Hittites, Perizzites,

21 Hivites, and Jebusites, who did not belong to Israel—that is their descendants who survived in the land, wherever the Israelites had been unable to annihilate them—were employed by Solomon on perpetual

22 forced labour, as they still are. But Solomon put none of the Israelites to forced labour; they were his fighting men,*d* his captains and lieutenants, and the commanders of his chariots and of his cavalry.

23 The number of officers in charge of the foremen over Solomon's work was five hundred and fifty; these superintended the people engaged on the work.

24   Then Solomon brought Pharaoh's daughter up*e* from the City of David to her own house which he had built for her; later on he built the Millo.

25   Three times a year Solomon used to offer whole-offerings and shared-offerings on the altar which he had built to the LORD, making smoke-offerings*f* before the LORD. So he completed the house.

26   King Solomon built a fleet of ships at Ezion-geber, near Eloth*g* on

27 the shore of the Red Sea,*h* in Edom. Hiram sent men of his own to serve with the fleet, experienced seamen, to work with Solomon's men;

28 and they went to Ophir and brought back four hundred and twenty talents of gold, which they delivered to King Solomon.

10 1*i* THE QUEEN OF SHEBA heard of Solomon's fame*j* and came to test

2 him with hard questions. She arrived in Jerusalem with a very large retinue, camels laden with spices, gold in great quantity, and precious

---

[a] *That is* Sterile Land.   [b] *Or, as otherwise read,* Tadmor.   [c] *So Sept.; Heb. adds* in the land.   [d] *Prob. rdg.; Heb. adds* and his servants.   [e] Then...daughter up: *so Sept.; Heb.* However, Pharaoh's daughter had gone up.   [f] *So Sept.; Heb. adds* with it which.   [g] *Or* Elath.   [h] *Or* the Sea of Reeds.   [i] *Verses 1–25: cp.* 2 Chr. 9. 1–24.   [j] *Prob. rdg., cp.* 2 Chr. 9. 1; *Heb. adds* to the name of the LORD.

stones. When she came to Solomon, she told him everything she had
in her mind, and Solomon answered all her questions; not one of them ₃
was too abstruse for the king to answer. When the queen of Sheba saw ₄
all the wisdom of Solomon, the house which he had built, the food on ₅
his table, the courtiers sitting round him, and his attendants standing
behind in their livery, his cupbearers, and the whole-offerings which he
used to offer in the house of the LORD, there was no more spirit left in
her. Then she said to the king, 'The report which I heard in my own ₆
country about you*a* and your wisdom was true, but I did not believe it ₇
until I came and saw for myself. Indeed I was not told half of it; your
wisdom and your prosperity go far beyond the report which I had of
them. Happy are your wives,*b* happy these courtiers of yours who wait ₈
on you every day and hear your wisdom! Blessed be the LORD your God ₉
who has delighted in you and has set you on the throne of Israel;
because he loves Israel for ever, he has made you their king to maintain
law and justice.' Then she gave the king a hundred and twenty talents ₁₀
of gold, spices in great abundance, and precious stones. Never again came
such a quantity of spices as the queen of Sheba gave to King Solomon.

Besides all this, Hiram's fleet of ships, which had brought gold from ₁₁
Ophir, brought in also from Ophir cargoes of almug wood and precious
stones. The king used the wood to make stools*c* for the house of the ₁₂
LORD and for the royal palace, as well as harps and lutes for the
singers. No such almug wood has ever been imported or even seen
since that time.

And King Solomon gave the queen of Sheba all she desired, what- ₁₃
ever she asked, in addition to all that he gave her of his royal bounty.
So she departed and returned with her retinue to her own land.

Now the weight of gold which Solomon received yearly was six ₁₄
hundred and sixty-six talents, in addition to the tolls levied by*d* the ₁₅
customs officers and profits on foreign trade, and the tribute of*e* the
kings of Arabia and the regional governors.

King Solomon made two hundred shields of beaten gold, and six ₁₆
hundred shekels of gold went to the making of each one; he also made ₁₇
three hundred bucklers of beaten gold, and three minas of gold went to
the making of each buckler. The king put these into the House of the
Forest of Lebanon.

The king also made a great throne of ivory and overlaid it with fine ₁₈
gold. Six steps led up to the throne; at the back of the throne there was ₁₉
the head of a calf. There were arms on each side of the seat, with a lion
standing beside each of them, and twelve lions stood on the six steps, ₂₀
one at either end of each step. Nothing like it had ever been made for

[a] *Lit.* your affairs. [b] *So Sept.; Heb.* men. [c] *Mng. of Heb. word uncertain.*
[d] tolls levied by: *so Sept.; Heb.* men of. [e] and the tribute of: *prob. rdg.; Heb.* and all.

21 any monarch. All Solomon's drinking vessels were of gold, and all the plate in the House of the Forest of Lebanon was of red gold; no silver
22 was used, for it was reckoned of no value in the days of Solomon. The king had a fleet of merchantmen[a] at sea with Hiram's fleet; once every three years this fleet of merchantmen came home, bringing gold and silver, ivory, apes and monkeys.
23   Thus King Solomon outdid all the kings of the earth in wealth and
24 wisdom, and all the world courted him, to hear the wisdom which God
25 had put in his heart. Each brought his gift with him, vessels of silver and gold, garments, perfumes and spices, horses and mules, so much year by year.
26[b]   And Solomon got together many chariots and horses; he had fourteen hundred chariots and twelve thousand horses, and he stabled some in the chariot-towns and kept others at hand in Jerusalem.
27 The king made silver as common in Jerusalem as stones, and cedar as
28 plentiful as sycomore-fig in the Shephelah. Horses were imported from Egypt and Coa for Solomon; the royal merchants obtained them from
29 Coa by purchase. Chariots were imported from Egypt for six hundred silver shekels each, and horses for a hundred and fifty; in the same way the merchants obtained them for export from all the kings of the Hittites and the kings of Aram.
11   King Solomon was a lover of women, and besides Pharaoh's daughter he married many foreign women, Moabite, Ammonite, Edomite,
2 Sidonian, and Hittite, from the nations with whom the LORD had forbidden the Israelites to intermarry, 'because', he said, 'they will entice you to serve their gods.' But Solomon was devoted to them and
3 loved them dearly. He had seven hundred wives, who were princesses, and three hundred concubines, and they turned his heart from the
4 truth. When he grew old, his wives turned his heart to follow other gods, and he did not remain wholly loyal to the LORD his God as his
5 father David had been. He followed Ashtoreth, goddess of the
6 Sidonians, and Milcom, the loathsome god of the Ammonites. Thus Solomon did what was wrong in the eyes of the LORD, and was not
7 loyal to the LORD like his father David. He built a hill-shrine for Kemosh, the loathsome god of Moab, on the height to the east of
8 Jerusalem, and for Molech, the loathsome god of the Ammonites. Thus he did for the gods to which all his foreign wives burnt offerings and
9 made sacrifices. The LORD was angry with Solomon because his heart had turned away from the LORD the God of Israel, who had appeared
10 to him twice and had strictly commanded him not to follow other gods;
11 but he disobeyed the LORD's command. The LORD therefore said to Solomon, 'Because you have done this and have not kept my covenant

[a] *Lit.* ships of Tarshish.   [b] *Verses 26–29: cp. 2 Chr. 1. 14–17; 9. 25–28.*

and my statutes as I commanded you, I will tear the kingdom from you
and give it to your servant. Nevertheless, for the sake of your father 12
David I will not do this in your day; I will tear it out of your son's hand.
Even so not the whole kingdom; I will leave him one tribe for the sake 13
of my servant David and for the sake of Jerusalem, my chosen city.'
   Then the LORD raised up an adversary for Solomon, Hadad the 14
Edomite, of the royal house of Edom. At the time when David reduced 15
Edom, his commander-in-chief Joab had destroyed every male in the
country when he went into it to bury the slain. He and the armies of 16
Israel remained there for six months, until he had destroyed every male
in Edom. Then Hadad, who was still a boy, fled the country with some 17
of his father's Edomite servants, intending to enter Egypt. They set out 18
from Midian, made their way to Paran and, taking some men from
there, came to Pharaoh king of Egypt, who assigned Hadad a house and
maintenance and made him a grant of land. Hadad found great favour 19
with Pharaoh, who gave him in marriage a sister of Queen Tahpenes
his wife. She bore him his son Genubath; Tahpenes weaned the child 20
in Pharaoh's house, and he lived there along with Pharaoh's children.
When Hadad heard in Egypt that David rested with his forefathers 21
and that his commander-in-chief Joab was also dead, he said to
Pharaoh, 'Let me go so that I may return to my own country.' 'What 22
is it that you find wanting in my country', said Pharaoh, 'that you want
to go back to your own?' 'Nothing,' said Hadad, 'but do, pray, let
me go.' He remained an adversary for Israel all through Solomon's 25
reign. This*a* is the harm that Hadad caused: he maintained a strangle-
hold on*b* Israel and became king of Edom.*c*
   Then God raised up another adversary against Solomon, Rezon son 23
of Eliada, who had fled from his master Hadadezer king of Zobah. He 24
gathered men about him and became a captain of freebooters,*d* who
came to Damascus and occupied it; he*e* became king there.
   Jeroboam son of Nebat, one of Solomon's courtiers, an Ephrathite 26*f*
from Zeredah, whose widowed mother was named Zeruah, rebelled
against the king. And this is the story of his rebellion. Solomon had 27
built the Millo and closed the breach in the wall of the city of his father
David. Now this Jeroboam was a man of great energy; and Solomon, 28
seeing how the young man worked, had put him in charge of all the
labour-gangs in the tribal district of Joseph. On one occasion Jeroboam 29
had left Jerusalem, and the prophet Ahijah from Shiloh met him on the
road. The prophet was wrapped in a new cloak, and the two of them
were alone in the open country. Then Ahijah took hold of the new cloak 30

[a] *So Sept.; Heb. obscure.* [b] maintained...on: *so Pesh.; Heb.* loathed. [c] *So Sept.;
Heb.* Aram. [d] *So Sept.; Heb. adds* when David killed them. [e] *So Sept.; Heb.* they.
[f] *Verse 25 transposed to follow verse 22.*

31 he was wearing, tore it into twelve pieces and said to Jeroboam, 'Take ten pieces, for this is the word of the LORD the God of Israel: "I am going to tear the kingdom from the hand of Solomon and give you ten
32 tribes. But one tribe will remain his, for the sake of my servant David and for the sake of Jerusalem, the city I have chosen out of all the tribes
33 of Israel. I have done this because Solomon has[a] forsaken me; he has[a] prostrated himself before Ashtoreth goddess of the Sidonians, Kemosh god of Moab, and Milcom god of the Ammonites, and has[a] not conformed to my ways. He has not done what is right in my eyes or observed
34 my statutes and judgements as David his father did. Nevertheless I will not take the whole kingdom from him, but will maintain his rule as long as he lives, for the sake of my chosen servant David, who did
35 observe my commandments and statutes. But I will take the kingdom,
36 that is the ten tribes, from his son and give it to you. One tribe I will give to his son, that my servant David may always have a flame burning before me in Jerusalem, the city which I chose to receive my Name.
37 But I will appoint you to rule over all that you can desire, and to be
38 king over Israel. If you pay heed to all my commands, if you conform to my ways and do what is right in my eyes, observing my statutes and commandments as my servant David did, then I will be with you. I will establish your family for ever as I did for David; I will give
39 Israel to you, and punish David's descendants as they have deserved, but not for ever."'
40 After this Solomon sought to kill Jeroboam, but he fled to King Shishak in Egypt and remained there till Solomon's death.
41[b] The other acts and events of Solomon's reign, and all his wisdom,
42 are recorded in the annals of Solomon. The reign of King Solomon in
43 Jerusalem over the whole of Israel lasted forty years. Then he rested with his forefathers and was buried in the city of David his father, and he was succeeded by his son Rehoboam.

The divided kingdom

12 1[c] REHOBOAM WENT to Shechem, for all Israel had gone there to
2 make him king. When Jeroboam son of Nebat, who was still in Egypt, heard of it, he remained[d] there, having taken refuge there to
3 escape King Solomon. They now recalled him, and he and all the
4 assembly of Israel came to Rehoboam and said, 'Your father laid a cruel yoke upon us; but if you will now lighten the cruel slavery he imposed

[a] has: *so Sept.; Heb. has plural.* [b] *Verses 41–43: cp. 2 Chr. 9. 29–31.* [c] *Verses 1–19: cp. 2 Chr. 10. 1–19.* [d] *Or, with Sept. and 2 Chr. 10. 2, returned from.*

on us and the heavy yoke he laid on us, we will serve you.' 'Give me 5
three days,' he said, 'and come back again.' So the people went away.
King Rehoboam then consulted the elders who had been in attendance 6
on his father Solomon while he lived: 'What answer do you advise me
to give to this people?' And they said, 'If today you are willing to serve 7
this people, show yourself their servant now and speak kindly to them,
and they will be your servants ever after.' But he rejected the advice 8
which the elders gave him. He next consulted those who had grown up
with him, the young men in attendance, and asked them, 'What answer 9
do you advise me to give to this people's request that I should lighten
the yoke which my father laid on them?' The young men replied, 'Give 10
this answer to the people who say that your father made their yoke
heavy and ask you to lighten it; tell them: "My little finger is thicker
than my father's loins. My father laid a heavy yoke on you; I will make 11
it heavier. My father used the whip on you; but I will use the lash."'
Jeroboam and the people all came back to Rehoboam on the third day, 12
as the king had ordered. And the king gave them a harsh answer. He 13
rejected the advice which the elders had given him and spoke to the 14
people as the young men had advised: 'My father made your yoke
heavy; I will make it heavier. My father used the whip on you; but
I will use the lash.' So the king would not listen to the people; for the 15
LORD had given this turn to the affair, in order that the word he had
spoken by Ahijah of Shiloh to Jeroboam son of Nebat might be fulfilled.
When all Israel saw that the king would not listen to them, they 16
answered:

> What share have we in David?
> We have no lot in the son of Jesse.
> Away to your homes, O Israel;
> now see to your own house, David.

So Israel went to their homes, and Rehoboam ruled over those Israelites 17
who lived in the cities of Judah.

Then King Rehoboam sent out Adoram, the commander of the 18
forced levies, but the Israelites stoned him to death; thereupon King
Rehoboam mounted his chariot in haste and fled to Jerusalem. From 19
that day to this, the whole of Israel has been in rebellion against the
house of David.

When the men of Israel heard that Jeroboam had returned, they sent 20
and called him to the assembly and made him king over the whole of
Israel. The tribe of Judah alone followed the house of David.

When Rehoboam reached Jerusalem, he assembled all the house of 21[a]
Judah, the tribe of Benjamin also, a hundred and eighty thousand
chosen warriors, to fight against the house of Israel and recover his

[a] *Verses 21–24: cp. 2 Chr. 11. 1–4.*

22 kingdom. But the word of God came to Shemaiah the man of God:
23 'Say to Rehoboam son of Solomon, king of Judah, and to the house of
24 Judah and to Benjamin and the rest of the people, "This is the word of
the LORD: You shall not go up to make war on your kinsmen the
Israelites. Return to your homes, for this is my will."' So they listened
to the word of the LORD and returned home, as the LORD had told them.

25 THEN JEROBOAM REBUILT Shechem in the hill-country of Ephraim
and took up residence there; from there he went out and built Penuel.
26 'As things now stand,' he said to himself, 'the kingdom will revert to
27 the house of David. If this people go up to sacrifice in the house of the
LORD in Jerusalem, it will revive their allegiance to their lord Rehoboam
king of Judah, and they will kill me and return to King Rehoboam.'
28 After giving thought to the matter he made two calves of gold and said
to the people, 'It is too much trouble for you to go up to Jerusalem;
29 here are your gods, Israel, that brought you up from Egypt.' One he
30 set up at Bethel and the other he put at Dan, and this thing became a
sin in Israel; the people[a] went to Bethel to worship the one, and[a] all the
31 way to Dan to worship the other. He set up shrines on the hill-tops
also and appointed priests from every class of the people, who did not
32 belong to the Levites. He instituted a pilgrim-feast on the fifteenth day
of the eighth month like that in Judah, and he offered sacrifices upon
the altar. This he did at Bethel, sacrificing to the calves that he had
made and compelling the priests of the hill-shrines, which he had set up,
33 to serve at Bethel. So he went up to the altar that he had made at
Bethel on the fifteenth day of the eighth month; there, in a month of his
own choosing, he instituted for the Israelites a pilgrim-feast and
himself went up to the altar to burn the sacrifice.

13   As Jeroboam stood by the altar to burn the sacrifice, a man of God
from Judah, moved by the word of the LORD, appeared at Bethel.
2   He inveighed against the altar in the LORD's name, crying out, 'O altar,
altar! This is the word of the LORD: "Listen! A child shall be born to
the house of David, named Josiah. He will sacrifice upon you the priests
of the hill-shrines who make offerings upon you, and he[b] will burn
3   human bones upon you."' He gave a sign the same day: 'This is the
sign which the LORD has ordained: This altar will be rent in pieces
4   and the ashes upon it will be spilt.' When King Jeroboam heard the
sentence which the man of God pronounced against the altar at Bethel,
he pointed to him from the altar and said, 'Seize that man!' Immediately the hand which he had pointed at him became paralysed, so
5   that he could not draw it back. The altar too was rent in pieces and the
ashes were spilt, in fulfilment of the sign that the man of God had given

[a] *in Israel...one, and: so Luc. Sept.; Heb.* the people went.   [b] *So Sept.; Heb.* they.

at the LORD's command. The king appealed to the man of God to 6
pacify the LORD his God and pray for him that his hand might be
restored. The man of God did as he asked; his hand was restored and
became as it had been before. Then the king said to the man of God, 7
'Come home and take refreshment at my table, and let me give you
a present.' But the man of God answered, 'If you were to give me half 8
your house, I would not enter it with you: I will eat and drink nothing
in this place, for the LORD's command to me was to eat and drink 9
nothing, and not to go back by the way I came.' So he went back 10
another way; he did not return by the road he had taken to Bethel.

At that time there was an aged prophet living in Bethel. His sons 11
came*a* and recounted to him all that the man of God had done in Bethel
that day; they also told their father what he had said to the king. Their 12
father said to them, 'Which road did he take?' They pointed out the
road taken by the man of God who had come from Judah. He said to 13
his sons, 'Saddle an ass for me.' They saddled the ass, and he mounted
it and went after the man of God. He found him seated under a 14
terebinth and said to him, 'Are you the man of God who came from
Judah?' And he said, 'Yes, I am.' 'Come home and eat with me', said 15
the prophet. 'I cannot go back with you or enter your house,' said the 16
other; 'I can neither eat nor drink with you in this place, for it was 17
told me by the word of the LORD: "You shall eat and drink nothing
there, nor shall you go back the way you came."' And the old man said 18
to him, 'I also am a prophet, as you are; and an angel commanded me
by the word of the LORD to bring you home with me to eat and drink
with me.' He was lying; but the man of Judah went back with him and 19
ate and drank in his house. While they were still seated at table the 20
word of the LORD came to the prophet who had brought him back, and 21
he cried out to the man of God from Judah, 'This is the word of the
LORD: "You have defied the word of the LORD your God and have not
obeyed his command; you have come back to eat and to drink in the 22
place where he forbade it; therefore your body shall not be laid in the
grave of your forefathers."'

After they had eaten and drunk, he saddled an ass for the prophet whom 23
he had brought back. As he went on his way a lion met him and killed 24
him, and his body was left lying in the road, with the ass and the lion
both standing beside it. Some passers-by saw the body lying in the road 25
and the lion standing beside it, and they brought the news to the city
where the old prophet lived. When the prophet who had caused him 26
to break his journey heard it, he said, 'It is the man of God who defied
the word of the LORD. The LORD has given him to the lion, and it has
broken his neck and killed him in fulfilment of the word of the LORD.'

[a] *So Sept.; Heb.* His son came.

27 He told his sons to saddle an ass and, when they had saddled it,
28 he set out and found the body lying in the road with the ass and the
lion standing beside it; the lion had neither devoured the body nor
29 broken the back of the ass. Then the prophet lifted the body of the man
of God, laid it on the ass and brought it back to his own city to mourn
30 over it and bury it. He laid the body in his own grave and they mourned
31 for him, saying, 'My brother, my brother!' After burying him, he
said to his sons, 'When I die, bury me in the grave where the man of
32 God lies buried; lay my bones beside his; for the sentence which he
pronounced at the LORD's command against the altar in Bethel and all
the hill-shrines of Samaria shall be carried out.'

33   After this Jeroboam still did not abandon his evil ways but went on
appointing priests for the hill-shrines from all classes of the people; any
man who offered himself he would consecrate to be priest of a hill-
34 shrine. By doing this he brought guilt upon his own house and doomed
it to utter destruction.

14 1,2   At that time Jeroboam's son Abijah fell ill, and Jeroboam said to his
wife, 'Come now, disguise yourself so that people may not be able to
recognize you as my wife, and go to Shiloh. Ahijah the prophet is
3 there, the man who said I was to be king over this people. Take with
you ten loaves, some raisins, and a flask of syrup, and go to him; he
4 will tell you what will happen to the child.' Jeroboam's wife did so; she
set off at once for Shiloh and came to Ahijah's house. Now Ahijah
could not see, for his eyes were fixed in the blindness of old age,
5 and the LORD had said to him, 'The wife of Jeroboam is on her way to
consult you about her son, who is ill; you shall give her such and such an
6 answer.' When she came in, concealing who she was, and Ahijah heard
her footsteps at the door, he said, 'Come in, wife of Jeroboam. Why
7 conceal who you are? I have heavy news for you. Go and tell Jeroboam:
"This is the word of the LORD the God of Israel: I raised you out of the
8 people and appointed you prince over my people Israel; I tore away
the kingdom from the house of David and gave it to you; but you have
not been like my servant David, who kept my commands and followed
9 me with his whole heart, doing only what was right in my eyes. You
have outdone all your predecessors in wickedness; you have provoked
me to anger by making for yourself other gods and images of cast
10 metal; and you have turned your back on me. For this I will bring
disaster on the house of Jeroboam and I will destroy them all, every
mother's son, whether still under the protection of the family or not,
and I will sweep away the house of Jeroboam in Israel, as a man sweeps
11 up dung until none is left. Those of that house who die in the city shall
be food for the dogs, and those who die in the country shall be food for
the birds. It is the word of the LORD."

'You must go home now; the moment you set foot in the city, the 12
child will die. All Israel will mourn for him and bury him; he alone of 13
all Jeroboam's family will have proper burial, because in him alone
could the LORD the God of Israel find anything good. Then the LORD 14
will set up a king over Israel who shall put an end to the house of
Jeroboam. This first; and what next*a*? The LORD will strike Israel, till 15
it trembles like a reed in the water; he will uproot its people from this
good land which he gave to their forefathers and scatter them beyond
the Euphrates, because they have made their sacred poles*b* and
provoked the LORD's anger. And he will abandon Israel for the sins 16
that Jeroboam has committed and has led Israel to commit.' Jeroboam's 17
wife went home at once to Tirzah and, as she crossed the threshold of
the house, the boy died. They buried him, and all Israel mourned 18
over him; and thus the word of the LORD was fulfilled which he had
spoken through his servant Ahijah the prophet.

The other events of Jeroboam's reign, in war and peace, are recorded 19
in the annals of the kings of Israel. He reigned twenty-two years; then 20
he rested with his forefathers and was succeeded by his son Nadab.

IN JUDAH Rehoboam son of Solomon had become king. He was 21
forty-one years old when he came to the throne, and he reigned for
seventeen years in Jerusalem, the city which the LORD had chosen out
of all the tribes of Israel to receive his Name. Rehoboam's mother was
a woman of Ammon called Naamah. Judah did what was wrong in the 22
eyes of the LORD, rousing his jealous indignation by the sins they
committed, beyond anything that their forefathers had done. They 23
erected hill-shrines, sacred pillars, and sacred poles, on every high hill
and under every spreading tree. Worse still, all over the country there 24
were male prostitutes attached to the shrines, and the people adopted
all the abominable practices of the nations whom the LORD had
dispossessed in favour of Israel.

In the fifth year of Rehoboam's reign Shishak king of Egypt attacked 25*c*
Jerusalem. He removed the treasures of the house of the LORD and of 26
the royal palace, and seized everything, including all the shields of gold
that Solomon had made. King Rehoboam replaced them with bronze 27
shields and entrusted them to the officers of the escort who guarded
the entrance of the royal palace. Whenever the king entered the house 28
of the LORD, the escort carried them; afterwards they returned them
to the guard-room.

The other acts and events of Rehoboam's reign are recorded in the 29*d*
annals of the kings of Judah. There was continual fighting between him 30

[*a*] next: so *Targ.; Heb.* now.   [*b*] *Heb.* asherim.   [*c*] *Verses 25–28: cp. 2 Chr. 12.9–11.*
[*d*] *Verses 29–31: cp. 2 Chr. 12. 13–16.*

31 and Jeroboam. He rested with his forefathers and was buried with them in the city of David. (His mother was a woman of Ammon, whose name was Naamah.) He was succeeded by his son Abijam.

15   In the eighteenth year of the reign of Jeroboam son of Nebat,
2 Abijam became king of Judah. He reigned in Jerusalem for three years;
3 his mother was Maacah granddaughter*a* of Abishalom. All the sins that his father had committed before him he committed too, nor was
4 he faithful to the LORD his God as his ancestor David had been. But for David's sake the LORD his God gave him a flame to burn in Jerusalem, by establishing his dynasty and making Jerusalem secure,
5 because David had done what was right in the eyes of the LORD and had not disobeyed any of his commandments all his life, except in the
7 matter of Uriah the Hittite.*b* The other acts and events of Abijam's reign are recorded in the annals of the kings of Judah. There was
8 fighting between Abijam and Jeroboam. And Abijam rested with his forefathers and was buried in the city of David; and he was succeeded by his son Asa.

9   In the twentieth year of Jeroboam king of Israel, Asa became king
10 of Judah. He reigned in Jerusalem for forty-one years; his grand-
11 mother*c* was Maacah granddaughter*a* of Abishalom. Asa did what was
12 right in the eyes of the LORD, like his ancestor David. He expelled from the land the male prostitutes attached to the shrines and did away
13*d* with all the idols which his predecessors had made. He even deprived his own grandmother*c* Maacah of her rank as queen mother because she had an obscene object made for the worship of Asherah; Asa cut
14 it down and burnt it in the gorge of the Kidron. Although the hill-shrines were allowed to remain, Asa himself remained faithful to the
15 LORD all his life. He brought into the house of the LORD all his father's votive offerings and his own, gold and silver and sacred vessels.

16   Asa was at war with Baasha king of Israel all through their reigns.
17*e* Baasha king of Israel invaded Judah and fortified Ramah to cut off all
18 access to Asa king of Judah. So Asa took all the gold and silver that remained in the treasuries of the house of the LORD and of the royal palace, and sent his servants with them to Ben-hadad son of Tabrimmon, son of Hezion, king of Aram, whose capital was Damascus, with
19 instructions to say, 'There is an alliance between us, as there was between our fathers. I now send you this present of silver and gold; break off your alliance with Baasha king of Israel, so that he may
20 abandon his campaign against me.' Ben-hadad listened willingly to King Asa; he ordered the commanders of his armies to move against

---

[a] *Lit.* daughter.   [b] *Prob. rdg.; Heb. adds* (6) There was war between Rehoboam and Jeroboam all his days (*cp. 14. 30*).   [c] *Lit.* mother.   [d] *Verses 13–15: cp. 2 Chr. 15. 16–18.*   [e] *Verses 17–22: cp. 2 Chr. 16. 1–6.*

the cities of Israel, and they attacked Iyyon, Dan, Abel-beth-maacah, and that part of Kinnereth which marches with the land of Naphtali. When Baasha heard of it, he stopped fortifying Ramah and fell back 21 on Tirzah. Then King Asa issued a proclamation requiring every man 22 in Judah to join in removing the stones of Ramah and the timbers with which Baasha had fortified it; no one was exempted; and he used them to fortify Geba of Benjamin and Mizpah.

All the other events of Asa's reign, his exploits and his achievements, 23[a] and the cities he built, are recorded in the annals of the kings of Judah. But in his old age his feet were crippled by disease. He rested with his 24 forefathers and was buried with them in the city of his ancestor David; and he was succeeded by his son Jehoshaphat.

Nadab son of Jeroboam became king of Israel in the second year of 25 Asa king of Judah, and he reigned for two years. He did what was 26 wrong in the eyes of the LORD and followed in his father's footsteps, repeating the sin which he had led Israel to commit. Baasha son of 27 Ahijah, of the house of Issachar, conspired against him and attacked him at Gibbethon, a Philistine city, which Nadab was besieging with all his forces. And Baasha slew him and usurped the throne in the 28 third year of Asa king of Judah. As soon as he became king, he struck 29 down all the family of Jeroboam, destroying every living soul and leaving not one survivor. Thus the word of the LORD was fulfilled which he spoke through his servant Ahijah the Shilonite. This happened 30 because of the sins of Jeroboam and the sins which he led Israel to commit, and because he had provoked the anger of the LORD the God of Israel. The other events of Nadab's reign and all his acts are 31 recorded in the annals of the kings of Israel. Asa was at war with 32 Baasha king of Israel all through their reigns.

In the third year of Asa king of Judah, Baasha son of Ahijah became 33 king of all Israel in Tirzah and reigned twenty-four years. He did what 34 was wrong in the eyes of the LORD and followed in Jeroboam's foot-steps, repeating the sin which he had led Israel to commit. Then the 16 word of the LORD came to Jehu son of Hanani concerning Baasha: 'I 2 raised you from the dust and made you a prince over my people Israel, but you have followed in the footsteps of Jeroboam and have led my people Israel into sin, and have provoked me to anger with their sins. Therefore I will sweep away Baasha and his house and will deal 3 with it as I dealt with the house of Jeroboam son of Nebat. Those of 4 Baasha's family who die in the city shall be food for the dogs, and those who die in the country shall be food for the birds.' The other events of 5 Baasha's reign, his achievements and his exploits, are recorded in the annals of the kings of Israel. Baasha rested with his forefathers and 6

[a] *Verses 23, 24: cp. 2 Chr. 16. 11–14.*

7 was buried in Tirzah; and he was succeeded by his son Elah. Moreover the word of the LORD concerning Baasha and his family came through the prophet Jehu son of Hanani, because of all the wrong that he had done in the eyes of the LORD, thereby provoking his anger: because he had not only sinned like the house of Jeroboam, but had also brought destruction upon it.

8 In the twenty-sixth year of Asa king of Judah, Elah son of Baasha
9 became king of Israel and he reigned in Tirzah two years. Zimri, who was in his service commanding half the chariotry, plotted against him. The king was in Tirzah drinking himself drunk in the house of Arza,
10 comptroller of the household there, when Zimri broke in and attacked him, assassinated him and made himself king. This took place in the
11 twenty-seventh year of Asa king of Judah. As soon as he had become king and was enthroned, he struck down all the family of Baasha and
12 left not a single mother's son alive, kinsman or friend. He destroyed the whole family of Baasha, and thus fulfilled the word of the LORD
13 concerning Baasha, spoken through the prophet Jehu. This was what came of all the sins which Baasha and his son Elah had committed and the sins into which they had led Israel, provoking the anger of the
14 LORD the God of Israel with their worthless idols. The other events and acts of Elah's reign are recorded in the annals of the kings of Israel.

15 In the twenty-seventh year of Asa king of Judah, Zimri reigned in Tirzah for seven days. At the time the army was investing the Philistine
16 city of Gibbethon. When the Israelite troops in the field heard of Zimri's conspiracy and the murder of the king, there and then in the camp they made their commander Omri king of Israel by common
17 consent. Then Omri and his whole force withdrew from Gibbethon
18 and laid siege to Tirzah. Zimri, as soon as he saw that the city had fallen, retreated to the keep of the royal palace, set the whole of it on
19 fire over his head and so perished. This was what came of the sin he had committed by doing what was wrong in the eyes of the LORD and following in the footsteps of Jeroboam, repeating the sin into which he
20 had led Israel. The other events of Zimri's reign, and his conspiracy, are recorded in the annals of the kings of Israel.

21 Thereafter the people of Israel were split into two factions: one supported Tibni son of Ginath, determined to make him king; the
22 other supported Omri. Omri's party proved the stronger; Tibni lost his life and Omri became king.

23 It was in the thirty-first year of Asa king of Judah that Omri became
24 king of Israel and he reigned twelve years, six of them in Tirzah. He bought the hill of Samaria from Shemer for two talents of silver and built a city on it which he named Samaria after Shemer the owner of
25 the hill. Omri did what was wrong in the eyes of the LORD; he outdid all

his predecessors in wickedness. He followed in the footsteps of 26
Jeroboam son of Nebat, repeating the sins which he had led Israel to
commit, so that they provoked the anger of the LORD their God with
their worthless idols. The other events of Omri's reign, and his exploits, 27
are recorded in the annals of the kings of Israel. So Omri rested with 28
his forefathers and was buried in Samaria; and he was succeeded by his
son Ahab.

Ahab and Elijah

AHAB SON OF OMRI became king of Israel in the thirty-eighth 29
year of Asa king of Judah, and he reigned over Israel in Samaria
for twenty-two years. He did more that was wrong in the eyes of the 30
LORD than all his predecessors. As if it were not enough for him to follow 31
the sinful ways of Jeroboam son of Nebat, he contracted a marriage with
Jezebel daughter of Ethbaal king of Sidon, and went and worshipped
Baal; he prostrated himself before him and erected an altar to him in the 32
temple of Baal which he built in Samaria. He also set up a sacred pole; 33
indeed he did more to provoke the anger of the LORD the God of Israel
than all the kings of Israel before him. In his days Hiel of Bethel 34
rebuilt Jericho; laying its foundations cost him his eldest son Abiram,
and the setting up of its gates cost him Segub his youngest son. Thus
was fulfilled what the LORD had spoken through Joshua son of Nun.

Elijah the Tishbite, of Tishbe in Gilead, said to Ahab, 'I swear by 17
the life of the LORD the God of Israel, whose servant I am, that there
shall be neither dew nor rain these coming years unless I give the
word.' Then the word of the LORD came to him: 'Leave this place 2,3
and turn eastwards; and go into hiding in the ravine of Kerith east of
the Jordan. You shall drink from the stream, and I have commanded 4
the ravens to feed you there.' He did as the LORD had told him: he went 5
and stayed in the ravine of Kerith east of the Jordan, and the ravens 6
brought him bread and meat morning and evening, and he drank from
the stream. After a while the stream dried up, for there had been no 7
rain in the land. Then the word of the LORD came to him: 'Go now to 8,9
Zarephath, a village of Sidon, and stay there; I have commanded
a widow there to feed you.' So he went off to Zarephath. When he 10
reached the entrance to the village, he saw a widow gathering sticks,
and he called to her and said, 'Please bring me a little water in a pitcher
to drink.' As she went to fetch it, he called after her, 'Bring me, please, a 11
piece of bread as well.' But she said, 'As the LORD your God lives, I have 12
no food to sustain me except a handful of flour in a jar and a little oil in a
flask. Here I am, gathering two or three sticks to go and cook something

13 for my son and myself before we die.' 'Never fear,' said Elijah; 'go and
do as you say; but first make me a small cake from what you have and
bring it out to me; and after that make something for your son and
14 yourself. For this is the word of the LORD the God of Israel: "The jar
of flour shall not give out nor the flask of oil fail, until the LORD sends
15 rain on the land."' She went and did as Elijah had said, and there was
16 food for him and for her and her family for a long time. The jar of
flour did not give out nor did the flask of oil fail, as the word of the
LORD foretold through Elijah.

17   Afterwards the son of this woman, the mistress of the house, fell ill
18 and grew worse and worse, until at last his breathing ceased. Then she
said to Elijah, 'What made you interfere, you man of God? You came
19 here to bring my sins to light and kill my son!' 'Give me your son', he
said. He took the boy from her arms and carried him up to the roof-
20 chamber where his lodging was, and laid him on his own bed. Then he
called out to the LORD, 'O LORD my God, is this thy care for the widow
21 with whom I lodge, that thou hast been so cruel to her son?' Then he
breathed deeply*a* upon the child three times and called on the LORD, 'O
LORD my God, let the breath of life, I pray, return to the body of this
22 child.' The LORD listened to Elijah's cry, and the breath of life returned
23 to the child's body, and he revived; Elijah lifted him up and took him
down from the roof into the house, gave him to his mother and said,
24 'Look, your son is alive.' Then she said to Elijah, 'Now I know for
certain that you are a man of God and that the word of the LORD on
your lips is truth.'

18   Time went by, and in the third year the word of the LORD came to
Elijah: 'Go and show yourself to Ahab, and I will send rain upon the
2 land.' So he went to show himself to Ahab. At this time the famine in
3 Samaria was at its height, and Ahab summoned Obadiah, the comp-
4 troller of his household, a devout worshipper of the LORD. When
Jezebel massacred the prophets of the LORD, he had taken a hundred
of them and hidden them in caves, fifty by fifty, giving them food and
5 drink to keep them alive. Ahab said to Obadiah, 'Let us go through*b*
the land, both of us, to every spring and gully; if we can find enough
grass we may keep the horses and mules alive and lose none of our
6 cattle.' They divided the land between them for their survey, Ahab
going one way by himself and Obadiah another.

7   As Obadiah was on his way, Elijah met him. Obadiah recognized
him and fell prostrate before him and said, 'Can it be you, my lord
8 Elijah?' 'Yes,' he said, 'it is I; go and tell your master that Elijah is
9 here.' 'What wrong have I done?' said Obadiah. 'Why should you
10 give me into Ahab's hands? He will put me to death. As the LORD your

[a] *Or* stretched himself.   [b] Let us go through: *so Sept.; Heb.* Go into...

God lives, there is no nation or kingdom to which my master has not sent in search of you. If they said, "He is not here", he made that kingdom or nation swear on oath that they could not find you. Yet now 11 you say, "Go and tell your master that Elijah is here." What will 12 happen? As soon as I leave you, the spirit of the LORD will carry you away, who knows where? I shall go and tell Ahab, and when he fails to find you, he will kill me. Yet I have been a worshipper of the LORD from boyhood. Have you not been told, my lord, what I did when 13 Jezebel put the LORD's prophets to death, how I hid a hundred of them in caves, fifty by fifty, and kept them alive with food and drink? And now you say, "Go and tell your master that Elijah is here"! He will 14 kill me.' Elijah answered, 'As the LORD of Hosts lives, whose servant 15 I am, I swear that I will show myself to him this very day.' So Obadiah 16 went to find Ahab and gave him the message, and Ahab went to meet Elijah.

As soon as Ahab saw Elijah, he said to him, 'Is it you, you troubler of 17 Israel?' 'It is not I who have troubled Israel,' he replied, 'but you and 18 your father's family, by forsaking the commandments of the LORD and following Baal. But now, send and summon all Israel to meet me on 19 Mount Carmel, and the four hundred and fifty prophets of Baal with them and the four hundred prophets of the goddess Asherah, who are Jezebel's pensioners.'*a* So Ahab sent out to all the Israelites and 20 assembled the prophets on Mount Carmel. Elijah stepped forward and 21 said to the people, 'How long will you sit on the fence*b*? If the LORD is God, follow him; but if Baal, then follow him.' Not a word did they answer. Then Elijah said to the people, 'I am the only prophet of the 22 LORD still left, but there are four hundred and fifty prophets of Baal. Bring two bulls; let them choose one for themselves, cut it up and lay 23 it on the wood without setting fire to it, and I will prepare the other and lay it on the wood without setting fire to it. You shall invoke your 24 god by name and I will invoke the LORD by name; and the god who answers by fire, he is God.' And all the people shouted their approval.

Then Elijah said to the prophets of Baal, 'Choose one of the bulls 25 and offer it first, for there are more of you; invoke your god by name, but do not set fire to the wood.' So they took the bull provided for them 26 and offered it, and they invoked Baal by name from morning until noon, crying, 'Baal, Baal, answer us'; but there was no sound, no answer. They danced wildly beside the altar they had set up. At midday 27 Elijah mocked them: 'Call louder, for he is a god; it may be he is deep in thought, or engaged, or on a journey; or he may have gone to sleep and must be woken up.' They cried still louder and, as was their 28 custom, gashed themselves with swords and spears until the blood ran.

[a] *Lit.* who sit at Jezebel's table.   [b] sit on the fence: *lit.* bestride two branches.

29 All afternoon they raved and ranted till the hour of the regular sacrifice, but still there was no sound, no answer, no sign of attention.

30 Then Elijah said to all the people, 'Come here to me.' They all came,
31 and he repaired the altar of the LORD which had been torn down. He took twelve stones, one for each tribe of the sons of Jacob, the man
32 named Israel by the word of the LORD. With these stones he built an altar in the name of the LORD; he dug a trench round it big enough to
33 hold two measures*a* of seed; he arranged the wood, cut up the bull
34 and laid it on the wood. Then he said, 'Fill four jars with water and pour it on the whole-offering and on the wood.' They did so,*b* and he said, 'Do it again.' They did it again, and he said, 'Do it a third time.'
35 They did it a third time, and the water ran all round the altar and even
36 filled the trench. At the hour of the regular sacrifice the prophet Elijah came forward and said, 'LORD God of Abraham, of Isaac, and of Israel, let it be known today that thou art God in Israel and that I am
37 thy servant and have done all these things at thy command. Answer me, O LORD, answer me and let this people know that thou, LORD, art God and that it is thou that hast caused them to be backsliders.'*c*
38 Then the fire of the LORD fell. It consumed the whole-offering, the wood, the stones, and the earth, and licked up the water in the trench.
39 When all the people saw it, they fell prostrate and cried, 'The LORD is
40 God, the LORD is God.' Then Elijah said to them, 'Seize the prophets of Baal; let not one of them escape.' They seized them, and Elijah took them down to the Kishon and slaughtered them there in the valley.

41 Elijah said to Ahab, 'Go back now, eat and drink, for I hear the
42 sound of coming rain.' He did so, while Elijah himself climbed to the crest of Carmel. There he crouched on the ground with his face
43 between his knees. He said to his servant, 'Go and look out to the west.' He went and looked; 'There is nothing to see', he said. Seven times
44 Elijah ordered him back, and seven times he went.*d* The seventh time he said, 'I see a cloud no bigger than a man's hand, coming up from the west.' 'Now go', said Elijah, 'and tell Ahab to harness his
45 chariot and be off, or the rain will stop him.' Meanwhile the sky had grown black with clouds, the wind rose, and heavy rain began to fall.
46 Ahab mounted his chariot and set off for Jezreel; but the power of the LORD had come upon Elijah: he tucked up his robe and ran before Ahab all the way to Jezreel.

19 Ahab told Jezebel all that Elijah had done and how he had put all
2 the prophets to death with the sword. Jezebel then sent a messenger to Elijah to say, 'The gods do the same to me and more, unless by this
3 time tomorrow I have taken your life as you took theirs.' He was afraid

[a] *The Heb. measure called* seah. [b] They did so: *so Sept.; Heb. om.* [c] *Or* thou that dost bring them back to their allegiance. [d] and seven times he went: *so Sept.; Heb. om.*

and fled for his life. When he reached Beersheba in Judah, he left his
servant there and himself went a day's journey into the wilderness. He 4
came upon a broom-bush, and sat down under it and prayed for death:
'It is enough,' he said; 'now, LORD, take my life, for I am no better
than my fathers before me.' He lay down under the bush and, while he 5
slept, an angel touched him and said, 'Rise and eat.' He looked, and 6
there at his head was a cake baked on hot stones, and a pitcher of water.
He ate and drank and lay down again. The angel of the LORD came 7
again and touched him a second time, saying, 'Rise and eat; the
journey is too much for you.' He rose and ate and drank and, sustained 8
by this food, he went on for forty days and forty nights to Horeb, the
mount of God. He entered a cave and there he spent the night. 9

Suddenly the word of the LORD came to him: 'Why are you here,
Elijah?' 'Because of my great zeal for the LORD the God of Hosts', he 10
said. 'The people of Israel have forsaken thy covenant, torn down thy
altars and put thy prophets to death with the sword. I alone am left,
and they seek to take my life.' The answer came: 'Go and stand on the 11
mount before the LORD.' For the LORD was passing by: a great and
strong wind came rending mountains and shattering rocks before him,
but the LORD was not in the wind; and after the wind there was an
earthquake, but the LORD was not in the earthquake; and after the 12
earthquake fire, but the LORD was not in the fire; and after the fire a low
murmuring sound. When Elijah heard it, he muffled his face in his 13
cloak and went out and stood at the entrance of the cave. Then there
came a voice: 'Why are you here, Elijah?' 'Because of my great zeal 14
for the LORD the God of Hosts', he said. 'The people of Israel have
forsaken thy covenant, torn down thy altars and put thy prophets to
death with the sword. I alone am left, and they seek to take my life.'

The LORD said to him, 'Go back by way of the wilderness of 15
Damascus, enter the city and anoint Hazael to be king of Aram; anoint 16
Jehu son*a* of Nimshi to be king of Israel, and Elisha son of Shaphat of
Abel-meholah to be prophet in your place. Anyone who escapes the 17
sword of Hazael Jehu will slay, and anyone who escapes the sword
of Jehu Elisha will slay. But I will leave seven thousand in Israel, 18
all who have not bent the knee to Baal, all whose lips have not kissed
him.'

Elijah departed and found Elisha son of Shaphat ploughing; there 19
were twelve pair of oxen ahead of him, and he himself was with the last
of them. As Elijah passed, he threw his cloak over him, and Elisha, 20
leaving his oxen, ran after Elijah and said, 'Let me kiss my father and
mother goodbye, and then I will follow you.' 'Go back,' he replied;
'what have I done to prevent you?' He followed him no further but 21

[a] Or grandson (*cp. 2 Kgs. 9. 2*).

481

went home, took his pair of oxen, slaughtered them and burnt the wooden gear to cook the flesh, which he gave to the people to eat. Then he followed Elijah and became his disciple.

20 BEN-HADAD KING OF ARAM, having mustered all his forces, and taking with him thirty-two kings with their horses and chariots,
2 marched against Samaria to take it by siege or assault. He sent envoys
3 into the city to Ahab king of Israel to say, 'Hear what Ben-hadad says: Your silver and gold are mine, your wives and your splendid sons are
4 mine.'*a* The king of Israel answered, 'As you say, my lord king, I am
5 yours and all that I have.' The envoys came again and said, 'Hear what Ben-hadad says: I demand that you hand over your silver and gold,
6 your wives and your sons. This time tomorrow I will send my servants to search your house and your subjects' houses and to take possession
7 of everything you prize, and remove it.' The king of Israel then summoned all the elders of the land and said, 'You see this? The man is plainly picking a quarrel; for I did not demur when he sent to
8 claim my wives and my sons, my silver and gold.'*b* All the elders and all the people answered, 'Do not listen to him; you must not consent.'
9 So he gave this reply to Ben-hadad's envoys: 'Say to my lord the king: I accepted your majesty's demands on the first occasion; but what you now ask I cannot do.' The envoys went away and reported to their
10 master, and Ben-hadad sent back word: 'The gods do the same to me and more, if there is enough dust in Samaria to provide a handful for
11 each of my men.' The king of Israel made reply, 'Remind him of the saying: "The lame must not think himself a match for the nimble."'
12 This message reached Ben-hadad while he and the kings were drinking in their quarters.*c* At once he ordered his men to attack the city, and they did so.
13   Meanwhile a prophet had come to Ahab king of Israel and said to him, 'This is the word of the LORD: "You see this great rabble? Today I will give it into your hands and you shall know that I am the LORD."'
14 'Whom will you use for that?' asked Ahab. 'The young men who serve the district officers', was the answer. 'Who will draw up the line of
15 battle?' asked the king. 'You', said the prophet. Then Ahab called up these young men, two hundred and thirty-two all told, and behind
16 them the people of Israel, seven thousand in all. They went out at midday, while Ben-hadad and his allies, those thirty-two kings, were
17 drinking themselves drunk in their quarters.*c* The young men sallied out first, and word was sent to Ben-hadad that a party had come out of

[a] *Or* are your wives and your sons any good to me? [b] for I did not...gold: *or, with Sept.,* for he sent to demand my wives and children; my silver and gold I did not refuse. [c] in their quarters: *or* at Succoth.

Samaria. 'If they have come out for peace,' he said, 'take them alive; 18
if for battle, take them alive.'

So out of the city the young men went, and the army behind them; 19
each struck down his man, and the Aramaeans fled. The Israelites 20
pursued them, but Ben-hadad king of Aram escaped on horseback
with some of the cavalry. Then the king of Israel advanced and 21
captured[a] the horses and chariots, inflicting a heavy defeat on the
Aramaeans.

Then the prophet came to the king of Israel and said to him, 'Build 22
up your forces; you know what you must do. At the turn of the year
the king of Aram will renew the attack.' But the king of Aram's ministers 23
gave him this advice: 'Their gods are gods of the hills; that is why they
defeated us. Let us fight them in the plain; and then we shall have the
upper hand. What you must do is to relieve the kings of their command 24
and appoint other officers in their place. Raise another army like the 25
one you have lost. Bring your cavalry and chariots up to their former
strength, and then let us fight them in the plain, and we shall have the
upper hand.' He listened to their advice and acted on it.

At the turn of the year Ben-hadad mustered the Aramaeans and 26
advanced to Aphek to attack Israel. The Israelites too were mustered 27
and formed into companies, and then went out to meet them and
encamped opposite them. They seemed no better than a pair of new-born
kids, while the Aramaeans covered the country-side. The man of God 28
came to the king of Israel and said, 'This is the word of the LORD: The
Aramaeans may think that the LORD is a god of the hills and not a god
of the valleys; but I will give all this great rabble into your hands and
you shall know that I am the LORD.'

They lay in camp opposite one another for seven days; on the seventh 29
day battle was joined and the Israelites destroyed a hundred thousand
of the Aramaean infantry in one day. The survivors fled to Aphek, into 30
the citadel, and the city wall fell upon the twenty-seven thousand men
who were left. Ben-hadad took refuge in the citadel, retreating into
an inner room; and his attendants said to him, 'Listen; we have 31
heard that the kings of Israel are men to be trusted. Let us therefore
put sackcloth round our waists and wind rough cord round our heads
and go out to the king of Israel. It may be that he will spare your life.'
So they fastened on the sackcloth and the cord, and went to the king of 32
Israel and said, 'Your servant Ben-hadad pleads for his life.' 'My royal
cousin,' he said, 'is he still alive?' The men, taking the word for a 33
favourable omen, caught it up at once and said, 'Your cousin, yes,
Ben-hadad.' 'Go and fetch him', he said. Then Ben-hadad came out
and Ahab invited him into his chariot. And Ben-hadad said to him, 34

[a] *So Sept.; Heb.* destroyed.

483

'I will restore the cities which my father took from your father, and you may establish for yourself a trading quarter in Damascus, as my father did in Samaria.' 'On these terms', said Ahab, 'I will let you go.' So he granted him a treaty and let him go.

35 One of a company of prophets, at the command of the LORD,
36 ordered a certain man to strike him, but the man refused. 'Because you have not obeyed the LORD,' said the prophet, 'when you leave me, a lion will attack you.' When the man left, a lion did meet him and attacked
37 him. The prophet fell in with another man and ordered him to strike
38 him. He struck and wounded him. Then the prophet went off, with a bandage over his eyes, and thus disguised waited by the wayside for
39 the king. As the king was passing, he called out to him, 'Sir, I went into the thick of the battle, and a soldier came over to me with a prisoner and said, "Take charge of this fellow. If by any chance he gets away, your life shall be forfeit, or you shall pay a talent of silver."
40 As I was busy with one thing and another, sir, he disappeared.' The king of Israel said to him, 'You deserve to die.' And he said to the king
41 of Israel,[a] 'You have passed sentence on yourself.' Then he tore the bandage from his eyes, and the king of Israel saw that he was one of the
42 prophets. And he said to the king, 'This is the word of the LORD: "Because you let that man go when I had put him under a ban, your
43 life shall be forfeit for his life, your people for his people."' The king of Israel went home sullen and angry and entered Samaria.

21 NABOTH OF JEZREEL had a vineyard[b] near the palace of Ahab king
2   of Samaria. One day Ahab made a proposal to Naboth: 'Your vineyard is close to my palace; let me have it for a garden; I will give you a better
3   vineyard in exchange for it or, if you prefer, its value in silver.' But Naboth answered, 'The LORD forbid that I should let you have land
4   which has always been in my family.' So Ahab went home sullen and angry because Naboth would not let him have his ancestral land. He
5   lay down on his bed, covered his face and refused to eat. His wife Jezebel came in to him and said, 'What makes you so sullen and why
6   do you refuse to eat?' He told her, 'I proposed to Naboth of Jezreel that he should let me have his vineyard at its value or, if he liked, in exchange for another; but he would not let me have the vineyard.'
7   'Are you or are you not king in Israel?' said Jezebel. 'Come, eat and take heart; I will make you a gift of the vineyard of Naboth of Jezreel.'
8   So she wrote a letter in Ahab's name, sealed it with his seal and sent it to the elders and notables of Naboth's city, who sat in council with him.
9   She wrote: 'Proclaim a fast and give Naboth the seat of honour among

[a] You deserve...Israel: *prob. rdg.; Heb. om.* [b] *So Sept.; Heb. adds* which was in Jezreel.

the people. And see that two scoundrels are seated opposite him to 10
charge him with cursing[a] God and the king, then take him out and stone
him to death.' So the elders and notables of Naboth's city, who sat 11
with him in council, carried out the instructions Jezebel had sent them
in her letter: they proclaimed a fast and gave Naboth the seat of 12
honour, and these two scoundrels came in, sat opposite him and 13
charged him publicly with cursing[a] God and the king. Then they took
him outside the city and stoned him, and sent word to Jezebel that 14
Naboth had been stoned to death.

As soon as Jezebel heard that Naboth had been stoned and was dead, 15
she said to Ahab, 'Get up and take possession of the vineyard which
Naboth refused to sell you, for he is no longer alive; Naboth of Jezreel
is dead.' When Ahab heard that Naboth was dead, he got up and went 16
to the vineyard to take possession. Then the word of the LORD came to 17
Elijah the Tishbite: 'Go down at once to Ahab king of Israel, who is in 18
Samaria; you will find him in Naboth's vineyard, where he has gone to
take possession. Say to him, "This is the word of the LORD: Have you 19
killed your man, and taken his land as well?" Say to him, "This is the
word of the LORD: Where dogs licked the blood of Naboth, there dogs
shall lick your blood."' Ahab said to Elijah, 'Have you found me, my 20
enemy?' 'I have found you', he said, 'because you have sold yourself
to do what is wrong in the eyes of the LORD. I will bring[b] disaster upon 21
you; I will sweep you away and destroy every mother's son of the house
of Ahab in Israel, whether under protection of the family or not. And 22
I will deal with your house as I did with the house of Jeroboam son of
Nebat and of Baasha son of Ahijah, because you have provoked my
anger and led Israel into sin.' And the LORD went on to say of Jezebel, 23
'Jezebel shall be eaten by dogs by the rampart of[c] Jezreel. Of the house 24
of Ahab, those who die in the city shall be food for the dogs, and those
who die in the country shall be food for the birds.' (Never was a man 25
who sold himself to do what is wrong in the LORD's eyes as Ahab did,
and all at the prompting of Jezebel his wife. He committed gross 26
abominations in going after false gods, doing everything that the
Amorites did, whom the LORD had dispossessed in favour of Israel.)
When Ahab heard this, he rent his clothes, put on sackcloth and fasted; 27
he lay down in his sackcloth and went about muttering to himself.
Then the word of the LORD came to Elijah the Tishbite: 'Have you 28, 29
seen how Ahab has humbled himself before me? Because he has thus
humbled himself, I will not bring disaster upon his house in his own
lifetime, but in his son's.'

[a] cursing: *lit.* bidding farewell to. [b] he said,...bring: *or* he said. 'Because you...
LORD, I am bringing... [c] by the rampart of: *or, with some MSS.*, in the plot of ground
at (*cp. 2 Kgs. 9. 36*).

22 FOR THREE YEARS there was no war between the Aramaeans and the
2*a* Israelites, but in the third year Jehoshaphat king of Judah went down
3 to visit the king of Israel. The latter said to his courtiers, 'You know
that Ramoth-gilead belongs to us, and yet we do nothing to recover it
4 from the king of Aram.' He said to Jehoshaphat, 'Will you join me in
attacking Ramoth-gilead?' Jehoshaphat said to the king of Israel,
5 'What is mine is yours: myself, my people, and my horses.' Then
Jehoshaphat said to the king of Israel, 'First let us seek counsel from
6 the LORD.' The king of Israel assembled the prophets, some four
hundred of them, and asked them, 'Shall I attack Ramoth-gilead or
shall I refrain?' 'Attack,' they answered; 'the Lord will deliver it into
7 your hands.' Jehoshaphat asked, 'Is there no other prophet of the LORD
8 here through whom we may seek guidance?' 'There is one more',
the king of Israel answered, 'through whom we may seek guidance of
the LORD, but I hate the man, because he prophesies no good for me;
never anything but evil. His name is Micaiah son of Imlah.' Jehoshaphat
9 exclaimed, 'My lord king, let no such word pass your lips!' So the
king of Israel called one of his eunuchs and told him to fetch Micaiah
son of Imlah with all speed.

10   The king of Israel and Jehoshaphat king of Judah were seated on their
thrones, in shining armour,*b* at the entrance to the gate of Samaria,
11 and all the prophets were prophesying before them. One of them,
Zedekiah son of Kenaanah, made himself horns of iron and said, 'This
is the word of the LORD: "With horns like these you shall gore the
12 Aramaeans and make an end of them."' In the same vein all the
prophets prophesied, 'Attack Ramoth-gilead and win the day; the
13 LORD will deliver it into your hands.' The messenger sent to fetch
Micaiah told him that the prophets had with one voice given the king a
favourable answer. 'And mind you agree with them', he added.
14 'As the LORD lives,' said Micaiah, 'I will say only what the LORD tells
me to say.'

15   When Micaiah came into the king's presence, the king said to him,
'Micaiah, shall we attack Ramoth-gilead or shall we refrain?' 'Attack
and win the day,' he said; 'the LORD will deliver it into your hands.'
16 'How often must I adjure you', said the king, 'to tell me nothing but the
17 truth in the name of the LORD?' Then Micaiah said, 'I saw all Israel
scattered on the mountains, like sheep without a shepherd; and I heard
the LORD say, "They have no master, let them go home in peace."'
18 The king of Israel said to Jehoshaphat, 'Did I not tell you that he
19 never prophesies good for me, nothing but evil?' Micaiah went on,
'Listen now to the word of the LORD. I saw the LORD seated on his
throne, with all the host of heaven in attendance on his right and on

[*a*] *Verses 2-35: cp. 2 Chr. 18. 2-34.*   [*b*] *So Sept.; Heb. adds* robes.

his left. The LORD said, "Who will entice Ahab to attack and fall on^a 20
Ramoth-gilead?" One said one thing and one said another; then a 21
spirit came forward and stood before the LORD and said, "I will
entice him." "How?" said the LORD. "I will go out", he said, "and be a 22
lying spirit in the mouth of all his prophets." "You shall entice him,"
said the LORD, "and you shall succeed; go and do it." You see, then, 23
how the LORD has put a lying spirit in the mouth of all these prophets
of yours, because he has decreed disaster for you.' Then Zedekiah son 24
of Kenaanah came up to Micaiah and struck him in the face: 'And how
did the spirit of the LORD pass from me to speak to you?' he said.
Micaiah answered, 'That you will find out on the day when you run 25
into an inner room to hide yourself.' Then the king of Israel ordered 26
Micaiah to be arrested and committed to the custody of Amon the
governor of the city and Joash the king's son.^{b} 'Lock this fellow up', he 27
said, 'and give him prison diet of bread and water until I come home in
safety.' Micaiah retorted, 'If you do return in safety, the LORD has not 28
spoken by me.'^{c}

So the king of Israel and Jehoshaphat king of Judah marched on 29
Ramoth-gilead, and the king of Israel said to Jehoshaphat, 'I will 30
disguise myself to go into battle, but you shall wear your royal robes.'
So he went into battle in disguise. Now the king of Aram had com- 31
manded the thirty-two captains of his chariots not to engage all and
sundry but the king of Israel alone. When the captains saw Jehoshaphat, 32
they thought he was the king of Israel and turned to attack him. But
Jehoshaphat cried out and, when the captains saw that he was not the 33
king of Israel, they broke off the attack on him. But one man drew his 34
bow at random and hit the king of Israel where the breastplate joins
the plates of the armour. So he said to his driver, 'Wheel round and
take me out of the line; I am wounded.' When the day's fighting 35
reached its height, the king was facing the Aramaeans propped up in
his chariot, and the blood from his wound flowed down upon the floor
of the chariot; and in the evening he died. At sunset the herald went 36
through the ranks, crying, 'Every man to his city, every man to his
country.' Thus died the king. He was brought to Samaria and they 37
buried him there. The chariot was swilled out at the pool of Samaria, 38
and the dogs licked up the blood, and the prostitutes washed themselves in it, in fulfilment of the word the LORD had spoken.

Now the other acts and events of Ahab's reign, the ivory house and 39
all the cities he built, are recorded in the annals of the kings of Israel.
So Ahab rested with his forefathers and was succeeded by his son 40
Ahaziah.

[a] *Or* at. [b] son: *or* deputy. [c] *So Sept.; Heb. adds* and he said, 'Listen, peoples, all together.'

41[a] Jehoshaphat son of Asa had become king of Judah in the fourth year
42 of Ahab king of Israel. He was thirty-five years old when he came to the
throne, and he reigned in Jerusalem for twenty-five years; his mother
43 was Azubah daughter of Shilhi. He followed in the footsteps of Asa
his father and did not swerve from them; he did what was right in the
eyes of the LORD. [b]But the hill-shrines were allowed to remain; the people
44 continued to slaughter and burn sacrifices there. Jehoshaphat remained
45 at peace with the king of Israel. The other events of Jehoshaphat's
reign, his exploits and his wars, are recorded in the annals of the kings
46 of Judah. But he did away with such of the male prostitutes attached
to the shrines as were still left over from the days of Asa his father.
47,48 There was no king in Edom, only[c] a viceroy of Jehoshaphat; he
built merchantmen[d] to sail to Ophir for gold, but they never made the
49 journey because they were wrecked at Ezion-geber. Ahaziah son of
Ahab proposed to Jehoshaphat that his own men should go to sea with
his; but Jehoshaphat would not consent.
50 Jehoshaphat rested with his forefathers and was buried with them
in the city of David his father, and was succeeded by his son Joram.
51 Ahaziah son of Ahab became king of Israel in Samaria in the
seventeenth year of Jehoshaphat king of Judah, and reigned over Israel
52 for two years. He did what was wrong in the eyes of the LORD, following
in the footsteps of his father and mother and in those of Jeroboam son
53 of Nebat, who had led Israel into sin. He served Baal and worshipped
him, and provoked the anger of the LORD the God of Israel, as his
father had done.

[a] *Verses 41–43: cp. 2 Chr. 20. 31–33.* [b] But...there: *verse 44 in Heb.* [c] only: *prob.
rdg.; Heb. om.* [d] *Lit.* ships of Tarshish.

THE SECOND BOOK OF
KINGS

Elisha and the end of the house of Ahab

AFTER AHAB'S DEATH Moab rebelled against Israel. **1**
Ahaziah fell through a latticed window in his roof-chamber **2**
in Samaria and injured himself; he sent messengers to inquire
of Baal-zebub the god of Ekron whether he would recover from his
illness. The angel of the LORD ordered Elijah the Tishbite to go and **3**
meet the messengers of the king of Samaria and say to them, 'Is there
no god in Israel, that you go to inquire of Baal-zebub the god of
Ekron? This is the word of the LORD to your master: "You shall not **4**
rise from the bed where you are lying; you will die."' Then Elijah
departed. The messengers went back to the king. When asked why they **5**
had returned, they answered that a man had come to meet them and **6**
had ordered them to return and say to the king who had sent them,
'This is the word of the LORD: "Is there no god in Israel, that you
send to inquire of Baal-zebub the god of Ekron? In consequence, you
shall not rise from the bed where you are lying; you will die."' The **7**
king asked them what kind of man it was who had met them and said
this. 'A hairy man', they answered, 'with a leather apron round his **8**
waist.' 'It is Elijah the Tishbite', said the king.

Then the king sent a captain to him with his company of fifty. He **9**
went up and found the prophet sitting on a hill-top and said to him,
'Man of God, the king orders you to come down.' Elijah answered the **10**
captain, 'If I am a man of God, may fire fall from heaven and consume
you and your company!' Fire fell from heaven and consumed the
officer and his fifty men. The king sent another captain of fifty with **11**
his company, and he went up[a] and said to the prophet, 'Man of God,
this is the king's command: Come down at once.' Elijah answered, **12**
'If I am a man of God, may fire fall from heaven and consume you and
your company!' God's fire fell from heaven and consumed the man and
his company. The king sent the captain of a third company with his **13**
fifty men, and this third captain went up the hill to Elijah and knelt
down before him and pleaded with him: 'Man of God, consider me
and these fifty servants of yours, and set some value on our lives. Fire **14**
fell from heaven and consumed the other two captains of fifty and their
companies; but let my life have some value in your eyes.' The angel of **15**

[a] So Luc. Sept.; Heb. answered.

the LORD said to Elijah, 'Go down with him. Do not be afraid.' So he
16 rose and went down with him to the king, and he said, 'This is the
word of the LORD: "You have sent to inquire of Baal-zebub the god of
Ekron,^a and therefore you shall not rise from the bed where you are
17 lying; you will die."' The word of the LORD which Elijah had spoken
was fulfilled, and Ahaziah died; and because he had no son, his
brother^b Jehoram succeeded him in the second year of Joram son of
Jehoshaphat king of Judah.
18   The other events of Ahaziah's reign are recorded in the annals of the
kings of Israel.

2   The time came when the LORD would take Elijah up to heaven in
2 a whirlwind. Elijah and Elisha left Gilgal, and Elijah said to Elisha,
'Stay here; for the LORD has sent me to Bethel.' But Elisha said, 'As the
LORD lives, your life upon it, I will not leave you.' So they went down
3 country to Bethel. There a company of prophets came out to Elisha
and said to him, 'Do you know that the LORD is going to take your lord
and master from you today?' 'I do know,' he replied; 'say no more.'
4 Then Elijah said to him, 'Stay here, Elisha; for the LORD has sent me
to Jericho.' But he replied, 'As the LORD lives, your life upon it, I will
5 not leave you.' So they went to Jericho. There a company of prophets
came up to Elisha and said to him, 'Do you know that the LORD is
going to take your lord and master from you today?' 'I do know,'
6 he said; 'say no more.' Then Elijah said to him, 'Stay here; for the
LORD has sent me to the Jordan.' The other replied, 'As the LORD
lives, your life upon it, I will not leave you.' So the two of them went on.
7   Fifty of the prophets followed them, and stood watching from a
8 distance as the two of them stopped by the Jordan. Elijah took his
cloak, rolled it up and struck the water with it. The water divided to
9 right and left, and they both crossed over on dry ground. While they
were crossing, Elijah said to Elisha, 'Tell me what I can do for you
before I am taken from you.' Elisha said, 'Let me inherit a double
10 share of your spirit.' 'You have asked a hard thing', said Elijah. 'If
you see me taken from you, may your wish be granted; if you do not,
11 it shall not be granted.' They went on, talking as they went, and
suddenly there appeared chariots of fire and horses of fire, which
separated them one from the other, and Elijah was carried up in the
12 whirlwind to heaven. When Elisha saw it, he cried, 'My father, my
father, the chariots and the horsemen of Israel!', and he saw him no
13 more. Then he took hold of his mantle and rent it in two, and he picked
up the cloak which had fallen from Elijah, and came back and stood on
14 the bank of the Jordan. There he too struck the water with Elijah's

[a] So Sept.; Heb. adds is it because there is no god in Israel of whom you may inquire?
[b] his brother: so Luc. Sept.; Heb. om.

cloak and said, 'Where is the LORD the God of Elijah?' When he struck
the water, it was again divided to right and left, and he crossed over.
The prophets from Jericho, who were watching, saw him and said, 15
'The spirit of Elijah has settled on Elisha.' So they came to meet him,
and fell on their faces before him and said, 'Your servants have fifty 16
stalwart men. Let them go and search for your master; perhaps the
spirit of the LORD has lifted him up and cast him on some mountain or
into some valley.' But he said, 'No, you must not send them.' They 17
pressed him, however, until he had not the heart to refuse. So they sent
out the fifty men but, though they searched for three days, they did not
find him. When they came back to Elisha, who had remained at 18
Jericho, he said to them, 'Did I not tell you not to go?'

The people of the city said to Elisha, 'You can see how pleasantly 19
our city is situated, but the water is polluted and the country is troubled
with miscarriages.' He said, 'Fetch me a new bowl and put some salt 20
in it.' When they had fetched it, he went out to the spring and, throwing 21
the salt into it, he said, 'This is the word of the LORD: "I purify this
water. It shall cause no more death or miscarriage."' The water has 22
remained pure till this day, in fulfilment of Elisha's word.

He went up from there to Bethel and, as he was on his way, some 23
small boys came out of the city and jeered at him, saying, 'Get along
with you, bald head, get along.' He turned round and looked at them 24
and he cursed them in the name of the LORD; and two she-bears came
out of a wood and mauled forty-two of them. From there he went on 25
to Mount Carmel, and thence back to Samaria.

In the eighteenth year of Jehoshaphat king of Judah, Jehoram son 3
of Ahab became king of Israel in Samaria, and he reigned for twelve
years. He did what was wrong in the eyes of the LORD, though not as 2
his father and his mother had done; he did remove the sacred pillar of
the Baal which his father had made. Yet he persisted in the sins into 3
which Jeroboam son of Nebat had led Israel, and did not give them up.

Mesha king of Moab was a sheep-breeder, and he used to supply the 4
king of Israel regularly with the wool of a hundred thousand lambs and
a hundred thousand rams. When Ahab died, the king of Moab rebelled 5
against the king of Israel. Then King Jehoram came from Samaria and 6
mustered all Israel. He also sent this message to Jehoshaphat king of 7
Judah: 'The king of Moab has rebelled against me. Will you join me
in attacking Moab?' 'I will,' he replied; 'what is mine is yours: myself,
my people, and my horses.' 'From which direction shall we attack?' 8
Jehoram asked. 'Through the wilderness of Edom', replied the other.
So the king of Israel set out with the king of Judah and the king of 9
Edom. When they had been seven days on the march, they had no
water left for the army or the pack-animals. Then the king of Israel 10

said, 'Alas, the LORD has brought together three kings, only to put us
11 at the mercy of the Moabites.' But Jehoshaphat said, 'Is there not a
prophet of the LORD here through whom we may seek guidance of the
LORD?' One of the officers of the king of Israel answered, 'Elisha son
of Shaphat is here, the man who poured water on Elijah's hands.'
12 'The word of the LORD is with him', said Jehoshaphat. So the king of
Israel and Jehoshaphat and the king of Edom went down to Elisha.
13 Elisha said to the king of Israel, 'Why do you come to me? Go to the
prophets of your father and your mother.' But the king of Israel said
to him, 'No; the LORD has called us three kings out to put us at the
14 mercy of the Moabites.' 'As the LORD of Hosts lives, whom I serve,'
said Elisha, 'I would not spare a look or a glance for you, if it were not
15 for my regard for Jehoshaphat king of Judah. But now, fetch me a
minstrel.' They fetched a minstrel,^a and while he was playing, the power
16 of the LORD came upon Elisha and he said, 'This is the word of the
17 LORD: "Pools will form all over this ravine." The LORD has decreed
that you shall see neither wind nor rain, yet this ravine shall be filled
with water for you and your army^b and your pack-animals to drink.
18 But that is a mere trifle in the sight of the LORD; what he will also do,
19 is to put Moab at your mercy. You will raze to the ground every
fortified town and every noble city; you will cut down all their fine
trees; you will stop up all the springs of water; and you will spoil every
20 good piece of land by littering it with stones.' In the morning at the
hour of the regular sacrifice they saw water flowing in from the
direction of Edom, and the land was flooded.
21   Meanwhile all Moab had heard that the kings had come up to fight
against them, and every man, young and old, who could carry arms, was
22 called out and stationed on the frontier. When they got up next morning
and the sun had risen over the water, the Moabites saw the water in
23 front of them red like blood and cried out, 'It is blood. The kings must
have quarrelled and attacked one another. Now to the plunder, Moab!'
24 When they came to the Israelite camp, the Israelites turned out and
attacked them and drove the Moabites headlong in flight, and them-
25 selves entered^c the land of Moab, destroying as they went. They razed
the cities to the ground; they littered every good piece of land with
stones, each man casting one stone on to it; they stopped up every
spring of water; they cut down all their fine trees; and they harried
Moab^d until only in Kir-hareseth were any buildings left standing,
and even this city the slingers surrounded and attacked.
26   When the king of Moab saw that the war had gone against him, he
took seven hundred men with him, armed with swords, to cut a way

[a] They fetched a minstrel: *so Luc. Sept.; Heb. om.* [b] *So Luc. Sept.; Heb.* cattle.
[c] *So Sept.; Heb.* destroyed. [d] and...Moab: *so Luc. Sept.; Heb. om.*

through to the king of Aram,*[a]* but they failed in the attempt. Then he 27
took his eldest son, who would have succeeded him, and offered him
as a whole-offering upon the city wall. The Israelites were filled with
such consternation at this sight,*[b]* that they struck camp and returned
to their own land.

The wife of a member of a company of prophets appealed to Elisha. 4
'My husband, your servant, has died', she said. 'You know that he
was a man who feared the LORD; but a creditor has come to take away
my two boys as his slaves.' Elisha said to her, 'How can I help you? 2
Tell me what you have in the house.' 'Nothing at all', she answered,
'except a flask of oil.' 'Go out then', he said, 'and borrow vessels from 3
all your neighbours; get as many empty ones as you can. Then, when 4
you come home, shut yourself in with your sons, pour from the flask
into all these vessels and, as they are filled, set them aside.' She left 5
him and shut herself in with her sons. As they brought her the vessels
she filled them. When they were all full, she said to one of her sons, 6
'Bring me another.' 'There is not one left', he said. Then the flow of
oil ceased. She came out and told the man of God, and he said, 'Go and 7
sell the oil and redeem your boys who are being taken as pledges,*[c]* and
you and they can live on what is left.'

It happened once that Elisha went over to Shunem. There was a great 8
lady there who pressed him to accept her hospitality, and so, whenever
he came that way, he stopped to take food there. One day she said to 9
her husband, 'I know that this man who comes here regularly is a holy
man of God. Why not build up the wall to make him a little roof- 10
chamber, and put in it a bed, a table, a seat, and a lamp, and let him
stay there whenever he comes to us?' Once when he arrived and went 11
to this roof-chamber and lay down to rest, he said to Gehazi, his 12
servant, 'Call this Shunammite woman.' He called her and, when she
appeared before the prophet, he said to his servant, 'Say to her, "You 13
have taken all this trouble for us. What can I do for you? Shall I
speak for you to the king or to the commander-in-chief?"' But she
replied, 'I am content where I am, among my own people.' He said, 14
'Then what can be done for her?' Gehazi said, 'There is only this:
she has no child and her husband is old.' 'Call her back', Elisha said. 15
When she was called, she appeared in the doorway, and he said, 'In due 16
season, this time next year, you shall have a son in your arms.' But she
said, 'No, no, my lord, you are a man of God and would not lie to your
servant.' Next year in due season the woman conceived and bore a son, 17
as Elisha had foretold.

When the child was old enough, he went out one day to the reapers 18

[a] *So Old Latin; Heb.* Edom.   [b] The Israelites...sight: *or* There was such great anger
against the Israelites...   [c] redeem...pledges: *or* pay off your debt.

19 where his father was. All of a sudden he cried out to his father, 'O my head, my head!' His father told a servant to carry him to his mother.
20 He brought him to his mother; the boy sat on her lap till midday, and
21 then he died. She went up and laid him on the bed of the man of God,
22 shut the door and went out. She called her husband and said, 'Send me one of the servants and a she-ass, I must go to the man of God as
23 fast as I can, and come straight back.' 'Why go to him today?' he asked. 'It is neither new moon nor sabbath.'*a* 'Never mind that', she
24 answered. When the ass was saddled, she said to her servant, 'Lead on
25 and do not slacken pace unless I tell you.' So she set out and came to the man of God on Mount Carmel. The man of God spied her in the distance and said to Gehazi, his servant, 'That is the Shunammite
26 woman coming. Run and meet her, and ask, "Is all well with you? Is all well with your husband? Is all well with the boy?"' She answered,
27 'All is well.' When she reached the man of God on the hill, she clutched his feet. Gehazi came forward to push her away, but the man of God said, 'Let her alone; she is in great distress, and the LORD has concealed
28 it from me and not told me.' 'My lord,' she said, 'did I ask for a son?
29 Did I not beg you not to raise my hopes and then dash them?' Then he turned to Gehazi: 'Hitch up your cloak; take my staff with you and run. If you meet anyone on the way, do not stop to greet him; if anyone greets you, do not answer him. Lay my staff on the boy's face.'
30 But the mother cried, 'As the LORD lives, your life upon it, I will not leave you.' So he got up and followed her.*b*
31   Gehazi went on ahead of them and laid the staff on the boy's face, but there was no sound and no sign of life. So he went back to meet
32 Elisha and told him that the boy had not roused. When Elisha entered the house, there was the boy dead, on the bed where he had been laid.
33 He went into the room, shut the door on the two of them and prayed
34 to the LORD. Then, getting on to the bed, he lay upon the child, put his mouth to the child's mouth, his eyes to his eyes and his hands to his hands; and, as he pressed*c* upon him, the child's body grew warm.
35 Elisha got up and walked once up and down the room; then, getting on to the bed again, he pressed*c* upon him and breathed into him*d*
36 seven times; and the boy opened his eyes. The prophet summoned Gehazi and said, 'Call this Shunammite woman.' She answered his
37 call and the prophet said, 'Take your child.' She came in and fell prostrate before him. Then she took up her son and went out.
38   Elisha returned to Gilgal at a time when there was a famine in the land. One day, when a group of prophets was sitting at his feet, he said to his servant, 'Set the big pot on the fire and prepare some broth for

[a] *Or* full moon.   [b] *Or* went with her.   [c] *Prob. rdg.; Heb.* crouched.   [d] and breathed into him: *or* and the boy sneezed.

the company.' One of them went out into the fields to gather herbs and ³⁹
found a wild vine, and filled the skirt of his garment with bitter-
apples.ᵃ He came back and sliced them into the pot, not knowing
what they were. They poured it out for the men to eat, but, when they ⁴⁰
tasted it, they cried out, 'Man of God, there is death in the pot', and
they could not eat it. The prophet said, 'Fetch some meal.' He threw ⁴¹
it into the pot and said, 'Now pour out for the men to eat.' This time
there was no harm in the pot.

A man came from Baal-shalisha, bringing the man of God some of ⁴²
the new season's bread, twenty barley loaves, and fresh ripe ears of
corn.ᵇ Elisha said, 'Give this to the people to eat.' But his disciple ⁴³
protested, 'I cannot set this before a hundred men.' Still he repeated,
'Give it to the people to eat; for this is the word of the LORD: "They
will eat and there will be some left over."' So he set it before them, and ⁴⁴
they ate and left some over, as the LORD had said.

NAAMAN, COMMANDER of the king of Aram's army, was a great 5
man highly esteemed by his master, because by his means the LORD
had given victory to Aram; but he was a leper.ᶜ ᵈ On one of their raids ²
the Aramaeans brought back as a captive from the land of Israel a little
girl, who became a servant to Naaman's wife. She said to her mistress, ³
'If only my master could meet the prophet who lives in Samaria, he
would get rid of the disease for him.' Naaman went in and reported to ⁴
his master word for word what the girl from the land of Israel had said.
'Very well, you may go,' said the king of Aram, 'and I will send a letter ⁵
to the king of Israel.' So Naaman went, taking with him ten talents of
silver, six thousand shekels of gold, and ten changes of clothing. He ⁶
delivered the letter to the king of Israel, which read thus: 'This letter
is to inform you that I am sending to you my servant Naaman, and
I beg you to rid him of his disease.' When the king of Israel read the ⁷
letter, he rent his clothes and said, 'Am I a godᵉ to kill and to make alive,
that this fellow sends to me to cure a man of his disease? Surely you
must see that he is picking a quarrel with me.' When Elisha, the man ⁸
of God, heard how the king of Israel had rent his clothes, he sent to
him saying, 'Why did you rend your clothes? Let the man come to me,
and he will know that there is a prophet in Israel.' So Naaman came ⁹
with his horses and chariots and stood at the entrance to Elisha's house.
Elisha sent out a messenger to say to him, 'If you will go and wash seven ¹⁰
times in the Jordan, your flesh will be restored and you will be clean.'
Naaman was furious and went away, saying, 'I thought he would at ¹¹

[a] Or poisonous wild gourds. [b] fresh...corn: prob. rdg.; Heb. unintelligible. [c] he was
a leper: or his skin was diseased. [d] So Luc. Sept.; Heb. adds a mighty warrior. [e] Or
Am I God.

least have come out and stood, and invoked the LORD his God by name,
12 waved his hand over the place and so rid me of the disease. Are not
Abana and Pharpar, rivers of Damascus, better than all the waters of
Israel? Can I not wash in them and be clean?' So he turned and went
13 off in a rage. But his servants came up to him and said, 'If the prophet
had bidden you do something difficult, would you not do it? How much
14 more then, if he tells you to wash and be clean?' So he went down and
dipped himself in the Jordan seven times as the man of God had told
him, and his flesh was restored as a little child's, and he was clean.

15   Then he and his retinue went back to the man of God and stood
before him; and he said, 'Now I know that there is no god anywhere
on earth except in Israel. Will you accept a token of gratitude from
16 your servant?' 'As the LORD lives, whom I serve,' said the prophet,
17 'I will accept nothing.' He was pressed to accept, but he refused. 'Then
if you will not,' said Naaman, 'let me, sir, have two mules' load of
earth. For I will no longer offer whole-offering or sacrifice to any god
18 but the LORD. In this one matter only may the LORD pardon me: when
my master goes to the temple of Rimmon to worship, leaning on my
arm, and I worship in the temple of Rimmon when he worships[a] there,
19 for this let the LORD pardon me.' And Elisha bade him farewell.

20   Naaman had gone only a short distance on his way, when Gehazi,
the servant of Elisha the man of God, said to himself, 'What? Has my
master let this Aramaean, Naaman, go scot-free, and not accepted
what he brought? As the LORD lives, I will run after him and get
21 something from him.' So Gehazi hurried after Naaman. When Naaman
saw him running after him, he jumped down from his chariot to meet
22 him and said, 'Is anything wrong?' 'Nothing,' said Gehazi, 'but my
master sent me to say that two young men of the company of prophets
from the hill-country of Ephraim have just arrived. Could you provide
23 them with a talent of silver and two changes of clothing?' Naaman said,
'By all means; take two talents.' He pressed[b] him to take them; so he
tied up the two talents of silver in two bags, and the two changes of
clothing, and gave them to his two servants, and they walked ahead
24 carrying them. When Gehazi came to the citadel[c] he took them from
the two servants, deposited them in the house and dismissed the men;
25 and they departed. When he went in and stood before his master,
Elisha said, 'Where have you been, Gehazi?' 'Nowhere', said Gehazi.
26 But he said to him, 'Was I not with you[d] in spirit when the man turned
back from his chariot to meet you? Is it not true that you have the
money? You may buy gardens with it,[e][f] and olive-trees and vineyards,

[a] So Sept.; Heb. I worship.   [b] Prob. rdg.; Heb. broke out on.   [c] Or hill.   [d] with
you: so Sept.; Heb. om.   [e] gardens with it: prob. rdg.; Heb. garments.   [f] Is it not...
with it: or Was it a time to get the money and to get garments?

sheep and oxen, slaves and slave-girls; but the disease of Naaman will 27 fasten on you and on your descendants for ever.' Gehazi left his presence, his skin diseased, white as snow.

A COMPANY OF PROPHETS said to Elisha, 'You can see that this 6 place where our community is living, under you as its head, is too small for us. Let us go to the Jordan and each fetch a log, and make ourselves*[a]* 2 a place to live in.' The prophet agreed. Then one of them said, 'Please, 3 sir, come with us.' 'I will', he said, and he went with them. When they 4 reached the Jordan, they began cutting down trees; but it chanced 5 that, as one man was felling a trunk, the head of his axe flew off into the water. 'Oh, master!' he exclaimed, 'it was a borrowed one.' 'Where 6 did it fall?' asked the man of God. When he was shown the place, he cut off a piece of wood and threw it in and made the iron float. Then he 7 said, 'There you are, lift it out.' So he stretched out his hand and took it.

Once, when the king of Aram was making war on Israel, he held a 8 conference with his staff at which he said, 'I mean to attack in such and such a direction.' But the man of God warned the king of Israel: 'Take 9 care to avoid this place, for the Aramaeans are going down that way.' So the king of Israel sent to the place about which the man of God had 10 given him this warning; and the king took special precautions every time he found himself near that place. The king of Aram was greatly 11 perturbed at this and, summoning his staff, he said to them, 'Tell me, one of you, who has betrayed us*[b]* to the king of Israel?' 'None of us, 12 my lord king,' said one of his staff; 'but Elisha, the prophet in Israel, tells the king of Israel the very words you speak in your bedchamber.' 'Go and find out where he is,' said the king, 'and I will send and seize 13 him.' He was told that the prophet was at Dothan, and he sent a strong 14 force there with horses and chariots. They came by night and surrounded the city.

When the disciple of the man of God rose early in the morning and 15 went out, he saw a force with horses and chariots surrounding the city. 'Oh, master,' he said, 'which way are we to turn?' He answered, 'Do 16 not be afraid, for those who are on our side are more than those on theirs.' Then Elisha offered this prayer: 'O Lord, open his eyes and let him 17 see.' And the Lord opened the young man's eyes, and he saw the hills covered with horses and chariots of fire all round Elisha. As they came 18 down towards him, Elisha prayed to the Lord: 'Strike this host, I pray thee, with blindness'; and he struck them blind as Elisha had asked. Then Elisha said to them, 'You are on the wrong road; this is 19 not the city. Follow me and I will lead you to the man you are looking for.' And he led them to Samaria. As soon as they had entered Samaria, 20

[a] *So Pesh.; Heb. adds* there.   [b] who...us: *so Luc. Sept.; Heb.* who of ours.

Elisha prayed, 'O LORD, open the eyes of these men and let them see again.' And he opened their eyes and they saw that they were inside

21 Samaria. When the king of Israel saw them, he said to Elisha, 'My

22 father, am I to destroy them?' 'No, you must not do that', he answered. 'You may destroy[a] those whom you have taken prisoner with your own sword and bow, but as for these men, give them food and water, and let

23 them eat and drink, and then go back to their master.' So he prepared a great feast for them, and they ate and drank and then went back to their master. And Aramaean raids on Israel ceased.

24 But later, Ben-hadad king of Aram called up his entire army and

25 marched to the siege of Samaria. The city was near starvation, and they[b] besieged it so closely that a donkey's head was sold for eighty shekels of silver, and a quarter of a kab of locust-beans for five shekels.

26 One day, as the king of Israel was walking along the city wall, a woman

27 called to him, 'Help, my lord king!' He said, 'If the LORD will not[c] bring you help, where can I find any for you? From threshing-floor

28 or from winepress? What is your trouble?' She replied, 'This woman said to me, "Give up your child for us to eat today, and we will eat

29 mine tomorrow." So we cooked my son and ate him; but when I said to her the next day, "Now give up your child for us to eat", she had hidden

30 him.' When he heard the woman's story, the king rent his clothes. He was walking along the wall at the time, and when the people looked,

31 they saw that he had sackcloth underneath, next to his skin. Then he said, 'The LORD do the same to me and more, if the head of Elisha son of Shaphat stays on his shoulders today.'

32 Elisha was sitting at home, the elders with him. The king had dispatched one of his retinue but, before the messenger arrived, Elisha said to the elders, 'See how this son of a murderer has sent to behead me! Take care, when the messenger comes, to shut the door and hold it fast against him. Can you not hear his master following on his heels?'

33 While he was still speaking, the king[d] arrived and said, 'Look at our plight! This is the LORD's doing. Why should I wait any longer for

7 him to help us?' But Elisha answered, 'Hear this word of the LORD: By this time tomorrow a shekel will buy a measure[e] of flour or two

2 measures of barley in the gateway of Samaria.' Then the lieutenant on whose arm the king leaned said to the man of God, 'Even if the LORD were to open windows in the sky, such a thing could not happen!' He answered, 'You will see it with your own eyes, but none of it will you eat.'

3 At the city gate were four lepers.[f] They said to one another, 'Why

[a] *Prob. rdg.; Heb.* Would you destroy. [b] they: *so some MSS.; others om.* [c] If the LORD will not: *so Targ.; Heb.* Let not the LORD. [d] *Prob. rdg.; Heb.* messenger. [e] *Heb.* seah. [f] *Or* men suffering from skin-disease.

should we stay here and wait for death? If we say we will go into the 4
city, there is famine there, and we shall die; if we say we will stay here,
we shall die just the same. Well then, let us go to the camp of the
Aramaeans and give ourselves up: if they spare us, we shall live; if
they put us to death, we can but die.' And so in the twilight they set 5
out for the Aramaean camp; but when they reached the outskirts, they
found no one there; for the Lord had caused the Aramaean army to 6
hear a sound like that of chariots and horses and of a great host, so that
the word went round: 'The king of Israel has hired the kings of the
Hittites and the kings of Egypt to attack us.' They had fled at once in 7
the twilight, abandoning their tents, their horses and asses, and leaving
the camp as it stood, while they fled for their lives. When the four men 8
came to the outskirts of the camp, they went into a tent and ate and
drank and looted silver and gold and clothing, and made off and hid
them. Then they came back, went into another tent and rifled it, and
made off and hid the loot. Then they said to one another, 'What we are 9
doing is not right. This is a day of good news and we are keeping it to
ourselves. If we wait till morning, we shall be held to blame. We must
go now and give the news to the king's household.' So they came and 10
called to the watch at the city gate and described how they had gone
to the Aramaean camp and found not a single man in it and had heard
no sound: nothing but horses and asses tethered, and the tents left as
they were. Then the watch called out and gave the news to the king's 11
household in the palace. The king rose in the night and said to his staff, 12
'I will tell you what the Aramaeans have done. They know that we are
starving, and they have left their camp to go and hide in the open
country, expecting us to come out, and then they can take us alive
and enter the city.' One of his staff said, 'Send out a party of men with 13
some of the horses that are left; if they live, they will be as well off as
all the other Israelites who are still left; if they die,*a* they will be no
worse off than all those who have already perished. Let them go and
see what has happened.' So they picked two mounted men,*b* and the 14
king dispatched them in the track of the Aramaean army with the order
to go and find out what had happened. They followed as far as the 15
Jordan and found the whole road littered with clothing and equipment
which the Aramaeans had flung aside in their haste. The messengers
returned and reported this to the king. Then the people went out and 16
plundered the Aramaean camp, and a measure of flour was sold for a
shekel and two measures of barley for a shekel, so that the word of the
LORD came true. Now the king had appointed the lieutenant on whose 17
arm he leaned to take charge of the gate, and the people trampled him

[a] if they live...if they die: *prob. rdg.; Heb. obscure.*   [b] two mounted men: *so Sept.; Heb.*
two horse-chariots.

to death there, just as the man of God had foretold[a] when the king
18 visited him. For when the man of God said to the king, 'By this time tomorrow a shekel will buy two measures of barley or one measure of
19 flour in the gateway of Samaria', the lieutenant had answered, 'Even if the LORD were to open windows in the sky, such a thing could not happen!' And the man of God had said, 'You will see it with your own
20 eyes, but none of it will you eat.' And this is just what happened to him: the people trampled him to death at the gate.

8 Elisha said to the woman whose son he had restored to life, 'Go away at once with your household and find lodging where you can, for the LORD has decreed a seven years' famine and it has already come
2 upon the land.' The woman acted at once on the word of the man of God and went away with her household; and she stayed in the Philis-
3 tine country for seven years. When she came back at the end of the seven years, she sought an audience of the king to appeal for the return
4 of her house and land. Now the king was questioning Gehazi, the servant of the man of God, about all the great things Elisha had done;
5 and, as he was describing to the king how he had brought the dead to life, the selfsame woman began appealing to the king for her house and her land. 'My lord king,' said Gehazi, 'this is the very woman, and this
6 is her son whom Elisha brought to life.' The king asked the woman about it, and she told him. Then he entrusted the case to a eunuch and ordered him to restore all her property to her, with all the revenues from her land from the time she left the country till that day.

7 Elisha came to Damascus, at a time when Ben-hadad king of Aram
8 was ill; and when he was told that the man of God had arrived, he bade Hazael take a gift with him and go to the man of God and inquire of the LORD through him whether he would recover from his illness.
9 Hazael went, taking with him as a gift all kinds of wares of Damascus, forty camel-loads. When he came into the prophet's presence, he said, 'Your son Ben-hadad king of Aram has sent me to you to ask whether
10 he will recover from his illness.' 'Go and tell him that he will recover,' he answered; 'but the LORD has revealed to me that in fact he will die.'
11 The man of God stood there with set face like a man stunned, until he
12 could bear it no longer; then he wept. 'Why do you weep, my lord?' said Hazael. He answered, 'Because I know the harm you will do to the Israelites: you will set their fortresses on fire and put their young men to the sword; you will dash their children to the ground and you
13 will rip open their pregnant women.' But Hazael said, 'But I am a dog, a mere nobody; how can I do this great thing?' Elisha answered, 'The
14 LORD has revealed to me that you will be king of Aram.' Hazael left Elisha and returned to his master, who asked him what Elisha had said.

[a] *So Pesh.; Heb. adds* which he had foretold.

'He told me that you would recover', he replied. But the next day he 15
took a blanket and, after dipping it in water, laid it over the king's face,
and he died; and Hazael succeeded him.

In the fifth year of Jehoram son of Ahab king of Israel,[a] Joram son 16
of Jehoshaphat king of Judah became king. He was thirty-two years old 17[b]
when he came to the throne, and he reigned in Jerusalem for eight
years. He followed the practices of the kings of Israel as the house of 18
Ahab had done, for he had married Ahab's daughter; and he did what
was wrong in the eyes of the LORD. But for his servant David's sake 19
the LORD was unwilling to destroy Judah, since he had promised to
give him and[c] his sons a flame, to burn for all time.

During his reign Edom revolted against Judah and set up its own 20
king. Joram crossed over to Zair with all his chariots. He and his 21
chariot-commanders set out by night, but they were surrounded by
the Edomites and defeated,[d] whereupon the people fled to their tents.
So Edom has remained independent of Judah to this day; Libnah also 22
revolted at the same time. The other acts and events of Joram's reign 23
are recorded in the annals of the kings of Judah. So Joram rested with 24
his forefathers and was buried with them in the city of David, and his
son Ahaziah succeeded him.

In the twelfth year of Jehoram son of Ahab king of Israel, Ahaziah 25[e]
son of Joram king of Judah became king. Ahaziah was twenty-two years 26
old when he came to the throne, and he reigned in Jerusalem for
one year; his mother was Athaliah granddaughter[f] of Omri king of
Israel. He followed the practices of the house of Ahab and did what 27
was wrong in the eyes of the LORD like the house of Ahab, for he was
connected with that house by marriage. He allied himself with Jehoram 28
son of Ahab to fight against Hazael king of Aram at Ramoth-gilead;
but King Jehoram was wounded by the Aramaeans, and returned to 29
Jezreel to recover from the wounds which were inflicted on him
at Ramoth[g] in battle with Hazael king of Aram; and because of his
illness Ahaziah son of Joram king of Judah went down to Jezreel to
visit him.

ELISHA THE PROPHET summoned one of the company of prophets 9
and said to him, 'Hitch up your cloak, take this flask of oil with you
and go to Ramoth-gilead. When you arrive, you will find Jehu son of 2
Jehoshaphat, son of Nimshi; go in and call him aside from his fellow-
officers, and lead him through to an inner room. Then take the flask 3

[a] *So some Sept. MSS.; Heb. adds* and Jehoshaphat king of Judah. [b] *Verses 17–22:
cp. 2 Chr. 21. 5–10.* [c] *So many MSS.; others om.* [d] and defeated: *prob. rdg.; Heb.*
and he defeated Edom. [e] *Verses 25–29: cp. 2 Chr. 22. 1–6.* [f] *Lit.* daughter. [g] *So
Sept.; Heb.* Ramah.

and pour the oil on his head and say, "This is the word of the LORD: I anoint you king over Israel"; then open the door and flee for your life.'

4,5 So the young prophet went to Ramoth-gilead. When he arrived, he found the officers sitting together and said, 'Sir, I have a word for

6 you.' 'For which of us?' asked Jehu. 'For you, sir', he said. He rose and went into the house, and the prophet poured the oil on his head, saying, 'This is the word of the LORD the God of Israel: "I anoint you

7 king over Israel, the people of the LORD. You shall strike down the house of Ahab your master, and I will take vengeance on Jezebel for the blood of my servants the prophets and for the blood of all the

8 LORD's servants. All the house of Ahab shall perish and I will destroy every mother's son of his house in Israel, whether under the protection

9 of the family or not. And I will make the house of Ahab like the house of Jeroboam son of Nebat and the house of Baasha son of Ahijah.

10 Jezebel shall be devoured by dogs in the plot of ground at Jezreel and

11 no one will bury her."' Then he opened the door and fled. When Jehu rejoined the king's officers, they said to him, 'Is all well? What did this crazy fellow want with you?' 'You know him and the way his thoughts

12 run', he said. 'Nonsense!' they replied; 'tell us what happened.' 'I will tell you exactly what he said: "This is the word of the LORD: I anoint

13 you king over Israel."' They snatched up their cloaks and spread them under him on the stones*a* of the steps, and sounded the trumpet and shouted, 'Jehu is king.'

14   Then Jehu son of Jehoshaphat, son of Nimshi, laid his plans against Jehoram, while Jehoram and the Israelites were defending Ramoth-

15 gilead against Hazael king of Aram. King Jehoram had returned to Jezreel to recover from the wounds inflicted on him by the Aramaeans when he fought against Hazael king of Aram. Jehu said to them, 'If you are on my side,*b* see that no one escapes from the city to tell the news in

16 Jezreel.' He mounted his chariot and drove to Jezreel, for Jehoram was laid up there, and Ahaziah king of Judah had gone down to visit him.

17   The watchman standing on the watch-tower in Jezreel saw Jehu and his troop approaching and called out, 'I see a troop of men.' Then Jehoram said, 'Fetch a horseman and send to find out if they come

18 peaceably.' The horseman went to meet him and said, 'The king asks, "Is it peace?"' Jehu said, 'Peace? What is peace to you? Fall in behind me.' Thereupon the watchman reported, 'The messenger has

19 met them but he is not coming back.' A second horseman was sent; when he met them, he also said, 'The king asks, "Is it peace?"' 'Peace?'

20 said Jehu. 'What is peace to you? Fall in behind me.' Then the watchman reported, 'He has met them but he is not coming back. The driving is like the driving of Jehu son*c* of Nimshi, for he drives

[*a*] *Prob. rdg.; Heb. obscure.*   [*b*] on my side: *so Sept.; Heb. om.*   [*c*] *Or* grandson (*cp. verse 2*).

furiously.' 'Harness my chariot', said Jehoram. They harnessed it, and 21
Jehoram king of Israel and Ahaziah king of Judah went out each in his
own chariot to meet Jehu, and met him by the plot of Naboth of
Jezreel. When Jehoram saw Jehu, he said, 'Is it peace, Jehu?' But he 22
replied, 'Do you call it peace while your mother Jezebel keeps up her
obscene idol-worship and monstrous sorceries?' Jehoram wheeled 23
about and fled, crying out to Ahaziah, 'Treachery, Ahaziah!' Jehu 24
seized his bow and shot Jehoram between the shoulders; the arrow
pierced his heart and he sank down in his chariot. Then Jehu said to 25
Bidkar, his lieutenant, 'Pick him up and throw him into the plot of
land belonging to Naboth of Jezreel; remember how, when you and
I were riding side by side behind Ahab his father, the LORD pronounced this sentence against him: "It is the very word of the LORD: 26
as surely as I saw yesterday the blood of Naboth and the blood of his
sons, I will requite you in this plot." So pick him up and throw him
into it and thus fulfil the word of the LORD.' When Ahaziah king of 27
Judah saw this, he fled by the road to Beth-haggan. Jehu went after
him and said, 'Make sure of him too.' They shot him down*ᵃ* in his
chariot on the road up the valley*ᵇ* near Ibleam, but he escaped to
Megiddo and died there. His servants conveyed his body to Jerusalem 28
and buried him in his tomb with his forefathers in the city of David.

In the eleventh year of Jehoram son of Ahab, Ahaziah became king 29
over Judah.

Jehu came to Jezreel. Now Jezebel had heard what had happened; 30
she had painted her eyes and dressed her hair, and she stood looking
down from a window. As Jehu entered the gate, she said, 'Is it peace, 31
you Zimri, you murderer of your master?' He looked up at the window 32
and said, 'Who is on my side, who?' Two or three eunuchs looked out,
and he said, 'Throw her down.' They threw her down, and some of her 33
blood splashed on to the wall and the horses, which trampled her
underfoot. Then he went in and ate and drank. 'See to this accursed 34
woman', he said, 'and bury her; for she is a king's daughter.' But 35
when they went to bury her they found nothing of her but the skull, the
feet, and the palms of the hands; and they went back and told him. 36
Jehu said, 'It is the word of the LORD which his servant Elijah the
Tishbite spoke, when he said, "In the plot of ground at Jezreel the
dogs shall devour the flesh of Jezebel, and Jezebel's corpse shall lie 37
like dung upon the ground in the plot at Jezreel so that no one will be
able to say: This is Jezebel."'

Now seventy sons of Ahab were left in Samaria. Jehu therefore sent 10
a letter to Samaria, to the elders, the rulers of the city,*ᶜ* and to the tutors

[a] They...down: *so Pesh.; Heb. om.*   [b] the valley: *prob. rdg.; Heb.* to Gur.   [c] *So Luc.*
Sept.; Heb. of Jezreel.

2 of Ahab's children,*a* in which he wrote: 'Now, when this letter reaches you, since you have in your care your master's family as well as his
3 chariots and horses, fortified cities*b* and weapons, choose the best and the most suitable of your master's family, set him on his father's
4 throne, and fight for your master's house.' They were panic-stricken and said, 'The two kings could not stand against him; what hope is
5 there that we can?' Therefore the comptroller of the household and the governor of the city, with the elders and the tutors, sent this message to Jehu: 'We are your servants. Whatever you tell us we will do; but
6 we will not make anyone king. Do as you think fit.' Then he wrote them a second letter: 'If you are on my side and will obey my orders, then bring the heads of*c* your master's sons to me at Jezreel by this time tomorrow.' Now the royal princes, seventy in all, were with the
7 nobles of the city who were bringing them up. When the letter reached them, they took the royal princes and killed all seventy; they put their
8 heads in baskets and sent them to Jehu in Jezreel. When the messenger came to him and reported that they had brought the heads of the royal princes, he ordered them to be put in two heaps and left at the entrance
9 of the city gate till morning. In the morning he went out, stood there and said to all the people, 'You are fair judges. If I conspired against
10 my master and killed him, who put all these to death? Be sure then that every word which the LORD has spoken against the house of Ahab shall be fulfilled, and that the LORD has now done what he spoke
11 through his servant Elijah.' So Jehu put to death all who were left of the house of Ahab in Jezreel, as well as all his nobles, his close friends, and his priests, until he had left not one survivor.

12   Then he set out for Samaria, and on the way there, when he had
13 reached a shepherds' shelter,*d* he came upon the kinsmen of Ahaziah king of Judah and said, 'Who are you?' 'We are kinsmen of Ahaziah,' they replied; 'and we have come down to greet the families of the
14 king and of the queen mother.' 'Take them alive', he said. So they took them alive; then they slew them and flung them into the pit that was there, forty-two of them; they did not leave a single survivor.

15   When he had left that place, he found Jehonadab son of Rechab coming to meet him. He greeted him and said, 'Are you with me heart and soul, as I am with you?' 'I am', said Jehonadab. 'Then if you are,' said Jehu,*e* 'give me your hand.' He gave him his hand and Jehu
16 helped him up into his chariot. 'Come with me,' he said, 'and you will see my zeal for the LORD.' So he*f* took him with him in his chariot.
17 When he came to Samaria, he put to death all of Ahab's house who were

[*a*] children: *so some Sept. MSS.; Heb. om.*   [*b*] *So some MSS.; others* city.   [*c*] *So Luc. Sept.; Heb. adds* the men of.   [*d*] a shepherds' shelter: *or* Beth-eker of the Shepherds. [*e*] said Jehu: *so Sept.; Heb. om.*   [*f*] *So Sept.; Heb.* they.

left there and so blotted it out, in fulfilment of the word which the LORD
had spoken to Elijah. Then Jehu called all the people together and said 18
to them, 'Ahab served the Baal a little; Jehu will serve him much. Now, 19
summon all the prophets of Baal, all his ministers and priests; not one
must be missing. For I am holding a great sacrifice to Baal, and no one
who is missing from it shall live.' In this way Jehu outwitted the
ministers of Baal in order to destroy them. So Jehu said, 'Let a sacred 20
ceremony for Baal be held.' They did so, and Jehu himself sent word 21
throughout Israel, and all the ministers of Baal came; there was not a
man left who did not come. They went into the temple of Baal and it
was filled from end to end. Then he said to the person who had charge 22
of the wardrobe, 'Bring out robes for all the ministers of Baal'; and he
brought them out. Then Jehu and Jehonadab son of Rechab went into 23
the temple of Baal and said to the ministers of Baal, 'Look carefully
and make sure that there are no servants of the LORD here with you,
but only the ministers of Baal.' Then they went in to offer sacrifices and 24
whole-offerings. Now Jehu had stationed eighty men outside and said
to them, 'I am putting these men in your charge, and any man who lets
one escape shall answer for it with his life.' When he had finished 25
offering the whole-offering, Jehu ordered the guards and the lieutenants
to go and cut them all down, and let not one of them escape; so they
slew them without quarter. The escort and the lieutenants then rushed
into the keep of the temple of Baal and brought out the sacred pole[a] from 26
the temple of Baal and burnt it; and they pulled down the sacred pillar 27
of the Baal and the temple itself and made a privy of it—as it is today.
Thus Jehu stamped out the worship of Baal in Israel. He did not how- 28, 29
ever abandon the sins of Jeroboam son of Nebat who led Israel into sin,
but he maintained the worship of the golden calves of Bethel and Dan.

Then the LORD said to Jehu, 'You have done well what is right in my 30
eyes and have done to the house of Ahab all that it was in my mind to
do. Therefore your sons to the fourth generation shall sit on the throne
of Israel.' But Jehu was not careful to follow the law of the LORD the 31
God of Israel with all his heart; he did not abandon the sins of Jeroboam who led Israel into sin.

In those days the LORD began to work havoc on Israel, and Hazael 32
struck at them in every corner of their territory eastwards from the 33
Jordan: all the land of Gilead, Gad, Reuben, and Manasseh, from
Aroer which is by the gorge of the Arnon, including Gilead and Bashan.

The other events of Jehu's reign, his achievements and his exploits, 34
are recorded in the annals of the kings of Israel. So Jehu rested with his 35
forefathers and was buried in Samaria; and he was succeeded by his son
Jehoahaz. Jehu reigned over Israel in Samaria for twenty-eight years. 36

[a] *Prob. rdg.; Heb.* sacred pillars.

Kings of Israel and Judah

11 1[a] A S SOON AS ATHALIAH mother of Ahaziah saw that her son was
2 dead, she set out to destroy all the royal line. But Jehosheba
daughter of King Joram, sister of Ahaziah, took Ahaziah's son Joash
and stole him away from among the princes who were being murdered;
she put[b] him and his nurse in a bedchamber where he was hidden
3 from Athaliah and was not put to death. He remained concealed with
her in the house of the LORD for six years, while Athaliah ruled the
4 country. In the seventh year Jehoiada sent for the captains of units of
a hundred, both of the Carites and of the guards, and he brought them
into the house of the LORD; he made an agreement with them and put
them on their oath in the house of the LORD, and showed them the
5 king's son, and gave them the following orders: 'One third of you who
6 are on duty on the sabbath are to be on guard[c] in the palace; the rest
of you are to be on special duty in the house of the LORD, one third at
7 the Sur Gate and the other third at the gate with[d] the outrunners. Your
two companies who are off duty on the sabbath shall be on duty for the
8 king in the house of the LORD. So you shall be on guard round the king,
each man with his arms at the ready, and anyone who comes near the
ranks is to be put to death; you must be with the king wherever he
goes.'
9 The captains carried out the orders of Jehoiada the priest to the
letter. Each took his men, both those who came on duty on the sabbath
10 and those who came off, and came to Jehoiada. The priest handed out
to the captains King David's spears[e] and shields, which were in the
11 house of the LORD. Then the guards took up their stations, each man
carrying his arms at the ready, from corner to corner of the house to
12 north and south,[f] surrounding the king. Then he brought out the king's
son, put the crown on his head, handed him the warrant and anointed
him king. The people[g] clapped their hands and shouted, 'Long live
13 the king.' When Athaliah heard the noise made by the guards and[h] the
14 people, she came into the house of the LORD where the people were and
found the king standing, as was the custom, on the dais,[i] amidst outbursts of song and fanfares of trumpets in his honour, and all the
populace rejoicing and blowing trumpets. Then Athaliah rent her
15 clothes and cried, 'Treason! Treason!' Jehoiada the priest gave orders

[a] *Verses 1–20: cp. 2 Chr. 22. 10–23. 21.* [b] she put: *prob. rdg., cp. 2 Chr. 22. 11; Heb. om.*
[c] are to be on guard: *so Pesh.; Heb. who keep guard.* [d] *Or behind.* [e] *So Sept.,
cp. 2 Chr. 23. 9; Heb. spear.* [f] *Prob. rdg.; Heb. adds of the altar and the house.* [g] *So
Luc. Sept.; Heb. om.* [h] *So Pesh.; Heb. om.* [i] *Or by the pillar.*

to the captains in command of the troops: 'Bring her outside the precincts and put to the sword anyone in attendance on her'; for the priest said, 'She shall not be put to death in the house of the LORD.' So they laid hands on her and took her out by the entry for horses to ¹⁶ the royal palace, and there she was put to death.

Then Jehoiada made a covenant between the LORD and the king and ¹⁷ people that they should be the LORD's people, and also between the king and the people. And all the people went into the temple of Baal ¹⁸ and pulled it down; they smashed to pieces its altars and images, and they slew Mattan the priest of Baal before the altars. Then Jehoiada set a watch over the house of the LORD; he took the captains of units ¹⁹ of a hundred, the Carites and the guards and all the people, and they escorted the king from the house of the LORD through the Gate of the Guards to the royal palace, and seated him on the royal throne. The ²⁰ whole people rejoiced and the city was tranquil. That is how Athaliah was put to the sword in the royal palace.

Joash was seven years old when he became king. In the seventh year of ²¹;[a][b]12 Jehu, Joash became king, and he reigned in Jerusalem for forty years; his mother was Zibiah of Beersheba. He did what was right in the eyes ² of the LORD all his days, as Jehoiada the priest had taught him. The ³ hill-shrines, however, were allowed to remain; the people still continued to sacrifice and make smoke-offerings there.

Then Joash ordered the priests to take[c] all the silver brought as holy- ⁴ gifts into the house of the LORD, the silver for which each man was assessed,[d] the silver for the persons assessed under his name, and any silver which any man brought voluntarily to the house of the LORD. He ⁵ ordered the priests, also, each to make a contribution from his own funds, and to repair the house wherever it was found necessary. But in ⁶ the twenty-third year of the reign of Joash the priests had still not carried out the repairs to the house. King Joash summoned Jehoiada ⁷ the priest and the other priests and said to them, 'Why are you not repairing the house? Henceforth you need not contribute from your own funds for the repair of the house.' So the priests agreed neither to ⁸ receive money from the people nor to undertake the repairs of the house. Then Jehoiada the priest took a chest and bored a hole in the ⁹ lid and put it beside the altar on the right side going into the house of the LORD, and the priests on duty at the entrance put in it all the money brought into the house of the LORD. And whenever they saw ¹⁰ that the chest was well filled, the king's secretary and the high priest came and melted down the silver found in the house of the LORD and weighed it. When it had been checked, they gave the silver to the ¹¹

[a] *12. 1 in Heb.*   [b] *11. 21–12. 15: cp. 2 Chr. 24. 1–14.*   [c] to take: *so Sept.; Heb. om.*
[d] the silver...assessed: *prob. rdg.; Heb. obscure.*

foremen over the work in the house of the LORD and they paid the
12 carpenters and the builders working on the temple and the masons
and the stone-cutters; they used it also to buy timber and hewn stone
13 for the repairs and for all other expenses connected with them. They
did not use the silver brought into the house of the LORD to make silver
cups, snuffers, tossing-bowls, trumpets, or any gold or silver vessels;
14, 15 but they paid it to the workmen and used it for the repairs. No account
was demanded from the foremen to whom the money was given for the
16 payment of the workmen, for they were acting on trust. Money from
guilt-offerings and sin-offerings was not brought into the house of the
LORD: it belonged to the priests.

17   Then Hazael king of Aram came up and attacked Gath and took it;
18 and he moved on against Jerusalem. But Joash king of Judah took all
the holy-gifts that Jehoshaphat, Joram, and Ahaziah his forefathers,
kings of Judah, had dedicated, and his own holy-gifts, and all the gold
that was found in the treasuries of the house of the LORD and in the
royal palace, and sent them to Hazael king of Aram; and he withdrew
from Jerusalem.

19   The other acts and events of the reign of Joash are recorded in the
20*a* annals of the kings of Judah. His servants revolted against him and
21 struck him down in the house of Millo on the descent to Silla. It was
his servants Jozachar*b* son of Shimeath and Jehozabad son of Shomer
who struck the fatal blow; and he was buried with his forefathers in the
city of David. He was succeeded by his son Amaziah.

13   In the twenty-third year of Joash son of Ahaziah king of Judah,
Jehoahaz son of Jehu became king over Israel in Samaria and he
2 reigned seventeen years. He did what was wrong in the eyes of the
LORD and continued the sinful practices of Jeroboam son of Nebat who
3 led Israel into sin, and did not give them up. So the LORD was roused
to anger against Israel and he made them subject for some years to
4 Hazael king of Aram and Ben-hadad son of Hazael. Then Jehoahaz
sought to placate the LORD, and the LORD heard his prayer, for he saw
5 how the king of Aram oppressed Israel. The LORD appointed a
deliverer for Israel, who rescued them from*c* the power of Aram, and
6 the Israelites settled down again in their own homes. But they did not
give up the sinful practices of the house of Jeroboam who led Israel
into sin, but continued*d* in them; the goddess Asherah*e* remained in
7 Samaria. Hazael had left Jehoahaz no armed force except fifty horsemen, ten chariots, and ten thousand infantry; all the rest the king of
Aram had destroyed and made like dust under foot.

[a] *Verses 20, 21: cp. 2 Chr. 24. 25–27.*   [b] *So some MSS.; others* Jozabad.   [c] who
rescued them from: *so Luc. Sept.; Heb.* they came out of.   [d] *So Sept.; Heb.* he continued.
[e] the goddess Asherah: *or* the sacred pole.

The other events of the reign of Jehoahaz, and all his achievements 8
and his exploits, are recorded in the annals of the kings of Israel.
So Jehoahaz rested with his forefathers and was buried in Samaria; 9
and he was succeeded by his son Jehoash.

In the thirty-ninth*a* year of Joash king of Judah, Jehoash son of 10
Jehoahaz became king over Israel in Samaria and reigned sixteen years.
He did what was wrong in the eyes of the LORD; he did not give up any 11
of the sinful practices of Jeroboam son of Nebat who led Israel into sin,
but continued in them. The other events of the reign of Jehoash, all 12
his achievements, his exploits and his war with Amaziah king of Judah,
are recorded in the annals of the kings of Israel. So Jehoash rested with 13
his forefathers and was buried in Samaria with the kings of Israel, and
Jeroboam sat upon his throne.

Elisha fell ill and lay on his deathbed, and Jehoash king of Israel 14
went down to him and wept over him and said, 'My father! My
father, the chariots and the horsemen of Israel!' 'Take bow and arrows', 15
said Elisha, and he took bow and arrows. 'Put your hand to the bow', 16
said the prophet. He did so, and Elisha laid his hands on those of the
king. Then he said, 'Open the window toward the east'; he opened it 17
and Elisha told him to shoot, and he shot. Then the prophet said, 'An
arrow for the LORD's victory, an arrow for victory over Aram! You will
defeat Aram utterly at Aphek'; and he added, 'Now take up your 18
arrows.' When the king had taken them, Elisha said, 'Strike the ground
with them.' He struck three times and stopped. The man of God was 19
furious with him and said, 'You should have struck five or six times;
then you would have defeated Aram utterly; as it is, you will strike
Aram three times and no more.'

Then Elisha died and was buried. 20

Year by year Moabite raiders used to invade the land. Once some men 21
were burying a dead man when they caught sight of the raiders. They
threw the body into the grave of Elisha and made off;*b* when the body
touched the prophet's bones, the man came to life and rose to his feet.

All through the reign of Jehoahaz, Hazael king of Aram oppressed 22
Israel. But the LORD was gracious and took pity on them; because of 23
his covenant with Abraham, Isaac, and Jacob, he looked on them with
favour and was unwilling to destroy them; nor has he even yet banished
them from his sight. When Hazael king of Aram died and was succeeded 24
by his son Ben-hadad, Jehoash son of Jehoahaz recaptured the cities 25
which Ben-hadad had taken in war from Jehoahaz his father; three
times Jehoash defeated him and recovered the cities of Israel.

In the second year of Jehoash son of Jehoahaz king of Israel, **14** 1*c*

[a] *So some Sept. MSS.; Heb.* thirty-seventh.   [b] *So Luc. Sept.; Heb.* and he made off.
[c] *Verses 1–6: cp. 2 Chr. 25. 1–4.*

2 Amaziah son of Joash king of Judah succeeded his father. He was twenty-five years old when he came to the throne, and he reigned in Jerusalem for twenty-nine years; his mother was Jehoaddin of 3 Jerusalem. He did what was right in the eyes of the LORD, yet not as his forefather David had done; he followed his father Joash in every-4 thing. The hill-shrines were allowed to remain; the people continued 5 to slaughter and burn sacrifices there. When the royal power was firmly in his grasp, he put to death those of his servants who had 6 murdered the king his father; but he spared the murderers' children in obedience to the LORD's command written in the law of Moses: 'Fathers shall not be put to death for their children, nor children for 7 their fathers; a man shall be put to death only for his own sin.' He defeated ten thousand Edomites in the Valley of Salt and captured Sela; he gave it the name Joktheel, which it still bears.

8^a　　Then Amaziah sent messengers to Jehoash son of Jehoahaz, son of 9 Jehu, king of Israel, to propose a meeting. But Jehoash king of Israel sent this answer to Amaziah king of Judah: 'A thistle in Lebanon sent to a cedar in Lebanon to say, "Give your daughter in marriage to my son." But a wild beast in Lebanon, passing by, trampled on the thistle. 10 You have defeated Edom, it is true; and it has gone to your head. Stay at home and enjoy your triumph. Why should you involve yourself in disaster and bring yourself to the ground, and Judah with you?'

11　　But Amaziah would not listen; so Jehoash king of Israel marched out, and he and Amaziah king of Judah met one another at Beth-shemesh 12 in Judah. The men of Judah were routed by Israel and fled to their 13 homes. But Jehoash king of Israel captured Amaziah king of Judah, son of Joash, son of Ahaziah, at Beth-shemesh. He went to Jerusalem and broke down the city wall from the Gate of Ephraim to the Corner Gate, 14 a distance of four hundred cubits. He also took all the gold and silver and all the vessels found in the house of the LORD and in the treasuries of the royal palace, as well as hostages, and returned to Samaria.

15　　The other events of the reign of Jehoash, and all his achievements, his exploits and his wars with Amaziah king of Judah, are recorded in 16 the annals of the kings of Israel. So Jehoash rested with his forefathers and was buried in Samaria with the kings of Israel; and he was succeeded by his son Jeroboam.

17^b　　Amaziah son of Joash, king of Judah, outlived Jehoash son of 18 Jehoahaz, king of Israel, by fifteen years. The other events of Amaziah's 19 reign are recorded in the annals of the kings of Judah. A conspiracy was formed against him in Jerusalem and he fled to Lachish; but they sent 20 after him to Lachish and put him to death there. Then his body was conveyed on horseback to Jerusalem, and there he was buried with his

[a] *Verses 8–14: cp. 2 Chr. 25. 17–24.*　　[b] *Verses 17–22: cp. 2 Chr. 25. 25–26. 2.*

forefathers in the city of David. The people of Judah took Azariah, 21
now sixteen years old, and made him king in succession to his father
Amaziah. It was he who built Elath and restored it to Judah after the 22
king rested with his forefathers.

In the fifteenth year of Amaziah son of Joash king of Judah, Jeroboam 23
son of Jehoash king of Israel became king in Samaria and reigned for
forty-one years. He did what was wrong in the eyes of the LORD; he 24
did not give up the sinful practices of Jeroboam son of Nebat who led
Israel into sin. He re-established the frontiers of Israel from Lebo- 25
hamath to the Sea of the Arabah, in fulfilment of the word of the LORD
the God of Israel spoken by his servant the prophet Jonah son of
Amittai, of Gath-hepher. For the LORD had seen how bitterly Israel 26
had suffered; no one was safe, whether under the protection of his
family or not, and Israel was left defenceless. But the LORD had made 27
no threat to blot out the name of Israel under heaven, and he saved
them through Jeroboam son of Jehoash. The other events of Jero- 28
boam's reign, and all his achievements, his exploits, the wars he fought
and how he recovered Damascus and Hamath in Jaudi for*ᵃ* Israel, are
recorded in the annals of the kings of Israel. So Jeroboam rested with 29
his forefathers the kings of Israel; and he was succeeded by his son
Zechariah.

In the twenty-seventh year of Jeroboam king of Israel, Azariah*ᵇ* son **15**
of Amaziah king of Judah became king. He was sixteen years old when 2*ᶜ*
he came to the throne, and he reigned in Jerusalem for fifty-two years;
his mother was Jecoliah of Jerusalem. He did what was right in the 3
eyes of the LORD, as Amaziah his father had done. But the hill-shrines 4
were allowed to remain; the people still continued to slaughter and
burn sacrifices there. The LORD struck the king with leprosy,*ᵈ* which 5*ᵉ*
he had till the day of his death; he was relieved of all duties and lived
in his own house, while his son Jotham was comptroller of the household and regent. The other acts and events of Azariah's reign are 6
recorded in the annals of the kings of Judah. So he rested with his 7
forefathers and was buried with them in the city of David; and he was
succeeded by his son Jotham.

In the thirty-eighth year of Azariah king of Judah, Zechariah son of 8
Jeroboam became king over Israel in Samaria and reigned six months.
He did what was wrong in the eyes of the LORD, as his forefathers had 9
done; he did not give up the sinful practices of Jeroboam son of Nebat
who led Israel into sin. Shallum son of Jabesh formed a conspiracy 10
against him, attacked him in Ibleam,*ᶠ* killed him and usurped the

[*a*] in Jaudi for: *prob. rdg.; Heb.* to Judah in.   [*b*] Uzziah *in verses 13,30, 32,34.*   [*c*] *Verses 2,
3: cp. 2 Chr. 26. 3, 4.*   [*d*] *Or* a skin-disease.   [*e*] *Verses 5–7: cp. 2 Chr. 26. 21–23.*   [*f*] *So
Luc. Sept.; Heb.* before people.

11 throne. The other events of Zechariah's reign are recorded in the
12 annals of the kings of Israel. Thus the word of the LORD spoken to
    Jehu was fulfilled: 'Your sons to the fourth generation shall sit on the
    throne of Israel.'

13   Shallum son of Jabesh became king in the thirty-ninth year of
    Uzziah king of Judah, and he reigned one full month in Samaria.
14 Then Menahem son of Gadi came up from Tirzah to Samaria, attacked
    Shallum son of Jabesh there, killed him and usurped the throne.
15 The other events of Shallum's reign and the conspiracy that he formed
    are recorded in the annals of the kings of Israel.

16   Then Menahem, starting out from Tirzah, destroyed Tappuah[a] and
    everything in it and ravaged its territory; he ravaged it because it had
    not opened its gates to him, and he ripped open all the pregnant
    women.

17   In the thirty-ninth year of Azariah king of Judah, Menahem son of
    Gadi became king over Israel and he reigned in Samaria for ten years.
18 He did what was wrong in the eyes of the LORD; he did not give up the
    sinful practices of Jeroboam son of Nebat who led Israel into sin.
19 In his days[b] Pul king of Assyria invaded the country, and Menahem
    gave him a thousand talents of silver to obtain his help in strengthening
20 his hold on the kingdom. Menahem laid a levy on all the men of wealth
    in Israel, and each had to give the king of Assyria fifty silver shekels.
    Then the king of Assyria withdrew without occupying the country.
21 The other acts and events of Menahem's reign are recorded in the
22 annals of the kings of Israel. So Menahem rested with his forefathers;
    and he was succeeded by his son Pekahiah.

23   In the fiftieth year of Azariah king of Judah, Pekahiah son of
    Menahem became king over Israel in Samaria and reigned for two years.
24 He did what was wrong in the eyes of the LORD; he did not give up the
    sinful practices of Jeroboam son of Nebat who led Israel into sin.
25 Pekah son of Remaliah, his lieutenant, formed a conspiracy against him
    and, with the help of fifty Gileadites, attacked him in Samaria in the
26 citadel of the royal palace,[c] killed him and usurped the throne. The
    other acts and events of Pekahiah's reign are recorded in the annals of
    the kings of Israel.

27   In the fifty-second year of Azariah king of Judah, Pekah son of
    Remaliah became king over Israel in Samaria and reigned for twenty
28 years. He did what was wrong in the eyes of the LORD; he did not give
    up the sinful practices of Jeroboam son of Nebat who led Israel into
29 sin. In the days of Pekah king of Israel, Tiglath-pileser king of Assyria
    came and seized Iyyon, Abel-beth-maacah, Janoah, Kedesh, Hazor,

---

[a] *So Luc. Sept.; Heb.* Tiphsah.   [b] In his days: *so Sept.; Heb.* All his days.   [c] *Prob.
rdg.; Heb. adds* Argob and Arieh.

Gilead, and Galilee, with all the land of Naphtali, and deported the people to Assyria. Then Hoshea son of Elah formed a conspiracy 30 against Pekah son of Remaliah, attacked him, killed him and usurped the throne in the twentieth year of Jotham son of Uzziah. The other 31 acts and events of Pekah's reign are recorded in the annals of the kings of Israel.

In the second year of Pekah son of Remaliah king of Israel, Jotham 32 son of Uzziah king of Judah became king. He was twenty-five years old 33[a] when he came to the throne, and he reigned in Jerusalem for sixteen years; his mother was Jerusha daughter of Zadok. He did what was 34 right in the eyes of the LORD, as his father Uzziah had done;[b] but the 35 hill-shrines were allowed to remain and the people continued to slaughter and burn sacrifices there. It was he who constructed the upper gate of the house of the LORD. The other acts and events of 36 Jotham's reign are recorded in the annals of the kings of Judah. In those days the LORD began to make Rezin king of Aram and Pekah 37 son of Remaliah attack Judah. And Jotham rested with his forefathers 38 and was buried with them in the city of David his forefather; and he was succeeded by his son Ahaz.

Downfall of the northern kingdom

IN THE SEVENTEENTH YEAR of Pekah son of Remaliah, Ahaz son 16 of Jotham king of Judah became king. Ahaz was twenty years old 2[c] when he came to the throne, and he reigned in Jerusalem for sixteen years. He did not do what was right in the eyes of the LORD his God like his forefather David, but followed in the footsteps of the kings of 3 Israel; he even passed his son through the fire, adopting the abominable practice of the nations whom the LORD had dispossessed in favour of the Israelites. He slaughtered and burnt sacrifices at the hill-shrines and on 4 the hill-tops and under every spreading tree.

Then Rezin king of Aram and Pekah son of Remaliah king of Israel 5 attacked Jerusalem and besieged Ahaz but could not bring him to battle. At that time the king of Edom[d] recovered Elath and drove the 6 Judaeans out of it; so the Edomites entered the city and have occupied it to this day. Ahaz sent messengers to Tiglath-pileser king of Assyria 7 to say, 'I am your servant and your son. Come and save me from the king of Aram and from the king of Israel who are attacking me.' Ahaz 8 took the silver and gold found in the house of the LORD and in the

[a] *Verses 33–35: cp. 2 Chr. 27. 1–3.* [b] *So some MSS.; others repeat* had done. [c] *Verses 2–4: cp. 2 Chr. 28. 1–4.* [d] the king of Edom: *prob. rdg.; Heb.* Rezin king of Aram.

treasuries of the royal palace and sent them to the king of Assyria as a
9 bribe. The king of Assyria listened to him; he advanced on Damascus,
captured it, deported its inhabitants to Kir and put Rezin to death.
10 When King Ahaz went to meet Tiglath-pileser king of Assyria at
Damascus, he saw there an altar of which he sent a sketch and a detailed
11 plan to Uriah the priest. Accordingly, Uriah built an altar, following all
the instructions that the king had sent him from Damascus, and had it
12 ready against the king's return. When the king returned from Damascus,
13 he saw the altar, approached it and mounted the steps; there he burnt
his whole-offering and his grain-offering and poured out his drink-
offering, and he flung the blood of his shared-offerings against it.
14 The bronze altar that was before the LORD he removed from the front
of the house, from between this altar and the house of the LORD, and
15 put it on the north side of this altar. Then King Ahaz gave these
instructions to Uriah the priest: 'Burn on the great altar the morning
whole-offering and the evening grain-offering, and the king's whole-
offering and his grain-offering, and the whole-offering of all the people
of the land, their grain-offering and their drink-offerings, and fling
against it all the blood of the sacrifices. But the bronze altar shall be
16 mine, to offer morning sacrifice.' Uriah the priest did all that the king
17 told him. Then King Ahaz broke up the trolleys and removed the
panels, and he took down the basin and the Sea of bronze from the
18 oxen which supported it and put it on a stone base. In the house of
the LORD he turned round the structure[a] they had erected for use on the
sabbath, and the outer gate for the king, to satisfy the king of Assyria.
19[b] The other acts and events of the reign of Ahaz are recorded in the
20 annals of the kings of Judah. So Ahaz rested with his forefathers and
was buried with them in the city of David; and he was succeeded by
his son Hezekiah.

17 In the twelfth year of Ahaz king of Judah, Hoshea son of Elah
2 became king over Israel in Samaria and reigned nine years. He did
what was wrong in the eyes of the LORD, but not as the previous kings
3 of Israel had done. Shalmaneser king of Assyria made war upon him
4 and Hoshea became tributary to him. But when the king of Assyria
discovered that Hoshea was being disloyal to him, sending messengers
to the king of Egypt at So,[c] and withholding the tribute which he had
been paying year by year, the king of Assyria arrested him and put him
5 in prison. Then he invaded the whole country and, reaching Samaria,
6 beseiged it for three years. In the ninth year of Hoshea he captured
Samaria and deported its people to Assyria and settled them in Halah
and on the Habor, the river of Gozan, and in the cities of Media.

[a] structure: *mng. uncertain.* [b] *Verses 19, 20: cp. 2 Chr. 28. 26, 27.* [c] *to the king of
Egypt at So: prob. rdg.; Heb.* to So king of Egypt.

All this happened to the Israelites because they had sinned against 7 the LORD their God who brought them up from Egypt, from the rule of Pharaoh king of Egypt; they paid homage to other gods and observed 8 the laws and customs of the nations whom the LORD had dispossessed before them[a] and uttered blasphemies against the LORD their God; 9 they built hill-shrines for themselves in all their settlements, from watch-tower to fortified city, and set up sacred pillars and sacred poles 10 on every high hill and under every spreading tree, and burnt sacrifices 11 at all the hill-shrines there, as the nations did whom the LORD had displaced before them. By this wickedness of theirs they provoked the LORD's anger. They worshipped idols, a thing which the LORD had 12 forbidden them to do. Still the LORD solemnly charged Israel and 13 Judah by every prophet and seer, saying, 'Give up your evil ways; keep my commandments and statutes given in the law which I enjoined on your forefathers and delivered to you through my servants the prophets.' They would not listen, however, but were as stubborn 14 and rebellious as their forefathers had been, who refused to put their trust in the LORD their God; they rejected his statutes and the covenant 15 which he had made with their forefathers and the solemn warnings which he had given to them; they followed worthless idols and became worthless themselves; they imitated the nations round about them, a thing which the LORD had forbidden them to do. Forsaking every 16 commandment of the LORD their God, they made themselves images of cast metal, two calves, and also a sacred pole; they prostrated themselves to all the host of heaven and worshipped the Baal, and they made 17 their sons and daughters pass through the fire. They practised augury and divination; they sold themselves to do what was wrong in the eyes of the LORD and so provoked his anger.

Thus it was that the LORD was incensed against Israel and banished 18 them from his presence; only the tribe of Judah was left. Even Judah 19 did not keep the commandments of the LORD their God but followed the practices adopted by Israel; so the LORD rejected the whole race of 20 Israel and punished them and gave them over to plunderers and finally flung them out of his sight. When he tore Israel from the house of 21 David, they made Jeroboam son of Nebat king, who seduced Israel from their allegiance to the LORD and led them into grave sin. The 22 Israelites persisted in all the sins that Jeroboam had committed and did not give them up, until finally the LORD banished the Israelites 23 from his presence, as he had threatened through his servants the prophets, and they were carried into exile from their own land to Assyria; and there they are to this day.

Then the king of Assyria brought people from Babylon, Cuthah, 24

[a] *So Pesh.; Heb. adds* those of the kings of Egypt which they practised.

Avva, Hamath, and Sepharvaim, and settled them in the cities of
Samaria in place of the Israelites; so they occupied Samaria and lived
25 in its cities. In the early years of their settlement they did not pay
homage to the LORD; and the LORD sent lions among them, and the
26 lions preyed upon them. The king was told that the deported peoples
whom he had settled in the cities of Samaria did not know the established
usage of the god of the country, and that he had sent lions among them
27 which were preying upon them because they did not know this. The
king of Assyria, therefore, gave orders that one of the priests deported
from Samaria should be sent back to live there and teach the people
28 the usage of the god of the country. So one of the deported priests came
and lived at Bethel, and taught them how they should pay their homage
29 to the LORD. But each of the nations made its own god, and they set
them up within*a* the hill-shrines which the Samaritans had made, each
30 nation in its own settlements. Succoth-benoth was worshipped by the
men of Babylon, Nergal by the men of Cuth, Ashima by the men of
31 Hamath, Nibhaz and Tartak by the Avvites; and the Sepharvites burnt
their children as offerings to Adrammelech and Anammelech, the gods
32 of Sepharvaim. While still paying homage to the LORD, they appointed
people from every class to act as priests of the hill-shrines and they
33 resorted to them there. They paid homage to the LORD while at the
same time they served their own gods, according to the custom of the
nations from which they had been carried into exile.

34   They keep up these old practices to this day; they do not pay homage
to the LORD, for they do not keep his*b* statutes and his*b* judgements,
the law and commandment, which he enjoined upon the descendants
35 of Jacob whom he named Israel. When the LORD made a covenant
with them, he gave them this commandment: 'You shall not pay
homage to other gods or bow down to them or serve them or sacrifice
36 to them, but you shall pay homage to the LORD who brought you up
from Egypt with great power and with outstretched arm; to him you
37 shall bow down, to him you shall offer sacrifice. You shall faithfully
keep the statutes, the judgements, the law, and the commandments
which he wrote for you, and you shall not pay homage to other gods.
38 You shall not forget the covenant which I made with you; you shall
39 not pay homage to other gods. But to the LORD your God you shall pay
40 homage, and he will preserve you from all your enemies.' However,
41 they would not listen but continued their former practices. While
these nations paid homage to the LORD they continued to serve their
images, and their children and their children's children have maintained the practice of their forefathers to this day.

[a] *Or* in niches at.   [b] *Prob. rdg.; Heb.* their.

IN THE THIRD YEAR of Hoshea son of Elah king of Israel, Hezekiah 18 1[a]
son of Ahaz king of Judah became king. He was twenty-five years old 2
when he came to the throne, and he reigned in Jerusalem for twenty-
nine years; his mother was Abi daughter of Zechariah. He did what 3
was right in the eyes of the LORD, as David his forefather had done.
It was he who suppressed the hill-shrines, smashed the sacred pillars, 4
cut down every sacred pole and broke up the bronze serpent that
Moses had made; for up to that time the Israelites had been burning
sacrifices to it; they called it Nehushtan. He put his trust in the LORD 5
the God of Israel; there was nobody like him among all the kings of
Judah who succeeded him or among those who had gone before him. He 6
remained loyal to the LORD and did not fail in his allegiance to him, and
he kept the commandments which the LORD had given to Moses. So the 7
LORD was with him and he prospered in all that he undertook; he
rebelled against the king of Assyria and was no longer subject to him.
He conquered the Philistine country as far as Gaza and its boundaries, 8
alike the watch-tower and the fortified city.

In the fourth year of Hezekiah's reign (that was the seventh year of 9
Hoshea son of Elah king of Israel) Shalmaneser king of Assyria made
an attack on Samaria, invested it and captured it after a siege of three 10
years; it was in the sixth year of Hezekiah (the ninth year of Hoshea
king of Israel) that Samaria was captured. The king of Assyria deported 11
the Israelites to Assyria and settled them in Halah and on the Habor,
the river of Gozan, and in the cities of Media, because they did not 12
obey the LORD their God but violated his covenant and every commandment that Moses the servant of the LORD had given them; they would
not listen and they would not obey.

In the fourteenth[b] year of the reign of Hezekiah, Sennacherib king 13[c]
of Assyria attacked and took all the fortified cities of Judah. Hezekiah 14
king of Judah sent a message to the king of Assyria at Lachish: 'I have
done wrong; withdraw from my land, and I will pay any penalty you
impose upon me.' So the king of Assyria laid on Hezekiah king of
Judah a penalty of three hundred talents of silver and thirty talents
of gold; and Hezekiah gave him all the silver found in the house 15
of the LORD and in the treasuries of the royal palace. At that time 16
Hezekiah broke up the doors of the temple of the LORD and the
door-frames which he himself had plated, and gave them to the king
of Assyria.

From Lachish the king of Assyria sent the commander-in-chief, 17
the chief eunuch, and the chief officer[d] with a strong force to King

---

[a] *Verses 1–3: cp. 2 Chr. 29. 1, 2.* [b] *Possibly an error for* twenty-fourth [c] *Verses 13–37:
cp. Isa. 36. 1–22; 2 Chr. 32. 1–19.* [d] the commander-in-chief, the chief eunuch, and
the chief officer: *or* Tartan, Rab-saris, and Rab-shakeh.

Hezekiah at Jerusalem, and they went up and came to Jerusalem*ᵃ* and
halted by the conduit of the Upper Pool on the causeway which leads
18 to the Fuller's Field. When they called for the king, Eliakim son of
Hilkiah, the comptroller of the household, came out to them, with
Shebna the adjutant-general and Joah son of Asaph, the secretary of
19 state. The chief officer said to them, 'Tell Hezekiah that this is the
message of the Great King, the king of Assyria: "What ground have
20 you for this confidence of yours? Do you think fine words can take the
place of skill and numbers? On whom then do you rely for support in
21 your rebellion against me? On Egypt? Egypt is a splintered cane that
will run into a man's hand and pierce it if he leans on it. That is what
22 Pharaoh king of Egypt proves to all who rely on him. And if you tell
me that you are relying on the LORD your God, is he not the god whose
hill-shrines and altars Hezekiah has suppressed, telling Judah and
Jerusalem that they must prostrate themselves before this altar in
Jerusalem?"

23 'Now, make a bargain with my master the king of Assyria: I will
24 give you two thousand horses if you can find riders for them. Will you
reject the authority of even the least of my master's servants and rely
25 on Egypt for chariots and horsemen? Do you think that I have come to
attack this place and destroy it without the consent of the LORD? No;
the LORD himself said to me, "Attack this land and destroy it."'

26 Eliakim son of Hilkiah, Shebna, and Joah said to the chief officer,
'Please speak to us in Aramaic, for we understand it; do not speak
27 Hebrew to us within earshot of the people on the city wall.' The chief
officer answered, 'Is it to your master and to you that my master has
sent me to say this? Is it not to the people sitting on the wall who, like
you, will have to eat their own dung and drink their own urine?'
28 Then he stood and shouted in Hebrew, 'Hear the message of the Great
29 King, the king of Assyria. These are the king's words: "Do not be taken
30 in by Hezekiah. He cannot save you from me. Do not let him persuade
you to rely on the LORD, and tell you that the LORD will save you and
31 that this city will never be surrendered to the king of Assyria." Do not
listen to Hezekiah; these are the words of the king of Assyria: "Make
peace with me. Come out to me, and then you shall each eat the fruit
of his own vine and his own fig-tree, and drink the water of his own
32 cistern, until I come and take you to a land like your own, a land of
grain and new wine, of corn and vineyards, of olives, fine oil, and
honey—life for you all, instead of death. Do not listen to Hezekiah;
he will only mislead you by telling you that the LORD will save you.
33 Did the god of any of these nations save his land from the king of
34 Assyria? Where are the gods of Hamath and Arpad? Where are the

[a] *So Sept.; Heb. adds* and went up and came.

gods of Sepharvaim, Hena, and Ivvah? Where are the gods of
Samaria?[a] Did they save Samaria from me? Among all the gods of 35
the nations is there one who saved his land from me? And how is the
LORD to save Jerusalem?"'

The people were silent and answered not a word, for the king had 36
given orders that no one was to answer him. Eliakim son of Hilkiah, 37
comptroller of the household, Shebna the adjutant-general, and Joah
son of Asaph, secretary of state, came to Hezekiah with their clothes
rent and reported what the chief officer had said.

When King Hezekiah heard their report, he rent his clothes and 19 1[b]
wrapped himself in sackcloth, and went into the house of the LORD. He 2
sent Eliakim comptroller of the household, Shebna the adjutant-general,
and the senior priests, all covered in sackcloth, to the prophet Isaiah
son of Amoz, to give him this message from the king: 'This day is a 3
day of trouble for us, a day of reproof and contempt. We are like a
woman who has no strength to bear the child that is coming to the
birth. It may be that the LORD your God heard all the words of the 4
chief officer whom his master the king of Assyria sent to taunt the
living God, and will confute what he, the LORD your God, heard. Offer
a prayer for those who still survive.' King Hezekiah's servants came to 5
Isaiah, and he told them to say this to their master: 'This is the word 6
of the LORD: "Do not be alarmed at what you heard when the lackeys of
the king of Assyria blasphemed me. I will put a spirit in him and he 7
shall hear a rumour and withdraw to his own country; and there I will
make him fall by the sword."'

So the chief officer withdrew. He heard that the king of Assyria had 8
left Lachish, and he found him attacking Libnah. But when the king 9
learnt that Tirhakah king of Cush was on the way to make war on him,
he sent messengers again to Hezekiah king of Judah, to say to him, 10
'How can you be deluded by your god on whom you rely when he
promises that Jerusalem shall not fall into the hands of the king of
Assyria? Surely you have heard what the kings of Assyria have done 11
to all countries, exterminating their people; can you then hope to
escape? Did their gods save the nations which my forefathers destroyed, 12
Gozan, Harran, Rezeph, and the people of Beth-eden living in
Telassar? Where are the kings of Hamath, of Arpad, and of Lahir, 13
Sepharvaim, Hena, and Ivvah?'

Hezekiah took the letter from the messengers and read it; then he 14
went up into the house of the LORD, spread it out before the LORD
and offered this prayer: 'O LORD God of Israel, enthroned on the 15
cherubim, thou alone art God of all the kingdoms of the earth; thou

[a] Where are the gods of Samaria?: *so Luc. Sept.; Heb. om.*   [b] *Verses 1–37: cp. Isa.
37. 1–38; 2 Chr. 32. 20–22.*

16 hast made heaven and earth. Turn thy ear to me, O Lord, and listen; open thine eyes, O Lord, and see; hear the message that Sennacherib
17 has sent to taunt the living God. It is true, O Lord, that the kings of
18 Assyria have ravaged the nations and their lands, that they have consigned their gods to the fire and destroyed them; for they were no
19 gods but the work of men's hands, mere wood and stone. But now, O Lord our God, save us from his power, so that all the kingdoms of the earth may know that thou, O Lord, alone art God.'
20   Isaiah son of Amoz sent to Hezekiah and said, 'This is the word of the Lord the God of Israel: I have heard your prayer to me concerning
21 Sennacherib king of Assyria. This is the word which the Lord has spoken concerning him:

> The virgin daughter of Zion disdains you,
>> she laughs you to scorn;
> the daughter of Jerusalem tosses her head
>> as you retreat.

22   Whom have you taunted and blasphemed?
>> Against whom have you clamoured,
> casting haughty glances at the Holy One of Israel?

23   You have sent your messengers to taunt the Lord,
>> and said:
> I have mounted my chariot and done mighty deeds:[a]
> I have gone high up in the mountains,
>> into the recesses of Lebanon.
> I have cut down its tallest cedars,
>> the best of its pines,
> I have reached its farthest corners,
>> forest and meadow.[b]

24   I have dug wells
> and drunk the waters of a foreign land,
> and with the soles of my feet I have dried up
>> all the streams of Egypt.

25   Have you not heard long ago?
>> I did it all.
> In days gone by I planned it
> and now I have brought it about,
> making fortified cities tumble down
>> into heaps of rubble.[c]

26   Their citizens, shorn of strength,
>> disheartened and ashamed,

---

[a] and done mighty deeds: *so Luc. Sept.; Heb. om.*   [b] forest and meadow: *so Sept.; Heb. forest of its meadow.*   [c] heaps of rubble: *prob. rdg., cp. Isa. 37. 26; Heb. obscure.*

> were but as plants in the field, as green herbs,
> as grass on the roof-tops blasted before the east wind.[a]
> I know your rising up[b] and your sitting down,   27
>   your going out and your coming in.
> The frenzy of your rage against me[c] and your arrogance   28
>   have come to my ears.
> I will put a ring in your nose
>   and a hook in your lips,
> and I will take you back by the road
>   on which you have come.

This shall be the sign for you: this year you shall eat shed grain and in 29
the second year what is self-sown; but in the third year sow and reap,
plant vineyards and eat their fruit. The survivors left in Judah shall 30
strike fresh root under ground and yield fruit above ground, for a 31
remnant shall come out of Jerusalem and survivors from Mount Zion.
The zeal of the LORD will perform this.

'Therefore, this is the word of the LORD concerning the king of 32
Assyria:

> He shall not enter this city
>   nor shoot an arrow there,
> he shall not advance against it with shield
>   nor cast up a siege-ramp against it.
> By the way on which he came[d] he shall go back;   33
>   this city he shall not enter.
>   This is the very word of the LORD.
> I will shield this city to deliver it,   34
> for my own sake and for the sake of my servant David.'

That night the angel of the LORD went out and struck down a 35
hundred and eighty-five thousand men in the Assyrian camp; when
morning dawned, they all lay dead. So Sennacherib king of Assyria 36
broke camp, went back to Nineveh and stayed there. One day, while he 37
was worshipping in the temple of his god Nisroch, Adrammelech and
Sharezer his sons murdered him and escaped to the land of Ararat.
He was succeeded by his son Esarhaddon.

At this time Hezekiah fell dangerously ill and the prophet Isaiah son 20 1[e]
of Amoz came to him and said, 'This is the word of the LORD: Give
your last instructions to your household, for you are a dying man and
will not recover.' Hezekiah turned his face to the wall and offered this 2

---

[a] the east wind: *prob. rdg., cp. Isa. 37. 27; Heb.* it is mature. [b] your rising up: *prob.
rdg., cp. Isa. 37. 28; Heb. om.* [c] *Prob. rdg., cp. Isa. 37. 29; Heb. repeats* the frenzy of your
rage against me. [d] *So some MSS.; others* comes. [e] *Verses 1–11: cp. Isa. 38. 1–8, 21, 22.*

3 prayer to the LORD: 'O LORD, remember how I have lived before thee, faithful and loyal in thy service, always doing what was good in thine
4 eyes.' And he wept bitterly. But before Isaiah had left the citadel, the
5 word of the LORD came to him: 'Go back and say to Hezekiah, the prince of my people: "This is the word of the LORD the God of your father David: I have heard your prayer and seen your tears; I will heal you and on the third day you shall go up to the house of the LORD.
6 I will add fifteen years to your life and deliver you and this city from the king of Assyria, and I will protect this city for my own sake and for
7 my servant David's sake."' Then Isaiah told them to apply a fig-plaster;
8 so they made one and applied it to the boil, and he recovered. Then Hezekiah asked Isaiah what sign the LORD would give him that he would be cured and would go up into the house of the LORD on the
9 third day. And Isaiah said, 'This shall be your sign from the LORD that he will do what he has promised; shall the shadow go[a] forward ten
10 steps or back ten steps?' Hezekiah answered, 'It is an easy thing for the shadow to move forward ten steps; rather let it go back ten steps.'
11 Isaiah the prophet called to the LORD, and he made the shadow go back ten steps where it had advanced down the stairway of Ahaz.
12[b]   At this time Merodach[c]-baladan son of Baladan king of Babylon sent envoys with a gift to Hezekiah; for he had heard that he had been ill.
13 Hezekiah welcomed[d] them and showed them all his treasury, silver and gold, spices and fragrant oil, his armoury and everything to be found among his treasures; there was nothing in his house and in
14 all his realm that Hezekiah did not show them. Then the prophet Isaiah came to King Hezekiah and asked him, 'What did these men say and where have they come from?' 'They have come from a
15 far-off country,' Hezekiah answered, 'from Babylon.' Then Isaiah asked, 'What did they see in your house?' 'They saw everything,' Hezekiah replied; 'there was nothing among my treasures that I did
16 not show them.' Then Isaiah said to Hezekiah, 'Hear the word of the
17 LORD: The time is coming, says the LORD, when everything in your house, and all that your forefathers have amassed till the present day,
18 will be carried away to Babylon; not a thing shall be left. And some of the sons who will be born to you, sons of your own begetting, shall be taken and shall be made eunuchs in the palace of the king of Babylon.'
19 Hezekiah answered, 'The word of the LORD which you have spoken is good'; thinking to himself that peace and security would last out his lifetime.
20   The other events of Hezekiah's reign, his exploits, and how he made

[a] shall...go: so *Targ.; Heb.* has...gone. [b] *Verses 12–19: cp. Isa. 39. 1–8.* [c] *So some MSS., cp. Isa. 39. 1; others* Berodach. [d] *So some MSS., cp. Isa. 39. 2; others* heard.

522

the pool and the conduit and brought water into the city, are recorded
in the annals of the kings of Judah. So Hezekiah rested with his fore- 21
fathers and was succeeded by his son Manasseh.

The last kings of Judah

MANASSEH WAS twelve years old when he came to the throne, 21 1ᵃ
and he reigned in Jerusalem for fifty-five years; his mother was
Hephzi-bah. He did what was wrong in the eyes of the LORD, in 2
following the abominable practices of the nations which the LORD had
dispossessed in favour of the Israelites. He rebuilt the hill-shrines 3
which his father Hezekiah had destroyed, he erected altars to the Baal
and made a sacred pole as Ahab king of Israel had done, and prostrated
himself before all the host of heaven and worshipped them. He built 4
altars in the house of the LORD, that house of which the LORD had said,
'Jerusalem shall receive my Name.' He built altars for all the host of 5
heaven in the two courts of the house of the LORD; he made his son 6
pass through the fire, he practised soothsaying and divination, and dealt
with ghosts and spirits. He did much wrong in the eyes of the LORD
and provoked his anger; and the image that he had made of the goddess 7
Asherah he put in the house, the place of which the LORD had said to
David and Solomon his son, 'This house and Jerusalem, which I chose
out of all the tribes of Israel, shall receive my Name for all time. I will 8
not again make Israel outcasts from the land which I gave to their
forefathers, if only they will be careful to observe all my commands
and all the law that my servant Moses gave them.' But they did not 9
obey, and Manasseh misled them into wickedness far worse than that
of the nations which the LORD had exterminated in favour of the
Israelites.

Then the LORD spoke through his servants the prophets: 'Because 10, 11
Manasseh king of Judah has done these abominable things, outdoing
the Amorites before him in wickedness, and because he has led Judah
into sin with his idols, this is the word of the LORD the God of Israel: 12
I will bring disaster on Jerusalem and Judah, disaster which will ring
in the ears of all who hear of it. I will mark down every stone of 13
Jerusalem with the plumb-line of Samaria and the plummet of the
house of Ahab; I will wipe away Jerusalem as when a man wipes his
plate and turns it upside down, and I will cast off what is left of my 14
people, my own possession, and hand them over to their enemies. They
shall be plundered and fall a prey to all their enemies; for they have 15

[a] *Verses 1–9: cp. 2 Chr. 33. 1–9.*

523

done what is wrong in my eyes and have provoked my anger from the
16 day their forefathers left Egypt up to the present day. And this
Manasseh shed so much innocent blood that he filled Jerusalem full to
the brim, not to mention the sin into which he led Judah by doing
17 what is wrong in my eyes.' The other events and acts of Manasseh's
reign, and the sin that he committed, are recorded in the annals of the
18 kings of Judah. So Manasseh rested with his forefathers and was buried
in the garden-tomb of his family, in the garden of Uzza; he was
succeeded by his son Amon.

19[a]   Amon was twenty-two years old when he came to the throne, and he
reigned in Jerusalem for two years; his mother was Meshullemeth
20 daughter of Haruz of Jotbah. He did what was wrong in the eyes of the
21 LORD as his father Manasseh had done. He followed in his father's
footsteps and served the idols that his father had served and prostrated
22 himself before them. He forsook the LORD the God of his fathers and
23 did not conform to his ways. King Amon's courtiers conspired against
24 him and murdered him in his house; but the people of the land killed
25 all the conspirators and made his son Josiah king in his place. The other
events of Amon's reign are recorded in the annals of the kings of Judah.
26 He was buried in his grave in the garden of Uzza; he was succeeded by
his son Josiah.

22 1[b]   Josiah was eight years old when he came to the throne, and he reigned
in Jerusalem for thirty-one years; his mother was Jedidah daughter of
2 Adaiah of Bozkath. He did what was right in the eyes of the LORD;
he followed closely in the footsteps of his forefather David, swerving
neither right nor left.

3[c]   In the eighteenth year of his reign Josiah sent Shaphan son of
Azaliah, son of Meshullam, the adjutant-general, to the house of the
4 LORD. 'Go to the high priest Hilkiah,' he said, 'and tell him to melt
down[d] the silver that has been brought into the house of the LORD,
which those on duty at the entrance have received from the people,
5 and to hand it over to the foremen in the house of the LORD, to pay
6 the workmen who are carrying out repairs in it, the carpenters,
builders, and masons, and to purchase timber and hewn stones for its
7 repair. They are not to be asked to account for the money that has been
8 given them; they are acting on trust.' The high priest Hilkiah told
Shaphan the adjutant-general that he had discovered the book of the
law in the house of the LORD, and he gave it to him, and Shaphan read
9 it. Then Shaphan came to report to the king and told him that his
servants had melted down the silver in the house of the LORD and
10 handed it over to the foremen there. Then Shaphan the adjutant-

[a] *Verses 19–24: cp. 2 Chr. 33. 21–25.*   [b] *Verses 1, 2: cp. 2 Chr. 34. 1, 2.*   [c] *Verses*
3–20: cp. 2 Chr. 34. 8–28.   [d] *So Targ.; Heb.* to count.

general told the king that the high priest Hilkiah had given him a book, and he read it out in the king's presence. When the king heard what 11 was in the book of the law, he rent his clothes, and ordered the priest 12 Hilkiah, Ahikam son of Shaphan, Akbor son of Micaiah, Shaphan the adjutant-general, and Asaiah the king's attendant, to go and seek 13 guidance of the LORD for himself, for the people, and for all Judah, about what was written in this book that had been discovered. 'Great is the wrath of the LORD', he said, 'that has been kindled against us, because our forefathers did not obey the commands in this book and do all that is laid upon us.'

So Hilkiah the priest, Ahikam, Akbor, Shaphan, and Asaiah went 14 to Huldah the prophetess, wife of Shallum son of Tikvah, son of Harhas, the keeper of the wardrobe, and consulted her at her home in the second quarter of Jerusalem. 'This is the word of the LORD the 15 God of Israel,' she answered: 'Say to the man who sent you to me, "This is the word of the LORD: I am bringing disaster on this place and 16 its inhabitants as foretold in the book which the king of Judah has read, because they have forsaken me and burnt sacrifices to other gods, pro- 17 voking my anger with all the idols they have made with their own hands; therefore, my wrath is kindled against this place and will not be quenched." This is what you shall say to the king of Judah who sent 18 you to seek guidance of the LORD: "This is the word of the LORD the God of Israel: You have listened to my words and shown a willing 19 heart, you humbled yourself before the LORD when you heard me say that this place and its inhabitants would become objects of loathing and scorn, you rent your clothes and wept before me. Because of all this,*a* I for my part have heard you. This is the very word of the LORD. Therefore, I will gather you to your forefathers, and you will be 20 gathered to your grave in peace; you will not live to see all the disaster which I am bringing upon this place."' So they brought back word to the king.

Then the king sent and called all the elders of Judah and Jerusalem 23 1*b* together, and went up to the house of the LORD; he took with him the 2 men of Judah and the inhabitants of Jerusalem, the priests and the prophets, the whole population, high and low. There he read out to them all the book of the covenant discovered in the house of the LORD; and then, standing on the dais,*c* the king made a covenant before the 3 LORD to obey him and keep his commandments, his testimonies, and his statutes, with all his heart and soul, and so fulfil the terms of the covenant written in this book. And all the people pledged themselves to the covenant.

[*a*] Because of all this: *prob. rdg., cp. Luc. Sept.; Heb. om.* [*b*] *Verses 1–3: cp. 2 Chr. 34. 29–32.* [*c*] *Or* by the pillar.

4   Next, the king ordered the high priest Hilkiah, the deputy high priest,[a] and those on duty at the entrance, to remove from the house of the LORD all the objects made for Baal and Asherah and all the host of heaven; he burnt these outside Jerusalem, in the open country by the
5   Kidron, and carried the ashes to Bethel. He suppressed the heathen priests whom the kings of Judah had appointed to burn[b] sacrifices at the hill-shrines in the cities of Judah and in the neighbourhood of Jerusalem, as well as those who burnt sacrifices to Baal, to the sun and
6   moon and planets and all the host of heaven. He took the symbol of Asherah[c] from the house of the LORD to the gorge of the Kidron outside Jerusalem, burnt it there and pounded it to dust, which was then
7   scattered over the common burial-ground. He also pulled down the houses of the male prostitutes attached to the house of the LORD, where the women wove vestments in honour of Asherah.
8   He brought in all the priests from the cities of Judah and desecrated the hill-shrines where they had burnt sacrifices, from Geba to Beer-sheba, and dismantled the hill-shrines of the demons[d] in front of the gate of Joshua, the governor of the city, to the left of the city gate.
9   These priests, however, never came up to the altar of the LORD in Jerusalem but used to eat unleavened bread with the priests of their
10   clan. He desecrated Topheth in the Valley of Ben-hinnom, so that no one might make his son or daughter pass through the fire in honour of
11   Molech.[e] He destroyed the horses that the kings of Judah had set up in honour of the sun at the entrance to the house of the LORD, beside the room of Nathan-melek the eunuch in the colonnade, and he burnt
12   the chariots of the sun. He pulled down the altars made by the kings of Judah on the roof by the upper chamber of Ahaz and the altars made by Manasseh in the two courts of the house of the LORD; he pounded
13   them to dust and threw it into the gorge of the Kidron. Also, on the east of Jerusalem, to the south of the Mount of Olives,[f] the king desecrated the hill-shrines which Solomon the king of Israel had built for Ashtoreth the loathsome goddess of the Sidonians, and for Kemosh the loathsome god of Moab, and for Milcom the abominable god of the
14   Ammonites; he broke down the sacred pillars and cut down the sacred poles and filled the places where they had stood with human bones.
15   At Bethel he dismantled the altar by[g] the hill-shrine made by Jeroboam son of Nebat who led Israel into sin, together with the hill-shrine itself; he broke its stones in pieces,[h] crushed them to dust and
16   burnt the sacred pole. When Josiah set eyes on the graves which were

[a] *Prob. rdg.; Heb.* priests.   [b] *So Luc. Sept.; Heb.* and he burnt.   [c] symbol of Asherah: *or* sacred pole.   [d] *Or* satyrs.   [e] in honour of Molech: *or* for an offering.   [f] *So Targ.; Heb.* Mount of the Destroyer.   [g] *Prob. rdg.; Heb. om.*   [h] he broke...pieces: *so Sept.; Heb.* he burnt the hill-shrine.

there on the hill, he sent and took the bones from them and burnt them on the altar to desecrate it, thus fulfilling the word of the LORD announced by the man of God when Jeroboam stood by the altar at the feast. But when he caught sight of the grave of the man of God[a] who had foretold these things, he asked, 'What is that monument I see 17 there?' The people of the city answered, 'The grave of the man of God who came from Judah and foretold all that you have done to the altar at Bethel.' 'Leave it alone,' he said; 'let no one disturb his bones.' 18 So they spared his bones and also those of the prophet who came from Samaria. Further, Josiah suppressed all the hill-shrines in the cities of 19 Samaria, which the kings of Israel had set up and thereby provoked the LORD's[b] anger, and he did to them what he had done at Bethel. He 20 slaughtered on the altars all the priests of the hill-shrines who were there, and he burnt human bones upon them. Then he went back to Jerusalem.

The king ordered all the people to keep the Passover to the LORD 21 their God, as this book of the covenant prescribed; no such Passover 22 had been kept either when the judges were ruling Israel or during the times of the kings of Israel and Judah. But in the eighteenth year of 23 Josiah's reign this Passover was kept to the LORD in Jerusalem. Further, Josiah got rid of all who called up ghosts and spirits, of all 24 household gods[c] and idols and all the loathsome objects seen in the land of Judah and in Jerusalem, so that he might fulfil the requirements of the law written in the book which the priest Hilkiah had discovered in the house of the LORD. No king before him had turned 25 to the LORD as he did, with all his heart and soul and strength, following the whole law of Moses; nor did any king like him appear again.

Yet the LORD did not abate his fierce anger; it still burned against 26 Judah because of all the provocation which Manasseh had given him. 'Judah also I will banish from my presence', he declared, 'as I banished 27 Israel; and I will cast off this city of Jerusalem which once I chose, and the house where I promised that my Name should be.'

The other events and acts of Josiah's reign are recorded in the annals 28 of the kings of Judah. It was in his reign that Pharaoh Necho king of 29 Egypt set out for the river Euphrates to help the king of Assyria. King Josiah went to meet him; and when they met at Megiddo, Pharaoh Necho slew him. His attendants conveyed his body in a chariot from 30[d] Megiddo to Jerusalem and buried him in his own burial place. Then the people of the land took Josiah's son Jehoahaz and anointed him king in place of his father.

Jehoahaz was twenty-three years old when he came to the throne, 31

[a] when Jeroboam...man of God: *so Sept.; Heb. om.*   [b] the LORD's: *so Sept.; Heb. om.*
[c] *Heb.* teraphim.   [d] *Verses 30–34: cp. 2 Chr. 36. 1–4.*

and he reigned in Jerusalem for three months; his mother was Hamutal
32 daughter of Jeremiah of Libnah. He did what was wrong in the eyes of
33 the LORD, as his forefathers had done. Pharaoh Necho removed him
from the throne^a in Jerusalem, and imposed on the land a fine of
34 a hundred talents of silver and one talent of gold. Pharaoh Necho made
Josiah's son Eliakim king in place of his father and changed his name
to Jehoiakim. He took Jehoahaz and brought him to Egypt, where he
35 died. Jehoiakim paid the silver and gold to Pharaoh, taxing the
country to meet Pharaoh's demands; he exacted it from the people,
from every man according to his assessment, so that he could pay
Pharaoh Necho.

36 　　Jehoiakim was twenty-five years old when he came to the throne,
and he reigned in Jerusalem for eleven years; his mother was Zebidah
37 daughter of Pedaiah of Rumah. He did what was wrong in the eyes of
24 the LORD, as his forefathers had done. During his reign Nebuchadnezzar king of Babylon took the field, and Jehoiakim became his
2 vassal; but three years later he broke with him and revolted. The LORD
launched against him raiding-parties of Chaldaeans, Aramaeans,
Moabites, and Ammonites, letting them range through Judah and
ravage it, as the LORD had foretold through his servants the prophets.
3 All this happened to Judah in fulfilment of the LORD's purpose to
banish them from his presence, because of all the sin that Manasseh
4 had committed and because of the innocent blood that he had shed;
he had drenched Jerusalem with innocent blood, and the LORD would
5 not forgive him. The other events and acts of Jehoiakim's reign are
6 recorded in the annals of the kings of Judah. He rested with his fore-
7 fathers, and was succeeded by his son Jehoiachin. The king of Egypt
did not leave his own land again, because the king of Babylon had
stripped him of all his possessions, from the Torrent of Egypt to the
river Euphrates.

Downfall of the southern kingdom

8^b　JEHOIACHIN WAS eighteen years old when he came to the throne,
　　and he reigned in Jerusalem for three months; his mother was
9 Nehushta daughter of Elnathan of Jerusalem. He did what was wrong
10 in the eyes of the LORD, as his father had done. At that time the troops
of Nebuchadnezzar king of Babylon advanced on Jerusalem and
11 besieged the city. Nebuchadnezzar arrived while his troops were

[a] removed...throne: *prob. rdg.*, *cp.* 2 *Chr.* 36. 3; *Heb.* bound him at Riblah in the land
of Hamath when he was king... 　[b] *Verses 8–17: cp.* 2 *Chr.* 36. 9, 10.

besieging it, and Jehoiachin king of Judah, his mother, his courtiers, his 12
officers, and his eunuchs, all surrendered to the king of Babylon. The
king of Babylon, now in the eighth year of his reign, took him prisoner;
and, as the LORD had foretold, he carried off all the treasures of the 13
house of the LORD and of the royal palace and broke up all the vessels of
gold which Solomon king of Israel had made for the temple of the
LORD. He carried the people of Jerusalem into exile, the officers and 14
the fighting men, ten thousand in number, together with all the craftsmen and smiths; only the weakest class of people were left. He deported 15
Jehoiachin to Babylon; he also took into exile from Jerusalem to
Babylon the king's mother and his wives, his eunuchs and the foremost
men of the land. He also deported to Babylon all the men of substance, 16
seven thousand in number, and a thousand craftsmen and smiths, all
of them able-bodied men and skilled armourers. He made Mattaniah, 17
uncle of Jehoiachin, king in his place and changed his name to
Zedekiah.

   Zedekiah was twenty-one years old when he came to the throne, and 18*a*
he reigned in Jerusalem for eleven years; his mother was Hamutal
daughter of Jeremiah of Libnah. He did what was wrong in the eyes 19
of the LORD, as Jehoiakim had done. Jerusalem and Judah so angered 20
the LORD that in the end he banished them from his sight; and Zedekiah rebelled against the king of Babylon.

   In the ninth year of his reign, in the tenth month, on the tenth day 25 1*b*
of the month, Nebuchadnezzar king of Babylon advanced with all his
army against Jerusalem, invested it and erected watch-towers against
it on every side; the siege lasted till the eleventh year of King Zedekiah. 2
In the fourth month of that year,*c* on the ninth day of the month, when 3
famine was severe in the city and there was no food for the common
people, the city was thrown open. When Zedekiah king of Judah saw 4
this,*d* he and all his armed escort left the city and fled*e* by night through
the gate called Between the Two Walls, near the king's garden. They
escaped towards the Arabah, although the Chaldaeans were surrounding the city. But the Chaldaean army pursued the king and overtook 5
him in the lowlands of Jericho; and all his company was dispersed.
The king was seized and brought before the king of Babylon at Riblah, 6
where he*f* pleaded his case before him. Zedekiah's sons were slain 7
before his eyes; then his eyes were put out, and he was brought to
Babylon in fetters of bronze.

   In the fifth month, on the seventh day of the month, in the nine- 8

[*a*] 24. *18–25. 21*: cp. *Jer. 52. 1–27*. [*b*] *Verses 1–12*: cp. *Jer. 39. 1–10; verses 1–17*:
cp. *2 Chr. 36. 17–20*. [*c*] In...year: *prob. rdg., cp. Jer. 52. 6; Heb. om.* [*d*] When...this:
prob. rdg., cp. Jer. 39. 4; Heb. om. [*e*] left...fled: *so Pesh., cp. Jer. 52. 7; Heb. om.* [*f*] So
some MSS.; *others* they.

teenth year of Nebuchadnezzar king of Babylon, Nebuzaradan, captain
9 of the king's bodyguard, came to Jerusalem and set fire to the house of
the LORD and the royal palace; all the houses in the city, including the
10 mansion of Gedaliah,[a] were burnt down. The Chaldaean forces with[b]
the captain of the guard pulled down the walls all round Jerusalem.
11 Nebuzaradan captain of the guard deported the rest of the people left
in the city, those who had deserted to the king of Babylon and any
12 remaining artisans.[c] He left only the weakest class of people to be
vine-dressers and labourers.

13 The Chaldaeans broke up the pillars of bronze in the house of the
LORD, the trolleys, and the Sea of bronze, and took the metal to
14 Babylon. They took also the pots, shovels, snuffers, saucers, and all the
15 vessels of bronze used in the service of the temple. The captain of the
guard took away the precious metal, whether gold or silver, of which
16 the firepans and the tossing-bowls were made. The bronze of the two
pillars, the one Sea, and the trolleys, which Solomon had made for the
17 house of the LORD, was beyond weighing. The one pillar was eighteen
cubits high and its capital was bronze; the capital was three cubits high,
and a decoration of network and pomegranates ran all round it, wholly
of bronze. The other pillar, with its network, was exactly like it.

18 The captain of the guard took Seraiah the chief priest and Zephaniah
19 the deputy chief priest and the three on duty at the entrance; he took
also from the city a eunuch who was in charge of the fighting men, five
of those with right of access to the king who were still in the city, the
adjutant-general[d] whose duty was to muster the people for war, and
20 sixty men of the people who were still there. These Nebuzaradan
21 captain of the guard brought to the king of Babylon at Riblah. There,
in the land of Hamath, the king of Babylon had them flogged and put
to death. So Judah went into exile from their own land.

22 Nebuchadnezzar king of Babylon appointed Gedaliah son of Ahikam,
son of Shaphan, governor over the few people whom he had left in
23 Judah. When the captains of the armed bands and their men heard
that the king of Babylon had appointed Gedaliah governor, they all
came to him at Mizpah: Ishmael son of Nethaniah, Johanan son of
Kareah, Seraiah son of Tanhumeth of Netophah, and Jaazaniah of
24 Beth-maacah. Then Gedaliah gave them and their men this assurance:
'Have no fear of the Chaldaean officers. Settle down in the land and
25 serve the king of Babylon; and then all will be well with you.' But in
the seventh month Ishmael son of Nethaniah, son of Elishama, who
was a member of the royal house, came with ten men and murdered

---

[a] Gedaliah: *prob. rdg.; Heb.* a great man.   [b] *So many MSS., cp. Jer. 52. 14; others om.*
[c] any remaining artisans: *prob. rdg., cp. Jer. 52. 15; Heb.* the remaining crowd.   [d] *Prob. rdg.; Heb. adds* commander-in-chief.

Gedaliah and the Jews and Chaldaeans who were with him at Mizpah.
Thereupon all the people, high and low, and the captains of the armed   26
bands, fled to Egypt for fear of the Chaldaeans.

In the thirty-seventh year of the exile of Jehoiachin king of Judah,   27[a]
on the twenty-seventh day of the twelfth month, Evil-merodach[b] king
of Babylon in the year of his accession showed favour to Jehoiachin
king of Judah. He brought him[c] out of prison, treated him kindly and   28
gave him a seat at table above the kings with him in Babylon. So   29
Jehoiachin discarded his prison clothes and lived as a pensioner of the
king for the rest of his life. For his maintenance, a regular daily   30
allowance was given him by the king as long as he lived.

[a] *Verses 27–30: cp. Jer. 52. 31–34.*   [b] *Or* Ewil-marduk.   [c] He brought him: *so Sept.*,
cp. Jer. 52. 32; Heb. om.

THE FIRST BOOK OF THE
CHRONICLES

Genealogies from Adam to Saul

1 1,2,^a3 ADAM, SETH, ENOSH, Kenan, Mahalalel, Jared, Enoch,
4 Methuselah, Lamech, Noah.
The sons of Noah:[b] Shem, Ham and Japheth.
5[c] The sons of Japheth: Gomer, Magog, Madai, Javan,[d] Tubal,
6 Meshech and Tiras. The sons of Gomer: Ashkenaz, Diphath[e] and
7 Togarmah. The sons of Javan: Elishah, Tarshish, Kittim[f] and
Rodanim.[g]
8,[h]9 The sons of Ham: Cush, Mizraim,[i] Put and Canaan. The sons of
Cush: Seba, Havilah, Sabta, Raama and Sabtecha. The sons of
10 Raama: Sheba and Dedan. Cush was the father of Nimrod, who began
11[j] to show himself a man of might on earth. From Mizraim sprang the
12 Lydians, Anamites, Lehabites, Naphtuhites, Pathrusites, Casluhites,
and the Caphtorites,[k] from whom the Philistines were descended.
13 Canaan was the father of Sidon, who was his eldest son, and Heth,[l]
14,15 the Jebusites, the Amorites, the Girgashites, the Hivites, the Arkites,
16 the Sinites, the Arvadites, the Zemarites, and the Hamathites.
17[m] The sons of Shem: Elam, Asshur, Arphaxad, Lud[n] and Aram. The
18 sons of Aram:[o] Uz, Hul, Gether and Mash.[p] Arphaxad was the father
19 of Shelah, and Shelah the father of Eber. Eber had two sons: one was
named Peleg,[q] because in his time the earth was divided, and his
20 brother's name was Joktan. Joktan was the father of Almodad, Sheleph,
21,22 Hazarmoth, Jerah, Hadoram, Uzal, Diklah, Ebal,[r] Abimael, Sheba,
23 Ophir, Havilah and Jobab. All these were sons of Joktan.
24,[s]25,26 The line of[t] Shem: Arphaxad, Shelah, Eber, Peleg, Reu, Serug,
27,28 Nahor, Terah, Abram, also known as Abraham, whose sons were Isaac
and Ishmael.
29[u] The sons of[v] Ishmael in the order of their birth: Nebaioth the eldest,

[a] *Verses 2–4: cp. Gen. 5. 9–32.* [b] The sons of Noah: *so Sept.; Heb. om.* [c] *Verses 5–7:
cp. Gen. 10. 2–4.* [d] *Or* Greece. [e] *Or, with many MSS.,* Riphath (*cp. Gen. 10. 3*).
[f] *Or* Tarshish of the Kittians. [g] *Or, with many MSS.,* Dodanim (*cp. Gen. 10. 4*).
[h] *Verses 8–10: cp. Gen. 10. 6–8.* [i] *Or* Egypt. [j] *Verses 11–16: cp. Gen. 10. 13–18.*
[k] and the Caphtorites: *transposed from end of verse; cp. Amos 9. 7.* [l] *Or* the Hittites.
[m] *Verses 17–23: cp. Gen. 10. 22–29.* [n] *Or* the Lydians. [o] The sons of Aram: *so one
MS., cp. Gen. 10. 23; others om.* [p] *So some MSS., cp. Gen. 10. 23; others* Meshech.
[q] *That is* Division. [r] *Or* Obal, *cp. Gen. 10. 28.* [s] *Verses 24–27: cp. Gen. 11. 10–
26.* [t] The line of: *prob. rdg.; Heb. om.* [u] *Verses 29–31: cp. Gen. 25. 13–16.* [v] The
sons of: *prob. rdg., cp. Gen. 25. 13; Heb. om.*

then Kedar, Adbeel, Mibsam, Mishma, Dumah, Massa, Hadad,*a* 30
Teman,*b* Jetur, Naphish and Kedemah. These were Ishmael's sons. 31

The sons of Keturah, Abraham's concubine: she bore him Zimran, 32*c*
Jokshan, Medan, Midian, Ishbak and Shuah. The sons of Jokshan:
Sheba and Dedan. The sons of Midian: Ephah, Epher, Enoch, Abida 33
and Eldaah. All these were descendants of Keturah.

Abraham was the father of Isaac, and Isaac's sons were Esau and 34
Israel. The sons of Esau: Eliphaz, Reuel, Jeush, Jalam and Korah. 35*d*
The sons of Eliphaz: Teman, Omar, Zephi, Gatam, Kenaz, Timna 36
and Amalek. The sons of Reuel: Nahath, Zerah, Shammah and Mizzah. 37

The sons of Seir: Lotan, Shobal, Zibeon, Anah, Dishon, Ezer and 38*e*
Dishan. The sons of Lotan: Hori and Homam; and Lotan had a sister 39
named Timna. The sons of Shobal: Alvan,*f* Manahath, Ebal, Shephi 40
and Onam. The sons of Zibeon: Aiah and Anah. The son*g* of Anah: 41
Dishon. The sons of Dishon: Amram, Eshban, Ithran and Cheran. The 42
sons of Ezer: Bilhan, Zavan and Akan.*h* The sons of Dishan: Uz and
Aran.

These are the kings who ruled over Edom before there were kings in 43*i*
Israel: Bela son of Beor, whose city was named Dinhabah. When he 44
died, he was succeeded by Jobab son of Zerah of Bozrah. When Jobab 45
died, he was succeeded by Husham of Teman. When Husham died, he 46
was succeeded by Hadad son of Bedad, who defeated Midian in
Moabite country. His city was named Avith. When Hadad died, he was 47
succeeded by Samlah of Masrekah. When Samlah died, he was suc- 48
ceeded by Saul of Rehoboth on the River. When Saul died, he was 49
succeeded by Baal-hanan son of Akbor. When Baal-hanan died, he 50
was succeeded by Hadad. His city was named Pai; his wife's name
was Mehetabel daughter of Matred a woman of Me-zahab.*j*

After Hadad died the chiefs in Edom were: chief Timna, chief Aliah, 51
chief Jetheth, chief Oholibamah, chief Elah, chief Pinon, chief Kenaz, 52, 53
chief Teman, chief Mibzar, chief Magdiel and chief Iram. These were 54
the chiefs of Edom.

These were the sons of Israel: Reuben, Simeon, Levi, Judah, 2
Issachar, Zebulun, Dan, Joseph, Benjamin, Naphtali, Gad and Asher. 2

The sons of Judah: Er, Onan and Shelah; the mother of these three 3
was a Canaanite woman, Bathshua.*k* Er, Judah's eldest son, displeased
the LORD and the LORD slew him. Then Tamar, Judah's daughter-in- 4
law, bore him Perez and Zerah, making in all five sons of Judah.

[a] *Or, possibly,* Harar, *cp. Gen. 25. 15.* [b] *So Sept.; Heb.* Tema. [c] *Verses 32, 33:*
cp. Gen. 25. 1–4. [d] *Verses 35–37: cp. Gen. 36. 4, 5, 9–13.* [e] *Verses 38–42: cp. Gen. 36.*
20–28. [f] *So many MSS., cp. Gen. 36. 23; others* Alian. [g] *Prob. rdg.; Heb.* sons; *the*
same correction is made in several other places in chs. 1–9. [h] *and* Akan: *so many MSS.,*
cp. Gen. 36. 27; others Jakan. [i] *Verses 43–54: cp. Gen. 36. 31–43.* [j] *Or* daughter of
Mezahab. [k] Bathshua: *or* daughter of Shua.

5,6 The sons of Perez: Hezron and Hamul. The sons of Zerah: Zimri,
7 Ethan, Heman, Calcol and Darda,*a* five in all. The son of Zimri:
Carmi.*b* The son of Carmi: Achar, who troubled Israel by his violation
8,9 of the sacred ban. The son of Ethan: Azariah. The sons of Hezron:
10 Jerahmeel, Ram and Caleb.*c* Ram was the father of Amminadab,
11 Amminadab father of Nahshon prince of Judah. Nahshon was the
12 father of Salma, Salma father of Boaz, Boaz father of Obed, Obed
13 father of Jesse. The eldest son of Jesse was Eliab, the second Abinadab,
14,15 the third Shimea, the fourth Nethaneel, the fifth Raddai, the sixth
16 Ozem, the seventh David; their sisters were Zeruiah and Abigail. The
17 sons of Zeruiah: Abishai, Joab and Asahel, three in all. Abigail was the
mother of Amasa; his father was Jether the Ishmaelite.

18 Caleb son of Hezron had Jerioth by Azubah his wife;*d* these were
19 her sons: Jesher, Shobab and Ardon. When Azubah died, Caleb
20 married Ephrath, who bore him Hur. Hur was the father of Uri, and
21 Uri father of Bezalel. Later, Hezron, then sixty years of age, had intercourse with the daughter of Machir father of Gilead, having married
22 her, and she bore Segub. Segub was the father of Jair, who had twenty-
23 three cities in Gilead. Geshur and Aram took from them Havvoth-jair,
and Kenath and its dependent villages, a total of sixty towns. All these
24 were descendants of Machir father of Gilead. After the death of Hezron,
Caleb had intercourse*e* with Ephrathah*f* and she bore him Ashhur the
founder*g* of Tekoa.

25 The sons of Jerahmeel eldest son of Hezron by*h* Ahijah were Ram
26 the eldest, Bunah, Oren and Ozem. Jerahmeel had another wife, whose
27 name was Atarah; she was the mother of Onam. The sons of Ram
28 eldest son of Jerahmeel: Maaz, Jamin and Eker. The sons of Onam:
29 Shammai and Jada. The sons of Shammai: Nadab and Abishur. The
name of Abishur's wife was Abihail; she bore him Ahban and Molid.
30 The sons of Nadab: Seled and Ephraim;*i* Seled died without children.
31,32 Ephraim's son was Ishi, Ishi's son Sheshan, Sheshan's son Ahlai. The
sons of Jada brother of Shammai: Jether and Jonathan; Jether died
33 without children. The sons of Jonathan: Peleth and Zaza. These were
the descendants of Jerahmeel.

34 Sheshan had daughters but no sons. He had an Egyptian servant
35 named Jarha; he gave his daughter in marriage to this Jarha, and she
36 bore him Attai. Attai was the father of Nathan, Nathan father of Zabad,
37,38 Zabad father of Ephlal, Ephlal father of Obed, Obed father of Jehu,
39 Jehu father of Azariah, Azariah father of Helez, Helez father of Elasah,

[a] *So many MSS.; others* Dara.   [b] The son...Carmi: *prob. rdg. (cp. Josh. 7. 1, 18); Heb.*
om.   [c] *So Sept.; Heb.* Celubai.   [d] his wife: *prob. rdg.; Heb.* a woman and.   [e] Caleb
had intercourse: *so Sept.; Heb.* in Caleb.   [f] *So Pesh.; Heb. adds* and Abiah Hezron's wife.
[g] *Lit.* father *and similarly several times in chs.* 2–4.   [h] by: *prob. rdg.; Heb. om.*   [i] *So*
one MS.; others Appaim.

Elasah father of Sisamai, Sisamai father of Shallum, Shallum father of 40, 41
Jekamiah, and Jekamiah father of Elishama.

The sons of Caleb brother of Jerahmeel: Mesha the eldest, founder 42
of Ziph, and*a* Mareshah founder of Hebron. The sons of Hebron: 43
Korah, Tappuah, Rekem and Shema. Shema was the father of Raham 44
father of Jorkoam, and Rekem was the father of Shammai. The son of 45
Shammai was Maon, and Maon was the founder of Beth-zur. Ephah, 46
Caleb's concubine, was the mother of Haran, Moza and Gazez; Haran
was the father of Gazez. The sons of Jahdai: Regem, Jotham, Geshan, 47
Pelet, Ephah and Shaaph. Maacah, Caleb's concubine, was the mother 48
of Sheber and Tirhanah; she bore also Shaaph founder of Madmannah, 49
and Sheva founder of Machbenah and Gibea. Caleb also had a daughter
named Achsah.

The descendants of Caleb: the sons*b* of Hur, the eldest son of 50
Ephrathah: Shobal the founder of Kiriath-jearim, Salma the founder 51
of Bethlehem, and Hareph the founder of Beth-gader. Shobal the 52
founder of Kiriath-jearim was the father of Reaiah*c* and the ancestor
of half the Manahethites.*d*

The clans of Kiriath-jearim: Ithrites, Puhites, Shumathites, and 53
Mishraites, from whom were descended the Zareathites and the
Eshtaulites.

The descendants of Salma: Bethlehem, the Netophathites, Ataroth, 54
Beth-joab, half the Manahethites, and the Zorites.

The clans of Sophrites*e* living at Jabez: Tirathites, Shimeathites, 55
and Suchathites. These were Kenites*f* who were connected by marriage
with the ancestor of the Rechabites.

These were the sons of David, born at Hebron: the eldest Amnon, 3 1*g*
whose mother was Ahinoam of Jezreel; the second Daniel, whose mother
was Abigail of Carmel; the third Absalom, whose mother was Maacah 2
daughter of Talmai king of Geshur; the fourth Adonijah, whose mother
was Haggith; the fifth Shephatiah, whose mother was Abital; the sixth 3
Ithream, whose mother was David's wife Eglah. These six were born 4
at Hebron, where David reigned seven years and six months. In
Jerusalem he reigned thirty-three years, and there the following sons 5*h*
were born to him: Shimea, Shobab, Nathan and Solomon; these four
were sons of Bathsheba*i* daughter of Ammiel. There were nine others: 6
Ibhar, Elishama, Eliphelet, Nogah, Nepheg, Japhia, Elishama, Eliada 7, 8
and Eliphelet. These were all the sons of David, with their sister Tamar, 9
in addition to his sons by concubines.

[*a*] *Prob. rdg.; Heb. adds* the sons of.   [*b*] *So Sept.; Heb.* son.   [*c*] *Prob. rdg., cp. 4. 2; Heb.*
the seer.   [*d*] *Prob. rdg., cp. verse 54; Heb.* Menuhoth.   [*e*] *Or* secretaries.   [*f*] *Lit.* Kinites.
[*g*] *Verses 1–4: cp. 2 Sam. 3. 2–5.*   [*h*] *Verses 5–8: cp. 14. 4–7; 2 Sam. 5. 14–16.*   [*i*] *So*
Vulg.; Heb. Bathshua.

10 Solomon's son was Rehoboam, his son Abia, his son Asa, his son
11, 12 Jehoshaphat, his son Joram, his son Ahaziah, his son Joash, his son
13 Amaziah, his son Azariah, his son Jotham, his son Ahaz, his son Hezekiah,
14, 15 his son Manasseh, his son Amon, and his son Josiah. The sons of Josiah:
the eldest was Johanan, the second Jehoiakim, the third Zedekiah, the
16, 17 fourth Shallum. The sons of Jehoiakim: Jeconiah and Zedekiah. The
18 sons of Jeconiah, a prisoner:*a* Shealtiel,*b* Malchiram, Pedaiah, She-
19 nazzar, Jekamiah, Hoshama and Nedabiah. The sons of Pedaiah:
Zerubbabel and Shimei. The sons*c* of Zerubbabel: Meshullam and
20 Hananiah; they had a sister, Shelomith. There were five others:
21 Hashubah, Ohel, Berechiah, Hasadiah and Jushab-hesed. The sons
of Hananiah: Pelatiah and Isaiah; his son was*d* Rephaiah, his son
22 Arnan, his son Obadiah, his son Shecaniah. The sons of Shecaniah:
Shemaiah,*e* Hattush, Igeal, Bariah, Neariah and Shaphat, six in all.
23, 24 The sons of Neariah: Elioenai, Hezekiah and Azrikam, three in all. The
sons of Elioenai: Hodaiah, Eliashib, Pelaiah, Akkub, Johanan, Dalaiah
and Anani, seven in all.

4 1, 2 The sons of Judah: Perez, Hezron, Carmi, Hur and Shobal. Reaiah
son of Shobal was the father of Jahath, Jahath father of Ahumai and
Lahad. These were the clans of the Zorathites.

3-4 The sons*f* of Etam: Jezreel, Ishma, Idbash, Penuel the founder of
Gedor, and Ezer the founder of Hushah; they had a sister named
Hazelelponi. These were the sons of Hur: Ephrathah the eldest, the
founder of Bethlehem.

5 Ashhur the founder of Tekoa had two wives, Helah and Naarah.
6 Naarah bore him Ahuzam, Hepher, Temeni and Haahashtari.*g* These
7 were the sons of Naarah. The sons of Helah: Zereth, Jezoar, Ethnan
8 and Coz.*h* Coz was the father of Anub and Zobebah and the clans of
Aharhel son of Harum.

9 Jabez ranked higher than his brothers; his mother called him Jabez
10 because, as she said, she had borne him in pain. Jabez called upon the
God of Israel and said, 'I pray thee, bless me and grant me wide
territories. May thy hand be with me, and do me no harm, I pray thee,
and let me be free from pain'; and God granted his petition.

11 Kelub brother of Shuah was the father of Mehir the father of Eshton.
12 Eshton was the father of Beth-rapha, Paseah, and Tehinnah father of
Ir-nahash. These were the men of Rechah.

13 The sons of Kenaz: Othniel and Seraiah. The sons of Othniel:
Hathath and Meonothai.*i*

[a] Jeconiah, a prisoner: *or* Jeconiah: Assir, ... [b] *So Sept.; Heb. adds* his son. [c] *So
some MSS.; others* son. [d] his son was: *so Sept., throughout verse; Heb.* the sons of.
[e] *Prob. rdg.; Heb. adds* and the sons of Shemaiah. [f] *So Sept.; Heb.* father. [g] Temeni
and Haahashtari: *or* the Temanite and the Ahashtarite. [h] and Coz: *so Targ.; Heb. om.*
[i] The sons of Othniel...Meonothai: *so Vulg.; Heb.* The son of Othniel: Hathath.

Meonothai was the father of Ophrah.   14

Seraiah was the father of Joab founder of Ge-harashim,[a] for they were craftsmen.

The sons of Caleb son of Jephunneh: Iru, Elah and Naam. The son 15 of Elah: Kenaz.[b]

The sons of Jehaleleel: Ziph and Ziphah, Tiria and Asareel.   16

The sons of Ezra: Jether, Mered, Epher and Jalon. These were the 17-18 sons of Bithiah daughter of Pharaoh, whom Mered had married; she conceived and gave birth to[c] Miriam, Shammai and Ishbah founder of Eshtemoa. His Jewish wife was the mother of Jered founder of Gedor, Heber founder of Soco, and Jekuthiel founder of Zanoah. The sons of 19 his[d] wife Hodiah sister of Naham were Daliah[e] father of Keilah the Garmite, and Eshtemoa the Maacathite.

The sons of Shimon: Amnon, Rinnah, Ben-hanan and Tilon.   20

The sons of Ishi: Zoheth and Ben-zoheth.

The sons of Shelah son of Judah: Er founder of Lecah, Laadah 21 founder of Mareshah, the clans of the guild of linen-workers at Ashbea, Jokim, the men of Kozeba, Joash, and Saraph who fell out 22 with Moab and came back to Bethlehem.[f] (The records are ancient.) They were the potters, and those who lived at Netaim and Gederah 23 were there on the king's service.

The sons of Simeon: Nemuel, Jamin, Jarib, Zerah, Saul, his son 24, 25 Shallum, his son Mibsam and his son Mishma. The sons of Mishma: 26 his son Hamuel, his son Zaccur and his son Shimei. Shimei had sixteen 27 sons and six daughters, but others of his family had fewer children, and the clan as a whole did not increase as much as the tribe of Judah. They lived at Beersheba, Moladah, Hazar-shual, Bilhah, Ezem, Tolad, 28, 29 Bethuel, Hormah, Ziklag, Beth-marcaboth, Hazar-susim, Beth-birei, 30, 31 and Shaaraim. These were their cities until David came to the throne. Their settlements[g] were Etam, Ain, Rimmon, Tochen, and Ashan, 32 five cities in all. They had also hamlets round these cities as far as Baal. 33 These were the places where they lived.

The names on their register were: Meshobab, Jamlech, Joshah son 34 of Amaziah, Joel, Jehu son of Josibiah, son of Seraiah, son of Asiel, 35 Elioenai, Jaakobah, Jeshohaiah, Asaiah, Adiel, Jesimiel, Benaiah, Ziza 36, 37 son of Shiphi, son of Allon, son of Jedaiah, son of Shimri, son of Shemaiah, whose names are recorded as princes in their clans, and their 38 families had greatly increased. They then went from the approaches to 39 Gedor east of the valley in search of pasture for their flocks. They 40 found rich and good pasture in a wide stretch of open country where

---

[a] *Or* the Valley of Craftsmen. [b] *So some MSS.; others* and Kenaz. [c] and gave birth to: *prob. rdg.; Heb. om.* [d] his: *prob. rdg.; Heb. om.* [e] *So Sept.; Heb. om.* [f] and came...Bethlehem: *prob. rdg.; Heb. unintelligible.* [g] *Prob. rdg.; Heb.* hamlets.

everything was quiet and peaceful; before then it had been occupied
41 by Hamites. During the reign of Hezekiah king of Judah these whose
names are written above came and destroyed the tribes of Ham*a* and
the Meunites whom they found there. They annihilated them so that
no trace of them has remained to this day; and they occupied the land
42 in their place, for there was pasture for their flocks. Of their number
five hundred Simeonites invaded the hill-country of Seir, led by
43 Pelatiah, Neariah, Rephaiah, and Uzziel, the sons of Ishi. They
destroyed all who were left of the surviving Amalekites; and they live
there still.

5   The sons of Reuben, the eldest of Israel's sons. (He was, in fact, the
first son born, but because he had committed incest with a wife of his
father's the rank of the eldest was transferred to the sons of Joseph,
Israel's son, who, however, could not be registered as the eldest son.
2 Judah held the leading place among his brothers because he fathered a
3 ruler, and the rank of the eldest was his, not*b* Joseph's.) The sons of
Reuben, the eldest of Israel's sons: Enoch, Pallu, Hezron and Carmi.
4 The sons of Joel: his son Shemaiah, his son Gog, his son Shimei,
5,6 his son Micah, his son Reaia, his son Baal, his son Beerah, whom
Tiglath-pileser*c* king of Assyria carried away into exile; he was a
7 prince of the Reubenites. His kinsmen, family by family, as registered
8 in their tribal lists: Jeiel the chief, Zechariah, Bela son of Azaz, son of
Shema, son of Joel. They lived in Aroer, and their lands stretched as
9 far as Nebo and Baal-meon. Eastwards they occupied territory as far
as the edge of the desert which stretches from the river Euphrates,
10 for they had large numbers of cattle in Gilead. During Saul's reign
they made war on the Hagarites, whom they conquered, occupying
their encampments over all the country east of Gilead.
11   Adjoining them were the Gadites, occupying the district of Bashan
12 as far as Salcah: Joel the chief; second in rank, Shapham; then Jaanai
13 and Shaphat in Bashan. Their fellow-tribesmen belonged to the
families of Michael, Meshullam, Sheba, Jorai, Jachan, Zia and Heber,
14 seven in all. These were the sons of Abihail son of Huri, son of Jaroah,
son of Gilead, son of Michael, son of Jeshishai, son of Jahdo, son of
15,16 Buz. Ahi son of Abdiel, son of Guni, was head of their family; they
lived in Gilead, in Bashan and its villages, in all the common land of
17 Sharon as far as*d* it stretched. These registers were all compiled in the
reigns of Jotham king of Judah and Jeroboam king of Israel.
18   The sons of Reuben, Gad, and half the tribe of Manasseh: of their
fighting men armed with shield and sword, their archers and their
battle-trained soldiers, forty-four thousand seven hundred and sixty

[a] the tribes of Ham: *prob. rdg., cp. verse 40;* Heb. their tribes. [b] his, not: *prob. rdg.;*
Heb. om. [c] So Luc. Sept.; Heb. Tilgath-pilneser. [d] as far as: *so Sept.;* Heb. upon.

were ready for active service. They made war on the Hagarites, Jetur, 19
Nephish, and Nodab. They were given help against them, for they cried 20
to their God for help in the battle, and because they trusted him he
listened to their prayer, and the Hagarites and all their allies surrendered to them.*a* They drove off their cattle, fifty thousand camels, 21
two hundred and fifty thousand sheep, and two thousand asses, and
they took a hundred thousand captives. Many had been killed, for the 22
war was of God's making, and they occupied the land instead of them
until the exile.

Half the tribe of Manasseh lived in the land from Bashan to Baal- 23
hermon, Senir, and Mount Hermon, and were numerous also in
Lebanon.*b* The heads of their families were: Epher,*c* Ishi, Eliel, 24
Azriel, Jeremiah, Hodaviah, and Jahdiel, all men of ability and repute,
heads of their families. But they sinned against the God of their fathers, 25
and turned wantonly to worship the gods of the peoples whom God had
destroyed before them. So the God of Israel stirred up Pul king of 26
Assyria, that is Tiglath-pileser*d* king of Assyria, and he carried into
exile Reuben, Gad, and half the tribe of Manasseh. He took them to
Halah, Habor, Hara, and the river Gozan, where they are to this day.

THE SONS OF LEVI: Gershon,*e* Kohath and Merari. The sons of 6 1,*f*2
Kohath: Amram, Izhar, Hebron and Uzziel. The children of Amram: 3
Aaron, Moses and Miriam. The sons of Aaron: Nadab, Abihu,
Eleazar and Ithamar. Eleazar was the father of Phinehas, Phinehas 4*g*
father of Abishua, Abishua father of Bukki, Bukki father of Uzzi, 5
Uzzi father of Zerahiah, Zerahiah father of Meraioth, Meraioth father 6,7
of Amariah, Amariah father of Ahitub, Ahitub father of Zadok, Zadok 8
father of Ahimaaz, Ahimaaz father of Azariah, Azariah father of 9
Johanan, and Johanan father of Azariah, the priest who officiated in 10
the LORD's house which Solomon built at Jerusalem. Azariah was the 11
father of Amariah, Amariah father of Ahitub, Ahitub father of Zadok, 12
Zadok father of Shallum, Shallum father of Hilkiah, Hilkiah father of 13
Azariah, Azariah father of Seraiah, and Seraiah father of Jehozadak. 14
Jehozadak went into exile when the LORD sent Judah and Jerusalem 15
into exile under Nebuchadnezzar.

The sons of Levi: Gershom, Kohath and Merari. The sons of 16,*h i* 17
Gershom: Libni and Shimei. The sons of Kohath: Amram, Izhar, 18
Hebron and Uzziel. The sons of Merari: Mahli and Mushi. The clans 19

[*a*] They were...surrendered to them: *or* They attacked them boldly, and the Hagarites and
all their allies surrendered to them, for they cried...to their prayer.   [*b*] in Lebanon: *so
Sept.; Heb. om.*   [*c*] *So Sept.; Heb.* and Epher.   [*d*] *So Pesh.; Heb.* Tilgath-pilneser.
[*e*] Gershom *in verses 16 and 17.*   [*f*] *5. 27 in Heb.*   [*g*] *Verses 4–8: cp. verses 50–53.*
[*h*] *6. 1 in Heb.*   [*i*] *Verses 16–19: cp. Exod. 6. 16–19.*

20^{*a*} of Levi, family by family: Gershom: his son Libni, his son Jahath,
21 his son Zimmah, his son Joah, his son Iddo, his son Zerah, his son
22^{*b*} Jeaterai. The sons of Kohath: his son Amminadab, his son Korah, his
23,24 son Assir, his son Elkanah, his son Ebiasaph, his son Assir, his son
25 Tahath, his son Uriel, his son Uzziah, his son Saul. The sons of
26 Elkanah: Amasai and Ahimoth, his son Elkanah,^{*c*} his son Zophai, his
27,28 son Nahath, his son Eliab, his son Jeroham, his son Elkanah. The sons
29 of Samuel: Joel the eldest and Abiah the second.^{*d*} The sons of Merari:
30 his son^{*e*} Mahli, his son Libni, his son Shimei, his son Uzza, his son
Shimea, his son Haggiah, his son Asaiah.

31 These are the men whom David appointed to take charge of the
music in the house of the LORD when the Ark should be deposited
32 there. They performed their musical duties before the Tent of the
Presence until Solomon built the house of the LORD in Jerusalem, and
33 took their regular turns of duty there. The following, with their
descendants, took this duty. Of the line of Kohath: Heman the
34 musician, son of Joel, son of Samuel, son of Elkanah, son of Jeroham,
35 son of Eliel, son of Toah, son of Zuph, son of Elkanah, son of Mahath,
36 son of Amasai, son of Elkanah, son of Joel, son of Azariah, son of
37 Zephaniah, son of Tahath, son of Assir, son of Ebiasaph, son of Korah,
38,39 son of Izhar, son of Kohath, son of Levi, son of Israel. Heman's
colleague Asaph stood at his right hand. He was the son of Berachiah,
40 son of Shimea, son of Michael, son of Baaseiah, son of Malchiah,
41,^{*f*}42 son of Ethni, son of Zerah, son of Adaiah, son of Ethan, son of Zimmah,
43,44 son of Shimei, son of Jahath, son of Gershom, son of Levi. On their
left stood their colleague of the line of Merari: Ethan son of Kishi, son
45 of Abdi, son of Malluch, son of Hashabiah, son of Amaziah, son of
46,47 Hilkiah, son of Amzi, son of Bani, son of Shamer, son of Mahli, son of
48 Mushi, son of Merari, son of Levi. Their kinsmen the Levites were
dedicated to all the service of the Tabernacle, the house of God.

49 But it was Aaron and his descendants who burnt the sacrifices on the
altar of whole-offering and the altar of incense, in fulfilment of all the
duties connected with the most sacred gifts, and to make expiation for
50^{*g*} Israel, exactly as Moses the servant of God had commanded. The sons
51 of Aaron: his son Eleazar, his son Phinehas, his son Abishua, his son
52 Bukki, his son Uzzi, his son Zerahiah, his son Meraioth, his son
53 Amariah, his son Ahitub, his son Zadok, his son Ahimaaz.

54 These are their settlements in encampments in the districts assigned
to the descendants of Aaron, to the clan of Kohath, for it was to them

[*a*] *Verses 20, 21: cp. verses 41–43.* [*b*] *Verses 22–28: cp. verses 33–38.* [*c*] *his son Elkanah:
so Sept.; Heb. Elkanah, the sons of Elkanah.* [*d*] *Joel...the second: so Luc. Sept.; Heb.
the eldest Vashni and Abiah.* [*e*] *his son: so Pesh.; Heb. om.* [*f*] *Verses 41–43: cp.
verses 20, 21.* [*g*] *Verses 50–53: cp. verses 4–8.*

that the lot had fallen: they gave them Hebron in Judah, with the 55
common land round it, but they assigned to Caleb son of Jephunneh 56
the open country belonging to the town and its hamlets. They gave to 57ᵃ
the sons of Aaron: Hebron the city*b* of refuge, Libnah, Jattir, Eshtemoa,
Hilen,*c* Debir, Ashan, and Beth-shemesh, each with its common land. 58, 59
And from the tribe of Benjamin: Geba, Alemeth, and Anathoth, each 60
with its common land, making thirteen cities in all by their clans.

They gave to the remaining clans of the sons of Kohath ten cities by 61
lot from the half tribe*d* of Manasseh. To the sons of Gershom according 62
to their clans they gave thirteen cities from the tribes of Issachar,
Asher, Naphtali, and Manasseh in Bashan. To the sons of Merari 63
according to their clans they gave by lot twelve cities from the tribes of
Reuben, Gad, and Zebulun. Israel gave these cities, each with its common 64
land, to the Levites. (The cities mentioned above, from the tribes of 65
Judah, Simeon, and Benjamin, were assigned by lot.)

Some of the clans of Kohath had cities allotted*e* to them. They gave 66, 67
them the city*f* of refuge, Shechem in the hill-country of Ephraim,
Gezer, Jokmeam, Beth-horon, Aijalon, and Gath-rimmon, each with 68, 69
its common land. From the half tribe of Manasseh, Aner and Bileam, 70
each with its common land, were given to the rest of the clans of Kohath.

To the sons of Gershom they gave from the half tribe of Manasseh: 71
Golan in Bashan, and Ashtaroth, each with its common land. From the 72
tribe of Issachar: Kedesh, Daberath, Ramoth, and Anem, each with its 73
common land. From the tribe of Asher: Mashal, Abdon, Hukok, and 74, 75
Rehob, each with its common land. From the tribe of Naphtali: Kedesh 76
in Galilee, Hammon, and Kiriathaim, each with its common land.

To the rest of the sons of Merari they gave from the tribe of Zebulun: 77
Rimmon*g* and Tabor, each with its common land. On the east of Jordan, 78
opposite Jericho, from the tribe of Reuben: Bezer-in-the-wilderness,
Jahzah, Kedemoth, and Mephaath, each with its common land. From 79, 80
the tribe of Gad: Ramoth in Gilead, Mahanaim, Heshbon, and Jazer, 81
each with its common land.

The sons of*h* Issachar: Tola, Pua, Jashub and Shimron, four. 7 1ⁱ
The sons of Tola: Uzzi, Rephaiah, Jeriel, Jahmai, Jibsam, and Samuel, 2
all able men and heads of families by paternal descent from Tola
according to their tribal lists; their number in David's time was
twenty-two thousand six hundred. The son of Uzzi: Izrahiah. The sons 3
of Izrahiah: Michael, Obadiah, Joel and Isshiah, making a total of five,

---

[a] *Verses 57–81: cp. Josh. 21. 13–39.*   [b] *Prob. rdg., cp. Josh. 21. 13; Heb.* cities.   [c] *So
many MSS.; others* Hilez.   [d] *So Vulg.; Heb. adds* half.   [e] allotted: *prob. rdg., cp. Josh. 21.
20; Heb.* of their frontier.   [f] *Prob. rdg., cp. Josh. 21. 21; Heb.* cities.   [g] *So Sept.; Heb.*
his Rimmon.   [h] *So Pesh.; Heb.* To the sons of.   [i] *Verses 1, 6, 13, 30 and 8. 1–5: cp.
Gen. 46. 13, 17, 21–24.*

4 all of them chiefs. In addition there were bands of fighting men recorded by families according to the tribal lists to the number of
5 thirty-six thousand, for they had many wives and children. Their fellow-tribesmen in all the clans of Issachar were able men, eighty-seven thousand; every one of them was registered.

6,7   The sons of[a] Benjamin: Bela, Becher and Jediael, three. The sons of Bela: Ezbon, Uzzi, Uzziel, Jerimoth and Iri, five. They were heads of their families and able men; the number registered was twenty-two
8 thousand and thirty-four. The sons of Becher: Zemira, Joash, Eliezer, Elioenai, Omri, Jeremoth, Abiah, Anathoth and Alemeth; all
9 these were sons of Becher according to their tribal lists, heads of their families and able men; and the number registered was twenty thousand
10 two hundred. The son of Jediael: Bilhan. The sons of Bilhan: Jeush,
11 Benjamin, Ehud, Kenaanah, Zethan, Tarshish and Ahishahar. All these were descendants of Jediael, heads of[b] families and able men. The number was seventeen thousand two hundred men, fit for active service in war.

12   The sons of Dan:[c] Hushim and the sons of Aher.[d]

13   The sons of Naphtali: Jahziel, Guni, Jezer, Shallum. These were sons of Bilhah.

14[e]   The sons of Manasseh,[f] born of his concubine, an Aramaean:
15 Machir father of Gilead. Machir married a woman whose name was[g] Maacah. The second son was named Zelophehad, and Zelophehad had
16 daughters.[h] Maacah wife of Machir had a son whom she named Peresh. His brother's name was Sheresh, and his sons were Ulam and Rakem.
17 The son of Ulam: Bedan. These were the sons of Gilead son of Machir,
18 son of Manasseh. His sister Hammoleketh was the mother of Ishhod,
19 Abiezer and Mahalah. The sons of Shemida: Ahian, Shechem, Likhi and Aniam.

20   The sons of Ephraim: Shuthelah, his son Bered, his son Tahath, his
21 son Eladah, his son Tahath, his son Zabad, his son Shuthelah. Ephraim's other sons Ezer and Elead were killed by the native Gittites
22 when they came down to lift their cattle. Their father Ephraim long
23 mourned for them, and his kinsmen came to comfort him. Then he had intercourse with his wife; she conceived and had a son whom he named
24 Beriah (because disaster[i] had come on his family). He had a daughter named Sherah; she built Lower and Upper Beth-horon and Uzzen-
25 sherah. He also had a son named Rephah; his son was[j] Resheph, his

---

[a] The sons of: *so some MSS.; others om.*   [b] *Prob. rdg.; Heb.* to the heads of.   [c] The sons of Dan: *prob. rdg., cp. Gen. 46. 23; Heb.* And Shuppim and Huppim, the sons of Ir.
[d] *Or* another.   [e] *Verses 14–19: cp. Num. 26. 29–33.*   [f] *Prob. rdg.; Heb. adds* Asriel.
[g] whose name was: *prob. rdg.; Heb.* to Huppim and Shuppim, and his sister's name was...
[h] The second...daughters: *possibly to be transposed to follow* Gilead *at the end of verse 14.*
[i] *Heb.* beraah.   [j] his son was: *so Luc. Sept.; Heb. om.*

son Telah, his son Tahan, his son Laadan, his son Ammihud, his son 26
Elishama, his son Nun, his son Joshua.   27

Their lands and settlements were: Bethel and its dependent villages, 28
to the east Naaran, to the west Gezer, Shechem, and Gaza,*a* with their
villages. In the possession of Manasseh were Beth-shean, Taanach, 29
Megiddo, and Dor, with their villages. In all of these lived the
descendants of Joseph the son of Israel.

The sons of Asher: Imnah, Ishvah, Ishvi and Beriah, together with 30
their sister Serah. The sons of Beriah: Heber and Malchiel father of 31
Birzavith. Heber was the father of Japhlet, Shomer, Hotham, and their 32
sister Shua. The sons of Japhlet: Pasach, Bimhal and Ashvath. These 33
were the sons of Japhlet. The sons of Shomer: Ahi, Rohgah, Jehubbah 34
and Aram. The sons of his brother Hotham:*b* Zophah, Imna, Shelesh 35
and Amal. The sons of Zophah: Suah, Harnepher, Shual, Beri, 36
Imrah, Bezer, Hod, Shamma, Shilshah, Ithran and Beera. The sons 37, 38
of Jether: Jephunneh, Pispah and Ara. The sons of Ulla: Arah, 39
Haniel and Rezia. All these were descendants of Asher, heads of 40
families, picked men of ability, leading princes. They were enrolled
among the fighting troops; the total number was twenty-six thousand
men.

The sons of Benjamin were: the eldest Bela, the second Ashbel, the **8**
third Aharah, the fourth Nohah and the fifth Rapha. The sons of Bela: 2, 3
Addar, Gera father of Ehud,*c* Abishua, Naaman, Ahoah, Gera, 4, 5
Shephuphan and Huram. These were the sons of Ehud, heads of 6
families living in Geba, who were removed to Manahath: Naaman, 7
Ahiah, and Gera—he it was who removed them. He was the father of
Uzza and Ahihud. Shaharaim had sons born to him in Moabite country, 8
after putting away his wives Mahasham*d* and Baara. By his wife 9
Hodesh he had Jobab, Zibia, Mesha, Malcham, Jeuz, Shachia and 10
Mirmah. These were his sons, heads of families. By Mahasham*e* he 11
had had Abitub and Elpaal. The sons of Elpaal: Eber, Misham, Shamed 12
who built Ono and Lod with its villages, also Beriah and Shema who 13
were heads of families living in Aijalon, having expelled the inhabitants
of Gath. Ahio, Shashak, Jeremoth, Zebadiah, Arad, Ader, Michael, 14, 15, 16
Ispah, and Joha were sons of Beriah; Zebadiah, Meshullam, Hezeki, 17
Heber, Ishmerai, Jezliah, and Jobab were sons of Elpaal; Jakim, 18, 19
Zichri, Zabdi, Elienai, Zilthai, Eliel, Adaiah, Beraiah, and Shimrath 20, 21
were sons of Shimei; Ishpan, Heber, Eliel, Abdon, Zichri, Hanan, 22, 23
Hananiah, Elam, Antothiah, Iphedeiah, and Penuel were sons of 24, 25
Shashak; Shamsherai, Shehariah, Athaliah, Jaresiah, Eliah, and Zichri 26, 27

[*a*] *So some MSS.; others* Aiah.   [*b*] *Prob. rdg., cp. verse 32; Heb.* Helem.   [*c*] father of
Ehud: *prob. rdg., cp. Judg. 3. 15; Heb.* Abihud.   [*d*] Mahasham: *prob. rdg., cp. Luc. Sept.
in verse 11; Heb.* Hushim.   [*e*] Mahasham: *prob. rdg., cp. Luc. Sept.; Heb.* Hushim.

28 were sons of Jeroham. These were enrolled in the tribal lists as heads of families, chiefs living in Jerusalem.

29[a] Jehiel[b] founder of Gibeon lived at Gibeon; his wife's name was
30 Maacah. His eldest son was Abdon, followed by Zur, Kish, Baal,
31,32 Nadab, Gedor, Ahio, Zacher and Mikloth.[c] Mikloth was the father of Shimeah; they lived alongside their kinsmen in Jerusalem.[d]

33 Ner was the father of Kish, Kish father of Saul, Saul father of
34 Jonathan, Malchishua, Abinadab and Eshbaal. Jonathan's son was
35 Meribbaal, and he was the father of Micah. The sons of Micah: Pithon,
36 Melech, Tarea and Ahaz. Ahaz was the father of Jehoaddah, Jehoaddah father of Alemeth, Azmoth and Zimri. Zimri was the father of Moza,
37 and Moza father of Binea; his son was Raphah, his son Elasah, and his
38 son Azel. Azel had six sons, whose names were Azrikam, Bocheru, Ishmael, Sheariah, Obadiah and Hanan. All these were sons of Azel.
39 The sons of his brother Eshek: the eldest Ulam, the second Jeush, the
40 third Eliphelet. The sons of Ulam were able men, archers, and had many sons and grandsons, a hundred and fifty. All these were descendants of Benjamin.

The restored community

9 SO ALL ISRAEL were registered and recorded in the book of the kings of Israel; but Judah for their sins were carried away to exile
2[e] in Babylon. The first to occupy their ancestral land in their cities were
3 lay Israelites, priests, Levites, and temple-servitors.[f] Jerusalem was occupied partly by Judahites, partly by Benjamites, and partly by men
4 of Ephraim and Manasseh. Judahites:[g] Uthai son of Ammihud, son of Omri, son of Imri, son of Bani, a descendant of Perez son of Judah.
5,6 Shelanites: Asaiah the eldest and his sons. The sons of Zerah: Jeuel
7 and six hundred and ninety of their kinsmen. Benjamites: Sallu son of
8 Meshullam, son of Hodaviah, son of Hassenuah, Ibneiah son of Jeroham, Elah son of Uzzi, son of Micri, Meshullam son of Shephatiah,
9 son of Reuel, son of Ibniah, and their recorded kinsmen numbering nine hundred and fifty-six, all heads of families.
10,11 Priests: Jedaiah, Jehoiarib, Jachin, Azariah son of Hilkiah, son of Meshullam, son of Zadok, son of Meraioth, son of Ahitub, the officer in
12 charge of the house of God, Adaiah son of Jeroham, son of Pashhur, son of Malchiah, Maasai son of Adiel, son of Jahzerah, son of Meshul-

---

[a] *Verses 29–38: cp. 9. 35–44.* [b] *So Luc. Sept., cp. 9. 35; Heb. om.* [c] and Mikloth: *so Sept., cp. 9. 37; Heb. om.* [d] *So Pesh.; Heb. adds* with their kinsmen. [e] *Verses 2–22: cp. Neh. 11. 3–22.* [f] *Heb.* Nethinim. [g] *Prob. rdg.; Heb. om.*

lam, son of Meshillemith, son of Immer, and their colleagues, heads of 13
families numbering one thousand seven hundred and sixty, men of
substance and fit for the work connected with the service of the house of
God.

Levites: Shemaiah son of Hasshub, son of Azrikam, son of Hasha- 14
biah, a descendant of Merari, Bakbakkar, Heresh, Galal, Mattaniah 15
son of Mica, son of Zichri, son of Asaph, Obadiah son of Shemaiah, 16
son of Galal, son of Jeduthun, and Berechiah son of Asa, son of Elkanah,
who lived in the hamlets of the Netophathites.

The door-keepers were Shallum, Akkub, Talmon, and Ahiman; 17
their brother Shallum was the chief. Until then they had all been door- 18
keepers in the quarters of the Levites at the king's gate, on the east.
Shallum son of Kore, son of Ebiasaph, son of Korah, and his kinsmen 19
of the Korahite family were responsible for service as guards of the
thresholds of the Tabernacle;*a* their ancestors had performed the duty
of guarding the entrances to the camp of the LORD. Phinehas son of 20
Eleazar had been their overseer in the past—the LORD be with him!
Zechariah son of Meshelemiah was the door-keeper of the Tent of the 21
Presence. Those picked to be door-keepers numbered*b* two hundred 22
and twelve in all, registered in their hamlets. David and Samuel the
seer had installed them because they were trustworthy. They and their 23
sons had charge, by watches, of the gates of the house, the tent-dwelling
of the LORD. The door-keepers were to be on four sides, east, west, 24
north, and south. Their kinsmen from their hamlets had to come on 25
duty with them for seven days at a time in turn. The four principal 26
door-keepers were chosen for their trustworthiness; they were
Levites and had charge of the rooms and the stores in the house of
God. They always slept in the precincts of the house of God (for the 27
watch was their duty) and they had charge of the key for opening the
gates every morning. Some of them had charge of the vessels used in 28
the service of the temple, keeping count of them as they were brought
in and taken out. Some of them were detailed to take charge of the 29
furniture and all the sacred vessels, the flour, the wine, the oil, the
incense, and the spices.

Some of the priests compounded the ointment for the spices. 30
Mattithiah the Levite, the eldest son of Shallum the Korahite, was in 31
charge of the preparation of the wafers because he was trustworthy.
Some of their Kohathite kinsmen were in charge of setting out the 32
rows of the Bread of the Presence every sabbath.

These, the musicians, heads of Levite families, were lodged in rooms 33
set apart for them, because they were liable for duty by day and by
night.

[a] *Lit.* Tent. [b] numbered: *so Pesh.; Heb.* at the thresholds.

34 These are the heads of Levite families, chiefs according to their tribal lists, living in Jerusalem.

35[a] Jehiel founder of Gibeon lived at Gibeon; his wife's name was
36 Maacah, and his sons were Abdon the eldest, Zur, Kish, Baal, Ner,
37,38 Nadab, Gedor, Ahio, Zechariah and Mikloth. Mikloth was the father
39 of Shimeam; they lived alongside their kinsmen in Jerusalem.[b] Ner was the father of Kish, Kish father of Saul, Saul father of Jonathan,
40 Malchishua, Abinadab and Eshbaal. The son of Jonathan was Merib-
41 baal, and Meribbaal was the father of Micah. The sons of Micah:
42 Pithon, Melech, Tahrea and Ahaz.[c] Ahaz was the father of Jarah, Jarah father of Alemeth, Azmoth, and Zimri; Zimri father of Moza,
43 and Moza father of Binea; his son was Rephaiah, his son Elasah, his son
44 Azel. Azel had six sons, whose names were Azrikam, Bocheru, Ishmael, Sheariah, Obadiah and Hanan. These were the sons of Azel.

The death of Saul

10 1[d] THE PHILISTINES fought a battle against Israel, and the men of
2 Israel were routed, leaving their dead on Mount Gilboa. The Philistines hotly pursued Saul and his sons and killed the three sons,
3 Jonathan, Abinadab and Malchishua. The battle went hard for Saul,
4 for some archers came upon him and he was wounded by them. So he said to his armour-bearer, 'Draw your sword and run me through, so that these uncircumcised brutes may not come and make sport of me.' But the armour-bearer refused, he dared not; whereupon Saul took his
5 own sword and fell on it. When the armour-bearer saw that Saul was
6 dead, he too fell on his sword and died. Thus Saul died and his three
7 sons; his whole house perished at one and the same time. And all the Israelites in the Vale, when they saw that their army had fled and that Saul and his sons had perished, fled likewise, abandoning their cities, and the Philistines went in and occupied them.

8 Next day, when the Philistines came to strip the slain, they found
9 Saul and his sons lying dead on Mount Gilboa. They stripped him, cut off his head and took away his armour; then they sent messengers through the length and breadth of their land to take the good news to
10 idols and people alike. They deposited his armour in the temple of
11 their god,[e] and nailed up his skull in the temple of Dagon. When the people of Jabesh-gilead heard all that the Philistines had done to Saul,
12 the bravest of them set out together to recover the bodies of Saul and

[a] *Verses 35–44: cp. 8. 29–38.* [b] *Prob. rdg.; Heb. adds* with their kinsmen. [c] *and Ahaz: so Luc. Sept., cp. 8. 35; Heb. om.* [d] *Verses 1–12: cp. 1 Sam. 31. 1–13.* [e] *Or* gods.

his sons; they brought them back to Jabesh and buried their bones under the oak-tree there, and fasted for seven days. Thus Saul paid 13 with his life for his unfaithfulness: he had disobeyed the word of the LORD and had resorted to ghosts for guidance. He had not sought 14 guidance of the LORD, who therefore destroyed him and transferred the kingdom to David son of Jesse.

David king over Israel

THEN ALL ISRAEL assembled at Hebron to wait upon David. 11 1*ª* 'We are your own flesh and blood', they said. 'In the past, while 2 Saul was still king, you led the forces of Israel to war, and you brought them home again. And the LORD your God said to you, "You shall be shepherd of my people Israel, you shall be their prince."' All the elders 3 of Israel came to the king at Hebron; there David made a covenant with them before the LORD, and they anointed David king over Israel, as the LORD had said through the lips of Samuel.

Then David and all Israel went to Jerusalem (that is Jebus, where the 4 Jebusites, the inhabitants of the land, lived). The people of Jebus said 5 to David, 'Never shall you come in here'; none the less David did capture the stronghold of Zion, and it is now known as the City of David. David said, 'The first man to kill a Jebusite shall become a commander 6 or an officer', and the first man to go up was Joab son of Zeruiah; so he was given the command.

David took up his residence in the stronghold: that is why they called 7 it the City of David. He built the city round it, starting at the Millo and 8 including its neighbourhood, while Joab reconstructed the rest of the city. So David steadily grew stronger, for the LORD of Hosts was with him. 9

Of David's heroes these were the chief, men who lent their full 10*ᵇ* strength to his government and, with all Israel, joined in making him king; such was the LORD's decree for Israel. First came Jashoboam*ᶜ* 11 the Hachmonite, chief of the three;*ᵈ* he it was who brandished his spear over three hundred, all slain at one time. Next to him was 12 Eleazar son of Dodo the Ahohite, one of the heroic three. He was with 13 David at Pas-dammim where the Philistines had gathered for battle in a field carrying a good crop of barley; and when the people had fled from the Philistines he stood his ground*ᵉ* in the field, saved it*ᶠ* and 14 defeated them. So the LORD brought about a great victory.

[a] *Verses 1–9: cp. 2 Sam. 5. 1–3, 6–10.* [b] *Verses 10–41: cp. 2 Sam. 23. 8–39.* [c] *Some Sept. MSS. have* Ishbaal. [d] *So Luc. Sept.; Heb.* thirty *or* lieutenants. [e] *So Sept., cp. 2 Sam. 23. 12; Heb.* they stood their ground. [f] saved it: *or* cleared it of the Philistines.

15 Three of the thirty chiefs went down to the rock to join David at the cave of Adullam, while the Philistines were encamped in the Vale of
16 Rephaim. At that time David was in the stronghold, and a Philistine
17 garrison held Bethlehem. One day a longing came over David, and he exclaimed, 'If only I could have a drink of water from the well*a* by
18 the gate of Bethlehem!' At this the three made their way through the Philistine lines and drew water from the well by the gate of Bethlehem, and brought it to David. But David refused to drink it; he poured it
19 out to the LORD and said, 'God forbid that I should do such a thing! Can I drink the blood of these men*b*? They have brought it at the risk of their lives.' So he would not drink it. Such were the exploits of the heroic three.

20 Abishai the brother of Joab was chief of the thirty.*c* He once brandished his spear over three hundred dead, and he was famous
21 among the thirty.*c* He held higher rank than the rest of the thirty*c* and
22 became their captain, but he did not rival the three. Benaiah son of Jehoiada, from Kabzeel, was*d* a hero of many exploits. It was he who smote the two champions of Moab, and who went down into a pit and
23 killed a lion on a snowy day. It was he who also killed the Egyptian, a giant seven and a half feet*e* high armed with a spear as big as the beam of a loom; he went to meet him with a club, snatched the spear out of
24 the Egyptian's hand and killed him with his own weapon. Such were the exploits of Benaiah son of Jehoiada, famous among the heroic thirty.*f*
25 He was more famous than the rest of the thirty, but did not rival the three. David appointed him to his household.

26 These were his valiant heroes: Asahel the brother of Joab, and
27 Elhanan son of Dodo from Bethlehem; Shammoth from Harod,*g* and
28 Helez from a place unknown; Ira son of Ikkesh from Tekoa, and
29 Abiezer from Anathoth; Sibbecai from Hushah, and Ilai the Ahohite;
30 Maharai from Netophah, and Heled son of Baanah from Netophah;
31 Ithai son of Ribai from Gibeah of Benjamin, and Benaiah from Pira-
32 thon; Hurai from the ravines of Gaash, and Abiel from Beth-arabah;
33, 34 Azmoth from Bahurim, and Eliahba from Shaalbon; Hashem*h* the
35 Gizonite, and Jonathan son of Shage the Hararite; Ahiam son of Sacar
36 the Hararite, and Eliphal son of Ur; Hepher from Mecherah, and
37 Ahijah from a place unknown; Hezro from Carmel, and Naarai son of
38 Ezbai; Joel the brother of Nathan, and Mibhar the son of Haggeri;
39 Zelek the Ammonite, and Naharai from Beeroth, armour-bearer to
40, 41 Joab son of Zeruiah; Ira the Ithrite, and Gareb the Ithrite; Uriah the
42 Hittite, and Zabad son of Ahlai. Adina son of Shiza the Reubenite, a chief

[a] *Or* cistern. [b] *So Vulg.; Heb. adds* at the risk of their lives. [c] *So Pesh.; Heb.* three.
[d] *So Pesh.; Heb. adds* the son of. [e] *Lit.* five cubits. [f] *Prob. rdg.; Heb.* three.
[g] *Prob. rdg., cp. 2 Sam. 23. 25; Heb.* Haror. [h] *So some Sept. MSS., cp. 2 Sam. 23. 32; Heb.* the sons of Hashem.

of the Reubenites, was over these thirty.ᵃ Also Hanan son of Maacah, 43
and Joshaphat the Mithnite; Uzzia from Ashtaroth, Shama and Jeiel 44
the sons of Hotham from Aroer; Jediael son of Shimri, and Joha his 45
brother, the Tizite; Eliel the Mahavite, and Jeribai and Joshaviah sons 46
of Elnaam, and Ithmah the Moabite; Eliel, Obed, and Jasiel, from 47
Zobah.ᵇ

These are the men who joined David at Ziklag while he was banned 12
from the presence of Saul son of Kish. They ranked among the warriors
valiant in battle. They carried bows and could sling stones or shoot 2
arrows with the left hand or the right; they were Benjamites, kinsmen
of Saul. The foremost were Ahiezer and Joash, the sons of Shemaah 3
the Gibeathite; Jeziel and Pelet, men of Beth-azmoth;ᶜ Berachah and
Jehu of Anathoth; Ishmaiah the Gibeonite, a hero among the thirty 4ᵈ
and a chief among them; Jeremiah, Jahaziel, Johanan, and Josabad of
Gederah; Eluzai, Jerimoth, Bealiah, Shemariah, and Shephatiah the 5ᵉ
Haruphite; Elkanah, Isshiah, Azareel, Joezer, Jashobeam, the Kora- 6
hites; and Joelah and Zebadiah sons of Jeroham, of Gedor. 7

Some Gadites also joined David at the stronghold in the wilderness, 8
valiant men trained for war, who could handle the heavy shield and
spear, grim as lions and swift as gazelles on the hills. Ezer was their 9
chief, Obadiah the second, Eliab the third; Mishmannah the fourth and 10
Jeremiah the fifth; Attai the sixth and Eliel the seventh; Johanan the 11, 12
eighth and Elzabad the ninth; Jeremiah the tenth and Machbanai the 13
eleventh. These were chiefs of the Gadites in the army, the least of 14
them a match for a hundred, the greatest a match for a thousand. These 15
were the men who in the first month crossed the Jordan, which was in
full flood in all its reaches, and wrought havoc in the valleys, east and
west.

Some men of Benjamin and Judah came to David at the stronghold. 16
David went out to them and said, 'If you come as friends to help me, 17
join me and welcome; but if you come to betray me to my enemies,
innocent though I am of any crime of violence, may the God of our
fathers see and judge.' At that a spirit took possession ofᶠ Amasai, the 18
chief of the thirty, and he said:ᵍ

> We are on your side, David!
> We are with you, son of Jesse!
> Greetings, greetings to you
> and greetings to your ally!
> For your God is your ally.

[a] was over these thirty: *so Pesh.; Heb.* had thirty over him. [b] from Zobah: *prob. rdg.;*
Heb. obscure. [c] men of Beth-azmoth: *lit.* sons of Azmoth. [d] *Verses 4 and 5 in Heb.*
[e] *Verse 6 in Heb.* [f] took possession of: *lit.* clothed itself with. [g] and he said: *so*
Sept.; Heb. om.

So David welcomed them and attached them to the columns of his raiding parties.

19 Some men of Manasseh had deserted to David when he went with the Philistines to war against Saul, though he did not, in fact, fight on the side of the Philistines. Their princes brusquely dismissed him, saying to themselves that he would desert them for his master Saul,
20 and that would cost them their heads. The men of Manasseh who deserted to him when he went to Ziklag were these: Adnah, Jozabad, Jediael, Michael, Jozabad, Elihu, and Zilthai, each commanding his
21 thousand in Manasseh. It was they who stood valiantly by David against the raiders, for they were all good fighters, and they were given
22 commands in his forces. From day to day men came in to help David, until he had gathered an immense army.[a]

23 These are the numbers of the armed bands which joined David at Hebron to transfer Saul's sovereignty to him, as the LORD had said:
24 men of Judah, bearing heavy shield and spear, six thousand eight
25 hundred, drafted for active service; of Simeon, fighting men drafted
26 for active service, seven thousand one hundred; of Levi, four thousand
27 six hundred, together with Jehoiada prince of the house of Aaron and
28 three thousand seven hundred men, and Zadok a valiant fighter, with
29 twenty-two officers of[b] his own clan; of Benjamin, Saul's kinsmen, three thousand, though most of them had hitherto remained loyal to
30 the house of Saul; of Ephraim, twenty thousand eight hundred,
31 fighting men, famous in their own clans; of the half tribe of Manasseh, eighteen thousand, who had been nominated to come and make David
32 king; of Issachar, whose tribesmen were skilled in reading the signs of the times to discover what course Israel should follow, two hundred
33 chiefs, with all their kinsmen under their command; of Zebulun, fifty thousand troops well-drilled for battle, armed with every kind of
34 weapon, bold and single-minded; of Naphtali, a thousand officers
35 with thirty-seven thousand men bearing heavy shield and spear; of the Danites, twenty-eight thousand six hundred well-drilled for
36, 37 battle; of Asher, forty thousand troops well-drilled for battle; of the Reubenites and the Gadites and the half tribe of Manasseh east of Jordan, a hundred and twenty thousand, armed with every kind of weapon.

38 All these warriors, bold men in battle, came to Hebron, loyally determined to make David king over the whole of Israel; the rest of
39 Israel, too, had but one thought, to make him king. They spent three days there with David, eating and drinking, for their kinsmen made
40 provision for them. Their neighbours also round about, as far away as Issachar, Zebulun, and Naphtali, brought food on asses and camels,

[a] an immense army: *lit.* a great army like the army of God. [b] of: *so Sept.; Heb. om.*

on mules and oxen, supplies of meal, fig-cakes, raisin-cakes, wine and oil, oxen and sheep, in plenty; for there was rejoicing in Israel.

DAVID CONSULTED the officers over units of a thousand and a 13 hundred on every matter brought forward. Then he said to the whole 2 assembly of Israel, 'If you approve, and if the LORD our God opens a way, let us*a* send to our kinsmen who have stayed behind, in all the districts of Israel, and also to the priests and Levites in the cities where they have common lands, bidding them join us. Let us fetch the Ark 3 of our God, for while Saul lived we never resorted to it.' The whole 4 assembly resolved to do this; the entire nation approved it.

So David assembled all Israel from the Shihor in Egypt to Lebo- 5 hamath, in order to fetch the Ark of God from Kiriath-jearim. Then 6*b* David and all Israel went up to Baalah, to Kiriath-jearim, which belonged to Judah, to fetch the Ark of God, the LORD enthroned upon the cherubim, the Ark which bore his name.*c* And they conveyed the 7 Ark of God on a new cart from the house of Abinadab, with Uzza and Ahio guiding the cart. David and all Israel danced for joy before God 8 without restraint to the sound of singing, of harps and lutes, of tambourines, and cymbals and trumpets. But when they came to the 9 threshing-floor of Kidon, the oxen stumbled, and Uzza put out his hand to hold the Ark. The LORD was angry with Uzza and struck him down 10 because he had put out his hand to the Ark. So he died there before God. David was vexed because the LORD's anger had broken out upon 11 Uzza, and he called the place Perez-uzza,*d* the name it still bears. David was afraid of God that day and said, 'How can I harbour the 12 Ark of God after this?' So he did not take the Ark with him into the 13 City of David, but turned aside and carried it to the house of Obed-edom the Gittite. Thus the Ark of God remained beside the house of 14 Obed-edom, in its tent,*e* for three months, and the LORD blessed the family of Obed-edom and all that he had.

Hiram king of Tyre sent an embassy to David; he sent cedar logs, 14 1*f* and masons and carpenters with them to build him a house. David 2 knew by now that the LORD had confirmed him as king over Israel and*g* had made his royal power stand higher for the sake of his people Israel.

David married more wives in Jerusalem, and more sons and daughters 3 were born to him. These are the names of the children born to him in 4*h* Jerusalem: Shammua, Shobab, Nathan, Solomon, Ibhar, Elishua, 5 Elpelet, Nogah, Nepheg, Japhia, Elishama, Beeliada and Eliphelet.   6, 7

[a] and if. . .let us: *or* and if it is from the LORD our God, let us seize the opportunity and. . .
[b] *Verses 6–14: cp. 2 Sam. 6. 2–11.*   [c] which bore his name: *prob. rdg.; Heb. obscure.*
[d] *That is* Outbreak on Uzza.   [e] *Or* in his tent.   [f] *Verses 1–16: cp. 2 Sam. 5. 11–25.*
[g] and: *so Targ., cp. 2 Sam. 5. 12; Heb. om.*   [h] *Verses 4–7: cp. 3. 5–8.*

8 When the Philistines learnt that David had been anointed king over the whole of Israel, they came up in force to seek him out. David,
9 hearing of this, went out to face them. Now the Philistines had come
10 and raided the Vale of Rephaim. So David inquired of God, 'If I attack the Philistines, wilt thou deliver them into my hands?' And the
11 LORD answered, 'Go; I will deliver them into your hands.' So he*a* went up and attacked them at Baal-perazim and defeated them there. 'God has used me to break through my enemies' lines,' David said, 'as a river breaks its banks'; that is why the place was named Baal-perazim.*b*
12 The Philistines left their gods behind them there, and by David's orders these were burnt.
13, 14 The Philistines made another raid on the Vale. Again David inquired of God, and God said to him, 'No, you must go up towards their rear; wheel round without making contact and*c* come upon them opposite
15 the aspens. Then, as soon as you hear a rustling sound in the tree-tops, you shall give battle, for God will have gone out before you to defeat
16 the Philistine army.' David did as God commanded, and they drove the
17 Philistine army in flight all the way from Gibeon to Gezer. So David's fame spread through every land, and the LORD inspired all nations with dread of him.

15 DAVID BUILT HIMSELF QUARTERS in the City of David, and
2 prepared a place for the Ark of God and pitched a tent for it. Then he decreed that only Levites should carry the Ark of God, since they had
3 been chosen by the LORD to carry it and to serve him*d* for ever. Next David assembled all Israel at Jerusalem, to bring up the Ark of the
4 LORD to the place he had prepared for it. He gathered together the
5 sons of Aaron and the Levites: of the sons of Kohath, Uriel the chief
6 with a hundred and twenty of his kinsmen; of the sons of Merari,
7 Asaiah the chief with two hundred and twenty of his kinsmen; of the sons of Gershom, Joel the chief with a hundred and thirty of his
8 kinsmen; of the sons of Elizaphan, Shemaiah the chief with two
9 hundred of his kinsmen; of the sons of Hebron, Eliel the chief with
10 eighty of his kinsmen; of the sons of Uzziel, Amminadab the chief with
11 a hundred and twelve of his kinsmen. And David summoned Zadok and Abiathar the priests, together with the Levites, Uriel, Asaiah, Joel,
12 Shemaiah, Eliel, and Amminadab, and said to them, 'You who are heads of families of the Levites, hallow yourselves, you and your kinsmen, and bring up the Ark of the LORD the God of Israel to the
13 place which I have prepared for it. It was because you were not present

[a] *So Sept., cp. 2 Sam. 5. 20.; Heb.* they. [b] *That is* Baal of Break-through.
[c] No...contact and: *or* Do not go up to the attack; withdraw from them and then...
[d] *Or* it.

the first time, that the LORD our God broke out upon us. For we had not sought his guidance as we should have done.' So the priests and the 14 Levites hallowed themselves to bring up the Ark of the LORD the God of Israel, and the Levites carried the Ark of God, bearing it on their 15 shoulders with poles as Moses had prescribed at the command of the LORD.

David also ordered the chiefs of the Levites to install as musicians 16 those of their kinsmen who were players skilled in making joyful music on their instruments, lutes and harps and cymbals. So the Levites 17 installed Heman son of Joel and, from his kinsmen, Asaph son of Berechiah; and from their kinsmen the Merarites, Ethan son of Kushaiah, together with their kinsmen of the second degree, Zechariah,ᵃ 18 Jaaziel, Shemiramoth, Jehiel, Unni, Eliab, Benaiah, Maaseiah, Matti-thiah, Eliphelehu, and Mikneiah, and the door-keepers Obed-edom and Jeiel. They installed the musicians Heman, Asaph, and Ethan to 19 sound the cymbals of bronze; Zechariah, Jaaziel, Shemiramoth, Jehiel, 20 Unni, Eliab, Maaseiah, and Benaiah to play on lutes;ᵇ Mattithiah, 21 Eliphelehu, Mikneiah, Obed-edom, Jeiel, and Azaziah to play on harps.ᶜ Kenaniah, officer of the Levites, was precentor in charge of the 22 music because of his proficiency. Berechiah and Elkanah were door- 23 keepers for the Ark, while the priests Shebaniah, Jehoshaphat, 24 Nethaneel, Amasai, Zechariah, Benaiah, and Eliezer sounded the trumpets before the Ark of God; and Obed-edom and Jehiah also were door-keepers for the Ark.

Then David and the elders of Israel and the captains of units of a 25ᵈ thousand went to bring up the Ark of the Covenant of the LORD with much rejoicing from the house of Obed-edom. Because God had 26 helped the Levites who carried the Ark of the Covenant of the LORD, they sacrificed seven bulls and seven rams.

Now David and all the Levites who carried the Ark, and the 27 musicians, and Kenaniah the precentor,ᵉ were arrayed in robes of fine linen; and David had on a linen ephod. All Israel escorted the Ark of 28 the Covenant of the LORD with shouts of acclamation, blowing on horns and trumpets, clashing cymbals and playing on lutes and harps. But as the Ark of the Covenant of the LORD was entering the city of 29 David, Saul's daughter Michal looked down through a window and saw King David dancing and making merry, and she despised him in her heart.

When they had brought in the Ark of God, they put it inside the 16 1ᶠ

[a] *So some MSS., cp. verse 20; others add* a son. [b] *Prob. rdg.; Heb. adds* al alamoth, *possibly a musical term.* [c] *Prob. rdg.; Heb. adds* al hashsheminith lenasseah, *possibly musical terms.* [d] *Verses 25–29: cp. 2 Sam. 6. 12–16.* [e] *the precentor: prob. rdg.; Heb. obscure.* [f] *Verses 1–3: cp. 2 Sam. 6. 17–19.*

tent that David had pitched for it, and they offered whole-offerings
2 and shared-offerings before God. After David had completed these
3 sacrifices, he blessed the people in the name of the LORD and gave food,
a loaf of bread, a portion of meat,[a] and a cake of raisins, to each
4 Israelite, man or woman. He appointed certain Levites to serve before
the Ark of the LORD, to repeat the Name, to confess and to praise the
5 LORD the God of Israel. Their leader was Asaph; second to him was
Zechariah; then came Jaaziel,[b] Shemiramoth, Jehiel, Mattithiah, Eliab,
Benaiah, Obed-edom, and Jeiel, with lutes and harps, Asaph, who
6 sounded the cymbals; and Benaiah and Jahaziel the priests, who blew
the trumpets before the Ark of the Covenant of God continuously
7 throughout that day. It was then that David first ordained the offering
of thanks to the LORD by Asaph and his kinsmen:

8[c]   Give the LORD thanks and invoke him by name,
       make his deeds known in the world around.
9   Pay him honour with song and psalm
       and think upon all his wonders.
10   Exult in his hallowed name;
       let those who seek the LORD be joyful in heart.
11   Turn to the LORD, your strength,[d]
       seek his presence always.
12   Remember the wonders that he has wrought,
       his portents and the judgements he has given,
13   O offspring of Israel his servants, O chosen sons of Jacob.

14   He is the LORD our God;
       his judgements fill the earth.
15   He called to mind[e] his covenant from long ago,[f]
       the promise he extended to a thousand generations—
16   the covenant made with Abraham,
       his oath given to Isaac,
17   the decree by which he bound himself for Jacob,
       his everlasting covenant with Israel:
18   'I will give you the land of Canaan', he said,
       'to be your possession, your patrimony.'
19   A small company it was,[g]
       few in number, strangers in that land,
20   roaming from nation to nation,
       from one kingdom to another;
21   but he let no man ill-treat them,

[a] portion of meat: *mng. of Heb. word uncertain.* [b] *Prob. rdg., cp. 15. 18, 20; Heb.* Jeiel.
[c] *Verses 8–22: cp. Ps. 105. 1–15.* [d] your strength: *or the symbol of his strength; lit. and
his strength.* [e] He called to mind: *so some Sept. MSS., cp. Ps. 105. 8; Heb.* Call to mind.
[f] from long ago: *or for ever.* [g] it was: *so some MSS., cp. Ps. 105. 12; others* you were.

for their sake he admonished kings:
   'Touch not my anointed servants,   22
   do my prophets no harm.'

Sing to the LORD, all men on earth,   23[a]
   proclaim his triumph day by day.
Declare his glory among the nations,   24
   his marvellous deeds among all peoples.
Great is the LORD and worthy of all praise;   25
   he is more to be feared than all gods.
For the gods of the nations are idols every one;   26
   but the LORD made the heavens.
Majesty and splendour attend him,   27
   might and joy are in his dwelling.

Ascribe to the LORD, you families of nations,   28
ascribe to the LORD glory and might;
   ascribe to the LORD the glory due to his name,   29
bring a gift and come before him.
   Bow down to the LORD in the splendour of holiness,[b]
     and dance in his honour, all men on earth.   30
     He has fixed the earth firm, immovable.
Let the heavens rejoice and the earth exult,   31
let men declare among the nations, 'The LORD is king.'
   Let the sea roar and all the creatures in it,   32
   let the fields exult and all that is in them;
   then let the trees of the forest shout for joy   33
   before the LORD when he comes to judge the earth.

It is good to give thanks to the LORD,   34[c]
   for his love endures for ever.
Cry, 'Deliver us, O God our saviour,   35[d]
gather us in and save us from the nations
   that we may give thanks to thy holy name
   and make thy praise our pride.'

Blessed be the LORD the God of Israel   36
   from everlasting to everlasting.

And all the people said 'Amen' and 'Praise the LORD.'

   David left Asaph and his kinsmen there before the Ark of the   37
Covenant of the LORD, to perform regular service before the Ark as
each day's duty required; as door-keepers he left Obed-edom son of   38
Jeduthun, and Hosah. (Obed-edom and his[e] kinsmen were sixty-eight

[a] *Verses 23–33: cp. Ps. 96. 1–13.*   [b] *Or* in holy vestments.   [c] *Verse 34: cp. Ps. 107. 1.*
[d] *Verses 35, 36: cp. Ps. 106. 47, 48.*   [e] *So Sept.; Heb.* their.

39 in number.) He left Zadok the priest and his kinsmen the priests before
40 the Tabernacle of the LORD at the hill-shrine in Gibeon, to make
offerings there to the LORD upon the altar of whole-offering regularly
morning and evening, exactly as it is written in the law enjoined by the
41 LORD upon Israel. With them he left Heman and Jeduthun and the
other men chosen and nominated to give thanks to the LORD, 'for his love
42 endures for ever.' They[a] had trumpets and cymbals for the players,
and the instruments used for sacred song. The sons of Jeduthun kept
the gate.
43 So all the people went home, and David returned to greet his
household.

17 1[b] AS SOON AS DAVID was established in his house, he said to Nathan the
prophet, 'Here I live in a house of cedar, while the Ark of the Covenant
2 of the LORD is housed in curtains.' Nathan answered David, 'Do what-
3 ever you have in mind, for God is with you.' But that night the word
4 of God came to Nathan: 'Go and say to David my servant, "This is the
word of the LORD: It is not you who shall build me a house to dwell in.
5 Down to this day I have never dwelt in a house since I brought Israel
6 up from Egypt; I lived in a tent and a tabernacle.[c] Wherever I journeyed
with Israel, did I ever ask any of the judges whom I appointed shep-
7 herds of my people why they had not built me a house of cedar?" Then
say this to my servant David: "This is the word of the LORD of Hosts:
I took you from the pastures, and from following the sheep, to be
8 prince over my people Israel. I have been with you wherever you have
gone, and have destroyed all the enemies in your path. I will make you
9 as famous as the great ones of the earth. I will assign a place for my
people Israel; there I will plant them, and they shall dwell in their own
land. They shall be disturbed no more, never again shall wicked men
10 wear them down as they did from the time when I first appointed
judges over Israel my people, and I will subdue all your enemies. But
I will make you great and the LORD shall build up your royal house.
11 When your life ends and you go to join your forefathers, I will set up
one of your family, one of your own sons, to succeed you, and I will
12 establish his kingdom. It is he shall build me a house, and I will
13 establish his throne for all time. I will be his father, and he shall be my
son. I will never withdraw my love from him as I withdrew it from
14 your predecessor. But I will give him a sure place in my house and
kingdom for all time, and his throne shall be established for ever."'
15 Nathan recounted to David all that had been said to him and all that
16 had been revealed. Then King David went into the presence of the

---

[a] *So Sept.; Heb.* adds Heman and Jeduthun. [b] *Verses 1–27: cp. 2 Sam. 7. 1–29.* [c] I
lived...tabernacle: *prob. rdg.; Heb.* I have been from tent to tent and from a tabernacle.

LORD and took his place there and said, 'What am I, LORD God, and what is my family, that thou hast brought me thus far? It was a small 17 thing in thy sight, O God, to have planned for thy servant's house in days long past, and now thou lookest upon me as a man already embarked on a high career, O LORD God. What more can David say to 18 thee of the honour thou hast done thy servant, well though thou knowest him? For the sake of thy servant, LORD, and according to thy 19 purpose, thou hast brought me to all this greatness.*a* O LORD, we have 20 never heard of one like thee; there is no god but thee. And thy people 21 Israel, to whom can they be compared? Is there any other*b* nation on earth whom God has gone out to redeem from slavery, to make them his people? Thou hast won a name for thyself by great and terrible deeds, driving out nations before thy people whom thou didst redeem from Egypt. Thou hast made thy people Israel thy own for ever, and 22 thou, O LORD, hast become their God. But now, LORD, let what thou 23 hast promised for thy servant and his house stand fast for all time; make good what thou hast said. Let it stand fast, that thy fame may be great 24 for ever, and let men say, "The LORD of Hosts, the God of Israel, is Israel's God." So shall the house of thy servant David be established before thee. Thou, my God, hast shown me thy purpose to build up 25 thy servant's house; therefore I have been able to pray before thee. Thou, O LORD, art God, and thou hast made these noble promises to 26 thy servant; thou hast been pleased to bless thy servant's house, that it 27 may continue always before thee; thou it is who hast blessed it, and it shall be blessed for ever.'

After this David defeated the Philistines and conquered them, and 18 1*c* took from them Gath with its villages; he defeated the Moabites, and 2 they became subject to him and paid him tribute. He also defeated 3 Hadadezer king of Zobah-hamath, who was on his way to set up a monument of victory by the river Euphrates. From him David 4 captured a thousand chariots, seven thousand horsemen and twenty thousand foot; he hamstrung all the chariot-horses, except a hundred which he retained. When the Aramaeans of Damascus came to the 5 help of Hadadezer king of Zobah, David destroyed twenty-two thousand of them, and established garrisons among these Aramaeans; 6 they became subject to him and paid him tribute. Thus the LORD gave David victory wherever he went. David took the gold quivers 7 borne by Hadadezer's servants and brought them to Jerusalem. He also 8 took a great quantity of bronze*d* from Hadadezer's cities, Tibhath and Kun; from this Solomon made the Sea of bronze,*d* the pillars, and the bronze*d* vessels.

[a] *So Sept.; Heb. adds* by making known all the great things. [b] any other: *so Sept.; Heb.* one. [c] *Verses 1–13: cp. 2 Sam. 8. 1–14.* [d] *Or* copper.

9 When Tou king of Hamath heard that David had defeated the entire
10 army of Hadadezer king of Zobah, he sent his son Hadoram to King
David to greet him and to congratulate him on defeating Hadadezer
in battle (for Hadadezer had been at war with Tou); and he brought
11 with him[a] vessels[b] of gold, silver, and copper, which King David
dedicated to the LORD. He dedicated also the silver and the gold which
he had carried away from all the other nations, from Edom and Moab,
from the Ammonites and the Philistines, and from Amalek.

12 Edom was defeated by Abishai son of Zeruiah, who destroyed
13 eighteen thousand of them in the Valley of Salt and stationed garrisons
in the country. All the Edomites now became subject to David. Thus
the LORD gave victory to David wherever he went.

14[c] David ruled over the whole of Israel and maintained law and justice
15 among all his people. Joab son of Zeruiah was in command of the army;
16 Jehoshaphat son of Ahilud was secretary of state; Zadok and Abiathar
son of Ahimelech, son of Ahitub,[d] were priests; Shavsha was adjutant-
17 general; Benaiah son of Jehoiada commanded the Kerethite and
Pelethite guards. The eldest sons of David were in attendance on the
king.

19 1[e] Some time afterwards Nahash king of the Ammonites died and was
2 succeeded by his son. David said, 'I must keep up the same loyal
friendship with Hanun son of Nahash as his father showed me', and
he sent a mission to condole with him on the death of his father. But
when David's envoys entered the country of the Ammonites to condole
3 with Hanun, the Ammonite princes said to Hanun, 'Do you suppose
David means to do honour to your father when he sends you his
condolences? These men of his are spies whom he has sent to find out
4 how to overthrow the country.' So Hanun took David's servants, and
he shaved them, cut off half their garments up to the hips, and dismissed
5 them. When David heard how they had been treated, he sent to meet
them, for they were deeply humiliated, and ordered them to wait in
6 Jericho and not to return until their beards had grown again. The
Ammonites knew that they had brought themselves into bad odour
with David, so Hanun and the Ammonites sent a thousand talents of
silver to hire chariots and horsemen from Aram-naharaim,[f] Maacah,
7 and Aram-zobah.[g] They hired thirty-two thousand chariots and the
king of Maacah and his people, who came and encamped before
Medeba, while the Ammonites came from their cities and mustered for

[a] he brought with him: *so Pesh. and 2 Sam. 8. 10; Heb. om.* [b] *So Pesh. and 2 Sam. 8. 10; Heb. all vessels.* [c] *Verses 14–17: cp. 2 Sam. 8. 15–18; 20. 23–26; 1 Kgs. 4. 2–4.* [d] *and Abiathar...Ahitub: prob. rdg., cp. 2 Sam. 8. 17; Heb. son of Ahitub and Abimelech son of Abiathar.* [e] *Verses 1–19: cp. 2 Sam. 10. 1–19.* [f] *That is Aram of Two Rivers.* [g] *Maacah, and Aram-zobah: prob. rdg.; Heb. Aram-maacah, and Zobah.*

battle. When David heard of it, he sent out Joab and all the fighting 8
men. The Ammonites came and took up their position at the entrance 9
to the city, while the allied kings took up theirs in the open country.
When Joab saw that he was threatened both front and rear, he detailed 10
some picked Israelite troops and drew them up facing the Aramaeans.
The rest of his forces he put under his brother Abishai, who took up 11
a position facing the Ammonites. 'If the Aramaeans prove too strong 12
for me,' he said, 'you must come to my relief; and if the Ammonites
prove too strong for you, I will relieve you. Courage! Let us fight 13
bravely for our people and for the cities*a* of our God. And the LORD's
will be done.' But when Joab and his men came to close quarters with 14
the Aramaeans, they put them to flight; and when the Ammonites saw 15
them in flight, they too fled before his brother Abishai and entered the
city. Then Joab came to Jerusalem. The Aramaeans saw that they had 16
been worsted by Israel, and they sent messengers to summon other
Aramaeans from the Great Bend of the Euphrates under Shophach,
commander of Hadadezer's army. Their movement was reported to 17
David, who immediately mustered all the forces of Israel, crossed the
Jordan and advanced against them and took up battle positions. The
Aramaeans likewise took up positions facing David and engaged him,*b*
but were put to flight by Israel. David slew seven thousand Aramaeans 18
in chariots and forty thousand infantry, killing Shophach the commander of the army. When Hadadezer's men saw that they had been 19
worsted by Israel, they sued for peace and submitted to David. The
Aramaeans were never again willing to give support to the Ammonites.

AT THE TURN OF THE YEAR, when kings take the field, Joab led 20 1*c*
the army out and ravaged the Ammonite country. He came to Rabbah
and laid siege to it, while David remained in Jerusalem; he reduced
the city and razed it to the ground. David took the crown from the head 2
of Milcom and found that it weighed a talent of gold and was set with
a precious stone, and this he placed on his own head. He also removed
a great quantity of booty from the city; he took its inhabitants and set 3
them to work with saws and other iron tools, sharp and toothed.*d*
David did this to all the cities of the Ammonites; then he and all his
people returned to Jerusalem.

Some time later war with the Philistines broke out in Gezer; it was 4*e*
then that Sibbechai of Hushah killed Sippai, a descendant of the
Rephaim, and the Philistines were reduced to submission. In another 5
war with the Philistines, Elhanan son of Jair killed Lahmi brother of

---

[*a*] *Or* altars. [*b*] The Aramaeans...him: *so Sept.; Heb.* When David had taken up position
facing the Aramaeans, they engaged him. [*c*] *Verses 1–3: cp. 2 Sam. 12. 26–31.* [*d*] toothed:
so one MS., cp. 2 Sam. 12. 31; others saws. [*e*] *Verses 4–7: cp. 2 Sam. 21. 18–22.*

6 Goliath of Gath, whose spear had a shaft like a weaver's beam. In yet another war in Gath, there appeared a giant with six fingers on each hand and six toes on each foot, twenty-four in all; he too was descended

7 from the Rephaim, and, when he defied Israel, Jonathan son of David's

8 brother Shimea killed him. These giants were the descendants of the Rephaim in Gath, and they all fell at the hands of David and his men.

21 1*a* NOW SATAN, setting himself against Israel, incited David to count the

2 people. So he instructed Joab and his public officers to go out and number Israel, from Beersheba to Dan, and to report the number to

3 him. Joab answered, 'Even if the LORD should increase his people a hundredfold, would not your majesty still be king and all the people your slaves? Why should your majesty want to do this? It will only

4 bring guilt on Israel.' But Joab was overruled by the king; he set out and went up and down the whole country. He then came to Jerusalem

5 and reported to David the numbers recorded: those capable of bearing arms were one million one hundred thousand in Israel, and four

6 hundred and seventy thousand in Judah. Levi and Benjamin were not counted by Joab, so deep was his repugnance against the king's order.

7 God was displeased with all this and proceeded to punish Israel.

8 David said to God, 'I have done a very wicked thing: I pray thee

9 remove thy servant's guilt, for I have been very foolish.' And the LORD

10 said to Gad, David's seer, 'Go and tell David, "This is the word of the LORD: I have three things to offer you; choose one of them and I will

11 bring it upon you."' So Gad came to David and said to him, 'This is

12 the word of the LORD: "Make your choice: three years of famine, three months of harrying by your foes and close pursuit by the sword of your enemy, or three days of the LORD's own sword, bringing pestilence throughout the country, and the LORD's angel working destruction in all the territory of Israel." Consider now what answer I am to take back

13 to him who sent me.' Thereupon David said to Gad, 'I am in a desperate plight; let me fall into the hands of the LORD, for his mercy is

14 very great; and let me not fall into the hands of man.' So the LORD sent a pestilence throughout Israel, and seventy thousand men of

15 Israel died. And God sent an angel to Jerusalem to destroy it; but, as he was destroying it, the LORD saw and repented of the evil, and said to the destroying angel at the moment when he was standing beside the threshing-floor of Ornan the Jebusite, 'Enough! Stay your hand.'

16 When David looked up and saw the angel of the LORD standing between earth and heaven, with his sword drawn in his hand and stretched out over Jerusalem, he and the elders, clothed in sackcloth,

17 fell prostrate to the ground; and David said to God, 'It was I who gave

[a] *Verses 1–27: cp. 2 Sam. 24. 1–25.*

the order to count the people. It was I who sinned, I, the shepherd,[a] who did wrong. But these poor sheep, what have they done? O LORD my God, let thy hand fall upon me and upon my family, but check this plague on the people.'[b]

The angel of the LORD, speaking through the lips of Gad, com- 18 manded David to go to the threshing-floor of Ornan the Jebusite and to set up there an altar to the LORD. David went up as Gad had bidden 19 him in the LORD's name. Ornan's four sons who were with him hid 20 themselves, but he was busy threshing his wheat when he turned and saw the angel. As David approached, Ornan looked up and, seeing the 21 king, came out from the threshing-floor and prostrated himself before him. David said to Ornan, 'Let me have the site of the threshing-floor 22 that I may build on it an altar to the LORD; sell it me at the full price, that the plague which has attacked my people may be stopped.' Ornan 23 answered David, 'Take it and let your majesty do as he thinks fit; see, here are the oxen for whole-offerings, the threshing-sledges for the fuel, and the wheat for the grain-offering; I give you everything.' But King David said to Ornan, 'No, I will pay the full price; I will not 24 present to the LORD what is yours, or offer a whole-offering which has cost me nothing.' So David gave Ornan six hundred shekels of gold 25 for the site, and built an altar to the LORD there; on this he offered 26 whole-offerings and shared-offerings, and called upon the LORD, who answered him with fire falling from heaven on the altar of whole-offering. Then, at the LORD's command, the angel sheathed his sword. 27

It was when David saw that the LORD had answered him at the 28 threshing-floor of Ornan the Jebusite that he offered sacrifice there. The 29 tabernacle of the LORD and the altar of whole-offering which Moses had made in the wilderness were then at the hill-shrine in Gibeon; but 30 David had been unable to go there and seek God's guidance, so shocked and shaken was he at the sight of the angel's sword. Then 22 David said, 'This is to be the house of the LORD God, and this is to be an altar of whole-offering for Israel.'

The temple and its organization

DAVID NOW GAVE ORDERS to assemble the aliens resident in 2 Israel, and he set them as masons to dress hewn stones and to build the house of God. He laid in a great store of iron to make nails 3 and clamps for the doors, more bronze than could be weighed and 4

[a] I, the shepherd: *prob. rdg.*; *Heb.* doing wrong.   [b] check...people: *prob. rdg.*; *Heb.* among thy people, not for a plague.

cedar-wood without limit; the men of Sidon and Tyre brought David
5 an ample supply of cedar. David said, 'My son Solomon is a boy of
tender years, and the house that is to be built to the LORD must be
exceedingly magnificent, renowned and celebrated in every land;
therefore I must make preparations for it myself.' So David made
abundant preparation before his death.

6 He sent for Solomon his son and charged him to build a house for
7 the LORD the God of Israel. 'Solomon, my son,' he said, 'I had intended
8 to build a house in honour of the name of the LORD my God; but the
LORD forbade me and said, "You have shed much blood in my sight
and waged great wars; for this reason you shall not build a house in
9ᵃ honour of my name. But you shall have a son who shall be a man of
peace; I will give him peace from all his enemies on every side; his
name shall be Solomon, 'Man of Peace', and I will grant peaceᵇ and
10 quiet to Israel in his days. He shall build a house in honour of my name;
he shall be my son and I will be a father to him, and I will establish
11 the throne of his sovereignty over Israel for ever." Now, Solomon my
son, the LORD be with you! May you prosper and build the house of the
12 LORD your God, as he promised you should. But may the LORD grant
you wisdom and discretion, so that when he gives you authority in
13 Israel you may keep the law of the LORD your God. You will prosper
only if you are careful to observe the decrees and ordinances which the
LORD enjoined upon Moses for Israel; be strong and resolute, neither
faint-hearted nor dismayed.

14 'In spite of all my troubles, I have here ready for the house of the
LORD a hundred thousand talents of gold and a million talents of silver,
with great quantities of bronze and iron, more than can be weighed;
timber and stone, too, I have got ready; and you may add to them.
15 Besides, you have a large force of workmen, masons, sculptors, and
16 carpenters, and countless men skilled in work of every kind, in gold and
silver, bronze and iron. So now to work, and the LORD be with you!'
17 David ordered all the officers of Israel to help Solomon his son:
18 'Is not the LORD your God with you? Will he not give you peace on
every side? For he has given the inhabitants of the land into my power,
19 and they will be subject to the LORD and his people. Devote yourselves,
therefore, heart and soul, to seeking guidance of the LORD your God,
and set about building his sanctuary, so that the Ark of the Covenant
of the LORD and God's holy vessels may be brought into a house built
in honour of his name.'

23 David was now an old man, weighed down with years, and he
2 appointed Solomon his son king over Israel. He gathered together all
3 the officers of Israel, the priests, and the Levites. The Levites were

[a] *Verse 9: cp. 1 Kgs. 5. 4.*   [b] *Heb.* shalom.

enrolled from the age of thirty upwards, their males being thirty-eight
thousand in all. Of these, twenty-four thousand were to be responsible 4
for the maintenance and service of the house of the LORD, six thousand
to act as officers and magistrates, four thousand to be door-keepers, 5
and four thousand to praise the LORD on the musical instruments which
David[a] had made for the service of praise. David organized them in 6
divisions, called after Gershon, Kohath, and Merari, the sons of Levi.

The sons of Gershon: Laadan and Shimei. The sons of Laadan: 7,8
Jehiel the chief, Zetham and Joel, three.[b] These were the heads of the 9
families grouped under Laadan. The sons of Shimei: Jahath, Ziza,[c] 10
Jeush and Beriah, four. Jahath was the chief and Ziza the second, but 11
Jeush and Beriah, having few children, were reckoned for duty as a
single family.

The sons of Kohath: Amram, Izhar, Hebron and Uzziel, four. The 12,13
sons of Amram: Aaron and Moses. Aaron was set apart, he and his sons
in perpetuity, to dedicate the most holy gifts,[d] to burn sacrifices before
the LORD, to serve him, and to give the blessing in his name for ever,
but the sons of Moses, the man of God, were to keep the name of 14
Levite. The sons of Moses: Gershom and Eliezer. The sons of 15,16
Gershom: Shubael[e] the chief. The sons of Eliezer: Rehabiah the chief. 17
Eliezer had no other sons, but Rehabiah had very many. The sons of 18
Izhar: Shelomoth[f] the chief. The sons of Hebron: Jeriah the chief, 19
Amariah the second, Jahaziel the third and Jekameam the fourth.
The sons of Uzziel: Micah the chief and Isshiah the second. 20

The sons of Merari: Mahli and Mushi. The sons of Mahli: Eleazar 21
and Kish. When Eleazar died, he left daughters but no sons, and their 22
cousins, the sons of Kish, married them. The sons of Mushi: Mahli, 23
Eder and Jeremoth, three.

Such were the Levites, grouped by families in the father's line whose 24
heads were entered in the detailed list; they performed duties in the
service of the house of the LORD, from the age of twenty upwards. For 25
David said, 'The LORD the God of Israel has given his people peace
and has made his abode in Jerusalem for ever. The Levites will no 26
longer have to carry the Tabernacle or any of the vessels for its service.'
By these last words of David the Levites were enrolled from the age of 27
twenty upwards. Their duty was to help the sons of Aaron in the service 28
of the house of the LORD: they were responsible for the care of the
courts and the rooms, for the cleansing of all holy things, and the
general service of the house of God; for the rows of the Bread of the 29
Presence, the flour for the grain-offerings, unleavened wafers, cakes

---

[a] *So Sept.; Heb.* I.   [b] *Prob. rdg.; Heb. adds* The sons of Shimei: Shelomith, Haziel and
Haran, three.   [c] *So Sept.; Heb.* Zina.   [d] to dedicate...gifts: *or* to be hallowed as most
holy.   [e] *So Sept.; Heb.* Shebuel.   [f] *So one MS.; others* Shelomith.

baked on the griddle, and pastry, and for the weights and measures.
30 They were to be on duty continually before the LORD every morning
31 and evening, giving thanks and praise to him, and at every offering of
whole-offerings to the LORD, on sabbaths, new moons and at the
32 appointed seasons, according to their prescribed number. The Levites
were to have charge of the Tent of the Presence and of the sanctuary,
but the sons of Aaron their kinsmen were charged with the service of
worship in the house of the LORD.

24 The divisions of the sons of Aaron: his sons were Nadab and Abihu,
2 Eleazar and Ithamar. Nadab and Abihu died before their father,
leaving no sons; therefore Eleazar and Ithamar held the office of priest.
3 David, acting with Zadok of the sons of Eleazar and with Ahimelech of
the sons of Ithamar, organized them in divisions for the discharge of
4 the duties of their office. The male heads of families proved to be more
numerous in the line of Eleazar than in that of Ithamar, so that sixteen
heads of families were grouped under the line of Eleazar and eight
5 under that of Ithamar. He organized them by drawing lots among them,
for there were sacred officers*a* and officers of God in the line of Eleazar
6 and in that of Ithamar. Shemaiah the clerk, a Levite, son of Nethaneel,
wrote down the names in the presence of the king, the officers, Zadok
the priest, and Ahimelech son of Abiathar, and of the heads of the
priestly and levitical families, one priestly family being taken from the
7 line of Eleazar and one*b* from that of Ithamar. The first lot fell to
8 Jehoiarib, the second to Jedaiah, the third to Harim, the fourth to
9, 10 Seorim, the fifth to Malchiah, the sixth to Mijamin, the seventh to
11 Hakkoz, the eighth to Abiah, the ninth to Jeshua, the tenth to She-
12, 13 caniah, the eleventh to Eliashib, the twelfth to Jakim, the thirteenth to
14 Huppah, the fourteenth to Jeshebeab,*c* the fifteenth to Bilgah, the
15 sixteenth to Immer, the seventeenth to Hezir, the eighteenth to Aphses,
16, 17 the nineteenth to Pethahiah, the twentieth to Jehezekel, the twenty-
18 first to Jachin, the twenty-second to Gamul, the twenty-third to
19 Delaiah, and the twenty-fourth to Maaziah. This was their order of
duty for the discharge of their service when they entered the house of
the LORD, according to the rule prescribed for them by their ancestor
Aaron, who had received his instructions from the LORD the God of
Israel.

20 Of the remaining Levites: of the sons of Amram: Shubael. Of the
21 sons of Shubael: Jehdeiah. Of Rehabiah: Isshiah, the chief of Rehabiah's
22 sons. Of the line of Izhar: Shelomoth. Of the sons of Shelomoth:
23 Jahath. The sons of Hebron:*d* Jeriah the chief,*e* Amariah the second,

[a] sacred officers: *or* officers of the sanctuary. [b] one: *so some MSS.; others* taken.
[c] *One form of Sept. has* Ishbaal. [d] Hebron: *so one MS.; others om.* [e] the chief: *so
Luc. Sept.; Heb. om.*

Jahaziel the third and Jekameam the fourth. The sons of Uzziel: 24
Micah. Of the sons of Micah: Shamir; Micah's brother: Isshiah. Of the 25
sons of Isshiah: Zechariah. The sons of Merari: Mahli and Mushi and 26
also*a* Jaaziah his son. The sons of Merari: of Jaaziah: Beno, Shoham, 27
Zaccur and Ibri. Of Mahli: Eleazar, who had no sons; of Kish: the 28, 29
sons of Kish: Jerahmeel; and the sons of Mushi: Mahli, Eder and 30
Jerimoth. These were the Levites by families. These also, side by side 31
with their kinsmen the sons of Aaron, cast lots in the presence of King
David, Zadok, Ahimelech, and the heads of the priestly and levitical
families, the senior and junior houses casting lots side by side.

David and his chief officers assigned special duties to the sons of 25
Asaph, of Heman, and of Jeduthun, leaders in inspired prophecy to the
accompaniment of harps, lutes, and cymbals; the number of the men
who performed this work in the temple was as follows. Of the sons of 2
Asaph: Zaccur, Joseph, Nethaniah and Asarelah; these were under
Asaph, a leader in inspired prophecy under the king. Of the sons of 3
Jeduthun: Gedaliah, Izri,*b* Isaiah, Shimei,*c* Hashabiah, Mattithiah,
these six under their father Jeduthun, a leader in inspired prophecy to
the accompaniment of the harp, giving thanks and praise to the LORD.
Of the sons of Heman: Bukkiah, Mattaniah, Uzziel, Shubael,*d* Jeri- 4
moth, Hananiah, Hanani, Eliathah, Giddalti, Romamti-ezer, Joshbekashah, Mallothi, Hothir, and Mahazioth;*e* all these were sons of 5
Heman the king's seer, given to him through the promises of God for
his greater glory. God had given Heman fourteen sons and three
daughters, and they all served under their father for the singing in the 6
house of the LORD; they took part in the service of the house of God,
with cymbals, lutes, and harps, while Asaph, Jeduthun, and Heman
were under the king. Reckoned with their kinsmen, trained singers of 7
the LORD, they brought the total number of skilled musicians up to
two hundred and eighty-eight. They cast lots for their duties, young 8
and old, master-singer and apprentice side by side.

The first lot fell*f* to Joseph: he and his brothers and his sons, twelve.*g* 9
The second to Gedaliah: he and his brothers and his sons, twelve.
The third to Zaccur: his sons and his brothers, twelve. The fourth to 10, 11
Izri: his sons and his brothers, twelve. The fifth to Nethaniah: his 12
sons and his brothers, twelve. The sixth to Bukkiah: his sons and his 13
brothers, twelve. The seventh to Asarelah:*h* his sons and his brothers, 14

[a] and also: *prob. rdg.; Heb.* the sons of. [b] *Prob. rdg., cp. verse 11; Heb.* Zeri. [c] *So
one MS.; others om.* [d] *So Sept., cp. verse 20; Heb.* Shebuel. [e] Hananiah...Mahazioth:
*these nine proper names were probably originally the words of a prayer, which may have had its
place immediately after verse 3:* Be gracious to me, O LORD, be gracious to me; my God
art thou; I will magnify and exalt thee, my helper. Lingering in hardship, I faint. Grant
me vision after vision. [f] *Prob. rdg.; Heb. adds* to Asaph. [g] he...twelve: *prob. rdg.;
Heb. om.* [h] *So one form of Sept., cp. verse 2; Heb.* Yesarelah.

15 twelve. The eighth to Isaiah: his sons and his brothers, twelve.
16, 17 The ninth to Mattaniah: his sons and his brothers, twelve. The tenth
18 to Shimei: his sons and his brothers, twelve. The eleventh to Azareel:
19 his sons and his brothers, twelve. The twelfth to Hashabiah: his sons
20 and his brothers, twelve. The thirteenth to Shubael: his sons and his
21 brothers, twelve. The fourteenth to Mattithiah: his sons and his
22 brothers, twelve. The fifteenth to Jeremoth: his sons and his brothers,
23 twelve. The sixteenth to Hananiah: his sons and his brothers, twelve.
24 The seventeenth to Joshbekashah: his sons and his brothers, twelve.
25, 26 The eighteenth to Hanani: his sons and his brothers, twelve. The
27 nineteenth to Mallothi: his sons and his brothers, twelve. The twenti-
28 eth to Eliathah: his sons and his brothers, twelve. The twenty-first
29 to Hothir: his sons and his brothers, twelve. The twenty-second to
30 Giddalti: his sons and his brothers, twelve. The twenty-third to
31 Mahazioth: his sons and his brothers, twelve. The twenty-fourth to
Romamti-ezer: his sons and his brothers, twelve.

26 The divisions of the door-keepers: Korahites: Meshelemiah son of
2 Kore, son of Ebiasaph.[a] Sons of Meshelemiah: Zechariah the eldest,
3 Jediael the second, Zebediah the third, Jathniel the fourth, Elam the
4 fifth, Jehohanan the sixth, Elioenai the seventh. Sons of Obed-edom:
Shemaiah the eldest, Jehozabad the second, Joah the third, Sacar the
5 fourth, Nethaneel the fifth, Ammiel the sixth, Issachar the seventh,
6 Peulthai the eighth (for God had blessed him). Shemaiah, his son, was
the father of sons who had authority in their family, for they were men
7 of great ability. Sons of Shemaiah: Othni, Rephael, Obed, Elzabad and[b]
8 his brothers Elihu and Semachiah, men of ability. All these belonged to
the family of Obed-edom; they, their sons and brothers, were men of
9 ability, fit for service in the temple; total: sixty-two. Sons and brothers
10 of Meshelemiah, all men of ability, eighteen. Sons of Hosah, a
Merarite: Shimri the chief (he was not the eldest, but his father had
11 made him chief), Hilkiah the second, Tebaliah the third, Zechariah the
fourth. Total of Hosah's sons and brothers: thirteen.
12 The male heads of families constituted the divisions of the door-
keepers; their duty was to serve in the house of the LORD side by side
13 with their kinsmen. Young and old, family by family, they cast lots for
14 the gates. The lot for the east gate fell to Shelemiah; then lots were cast
for his son Zechariah, a prudent counsellor, and he was allotted the
15 north gate. To Obed-edom was allotted the south gate, and the gate-
16 house to his sons. Hosah[c] was allotted the west gate, together with the
Shallecheth gate on the ascending causeway. Guard corresponded to
17 guard. Six Levites were on duty daily on the east side, four on the

[a] son of Ebiasaph: *prob. rdg.; Heb.* from the sons of Asaph. [b] and: *so some MSS.; others om.* [c] Hosah: *prob. rdg.; Heb.* Shuppim and Hosah.

north and four on the south, and two at each gatehouse; at the western 18
colonnade there were four at the causeway and two at the colonnade
itself. These were the divisions of the door-keepers, Korahites and 19
Merarites.

Fellow-Levites[a] were in charge of the stores of the house of God and 20
of the stores of sacred gifts. Of the children of Laadan, descendants 21
of the Gershonite line through Laadan, heads of families in the group
of Laadan the Gershonite, Jehiel and[b] his brothers Zetham and Joel 22
were in charge of the stores of the house of the LORD. Of the families of 23
Amram, Izhar, Hebron and Uzziel, Shubael[c] son of Gershom, son of 24
Moses, was overseer of the stores. The line of Eliezer his brother:[d] his 25
son Rehabiah, his son Isaiah, his son Joram, his son Zichri, and his son
Shelomoth. This Shelomoth and his kinsmen were in charge of all the 26
stores of the sacred gifts dedicated by David the king, the heads of
families, the officers over units of a thousand and a hundred, and other
officers of the army. They had dedicated some of the spoils taken in the 27
wars for the upkeep of the house of the LORD. Everything which 28
Samuel the seer, Saul son of Kish, Abner son of Ner, and Joab son of
Zeruiah had dedicated, in short every sacred gift, was under the charge
of Shelomoth and his kinsmen. Of the family of Izhar, Kenaniah and 29
his sons acted as clerks and magistrates in the secular affairs of Israel.
Of the family of Hebron, Hashabiah and his kinsmen, men of ability to 30
the number of seventeen hundred, had the oversight of Israel west of the
Jordan, both in the work of the LORD and in the service of the king.
Also of the family of Hebron, Jeriah was the chief. (In the fortieth year 31
of David's reign search was made in the family histories of the Hebron-
ites, and men of great ability were found among them at Jazer in
Gilead.) His kinsmen, all men of ability, two thousand seven hundred 32
of them, heads of families, were charged by King David with the
oversight of the Reubenites, the Gadites, and the half tribe of
Manasseh, in religious and civil affairs alike.

THE NUMBER OF THE ISRAELITES—that is to say, of the heads of 27
families, the officers over units of a thousand and a hundred, and the
clerks who had their share in the king's service in the various divisions
which took monthly turns of duty throughout the year—was twenty-
four thousand in each division.

First, Jashobeam son of Zabdiel commanded the division for the 2
first month with twenty-four thousand in his division; a member of 3
the house of Perez, he was chief officer of the temple staff for the first

---

[a] Fellow-Levites: *so Sept.; Heb.* Levites, Ahijah.   [b] Jehiel and: *prob. rdg.; Heb.* Jehieli.
The sons of Jehieli...   [c] *So Vulg.; Heb.* Shebuel.   [d] The line...brother: *so Sept.;
Heb. obscure.*

4 month. Eleazar son of[a] Dodai the Ahohite[b] commanded the division for the second month with twenty-four thousand in his division.
5 Third, Benaiah son of Jehoiada the chief priest, commander of the army, was the officer for the third month with twenty-four thousand in
6 his division (he was the Benaiah who was one of the thirty warriors and was a chief among the thirty); but his son Ammizabad commanded[c]
7 his division. Fourth, Asahel, the brother of Joab, was the officer commanding for the fourth month with twenty-four thousand in his
8 division; and his successor was Zebediah his son. Fifth, Shamhuth the Zerahite[d] was the officer commanding for the fifth month with twenty-
9 four thousand in his division. Sixth, Ira son of Ikkesh, a man of Tekoa, was the officer commanding for the sixth month with twenty-
10 four thousand in his division. Seventh, Helez an Ephraimite, from a place unknown, was the officer commanding for the seventh month
11 with twenty-four thousand in his division. Eighth, Sibbecai the Hushathite, of the family of Zerah, was the officer commanding for the
12 eighth month with twenty-four thousand in his division. Ninth, Abiezer, from Anathoth in Benjamin, was the officer commanding for
13 the ninth month with twenty-four thousand in his division. Tenth, Maharai the Netophathite, of the family of Zerah, was the officer commanding for the tenth month with twenty-four thousand in his
14 division. Eleventh, Benaiah the Pirathonite, from Ephraim, was the officer commanding for the eleventh month with twenty-four thousand
15 in his division. Twelfth, Heldai the Netophathite, of the family of Othniel, was the officer commanding for the twelfth month with twenty-four thousand in his division.

16 The following were the principal officers in charge of the tribes of Israel: of Reuben, Eliezer son of Zichri; of Simeon, Shephatiah son of
17, 18 Maacah; of Levi, Hashabiah son of Kemuel; of Aaron, Zadok; of Judah,
19 Elihu a kinsman of David; of Issachar, Omri son of Michael; of Zebulun,
20 Ishmaiah son of Obadiah; of Naphtali, Jerimoth son of Azriel; of Ephraim, Hoshea son of Azaziah; of the half tribe of Manasseh, Joel
21 son of Pedaiah; of the half of Manasseh in Gilead, Iddo son of
22 Zechariah; of Benjamin, Jaasiel son of Abner; of Dan, Azareel son of Jeroham. These were the officers in charge of the tribes of Israel.

23 David took no census of those under twenty years of age, for the LORD had promised to make the Israelites as many as the stars in the
24 heavens. Joab son of Zeruiah did begin to take a census but he did not finish it; this brought harm upon Israel, and the census was not entered in the chronicle of King David's reign.

[a] Eleazar son of: *prob. rdg.*, *cp. 11. 12*; *Heb. om.* [b] *So Sept.*; *Heb. adds* and his division and Mikloth the prince. [c] commanded: *so Sept.*; *Heb. om.* [d] the Zerahite: *prob. rdg.*; *Heb.* the Izrah.

Azmoth son of Adiel was in charge of the king's stores; Jonathan 25
son of Uzziah was in charge of the stores in the country, in the cities,
in the villages and in the fortresses. Ezri son of Kelub had oversight 26
of the workers on the land; Shimei of Ramah was in charge of the 27
vine-dressers, while Zabdi of Shephem had charge of the produce of
the vineyards for the wine-cellars. Baal-hanan the Gederite supervised 28
the wild olives and the sycomore-figs in the Shephelah; Joash was in
charge of the oil-stores. Shitrai of Sharon was in charge of the herds 29
grazing in Sharon, Shaphat son of Adlai of the herds in the vales.
Obil the Ishmaelite was in charge of the camels, Jehdeiah the Merono- 30
thite of the asses. Jaziz the Hagerite was in charge of the flocks. All 31
these were the officers in charge of King David's possessions. David's 32
favourite nephew Jonathan, a counsellor, a discreet and learned man,
and Jehiel the Hachmonite, were tutors to the king's sons. Ahithophel 33
was a king's counsellor; Hushai the Archite was the King's Friend.
Ahithophel was succeeded by Jehoiada son of Benaiah, and Abiathar. 34
Joab was commander of the army.

DAVID ASSEMBLED at Jerusalem all the officers of Israel, the officers **28**
over the tribes, over the divisions engaged in the king's service, over
the units of a thousand and a hundred, and those in charge of all the
property and the cattle of the king and of his sons, as well as the
eunuchs, the heroes and all the men of ability. Then King David rose 2
to his feet and said, 'Hear me, kinsmen and people. I had in mind to
build a house as a resting-place for the Ark of the Covenant of the LORD
which might serve as a footstool for the feet of our God, and I made
preparations to build it. But God said to me, "You shall not build a 3
house in honour of my name, for you have been a fighting man and
you have shed blood." Nevertheless, the LORD the God of Israel chose 4
me out of all my father's family to be king over Israel in perpetuity;
for it was Judah that he chose as ruling tribe, and, out of the house of
Judah, my father's family; and among my father's sons it was I whom
he was pleased to make king over all Israel. And out of all my sons— 5
for the LORD gave me many sons—he chose Solomon to sit upon the
throne of the LORD's sovereignty over Israel; and he said to me, "It is 6
Solomon your son who shall build my house and my courts, for I have
chosen him to be a son to me and I will be a father to him. I will 7
establish his sovereignty in perpetuity, if only he steadfastly obeys my
commandments and my laws as they are now obeyed." Now therefore, 8
in the presence of all Israel, the assembly of the LORD, and within the
hearing of our God, I bid you all study carefully the commandments
of the LORD your God, that you may possess this good land and hand
it down as an inheritance for all time to your children after you. And 9

you, Solomon my son, acknowledge your father's God and serve him
with whole heart and willing mind, for the LORD searches all hearts
and discerns every invention of men's thoughts. If you search for him,
he will let you find him, but if you forsake him, he will cast you off for

10 ever. Remember, then, that the LORD has chosen you to build a house
for a sanctuary: be steadfast and do it.'

11 David gave Solomon his son the plan of the porch of the temple*a* and
its buildings, strong-rooms, roof-chambers and inner courts, and the

12 shrine of expiation;*b* also the plans of all he had in mind for the courts
of the house of the LORD and for all the rooms around it, for the stores

13 of God's house and for the stores of the sacred gifts, for the divisions
of the priests and the Levites, for all the work connected with the
service of the house of the LORD and for all the vessels used in its

14 service. He prescribed the weight of gold for all the gold vessels*c* used
in the various services, and the weight of silver*d* for all the silver vessels

15 used in the various services; and the weight of gold for the gold lamp-
stands and their lamps; and the weight of silver for the silver lamp-
stands, the weight required for each lamp-stand and its lamps according

16 to the use of each; and the weight of gold for each of the tables for the
rows of the Bread of the Presence, and of silver for the silver tables.

17 He prescribed also the weight of pure gold for the forks, tossing-bowls
and cups, the weight of gold for each of the golden dishes and of silver*d*

18 for each of the silver dishes; the weight also of refined gold for the altar
of incense, and of gold for the model of the chariot, that is the cherubim
with their wings outspread to screen the Ark of the Covenant of the

19 LORD. 'All this was drafted by the LORD's own hand,' said David;
'my part was to consider the detailed working out of the plan.'

20 Then David said to Solomon his son, 'Be steadfast and resolute and
do it; be neither faint-hearted nor dismayed, for the LORD God, my
God, will be with you; he will neither fail you nor forsake you, until
you have finished all the work needed for the service of the house of the

21 LORD. Here are the divisions of the priests and the Levites, ready for all
the service of the house of God. In all the work you will have the help
of every willing craftsman for any task; and the officers and all the
people will be entirely at your command.'

29 King David then said to the whole assembly, 'My son Solomon is the
one chosen by God, Solomon alone, a boy of tender years; and this is
a great work, for it is a palace not for man but for the LORD God.

2 Now to the best of my strength I have made ready for the house of my
God gold for the gold work, silver for the silver, bronze for the bronze,
iron for the iron, and wood for the woodwork, together with cornelian

[a] of the temple: *prob. rdg.; Heb. om.*   [b] the shrine...expiation: *or* the place for the Ark
with its cover.   [c] for...vessels: *prob. rdg.; Heb.* for gold.   [d] of silver: *prob. rdg.; Heb. om.*

and other gems for setting, stones for mosaic work, precious stones of every sort, and marble in plenty. Further, because I delight in the house 3 of my God, I give my own private store of gold and silver for the house of my God—over and above all the store which I have collected for the sanctuary—namely three thousand talents of gold, gold from Ophir, 4 and seven thousand talents of fine silver for overlaying the walls of the buildings, for providing gold for the gold work, silver for the silver, and 5 for any work to be done by skilled craftsmen. Now who is willing to give with open hand to the LORD today?'

Then the heads of families, the officers administering the tribes of 6 Israel, the officers over units of a thousand and a hundred, and the officers in charge of the king's service, responded willingly and gave 7 for the work of the house of God five thousand talents of gold, ten thousand darics, ten thousand talents of silver, eighteen thousand talents of bronze, and a hundred thousand talents of iron. Further, those who 8 possessed precious stones gave them to the treasury of the house of the LORD, into the charge of Jehiel the Gershonite. The people rejoiced at 9 this willing response, because in the loyalty of their hearts they had given willingly to the LORD; King David also was full of joy, and he 10 blessed the LORD in the presence of all the assembly and said, 'Blessed art thou, LORD God of our father Israel, from of old and for ever. Thine, O LORD, is the greatness, the power, the glory, the splendour, 11 and the majesty; for everything in heaven and on earth is thine;[a] thine, O LORD, is the sovereignty, and thou art exalted over all as head. Wealth and honour come from thee; thou rulest over all; might and 12 power are of thy disposing; thine it is to give power and strength to all. And now, we give thee thanks, our God, and praise thy glorious name. 13

'But what am I, and what is my people, that we should be able to 14 give willingly like this? For everything comes from thee, and it is only of thy gifts that we give to thee. We are aliens before thee and settlers, 15 as were all our fathers; our days on earth are like a shadow, we have no abiding place. O LORD our God, from thee comes all this wealth 16 that we have laid up to build a house in honour of thy holy name, and everything is thine. I know, O my God, that thou dost test the heart 17 and that plain honesty pleases thee; with an honest heart I have given all these gifts willingly, and have rejoiced now to see thy people here present give willingly to thee. O LORD God of Abraham, Isaac and 18 Israel our fathers, maintain this purpose for ever in thy people's thoughts and direct their hearts toward thyself. Grant that Solomon 19 my son may loyally keep thy commandments, thy solemn charge, and thy statutes, that he may fulfil them all and build the palace for which I have prepared.'

[a] is thine: *prob. rdg.; Heb. om.*

20 Then, turning to the whole assembly, David said, 'Now bless the LORD your God.' So all the assembly blessed the LORD the God of their fathers, bowing low and prostrating themselves before the LORD and
21 the king. The next day they sacrificed to the LORD and offered whole-offerings to him, a thousand oxen, a thousand rams, a thousand lambs, with the prescribed drink-offerings, and abundant sacrifices for all
22 Israel. So they ate and drank before the LORD that day with great rejoicing. They then appointed Solomon, David's son, king a second
23 time and anointed him as the LORD's prince, and Zadok as priest. So Solomon sat on the LORD's throne as king in place of his father David,
24 and he prospered and all Israel obeyed him. All the officers and the warriors, as well as all the sons of King David, swore fealty to King
25 Solomon. The LORD made Solomon stand very high in the eyes of all Israel, and bestowed upon him sovereignty such as no king in Israel had had before him.
26, 27 David son of Jesse had ruled over the whole of Israel, and the length of his reign over Israel was forty years; he ruled for seven years in
28 Hebron, and for thirty-three in Jerusalem. He died in ripe old age, full of years, wealth, and honour; and Solomon his son ruled in his place.
29 The events of King David's reign from first to last are recorded in the books of Samuel the seer, of Nathan the prophet, and of Gad the seer,
30 with a full account of his reign, his prowess, and of the times through which he and Israel and all the kingdoms of the world had passed.

THE SECOND BOOK OF THE
CHRONICLES

The reign of Solomon and dedication of the temple

K ING SOLOMON, David's son, strengthened his hold on 1
the kingdom, for the LORD his God was with him and made
him very great.

Solomon spoke to all Israel, to the officers over units of a thousand 2
and of a hundred, the judges and all the leading men of Israel, the
heads of families; and he, together with all the assembled people, went 3
to the hill-shrine at Gibeon; for the Tent of God's Presence, which
Moses the LORD's servant had made in the wilderness, was there.
(But David had brought up the Ark of God from Kiriath-jearim to the 4
place which he had prepared for it, for he had pitched a tent for it in
Jerusalem.) The altar of bronze also, which Bezalel son of Uri, son of 5
Hur, had made, was there*[a]* in front of the Tabernacle of the LORD;
and Solomon and the assembly resorted to it.*[b]* There Solomon went up 6
to the altar of bronze before the LORD in the Tent of the Presence and
offered on it a thousand whole-offerings. That night God appeared to 7*[c]*
Solomon and said, 'What shall I give you? Tell me.' Solomon answered, 8
'Thou didst show great and constant love to David my father and thou
hast made me king in his place. Now, O LORD God, let thy word to 9
David my father be confirmed, for thou hast made me king over a
people as numerous as the dust on the earth. Give me now wisdom and 10
knowledge, that I may lead this people; for who is fit to govern this
great people of thine?' God answered Solomon, 'Because this is what 11
you desire, because you have not asked for wealth or possessions or
honour*[d]* or the lives of your enemies or even long life for yourself, but
have asked for wisdom and knowledge to govern my people over
whom I have made you king, wisdom and knowledge are given to you; 12
I shall also give you wealth and possessions and honour*[d]* such as no
king has had before you and none shall have after you.' Then Solomon 13
returned from the hill-shrine at Gibeon, from before the Tent of the
Presence, to Jerusalem and ruled over Israel.

Solomon got together many chariots and horses; he had fourteen 14*[e]*
hundred chariots and twelve thousand horses, and he stabled some in

[a] was there: *so many MSS.; others* he placed. [b] resorted to it: *or* worshipped him.
[c] *Verses 7–12: cp. 1 Kgs. 3. 5–14.* [d] *Or* riches. [e] *Verses 14–17: cp. 9. 25–28; 1 Kgs.*
10. 26–29.

15 the chariot-towns and kept others at hand in Jerusalem. The king made silver and gold as common in Jerusalem as stones, and cedar as
16 plentiful as sycomore-fig in the Shephelah. Horses were imported from Egypt and Coa for Solomon; the royal merchants obtained them
17 from Coa by purchase. Chariots were imported from Egypt for six hundred silver shekels each, and horses for a hundred and fifty; in the same way the merchants obtained them for export from all the kings of the Hittites and the kings of Aram.

2 1^a Solomon resolved to build a house in honour of the name of the
2^b LORD, and a royal palace for himself. He engaged seventy thousand hauliers and eighty thousand quarrymen, and three thousand six
3^c hundred men to superintend them. Then Solomon sent this message to Huram king of Tyre: 'You were so good as to send my father David
4 cedar-wood to build his royal residence. Now I am about to build a house in honour of the name of the LORD my God and to consecrate it to him, so that I may burn fragrant incense in it before him, and present the rows of the Bread of the Presence regularly, and whole-offerings morning and evening, on the sabbaths and the new moons and the appointed festivals of the LORD our God; for this is a duty laid upon
5 Israel for ever. The house I am about to build will be a great house,
6 because our God is greater than all gods. But who is able to build him a house when heaven itself, the highest heaven, cannot contain him? And who am I that I should build him a house, except that I may burn
7 sacrifices before him? Send me then a skilled craftsman, a man able to work in gold and silver, copper^d and iron, and in purple, crimson, and violet yarn, who is also an expert engraver and will work with my skilled workmen in Judah and in Jerusalem who were provided by
8 David my father. Send me also cedar, pine, and algum^e timber from Lebanon, for I know that your men are expert at felling the trees of
9 Lebanon; my men will work with yours to get an ample supply of timber ready for me, for the house which I shall build will be great and
10 wonderful. I will supply provisions^f for your servants, the woodmen who fell the trees: twenty thousand kor of wheat and twenty thousand kor of barley, with twenty thousand bath of wine and twenty thousand bath of oil.'
11 Huram king of Tyre sent this answer by letter to Solomon: 'It is because of the love which the LORD has for his people that he has made
12 you king over them.' The letter went on to say, 'Blessed is the LORD the God of Israel, maker of heaven and earth, who has given to King David a wise son, endowed with intelligence and understanding, to
13 build a house for the LORD and a royal palace for himself. I now send

[a] *1. 18 in Heb.* [b] *2. 1 in Heb.* [c] *Verses 3–16: cp. 1 Kgs. 5. 2–11.* [d] *Or* bronze.
[e] almug *in 1 Kgs. 10. 11.* [f] provisions: *so Vulg., cp. 1 Kgs. 5. 11; Heb.* plagues.

you a skilful and experienced craftsman, master Huram. He is the son 14
of a Danite woman, his father a Tyrian; he is an experienced worker
in gold and silver, copper*a* and iron, stone and wood, as well as in
purple, violet, and crimson yarn, and in fine linen; he is also a trained
engraver who will be able to work with your own skilled craftsmen and
those of my lord David your father, to any design submitted to him.
Now then, let my lord send his servants the wheat and the barley, the 15
oil and the wine, which he promised; we will fell all the timber in 16
Lebanon that you need and float it as rafts to the roadstead at Joppa,
and you will convey it from there up to Jerusalem.'

Solomon took a census of all the aliens resident in Israel, similar to 17
the census which David his father had taken; these were found to be
a hundred and fifty-three thousand six hundred. He made seventy 18
thousand of them hauliers and eighty thousand quarrymen, and three
thousand six hundred superintendents to make the people work.

Then Solomon began to build the house of the LORD in Jerusalem 3
on Mount Moriah, where the LORD had appeared to his father David,
on the site which David had prepared*b* on the threshing-floor of Ornan
the Jebusite. He began to build in the second month*c* of the fourth year 2*d*
of his reign. These are the foundations which Solomon laid for building 3
the house of God: the length, according to the old standard of measurement, was sixty cubits and the breadth twenty. The vestibule in front 4
of the house*e* was twenty cubits long, spanning the whole breadth of
the house, and its height was twenty;*f* on the inside he overlaid it with
pure gold. He panelled the large chamber with pine, covered it with fine 5
gold and carved on it palm-trees and chain-work. He adorned the 6
house with precious stones for decoration, and the gold he used was
from Parvaim. He covered the whole house with gold, its rafters and 7
frames, its walls and doors; and he carved cherubim on the walls.

He made the Most Holy Place twenty cubits long, corresponding to 8
the breadth of the house, and twenty cubits broad. He covered it all
with six hundred talents of fine gold, and the weight of the nails was 9
fifty shekels of gold. He also covered the upper chambers with gold.

In the Most Holy Place he carved two images*g* of cherubim and 10*h*
overlaid them with gold. The total span of the wings of the cherubim 11
was twenty cubits. A wing of the one cherub extended five cubits to
reach the wall of the house, while its other wing reached out five cubits
to meet a wing of the other cherub. Similarly, a wing of the second 12
cherub extended five cubits to reach the other wall of the house, while

---

[*a*] *Or* bronze.   [*b*] on...prepared: *so Sept.; Heb.* which he had prepared on David's site.
[*c*] *So some MSS.; others add* on the second.   [*d*] *Verses 2–4: cp. 1 Kgs. 6. 1–3.*   [*e*] house:
prob. rdg.; Heb. length.   [*f*] *So Sept.; Heb.* a hundred and twenty.   [*g*] *Mng. of Heb.
word uncertain.*   [*h*] *Verses 10–13: cp. 1 Kgs. 6. 23–28.*

13 its other wing met a wing of the first cherub. The wings of these cherubim extended twenty cubits; they stood with their feet on the

14 ground, facing the outer chamber. He made the Veil of violet, purple, and crimson yarn, and fine linen, and embroidered cherubim on it.

15[a] In front of the house he erected two pillars eighteen[b] cubits high,

16 with an architrave five cubits high on top of each. He made chain-work like a necklace[c] and set it round the tops of the pillars, and he carved

17 a hundred pomegranates and set them in the chain-work. He erected the two pillars in front of the temple, one on the right and one on the left; the one on the right he named Jachin[d] and the one on the left Boaz.[e]

4 He then made an altar of bronze, twenty cubits long, twenty cubits

2[f] broad, and ten cubits high. He also made the Sea of cast metal; it was round in shape, the diameter from rim to rim being ten cubits; it stood five cubits high, and it took a line thirty cubits long to go round it.

3 Under the Sea, on every side, completely surrounding the thirty[g] cubits of its circumference, were what looked like gourds,[h] two rows

4 of them, cast in one piece with the Sea itself. It was mounted on twelve oxen, three facing north, three west, three south, and three east, their

5 hind quarters turned inwards; the Sea rested on top of them. Its thickness was a hand-breadth; its rim was made like that of a cup, shaped like the calyx of a lily; when full it held three thousand bath.

6 He also made ten basins for washing, setting five on the left side and five on the right; in these they rinsed everything used for the whole-offering. The Sea was made for the priests to wash in.

7 He made ten golden lamp-stands in the prescribed manner and set

8 them in the temple, five on the right side and five on the left. He also made ten tables and placed them in the temple, five on the right and

9 five on the left; and he made a hundred golden tossing-bowls. He made the court of the priests and the great precinct and the doors for it, and

10 overlaid the doors of both with copper; he put the Sea at the right side, at the south-east corner of the temple.

11[i] Huram made the pots, the shovels, and the tossing-bowls. So he finished the work which he had undertaken for King Solomon on the

12 house of God. The two pillars; the two bowl-shaped capitals[j] on the tops of the pillars; the two ornamental networks to cover the two bowl-

13 shaped capitals on the tops of the pillars; the four hundred pomegranates for the two networks, two rows of pomegranates for each network, to

---

[a] *Verses 15–17: cp. 1 Kgs. 7. 15–21.* [b] *So Pesh., cp. 1 Kgs. 7. 15; Heb.* thirty-five.
[c] necklace: *prob. rdg.; Heb. obscure.* [d] *Or* Jachun, *meaning* It shall stand. [e] *Or* Booz, *meaning* In strength. [f] *Verses 2–5: cp. 1 Kgs. 7. 23–26.* [g] *Prob. rdg.; Heb.* ten.
[h] *Prob. rdg., cp. 1 Kgs. 7. 24; Heb.* oxen. [i] *4. 11–5. 1: cp. 1 Kgs. 7. 40–51.* [j] bowl-shaped capitals: *prob. rdg., cp. 1 Kgs. 7. 41; Heb.* the bowls and the capitals.

cover the two bowl-shaped capitals on the two^a pillars; the ten^b 14
trolleys and the ten^b basins on the trolleys; the one Sea and the twelve 15
oxen which supported it; the pots, the shovels, and the tossing-bowls^c— 16
all these^d objects master Huram made of bronze, burnished work for
King Solomon for the house of the LORD. In the Plain of the Jordan 17
the king cast them, in the foundry between Succoth and Zeredah.
Solomon made great quantities of all these objects; the weight of the 18
copper^e used was beyond reckoning.

Solomon made also all the furnishings for the house of God: the 19
golden altar, the tables upon which was set the Bread of the Presence,
the lamp-stands of red gold whose lamps burned before the inner 20
shrine in the prescribed manner, the flowers and lamps and tongs of 21
solid^f gold, the snuffers, tossing-bowls, saucers, and firepans of red gold, 22
and, at the entrance to the house, the inner doors leading to the Most
Holy Place and those leading to the sanctuary, of gold.

When all the work which Solomon did for the house of the LORD 5
was completed, he brought in the sacred treasures of his father David,
the silver, the gold, and the vessels, and deposited them in the storehouses of the house of God.

THEN SOLOMON SUMMONED the elders of Israel, and all the heads 2^g
of the tribes who were chiefs of families in Israel, to assemble in
Jerusalem, in order to bring up the Ark of the Covenant of the LORD
from the City of David, which is called Zion. All the men of Israel 3
assembled in the king's presence at the pilgrim-feast in the seventh
month. When the elders of Israel had all come, the Levites took the 4
Ark and carried it up with the Tent of the Presence and all the sacred 5
furnishings of the Tent: it was the priests and^h the Levites together
who carried them up. King Solomon and the whole congregation of 6
Israel, assembled with him before the Ark, sacrificed sheep and oxen
in numbers past counting or reckoning. Then the priests brought in the 7
Ark of the Covenant of the LORD to its place, the inner shrine of the
house, the Most Holy Place, beneath the wings of the cherubim. The 8
cherubim spread their wings over the place of the Ark, and formed a
covering above the Ark and its poles. The poles projected, and their 9
ends could be seen from the Holy Placeⁱ immediately in front of the
inner shrine, but from nowhere else outside; they are^j there to this
day. There was nothing inside the Ark but the two tablets which 10

[a] two: *prob. rdg., cp. 1 Kgs. 7. 42; Heb.* surface of the.   [b] the ten: *prob. rdg., cp.*
1 Kgs. 7. 43; Heb. he made the...   [c] tossing-bowls: *prob. rdg., cp. 1 Kgs. 7. 45; Heb.* forks.
[d] *Prob. rdg., cp. 1 Kgs. 7. 45; Heb.* their.   [e] *Or* bronze.   [f] *Mng. of Heb. word un-*
certain.   [g] *Verses 2–10: cp. 1 Kgs. 8. 1–9.*   [h] and: *so some MSS.; others om.*   [i] Holy
Place: *so Sept.; Heb.* Ark.   [j] *So many MSS.; others* it is.

Moses had put there at Horeb, the tablets of the covenant*a* which the
LORD made with the Israelites when they left Egypt.

11   Now when the priests came out of the Holy Place (for all the priests
who were present had hallowed themselves without keeping to their
12 divisions), all the levitical singers, Asaph, Heman, and Jeduthun, their
sons and their kinsmen, clothed in fine linen, stood with cymbals, lutes,
and harps, to the east of the altar, together with a hundred and twenty
13 priests who blew trumpets. Now the trumpeters and the singers joined
in unison to sound forth praise and thanksgiving to the LORD, and the
song was raised with trumpets, cymbals, and musical instruments, in
praise of the LORD, because 'that*b* is good, for his love endures for ever';
and the house was filled with the cloud of the glory*c* of the LORD.
14 The priests could not continue to minister because of the cloud, for the
6 1*d* glory of the LORD filled the house of God. Then Solomon said:

> O LORD who hast chosen to dwell in thick darkness,
2 > here have I built thee a lofty house,
> a habitation for thee to occupy for ever.

3   And as they stood waiting, the king turned round and blessed all the
4 assembly of Israel in these words: 'Blessed be the LORD the God of
Israel who spoke directly to my father David and has himself fulfilled
5 his promise. For he said, "From the day when I brought my people
out of Egypt, I chose no city out of all the tribes of Israel where I should
build a house for my Name to be there, nor did I choose any man to
6 be prince over my people Israel. But I chose Jerusalem for my Name
7 to be there, and I chose David to be over my people Israel." My father
David had in mind to build a house in honour of the name of the LORD
8 the God of Israel, but the LORD said to him, "You purposed to build a
9 house in honour of my name; and your purpose was good. Nevertheless, you shall not build it; but the son who is to be born to you, he
10 shall build the house in honour of my name." The LORD has now
fulfilled his promise: I have succeeded my father David and taken his
place on the throne of Israel, as the LORD promised; and I have built
11 the house in honour of the name of the LORD the God of Israel. I have
installed there the Ark containing the covenant of the LORD which he
made with Israel.'

12   Then Solomon, standing in front of the altar of the LORD, in the
13 presence of the whole assembly of Israel, spread out his hands. He had
made a bronze*e* platform, five cubits long, five cubits broad, and three
cubits high, and had placed it in the centre of the precinct. He mounted
it and knelt down in the presence of the assembly, and, spreading out

[a] the tablets of the covenant: *prob. rdg., cp. 1 Kgs. 8. 9; Heb. om.* [b] *Or* he. [c] glory:
so Sept.; Heb. house. [d] *Verses 1–39: cp. 1 Kgs. 8. 12–50.* [e] *Or* copper.

his hands towards heaven, he said, 'O LORD God of Israel, there is no 14
god like thee in heaven or on earth, keeping covenant with thy servants
and showing them constant love while they continue faithful to thee
in heart and soul. Thou hast kept thy promise to thy servant David 15
my father; by thy deeds this day thou hast fulfilled what thou didst say
to him in words. Now, therefore, O LORD God of Israel, keep this 16
promise of thine to thy servant David my father: "You shall never
want for a man appointed by me to sit on the throne of Israel, if only
your sons look to their ways and conform to my law, as you have done
in my sight." And now, O LORD God of Israel, let the word which thou 17
didst speak to thy servant David be confirmed.

'But can God indeed dwell with man on the earth? Heaven itself, 18
the highest heaven, cannot contain thee; how much less this house that
I have built! Yet attend to the prayer and the supplication of thy 19
servant, O LORD my God; listen to the cry and the prayer which thy
servant utters before thee, that thine eyes may ever be upon this house 20
day and night, this place of which thou didst say, "It shall receive my
Name"; so mayest thou hear thy servant when he prays towards this
place. Hear thou the supplications of thy servant and of thy people 21
Israel when they pray towards this place. Hear from heaven thy
dwelling and, when thou hearest, forgive.

'When a man wrongs his neighbour and he is adjured to take an 22
oath, and the adjuration is made before thy altar in this house, then do 23
thou hear from heaven and act: be thou thy servants' judge, requiting
the guilty man and bringing his deeds upon his own head, acquitting
the innocent and rewarding him as his innocence may deserve.

'When thy people Israel are defeated by an enemy because they have 24
sinned against thee, and they turn back to thee, confessing thy name
and making their prayer and supplication before thee in this house, do 25
thou hear from heaven; forgive the sin of thy people Israel and restore
them to the land which thou gavest to them and to their forefathers.

'When the heavens are shut up and there is no rain, because thy 26
servant*a* and thy people Israel have sinned against thee, and when they
pray towards this place, confessing thy name and forsaking their sin
when they feel thy punishment, do thou hear in*b* heaven and forgive 27
their sin; so mayest thou teach them the good way which they should
follow, and grant rain to thy land which thou hast given to thy people
as their own possession.

'If there is famine in the land, or pestilence, or black blight or red, 28
or locusts new-sloughed or fully grown, or if their enemies besiege
them in any*c* of their cities, or if plague or sickness befall them,

[a] *So Pesh.; Heb.* servants.   [b] *Or, with Sept.,* from.   [c] in any: *prob. rdg.; Heb.* in the land.

29 then hear the prayer or supplication of every man among thy people Israel, as each one, prompted by his own suffering and misery, spreads
30 out his hands towards this house; hear it from heaven thy dwelling and forgive. And, as thou knowest a man's heart, reward him according to
31 his deeds, for thou alone knowest the hearts of all men; and so they will fear and obey thee all their lives in the land thou gavest to our fore-fathers.

32 'The foreigner too, the man who does not belong to thy people Israel, but has come from a distant land because of thy great fame and thy strong hand and arm outstretched, when he comes and prays
33 towards this house, hear from heaven thy dwelling and respond to the call which the foreigner makes to thee, so that like thy people Israel all peoples of the earth may know thy fame and fear thee, and learn that this house which I have built bears thy name.

34 'When thy people go to war with their enemies, wherever thou dost send them, and they pray to thee, turning towards this city which thou hast chosen and towards this house which I have built in honour of thy
35 name, do thou from heaven hear their prayer and supplication, and grant them justice.

36 'Should they sin against thee (and what man is free from sin?) and shouldst thou in thy anger give them over to an enemy, who carries them
37 captive to a land far or near; if in the land of their captivity they learn their lesson and turn back and make supplication to thee in that land
38 and say, "We have sinned and acted perversely and wickedly", if they turn back to thee with heart and soul in the land of their captivity to which they have been taken, and pray, turning towards their land which thou gavest to their forefathers and towards this city which thou didst choose and this house which I have built in honour of thy name;
39 then from heaven thy dwelling do thou hear their prayer and suppli-cations and grant them justice. Forgive thy people their sins against
40 thee. Now, O my God, let thine eyes be open and thy ears attentive to
41 the prayer made in this place. Arise now, O LORD God, and come to thy place of rest, thou and the Ark of thy might. Let thy priests, O LORD God, be clothed with salvation and thy saints rejoice in prosperity.
42 O LORD God, reject not thy anointed prince;[a] remember thy servant David's loyal service.'[b]

7 When Solomon had finished this prayer, fire came down from heaven and consumed the whole-offering and the sacrifices, while the glory of
2 the LORD filled the house. The priests were unable to enter the house of
3 the LORD because the glory of the LORD had filled it. All the Israelites were watching as the fire came down with the glory of the LORD on the

[a] *So many MSS.; others* princes. [b] thy servant...service: *or* thy constant love for David thy servant.

house, and where they stood on the paved court they bowed low to the ground and worshipped and gave thanks to the LORD, because 'that*ᵃ* is good, for his love endures for ever.'

Then the king and all the people offered sacrifice before the LORD. 4 King Solomon offered a sacrifice of twenty-two thousand oxen and a 5 hundred and twenty thousand sheep; in this way the king and all the people dedicated the house of God. The priests stood at their appointed 6 posts; so too the Levites with their musical instruments for the LORD's service, which King David had made for giving thanks to the LORD— 'for his love endures for ever'—whenever he rendered praise with their help; opposite them, the priests sounded their trumpets; and all the Israelites were standing there.

Then Solomon consecrated the centre of the court which lay in 7*ᵇ* front*ᶜ* of the house of the LORD; there he offered the whole-offerings and the fat portions of the shared-offerings, because the bronze altar which he had made could not take the whole-offering, the grain-offering, and the fat portions. So Solomon and all Israel with him, a 8 very great assembly from Lebo-hamath to the Torrent of Egypt, celebrated the pilgrim-feast at that time for seven days. On the eighth 9 day they held a closing ceremony; for they had celebrated the dedication of the altar for seven days; the pilgrim-feast lasted seven days. On the twenty-third day of the seventh month he sent the people to 10 their homes, happy and glad at heart for all the prosperity granted by the LORD to David and Solomon and to his people Israel.

When Solomon had finished the house of the LORD and the royal 11 palace and had successfully carried out all that he had planned for the house of the LORD and the palace, the LORD appeared to him by night 12 and said, 'I have heard your prayer and I have chosen this place to be my place of sacrifice. When I shut up the heavens and there is no rain, 13 or command the locusts to consume the land, or send a pestilence against my people, if my people whom I have named my own submit 14 and pray to me and seek me and turn back from their evil ways, I will hear from heaven and forgive their sins and heal their land. Now my 15 eyes will be open and my ears attentive to the prayers which are made in this place. I have chosen and consecrated this house, that my Name 16 may be there for all time and my eyes and my heart be fixed on it for ever. And if you, on your part, live in my sight as your father David 17 lived, doing all I command you, and observing my statutes and my judgements, then I will establish your royal throne, as I promised by a 18 covenant granted to your father David when I said, "You shall never want for a man to rule over Israel." But if you turn away and forsake 19 my statutes and my commandments which I have set before you, and

[*a*] *Or* he.   [*b*] *Verses 7–22: cp. 1 Kgs. 8. 64–9. 9.*   [*c*] *Or to the east.*

if you go and serve other gods and prostrate yourselves before them,
20 then I will uproot you[a] from my land which I gave you,[a] I will reject
this house which I have consecrated in honour of my name, and make
21 it a byword and an object-lesson among all peoples. And this house
will become a ruin;[b] every passer-by will be appalled at the sight of it,
and they will ask, "Why has the LORD so treated this land and this
22 house?" The answer will be, "Because they forsook the LORD the God
of their fathers, who brought them out of Egypt, and clung to other
gods, prostrating themselves before them and serving them; that is why
the LORD has brought this great evil on them."'

8 1[c]   Solomon had taken twenty years to build the house of the LORD and
2 his own palace, and he rebuilt the cities which Huram had given him
3 and settled Israelites in them. He went to Hamath-zobah and seized it,
4 and rebuilt Tadmor in the wilderness and all the store-cities which he
5 had built in Hamath. He also built Upper Beth-horon and Lower
6 Beth-horon as fortified cities with walls and barred gates, and Baalath,
as well as all his store-cities, and all the towns where he quartered his
chariots and horses; and he carried out all his cherished plans for
building in Jerusalem, in the Lebanon, and throughout his whole
7 dominion. All the survivors of the Hittites, Amorites, Perizzites,
8 Hivites, and Jebusites, who did not belong to Israel—that is their
descendants who survived in the land, wherever the Israelites had been
unable to exterminate them—were employed by Solomon on forced
9 labour, as they still are. He put none of the Israelites to forced labour
for his public works; they were his fighting men, his captains and
lieutenants,[d] and the commanders of his chariots and of his cavalry.
10 These were King Solomon's officers, two hundred and fifty of them, in
charge of the foremen who superintended the people.
11   Solomon brought Pharaoh's daughter up from the City of David to
the house he had built for her, for he said, 'No wife of mine shall live
in the house of David king of Israel, because this place which the Ark
of the LORD has entered is[e] holy.'
12   Then Solomon offered whole-offerings to the LORD on the altar
13 which he had built to the east of the vestibule, according to what was
required for each day, making offerings according to the law of Moses
for the sabbaths, the new moons, and the three annual appointed
feasts—the pilgrim-feasts of Unleavened Bread, of Weeks, and of
14 Tabernacles.[f] Following the practice of his father David, he drew up
the roster of service for the priests and that for the Levites for leading
the praise and for waiting upon the priests, as each day required, and

[a] So Sept.; Heb. them.   [b] will become a ruin: so Pesh.; Heb. which was high.   [c] Verses
1–18: cp. 1 Kgs. 9. 10–28.   [d] his captains and lieutenants: so Sept.; Heb. the captains
of his lieutenants.   [e] this place which...is: prob. rdg.; Heb. those which...are.   [f] Or
Booths.

that for the door-keepers at each gate; for such was the instruction
which David the man of God had given. The instructions which David 15
had given concerning the priests and the Levites and concerning the
treasuries were not forgotten.

By this time all Solomon's work was achieved, from the foundation 16
of the house of the LORD to its completion; the house of the LORD
was perfect. Then Solomon went to Ezion-geber and to Eloth on the 17
coast of Edom, and Huram sent ships under the command of his own 18
officers and manned by crews of experienced seamen; and these, in
company with Solomon's servants, went to Ophir and brought back four
hundred and fifty talents of gold, which they delivered to King Solomon.

THE QUEEN OF SHEBA heard of Solomon's fame and came to test 9 1*a*
him with hard questions. She arrived in Jerusalem with a very large
retinue, camels laden with spices, gold in abundance, and precious
stones. When she came to Solomon, she told him everything she had
in her mind, and Solomon answered all her questions; not one of them 2
was too abstruse for him to answer. When the queen of Sheba saw the 3
wisdom of Solomon, the house which he had built, the food on his 4
table, the courtiers sitting round him, his attendants and his cupbearers in their livery standing behind, and the stairs by which he
went up to*b* the house of the LORD, there was no more spirit left in her.
Then she said to the king, 'The report which I heard in my own 5
country about you*c* and your wisdom was true, but I did not believe 6
what they told me until I came and saw for myself. Indeed, I was not
told half of the greatness of your wisdom; you surpass the report which
I had of you. Happy are your wives,*d* happy these courtiers of yours 7
who wait on you every day and hear your wisdom! Blessed be the LORD 8
your God who has delighted in you and has set you on his throne as his
king; because in his love your God has elected Israel to make it endure
for ever, he has made you king over it to maintain law and justice.'
Then she gave the king a hundred and twenty talents of gold, spices in 9
great abundance, and precious stones. There had never been any spices
to equal those which the queen of Sheba gave to King Solomon.

Besides all this, the servants of Huram and of Solomon, who had 10
brought gold from Ophir, brought also cargoes of algum wood and
precious stones. The king used the wood to make stands*e* for the 11
house of the LORD and for the royal palace, as well as harps and lutes
for the singers. The like of them had never before been seen in the
land of Judah.

King Solomon gave the queen of Sheba all she desired, whatever she 12

[a] *Verses 1–24: cp. 1 Kgs. 10. 1–25.* [b] stairs...up to: *or, with Sept.,* whole-offerings
which he used to offer in... [c] *Lit.* your affairs. [d] *So Luc. Sept.; Heb.* men. [e] *Mng.
of Heb. word uncertain.*

asked, besides his gifts in return for[a] what she had brought him. Then she departed and returned with her retinue to her own land.

13 Now the weight of gold which Solomon received yearly was six
14 hundred and sixty-six talents, in addition to the tolls[b] levied on merchants and on traders who imported goods; all the kings of Arabia and the regional governors also[c] brought gold and silver to the king.

15 King Solomon made two hundred shields of beaten gold, and six
16 hundred shekels of gold went to the making of each one; he also made three hundred bucklers of beaten gold, and three hundred shekels of gold went to the making of each buckler. The king put these into the House of the Forest of Lebanon.

17 The king also made a great throne of ivory and overlaid it with pure
18 gold. Six steps and a footstool for the throne were all encased in gold. There were arms on each side of the seat, with a lion standing beside
19 each of them, and twelve lions stood on the six steps, one at either end of each step. Nothing like it had ever been made for any monarch.
20 All Solomon's drinking vessels were of gold, and all the plate in the House of the Forest of Lebanon was of red gold; silver was reckoned
21 of no value in the days of Solomon. The king had a fleet of ships plying to Tarshish with Huram's men; once every three years this fleet of merchantmen[d] came home, bringing gold and silver, ivory, apes, and monkeys.

22 Thus King Solomon outdid all the kings of the earth in wealth and
23 wisdom, and all the kings of the earth courted him, to hear the wisdom
24 which God had put in his heart. Each brought his gift with him, vessels of silver and gold, garments, perfumes and spices, horses and mules, so much year by year.

25[e] Solomon had standing for four thousand horses and chariots, and twelve thousand cavalry horses, and he stabled some in the chariot-
26 towns and kept others at hand in Jerusalem. He ruled over all the kings from the Euphrates to the land of the Philistines and the border of
27 Egypt. He made silver as common in Jerusalem as stones, and cedar
28 as plentiful as sycomore-fig in the Shephelah. Horses were imported from Egypt and from all countries for Solomon.

29[f] The rest of the acts of Solomon's reign, from first to last, are recorded in the history of Nathan the prophet, in the prophecy of Ahijah of Shiloh, and in the visions of Iddo the seer concerning Jeroboam son
30 of Nebat. Solomon ruled in Jerusalem over the whole of Israel for forty
31 years. Then he rested with his forefathers and was buried in the city of David his father, and he was succeeded by his son Rehoboam.

[a] his gifts...for: *prob. rdg.; Heb. om.* [b] *So Pesh.; Heb.* men. [c] all...also: *or* and on all the kings of Arabia and the regional governors who... [d] *Lit.* ships of Tarshish. [e] *Verses 25–28: cp. 1. 14–17; 1 Kgs. 10. 26–29.* [f] *Verses 29–31: cp. 1 Kgs. 11. 41–43.*

The kings of Judah from Rehoboam to Ahaz

R EHOBOAM WENT TO SHECHEM, for all Israel had gone there to 10 1*ᵃ* make him king. When Jeroboam son of Nebat heard of it in Egypt, 2 where he had taken refuge to escape Solomon, he returned from Egypt. They now recalled him, and he and all Israel came to Rehoboam and 3 said, 'Your father laid a cruel yoke upon us; but if you will now lighten 4 the cruel slavery he imposed on us and the heavy yoke he laid on us, we will serve you.' 'Give me three days,' he said, 'and come back again.' 5 So the people went away. King Rehoboam then consulted the elders 6 who had been in attendance on his father Solomon while he lived: 'What answer do you advise me to give to this people?' And they said, 7 'If you show yourself well-disposed to this people and gratify them by speaking kindly to them, they will be your servants ever after.' But he 8 rejected the advice which the elders gave him. He next consulted those who had grown up with him, the young men in attendance, and asked 9 them, 'What answer do you advise me to give to this people's request that I should lighten the yoke which my father laid on them?' The 10 young men replied, 'Give this answer to the people who say that your father made their yoke heavy and ask you to lighten it; tell them: "My little finger is thicker than my father's loins. My father laid a heavy yoke 11 on you; I will make it heavier. My father used the whip on you; but I will use the lash."' Jeroboam and the people all came back to Reho- 12 boam on the third day, as the king had ordered. And the king gave them 13 a harsh answer. He rejected the advice which the elders had given him and spoke to the people as the young men had advised: 'My father 14 made*ᵇ* your yoke heavy; I will make it heavier. My father used the whip on you; but I will use the lash.' So the king would not listen to the 15 people; for the LORD had given this turn to the affair, in order that the word he had spoken by Ahijah of Shiloh to Jeroboam son of Nebat might be fulfilled.

When all Israel saw*ᶜ* that the king would not listen to them, they 16 answered:

What share have we in David?
We have no lot in the son of Jesse.
Away to your homes, O Israel;
now see to your own house, David.

So all Israel went to their homes, and Rehoboam ruled over those 17 Israelites who lived in the cities of Judah.

---

[a] *Verses 1–19: cp. 1 Kgs. 12. 1–19.* [b] My father made: *so some MSS.; others* I will make.
[c] saw: *prob. rdg., cp. 1 Kgs. 12. 16; Heb. om.*

18 Then King Rehoboam sent out Hadoram, the commander of the forced levies, but the Israelites stoned him to death; whereupon King
19 Rehoboam mounted his chariot in haste and fled to Jerusalem. From that day to this, Israel has been in rebellion against the house of David.

11 1^a When Rehoboam reached Jerusalem, he assembled the tribes of Judah and Benjamin, a hundred and eighty thousand chosen warriors,
2 to fight against Israel and recover his kingdom. But the word of the
3 LORD came to Shemaiah the man of God: 'Say to Rehoboam son of Solomon, king of Judah, and to all the Israelites in Judah and Benjamin,
4 "This is the word of the LORD: You shall not go up to make war on your kinsmen. Return to your homes, for this is my will."' So they listened to the word of the LORD and abandoned their campaign against Jeroboam.
5 Rehoboam resided in Jerusalem and built up the defences of certain
6 cities in Judah. The cities in Judah and Benjamin which he fortified
7,8 were Bethlehem, Etam, Tekoa, Beth-zur, Soco, Adullam, Gath,
9,10 Mareshah, Ziph, Adoraim, Lachish, Azekah, Zorah, Aijalon, and
11 Hebron. He strengthened the fortifications of these fortified cities, and put governors in them, as well as supplies of food, oil, and wine.
12 Also he stored shields and spears in every one of the cities, and strengthened their fortifications. Thus he retained possession of Judah and Benjamin.
13 Now the priests and the Levites throughout the whole of Israel
14 resorted to Rehoboam from all their territories; for the Levites had left all their common land and their own patrimony and had gone to Judah and Jerusalem, because Jeroboam and his successors rejected their
15 services as priests of the LORD, and he appointed his own priests for the hill-shrines, for the demons,^b and for the calves which he had made.
16 Those, from all the tribes of Israel, who were resolved to seek the LORD the God of Israel followed the Levites to Jerusalem to sacrifice to the
17 LORD the God of their fathers. So they strengthened the kingdom of Judah and for three years made Rehoboam son of Solomon secure, because he^c followed the example of David and Solomon during that time.
18 Rehoboam married Mahalath, whose father was Jerimoth son of David and whose mother was Abihail daughter of Eliab son of Jesse.
19,20 His sons by her were: Jeush, Shemariah and Zaham. Next he married Maacah granddaughter^d of Absalom, who bore him Abijah, Attai, Ziza
21 and Shelomith. Of all his wives and concubines, Rehoboam loved Maacah most; he had in all eighteen wives and sixty concubines and
22 became the father of twenty-eight sons and sixty daughters. He

[a] *Verses 1–4: cp. 1 Kgs. 12. 21–24.* [b] *Or* satyrs. [c] *So Sept.; Heb.* they. [d] *Lit.* daughter.

appointed Abijah son of Maacah chief among his brothers, making him crown prince and planning*a* to make him his successor on the throne. He   23 showed discretion in detailing his sons to take charge of all the fortified cities throughout the whole territory of Judah and Benjamin; he also made generous provision for them and procured them*b* wives.

When the kingdom of Rehoboam was on a firm footing and he   12 became strong, he forsook the law of the LORD, he and all Israel with him. In the fifth year of Rehoboam's reign, because of this disloyalty to   2 the LORD, Shishak king of Egypt attacked Jerusalem with twelve   3 hundred chariots and sixty thousand horsemen, and brought with him from Egypt an innumerable following of Libyans, Sukkites, and Cushites.*c* He captured the fortified cities of Judah and reached   4 Jerusalem. Then Shemaiah the prophet came to Rehoboam and the   5 leading men of Judah, who had assembled in Jerusalem before the advance of Shishak, and said to them, 'This is the word of the LORD: You have abandoned me; therefore I now abandon you to Shishak.' The princes of Israel and the king submitted and said, 'The LORD is   6 just.' When the LORD saw that they had submitted, there came from   7 him this word to Shemaiah: 'Because they have submitted I will not destroy them, I will let them barely escape; my wrath shall not be poured out on Jerusalem by means of Shishak, but they shall become   8 his servants; then they will know the difference between serving me and serving the rulers of other countries.' Shishak king of Egypt in his   9*d* attack on Jerusalem removed the treasures of the house of the LORD and of the royal palace. He seized everything, including the shields of gold that Solomon had made. King Rehoboam replaced them with   10 bronze shields and entrusted them to the officers of the escort who guarded the entrance of the royal palace. Whenever the king entered   11 the house of the LORD, the escort entered, carrying the shields; afterwards they returned them to the guard-room. Because Rehoboam   12 submitted, the LORD's wrath was averted from him, and he was not utterly destroyed; Judah enjoyed prosperity.

Thus King Rehoboam increased his power in Jerusalem. He was   13*e* forty-one years old when he came to the throne, and he reigned for seventeen years in Jerusalem, the city which the LORD had chosen out of all the tribes of Israel as the place to receive his Name. Rehoboam's mother was a woman of Ammon called Naamah. He did what was wrong,   14 he did not make a practice of seeking guidance of the LORD. The events   15 of Rehoboam's reign, from first to last, are recorded in the histories of Shemaiah the prophet and Iddo the seer.*f* There was continual fighting

[a] planning: *so Vulg.; Heb. om.*   [b] procured them: *prob. rdg.; Heb.* asked for a multitude of...   [c] *Or* Nubians.   [d] *Verses 9–11: cp. 1 Kgs. 14. 25–28.*   [e] *Verses 13–16: cp. 1 Kgs. 14. 29–31.*   [f] *Prob. rdg.; Heb. adds* to be enrolled by genealogy.

16 between Rehoboam and Jeroboam. He rested with his forefathers and was buried in the city of David; and he was succeeded by his son Abijah.

13 IN THE EIGHTEENTH YEAR of King Jeroboam's reign Abijah
2 became king of Judah. He reigned in Jerusalem for three years; his mother was Maacah[a] daughter of Uriel of Gibeah. There was fighting
3 between Abijah and Jeroboam. Abijah drew up his army of four hundred thousand picked troops in order of battle, while Jeroboam formed up against him with eight hundred thousand picked troops.
4 Abijah took up position on the slopes of Mount Zemaraim in the hill-country of Ephraim and called out, 'Hear me, Jeroboam and all Israel:
5 Ought you not to know that the LORD the God of Israel gave the kingship over Israel to David and his descendants in perpetuity by a
6 covenant of salt? Yet Jeroboam son of Nebat, the servant of Solomon
7 son of David, rose in rebellion against his lord, and certain worthless scoundrels gathered round him, who stubbornly opposed Solomon's son Rehoboam when he was young and inexperienced, and he was no
8 match for them. Now you propose to match yourselves against the kingdom of the LORD as ruled by David's sons, you and your mob of supporters and the golden calves which Jeroboam has made to be your
9 gods. Have you not dismissed from office the Aaronites, priests of the LORD, and the Levites, and followed the practice of other lands in appointing priests? Now, if any man comes for consecration with an offering of a young bull and seven rams, you accept him as a priest to
10 a god that is no god. But as for us, the LORD is our God and we have not forsaken him; we have Aaronites as priests ministering to the LORD
11 with the Levites, duly discharging their office.[b] Morning and evening, these burn whole-offerings and fragrant incense to the LORD and offer the Bread of the Presence arranged in rows on a table ritually clean; they also kindle the lamps on the golden lamp-stand every evening. Thus we do indeed keep the charge of the LORD our God, whereas you
12 have forsaken him. God is with us at our head, and his priests stand there with trumpets to signal the battle-cry against you. Men of Israel, do not fight the LORD the God of your fathers; you will have no success.'
13 Jeroboam sent a detachment of his troops to go round and lay an ambush in the rear, so that his main body faced Judah while the
14 ambush lay behind them. The men of Judah turned to find that they were engaged front and rear. Then they cried to the LORD for help.
15 The priests sounded their trumpets, and the men of Judah raised a shout, and when they did so, God put Jeroboam and all Israel to rout

[a] So Sept., cp. 1 Kgs. 15. 2; Heb. Micaiah.   [b] duly...office: so Sept.; Heb. in the work

before Abijah and Judah. The Israelites fled before the men of Judah, 16
and God delivered them into their power. So Abijah and his men 17
defeated them with very heavy losses, and five hundred thousand picked
Israelites fell in the battle. After this, the Israelites were reduced to 18
submission, and Judah prevailed because they relied on the LORD the
God of their fathers. Abijah followed up his victory over Jeroboam and 19
captured from him the cities of Bethel, Jeshanah, and Ephron, with
their villages. Jeroboam did not regain his power during the days of 20
Abijah; finally the LORD struck him down and he died.

But Abijah established his position; he married fourteen wives and 21
became the father of twenty-two sons and sixteen daughters. The other 22
events of Abijah's reign, both what he said and what he did, are recorded
in the story of the prophet Iddo. Abijah rested with his forefathers and 14 1*a*
was buried in the city of David; and he was succeeded on the throne by
his son Asa. In his days the land was at peace for ten years.

Asa did what was good and right in the eyes of the LORD his God. 2*b*
He suppressed the foreign altars and the hill-shrines, smashed the sacred 3
pillars and hacked down the sacred poles, and ordered Judah to seek 4
guidance of the LORD the God of their fathers and to keep the law and
the commandments. He also suppressed the hill-shrines and the 5
incense-altars in all the cities, and the kingdom was at peace under him.
He built fortified cities in Judah, for the land was at peace. He had no 6
war to fight during those years, because the LORD had given him
security. He said to the men of Judah, 'Let us build these cities and 7
fortify them, with walls round them, and towers and barred gates. The
land still lies open before us. Because we have sought guidance of the
LORD our God, he has sought us and given us security on every side.'
So they built and prospered.

Asa had an army equipped with shields and spears; three hundred 8
thousand men came from Judah, and two hundred and eighty thousand
from Benjamin, shield-bearers and archers; all were valiant warriors.
Zerah the Cushite came out against them with an army a million strong 9
and three hundred chariots. When he reached Mareshah, Asa came out 10
to meet him and they took up position in the valley of Zephathah at
Mareshah. Asa called upon the LORD his God and said, 'There is none 11
like thee, O LORD, to help men, whether strong or weak; help us,
O LORD our God, for on thee we rely and in thy name we have come out
against this horde. O LORD, thou art our God, how can man vie with
thee?' So the LORD gave Asa and Judah victory over the Cushites and 12
they fled, and Asa and his men pursued them as far as Gerar. The 13
Cushites broke before the LORD and his army, and many of them fell
mortally wounded; and Judah carried off great loads of spoil. They 14

[*a*] *13. 23 in Heb.*   [*b*] *14. 1 in Heb.*

destroyed all the cities around Gerar, for the LORD had struck the people with panic; and they plundered the cities, finding rich spoil in
15 them all. They also killed the herdsmen and seized many sheep and camels, and then they returned to Jerusalem.

15 1, 2 The spirit of God came upon Azariah son of Oded, and he went out to meet Asa and said to him, 'Hear me, Asa and all Judah and Benjamin. The LORD is with you when you are with him; if you look for him, he
3 will let himself be found; if you forsake him, he will forsake you. For a long time Israel was without the true God, without a priest to inter-
4 pret the law and without law.[a] But when, in their distress, they turned to the LORD the God of Israel and sought him, he let himself be found
5 by them. At those times there was no safety for people as they went about their business; the inhabitants of every land had their fill of
6 trouble; there was ruin on every side, nation at odds with nation, city
7 with city, for God harassed them with every kind of distress. But now you must be strong and not let your courage fail; for your work will be
8 rewarded.' When Asa heard these words,[b] he resolutely suppressed the loathsome idols in all Judah and Benjamin and in the cities which he had captured in the hill-country of Ephraim; and he repaired the altar of the LORD which stood before the vestibule of the LORD's house.[c]
9 Then he assembled all Judah and Benjamin and all who had come from Ephraim, Manasseh, and Simeon to reside among them; for great numbers had come over to him from Israel, when they saw that the
10 LORD his God was with him. So they assembled at Jerusalem in the
11 third month of the fifteenth year of Asa's reign, and that day they sacrificed to the LORD seven hundred oxen and seven thousand sheep
12 from the spoil which they had brought. And they entered into a covenant to seek guidance of the LORD the God of their fathers with all
13 their heart and soul; all who would not seek the LORD the God of Israel were to be put to death, young and old, men and women alike.
14 Then they bound themselves by an oath to the LORD, with loud shouts
15 of acclamation while trumpets and horns sounded; and all Judah rejoiced at the oath, because they had bound themselves with all their heart and had sought him earnestly, and he had let himself be found by
16[d] them. So the LORD gave them security on every side. King Asa also deprived Maacah his grandmother[e] of her rank as queen mother because she had an obscene object made for the worship of Asherah; Asa cut it down, ground it to powder and burnt it in the gorge of the
17 Kidron. Although the hill-shrines were allowed to remain in Israel,
18 Asa himself remained faithful all his life. He brought into the house of

[a] without law: *or* without the law.   [b] *Prob. rdg.; Heb. adds* and the prophecy, Oded the prophet.   [c] house: *prob. rdg.; Heb. om.*   [d] *Verses 16–18: cp. 1 Kgs. 15. 13–15.*   [e] *Lit.* mother.

God all his father's votive offerings and his own, gold and silver and
sacred vessels. And there was no more war until the thirty-fifth year of 19
Asa's reign.

In the thirty-sixth year of the reign of Asa, Baasha king of Israel 16 1*a*
invaded Judah and fortified Ramah to cut off all access to Asa king of
Judah. So Asa brought out silver and gold from the treasuries of the 2
house of the LORD and the royal palace, and sent this request to Ben-
hadad king of Aram, whose capital was Damascus: 'There is an 3
alliance between us, as there was between our fathers. I now send you
herewith silver and gold; break off your alliance with Baasha king of
Israel, so that he may abandon his campaign against me.' Ben-hadad 4
listened willingly to King Asa and ordered the commanders of his
armies to move against the cities of Israel, and they attacked Iyyon,
Dan, Abel-mayim, and all the store-cities of Naphtali. When Baasha 5
heard of it, he ceased fortifying Ramah and stopped all work on it.
Then King Asa took with him all the men of Judah and they carried 6
away the stones of Ramah and the timbers with which Baasha had
fortified it; and he used them to fortify Geba and Mizpah.

At that time the seer Hanani came to Asa king of Judah and said to 7
him, 'Because you relied on the king of Aram and not on the LORD
your God, the army of the king of Israel*b* has escaped. The Cushites and 8
the Libyans, were they not a great army with a vast number of chariots
and horsemen? Yet, because you relied on the LORD, he delivered them
into your power. The eyes of the LORD range through the whole earth, 9
to bring aid and comfort to those whose hearts are loyal to him. You
have acted foolishly in this affair; you will have wars from now on.'
Asa was angry with the seer and put him in the stocks; for these words 10
of his had made the king very indignant. At the same time he treated
some of the people with great brutality.

The events of Asa's reign, from first to last, are recorded in the 11*c*
annals of the kings of Judah and Israel. In the thirty-ninth year of his 12
reign Asa became gravely affected with gangrene in his feet; he did not
seek guidance of the LORD but resorted to physicians. He rested with 13
his forefathers, in the forty-first year of his reign, and was buried in the 14
tomb which he had bought*d* for himself in the city of David, being laid
on a bier*e* which had been heaped with all kinds of spices skilfully
compounded; and they kindled a great fire in his honour.

ASA WAS SUCCEEDED by his son Jehoshaphat, who determined to 17
resist Israel by force. He posted troops in all the fortified cities of 2
Judah and stationed officers*f* throughout Judah and in the cities of

[*a*] *Verses 1–6: cp. 1 Kgs. 15. 17–22.* [*b*] Israel: *so Luc. Sept.; Heb.* Aram. [*c*] *Verses 11–*
14: cp. 1 Kgs. 15. 23, 24. [*d*] *Or* dug. [*e*] *Or* in a niche. [*f*] *Or* garrisons.

3 Ephraim which his father Asa had captured. The LORD was with Jehoshaphat, for he followed the example his father*a* had set in his early
4 years and did not resort to the Baalim; he sought guidance of the God of his father and obeyed his commandments and did not follow the
5 practices of Israel. So the LORD established the kingdom under his rule, and all Judah brought him gifts, and his wealth and fame*b* became very
6 great. He took pride in the service of the LORD; he also suppressed the hill-shrines and the sacred poles in Judah.

7   In the third year of his reign he sent his officers, Ben-hayil, Obadiah, Zechariah, Nethaneel, and Micaiah, to teach in the cities of Judah,
8 together with the Levites, Shemaiah, Nethaniah, Zebadiah, Asahel, Shemiramoth, Jehonathan, Adonijah, Tobiah, and Tob-adonijah,*c*
9 accompanied by the priests Elishama and Jehoram. They taught in Judah, having with them the book of the law of the LORD; they went round the cities of Judah, teaching the people.

10   So the dread of the LORD fell upon all the rulers of the lands sur-
11 rounding Judah, and they did not make war on Jehoshaphat. Certain Philistines brought a gift, a great quantity of silver, to Jehoshaphat; the Arabs too brought him seven thousand seven hundred rams and seven
12 thousand seven hundred he-goats. Jehoshaphat became ever more
13 powerful and built fortresses and store-cities in Judah; and he had much work on hand in the cities of Judah. He had regular, seasoned
14 troops in Jerusalem, enrolled according to their clans in this way: of Judah, the officers over units of a thousand: Adnah the commander,
15 together with three hundred thousand seasoned troops; and next to him
16 the commander Johanan, with two hundred and eighty thousand; and next to him Amasiah son of Zichri, who had volunteered for the service
17 of the LORD, with two hundred thousand seasoned troops; and of Benjamin: an experienced soldier Eliada, with two hundred thousand
18 men armed with bows and shields; next to him Jehozabad, with a
19 hundred and eighty thousand fully-armed men. These were the men who served the king, apart from those whom the king had posted in the fortified cities throughout Judah.

18   When Jehoshaphat had become very wealthy and famous,*d* he allied
2*e* himself with Ahab by marriage. Some years afterwards he went down to visit Ahab in Samaria, and Ahab slaughtered many sheep and oxen for him and his retinue, and incited him to attack Ramoth-gilead.
3 What Ahab king of Israel said to Jehoshaphat king of Judah was this: 'Will you join me in attacking Ramoth-gilead?' And he answered, 'What is mine is yours, myself and my people; I will join with you in
4 the war.' Then Jehoshaphat said to the king of Israel, 'First let us seek

[*a*] *So some MSS.; others add* David.   [*b*] *Or* riches.   [*c*] *Prob. rdg.; Heb. adds* the Levites. [*d*] *Or* rich.   [*e*] *Verses 2–34: cp. 1 Kgs. 22. 2–35.*

counsel from the LORD.' The king of Israel assembled the prophets, 5
some four hundred of them, and asked them, 'Shall I*a* attack Ramoth-
gilead or shall I refrain?' 'Attack,' they answered; 'God will deliver it
into your hands.' Jehoshaphat asked, 'Is there no other prophet of the 6
LORD here through whom we may seek guidance?' 'There is one more', 7
the king of Israel answered, 'through whom we may seek guidance of
the LORD, but I hate the man, because he never prophesies any good
for me; never anything but evil. His name is Micaiah son of Imla.'
Jehoshaphat exclaimed, 'My lord king, let no such word pass your
lips!' So the king of Israel called one of his eunuchs and told him to 8
fetch Micaiah son of Imla with all speed.

The king of Israel and Jehoshaphat king of Judah were seated on 9
their thrones, clothed in their royal robes and in shining armour, at the
entrance to the gate of Samaria, and all the prophets were prophesying
before them. One of them, Zedekiah son of Kenaanah, made himself 10
horns of iron and said, 'This is the word of the LORD: "With horns
like these you shall gore the Aramaeans and make an end of them."'
In the same vein all the prophets prophesied, 'Attack Ramoth-gilead 11
and win the day; the LORD will deliver it into your hands.' The 12
messenger sent to fetch Micaiah told him that the prophets had with
one voice given the king a favourable answer. 'And mind you agree with
them', he added. 'As the LORD lives,' said Micaiah, 'I will say only 13
what my God tells me to say.'

When Micaiah came into the king's presence, the king said to him, 14
'Micaiah, shall I attack Ramoth-gilead or shall I refrain?' 'Attack and
win the day,' he said, 'and it will fall into your hands.' 'How often 15
must I adjure you', said the king, 'to tell me nothing but the truth in the
name of the LORD?' Then Micaiah said, 'I saw all Israel scattered on 16
the mountains, like sheep without a shepherd; and I heard the LORD
say, "They have no master; let them go home in peace."' The king of 17
Israel said to Jehoshaphat, 'Did I not tell you that he never prophesies
good for me, nothing but evil?' Micaiah went on, 'Listen now to the 18
word of the LORD: I saw the LORD seated on his throne, with all the
host of heaven in attendance on his right and on his left. The LORD 19
said, "Who will entice Ahab to attack and fall on*b* Ramoth-gilead?" One
said one thing and one said another; then a spirit came forward and 20
stood before the LORD and said, "I will entice him." "How?" said the
LORD. "I will go out", he said, "and be a lying spirit in the mouth of all 21
his prophets." "You shall entice him," said the LORD, "and you shall
succeed; go and do it." You see, then, how the LORD has put a lying 22
spirit in the mouth of all these prophets of yours, because he has
decreed disaster for you.' Then Zedekiah son of Kenaanah came up to 23

[a] *So Sept.; Heb.* we (*and similarly in verse 14*).   [b] *Or at.*

Micaiah and struck him in the face: 'And how did the spirit of the
24 LORD pass from me to speak to you?' he said. Micaiah answered, 'That
you will find out on the day when you run into an inner room to hide
25 yourself.' Then the king of Israel ordered Micaiah to be arrested and
committed to the custody of Amon the governor of the city and Joash
26 the king's son.*a* 'Lock this fellow up', he said, 'and give him prison diet
27 of bread and water until I come home in safety.' Micaiah retorted, 'If
you do return in safety, the LORD has not spoken by me.'*b*

28 So the king of Israel and Jehoshaphat king of Judah marched on
29 Ramoth-gilead, and the king of Israel said to Jehoshaphat, 'I will
disguise myself to go into battle, but you shall wear your royal robes.'
30 So he went into battle in disguise. Now the king of Aram had commanded the captains of his chariots not to engage all and sundry but the
31 king of Israel alone. When the captains saw Jehoshaphat, they thought
he was the king of Israel and wheeled to attack him. But Jehoshaphat
cried out, and the LORD came to his help; and God drew them away
32 from him. When the captains saw that he was not the king of Israel,
33 they broke off the attack on him. But one man drew his bow at random
and hit the king of Israel where the breastplate joins the plates of the
armour. So he said to his driver, 'Wheel round and take me out of the
34 line; I am wounded.' When the day's fighting reached its height, the
king of Israel was facing the Aramaeans, propped up in his chariot;
he remained so till evening, and at sunset he died.

19 As Jehoshaphat king of Judah returned in safety to his home in
2 Jerusalem, Jehu son of Hanani, the seer, went out to meet him and
said, 'Do you take delight in helping the wicked and befriending the
3 enemies of the LORD? The LORD will make you suffer for this.*c* Yet
there is some good in you, for you have swept away the sacred poles
from the land and have made a practice of seeking guidance of God.'
4 Jehoshaphat had his residence in Jerusalem, but he went out again
among his people from Beersheba to the hill-country of Ephraim and
5 brought them back to the LORD the God of their fathers. He appointed
judges throughout the land, one in each of the fortified cities of Judah,
6 and said to them, 'Be careful what you do; you are there as judges, to
please not man but the LORD, who is with you when you pass sentence.
7 Let the dread of the LORD be upon you, then; take care what you do, for
the LORD our God will not tolerate injustice, partiality, or bribery.'
8 In Jerusalem Jehoshaphat appointed some of the Levites and priests
and some heads of families by paternal descent in Israel to administer
the law of the LORD and to arbitrate in lawsuits among the inhabitants*d*

[*a*] son: *or* deputy.   [*b*] *Prob. rdg.; Heb. adds* and he said, 'Listen, peoples, all together.'
[*c*] The LORD...for this: *lit.* wrath from the LORD will come upon you.   [*d*] in...in-
habitants: *prob. rdg., cp. Sept.; Heb. obscure.*

of the city, and he gave them these instructions: 'You must always act 9
in the fear of the LORD, faithfully and with singleness of mind. In every 10
suit which comes before you from your kinsmen, in whatever city they
live, whether cases of bloodshed or offences against the law or the
commandments, against statutes or regulations, you shall warn them
to commit no offence against the LORD; otherwise you and your kinsmen will suffer for it.*a* If you act thus, you will be free of all offence.
Your authority in all matters which concern the LORD is Amariah the 11
chief priest, and in those which concern the king it is Zebediah
son of Ishmael, the prince of the house of Judah; the Levites are your
officers. Be strong and resolute, and may the LORD be on the side of
the good!'

It happened some time afterwards that the Moabites, the Ammonites, 20
and some of the Meunites*b* made war on Jehoshaphat. News was 2
brought to him that a great horde of them was attacking him from
beyond the Dead Sea, from Edom,*c* and was already at Hazazon-
tamar, which is En-gedi. Jehoshaphat in his alarm resolved to seek 3
guidance of the LORD and proclaimed a fast for all Judah. Judah 4
gathered together to ask counsel of the LORD; from every city of the
land they came to consult him. Jehoshaphat stood up in the assembly 5
of Judah and Jerusalem in the house of the LORD, in front of the New
Court, and said, 'O LORD God of our fathers, art not thou God in 6
heaven? Thou rulest over all the kingdoms of the nations; in thy hand
are strength and power, and there is none who can withstand thee.
Didst not thou, O God our God, dispossess the inhabitants of this land 7
in favour of thy people Israel, and give it for ever to the descendants of
Abraham thy friend? So they lived in it and have built a sanctuary in it 8
in honour of thy name and said, "Should evil come upon us, war or 9
flood,*d* pestilence or famine, we will stand before this house and before
thee, for in this house is thy Name, and we will cry to thee in our
distress and thou wilt hear and save." Thou didst not allow Israel, 10
when they came out of Egypt, to enter the land of the Ammonites, the
Moabites, and the people of the hill-country of Seir, so they turned
aside and left them alone and did not destroy them. Now see how these 11
people repay us: they are coming to drive us out of thy possession which
thou didst give to us. Judge them, O God our God, for we have no 12
strength to face this great horde which is invading our land; we know
not what we ought to do; we lift our eyes to thee.'

So all Judah stood there before the LORD, with their dependants, 13
their wives and their children. Then, in the midst of the assembly, the 14
spirit of the LORD came upon Jahaziel son of Zechariah, son of Benaiah,

---

[*a*] *Lit.* otherwise wrath will come upon you and your kinsmen.   [*b*] *Prob. rdg., cp.* Sept.;
Heb. Ammonites.   [*c*] *So one MS.; others* Aram.   [*d*] *Prob. rdg.; Heb.* judgement.

15 son of Jeiel, son of Mattaniah, a Levite of the line of Asaph, and he said, 'Attend, all Judah, all inhabitants of Jerusalem, and King Jehoshaphat; this is the word of the LORD to you: "Have no fear; do not be dismayed by this great horde, for the battle is in God's hands,
16 not yours. Go down to meet them tomorrow; they will come up by the Ascent of Ziz. You will find them at the end of the valley, east of the
17 wilderness of Jeruel. It is not you who will fight this battle; stand firm and wait, and you will see the deliverance worked by the LORD: he is on your side, O Judah and Jerusalem. Do not fear or be dismayed; go
18 out tomorrow to face them; for the LORD is on your side."' Jehoshaphat bowed his face to the ground, and all Judah and the inhabitants of
19 Jerusalem fell down before the LORD to make obeisance to him. Then the Levites of the lines of Kohath and Korah stood up and praised the LORD the God of Israel with a mighty shout.

20   So they rose early in the morning and went out to the wilderness of Tekoa; and, as they were starting, Jehoshaphat took his stand and said, 'Hear me, O Judah and inhabitants of Jerusalem: hold firmly to your faith in the LORD your God and you will be upheld; have faith in his
21 prophets and you will prosper.' After consulting with the people, he appointed men to sing to the LORD and praise the splendour of his holiness*a* as they went before the armed troops, and they sang:

> Give thanks to the LORD,
> for his love endures for ever.

22 As soon as their loud shouts of praise were heard, the LORD deluded the Ammonites and Moabites and the men of the hill-country of Seir, who
23 were invading Judah, and they were defeated. It turned out that the Ammonites and Moabites had taken up a position against the men of the hill-country of Seir, and set themselves to annihilate and destroy them; and when they had exterminated the men of Seir, they savagely
24 attacked one another. So when Judah came to the watch-tower in the wilderness and looked towards the enemy horde, there they were all
25 lying dead upon the ground; none had escaped. When Jehoshaphat and his men came to collect the booty, they found a large number of cattle,*b* goods, clothing,*c* and precious things, which they plundered until they could carry away no more. They spent three days collecting the booty,
26 there was so much of it. On the fourth day they assembled in the Valley of Berakah,*d* the name that it bears to this day because they blessed the
27 LORD there. Then all the men of Judah and Jerusalem, with Jehoshaphat at their head, returned home to the city in triumph; for the LORD had
28 given them cause to triumph over their enemies. They entered Jeru-

[a] *Or* singers in sacred vestments to praise the LORD.   [b] of cattle: *so Sept.; Heb.* among them.   [c] *So some MSS.; others* effigies.   [d] *That is* Valley of Blessing.

salem with lutes, harps, and trumpets playing, and went into the house
of the LORD. So the dread of God fell upon the rulers of every country, 29
when they heard that the LORD had fought against the enemies of
Israel; and the realm of Jehoshaphat was at peace, God giving him 30
security on all sides.

Thus Jehoshaphat reigned over Judah. He was thirty-five years old 31*a*
when he came to the throne, and he reigned in Jerusalem for twenty-
five years; his mother was Azubah daughter of Shilhi. He followed in 32
the footsteps of Asa his father and did not swerve from them; he did
what was right in the eyes of the LORD. But the hill-shrines were 33
allowed to remain, and the people did not set their hearts upon the God
of their fathers. The other events of Jehoshaphat's reign, from first to 34
last, are recorded in the history of Jehu son of Hanani, which is
included in the annals of the kings of Israel.

Later Jehoshaphat king of Judah allied himself with Ahaziah king of 35
Israel; he did wrong in joining with him to build ships for trade with 36
Tarshish; these were built in Ezion-geber. But Eliezer son of Doda- 37
vahu of Mareshah denounced Jehoshaphat with this prophecy: 'Because
you have joined with Ahaziah, the LORD will bring your work to
nothing.' So the ships were wrecked and could not make the voyage to
Tarshish.

JEHOSHAPHAT rested with his forefathers and was buried with them 21
in the city of David. He was succeeded by his son Joram, whose 2
brothers were Azariah, Jehiel, Zechariah, Azariah, Michael, and
Shephatiah, sons of Jehoshaphat. All of them were sons of Jehoshaphat
king of Judah,*b* and their father gave them many gifts, silver and gold 3
and other costly things, as well as fortified cities in Judah; but the
kingship he gave to Joram because he was the eldest.

When Joram was firmly established on his father's throne, he put 4
to the sword all his brothers and also some of the princes of Israel. He 5*c*
was thirty-two years old when he came to the throne, and he reigned
in Jerusalem for eight years. He followed the practices of the kings of 6
Israel as the house of Ahab had done, for he had married Ahab's
daughter; and he did what was wrong in the eyes of the LORD. But for 7
the sake of the covenant which he had made with David, the LORD was
unwilling to destroy the house of David, since he had promised to give
him and his sons a flame, to burn for all time.

During his reign Edom revolted against Judah and set up its own 8
king. Joram, with his commanders and all his chariots, advanced into 9
Edom. He and his chariot-commanders set out by night, but they were

[*a*] *Verses 31–33: cp. 1 Kgs. 22. 41–43.*   [*b*] *So many MSS.; others* Israel.   [*c*] *Verses 5–10:
cp. 2 Kgs. 8. 17–22.*

597

10 surrounded by the Edomites and defeated.*a* So Edom has remained independent of Judah to this day. Libnah revolted against him at the same time, because he had forsaken the LORD the God of his fathers,
11 and because he had built hill-shrines in the hill-country of Judah and had seduced the inhabitants of Jerusalem into idolatrous practices and corrupted Judah.
12 A letter reached Joram from Elijah the prophet, which ran thus: 'This is the word of the LORD the God of David your father: "You have not followed in the footsteps of Jehoshaphat your father and of Asa king
13 of Judah, but have followed the kings of Israel and have seduced Judah and the inhabitants of Jerusalem, as the house of Ahab did; and you have put to death your own brothers, sons of your father's house, men
14 better than yourself. Because of all this, the LORD is about to strike a heavy blow at your people, your children, your wives, and all your
15 possessions, and you yourself will suffer from a chronic disease of the bowels, until they prolapse and become severely ulcerated."'
16 Then the LORD aroused against Joram the anger of the Philistines
17 and of the Arabs who live near the Cushites, and they invaded Judah and made their way right through it, carrying off all the property which they found in the king's palace, as well as his sons and
18 wives; not a son was left to him except the youngest, Jehoahaz. It was after all this that the LORD struck down the king with an incurable
19 disease of the bowels. It continued for some time, and towards the end of the second year the disease caused his bowels to prolapse, and the painful ulceration brought on his death. But his people kindled
20 no fire in his honour as they had done for his fathers. He was thirty-two years old when he became king, and he reigned in Jerusalem for eight years. His passing went unsung, and he was buried in the city of David, but not in the burial-place of the kings.
22 1*b* Then the inhabitants of Jerusalem made Ahaziah, his youngest son, king in his place, for the raiders who had joined the Arabs in the campaign*c* had killed all the elder sons. So Ahaziah son of Joram became
2 king of Judah. He was forty-two years old when he came to the throne, and he reigned in Jerusalem for one year; his mother was Athaliah
3 granddaughter*d* of Omri. He too followed the practices of the house of
4 Ahab, for his mother was his counsellor in wickedness. He did what was wrong in the eyes of the LORD like the house of Ahab, for they had been
5 his counsellors after his father's death, to his undoing. He followed their counsel also in the alliance he made with Jehoram son of Ahab king of Israel, to fight against Hazael king of Aram at Ramoth-gilead. But
6 Jehoram was wounded by the Aramaeans, and returned to Jezreel to

[*a*] and defeated: *prob. rdg.; Heb.* and he defeated them.   [*b*] *Verses 1–6: cp. 2 Kgs. 8. 25–29.*
[*c*] *Lit.* camp.   [*d*] *Lit.* daughter.

recover from[a] the wounds which were inflicted on him at Ramoth[b] in battle with Hazael king of Aram.

Because of Jehoram's illness Ahaziah[c] son of Joram king of Judah went down to Jezreel to visit him. It was God's will that the visit of 7 Ahaziah to Jehoram should be the occasion of his downfall. During the visit he went out with Jehoram to meet Jehu son of Nimshi, whom the LORD had anointed to bring the house of Ahab to an end. So it came 8 about that Jehu, who was then at variance with the house of Ahab, found the officers of Judah and[d] the kinsmen of Ahaziah who were his attendants, and killed them. Then he searched out Ahaziah himself, and 9 his men captured him in Samaria, where he had gone into hiding. They brought him to Jehu and put him to death; they gave him burial, for they said, 'He was a son of Jehoshaphat who sought the guidance of the LORD with his whole heart.' Then the house of Ahaziah had no one strong enough to rule.

As soon as Athaliah mother of Ahaziah saw that her son was dead, 10[e] she set out to extirpate the royal line of the house of Judah. But 11 Jehosheba[f] daughter of King Joram took Ahaziah's son Joash and stole him away from among the princes who were being murdered; she put him and his nurse in a bedchamber. Thus Jehosheba[f] daughter of King Joram and wife of Jehoiada the priest, because she was Ahaziah's sister, hid Joash from Athaliah so that she did not put him to death. He 12 remained concealed with them in the house of God for six years, while Athaliah ruled the country.

In the seventh year Jehoiada felt himself strong enough to make an 23 agreement with Azariah son of Jeroham, Ishmael son of Jehohanan, Azariah son of Obed, Maaseiah son of Adaiah, and Elishaphat son of Zichri, all captains of units of a hundred. They went all through Judah 2 and gathered to Jerusalem the Levites from the cities of Judah and the heads of clans in Israel, and they came to Jerusalem. All the assembly 3 made a compact with the king in the house of God, and Jehoiada said to them, 'Here is the king's son! He shall be king, as the LORD promised that the sons of David should be. This is what you must do: a third of 4 you, priests and Levites, as you come on duty on the sabbath, are to be on guard at the threshold gates, another third are to be in the royal 5 palace, and another third are to be at the Foundation Gate, while all the people will be in the courts of the house of the LORD. Let no one 6 enter the house of the LORD except the priests and the attendant Levites; they may enter, for they are holy, but all the people shall continue to keep the LORD's charge. The Levites shall mount guard 7

[a] *So some MSS.; others* because... [b] *So Luc. Sept.; Heb.* Ramah. [c] *So some MSS.,* cp. 2 Kgs. 8. 29; others Azariah. [d] *So Sept.; Heb. adds* the sons of. [e] 22. 10 – 23. 21: cp. 2 Kgs. 11. 1-20. [f] *So Sept., cp.* 2 Kgs. 11. 2; *Heb.* Jehoshabeath.

round the king, each with his weapons at the ready; anyone who tries to enter the house is to be put to death. They shall stay with the king wherever he goes.'

8 The Levites and all Judah carried out the orders of Jehoiada the priest to the letter. Each captain took his men, both those who came on duty on the sabbath and those who came off, for Jehoiada the priest

9 had not released the outgoing divisions. And Jehoiada the priest handed out to the captains King David's spears, shields, and bucklers,^a

10 which were in the house of God; and he posted all the people, each man carrying his weapon at the ready, from corner to corner of the

11 house to north and south,^b surrounding the king. Then they brought out the king's son, put the crown on his head, handed him the warrant and proclaimed him king, and Jehoiada and his sons anointed him; and

12 a shout went up: 'Long live the king.' When Athaliah heard the noise of the people as they ran about cheering for the king, she came into the

13 house of the LORD where the people were and found the king standing on the dais^c at the entrance, amidst outbursts of song and fanfares of trumpets in his honour; all the populace were rejoicing and blowing trumpets, and singers with musical instruments were leading the celebrations. Athaliah rent her clothes and cried, 'Treason! Treason!'

14 Jehoiada the priest gave orders to^d the captains in command of the troops: 'Bring her outside the precincts and let anyone in attendance on her be put to the sword'; for the priest said, 'Do not kill her in the

15 house of the LORD.' So they laid hands on her and took her to the royal palace and killed her there at the passage to the Horse Gate.

16 Then Jehoiada made a covenant between the LORD^e and the whole

17 people and the king, that they should be the LORD's people. And all the people went into the temple of Baal and pulled it down; they smashed its altars and images, and they slew Mattan the priest of Baal

18 before the altars. Then Jehoiada committed the supervision of the house of the LORD to the charge of the priests and^f the Levites whom David had allocated to the house of the LORD, to offer whole-offerings to the LORD as prescribed in the law of Moses, with the singing and

19 rejoicing as handed down from David. He stationed the door-keepers at the gates of the house of the LORD, to prevent anyone entering who

20 was in any way unclean. Then he took the captains of units of a hundred, the nobles, and the governors of the people, and all the people of the land, and they escorted the king from the house of the LORD through the Upper Gate to the royal palace, and seated him on the royal throne.

[a] *Mng. of Heb. word uncertain.* [b] *Prob. rdg.; Heb. adds of the altar and the house.*
[c] *Prob. rdg., cp. 2 Kgs. 11. 14; Heb. by his pillar.* [d] *gave orders to: prob. rdg., cp.*
2 Kgs. 11. 15; Heb. brought out. [e] *the* LORD: *prob. rdg., cp. 2 Kgs. 11. 17; Heb. him.*
[f] *and: so some MSS.; others om.*

The whole people rejoiced and the city was tranquil. That is how 21
Athaliah was put to the sword.

Joash was seven years old when he became king, and he reigned in 24 1*a*
Jerusalem for forty years; his mother was Zibiah of Beersheba. He did 2
what was right in the eyes of the LORD as long as Jehoiada the priest
was alive. Jehoiada chose him two wives, and he had a family of sons 3
and daughters.

Some time after this, Joash decided to repair the house of the LORD. 4
So he assembled the priests and the Levites and said to them, 'Go 5
through the cities of Judah and collect the annual tax from all the
Israelites for the restoration of the house of your God, and do it
quickly.' But the Levites did not act quickly. The king then called for 6
Jehoiada the chief priest and said to him, 'Why have you not required
the Levites to bring in from Judah and Jerusalem the tax imposed by
Moses the servant of the LORD and by the assembly of Israel for the
Tent of the Tokens?' For the wicked Athaliah and*b* her adherents*c* had 7
broken into the house of God and had devoted all its holy things to the
service of the Baalim. So the king ordered them to make a chest and to 8
put it outside the gate of the house of the LORD; and proclamation was 9
made throughout Judah and Jerusalem that the people should bring
to the LORD the tax imposed on Israel in the wilderness by Moses the
servant of God. And all the leaders and all the people gladly brought 10
their taxes and cast them into the chest until it was full. Whenever the 11
chest was brought to the king's officers by the Levites and they saw that
it was well filled, the king's secretary and the chief priest's officer would
come to empty it, after which it was carried back to its place. This
they did daily, and they collected a great sum of money. The king and 12
Jehoiada gave it to those responsible for carrying out the work in the
house of the LORD, and they hired masons and carpenters to do the
repairs, as well as craftsmen in iron and copper*d* to restore the house. So 13
the workmen proceeded with their task and the new work progressed
under their hands; they restored the house of God according to its
original design and strengthened it. When they had finished, they 14
brought what was left of the money to the king and to Jehoiada, and it
was made into vessels for the house of the LORD, both for service and
for sacrificing, saucers and other vessels of gold and silver. While
Jehoiada lived, whole-offerings were offered in the house of the LORD
continually.

Jehoiada, now old and weighed down with years, died at the age of a 15
hundred and thirty and was buried with the kings in the city of David, 16
because he had done good in Israel and served God and his house.

[*a*] *Verses 1–14: cp. 2 Kgs. 11. 21–12. 15.* [*b*] and: *so Sept.; Heb. om.* [*c*] her adherents:
lit. her sons. [*d*] *Or* bronze.

17 After the death of Jehoiada the leading men of Judah came and made
18 obeisance to the king. He listened to them, and they forsook the house
of the LORD the God of their fathers and worshipped sacred poles and
19 idols. And Judah and Jerusalem suffered for this wickedness. But the
LORD sent prophets to bring them back to himself, prophets who
20 denounced them and were not heeded. Then the spirit of God took
possession of[a] Zechariah son of Jehoiada the priest, and he stood looking
down on the people and said to them, 'This is the word of God: "Why
do you disobey the commands of the LORD and court disaster? Because
21 you have forsaken the LORD, he has forsaken you."' But they made
common cause against him, and on orders from the king they stoned
22 him to death in the court of the house of the LORD. King Joash did not
remember the loyalty of Zechariah's father Jehoiada but killed his son,
who said as he was dying, 'May the LORD see this and exact the
penalty.'
23 At the turn of the year an Aramaean army advanced against Joash;
they invaded Judah and Jerusalem and massacred all the officers, so
that the army ceased to exist, and sent all their spoil to the king of
24 Damascus. Although the Aramaeans had invaded with a small force,
the LORD delivered a very great army into their hands, because the
people had forsaken the LORD the God of their fathers; and Joash
suffered just punishment.
25[b] When the Aramaeans had withdrawn, leaving the king severely
wounded, his servants conspired against him to avenge the death of
the son[c] of Jehoiada the priest; and they killed him on his bed. Thus he
died and was buried in the city of David, but not in the burial-place of
26 the kings. The conspirators were Zabad son of Shimeath an Ammonite
27 woman and Jehozabad son of Shimrith a Moabite woman. His
children, the many oracles about him, and his reconstruction of the
house of God are all on record in the story given in the annals of the
kings. He was succeeded by his son Amaziah.

25 1[d] AMAZIAH WAS TWENTY-FIVE YEARS OLD when he came to the
throne, and he reigned in Jerusalem for twenty-nine years; his mother
2 was Jehoaddan of Jerusalem. He did what was right in the eyes of the
3 LORD, but not whole-heartedly. When the royal power was firmly in
his grasp, he put to death those of his servants who had murdered the
4 king his father; but he spared their children, in obedience to the LORD's
command written in the law of Moses: 'Fathers shall not die for their
children, nor children for their fathers; a man shall die only for his
own sin.'

[a] took possession of: *lit.* clothed itself with.   [b] *Verses 25–27: cp. 2 Kgs. 12. 20, 21.*
[c] *So Sept.; Heb.* sons.   [d] *Verses 1–4: cp. 2 Kgs. 14. 1–6.*

Then Amaziah assembled the men of Judah and drew them up by 5
families, all Judah and Benjamin as well, under officers over units of
a thousand and a hundred. He mustered those of twenty years old and
upwards and found their number to be three hundred thousand, all
picked troops ready for service, able to handle spear and shield. He also 6
hired a hundred thousand seasoned troops from Israel for a hundred
talents of silver. But a man of God came to him and said, 'My lord 7
king, do not let the Israelite army march with you; the LORD is not
with Israel—all these Ephraimites! For, if you make these people*a* your 8
allies in the war, God will overthrow you in battle; he has power to help
or to overthrow.' Then Amaziah said to the man of God, 'What am 9
I to do about the hundred talents which I have spent on the Israelite
army?' The man of God answered, 'It is in the LORD's power to give
you much more than that.' So Amaziah detached the troops which had 10
come to him from Ephraim and sent them home; that infuriated them
against Judah and they went home in a rage.

Then Amaziah took heart and led his men to the Valley of Salt and 11
there killed ten thousand men of Seir. The men of Judah captured 12
another*b* ten thousand men alive, brought them to the top of a cliff*b*
and hurled them over so that they were all dashed to pieces. Mean- 13
while the troops which Amaziah had sent home without allowing them
to take part in the battle raided the cities of Judah from Samaria to
Beth-horon, massacred three thousand people in them and carried off
quantities of booty.

After Amaziah had returned from the defeat of the Edomites, he 14
brought the gods of the people of Seir and, setting them up as his own
gods, worshipped them and burnt sacrifices to them. The LORD was 15
angry with Amaziah for this and sent a prophet who said to him,
'Why have you resorted to gods who could not save their own people
from you?' But while he was speaking, the king said to him, 'Have we 16
appointed you counsellor to the king? Stop! Why risk your life?' The
prophet did stop, but first he said, 'I know that God has determined to
destroy you because you have done this and have not listened to my
counsel.'

Then Amaziah king of Judah, after consultation, sent messengers to 17*c*
Jehoash son of Jehoahaz, son of Jehu, king of Israel, to propose a
meeting. But Jehoash king of Israel sent this answer to Amaziah king 18
of Judah: 'A thistle in Lebanon sent to a cedar in Lebanon to say,
"Give your daughter in marriage to my son." But a wild beast in
Lebanon, passing by, trampled on the thistle. You have defeated Edom, 19
you say, but it has gone to your head. Enjoy your glory at home and

[*a*] these people: *prob. rdg.; Heb. obscure.*   [*b*] a cliff: *or* Sela.   [*c*] *Verses 17–24: cp. 2 Kgs.
14. 8–14.*

stay there. Why should you involve yourself in disaster and bring yourself to the ground, and Judah with you?'

20 But Amaziah would not listen; and this was God's doing in order to
give Judah into the power of Jehoash,*a* because they had resorted to the
21 gods of Edom. So Jehoash king of Israel marched out, and he and
22 Amaziah king of Judah met one another at Beth-shemesh in Judah. The
23 men of Judah were routed by Israel and fled to their homes. But Jehoash
king of Israel captured Amaziah king of Judah, son of Joash, son of
Jehoahaz, at Beth-shemesh, and brought him to Jerusalem. There he
broke down the city wall from the Gate of Ephraim to the Corner Gate,
24 a distance of four hundred cubits; he also took*b* all the gold and silver
and all the vessels found in the house of God, in the care of Obed-
edom, and the treasures of the royal palace, as well as hostages, and
returned to Samaria.

25*c* Amaziah son of Joash, king of Judah, outlived Jehoash son of
26 Jehoahaz, king of Israel, by fifteen years. The other events of Amaziah's
reign, from first to last, are recorded in the annals of the kings of Judah
27 and Israel. From the time when he turned away from the LORD, there
was conspiracy against him in Jerusalem and he fled to Lachish; but
28 they sent after him to Lachish and put him to death there. Then his
body was conveyed on horseback to Jerusalem, and there he was buried
with his forefathers in the city of David.*d*

26 All the people of Judah took Uzziah, now sixteen years old, and made
2 him king in succession to his father Amaziah. It was he who built
Eloth and restored it to Judah after the king rested with his forefathers.

3*e* Uzziah was sixteen years old when he came to the throne, and he
reigned in Jerusalem for fifty-two years; his mother was Jecoliah of
4 Jerusalem. He did what was right in the eyes of the LORD, as Amaziah
5 his father had done. He set himself to seek the guidance of God in the
days of Zechariah, who instructed him in the fear of*f* God; as long as
he sought guidance of the LORD, God caused him to prosper.

6 He took the field against the Philistines and broke down the walls of
Gath, Jabneh, and Ashdod; and he built cities in the territory of
7 Ashdod and among the Philistines. God aided him against them,
against the Arabs who lived in Gur-baal, and against the Meunites.
8 The Ammonites brought gifts to Uzziah and his fame spread to the
9 borders of Egypt, for he had become very powerful. Besides, he built
towers in Jerusalem at the Corner Gate, at the Valley Gate, and at the
10 escarpment, and fortified them. He built other towers in the wilderness

---

[a] of Jehoash: *so Luc. Sept.; Heb. om.* [b] he also took: *prob. rdg., cp. 2 Kgs. 14. 14; Heb.*
om. [c] *25. 25 – 26. 2: cp. 2 Kgs. 14. 17–22.* [d] *So some MSS.; others* the city of Judah.
[e] *Verses 3, 4: cp. 2 Kgs. 15. 2, 3.* [f] *in the fear of: so some MSS.; others* on seeing.

and dug many cisterns, for he had large herds of cattle both in the Shephelah and in the plain. He also had farmers and vine-dressers in the hill-country and in the fertile lands, for he loved the soil.

Uzziah had an army of soldiers trained and ready for service, grouped 11 according to the census made by Jeiel the adjutant-general and Maaseiah the clerk under the direction of Hananiah, one of the king's commanders. The total number of heads of families which supplied 12 seasoned warriors was two thousand six hundred. Under their command 13 was an army of three hundred and seven thousand five hundred, a powerful fighting force to aid the king against his enemies. Uzziah 14 prepared for the whole army shields, spears, helmets, coats of mail, bows, and*a* sling-stones. In Jerusalem he had machines designed by 15 engineers for use upon towers and bastions, made to discharge arrows and large stones. His fame spread far and wide, for he was so wonderfully gifted that he became very powerful.

But when he grew powerful his pride led to his own undoing:*b* he 16 offended against the LORD his God by entering the temple of the LORD to burn incense on the altar of incense. Azariah the priest and eighty 17 others of the LORD's priests, courageous men, went in after King Uzziah, confronted him and said, 'It is not for you, Uzziah, to burn 18 incense to the LORD, but for the Aaronite priests who have been consecrated for that office. Leave the sanctuary; for you have offended, and that will certainly bring you no honour from the LORD God.' The king, who had a censer in his hand ready to burn incense, was 19 indignant; and because of his indignation at the priests, leprosy broke out on his forehead in the presence of the priests, there in the house of the LORD, beside the altar of incense. When Azariah the chief priest 20 and the other priests looked towards him, they saw that he had leprosy on his forehead and they hurried him out of the temple, and indeed he himself hastened to leave, because the LORD had struck him with the disease. And King Uzziah remained a leper till the day of his death; 21*c* he lived in his own house as a leper, relieved of all duties and excluded from the house of the LORD, while his son Jotham was comptroller of the household and regent. The other events of Uzziah's reign, from 22 first to last, are recorded by the prophet Isaiah son of Amoz. So he 23 rested with his forefathers and was buried in a burial-ground, but not that of the kings;*d* for they said, 'He is a leper'; and he was succeeded by his son Jotham.

Jotham was twenty-five years old when he came to the throne, and 27 1*e*

[a] *Prob. rdg.; Heb. adds* for.   [b] his pride...undoing: *or* he became so proud that he acted corruptly.   [c] *Verses 21–23: cp.* 2 *Kgs.* 15. 5–7.   [d] in a...kings: *so Pesh.; Heb.* with his forefathers in the burial-ground belonging to the kings.   [e] *Verses 1–3: cp.* 2 *Kgs.* 15. 33–35.

he reigned in Jerusalem for sixteen years; his mother was Jerushah
2 daughter of Zadok. He did what was right in the eyes of the LORD, as
his father Uzziah had done, but unlike him he did not enter the temple
of the LORD; the people, however, continued their corrupt practices.
3 He constructed the upper gate of the house of the LORD and built
4 extensively on the wall at Ophel. He built cities in the hill-country of
5 Judah, and forts and towers on the wooded hills. He made war on the
king of the Ammonites and defeated him; and that year the Ammonites
gave him a hundred talents of silver, ten thousand kor of wheat and ten
thousand of barley. They paid him the same tribute in the second and
6 third years. Jotham became very powerful because he maintained a
7 steady course of obedience to the LORD his God. The other events of
Jotham's reign, all that he did in war and in peace, are recorded in the
8 annals of the kings of Israel and Judah. He was twenty-five years old
when he came to the throne, and he reigned in Jerusalem for sixteen
9 years. He rested with his forefathers and was buried in the city of
David; and he was succeeded by his son Ahaz.

28 1*a* AHAZ WAS TWENTY YEARS OLD when he came to the throne, and he
reigned in Jerusalem for sixteen years. He did not do what was right
2 in the eyes of the LORD like his forefather David, but followed in the
footsteps of the kings of Israel, and cast metal images for the Baalim.
3 He also burnt sacrifices in the Valley of Ben-hinnom; he even burnt his
sons in*b* the fire according to the abominable practice of the nations
4 whom the LORD had dispossessed in favour of the Israelites. He
slaughtered and burnt sacrifices at the hill-shrines and on the hill-tops
and under every spreading tree.

5   The LORD his God let him suffer at the hands of the king of Aram,
and the Aramaeans defeated him, took many captives and brought them
to Damascus; he was also made to suffer at the hands of the king of
6 Israel, who inflicted a severe defeat on him. This was Pekah son of
Remaliah, who killed in one day a hundred and twenty thousand men of
Judah, seasoned troops, because they had forsaken the LORD the God
7 of their fathers. And Zichri, an Ephraimite hero, killed Maaseiah the
king's son*c* and Azrikam the comptroller of the household and Elkanah
8 the king's chief minister. The Israelites took captive from their kinsmen
two hundred thousand women and children; they also took a large
amount of booty and brought it to Samaria.

9   A prophet of the LORD was there, Oded by name; he went out to
meet the army as it returned to Samaria and said to them, 'It is because
the LORD the God of your fathers is angry with Judah that he has

[*a*] *Verses 1–4: cp. 2 Kgs. 16. 2–4.*   [*b*] burnt his sons in: *or, with one MS.,* passed his sons
through.   [*c*] son: *or* deputy.

given them into your power; and you have massacred them in a rage
that has towered up to heaven. Now you propose to force the people of 10
Judah and Jerusalem, male and female, into slavery. Are not you also
guilty men before the LORD your God? Now, listen to me. Send back 11
those you have taken captive from your kinsmen, for the anger of the
LORD is roused against you.' Next, some Ephraimite chiefs, Azariah 12
son of Jehohanan, Berechiah son of Meshillemoth, Hezekiah[a] son of
Shallum, and Amasa son of Hadlai, met those who were returning
from the war and said to them, 'You must not bring these captives 13
into our country; what you are proposing would make us guilty before
the LORD and add to our sins and transgressions. We are guilty enough
already, and there is fierce anger against Israel.' So the armed men left 14
the captives and the spoil with the officers and the assembled people. The 15
captives were put in charge of men nominated for this duty, who found
clothes from the spoil for all who were naked. They clothed them and
shod them, gave them food and drink, and anointed them; those who
were tottering from exhaustion they conveyed on the backs of asses,
and so brought them to their kinsmen in Jericho, in the Vale of Palm
Trees. Then they themselves returned to Samaria.

At that time King Ahaz sent to the king[b] of Assyria for help. The 16, 17
Edomites had invaded again and defeated Judah and taken away
prisoners; and the Philistines had raided the cities of the Shephelah 18
and of the Negeb of Judah and had captured Beth-shemesh, Aijalon,
and Gederoth, as well as Soco, Timnah, and Gimzo with their villages,
and occupied them. The LORD had reduced Judah to submission because 19
of Ahaz king of Judah;[c] for his actions in Judah had been unbridled
and he had been grossly unfaithful to the LORD. Then Tiglath-pileser[d] 20
king of Assyria marched against him and, so far from assisting him,
pressed him hard. Ahaz stripped the house of the LORD, the king's 21
palace and the houses of his officers, and gave the plunder to the king
of Assyria; but all to no purpose.

This King Ahaz, when hard pressed, became more and more un- 22
faithful to the LORD; he sacrificed to the gods of Damascus who had 23
defeated him and said, 'The gods of the kings of Aram helped them;
I will sacrifice to them so that they may help me.' But in fact they
caused his downfall and that of all Israel. Then Ahaz gathered together 24
the vessels of the house of God and broke them up, and shut the doors
of the house of the LORD; he made himself altars at every corner in
Jerusalem, and at every single city of Judah he made hill-shrines to 25
burn sacrifices to other gods and provoked the anger of the LORD the
God of his fathers.

[a] *Or* Jehizkiah.   [b] *So Sept.; Heb.* kings.   [c] *So some MSS.; others* Israel.   [d] *So
Pesh.; Heb.* Tilgath-pilneser.

26ᵃ   The other acts and all the events of his reign, from first to last, are
27 recorded in the annals of the kings of Judah and Israel. So Ahaz rested
with his forefathers and was buried in the city of Jerusalem, but was
not given burial with the kings of Judah.ᵇ He was succeeded by his son
Hezekiah.

The kings of Judah from Hezekiah to the exile

29 1ᶜ   HEZEKIAH WAS TWENTY-FIVE YEARS OLD when he came to
the throne, and he reigned in Jerusalem for twenty-nine years;
2 his mother was Abijah daughter of Zechariah. He did what was right
in the eyes of the LORD, as David his forefather had done.
3   In the first year of his reign, in the first month, he opened the gates
4 of the house of the LORD and repaired them. He brought in the priests
and the Levites and gathered them together in the square on the east
5 side, and said to them, 'Levites, listen to me. Hallow yourselves now,
hallow the house of the LORD the God of your fathers, and remove the
6 pollution from the sanctuary. For our forefathers were unfaithful and
did what was wrong in the eyes of the LORD our God: they forsook
him, they would have nothing to do with his dwelling-place, they
7 turned their backs on it. They shut the doors of the porch and
extinguished the lamps, they ceased to burn incense and offer whole-
8 offerings in the sanctuary to the God of Israel. Therefore the anger of
the LORD fell upon Judah and Jerusalem and he made them repugnant,
9 an object of horror and derision, as you see for yourselves. Hence it is
that our fathers have fallen by the sword, our sons and daughters and
10 our wives are in captivity. Now I intend that we should pledge ourselves
to the LORD the God of Israel, in order that his anger may be averted
11 from us. So, my sons, let no time be lost; for the LORD has chosen you
to serve him and to minister to him, to be his ministers and to burn
sacrifices.'
12   Then the Levites set to work—Mahath son of Amasai and Joel son
of Azariah of the family of Kohath; of the family of Merari, Kish son
of Abdi and Azariah son of Jehalelel; of the family of Gershon, Joah
13 son of Zimmah and Eden son of Joah; of the family of Elizaphan,
Shimri and Jeiel; of the family of Asaph, Zechariah and Mattaniah;
14 of the family of Heman, Jehiel and Shimei; and of the family of
15 Jeduthun, Shemaiah and Uzziel. They assembled their kinsmen and
hallowed themselves, and then went in, as the king had instructed
16 them at the LORD's command, to purify the house of the LORD. The

[a] *Verses 26, 27: cp. 2 Kgs. 16. 19, 20.*   [b] *So Pesh.; Heb. Israel.*   [c] *Verses 1, 2: cp.*
2 Kgs. 18. 1–3.

priests went inside to purify the house of the LORD; they removed all the pollution which they found in the temple into the court of the house of the LORD, and the Levites took it from them and carried it outside to the gorge of the Kidron. They began the rites on the first day of the 17 first month, and on the eighth day they reached the porch; then for eight days they consecrated the house of the LORD, and on the sixteenth day of the first month they finished. Then they went into the palace*a* 18 and said to King Hezekiah, 'We have purified the whole of the house of the LORD, the altar of whole-offering with all its vessels, and the table for the Bread of the Presence arranged in rows with all its vessels; and we have put in order and consecrated all the vessels which 19 King Ahaz cast aside during his reign, when he was unfaithful. They are now in place before the altar of the LORD.'

Then King Hezekiah rose early, assembled the officers of the city 20 and went up to the house of the LORD. They brought seven bulls, seven 21 rams, and seven lambs for the whole-offering,*b* and seven he-goats as a sin-offering for the kingdom, for the sanctuary, and for Judah; these he commanded the priests of Aaron's line to offer on the altar of the LORD. So the bulls were slaughtered, and the priests took their blood 22 and flung it against the altar; the rams were slaughtered, and their blood was flung against the altar; the lambs were slaughtered, and their blood was flung against the altar. Then the he-goats for the sin-offering 23 were brought before the king and the assembly, who laid their hands on them; and the priests slaughtered them and used their blood as a sin- 24 offering on the altar to make expiation for all Israel. For the king had commanded that the whole-offering and the sin-offering should be made for all Israel.

He posted the Levites in the house of the LORD with cymbals, lutes, 25 and harps, according to the rule prescribed by David, by Gad the king's seer and Nathan the prophet; for this rule had come from the LORD through his prophets. The Levites stood ready with the instruments of 26 David, and the priests with the trumpets. Hezekiah gave the order that 27 the whole-offering should be offered on the altar. At the moment when the whole-offering began, the song to the LORD began too, with the trumpets, led by the instruments of David king of Israel. The whole 28 assembly prostrated themselves, the singers sang and the trumpeters sounded; all this continued until the whole-offering was complete. When the offering was complete, the king and all his company bowed 29 down and prostrated themselves. And King Hezekiah and his officers 30 commanded the Levites to praise the LORD in the words of David and of Asaph the seer. So they praised him most joyfully and bowed down and prostrated themselves.

[*a*] into the palace: *lit.* within.   [*b*] for the whole-offering: *prob. rdg.; Heb. om.*

31 Then Hezekiah said, 'You have now given to the LORD with open hands; approach with your sacrifices and thank-offerings for the house of the LORD.' So the assembly brought sacrifices and thank-offerings;
32 and every man of willing spirit brought whole-offerings. The number of whole-offerings which the assembly brought was seventy bulls, a hundred rams, and two hundred lambs; all these made a whole-
33 offering to the LORD. And the consecrated offerings were six hundred
34 bulls and three thousand sheep. But the priests were too few and could not flay all the whole-offerings; so their colleagues the Levites helped them until the work was completed and all the priests had hallowed themselves—for the Levites had been more scrupulous than the priests
35 in hallowing themselves. There were indeed whole-offerings in abundance, besides the fat of the shared-offerings and the drink-offerings for the whole-offerings. In this way the service of the house of
36 the LORD was restored; and Hezekiah and all the people rejoiced over what God had done for the people and because it had come about so suddenly.

30 Then Hezekiah sent word to all Israel and Judah, and also wrote letters to Ephraim and Manasseh, inviting them to come to the house of the LORD in Jerusalem to keep the Passover of the LORD the God of
2 Israel. The king and his officers and all the assembly in Jerusalem had
3 agreed to keep the Passover in the second month, but they had not been able to keep it at that time, because not enough priests had hallowed
4 themselves and the people had not assembled in Jerusalem. The
5 proposal was acceptable to the king and the whole assembly. So they resolved to make a proclamation throughout all Israel, from Beersheba to Dan, that the people should come to Jerusalem to keep the Passover of the LORD the God of Israel. Never before had so many kept it
6 according to the prescribed form. Couriers went throughout all Israel and Judah with letters from the king and his officers, proclaiming the royal command: 'Turn back, men of Israel, to the LORD the God of Abraham, Isaac, and Israel, so that he may turn back to those of you
7 who escaped capture by the kings of Assyria. Do not be like your fore-fathers and your kinsmen, who were unfaithful to the LORD the God of their fathers, so that he made them an object of horror, as you your-
8 selves saw. Do not be stubborn as your forefathers were; submit yourselves to the LORD and enter his sanctuary which he has sanctified for ever, and worship the LORD your God, so that his anger may be
9 averted from you. For when you turn back to the LORD, your kinsmen and your children will win compassion from their captors and return to this land. The LORD your God is gracious and compassionate, and he will not turn away from you if you turn back to him.'
10 So the couriers passed from city to city through the land of

Ephraim and Manasseh and as far as Zebulun, but they were treated
with scorn and ridicule. However, a few men of Asher, Manasseh, and   11
Zebulun submitted and came to Jerusalem. Further, the hand of God   12
moved the people in Judah with one accord to carry out what the king
and his officers had ordered at the LORD's command.

Many people, a very great assembly, came together in Jerusalem to   13
keep the pilgrim-feast of Unleavened Bread in the second month. They   14
began by removing the altars in Jerusalem; they removed the altars for
burning sacrifices and threw them into the gorge of the Kidron. They   15
killed the passover lamb on the fourteenth day of the second month;
and the priests and the Levites were bitterly ashamed. They hallowed
themselves and brought whole-offerings to the house of the LORD. They   16
took their accustomed places, according to the direction laid down for
them in the law of Moses the man of God; the priests flung against the
altar the blood which they received from the Levites. But many in the   17
assembly had not hallowed themselves; therefore the Levites had to kill
the passover lamb for every one who was unclean, in order to hallow
him to the LORD. For a majority of the people, many from Ephraim,   18
Manasseh, Issachar, and Zebulun, had not kept themselves ritually
clean, and therefore kept the Passover irregularly. But Hezekiah prayed
for them, saying, 'May the good LORD grant pardon to every one who   19
makes a practice of seeking guidance of God, the LORD the God of his
fathers, even if he has not observed the rules for the purification of the
sanctuary.' The LORD heard Hezekiah and healed the people. And the   20, 21
Israelites who were present in Jerusalem kept the feast of Unleavened
Bread for seven days with great rejoicing, and the Levites and the
priests praised the LORD every day with unrestrained fervour.*a* Hezekiah   22
spoke encouragingly to all the Levites who had shown true understanding in the service of the LORD. So they spent the seven days of the
festival sacrificing shared-offerings and making confession to*b* the LORD
the God of their fathers.

Then the whole assembly agreed to keep the feast for another seven   23
days; so they kept it for another seven days with general rejoicing.
For Hezekiah king of Judah set aside for the assembly a thousand bulls   24
and seven thousand sheep, and his officers set aside for the assembly
a thousand bulls and ten thousand sheep; and priests hallowed themselves in great numbers. So the whole assembly of Judah, including the   25
priests and the Levites, rejoiced, together with all the assembly which
came out of Israel, and the resident aliens from Israel and those who
lived in Judah. There was great rejoicing in Jerusalem, the like of which   26
had not been known there since the days of Solomon son of David king

---

[a] with unrestrained fervour: *prob. rdg.; Heb.* with powerful instruments.   [b] making
confession to: *or* confessing.

27 of Israel. Then the priests and*ᵃ* the Levites stood to bless the people; the LORD listened to their cry,*ᵇ* and their prayer came to God's holy dwelling-place in heaven.

31   When this was over, all the Israelites present went out to the cities of Judah and smashed the sacred pillars, hacked down the sacred poles and broke up the hill-shrines and the altars throughout Judah and Benjamin, Ephraim and Manasseh, until they had made an end of them. That done, the Israelites returned, each to his own patrimony in his own city.

2   Then Hezekiah installed the priests and the Levites in office, division by division, allotting to each priest or Levite his own particular duty, for whole-offerings or shared-offerings, to give thanks or to sing praise, or to serve*ᶜ* in the gates of the several quarters in the LORD's house.*ᵈ*

3   The king provided from his own resources, as the share due from him, the whole-offerings for both morning and evening, and for sabbaths, new moons, and appointed seasons, as prescribed in the law

4 of the LORD. He ordered the people living in Jerusalem to provide the share due from the priests and the Levites, so that they might devote

5 themselves entirely to the law of the LORD. As soon as the king's order was issued to the Israelites, they gave generously from the firstfruits of their corn and new wine, oil and honey, all the produce of their land;

6 they brought a full tithe of everything. The Israelites and the Judaeans living in the cities of Judah also brought a tithe of cattle and sheep, and a tithe of all produce as offerings*ᵉ* dedicated to the LORD their God, and

7 they stacked the produce in heaps. They began to deposit the heaps in

8 the third month and completed them in the seventh. When Hezekiah and his officers came and saw the heaps, they blessed the LORD and his

9 people Israel. Hezekiah asked the priests and the Levites about these

10 heaps, and Azariah the chief priest, who was of the line of Zadok, answered, 'From the time when the people began to bring their contribution into the house of the LORD, they have had enough to eat, enough and to spare; indeed, the LORD has so greatly blessed them that they have this great store left over.'

11   Then Hezekiah ordered store-rooms to be prepared in the house of

12 the LORD, and this was done; and the people honestly brought in their contributions, the tithe, and their dedicated gifts. The overseer in charge of them was Conaniah the Levite, with Shimei his brother as his

13 deputy; Jehiel, Azaziah, Nahath, Asahel, Jerimoth, Jozabad, Eliel, Ismachiah, Mahath, and Benaiah were appointed by King Hezekiah and Azariah, the chief overseer of the house of God, to assist Conaniah and

---

[*a*] and: *so many MSS.; others om.*   [*b*] the LORD...cry: *so Pesh.; Heb.* their cry was heard.
[*c*] to serve: *transposed from before* to give thanks.   [*d*] in the LORD's house: *so Sept.; Heb.*
of the LORD.   [*e*] tithe of all produce as offerings: *lit.* tithe of offerings.

Shimei his brother. And Kore son of Imnah the Levite, keeper of the 14
East Gate, was in charge of the freewill offerings to God, to apportion
the contributions made to the LORD and the most sacred offerings. Eden, 15
Miniamin, Jeshua, Shemaiah, Amariah, and Shecaniah in the priestly
cities assisted him in the fair distribution of portions to their kinsmen,
young and old^a alike, by divisions. Irrespective of their registration, 16
shares were distributed to all males three years of age and upwards who
entered the house of the LORD to take their daily part in the service,
according to their divisions, as their office demanded. The priests were 17
registered by families, the Levites from twenty years of age and upwards
by their offices in their divisions. They were registered with all their 18
dependants, their wives, their sons, and their daughters, the whole
company of them, because in virtue of their permanent standing they
had to keep themselves duly hallowed. As for the priests of Aaron's line 19
in the common lands attached to their cities, in every city men were
nominated to distribute portions to every male among the priests and
to every one who was registered with the Levites.

Such was the action taken by Hezekiah throughout Judah; he did 20
what was good and right and loyal in the sight of the LORD his God.
Whatever he undertook in the service of the house of God and in 21
obedience to the law and the commandment to seek guidance of his
God, he did with all his heart, and he prospered.

After these events and this example of loyal conduct, Sennacherib 32 1^b
king of Assyria invaded Judah and encamped against the fortified cities,
believing that he could attach them to himself. When Hezekiah saw that 2
he had come and was determined to attack Jerusalem, he consulted his 3
civil and military officers about blocking up the springs outside the
city; and they encouraged him. They gathered together a large number 4
of people and blocked up all the springs and the stream which flowed
through the land. 'Why', they said, 'should Assyrian kings come here
and find plenty of water?' Then the king acted boldly; he made good 5
every breach in the city wall and erected towers on it;^c he built another
wall outside it and strengthened the Millo of the city of David; he also
collected a great quantity of weapons and shields. He appointed 6
military commanders over the people and assembled them in the square
by the city gate and spoke encouragingly to them in these words: 'Be 7
strong; be brave. Do not let the king of Assyria or the rabble he has
brought with him strike terror or panic into your hearts. We have more
on our side than he has. He has human strength; but we have the LORD 8
our God to help us and to fight our battles.' So spoke Hezekiah king of
Judah, and the people were buoyed up by his words.

[a] *Or* high and low.   [b] *Verses 1–19: cp. 2 Kgs. 18. 13–37; Isa. 36. 1–22.*   [c] towers on
it: *so Targ.; Heb.* on the towers.

9 After this, Sennacherib king of Assyria, while he and his high command were at Lachish, sent envoys to Jerusalem to deliver this message to Hezekiah king of Judah and to all the Judaeans in Jeru-
10 salem: 'Sennacherib king of Assyria says, "What gives you confidence
11 to stay in Jerusalem under siege? Hezekiah is misleading you into risking death by famine or thirst where you are, when he tells you that the LORD your God will save you from the grip of the Assyrian king.
12 Was it not Hezekiah himself who suppressed the LORD's hill-shrines and altars and told the people of Judah and Jerusalem that they must prostrate themselves before one altar only and burn sacrifices there?
13 You know very well what I and my forefathers have done to all the peoples of the lands. Were the gods of these nations able to save their
14 lands from me? Not one of the gods of these nations, which my fore-fathers exterminated, was able to save his people from me. Much less
15 will your god save you! How, then, can Hezekiah deceive you or mislead you like this? How can you believe him, for no god of any nation or kingdom has been able to save his people from me or my forefathers? Much less will your gods save you[a]!"'
16 The envoys of Sennacherib spoke still more against the LORD God
17 and against his servant Hezekiah. And the king himself wrote a letter to defy the LORD the God of Israel, in these terms: 'Just as the gods of other nations could not save their people from me, so the god of
18 Hezekiah will not save his people from me.' Then they shouted in Hebrew at the top of their voices at the people of Jerusalem on the wall,
19 to strike them with fear and terror, hoping thus to capture the city. They described the god[b] of Jerusalem as being like the gods of the other peoples of the earth—things made by the hands of men.
20[c] In this plight King Hezekiah and the prophet Isaiah son of Amoz
21 cried to heaven in prayer. So the LORD sent an angel who cut down all the fighting men, as well as the leaders and the commanders, in the camp of the king of Assyria, so that he went home disgraced to his own land. When he entered the temple of his god, certain of his own sons struck him down with their swords.
22 Thus the LORD saved Hezekiah and the inhabitants of Jerusalem from Sennacherib king of Assyria and all their enemies; and he gave
23 them respite on every side. Many people brought to Jerusalem offerings for the LORD and costly gifts for Hezekiah king of Judah. From then on he was held in high honour by all the nations.
24 About this time Hezekiah fell dangerously ill and prayed to the LORD; the LORD said, 'I will heal you',[d] and granted him a sign.
25 But, being a proud man, he was not grateful for the good done to him,

[a] Or, with some MSS., will your god save you. [b] Or gods. [c] Verses 20-22: cp. 2 Kgs. 19. 1-37; Isa. 37. 1-38. [d] I will heal you: prob. rdg., cp. 2 Kgs. 20. 5; Heb. om.

and Judah and Jerusalem suffered for it. Then, proud as he was, 26
Hezekiah submitted, and the people of Jerusalem with him, and the
LORD's anger did not fall on them again in Hezekiah's time.

Hezekiah enjoyed great wealth and fame.*a* He built for himself 27
treasuries for silver and gold, precious stones and spices, shields and
other costly things; and barns for the harvests of corn, new wine, and 28
oil; and stalls for every kind of cattle, as well as sheepfolds.*b* He 29
amassed*c* a great many flocks and herds; God had indeed given him
vast riches. It was this same Hezekiah who blocked the upper outflow 30
of the waters of Gihon and directed them downwards and westwards
to the city of David. In fact, Hezekiah was successful in everything he
attempted, even in the affair of the envoys sent by the king*d* of 31
Babylon—the envoys who came to inquire about the portent which
had been seen in the land at the time when God left him to himself, to
test him and to discover all that was in his heart.

The other events of Hezekiah's reign, and his works of piety, are 32
recorded in the vision of the prophet Isaiah son of Amoz and*e* in the
annals of the kings of Judah and Israel. So Hezekiah rested with his 33
forefathers and was buried in the uppermost of the graves of David's
sons; all Judah and the people of Jerusalem paid him honour when he
died, and he was succeeded by his son Manasseh.

MANASSEH WAS TWELVE YEARS OLD when he came to the throne, 33 1*f*
and he reigned in Jerusalem for fifty-five years. He did what was 2
wrong in the eyes of the LORD, in following the abominable practices
of the nations which the LORD had dispossessed in favour of the
Israelites. He rebuilt the hill-shrines which his father Hezekiah had 3
dismantled, he erected altars to the Baalim and made sacred poles, he
prostrated himself before all the host of heaven and worshipped them.
He built altars in the house of the LORD, that house of which the LORD 4
had said, 'In Jerusalem shall my Name be for ever.' He built altars for 5
all the host of heaven in the two courts of the house of the LORD;
he made his sons pass through the fire in the Valley of Ben-hinnom, 6
he practised soothsaying, divination, and sorcery, and dealt with ghosts
and spirits. He did much wrong in the eyes of the LORD and provoked
his anger; and the image that he had had carved in relief he put in the 7
house of God, the place of which God had said to David and Solomon
his son, 'This house and Jerusalem, which I chose out of all the tribes
of Israel, shall receive my Name for all time. I will not again displace 8
Israel from the land which I assigned to their forefathers, if only they

[*a*] *Or* riches. [*b*] sheepfolds: *so Sept.; Heb.* sheep for the folds. [*c*] *Prob. rdg.; Heb.*
adds cities. [*d*] *Prob. rdg., cp. 2 Kgs. 20. 12; Heb.* officers. [*e*] and: *so Sept.; Heb. om.*
[*f*] *Verses 1–9: cp. 2 Kgs. 21. 1–9.*

will be careful to observe all that I commanded them through Moses,
9 all the law, the statutes, and the rules.' But Manasseh misled Judah and
the inhabitants of Jerusalem into wickedness far worse than that of the
nations which the LORD had exterminated in favour of the Israelites.
10 The LORD spoke to Manasseh and to his people, but they paid no
11 heed. So the LORD brought against them the commanders of the army
of the king of Assyria; they captured Manasseh with spiked weapons,
12 and bound him with fetters, and brought him to Babylon. In his
distress he prayed to the LORD his God and sought to placate him, and
13 made his humble submission before the God of his fathers. He prayed,
and God accepted his petition and heard his supplication. He brought
him back to Jerusalem and restored him to the throne; and thus
Manasseh learnt that the LORD was God.
14 After this he built an outer wall for the city of David, west of Gihon
in the gorge, and extended it to the entrance by the Fish Gate, en-
closing Ophel; and he raised it to a great height. He also put military
15 commanders in all the fortified cities of Judah. He removed the foreign
gods and the carved image from the house of the LORD and all the altars
which he had built on the temple mount[a] and in Jerusalem, and threw
16 them out of the city. Moreover, he repaired the altar of the LORD and
sacrificed at it shared-offerings and thank-offerings, and commanded
17 Judah to serve the LORD the God of Israel. But the people still continued to sacrifice at the hill-shrines, though only to the LORD their God.
18 The rest of the acts of Manasseh, his prayer to his God, and the
discourses of the seers who spoke to him in the name of the LORD the
God of Israel, are recorded in the chronicles of the kings of Israel.
19 His prayer and the answer he received to it, and all his sin and unfaithfulness, and the places where he built hill-shrines and set up sacred
poles and carved idols, before he submitted, are recorded in the
20 chronicles of the seers.[b] So Manasseh rested with his forefathers and
was buried in the garden-tomb of[c] his family; he was succeeded by
his son Amon.
21[d] Amon was twenty-two years old when he came to the throne, and he
22 reigned in Jerusalem for two years. He did what was wrong in the eyes
of the LORD as his father Manasseh had done. He sacrificed to all the
23 images that his father Manasseh had made, and worshipped them. He
was not submissive before the LORD like his father Manasseh; his guilt
24 was much greater. His courtiers conspired against him and murdered
25 him in his house; but the people of the land killed all the conspirators
and made his son Josiah king in his place.

[a] temple mount: *lit.* mount of the house of the LORD. [b] *So one MS.; others* my seers.
[c] the garden-tomb of: *prob. rdg., cp. 2 Kgs. 21. 18; Heb. om.* [d] *Verses 21–25: cp. 2 Kgs.
21. 19–24.*

JOSIAH WAS EIGHT YEARS OLD when he came to the throne, and he 34 1*a*
reigned in Jerusalem for thirty-one years. He did what was right in the 2
eyes of the LORD; he followed in the footsteps of his forefather David,
swerving neither right nor left. In the eighth year of his reign, when he 3
was still a boy, he began to seek guidance of the God of his forefather
David; and in the twelfth year he began to purge Judah and Jerusalem
of the hill-shrines and the sacred poles, and the carved idols and the
images of metal. He saw to it that the altars for the Baalim were 4
destroyed and he hacked down the incense-altars which stood above
them; he broke in pieces the sacred poles and the carved and metal
images, grinding them to powder and scattering it on the graves of
those who had sacrificed to them. He also burnt the bones of the priests 5
on their altars and purged Judah and Jerusalem. In the cities of 6
Manasseh, Ephraim, and Simeon, and as far as Naphtali, he burnt
down their houses wherever he found them; he destroyed the altars 7
and the sacred poles, ground the idols to powder, and hacked down the
incense-altars throughout the land of Israel. Then he returned to
Jerusalem.

In the eighteenth year of his reign, after he had purified the land and 8*b*
the house, he sent Shaphan son of Azaliah and Maaseiah the governor
of the city and Joah son of Joahaz the secretary of state to repair the
house of the LORD his God. They came to Hilkiah the high priest and 9
gave him the silver that had been brought to the house of God, the
silver which the Levites, on duty at the threshold, had gathered from
Manasseh, Ephraim, and all the rest of Israel, as well as from Judah
and Benjamin and the inhabitants of Jerusalem. It was then handed 10
over to the foremen in charge of the work in the house of the LORD,
and these men, working in the house, used it for repairing and
strengthening the fabric; they gave it also to the carpenters and builders 11
to buy hewn stone, and timber for rafters and beams, for the buildings
which the kings of Judah had allowed to fall into ruin. The men did 12–13
their work honestly under the direction of Jahath and Obadiah,
Levites of the line of Merari, and Zechariah and Meshullam, members
of the family of Kohath. These also had control of the porters and
directed the workmen of every trade. The Levites were all skilled
musicians, and some of them were secretaries, clerks, or door-keepers.
When they fetched the silver which had been brought to the house of 14
the LORD, the priest Hilkiah discovered the book of the law of the LORD
which had been given through Moses. Then Hilkiah told Shaphan the 15
adjutant-general, 'I have discovered the book of the law in the house
of the LORD.' Hilkiah gave the book to Shaphan, and he brought it to 16
the king and reported to him: 'Your servants are doing all that was

[*a*] *Verses 1, 2: cp. 2 Kgs. 22. 1, 2.*   [*b*] *Verses 8–32: cp. 2 Kgs. 22. 3–23. 3.*

17 entrusted to them. They have melted down the silver in the house of the LORD and have handed it over to the foremen and the workmen.'

18 Shaphan the adjutant-general also told the king that the priest Hilkiah had given him a book; and he read it out in the king's presence.

19 When the king heard what was in the book of the law, he rent his

20 clothes, and ordered Hilkiah, Ahikam son of Shaphan, Abdon son of Micah, Shaphan the adjutant-general, and Asaiah the king's attendant,

21 to go and seek guidance of the LORD, for himself and for all who still remained in Israel and Judah, about the contents of the book that had been discovered. 'Great is the wrath of the LORD,' he said, 'and it has been poured out upon us because our forefathers did not observe the command of the LORD and do all that is written in this book.'

22 So Hilkiah and those whom the king had instructed*a* went to Huldah the prophetess, wife of Shallum son of Tikvah,*b* son of Hasrah, the keeper of the wardrobe, and consulted her at her home in the second

23 quarter of Jerusalem. 'This is the word of the LORD the God of Israel,'

24 she answered: 'Say to the man who sent you to me, "This is the word of the LORD: I am bringing disaster on this place and its inhabitants, fulfilling all the imprecations recorded in the book which was read in

25 the presence of the king of Judah, because they have forsaken me and burnt sacrifices to other gods, provoking my anger with all the idols they have made with their own hands; therefore my wrath is poured

26 out upon this place and will not be quenched." This is what you shall say to the king of Judah who sent you to seek guidance of the LORD: "This is the word of the LORD the God of Israel: You have listened to

27 my words and shown a willing heart, you humbled yourself before God when you heard what I said about this place and its inhabitants; you humbled yourself and rent your clothes and wept before me. Because of all this,*c* I for my part have heard you. This is the very word of the

28 LORD. Therefore, I will gather you to your forefathers, and you will be gathered to your grave in peace; you will not live to see all the disaster which I am bringing upon this place and upon its inhabitants."' So they brought back word to the king.

29 Then the king sent and called all the elders of Judah and Jerusalem

30 together, and went up to the house of the LORD; he took with him all the men of Judah and the inhabitants of Jerusalem, the priests and the Levites, the whole population, high and low. There he read them the

31 whole book of the covenant discovered in the house of the LORD; and then, standing on the dais,*d* the king made a covenant before the LORD to obey him and keep his commandments, his testimonies, and his statutes, with all his heart and soul, and so fulfil the terms of the covenant

[a] had instructed: *so Sept.; Heb. om.* [b] *Prob. rdg., cp. 2 Kgs. 22. 14; Heb.* Tokhath. [c] Because of all this: *prob. rdg.; Heb. om.* [d] on the dais: *so Sept.; Heb. in his place.*

written in this book. Then he swore an oath with all who were present 32
in Jerusalem to keep the covenant.*a* Thereafter the inhabitants of
Jerusalem did obey the covenant of God, the God of their fathers.
Josiah removed all abominable things from all the territories of the 33
Israelites, so that everyone living in Israel might serve the LORD his
God. As long as he lived they did not fail in their allegiance to the LORD
the God of their fathers.

Josiah kept a Passover to the LORD in Jerusalem, and the passover 35
lamb was killed on the fourteenth day of the first month. He appointed 2
the priests to their offices and encouraged them to perform the service
of the house of the LORD. He said to the Levites, the teachers of Israel, 3
who were dedicated to the LORD, 'Put the holy Ark in the house
which Solomon son of David king of Israel built; it is not to be carried
about on your shoulders. Now is the time to serve the LORD your God
and his people Israel: prepare yourselves by families according to your 4
divisions, following the written instructions of David king of Israel and
those of Solomon his son; and stand in the Holy Place as representatives 5
of the family groups of the lay people, your brothers, one division of
Levites to each family group. Kill the passover lamb and hallow your- 6
selves and prepare for your brothers to fulfil the word of the LORD
given through Moses.'

Josiah contributed on behalf of all the lay people present thirty 7
thousand small cattle, that is young rams and goats, for the Passover, in
addition to three thousand bulls; all these were from the king's own
resources. And his officers contributed willingly for the people, the 8
priests, and the Levites. Hilkiah, Zechariah, and Jehiel, the chief
officers of the house of God, gave on behalf of the priests two thousand
six hundred small cattle for the Passover, in addition to three hundred
bulls. And Conaniah, Shemaiah and Nethaneel his brothers, and 9
Hashabiah, Jeiel, and Jozabad, the chiefs of the Levites, gave on behalf
of the Levites for the Passover five thousand small cattle in addition
to five hundred bulls.

When the service had been arranged, the priests stood in their 10
places and the Levites in their divisions, according to the king's
command. They killed the passover victim, and the priests flung the 11
blood*b* against the altar as the Levites flayed the animals. Then they 12
removed the fat flesh,*c* which they allocated to the people by groups of
families for them to offer to the LORD, as prescribed in the book of
Moses; and so with the bulls. They cooked the passover victim over the 13
fire according to custom, and boiled the holy offerings in pots, cauldrons,
and pans, and served them quickly to all the people. After that they 14

[a] to keep the covenant: *prob. rdg., cp. 2 Kgs. 23. 3; Heb.* and Benjamin.   [b] the blood:
so Pesh.; Heb. from their hand.   [c] fat flesh: *or* whole-offering.

made the necessary preparations for themselves and the priests, because the priests of Aaron's line were engaged till nightfall in offering whole-offerings and the fat portions; so the Levites made the necessary
15 preparations for themselves and for the priests of Aaron's line. The singers, the sons of Asaph, were in their places according to the rules laid down by David and by Asaph, Heman, and Jeduthun, the king's seers.*a* The door-keepers stood, each at his gate; there was no need for them to leave their posts, because their kinsmen the Levites had made the preparations for them.
16 In this manner all the service of the LORD was arranged that day, to keep the Passover and to offer whole-offerings on the altar of the LORD,
17 according to the command of King Josiah. The people of Israel who were present kept the Passover at that time and the pilgrim-feast of
18 Unleavened Bread for seven days. No Passover like it had been kept in Israel since the days of the prophet Samuel; none of the kings of Israel had ever kept such a Passover as Josiah kept, with the priests and Levites and all Judah and Israel who were present and the inhabitants of Jeru-
19 salem. In the eighteenth year of Josiah's reign this Passover was kept.
20 After Josiah had thus organized all the service of the house, Necho king of Egypt marched up to attack Carchemish on the Euphrates; and
21 Josiah went out to confront him. But Necho sent envoys to him, saying, 'What do you want with me, king of Judah? I have no quarrel with you today, only with those with whom I am at war. God has purposed to speed me on my way, and God is on my side; do not stand in his
22 way, or he will destroy you.' Josiah would not be deflected from his purpose but insisted on fighting; he refused to listen to Necho's words spoken at God's command, and he sallied out to join battle in the vale
23 of Megiddo. The archers shot at him; he was severely wounded and
24 told his bodyguard to carry him off. They lifted him out of his chariot and carried him in his viceroy's chariot to Jerusalem. There he died and was buried among the tombs of his ancestors, and all Judah and
25 Jerusalem mourned for him. Jeremiah also made a lament for Josiah; and to this day the minstrels, both men and women, commemorate Josiah in their lamentations. Such laments have become traditional in Israel, and they are found in the written collections.
26 The other events of Josiah's reign, and his works of piety, all performed in accordance with what is laid down in the law of the LORD,
27 and his acts, from first to last, are recorded in the annals of the kings of Israel and Judah.

36 1*b* THE PEOPLE OF THE LAND took Josiah's son Jehoahaz and made
2 him king in place of his father in Jerusalem. He was twenty-three years

[a] *So some MSS.; others* seer.   [b] *Verses 1–4: cp. 2 Kgs. 23. 30–34.*

old when he came to the throne, and he reigned in Jerusalem for three months. Then Necho king of Egypt deposed him and fined the 3 country a hundred talents of silver and one talent of gold, and made 4 his brother Eliakim king over Judah and Jerusalem in his place, changing his name to Jehoiakim; he also carried away his brother Jehoahaz to Egypt. Jehoiakim was twenty-five years old when he came 5 to the throne, and he reigned in Jerusalem for eleven years. He did what was wrong in the eyes of the LORD his God. So Nebuchadnezzar 6 king of Babylon marched against him and put him in fetters and took him to Babylon. He also removed to Babylon some of the vessels of 7 the house of the LORD and put them into his own palace there. The other 8 events of Jehoiakim's reign, including the abominations he committed, and everything of which he was held guilty, are recorded in the annals of the kings of Israel and Judah. He was succeeded by his son Jehoiachin.

Jehoiachin was eight years old when he came to the throne, and he 9[a] reigned in Jerusalem for three months and ten days. He did what was wrong in the eyes of the LORD. At the turn of the year King Nebuchad- 10 nezzar sent and brought him to Babylon, together with the choicest vessels of the house of the LORD, and made his father's brother[b] Zedekiah king over Judah and Jerusalem.

Zedekiah was twenty-one years old when he came to the throne, and 11 he reigned in Jerusalem for eleven years. He did what was wrong in the 12 eyes of the LORD his God; he did not defer to the guidance of the prophet Jeremiah, the spokesman of the LORD. He also rebelled against 13 King Nebuchadnezzar, who had laid on him a solemn oath of allegiance. He was obstinate and stubborn and refused to return to the LORD the God of Israel. All the chiefs of Judah and[c] the priests and the 14 people became more and more unfaithful, following all the abominable practices of the other nations; and they defiled the house of the LORD which he had hallowed in Jerusalem. The LORD God of their fathers 15 had warned them betimes through his messengers, for he took pity on his people and on his dwelling-place; but they never ceased to deride 16 his messengers, scorn his words and scoff at his prophets, until the anger of the LORD burst out against his people and could not be appeased. So he brought against them the king of the Chaldaeans, who 17[d] put their young men to the sword in the sanctuary and spared neither young man nor maiden, neither the old nor the weak; God gave them all into his power. And he brought all the vessels of the house of God, 18 great and small, and the treasures of the house of the LORD and of the king and his officers—all these he brought to Babylon. And they burnt 19

[a] *Verses 9, 10: cp. 2 Kgs. 24. 8–17.*   [b] father's brother: *so Sept.;* Heb. brother.   [c] Judah and: *so Sept.;* Heb. om.   [d] *Verses 17–20: cp. 2 Kgs. 25. 1–17.*

down the house of God, razed the city wall of Jerusalem and burnt
down all its stately mansions and all their precious possessions until
20 everything was destroyed. Those who escaped the sword he took
captive to Babylon, and they became slaves to him and his sons until
21 the sovereignty passed to the Persians, while the land of Israel ran the
full term of its sabbaths. All the time that it lay desolate it kept the
sabbath rest, to complete seventy years in fulfilment of the word of the
Lord by the prophet Jeremiah.

22ᵃ   Now in the first year of Cyrus king of Persia, so that the word of the
Lord spoken through Jeremiah might be fulfilled, the Lord stirred up
the heart of Cyrus king of Persia; and he issued a proclamation
throughout his kingdom, both by word of mouth and in writing, to this
effect:

23   This is the word of Cyrus king of Persia: The Lord the God of
heaven has given me all the kingdoms of the earth, and he himself
has charged me to build him a house at Jerusalem in Judah. To every
man of his people now among you I say, the Lord his God be*ᵇ* with
him, and let him go up.

[a] *Verses 22, 23: cp. Ezra 1. 1–3.*   [b] be: *prob. rdg., cp. Ezra 1. 3; Heb. om.*

THE BOOK OF

EZRA

The return of the exiles to Jerusalem

NOW IN THE FIRST YEAR of Cyrus king of Persia, 1
so that the word of the LORD spoken through Jeremiah might
be fulfilled, the LORD stirred up the heart of Cyrus king of
Persia; and he issued a proclamation throughout his kingdom, both by
word of mouth and in writing, to this effect:

This is the word of Cyrus king of Persia: The LORD the God of 2
heaven has given me all the kingdoms of the earth, and he himself
has charged me to build him a house at Jerusalem in Judah. To every 3
man of his people now among you I say, God be with him, and let
him go up to Jerusalem in Judah, and rebuild the house of the LORD
the God of Israel, the God whose city is Jerusalem. And every 4
remaining Jew, wherever he may be living, may claim aid from his
neighbours in that place, silver and gold, goods*a* and cattle, in
addition to the voluntary offerings for the house of God in Jerusalem.

Thereupon the heads of families of Judah and Benjamin, and the 5
priests and the Levites, answered the summons, all whom God had
moved to go up to rebuild the house of the LORD in Jerusalem. Their 6
neighbours all assisted them with gifts of every kind, silver*b* and gold,
goods*a* and cattle and valuable gifts in abundance,*c* in addition to any
voluntary service. Moreover, Cyrus king of Persia produced the vessels 7
of the house of the LORD which Nebuchadnezzar had removed from
Jerusalem and placed in the temple of his god; and he handed them 8
over into the charge of Mithredath the treasurer, who made an
inventory of them for Sheshbazzar the ruler of Judah. This was the 9
list: thirty gold basins, a thousand silver basins, twenty-nine vessels of
various kinds, thirty golden bowls, four hundred and ten silver bowls 10
of various types, and a thousand other vessels. The vessels of gold and 11
silver amounted in all to five thousand four hundred; and Sheshbazzar
took them all up to Jerusalem, when the exiles were brought back from
Babylon.

Of the captives whom Nebuchadnezzar king of Babylon had taken 2 1*d*
into exile in Babylon, these were the people of the province who

[*a*] Or pack-animals.　[*b*] with gifts...silver: *prob. rdg., cp. 1 Esdras 2. 9; Heb.* with vessels
of silver.　[*c*] in abundance: *prob. rdg., cp. 1 Esdras 2. 9; Heb.* apart.　[*d*] *Verses 1–70:
cp. Neh. 7. 6–73.*

2 returned to Jerusalem and Judah, each to his own city, led by Zerubbabel, Jeshua,[a] Nehemiah, Seraiah, Reelaiah, Mordecai, Bilshan,
Mispar, Bigvai, Rehum and Baanah.

3   The roll of the men of the people of Israel: the family of Parosh, two
4 thousand one hundred and seventy-two; the family of Shephatiah,
5 three hundred and seventy-two; the family of Arah, seven hundred and
6 seventy-five; the family of Pahath-moab, namely the families of Jeshua
7 and[b] Joab, two thousand eight hundred and twelve; the family of Elam,
8 one thousand two hundred and fifty-four; the family of Zattu, nine
9 hundred and forty-five; the family of Zaccai, seven hundred and sixty;
10, 11 the family of Bani, six hundred and forty-two; the family of Bebai, six
12 hundred and twenty-three; the family of Azgad, one thousand two
13 hundred and twenty-two; the family of Adonikam, six hundred and
14, 15 sixty-six; the family of Bigvai, two thousand and fifty-six; the family
16 of Adin, four hundred and fifty-four; the family of Ater, namely that of
17 Hezekiah, ninety-eight; the family of Bezai, three hundred and twenty-
18, 19 three; the family of Jorah, one hundred and twelve; the family of
20 Hashum, two hundred and twenty-three; the family of Gibbar,
21 ninety-five. The men[c] of Bethlehem, one hundred and twenty-three;
22, 23 the men of Netophah, fifty-six; the men of Anathoth, one hundred and
24, 25 twenty-eight; the men of Beth-azmoth,[d] forty-two; the men of Kiriath-
26 jearim,[e] Kephirah, and Beeroth, seven hundred and forty-three; the
27 men[f] of Ramah and Geba, six hundred and twenty-one; the men of
28 Michmas, one hundred and twenty-two; the men of Bethel and Ai, two
29, 30 hundred and twenty-three; the men[g] of Nebo, fifty-two; the men of
31 Magbish, one hundred and fifty-six; the men of the other Elam, one
32 thousand two hundred and fifty-four; the men of Harim, three hundred
33 and twenty; the men of Lod, Hadid, and Ono, seven hundred and
34, 35 twenty-five; the men of Jericho, three hundred and forty-five; the men
of Senaah, three thousand six hundred and thirty.

36   Priests: the family of Jedaiah, of the line of Jeshua, nine hundred and
37, 38 seventy-three; the family of Immer, one thousand and fifty-two; the
39 family of Pashhur, one thousand two hundred and forty-seven; the
family of Harim, one thousand and seventeen.

40   Levites: the families of Jeshua and Kadmiel, of the line of Hodaviah,
41 seventy-four. Singers: the family of Asaph, one hundred and twenty-
42 eight. The guild of door-keepers: the family of Shallum, the family of
Ater, the family of Talmon, the family of Akkub, the family of Hatita,
and the family of Shobai, one hundred and thirty-nine in all.

[a] Or Joshua (cp. Hag. 1. 1). [b] and: prob. rdg., cp. Neh. 7. 11; Heb. om. [c] Prob. rdg.,
cp. Neh. 7. 26; Heb. family. [d] Prob. rdg., cp. Neh. 7. 28; Heb. the family of Azmoth.
[e] Prob. rdg., cp. Neh. 7. 29; Heb. the family of Kiriath-arim. [f] Prob. rdg., cp. Neh. 7.
30; Heb. family. [g] Prob. rdg.; Heb. family (also in verses 30–35).

Temple-servitors:[a] the family of Ziha, the family of Hasupha, the 43
family of Tabbaoth, the family of Keros, the family of Siaha, the family 44
of Padon, the family of Lebanah, the family of Hagabah, the family of 45
Akkub, the family of Hagab, the family of Shamlai,[b] the family of 46
Hanan, the family of Giddel, the family of Gahar, the family of Reaiah, 47
the family of Rezin, the family of Nekoda, the family of Gazzam, 48
the family of Uzza, the family of Paseah, the family of Besai, the family 49, 50
of Asnah, the family of the Meunim,[c] the family of the Nephusim,[d]
the family of Bakbuk, the family of Hakupha, the family of Harhur, the 51, 52
family of Bazluth, the family of Mehida, the family of Harsha, the 53
family of Barkos, the family of Sisera, the family of Temah, the family 54
of Neziah, and the family of Hatipha.

Descendants of Solomon's servants: the family of Sotai, the family of 55
Hassophereth, the family of Peruda, the family of Jaalah, the family 56
of Darkon, the family of Giddel, the family of Shephatiah, the family of 57
Hattil, the family of Pochereth-hazzebaim, and the family of Ami.

The temple-servitors and the descendants of Solomon's servants 58
amounted to three hundred and ninety-two in all.

The following were those who returned from Tel-melah, Tel-harsha, 59
Kerub, Addan, and Immer, but could not establish their father's family
nor whether by descent they belonged to Israel: the family of Delaiah, 60
the family of Tobiah, and the family of Nekoda, six hundred and
fifty-two. Also of the priests: the family of Hobaiah, the family of 61
Hakkoz, and the family of Barzillai who had married a daughter of
Barzillai the Gileadite and went by his[e] name. These searched for their 62
names among those enrolled in the genealogies, but they could not be
found; they were disqualified for the priesthood as unclean, and the 63
governor forbade them to partake of the most sacred food until there
should be a priest able to consult the Urim and the Thummim.

The whole assembled people numbered forty-two thousand three 64
hundred and sixty, apart from their slaves, male and female, of whom 65
there were seven thousand three hundred and thirty-seven; and they
had two hundred singers, men and women. Their horses numbered 66
seven hundred and thirty-six, their mules two hundred and forty-five,
their camels four hundred and thirty-five, and their asses six thousand 67
seven hundred and twenty.

When they came to the house of the LORD in Jerusalem, some of the 68
heads of families volunteered to rebuild the house of God on its original
site. According to their resources they gave for the fabric fund a total 69
of sixty-one thousand drachmas of gold, five thousand minas of silver,
and one hundred priestly robes.

[a] *Heb.* Nethinim.　[b] *Or* Shalmai (*cp. Neh. 7. 48*).　[c] *Or* Meinim.　[d] *Or* Nephisim.
[e] *Prob. rdg., cp. 1 Esdras 5. 38; Heb.* their.

70   The priests, the Levites, and some of the people lived in Jerusalem and its suburbs;[a] the singers, the door-keepers, and temple-servitors,[b] and all other Israelites, lived in their own towns.

Worship restored and the temple rebuilt

3   WHEN THE SEVENTH MONTH CAME, the Israelites now being settled in their towns, the people assembled as one man in
2 Jerusalem. Then Jeshua son of Jozadak and his fellow-priests, and Zerubbabel son of Shealtiel and his kinsmen, set to work and built the altar of the God of Israel, in order to offer upon it whole-offerings as
3 prescribed in the law of Moses the man of God. They put the altar in place first, because they lived in fear of the foreign population; and they offered upon it whole-offerings to the LORD, both morning and
4 evening offerings. They kept the pilgrim-feast of Tabernacles[c] as ordained, and offered whole-offerings every day in the number
5 prescribed for each day, and, in addition to these, the regular whole-offerings and the offerings for sabbaths,[d] for new moons and for all the sacred seasons appointed by the LORD, and all voluntary offerings
6 brought to the LORD. The offering of whole-offerings began from the first day of the seventh month, although the foundation of the temple
7 of the LORD had not yet been laid. They gave money for the masons and carpenters, and food and drink and oil for the Sidonians and the Tyrians to fetch cedar-wood from the Lebanon to the roadstead at Joppa, by licence from Cyrus king of Persia.
8   In the second year after their return to the house of God in Jerusalem, and in the second month, Zerubbabel son of Shealtiel and Jeshua son of Jozadak started work, aided by all their fellow-Israelites, the priests and the Levites and all who had returned from captivity to Jerusalem. They appointed Levites from the age of twenty years and
9 upwards to supervise the work of the house of the LORD. Jeshua with his sons and his kinsmen, Kadmiel, Binnui, and Hodaviah,[e] together assumed control of those responsible for the work on the house of God.[f]
10   When the builders had laid the foundation of the temple of the LORD, the priests in their robes took their places with their trumpets, and the Levites, the sons of Asaph, with their cymbals, to praise the
11 LORD in the manner prescribed by David king of Israel; and they

[a] in Jerusalem and its suburbs: *prob. rdg., cp. 1 Esdras 5. 46; Heb. om.*   [b] *Prob. rdg.; Heb. adds* in their towns.   [c] *Or* Booths.   [d] for sabbaths: *prob. rdg., cp. 1 Esdras 5. 52; Heb. om.* [e] Binnui, and Hodaviah: *prob. rdg.; Heb.* and his sons the family of Judah.   [f] *Prob. rdg.; Heb. adds* the family of Henadad, their family and their kinsmen the Levites.

chanted praises and thanksgiving to the LORD, singing, 'It is good to give thanks to the LORD,*a* for his love towards Israel endures for ever.' All the people raised a great shout of praise to the LORD because the foundation of the house of the LORD had been laid. But many of the 12 priests and Levites and heads of families, who were old enough to have seen the former house, wept and wailed aloud when they saw the foundation of this house laid, while many others shouted for joy at the top of their voice. The people could not distinguish the sound of the 13 shout of joy from that of the weeping and wailing, so great was the shout which the people were raising, and the sound could be heard a long way off.

When the enemies of Judah and Benjamin heard that the returned 4 exiles were building a temple to the LORD the God of Israel, they 2 approached Zerubbabel and Jeshua*b* and the heads of families and said to them, 'Let us join you in building, for like you we seek your God, and we have been sacrificing to him ever*c* since the days of Esarhaddon king of Assyria, who brought us here.' But Zerubbabel and Jeshua and 3 the rest of the heads of families in Israel said to them, 'The house which we are building for our God is no concern of yours. We alone will build it for the LORD the God of Israel, as his majesty Cyrus king of Persia commanded us.'

Then the people of the land caused the Jews to lose heart and made 4 them afraid to continue building; and in order to defeat their purpose 5 they bribed officials at court to act against them. This continued throughout the reign of Cyrus and into the reign of Darius king of Persia.

At the beginning of the reign of Ahasuerus, the people of the land 6 brought a charge in writing against the inhabitants of Judah and Jerusalem.

And in the days of Artaxerxes king of Persia, with the agreement of 7 Mithredath, Tabeel and all his colleagues wrote to him; the letter was written in Aramaic and read aloud in Aramaic.

Rehum the high commissioner and Shimshai the secretary wrote a 8*d* letter to King Artaxerxes concerning Jerusalem in the following terms:

From Rehum the high commissioner, Shimshai the secretary, and 9 all their colleagues, the judges, the commissioners, the overseers, and chief officers, the men of Erech and Babylon, and the Elamites in Susa, and the other peoples whom the great and renowned Asnappar*e* 10 deported and settled in the city of Samaria and in the rest of the province of Beyond-Euphrates.

[a] to give thanks to the LORD: *prob. rdg., cp. Ps. 106. 1; Heb. om.* [b] and Jeshua: *prob. rdg., cp. 1 Esdras 5. 68; Heb. om.* [c] and we...ever: *or, as otherwise read,* but we have not sacrificed. [d] *From 4. 8 to 6. 18 the text is in Aramaic.* [e] *Or* Osnappar.

11 Here follows the text of their letter:

To King Artaxerxes from his servants, the men of the province of Beyond-Euphrates:

12 Be it known to Your Majesty that the Jews who left you and came to these parts have reached Jerusalem and are rebuilding that wicked and rebellious city; they have surveyed*a* the foundations and are

13 completing*b* the walls. Be it known to Your Majesty that, if their city is rebuilt and the walls are completed, they will pay neither general levy, nor poll-tax, nor land-tax, and in the end*c* they will harm the

14 monarchy. Now, because we eat the king's salt and it is not right that we should witness the king's dishonour, therefore we have sent to

15 inform Your Majesty, in order that search may be made in the annals of your predecessors. You will discover by searching through the annals that this has been a rebellious city, harmful to the monarchy and its provinces, and that sedition has long been rife within its walls.

16 That is why the city was laid waste. We submit to Your Majesty that, if it is rebuilt and its walls are completed, the result will be that you will have no more footing in the province of Beyond-Euphrates.

17 The king sent this answer:

To Rehum the high commissioner, Shimshai the secretary, and all your colleagues resident in Samaria and in the rest of the province

18 of Beyond-Euphrates, greeting. The letter which you sent to me has

19 now been read clearly in my presence. I have given orders and search has been made, and it has been found that the city in question has a long history of revolt against the monarchy, and that rebellion and

20 sedition have been rife in it. Powerful kings have ruled in Jerusalem, exercising authority over the whole province of Beyond-Euphrates,

21 and general levy, poll-tax, and land-tax have been paid to them. Therefore, issue orders that these men must desist. This city is not to be

22 rebuilt until a decree to that effect is issued by me. See that you do not neglect your duty in this matter, lest more damage and harm be done to the monarchy.

23 When the text of the letter from King Artaxerxes was read before Rehum the high commissioner,*d* Shimshai the secretary, and their colleagues, they hurried to Jerusalem and forcibly compelled the Jews

24 to stop work. From then onwards the work on the house of God in Jerusalem stopped; and it remained at a standstill till the second year of the reign of Darius king of Persia.

[*a*] have surveyed: *prob. rdg.; Aram.* are surveying. [*b*] are completing: *so Vulg.; Aram.* have completed. [*c*] in the end: *or* certainly. [*d*] the high commissioner: *so Pesh.; Aram.* om.

But the prophets Haggai[a] and Zechariah grandson[b] of Iddo up- 5
braided the Jews in Judah and Jerusalem, prophesying in the name of
the God of Israel. Then Zerubbabel son of Shealtiel and Jeshua son 2
of Jozadak at once began to rebuild the house of God in Jerusalem, and
the prophets of God were with them and supported them. Tattenai, 3
governor of the province of Beyond-Euphrates, Shethar-bozenai, and
their colleagues promptly came to them and said, 'Who issued a decree
permitting you to rebuild this house and complete its furnishings?'
They[c] also asked them for the names of the men engaged in the building. 4
But the elders of the Jews were under God's watchful eye, and they 5
were not prevented from continuing the work, until such time as a
report should reach Darius and a royal letter should be received in
answer.

Here follows the text of the letter sent by Tattenai, governor of the 6
province of Beyond-Euphrates, Shethar-bozenai, and his colleagues,
the inspectors in the province of Beyond-Euphrates, to King Darius.
This is the written report that they sent: 7

To King Darius, all greetings. Be it known to Your Majesty that 8
we went to the province of Judah and found the house of the great
God being rebuilt by the Jewish elders,[d] with massive stones and
timbers laid in the walls. The work was being done thoroughly and
was making good progress under their direction. We asked these 9
elders who had issued a decree for the rebuilding of this house and
the completion of the furnishings. We also asked them for their names, 10
so that we might make a list of the leaders for your information. This 11
was their reply: 'We are the servants of the God of heaven and earth,
and we are rebuilding the house originally built many years ago;
a great king of Israel built it and completed it. But because our fore- 12
fathers provoked the anger of the God of heaven, he put them into
the power of Nebuchadnezzar the Chaldaean, king of Babylon, who
pulled down this house and carried the people captive to Babylon.
However, Cyrus king of Babylon in the first year of his reign issued 13
a decree that this house of God should be rebuilt. Moreover, there 14
were gold and silver vessels of the house of God, which Nebuchadnezzar had taken from the temple in Jerusalem and put in the
temple in Babylon; and these King Cyrus took out of the temple in
Babylon. He gave them to a man named Sheshbazzar, whom he had
appointed governor, and said to him, "Take these vessels; go and 15
restore them to the temple in Jerusalem, and let the house of God
there be rebuilt on its original site." Then this Sheshbazzar came and 16

[a] *Prob. rdg., cp. 1 Esdras 6. 1; Aram. adds* the prophet.　[b] *Lit.* son.　[c] *So Pesh.; Aram.*
We.　[d] by...elders: *prob. rdg., cp. 1 Esdras 6. 8; Aram. om.*

laid the foundation of the house of God in Jerusalem; and from that time until now the rebuilding has continued, but it is not yet finished.'

17 Now, therefore, if it please Your Majesty, let search be made in the royal archives in Babylon, to discover whether a decree was issued by King Cyrus for the rebuilding of this house of God in Jerusalem. Then let the king send us his wishes in the matter.

6 Then King Darius issued an order, and search was made in the
2 archives where the treasures were deposited in Babylon. But it was in Ecbatana, in the royal residence in the province of Media, that a scroll was found, on which was written the following memorandum:

3 In the first year of King Cyrus, the king issued this decree concerning the house of God in Jerusalem: Let the house be rebuilt as a place where sacrifices are offered and fire-offerings brought. Its
4 height shall be sixty cubits and its breadth sixty cubits, with three courses of massive stones and one[a] course of timber, the cost to be
5 defrayed from the royal treasury. Also the gold and silver vessels of the house of God, which Nebuchadnezzar took out of the temple in Jerusalem and brought to Babylon, shall be restored; they shall all be taken back to the temple in Jerusalem, and restored each to its place in the house of God.

6 Then King Darius issued this order:[b]

Now, Tattenai, governor of the province of Beyond-Euphrates, Shethar-bozenai, and your colleagues, the inspectors in the province
7 of Beyond-Euphrates, you are to keep away from the place, and to leave the governor of the Jews and their elders free to rebuild this
8 house of God; let them rebuild it on its original site. I also issue an order prescribing what you are to do for these elders of the Jews, so that the said house of God may be rebuilt. Their expenses are to be defrayed in full from the royal funds accruing from the taxes of the province of Beyond-Euphrates, so that the work may not be brought
9 to a standstill. And let them have daily without fail whatever they want, young bulls, rams, or lambs as whole-offerings for the God of heaven, or wheat, salt, wine, or oil, as the priests in Jerusalem demand,
10 so that they may offer soothing sacrifices to the God of heaven, and
11 pray for the life of the king and his sons. Furthermore, I decree that, if any man tampers with this edict, a beam shall be pulled out of his house and he shall be fastened erect to it and flogged; and, in
12 addition, his house shall be forfeit.[c] And may the God who made that place a dwelling for his Name overthrow any king or people that

[a] *Prob. rdg., cp. 1 Esdras 6. 25; Aram.* a new. [b] Then...order: *prob. rdg., cp. 1 Esdras 6. 27; Aram. om.* [c] *Or* made into a dunghill (*mng. of Aram. word uncertain*).

shall presume to tamper with this edict or to destroy this house of God in Jerusalem. I Darius have issued a decree; it is to be carried out to the letter.

Then Tattenai, governor of the province of Beyond-Euphrates, 13 Shethar-bozenai, and their colleagues carried out to the letter the instructions which King Darius had sent them, and the elders of the 14 Jews went on with the rebuilding. As a result of the prophecies of Haggai the prophet and Zechariah grandson[a] of Iddo they had good success and finished the rebuilding as commanded by the God of Israel and according to the decrees of Cyrus and Darius;[b] and the house was 15 completed on the twenty-third[c] day of the month Adar, in the sixth year of King Darius.

Then the people of Israel, the priests and the Levites and all the other 16 exiles who had returned, celebrated the dedication of the house of God with great rejoicing. For its dedication they offered one hundred bulls, 17 two hundred rams, and four hundred lambs, and as a sin-offering for all Israel twelve he-goats, corresponding to the number of the tribes of Israel. And they re-established the priests in their groups and the 18 Levites in their divisions for the service of God in Jerusalem, as prescribed in the book of Moses.

On the fourteenth day of the first month the exiles who had returned 19 kept the Passover. The priests and the Levites, one and all, had purified 20 themselves; all of them were ritually clean, and they killed the passover lamb for all the exiles who had returned, for their fellow-priests and for themselves. It was eaten by the Israelites who had come back from 21 exile and by all who had separated themselves from the peoples of the land and their uncleanness and sought the Lord the God of Israel. And 22 they kept the pilgrim-feast of Unleavened Bread for seven days with rejoicing; for the Lord had given them cause for joy by changing the disposition of the king of Assyria towards them, so that he encouraged them in the work of the house of God, the God of Israel.

Ezra's mission to Jerusalem

NOW AFTER THESE EVENTS, in the reign of Artaxerxes king of 7 Persia, there came up from Babylon one Ezra son of Seraiah, son of Azariah, son of Hilkiah, son of Shallum, son of Zadok, son[d] 2 of Ahitub, son of Amariah, son of Azariah, son of Meraioth, son of 3, 4

[a] *Lit.* son.   [b] *Prob. rdg.; Aram. adds* and Artaxerxes king of Persia.   [c] *Prob. rdg.,* cp. 1 Esdras 7. 5; Aram. third.   [d] *Or* grandson.

5 Zerahiah, son of Uzzi, son of Bukki, son of Abishua, son of Phinehas,
6 son of Eleazar, son of Aaron the chief priest. He was a scribe*a* learned
in the law of Moses which the LORD the God of Israel had given them;
and the king granted him all that he asked, for the hand of the LORD his
7 God was upon him. In the seventh year of King Artaxerxes, other
Israelites, priests, Levites, singers, door-keepers, and temple-servitors
8 went up with him to Jerusalem; and they reached Jerusalem in the
9 fifth month, in the seventh year of the king. On the first day of the first
month Ezra fixed the day for departure from Babylon, and on the first
day of the fifth month he arrived at Jerusalem, for the gracious hand of
10 his God was upon him. For Ezra had devoted himself to the study and
observance of the law of the LORD and to teaching statute and ordinance
in Israel.

11   This is a copy of the royal letter which King Artaxerxes had given to
Ezra the priest and scribe, a scribe versed in questions concerning the
commandments and the statutes of the LORD laid upon Israel:

12*b*   Artaxerxes, king of kings, to Ezra the priest and scribe learned in
        the law of the God of heaven:
13   This is my decision. I hereby issue a decree that any of the people
        of Israel or of its priests or Levites in my kingdom who volunteer
14   to go to Jerusalem may go with you. You are sent by the king and his
        seven counsellors to find out how things stand in Judah and Jeru-
        salem with regard to the law of your God with which you are
15   entrusted. You are also to convey the silver and gold which the king
        and his counsellors have freely offered to the God of Israel whose
16   dwelling is in Jerusalem, together with any silver and gold that you
        may find throughout the province of Babylon, and the voluntary
        offerings of the people and of the priests which they freely offer for
17   the house of their God in Jerusalem. In pursuance of this decree you
        shall use the money solely for the purchase of bulls, rams, and lambs,
        and the proper grain-offerings and drink-offerings, to be offered on
18   the altar in the house of your God in Jerusalem. Further, should any
        silver and gold be left over, you and your colleagues may use it at
19   your discretion according to the will of your God. The vessels which
        have been given you for the service of the house of your God you
20   shall hand over to the God of Jerusalem; and if anything else should
        be required for the house of your God, which it may fall to you to
        provide, you may provide it out of the king's treasury.
21   And I, King Artaxerxes, issue an order to all treasurers in the
        province of Beyond-Euphrates that whatever is demanded of you by
        Ezra the priest, a scribe learned in the law of the God of heaven, is to

[*a*] *Or* doctor of the law.   [*b*] *The text of verses 12–26 is in Aramaic.*

be supplied exactly, up to a hundred talents of silver, a hundred kor 22
of wheat, a hundred bath of wine, a hundred bath of oil, and salt
without reckoning. Whatever is demanded by the God of heaven, let 23
it be diligently carried out for the house of the God of heaven; otherwise wrath may fall upon the realm of the king and his sons. We 24
also make known to you that you have no authority to impose general
levy, poll-tax, or land-tax on any of the priests, Levites, musicians,
door-keepers, temple-servitors, or other servants of this house of God.

And you, Ezra, in accordance with the wisdom of your God with 25
which you are entrusted, are to appoint arbitrators and judges to
judge all your people in the province of Beyond-Euphrates, all who
acknowledge the laws of your God;*a* and you and they are to instruct
those who do not acknowledge them. Whoever will not obey the law 26
of your God and the law of the king, let judgement be rigorously
executed upon him, be it death, banishment, confiscation of property,
or imprisonment.

Then Ezra said,*b* 'Blessed be the LORD the God of our fathers who 27
has prompted the king thus to add glory to the house of the LORD in
Jerusalem, and has made the king and his counsellors and all his high 28
officers well disposed towards me!'

So, knowing that the hand of the LORD my God was upon me,
I took courage and assembled leading men out of Israel to go up with me.

These are the heads of families, as registered, family by family, of 8
those who went up with me from Babylon in the reign of King Artaxerxes: of the family of Phinehas, Gershom; of the family of Ithamar, 2
Daniel; of the family of David, Hattush son of*c* Shecaniah; of the 3
family of Parosh, Zechariah, and with him a hundred and fifty males in
the register; of the family of Pahath-moab, Elihoenai son of Zerahiah, 4
and with him two hundred males; of the family of Zattu,*d* Shecaniah 5
son of Jahaziel, and with him three hundred males; of the family 6
of Adin, Ebed son of Jonathan, and with him fifty males; of the 7
family of Elam, Isaiah son of Athaliah, and with him seventy males; of 8
the family of Shephatiah, Zebadiah son of Michael, and with him eighty
males; of the family of Joab, Obadiah son of Jehiel, and with him two 9
hundred and eighteen males; of the family of Bani,*e* Shelomith son 10
of Josiphiah, and with him a hundred and sixty males; of the family of 11
Bebai, Zechariah son of Bebai, and with him twenty-eight males; of 12
the family of Azgad, Johanan son of Hakkatan, and with him a
hundred and ten males. The last were the family of Adonikam, and 13

[a] to judge...your God: *or* all of them versed in the laws of your God, to judge all the
people in the province of Beyond-Euphrates. [b] Then Ezra said: *prob. rdg., cp. 1 Esdras
8. 25; Heb. om.* [c] son of: *prob. rdg.; Heb.* of the family of. [d] of Zattu: *prob. rdg., cp.
1 Esdras 8. 32; Heb. om.* [e] of Bani: *prob. rdg., cp. 1 Esdras 8. 36; Heb. om.*

these were their names: Eliphelet, Jeiel, and Shemaiah, and with them
14 sixty males; and the family of Bigvai, Uthai and Zabbud, and with them seventy males.

15 I assembled them by the river which flows toward Ahava; and we encamped there three days. When I reviewed the people and the priests,
16 I found no Levite there. So I sent Eliezer, Ariel, Shemaiah, Elnathan, Jarib, Elnathan, Nathan, Zechariah, and Meshullam, prominent men,
17 and Joiarib and Elnathan, men of discretion, with instructions to go to Iddo, the chief man of the settlement at Casiphia; and I gave them a message for him and[a] his kinsmen, the temple-servitors there, asking
18 for servitors for the house of our God to be sent to us. And, because the gracious hand of our God was upon us, they let us have Sherebiah, a man of discretion, of the family of Mahli son of Levi, son of Israel,
19 together with his sons and kinsmen, eighteen men; also Hashabiah, together with Isaiah of the family of Merari, his kinsmen and their
20 sons, twenty men; besides two hundred and twenty temple-servitors (this was an order instituted by David and his officers to assist the Levites). These were all indicated by name.

21 Then I proclaimed a fast there by the river Ahava, so that we might mortify ourselves before our God and ask from him a safe journey for
22 ourselves, our dependants, and all our possessions. For I was ashamed to ask the king for an escort of soldiers and horsemen to help us against enemies on the way, because we had said to the king, 'The hand of our God is upon all who seek him, working their good; but his fierce
23 anger is on all who forsake him.' So we fasted and asked our God for a safe journey, and he answered our prayer.

24 Then I separated twelve of the chiefs of the priests, together with[b]
25 Sherebiah and Hashabiah and ten of their kinsmen, and handed over to them the silver and gold and the vessels which had been set aside by the king, his counsellors and his officers and all the Israelites who were
26 present, as their contribution to the house of our God. I handed over to them six hundred and fifty talents of silver, a hundred silver vessels
27 weighing two talents, a hundred talents of gold, twenty golden bowls worth a thousand drachmas, and two vessels of a fine red copper,[c]
28 precious as gold. And I said to the men, 'You are dedicated to the LORD, and the vessels too are sacred; the silver and gold are a voluntary
29 offering to the LORD the God of your fathers. Watch over them and guard them, until you hand them over in the presence of the chiefs of the priests and the Levites and the heads of families of Israel in Jerusalem, in the rooms of the house of the LORD.'
30 So the priests and Levites received the consignment of silver and gold

[a] and: *so Vulg.; Heb. om.* [b] together with: *prob. rdg., cp. 1 Esdras 8. 54; Heb. om.*
[c] red copper: *or* orichalc.

634

and vessels, to be taken to the house of our God in Jerusalem; and on 31
the twelfth day of the first month we left the river Ahava bound for
Jerusalem. The hand of our God was upon us, and he saved us from
enemy attack and from ambush on the way. When we arrived at 32
Jerusalem, we rested for three days. And on the fourth day the silver 33
and gold and the vessels were deposited in the house of our God in the
charge of Meremoth son of Uriah the priest, who had with him Eleazar
son of Phinehas, and they had with them the Levites Jozabad son of
Jeshua and Noadiah son of Binnui. Everything was checked as it was 34
handed over, and at the same time a written record was made of the
whole consignment. Then those who had come home from captivity, 35
the exiles who had returned, offered as whole-offerings to the God of
Israel twelve bulls for all Israel, ninety-six rams and seventy-two[a]
lambs, with twelve he-goats as a sin-offering; all these were offered as
a whole-offering to the LORD. They also delivered the king's commis- 36
sion to the royal satraps and governors in the province of Beyond-
Euphrates; and these gave support to the people and the house of God.

When all this had been done, some of the leaders approached me and 9
said, 'The people of Israel, including priests and Levites, have not
kept themselves apart from the foreign population and from the
abominable practices of the Canaanites, the Hittites, the Perizzites, the
Jebusites, the Ammonites, the Moabites, the Egyptians, and the
Amorites. They have taken women of these nations as wives for 2
themselves and their sons, so that the holy race has become mixed
with the foreign population; and the leaders and magistrates have been
the chief offenders.' When I heard this news, I rent my robe and mantle, 3
and tore my hair and my beard, and I sat dumbfounded; and all who 4
went in fear of the words of the God of Israel rallied to me because of
the offence of these exiles. I sat there dumbfounded till the evening
sacrifice.

Then, at the evening sacrifice, I rose from my humiliation and, in my 5
rent robe and mantle, I knelt down and spread out my hands to the
LORD my God and said, 'O my God, I am humiliated, I am ashamed 6
to lift my face to thee, my God; for we are sunk in our iniquities, and
our guilt is so great that it reaches high heaven. From the days of our 7
fathers down to this present day our guilt has been great. For our
iniquities we, our kings, and our priests have been subject to death,
captivity, pillage, and shameful humiliation at the hands of foreign
kings, and such is our present plight. But now, for a brief moment, the 8
LORD our God has been gracious to us, leaving us some survivors and
giving us a foothold in his holy place. He has brought light to our eyes
again and given us some chance to renew our lives in our slavery.

[a] *Prob. rdg., cp. 1 Esdras 8. 65; Heb.* seventy-seven.

9 For slaves we are; nevertheless, our God has not forsaken us in our slavery, but has made the kings of Persia so well disposed towards us as to give us the means of renewal, so that we may repair the house of our God and rebuild its ruins, and to give us a wall of defence in[a] Judah
10 and Jerusalem. Now, O our God, what are we to say after this? For we
11 have neglected the commands which thou gavest through thy servants the prophets, when thou saidst, "The land which you are entering and will possess is a polluted land, polluted by the foreign population with their abominable practices, which have made it unclean from end to end.
12 Therefore, do not give your daughters in marriage to their sons, and do not marry your sons to their daughters, and never seek their welfare or prosperity. Thus you will be strong and enjoy the good things of the land, and pass it on to your children as an everlasting possession."
13 Now, after all that we have suffered for our evil deeds and for our great guilt—although thou, our God, hast punished us less than our iniquities
14 deserved and hast allowed us to survive as now we do—shall we again disobey thy commands and join in marriage with peoples who indulge in such abominable practices? Would not thy anger against us be un-
15 relenting, until no remnant, no survivor was left? O LORD God of Israel, thou art righteous; now as before, we are only a remnant that has survived. Look upon us, guilty as we are in thy sight; for because of our guilt none of us can stand in thy presence.'

10 While Ezra was praying and making confession, prostrate in tears before the house of God, a very great crowd of Israelites assembled
2 round him, men, women, and children, and they all wept bitterly. Then Shecaniah son of Jehiel, one of the family of Elam, spoke up and said to Ezra, 'We have committed an offence against our God in marrying foreign wives, daughters of the foreign population. But in spite of
3 this, there is still hope for Israel. Now, therefore, let us pledge our-selves to our God to dismiss all these women and their brood, according to your advice, my lord, and the advice of those who go in fear of the command of our God; and let us act as the law prescribes.
4 Up now, the task is yours, and we will support you. Take courage and act.'
5 Ezra stood up and made the chiefs of the priests, the Levites, and all the Israelites swear to do as had been said; and they took the oath.
6 Then Ezra left his place in front of the house of God and went to the room of Jehohanan grandson[b] of Eliashib and lodged[c] there; he neither ate bread nor drank water, for he was mourning for the offence
7 committed by the exiles who had returned. Next, there was issued throughout Judah and Jerusalem a proclamation that all the exiles

[a] *Or* thereby giving us a wall of defence for...   [b] *Lit.* son.   [c] *Prob. rdg., cp. 1 Esdras* 9. 2; *Heb.* went.

should assemble in Jerusalem, and that if anyone did not arrive within 8
three days, it should be within the discretion of the chief officers and
the elders to confiscate*a* all his property and to exclude him from the
community of the exiles. So all the men of Judah and Benjamin 9
assembled in Jerusalem within the three days; and on the twentieth
day of the ninth month the people all sat in the forecourt of the house
of God, trembling with apprehension and shivering in the heavy rain.
Ezra the priest stood up and said, 'You have committed an offence in 10
marrying foreign wives and have added to Israel's guilt. Make your 11
confession now to the LORD the God of your fathers and do his will,
and separate yourselves from the foreign population and from your
foreign wives.' Then all the assembled people shouted in reply, 'Yes; 12
we must do what you say. But there is a great crowd of us here, and it 13
is the rainy season; we cannot go on standing out here in the open.
Besides, this business will not be finished in one day or even two,
because we have committed so grave an offence in this matter. Let our 14
leading men act for the whole assembly, and let all in our cities who
have married foreign women present themselves at appointed times,
each man with the elders and judges of his own city, until God's anger
against us on this account*b* is averted.' Only Jonathan son of Asahel 15
and Jahzeiah son of Tikvah, supported by Meshullam and Shabbethai
the Levite, opposed this.

So the exiles acted as agreed, and Ezra the priest selected*c* certain 16
men, heads of households representing their families, all of them
designated by name. They began their formal inquiry into the matter
on the first day of the tenth month, and by the first day of the first 17
month they had finished their inquiry into all the marriages with
foreign women.

Among the members of priestly families who had married foreign 18
women were found Maaseiah, Eliezer, Jarib, and Gedaliah of the family
of Jeshua son of Jozadak and his brothers. They pledged themselves 19
to dismiss their wives, and they brought a ram from the flock as a guilt-
offering for their sins. Of the family of Immer: Hanani and Zebadiah. 20
Of the family of Harim: Maaseiah, Elijah, Shemaiah, Jehiel and Uzziah. 21
Of the family of Pashhur: Elioenai, Maaseiah, Ishmael, Nethaneel, 22
Jozabad and Elasah.

Of the Levites: Jozabad, Shimei, Kelaiah (that is Kelita), Pethahiah, 23
Judah and Eliezer. Of the singers: Eliashib. Of the door-keepers: 24
Shallum, Telem and Uri.

And of Israel: of the family of Parosh: Ramiah, Izziah, Malchiah, 25
Mijamin, Eleazar, Malchiah and Benaiah. Of the family of Elam: 26

[*a*] *Lit.* to devote.   [*b*] on this account: *so Pesh.; Heb.* as far as this.   [*c*] *and Ezra the priest selected: prob. rdg., cp. 1 Esdras 9. 16; Heb. obscure.*

27 Mattaniah, Zechariah, Jehiel, Abdi, Jeremoth and Elijah. Of the
   family of Zattu: Elioenai, Eliashib, Mattaniah, Jeremoth, Zabad and
28 Aziza. Of the family of Bebai: Jehohanan, Hananiah, Zabbai and
29 Athlai. Of the family of Bani: Meshullam, Malluch, Adaiah, Jashub,
30 Sheal and Jeremoth. Of the family of Pahath-moab: Adna, Kelal,
   Benaiah, Maaseiah, Mattaniah, Bezalel, Binnui and Manasseh.
31 Of*a* the family of Harim: Eliezer, Isshijah, Malchiah, Shemaiah,
32,33 Simeon, Benjamin, Malluch and Shemariah. Of the family of Hashum:
   Mattenai, Mattattah, Zabad, Eliphelet, Jeremai, Manasseh and Shimei.
34,35 Of the family of Bani: Maadai, Amram and Uel, Benaiah, Bedeiah and
36,37 Keluhi, Vaniah, Meremoth, Eliashib, Mattaniah, Mattenai and Jaasau.
38,39 Of the family of*b* Binnui: Shimei, Shelemiah, Nathan and Adaiah,
40,41 Maknadebai, Shashai and Sharai, Azareel, Shelemiah and Shemariah,
42,43 Shallum, Amariah and Joseph. Of the family of Nebo: Jeiel, Matti-
44 thiah, Zabad, Zebina, Jaddai, Joel and Benaiah. All these had married
   foreign women, and they dismissed them, together with their children.*c*

[a] *So many MSS.; others om.*   [b] Of the family of: *prob. rdg., cp. 1 Esdras 9. 34;* Heb.
and Bani and.   [c] and they...children: *prob. rdg., cp. 1 Esdras 9. 36;* Heb. and some of
them were women; and they had borne sons.

THE BOOK OF

NEHEMIAH

Nehemiah's commission

THE NARRATIVE OF NEHEMIAH son of Hacaliah. 1
In the month Kislev in the twentieth year, when I was in
Susa the capital city, it happened that one of my brothers, 2
Hanani, arrived with some others from Judah; and I asked them about
Jerusalem and about the Jews, the families still remaining of those who
survived the captivity. They told me that those still remaining in the 3
province who had survived the captivity were facing great trouble and
reproach; the wall of Jerusalem was broken down and the gates had
been destroyed by fire. When I heard this news, I sat down and wept; 4
I mourned for some days, fasting and praying to the God of heaven. This 5
was my prayer: 'O LORD God of heaven, O great and terrible God who
faithfully keepest covenant with those who love thee and observe thy
commandments, let thy ear be attentive and thine eyes open, to hear my 6
humble prayer which I make to thee day and night on behalf of thy
servants the sons of Israel. I confess the sins which we Israelites have
all committed against thee, and of which I and my father's house are
also guilty. We have wronged thee and have not observed the 7
commandments, statutes, and rules which thou didst enjoin upon thy
servant Moses. Remember what thou didst impress upon him in these 8
words: "If you are unfaithful, I will disperse you among the nations;
but if you return to me and observe my commandments and fulfil them, 9
I will gather your children who have been scattered to the ends of the
earth and will bring them home to the place which I have chosen
as a dwelling for my Name." They are thy servants and thy people, 10
whom thou hast redeemed with thy great might and thy strong hand.
O Lord, let thy ear be attentive to my humble prayer, and to the 11
prayer of thy servants who delight to revere thy name. Grant me
good success this day, and put it into this man's heart to show me
kindness.'

Now I was the king's cupbearer, and one day, in the month Nisan, 2
in the twentieth year of King Artaxerxes, when his wine was ready,
I took it up and handed it to the king, and as I stood before him I was
feeling very unhappy. He said to me, 'Why do you look so unhappy? 2
You are not ill; it can be nothing but unhappiness.' I was much afraid
and answered, 'The king will live for ever. But how can I help looking 3

unhappy when the city where my forefathers are buried lies waste and
4 its gates are burnt?' 'What are you asking of me?' said the king.
5 I prayed to the God of heaven, and then I answered, 'If it please your
majesty, and if I enjoy your favour, I beg you to send me to Judah, to
6 the city where my forefathers are buried, so that I may rebuild it.' The
king, with the queen consort sitting beside him, asked me, 'How long
will the journey last, and when will you return?' Then the king
approved the request and let me go, and I told him how long I should be.
7 Then I said to the king, 'If it please your majesty, let letters be given
me for the governors in the province of Beyond-Euphrates with orders
8 to grant me all the help I need for my journey to Judah. Let me have
also a letter for Asaph, the keeper of your royal forests, instructing him
to supply me with timber to make beams for the gates of the citadel,
which adjoins the palace, and for the city wall, and for the palace
which I shall occupy.' The king granted my requests, for the gracious
9 hand of my God was upon me. I came in due course to the governors
in the province of Beyond-Euphrates and presented to them the king's
letters; the king had given me an escort of army officers with cavalry.
10 But when Sanballat the Horonite and the slave Tobiah, an Ammonite,
heard this, they were much vexed that someone should have come to
promote the interests of the Israelites.

The walls of Jerusalem rebuilt

11,12 WHEN I ARRIVED in Jerusalem, I waited three days. Then I set
out by night, taking a few men with me; but I told no one what
my God was prompting me to do for Jerusalem. I had no beast with
13 me except the one on which I myself rode. I went out by night through
the Valley Gate towards the Dragon Spring and the Dung Gate, and
I inspected the places where the walls of Jerusalem had been broken
14 down and her gates burnt. Then I passed on to the Fountain Gate and
the King's Pool; but there was no room for me to ride through.
15 I went up the valley in the night and inspected the city wall; then
16 I re-entered the city by the Valley Gate. So I arrived back without the
magistrates knowing where I had been or what I was doing. I had not
yet told the Jews, the priests, the nobles, the magistrates, or any of
those who would be responsible for the work.
17 Then I said to them, 'You see our wretched plight. Jerusalem lies in
ruins, its gates destroyed by fire. Come, let us rebuild the wall of
18 Jerusalem and be rid of the reproach.' I told them how the gracious
hand of my God had been upon me and also what the king had said

to me. They replied, 'Let us start the rebuilding.' So they set about the work vigorously and to good purpose.

But when Sanballat the Horonite, Tobiah the Ammonite slave, and 19 Geshem the Arab heard of it, they jeered at us, asking contemptuously, 'What is this you are doing? Is this a rebellion against the king?' But I answered them, 'The God of heaven will give us success. We, 20 his servants, are making a start with the rebuilding. You have no stake, or claim, or traditional right in Jerusalem.'

Eliashib the high priest and his fellow-priests started work and 3 rebuilt the Sheep Gate. They laid its beams*a* and set its doors in place; they carried the work as far as the Tower of the Hundred, as far as the Tower of Hananel, and consecrated it. Next to Eliashib the 2 men of Jericho worked; and next to them Zaccur son of Imri.

The Fish Gate was built by the sons of Hassenaah; they laid its 3 tie-beams and set its doors in place with their bolts and bars. Next to 4 them Meremoth son of Uriah, son of Hakkoz, repaired his section; next to them Meshullam son of Berechiah, son of Meshezabel; next to them Zadok son of Baana did the repairs; and next again the men of 5 Tekoa did the repairs, but their nobles would not demean themselves to serve their governor.

The Jeshanah Gate*b* was repaired by Joiada son of Paseah and 6 Meshullam son of Besodeiah; they laid its tie-beams and set its doors in place with their bolts and bars. Next to them Melatiah the Gibeonite 7 and Jadon the Meronothite, the men of Gibeon and Mizpah, did the repairs as far as the seat of the governor of the province of Beyond-Euphrates. Next to them Uzziel son of Harhaiah, a goldsmith,*c* did the 8 repairs, and next Hananiah, a perfumer; they reconstructed Jerusalem as far as the Broad Wall. Next to them Rephaiah son of Hur, ruler of 9 half the district of Jerusalem, did the repairs. Next to them Jedaiah 10 son of Harumaph did the repairs opposite his own house; and next Hattush son of Hashabniah. Malchiah son of Harim and Hasshub son 11 of Pahath-moab repaired a second section including the Tower of the Ovens.*d* Next to them Shallum son of Hallohesh, ruler of half the 12 district of Jerusalem, did the repairs with the help of his daughters.

The Valley Gate was repaired by Hanun and the inhabitants of 13 Zanoah; they rebuilt it and set its doors in place with their bolts and bars, and they repaired a thousand cubits of the wall as far as the Dung Gate. The Dung Gate itself was repaired by Malchiah son of Rechab, 14 ruler of the district of Beth-hakkerem; he rebuilt*e* it and set its doors in place with their bolts and bars. The Fountain Gate was repaired by 15

[*a*] laid its beams: *prob. rdg.; Heb.* consecrated it.   [*b*] The Jeshanah Gate: *or* The gate of the Old City.   [*c*] a goldsmith: *so Pesh.; Heb.* goldsmiths.   [*d*] *Or* Furnaces.   [*e*] *Prob. rdg.; Heb.* he will rebuild.

Shallun[a] son of Col-hozeh, ruler of the district of Mizpah; he rebuilt[b] it and roofed it and set its doors in place with their bolts and bars; and he built the wall of the Pool of Shelah next to the king's garden and onwards as far as the steps leading down from the City of David.

16 After him Nehemiah son of Azbuk, ruler of half the district of Beth-zur, did the repairs as far as a point opposite the burial-place of David,
17 as far as the artificial pool and the House of the Heroes.[c] After him the Levites did the repairs: Rehum son of Bani and next to him Hashabiah, ruler of half the district of Keilah, did the repairs for his district.
18 After him their kinsmen did the repairs: Binnui[d] son of Henadad, ruler
19 of half the district of Keilah; next to him Ezer son of Jeshua, ruler of Mizpah, repaired a second section opposite the point at which the
20 ascent meets the escarpment; after him Baruch son of Zabbai[e] repaired a second section, from the escarpment to the door of the house of
21 Eliashib the high priest. After him Meremoth son of Uriah, son of Hakkoz, repaired a second section, from the door of the house of Eliashib to the end of the house of Eliashib.
22 After him the priests of the neighbourhood of Jerusalem did the
23 repairs. Next Benjamin and Hasshub did the repairs opposite their own house; and next Azariah son of Maaseiah, son of Ananiah, did the
24 repairs beside his house. After him Binnui son of Henadad repaired a second section, from the house of Azariah as far as the escarpment and
25 the corner. Palal son of Uzai worked opposite the escarpment and the upper tower which projects from the king's house and belongs to the
26 court of the guard. After him Pedaiah son of Parosh[f] worked as far as a point on the east opposite the Water Gate and the projecting tower.
27 Next the men of Tekoa repaired a second section, from a point opposite the great projecting tower as far as the wall of Ophel.
28 Above the Horse Gate the priests did the repairs opposite their own
29 houses. After them Zadok son of Immer did the repairs opposite his own house; after him Shemaiah son of Shecaniah, the keeper of the
30 East Gate, did the repairs. After him Hananiah son of Shelemiah and Hanun, sixth son of Zalaph, repaired a second section. After him
31 Meshullam son of Berechiah did the repairs opposite his room. After him Malchiah, a goldsmith, did the repairs as far as the house of the temple-servitors[g] and the merchants, opposite the Mustering Gate, as
32 far as the roof-chamber at the corner. Between the roof-chamber at the corner and the Sheep Gate the goldsmiths and merchants did the repairs.

[a] *Or, with some MSS.,* Shallum. [b] *Prob. rdg.; Heb.* he will rebuild. [c] *Or* and the bar-racks. [d] *So some MSS.; others* Bavvai. [e] *So some MSS.; others add* inflamed. [f] *Prob. rdg.; Heb. adds* and the temple-servitors lodged on Ophel (*cp. 11. 21*). [g] *Heb.* Nethinim.

WHEN SANBALLAT HEARD that we were rebuilding the wall, he was 4 1*a*
very indignant; in his anger he jeered at the Jews and said in front of 2
his companions and of the garrison in Samaria, 'What do these feeble
Jews think they are doing? Do they mean to reconstruct the place?
Do they hope to offer sacrifice and finish the work in a day? Can they
make stones again out of heaps of rubble, and burnt at that?' Tobiah 3
the Ammonite, who was beside him, said, 'Whatever it is they are
building, if a fox climbs up their stone walls, it will break them down.'

Hear us, our God, for they treat us with contempt. Turn back their 4
reproach upon their own heads and let them become objects of
contempt in a land of captivity. Do not condone their guilt or let their 5
sin be struck off the record, for they have openly provoked the builders.

We built up the wall until it was continuous all round up to half its 6
height; and the people worked with a will. But when Sanballat and 7*b*
Tobiah, the Arabs and Ammonites and Ashdodites, heard that the new
work on the walls of Jerusalem had made progress and that the filling
of the breaches had begun, they were very angry; and they all banded 8
together to come and attack Jerusalem and to create confusion. So we 9
prayed to our God, and posted a guard day and night against them.

But the men of Judah said, 'The labourers' strength has failed, and 10
there is too much rubble; we shall never be able to rebuild the wall by
ourselves.' And our adversaries said, 'Before they know it or see any- 11
thing, we shall be upon them and kill them, and so put an end to the
work.' When the Jews who lived among them came in to the city, they 12
warned us many*c* times that they would gather from every place where
they lived to attack us, and that they would station themselves*d* on the 13
lowest levels below the wall, on patches of open ground. Accordingly
I posted my people by families, armed with swords, spears, and bows.
Then I surveyed the position and at once addressed the nobles, the 14
magistrates, and all the people. 'Do not be afraid of them', I said.
'Remember the Lord, great and terrible, and fight for your brothers,
your sons and daughters, your wives and your homes.' Our enemies 15
heard that everything was known to us, and that God had frustrated
their plans; and we all returned to our work on the wall.

From that day forward half the men under me were engaged in the 16
actual building, while the other half stood by holding their spears,
shields, and bows, and wearing coats of mail; and officers supervised all
the people of Judah who were engaged on the wall. The porters 17
carrying the loads had one hand on the load and a weapon in the other.
The builders had their swords attached to their belts as they built; the 18
trumpeter was beside me. I addressed the nobles, the magistrates, 19

[*a*] *3. 33 in Heb.* [*b*] *4. 1 in Heb.* [*c*] *Lit.* ten. [*d*] where...themselves: *so Sept.; Heb.*
which you return against us and I stationed.

and all the people: 'The work is great and covers much ground', I said.
'We are isolated on the wall, each man at some distance from his neigh-
20 bour. Wherever the trumpet sounds, rally to us there, and our God will
21 fight for us.' So we continued with the work, half the men holding
22 the spears, from daybreak until the stars came out. At the same time I
had said to the people, 'Let every man and his servant pass the night in
Jerusalem, to act as a guard for us by night and a working party by day.'
23 So neither I nor my kinsmen nor the men under me nor my bodyguard
ever took off our clothes, each keeping his right hand on*a* his weapon.

5 THERE CAME A TIME when the common people, both men and
2 women, raised a great outcry against their fellow-Jews. Some complained that they were giving their sons and daughters as pledges*b* for
3 food to keep themselves alive; others that they were mortgaging their
4 fields, vineyards, and houses to buy corn in the famine; others again
that they were borrowing money on*c* their fields and vineyards to pay
5 the king's tax. 'But', they said, 'our bodily needs are the same as other
people's, our children are as good as theirs; yet here we are, forcing our
sons and daughters to become slaves. Some of our daughters are
already enslaved, and there is nothing we can do, because our fields and
6 vineyards now belong to others.' I was very angry when I heard their
7 outcry and the story they told. I mastered my feelings and reasoned
with the nobles and the magistrates. I said to them, 'You are holding
8 your fellow-Jews as pledges for debt.' I rebuked them severely and said,
'As far as we have been able, we have bought back our fellow-Jews who
had been sold to other nations; but you are now selling your own
fellow-countrymen, and they will have to be bought back by us!' They
9 were silent and had not a word to say. I went on, 'What you are doing
is wrong. You ought to live so much in the fear of God that you are
above reproach in the eyes of the nations who are our enemies.
10 Speaking for myself, I and my kinsmen and the men under me are
advancing them money and corn. Let us give up this taking of persons
11 as pledges for debt. Give back today to your debtors their fields and
vineyards, their olive-groves and houses, as well as the income*d* in
12 money, and in corn, new wine, and oil.' 'We will give them back', they
promised, 'and exact nothing more. We will do what you say.' So,
summoning the priests, I put the offenders on oath to do as they had
13 promised. Then I shook out the fold of my robe and said, 'So may God
shake out from his house and from his property every man who does not
fulfil this promise. May he be shaken out like this and emptied!' And

[a] keeping his right hand on: *prob. rdg.; Heb.* obscure.   [b] that they...as pledges: *prob.
rdg.; Heb.* that they, their sons and daughters were many.   [c] on: *so I uc. Sept.; Heb. om.*
[d] *Prob. rdg.; Heb.* hundredth.

all the assembled people said 'Amen' and praised the LORD. And they did as they had promised.

Moreover, from the time when I was appointed governor in the land 14 of Judah, from the twentieth to the thirty-second year of King Artaxerxes, a period of twelve years, neither I nor my kinsmen drew the governor's allowance of food. Former governors had laid a heavy burden 15 on the people, exacting from them a daily toll*a* of bread and wine to the value of forty shekels of silver. Further, the men under them had tyrannized over the people; but, for fear of God, I did not behave like this. I also put all my energy into the work on this wall, and I*b* acquired 16 no land; and all my men were gathered there for the work. Also I had 17 as guests at my table a hundred and fifty Jews, including the magistrates, as well as men who came to us from the surrounding nations. The 18 provision which had to be made each day was an ox and six prime sheep; fowls also were prepared for me, and every ten days skins*c* of wine in abundance. Yet, in spite of all this, I did not draw the governor's allowance, because the people were so heavily burdened. Remember 19 for my good, O God, all that I have done for this people.

When the news came to Sanballat, Tobiah, Geshem the Arab, and 6 the rest of our enemies, that I had rebuilt the wall and that not a single breach remained in it, although I had not yet set up the doors in the gates, Sanballat and Geshem sent me an invitation to come and confer 2 with them at Hakkephirim in the plain of Ono; this was a ruse on their part to do me harm. So I sent messengers to them with this reply: 3 'I have important work on my hands at the moment; I cannot come down. Why should the work be brought to a standstill while I leave it and come down to you?' They sent me a similar invitation four times, 4 and each time I gave them the same answer. On a fifth occasion San- 5 ballat made a similar approach, but this time his messenger came with an open letter. It ran as follows: 'It is reported among the nations—and 6 Gashmu*d* confirms it—that you and the Jews are plotting rebellion, and it is for this reason that you are rebuilding the wall, and—so the report goes—that you yourself want to be king. You are also said to 7 have put up prophets to proclaim in Jerusalem that Judah has a king, meaning yourself. The king will certainly hear of this. So come at once and let us talk the matter over.' Here is the reply I sent: 'No such 8 thing as you allege has taken place; you have made up the whole story.' They were all trying to intimidate us, in the hope that we should then 9 relax our efforts and that the work would never be finished. So I applied myself to it with greater energy.*e*

[a] a daily toll: *prob. rdg.; Heb. obscure.* [b] *So some MSS.; others* we. [c] skins: *so some MSS.; others* with every kind. [d] Geshem *in 2. 19 and 6. 1, 2.* [e] I applied...energy: *so Sept.; Heb.* strengthen me for the work.

10 One day I went to the house of Shemaiah son of Delaiah, son of Mehetabel, for he was confined to his house. He said, 'Let us meet in the house of God, within the sanctuary, and let us shut the doors, for
11 they are coming to kill you—they are coming to kill you by night.' But I said, 'Should a man like me run away? And can a man like me go into
12 the sanctuary and survive*a*? I will not go in.' Then it dawned on me: God had not sent him. His prophecy aimed at harming me, and Tobiah
13 and Sanballat had bribed him to utter it. He had been bribed to frighten me into compliance and into committing sin; then they could give me
14 a bad name and discredit me. Remember Tobiah and Sanballat, O God, for what they have done, and also the prophetess Noadiah and all the other prophets who have tried to intimidate me.

15 On the twenty-fifth day of the month Elul the wall was finished; it
16 had taken fifty-two days. When our enemies heard of it, and all the surrounding nations saw it,*b* they thought it a very wonderful achievement,*c* and they recognized that this work had been accomplished by the help of our God.

17 All this time the nobles in Judah were sending many letters to
18 Tobiah, and receiving replies from him. For many in Judah were in league with him, because he was a son-in-law of Shecaniah son of Arah, and his son Jehohanan had married a daughter of Meshullam
19 son of Berechiah. They were always praising*d* him in my presence and repeating to him what I said. Tobiah also wrote to me to intimidate me.

7 NOW WHEN THE WALL had been rebuilt, and I had set the doors in
2 place and the gate-keepers*e* had been appointed, I gave the charge of Jerusalem to my brother Hanani, and to Hananiah, the governor of the citadel, for he was trustworthy and God-fearing above other men.
3 And I said to them, 'The entrances to Jerusalem are not to be left open during the heat of the day; the gates must be kept shut and barred while the gate-keepers are standing at ease. Appoint guards from among the inhabitants of Jerusalem, some on sentry-duty and others posted in front of their own homes.'

4 The city was large and spacious; there were few people in it and no
5 houses had yet been rebuilt. Then God prompted me to assemble the nobles, the magistrates, and the people, to be enrolled family by family. And I found the book of the genealogies of those who had been the
6*f* first to come back. This is what I found written in it: Of the captives whom Nebuchadnezzar king of Babylon had taken into exile, these are the people of the province who have returned to Jerusalem and

[*a*] and survive: *or* to save his life. [*b*] *Or* were afraid. [*c*] they thought...achievement: *prob. rdg.; Heb.* they fell very much in their own eyes. [*d*] *Or* repeating rumours about... [*e*] *Prob. rdg.; Heb. adds* the singers and the Levites. [*f*] *Verses 6–73: cp. Ezra 2. 1–70.*

Judah, each to his own town, led by Zerubbabel, Jeshua,[a] Nehemiah, 7
Azariah, Raamiah, Nahamani, Mordecai, Bilshan, Mispereth, Bigvai,
Nehum and Baanah.

The roll of the men of the people of Israel: the family of Parosh, two 8
thousand one hundred and seventy-two; the family of Shephatiah, three 9
hundred and seventy-two; the family of Arah, six hundred and fifty- 10
two; the family of Pahath-moab, namely the families of Jeshua and 11
Joab, two thousand eight hundred and eighteen; the family of Elam, 12
one thousand two hundred and fifty-four; the family of Zattu, eight 13
hundred and forty-five; the family of Zaccai, seven hundred and sixty; 14
the family of Binnui, six hundred and forty-eight; the family of Bebai, 15, 16
six hundred and twenty-eight; the family of Azgad, two thousand three 17
hundred and twenty-two; the family of Adonikam, six hundred and 18
sixty-seven; the family of Bigvai, two thousand and sixty-seven; the 19, 20
family of Adin, six hundred and fifty-five; the family of Ater, namely 21
that of Hezekiah, ninety-eight; the family of Hashum, three hundred 22
and twenty-eight; the family of Bezai, three hundred and twenty-four; 23
the family of Harif, one hundred and twelve; the family of Gibeon, 24, 25
ninety-five. The men of Bethlehem and Netophah, one hundred and 26
eighty-eight; the men of Anathoth, one hundred and twenty-eight; 27
the men of Beth-azmoth, forty-two; the men of Kiriath-jearim, 28, 29
Kephirah, and Beeroth, seven hundred and forty-three; the men of 30
Ramah and Geba, six hundred and twenty-one; the men of Michmas, 31
one hundred and twenty-two; the men of Bethel and Ai, one hundred 32
and twenty-three; the men of[b] Nebo, fifty-two; the men[c] of the other 33, 34
Elam, one thousand two hundred and fifty-four; the men of Harim, 35
three hundred and twenty; the men of Jericho, three hundred 36
and forty-five; the men of Lod, Hadid, and Ono, seven hundred and 37
twenty-one; the men of Senaah, three thousand nine hundred and 38
thirty.

Priests: the family of Jedaiah, of the line of Jeshua, nine hundred 39
and seventy-three; the family of Immer, one thousand and fifty-two; 40
the family of Pashhur, one thousand two hundred and forty-seven; 41
the family of Harim, one thousand and seventeen.   42

Levites: the families of Jeshua and[d] Kadmiel, of the line of Hodvah, 43
seventy-four. Singers: the family of Asaph, one hundred and forty- 44
eight. Door-keepers: the family of Shallum, the family of Ater, the 45
family of Talmon, the family of Akkub, the family of Hatita, and the
family of Shobai, one hundred and thirty-eight in all.

Temple-servitors: the family of Ziha, the family of Hasupha, the 46

[a] *Or* Joshua (*cp. Hag. 1. 1*). [b] *Prob. rdg., cp. Ezra 2. 29; Heb. adds* the other.
[c] *Prob. rdg.; Heb.* family (*also in verses 35–38*). [d] *and: prob. rdg., cp. Ezra 2. 40;
Heb.* to.

47 family of Tabbaoth, the family of Keros, the family of Sia, the family
48 of Padon, the family of Lebanah, the family of Hagabah, the family of
49 Shalmai, the family of Hanan, the family of Giddel, the family of
50 Gahar, the family of Reaiah, the family of Rezin, the family of Nekoda,
51 the family of Gazzam, the family of Uzza, the family of Paseah,
52 the family of Besai, the family of the Meunim, the family of the
53 Nephishesim,*a* the family of Bakbuk, the family of Hakupha, the family
54 of Harhur, the family of Bazlith,*b* the family of Mehida,*c* the family of
55 Harsha, the family of Barkos, the family of Sisera, the family of Temah,
56 the family of Neziah, and the family of Hatipha.

57   Descendants of Solomon's servants: the family of Sotai, the family
58 of Sophereth, the family of Perida, the family of Jaalah, the family of
59 Darkon, the family of Giddel, the family of Shephatiah, the family of
Hattil, the family of Pochereth-hazzebaim, and the family of Amon.

60   The temple-servitors and the descendants of Solomon's servants
amounted to three hundred and ninety-two in all.

61   The following were those who returned from Tel-melah, Tel-harsha,
Kerub, Addon, and Immer, but could not establish their father's
62 family nor whether by descent they belonged to Israel: the family of
Delaiah, the family of Tobiah, the family of Nekoda, six hundred and
63 forty-two. Also of the priests: the family of Hobaiah, the family of
Hakkoz, and the family of Barzillai who had married a daughter of
64 Barzillai the Gileadite and went by his*d* name. These searched for their
names among those enrolled in the genealogies, but they could not be
65 found; they were disqualified for the priesthood as unclean, and the
governor forbade them to partake of the most sacred food until there
should be a priest able to consult the Urim and the Thummim.

66   The whole assembled people numbered forty-two thousand three
67 hundred and sixty, apart from their slaves, male and female, of whom
there were seven thousand three hundred and thirty-seven; and they
68 had two hundred and forty-five singers, men and women. Their horses
numbered seven hundred and thirty-six, their mules two hundred and
69 forty-five,*e* their camels four hundred and thirty-five, and their asses
six thousand seven hundred and twenty.

70   Some of the heads of families gave contributions for the work. The
governor gave to the treasury a thousand drachmas of gold, fifty
71 tossing-bowls, and five hundred and thirty priestly robes. Some of the
heads of families gave for the fabric fund twenty thousand drachmas of
72 gold and two thousand two hundred minas of silver. What the rest of
the people gave was twenty thousand drachmas of gold, two thousand
minas of silver, and sixty-seven priestly robes.

[a] *Or* Nephushesim.   [b] *Or* Bazluth (*cp. Ezra 2. 52*).   [c] Mehira *in some MSS.*   [d] *Prob.*
rdg., cp. 1 Esdras 5. 38; Heb. their.   [e] Their horses . . . forty-five: *so some MSS.; others om.*

The priests, the Levites, and some of the people lived in Jerusalem 73 and its suburbs;*ᵃ* the door-keepers, the singers, the temple-servitors, and all other Israelites, lived in their own towns.

The law read by Ezra and the covenant renewed

WHEN THE SEVENTH MONTH CAME, and the Israelites were now settled in their towns, the people assembled as one man in 8 the square in front of the Water Gate, and Ezra the scribe*ᵇ* was asked to bring the book of the law of Moses, which the LORD had enjoined upon Israel. On the first day of the seventh month, Ezra the priest 2 brought the law before the assembly, every man and woman, and all who were capable of understanding what they heard.*ᶜ* He read from it, 3 facing the square in front of the Water Gate, from early morning till noon, in the presence of the men and the women, and those who could understand;*ᵈ* all the people listened attentively to the book of the law. Ezra the scribe stood on a wooden platform made for the purpose,*ᵉ* and 4 beside him stood Mattithiah, Shema, Anaiah, Uriah, Hilkiah, and Maaseiah on his right hand; and on his left Pedaiah, Mishael, Malchiah, Hashum, Hashbaddanah, Zechariah and Meshullam. Ezra opened the 5 book in the sight of all the people, for he was standing above them; and when he opened it, they all stood. Ezra blessed the LORD, the great God, 6 and all the people raised their hands and answered, 'Amen, Amen'; and they bowed their heads and prostrated themselves humbly before the LORD. Jeshua, Bani, Sherebiah, Jamin, Akkub, Shabbethai, Hodiah, 7 Maaseiah, Kelita, Azariah, Jozabad, Hanan, Pelaiah, the Levites,*ᶠ* expounded the law to the people while they remained in their places. They read from the book of the law of God clearly, made its sense 8 plain and gave instruction in what was read.

Then Nehemiah the governor and Ezra the priest and scribe, and 9 the Levites who instructed the people, said to them all, 'This day is holy to the LORD your God; do not mourn or weep.' For all the people had been weeping while they listened to the words of the law. Then he 10 said to them, 'You may go now; refresh yourselves with rich food and sweet drinks, and send a share to all who cannot provide for themselves; for this day is holy to our Lord. Let there be no sadness, for joy in the LORD is your strength.' The Levites silenced the people, saying, 'Be 11 quiet, for this day is holy; let there be no sadness.' So all the people 12

[a] in Jerusalem and its suburbs: *prob. rdg., cp. 1 Esdras 5. 46; Heb. om.* [b] *Or* doctor of the law. [c] were capable...heard: *or* would teach them to understand. [d] could understand: *or* were to instruct. [e] *Or* for the address. [f] *Prob. rdg.; Heb.* and the Levites.

went away to eat and to drink, to send shares to others and to celebrate the day with great rejoicing, because they had understood what had been explained to them.

13 On the second day the heads of families of the whole people, with the priests and the Levites, assembled before Ezra the scribe to study 14 the law. And they found written in the law that the LORD had given commandment through Moses that the Israelites should live in 15 arbours*a* during the feast of the seventh month, and that they should make proclamation throughout all their cities and in Jerusalem: 'Go out into the hills and fetch branches of olive and wild olive, myrtle and 16 palm, and other leafy boughs to make arbours, as prescribed.' So the people went out and fetched them and made arbours for themselves, each on his own roof, and in their courts and in the courts of the house of God, and in the square at the Water Gate and the square at the 17 Ephraim Gate. And the whole community of those who had returned from the captivity made arbours and lived in them, a thing that the Israelites had not done from the days of Joshua*b* son of Nun to that 18 day; and there was very great rejoicing. And day by day, from the first day to the last, the book of the law of God was read. They kept the feast for seven days, and on the eighth day there was a closing ceremony, according to the rule.

9 ON THE TWENTY-FOURTH DAY of this month the Israelites assembled for a fast, clothed in sackcloth and with earth on their heads. 2 Those who were of Israelite descent separated themselves from all the foreigners; they took their places and confessed their sins and the 3 iniquities of their forefathers. Then they stood up in their places, and the book of the law of the LORD their God was read for one fourth of the day, and for another fourth they confessed and did obeisance to the 4 LORD their God. Upon the steps assigned to the Levites stood Jeshua, Bani, Kadmiel, Shebaniah, Bunni, Sherebiah, Bani, and Kenani, and 5 they cried aloud to the LORD their God. Then the Levites, Jeshua, Kadmiel, Bani, Hashabniah, Sherebiah, Hodiah, Shebaniah, and Pethahiah, said, 'Stand up and bless the LORD your God, saying: From everlasting to everlasting thy glorious name is blessed*c* and exalted 6 above all blessing and praise. Thou alone art the LORD; thou hast made heaven, the highest heaven with all its host, the earth and all that is on it, the seas and all that is in them. Thou preservest all of them, and the 7 host of heaven worships thee. Thou art the LORD, the God who chose Abram and brought him out of Ur of the Chaldees and named him 8 Abraham. Thou didst find him faithful to thee and didst make a cove-

[a] Or tabernacles or booths. [b] Heb. Jeshua. [c] thy glorious name is blessed: *prob. rdg.; Heb.* and let them bless thy glorious name.

nant with him to give to him and[a] to his descendants the land of the
Canaanites, the Hittites, the Amorites, the Perizzites, the Jebusites,
and the Girgashites; and thou didst fulfil thy promise, for thou art just.

'And thou didst see the misery of our forefathers in Egypt and didst 9
hear their cry for help at the Red Sea,[b] and didst work signs and 10
portents against Pharaoh, all his courtiers and all the people of his land,
knowing how arrogantly they treated our forefathers, and thou didst
win for thyself a name that lives on to this day. Thou didst tear the sea 11
apart before them so that they went through the middle of it on dry
ground; but thou didst cast their pursuers into the depths, like a stone
cast into turbulent waters. Thou didst guide them by a pillar of cloud 12
in the day-time and by a pillar of fire at night to give them light on the
road by which they travelled. Thou didst descend upon Mount Sinai 13
and speak with them from heaven, and give them right judgements and
true laws, and statutes and commandments which were good, and thou 14
didst make known to them thy holy sabbath and give them commandments, statutes, and laws through thy servant Moses. Thou gavest them 15
bread from heaven to stay their hunger and thou broughtest water out
from a rock for them to quench their thirst, and thou didst bid them
enter and take possession of the land which thou hadst solemnly sworn
to give them. But they, our forefathers, were arrogant and stubborn, 16
and disobeyed thy commandments. They refused to obey and did not 17
remember the miracles which thou didst accomplish among them; they
remained stubborn, and they appointed a man to lead them back to
slavery in Egypt.[c] But thou art a forgiving god, gracious and compassionate, long-suffering and ever constant, and thou didst not forsake
them. Even when they made the image of a bull-calf in metal and said, 18
"This is your god who brought you up from Egypt", and were guilty of
great blasphemies, thou in thy great compassion didst not forsake them 19
in the wilderness. The pillar of cloud did not fail to guide them on their
journey by day nor the pillar of fire by night to give them light on the
road by which they travelled. Thou gavest thy good spirit to instruct 20
them; thy manna thou didst not withhold from them, and thou gavest
them water to quench their thirst. Forty years long thou didst sustain 21
them in the wilderness, and they lacked nothing; their clothes did not
wear out and their feet were not swollen.

'Thou gavest them kingdoms and peoples, allotting these to them 22
as spoils of war. Thus they took possession of the land of Sihon[d] king
of Heshbon and the land of Og king of Bashan. Thou didst multiply 23
their descendants so that they became countless as the stars in the sky,
bringing them into the land which thou didst promise to give to their

[a] to him and: *so Sept.; Heb. om.*   [b] *Or* the Sea of Reeds.   [c] in Egypt: *so some MSS.;
others* in their rebellion.   [d] *So one MS.; others add* and the land of.

24 forefathers as their possession. When their descendants entered the land and took possession of it, thou didst subdue before them the Canaanites who inhabited it and gavest these, kings and peoples alike, into their
25 hands to do with them whatever they wished. They captured fortified cities and a fertile land and took possession of houses full of all good things, rock-hewn cisterns, vineyards, olive-trees, and fruit-trees in abundance; so they ate and were satisfied and grew fat and found
26 delight in thy great goodness. But they were defiant and rebelled against thee; they turned their backs on thy law and killed thy prophets, who solemnly warned them to return to thee, and they were guilty of
27 great blasphemies. Because of this thou didst hand them over to their enemies who oppressed them. But when, in the time of their oppression, they cried to thee for help, thou heardest them from heaven and in thy great compassion didst send them saviours to save them from
28 their enemies. But when they had had a respite, they once more did what was wrong in thine eyes; and thou didst abandon them to their enemies who held them in subjection. But again they cried to thee for help, and many times over thou heardest them from heaven and in thy
29 compassion didst save them. Thou didst solemnly warn them to return to thy law, but they grew arrogant and did not heed thy commandments; they sinned against thy ordinances, which bring life to him who keeps them. Stubbornly they turned away in mulish obstinacy and would not
30 obey. Many years thou wast patient with them and didst warn them by thy spirit through thy prophets; but they would not listen. Therefore
31 thou didst hand them over to foreign peoples. Yet in thy great compassion thou didst not make an end of them nor forsake them; for thou art a gracious and compassionate god.

32 'Now therefore, our God, thou great and mighty and terrible God, who faithfully keepest covenant, do not make light of the hardships that have befallen us—our kings, our princes, our priests, our prophets, our forefathers, and all thy people—from the days of the kings of
33 Assyria to this day. In all that has befallen us thou hast been just, thou
34 hast kept faith, but we have done wrong. Our kings, our princes, our priests, and our forefathers did not keep thy law nor heed thy command-
35 ments and the warnings which thou gavest them. Even under their own kings, while they were enjoying the great prosperity which thou gavest them and the broad and fertile land which thou didst bestow upon them, they did not serve thee; they did not abandon their evil ways.
36 Today we are slaves, slaves here in the land which thou gavest to our forefathers so that they might eat its fruits and enjoy its good things.
37 All its produce now goes to the kings whom thou hast set over us because of our sins. They have power over our bodies, and they do as they please with our beasts, while we are in dire distress.

'Because of all this we make a binding declaration in writing, and 38ᵃ our princes, our Levites, and our priests witness the sealing.

'Those who witness the sealing are Nehemiah the governor, son of 10 Hacaliah, Zedekiah, Seraiah, Azariah, Jeremiah, Pashhur, Amariah, 2,3 Malchiah, Hattush, Shebaniah,ᵇ Malluch, Harim, Meremoth, Obadiah, 4,5 Daniel, Ginnethon, Baruch, Meshullam, Abiah, Mijamin, Maaziah, 6,7,8 Bilgai, Shemaiah; these are the priests. The Levites: Jeshuaᶜ son 9 of Azaniah, Binnui of the family of Henadad, Kadmiel; and their 10 brethren, Shebaniah, Hodiah,ᵈ Kelita, Pelaiah, Hanan, Mica, Rehob, 11 Hashabiah, Zaccur, Sherebiah, Shebaniah, Hodiah, Bani, Beninu.ᵉ 12,13 The chiefs of the people: Parosh, Pahath-moab, Elam, Zattu, Bani, 14 Bunni, Azgad, Bebai, Adonijah, Bigvai, Adin, Ater, Hezekiah, 15,16,17 Azzur, Hodiah, Hashum, Bezai, Hariph, Anathoth, Nebai,ᶠ Magpiash, 18,19,20 Meshullam, Hezir, Meshezabel, Zadok, Jaddua, Pelatiah, Hanan, 21,22 Anaiah, Hoshea, Hananiah, Hasshub, Hallohesh, Pilha, Shobek, 23,24 Rehum, Hashabnah, Maaseiah, Ahiah, Hanan, Anan, Malluch, 25,26,27 Harim, Baanah.

'The rest of the people, the priests, the Levites, the door-keepers, 28 the singers, the temple-servitors, with their wives, their sons, and their daughters, all who are capable of understanding, all who for the sake of the law of God have kept themselves apart from the foreign population, join with the leading brethren,ᵍ when the oath is put to them, in 29 swearing to obey God's law given by Moses the servant of God, and to observe and fulfil all the commandments of the LORD our Lord, his rules and his statutes.

'We will not give our daughters in marriage to the foreign population 30 or take their daughters for our sons. If on the sabbath these people 31 bring in merchandise, especially corn, for sale, we will not buy from them on the sabbath or on any holy day. We will forgo the crops of the seventh year and release every person still held as a pledge for debt.

'We hereby undertake the duty of giving yearly the third of a shekel 32 for the service of the house of our God, for the Bread of the Presence, 33 the regular grain-offering and whole-offering, the sabbaths, the new moons, the appointed seasons, the holy-gifts, and the sin-offerings to make expiation on behalf of Israel, and for all else that has to be done in the house of our God. We, the priests, the Levites, and the people, 34 have cast lots for the wood-offering, so that it may be brought into the house of our God by each family in turn, at appointed times, year by year, to burn upon the altar of the LORD our God, as prescribed in the law. We undertake to bring the firstfruits of our land and the firstfruits 35

[a] *10. 1 in Heb.* [b] *Or, with some MSS.*, Shecaniah. [c] *Prob. rdg.; Heb.* and Jeshua. [d] *Or, with Ezra 2. 40*, Hodaviah. [e] *Or, with slight change*, Kenani, *cp. 9. 4.* [f] *Or* Nobai. [g] the leading brethren: *prob. rdg.; Heb.* their brethren, their leading men.

36 of every fruit-tree, year by year, to the house of the LORD; also to bring to the house of our God, to the priests who minister in the house of our God, the first-born of our sons and of our cattle, as prescribed in
37 the law, and the first-born of our herds and of our flocks; and to bring to the priests the first kneading of our dough,^a and the first of the fruit of every tree, of the new wine and of the oil, to the store-rooms in the house of our God; and to bring to the Levites the tithes from our land, for it is the Levites who collect the tithes in all our farming villages.
38 The Aaronite priest shall be with the Levites when they collect the tithes; and the Levites shall bring up one tenth of the tithes to the house
39 of our God, to the appropriate rooms in the storehouse. For the Israelites and the Levites shall bring the contribution of corn, new wine, and oil to the rooms where the vessels of the sanctuary are kept, and where the ministering priests, the door-keepers, and the singers are lodged. We will not neglect the house of our God.'

11 THE LEADERS OF THE PEOPLE settled in Jerusalem; and the rest of the people cast lots to bring one in every ten to live in Jerusalem, the
2 holy city, while the remaining nine lived in other towns. And the people were grateful to all those who volunteered to live in Jerusalem.
3   These are the chiefs of the province who lived in Jerusalem; but, in the towns of Judah, other Israelites, priests, Levites, temple-servitors, and descendants of Solomon's servants lived on their own property,
4 in their own towns. Some members of the tribes of Judah and Benjamin lived in Jerusalem. Of Judah: Athaiah son of Uzziah, son of Zechariah, son of Amariah, son of Shephatiah, son of Mahalalel of the family of
6 Perez, all of whose family, to the number of four hundred and sixty-
5 eight men of substance, lived in Jerusalem; and Maaseiah son of Baruch, son of Col-hozeh, son of Hazaiah, son of Adaiah, son of Joiarib, son of Zechariah of the Shelanite family.
7   These were the Benjamites: Sallu son of Meshullam, son of Joed, son of Pedaiah, son of Kolaiah, son of Maaseiah, son of Ithiel, son of
8 Isaiah, and his kinsmen^b Gabbai and Sallai,^c nine hundred and twenty-
9 eight in all. Joel son of Zichri was their overseer, and Judah son of Hassenuah was second over the city.^d
10, 11   Of the priests: Jedaiah son of Joiarib, son of^e Seraiah, son of Hilkiah, son of Meshullam, son of Zadok, son of Meraioth, son of
12 Ahitub, supervisor of the house of God, and his^f brethren responsible for the work in the temple, eight hundred and twenty-two in all; and

[a] *So Sept.; Heb. adds* and our contributions.   [b] his kinsmen: *so Luc. Sept.; Heb. after* him.   [c] Gabbai and Sallai: *these names are uncertain.*   [d] second over the city: *or over* the second quarter of the city.   [e] son of: *prob. rdg.; Heb. obscure.*   [f] *Prob. rdg.; Heb.* their.

Adaiah son of Jeroham, son of Pelaliah, son of Amzi, son of Zechariah, son of Pashhur, son of Malchiah, and his brethren, heads of fathers' 13 houses, two hundred and forty-two in all; and Amasai*a* son of Azarel, son of Ahzai, son of Meshillemoth, son of Immer, and his*b* brethren, 14 men of substance, a hundred and twenty-eight in all; their overseer was Zabdiel son of Haggedolim.

And of the Levites: Shemaiah son of Hasshub, son of Azrikam, son 15 of Hashabiah, son of Bunni; and Shabbethai and Jozabad of the chiefs 16 of the Levites, who had charge of the external business of the house of God; and Mattaniah son of Micah, son of Zabdi,*c* son of Asaph, who 17 as precentor led the prayer of thanksgiving,*d* and Bakbukiah who held the second place among his brethren; and Abda son of Shammua, son of Galal, son of Jeduthun. The number of Levites in the holy city was 18 two hundred and eighty-four in all.

The gate-keepers who kept guard at the gates were Akkub, Talmon, 19 and their brethren, a hundred and seventy-two. The rest of the 20 Israelites*e* were in all the towns of Judah, each man on his own inherited property. But the temple-servitors lodged on Ophel, and Ziha 21 and Gishpa were in charge of them.

The overseer of the Levites in Jerusalem was Uzzi son of Bani, son 22 of Hashabiah, son of Mattaniah, son of Mica, of the family of Asaph the singers, for the supervision of the business of the house of God. For they were under the king's orders, and there was obligatory duty 23 for the singers every day. Pethahiah son of Meshezabel, of the family 24 of Zerah son of Judah, was the king's adviser on all matters affecting the people.

As for the hamlets with their surrounding fields: some of the men 25 of Judah lived in Kiriath-arba and its villages, in Dibon and its villages, and in Jekabzeel*f* and its hamlets, in Jeshua, Moladah, and 26 Bethpelet, in Hazar-shual, and in Beersheba and its villages, in Ziklag 27, 28 and in Meconah and its villages, in Enrimmon, Zorah, and Jarmuth, 29 in Zanoah, Adullam, and their hamlets, in Lachish and its fields and 30 Azekah and its villages. Thus they occupied the country from Beersheba to the Valley of Hinnom.

The men of Benjamin lived in*g* Geba, Michmash, Aiah, and Bethel 31 with its villages, in Anathoth, Nob, and Ananiah, in Hazor, Ramah, and 32, 33 Gittaim, in Hadid, Zeboim, and Neballat, in Lod, Ono, and*h* Ge- 34, 35 harashim.*i* And certain divisions of the Levites in Judah were attached 36 to Benjamin.

[*a*] *Prob. rdg.; Heb.* Amashsai. [*b*] *So Sept.; Heb.* their. [*c*] *Or, with Luc. Sept.,* Zichri. [*d*] *as precentor . . . thanksgiving: mng. uncertain.* [*e*] *Prob. rdg.; Heb. adds* the levitical priests. [*f*] Kabzeel *in 1 Chr. 11. 22.* [*g*] *Prob. rdg.; Heb.* from. [*h*] *and: prob. rdg.; Heb. om.* [*i*] *Or* and the Valley of Woods *or* and the Valley of Craftsmen.

12 These are the priests and the Levites who came back with Zerubbabel
2 son of Shealtiel, and Jeshua:[a] Seraiah, Jeremiah, Ezra, Amariah,
3,4 Malluch, Hattush, Shecaniah, Rehum, Meremoth, Iddo, Ginnethon,[b]
5,6 Abiah, Mijamin, Maadiah, Bilgah, Shemaiah, Joiarib, Jedaiah,
7 Sallu, Amok, Hilkiah, Jedaiah. These were the chiefs of the priests and
of their brethren in the days of Jeshua.

8 And the Levites: Jeshua, Binnui, Kadmiel, Sherebiah, Judah, and
Mattaniah, who with his brethren was in charge of the songs of thanks-
9 giving. And Bakbukiah and Unni their brethren stood opposite them
10 in the service. And Jeshua was the father of Joiakim, Joiakim the
11 father of Eliashib, Eliashib of Joiada, Joiada the father of Jonathan,[c]
12 and Jonathan the father of Jaddua. And in the days of Joiakim the
priests who were heads of families were: of Seraiah, Meraiah; of
13 Jeremiah, Hananiah; of Ezra, Meshullam; of Amariah, Jehohanan;
14,15 of Malluch,[d] Jonathan; of Shebaniah, Joseph; of Harim, Adna; of
16 Meraioth,[e] Helkai; of Iddo, Zechariah; of Ginnethon, Meshullam;
17,18 of Abiah, Zichri; of Miniamin[f]; of Moadiah, Piltai; of Bilgah, Sham-
19 mua; of Shemaiah, Jehonathan; of Joiarib, Mattenai; of Jedaiah,
20,21 Uzzi; of Sallu,[g] Kallai; of Amok, Eber; of Hilkiah, Hashabiah; of
Jedaiah, Nethaneel.

22 [h]The heads of the priestly families[i] in the days of Eliashib, Joiada,
Johanan, and Jaddua were recorded down to[j] the reign of Darius the
23 Persian. The heads of the levitical families were recorded in the annals
24 only down to the days of Johanan the grandson[k] of Eliashib. And the
chiefs of the Levites: Hashabiah, Sherebiah, Jeshua, Binnui,[l] Kadmiel,
with their brethren in the other turn of duty, to praise and to give
thanks, according to the commandment of David the man of God, turn
25 by turn. Mattaniah, Bakbukiah, Obadiah, Meshullam, Talmon, and
26 Akkub were gate-keepers standing guard at the gatehouses. This was the
arrangement in the days of Joiakim son of Jeshua, son of Jozadak, and
in the days of Nehemiah the governor and of Ezra the priest and scribe.

27 At the dedication of the wall of Jerusalem they sought out the Levites
in all their settlements, and brought them to Jerusalem to celebrate the
dedication with[m] rejoicing, with thanksgiving and song, to the accom-
28 paniment of cymbals, lutes, and harps. And the Levites,[n] the singers,
were assembled from[o] the district round Jerusalem and from the
29 hamlets of the Netophathites; also from Beth-gilgal and from the

[a] Or Joshua. [b] So many MSS.; others Ginnethoi. [c] Johanan in verse 22. [d] Prob.
rdg.; Heb. Malluchi, or Melichu. [e] Meremoth in Luc. Sept. (cp. verse 3). [f] A name is
missing here. [g] Prob. rdg., cp. verse 7; Heb. Sallai. [h] Prob. rdg.; Heb. prefixes The
Levites. [i] heads...families: prob. rdg.; Heb. heads of the families and the priests.
[j] down to: so many MSS.; others upon. [k] Lit. son. [l] Jeshua, Binnui: prob. rdg.;
Heb. and Jeshua son of. [m] Prob. rdg.; Heb. and. [n] the Levites: prob. rdg.; Heb. the
sons of. [o] So Luc. Sept.; Heb. and from.

region of Geba and Beth-azmoth;*[a]* for the singers had built themselves
hamlets in the neighbourhood of Jerusalem. The priests and the 30
Levites purified themselves; and they purified the people, the gates,
and the wall. Then I brought the leading men of Judah up on to the 31
city wall, and appointed two great choirs to give thanks. One went in
procession*[b]* to the right, going along the wall to the Dung Gate; and 32
after it went Hoshaiah with half the leading men of Judah, and Azariah, 33
Ezra, Meshullam, Judah, Benjamin, Shemaiah, and Jeremiah; and 34,35
certain of the priests with trumpets: Zechariah son of Jonathan, son of
Shemaiah, son of Mattanaiah, son of Micaiah, son of Zaccur, son of
Asaph, and his kinsmen, Shemaiah, Azarel, Milalai, Gilalai, Maai, 36
Nethaneel, Judah, and Hanani, with the musical instruments of David
the man of God; and Ezra the scribe led them. They went past the 37
Fountain Gate and thence straight forward by the steps up to the City
of David, by the ascent to the city wall, past the house of David, and
on to the Water Gate on the east. The other thanksgiving choir went to 38
the left,*[c]* and I followed it with half the leading men of*[d]* the people,
continuing along the wall, past the Tower of the Ovens*[e]* to the Broad
Wall, and past the Ephraim Gate, and over the Jeshanah Gate,*[f]* and 39
over the Fish Gate, taking in the Tower of Hananel and the Tower of
the Hundred, as far as the Sheep Gate; and they halted at the Gate of
the Guardhouse. So the two thanksgiving choirs took their place in the 40
house of God, and I and half the magistrates with me; and the priests 41
Eliakim, Maaseiah, Miniamin, Micaiah, Elioenai, Zechariah, and
Hananiah, with trumpets; and Maaseiah, Shemaiah, Eleazar, Uzzi, 42
Jehohanan, Malchiah, Elam, and Ezer. The singers, led by Izrahiah,
raised their voices. A great sacrifice was celebrated that day, and they 43
all rejoiced because God had given them great cause for rejoicing; the
women and children rejoiced with them. And the rejoicing in Jerusalem
was heard a long way off.

On that day men were appointed to take charge of the store-rooms 44
for the contributions, the firstfruits, and the tithes, to gather in the
portions required by the law for the priests and Levites according to
the extent of the farmlands round the towns; for all Judah was full of
rejoicing at the ministry of the priests and Levites. And they performed 45
the service of their God and the service of purification, as did the
singers and the door-keepers, according to the rules laid down by
David and*[g]* his son Solomon. For it was in the days of David that 46
Asaph took the lead as chief of the singers and director*[h]* of praise and

[a] Beth-azmoth: *prob. rdg.*, *cp. 7. 28*; *Heb.* Azmoth.   [b] One...procession: *prob. rdg.;*
Heb. Processions.   [c] to the left: *prob. rdg.; Heb.* to the front.   [d] the leading men of:
prob. rdg.; Heb. om.   [e] *Or* Furnaces.   [f] the Jeshanah Gate: *or* the gate of the Old City.
[g] *So many MSS.; others om.*   [h] *Prob. rdg.; Heb.* song.

47 thanksgiving to God. And in the days of Zerubbabel and of Nehemiah all Israel gave the portions for the singers and the door-keepers as each day required; and they set apart the portion for the Levites, and the Levites set apart the portion for the Aaronites.

Nehemiah's reforms

13 ON THAT DAY at the public reading from the book of Moses, it was found to be laid down that no Ammonite or Moabite should
2 ever enter the assembly of God, because they did not meet the Israelites with food and water but hired Balaam to curse them, though our God
3 turned the curse into a blessing. When the people heard the law, they separated from Israel all who were of mixed blood.
4   But before this, Eliashib the priest, who was appointed over the store-rooms of the house of our God, and who was connected by
5 marriage with Tobiah, had provided for his use a large room where formerly they had kept the grain-offering, the incense, the temple vessels, the tithes of corn, new wine, and oil prescribed for the Levites,
6 singers, and door-keepers, and the contributions for the priests. All this time I was not in Jerusalem because, in the thirty-second year of Artaxerxes king of Babylon, I had gone to the king. Some time later,
7 I asked permission from him and returned to Jerusalem. There I discovered the wicked thing that Eliashib had done for Tobiah's sake
8 in providing him with a room in the courts of the house of God. I was greatly displeased and threw all Tobiah's belongings out of the room.
9 Then I gave orders that the room should be purified, and that the vessels of the house of God, with the grain-offering and incense, should be put back into it.
10   I also learnt that the Levites had not been given their portions; both they and the singers, who were responsible for their respective duties,
11 had made off to their farms. So I remonstrated with the magistrates and said, 'Why is the house of God deserted?' And I recalled the men
12 and restored them to their places. Then all Judah brought the tithes of
13 corn, new wine, and oil into the storehouses; and I put in charge of them Shelemiah the priest, Zadok the accountant, and Pedaiah a Levite, with Hanan son of Zaccur, son of Mattaniah, as their assistant, for they were considered trustworthy men; their duty was the distri-
14 bution of their shares to their brethren. Remember this, O God, to my credit, and do not wipe out of thy memory the devotion which I have shown in the house of my God and in his service.
15   In those days I saw men in Judah treading winepresses on the

sabbath, collecting quantities of produce and piling it on asses—wine, grapes, figs, and every kind of load, which they brought into Jerusalem on the sabbath; and I protested to them about selling food on that day. Tyrians living in Jerusalem also brought in fish and all kinds of 16 merchandise and sold them on the sabbath to the people of Judah, even in Jerusalem. Then I complained to the nobles of Judah and said to 17 them, 'How dare you profane the sabbath in this wicked way? Is not 18 this just what your fathers did, so that our God has brought all this evil on us and on this city? Now you are bringing more wrath upon Israel by profaning the sabbath.' When the entrances to Jerusalem had 19 been cleared in preparation for the sabbath, I gave orders that the gates should be shut and not opened until after the sabbath. And I appointed some of the men under me to have charge of the gates so that no load might enter on the sabbath. Then on one or two occasions the merchants 20 and all kinds of traders camped just outside Jerusalem, but I cautioned 21 them. 'Why are you camping in front of the city wall?' I asked. 'If you do it again, I will take action against you.' After that they did not come on the sabbath again. And I commanded the Levites who were to 22 purify themselves and take up duty as guards at the gates, to ensure that the sabbath was kept holy. Remember this also to my credit, O God, and spare me in thy great love.

In those days also I saw that some Jews had married women from 23 Ashdod, Ammon, and Moab. Half their children spoke the language of 24 Ashdod or of the other peoples and could not speak the language of the Jews. I argued with them and reviled them, I beat them and tore out 25 their hair; and I made them swear in the name of God: 'We will not marry our daughters to their sons, or take any of their daughters in marriage for our sons or for ourselves.' 'Was it not for such women', 26 I said, 'that King Solomon of Israel sinned? Among all the nations there was no king like him; he was loved by his God, and God made him king over all Israel; nevertheless even he was led by foreign women into sin. Are we then to follow your example and commit this grave 27 offence, breaking faith with our God by marrying foreign women?'

Now one of the sons of Joiada son of Eliashib the high priest had 28 married a daughter of Sanballat the Horonite; therefore I drove him out of my presence. Remember, O God, to their shame that they have 29 defiled the priesthood and the covenant of the priests[a] and the Levites.

Thus I purified them from everything foreign, and I made the 30 Levites and the priests resume the duties of their office; I also made 31 provision for the wood-offering, at appointed times, and for the first-fruits. Remember me for my good, O God.

[a] *Or* priesthood.

ESTHER

Esther chosen as queen by the Persian king

1 THE EVENTS HERE RELATED happened in the days
of Ahasuerus, the Ahasuerus who ruled from India to Ethiopia,*a*
2 a hundred and twenty-seven provinces. At this time he sat on
3 his royal throne in Susa the capital city. In the third year of his reign
he gave a banquet for all his officers and his courtiers; and when his
army of Persians and Medes, with his nobles and provincial governors,
4 were in attendance, he displayed the wealth of his kingdom and the
pomp and splendour of his majesty for many days, a hundred and
5 eighty in all. When these days were over, the king gave a banquet for all
the people present in Susa the capital city, both high and low; it was
held in the garden court of the royal pavilion and lasted seven days.
6 There were white curtains and violet hangings fastened to silver rings
with bands of fine linen and purple;*b* there were alabaster pillars and
couches of gold and silver set on a mosaic pavement of malachite and
7 alabaster, of mother-of-pearl and turquoise. Wine was served in golden
cups of various patterns: the king's wine flowed freely as befitted
8 a king, and the law of the drinking was that there should be no com-
pulsion, for the king had laid it down that all the stewards of his palace
9 should respect each man's wishes. In addition, Queen Vashti gave a
banquet for the women in the royal apartments of King Ahasuerus.
10 On the seventh day, when he was merry with wine, the king ordered
Mehuman, Biztha, Harbona, Bigtha, Abagtha, Zethar, and Carcas, the
11 seven eunuchs who were in attendance on the king's person, to bring
Queen Vashti before him wearing her royal crown, in order to display
her beauty to the people and the officers; for she was indeed a beautiful
12 woman. But Queen Vashti refused to come in answer to the royal
command conveyed by the eunuchs. This greatly incensed the king,
and he grew hot with anger.
13 Then the king conferred with his wise men versed in misdemeanours;*c*
for it was his royal custom to consult all who were versed in law and
14 religion, those closest to him being Carshena, Shethar, Admatha,
Tarshish, Meres, Marsena, and Memucan, the seven princes of Persia
and Media who had access to the king and held first place in the
15 kingdom. He asked them, 'What does the law require to be done with

[*a*] *Heb.* Cush.   [*b*] bands...purple: *or* white and purple cords.   [*c*] *Or* times.

Queen Vashti for disobeying the command of King Ahasuerus brought to her by the eunuchs?' Then Memucan made answer before the king 16 and the princes: 'Queen Vashti has done wrong, and not to the king alone, but also to all the officers and to all the peoples in all the provinces of King Ahasuerus. Every woman will come to know what 17 the queen has done, and this will make them treat their husbands with contempt; they will say, "King Ahasuerus ordered Queen Vashti to be brought before him and she did not come." The great ladies of 18 Persia and Media, who have heard of the queen's conduct, will tell all the king's officers about this day, and there will be endless disrespect and insolence! If it please your majesty, let a royal decree go out from 19 you and let it be inscribed in the laws of the Persians and Medes, never to be revoked, that Vashti shall not again appear before King Ahasuerus; and let the king give her place as queen to another woman who is more worthy of it than she. Thus when this royal edict is heard through the 20 length and breadth of the kingdom, all women will give honour to their husbands, high and low alike.' Memucan's advice pleased the king and 21 the princes, and the king did as he had proposed. Letters were sent to 22 all the royal provinces, to every province in its own script and to every people in their own language, in order that each man might be master in his own house and control all his own womenfolk.[a]

Later, when the anger of King Ahasuerus had died down, he 2 remembered Vashti and what she had done and what had been decreed against her. So the king's attendants said, 'Let beautiful young virgins 2 be sought out for your majesty; and let your majesty appoint commis- 3 sioners in all the provinces of your kingdom to bring all these beautiful young virgins into the women's quarters in Susa the capital city. Let them be committed to the care of Hegai, the king's eunuch in charge of the women, and let cosmetics be provided for them; and let the one 4 who is most acceptable to the king become queen in place of Vashti.' This idea pleased the king and he acted on it.

Now there was in Susa the capital city a Jew named Mordecai son 5 of Jair, son of Shimei, son of Kish, a Benjamite; he had been carried 6 into exile from Jerusalem among those whom Nebuchadnezzar king of Babylon had carried away with Jeconiah king of Judah. He had a foster- 7 child Hadassah, that is Esther, his uncle's daughter, who had neither father nor mother. She was a beautiful and charming girl, and after the death of her father and mother Mordecai had adopted her as his own daughter. When the king's order and his edict were published, and 8 many girls were brought to Susa the capital city to be committed to the care of Hegai, Esther too was taken to the king's palace to be entrusted to Hegai, who had charge of the women. She attracted his notice and 9

[a] and control...womenfolk: *prob. rdg.; Heb.* and speak in his own language.

received his special favour: he readily provided her with her cosmetics and her allowance of food, and also with seven picked maids from the king's palace, and he gave her and her maids privileges in the women's quarters.

10 Esther had not disclosed her race or her family, because Mordecai
11 had forbidden her to do so. Every day Mordecai passed along by the forecourt of the women's quarters to learn how Esther was faring and what was happening to her.

12 The full period of preparation prescribed for the women was twelve months, six months with oil and myrrh and six months with perfumes and cosmetics. When the period was complete, each girl's turn came to go
13 to King Ahasuerus, and she was allowed to take with her whatever she asked, when she went from the women's quarters to the king's palace.
14 She went into the palace in the evening and returned in the morning to another part of the women's quarters, to be under the care of Shaashgaz, the king's eunuch in charge of the concubines. She did not again go to the king unless he expressed a wish for her; then she was summoned by name.

15 When the turn came for Esther, daughter of Abihail the uncle of Mordecai her adoptive father, to go to the king, she asked for nothing to take with her except what was advised by Hegai, the king's eunuch in
16 charge of the women; and Esther charmed all who saw her. When she was taken to King Ahasuerus in the royal palace, in the seventh year of
17 his reign, in the tenth month, that is the month Tebeth, the king loved her more than any of his other women and treated her with greater favour and kindness than the rest of the virgins. He put a royal crown
18 on her head and made her queen in place of Vashti. Then the king gave a great banquet for all his officers and courtiers, a banquet in honour of Esther. He also proclaimed a holiday*a* throughout the provinces and distributed gifts worthy of a king.

19, 20 Mordecai was in attendance at court;*b* on his instructions Esther had not disclosed her family or her race, she had done what Mordecai told
21 her, as she did when she was his ward. One day when Mordecai was in attendance at court, Bigthan and Teresh, two of the king's eunuchs, keepers of the threshold, who were disaffected, were plotting to lay hands
22 on King Ahasuerus. This became known to Mordecai, who told Queen
23 Esther; and she told the king, mentioning Mordecai by name. The affair was investigated and the report confirmed; the two men were hanged on the gallows. All this was recorded in the royal chronicle in the presence of the king.

[*a*] *Or* an amnesty. [*b*] *So Sept.; Heb. adds* when the virgins were brought in a second time.

Haman's plot against the Jews

AFTER THIS, King Ahasuerus promoted Haman son of Hammedatha 3 the Agagite, advancing him and giving him precedence above all his fellow-officers. So the king's attendants at court all bowed down to 2 Haman and did obeisance, for so the king had commanded; but Mordecai did not bow down to him or do obeisance. Then the 3 attendants at court said to Mordecai, 'Why do you flout his majesty's command?' Day by day they challenged him, but he refused to listen 4 to them; so they informed Haman, in order to discover if Mordecai's refusal would be tolerated, for he had told them that he was a Jew. When Haman saw that Mordecai was not bowing down to him or doing 5 obeisance, he was infuriated. On learning who Mordecai's people were, 6 he scorned to lay hands on him alone, and looked for a way to destroy all the Jews throughout the whole kingdom of Ahasuerus, Mordecai and all his race.

In the twelfth year of King Ahasuerus, in the first month, Nisan, 7 they cast lots, Pur as it is called, in the presence of Haman, taking day by day and month by month, and the lot fell on the thirteenth day of the twelfth month,[a] the month Adar. Then Haman said to King Ahasuerus, 8 'There is a certain people, dispersed among the many peoples in all the provinces of your kingdom, who keep themselves apart. Their laws are different from those of every other people; they do not keep your majesty's laws. It does not befit your majesty to tolerate them. If it 9 please your majesty, let an order be made in writing for their destruction; and I will pay ten thousand talents of silver to your majesty's officials, to be deposited in the royal treasury.' So the king took the 10 signet-ring from his hand and gave it to Haman son of Hammedatha the Agagite, the enemy of the Jews; and he said to him, 'The money 11 and the people are yours; deal with them as you wish.'

On the thirteenth day of the first month the king's secretaries were 12 summoned and, in accordance with Haman's instructions, a writ was issued to the king's satraps and the governor of every province, and to the officers over each separate people: for each province in its own script and for each people in their own language. It was drawn up in the name of King Ahasuerus and sealed with the king's signet. Thus letters 13 were sent by courier to all the king's provinces with orders to destroy, slay, and exterminate all Jews, young and old, women and children, in one day, the thirteenth day of the twelfth month, the month Adar, and to plunder their possessions. A copy of the writ was to be issued as a 14

[a] and the lot...twelfth month: *prob. rdg., cp. verse 13; Heb.* the twelfth.

decree in every province and to be published to all the peoples, so that
15 they might be ready for that day. The couriers were dispatched post-
haste at the king's command, and the decree was issued in Susa the
capital city. The king and Haman sat down to drink; but the city of
Susa was thrown into confusion.

4 When Mordecai learnt all that had been done, he rent his clothes,
put on sackcloth and ashes, and went through the city crying loudly
2 and bitterly. He came within sight of the palace gate, because no one
3 clothed with sackcloth was allowed to pass through the gate. In every
province reached by the royal command and decree there was great
mourning among the Jews, with fasting and weeping and beating of the
4 breast. Most of them made their beds of sackcloth and ashes. When
Queen Esther's maids and eunuchs came and told her, she was distraught, and sent garments for Mordecai, so that they might take off
the sackcloth and clothe him with them; but he would not accept them.
5 Then Esther summoned Hathach, one of the king's eunuchs who had
been appointed to wait upon her, and ordered him to find out from
6 Mordecai what the trouble was and what it meant. Hathach went to
7 Mordecai in the city square in front of the palace gate, and Mordecai
told him all that had happened to him and how much money Haman
had offered to pay into the royal treasury for the destruction of the
8 Jews. He also gave him a copy of the writ for their destruction issued
in Susa, so that he might show it to Esther and tell her about it, bidding
her go to the king to plead for his favour and entreat him for her
9, 10 people. Hathach went and told Esther what Mordecai had said, and she
11 sent him back with this message: 'All the king's courtiers and the people
of the provinces are aware that if any person, man or woman, enters the
king's presence in the inner court unbidden, there is one law only: that
person shall be put to death, unless the king stretches out to him the
golden sceptre; then and then only shall he live. It is now thirty days
12 since I myself was called to go to the king.' But when they told
13 Mordecai what Esther had said, he bade them go back to her and say,
'Do not imagine that you alone of all the Jews will escape because you
14 are in the royal palace. If you remain silent at such a time as this, relief
and deliverance for the Jews will appear from another quarter, but you
and your father's family will perish. Who knows whether it is not for
15 such a time as this that you have come to royal estate?' Esther gave
16 them this answer to take back to Mordecai: 'Go and assemble all the
Jews to be found in Susa and fast for me; take neither food nor drink
for three days, night or day, and I and my maids will fast as you do.
After that I will go to the king, although it is against the law; and if
17 I perish, I perish.' So Mordecai went away and did exactly as Esther
had bidden him.

On the third day Esther put on her royal robes and stood in the 5 inner court of the king's palace, facing the palace itself; the king was seated on his royal throne in the palace, facing the entrance. When the 2 king caught sight of Queen Esther standing in the court, she won his favour and he stretched out to her the golden sceptre which he was holding. Thereupon Esther approached and touched the head of the sceptre. Then the king said to her, 'What is it, Queen Esther? What- 3 ever you ask of me, up to half my kingdom, shall be given to you.' 'If it 4 please your majesty,' said Esther, 'will you come today, sire, and Haman with you, to a banquet which I have made ready for you?' The 5 king gave orders that Haman should be fetched quickly, so that Esther's wish might be fulfilled; and the king and Haman went to the banquet which she had prepared. Over the wine the king said to 6 Esther, 'Whatever you ask of me shall be given to you. Whatever you request of me, up to half my kingdom, it shall be done.' Esther said in 7 answer, 'What I ask and request of you is this. If I have won your 8 majesty's favour, and if it please you, sire, to give me what I ask and to grant my request, will your majesty and Haman come tomorrow[a] to the banquet which I shall prepare for you both? Tomorrow I will do as your majesty has said.'

So Haman went away that day in good spirits and well pleased with 9 himself. But when he saw Mordecai in attendance at court and how he did not rise nor defer to him, he was filled with rage; but he kept 10 control of himself and went home. Then he sent for his friends and his wife Zeresh and held forth to them about the splendour of his wealth 11 and his many sons, and how the king had promoted him and advanced him above the other officers and courtiers. 'That is not all,' said 12 Haman; 'Queen Esther invited no one but myself to accompany the king to the banquet which she had prepared; and she has invited me again tomorrow with the king. Yet all this means nothing to me so long 13 as I see that Jew Mordecai in attendance at court.' Then his wife 14 Zeresh and all his friends said to him, 'Let a gallows seventy-five feet[b] high be set up, and recommend to the king in the morning to have Mordecai hanged upon it. Then go with the king to the banquet in good spirits.' Haman thought this an excellent plan, and he set up the gallows.

[a] So Sept.; Heb. om.   [b] Lit. fifty cubits.

665

Haman's downfall and Mordecai's triumph

6 THAT NIGHT sleep eluded the king, so he ordered the chronicle of
2 daily events to be brought; and it was read to him. Therein was
recorded that Mordecai had given information about Bigthana and
Teresh, the two royal eunuchs among the keepers of the threshold who
3 had plotted to lay hands on King Ahasuerus. Whereupon the king
said, 'What honour or dignity has been conferred on Mordecai for
this?' The king's courtiers who were in attendance told him that
4 nothing had been done for Mordecai. The king asked, 'Who is that in
the court?' Now Haman had just entered the outer court of the palace
to recommend to the king that Mordecai should be hanged on the
5 gallows which he had prepared for him. The king's servants answered,
6 'It is Haman standing there'; and the king bade him enter. He came
in, and the king said to him, 'What should be done for the man whom
the king wishes to honour?' Haman said to himself, 'Whom would the
7 king wish to honour more than me?' And he said to the king, 'For the
8 man whom the king wishes to honour, let there be brought royal robes
which the king himself wears, and a horse which the king rides, with
9 a royal crown upon its head. And let the robes and the horse be delivered
to one of the king's most honourable officers, and let him attire the
man whom the king wishes to honour and lead him mounted on the
horse through the city square, calling out as he goes: "See what is done
10 for the man whom the king wishes to honour."' Then the king said to
Haman, 'Fetch the robes and the horse at once, as you have said, and do
all this for Mordecai the Jew who is in attendance at court. Leave nothing
11 undone of all that you have said.' So Haman took the robes and the
horse, attired Mordecai, and led him mounted through the city square,
calling out as he went: 'See what is done for the man whom the king
wishes to honour.'

12 Then Mordecai returned to court and Haman hurried off home
13 mourning, with head uncovered. He told his wife Zeresh and all his
friends everything that had happened to him. And this was the reply
of his friends[a] and his wife Zeresh: 'If Mordecai, in face of whom your
fortunes begin to fall, belongs to the Jewish race, you will not get the
better of him; he will see your utter downfall.'

14 While they were still talking with Haman, the king's eunuchs
arrived and hurried him away to the banquet which Esther had
prepared.

7 1,2 So the king and Haman went to dine with Queen Esther. Again on

[a] *So Sept.; Heb.* his wise men.

that second day, over the wine, the king said, 'Whatever you ask of me will be given to you, Queen Esther. Whatever you request of me, up to half my kingdom, it shall be done.' Queen Esther answered, 'If I have ³ found favour with your majesty, and if it please your majesty, my request and petition is that my own life and the lives of my people may be spared. For we have been sold, I and my people, to be destroyed, ⁴ slain, and exterminated. If it had been a matter of selling us, men and women alike, into slavery, I should have kept silence; for then our plight would not be such as to injure the king's interests.' Then King ⁵ Ahasuerus said to Queen Esther, 'Who is he, and where is he, who has presumed to do such a thing as this?' 'An adversary and an enemy,' ⁶ said Esther, 'this wicked Haman.' At that Haman was dumbfounded in the presence of the king and the queen. The king rose from the ⁷ banquet in a rage and went to the garden of the pavilion, while Haman remained where he was, to plead for his life with Queen Esther; for he saw that in the king's mind his fate was determined. When the king ⁸ returned from the garden to the banqueting hall, Haman had flung himself across the couch on which Esther was reclining. The king exclaimed, 'Will he even assault the queen here in my presence?' No sooner had the words left the king's mouth than Haman hid his face in despair.[a] Then Harbona, one of the eunuchs in attendance on the king, ⁹ said, 'At Haman's house stands the gallows, seventy-five feet[b] high, which he himself has prepared for Mordecai, who once served the king well.' 'Hang Haman on it', said the king. So they hanged him on the ¹⁰ gallows that he himself had prepared for Mordecai. After that the king's rage abated.

On that day King Ahasuerus gave Queen Esther the house of **8** Haman, enemy of the Jews; and Mordecai came into the king's presence, for Esther had told him how he was related to her. Then the king took ² off his signet-ring, which he had taken back from Haman, and gave it to Mordecai. And Esther put Mordecai in charge of Haman's house.

Once again Esther spoke before the king, falling at his feet in tears ³ and pleading with him to avert the calamity planned by Haman the Agagite and to frustrate his plot against the Jews. The king stretched ⁴ out the golden sceptre to Esther, and she rose and stood before the king, and said, 'May it please your majesty: if I have found favour with ⁵ you, and if the proposal seems right to your majesty and I have won your approval, let a writ be issued to recall the letters which Haman son of Hammedatha the Agagite wrote in pursuance of his plan to destroy the Jews in all the royal provinces. For how can I bear to see ⁶ the calamity which is coming upon my race? Or how can I bear to see the destruction of my family?' Then King Ahasuerus said to Queen ⁷

[a] Haman...despair: *prob. rdg.; Heb.* they covered Haman's face.   [b] *Lit.* fifty cubits.

Esther and to Mordecai the Jew, 'I have given Haman's house to Esther, and he has been hanged on the gallows, because he threatened

8 the lives of the Jews. Now you shall issue a writ concerning the Jews in my name, in whatever terms you think fit, and seal it with the royal signet; for an order written in the name of the king and sealed with the royal signet cannot be revoked.'

9 And so, on the twenty-third day of the third month, the month Sivan, the king's secretaries were summoned; and a writ was issued to the Jews, exactly as Mordecai directed, and to the satraps, the governors, and the officers in the provinces from India to Ethiopia, a hundred and twenty-seven provinces, for each province in its own script and for each people in their own language, and also for the Jews

10 in their own script and language. The writ was drawn up in the name of King Ahasuerus and sealed with the royal signet, and letters were

11 sent by mounted couriers riding on horses from the royal stables. By these letters the king granted permission to the Jews in every city to unite and defend themselves, and to destroy, slay, and exterminate the whole strength of any people or province which might attack them,

12 women and children too, and to plunder their possessions, throughout all the provinces of King Ahasuerus, in one day, the thirteenth day of

13 the twelfth month, the month Adar. A copy of the writ was to be issued as a decree in every province and published to all peoples, and the Jews were to be ready for that day, the day of vengeance on their

14 enemies. So the couriers, mounted on their royal horses, were dispatched post-haste at the king's urgent command; and the decree was issued also in Susa the capital city.

15 Mordecai left the king's presence in royal robes of violet and white, wearing a great golden crown and a cloak of fine linen and purple, and

16 all the city of Susa shouted for joy. For the Jews there was light and

17 joy, gladness and honour. In every province and every city reached by the royal command and decree, there was joy and gladness for the Jews, feasting and holiday. And many of the peoples of the land professed themselves Jews, because fear of the Jews had seized them.

9 ON THE THIRTEENTH DAY of the twelfth month, the month Adar, the time came for the king's command and his edict to be carried out. The very day on which the enemies of the Jews had hoped to gain the upper hand over them was to become the day when the Jews should

2 gain the upper hand over those who hated them. On that day the Jews united in their cities in all the provinces of King Ahasuerus to fall upon those who had planned their ruin. No one could resist them,

3 because fear of them had seized all peoples. All the officers of the provinces, the satraps and the governors, and all the royal officials,

aided the Jews, because fear of Mordecai had seized them. Mordecai 4
had become a great personage in the royal palace; his fame had spread
throughout all the provinces as the power of the man grew steadily
greater. So the Jews put their enemies to the sword, with great 5
slaughter and destruction; they worked their will on those who hated
them. In Susa, the capital city, the Jews killed five hundred men 6
and destroyed them; and they killed also Parshandatha, Dalphon and 7
Aspatha, Poratha, Adalia and Aridatha, Parmashta, Arisai, Aridai and 8,9
Vaizatha, the ten sons of Haman son of Hammedatha, the enemy of the 10
Jews; but they did not touch the plunder.

That day when the number of those killed in Susa the capital city 11
came to the notice of the king, he said to Queen Esther, 'In Susa, the 12
capital city, the Jews have killed and destroyed five hundred men and
the ten sons of Haman. What have they done in the rest of the king's
provinces? Whatever you ask further will be given to you; whatever
more you seek shall be done.' Esther answered him, 'If it please your 13
majesty, let tomorrow be granted to the Jews in Susa to do according
to the edict for today; and let the bodies of Haman's ten sons be hung
up on the gallows.' The king gave orders for this to be done; the edict 14
was issued in Susa and Haman's ten sons were hung up on the gallows.
The Jews in Susa united again on the fourteenth day of the month 15
Adar and killed three hundred men in Susa; but they did not touch the
plunder.

The rest of the Jews in the king's provinces had united to defend 16
themselves; they took vengeance on[a] their enemies by killing seventy-
five thousand of those who hated them; but they did not touch the
plunder. This was on the thirteenth day of the month Adar, and they 17
rested on the fourteenth day and made that a day of feasting and joy.
The Jews in Susa had united on the thirteenth and fourteenth days of 18
the month, and rested on the fifteenth day and made that a day of
feasting and joy. This is why isolated Jews who live in remote villages 19
keep the fourteenth day of the month Adar in joy and feasting, as a
holiday on which they send presents of food to one another.

Then Mordecai set these things on record and sent letters to all the 20
Jews in all the provinces of King Ahasuerus, far and near, binding them 21
to keep the fourteenth and fifteenth days of the month Adar, year by
year, as the days on which the Jews obtained relief from their enemies 22
and as the month which was changed for them from sorrow into joy,
from a time of mourning to a holiday. They were to keep them as days
of feasting and joy, days for sending presents of food to one another
and gifts to the poor.

So the Jews undertook to continue the practice that they had begun 23

[a] *Prob. rdg.; Heb.* got respite from.

24 in accordance with Mordecai's letter. This they did because Haman son of Hammedatha the Agagite, the enemy of all the Jews, had plotted to destroy the Jews and had cast lots, Pur as it is called, with intent to
25 crush and destroy them. But when the matter came before the king, he issued written orders that the wicked plot which Haman had devised against the Jews should recoil on his own head, and that he and his
26 sons should be hanged on the gallows. Therefore, these days were named Purim after the word Pur. Accordingly, because of all that was written in this letter, because of all they had seen and experienced in
27 this affair, the Jews resolved and undertook, on behalf of themselves, their descendants, and all who should join them, that they would without fail keep these two days as a yearly festival in the prescribed
28 manner and at the appointed time; that these days should be remembered and kept, generation after generation, in every family, province, and city, that the days of Purim should always be observed among the Jews, and that the memory of them should never cease among their descendants.

29 Queen Esther daughter of Abihail gave full authority in writing to[a]
30 Mordecai the Jew, to confirm this second letter about Purim. Letters wishing peace and security were sent to all the Jews in the hundred and
31 twenty-seven provinces of King Ahasuerus, making the observance of these days of Purim at their appointed time binding on them, as Mordecai the Jew[b] had prescribed. In the same way they had prescribed regulations for fasts and lamentations for themselves and their
32 descendants. The command of Esther confirmed these regulations for Purim, and the record is preserved in writing.

10 King Ahasuerus imposed forced labour on the land and the coasts
2 and islands. All the king's acts of authority and power, and the dignities which he conferred on Mordecai, are written in the annals of the kings
3 of Media and Persia. For Mordecai the Jew was second only to King Ahasuerus; he was a great man among the Jews and was popular with the mass of his countrymen, for he sought the good of his people and promoted the welfare of all their descendants.[c]

[a] *Prob. rdg.; Heb.* and. [b] *Prob. rdg.; Heb. adds* and Queen Esther. [c] *Or* and was in friendly relations with all his race.

THE BOOK OF

JOB

Prologue

THERE LIVED in the land of Uz a man of blameless and 1
upright life named Job, who feared God and set his face against
wrongdoing. He had seven sons and three daughters; and he 2,3
owned seven thousand sheep and three thousand camels, five hundred
yoke of oxen and five hundred asses, with a large number of slaves.
Thus Job was the greatest man in all the East.

Now his sons used to foregather and give, each in turn, a feast in his 4
own house; and they used to send and invite their three sisters to eat
and drink with them. Then, when a round of feasts was finished, Job 5
sent for his children and sanctified them, rising early in the morning
and sacrificing a whole-offering for each of them; for he thought that
they might somehow have sinned against God and committed
blasphemy in their hearts. This he always did.

The day came when the members of the court of heaven*a* took their 6
places in the presence of the LORD, and Satan*b* was there among them.
The LORD asked him where he had been. 'Ranging over the earth', he 7
said, 'from end to end.' Then the LORD asked Satan, 'Have you 8
considered my servant Job? You will find no one like him on earth,
a man of blameless and upright life, who fears God and sets his face
against wrongdoing.' Satan answered the LORD, 'Has not Job good 9
reason to be God-fearing? Have you not hedged him round on every 10
side with your protection, him and his family and all his possessions?
Whatever he does you have blessed, and his herds have increased
beyond measure. But stretch out your hand and touch all that he has, 11
and then he will curse you to your face.' Then the LORD said to Satan, 12
'So be it. All that he has is in your hands; only Job himself you must
not touch.' And Satan left the LORD's presence.

When the day came that Job's sons and daughters were eating and 13
drinking in the eldest brother's house, a messenger came running to 14
Job and said, 'The oxen were ploughing and the asses were grazing
near them, when the Sabaeans swooped down and carried them off, 15
after putting the herdsmen to the sword; and I am the only one to
escape and tell the tale.' While he was still speaking, another messenger 16
arrived and said, 'God's fire flashed from heaven. It struck the sheep

[a] members of the court of heaven: *lit.* sons of God. [b] *Or* the adversary.

671

and the shepherds and burnt them up; and I am the only one to escape
17 and tell the tale.' While he was still speaking, another arrived and said,
'The Chaldaeans, three bands of them, have made a raid on the camels
and carried them off, after putting the drivers to the sword; and I am
18 the only one to escape and tell the tale.' While this man was speaking,
yet another arrived and said, 'Your sons and daughters were eating and
19 drinking in the eldest brother's house, when suddenly a whirlwind
swept across from the desert and struck the four corners of the house,
and it fell on the young people and killed them; and I am the only one
20 to escape and tell the tale.' At this Job stood up and rent his cloak; then
21 he shaved his head and fell prostrate on the ground, saying:

> Naked I came from the womb,[a]
> naked I shall return whence I came.
> The LORD gives and the LORD takes away;
> blessed be the name of the LORD.

22 Throughout all this Job did not sin; he did not charge God with
unreason.

2 Once again the day came when the members of the court of heaven
took their places in the presence of the LORD, and Satan was there
2 among them. The LORD asked him where he had been. 'Ranging over
3 the earth', he said, 'from end to end.' Then the LORD asked Satan,
'Have you considered my servant Job? You will find no one like him
on earth, a man of blameless and upright life, who fears God and sets
his face against wrongdoing. You incited me to ruin him without a
4 cause, but his integrity is still unshaken.' Satan answered the LORD, 'Skin
5 for skin! There is nothing the man will grudge to save himself. But
stretch out your hand and touch his bone and his flesh, and see if he
will not curse you to your face.'

6 Then the LORD said to Satan, 'So be it. He is in your hands; but
7 spare his life.' And Satan left the LORD's presence, and he smote Job
8 with running sores from head to foot, so that he took a piece of a
9 broken pot to scratch himself as he sat among the ashes. Then his wife
said to him, 'Are you still unshaken in your integrity? Curse God and
10 die!' But he answered, 'You talk as any wicked fool of a woman might
talk. If we accept good from God, shall we not accept evil?' Throughout
all this, Job did not utter one sinful word.

11 When Job's three friends, Eliphaz of Teman, Bildad of Shuah, and
Zophar of Naamah, heard of all these calamities which had overtaken
him, they left their homes and arranged to come and condole with him
12 and comfort him. But when they first saw him from a distance, they
did not recognize him; and they wept aloud, rent their cloaks and tossed

[a] *Lit.* my mother's womb (*cp. Eccles. 5. 15*).

dust into the air over their heads. For seven days and seven nights they 13
sat beside him on the ground, and none of them said a word to him;
for they saw that his suffering was very great.

Job's complaint to God

After this Job broke silence and cursed the day of his birth: **3** 1–2

Perish the day when I was born   3
and the night which said, 'A man is conceived'!
May that day turn to darkness; may God above not look for it,   4
nor light of dawn shine on it.
May blackness sully it, and murk and gloom,   5
cloud smother that day, swift darkness eclipse its sun.
Blind darkness swallow up that night;   6
count it not among the days of the year,
reckon it not in the cycle of the months.
That night, may it be barren for ever,   7
no cry of joy be heard in it.
Cursed be it by those whose magic binds even the monster of the   8
    deep,
who are ready to tame Leviathan himself with spells.
May no star shine out in its twilight;   9
may it wait for a dawn that never comes,
nor ever see the eyelids of the morning,
because it did not shut the doors of the womb that bore me   10
and keep trouble away from my sight.
Why was I not still-born,   11
why did I not die when I came out of the womb?
Why was I ever laid on my mother's knees   12
or put to suck at her breasts?
Why was I not hidden like an untimely birth,   16
like an infant that has not lived to see the light?
For then I should be lying in the quiet grave,   13
asleep in death, at rest,
with kings and their ministers   14
who built themselves palaces,
with princes rich in gold   15
who filled their houses with silver.
There the wicked man chafes no more,   17*a*

[a] *Verse 16 transposed to follow verse 12.*

there the tired labourer rests;
18 the captive too finds peace there
and hears no taskmaster's voice;
19 high and low are there,
even the slave, free from his master.
20 Why should the sufferer be born to see the light?
Why is life given to men who find it so bitter?
21 They wait for death but it does not come,
they seek it more eagerly than^a hidden treasure.
22 They are glad when they reach the tomb,
and when they come to the grave they exult.
23 Why should a man be born to wander blindly,
hedged in by God on every side?
24 My sighing is all my food,
and groans pour from me in a torrent.
25 Every terror that haunted me has caught up with me,
and all that I feared has come upon me.
26 There is no peace of mind nor quiet for me;
I chafe in torment and have no rest.

First cycle of speeches

4 Then Eliphaz the Temanite began:

2 If one ventures to speak with you, will you lose patience?
For who could hold his tongue any longer?
3 Think how once you encouraged those who faltered,
how you braced feeble arms,
4 how a word from you upheld the stumblers
and put strength into weak knees.
5 But now that adversity comes upon you, you lose patience;
it touches you, and you are unmanned.
6 Is your religion no comfort to you?
Does your blameless life give you no hope?
7 For consider, what innocent man has ever perished?
Where have you seen the upright destroyed?
8 This I know, that those who plough mischief and sow trouble
reap as they have sown;
9 they perish at the blast of God
and are shrivelled by the breath of his nostrils.

^u [a] *Or* seek it among...

The roar of the lion, the whimpering of his cubs, fall silent;   10
the teeth of the young lions are broken;
the lion perishes for lack of prey   11
and the whelps of the lioness are abandoned.

A word stole into my ears,   12
and they caught the whisper of it;
in the anxious visions of the night,   13
when a man sinks into deepest sleep,
terror seized me and shuddering;   14
the trembling of my body frightened me.
A wind brushed my face   15
and made the hairs bristle on my flesh;
and a figure stood there whose shape I could not discern,   16
an apparition loomed before me,
and I heard the sound of a low voice:
'Can mortal man be more righteous than God,   17
or the creature purer than his Maker?
If God mistrusts his own servants   18
and finds his messengers at fault,
how much more those that dwell in houses whose walls are   19
    clay,
whose foundations are dust,
which can be crushed like a bird's nest
or torn down between dawn and dark,   20
how much more shall such men perish outright and unheeded,
^adie, without ever finding wisdom?'   21

Call if you will; is there any to answer you?   5
To which of the holy ones will you turn?
The fool is destroyed by his own angry passions,   2
and the end of childish resentment is death.
I have seen it for myself: a fool uprooted,   3
his home in sudden ruin about him,^b
his children past help,   4
browbeaten in court^c with none to save them.
^dTheir rich possessions are snatched from them;   5
what they have harvested others hungrily devour;
the stronger man seizes it from the panniers,
panting, thirsting for their wealth.
Mischief does not grow out of the soil   6

[a] *Prob. rdg., transposing* Their rich possessions are snatched from them *to follow 5. 4.*
[b] ruin about him: *prob. rdg.; Heb. obscure.*   [c] in court: *lit.* in the gate.   [d] *Line transposed from 4. 21.*

nor trouble spring from the earth;
7   man is born to trouble,
     as surely as birds fly*a* upwards.

8   For my part, I would make my petition to God
     and lay my cause before him,
9   who does great and unsearchable things,
     marvels without number.
10   He gives rain to the earth
     and sends water on the fields;
11   he raises the lowly to the heights,
     the mourners are uplifted by victory;
12   he frustrates the plots of the crafty,
     and they win no success,
13   he traps the cunning in their craftiness,
     and the schemers' plans are thrown into confusion.
14   In the daylight they run into darkness,
     and grope at midday as though it were night.
15   He saves the destitute from their greed,*b*
     and the needy from the grip of the strong;
16   so the poor hope again,
     and the unjust are sickened.

17   Happy the man whom God rebukes!
     therefore do not reject the discipline of the Almighty.
18   For, though he wounds, he will bind up;
     the hands that smite will heal.
19   You may meet disaster six times, and he will save you;
     seven times, and no harm shall touch you.
20   In time of famine he will save you from death,
     in battle from the sword.
21   You will be shielded from the lash of slander,*c*
     and when violence comes you need not fear.
22   You will laugh at violence and starvation
     and have no need to fear wild beasts;
23   for you have a covenant with the stones to spare your fields.
     and the weeds have been constrained to leave you at peace.
24   You will know that all is well with your household,
     you will look round your home and find nothing amiss;
25   you will know, too, that your descendants will be many
     and your offspring like grass, thick upon the earth.
26   You will come in sturdy old age to the grave
     as sheaves come in due season to the threshing-floor.

[a] *Or* as sparks shoot.   [b] *Lit.* mouths.   [c] from...slander: *or* when slander is rife.

We have inquired into all this, and so it is;   27
this we have heard, and you may know it for the truth.

Then Job answered: 6

O that the grounds for my resentment might be weighed,   2
and my misfortunes set with them on the scales!
For they would outweigh the sands of the sea: 3
what wonder if my words are wild?[a]
The arrows of the Almighty find their mark in me,   4
and their poison soaks into my spirit;
God's onslaughts wear me away.
Does the wild ass bray when he has grass   5
or the ox low when he has fodder?
Can a man eat tasteless food unseasoned with salt,   6
or find any flavour in the juice of mallows?
Food that should nourish me sticks in my throat,   7
and my bowels rumble with an echoing sound.

O that I might have my request,   8
that God would grant what I hope for:
that he would be pleased to crush me,   9
to snatch me away with his hand and cut me off!
For that would bring me relief,   10
and in the face of unsparing anguish I would leap for joy.[b]
Have I the strength to wait?   11
What end have I to expect, that I should be patient?
Is my strength the strength of stone,   12
or is my flesh bronze?
Oh how shall I find help within myself?   13
The power to aid myself is put out of my reach.

Devotion is due from his friends   14
to one who despairs and loses faith in the Almighty;
but my brothers have been treacherous as a mountain stream,   15
like the channels of streams that run dry,
which turn dark with ice   16
or are hidden with piled-up snow;
or they vanish the moment they are in spate,   17
dwindle in the heat and are gone.
Then the caravans, winding hither and thither,   18
go up into the wilderness and perish;[c]
the caravans of Tema look for their waters,   19

[a] what...wild?: *or* therefore words fail me.   [b] *Prob. rdg.; Heb. adds* I have not denied
the words of the Holy One.   [c] *Or* and are lost.

travelling merchants of Sheba hope for them;
20 but they are disappointed, for all their confidence,
    they reach them only to be balked.
21 So treacherous have you now been to me:[a]
    you felt dismay and were afraid.
22 Did I ever say, 'Give me this or that;
    open your purses to save my life;
23 rescue me from my enemy;
    ransom me out of the hands of ruthless men'?
24 Tell me plainly, and I will listen in silence;
    show me where I have erred.
25 How harsh are the words of the upright man!
    What do the arguments of wise men[b] prove?
26 Do you mean to argue about words
    or to sift the utterance of a man past hope?
27 Would you assail an orphan[c]?
    Would you hurl yourselves on a friend?
28 So now, I beg you, turn and look at me:
    am I likely to lie to your faces?
29 Think again, let me have no more injustice;
    think again, for my integrity is in question.
30 Do I ever give voice to injustice?
    Does my sense not warn me when my words are wild?

7   Has not man hard service on earth,
    and are not his days like those of a hired labourer,
2   like those of a slave longing for the shade
    or a servant kept waiting for his wages?
3   So months of futility are my portion,
    troubled nights are my lot.
4   When I lie down, I think,
    'When will it be day that[d] I may rise?'
    When the evening grows long and I lie down,[e]
    I do nothing but toss till morning twilight.
5   My body is infested with worms,
    and scabs cover my skin.[f]
6   My days are swifter than a shuttle[g]
    and come to an end as the thread runs out.[h]
7   Remember, my life is but a breath of wind;
    I shall never again see good days.

[a] So...to me: *prob. rdg.; Heb. obscure.*   [b] wise men: *prob. rdg.; Heb. unintelligible.*
[c] *Or* a blameless man.   [d] day that: *so Sept.; Heb. om.*   [e] and I lie down: *prob. rdg.,
cp. Pesh.; Heb. om.*   [f] *Prob. rdg.; Heb. adds* it is cracked and discharging.   [g] *Or* a
fleeting odour.   [h] as...out: *or* without hope.

Thou wilt behold me no more with a seeing eye;   8
under thy very eyes I shall disappear.
As clouds break up and disperse,   9
so he that goes down to Sheol never comes back;
he never returns home again,   10
and his place will know him no more.*a*

But I will not hold my peace;   11
I will speak out in the distress of my mind
and complain in the bitterness of my soul.
Am I the monster of the deep, am I the sea-serpent,   12
that thou settest a watch over me?
When I think that my bed will comfort me,   13
that sleep will relieve my complaining,
thou dost terrify me with dreams   14
and affright me with visions.
I would rather be choked outright;   15
I would prefer death to all my sufferings.
I am in despair, I would not go on living;   16
leave me alone, for my life is but a vapour.
What is man that thou makest much of him   17
and turnest thy thoughts towards him,
only to punish him morning by morning   18
or to test him every hour of the day?
Wilt thou not look away from me for an instant?   19
Wilt thou not let me be while I swallow my spittle?
If I have sinned, how do I injure thee,   20
thou watcher of the hearts*b* of men?
Why hast thou made me thy butt,
and why have I become thy*c* target?
Why dost thou not pardon my offence   21
and take away my guilt?
But now I shall lie down in the grave;
seek me, and I shall not be.

Then Bildad the Shuhite began: **8**

How long will you say such things,   2
the long-winded ramblings of an old man?
Does God pervert judgement?   3
Does the Almighty pervert justice?
Your sons sinned against him,   4
so he left them to be victims of their own iniquity.

[*a*] *Or* and he will not be noticed any more in his place.   [*b*] of the hearts: *so Sept.; Heb. om.*
[*c*] *So some MSS., cp. Sept.; others* my.

679

5   If only you will seek God betimes
      and plead for the favour of the Almighty,

6   if you are innocent and upright,
      then indeed will he watch over you
      and see your just intent fulfilled.

7   Then, though your beginnings were humble,
      your end will be great.

8   Inquire now of older generations
      and consider the experience of their fathers;

9   for we ourselves are of yesterday and are transient;
      our days on earth are a shadow.

10   Will not they speak to you and teach you
      and pour out the wisdom of their hearts?

11   Can rushes grow where there is no marsh?
      Can reeds flourish without water?

12   While they are still in flower and not ready to cut,[a]
      they wither earlier than[b] any green plant.

13   Such is the fate of all who forget God;
      the godless man's life-thread breaks off;

14   his confidence is gossamer,
      and the ground of his trust a spider's web.

15   He leans against his house but it does not stand;
      he clutches at it but it does not hold firm.

16   His is the lush growth of a plant in the sun,
      pushing out shoots over the garden;

17   but its roots become entangled in a stony patch
      and run against a bed of rock.

18   Then someone uproots it from its place,
      which[c] disowns it and says, 'I have never known you.'

19   That is how its life withers away,
      and other plants spring up from the earth.

20   Be sure, God will not spurn the blameless man,
      nor will he grasp the hand of the wrongdoer.

21   He will yet fill your mouth with laughter,
      and shouts of joy will be on your lips;

22   your enemies shall be wrapped in confusion,
      and the tents of the wicked shall vanish away.

9 Then Job answered:

2   Indeed this I know for the truth,
      that no man can win his case against God.

[a] and...cut: *or* they are surely cut. [b] *Or* wither like... [c] *Or* and.

If a man chooses to argue with him, 3
God will not answer one question in a thousand.[a]
He is wise, he is powerful; 4
what man has stubbornly resisted him and survived?
It is God who moves mountains, giving them no rest, 5
turning them over in his wrath;
who makes the earth start from its place 6
so that its pillars are convulsed;
who commands the sun's orb not to rise 7
and shuts up the stars under his seal;
who by himself spread out the heavens 8
and trod on the sea-monster's back;[b]
who made Aldebaran and Orion, 9
the Pleiades and the circle of the southern stars;
who does great and unsearchable things, 10
marvels without number.

He passes by me, and I do not see him; 11
he moves on his way undiscerned by me;
if he hurries on,[c] who can bring him back? 12
Who will ask him what he does?
God does not turn back his wrath; 13
the partisans of Rahab lie prostrate at his feet.
How much less can I answer him 14
or find words to dispute with him?
Though I am right, I get no answer, 15
though I plead with my accuser for mercy.
If I summoned him to court and he responded, 16
I do not believe that he would listen to my plea—
for he bears hard upon me for a trifle[d] 17
and rains blows on me without cause;
he leaves me no respite to recover my breath 18
but fills me with bitter thoughts.
If the appeal is to force, see how strong he is; 19
if to justice, who can compel him[e] to give me a hearing?
Though I am right, he condemns me out of my own mouth; 20
though I am blameless, he twists my words.
Blameless, I say; of myself 21
I reck nothing, I hold my life cheap.
But it is all one; therefore I say, 22
'He destroys blameless and wicked alike.'

[a] If a man...thousand: *or* If God is pleased to argue with him, man cannot answer one
question in a thousand. [b] *Or* on the crests of the waves. [c] *So some MSS.; others*
seizes. [d] *Lit.* a hair. [e] *So Sept.; Heb.* me.

23   When a sudden flood brings death,
       he mocks the plight of the innocent.

24   The land is given over to the power of the wicked,
       and the eyes of its judges are blindfold.[a]

25   My days have been swifter than a runner,
       they have slipped away and seen no prosperity;

26   they have raced by like reed-built skiffs,
       swift as vultures swooping on carrion.

27   If I think, 'I will forget my griefs,
       I will show a cheerful face and smile',

28   I tremble in every nerve;[b]
       I know that thou wilt not hold me innocent.

29   If I am to be accounted guilty,
       why do I labour in vain?

30   Though I wash myself with soap
       or cleanse my hands with lye,

31   thou wilt thrust me into the mud
       and my clothes will make me loathsome.

32   He is not a man as I am, that I can answer him
       or that we can confront one another in court.

33   If only there were one to arbitrate between us
       and impose his authority on us both,

34   so that God might take his rod from my back,
       and terror of him might not come on me suddenly.

35   I would then speak without fear of him;
       for I know I am not what I am thought to be.

10   I am sickened of life;
       I will give free rein to my griefs,
       I will speak out in bitterness of soul.

2   I will say to God, 'Do not condemn me,
       but tell me the ground of thy complaint against me.

3   Dost thou find any advantage in oppression,
       in spurning the fruit of all thy labour
       and smiling on the policy of wicked men?

4   Hast thou eyes of flesh
       or dost thou see as mortal man sees?

5   Are thy days as those of a mortal
       or thy years as the life of a man,

6   that thou lookest for guilt in me
       and dost seek in me for sin,

---

[a] *Prob. rdg.; Heb. adds* if not he, then who?   [b] *Or* I am afraid of all that I must suffer.

though thou knowest that I am guiltless   7
and have none to save me from thee?

'Thy hands gave me shape and made me;   8
and dost thou at once turn and destroy me?
Remember that thou didst knead me like clay;   9
and wouldst thou turn me back into dust?
Didst thou not pour me out like milk   10
and curdle me like cheese,
clothe me with skin and flesh   11
and knit me together with bones and sinews?
Thou hast given me life and continuing favour,   12
and thy providence has watched over my spirit.
Yet this was the secret purpose of thy heart,   13
and I know that this was thy intent:
that, if I sinned, thou wouldst be watching me   14
and wouldst not acquit me of my guilt.
If I indeed am wicked, the worse for me!   15
If I am righteous, even so I may lift up my head;[a]
if I am[b] proud as a lion, thou dost hunt me down   16
and dost confront me again with marvellous power;
thou dost renew thy onslaught upon me,   17
and with mounting anger against me
bringest fresh forces to the attack.
Why didst thou bring me out of the womb?   18
O that I had ended there and no eye had seen me,
that I had been carried from the womb to the grave   19
and were as though I had not been born.
Is not my life short and fleeting?   20
Let me be, that I may be happy for a moment,
before I depart to a land of gloom,   21
a land of deep darkness, never to return,
a land of gathering shadows, of deepening darkness,   22
lit by no ray of light,[c] dark[d] upon dark.'

Then Zophar the Naamathite began: **11**

Should this spate of words not be answered?   2
Must a man of ready tongue be always right?
Is your endless talk to reduce men to silence?   3
Are you to talk nonsense and no one rebuke you?
You claim that your opinions are sound;   4

[a] *Prob. rdg.; Heb. adds* filled with shame and steeped in my affliction. [b] *So Sept.; Heb.*
if he is. [c] lit...light: *or* a place of disorder. [d] *Prob. rdg.; Heb. obscure.*

you say to God, 'I am spotless in thy sight.'
5   But if only he would speak
and open his lips to talk with you,
6   and expound to you the secrets of wisdom,
for wonderful are its effects!
[Know then that God exacts from you less than your sin deserves.]
7   Can you fathom the mystery of God,
can you fathom the perfection of the Almighty?
8   It is higher than heaven;*a* you can do nothing.
It is deeper than Sheol; you can know nothing.
9   Its measure is longer than the earth
and broader than the sea.
10 If he passes by, he may keep secret his passing;
if he proclaims it, who can turn him back?
11 He surely knows which men are false,
and when he sees iniquity, does he not take note of it?*b*
12 Can a fool grow wise?
can a wild ass's foal be born a man?
13 If only you had directed your heart rightly
and spread out your hands to pray to him!
14 If you have wrongdoing in hand, thrust it away;
let no iniquity make its home with you.
15 Then you could hold up your head without fault,
a man of iron, knowing no fear.
16 Then you will forget your trouble;
you will remember it only as flood-waters that have passed;
17 life will be lasting, bright as noonday,
and darkness will be turned to morning.
18 You will be confident, because there is hope;
sure of protection, you will lie down in confidence;*c*
19 great men will seek your favour.
20 Blindness will fall on the wicked;
the ways of escape are closed to them,
and their hope is despair.

12 Then Job answered:

2   No doubt you are perfect men*d*
and absolute wisdom is yours*e*!
3   But I have sense as well as you;

[a] It is...heaven: *so Vulg.; Heb.* The heights of heaven. [b] does...of it?: *or* he does not stand aloof. [c] *Prob. rdg.; Heb. adds* and you will lie down unafraid. [d] *Prob. rdg.; Heb.* No doubt you are people. [e] *So Aq. and Symm.; Heb.* and wisdom will die with you.

in nothing do I fall short of you;
what gifts indeed have you that others have not?
Yet I am a laughing-stock to my friend—   4
a laughing-stock, though I am innocent and blameless,
one that called upon God, and he answered.*a*
Prosperity and ease look down on misfortune,   5
on the blow that fells the man who is already reeling,
while the marauders' tents are left undisturbed   6
and those who provoke God live safe and sound.*b*

Go and ask the cattle,   7
ask the birds of the air to inform you,
or tell the creatures that crawl to teach you,   8
and the fishes of the sea to give you instruction.
Who cannot learn from all these   9
that the LORD's own hand has done this?
(Does not the ear test what is spoken   11*c*
as the palate savours food?
There is wisdom, remember, in age,   12
and long life brings understanding.)

In God's hand are the souls of all that live,   10
the spirits of all human kind.
Wisdom and might are his,   13
with him are firmness and understanding.
If he pulls down, there is no rebuilding;   14
if he imprisons, there is no release.
If he holds up the waters, there is drought;   15
if he lets them go, they turn the land upside down.
Strength and success belong to him,   16
deceived and deceiver are his to use.
He makes counsellors behave like idiots   17
and drives judges mad;
he looses the bonds imposed by kings   18
and removes the girdle of office from their waists;
he makes priests behave like idiots   19
and overthrows men long in office;
those who are trusted he strikes dumb,   20
he takes away the judgement of old men;
he heaps scorn on princes   21
and abates the arrogance of nobles.
He leads peoples astray and destroys them,   23*d*

[a] *Or* and he afflicted me. [b] *Prob. rdg.; Heb. adds* He brings it in full measure to whom
he will (*cp. 21. 17*). [c] *Verse 10 transposed to follow verse 12.* [d] *Verse 22 transposed
to follow verse 25.*

he lays them low, and there they lie.
24 He takes away their wisdom from the rulers of the nations
and leaves them wandering in a pathless wilderness;
25 they grope in the darkness without light
and are left to wander like a drunkard.
22 He uncovers mysteries deep in obscurity
and into thick darkness he brings light.

13 All this I have seen with my own eyes,
with my own ears I have heard it, and understood it.
2 What you know, I also know;
in nothing do I fall short of you.
3 But for my part I would speak with the Almighty
and am ready to argue with God,
4 while you like fools are smearing truth with your falsehoods,
stitching a patchwork of lies, one and all.
5 Ah, if you would only be silent
and let silence be your wisdom!
6 Now listen to my arguments
and attend while I put my case.
7 Is it on God's behalf that you speak so wickedly,
or in his defence that you allege what is false?
8 Must you take God's part,
or put his case for him?
9 Will all be well when he examines you?
Will you quibble with him as you quibble with a man?
10 He will most surely expose you
if you take his part by falsely accusing me.
11 Will not God's majesty strike you with dread,
and terror of him overwhelm you?
12 Your pompous talk is dust and ashes,
your defences will crumble like clay.*a*
13 Be silent, leave me to speak my mind,
and let what may come upon me!
14 I will*b* put my neck in the noose*c*
and take my life in my hands.
15 If he would slay me, I should not hesitate;
I should still argue my cause to his face.
16 This at least assures my success,
that no godless man may appear before him.
17 Listen then, listen to my words,
and give a hearing to my exposition.

[a] your defences...clay: *lit.* the bosses of your shields are bosses of clay. [b] *So Sept.;*
Heb. Why shall I... [c] *Lit.* take my flesh in my teeth.

686

Be sure of this: once I have stated my case   18
I know that I shall be acquitted.
Who is there that can argue so forcibly with me   19
that he could reduce me straightway to silence and death?

Grant me these two conditions only,   20
and then I will not hide myself out of thy sight:
take thy heavy hand clean away from me   21
and let not the fear of thee strike me with dread.
Then summon me, and I will answer;   22
or I will speak first, and do thou answer me.
How many iniquities and sins are laid to my charge?   23
let me know my offences and my sin.
Why dost thou hide thy face   24
and treat me as thy enemy?
Wilt thou chase a driven leaf,   25
wilt thou pursue dry chaff,
prescribing punishment*a* for me   26
and making me heir to the iniquities of my youth,
putting my feet in the stocks*b*   27
and setting a slave-mark on the arches of my feet?*c*

Man born of woman is short-lived and full of disquiet.   **14**
He blossoms like a flower and then he withers;   2
he slips away like a shadow and does not stay;
*d*he is like a wine-skin that perishes
or a garment that moths have eaten.
Dost thou fix thine eyes on such a creature,   3
and wilt thou bring him into court to confront thee?*e*
The days of his life are determined,   5
and the number of his months is known to thee;
thou hast laid down a limit, which he cannot pass.
Look away from him therefore and leave him alone*f*   6
counting the hours day by day like a hired labourer.

If a tree is cut down,   7
there is hope that it will sprout again
and fresh shoots will not fail.
Though its roots grow old in the earth,   8
and its stump is dying in the ground,
if it scents water it may break into bud   9

[a] *So Pesh.; Heb.* bitter things. [b] *Prob. rdg.; Heb. adds* keeping a close watch on all I do.
[c] *Prob. rdg.; Heb. adds verse 28,* he is like...have eaten, *now transposed to follow 14. 2.*
[d] he is like...have eaten: *13. 28 transposed here.* [e] *So one Heb. MS.; others add* (4)
Who can produce pure out of unclean? No one. [f] and leave him alone: *so one MS.;*
others that he may cease.

687

and make new growth like a young plant.
10 But a man dies, and he disappears;[a]
man comes to his end, and where is he?
11 As the waters of a lake dwindle,
or as a river shrinks and runs dry,
12 so mortal man lies down, never to rise
until the very sky splits open.
If a man dies, can he live again?[b]
He shall never be roused from his sleep.
13 If only thou wouldst hide me in Sheol
and conceal me till thy anger turns aside,
if thou wouldst fix a limit for my time there, and then remember me!
14 [c]Then I would not lose hope, however long my service,
waiting for my relief to come.
15 Thou wouldst summon me, and I would answer thee;
thou wouldst long to see the creature thou hast made.
16 But now thou dost count every step I take,
watching all my course.
17 Every offence of mine is stored in thy bag;
thou dost keep my iniquity under seal.
18 Yet as a falling mountain-side is swept away,
and a rock is dislodged from its place,
19 as water wears away stones,
and a rain-storm scours the soil from the land,
so thou hast wiped out the hope of frail man;
20 thou dost overpower him finally, and he is gone;
his face is changed, and he is banished from thy sight.
22[d] His flesh upon him becomes black,
and his life-blood dries up within him.[e]
21 His sons rise to honour, and he sees nothing of it;
they sink into obscurity, and he knows it not.

Second cycle of speeches

15 Then Eliphaz the Temanite answered:

2 Would a man of sense give vent to such foolish notions
and answer with a bellyful of wind?
3 Would he bandy useless words

---

[a] *Or* and is powerless. [b] *Line transposed from beginning of verse 14.* [c] *See note on verse 12.* [d] *Verses 21 and 22 transposed.* [e] His flesh...within him: *or* His own kin, maybe, regret him, and his slaves mourn his loss.

and arguments so unprofitable?
Why! you even banish the fear of God from your mind,   4
usurping the sole right to speak in his presence;
your iniquity dictates what you say,   5
and deceit is the language of your choice.
You are condemned out of your own mouth, not by me;   6
your own lips give evidence against you.

Were you born first of mankind?   7
were you brought forth before the hills?
Do you listen in God's secret council   8
or usurp all wisdom for yourself alone?
What do you know that we do not know?   9
What insight have you that we do not share?
We have age and white hairs in our company,   10
men older than your father.
Does not the consolation of God suffice you,   11
a word whispered quietly in your ear?
What makes you so bold at heart,   12
and why do your eyes flash,
that you vent your anger on God   13
and pour out such a torrent of words?
What is frail man that he should be innocent,   14
or any child of woman that he should be justified?
If God puts no trust in his holy ones,   15
and the heavens are not innocent in his sight,
how much less so is man, who is loathsome and rotten   16
and laps up evil like water!

I will tell you, if only you will listen,   17
and I will describe what I have seen
[what has been handed down by wise men   18
and was not concealed from them by their fathers;
to them alone the land was given,   19
and no foreigner settled among them]:
the wicked are racked with anxiety all their days,   20
the ruthless man for all the years in store for him.
The noise of the hunter's scare rings in his ears,   21
and in time of peace the raider falls on him;
he cannot hope to escape from dark death;   22
he is marked down for the sword;
he is flung out as food for vultures;   23
such a man knows that his destruction is certain.
Suddenly a black day comes upon him,   24

distress and anxiety overwhelm him
[like a king ready for battle];
25   for he has lifted his hand against God
and is pitting himself against the Almighty,
26   charging him head down,
with the full weight of his bossed shield.

27   Heavy though his jowl is and gross,
and though his sides bulge with fat,
28   the city where he lives will lie in ruins,
his house will be deserted;
it will soon become a heap of rubble.
29   He will no longer be rich, his wealth will not last,
and he will strike no root*a* in the earth;*b*
30   scorching heat will shrivel his shoots,
and his blossom*c* will be shaken off by the wind.
31   He deceives himself, trusting in his high rank,
for all his dealings will come to nothing.
32   His palm-trees*d* will wither*e* unseasonably,
and his branches will not spread;
33   he will be like a vine that sheds its unripe grapes,
like an olive-tree that drops its blossom.
34   For the godless, one and all, are barren,
and their homes, enriched by bribery, are destroyed by fire;
35   they conceive mischief and give birth to trouble,
and the child of their womb is deceit.

16 Then Job answered:

2   I have heard such things often before,
you who make trouble, all of you, with every breath,
3   saying, 'Will this windbag never have done?
What makes him so stubborn in argument?'
4   If you and I were to change places,
I could talk like you;
how I could harangue you
and wag my head at you!
5   But no, I would speak words of encouragement,
and then my condolences would flow in streams.
6   If I speak, my pain is not eased;
if I am silent, it does not leave me.

[a] root: *prob. rdg., cp. Vulg.; Heb. unintelligible.* [b] *Prob. rdg.; Heb. adds* he will not escape from darkness. [c] *So Sept.; Heb.* mouth. [d] His palm-trees: *prob. rdg., cp. Sept.; Heb. om.* [e] *So Sept.; Heb.* will be filled.

Meanwhile, my friend wearies me with false sympathy;   7
they tear me to pieces,*a* he and his*b* fellows.   8
He has come forward to give evidence against me;
the liar*c* testifies against me to my face,
in his wrath he wears me down, his hatred is plain to see;   9
he grinds his teeth at me.

My enemies look daggers at me,
they bare their teeth to rend me,*d*   10
they slash my cheeks with knives;
they are all in league against me.
God has left me at the mercy of malefactors   11
and cast me into the clutches of wicked men.
I was at ease, but he set upon me and mauled me,   12
seized me by the neck and worried me.
He set me up as his target;
his arrows rained upon me from every side;   13
pitiless, he cut deep into my vitals,
he spilt my gall on the ground.
He made breach after breach in my defences;   14
he fell upon me like a fighting man.

I stitched sackcloth together to cover my body   15
and I buried my forelock in the dust;
my cheeks were flushed with weeping   16
and dark shadows were round my eyes,
yet my hands were free from violence   17
and my prayer was sincere.

O earth, cover not my blood   18
and let my cry for justice find no rest!
For look! my witness is in heaven;   19
there is one on high ready to answer for me.
My appeal will come*e* before God,   20
while my eyes turn again and again to him.
If only there were one to arbitrate between man and God,   21
as between a man and his neighbour!
For there are but few years to come   22
before I take the road from which I shall not return.

My mind is distraught, my days are numbered,   17
and the grave is waiting for me.
Wherever I turn, men taunt me,   2

[a] *So some MSS.; others* they seize me.   [b] *Prob. rdg.; Heb.* my.   [c] *So Vulg.; Heb.* my
falsehood.   [d] *Lit.* they open their mouth at me.   [e] *My...come: so Sept.; Heb.* My
intercessors are my friends.

and my day is darkened[a] by their sneers.

3   Be thou my surety with thyself,
for who else can pledge himself for me?

4   Thou wilt not let those men triumph,
whose minds thou hast sunk in ignorance;

5   if such a man denounces his friends to their ruin,
his sons' eyes shall grow dim.

6   I am held up as a byword in every land,
a portent for all to see;

7   my eyes are dim with grief,
my limbs wasted to a shadow.

8   Honest men are bewildered at this,
and the innocent are indignant at my plight.

9   In spite of all, the righteous man maintains his course,
and he whose hands are clean grows strong again.

10   But come on, one and all, try again!
I shall not find a wise man among you.

11   My days die away like an echo;
my heart-strings[b] are snapped.

12   Day is turned into night,
and morning[c] light is darkened before me.

13   If I measure Sheol for my house,
if I spread my couch in the darkness,

14   if I call the grave my father
and the worm my mother or my sister,

15   where, then, will my hope be,
and who will take account of my piety?

16   I cannot take them down to Sheol with me,[d]
nor can they descend with me into the earth.

18 Then Bildad the Shuhite answered:

2   How soon will you bridle[e] your tongue?
Do but think, and then we will talk.

3   What do you mean by treating us as cattle?
Are we nothing but brute beasts to you?[f]

4   Is the earth to be deserted to prove you right,
or the rocks to be moved from their place?

5   No, it is the wicked whose light is extinguished,
from whose fire no flame will rekindle;

[a] my...darkened: *lit.* my eyes are weary.   [b] *Prob. rdg.; Heb.* the desires of my heart.
[c] morning: *prob. rdg.; Heb.* near.   [d] to Sheol with me: *so Sept.; Heb. obscure.*   [e] bridle:
prob. rdg.; Heb. unintelligible.   [f] *Prob. rdg.; Heb. adds* rending himself in his anger.

the light fades in his tent,   6
and his lamp dies down and fails him.
In his iniquity his steps[a] totter,   7
and his disobedience trips him up;
he rushes headlong into a net   8
and steps through the hurdle that covers a pit;
his heel is caught in a snare,   9
the noose grips him tight;
a cord lies hidden in the ground for him   10
and a trap in the path.
The terrors of death suddenly beset him   11
and make him piss over his feet.
For all his vigour he is paralysed with fear;   12
strong as he is, disaster awaits him.
Disease eats away his skin,   13
Death's eldest child devours his limbs.
He is torn from the safety of his home,   14
and Death's terrors escort him to their king.[b]
Magic herbs lie strewn about his tent,   15
and his home is sprinkled with sulphur to protect it.
His roots beneath dry up,   16
and above, his branches wither.
His memory vanishes from the face of the earth   17
and he leaves no name in the world.
He is driven from light into darkness   18
and banished from the land of the living.
He leaves no issue or offspring among his people,   19
no survivor in his earthly home;
in the west men hear of his doom and are appalled;   20
in the east they shudder with horror.
Such is the fate of the dwellings of evildoers,   21
and of the homes of those who care nothing for God.

Then Job answered: **19**

How long will you exhaust me   2
and pulverize me with words?
Time and time again you have insulted me   3
and shamelessly done me wrong.[c]
If in fact I had erred,   4
the error would still be mine.

[a] In...steps: *so Pesh.; Heb.* The steps of his iniquity. [b] *Or* and you conduct him to
the king of terrors. [c] done me wrong: *so some MSS.; others* are astonished at me.

5   But if indeed you lord it over me
and try to justify the reproaches levelled at me,

6   I tell you, God himself has put me in the wrong,
he has drawn the net round me.

7   If I cry 'Murder!' no one answers;
if I appeal for help, I get no justice.

8   He has walled in my path so that I cannot break away,
and he has hedged in the road before me.

9   He has stripped me of all honour
and has taken the crown from my head.

10   On every side he beats me down and I am gone;
he has pulled up my tent-rope[a] like a tree.

11   His anger is hot against me
and he counts me his enemy.

12   His raiders gather in force[b]
and encamp about my tent.

13   My brothers hold aloof from me,
my friends are utterly estranged from me;

14-15   my kinsmen and intimates fall away,
my retainers have forgotten me;
my slave-girls treat me as a stranger,
I have become an alien in their eyes.

16   I summon my slave, but he does not answer,
though I entreat him as a favour.

17   My breath is noisome to my wife,
and I stink in the nostrils of my own family.

18   Mere children despise me
and, when I rise, turn their backs on me;

19   my intimate companions loathe me,
and those whom I love have turned against me.

20   My bones stick out through[c] my skin,[d]
and I gnaw my under-lip with my teeth.

21   Pity me, pity me, you that are my friends;
for the hand of God has touched me.

22   Why do you pursue me as God pursues me?
Have you not had your teeth in me long enough?

23   O that my words might be inscribed,
O that they might be engraved in an inscription,

24   cut with an iron tool and filled with lead
to be a witness[e] in hard rock!

[a] *Or* he has uprooted my hope. [b] *Prob. rdg.; Heb. adds* they raise an earthwork against me. [c] stick out through: *lit.* cling to. [d] *Prob. rdg.; Heb. adds* and my flesh. [e] to... witness: *or* for ever.

But in my heart I know that my vindicator lives   25
and that he will rise last to speak in court;
and I shall discern my witness standing at my side*a*   26
and see my defending counsel, even God himself,
whom I shall see with my own eyes,   27
I myself and no other.

My heart failed me when you said,   28
'What a train of disaster he has brought on himself!
The root of the trouble lies in him.'*b*
Beware of the sword that points at you,   29
the sword that sweeps away all iniquity;
then you will know that there is a judge.*c*

Then Zophar the Naamathite answered: **20**

My distress of mind forces me to reply,   2
and this is why*d* I hasten to speak:
I have heard arguments that are a reproach to me,   3
a spirit beyond my understanding gives me the answers.
Surely you know that this has been so since time began,   4
since man was first set on the earth:
the triumph of the wicked is short-lived,   5
the glee of the godless lasts but a moment?
Though he stands high as heaven,   6
and his head touches the clouds,
he will be swept utterly away like his own dung,   7
and all that saw him will say, 'Where is he?'
He will fly away like a dream and be lost,   8
driven off like a vision of the night;
the eye which glimpsed him shall do so no more   9
and shall never again see him in his place.
The youth and strength which filled his bones   11*e*
shall lie with him in the dust.
His sons will pay court to the poor,   10
and their*f* hands will give back his wealth.
Though evil tastes sweet in his mouth,   12
and he savours it, rolling it round his tongue,
though he lingers over it and will not let it go,   13
and holds it back on his palate,
yet his food turns in his stomach,   14
changing to asps' venom within him.

[a] my witness...side: *prob. rdg.; Heb. unintelligible.* [b] *So many MSS.; others* me.
[c] *Or* judgement. [d] this is why: *prob. rdg.; Heb. obscure.* [e] *Verses 10 and 11 transposed.*
[f] *Prob. rdg.; Heb.* his.

15   He gulps down wealth, then vomits it up,
     or God makes him discharge it.

16   He sucks the poison of asps,
     and the tongue of the viper kills him.

17   Not for him to swill down rivers of cream[a]
     or torrents of honey and curds;

18   he must give back his gains without swallowing them,
     and spew up his profit undigested;

19   for he has hounded and harassed the poor,
     he has seized houses which he did not build.

20   Because his appetite gave him no rest,
     and he cannot escape his own desires,

21   nothing is left for him to eat,
     and so his well-being does not last;

22   with every need satisfied his troubles begin,
     and the full force of hardship strikes him.

23   [b]God vents his anger upon him
     and rains on him cruel blows.

24   He is wounded by weapons of iron
     and pierced by a bronze-tipped arrow;

25   out at his back the point comes,
     the gleaming tip from his gall-bladder.[c]

26   Darkness unrelieved awaits him,[d]
     a fire that needs no fanning will consume him.
     [Woe betide any survivor in his tent!]

27   The heavens will lay bare his guilt,
     and earth will rise up to condemn him.

28   A flood will sweep away his house,
     rushing waters on the day of wrath.

29   Such is God's reward for the wicked man
     and the lot appointed for the rebel[e] by God.

21   Then Job answered:

2   Listen to me, do but listen,
     and let that be the comfort you offer me.

3   Bear with me while I have my say;
     when I have finished, you may mock.

4   May not I too voice[f] my thoughts?
     Have not I as good cause to be impatient?

[a] rivers of cream: *prob. rdg.; Heb. obscure.* [b] *So one Sept. MS.; Heb. prefixes* Let it be for filling his belly. [c] *So some MSS. of Sept.; Heb. adds* terrors upon him. [d] *So Sept.; Heb.* awaits his stored things. [e] the rebel: *prob. rdg.; Heb.* his word. [f] May...voice: *prob. rdg.; Heb. obscure.*

Look at my plight, and be aghast;　　　　　　　　　5
clap your hand to your mouth.
When I stop to think, I am filled with horror,　　　6
and my whole body is convulsed.

Why do the wicked enjoy long life,　　　　　　　　7
hale in old age, and great and powerful?
They live to see their children settled,　　　　　　8
their kinsfolk and descendants flourishing;
their families are secure and safe;　　　　　　　　9
the rod of God's justice does not reach them.
Their bull mounts and fails not of its purpose;　　10
their cow calves and does not miscarry.
Their children like lambs run out to play,　　　　11
and their little ones skip and dance;
they rejoice with*a* tambourine and harp　　　　　12
and make merry to the sound of the flute.
Their lives close in prosperity,　　　　　　　　　13
and they go down to Sheol in peace.
To God they say, 'Leave us alone;　　　　　　　14
we do not want to know your ways.
What is the Almighty that we should worship him,　15
or what should we gain by seeking his favour?'

Is not the prosperity of the wicked in their own hands?　16
Are not their purposes very different from God's*b*?
How often is the lamp of the wicked snuffed out,　17
and how often does their ruin come upon them?
How often does God in his anger deal out suffering,
bringing it in full measure to whom he will?*c*
How often is that man like a wisp of straw before the wind,　18
like chaff which the storm-wind whirls away?
You say, 'The trouble he has earned, God will keep for his sons';　19
no, let him be paid for it in full and be punished.
Let his own eyes see damnation come upon him,　20
and the wrath of the Almighty be the cup he drinks.
What joy shall he have in his children after him,　21
if his very months and days are numbered?
Can any man teach God,　　　　　　　　　　　22
God who judges even those in heaven above?

One man, I tell you, dies crowned with success,　23
lapped in security and comfort,

[a] with: *so some MSS.; others* as to.　[b] God's: *prob. rdg.; Heb.* mine.　[c] *Line transposed from 12. 6.*

24   his loins full of vigour
      and the marrow juicy in his bones;
25   another dies in bitterness of soul
      and never tastes prosperity;
26   side by side they are laid in earth,
      and worms are the shroud of both.

27   I know well what you are thinking
      and the arguments you are marshalling[a] against me;
28   I know you will ask, 'Where is the great man's home now,
      what has become of the home of the wicked?'
29   Have you never questioned travellers?
      Can you not learn from the signs they offer,
30   that the wicked is spared when disaster comes
      and conveyed to safety before the day of wrath?
31   No one denounces his conduct to his face,
      no one requites him for what he has done.
32-33 When he is carried to the grave,
      all the world escorts him, before and behind;
      the dust of earth is sweet to him,
      and thousands keep watch at his tomb.
34   How futile, then, is the comfort you offer me!
      How false your answers ring!

Third cycle of speeches

22   Then Eliphaz the Temanite answered:

2   Can man be any benefit to God?
      Can even a wise man benefit him?
3   Is it an asset to the Almighty if you are righteous?
      Does he gain if your conduct is perfect?
4   Do not think that he reproves you because you are pious,
      that on this count he brings you to trial.
5   No: it is because you are a very wicked man,
      and your depravity passes all bounds.
6   Without due cause you take a brother in pledge,
      you strip men of their clothes and leave them naked.
7   When a man is weary, you give him no water to drink
      and you refuse bread to the hungry.
8   Is the earth, then, the preserve of the strong

[a] *So Pesh.; Heb.* you do violence.

698

and a domain for the favoured few?
Widows you have sent away empty-handed, 9
orphans you have struck defenceless.
No wonder that there are pitfalls in your path, 10
that scares are set to fill you with sudden fear.
The light*a* is turned into darkness, and you cannot see; 11
the flood-waters cover you.
Surely God is at the zenith of the heavens 12
and looks down on all the stars, high as they are.
But you say, 'What does God know? 13
Can he see through thick darkness to judge?
His eyes cannot pierce the curtain of the clouds 14
as he walks to and fro on the vault of heaven.'
Consider the course of the wicked man, 15
the path the miscreant treads;
see how they are carried off before their time, 16
their very foundation flowing away like a river;
these men said to God, 'Leave us alone; 17
what can the Almighty do to us*b*?'
Yet it was he that filled their houses with good things, 18
although their purposes and his*c* were very different.
The righteous see their fate and exult, 19
the innocent make game of them;
for their riches*d* are swept away, 20
and the profusion of their wealth is destroyed by fire.

Come to terms with God and you will prosper; 21
that is the way to mend your fortune.
Take instruction from his mouth 22
and store his words in your heart.
If you come back to the Almighty in true sincerity, 23
if you banish wrongdoing from your home,
if you treat your precious metal as dust*e* 24
and the gold of Ophir as stones from the river-bed,
then the Almighty himself will be your precious metal; 25
he will be your silver in double measure.
Then, with sure trust in*f* the Almighty, 26
you will raise your face to God;
you will pray to him, and he will hear you, 27
and you will have cause to fulfil your vows.
In all your designs you will succeed, 28

[a] The light: *so Sept.; Heb.* Or. [b] *So Sept.; Heb.* them. [c] *So Sept.; Heb.* mine.
[d] *So Sept.; Heb. word unknown.* [e] *Prob. rdg.; Heb.* if you put your precious metal on dust.
[f] with...in: *or* delighting in.

and light will shine on your path;

29   but God brings down the pride of the haughty[a]
and keeps safe the man of modest looks.

30   He will deliver the innocent,[b]
and you will be delivered, because your hands are clean.

23   Then Job answered:

2   My thoughts today are resentful,
for God's[c] hand is heavy on me in my trouble.

3   If only I knew how to find him,
how to enter his court,

4   I would state my case before him
and set out my arguments in full;

5   then I should learn what answer he would give
and find out what he had to say.

6   Would he exert his great power to browbeat me?
No; God himself would never bring a charge against me.

7   There the upright are vindicated before him,
and I shall win from my judge an absolute discharge.

8   If I go forward,[d] he is not there;
if backward,[e] I cannot find him;

9   when I turn[f] left,[g] I do not descry him;
I face[h] right,[i] but I see him not.

10   But he knows me in action or at rest;[j]
when he tests me, I prove to be gold.

11   My feet have kept to the path he has set me,
I have followed his way and not turned from it.

12   I do not ignore the commands that come from his lips,
I have stored in my heart[k] what he says.

13   He decides,[l] and who can turn him from his purpose?
He does what his own heart desires.

14   What he determines,[m] that he carries out;
his mind is full of plans like these.

15   Therefore I am fearful of meeting him;
when I think about him,[n] I am afraid;

16   it is God who makes me faint-hearted
and the Almighty who fills me with fear,

[a] but...haughty: *prob. rdg.; Heb. obscure.* [b] *Prob. rdg.; Heb.* the not innocent.
[c] *So Sept.; Heb.* my. [d] *Or* east. [e] *Or* west. [f] *Prob. rdg.; Heb.* he turns. [g] *Or*
north. [h] *So Pesh.; Heb.* he faces. [i] *Or* south. [j] me...rest: *so Pesh.; Heb.* a way
with me. [k] in my heart: *so Sept.; Heb.* from my allotted portion. [l] He decides: *prob.
rdg.; Heb.* He in one. [m] *So Pesh.; Heb.* What I determine. [n] when...him: *or* I stand
aloof.

yet I am not reduced to silence by the darkness   17
nor[a] by the mystery which hides him.

[b]The day of reckoning is no secret to the Almighty,   24
though those who know him have no hint of its date.
Wicked men[c] move boundary-stones   2
and carry away flocks and their shepherds.[d]
In the field they reap what is not theirs,[e]   6[f]
and filch the late grapes from the rich[g] man's vineyard.
They drive off the orphan's ass   3
and lead away the widow's ox with a rope.
They snatch the fatherless infant from the breast   9
and take the poor man's child in pledge.
They jostle the poor out of the way;   4
the destitute huddle together, hiding from them.
The poor rise early like the wild ass,   5
when it scours the wilderness for food;
but though they work till nightfall,[h]
their children go hungry.[i]
Naked and bare they pass the night;   7
in the cold they have nothing to cover them.
They are drenched by rain-storms from the hills   8
and hug the rock, their only shelter.
Naked and bare they go about their work,   10
and hungry they carry the sheaves;
they press the oil in the shade where two walls meet,   11
they tread the winepress but themselves go thirsty.
Far from the city, they groan like dying men,   12
and like wounded men they cry out;
but God pays no heed to their prayer.
Some there are who rebel against the light of day,   13
who know nothing of its ways
and do not linger in the paths of light.
The murderer rises before daylight   14
to kill some miserable wretch.[j]
The seducer watches eagerly for twilight,   15
thinking, 'No eye will catch sight of me.'
The thief prowls[k] by night,[l]

---

[a] yet I am not...nor: *or* indeed I am...and... [b] *Prob. rdg.; Heb. prefixes* Why.
[c] Wicked men: *prob. rdg., cp. Sept.; Heb. obscure.* [d] and their shepherds: *so Sept.;
Heb.* and feed them. [e] *Lit.* his. [f] *Verses 3–9 re-arranged to restore the natural order.*
[g] *Or* wicked. [h] *Prob. rdg.; Heb.* Arabah. [i] go hungry: *prob. rdg.; Heb.* to it food.
[j] *See note on verse 15.* [k] The thief prowls: *prob. rdg.; Heb.* Let him be like a thief.
[l] *Line transposed from end of verse 14.*

his face covered with a mask,
16   and in the darkness breaks into houses
which he has*ᵃ* marked down in the day.
One and all,*ᵇ* they are strangers to the daylight,
17   but dark night is morning to them;
and in the welter of night they are at home.
18   Such men are scum on the surface of the water;
their fields have a bad name throughout the land,
and no labourer will go near their*ᶜ* vineyards.
19   As drought and heat make away with snow,
so the waters of Sheol*ᵈ* make away with the sinner.
20   The womb forgets him, the worm sucks him dry;
he will not be remembered ever after.*ᵉ*
21   He may have wronged*ᶠ* the barren childless woman
and been no help to the widow;
22   yet God in his strength carries off even the mighty;
they may rise, but they have no firm hope of life.
23   He lulls them into security and confidence;
but his eyes are fixed on their ways.
24   For a moment they rise to the heights, but are soon gone;
iniquity is snapped like a stick.*ᵍ*
They are laid low and wilt like a mallow-flower;
they droop like an ear of corn on the stalk.
25   If this is not so, who will prove me wrong
and make nonsense of my argument?

25 Then Bildad the Shuhite answered:

2   Authority and awe rest with him
who has established peace in his realm on high.
3   His squadrons are without number;
at whom will they not spring from ambush*ʰ*?
4   How then can a man be justified in God's sight,
or one born of woman be innocent?
5   If the circling moon is found wanting,
and the stars are not innocent in his eyes,
6   much more so man who is but a maggot,
mortal man who is only a worm.

---

[a] *So Pesh.; Heb.* they have. [b] One and all: *transposed from after* but *in next verse.*
[c] *Lit.* the. [d] snow...Sheol: *prob. rdg.; Heb.* snow-water, Sheol. [e] *Prob. rdg.; Heb.*
here adds iniquity is snapped like a stick (*see note on verse 24*). [f]He...wronged: *so Targ.;*
Heb. shepherd. [g] *Line transposed from end of verse 20.* [h] from ambush: *so Sept.;*
Heb. his light.

702

Then Job answered: **26**

What help you have given to the man without resource,   2
what deliverance you have brought to the powerless!
What counsel you offer to a man at his wit's end,   3
what sound advice to the foolish!
Who has prompted you to say such things,   4
and whose spirit is expressed in your speech?
In the underworld the shades writhe in fear,   5
the waters and all that live in them are struck with terror.[a]
Sheol is laid bare,   6
and Abaddon uncovered before him.
God spreads the canopy of the sky over chaos   7
and suspends earth in the void.
He keeps the waters penned in dense cloud-masses,   8
and the clouds do not burst open under their weight.
He covers the face of the full moon,[b]   9
unrolling his clouds across it.
He has fixed the horizon on the surface of the waters   10
at the farthest limit of light and darkness.
The pillars of heaven quake   11
and are aghast at his rebuke.
With his strong arm he cleft the sea-monster,   12
and struck down the Rahab by his skill.
At his breath the skies are clear,   13
and his hand breaks the twisting[c] sea-serpent.
These are but the fringe of his power;   14
and how faint the whisper that we hear of him!
[Who could fathom the thunder of his might?]

Then Job resumed his discourse: **27**

I swear by God, who has denied me justice,   2
and by the Almighty, who has filled me with bitterness:
so long as there is any life left in me   3
and God's breath is in my nostrils,
no untrue word shall pass my lips   4
and my tongue shall utter no falsehood.
God forbid that I should allow you to be right;   5
till death, I will not abandon my claim to innocence.
I will maintain the rightness of my cause, I will never give up; 6
so long as I live, I will not change.

[a] are struck with terror: *prob. rdg.; Heb. om.*   [b] *Or* He overlays the surface of his throne.
[c] *Or* primeval.

7   May my enemy meet the fate of the wicked,
and my antagonist the doom of the wrongdoer!

8^a What hope has a godless man, when he is cut off,^b
when God takes away his life?

9   Will God listen to his cry
when trouble overtakes him?

10 Will he trust himself to the Almighty
and call upon God at all times?

11 I will teach you what is in God's power,
I will not conceal the purpose of the Almighty.

12 If all of you have seen these things,
why then do you talk such empty nonsense?

13 This is the lot prescribed by God for the wicked,
and the ruthless man's reward from the Almighty.

14 He may have many sons, but they will fall by the sword,
and his offspring will go hungry;

15 the survivors will be brought to the grave by pestilence,
and no widows will weep for them.

16 He may heap up silver like dirt
and get himself piles of clothes;

17 he may get them, but the righteous will wear them,
and his silver will be shared among the innocent.

18 The house he builds is flimsy as a bird's nest
or a shelter put up by a watchman.

19 He may lie down rich one day, but never again;^c
he opens his eyes and all is gone.

20 Disaster overtakes him like a flood,
and a storm snatches him away in the night;

21 the east wind lifts him up and he is gone;
it whirls him far from home;

22 it flings itself on him without mercy,
and he is battered and buffeted by its force;

23 it snaps its fingers at him
and whistles over him wherever he may be.

[a] *It is possible that verses 8–23 are part of a speech by Zophar otherwise lost from the third cycle of speeches.* [b] *Or* What is a godless man's thread of life when it is cut... [c] *but* ...again: *so Sept.; Heb.* but he is not gathered in.

God's unfathomable wisdom

There are mines for silver   **28**
and places where men refine gold;
where iron is won from the earth   2
and copper smelted from the ore;
the end of the seam lies in darkness,   3
and it is followed to its farthest limit.*a*
Strangers cut the galleries;*b*   4
they are forgotten as they drive forward far from men.*c*
While corn is springing from the earth above,   5
what lies beneath is raked over like a fire,
and out of its rocks comes lapis lazuli,   6
dusted with flecks of gold.
No bird of prey knows the way there,   7
and the falcon's keen eye cannot descry it;
proud beasts do not set foot on it,   8
and no serpent comes that way.
Man sets his hand to the granite rock   9
and lays bare the roots of the mountains;
he cuts galleries in the rocks,   10
and gems of every kind meet his eye;
he dams up the sources of the streams   11
and brings the hidden riches of the earth to light.
But where can wisdom be found?   12
And where is the source of understanding?
No man knows the way to it;*d*   13
it is not found in the land of living men.
The depths of ocean say, 'It is not in us',   14
and the sea says, 'It is not with me.'
Red gold cannot buy it,   15
nor can its price be weighed out in silver;
it cannot be set in the scales against gold of Ophir,   16
against precious cornelian or lapis lazuli;
gold and crystal*e* are not to be matched with it,   17
no work in fine gold can be bartered for it;
black coral and alabaster are not worth mention,   18
and a parcel of wisdom fetches more than red coral;

[a] *Prob. rdg.; Heb. adds* stones of darkness and deep darkness.   [b] Strangers...galleries: *prob. rdg.; Heb. obscure.*   [c] *Prob. rdg.; Heb. adds* languishing without foothold.   [d] *So Sept.; Heb.* knows its value.   [e] *Lit.* glass.

19   topaz*ᵃ* from Ethiopia is not to be matched with it,
      it cannot be set in the scales against pure gold.

20   Where then does wisdom come from,
      and where is the source of understanding?

21   No creature on earth can see it,
      and it is hidden from the birds of the air.

22   Destruction*ᵇ* and death say,
      'We know of it only by report.'

23   But God understands the way to it,
      he alone knows its source;

24   for he can see to the ends of the earth
      and he surveys everything under heaven.

25   When he made a counterpoise for the wind
      and measured out the waters in proportion,

26   when he laid down a limit for the rain
      and a path for the thunderstorm,

27   even then he saw wisdom and took stock of it,
      he considered*ᶜ* it and fathomed its very depths.

28   And he said to man:
         The fear of the Lord is wisdom,
         and to turn from evil is understanding.

Job's final survey of his case

29   Then Job resumed his discourse:

2   If I could only go back to the old days,
         to the time when God was watching over me,

3   when his lamp shone above my head,
         and by its light I walked through the darkness!

4   If I could be as in the days of my prime,
         when God protected my home,*ᵈ*

5   while the Almighty was still there at my side,
         and my servants stood round me,

6   while my path flowed with milk,
         and the rocks streamed oil!

7   If I went through the gate out of the town
         to take my seat in the public square,

8   young men saw me and kept out of sight;
         old men rose to their feet,

[*a*] Or chrysolite.   [*b*] *Heb.* Abaddon, *cp. 26. 6.*   [*c*] *So some MSS.; others* established.
[*d*] when...home: *so Sept.; Heb.* in the secret council of God upon my home.

men in authority broke off their talk   9
and put their hands to their lips;
the voices of the nobles died away,   10
and every man held his tongue.
They listened to me expectantly   21[a]
and waited in silence for my opinion.
When I had spoken, no one spoke again;   22
my words fell gently on them;
they waited for them as for rain   23
and drank them in like showers in spring.
When I smiled on them, they took heart;   24
when my face lit up, they lost their gloomy looks.
I presided over them, planning their course,   25
like a king encamped with his troops.[b]

Whoever heard of me spoke in my favour,   11
and those who saw me bore witness to my merit,
how I saved the poor man when he called for help   12
and the orphan who had no protector.
The man threatened with ruin blessed me,   13
and I made the widow's heart sing for joy.
I put on righteousness as a garment and it clothed me;   14
justice, like a cloak or a turban, wrapped me round.
I was eyes to the blind   15
and feet to the lame;
I was a father to the needy,   16
and I took up the stranger's cause.
I broke the fangs of the miscreant   17
and rescued the prey from his teeth.
I thought, 'I shall die with my powers unimpaired   18
and my days uncounted as the grains of sand,[c]
with my roots spreading out to the water   19
and the dew lying on my branches,
with the bow always new in my grasp   20
and the arrow ever ready to my hand.'[d]

But now I am laughed to scorn   30
by men of a younger generation,
men whose fathers I would have disdained
to put with the dogs who kept my flock.
What use were their strong arms to me,   2
since their sturdy vigour had wasted away?

[a] *Verses 21–25 transposed to this point.* [b] *Prob. rdg.; Heb. adds* as when one comforts
mourners. [c] *Or* as those of the phoenix. [d] *Verses 21–25 transposed to follow verse 10.*

3   They gnawed roots^a in the desert,
    gaunt with want and hunger,^b

4   they plucked saltwort and wormwood
    and root of broom^c for their food.

5   Driven out from the society of men,^d
    pursued like thieves with hue and cry,

6   they lived in gullies and ravines,
    holes in the earth and rocky clefts;

7   they howled like beasts among the bushes,
    huddled together beneath the scrub,

8   vile base-born wretches,
    hounded from the haunts of men.

9   Now I have become the target of their taunts,
    my name is a byword among them.

10   They loathe me, they shrink from me,
    they dare to spit in my face.

11   They run wild and savage^e me;
    at sight of me they throw off all restraint.

12   On my right flank they attack in a mob;^f
    they raise their siege-ramps against me,

13   they tear down my crumbling defences to my undoing,
    and scramble up against me unhindered;

14   they burst in through the gaping breach;
    at the moment of the crash they come rolling in.

15   Terror upon terror overwhelms me,
    it sweeps away my resolution like the wind,
    and my hope of victory vanishes like a cloud.

16   So now my soul is in turmoil within me,^g
    and misery has me daily in its grip.

17   By night pain pierces my very bones,
    and there is ceaseless throbbing in my veins;

18   my garments are all bespattered with my phlegm,
    which chokes me like the collar of a shirt.

19   God himself^h has flung me down in the mud,
    no better than dust or ashes.

20   I call for thy help, but thou dost not answer;
    I stand up to plead, but thou sittest aloof;

21   thou hast turned cruelly against me

[a] roots: *prob. rdg.; Heb. om.* [b] *Prob. rdg.; Heb. adds* yesterday waste and derelict land.
[c] root of broom: *probably* fungus on broom root. [d] the society of men: *prob. rdg.; Heb. obscure.* [e] They run...savage: *prob. rdg.; Heb.* He runs...savages. [f] *Prob. rdg.; Heb. adds* they let loose my feet. [g] *Lit.* is poured out upon me. [h] God himself: *prob. rdg.; Heb. om.*

and with thy strong hand pursuest me in hatred;
thou dost snatch me up and set me astride the wind,   22
and the tempest*ᵃ* tosses me up and down.
I know that thou wilt hand me over to death,   23
to the place appointed for all mortal men.

Yet no beggar held out his hand   24
but was relieved*ᵇ* by me in his distress.
Did I not weep for the man whose life was hard?   25
Did not my heart grieve for the poor?
Evil has come though I expected good;   26
I looked for light but there came darkness.
My bowels are in ferment and know no peace;   27
days of misery stretch out before me.
I go about dejected and friendless;   28
I rise in the assembly, only to appeal for help.
The wolf is now my brother,   29
the owls of the desert have become my companions.
My blackened skin peels off,   30
and my body is scorched by the heat.
My harp has been tuned for a dirge,   31
my flute to the voice of those who weep.

What is the lot prescribed by God above,   31 2ᶜ
the reward from the Almighty on high?
Is not ruin prescribed for the miscreant   3
and calamity for the wrongdoer?
Yet does not God himself see my ways   4
and count my every step?

I swear I have had no dealings with falsehood   5
and have not embarked on a course of deceit.
I have come to terms with my eyes,   1
never to take notice of a girl.
Let God weigh me in the scales of justice,   6
and he will know that I am innocent!
If my steps have wandered from the way,   7
if my heart has followed my eyes,
or any dirt stuck to my hands,
may another eat what I sow,   8
and may my crops be pulled up by the roots!
If my heart has been enticed by a woman   9
or I have lain in wait at my neighbour's door,

[a] the tempest: *prob. rdg.; Heb. unintelligible.* [b] was relieved: *prob. rdg.; Heb. unintelligible.* [c] *Verse 1 transposed to follow verse 5.*

10   may my wife be another man's slave,^a
    and may other men enjoy her.

11   [But that is a wicked act, an offence before the law;

12   it would be a consuming and destructive fire,
    raging^b among my crops.]

13   If I have ever rejected the plea of my slave
    or of my slave-girl, when they brought their complaint to me,

14   what shall I do if God appears?
    What shall I answer if he intervenes?

15   Did not he who made me in the womb make them?
    Did not the same God create us in the belly?

16   If I have withheld their needs from the poor
    or let the widow's eye grow dim with tears,

17   if I have eaten my crust alone,
    and the orphan has not shared it with me—

18   the orphan who from boyhood honoured me like a father,
    whom I guided from the day of his^c birth—

19   if I have seen anyone perish for lack of clothing,
    or a poor man with nothing to cover him,

20   if his body had no cause to bless me,
    because he was not kept warm with a fleece from my flock,

21   if I have raised^d my hand against the innocent,^e
    knowing that men would side with me in court,^f

22   then may my shoulder-blade be torn from my shoulder,
    my arm be wrenched out of its socket!

23   But the terror of God was heavy upon me,^g
    and for fear of his majesty I could do none of these things.

24   If I have put my faith in gold
    and my trust in the gold of Nubia,

25   if I have rejoiced in my great wealth
    and in the increase of riches;

26   if I ever looked on the sun in splendour
    or the moon moving in her glory,

27   and was led astray in my secret heart
    and raised my hand in homage;

28   this would have been an offence before the law,
    for I should have been unfaithful to God on high.

38^h If my land has cried out in reproach at me,
    and its furrows have joined in weeping,

39   if I have eaten its produce without payment

---

[a] be...slave: *lit.* grind corn for another. [b] *Prob. rdg.; Heb.* uprooting. [c] *Prob. rdg.; Heb.* my. [d] *Or* waved. [e] *Or* orphan. [f] *Lit.* in the gate. [g] *Prob. rdg.; Heb.* A fear towards me is a disaster from God. [h] *Verses 38–40 transposed (but see note e, page 711).*

and have disappointed my creditors,
may thistles spring up instead of wheat,   40
and weeds instead of barley!

Have I rejoiced at the ruin of the man that hated me   29
or been filled with malice when trouble overtook him,
even though I did not allow my tongue*a* to sin   30
by demanding his life with a curse?
Have the men of my household*b* never said,   31
'Let none of us speak ill of him!
No stranger has spent the night in the street'?   32
For I have kept open house for the traveller.
Have I ever concealed my misdeeds as men do,   33
keeping my guilt to myself,
because I feared the gossip of the town   34
or dreaded the scorn of my fellow-citizens?
Let me but call a witness in my defence!   35
Let the Almighty state his case against me!
If my accuser had written out his indictment,
I would not keep silence and remain indoors.*c*
No! I would flaunt it on my shoulder   36
and wear it like a crown on my head;
I would plead the whole record of my life   37
and present that in court as my defence.*d*

           Job's speeches are finished.*e*

Speeches of Elihu

So these three men gave up answering Job; for he continued to think 32
himself righteous. Then Elihu son of Barakel the Buzite, of the family 2
of Ram, grew angry; angry because Job had made himself out more
righteous than God,*f* and angry with the three friends because they had 3
found no answer to Job and had let God appear wrong.*g* Now Elihu 4
had hung back while they were talking with Job because they were
older than he; but, when he saw that the three had no answer, he could 5
no longer contain his anger. So Elihu son of Barakel the Buzite began 6
to speak:

[*a*] *Lit.* palate. [*b*] *Lit.* tent. [*c*] *Line transposed from verse 34.* [*d*] *Verses 38–40 transposed to follow verse 28 (but see note e).* [*e*] *The last line of verse 40 retained here.* [*f*] *Or* had justified himself with God. [*g*] *Prob. original rdg., altered in Heb. to* and had not proved Job wrong.

I am young in years,
and you are old;
that is why I held back and shrank
from displaying my knowledge in front of you.

7 I said to myself, 'Let age speak,
and length of years expound wisdom.'

8 But the spirit of God himself[a] is in man,
and the breath of the Almighty gives him understanding;

9 it is not only the old who are wise
or the aged who understand what is right.

10 Therefore I say: Listen to me;
I too will display my knowledge.

11 Look, I have been waiting upon your words,
listening for the conclusions of your thoughts,
while you sought for phrases;

12 I have been giving thought to your conclusions,
but not one of you refutes Job or answers his arguments.

13 Take care then not to claim that you have found wisdom;
God will rebut him, not man.

14 I will not string[b] words together like you[c]
or answer him as you have done.

15 If these men are confounded and no longer answer,
if words fail them,

16 am I to wait because they do not speak,
because they stand there and no longer answer?

17 I, too, have a furrow to plough;
I will express my opinion;

18 for I am bursting with words,
a bellyful of wind gripes me.

19 My stomach is distended as if with wine,
bulging like a blacksmith's[d] bellows;

20 I must speak to find relief,
I must open my mouth and answer;

21 I will show no favour to anyone,
I will flatter no one, God or man;[e]

22 for I cannot use flattering titles,
or my Maker would soon do away with me.

33 Come now, Job, listen to my words
and attend carefully to everything I say.

---

[a] the spirit...himself: *so Symm.; Heb.* a spirit. [b] *Prob. rdg.; Heb.* He has not strung.
[c] *Prob. rdg.; Heb.* towards me. [d] *So Sept.; Heb.* like new. [e] *Prob. rdg.; Heb.* I will not flatter man.

Look, I am ready to answer;   2
the words are on the tip of my tongue.*a*
My heart assures me that I speak with knowledge,   3
and that my lips speak with sincerity.
For the spirit of God made me,   4
and the breath of the Almighty gave me life.
Answer me if you can,   5
marshal your arguments and confront me.
In God's sight*b* I am just what you are;   6
I too am only a handful of clay.
Fear of me need not abash you,   7
nor any pressure from me overawe you.
You have said your say and I heard you;   8
I have listened to the sound of your words:
'I am innocent', you said, 'and free from offence,   9
blameless and without guilt.
Yet God finds occasions to put me in the wrong*c*   10
and counts me his enemy;
he puts my feet in the stocks   11
and keeps a close watch on all I do.'

Well, this is my answer: You are wrong.   12
God is greater than man;
why then plead your case with him?   13
for no one can answer his arguments.
Indeed, once God has spoken   14
he does not speak a second time to confirm it.
In dreams, in visions of the night,   15
when deepest sleep falls upon men,
while they sleep on their beds, God makes them listen,   16
and his correction strikes them with terror.
To turn a man from reckless conduct,   17
to check the pride*d* of mortal man,
at the edge of the pit he holds him back alive   18
and stops him from crossing the river of death.
Or again, man learns his lesson on a bed of pain,   19
tormented by a ceaseless ague in his bones;
he turns from his food with loathing   20
and has no relish for the choicest meats;
his flesh hangs loose upon him,   21
his bones are loosened and out of joint,
his soul draws near to the pit,   22

[a] *Lit.* my tongue speaks with my palate.   [b] In God's sight: *or* In strength.   [c] *So Pesh.;*
Heb. finds ways of thwarting me.   [d] the pride: *prob. rdg.; Heb. obscure.*

713

his life to the ministers of death.

23 Yet if an angel, one of thousands, stands by him,
 a mediator between him and God,
 to expound what he has done right
 and to secure mortal man his due;[a]

24 if he speaks in the man's favour and says, 'Reprieve[b] him,
 let him not go down to the pit, I have the price of his release';

25 then that man will grow sturdier[c] than he was in youth,
 he will return to the days of his prime.

26 If he entreats God to show him favour,
 to let him see his face and shout for joy;[d]

27 if he declares before all men, 'I have sinned,
 turned right into wrong and thought nothing of it';

28 then he saves himself from going down to the pit,
 he lives and sees the light.

29 All these things God may do to a man,
 again and yet again,

30 bringing him back from the pit
 to enjoy the full light of life.

31 Listen, Job, and attend to me;
 be silent, and I myself will speak.

32 If you have any arguments, answer me;
 speak, and I would gladly find you proved right;

33 but if you have none, listen to me:
 keep silence, and I will teach you wisdom.

34 Then Elihu went on to say:

2 Mark my words, you wise men;
 you men of long experience, listen to me;

3 for the ear tests what is spoken
 as the palate savours food.

4 Let us then examine for ourselves what is right;
 let us together establish the true good.

5 Job has said, 'I am innocent,
 but God has deprived me of justice,

6 he has falsified[e] my case;
 my state is desperate, yet I have done no wrong.'

7 Was there ever a man like Job
 with his thirst for irreverent talk,

8 choosing bad company to share his journeys,

---

[a] *Line transposed from verse 26.* [b] *So some MSS.; others have an unknown word.*
[c] will grow sturdier: *prob. rdg.; Heb. unintelligible.* [d] *See note on verse 23.* [e] *So Sept.;*
Heb. am I falsifying.

a fellow-traveller with wicked men?
For he says that it brings a man no profit   9
to find favour with God.
But listen to me, you men of good sense.   10
   Far be it from God to do evil
   or the Almighty to play false!
For he pays a man according to his work   11
and sees that he gets what his conduct deserves.
The truth is, God does no wrong,   12
the Almighty does not pervert justice.
Who committed the earth to his keeping?   13
Who but he established the whole world?
If he were to turn his thoughts inwards   14
and recall his life-giving spirit,
all that lives would perish on the instant,   15
and man return again to dust.

Now Job, if you have the wit, consider this;   16
listen to the words I speak.
Can it be that a hater of justice holds the reins?   17
Do you disparage a sovereign whose rule is so fair,
who will say to a prince, 'You scoundrel',   18
and call his magnates blackguards to their faces;
who does not show special favour to those in office   19
and thinks no more of rich than of poor?
All alike are God's creatures,
who may die in a moment, in the middle of the night;   20
at his touch the rich are no more,
and the mighty vanish though no hand is laid on them.
His eyes are on the ways of men,   21
and he sees every step they take;
there is nowhere so dark, so deep in shadow,   22
that wrongdoers may hide from him.
Therefore he repudiates all that they do;   25
he turns on them in the night, and they are crushed.
There are no appointed days for men   23
to appear before God for judgement.
He holds no inquiry, but breaks the powerful   24
and sets up others in their place.
For their crimes he strikes them down*a*   26*b*
and makes them disgorge their bloated wealth,*c*
because they have ceased to obey him   27

[a] he strikes them down: *prob. rdg.; Heb. om.*   [b] *Verse 25 transposed to follow verse 22.*
[c] *Or* and chastises them where people see.

and pay no heed to his ways.

28 Then the cry of the poor reaches his ears,
and he hears the cry of the distressed.

29-30 [Even if he is silent, who can condemn him?
If he looks away, who can find fault?
What though he makes a godless man king
over a stubborn*ᵃ* nation and all its people?]

31 But suppose you were to say to God,
'I have overstepped the mark; I will do no more*ᵇ* mischief.

32 Vile wretch that I am, be thou my guide;
whatever wrong I have done, I will do wrong no more.'

33 Will he, at these words, condone your rejection of him?
It is for you to decide, not me:
but what can you answer?

34 Men of good sense will say,
any intelligent hearer will tell me,

35 'Job talks with no knowledge,
and there is no sense in what he says.

36 If only Job could be put to the test once and for all
for answers that are meant to make mischief*ᶜ*!

37 He is a sinner and a rebel as well*ᵈ*
with his endless ranting against God.'

35 Then Elihu went on to say:

2 Do you think that this is a sound plea
or maintain that you are in the right against God?—

3 if you say, 'What would be the advantage to me?
how much should I gain from sinning?'

4 I will bring arguments myself against you,
you and your three*ᵉ* friends.

5 Look up at the sky and then consider,
observe the rain-clouds towering above you.

6 How does it touch him if you have sinned?
However many your misdeeds, what does it mean to him?

7 If you do right, what good do you bring him,
or what does he gain from you?

8 Your wickedness touches only men, such as you are;
the right that you do affects none but mortal man.

9 Men will cry out beneath the burdens of oppression
and call for help against the power of the great;

[a] a stubborn: *so Sept.; Heb.* the snares of a . . .   [b] more: *prob. rdg.; Heb. obscure.*
[c] that . . . mischief: *so some MSS.; others* among mischief-makers.   [d] *Prob. rdg.; Heb.*
adds between us it is enough.   [e] *So Sept.; Heb. om.*

but none of them asks, 'Where is God my Maker   10
who gives protection by night,
who grants us more knowledge than the beasts of the earth   11
and makes us wiser than the birds of the air?'
So, when they cry out, he does not answer,   12
because they are self-willed and proud.
All to no purpose! God does not listen,   13
the Almighty does not see.

The worse for you when you say, 'He does*a* not see me'*b*!   14
Humble yourself*c* in his presence and wait for his word.
But now, because God does not grow angry and punish   15
and because he lets folly pass unheeded,
Job gives vent to windy nonsense   16
and makes a parade of empty words.

Then Elihu went on to say: 36

Be patient a little longer, and let me enlighten you;   2
there is still something more to be said on God's side.
I will search far and wide to support my conclusions,   3
as I defend the justice of my Maker.
There are no flaws in my reasoning;   4
before you stands one whose conclusions are sound.

God,*d* I say, repudiates the high and*e* mighty   5
and does not let the wicked prosper,   6
but allows the just claims of the poor and suffering;
he does not deprive the sufferer of his due.*f*   7
Look at kings on their thrones:
when God gives them sovereign power, they grow arrogant.
Next you may see them loaded with fetters,   8
held fast in captives' chains:
he denounces their conduct to them,   9
showing how insolence and tyranny was their offence;
his warnings sound in their ears   10
and summon them to turn back from their evil courses.
If they listen to him, they spend*g* their days in prosperity   11
and their years in comfort.
But, if they do not listen, they die, their lesson unlearnt,   12
and cross the river of death.

---

[a] *So Vulg.; Heb.* You do.   [b] *So some MSS.; others* him.   [c] Humble yourself: *prob. rdg.; Heb.* Judge.   [d] *Prob. rdg.; Heb. adds* a mighty one and not.   [e] and: *prob. rdg.; Heb. om.*   [f] deprive...due: *or* withdraw his gaze from the righteous.   [g] *Prob. rdg.; Heb. adds* they end.

13   Proud men rage against him
     and do not cry to him for help when caught in his toils;
14   so they die in their prime,
     like male prostitutes,*a* worn out.*b*
15   Those who suffer he rescues through suffering
     and teaches them by the discipline of affliction.
16   Beware, if you are tempted to exchange hardship for comfort,*c*
     for unlimited plenty spread before you,*d* and a generous table;
17   if you eat your fill of a rich man's fare
     when you are occupied with the business of the law,
18   do not be led astray by lavish gifts of wine
     and do not let bribery warp your judgement.
19   Will that wealth of yours, however great, avail you,
     or all the resources of your high position?
21*e* Take care not to turn to mischief;
     for that is why you are tried by affliction.
20   Have no fear if in the breathless terrors of the night
     you see nations vanish where they stand.
22   God towers in majesty above us;
     who wields such sovereign power as he?
23   Who has prescribed his course for him?
     Who has said to him, 'Thou hast done wrong'?
24   Remember then to sing the praises of his work,
     as men have always sung them.
25   All men stand back from*f* him;
     the race of mortals look on from afar.
26   Consider; God is so great that we cannot know him;
     the number of his years is beyond reckoning.
27   He draws up drops of water from the sea*g*
     and distils rain from the mist he has made;
28   the rain-clouds pour down in torrents,*h*
     they descend in showers on mankind;
31   thus he sustains the nations
     and gives them food in plenty.
29   Can any man read the secret of the sailing clouds,
     spread like a carpet under*i* his pavilion?
30   See how he unrolls the mist*j* across the waters,
     and its streamers*k* cover the sea.

[a] Cp. Deut. 23. 17.   [b] worn out: *prob. rdg.; Heb. unintelligible.*   [c] for comfort: *prob. rdg.; Heb. om.*   [d] *So one MS.; others* her.   [e] *Verses 20 and 21 transposed.*   [f] Or gaze at.   [g] from the sea: *prob. rdg.; Heb. om.*   [h] in torrents: *prob. rdg.; Heb.* which.   [i] spread...under: *prob. rdg.; Heb.* crashing noises.   [j] *So Targ.; Heb.* light.   [k] its streamers: *prob. rdg.; Heb.* the roots of.

He charges the thunderbolts with flame   32[a]
and launches them straight[b] at the mark;
in his anger he calls up the tempest,   33
and the thunder is the herald of its coming.[c]
This too makes my heart beat wildly   37
and start from its place.
Listen, listen to the thunder of God's voice   2
and the rumbling of his utterance.
Under the vault of heaven he lets it roll,   3
and his lightning reaches the ends of the earth;
there follows a sound of roaring   4
as he thunders with the voice of majesty.[d]
God's voice is marvellous in its working;[e]   5
he does great deeds that pass our knowledge.
For he says to the snow, 'Fall to earth',   6
and to the rainstorms, 'Be fierce.'
And when his voice is heard,
the floods of rain pour down unchecked.[f]
He shuts every man fast indoors,[g]   7
and all men whom he has made must stand idle;
the beasts withdraw into their lairs   8
and take refuge in their dens.
The hurricane bursts from its prison,   9
and the rain-winds bring bitter cold;
at the breath of God the ice-sheet is formed,   10
and the wide waters are frozen hard as iron.
He gives the dense clouds their load of moisture,   11
and the clouds spread his mist[h] abroad,
as they travel round in their courses,   12
steered by his guiding hand
to do his bidding
all over the habitable world.[i]

Listen, Job, to this argument;   14
stand still, and consider God's wonderful works.
Do you know how God assigns them their tasks,   15
how he sends light flashing from his clouds?
Do you know why the clouds hang poised overhead,   16
a wonderful work of his consummate skill,

[a] *Verse 31 transposed to follow verse 28.* [b] and…straight: *prob. rdg.; Heb.* and gives orders concerning it. [c] in his anger… coming: *prob. rdg.; Heb. obscure.* [d] *See note on verse 6.* [e] *Prob. rdg.; Heb.* thundering. [f] And when…unchecked: *prob. rdg.; some words in these lines transposed from verse 4.* [g] indoors: *prob. rdg.; Heb. obscure.* [h] *So Targ.; Heb.* light. [i] *Prob. rdg.; Heb. adds* (13) whether he makes him attain the rod, or his earth, or constant love.

17   sweating there in your stifling clothes,
     when the earth lies sultry under the south wind?
18   Can you beat out the vault of the skies, as he does,
     hard as a mirror of cast metal?
19   Teach us then what to say to him;
     for all is dark, and we cannot marshal our thoughts.
20   Can any man dictate to God when he is*a* to speak?
     or command him to make proclamation?
21   At one moment the light is not seen,
     it is overcast with clouds and rain;
     then the wind passes by and clears them away,
22   and a golden glow comes from the north.*b*
23   But the Almighty we cannot find; his power is beyond our ken,
     and his righteousness not slow to do justice.
24   Therefore mortal men pay him reverence,
     and all who are wise look to him.*c*

God's answer and Job's submission

38   Then the LORD answered Job out of the tempest:

2   Who is this whose ignorant words
     cloud my design in darkness?
3   Brace yourself and stand up like a man;
     I will ask questions, and you shall answer.
4   Where were you when I laid the earth's foundations?
     Tell me, if you know and understand.
5   Who settled its dimensions? Surely you should know.
     Who stretched his measuring-line over it?
6   On what do its supporting pillars rest?
     Who set its corner-stone in place,
7   when the morning stars sang together
     and all the sons of God shouted aloud?
8   Who watched over the birth of the sea,*d*
     when it burst in flood from the womb?—
9   when I wrapped it in a blanket of cloud
     and cradled*e* it in fog,
10   when I established its bounds,
     fixing its doors and bars in place,

[*a*] *Prob. rdg.; Heb.* I am.   [*b*] *Prob. rdg.; Heb. adds* this refers to God, terrible in majesty.
[*c*] to him: *so Sept.; Heb.* not.   [*d*] Who…sea: *prob. rdg.; Heb.* And he held back the
sea with two doors.   [*e*] *Lit.* swaddled.

and said, 'Thus far shall you come and no farther,　　11
and here your surging waves shall halt.'[a]
In all your life have you ever called up the dawn　　12
or shown the morning its place?
Have you taught it to grasp the fringes of the earth　　13
and shake the Dog-star from its place;[b]
to bring up the horizon in relief as clay under a seal,　　14
until all things stand out like the folds of a cloak,
when the light of the Dog-star is dimmed　　15
and the stars of the Navigator's Line go out one by one[c]?
Have you descended to the springs of the sea　　16
or walked in the unfathomable deep?
Have the gates of death been revealed to you?　　17
Have you ever seen the door-keepers of the place of darkness?
Have you comprehended the vast expanse of the world?　　18
Come, tell me all this, if you know.
Which is the way to the home of light　　19
and where does darkness dwell?
And can you then take each to its appointed bound　　20
and escort it on its homeward path?
Doubtless you know all this; for you were born already,　　21
so long is the span of your life!

Have you visited the storehouse of the snow　　22
or seen the arsenal where hail is stored,
which I have kept ready for the day of calamity,　　23
for war and for the hour of battle?
By what paths is the heat spread abroad　　24
or the east wind carried far and wide over the earth?
Who has cut channels for the downpour　　25
and cleared a passage for the thunderstorm,
for rain to fall on land where no man lives　　26
and on the deserted wilderness,
clothing lands waste and derelict with green　　27
and making grass grow on thirsty ground[d]?
Has the rain a father?　　28
Who sired the drops of dew?
Whose womb gave birth to the ice,　　29
and who was the mother of the frost from heaven,
which lays a stony cover over the waters　　30
and freezes the expanse of ocean?
Can you bind the cluster of the Pleiades　　31

[a] *Prob. rdg.; Heb.* here one shall set on your surging waves.　[b] *Lit.* the Dog-stars from it.
[c] *Lit.* and the high arm breaks up.　[d] thirsty ground: *prob. rdg.; Heb.* source.

or loose Orion's belt?

32 Can you bring out the signs of the zodiac in their season
or guide Aldebaran and its train?

33 Did you proclaim the rules that govern the heavens,
or determine the laws of nature on earth?

34 Can you command the dense clouds
to cover you with their weight of waters?

35 If you bid lightning speed on its way,
will it say to you, 'I am ready'?

36 Who put wisdom in depths of darkness
and veiled understanding in secrecy[a]?

37 Who is wise enough to marshal the rain-clouds
and empty the cisterns[b] of heaven,

38 when the dusty soil sets hard as iron,
and the clods of earth cling together?

39 Do you hunt her prey for the lioness
and satisfy the hunger of young lions,

40 as they crouch in the lair
or lie in wait in the covert?

41 Who provides the raven with its quarry
when its fledglings croak[c] for lack of food?

39 Do you know when the mountain-goats are born
or attend the wild doe when she is in labour?

2 Do you count the months that they carry their young
or know the time of their delivery,

3 when they crouch down to open their wombs
and bring their offspring to the birth,

4 when the fawns grow and thrive in the open forest,
and go forth and do not return?

5 Who has let the wild ass of Syria range at will
and given the wild ass of Arabia its freedom?—

6 whose home I have made in the wilderness
and its lair in the saltings;

7 it disdains the noise of the city
and is deaf to the driver's shouting;

8 it roams the hills as its pasture
and searches for anything green.

9 Does the wild ox consent to serve you,
does it spend the night in your stall?

10 Can you harness its strength[d] with ropes,
or will it harrow the furrows[d] after you?

[a] secrecy: *prob. rdg.; Heb. word unknown.*   [b] *Lit.* and tip up the water-skins...   [c] *Prob.
rdg.; Heb. adds* they cry to God.   [d] *Prob. rdg.; Heb. transposes* strength *and* furrows.

Can you depend on it, strong as it is, 11
or leave your labour to it?
Do you trust it to come back 12
and bring home your grain to*ᵃ* the threshing-floor?
The wings of the ostrich*ᵇ* are stunted;*ᶜ* 13
*ᵈ*her pinions and plumage are so scanty*ᵉ*
that she abandons her eggs to the ground, 14
letting them be kept warm by the sand.
She forgets that a foot may crush them, 15
or a wild beast trample on them;
she treats her chicks heartlessly as if they*ᶠ* were not hers, 16
not caring if her labour is wasted
(for God has denied her wisdom 17
and left her without sense),
while like a cock she struts*ᵍ* over the uplands, 18
scorning both horse and rider.

Did you give the horse his strength? 19
Did you clothe his neck with a mane?
Do you make him quiver like a locust's wings, 20
when his shrill neighing strikes terror?
He shows his mettle as he*ʰ* paws and prances; 21
he charges the armoured line with all his might.
He scorns alarms and knows no dismay; 22
he does not flinch before the sword.
The quiver rattles at his side, 23
the spear and sabre flash.
Trembling with eagerness, he devours the ground 24
and cannot be held in when he hears the horn;
at the blast of the horn he cries 'Aha!' 25
and from afar he scents the battle.*ⁱ*
Does your skill teach the hawk to use its pinions 26
and spread its wings towards the south?
Do you instruct the vulture to fly high 27
and build its nest aloft?
It dwells among the rocks and there it lodges; 28
its station is a crevice in the rock;
from there it searches for food, 29
keenly scanning the distance,
that its brood may be gorged with blood; 30

[a] *So Sept.; Heb. adds* and. [b] *Heb. word of uncertain mng.* [c] are stunted: *prob. rdg.;
Heb. unintelligible.* [d] *Prob. rdg.; Heb. prefixes* if. [e] *Prob. rdg.; Heb.* godly *or* stork.
[f] as if they: *so Vulg.; Heb.* those that. [g] *Lit.* while she plays the male. [h] *So Sept.;
Heb.* they. [i] *Prob. rdg.; Heb. adds* the thunder of the captains and the shouting.

and where the slain are, there the vulture is.

41 1^a   Can you pull out the whale^b with a gaff

or can you slip a noose round its tongue?

2   Can you pass a cord through its nose

or put a hook through its jaw?

3   Will it plead with you for mercy

or beg its life with soft words?

4   Will it enter into an agreement with you

to become your slave for life?

5   Will you toy with it as with a bird

or keep it on a string like a song-bird^c for your maidens?

6   Do trading-partners haggle over it

or merchants share it out?

40 Then the LORD said to Job:

2   Is it for a man who disputes with the Almighty to be stubborn?

Should he that argues with God answer back?

3 And Job answered the LORD:

4   What reply can I give thee, I who carry no weight?

I put my finger to my lips.

5   I have spoken once and now will not answer again;

twice have I spoken, and I will do so no more.

6 Then the LORD answered Job out of the tempest:

7   Brace yourself and stand up like a man;

I will ask questions, and you shall answer.

8   Dare you deny that I am just

or put me in the wrong that you may be right?

9   Have you an arm like God's arm,

can you thunder with a voice like his?

10   Deck yourself out, if you can, in pride and dignity,

array yourself in pomp and splendour;

11   unleash the fury of your wrath,

look upon the proud man and humble him;

12   look upon every proud man and bring him low,

throw down the wicked where they stand;

13   hide them in the dust together,

and shroud them in an unknown grave.

14   Then I in my turn will acknowledge

that your own right hand can save you.

[a] *41. 1–6 (in Heb. 40. 25–30) transposed to this point.* [b] *Or* Leviathan. [c] like a song-bird: *so Sept.; Heb. om.*

Consider the chief of the beasts, the crocodile,[a]   15
who devours cattle as if they were grass:[b]
what strength is in his loins!   16
what power in the muscles of his belly!
His tail is rigid as[c] a cedar,   17
the sinews of his flanks are closely knit,
his bones are tubes of bronze,   18
and his limbs like bars of iron.
He is the chief of God's works,[d]   19
made to be a tyrant over his peers;[e]
for he takes[f] the cattle of the hills for his prey   20
and in his jaws he crunches all wild beasts.
There under the thorny lotus he lies,   21
hidden in the reeds and the marsh;
the lotus conceals him in its shadow,   22
the poplars of the stream surround him.
If the river is in spate, he is not scared,   23
he sprawls at his ease though the stream[g] is in flood.
Can a man blind[h] his eyes and take him   24
or pierce his nose with the teeth of a trap?
Can you fill his skin with harpoons   **41** 7[i][j]
or his head with fish-hooks?
If ever you lift your hand against him,   8
think of the struggle that awaits you, and let be.

No, such a man is in desperate case,   9[k]
hurled headlong at the very sight of him.
How fierce he is when he is roused!   10
Who is there to stand up to him[l]?
Who has ever attacked him[m] unscathed[n]?   11
Not a man[o] under the wide heaven.
I will not pass over in silence his limbs,   12
his prowess and the grace of his proportions.
Who has ever undone his outer garment   13
or penetrated his doublet of hide?
Who has ever opened the portals of his face?   14
for there is terror in his arching teeth.
His back[p] is row upon row of shields,   15

[a] chief...crocodile: *prob. rdg.*; *Heb.* beasts (behemoth) which I have made with you.
[b] cattle...grass: *prob. rdg.*; *Heb.* grass like cattle. [c] *Or* He bends his tail like...
[d] *Lit.* ways. [e] *Prob. rdg.*; *Heb.* his sword. [f] *Prob. rdg.*; *Heb.* they take. [g] *Lit.*
Jordan. [h] Can a man blind: *prob. rdg.*; *Heb.* obscure. [i] *40. 31 in Heb.* [j] *Verses
1–6 transposed to follow 39. 30.* [k] *41. 1 in Heb.* [l] *So some MSS.*; *others* me. [m] *Prob.
rdg.*; *Heb.* me. [n] *So Sept.*; *Heb.* and I am safe. [o] *Prob. rdg.*; *Heb.* He is mine.
[p] *Prob. rdg.*; *Heb.* pride.

enclosed in a wall[a] of flints;
16 one presses so close on the other
    that air cannot pass between them,
17 each so firmly clamped to its neighbour
    that they hold and cannot spring apart.
18 His sneezing sends out sprays of light,
    and his eyes gleam like the shimmer of dawn.[b]
19 Firebrands shoot from his mouth,
    and sparks come streaming out;
20 his nostrils pour forth smoke
    like a cauldron on a fire blown to full heat.[c]
21 His breath sets burning coals ablaze,
    and flames flash from his mouth.
22 Strength is lodged in his neck,
    and untiring energy dances ahead of him.
23 Close knit is his underbelly,
    no pressure will make it yield.
24 His heart is firm as a rock,
    firm as the nether millstone.
25 When he raises himself, strong men[d] take fright,
    bewildered at the lashings of his tail.
26 Sword or spear, dagger or javelin,
    if they touch him, they have no effect.
27 Iron he counts as straw,
    and bronze as rotting wood.
28 No arrow can pierce him,
    and for him sling-stones are turned into chaff;
29 to him a club is a mere reed,[e]
    and he laughs at the swish of the sabre.
30 Armoured beneath with jagged sherds,
    he sprawls on the mud like a threshing-sledge.
31 He makes the deep water boil like a cauldron,
    he whips up the lake like ointment in a mixing-bowl.
32 He leaves a shining trail behind him,
    and the great river is like white hair in his wake.
33 He has no equal on earth;
    for he is made quite without fear.
34 He looks down on all creatures, even the highest;
    he is king over all proud beasts.

[a] *Prob. rdg.; Heb.* seal. [b] *Lit.* eyelids of the morning. [c] full heat: *so Pesh.; Heb.* rushes. [d] strong men: *or* leaders *or* gods. [e] a mere reed: *so Symm. and Theod.; Heb.* chaff.

Then Job answered the LORD: **42**

I know that thou canst do all things **2**
and that no purpose is beyond thee.
*a*But I have spoken of great*b* things which I have not understood, **3**
things too wonderful for me to know.*c*
I knew of thee then only by report, **5**
but now I see thee with my own eyes.
Therefore I melt away;*d* **6**
I repent in dust and ashes.

Epilogue

When the LORD had finished speaking to Job, he said to Eliphaz the **7**
Temanite, 'I am angry with you and your two friends, because you
have not spoken as you ought about me, as my servant Job has done.*e*
So now take seven bulls and seven rams, go to my servant Job and offer **8**
a whole-offering for yourselves, and he will intercede for you; I will
surely show him favour by not being harsh with you because you have
not spoken as you ought about me, as he has done.'*f* Then Eliphaz the **9**
Temanite and Bildad the Shuhite and*g* Zophar the Naamathite went
and carried out the LORD's command, and the LORD showed favour to
Job when he had interceded for his friends. So the LORD restored Job's **10**
fortunes and doubled all his possessions.

Then all Job's brothers and sisters and his former acquaintance **11**
came and feasted with him in his home, and they consoled and comforted him for all the misfortunes which the LORD had brought on
him; and each of them gave him a sheep*h* and a gold ring. Further- **12**
more, the LORD blessed the end of Job's life more than the beginning;
and he had fourteen thousand head of small cattle and six thousand
camels, a thousand yoke of oxen and as many she-asses. He had seven*i* **13**
sons and three daughters; and he named his eldest daughter Jemimah, **14**
the second Keziah and the third Keren-happuch. There were no women **15**
in all the world so beautiful as Job's daughters; and their father gave
them an inheritance with their brothers.

Thereafter Job lived another hundred and forty years, he saw his **16**
sons and his grandsons to four generations, and died at a very great age. **17**

[a] *So one form of Sept.; Heb. prefixes* Whoever conceals counsel without knowledge,
cp. 38. 2. [b] *So Sept.; Heb. om.* [c] *Prob. rdg.; Heb. adds* (4) O listen, and let me speak;
I will ask questions, and you shall answer. [d] *Or* despise myself. [e] *about...done:
so some MSS.; others* to me about my servant Job. [f] *about...done: so some MSS.; others*
to me about him. [g] *So many MSS.; others om.* [h] *Or* piece of money. [i] *Or* fourteen.

PSALMS

BOOK 1

1

1   Happy is the man
    who does not take the wicked for his guide
    nor walk the road that sinners tread
    nor take his seat among the scornful;
2   the law of the LORD is his delight,
  the law his meditation night and day.
3   He is like a tree
    planted beside a watercourse,
    which yields its fruit in season
      and its leaf never withers:
    in all that he does he prospers.
4   Wicked men are not like this;
    they are like chaff driven by the wind.
5   So when judgement comes the wicked shall not stand firm,
  nor shall sinners stand in the assembly of the righteous.
6   The LORD watches over the way of the righteous,
      but the way of the wicked is doomed.

2

1   Why are the nations in turmoil?
    Why do the peoples hatch their futile plots?
2   The kings of the earth stand ready,
    and the rulers conspire together
    against the LORD and his anointed king.
3   'Let us break their fetters,' they cry,
    'let us throw off their chains!'
4   The Lord who sits enthroned in heaven
      laughs them to scorn;
5   then he rebukes them in anger,
    he threatens them in his wrath.
6   Of me he says, 'I have enthroned my king
    on Zion my holy mountain.'

I will repeat*a* the LORD's decree: 7
'You are my son,' he said;
  'this day I become your father.
  Ask of me what you will: 8
  I will give you nations as your inheritance,
  the ends of the earth as your possession.
  You shall break them with a rod of iron,   9
  you shall shatter them like a clay pot.'
Be mindful then, you kings;   10
   learn your lesson, rulers of the earth:
  worship the LORD with reverence;   11–12
  tremble, and kiss the king,*b*
lest the LORD be angry and you are struck down in mid course;
  for his anger flares up in a moment.
    Happy are all who find refuge in him.

3

  LORD, how my enemies have multiplied!   1
  Many rise up against me,
  many there are who say of me,   2
  'God will not bring him victory.'
But thou, LORD, art a shield to cover me: 3
  thou art my glory, and thou dost raise my head high.
  I cry aloud to the LORD,   4
   and he answers me from his holy mountain.
  I lie down and sleep,   5
  and I wake again, for the LORD upholds me.
  I will not fear the nations in their myriads   6
  who set on me from all sides.

Rise up, LORD; save me, O my God.   7
  Thou dost strike all my foes across the face
   and breakest the teeth of the wicked.
   Thine is the victory, O LORD,   8
  and may*c* thy blessing rest upon thy people.

4

  Answer me when I call, O God, maintainer of my right, 1
I was hard pressed, and thou didst set me at large;
  be gracious to me now and hear my prayer.

[*a*] *So Sept.; Heb.* I will repeat unto...   [*b*] tremble...king: *prob. rdg.; lit.* tremble and kiss the mighty one; *Heb. obscure.*   [*c*] Thine...and may: *or* O LORD of salvation, may...

2 Mortal men, how long will you pay me not honour but dishonour,
   or set your heart on trifles and run after lies?

3 Know that the LORD has shown me^a his marvellous love;
   the LORD hears when I call to him.

4   However angry your hearts, do not do wrong;
   though you lie abed resentful,^b do not break silence:

5 pay your due of sacrifice, and trust in the LORD.

6 There are many who say, 'If only we might be prosperous again!
   But the light of thy presence has fled from us, O LORD.'

7   Yet in my heart thou hast put more happiness
   than they enjoyed when there was corn and wine in plenty.

8 Now I will lie down in peace, and sleep;
   for thou alone, O LORD, makest me live unafraid.

5

1   Listen to my words, O LORD,
           consider my inmost thoughts;

2 heed my cry for help, my king and my God.

3 In the morning, when I say my prayers,
           thou wilt hear me.
   I set out my morning sacrifice^c
           and watch for thee, O LORD.

4 For thou art not a God who welcomes wickedness;
           evil can be no guest of thine.^d

5   There is no place for arrogance before thee;
           thou hatest evildoers,

6   thou makest an end of all liars.

   The LORD detests traitors and men of blood.

7 But I, through thy great love, may come into thy house,
   and bow low toward thy holy temple in awe of thee.

8   Lead me, LORD, in thy righteousness,
           because my enemies are on the watch;
           give me a straight path to follow.

9   There is no trusting what they say,^e
           they are nothing but wind.
   Their throats are an open^f sepulchre;
           smooth talk runs off their tongues.

10   Bring ruin on them, O God;

---

[a] *Prob. rdg.; Heb.* him. [b] lie abed resentful: *prob. rdg.; Heb.* say on your beds. [c] *Or* plea. [d] who welcomes...thine: *or* who protects a wicked man; an evil man cannot be thy guest. [e] *So Sept.; Heb.* he says. [f] *Or* inscribed.

let them fall by their own devices.
Cast them out, after all their rebellions,
for they have defied thee.
But let all who take refuge in thee rejoice,   11
let them for ever break into shouts of joy;
shelter those who love thy name,
that they may exult in thee.
For thou, O Lord, wilt bless the righteous;   12
thou wilt hedge him round with favour as with a shield.

6

O Lord, do not condemn me in thy anger,   1
do not punish me in thy fury.
Be merciful to me, O Lord, for I am weak;   2
heal me, my very bones are shaken;
my soul quivers in dismay.   3
And thou, O Lord—how long?
Come back, O Lord; set my soul free,   4
deliver me for thy love's sake.
None talk of thee among the dead;   5
who praises thee in Sheol?

I am wearied with groaning;   6
all night long my pillow is wet with tears,
I soak my bed with weeping.
Grief dims my eyes;   7
they are worn out with all my woes.
Away from me, all you evildoers,   8
for the Lord has heard the sound of my weeping.
The Lord has heard my entreaty;   9
the Lord will accept my prayer.
All my enemies shall be confounded and dismayed;   10
they shall turn away in sudden confusion.

7

O Lord my God, in thee I find refuge;   1
save me, rescue me from my pursuers,
before they tear at my throat like a lion   2
and carry me off beyond hope of rescue.
O Lord my God, if I have done any of these things—   3
if I have stained my hands with guilt,
if I have repaid a friend evil for good   4

731

or set free an enemy who attacked me without cause,
5 may my adversary come after me and overtake me,
   trample my life to the ground
   and lay my honour in the dust!

6   Arise, O Lord, in thy anger,
         rouse thyself in wrath against my foes.
   Awake, my God who hast ordered that justice be done;
7   let the peoples assemble around thee,
         and take thou thy seat on high above them.
8   O Lord, thou who dost pass sentence on the nations,
         O Lord, judge me as my righteousness deserves,
         for I am clearly innocent.
9 Let wicked men do no more harm,
   establish the reign of righteousness,*a*
   thou who examinest both heart and mind,
         thou righteous God.

10 God, the High God, is my shield
    who saves men of honest heart.
11 God is a just judge,
    every day he requites the raging enemy.

12   He sharpens his sword,
         strings his bow and makes it ready.
13 He has prepared his deadly shafts
    and tipped his arrows with fire.
14   But the enemy is in labour with iniquity;
    he conceives mischief, and his brood is lies.
15 He has made a pit and dug it deep,
    and he himself shall fall into the hole that he has made.
16 His mischief shall recoil upon himself,
    and his violence fall on his own head.

17 I will praise the Lord for his righteousness
    and sing a psalm to the name of the Lord Most High.

8

1   O Lord our sovereign,
         how glorious is thy name in all the earth!
         Thy majesty is praised high as the heavens.
2   Out of the mouths of babes, of infants at the breast,
            thou hast rebuked*b* the mighty,

[a] the reign of righteousness: *or* the cause of the righteous.   [b] *Prob. rdg.; Heb.* founded.

silencing enmity and vengeance to teach thy foes a lesson.
When I look up at thy heavens, the work of thy fingers,   3
   the moon and the stars set in their place by thee,
   what is man that thou shouldst remember him,   4
      mortal man that thou shouldst care for him?
   Yet thou hast made him little less than a god,   5
   crowning him with glory and honour.
   Thou makest him master over all thy creatures;   6
   thou hast put everything under his feet:
all sheep and oxen, all the wild beasts,   7
   the birds in the air and the fish in the sea,   8
   and all that moves along the paths of ocean.
   O LORD our sovereign,   9
   how glorious is thy name in all the earth!

9–10

I will praise thee, O LORD,[a] with all my heart,   1
   I will tell the story of thy marvellous acts.
I will rejoice and exult in thee,   2
I will praise thy name in psalms, O thou Most High,
   when my enemies turn back,   3
when they fall headlong and perish at thy appearing;
for thou hast upheld my right and my cause,   4
   seated on thy throne, thou righteous judge.
Thou hast rebuked the nations and overwhelmed the ungodly,   5
thou hast blotted out their name for all time.
The strongholds of the enemy are thrown down for evermore;   6
thou hast laid their cities in ruins, all memory of them is lost.
The LORD thunders,[b] he sits enthroned for ever: 7
   he has set up his throne, his judgement-seat.
He it is who will judge the world with justice   8
   and try the cause of the peoples fairly.
So may the LORD be a tower of strength for the oppressed,   9
   a tower of strength in time of need,
that those who acknowledge thy name may trust in thee;   10
   for thou, LORD, dost not forsake those who seek thee.
Sing psalms to the LORD who dwells in Zion,   11
   proclaim his deeds among the nations.
For the Avenger of blood has remembered men's desire,   12
   and has not forgotten the cry of the poor.

[a] thee, O LORD: *so Sept.; Heb.* the LORD. [b] thunders: *prob. rdg.; Heb. unintelligible.*

13   Have pity on me, O Lord; look upon my affliction,
        thou who hast lifted me up*a* and caught me back from the
            gates of death,
14   that I may repeat all thy praise
    and exult at this deliverance in the gates of Zion's city.

15   The nations have plunged into a pit of their own making;
    their own feet are entangled in the net which they hid.
16   Now the Lord makes himself known. Justice is done:
        the wicked man is trapped in his own devices.
17   They rush blindly down to Sheol, the wicked,
        all the nations who are heedless of God.
18   But the poor shall not always be unheeded
    nor the hope of the destitute be always vain.
19   Arise, Lord, give man no chance to boast his strength;
        summon the nations before thee for judgement.
20   Strike them with fear, O Lord,
    let the nations know that they are but men.

10   Why stand so far off, Lord,
        hiding thyself in time of need?
2   The wicked man in his pride hunts down the poor:
        may his crafty schemes be his own undoing!
3   The wicked man is obsessed with his own desires,
        and in his greed gives wickedness*b* his blessing;
4   arrogant as he is, he scorns the Lord
        and leaves no place for God in all his schemes.
5   His ways are always devious;
        thy judgements are beyond his grasp,*c*
        and he scoffs at all restraint.
6   He says to himself, 'I shall never be shaken;
        no misfortune can check my course.'*d*
7   His mouth is full of lies and violence;
        mischief and trouble lurk under his tongue.
8   He lies in ambush in the villages
        and murders innocent men by stealth.
       He is watching*e* intently for some poor wretch;
9   he seizes him and drags him away in his net;
    he crouches stealthily, like a lion in its lair
        crouching to seize its victim;
10   the good man*f* is struck down and sinks to the ground,

[a] thou...me up: *prob. rdg.; Heb.* from those who hate me. [b] wickedness: *transposed from first line of verse 4.* [c] beyond his grasp: *prob. rdg.; Heb.* on high before him. [d] my course: *prob. rdg.; Heb.* which. [e] *Prob. rdg.; Heb.* storing up. [f] the good man: *prob. rdg.; Heb. om.*

and poor wretches fall into his toils.
He says to himself, 'God has forgotten;   11
he has hidden his face and has seen nothing.'

Arise, LORD, set^a thy hand to the task;   12
  do not forget the poor, O God.
Why, O God, has the wicked man rejected thee   13
  and said to himself that thou dost not care?
Thou seest that mischief and trouble are his companions,   14
  thou takest the matter into thy own hands.
  The poor victim commits himself to thee;
fatherless, he finds in thee his helper.
  Break the power of wickedness and wrong;   15
  hunt out all wickedness until thou canst find no more.

The LORD is king for ever and ever;   16
  the nations have vanished from his land.
  Thou hast heard the lament of the humble, O LORD,   17
  and art attentive to their heart's desire,
  bringing justice to the orphan and the downtrodden   18
that fear may never drive men from their homes again.

11

In the LORD I have found my refuge; why do you say to me,   1
  'Flee to the mountains like a bird;
see how the wicked string their bows   2
  and fit the arrow to the string,
  to shoot down honest men out of the darkness'?
When foundations are undermined, what can the good man do?   3
    The LORD is in his holy temple,   4
  the LORD's throne is in heaven.
His eye is upon mankind, he takes their measure at a glance.
The LORD weighs just and unjust   5
  and hates with all his soul the lover of violence.
  He shall rain down red-hot coals upon the wicked;   6
brimstone and scorching winds shall be the cup they drink.
For the LORD is just and loves just dealing;   7
  his face is turned towards the upright man.

[a] *Or* who settest.

735

12

1   Help, LORD, for loyalty is no more;
       good faith between man and man is over.
2   One man lies to another:
       they talk with smooth lip and double heart.
3   May the LORD make an end of such smooth lips
       and the tongue that talks so boastfully!
4   They said, 'Our tongue can win the day.
       Words are our ally; who can master us?'
5   'For the ruin of the poor, for the groans of the needy,
       now I will arise,' says the LORD,
       'I will place him in the safety for which he longs.'

6   The words of the LORD are pure words:
       silver refined in a crucible,
       gold[a] seven times purified.
7   Do thou, LORD, protect us[b]
       and guard us from a profligate and evil generation.[c]
8   The wicked flaunt themselves on every side,
       while profligacy stands high among mankind.

13

1   How long, O LORD, wilt thou quite forget me?
       How long wilt thou hide thy face from me?
2   How long must I suffer anguish in my soul,
       grief in my heart, day and night[d]?
       How long shall my enemy lord it over me?
3   Look now and answer me, O LORD my God.
       Give light to my eyes lest I sleep the sleep of death,
4   lest my adversary say, 'I have overthrown him',
       and my enemies rejoice at my downfall.
5   But for my part I trust in thy true love.
       My heart shall rejoice, for thou hast set me free.
6   I will sing to the LORD, who has granted all my desire.

14

1[e]   The impious fool says in his heart,
       'There is no God.'

[a] gold: *prob. rdg.; Heb.* to the earth.   [b] *So some MSS.; others* them.   [c] a profligate and evil generation: *prob. rdg.; Heb.* the generation which is for ever.   [d] and night: *so Sept.; Heb. om.*   [e] *Verses 1–7: cp. Ps. 53. 1–6.*

How vile men are, how depraved and loathsome;
   not one does anything good!
The LORD looks down from heaven   2
   on all mankind
to see if any act wisely,
   if any seek out God.
But all are disloyal, all are rotten to the core;   3
   not one does anything good,
   no, not even one.

   Shall they not rue it,   4
all evildoers who devour my people
   as men devour bread,
   and never call upon the LORD?
There they were in dire alarm;   5
for God was in the brotherhood of the godly.
   The resistance of their victim was too much for them,   6
   because the LORD was his refuge.
If only Israel's deliverance might come out of Zion!   7
   When the LORD restores his people's fortunes,
let Jacob rejoice, let Israel be glad.

15

O LORD, who may lodge in thy tabernacle?   1
Who may dwell on thy holy mountain?
The man of blameless life, who does what is right   2
and speaks the truth from his heart;
   who has no malice on his tongue,   3
who never wrongs a friend
and tells no tales against his neighbour;
the man who shows his scorn for the worthless   4
and honours all who fear the LORD;
who swears to his own hurt and does not retract;
who does not put his money out to usury   5
and takes no bribe against an innocent man.
He who does these things shall never be brought low.

16

Keep me, O God, for in thee have I found refuge.   1
   I have said to the LORD,   2
   'Thou, Lord, art my felicity.'
The gods whom earth holds sacred are all worthless,   3

and cursed are all who make them their delight;*[a]*

4 those who run after them*[b]* find trouble without end.
I will not offer them libations of blood
nor take their names upon my lips.

5 Thou, LORD, my allotted portion, thou my cup,
thou dost enlarge my boundaries:

6 the lines fall for me in pleasant places,
indeed I am well content with my inheritance.

7 I will bless the LORD who has given me counsel:
in the night-time wisdom comes to me in my inward parts.

8 I have set the LORD continually before me:
with him*[c]* at my right hand I cannot be shaken.

9 Therefore my heart exults
and my spirit rejoices,
my body too rests unafraid;

10 for thou wilt not abandon me to Sheol
nor suffer thy faithful servant to see the pit.

11 Thou wilt show me the path of life;
in thy presence is the fullness of joy,
in thy right hand pleasures for evermore.

17

1 Hear, LORD, my*[d]* plea for justice,
give my cry a hearing,
listen to my prayer,
for it is innocent of all deceit.

2 Let judgement in my cause issue from thy lips,
let thine eyes be fixed on justice.

3 Thou hast tested my heart and watched me all night long;
thou hast assayed me and found in me no mind to evil.

4 I will not speak of the deeds of men;
I have taken good note of all thy sayings.

5 I have not strayed from the course of duty;
I have followed thy path and never stumbled.

6 I call upon thee, O God, for thou wilt answer me.
Bend down thy ear to me, listen to my words.

7 Show me how marvellous thy true love can be,
who with thy hand dost save
all who seek sanctuary from their enemies.

8 Keep me like the apple of thine eye;

[a] are all worthless...delight: *prob. rdg.; Heb. obscure.* [b] after them: *prob. rdg.; Heb. obscure.* [c] with him: *prob. rdg.; Heb. om.* [d] my: *so Sept.; Heb. om.*

hide me in the shadow of thy wings
  from the wicked who obstruct me,   9
from deadly foes who throng round me.
  They have stifled all compassion;   10
  their mouths are full of pride;
  they press me hard,*a* now they hem me in,   11
on the watch to bring me*b* to the ground.
The enemy is like a lion eager for prey,   12
  like a young lion crouching in ambush.
Arise, LORD, meet him face to face and bring him down.   13
  Save my life from the wicked;
    make an end of them*c* with thy sword.   14
With thy hand, O LORD, make an end of them;*c*
  thrust them out of this world in the prime of their life,
gorged as they are with thy good things,
    blest with many sons
  and leaving their children wealth in plenty.
But my plea is just: I shall see thy face,   15
  and be blest with a vision of thee when I awake.

18

  I love thee, O LORD my strength.   1
The LORD is my stronghold, my fortress and my champion, 2*d*
  my God, my rock where I find safety,
my shield, my mountain refuge, my strong tower.
I will call on the LORD to whom all praise is due,   3
  and I shall be delivered from my enemies.
When the bonds of death held me fast,   4
  destructive torrents overtook me,
the bonds of Sheol tightened round me,   5
  the snares of death were set to catch me;
then in anguish of heart I cried to the LORD,   6
I called for help to my God;
  he heard me from his temple,
  and my cry reached his ears.
The earth heaved and quaked,   7
  the foundations of the mountains shook;
  they heaved, because he was angry.
Smoke rose from his nostrils,   8
  devouring fire came out of his mouth,

[a] they press me hard: *prob. rdg.; Heb.* our footsteps. [b] me: *so Pesh.; Heb. om.* [c] make
an end of them: *prob. rdg.; Heb. unintelligible.* [d] *Verses 2–50: cp. 2 Sam. 22. 2–51.*

glowing coals and searing heat.

9   He swept the skies aside as he descended,
     thick darkness lay under his feet.

10   He rode on a cherub, he flew through the air;
     he swooped on the wings of the wind.

11   He made darkness around him his hiding-place
     and dense[a] vapour his canopy.[b]

12   Thick clouds came out of the radiance before him,
     hailstones and glowing coals.

13   The LORD thundered from the heavens
     and the voice of the Most High spoke out.[c]

14   He loosed his arrows, he sped them far and wide,
     he shot forth lightning shafts and sent them echoing.

15   The channels of the sea-bed were revealed,
     the foundations of earth laid bare
     at the LORD's rebuke,
     at the blast of the breath of his[d] nostrils.

16   He reached down from the height and took me,
     he drew me out of mighty waters,

17   he rescued me from my enemies, strong as they were,
     from my foes when they grew too powerful for me.

18   They confronted me in the hour of my peril,
     but the LORD was my buttress.

19   He brought me out into an open place,
     he rescued me because he delighted in me.

20   The LORD rewarded me as my righteousness deserved;
     my hands were clean, and he requited me.

21   For I have followed the ways of the LORD
     and have not turned wickedly from my God;

22   all his laws are before my eyes,
     I have not failed to follow his decrees.

23   In his sight I was blameless
     and kept myself from wilful sin;

24   the LORD requited me as my righteousness deserved
     and the purity of my life in his eyes.

25   With the loyal thou showest thyself loyal
     and with the blameless man blameless.

26   With the savage man thou showest thyself savage,
     and[e] tortuous with the perverse.

---

[a] *Prob. rdg.*, *cp. 2 Sam. 22. 12; Heb.* dark.   [b] *Prob. rdg.; Heb. adds* thick clouds.   [c] *Prob. rdg.; Heb. adds* hailstones and glowing coals.   [d] *Prob. rdg.; Heb.* thy.   [e] With the savage...savage, and: *or* With the pure thou showest thyself pure, but...

Thou deliverest humble folk,   27
and bringest proud looks down to earth.
Thou, LORD, dost make my lamp burn bright,   28
and my God will lighten my darkness.
With thy help I leap over a bank,   29
by God's aid I spring over a wall.

The way of God is perfect,   30
the LORD's word has stood the test;
he is the shield of all who take refuge in him.
What god is there but the LORD?   31
What rock but our God?—
the God who girds me with strength   32
and makes my way blameless,
who makes me swift as a hind   33
and sets me secure on the*a* mountains;
who trains my hands for battle,   34
and my arms aim an arrow tipped with bronze.

Thou hast given me the shield of thy salvation,   35
thy hand sustains me, thy providence makes me great.
Thou givest me room for my steps,   36
my feet have not faltered.
I pursue my enemies and overtake them,   37
I do not return until I have made an end of them.
I strike them down and they will never rise again;   38
they fall beneath my feet.
Thou dost arm me with strength for the battle   39
and dost subdue my foes before me.
Thou settest my foot on my enemies' necks,   40
and I bring to nothing those that hate me.
They cry out and there is no one to help them,   41
they cry to the LORD and he does not answer.
I will pound them fine as dust before the wind,   42
like mud in the streets will I trample them.*b*
Thou dost deliver me from the clamour of the people,   43
and makest me master of the nations.
A people I never knew shall be my subjects;
as soon as they hear tell of me, they shall obey me,   44
and foreigners shall come cringing to me.
Foreigners shall be brought captive to me,   45
and emerge from their strongholds.

[*a*] *So Sept.; Heb.* my.   [*b*] *Prob. rdg., cp.* 2 Sam. 22. 43; *Heb.* will I empty them
out.

46 The LORD lives, blessed is my rock,
high above all is God who saves me.

47 O God, who grantest me vengeance,
who layest nations prostrate at my feet,

48 who dost rescue me from my foes and set me over my enemies,
thou dost deliver me from violent men.

49 Therefore, LORD, I will praise thee among the nations
and sing psalms to thy name,

50 to one who gives his king great victories
and in all his acts keeps faith with his anointed king,
with David and his descendants for ever.

19

1 The heavens tell out the glory of God,
the vault of heaven reveals his handiwork.

2 One day speaks to another,
night with night shares its knowledge,

3 and this without speech or language
or sound of any voice.

4 Their music goes out through all the earth,
their words reach to the end of the world.
In them a tent is fixed for the sun,

5 who comes out like a bridegroom from his wedding canopy,
rejoicing like a strong man to run his race.

6 His rising is at one end of the heavens,
his circuit touches their farthest ends;
and nothing is hidden from his heat.

7 The law of the LORD is perfect and revives the soul.
The LORD's instruction never fails,
and makes the simple wise.

8 The precepts of the LORD are right and rejoice the heart.
The commandment of the LORD shines clear
and gives light to the eyes.

9 The fear of the LORD is pure and abides for ever.
The LORD's decrees are true and righteous every one,

10 more to be desired than gold, pure gold in plenty,
sweeter than syrup or honey from the comb.

11 It is these that give thy servant warning,
and he who keeps them wins a great reward.

12 Who is aware of his unwitting sins?
Cleanse me of any secret fault.

Hold back thy servant also from sins of self-will,   13
    lest they get the better of me.
    Then I shall be blameless
and innocent of any great transgression.

May all that I say and think be acceptable to thee,   14
    O Lord, my rock and my redeemer!

20

May the Lord answer you in the hour of trouble!   1
The name of Jacob's God be your tower of strength,
give you help from the sanctuary   2
    and send you support from Zion!
    May he remember all your offerings   3
    and look with favour on your rich sacrifices,
give you your heart's desire   4
    and grant success to all your plans!
    Let us sing aloud in praise of your victory,   5
    let us do homage to the name of our God!
The Lord grant all you ask!

    Now I know   6
that the Lord has given victory to his anointed king:
    he will answer him from his holy heaven
    with the victorious might of his right hand.
Some boast of chariots and some of horses,   7
but our boast is the name of the Lord our God.
    They totter and fall,   8
but we rise up and are full of courage.
    O Lord, save the king,   9
    and answer us[a] in the hour of our calling.

21

The king rejoices in thy might, O Lord: 1
    well may he exult in thy victory,
    for thou hast given him his heart's desire   2
    and hast not refused him what he asked.
    Thou dost welcome him with blessings and prosperity 3
    and set a crown of fine gold upon his head.
He asked of thee life, and thou didst give it him,   4
    length of days for ever and ever.

[a] O Lord...answer us: *so Sept.; Heb.* Save, O Lord: let the king answer us.

5   Thy salvation has brought him great glory;
          thou dost invest him with majesty and honour,
6   for thou bestowest blessings on him for evermore
            and dost make him glad with joy in thy presence.
7   The king puts his trust in the LORD;
            the loving care of the Most High holds him unshaken.

8   Your hand shall reach all your enemies:
          your right hand shall reach those who hate you;
9   at your coming you shall plunge them into a fiery furnace;
            the LORD in his anger will strike them down,
              and fire shall consume them.
10   It will exterminate their offspring from the earth
            and rid mankind of their posterity.
11   For they have aimed wicked blows at you,
            they have plotted mischief but could not prevail;
12   but you will catch them round the shoulders*a*
            and will aim with your bow-strings at their faces.

13   Be exalted, O LORD, in thy might;
            we will sing a psalm of praise to thy power.

22

1   My God, my God, why hast thou forsaken me
            and art so far from saving me,*b* from heeding my groans?
2   O my God, I cry in the day-time but thou dost not answer,
            in the night I cry but get no respite.
3   And yet thou art enthroned in holiness,
              thou art he whose praises Israel sings.
4   In thee our fathers put their trust;
              they trusted, and thou didst rescue them.
5   Unto thee they cried and were delivered;
            in thee they trusted and were not put to shame.
6   But I am a worm, not a man,
              abused by all men, scorned by the people.
7   All who see me jeer at me,
          make mouths at me and wag their heads:
8   'He threw himself on the LORD for rescue;
            let the LORD deliver him, for he holds him dear!'
9   But thou art he who drew me from the womb,
              who laid me at my mother's breast.

[a] but you...shoulders: *mng. of Heb. words uncertain.*   [b] *Or, with slight change,* from my
cry.

Upon thee was I cast at birth;   10
from my mother's womb thou hast been my God.
   Be not far from me,   11
for trouble is near, and I have no helper.
   A herd of bulls surrounds me,   12
      great bulls*ᵃ* of Bashan beset me.
   Ravening and roaring lions   13
open their mouths wide against me.
      My strength drains away like water   14
      and all my bones are loose.
My heart has turned to wax and melts within me.
   My mouth*ᵇ* is dry as a potsherd,   15
and my tongue sticks to my jaw;
      I am laid*ᶜ* low in the dust of death.*ᵈ*
      The huntsmen are all about me;   16
      a band of ruffians rings me round,
and they have hacked off*ᵉ* my hands and my feet.
      I tell my tale of misery,   17
while they look on and gloat.
They share out my garments among them   18
and cast lots for my clothes.
But do not remain so far away, O LORD;   19
O my help, hasten to my aid.
Deliver my very self from the sword,   20
   my precious life from the axe.
      Save me from the lion's mouth,   21
      my poor body*ᶠ* from the horns of the wild ox.

I will declare thy fame to my brethren;   22
   I will praise thee in the midst of the assembly.
   Praise him, you who fear the LORD;   23
   all you sons of Jacob, do him honour;
stand in awe of him, all sons of Israel.
   For he has not scorned the downtrodden,   24
   nor shrunk in loathing from his plight,
nor hidden his face from him,
but gave heed to him when he cried out.
Thou dost inspire my praise in the full assembly;   25
and I will pay my vows before all who fear thee.
Let the humble eat and be satisfied.   26

[*a*] great bulls: *lit.* bisons. [*b*] *Prob. rdg.; Heb.* My strength. [*c*] I am laid: *prob. rdg.;*
Heb. thou wilt lay me. [*d*] I am…death: *should possibly follow verse 17.* [*e*] and they have
hacked off: *prob. rdg.; Heb.* like a lion. [*f*] my poor body: *prob. rdg.; Heb.* thou hast
answered me.

Let those who seek the LORD praise him
and be^a in good heart for ever.

27 Let all the ends of the earth remember and turn again to the LORD;
let all the families of the nations bow down before him.^b

28 For kingly power belongs to the LORD,
and dominion over the nations is his.

29 How can those buried in the earth do him homage,
how can those who go down to the grave bow before him?
But I shall live for his sake,

30 my posterity^c shall serve him.
This shall be told of the Lord to future generations;

31 and they shall justify him,
declaring to a people yet unborn
that this was his doing.

23

1 The LORD is my shepherd; I shall want nothing.

2 He makes me lie down in green pastures,
and leads me beside the waters of peace;

3 he renews life within me,
and for his name's sake guides me in the right path.

4 Even though I walk through a valley dark as death
I fear no evil, for thou art with me,
thy staff and thy crook are my comfort.

5 Thou spreadest a table for me in the sight of my enemies;
thou hast richly bathed my head with oil,
and my cup runs over.

6 Goodness and love unfailing, these will follow me
all the days of my life,
and I shall dwell in the house of the LORD
my whole life long.

24

1 The earth is the LORD's and all that is in it,
the world and those who dwell therein.

2 For it was he who founded it upon the seas
and planted it firm upon the waters beneath.

3 Who may go up the mountain of the LORD?
And who may stand in his holy place?

[a] and be: *so Sept.; Heb.* may you be. [b] *So Sept.; Heb.* thee. [c] But I...posterity: *prob. rdg.; Heb. obscure.*

He who has clean hands and a pure heart,   4
who has not set his mind on falsehood,
   and has not committed perjury.
He shall receive a blessing from the LORD,   5
   and justice from God his saviour.
   Such is the fortune of those who seek him,   6
   who seek the face of the God of Jacob.*a*

Lift up your heads, you gates,   7
   lift yourselves up, you everlasting doors,
that the king of glory may come in.
   Who is the king of glory?   8
   The LORD strong and mighty,
   the LORD mighty in battle.
Lift up your heads, you gates,   9
   lift them up, you everlasting doors,
   that the king of glory may come in.
Who then is the king of glory?   10
The king of glory is the LORD of Hosts.

25

Unto thee, O LORD my God, I lift up my heart.   1
In thee I trust: do not put me to shame,   2
   let not my enemies exult over me.
   No man who hopes in thee is put to shame;   3
but shame comes to all who break faith without cause.
     Make thy paths known to me, O LORD;   4
     teach me thy ways.
   Lead me in thy truth and teach me;   5
   thou art God my saviour.
   For thee I have waited all the day long,
   for the coming of thy goodness, LORD.*b*
Remember, LORD, thy tender care and thy love unfailing,   6
   shown from ages past.
Do not remember the sins and offences of my youth,   7
but remember me in thy unfailing love.
   The LORD is good and upright;   8
therefore he teaches sinners the way they should go.
   He guides the humble man in doing right,   9
   he teaches the humble his ways.

[a] the face...Jacob: *so Sept.; Heb.* your face, O Jacob. [b] for the coming...LORD:
transposed from end of verse 7.

10   All the ways of the LORD are loving and sure
        to men who keep his covenant and his charge.
11   For the honour of thy name, O LORD,
        forgive my wickedness, great as it is.
12   If there is any man who fears the LORD,
        he shall be shown the path that he should choose;
13   he shall enjoy lasting prosperity,
        and his children after him shall inherit the land.
14   The LORD confides his purposes to those who fear him,
        and his covenant is theirs to know.
15   My eyes are ever on the LORD,
    who alone can free my feet from the net.

16   Turn to me and show me thy favour,
        for I am lonely and oppressed.
17   Relieve the sorrows of my heart
        and bring me out of my distress.
18   Look at my misery and my trouble
        and forgive me every sin.
19   Look at my enemies, see how many they are
        and how violent their hatred for me.
20   Defend me and deliver me,
        do not put me to shame when I take refuge in thee.
21   Let integrity and uprightness protect me,
        for I have waited for thee, O LORD.[a]
22   O God, redeem Israel from all his sorrows.

26

1   Give me justice, O LORD,
        for I have lived my life without reproach,
        and put unfaltering trust in the LORD.
2   Test me, O LORD, and try me;
        put my heart and mind to the proof.
3   For thy constant love is before my eyes,
        and I live in thy truth.
4   I have not sat among worthless men,
        nor do I mix with hypocrites;
5   I hate the company of evildoers
        and will not sit among the ungodly.
6   I wash my hands in innocence
        to join in procession round thy altar, O LORD,

[a] O LORD: *so Sept.; Heb. om.*

singing of thy marvellous acts,   7
    recounting them all with thankful voice.
O LORD, I love the beauty[a] of thy house,   8
    the place where thy glory dwells.
Do not sweep me away with sinners,   9
nor cast me out with men who thirst for blood,
    whose fingers are active in mischief,   10
and their hands are full of bribes.
But I live my life without reproach;   11
redeem me, O LORD,[b] and show me thy favour.
When once my feet are planted on firm ground,   12
I will bless the LORD in the full assembly.

27

The LORD is my light and my salvation;   1
    whom should I fear?
The LORD is the refuge of my life;
    of whom then should I go in dread?
When evildoers close in on me to devour me,   2
    it is my enemies, my assailants,
        who stumble and fall.
If an army should encamp against me,   3
    my heart would feel no fear;
if armed men should fall upon me,
    even then I should be undismayed.
One thing I ask of the LORD,   4
    one thing I seek:
    that I may be constant in the house of the LORD
    all the days of my life,
    to gaze upon the beauty of the LORD
    and to seek him[c] in his temple.
For he will keep me safe beneath his roof[d]   5
    in the day of misfortune;
  he will hide me under the cover of his tent;
  he will raise me beyond reach of distress.
Now I can raise my head high   6
    above the enemy all about me;
  so will I acclaim him with sacrifice before his tent
    and sing a psalm of praise to the LORD.

[a] *So Sept.; Heb.* dwelling.   [b] O LORD: *so Sept.; Heb. om.*   [c] *Or* and to pay my
morning worship.   [d] *Lit.* in his arbour.

7   Hear, O LORD, when I call aloud;
            show me favour and answer me.
8   'Come,' my heart has said,
            'seek his face.'[a]
        I will seek thy face, O LORD;
9   do not hide it from me,
        nor in thy anger turn away thy servant,
            whose help thou hast been;
        do not cast me off or forsake me, O God my saviour.
10   Though my father and my mother forsake me,
            the LORD will take me into his care.
11–12   Teach me thy way, O LORD;
            do not give me up to the greed of my enemies;
        lead me by a level path
            to escape my watchful foes;
        liars stand up to give evidence against me,
            breathing malice.
13   Well I know[b] that I shall see the goodness of the LORD
            in the land of the living.

14   Wait for the LORD; be strong, take courage,
            and wait for the LORD.

28

1   To thee, O LORD, I call;
        O my Rock, be not deaf to my cry,
            lest, if thou answer me with silence,
        I become like those who go down to the abyss.
2   Hear my cry for mercy
            when I call to thee for help,
        when I lift my hands to thy holy shrine.
3   Do not drag me away with the ungodly, with evildoers,
        who speak civilly to neighbours, with malice in their hearts.
4   Reward them for their works, their evil deeds;
            reward them for what their hands have done;
            give them their deserts.
5   Because they pay no heed to the works of the LORD
            or to what his hands have done,
            may he tear them down and never build them up!

6   Blessed be the LORD,
            for he has heard my cry for mercy.

[a] seek his face: *prob. rdg.; Heb.* seek ye my face.   [b] Well I know: *so some MSS.; others* Had I not well known.

The LORD is my strength, my shield,   7
    in him my heart trusts;
so I am sustained, and my heart leaps for joy,
    and I praise him with my whole body.*a*
The LORD is strength to his people,*b*   8
a safe refuge for his anointed king.

O save thy people and bless thy own,   9
    shepherd them, carry them for ever.

29

Ascribe to the LORD, you gods,   1
ascribe to the LORD glory and might.
Ascribe to the LORD the glory due to his name;   2
bow down to the LORD in the splendour of holiness.*c*
    The God of glory thunders: 3
    the voice of the LORD echoes over the waters,
    the LORD is over the mighty waters.
    The voice of the LORD is power.   4
    The voice of the LORD is majesty.
The voice of the LORD breaks the cedars,   5
the LORD splinters the cedars of Lebanon.
He makes Lebanon skip like a calf,   6
Sirion like a young wild ox.
The voice of the LORD makes flames of fire burst forth, 7
the voice of the LORD makes the wilderness writhe in travail; 8
    the LORD makes the wilderness of Kadesh writhe.
The voice of the LORD makes the hinds calve   9
    and brings kids early to birth;
and in his temple all cry, 'Glory!'
    The LORD is king above*d* the flood,   10
the LORD has taken his royal seat as king for ever.
The LORD will give strength to his people;   11
the LORD will bless his people with peace.

30

I will exalt thee, O LORD;   1
    thou hast lifted me up
and hast not let my enemies make merry over me.
O LORD my God, I cried to thee and thou didst heal me. 2

[*a*] with my whole body: *prob. rdg.; Heb.* from my song. [*b*] *So some MSS.; others* to
them. [*c*] the splendour of holiness: *or* holy vestments. [*d*] *Or* since.

3   O Lord, thou hast brought me up from Sheol
            and saved my life as I was sinking into the abyss.*a*
4   Sing a psalm to the Lord, all you his loyal servants,
            and give thanks to his holy name.
5   In his anger is disquiet, in his favour there is life.
            Tears may linger at nightfall,
               but joy comes in the morning.
6   Carefree as I was, I had said,
            'I can never be shaken.'
7   But, Lord, it was thy will to shake my mountain refuge;
         thou didst hide thy face, and I was struck with dismay.
8   I called unto thee, O Lord,
            and I pleaded with thee, Lord,*b* for mercy:
9   'What profit in my death if I go down into the pit?
         Can the dust confess thee or proclaim thy truth?
10   Hear, O Lord, and be gracious to me;
            Lord, be my helper.'
11   Thou hast turned my laments into dancing;
         thou hast stripped off my sackcloth and clothed me with joy,
12   that my*c* spirit may sing psalms to thee and never cease.
       I will confess thee for ever, O Lord my God.

31

1   With thee, O Lord, I have sought shelter,
            let me never be put to shame.
            Deliver me in thy righteousness;
2   bow down and hear me,
            come quickly to my rescue;
         be thou my rock of refuge,
            a stronghold to keep me safe.
3   Thou art to me both rock and stronghold;
         lead me and guide me for the honour of thy name.
4   Set me free from the net men have hidden for me;
            thou art my refuge,
5   into thy keeping I commit my spirit.
       Thou hast redeemed me, O Lord thou God of truth.
6   Thou hatest*d* all who worship useless idols,
            but I put my trust in the Lord.
7   I will rejoice and be glad in thy unfailing love;

[a] and saved...abyss: *or* and rescued me alive from among those who go down to the
abyss.   [b] with thee, Lord: *lit.* with the Lord.   [c] my: *so Sept.; Heb. om.*   [d] *So Sept.;
Heb.* I hate.

for thou hast seen my affliction
and hast cared for me in my distress.
Thou hast not abandoned me to the power of the enemy   8
but hast set me free to range at will.
Be gracious to me, O Lord, for I am in distress,   9
and my eyes are dimmed with grief.*a*
My life is worn away with sorrow   10
and my years with sighing;
strong as I am, I stumble under my load of misery;*b*
there is disease in all my bones.
I have such enemies that all men scorn me;*c*   11
my neighbours find me a burden,
my friends shudder at me;
when they see me in the street they turn quickly away.
I am forgotten, like a dead man out of mind;   12
I have come to be like something lost.
For I hear many men whispering   13
threats from every side,
in league against me as they are
and plotting to take my life.
But, Lord, I put my trust in thee;   14
I say, 'Thou art my God.'
My fortunes are in thy hand;   15
rescue me from my enemies and those who persecute me.
Make thy face shine upon thy servant;   16
save me in thy unfailing love.
O Lord, do not put me to shame when I call upon thee;   17
let the wicked be ashamed, let them sink into Sheol.
Strike dumb the lying lips   18
which speak with contempt against the righteous
in pride and arrogance.
How great is thy goodness,   19
stored up for those who fear thee,
made manifest before the eyes of men
for all who turn to thee for shelter.
Thou wilt hide them under the cover of thy presence   20
from men in league together;
thou keepest them beneath thy roof,*d*
safe from contentious men.

Blessed be the Lord,   21
who worked a miracle of unfailing love for me

[a] *Prob. rdg.; Heb. adds* my soul and my body.   [b] *Prob. rdg., cp. Sept.; Heb.* iniquity.
[c] I have...scorn me: *or* I am scorned by all my enemies.   [d] *Lit.* in an arbour.

when I was in sore straits.[a]
22 In sudden alarm I said,
 'I am shut out from thy sight.'
 But thou didst hear my cry for mercy
 when I called to thee for help.
23 Love the LORD, all you his loyal servants.
 The LORD protects the faithful
 but pays the arrogant in full.
24 Be strong and take courage,
 all you whose hope is in the LORD.

32

1 Happy the man whose disobedience is forgiven,
 whose sin is put away!
2 Happy is a man when the LORD lays no guilt to his account,
 and in his spirit there is no deceit.

3 While I refused to speak, my body wasted away
 with moaning all day long.
4 For day and night
 thy hand was heavy upon me,
 the sap in me dried up as in summer drought.
5 Then I declared my sin, I did not conceal my guilt.
 I said, 'With sorrow I will confess
 my disobedience to the LORD';
 then thou didst remit the penalty of my sin.
6 So every faithful heart shall pray to thee
 in the hour of anxiety,[b] when great floods threaten.
 Thou art a refuge for me from distress
 so that it cannot touch me;[c]
7 thou dost guard me[d] and enfold me in salvation
 beyond all reach of harm.[e]

8 I will teach you, and guide you in the way you should go.
 I will keep you under my eye.
9 Do not behave like horse or mule, unreasoning creatures,
 whose course must be checked with bit and bridle.
10 Many are the torments of the ungodly;
 but unfailing love enfolds him who trusts in the LORD.
11 Rejoice in the LORD and be glad, you righteous men,
 and sing aloud, all men of upright heart.

[a] when...straits: *prob. rdg.; Heb.* like a city besieged. [b] of anxiety: *prob. rdg.; Heb. unintelligible.* [c] *Prob. rdg.; Heb.* him. [d] *Prob. rdg.; Heb. adds an unintelligible word.* [e] beyond...harm: *transposed from end of verse 9.*

33

Shout for joy before the LORD, you who are righteous;   1
praise comes well from the upright.
Give thanks to the LORD on the harp;   2
sing him psalms to the ten-stringed lute.
Sing to him a new song;   3
strike up with all your art and shout in triumph.
   The word of the LORD holds true,   4
   and all his work endures.
The LORD loves righteousness and justice,   5
his love unfailing filis the earth.
The LORD's word made the heavens,   6
all the host of heaven was made at his command.
He gathered the sea like water in a goatskin;[a]   7
he laid up the deep in his store-chambers.
Let the whole world fear the LORD   8
and all men on earth stand in awe of him.
For he spoke, and it was;   9
he commanded, and it stood firm.
The LORD brings the plans of nations to nothing;   10
   he frustrates the counsel of the peoples.
But the LORD's own plans shall stand for ever,   11
and his counsel endure for all generations.
Happy is the nation whose God is the LORD,   12
the people he has chosen for his own possession.
The LORD looks out from heaven,   13
he sees the whole race of men;
he surveys from his dwelling-place   14
   all the inhabitants of earth.
It is he who fashions the hearts of all men alike,   15
   who discerns all that they do.
A king is not saved by a great army,   16
nor a warrior delivered by great strength.
A man cannot trust his horse to save him,   17
   nor can it deliver him for all its strength.
The LORD's eyes are turned towards those who fear him,   18
   towards those who hope for his unfailing love
to deliver them from death,   19
   to keep them alive in famine.
We have waited eagerly for the LORD;   20
he is our help and our shield.

     [a] *So Sept.; Heb.* heap.

21   For in him our hearts are glad,
              because we have trusted in his holy name.
22   Let thy unfailing love, O LORD, rest upon us,
              as we have put our hope in thee.

34

1   I will bless the LORD continually;
             his praise shall be always on my lips.
2   In the LORD I will glory;
             the humble shall hear and be glad.
3   O glorify the LORD with me,
             and let us exalt his name together.
4   I sought the LORD's help and he answered me;
             he set me free from all my terrors.
5   Look towards him and shine with joy;
                no longer hang your[a] heads in shame.
6   Here was a poor wretch who cried to the LORD;
             he heard him and saved him from all his troubles.
7   The angel of the LORD is on guard
             round those who fear him, and rescues them.
8   Taste, then, and see that the LORD is good.
             Happy the man who finds refuge in him!
9   Fear the LORD, all you his holy people;
             for those who fear him lack nothing.
10   Unbelievers suffer want and go hungry,
             but those who seek the LORD lack no good thing.
11   Come, my children, listen to me:
             I will teach you the fear of the LORD.
12   Which of you delights in life
             and desires a long life to enjoy all good things?
13   Then keep your tongue from evil
             and your lips from uttering lies;
14   turn from evil and do good,
             seek peace and pursue it.
15   The eyes of the LORD are upon the righteous,
             and his ears are open to their cries.
16   The LORD sets his face against evildoers
             to blot out their memory from the earth.
17   When men cry for help, the LORD hears them
             and sets them free from all their troubles.
18   The LORD is close to those whose courage is broken

[a] *So Sept.; Heb.* let them no longer hang their...

and he saves those whose spirit is crushed.
The good man's misfortunes may be many,   19
the Lord delivers him out of them all.
     He guards every bone of his body,   20
and not one of them is broken.
Their own misdeeds are death to the wicked,   21
     and those who hate the righteous are brought to ruin.

The Lord ransoms the lives of his servants,   22
and none who seek refuge in him are brought to ruin.

35

Strive, O Lord, with those who strive against me;   1
     fight against those who fight me.
Grasp shield and buckler,   2
     and rise up to help me.
Uncover the spear and bar the way   3
against my pursuers.
Let me hear thee declare,
     'I am your salvation.'
Shame and disgrace be on those who seek my life;   4
and may those who plan to hurt me retreat in dismay!
     May they be like chaff before the wind,   5
     driven by the angel of the Lord!
Let their way be dark and slippery   6
     as the angel of the Lord pursues them!
For unprovoked they have hidden a net[a] for me,   7
unprovoked they have dug a pit to trap me.
May destruction unforeseen come on him;   8
may the net which he hid catch him;
may he crash headlong into it!
Then I shall rejoice in the Lord   9
     and delight in his salvation.
     My very bones cry out,   10
     'Lord, who is like thee?—
thou saviour of the poor from those too strong for them,
the poor and wretched from those who prey on them.'
     Malicious witnesses step forward;   11
     they question me on matters of which I know nothing.
They return me evil for good,   12
     lying in wait[b] to take my life.

[a] *Prob. rdg., transposing* a pit *from this line to follow* have dug.   [b] lying in wait: *prob. rdg.; Heb.* bereavement.

13   And yet when they were sick, I put on sackcloth,
      I mortified myself with fasting.
      When my prayer came back unanswered,
14   I walked with head bowed in grief as if for a brother;
      as one in sorrow for his mother I lay prostrate in mourning.
15   But when I stumbled, they crowded round rejoicing,
         they crowded about me;
         nameless ruffians*a* jeered at me
         and nothing would stop them.
16   When I slipped, brutes who would mock even a hunchback
      ground their teeth at me.
17   O Lord, how long wilt thou look on
         at those who hate me for no reason*b*?
      Rescue me out of their cruel grasp,
         save my precious life from the unbelievers.
18   Then I will praise thee before a great assembly,
      I will extol thee where many people meet.
19   Let no treacherous enemy gloat over me
         nor leer at me in triumph.*c*
20   No friendly greeting do they give
         to peaceable folk.
      They invent lie upon lie,
21   they open their mouths at me:
      'Hurrah!' they shout in their joy,
         feasting their eyes on me.
22   Thou hast seen all this, O Lord, do not keep silence;
      O Lord, be not far from me.
23   Awake, bestir thyself, to do me justice,
         to plead my cause, my Lord and my God.
24   Judge me, O Lord my God, as thou art true;
         do not let them gloat over me.
25   Do not let them say to themselves, 'Hurrah!
         We have swallowed him up at one gulp.'*d*
26   Let them all be disgraced and dismayed
         who rejoice at my fall;
      let them be covered with shame and dishonour
         who glory over me.
27   But let all who would see me righted shout for joy,
         let them cry continually,
         'All glory to the Lord
      who would see his servant thrive!'

[*a*] nameless ruffians: *or* ruffians who give me no rest.   [*b*] *Line transposed from verse 19.*
[*c*] *See note on verse 17.*   [*d*] *So Pesh.; Heb. adds* let them not say.

So shall I talk of thy justice   28
  and of thy praise all the day long.

36

Deep in his*a* heart, sin whispers to the wicked man   1
who cherishes no fear of God.
For he flatters himself in his own opinion   2
and, when he is found out, he does not mend his ways.*b*
All that he says is mischievous and false;   3
he has turned his back on wisdom;
in his bed he plots how best to do mischief.   4
So set is he on his wrong courses
  that he rejects nothing evil.
But thy unfailing love, O LORD, reaches to heaven,   5
  thy faithfulness to the skies.
  Thy righteousness is like the lofty mountains,*c*   6
thy judgements are like the great abyss;
O LORD, who savest man and beast,
  how precious is thy unfailing love!   7
Gods and men seek refuge in the shadow of thy wings.
  They are filled with the rich plenty of thy house,   8
  and thou givest them water from the flowing stream
      of thy delights;
  for with thee is the fountain of life,   9
and in thy light we are bathed with light.
Maintain thy love unfailing over those who know thee,   10
  and thy justice toward men of honest heart.
Let not the foot of pride come near me,   11
  no wicked hand disturb me.
There they lie, the evildoers,   12
they are hurled down and cannot rise.

37

Do not strive to outdo the evildoers   1
  or emulate those who do wrong.
For like grass they soon wither,   2
  and fade like the green of spring.
Trust in the LORD and do good;   3
settle in the land and find safe pasture.

[*a*] *So some MSS.; others* my.   [*b*] he does . . . ways: *prob. rdg.; Heb. unintelligible.*   [*c*] *Lit.*
the mountains of God.

4   Depend upon the LORD,
          and he will grant you your heart's desire.

5   Commit your life to the LORD;
          trust in him and he will act.

6   He will make your righteousness shine clear as the day
          and the justice of your cause like the sun at noon.

7   Wait quietly for the LORD, be patient till he comes;
          do not strive to outdo the successful
          nor envy him who gains his ends.

8   Be angry no more, have done with wrath;
          strive not to outdo in evildoing.

9   For evildoers will be destroyed,
          but they who hope in the LORD shall possess the land.

10   A little while, and the wicked will be no more;
        look well, and you will find their place is empty.

11   But the humble shall possess the land
         and enjoy untold prosperity.

12   The wicked mutter against the righteous man
         and grind their teeth at the sight of him;

13   the Lord shall laugh at them,
         for he sees that their time is coming.

14   The wicked have drawn their swords
          and strung their bows
        to bring low the poor and needy
        and to slaughter honest men.

15   Their swords shall pierce their own hearts
         and their bows be broken.

16   Better is the little which the righteous has
         than the great wealth of the wicked.

17   For the strong arm of the wicked shall be broken,
         but the LORD upholds the righteous.

18   The LORD knows each day of the good man's life,
         and his inheritance shall last for ever.

19   When times are bad, he shall not be distressed,
          and in days of famine he shall have enough.

20   But the wicked shall perish,
         and their children shall beg their bread.*a*
         The enemies of the LORD, like fuel in a furnace,*b*
         are consumed in smoke.

21   The wicked man borrows and does not pay back,
         but the righteous is a generous giver.

[a] *Line transposed from verse 25.* [b] like...furnace: *prob. rdg.; Heb.* like the worth of rams.

All whom the LORD has blessed shall possess the land,   22
    and all who are cursed by him shall be destroyed.
It is the LORD who directs a man's steps,   23
    he holds him firm and watches over his path.
    Though he may fall, he will not go headlong,   24
for the LORD grasps him by the hand.
I have been young and am now grown old,   25
    and never have I seen a righteous man forsaken.*
Day in, day out, he lends generously,   26
    and his children become a blessing.
Turn from evil and do good,   27
    and live at peace for ever;
    for the LORD is a lover of justice   28
    and will not forsake his loyal servants.
The lawless* are banished for ever
    and the children of the wicked destroyed.
The righteous shall possess the land   29
and shall live there at peace for ever.
The righteous man utters words of wisdom   30
and justice is always on his lips.
    The law of his God is in his heart,   31
    his steps do not falter.
The wicked watch for the righteous man   32
    and seek to take his life;
    but the LORD will not leave him in their power   33
    nor let him be condemned before his judges.
Wait for the LORD and hold to his way;   34
    he will keep you* safe from wicked men*
and will raise you to be master of the land.
When the wicked are destroyed, you shall be there to see.
I have watched a wicked man at his work,   35
rank as a spreading tree in its native soil.
I* passed by one day, and he was gone;   36
    I searched for him, but he could not be found.
Now look at the good man, watch him who is honest,   37
    for the man of peace leaves descendants;
    but transgressors are wiped out one and all,   38
    and the descendants of the wicked are destroyed.
Deliverance for the righteous comes from the LORD,   39
    their refuge in time of trouble.

[a] *See note on verse 20.* [b] The lawless: *prob. rdg., cp. Sept.; Heb. om.* [c] *Prob. rdg.;
Heb.* them. [d] he will...wicked men: *transposed from verse 40.* [e] *So Sept.; Heb.*
He.

761

40   The LORD will help them and deliver them;*a*
        he will save them because they seek shelter with him.

                              38

1   O LORD, do not rebuke me in thy anger,
            nor punish me in thy wrath.
2   For thou hast aimed thy arrows*b* at me,
            and thy hand weighs heavy upon me.
3   Thy indignation has left no part of my body unscarred;
            there is no health in my whole frame because of my sin.
4   For my iniquities have poured over my head;
        they are a load heavier than I can bear.
5   My wounds fester and stink because of my folly.
6   I am bowed down and utterly prostrate.
        All day long I go about as if in mourning,
7   for my loins burn with fever,
            and there is no wholesome flesh in me.
8   All battered and benumbed,
            I groan aloud in my heart's longing.
9   O Lord, all my lament lies open before thee
        and my sighing is no secret to thee.
10   My heart beats fast, my strength has ebbed away,
            and the light has gone out of my eyes.
11   My friends and my companions shun me in my sickness,
            and my kinsfolk keep far away.
12   Those who wish me dead defame me,
            those who mean to injure me spread cruel gossip
            and mutter slanders all day long.
13   But I am deaf, I do not listen;
            I am like a dumb man who cannot open his mouth.
14   I behave like a man who cannot hear
            and whose tongue offers no defence.
15   On thee, O LORD, I fix my hope;
        thou wilt answer, O Lord my God.
16   I said, 'Let them never rejoice over me
            who exult when my foot slips.'
17   I am indeed prone to stumble,
            and suffering is never far away.
18   I make no secret of my iniquity
            and am anxious at the thought of my sin.

[*a*] *See note on verse 34.* [*b*] thou...arrows: *prob. rdg.; Heb.* thy arrows have come down.

But many are my enemies, all without cause,[a]   19
and many those who hate me wrongfully.
Those who repay good with evil   20
oppose me because my purpose is good.
    But, Lord, do not thou forsake me;   21
keep not far from me, my God.
Hasten to my help, O Lord my salvation.   22

39

I said: I will keep close watch over myself   1
    that all I say may be free from sin.
I will keep a muzzle on my mouth,
    so long as wicked men confront me.
In dumb silence I held my peace.   2
So my agony was quickened,
    and my heart burned within me.   3
My mind wandered as the fever grew,
    and I began to speak:
Lord, let me know my end   4
    and the number of my days;
tell me how short my life must be.
I know thou hast made my days a mere span long,   5
    and my whole life is nothing in thy sight.
Man, though he stands upright, is but a puff of wind,
he moves like a phantom;   6
the riches[b] he piles up are no more than vapour,
he does not know who will enjoy them.
And now, Lord, what do I wait for?   7
My hope is in thee.
    Deliver me from all who do me wrong,   8
    make me no longer the butt of fools.
I am dumb, I will not open my mouth,   9
    because it is thy doing.
Plague me no more;   10
I am exhausted by thy blows.
When thou dost rebuke a man to punish his sin,   11
    all his charm festers and drains away;
        indeed man is only a puff of wind.
Hear my prayer, O Lord;   12
    listen to my cry,
    hold not thy peace at my tears;

[a] all...cause: *prob. rdg.; Heb.* living.   [b] the riches: *prob. rdg.; Heb.* they murmur.

    for I find shelter with thee,
    I am thy guest, as all my fathers were.
13   Frown on me no more and let me smile again,
    before I go away and cease to be.

40

1   I waited, waited for the LORD,
    he bent down to me and heard my cry.
2   He brought me up out of the muddy pit,
      out of the mire and the clay;
    he set my feet on a rock
      and gave me a firm footing;
3   and on my lips he put a new song,
      a song of praise to our God.
    Many when they see will be filled with awe
      and will learn to trust in the LORD:
4   happy is the man
    who makes the LORD his trust,
    and does not look to brutal and treacherous men.
5   Great things thou hast done,
      O LORD my God;
    thy wonderful purposes are all for our good;
      none can compare with thee;
    I would proclaim them and speak of them,
      but they are more than I can tell.
6   If thou hadst desired sacrifice and offering
      thou wouldst have given me ears to hear.
    If thou hadst asked for whole-offering and sin-offering
7   I would have said, 'Here I am.'[a]
8   My desire is to do thy will, O God,
      and thy law is in my heart.
9   In the great assembly I have proclaimed what is right,
    I do not hold back my words,
    as thou knowest, O LORD.
10   I have not kept thy goodness hidden in my heart;
    I have proclaimed thy faithfulness and saving power,
      and not concealed thy unfailing love and truth
      from the great assembly.
11   Thou, O LORD, dost not withhold
      thy tender care from me;
    thy unfailing love and truth for ever guard me.

[a] *Prob. rdg.; Heb. adds* in a scroll of a book it is prescribed for me.

For misfortunes beyond counting   12
 press on me from all sides;
 my iniquities have overtaken me,
 and my sight fails;
they are more than the hairs of my head,
 and my courage forsakes me.
Show me favour, O LORD, and save me;   13[a]
hasten to help me, O LORD.
 Let those who seek to take my life   14
 be put to shame and dismayed one and all;
let all who love to hurt me shrink back disgraced;
 let those who cry 'Hurrah!' at my downfall 15
 be horrified at their reward of shame.
 But let all those who seek thee   16
 be jubilant and rejoice in thee;
and let those who long for thy saving help ever cry,
 'All glory to the LORD!'

But I am poor and needy;   17
O Lord, think of me.[b]
Thou art my help and my salvation;
 O my God, make no delay.

<h1 style="text-align:center">41</h1>

Happy the man who has a concern for the helpless! 1
The LORD will save him in time of trouble.
The LORD protects him and gives him life,   2
 making him secure in the land;
the LORD never leaves him[c] to the greed of his enemies.
 He nurses him on his sick-bed;   3
he turns[d] his bed when he is ill.

But I said, 'LORD, be gracious to me;   4
heal me, for I have sinned against thee.'
'His case is desperate,' my enemies say;   5
'when will he die, and his line become extinct?'
All who visit me speak from an empty heart, 6
alert to gather bad news;
 then they go out to spread it abroad.
All who hate me whisper together about me 7
and love to make the worst of everything:

[a] *Verses 13–17: cp. Ps. 70. 1–5.* [b] O Lord...me: *prob. rdg.; Heb.* may the Lord think
of me. [c] never leaves him: *prob. rdg.; Heb.* do thou not give him up... [d] *Prob. rdg.,
cp. Pesh.; Heb.* thou hast turned.

8   'An evil spell is cast upon him;
        he is laid on his bed, and will rise no more.'
9   Even the friend whom I trusted, who ate at my table,[a]
        exults over my misfortune.
10   O LORD, be gracious and restore me,
        that I may pay them out to the full.[b]
11   Then I shall know that thou delightest in me
        and that my enemy will not triumph over me.
12   But I am upheld by thee because of my innocence;
        thou keepest me for ever in thy sight.

13   Blessed be the LORD, the God of Israel,
        from everlasting to everlasting.
                    Amen, Amen.

BOOK 2

42–43

1   As a hind longs for the running streams,
        so do I long for thee, O God.
2   With my whole being I thirst for God, the living God.
        When shall I come to God and appear in his presence?
3   Day and night, tears are my food;
        'Where is your God?' they ask me all day long.
4   As I pour out my soul in distress, I call to mind
        how I marched in the ranks of the great[c] to the house of God,
        among exultant shouts of praise, the clamour of the pilgrims.
5   How deep I am sunk in misery,
          groaning in my distress:
        yet I will wait for God;
        I will praise him continually,
          my[d] deliverer, my God.
6   I am sunk in misery, therefore will I remember thee,
          though from the Hermons and the springs of Jordan,
            and from the hill of Mizar,
7   deep calls to deep in the roar of thy cataracts,
        and all thy waves, all thy breakers, pass over me.
8   The LORD makes his unfailing love shine forth[e]

[a] who...table: *or* slanders me.   [b] to the full: *transposed from end of verse 9.*   [c] of the
great: *so some MSS.; others have an obscure word.*   [d] *So some MSS.; others* his.   [e] makes
...forth: *or* entrusts me to his unfailing love.

    alike by day and night;
  his praise on my lips is a prayer
    to the God of my life.
I will say to God my rock, 'Why hast thou forgotten me?'   9
Why must I go like a mourner because my foes oppress me?
My enemies taunt me, jeering^a at my misfortunes;   10
'Where is your God?' they ask me all day long.
  How deep I am sunk in misery,   11
  groaning in my distress:
  yet I will wait for God;
  I will praise him continually,
  my deliverer, my God.
Plead my cause and give me judgement against an impious race;   43
save me from malignant men and liars, O God.
Thou, O God, art my refuge; why hast thou rejected me?   2
Why must I go like a mourner because my foes oppress me?
Send forth thy light and thy truth to be my guide   3
and lead me to thy holy hill, to thy tabernacle,
then shall I come to the altar of God, the God of my^b joy,   4
and praise thee on the harp, O God, thou God of my delight.
  How deep I am sunk in misery,   5
  groaning in my distress:
  yet I will wait for God;
  I will praise him continually,
  my deliverer, my God.

44

O God, we have heard for ourselves,   1
  our fathers have told us
all the deeds which thou didst in their days,
all the work of thy hand in days of old.   2
Thou didst plant them in the land and drive the nations out,
thou didst make them strike root, breaking up the peoples;
it was not our fathers' swords won them the land,   3
nor their arm that gave them victory,
  but thy right hand and thy arm
  and the light of thy presence; such was thy favour to them.
Thou art my king and my God;   4
at thy bidding Jacob is victorious.
By thy help we will throw back our enemies,   5
in thy name we will trample down our adversaries.

    [*a*] jeering: *prob. rdg.; Heb. obscure.*   [*b*] my: *so one MS.; others om.*

6   I will not trust in my bow,
    nor will my sword win me the victory;
7   for thou dost deliver us from our foes
    and put all our enemies to shame.
8   In God have we gloried all day long,
    and we will praise thy name for ever.
9   But now thou hast rejected and humbled us
    and dost no longer lead our armies into battle.
10   Thou hast hurled us back before the enemy,
    and our foes plunder us as they will.
11   Thou hast given us up to be butchered like sheep
    and hast scattered us among the nations.
12   Thou hast sold thy people for next to nothing
    and had no profit from the sale.
13   Thou hast exposed us to the taunts of our neighbours,
    to the mockery and contempt of all around.
14   Thou hast made us a byword among the nations,
    and the peoples shake their heads at us;
15   so my disgrace confronts me all day long,
    and I am covered with shame
16   at the shouts of those who taunt and abuse me
    as the enemy takes his revenge.
17   All this has befallen us, but we do not forget thee
    and have not betrayed thy covenant;
18   we have not gone back on our purpose,
    nor have our feet strayed from thy path.
19   Yet thou hast crushed us as the sea-serpent[a] was crushed
    and covered us with the darkness of death.
20   If we had forgotten the name of our God
    and spread our hands in prayer to any other,
21   would not God find this out,
    for he knows the secrets of the heart?
22   Because of thee we are done to death all day long,
    and are treated as sheep for slaughter.
23   Bestir thyself, Lord; why dost thou sleep?
    Awake, do not reject us for ever.
24   Why dost thou hide thy face,
    heedless of our misery and our sufferings?
25   For we sink down to the dust
    and lie prone on the earth.
26   Arise and come to our help;
    for thy love's sake set us free.

[a] *So Pesh.; Heb.* the jackals.

45

My heart is stirred by a noble theme, 1
in a king's honour I utter the song I have made,
  and my tongue runs like the pen of an expert scribe.

You surpass all mankind in beauty, 2
  your lips are moulded in grace,
so you are blessed by God for ever.
With your sword ready at your side, warrior king, 3
your limbs resplendent[a] in their royal armour, 4
ride on to execute true sentence and just judgement.
  Your right hand shall show you a scene of terror:
  your sharp arrows flying, nations beneath your feet, 5
    the courage of the king's foes melting away![b]

Your throne is like God's throne, eternal, 6
  your royal sceptre a sceptre of righteousness.
You have loved right and hated wrong; 7
so God, your God, has anointed you
  above your fellows with oil, the token of joy.
Your robes are all fragrant with myrrh and powder of aloes, 8
    and the music of strings greets you
    from a palace panelled with ivory.
A princess[c] takes her place among the noblest of your women, 9
a royal lady at your side in gold of Ophir.

Listen, my daughter, hear my words 10
  and consider them:
forget your own people and your father's house;
and, when the king desires your beauty, 11
  remember that he is your lord.
Do him obeisance, daughter of Tyre, 12
and the richest in the land will court you with gifts.

In the palace honour awaits her;[d] 13
  she is a king's daughter,
  arrayed in cloth-of-gold richly embroidered. 14
Virgins shall follow her into the presence of the king;
  her companions shall be brought to her,[e]
escorted with the noise of revels and rejoicing 15
  as they enter the king's palace.

[a] your limbs resplendent: *prob. rdg.; Heb.* and in your pomp prosper. [b] the courage...
away: *prob. rdg.; Heb.* obscure. [c] *So Pesh.; Heb.* daughters of kings. [d] honour awaits
her: *prob. rdg.; Heb.* all honoured. [e] *So some MSS.; others* to you.

16   You shall have sons, O king, in place of your forefathers
           and will make them rulers over all the land.*ᵃ

17   I will declare your fame to all generations;
           therefore the nations will praise you for ever and ever.

46

1   God is our shelter and our refuge,
           a timely help in trouble;

2   so we are not afraid when the earth heaves
           and the mountains are hurled into the sea,

3   when its waters seethe in tumult
           and the mountains quake before his majesty.

4   There is a river whose streams gladden the city of God,ᵇ
           which the Most High has made his holy dwelling;ᶜ

5   God is in that city; she will not be overthrown,
           and he will help her at the break of day.

6   Nations are in tumult, kingdoms hurled down;
           when he thunders, the earth surges like the sea.

7   The Lᴏʀᴅ of Hosts is with us,
           the God of Jacob our high stronghold.

8   Come and see what the Lᴏʀᴅ has done,
           the devastation he has brought upon earth,

9   from end to end of the earth he stamps out war:
        he breaks the bow, he snaps the spear
           and burns the shield in the fire.

10   Let be then: learn that I am God,
        high over the nations, high above earth.

11   The Lᴏʀᴅ of Hosts is with us,
           the God of Jacob our high stronghold.

47

1   Clap your hands, all you nations;
           acclaim our God with shouts of joy.

2   How fearful is the Lᴏʀᴅ Most High,
           great sovereign over all the earth!

3   He lays the nations prostrate beneath us,
           he lays peoples under our feet;

4   he chose our patrimony for us,
           the pride of Jacob whom he loved.

[a] over all the land: *or* in all the earth.   [b] the city of God: *or* a wondrous city.   [c] which
...dwelling: *so Sept.; Heb.* the sanctuary of the dwellings of the Most High.

God has gone up with shouts of acclamation,   5
　the LORD has gone up with a fanfare of trumpets.
Praise God,*a* praise him with psalms;   6
praise our king, praise him with psalms.
God is king of all the earth;   7
　sing psalms with all your art.*b*
God reigns over the nations,   8
God is seated on his holy throne.
　The princes of the nations assemble   9
　with the families of Abraham's line;*c*
for the mighty ones of earth belong to God,
and he is raised above them all.

48

The LORD is great and worthy of our praise   1
　in the city of our God, upon his holy hill.
Fair and lofty, the joy of the whole earth   2
　is Zion's hill, like the farthest reaches of the north,*d*
　the hill of the great King's city.
In her palaces God is known for a tower of strength.   3
　See how the kings all gather round her,   4
　marching on in company.
They are struck with amazement when they see her,   5
　they are filled with alarm and panic;
they are seized with trembling,   6
　they toss in pain like a woman in labour,
　like the ships of Tarshish   7
when an east wind*e* wrecks them.
All we had heard we saw with our own eyes   8
　in the city of the LORD of Hosts,
　in the city of our God,
　the city which God plants firm for evermore.
O God, we re-enact the story of thy true love   9
　within thy temple;
　the praise thy name deserves, O God,   10
　is heard at earth's farthest bounds.
Thy hand is charged with justice,
　and the hill of Zion rejoices,   11
　Judah's daughter-cities exult
　in thy judgements.

[a] Praise God: *or* Praise, you gods.   [b] with all your art: *mng. of Heb. word uncertain.*
[c] the families of Abraham's line: *prob. rdg.; Heb.* the God of Abraham.   [d] *Or* of Zaphon.
[e] when...wind: *so some MSS.; others* with an east wind which...

12   Make the round of Zion in procession,
            count the number of her towers,
13   take good note of her ramparts,
            pass her palaces in review,
        that you may tell generations yet to come:
14   Such is God,
        our God for ever and ever;
            he shall be our guide eternally.[a]

<h2 style="text-align:center">49</h2>

1   Hear this, all you nations;
        listen, all who inhabit this world,
2   all mankind, every living man,
        rich and poor alike;
3   for the words that I speak are wise,
            my thoughtful heart is full of understanding.

4   I will set my ear to catch the moral of the story
        and tell on the harp how I read the riddle;
5   why should I be afraid in evil times,
        beset by the wickedness of treacherous foes,
6   who trust in their riches
            and boast of their great wealth?
7   Alas! no man can ever ransom himself
        nor pay God the price of that release;
8   his[b] ransom would cost too much,
            for ever beyond his power to pay,
9   the ransom that would let him live on always
            and never see the pit of death.

10   But remember this:[c] wise men must die;
        stupid men, brutish men, all perish.[d]
11   The grave[e] is their eternal home,
        their dwelling for all time to come;
        they may give their own names to estates,
        but they must leave their riches to others.[f]
12   For men are like oxen whose life cannot last,[g]
        they are like cattle whose time is short.
13   Such is the fate of foolish men
        and of all who seek to please them:

[a] *Poss. mng.; Heb. word uncertain.* [b] *So Sept.; Heb.* their. [c] But remember this:
prob. rdg.; Heb. But he will remember this. [d] *Line transposed from here to follow verse*
11. [e] *So Sept.; Heb.* Their inward parts. [f] *Line transposed from verse 10.* [g] whose
life cannot last: *Sept. has* who have no understanding (*see note on verse 20*).

like sheep they run headlong into Sheol, the land of Death;   14
he is their shepherd and urges them on;
    their flesh must rot away*a*
and their bodies be wasted by Sheol,
    stripped of all honour.
But God will ransom my life,   15
    he will take me from the power of Sheol.
Do not envy a man when he grows rich,   16
    when the wealth of his family increases;
for he will take nothing when he dies,   17
    and his wealth will not go with him.
Though in his lifetime he counts himself happy   18
and men praise him in his*b* prosperity,
he*c* will go to join the company of his forefathers   19
who will never again see the light.
For men are like oxen whose life cannot last,*d*   20
they are like cattle whose time is short.

50

God, the Lord God, has spoken   1
and summoned the world from the rising to the setting sun.
God shines out from Zion, perfect in beauty.   2
    Our God is coming and will not keep silence: 3
    consuming fire runs before him
    and wreathes him closely round.*e*
He summons heaven on high and earth   4
to the judgement of his people:
'Gather to me my loyal servants,   5
all who by sacrifice have made a covenant with me.'
The heavens proclaim his justice,   6
for God himself is the judge.

Listen, my people, and I will speak;   7
I will bear witness against you, O Israel:
I am God, your God,
    shall I not*f* find fault with your sacrifices, 8
though*g* your offerings are before me always?
I need take no young bull from your house,   9
    no he-goat from your folds;

[a] and urges...rot away: *prob. rdg.; Heb. obscure.* [b] him...his: *prob. rdg.; Heb.* you...
your. [c] he: *prob. rdg.; Heb.* you. [d] whose life cannot last: *so many MSS.; others* who
have no understanding. [e] and wreathes him closely round: *or* and rages round him.
[f] *Or* I will not. [g] *Or* for.

10   for all the beasts of the forest are mine
    and the cattle in thousands on my hills.
11   I know every bird on those hills,
    the teeming life of the fields is my care.
12   If I were hungry, I would not tell you,
    for the world and all that is in it are mine.
13   Shall I eat the flesh of your bulls[a]
    or drink the blood of he-goats?
14   Offer to God the sacrifice of thanksgiving
    and pay your vows to the Most High.
15   If you call upon me in time of trouble,
    I will come to your rescue, and you shall honour me.

16   God's word to the wicked man is this:
    What right have you to recite my laws
    and make so free with the words of my covenant,
17   you who hate correction
    and turn your back when I am speaking?
18   If you meet a thief, you choose him as your friend;
    you make common cause with adulterers;
19   you charge your mouth with wickedness
    and harness your tongue to slander.
20   You are for ever talking against your brother,
    stabbing your own mother's son in the back.
21   All this you have done, and shall I keep silence?
    You thought that I was another like yourself,
    but point by point I will rebuke you to your face.
22   Think well on this, you who forget God,
    or I will tear you in pieces and no one shall save you.
23   He who offers a sacrifice of thanksgiving
      does me due honour,
    and to him who follows my way[b]
    I will show the salvation of God.

51

1   Be gracious to me, O God, in thy true love;
    in the fullness of thy mercy blot out my misdeeds.

2   Wash away all my guilt
    and cleanse me from my sin.
3   For well I know my misdeeds,
    and my sins confront me all the day long.

[a] *Lit.* bisons.   [b] him who follows my way: *prob. rdg.; Heb.* him who puts a way.

Against thee, thee only, I have sinned   4
and done what displeases thee,
  so that thou mayest be proved right in thy charge
    and just in passing sentence.

In iniquity I was brought to birth   5
and my mother conceived me in sin;
  yet, though thou hast hidden the truth in darkness,   6
through this mystery thou dost teach me wisdom.
Take hyssop[a] and sprinkle me, that I may be clean;   7
wash me, that I may become whiter than snow;
  let me hear the sounds of joy and gladness,   8
let the bones dance which thou hast broken.
Turn away thy face from my sins   9
  and blot out all my guilt.

Create a pure heart in me, O God,   10
  and give me a new and steadfast spirit;
    do not drive me from thy presence   11
  or take thy holy spirit from me;
  revive in me the joy of thy deliverance   12
    and grant me a willing spirit to uphold me.

I will teach transgressors the ways that lead to thee,   13
and sinners shall return to thee again.
O Lord God, my deliverer, save me from bloodshed,[b]   14
and I will sing the praises of thy justice.
Open my lips, O Lord,   15
that my mouth may proclaim thy praise.
Thou hast no delight in sacrifice;   16
if I brought thee an offering, thou wouldst not accept it.
My sacrifice, O God, is a broken spirit;   17
a wounded[c] heart, O God, thou wilt not despise.

Let it be thy pleasure to do good to Zion,   18
  to build anew the walls of Jerusalem.
Then only shalt thou delight in the appointed sacrifices;[d]   19
then shall young bulls be offered on thy altar.

[a] *Or* marjoram. [b] *Or* from punishment by death. [c] *So Pesh.; Heb.* a broken and wounded. [d] *Prob. rdg.; Heb. adds* a whole-offering and one wholly consumed.

52

1-2   Why make your wickedness your boast, you man of might,
       forging wild lies all day against[a] God's loyal servant?
       Your slanderous tongue is sharp as a razor.

3   You love evil and not good,
             falsehood, not speaking the truth;

4   cruel gossip you love and slanderous talk.

5   So may God[b] pull you down to the ground,
             sweep you away, leave you ruined and homeless,
               uprooted from the land of the living.

6   The righteous will look on, awestruck,[c]
             and laugh at his plight:

7   'This is the man', they say,
               'who does not make God his refuge,
             but trusts in his great wealth
               and takes refuge in wild lies.'

8   But I am like a spreading olive-tree in God's house;
       for I trust in God's true love for ever and ever.

9   I will praise thee for ever for what thou hast done,
       and glorify thy name among thy loyal servants;
             for that is good.

53

1[d]   The impious fool says in his heart,
             'There is no God.'
       How vile men are, how depraved and loathsome;
             not one does anything good!

2   God looks down from heaven
             on all mankind
       to see if any act wisely,
             if any seek out God.

3   But all are unfaithful, all are rotten to the core;
             not one does anything good,
             no, not even one.

4   Shall they not rue it,
       these evildoers who devour my people
             as men devour bread,
             and never call upon God?

[a] against: *prob. rdg., cp. Pesh.; Heb. om.* [b] *Or So God will.* [c] *Or, with some MSS.,* rejoicing, *cp. Pss. 58. 10; 107. 42.* [d] *Verses 1–6: cp. Ps. 14. 1–7.*

There they were in dire alarm*a*   5
when God scattered them.
The crimes of the godless were frustrated;*b*
    for God had rejected them.
If only Israel's deliverance might come out of Zion!   6
    When God restores his people's fortunes,
let Jacob rejoice, let Israel be glad.

54

Save me, O God, by the power of thy name,   1
    and vindicate me through thy might.
O God, hear my prayer,   2
    listen to my supplication.
Insolent men*c* rise to attack me,   3
ruthless men seek my life;
they give no thought to God.

But God is my helper,   4
    the Lord the mainstay of my life.
May their own malice recoil on my watchful foes;   5
silence them by thy truth, O LORD.
I will offer thee a willing sacrifice   6
and praise thy name, for that is good;
God has rescued me from every trouble,   7
and I look on my enemies' downfall with delight.

55

Listen, O God, to my pleading,   1
do not hide thyself when I pray.
Hear me and answer,   2
    for my cares give me no peace.
I am panic-stricken at the shouts of my enemies,   3
    at the shrill clamour of the wicked;
for they heap trouble on me
    and they revile me in their anger.
My heart is torn with anguish   4
and the terrors of death come upon me.
Fear and trembling overwhelm me   5
    and I shudder from head to foot.

[*a*] *So some MSS.; others add* there was no fear.   [*b*] The crimes...frustrated: *prob. rdg.;*
Heb. obscure.   [*c*] Insolent men: *so some MSS.; others* Strangers.

6   *a*Oh that I had the wings of a dove
          to fly away and be at rest!
7   I should escape far away
          and find a refuge in the wilderness;
8   soon I should find myself a sanctuary
          from wind and storm,
9   from the blasts of calumny, O Lord,
          from my enemies' contentious tongues.
       I have seen violence and strife in the city;
10   day and night they encircle it,
          all along its walls;
       it is filled with trouble and mischief,
11   alive with rumour and scandal,
       and its public square is never free
          from violence and spite.
12   It was no enemy that taunted me,
          or I should have avoided him;
       no adversary that treated me with scorn,
          or I should have kept out of his way.
13   It was you, a man of my own sort,
          my comrade, my own dear friend,
14-15 with whom I kept pleasant company
          in the house of God.

       May death strike them,
       and may they*b* perish in confusion,
       may they go down alive into Sheol;
          for their homes are haunts of evil!

16   But I will call upon God;
          the LORD will save me.
17   Evening and morning and at noon
          I nurse my woes, and groan.
18   He has heard my cry, he rescued me
          and gave me back my peace,
       when they beset me like archers,*c*
          massing against me,
19   like Ishmael and the desert tribes
          and those who dwell in the East,
       who have no respect for an oath
          nor any fear of God.
20   Such men do violence to those at peace with them

[a] *Prob. rdg.; Heb. prefixes* And I said. [b] *Prob. rdg.; Heb.* we. [c] when…archers:
prob. rdg.; Heb. obscure.

and break their promised word;
their speech is smoother than butter   21
    but their thoughts are of war;
their words are slippery as oil
    but sharp as drawn swords.

Commit your fortunes to the LORD,   22
    and he will sustain you;
he will never let the righteous be shaken.
Cast them, O God, into the pit of destruction;   23
    bloodthirsty and treacherous,
they shall not live out half their days;
    but I will put my trust in thee.

56

Be gracious to me, O God, for the enemy persecute me,   1
    my assailants harass me all day long.
All the day long my watchful foes persecute me;   2
    countless are those who assail me.
Appear on high*ᵃ* in my day of fear;   3
    I put my trust in thee.
With God to help me I will shout defiance,   4
in God I trust and shall not be afraid;
    what can mortal men do to me?
All day long abuse of me is their only theme,   5
    all their thoughts are hostile.
In malice they are on the look-out, and watch for me,   6
    they dog my footsteps;
but, while they lie in wait for me,
it is they who will not*ᵇ* escape.   7
O God, in thy anger bring ruin on the nations.

Enter my lament in thy book,*ᶜ*   8
store every tear in thy flask.*ᵈ*
Then my enemies will turn back   9
    on the day when I call upon thee;*ᵉ*
for this I know, that God is on my side,
    with God to help me I will shout defiance.*ᶠ*   10

---

[a] Appear on high: *prob. rdg.; Heb.* Height.   [b] it is...not: *prob. rdg.; Heb.* for iniquity.
[c] Enter...book: *prob. rdg.; Heb. obscure.*   [d] *Prob. rdg.; Heb. adds* is it not in thy book?
[e] Enter...thee: *or* Thou hast entered my lament in thy book, my tears are put in thy
flask. Then my enemies turned back, when I called upon thee.   [f] *Prob. rdg.; Heb. adds*
With the LORD to help me I will shout defiance.

11 　　　In God I trust and shall not be afraid;
　　　　　what can man do to me?
12 　　　I have bound myself with vows to thee, O God,
　　　　　and will redeem them with due thank-offerings;
13 　　　for thou hast rescued me from death[a]
　　　　　to walk in thy presence, in the light of life.

57

1 　　　Be gracious to me, O God, be gracious;
　　　　　for I have made thee my refuge.
　　　　　I will take refuge in the shadow of thy wings
　　　　　　　until the storms are past.
2 　　　I will call upon God Most High,
　　　　　on God who fulfils his purpose for me.
3 　　　He will send his truth and his love that never fails,
　　　　　he will send from heaven and save me.
　　　　　God himself will frustrate my persecutors;
4 　　　for I lie down among lions, man-eaters,
　　　　　whose teeth are spears and arrows
　　　　　and whose tongues are sharp swords.
5 　　　Show thyself, O God, high above the heavens;
　　　　　let thy glory shine over all the earth.
6 　　　Men have prepared a net to catch me as I walk,
　　　　　but I bow my head to escape from it;
　　　　　they have dug a pit in my path
　　　　　but have fallen into it themselves.

7[b] 　　My heart is steadfast, O God,
　　　　　my heart is steadfast.
　　　　　I will sing and raise a psalm;
8 　　　　awake, my spirit,
　　　　awake, lute and harp,
　　　　　I will awake at dawn of day.[c]
9 　　　I will confess thee, O Lord, among the peoples,
　　　　　among the nations I will raise a psalm to thee,
10 　　　for thy unfailing love is wide as the heavens
　　　　　and thy truth reaches to the skies.
11 　　　Show thyself, O God, high above the heavens;
　　　　　let thy glory shine over all the earth.

[a] *Prob. rdg.; Heb. adds* is it not my feet from stumbling (*cp. Ps. 116. 8*).　[b] *Verses 7–11:*
cp. Ps. 108. 1–5.　[c] at dawn of day: *or* the dawn.

58

Answer, you rulers:[a] are your judgements just?   1
Do you decide impartially between man and man?
    Never! Your hearts devise all kinds of wickedness   2
    and survey the violence that you have done on earth.

Wicked men, from birth they have taken to devious ways; 3
liars, no sooner born than they go astray,
    venomous with the venom of serpents,   4
    of the deaf asp which stops its ears
    and will not listen to the sound of the charmer,   5
       however skilful his spells may be.

O God, break the teeth in their mouths.   6
Break, O Lord, the jaws of the unbelievers.[b]
May they melt, may they vanish like water,   7
may they wither like trodden grass,[c]
    like an abortive birth which melts away   8
    or a still-born child which never sees[d] the sun!
All unawares, may they be rooted up like[e] a thorn-bush,   9
    like weeds which a man angrily[f] clears away!

The righteous shall rejoice that he has seen vengeance done   10
    and shall wash his feet in the blood of the wicked,
       and men shall say,   11
    'There is after all a reward for the righteous;
after all, there is a God that judges on earth.'

59

Rescue me from my enemies, O my God,   1
be my tower of strength against all who assail me,
    rescue me from these evildoers,   2
    deliver me from men of blood.
Savage men lie in wait for me,   3
they lie in ambush ready to attack me;
for no fault or guilt of mine, O Lord,
innocent as I am,[g] they run to take post against me.   4-5
But thou, Lord God of Hosts, Israel's God,
    do thou bestir thyself at my call, and look:

[a] *Or* you gods. [b] the jaws of the unbelievers: *or* the lions' fangs. [c] like trodden grass: *prob. rdg.; Heb. obscure.* [d] sees: *prob. rdg.; Heb.* they see. [e] may they be rooted up like: *prob. rdg.; Heb.* your pots. [f] angrily: *prob. rdg.; Heb.* like anger. [g] as I am: *prob. rdg., cp. Targ.; Heb. om.*

awake, and punish all the nations.
Have no mercy on villains and traitors,

6   who run wild at nightfall like dogs,
snarling and prowling round the city,

15[a]   wandering to and fro in search of food,
and howling if they are not satisfied.

7   From their mouths comes a stream of nonsense;
'But who will hear?' they murmur.[b]

8   But thou, O Lord, dost laugh at them,
and deride all the nations.

9   O my[c] strength,[d] to thee I turn in the night-watches;
for thou,[e] O God, art my strong tower.

10   My God, in his true love, shall be my champion;
with God's help, I shall gloat over my watchful foes.

11   Wilt thou not kill them, lest my people forget?
Scatter them by thy might and bring them to ruin.

12   Deliver them,[f] O Lord, to be destroyed
by their own sinful words;
let what they have spoken entrap them in their pride.
Let them be cut off for their cursing and falsehood;

13   bring them to an end in thy wrath,
and they will be no more;
then they will know that God is ruler in Jacob,
even to earth's farthest limits.[g] [h]

16   But I will sing of thy strength,
and celebrate thy love when morning comes;
for thou hast been my strong tower
and a sure retreat in days of trouble.

17   O thou my strength, I will raise a psalm to thee;
for thou, O God, art[i] my strong tower.[j]

60

1   O God, thou hast cast us off and broken us;
thou hast been angry and rebuked us cruelly.

2   Thou hast made the land quake and torn it open;
it gives way and crumbles into pieces.

3   Thou hast made thy people drunk with a bitter draught,
thou hast given us wine that makes us stagger.

[a] *Verse transposed.* [b] they murmur: *so Symm.; Heb. om.* [c] my: *so Sept.; Heb.* his.
[d] *Or* refuge. [e] thou: *so Pesh.; Heb. om.* [f] Deliver them: *prob. rdg.; Heb.* Our shield.
[g] *Prob. rdg.; Heb. adds* (14) who run wild at nightfall like dogs, snarling and prowling
round the city (*cp. verse 6*). [h] *Verse 15 transposed to follow verse 6.* [i] thou...art:
so Pesh.; Heb. God is. [j] *So many MSS.; others add* God of my unfailing love.

But thou hast given a warning to those who fear thee,   4
    to make their escape before the sentence falls.*a*

Deliver those that are dear to thee;   5*b*
save them with thy right hand, and answer.
God has spoken from his sanctuary:*c*   6
    'I will go up now and measure out Shechem;
    I will divide the valley of Succoth into plots;
Gilead and Manasseh are mine;   7
Ephraim is my helmet,*d* Judah my sceptre;
Moab is my wash-bowl, I fling my shoes at Edom;   8
    Philistia is the target of my anger.'

Who can bring me to the fortified city,   9
    who can guide*e* me to Edom,
since thou, O God, hast abandoned us   10
    and goest not forth*f* with our armies?
Grant us help against the enemy,   11
    for deliverance by man is a vain hope.
With God's help we shall do valiantly,   12
    and God himself will tread our enemies under foot.

61

Hear my cry, O God, listen to my prayer.   1
From the end of the earth I call to thee with fainting heart;   2
    lift me up*g* and set me upon a rock.
For thou hast been my shelter,   3
    a tower for refuge from the enemy.
In thy tent will I make my home for ever   4
    and find my shelter under the cover of thy wings.
For thou, O God, hast heard my vows   5
    and granted the wish*h* of all who revere thy name.

To the king's life add length of days,   6
    year upon year for many generations;
    may he dwell in God's presence for ever,   7
    may true and constant love preserve*i* him.

So will I ever sing psalms in honour of thy name   8
    as I fulfil my vows day after day.

[*a*] *Lit.* before truth.   [*b*] *Verses 5–12: cp. Ps. 108. 6–13.*   [*c*] from his sanctuary: *or* in his holiness.   [*d*] my helmet: *lit.* the refuge of my head.   [*e*] *So Sept.; Heb.* has guided. [*f*] *So Pesh.; Heb.* adds O God.   [*g*] lift me up: *prob. rdg., cp. Sept.; Heb.* obscure. [*h*] *Prob. rdg.; Heb.* the inheritance.   [*i*] *So some MSS.; others add an unintelligible word.*

62

1   Truly my heart waits silently for God;
      my deliverance comes from him.

2   In truth he is my rock of deliverance,
      my tower of strength, so that I stand unshaken.

3   How long will you assail a man with your threats,
      all battering on a leaning wall?

4   In truth men plan to topple him from his height,
      and stamp on the fallen stones.*a*
    With their lips they bless him, the hypocrites,
      but revile him in their hearts.

5   Truly my heart waits silently for God;
      my hope of deliverance comes from him.

6   In truth he is my rock of deliverance,
      my tower of strength, so that I am unshaken.

7   My deliverance and my honour depend upon God,
    God who is my rock of refuge and my shelter.

8   Trust always in God, my people,
    pour out your hearts before him;
      God is our shelter.

9   In very truth men are a puff of wind,
      all men are faithless;
    put them in the balance and they can only rise,
      all of them lighter than wind.

10   Put no trust in extortion,
      do not be proud of stolen goods;
    though wealth breeds wealth, set not your heart on it.

11   One thing God has spoken,
      two things I have learnt:
    'Power belongs to God'

12   and 'True love, O Lord, is thine';
    thou dost requite a man for his deeds.

63

1   O God, thou art my God, I seek thee early
      with a heart that thirsts for thee
      and a body wasted with longing for thee,
    like a dry and thirsty land that has no water.

[a] the fallen stones: *transposed from end of verse 3.*

So longing, I come before thee in the sanctuary   2
to look upon thy power and glory.
Thy true love is better than life;   3
therefore I will sing thy praises.
And so I bless thee all my life   4
and in thy name lift my hands in prayer.
I am satisfied as with a rich and sumptuous feast   5
and wake the echoes with thy praise.
When I call thee to mind upon my bed   6
and think on thee in the watches of the night,
remembering how thou hast been my help   7
and that I am safe in the shadow of thy wings,
then I humbly follow thee with all my heart,   8
and thy right hand is my support.

Those who seek my life, bent on evil,   9
shall sink into the depths of the earth;
they shall be given over to the sword;   10
they shall be carrion for jackals.

The king shall rejoice in God,   11
and whoever swears by God's name shall exult;
the voice of falsehood shall be silenced.

64

Hear me, O God, hear my lament;   1
keep me safe from the threats*ᵃ* of the enemy.
Hide me from the factions of the wicked,   2
from the turbulent mob of evildoers,
who sharpen their tongues like swords   3
and wing their cruel words like arrows,*ᵇ*
to shoot down the innocent from cover,   4
shooting suddenly, themselves unseen.
They boldly*ᶜ* hide their snares,   5
sure that none will see them;
they hatch their secret plans*ᵈ* with skill and cunning,   6
with evil*ᵉ* purpose and deep design.
But God with his arrow shoots them down,   7
and sudden is their overthrow.

[a] *Lit.* scares.   [b] and wing...arrows: *prob. rdg.; Heb.* they tread their arrow a cruel word.
[c] *See first note on verse 8.*   [d] their secret plans: *prob. rdg.; Heb. unintelligible.*   [e] evil:
prob. rdg.; Heb. man.

8   They may repeat their wicked tales,^a
     but their mischievous tongues^b are their undoing.
     All who see their fate take fright at it,
9   every man is afraid;
         'This is God's work', they declare;
         they learn their lesson from what he has done.
10   The righteous rejoice and seek refuge in the LORD
         and all the upright exult.

65

1-2 We owe thee praise, O God, in Zion;
     thou hearest prayer, vows shall be paid to thee.
3   All men shall lay their guilt before thee:
         our sins are too heavy for us;^c
         only thou canst blot them out.
4   Happy is the man of thy choice, whom thou dost bring
         to dwell in thy courts;
         let us enjoy the blessing of thy house,
         thy holy temple.
5   By deeds of terror answer us with victory,
         O God of our deliverance,
     in whom men trust from the ends of the earth
         and far-off seas;
6   thou art girded with strength,
     and by thy might dost fix the mountains in their place,
7   dost calm the rage of the seas and their raging waves.^d
8   The dwellers at the ends of the earth
         hold thy signs in awe;
     thou makest morning and evening sing aloud in triumph.

9   Thou dost visit the earth and give it abundance,
         as often as thou dost enrich it
     with the waters of heaven, brimming in their channels,
         providing rain^e for men.
     For this is thy provision for it,
10   watering its furrows, levelling its ridges,
     softening it with showers and blessing its growth.
11   Thou dost crown the year with thy good gifts
         and the palm-trees drip with sweet juice;

[a] They...tales: *transposed from after* boldly *in verse 5.* [b] their mischievous tongues: *prob. rdg.; Heb.* against them their tongues. [c] *So Sept.; Heb.* me. [d] *Prob. rdg.; Heb. adds* and tumult of people. [e] *Or* corn.

the pastures in the wild are rich with blessing 12
and the hills wreathed in happiness,
the meadows are clothed with sheep 13
and the valleys mantled in corn,
    so that they shout, they break into song.

66

Acclaim our God, all men on earth; 1
    let psalms declare the glory of his name, 2
    make glorious his praise.
Say unto God, 'How fearful are thy works! 3
Thy foes cower before the greatness of thy strength.
All men on earth fall prostrate in thy presence, 4
and sing to thee, sing psalms in honour of thy name.'
    Come and see all that God has done, 5
    tremendous in his dealings with mankind.
He turned the waters into dry land 6
so that his people*^a* passed through the sea*^b* on foot;
there did we rejoice in him.*^c*

He rules for ever by his power, 7
his eye rests on the nations;
let no rebel rise in defiance.

Bless our God, all nations; 8
    let his praise be heard far and near.
He set us in the land of the living; 9
he keeps our feet from stumbling.
    For thou, O God, hast put us to the proof 10
    and refined us like silver.
    Thou hast caught us in a net, 11
thou hast bound our bodies fast;
thou hast let men ride over our heads. 12
We went through fire and water,
    but thou hast brought us out into liberty.*^d*

I will bring sacrifices into thy temple 13
and fulfil my vows to thee,
vows which I made with my own lips 14
and swore with my own mouth when in distress.
I will offer thee fat beasts as sacrifices 15

[a] his people: *Heb.* they. [b] *Lit.* river. [c] there...him: *or* where we see this, we will
rejoice in him. [d] *So Sept.; Heb.* moisture.

and burn rams as a savoury offering;
I will make ready oxen and he-goats.

16   Come, listen, all who fear God,
and I will tell you all that he has done for me;
17   I lifted up my voice in prayer,
his high praise was on my lips.*a*
18   If I had cherished evil thoughts,
the Lord would not have heard me;
19   but in truth God has heard
and given heed to my prayer.
20   Blessed is God
who has not withdrawn his love and care from me.

67

1   God be gracious to us and bless us,
God make his face shine upon us,
2   that his*b* ways may be known on earth
and his*b* saving power among all the nations.
3   Let the peoples praise thee, O God;
let all peoples praise thee.
4   Let all nations rejoice and shout in triumph;
for thou dost judge the peoples with justice
and guidest the nations of the earth.
5   Let the peoples praise thee, O God;
let all peoples praise thee.
6   The earth has given its increase
and God, our God, will bless us.

7   God grant us his blessing,
that all the ends of the earth may fear him.

68

1   God arises and his enemies are scattered;
those who hate him flee before him,
2   driven away like smoke in the wind;
like wax melting at the fire,
the wicked perish at the presence of God.
3   But the righteous are joyful, they exult before God,
they are jubilant and shout for joy.

[a] on my lips: *lit.* under my tongue.   [b] *So Pesh.; Heb.* thy.

Sing the praises of God, raise a psalm to his name,   4
  extol him who rides over the desert plains.*a*
Be joyful*b* and exult before him,
  father of the fatherless, the widow's champion—   5
  God in his holy dwelling-place.
God gives the friendless a home   6
  and brings out the prisoner safe and sound;
but rebels must live in the scorching desert.

O God, when thou didst go forth before thy people,   7
  marching across the wilderness,
earth trembled, the very heavens quaked   8
before God the lord of Sinai, before God the God of Israel.

Of thy bounty, O God, thou dost refresh with rain   9
  thy own land in its weariness,
  the land which thou thyself didst provide,
  where thy own people made their home,   10
which thou, O God, in thy goodness providest for the poor.

The Lord proclaims good news:*c*   11-13
'Kings with their armies have fled headlong.'
O mighty host, will you linger among the sheepfolds
  while the women in your tents divide the spoil—
  an image of a dove, its wings sheathed in silver
  and its pinions in yellow gold—
  while the Almighty scatters kings far and wide   14
  like snowflakes falling on Zalmon?

The hill of Bashan is a hill of God indeed,   15
  a hill of many peaks is Bashan's hill.
But, O hill of many peaks, why gaze in envy   16
at the hill where the LORD delights to dwell,
where the LORD himself will live for ever?
  Twice ten thousand were God's chariots, thousands upon   17
    thousands,*d*
when the Lord came in holiness from Sinai.*e*
Thou didst go up to thy lofty home with captives in thy train,   18
  having received tribute from men;
  in the presence of the LORD God no rebel could live.*f*

[a] over the desert plains: *or* on the plains. [b] Be joyful: *prob. rdg.; Heb.* In the LORD is
his name. [c] proclaims good news: *or* gives the word, women bearing good news.
[d] thousands upon thousands: *mng. of Heb. phrase uncertain.* [e] came...from Sinai:
prob. rdg.; Heb. obscure. [f] in the presence...live: *so Pesh.; Heb. unintelligible.*

19   Blessed is the Lord:
            he carries us day by day,
            God our salvation.

20   Our God is a God who saves us,
            in the Lord God's hand lies escape from death.[a]

21   God himself will smite[b] the head of his enemies,
            those proud sinners with their flowing locks.

22   The Lord says, 'I will return from the Dragon,[c]
            I will return from the depths of the sea,

23   that you may dabble your feet in blood,
            while the tongues of your dogs are eager[d] for it.'

24   Thy procession, O God, comes into view,
            the procession of my God and King into the sanctuary:

25   at its head the singers, next come minstrels,
            girls among them playing on tambourines.

26   In the great concourse they bless God,
            all Israel assembled[e] bless the Lord.

27   There is the little tribe of Benjamin leading them,
            there the company of Judah's princes,
            the princes of Zebulun and of Naphtali.

28   O God, in virtue of thy power[f]—
            that godlike power which has acted for us—

29   command kings to bring gifts to thee
            for the honour of thy temple in Jerusalem.

30   Rebuke those wild beasts of the reeds, that herd of bulls,
            the bull-calf warriors of the nations;[g]
            scatter these nations which revel in war;

31   make them bring tribute[h] from Egypt,
            precious stones and silver from Pathros;[i]
            let Nubia stretch out[j] her hands to God.

32   All you kingdoms of the world, sing praises to God,
            sing psalms to the Lord,

33   to him who rides on the heavens, the ancient heavens.
            Hark! he speaks in the mighty thunder.

34   Ascribe all might to God, Israel's High God,
            Israel's pride and might throned in the skies.

---

[a] in the Lord God's hand...death: *or* death is expelled by the Lord God.   [b] will smite: *or* smites.   [c] the Dragon: *or* Bashan.   [d] are eager: *prob. rdg.; Heb.* from enemies. [e] assembled: *prob. rdg.; Heb. obscure.*   [f] O God...power: *prob. rdg.; Heb.* Your God your power.   [g] *See second note on verse 31.*   [h] *Mng. of Heb. word uncertain.* [i] precious...Pathros: *prob. rdg., transposed from verse 30 and slightly altered.*   [j] stretch out: *prob. rdg.; Heb. obscure.*

Terrible is God as he comes from his*ᵃ* sanctuary;   35
he is Israel's own God,
who gives to his*ᵇ* people might and abundant power.
     Blessed be God.

69

Save me, O God;   1
for the waters have risen up to my neck.
I sink in muddy depths and have no foothold;   2
I am swept into deep water, and the flood carries me away.
I am wearied with crying out, my throat is sore,   3
my eyes grow dim as I wait for God to help me.
     Those who hate me without reason   4
     are more than the hairs of my head;
they outnumber my hairs, those who accuse me falsely.
How can I give back what I have not stolen?
O God, thou knowest how foolish I am,   5
and my guilty deeds are not hidden from thee.
Let none of those who look to thee be shamed on my account,   6
     O Lord GOD of Hosts;
     let none who seek thee be humbled through my fault,
     O God of Israel.
For in thy service I have suffered reproach;   7
I dare not show my face for shame.
I have become a stranger to my brothers,   8
     an alien to my own mother's sons;
     bitter enemies of thy temple tear me in pieces;*ᶜ*   9
those who reproach thee reproach me.
I have broken*ᵈ* my spirit with fasting,   10
only to lay myself open to many reproaches.
I have made sackcloth my clothing   11
and have become a byword among them.
Those who sit by the town gate talk about me;   12
drunkards sing songs about me*ᵉ* in their cups.
But I lift up this prayer to thee, O LORD: 13
accept me*ᶠ* now in thy great love,
answer me with thy sure deliverance, O God.
Rescue me from the mire, do not let me sink;   14
let me be rescued from the muddy depths,*ᵍ*

[*a*] his: *so Sept.; Heb.* thy.   [*b*] his: *so Sept.; Heb. om.*   [*c*] bitter...pieces: *or* zeal for thy
temple has eaten me up (*cp. John* 2. *17*).   [*d*] *So Scroll; Heb.* I wept.   [*e*] sing...me: *so
Sept.; Heb.* songs.   [*f*] *Prob. rdg.; Heb.* acceptance.   [*g*] from...depths: *prob. rdg.; Heb.*
from my haters and from the depths.

15   so that no flood may carry me away,
        no abyss swallow me up,
        no deep close over me.
16   Answer me, O Lord, in the goodness of thy unfailing love,
        turn towards me in thy great affection.
17   I am thy servant, do not hide thy face from me.
        Make haste to answer me, for I am in distress.
18   Come near to me and redeem me;
          ransom me, for I have many enemies.

19   Thou knowest what reproaches I bear,
        all my anguish is seen by thee.
20   Reproach has broken my heart,
        my shame and my dishonour*a* are past hope;
        I looked for consolation and received none,
          for comfort and did not find any.
21   They put poison in my food
        and gave me vinegar when I was thirsty.
22   May their own table be a snare to them
        and their sacred feasts lure them to their ruin;
23   may their eyes be darkened so that they do not see,
        let a continual ague shake their loins.
24   Pour out thine indignation upon them
          and let thy burning anger overtake them.
25   May their settlements be desolate,
        and no one living in their tents;
26   for they pursue him whom thou hast struck down
    and multiply*b* the torments of those*c* whom thou hast wounded.
27   Give them the punishment their sin deserves;*d*
          exclude them from thy righteous mercy;
28   let them be blotted out from the book of life
        and not be enrolled among the righteous.

29   But by thy saving power, O God, lift me high
        above my pain and my distress,
30   then I will praise God's name in song
        and glorify him with thanksgiving;
31   that will please the Lord more than the offering of a bull,
        a young bull with horn and cloven hoof.

32   See and rejoice,*e* you humble folk,
        take heart, you seekers after God;

[a] my shame and my dishonour: *transposed from after* reproaches *in verse 19.*   [b] *So Sept.;*
Heb. and recount.   [c] *Or, with one MS.,* him.   [d] Give them...deserves: *or* Add punishment to punishment.   [e] and rejoice: *prob. rdg., cp.* Pesh.; *Heb.* let them rejoice.

for the LORD listens to the poor   33
and does not despise those bound to his service.*a*
Let sky and earth praise him,   34
the seas and all that move in them,
for God will deliver Zion   35–36
   and rebuild the cities of Judah.
   His servants' children shall inherit them;
they shall dwell there in their own possession
   and all who love his name shall live in them.

70

Show me favour,*b* O God, and save me;   1*c*
hasten to help me, O LORD.
Let all who seek my life be brought to shame and dismay,   2
let all who love to hurt me shrink back disgraced;
   let those who cry 'Hurrah!' at my downfall*d*   3
turn back at the shame they incur,
     but let all who seek thee   4
     be jubilant and rejoice in thee,
and let those who long for thy saving help ever cry,
   'All glory to God!'

But I am poor and needy;   5
   O God, hasten to my aid.
Thou art my help, my salvation;
   O LORD, make no delay.

71

In thee, O LORD, I have taken refuge;   1
never let me be put to shame.
As thou art righteous rescue me and save my life;   2
hear me and set me free,
be a rock of refuge for me,   3
where I may ever find safety at thy call;
   for thou art my towering crag and stronghold.
   O God, keep my life safe from the wicked,   4
     from the clutches of unjust and cruel men.

Thou art my hope, O Lord,   5
   my trust, O LORD, since boyhood.

---

[a] those...service: *lit.* his prisoners.   [b] Show me favour: *prob. rdg., cp. Ps. 40. 13; Heb. om.*
[c] *Verses 1–5: cp. Ps. 40. 13–17.*   [d] at my downfall: *so Sept.; Heb. om.*

6 From birth I have leaned upon thee,
my protector since I left*ᵃ* my mother's womb.*ᵇ*
7 To many I seem a solemn warning;
but I have thee for my strong refuge.
8 My mouth shall be full of thy praises,
I shall tell of thy splendour all day long.
9 Do not cast me off when old age comes,
nor forsake me when my strength fails,
10 when my enemies' rancour bursts upon me*ᶜ*
and those who watch me whisper together,
11 saying, 'God has forsaken him;
after him! seize him; no one will rescue him.'
12 O God, do not stand aloof from me;
O my God, hasten to my help.
13 Let all my traducers be shamed and dishonoured,*ᵈ*
let all who seek my hurt be covered with scorn.*ᵉ*
14 But I will wait in continual hope,
I will praise thee again and yet again;
15 all day long thy righteousness,
thy saving acts, shall be upon my lips.
Thou shalt ever be the theme of my praise,*ᶠ*
although I have not the skill of a poet.
16 I will begin with a tale of great deeds, O Lord GOD,
and sing of thy righteousness, thine alone.
17 O God, thou hast taught me from boyhood,
all my life I have proclaimed thy marvellous works;
18 and now that I am old and my hairs are grey,
forsake me not, O God,
when I extol thy mighty arm to future generations,
19 thy power and righteousness, O God, to highest heaven;
for thou hast done great things.
Who is like thee, O God?
20 Thou hast made me pass through bitter and deep distress,
yet dost revive me once again
and lift me again from earth's watery depths.
21 Restore me to honour, turn and comfort me,
22 then I will praise thee on the lute
for thy faithfulness, O God;
I will sing psalms to thee with the harp,
thou Holy One of Israel;

[a] my...left: *or who didst bring me out from.* [b] *See note on verse 15.* [c] enemies'...
me: *prob. rdg.; Heb.* enemies say of me. [d] *So many MSS.; others* and waste away.
[e] *So Pesh.; Heb. adds* and dishonour. [f] *Line transposed from verse 6.*

> songs of joy shall be on my lips;   23
> I will sing thee psalms, because thou hast redeemed me.
> All day long my tongue shall tell of thy righteousness;   24
> shame and disgrace await those who seek my hurt.

72

> O God, endow the king with thy own justice,   1
> and give thy righteousness to a king's son,
> that he may judge thy people rightly   2
> and deal out justice to the poor and suffering.
> May hills and mountains afford thy people   3
> peace and prosperity in righteousness.
> He shall give judgement for the suffering   4
> and help those of the people that are needy;
> he shall crush the oppressor.
> He shall live as long^a as the sun endures,   5
> long as the moon, age after age.
> He shall be like rain falling on early crops,   6
> like showers watering^b the earth.
> In his days righteousness^c shall flourish,   7
> prosperity abound until the moon is no more.
> May he hold sway from sea to sea,   8
> from the River to the ends of the earth.
> Ethiopians shall crouch low before him;   9
> his enemies shall lick the dust.
> The kings of Tarshish and the islands shall bring gifts,   10
> the kings of Sheba and Seba shall present their tribute,
> and all kings shall pay him homage,   11
> all nations shall serve him.
> For he shall rescue the needy from their rich oppressors,   12
> the distressed who have no protector.
> May he have pity on the needy and the poor,   13
> deliver the poor from death;
> may he redeem them from oppression and violence   14
> and may their blood be precious in his eyes.

> May the king live long   15
> and receive gifts of gold^d from Sheba;
> prayer be made for him continually,
> blessings be his all the day long.
> May there be abundance of corn in the land,   16

[a] He...long: *so Sept.; Heb.* They shall fear thee.   [b] like showers watering: *prob. rdg.; Heb. unintelligible.*   [c] *So some MSS.; others* a righteous man.   [d] *Or* frankincense.

> growing in plenty to the tops of the hills;
> may the crops flourish like Lebanon,
>   and the sheaves*ᵃ* be numberless as blades of grass.

17
> Long may the king's name endure,
>   may it live for ever*ᵇ* like the sun;
> so shall all peoples*ᶜ* pray to be blessed as he was,
>   all nations tell of his happiness.

18
> Blessed be the Lᴏʀᴅ God, the God of Israel,
>   who alone does marvellous things;
19
> blessed be his glorious name for ever,
>   and may his glory fill all the earth.
>   Amen, Amen.

20
> Here end the prayers of David son of Jesse.

BOOK 3

73

1
> How good God is to the upright!*ᵈ*
>   How good to those who are pure in heart!

2
> My feet had almost slipped,
>   my foothold had all but given way,
3
> because the boasts of sinners roused my envy
>   when I saw how they prosper.
4
> No pain, no suffering is theirs;
>   they are sleek and sound in limb;
5
> they are not plunged in trouble as other men are,
>   nor do they suffer the torments of mortal men.
6
> Therefore pride is their collar of jewels
>   and violence the robe that wraps them round.
7
> Their eyes gleam through folds of fat;
>   while vain fancies pass through their minds.
8
> Their talk is all sneers and malice;
>   scornfully they spread their calumnies.
9
> Their slanders reach up to heaven,
>   while their tongues ply to and fro on earth.
10
> And so my*ᵉ* people follow their lead*ᶠ*

[a] the sheaves: *prob. rdg.; Heb.* from a city. [b] live for ever: *so Sept.; Heb. unintelligible.*
[c] all peoples: *prob. rdg., cp. Sept.; Heb. om.* [d] How...upright: *prob. rdg.; Heb.* How
good it is to Israel! [e] *So Sept.; Heb.* his. [f] their lead: *prob. rdg.; Heb.* hither.

and find nothing to blame in them,[a]
even though they say, 'What does God know?   11
The Most High neither knows nor cares.'
So wicked men talk, yet still they prosper,   12
and rogues[b] amass great wealth.

So it was all in vain that I kept my heart pure   13
and washed my hands in innocence.
For all day long I suffer torment   14
and am punished every morning.
Yet had I let myself talk on in this fashion,   15
I should have betrayed the family of God.[c]
So I set myself to think this out   16
but I found it too hard for me,
until I went into God's sacred courts;   17
there I saw clearly what their end would be.

How often thou dost set them on slippery ground   18
and drive them headlong into ruin!
Then in a moment how dreadful their end,   19
cut off root and branch by death with all its terrors,
like a dream when a man rouses himself, O Lord,   20
like images in sleep which are dismissed on waking!

When my heart was embittered   21
I felt the pangs of envy,
I would not understand, so brutish was I,   22
I was a mere beast in thy sight, O God.
Yet I am always with thee,   23
thou holdest my right hand;
thou dost guide me by thy counsel   24
and afterwards wilt receive me with glory.[d]
Whom have I in heaven but thee[e]?   25
And having thee,[f] I desire nothing else on earth.
Though heart and body fail,[g]   26
yet God is my possession for ever.
They who are far from thee are lost;   27
thou dost destroy all who wantonly forsake thee.
But my chief good is to be near thee, O God;   28
I have chosen thee, Lord GOD, to be my refuge.[h]

[a] and find...in them: *prob. rdg.; Heb. obscure.* [b] yet...rogues: *prob. rdg.; Heb.* those at ease for ever. [c] the family of God: *lit.* thy family. [d] and afterwards...glory: *or, with slight change of text,* and dost lead me along the path of honour. [e] but thee: *so Targ.; Heb. om.* [f] *Or* And compared with thee. [g] *So one MS.; others add* the rock of my heart. [h] *Prob. rdg.; Heb. adds* to tell all thy works.

74

1   Why hast thou cast us off, O God? Is it for ever?
     Why art thou so stern, so angry with the sheep of thy flock?
2   Remember the assembly of thy people,
           taken long since for thy own,*a*
     and Mount Zion, which was thy home.
3   Now at last*b* restore what was ruined beyond repair,
     the wreck that the foe has made of thy sanctuary.

4   The shouts of thy enemies filled the holy place,*c*
         they planted their standards there as tokens of victory.
5   They brought it crashing down,*d*
           like woodmen plying their axes in the forest;
6   they ripped*e* the carvings clean out,
         they smashed them with hatchet and pick.
7   They set fire to thy sanctuary,
         tore down and polluted the shrine sacred to thy name.
8   They said to themselves, 'We will sweep them away',*f*
     and all over the land they burnt God's holy places.*g*

9   We cannot see what lies before us,*h* we have no prophet now;
     we have no one who knows how long this is to last.
10   How long, O God, will the enemy taunt thee?
     Will the adversary pour scorn on thy name for ever?
11   Why dost thou hold back thy hand,
         why keep thy right hand within thy bosom?

12   But thou, O God, thou king from of old,
           thou mighty conqueror all the world over,
13   by thy power thou didst cleave the sea-monster in two
         and break the sea-serpent's heads above the waters;
14   thou didst crush Leviathan's many heads
         and throw him to the sharks*i* for food.
15   Thou didst open channels for spring and torrent;
         thou didst dry up rivers never known to fail.
16   The day is thine, and the night is thine also,
     thou didst ordain the light of moon and sun;
17   thou hast fixed all the regions of the earth;
     summer and winter, thou didst create them both.

[a] *Prob. rdg.; Heb. adds* thou didst redeem the tribe of thy possession. [b] Now at last: *prob. rdg.; Heb.* Thy steps. [c] the holy place: *or* thy meeting place. [d] They...down: *prob. rdg.; Heb. unintelligible.* [e] they ripped: *so Sept.; Heb.* and now. [f] We...away: *so Pesh.; Heb.* their offspring. [g] holy places: *or* meeting places. [h] what...us: *prob. rdg.; Heb.* our signs. [i] to the sharks: *prob. rdg.; Heb.* to a people, desert-dwellers.

Remember, O Lord, the taunts of the enemy,   18
the scorn a savage nation pours on thy name.
Cast not to the beasts the soul that confesses thee;*a*   19
forget not for ever the sufferings of thy servants.
Look upon thy creatures:*b* they are filled with hatred,   20
and earth is the haunt of violence.
Let not the oppressed be shamed and turned away;   21
let the poor and the downtrodden praise thy name.
Rise up, O God, maintain thy own cause;   22
remember how brutal men taunt thee all day long.
Ignore no longer the cries of thy assailants,   23
the mounting clamour of those who defy thee.

75

We give thee thanks, O God, we give thee thanks;   1
thy name is brought very near to us
in the story of thy wonderful deeds.

I seize the appointed time   2
and then I judge mankind with justice.
When the earth rocks, with all who live on it,   3
I make its pillars firm.
To the boastful I say, 'Boast no more',   4
and to the wicked, 'Do not toss your proud horns:
toss not your horns against high heaven   5
nor speak arrogantly against your Creator.'
No power from the east nor from the west,   6
no power from the wilderness, can raise a man up.
For God is judge;   7
he puts one man down and raises up another.
The Lord holds a cup in his hand,   8
and the wine foams in it, hot with spice;
he offers it to every man*c* for drink,
and all the wicked on earth must drain it to the dregs.
But I will glorify him for ever;   9
I will sing praises to the God of Jacob.

I will break off the horns of the wicked,   10
but the horns of the righteous shall be lifted high.

[a] that confesses thee: *so Sept.; Heb.* of thy turtle-dove. [b] thy creatures: *prob. rdg.; Heb.*
the covenant, because. [c] every man: *so Sept.; Heb.* from this.

76

<table>
<tr><td>1</td><td>In Judah God is known,
his name is great in Israel;</td></tr>
<tr><td>2</td><td>his tent is pitched in Salem,
in Zion his battle-quarters are set up.^a</td></tr>
<tr><td>3</td><td>He has broken the flashing arrows,
shield and sword and weapons of war.</td></tr>
</table>

1 In Judah God is known,
his name is great in Israel;
2 his tent is pitched in Salem,
in Zion his battle-quarters are set up.*a*

3 He has broken the flashing arrows,
shield and sword and weapons of war.

4 Thou art terrible,*b* O Lord, and mighty:
5 men that lust for plunder stand aghast,
the boldest swoon away,
and the strongest cannot lift a hand.
6   At thy rebuke, O God of Jacob,
rider and horse fall senseless.
7 Terrible art thou, O Lord;
who can stand in thy presence when thou art angry?
8 Thou didst give sentence out of heaven;
the earth was afraid and kept silence.
9 O God, at thy rising*c* in judgement
to deliver all humble men on the earth,
10 for all her fury Edom shall confess thee,
and the remnant left in Hamath shall dance in worship.

11 Make vows to the LORD your God, and pay them duly;
let the peoples all around him bring their tribute;*d*
12 for he breaks the spirit of princes,
he is the terror of the kings on earth.

77

1   I cried aloud to God,
I cried to God, and he heard me.
2 In the day of my distress I sought the Lord,
and by night I lifted*e* my outspread hands in prayer.
I lay sweating and nothing would cool me;
I refused all comfort.
3 When I called God to mind, I groaned;
as I lay thinking, darkness came over my spirit.
4 My eyelids were tightly closed;
I was dazed and I could not speak.

[a] are set up: *prob. rdg.; Heb.* thither (*at beginning of verse 3*).   [b] terrible: *so Theod.;*
Heb. illuminated.   [c] O God...rising: *prob. rdg.; Heb.* When God rises.   [d] *Prob. rdg.;*
Heb. adds for the terror (*cp. verse 12*).   [e] I lifted: *prob. rdg.; Heb. om.*

My thoughts went back to times long past,   5
　I remembered forgotten years;
all night long I was in deep distress,   6
as I lay thinking, my spirit was sunk in despair.

Will the Lord reject us for evermore   7
　and never again show favour?
Has his unfailing love now failed us utterly,   8
must his^a promise time and again be unfulfilled?
Has God forgotten to be gracious,   9
has he in anger withheld his mercies?
'Has his right hand', I said, 'lost its grasp?   10
　Does it hang powerless,^b the arm of the Most High?'

But then, O LORD, I call to mind thy deeds;^c   11
I recall thy wonderful acts in times gone by.
　I meditate upon thy works   12
　and muse on all that thou hast done.
O God, thy way is holy;   13
what god is so great as our God?
Thou art the God who workest miracles;   14
thou hast shown the nations thy power.
With thy strong arm thou didst redeem thy people,   15
　the sons of Jacob and Joseph.

　The waters saw thee, O God,   16
　they saw thee and writhed in anguish;
　the ocean was troubled to its depths.
The clouds poured water, the skies thundered,   17
　thy arrows flashed hither and thither.
　The sound of thy thunder was in the whirlwind,^d 18
　thy lightnings lit up the world,
　earth shook and quaked.
Thy path was through the sea, thy way through mighty waters, 19
　and no man marked thy footsteps.
　Thou didst guide thy people like a flock of sheep,   20
　under the hand of Moses and Aaron.

78

　Mark my teaching, O my people,   1
　listen to the words I am to speak.
　I will tell you a story with a meaning,   2

[a] his: *so Pesh.; Heb. om.*   [b] lost...powerless: *prob. rdg.; Heb. unintelligible.*   [c] *Prob. rdg.; Heb.* then I call to mind the deeds of the LORD, for.   [d] *Or* in the chariot-wheels.

I will expound the riddle of things past,

3   things that we have heard and know,
and our fathers have repeated to us.

4   From their sons we will not hide
the praises of the LORD and his might
nor the wonderful acts he has performed;
then they shall repeat them to the next generation.

5   He laid on Jacob a solemn charge
and established a law in Israel,
which he commanded our fathers
    to teach their sons,

6   that it might be known to a future generation,
    to children yet unborn,
and these would repeat it to their sons in turn.

7   He charged them to put their trust in God,
to hold his great acts ever in mind
    and to keep all his commandments;

8   not to do as their fathers did,
a disobedient and rebellious race,
a generation with no firm purpose,
with hearts not fixed steadfastly on God.

9   The men of Ephraim, bowmen all and marksmen,
    turned and ran in the hour of battle.

10   They had not kept God's covenant
and had refused to live by his law;

11   they forgot all that he had done
and the wonderful acts which he had shown them.

12   He did wonders in their fathers' sight
    in the land of Egypt, the country of Zoan:

13   he divided the sea and took them through it,
making the water stand up like banks on either side.

14   He led them with a cloud by day
and all night long with a glowing fire.

15   He cleft the rock in the wilderness
and gave them water to drink, abundant as the sea;

16   he brought streams out of the cliff
and made water run down like rivers.

17   But they sinned against him yet again:
in the desert they defied the Most High,

18   they tried God's patience wilfully,
demanding food to satisfy their hunger.

19   They vented their grievance against God and said,

'Can God spread a table in the wilderness?'
When he struck a rock, water gushed out   20
until the gullies overflowed;
they said, 'Can he give bread as well,
can he provide meat for his people?'
When he heard this, the LORD was filled with fury: 21
fire raged against Jacob,
anger blazed up against Israel,
because they put no trust in God   22
and had no faith in his power to save.
Then he gave orders to the skies above   23
and threw open heaven's doors,
he rained down manna for them to eat   24
and gave them the grain of heaven.
So men ate the bread of angels;   25
he sent them food to their heart's desire.
He let loose the east wind from heaven   26
and drove the south wind by his power;
he rained meat like a dust-storm upon them,   27
flying birds like the sand of the sea-shore,
which he made settle all over the camp   28
round the tents where they lived.
So the people ate and were well filled,   29
for he had given them what they craved.
Yet they did not abandon their complaints*a*   30
even while the food was in their mouths.
Then the anger of God blazed up against them;   31
he spread death among their stoutest men
and brought the young men of Israel to the ground.

In spite of all, they persisted in their sin   32
and had no faith in his wonderful acts.
So in one moment he snuffed out their lives   33
and ended their years in calamity.
When he struck them, they began to seek him,   34
they would turn and look eagerly for God;
they remembered that God was their Creator,   35
that God Most High was their deliverer.
But still they beguiled him with words   36
and deceived him with fine speeches;
they were not loyal to him in their hearts   37
nor were they faithful to his covenant.

[a] *Or* craving.

38   Yet he wiped out their guilt
      and did not smother his own[a] natural affection;
      often he restrained his wrath
      and did not rouse his anger to its height.
39   He remembered that they were only mortal men,
      who pass by like a wind and never return.

40   How often they rebelled against him in the wilderness
          and grieved him in the desert!
41   Again and again they tried God's patience
          and provoked the Holy One of Israel.
42   They did not remember his prowess
      on the day when he saved them from the enemy,
43   how he set his signs in Egypt,
          his portents in the land of Zoan.
44   He turned their streams into blood,
      and they could not drink the running water.
45   He sent swarms of flies which devoured them,
      and frogs which brought devastation;
46   he gave their harvest over to locusts
      and their produce to the grubs;
47   he killed their vines with hailstones
          and their figs[b] with torrents of rain;
48   he abandoned their cattle to the plague[c]
      and their beasts to the arrows of pestilence.
49   He loosed upon them the violence of his anger,
      wrath and enmity and rage,
      launching those messengers of evil
50–51 to open a way for his fury.
      He struck down all the first-born in Egypt,
      the flower of their manhood in the tents of Ham,
      not shielding their lives from death
      but abandoning their bodies to the plague.
52   But he led out his own people like sheep
      and guided them like a flock in the wilderness.
53   He led them in safety and they were not afraid,
      and the sea closed over their enemies.
54   He brought them to his holy mountain,
      the hill which his right hand had won;
55   he drove out nations before them,
      he allotted their lands to Israel as a possession

[a] his own: *prob. rdg.; Heb. om.* [b] *Lit.* sycomore-figs. [c] *So one MS.; others* hail.

and settled his tribes in their dwellings.

Yet they tried God's patience and rebelled against him;   56
they did not keep the commands of the Most High;
they were renegades, traitors like their fathers,   57
they changed, they went slack like a bow.

    They provoked him to anger with their hill-shrines   58
    and roused his jealousy with their carved images.
When God heard this, he put them out of mind   59
and utterly rejected Israel.

    He forsook his home at Shiloh,   60
the tabernacle in which he dwelt among men;
he surrendered the symbol of his strength*a* into captivity   61
    and his pride into enemy hands;
he gave his people over to the sword   62
    and put his own possession out of mind.
Fire devoured his young men,   63
and his maidens could raise no lament for them;
his priests fell by the sword,   64
and his widows could not weep.

Then the Lord awoke as a sleeper awakes,   65
like a warrior heated with wine;
he struck his foes in the back parts   66
and brought perpetual shame upon them.

    He despised the clan of Joseph   67
    and did not choose the tribe of Ephraim;
    he chose the tribe of Judah   68
    and Mount Zion which he loved;
he built his sanctuary high as the heavens,   69
founded like the earth to last for ever.
He chose David to be his servant   70
    and took him from the sheepfolds;
    he brought him from minding the ewes   71
to be the shepherd of his people Jacob;*b*
    and he shepherded them in singleness of heart   72
    and guided them with skilful hand.

79

    O God, the heathen have set foot in thy domain,   1
      defiled thy holy temple
    and laid Jerusalem in ruins.

[*a*] the symbol of his strength: *lit.* his strength. [*b*] *Prob. rdg.; Heb. adds* and Israel his possession.

2   They have thrown out the dead bodies of thy servants
         to feed the birds of the air;
       they have made thy loyal servants carrion for wild beasts.
3   Their blood is spilled all round Jerusalem like water,
         and there they lie unburied.
4   We suffer the contempt of our neighbours,
       the gibes and mockery of all around us.

5   How long, O LORD, wilt thou be roused to such fury?
       Must thy jealousy rage like a fire?
6   Pour out thy wrath over nations which do not know thee
     and over kingdoms which do not invoke thee by name;
7   see how they have devoured Jacob and laid waste his homesteads.
8   Do not remember against us the guilt of past generations
       but let thy compassion come swiftly to meet us,
         we have been brought so low.

9   Help us, O God our saviour, for the honour of thy name;
       for thy name's sake deliver us and wipe out our sins.
10   Why should the nations ask, 'Where is their God?'
       Let thy vengeance for the bloody slaughter of thy servants
       fall on those nations before our very eyes.

11   Let the groaning of the captives reach thy presence
       and in thy great might set free death's prisoners.
12   As for the contempt our neighbours pour on thee, O Lord,
       turn it back sevenfold on their own heads.
13   Then we thy people, the flock which thou dost shepherd,
       will give thee thanks for ever
     and repeat thy praise to every generation.

80

1   Hear us, O shepherd of Israel,
     who leadest Joseph like a flock of sheep.
       Show thyself, thou that art throned on the cherubim,
2   to Ephraim and to Benjamin.
       Rouse thy victorious might from slumber,[a]
       come to our rescue.
3   Restore us, O God,
     and make thy face shine upon us that we may be saved.
4   O LORD God of Hosts,
     how long wilt thou resist thy people's prayer?

[a] from slumber: *prob. rdg.; Heb.* and Manasseh.

    Thou hast made sorrow their daily bread   5
and tears of threefold grief their drink.
Thou hast humbled us before our neighbours,   6
and our enemies mock us to their hearts' content.
    O God of Hosts, restore us;   7
make thy face shine upon us that we may be saved.

Thou didst bring a vine out of Egypt;   8
thou didst drive out nations and plant it;
thou didst clear the ground before it,   9
so that it made good roots and filled the land.
The mountains were covered with its shade,   10
    and its branches were like those of mighty cedars.
It put out boughs all the way to the Sea   11
    and its shoots as far as the River.
Why hast thou broken down the wall round it   12
so that every passer-by can pluck its fruit?
The wild boar from the thickets gnaws it,   13
    and swarming insects from the fields feed on it.
O God of Hosts, once more look down from heaven,   14
take thought for this vine and tend it,
    this stock that thy right hand has planted.[a]   15
Let them that set fire to it or cut it down   16
    perish before thy angry face.
Let thy hand rest upon the man at thy right side,   17
the man whom thou hast made strong for thy service.
    We have not turned back from thee,   18
so grant us new life, and we will invoke thee by name.
LORD God of Hosts, restore us;   19
make thy face shine upon us that we may be saved.

81

Sing out in praise of God our refuge,[b]   1
    acclaim the God of Jacob.
Take pipe and tabor,   2
take tuneful harp and lute.
Blow the horn for the new month,   3
    for the full moon on the day of our pilgrim-feast.
This is a law for Israel,   4
    an ordinance of the God of Jacob,

[a] *Prob. rdg.; Heb. adds* and on the son whom thou hast made strong for thy service (*cp. verse 17*). [b] *Or* strength.

5   laid as a solemn charge on Joseph
         when he came out of Egypt.*a*

6   When I lifted the load from his shoulders,
         his hands let go the builder's basket.

7   When you cried to me in distress, I rescued you;
         unseen, I answered you in thunder.
     I tested you at the waters of Meribah,
         where I opened your mouths and filled them.*b*

16*c*   I fed Israel*d* with the finest wheat-flour
         and satisfied him*e* with honey from the rocks.

8   Listen, my people, while I give you a solemn charge—
         do but listen to me, O Israel:

9   you shall have no strange god
         nor bow down to any foreign god;

10   I am the Lord your God
         who brought you up from Egypt.*f*

11   But my people did not listen to my words
         and Israel would have none of me;

12   so I sent them off, stubborn as they were,
         to follow their own devices.

13   If my people would but listen to me,
         if Israel would only conform to my ways,

14   I would soon bring their enemies to their knees
         and lay a heavy hand upon their persecutors.

15   Let those who hate them*g* come cringing to them,
         and meet with everlasting troubles.*h*

82

1   God takes his stand in the court of heaven
         to deliver judgement among the gods themselves.

2   How long will you judge unjustly
         and show favour to the wicked?

3   You ought to give judgement for the weak and the orphan,
         and see right done to the destitute and downtrodden,

4   you ought to rescue the weak and the poor,
         and save them from the clutches of wicked men.

[a] *Prob. rdg.; Heb. adds* I hear an unfamiliar language. [b] *Line transposed from end of verse 10.* [c] *Verse transposed.* [d] I fed Israel: *prob. rdg.; Heb.* He fed him. [e] *So one MS.; others* you. [f] *See note on verse 7.* [g] those...them: *prob. rdg.; Heb.* those who hate the Lord. [h] *Verse 16 transposed to follow verse 7.*

But you know nothing, you understand nothing,   5
  you walk in the dark
  while earth's foundations are giving way.
This is my sentence: Gods you may be,   6
  sons all of you of a high god,*a*
yet you shall die as men die;*b*   7
princes fall, every one of them, and so shall you.

Arise, O God, and judge the earth;   8
  for thou dost pass all nations through thy sieve.

83

Rest not, O God;   1
O God, be neither silent nor still,
for thy enemies are making a tumult,   2
and those that hate thee carry their heads high.
They devise cunning schemes against thy people   3
and conspire against those thou hast made thy treasure:
  'Come, away with them,' they cry,   4
  'let them be a nation no longer,
let Israel's name be remembered no more.'
With one mind they have agreed together   5
  to make a league against thee:
    the families of Edom, the Ishmaelites,   6
    Moabites and Hagarenes,
Gebal, Ammon and Amalek,   7
  Philistia and the citizens of Tyre,
Asshur too their ally,   8
all of them lending aid to the descendants of Lot.
Deal with them as with Sisera,   9
  as with Jabin by the torrent of Kishon,
who fell vanquished as Midian*c* fell at En-harod,*d*   10
  and were spread on the battlefield like dung.
Make their princes like Oreb and Zeeb,   11
  make all their nobles like Zebah and Zalmunna;
for they said, 'We will seize for ourselves   12
  all the pastures of God's people.'
Scatter them, O God, like thistledown,   13
  like chaff before the wind.
Like fire raging through the forest   14
  or flames which blaze across the hills,

[a] *Or* of the Most High. [b] *Or* as Adam died. [c] as Midian: *transposed from previous*
verse. [d] En-harod: *prob. rdg., cp. Judg. 7. 1; Heb.* Endor.

15   hunt them down with thy tempest,
         and dismay them with thy storm-wind.
16   Heap shame upon their heads, O LORD,
         until they confess the greatness of thy name.
17   Let them be abashed, and live in perpetual dismay;
         let them feel their shame and perish.
18   So let them learn that thou^a alone art LORD,
         God Most High over all the earth.

84

1   How dear is thy dwelling-place,
         thou LORD of Hosts!
2   I pine, I faint with longing
         for the courts of the LORD's temple;
     my whole being cries out with joy
         to the living God.
3   Even the sparrow finds a home,
         and the swallow has her nest,
     where she rears her brood beside thy altars,
         O LORD of Hosts, my King and my God.
4   Happy are those who dwell in thy house;
         they never cease from praising thee.
5   Happy the men whose refuge is in thee,
         whose hearts are set on the pilgrim ways^b!
6   As they pass through the thirsty valley
         they find water from a spring;
     and the LORD provides even men who lose their way
         with pools to quench their thirst.^{c}
7   So they pass on from outer wall to inner,
     and the God of gods shows himself in Zion.

8   O LORD God of Hosts, hear my prayer;
         listen, O God of Jacob.
9   O God, look upon our lord the king
         and accept thy anointed prince with favour.

10   Better one day in thy courts
         than a thousand days at home;
     better to linger by the threshold of God's house
         than to live in the dwellings of the wicked.
11   The LORD God is a battlement and a shield;

[a] *So some MSS.; others add* thy name.   [b] are set...ways: *or* high praises fill.   [c] they find...thirst: *prob. rdg.; Heb. obscure.*

grace and honour are his to give.
The LORD will hold back no good thing
from those whose life is blameless.

O LORD of Hosts,   12
happy the man who trusts in thee!

85

LORD, thou hast been gracious to thy land   1
and turned the tide of Jacob's fortunes.
Thou hast forgiven the guilt of thy people   2
and put away all their sins.
Thou hast taken back all thy anger   3
and turned from thy bitter wrath.

Turn back to us, O God our saviour,   4
and cancel thy displeasure.
Wilt thou be angry with us for ever?   5
Must thy wrath last for all generations?
Wilt thou not give us new life   6
that thy people may rejoice in thee?
O LORD, show us thy true love   7
and grant us thy deliverance.

Let me hear the words of the LORD: 8
are they not[a] words of peace,
    peace to his people and his loyal servants
    and to all who turn and trust in him[b]?
Deliverance is near to those who worship him,   9
    so that glory may dwell in our land.
Love and fidelity have come together;   10
justice and peace join hands.
Fidelity springs up from earth   11
and justice looks down from heaven.
The LORD will add prosperity,   12
and our land shall yield its harvest.
Justice shall go in front of him   13
    and the path before his feet shall be peace.[c]

[a] of the LORD: are they not: *prob. rdg.; Heb.* of God the LORD.   [b] and to all...him:
so Sept.; Heb. and let them not lose hope.   [c] and the path...peace: *prob. rdg.; Heb.* so
that he may put his feet to the way.

86

1   Turn to me, LORD, and answer;
     I am downtrodden and poor.
2   Guard me, for I am constant and true;
     save thy servant who puts his trust in thee.
3   O Lord my God,[a] show me thy favour;
     I call to thee all day long.
4   Fill thy servant's heart with joy, O Lord,
     for I lift up my heart to thee.
5   Thou, O Lord, art kind and forgiving,
         full of true love for all who cry to thee.
6   Listen, O LORD, to my prayer
             and hear my pleading.
7   In the day of my distress I call on thee;
             for thou wilt answer me.

8   Among the gods not one is like thee, O Lord,
         no deeds are like thine.
9   All the nations thou hast made, O Lord, will come,
     will bow down before thee and honour thy name;
10   for thou art great, thy works are wonderful,
         thou alone art God.

11   Guide me, O LORD,
     that I may be true to thee and follow thy path;
         let me be one in heart
         with those who revere thy name.
12   I will praise thee, O Lord my God, with all my heart
         and honour thy name for ever.
13   For thy true love stands high above me;
     thou hast rescued my soul from the depths of Sheol.
14   O God, proud men attack me;
         a mob of ruffians seek my life
             and give no thought to thee.
15   Thou, Lord, art God, compassionate and gracious,
         forbearing, ever constant and true.
16   Turn towards me and show me thy favour;
         grant thy slave protection
             and rescue thy slave-girl's son.
17   Give me proof of thy kindness;
         let those who hate thee see to their shame
     that thou, O LORD, hast been my help and comfort.

[a] my God: *transposed from previous verse.*

87[a]

The LORD loves the gates of Zion   1–2
    more than all the dwellings of Jacob;
    her[b] foundations are laid upon holy hills,
and he has made her his home.[c]   4–5
I will count Egypt[d] and Babylon among my friends;
Philistine, Tyrian and Nubian shall be[e] there;
    and Zion shall be called a mother[f]
    in whom men of every race are born.
The LORD shall write against each in the roll of nations: 6
'This one was born in her.'
Singers and dancers alike all chant[g] your praises,   7
proclaiming glorious things of you, O city of God.   3

88

O LORD, my God, by day I call for help,[h]   1
by night I cry aloud in thy presence.
Let my prayer come before thee,   2
hear my loud lament;
for I have had my fill of woes,   3
and they have brought me to the threshold of Sheol.
I am numbered with those who go down to the abyss   4
and have become like a man beyond help,
    like[i] a man who lies dead[j]   5
    or the slain who sleep in the grave,
whom thou rememberest no more
because they are cut off from thy care.
    Thou hast plunged me into the lowest abyss,   6
    in dark places, in the depths.
Thy wrath rises against me,   7
thou hast turned on me the full force of thy anger.[k]
Thou hast taken all my friends far from me,   8
and made me loathsome to them.
    I am in prison and cannot escape;
    my eyes are failing and dim with anguish.   9

---

[a] *The text of this psalm is disordered, and several verses have been re-arranged.* [b] *Prob. rdg.; Heb.* his. [c] his home: *prob. rdg.; Heb.* most high. [d] Egypt: *Heb.* Rahab. [e] *Prob. rdg.; Heb. adds* this one was born (*cp. verse 6*). [f] a mother: *so Sept.; Heb. om.* [g] all chant: *prob. rdg.; Heb.* all my springs. [h] I call for help: *prob. rdg.; Heb.* my deliverance. [i] *So some MSS.; others* among. [j] who lies dead: *prob. rdg.; Heb. obscure.* [k] anger: *or* waves.

I have called upon thee, O Lord, every day
and spread out my hands in prayer to thee.

10   Dost thou work wonders for the dead?
Shall their company rise up and praise thee?
11   Will they speak of thy faithful love in the grave,
of thy sure help in the place of Destruction*[a]*?
12   Will thy wonders be known in the dark,
thy victories in the land of oblivion?

13   But, Lord, I cry to thee,
my prayer comes before thee in the morning.
14   Why hast thou cast me off, O Lord,
why dost thou hide thy face from me?
15   I have suffered from boyhood and come near to death;
I have borne thy terrors, I cower*[b]* beneath thy blows.
16   Thy burning fury has swept over me,
thy onslaughts have put me to silence;
17   all the day long they surge round me like a flood,
they engulf me in a moment.
18   Thou hast taken lover and friend far from me,
and parted me from*[c]* my companions.

89

1   I will sing the story of thy love, O Lord,*[d]* for ever;
I will proclaim thy faithfulness to all generations.
2   Thy true love is firm as the ancient earth,*[e]*
thy faithfulness fixed as the heavens.
5*[f]*   The heavens praise thy wonders, O Lord,
and the council of the holy ones exalts thy faithfulness.
6   In the skies who is there like the Lord,
who like the Lord in the court of heaven,
7   like God who is dreaded among the assembled holy ones,
great*[g]* and terrible above all who stand about him?
8   O Lord God of Hosts, who is like thee?
Thy strength*[h]* and faithfulness, O Lord, surround thee.
9   Thou rulest the surging sea,
calming the turmoil*[i]* of its waves.

---

[a] *Heb.* Abaddon.   [b] I cower: *so Vulg.; Heb. unintelligible.*   [c] parted me from: *prob. rdg., cp. Pesh.; Heb. unintelligible.*   [d] thy love, O Lord: *so Sept.; Heb.* the Lord's acts of love.   [e] Thy...earth: *prob. rdg.; Heb.* Thou hast said for ever true love shall be made firm.   [f] *Verses 3 and 4 transposed to follow* servants *in verse 19.*   [g] great: *so Sept.; Heb.* often.   [h] Thy strength: *prob. rdg.; Heb. obscure.*   [i] turmoil: *prob. rdg.; Heb. obscure.*

Thou didst crush the monster Rahab with a mortal blow[a]   10
   and scatter thy enemies with thy strong arm.
Thine are the heavens, the earth is thine also;   11
the world with all that is in it is of thy foundation.
Thou didst create Zaphon and Amanus;[b]   12
Tabor and Hermon echo thy name.
   Strength of arm and valour are thine;   13
thy hand is mighty, thy right hand lifted high;
   thy throne is built upon righteousness and justice,   14
true love and faithfulness herald thy coming.

Happy the people who have learnt to acclaim thee,   15
who walk, O LORD, in the light of thy presence!
In thy name they shall rejoice all day long;   16
   thy righteousness shall lift them up.
Thou art thyself the strength in which they glory;   17
   through thy favour we hold our heads high.
   The LORD, he is our shield;   18
   the Holy One of Israel, he is our king.

Then didst thou announce in a vision   19
and declare to thy faithful servants:
   I have made a covenant with him I have chosen,   3
   I have sworn to my servant David:
'I will establish your posterity for ever,   4
I will make your throne endure for all generations.'
I have endowed a warrior with princely gifts,
so that the youth I have chosen towers over his people.
I have discovered David my servant;   20
   I have anointed him with my holy oil.
My hand shall be ready to help him   21
   and my arm to give him strength.
No enemy shall strike at him   22
   and no rebel bring him low;
I will shatter his foes before him   23
   and vanquish those who hate him.
My faithfulness and true love shall be with him   24
and through my name he shall hold his head high.
I will extend his rule over the Sea   25
   and his dominion as far as the River.
He will say to me, 'Thou art my father,   26
   my God, my rock and my safe refuge.'

[a] with a mortal blow: *lit.* like one wounded *or* slain.   [b] Amanus: *prob. rdg.; Heb.* right hand *or* south.

27	And I will name him my first-born,
	highest among the kings of the earth.
28	I will maintain my love for him for ever
	and be faithful in my covenant with him.
29	I will establish his posterity for ever
	and his throne as long as the heavens endure.
30	If his sons forsake my law
	and do not conform to my judgements,
31	if they renounce my statutes
	and do not observe my commands,
32	I will punish their disobedience with the rod
	and their iniquity with lashes.
33	Yet I will not deprive him of my true love
	nor let my faithfulness prove false;
34	I will not renounce my covenant
	nor change my promised purpose.
35	I have sworn by my holiness once and for all,
	I will not break my word to David:
36	his posterity shall continue for ever,
	his throne before me like the sun;
37	it shall be sure for ever as the moon's return,
	faithful so long as the skies remain.[a]

38	Yet thou hast rejected thy anointed king,
	thou hast spurned him and raged against him,[b]
39	thou hast denounced the covenant with thy servant,
	defiled his crown and flung it to the ground.
40	Thou hast breached his walls
	and laid his fortresses in ruin;
41	all who pass by plunder him,
	and he suffers the taunts of his neighbours.
42	Thou hast increased the power of his enemies
	and brought joy to all his foes;
43	thou hast let his sharp sword be driven back
	and left him without help in the battle.
44	Thou hast put an end to his glorious rule[c]
	and hurled his throne to the ground;
45	thou hast cut short the days of his youth and vigour
	and covered him with shame.

| 46 | How long, O Lᴏʀᴅ, wilt thou hide thyself from sight? |
| | How long must thy wrath blaze like fire? |

[a] so long...remain: *prob. rdg.; Heb.* a witness in the skies.   [b] raged against him: *or* put him out of mind.   [c] his glorious rule: *prob. rdg.; Heb.* from his purity.

Remember that I shall not live for ever;[a]   47
hast thou created man in vain?
What man shall live and not see death   48
  or save himself from the power of Sheol?
Where are those former acts of thy love, O Lord,   49
  those faithful promises given to David?
Remember, O Lord, the taunts hurled at thy servant,[b]   50
how I have borne in my heart the calumnies of the nations;[c]
  so have thy enemies taunted us, O LORD,   51
  taunted the successors of thy anointed king.

Blessed is the LORD for ever.   52
              Amen, Amen.

BOOK 4

90

Lord, thou hast been our refuge   1
  from generation to generation.
Before the mountains were brought forth,   2
  or earth and world were born in travail,
from age to age everlasting thou art God.
  Thou turnest man back into dust;   3
  'Turn back,' thou sayest, 'you sons of men';
  for in thy sight a thousand years are as yesterday;   4
  a night-watch passes, and thou hast cut them off;   5
  they are like a dream at daybreak,
  they fade like grass which springs up[d] with the morning 6
  but when evening comes is parched and withered.
So we are brought to an end by thy anger   7
  and silenced by thy wrath.
  Thou dost lay bare our iniquities before thee   8
  and our lusts in the full light of thy presence.
All our days go by under the shadow of thy wrath;   9
  our years die away like a murmur.[e]
Seventy years is the span of our life,   10
  eighty if our strength holds;[f]
  the hurrying years are labour and sorrow,

[a] live for ever: *prob. rdg.; Heb. obscure*. [b] *So some MSS.; others* servants. [c] the
calumnies...nations: *prob. rdg.; Heb.* all of many peoples. [d] *Prob. rdg.; Heb. adds* and
passes away. [e] a murmur: *or, with some MSS.,* a task interrupted. [f] *Or* eighty at the
most.

so quickly they pass and are forgotten.
11 Who feels the power of thy anger,
who feels thy wrath like those that fear thee?
12 Teach us to order our days rightly,
that we may enter the gate of wisdom.
13 How long, O Lord?
Relent, and take pity on thy servants.
14 Satisfy us with thy love when morning breaks,
that we may sing for joy and be glad all our days.
15 Repay us days of gladness for our days of suffering,
for the years thou hast humbled us.
16 Show thy servants thy deeds
and their children thy majesty.
17 May all delightful things be ours, O Lord our God;
establish firmly all we do.*a*

91

1 You that live in the shelter of the Most High
and lodge under the shadow of the Almighty,
2 who say, 'The Lord is my safe retreat,
my God the fastness in which I trust';
3 he himself will snatch you away
from fowler's snare or raging tempest.
4 He will cover you with his pinions,
and you shall find safety beneath his wings;
5 you shall not fear the hunters' trap*b* by night
or the arrow that flies by day,
6 the pestilence that stalks in darkness
or the plague raging at noonday.
7 A thousand may fall at your side,
ten thousand close at hand,
but you it shall not touch;
his truth*c* will be your shield and your rampart.*d*
8 With your own eyes you shall see all this;
you shall watch the punishment of the wicked.
9 For you, the Lord is a*e* safe retreat;
you have made the Most High your refuge.
10 No disaster shall befall you,
no calamity shall come upon your home.

[a] *So some MSS.; others add* on us, and establish firmly all we do. [b] the hunters' trap:
lit. the scare. [c] *Or* his arm. [d] his truth...rampart: *transposed from end of verse 4.*
[e] *Prob. rdg.; Heb.* my.

For he has charged his angels 11
 to guard you wherever you go,
 to lift you on their hands 12
for fear you should strike your foot against a stone.
You shall step on asp and cobra, 13
you shall tread safely on snake and serpent.

Because his love is set on me, I will deliver him; 14
I will lift him beyond danger, for he knows me by my name.
 When he calls upon me, I will answer; 15
I will be with him in time of trouble;
 I will rescue him and bring him to honour.
I will satisfy him with long life 16
to enjoy the fullness of my salvation.

92

O LORD, it is good to give thee thanks, 1
to sing psalms to thy name, O Most High,
to declare thy love in the morning 2
 and thy constancy every night,
  to the music of a ten-stringed lute, 3
  to the sounding chords of the harp.
Thy acts, O LORD, fill me with exultation; 4
 I shout in triumph at thy mighty deeds.
How great are thy deeds, O LORD! 5
How fathomless thy thoughts!

He who does not know this is a brute, 6
a fool is he who does not understand this:
 that though the wicked grow like grass 7
and every evildoer prospers,
 they will be destroyed for ever.
While thou, LORD, dost reign on high eternally, 8
thy foes will surely perish,*a* 9
all evildoers will be scattered.

I lift my head high, like a wild ox tossing its horn; 10
I am anointed richly with oil.
I gloat over all who speak ill of me, 11
I listen for the downfall of my cruel foes.
 The righteous flourish like a palm-tree, 12
 they grow tall as a cedar on Lebanon;

 [a] *So Sept.; Heb. adds* for behold thy foes, O LORD.

13   planted as they are in the house of the LORD,
            they flourish in the courts of our God,
14   vigorous in old age like trees full of sap,
            luxuriant, wide-spreading,
15   eager to declare that the LORD is just,
            the LORD my rock,[a] in whom there is no unrighteousness.

93

1   The LORD is king; he is clothed in majesty;
    the LORD clothes himself with might and fastens on his belt of
      wrath.

    Thou hast fixed the earth immovable and firm,
2   thy throne firm from of old;
        from all eternity thou art God.[b]
3   O LORD, the ocean lifts up, the ocean lifts up its clamour;
        the ocean lifts up[c] its pounding waves.
4   The LORD on high is mightier far
        than the noise of great waters,
        mightier than the breakers of the sea.

5   Thy law stands firm, and holiness is the beauty of thy temple,
      while time shall last, O LORD.

94

1   O LORD, thou God of vengeance,
        thou God of vengeance, show thyself.
2   Rise up, judge of the earth;
      punish the arrogant as they deserve.
3   How long shall the wicked, O LORD,
      how long shall the wicked exult?
4   Evildoers are full of bluster,
      boasting and swaggering;
5   they beat down thy people, O LORD,
      and oppress thy chosen nation;
6   they murder the widow and the stranger
      and do the fatherless to death;
7   they say, 'The LORD does not see,
      the God of Jacob pays no heed.'
8   Pay heed yourselves, most brutish of the people;
      you fools, when will you be wise?

[a] *Or* creator. [b] God: *so Targ.; Heb. om.* [c] the ocean lifts up: *or* let the ocean lift up.

Does he that planted the ear not hear,   9
he that moulded the eye not see?
Shall not he that instructs the nations correct them?   10
The teacher of mankind, has he no^a knowledge?
The LORD knows the thoughts of man,   11
that they are but a puff of wind.

Happy the man whom thou dost instruct, O LORD,   12
and teach out of thy law,
giving him respite from adversity   13
until a pit is dug for the wicked.
The LORD will not abandon his people   14
nor forsake his chosen nation;
for righteousness still informs his judgement,^b   15
and all upright men follow it.

Who is on my side against these sinful men?   16
Who will stand up for me against these evildoers?
If the LORD had not been my helper,   17
I should soon have slept in the silent grave.
When I felt that my foot was slipping,   18
thy love, O LORD, held me up.
Anxious thoughts may fill my heart,   19
but thy presence is my joy and my consolation.
Shall sanctimonious calumny call thee partner,   20
or he that contrives a mischief under cover of law?
For they put the righteous on trial^c for his life   21
and condemn to death innocent men.
But the LORD has been my strong tower,   22
and God my rock of refuge;
our God requites the wicked for their injustice,   23
the LORD puts them to silence^d for their misdeeds.

95

Come! Let us raise a joyful song to the LORD,   1
a shout of triumph to the Rock of our salvation.
Let us come into his presence with thanksgiving,   2
and sing him psalms of triumph.
For the LORD is a great God,   3
a great king over all gods;

[a] no: *prob. rdg.; Heb. om.*   [b] for...judgement: *prob. rdg.; Heb.* for judgement will return as far as righteousness.   [c] they put...trial: *prob. rdg.; Heb.* they cut the righteous. [d] *So some MSS.; others repeat* puts them to silence.

4   the farthest places of the earth are in his hands,
       and the folds of the hills are his;
5   the sea is his, he made it;
       the dry land fashioned by his hands is his.
6   Come! Let us throw ourselves at his feet in homage,
       let us kneel before the Lord who made us;
7   for he is our God,
     we are his people, we the flock he shepherds.*a*
     You shall know*b* his power today
       if you will listen to his voice.

8   Do not grow stubborn, as you were at Meribah,*c*
       as at the time of Massah*d* in the wilderness,
9   when your forefathers challenged me,
       tested me and saw for themselves all that I did.
10   For forty years I was indignant
     with that generation, and I said:
     They are a people whose hearts are astray,
       and they will not discern my ways.
11   As I swore in my anger:
       They shall never enter my rest.

96

1*e* Sing a new song to the Lord;
       sing to the Lord, all men on earth.
2   Sing to the Lord and bless his name,
       proclaim his triumph day by day.
3   Declare his glory among the nations,
       his marvellous deeds among all peoples.
4   Great is the Lord and worthy of all praise;
       he is more to be feared than all gods.
5   For the gods of the nations are idols every one;
       but the Lord made the heavens.
6   Majesty and splendour attend him,
       might and beauty are in his sanctuary.

7   Ascribe to the Lord, you families of nations,
     ascribe to the Lord glory and might;
8   ascribe to the Lord the glory due to his name,
     bring a gift and come into his courts.

[*a*] his people...shepherds: *so one MS.*, cp. Ps. 79. 13; *others* the people of his shepherding and a flock. [*b*] You shall know: *prob. rdg.; Heb. om.* [*c*] *That is* Dispute. [*d*] *That is* Challenge. [*e*] *Verses 1–13: cp. 1 Chr. 16. 23–33.*

Bow down to the LORD in the splendour of holiness,[a]   9
and dance in his honour, all men on earth.
Declare among the nations, 'The LORD is king.   10
He has fixed the earth firm, immovable;
he will judge the peoples justly.'
Let the heavens rejoice and the earth exult,   11
let the sea roar and all the creatures in it,
let the fields exult and all that is in them;   12
then let all the trees of the forest shout for joy
before the LORD when he comes[b] to judge the earth.   13
He will judge the earth with righteousness
and the peoples in good faith.

97

The LORD is king, let the earth be glad,   1
let coasts and islands all rejoice.
Cloud and mist enfold him,   2
righteousness and justice
are the foundation of his throne.
Fire goes before him   3
and burns up his enemies[c] all around.
The world is lit up beneath his lightning-flash;   4
the earth sees it and writhes in pain.
The mountains melt like wax as the LORD approaches,   5
the Lord of all the earth.
The heavens proclaim his righteousness,   6
and all peoples see his glory.
Let all who worship images, who vaunt their idols,   7
be put to shame;
bow down, all gods,[d] before him.

Zion heard and rejoiced, the cities of Judah were glad   8
at thy judgements, O LORD.
For thou, LORD, art most high over all the earth,   9
far exalted above all gods.

The LORD loves[e] those who hate evil;   10
he keeps his loyal servants safe
and rescues them from the wicked.
A harvest of light is sown for the righteous,   11

---

[a] the splendour of holiness: *or* holy vestments.   [b] *So many MSS.; others repeat* when he comes.   [c] burns...enemies: *or, with slight change,* blazes on every side.   [d] bow...gods: *or* all gods bow down...   [e] The LORD loves: *prob. rdg.; Heb.* Lovers of the LORD.

and joy for all good men.
12   You that are righteous, rejoice in the Lord
and praise his holy name.

98

1   Sing a new song to the Lord,
for he has done marvellous deeds;
his right hand and holy arm have won him victory.
2   The Lord has made his victory known;
he has displayed his righteousness to all the nations.
3   He has remembered his constancy,
his love for the house of Israel.
All the ends of the earth have seen
the victory of our God.

4   Acclaim the Lord, all men on earth,
break into songs of joy, sing psalms.
5   Sing psalms in the Lord's honour with the harp,
with the harp and with the music of the psaltery.
6   With trumpet and echoing horn
acclaim the presence of the Lord our king.
7   Let the sea roar and all its creatures,
the world and those who dwell in it.
8   Let the rivers clap their hands,
let the hills sing aloud together
9   before the Lord; for he comes
to judge the earth.
He will judge the world with righteousness
and the peoples in justice.

99

1   The Lord is king, the peoples are perturbed;
he is throned on the cherubim, earth quivers.
2   The Lord is great in Zion;
he is exalted above all the peoples.
3   They extol his[a] name as great and terrible;
4   he is holy, he is mighty,
a king who loves justice.

Thou hast established justice and equity;
thou hast dealt righteously in Jacob.

[a] *Prob. rdg.; Heb.* thy.

Exalt the LORD our God,   5
   bow down before his footstool;
   he is holy.

Moses and Aaron among his priests,   6
   and Samuel among those who call on his name,
called to the LORD, and he answered.
   He spoke to them in a pillar of cloud;   7
they followed his teaching and kept the law he gave them.
Thou, O LORD our God, thou didst answer them;   8
thou wast a God who forgave all their misdeeds
   and held them innocent.
Exalt the LORD our God,   9
   bow down towards his holy hill;
   for the LORD our God is holy.

100

Acclaim the LORD, all men on earth,   1
   worship the LORD in gladness;   2
enter his presence with songs of exultation.
Know that the LORD is God;   3
he has made us and we are his own,
   his people, the flock which he shepherds.
Enter his gates with thanksgiving   4
   and his courts with praise.
Give thanks to him and bless his name;
for the LORD is good and his love is everlasting,   5
   his constancy endures to all generations.

101

I sing of loyalty and justice;   1
I will raise a psalm to thee, O LORD.[a]

I will follow a wise and blameless course,   2
whatever may befall me.[b]
I will go about my house in purity of heart.
I will set before myself no sordid aim;   3
I will hate disloyalty, I will have none of it.
I will reject all crooked thoughts;   4
   I will have no dealings with evil.

[a] I sing...O LORD: *or* I will follow a course of justice and loyalty; I will hold thee in
awe, O LORD. [b] whatever may befall me: *prob. rdg.; Heb.* when comest thou to me?

5   I will silence those who spread tales behind men's backs,
     I will not sit at table with proud, pompous men,
6   I will choose the most loyal for my companions;
     my servants shall be men whose lives are blameless.
7   No scandal-monger shall live in my household;
     no liar shall set himself up where I can see him.
8   Morning after morning I will put all wicked men to silence
     and will rid the LORD's city of all evildoers.

102

1   LORD, hear my prayer
     and let my cry for help reach thee.
2   Hide not thy face from me
     when I am in distress.
     Listen to my prayer
     and, when I call, answer me soon;
3   for my days vanish like smoke,
     my body is burnt up as in an oven.[a]
4   I am stricken, withered like grass;
     I cannot find the strength to eat.
5   Wasted away,[b] I groan aloud
     and my skin hangs on my bones.
6   I am like a desert-owl in the wilderness,
     an owl that lives among ruins.
7   Thin and meagre, I wail in solitude,[c]
     like a bird that flutters[d] on the roof-top.
8   My enemies insult me all the day long;
     mad with rage, they conspire against me.
9   I have eaten ashes for bread
     and mingled tears with my drink.
10   In thy wrath and fury
       thou hast taken me up and flung me aside.
11   My days decline as the shadows lengthen,
     and like grass I wither away.

12   But thou, LORD, art enthroned for ever
     and thy fame shall be known to all generations.
13   Thou wilt arise and have mercy on Zion;
     for the time is come[e] to pity her.

---

[a] as . . . oven: *or, with one MS., like* dried meat.   [b] Wasted away: *transposed from previous verse.*   [c] in solitude: *so Pesh.; Heb. om.*   [d] that flutters: *so some MSS.; others* in solitude.   [e] *Prob. rdg.; Heb. adds* season.

Her very stones are dear to thy servants,   14
   and even her dust moves them with pity.
Then shall the nations revere thy name, O Lord,   15
   and all the kings of the earth thy glory,
when the Lord builds up Zion again   16
   and shows himself in his glory.
He turns to hear the prayer of the destitute   17
   and does not scorn them when they pray.
This shall be written down for future generations,   18
and a people yet unborn shall praise the Lord.
The Lord looks down from his sanctuary on high,   19
   from heaven he surveys the earth
      to listen to the groaning of the prisoners   20
      and set free men under sentence of death;
so shall the Lord's name be on men's lips in Zion   21
   and his praise shall be told in Jerusalem,
when peoples are assembled together,   22
peoples and kingdoms, to serve the Lord.

My strength is broken in mid course;   23
the time allotted me is short.   24
   Snatch me not away before half my days are done,
   for thy years last through all generations.
Long ago thou didst lay the foundations of the earth,   25
   and the heavens were thy handiwork.
They shall pass away, but thou endurest;   26
like clothes they shall all grow old;
   thou shalt cast them off like a cloak,
   and they shall vanish;
but thou art the same and thy years shall have no end;   27
   thy servants' children shall continue,   28
and their posterity shall be established in thy presence.

103

Bless the Lord, my soul;   1
   my innermost heart, bless his holy name.
Bless the Lord, my soul,   2
   and forget none of his benefits.
   He pardons all my guilt   3
   and heals all my suffering.
He rescues me from the pit of death   4
and surrounds me with constant love,
   with tender affection;

5   he contents me with all good in the prime of life,
               and my youth is ever new like an eagle's.

6   The LORD is righteous in his acts;
               he brings justice to all who have been wronged.

7   He taught Moses to know his way
               and showed the Israelites what he could do.

8   The LORD is compassionate and gracious,
               long-suffering and for ever constant;

9   he will not always be the accuser
               or nurse his anger for all time.

10   He has not treated us as our sins deserve
               or requited us for our misdeeds.

11   For as the heaven stands high above the earth,
               so his strong love stands high over all who fear him.

12   Far as east is from west,
               so far has he put our offences away from us.

13   As a father has compassion on his children,
               so has the LORD compassion on all who fear him.

14   For he knows how we were made,
               he knows full well that we are dust.

15   Man's days are like the grass;
               he blossoms like the flowers of the field:

16   a wind passes over them, and they cease to be,
               and their place knows them no more.

17   But the LORD's love never fails those who fear him;
               his righteousness never fails their sons and their grandsons

18   who listen to his voice[a] and keep his covenant,
               who remember his commandments and obey them.

19   The LORD has established his throne in heaven,
               his kingly power over the whole world.

20   Bless the LORD, all his angels,
               creatures of might who do his bidding.

21   Bless the LORD, all his hosts,
               his ministers who serve his will.

22   Bless the LORD, all created things,
               in every place where he has dominion.

             Bless the LORD, my soul.

             [a] who listen to his voice: *transposed from end of verse 20.*

104

Bless the LORD, my soul: 1
O LORD my God, thou art great indeed,
  clothed in majesty and splendour,
  and wrapped in a robe of light.   2
  Thou hast spread out the heavens like a tent
  and on their waters laid the beams of thy pavilion;   3
  who takest the clouds for thy chariot,
  riding on the wings of the wind;
  who makest the winds thy messengers   4
  and flames of fire thy servants;
  thou didst fix the earth on its foundation   5
  so that it never can be shaken;
  the deep overspread it like a cloak,   6
  and the waters lay above the mountains.
  At thy rebuke they ran,   7
  at the sound of thy thunder they rushed away,
  flowing over the hills,   8
  pouring down into the valleys
  to the place appointed for them.
Thou didst fix a boundary which they might not pass;   9
  they shall not return to cover the earth.

Thou dost make springs break out in the gullies,   10
  so that their water runs between the hills.
  The wild beasts all drink from them,   11
  the wild asses quench their thirst;
  the birds of the air nest on their banks   12
  and sing among the leaves.

From thy high pavilion thou dost water the hills;   13
  the earth is enriched by thy provision.
  Thou makest grass grow for the cattle   14
    and green things for those who toil for man,
  bringing bread out of the earth
  and wine to gladden men's hearts,   15
  oil to make their faces shine
  and bread to sustain their strength.
    The trees of the LORD are green and leafy,   16
    the cedars of Lebanon which he planted;
  the birds build their nests in them,   17
  the stork makes her home in their tops.[a]

[a] in their tops: *prob. rdg.; Heb.* the pine-trees.

18   High hills are the haunt of the mountain-goat,
     and boulders a refuge for the rock-badger.

19   Thou hast made the moon to measure the year
     and taught the sun where to set.
20   When thou makest darkness and it is night,
     all the beasts of the forest come forth;
21   the young lions roar for prey,
       seeking their food from God.
22   When thou makest the sun rise, they slink away
       and go to rest in their lairs;
23   but man comes out to his work
       and to his labours until evening.
24   Countless are the things thou hast made, O LORD.
     Thou hast made all by thy wisdom;
     and the earth is full of thy creatures,
25   beasts great and small.

Here is the great immeasurable sea,
     in which move creatures beyond number.
26   Here ships sail to and fro,
   here is Leviathan whom thou hast made thy plaything.[a]

27   All of them look expectantly to thee
     to give them their food at the proper time;
28   what thou givest them they gather up;
     when thou openest thy hand, they eat their fill.
29   Then thou hidest thy face, and they are restless and
        troubled;
     when thou takest away their breath, they fail
  [and they return to the dust from which they came];
30   but when thou breathest into them, they recover;
     thou givest new life to the earth.

31   May the glory of the LORD stand for ever
     and may he rejoice in his works!
32   When he looks at the earth, it quakes;
     when he touches the hills, they pour forth smoke.

33   I will sing to the LORD as long as I live,
     all my life I will sing psalms to my God.
34   May my meditation please the LORD,
     as I show my joy in him!

[a] thy plaything: *or* that it may sport in it.

Away with all sinners from the earth   35
and may the wicked be no more!

Bless the LORD, my soul.

O praise the LORD.[a]

105

Give the LORD thanks and invoke him by name,   1[b]
  make his deeds known in the world around.
Pay him honour with song and psalm   2
  and think upon all his wonders.
Exult in his hallowed name;   3
  let those who seek the LORD be joyful in heart.
Turn to the LORD, your strength,[c]   4
seek his presence always.
Remember the wonders that he has wrought,   5
  his portents and the judgements he has given,
O offspring of Abraham his servant, O chosen sons of Jacob.   6

He is the LORD our God;   7
  his judgements fill the earth.
He called to mind his covenant from long ago,[d]   8
the promise he extended to a thousand generations—
  the covenant made with Abraham,   9
  his oath given to Isaac,
the decree by which he bound himself for Jacob,   10
his everlasting covenant with Israel:
'I will give you the land of Canaan', he said,   11
  'to be your possession, your patrimony.'
  A small company it was,   12
few in number, strangers in that land,
roaming from nation to nation,   13
from one kingdom to another;
but he let no one ill-treat them,   14
for their sake he admonished kings:
  'Touch not my anointed servants,   15
  do my prophets no harm.'

He called down famine on the land   16
and cut short their daily bread.[e]

[a] O praise the LORD: *Heb.* Hallelujah.   [b] *Verses 1–15: cp. 1 Chr. 16. 8–22.*   [c] your
strength: *lit.* and his strength.   [d] from long ago: *or* for ever.   [e] and cut...bread: *lit.*
and broke their stick of bread.

¹⁷   But he had sent on a man before them,
Joseph, who was sold into slavery;
¹⁸   he was kept a prisoner with fetters on his feet
and an iron collar clamped on his neck.
¹⁹   He was tested by the Lord's command
until what he foretold came true.
²⁰   Then the king sent and set him free,
the ruler of nations released him;
²¹   he made him master of his household
and ruler over all his possessions,
²²   to correct his officers at will
and teach his counsellors wisdom.
²³   Then Israel too went down into Egypt
and Jacob came to live in the land of Ham.
²⁴   There God made his people very fruitful,
he made them stronger than their enemies,
²⁵   whose hearts he turned to hatred of his people
and double-dealing with his servants.
²⁶   He sent his servant Moses
and Aaron whom he had chosen.
²⁷   They were his*a* mouthpiece to announce his signs,
his portents in the land of Ham.
²⁸   He sent darkness, and all was dark,
but still they resisted his commands.
²⁹   He turned their waters into blood
and killed all their fish.
³⁰   Their country swarmed with frogs,
even their princes' inner chambers.
³¹   At his command came swarms of flies
and maggots the whole land through.
³²   He changed their rain into hail
and flashed fire over their country.
³³   He blasted their vines and their fig-trees
and splintered the trees throughout the land.
³⁴   At his command came locusts,
hoppers past all number,
³⁵   they consumed every green thing in the land,
consumed all the produce of the soil.
³⁶   Then he struck down all the first-born in Egypt,*b*
the firstfruits of their manhood;
³⁷   he led Israel*c* out, laden with silver and gold,
and among all their tribes no man fell.

[a] *So Sept.; Heb.* their.   [b] in Egypt: *so some MSS.; others* in their land.   [c] *Lit.* them.

The Egyptians were glad when they went,   38
    for fear of Israel had taken hold of them.
He spread a cloud as a screen,   39
    and fire to light up the night.
They asked, and he sent them quails,   40
    he gave them bread from heaven in plenty.
He opened a rock and water gushed out,   41
    a river flowing in a parched land;
    for he had remembered his solemn promise   42
    given to his servant Abraham.
So he led out his people rejoicing,   43
    his chosen ones in triumph.
He gave them the lands of heathen nations   44
and they took possession where others had toiled,
    so that they might keep his statutes   45
    and obey his laws.

    O praise the LORD.

106

    O praise the LORD.   1

It is good to give thanks to the LORD;
    for his love endures for ever.
Who will tell of the LORD's mighty acts   2
    and make his praises heard?
    Happy are they who act justly   3
    and do right at all times!
Remember me, LORD, when thou showest favour to thy people, 4
    look upon me when thou savest them,
    that I may see the prosperity of thy chosen,   5
rejoice in thy nation's joy and exult with thy own people.

We have sinned like our forefathers,   6
we have erred and done wrong.
Our fathers in Egypt took no account of thy marvels,   7
    they did not remember thy many acts of faithful love,
    but in spite of all*[a]* they rebelled by the Red Sea.*[b]*
    Yet the LORD delivered them for his name's sake   8
    and so made known his mighty power.
He rebuked the Red Sea and it dried up,   9
he led his people through the deeps as through the wilderness.
    So he delivered them from those who hated them,   10

[a] in spite of all: *prob. rdg.; Heb. obscure.*   [b] *Or* the Sea of Reeds.

and claimed them back from the enemy's hand.

11 The waters closed over their adversaries,
not one of them survived.

12 Then they believed his promises and sang praises to him.

13 But they quickly forgot all he had done
and would not wait to hear his counsel;

14 their greed was insatiable in the wilderness,
they tried God's patience in the desert.

15 He gave them what they asked
but sent a wasting sickness among them.*

16 They were envious of Moses in the camp,
and of Aaron, who was consecrated to the LORD.

17 The earth opened and swallowed Dathan,
it closed over the company of Abiram;

18 fire raged through their company,
the wicked perished in flames.

19 At Horeb they made a calf
and bowed down to an image;

20 they exchanged their Glory*
for the image of a bull that feeds on grass.

21 They forgot God their deliverer,
who had done great deeds in Egypt,

22 marvels in the land of Ham,
terrible things at the Red Sea.

23 So his purpose was to destroy them,
but Moses, the man he had chosen,
threw himself into the breach
to turn back his wrath lest it destroy them.

24 They made light of the pleasant land,
disbelieving his promise;

25 they muttered treason in their tents
and would not obey the LORD.

26 So with uplifted hand he swore
to strike them down in the wilderness,

27 to scatter their descendants among the nations
and disperse them throughout the world.

28 They joined in worshipping the Baal of Peor
and ate meat sacrificed to lifeless gods.

[a] among them: *or* in their throats.   [b] their Glory: *or* the glory of God (*cp. Jer.* 2. 11; *Romans* 1. 23).

Their deeds provoked the LORD to anger,　　　　29
and plague broke out amongst them;
but Phinehas stood up and interceded,　　　　30
　so the plague was stopped.
This was counted to him as righteousness　　　　31
throughout all generations for ever.

They roused the LORD to anger at the waters of Meribah,　32
and Moses suffered because of them;
　for they had embittered his spirit　　　　33
　and he had spoken rashly.

They did not destroy the peoples round about,　　34
as the LORD had commanded them to do,
　but they mingled with the nations,　　　35
　learning their ways;
　they worshipped their idols　　　　36
and were ensnared by them.
　Their sons and their daughters　　　37
　they sacrificed to foreign demons;
they shed innocent blood,　　　　38
　the blood of sons and daughters
　offered to the gods of Canaan,
and the land was polluted with blood.
Thus they defiled themselves by their conduct　　39
and they followed their lusts and broke faith with God.
Then the LORD grew angry with his people　　40
　and loathed them, his own chosen nation;
　so he gave them into the hands of the nations,　41
and they were ruled by their foes;
　their enemies oppressed them　　　42
　and made them subject to their power.
Many times he came to their rescue,　　　43
but they were disobedient and rebellious still.[a]
And yet, when he heard them wail and cry aloud,　44
　he looked with pity on their distress;
he called to mind his covenant with them　　45
　and, in his boundless love, relented;
he roused compassion for them　　　46
　in the hearts of all their captors.

Deliver us, O LORD our God,　　　　47
　and gather us in from among the nations

[a] *Prob. rdg.; Heb. adds* and were brought low by their guilt.

> that we may give thanks to thy holy name
> and make thy praise our pride.

48   Blessed be the LORD the God of Israel
> from everlasting to everlasting;
> and let all the people say 'Amen.'

> O praise the LORD.

BOOK 5

107

1   It is good to give thanks to the LORD,
> for his love endures for ever.
2   So let them say who were redeemed by the LORD,
> redeemed by him from the power of the enemy
3   and gathered out of every land,
> from east and west, from north and south.[a]

4   Some lost their way in desert wastes;
> they found no road to a city to live in;
5   hungry and thirsty,
> their spirit sank within them.
6   So they cried to the LORD in their trouble,
> and he rescued them from their distress;
7   he led them by a straight and easy way
> until they came to a city to live in.
8   Let them thank the LORD for his enduring love
> and for the marvellous things he has done for men:
9   he has satisfied the thirsty
> and filled the hungry with good things.

10   Some sat in darkness, dark as death,
> prisoners bound fast in iron,
11   because they had rebelled against God's commands
> and flouted the purpose of the Most High.
12   Their spirit was subdued by hard labour;
> they stumbled and fell with none to help them.
13   So they cried to the LORD in their trouble,
> and he saved them from their distress;
14   he brought them out of darkness, dark as death,
> and broke their chains.

[a] and south: *prob. rdg., cp. Targ.; Heb.* and west.

Let them thank the LORD for his enduring love   15
  and for the marvellous things he has done for men:
he has shattered doors of bronze,   16
    bars of iron he has snapped in two.

Some were fools, they took to rebellious ways,   17
  and for their transgression they suffered punishment.
They sickened at the sight of food   18
  and drew near to the very gates of death.
So they cried to the LORD in their trouble,   19
  and he saved them from their distress;
he sent his word to heal them   20
  and bring them alive out of the pit of death.*a*
Let them thank the LORD for his enduring love   21
  and for the marvellous things he has done for men.
Let them offer sacrifices of thanksgiving   22
  and recite his deeds with shouts of joy.

Others there are who go to sea in ships   23
  and make their living on the wide waters.
These men have seen the acts of the LORD   24
  and his marvellous doings in the deep.
At his command the storm-wind rose   25
  and lifted the waves high.
Carried up to heaven, plunged down to the depths,   26
    tossed to and fro in peril,
they reeled and staggered like drunken men,   27
  and their seamanship was all in vain.
So they cried to the LORD in their trouble,   28
  and he brought them out of their distress.
The storm sank to a murmur   29
  and the waves of the sea were stilled.
They were glad then that all was calm,   30
  as he guided them to the harbour they desired.
Let them thank the LORD for his enduring love   31
  and for the marvellous things he has done for men.
Let them exalt him in the assembly of the people   32
  and praise him in the council of the elders.

He turns rivers into desert   33
  and springs of water into thirsty ground;
he turns fruitful land into salt waste,   34
    because the men who dwell there are so wicked.

[a] alive...death: *prob. rdg.; Heb.* from their corruption.

35   Desert he changes into standing pools,
          and parched land into springs of water.
36   There he gives the hungry a home,
          and they build themselves a city to live in;
37   they sow fields and plant vineyards
          and reap a fruitful harvest.
38   He blesses them and their numbers increase,
          and he does not let their herds lose strength.
39   Tyrants*a* lose their strength and are brought low
          in the grip of misfortune and sorrow;
40   he brings princes into contempt
          and leaves them wandering in a trackless waste.
41   But the poor man he lifts clear of his troubles
          and makes families increase like flocks of sheep.
42   The upright see it and are glad,
          while evildoers are filled with disgust.
43   Let the wise man lay these things to heart,
          and ponder the record of the LORD's enduring love.

108

1*b*   My heart is steadfast, O God,
          my heart is steadfast.*c*
        I will sing and raise a psalm;
          awake,*d* my spirit,
2   awake, lute and harp,
          I will awake at dawn of day.*e*
3   I will confess thee, O LORD, among the peoples,
          among the nations I will raise a psalm to thee;
4   for thy unfailing love is wider than the heavens
          and thy truth reaches to the skies.
5   Show thyself, O God, high above the heavens;
          let thy glory shine over all the earth.
6*f*   Deliver those that are dear to thee;
        save with thy right hand and answer.

7   God has spoken from his sanctuary:*g*
          'I will go up now and measure out Shechem;
          I will divide the valley of Succoth into plots;
8   Gilead and Manasseh are mine;

[*a*] *Prob. rdg.; Heb. om.* [*b*] *Verses 1–5: cp. Ps. 57. 7–11.* [*c*] my heart is steadfast: *so some MSS.; others om.* [*d*] awake: *prob. rdg.; Heb. also.* [*e*] at dawn of day: *or* the dawn. [*f*] *Verses 6–13: cp. Ps. 60. 5–12.* [*g*] from his sanctuary: *or* in his holiness.

Ephraim is my helmet,^a Judah my sceptre;
  Moab is my wash-bowl, I fling my shoes at Edom;   9
    Philistia is the target of my anger.'

Who can bring me to the impregnable city,   10
  who can guide^b me to Edom,
since thou, O God, hast abandoned us   11
  and goest not forth^c with our armies?
Grant us help against the enemy,   12
  for deliverance by man is a vain hope.
With God's help we shall do valiantly,   13
  and God himself will tread our enemies under foot.

109

O God of my praise, be silent no longer,   1
  for wicked men heap calumnies upon me.   2
They have lied to my face
  and ringed me round with words of hate.   3
They have attacked me without a cause^d
  and accused me though I have done nothing unseemly.^e   4
They have repaid me evil for good   5
  and hatred in return for my love.
They say, 'Put up some rascal to denounce him,   6
  an accuser to stand at his right side.'
But when judgement is given, that rascal will be exposed   7
  and his follies accounted a sin.
May his days be few;   8
  may his hoarded wealth^f fall to another!
May his children be fatherless,   9
  his wife a widow!
May his children be vagabonds and beggars,   10
  driven from their homes!
May the money-lender distrain on all his goods   11
  and strangers seize his earnings!
May none remain loyal to him,   12
  and none have mercy on his fatherless children!
May his line be doomed to extinction,   13
  may their name be wiped out within a generation!
May the sins of his forefathers be remembered^g   14

[a] my helmet: *lit.* the refuge of my head. [b] *So Sept.; Heb.* has guided. [c] *So some MSS.; others add* O God. [d] *Prob. rdg.; Heb. adds* in return for my love. [e] though... unseemly: *prob. rdg.; Heb. obscure.* [f] hoarded wealth: *or* charge, *cp. Acts 1. 20.* [g] *So Pesh.; Heb. adds* before the Lord.

and his mother's wickedness never be wiped out!
15 May they remain on record before the Lord,
but may he extinguish their name from the earth!
16 For that man never set himself
to be loyal to his friend
but persecuted the downtrodden and the poor
and hounded the broken-hearted to their death.
17 Curses he loved: may the curse fall on him!
He took no pleasure in blessing: may no blessing be his!
18 He clothed himself in cursing like a garment:
may it seep into his body like water
and into his bones like oil!
19 May it wrap him round like the clothes he puts on,
like the belt which he wears every day!
20 May the Lord so requite my accusers
and those who speak evil against me!

21 But thou, O Lord God,
deal with me as befits thy honour;
in[a] the goodness of thy unfailing love deliver me,
22 for I am downtrodden and poor,
and my heart within me is distracted.
23 I fade like a passing shadow,
I am shaken off like a locust.
24 My knees are weak with fasting
and my flesh wastes away, so meagre is my fare.
25 I have become the victim of their taunts;
when they see me they toss their heads.
26 Help me, O Lord my God;
save me, by thy unfailing love,
27 that men may know this is thy doing
and thou alone, O Lord, hast done it.
28 They may curse, but thou dost bless;
may my opponents be put to shame,[b]
but may thy servant rejoice!
29 May my accusers be clothed with dishonour,
wrapped in their shame as in a cloak!
30 I will lift up my voice to extol the Lord,
and before a great company I will praise him.
31 For he stands at the poor man's right side
to save him from his adversaries.[c]

[a] *Prob. rdg., cp. Targ.; Heb.* because of. [b] may my...shame: *so Sept.; Heb.* they rose up and were put to shame. [c] *Prob. rdg.; Heb.* his judges.

110

The LORD said to my lord,   1
  'You shall sit^a at my right hand
when^b I make your enemies the footstool under your feet.'
When the LORD from Zion hands you the sceptre, the symbol of   2
    your power,
  march forth through the ranks of^c your enemies.
At birth^d you were endowed with princely gifts   3
  and^e resplendent^f in holiness.
You have shone with the dew of youth since your mother bore you.
The LORD has sworn and will not change his purpose: 4
  'You are a priest for ever,
    in the succession of Melchizedek.'
The Lord at your right hand   5
has broken kings in the day of his anger.
So the king in his majesty,^g sovereign of a mighty land, 6
  will punish nations;^h
    he will drink from the torrent beside the path   7
    and therefore will hold his head high.

111

O praise the LORD.   1

With all my heart will I praise the LORD
in the company of good men, in the whole congregation.
Great are the doings of the LORD;   2
  all men study them for their delight.
His acts are full of majesty and splendour;   3
  righteousness is his for ever.
He has won a name by his marvellous deeds;   4
  the LORD is gracious and compassionate.
He gives food to those who fear him,   5
  he keeps his covenant always in mind.
He showed his people what his strength could do,   6
  bestowing on them the lands of other nations.
His works are truth and justice;   7
  his precepts all stand on firm foundations,
strongly based to endure for ever,   8

[a] You shall sit: or Sit. [b] Or until or while. [c] Or reign in the midst of. [d] At birth:
or On the day of your power. [e] you were...and: or your people offered themselves
willingly; mng. of Heb. uncertain. [f] Or apparelled. [g] So...majesty: poss. rdg.; Heb.
full of corpses, he crushed. [h] So...nations: or He shall punish the nations—heaps of
corpses, broken heads—over a wide expanse.

their fabric goodness and truth.
9 He sent and redeemed his people;
he decreed that his covenant should always endure.
Holy is his name, inspiring awe.
10 The fear of the Lord is the beginning[a] of wisdom,
and they who live by it[b] grow in understanding.
Praise will be his for ever.

112

1 O praise the Lord.

Happy is the man who fears the Lord
and finds great joy in his commandments.
2 His descendants shall be the mightiest in the land,
a blessed generation of good men.
3 His house shall be full of wealth and riches;
righteousness shall be his for ever.
4 He is gracious, compassionate, good,
a beacon in darkness for honest men.
5 It is right for a man to be gracious in his lending,
to order his affairs with judgement.
6 Nothing shall ever shake him;
his goodness shall be remembered for all time.
7 Bad news shall have no terrors for him,
because his heart is steadfast, trusting in the Lord.
8 His confidence is strongly based, he will have no fear;
and in the end he will gloat over his enemies.
9 He gives freely to the poor;
righteousness shall be his for ever;
in honour he carries his head high.
10 The wicked man shall see it with rising anger
and grind his teeth in despair;
the hopes of wicked men shall come to nothing.

113

1 O praise the Lord.

Praise the Lord, you that are his servants,
praise the name of the Lord.
2 Blessed be the name of the Lord
now and evermore.

[a] *Or* chief part. [b] *So Sept.; Heb.* them.

From the rising of the sun to its setting   3
     may the LORD's name be praised.
High is the LORD above all nations,   4
     his glory above the heavens.
There is none like the LORD our God   5–6
     in heaven or on earth,
who sets his throne so high
     but deigns to look down so low;
who lifts the weak out of the dust   7
     and raises the poor from the dunghill,
giving them a place among princes,   8
     among the princes of his people;
who makes the woman in a childless house   9
     a happy mother of children.*a*

114

O praise the LORD.*b*   1

When Israel came out of Egypt,
     Jacob from a people of outlandish speech,
Judah became his sanctuary,   2
     Israel his dominion.
The sea looked and ran away;   3
     Jordan turned back.
The mountains skipped like rams,   4
     the hills like young sheep.
What was it, sea? Why did you run?   5
     Jordan, why did you turn back?
Why, mountains, did you skip like rams,   6
     and you, hills, like young sheep?
Dance, O earth, at the presence of the Lord,   7
     at the presence of the God of Jacob,
who turned the rock into a pool of water,   8
     the granite cliff into a fountain.

115

Not to us, O LORD, not to us,   1
     but to thy name ascribe the glory,
     for thy true love and for thy constancy.

[*a*] O praise the LORD *transposed to the beginning of Ps. 114.*   [*b*] *See note on Ps. 113. 9.*

2   Why do the nations ask,
                   'Where then is their God?'

3   Our God is in high[a] heaven;
                   he does whatever pleases him.

4   Their idols are silver and gold,
                   made by the hands of men.

5   They have mouths that cannot speak,
                   and eyes that cannot see;

6   they have ears that cannot hear,
                   nostrils, and cannot smell;

7   with their hands they cannot feel,
                   with their feet they cannot walk,
                   and no sound comes from their throats.

8   Their makers grow to be like them,
                   and so do all who trust in them.

9   But Israel trusts in the LORD;
                   he is their helper and their shield.

10   The house of Aaron trusts in the LORD;
                   he is their helper and their shield.

11   Those who fear the LORD trust in the LORD;
                   he is their helper and their shield.

12   The LORD remembers us, and he will bless us;
                   he will bless the house of Israel,
                   he will bless the house of Aaron.

13   The LORD will bless all who fear him,
                   high and low alike.

14   May the LORD give you increase,
                   both you and your sons.

15   You are blessed by the LORD,
                   the LORD who made heaven and earth.

16   The heavens, they are the LORD's;
                   the earth he has given to all mankind.

17   It is not the dead who praise the LORD,
                   not those who go down into silence;

18   but we, the living,[b] bless the LORD,
                   now and for evermore.

               O praise the LORD.

[a] high: *so Sept.; Heb. om.*   [b] the living: *so Sept.; Heb. om.*

116

I love the LORD, for he has heard me   1
  and listens to my prayer;
for he has given me a hearing   2
  whenever I have cried to him.
The cords of death bound me,   3
  Sheol held me in its grip.
Anguish and torment held me fast;
  so I invoked the LORD by name,   4
'Deliver me, O LORD, I beseech thee;
  for I am thy slave.'*a*
Gracious is the LORD and righteous,   5
  our God is full of compassion.
The LORD preserves the simple-hearted;   6
  I was brought low and he saved me.
Be at rest once more, my heart,   7
  for the LORD has showered gifts upon you.
He has*b* rescued me from death   8
  and my feet from stumbling.*c*
I will walk in the presence of the LORD   9
  in the land of the living.

I was sure that I should be swept away,   10
  and my distress was bitter.
In panic I cried,   11
  'How faithless all men are!'
How can I repay the LORD   12
  for all his gifts to me?
I will take in my hands the cup of salvation   13
  and invoke the LORD by name.
I will pay my vows to the LORD   14
  in the presence of all his people.
A precious thing in the LORD's sight   15
  is the death of those who die faithful to him.
*d*I am thy slave, thy slave-girl's son;   16
  thou hast undone the bonds that bound me.
To thee will I bring a thank-offering   17
  and invoke the LORD by name.
I will pay my vows to the LORD   18
  in the presence of all his people,

[a] for...slave: *transposed from the beginning of verse 16; Heb. adds* O LORD. [b] *So Sept.;*
Heb. Thou hast. [c] *So Pesh.; Heb. adds* my eyes from weeping. [d] *Prob. rdg.; Heb.*
prefixes For I am thy slave, O LORD; *see note on verse 4.*

19
     in the courts of the Lord's house,
       in the midst of you, Jerusalem.

     O praise the Lord.

117

1
     Praise the Lord, all nations,
       extol him, all you peoples;
2
     for his love protecting us is strong,
       the Lord's constancy is everlasting.

     O praise the Lord.

118

1
     It is good to give thanks to the Lord,
       for his love endures for ever.
2
     Declare it, house of[a] Israel:
       his love endures for ever.
3
     Declare it, house of Aaron:
       his love endures for ever.
4
     Declare it, you that fear the Lord:
       his love endures for ever.
5
     When in my distress I called to the Lord,
       his answer was to set me free.
6
     The Lord is on my side, I have no fear;
       what can man do to me?
7
     The Lord is on my side, he is my helper,
       and I shall gloat over my enemies.
8
     It is better to find refuge in the Lord
       than to trust in men.
9
     It is better to find refuge in the Lord
       than to trust in princes.
10
     All nations surround me,
       but in the Lord's name I will drive them away.
11
     They surround me on this side and on that,
       but in the Lord's name I will drive them away.
12
     They surround me like bees at the honey;[b]
       they attack me, as fire attacks brushwood,
       but in the Lord's name I will drive them away.
13
     They thrust[c] hard against me so that I nearly fall;
       but the Lord has helped me.

[a] house of: *so Sept.; Heb. om.*   [b] at the honey: *so Sept.; Heb. om.*   [c] *So Sept.; Heb.* Thou dost thrust.

The LORD is my refuge and defence,   14
    and he has become my deliverer.
Hark! Shouts of deliverance   15
    in the camp of the victors[a]!
With his right hand the LORD does mighty deeds,
    the right hand of the LORD raises up.[b]   16
I shall not die but live   17
    to proclaim the works of the LORD.
The LORD did indeed chasten me,   18
    but he did not surrender me to Death.

Open to me the gates of victory;[c]   19
    I will enter by them and praise the LORD.
This is the gate of the LORD;   20
    the victors[a] shall make their entry through it.
I will praise thee, for thou hast answered me   21
    and hast become my deliverer.
The stone which the builders rejected   22
    has become the chief corner-stone.
This is the LORD's doing;   23
    it is marvellous in our eyes.
This is the day on which the LORD has acted:[d]   24
    let us exult and rejoice in it.
We pray thee, O LORD, deliver us;   25
    we pray thee, O LORD, send us prosperity.
Blessed in the name of the LORD are all who come;   26
    we bless you from the house of the LORD.
The LORD is God; he has given light to us,   27
the ordered line of pilgrims[e] by the horns of the altar.
Thou art my God and I will praise thee;   28
    my God, I will exalt thee.
It is good to give thanks to the LORD,   29
    for his love endures for ever.

119

Happy are they whose life is blameless,   1
    who conform to the law of the LORD.
Happy are they who obey his instruction,   2
    who set their heart on finding him;
who have done no wrong   3

[a] *Or* righteous. [b] *So some MSS.; others repeat* with his right hand the LORD does
mighty deeds. [c] *Or* righteousness. [d] *Or* which the LORD has made. [e] the...
pilgrims: *so Scroll; Heb.* bind the pilgrimage with cords.

and have lived according to his will.
4   Thou, Lord, hast laid down thy precepts
         for men to keep them faithfully.
5   If only I might hold a steady course,
         keeping thy statutes!
6   I shall never be put to shame
         if I fix my eyes on thy commandments.
7   I will praise thee in sincerity of heart
         as I learn thy just decrees.
8   Thy statutes will I keep faithfully;
         O do not leave me forsaken.

9   How shall a young man steer an honest course?
         By holding to thy word.
10   With all my heart I strive to find thee;
         let me not stray from thy commandments.
11   I treasure thy promise in my heart,
         for fear that I might sin against thee.
12   Blessed art thou, O Lord;
         teach me thy statutes.
13   I say them over, one by one,
         the decrees that thou hast proclaimed.
14   I have found more joy along the path of thy instruction
         than in*a* any kind of wealth.
15   I will meditate on thy precepts
         and keep thy paths ever before my eyes.
16   In thy statutes I find continual delight;
         I will not forget thy word.

17   Grant this to me, thy servant: let me live
         and, living, keep thy word.
18   Take the veil from my eyes, that I may see
         the marvels that spring from thy law.
19   I am but a stranger here on earth,*b*
         do not hide thy commandments from me.
20   My heart pines with longing
         day and night for thy decrees.
21   The proud have felt thy rebuke;
         cursed are those who turn from thy commandments.
22   Set me free from scorn and insult,
         for I have obeyed thy instruction.
23   The powers that be sit scheming together against me;
         but I, thy servant, will study thy statutes.

[a] So *Pesh.; Heb.* as in.   [b] *Or* in the land.

Thy instruction is my continual delight;   24
  I turn to it for counsel.

I lie prone in the dust;   25
  grant me life according to thy word.
I tell thee all I have done and thou dost answer me;   26
  teach me thy statutes.
Show me the way set out in thy precepts,   27
  and I will meditate on thy wonders.
I cannot rest for misery;   28
  renew my strength in accordance with thy word.
Keep falsehood far from me   29
  and grant me the grace of living by thy law.
I have chosen the path of truth   30
  and have set thy decrees before me.
I hold fast to thy instruction;   31
  O Lord, let me not be put to shame.
I will run the course set out in thy commandments,   32
  for they gladden my heart.

Teach me, O Lord, the way set out in thy statutes,   33
  and in keeping them I shall find my reward.
Give me the insight to obey thy law   34
  and to keep it with all my heart;
make me walk in the path of thy commandments,   35
  for that is my desire.
Dispose my heart toward thy instruction   36
  and not toward ill-gotten gains;
turn away my eyes from all that is vile,   37
  grant me life by thy word.[a]
Fulfil thy promise for thy servant,   38
  the promise made to those who fear thee.
Turn away the censure which I dread,   39
  for thy decrees are good.
How I long for thy precepts!   40
  In thy righteousness grant me life.

Thy love never fails; let it light on me, O Lord,   41
  and thy deliverance, for that was thy promise;
then I shall have my answer to the man who taunts me,   42
  because I trust in thy word.
Rob me not of my power to speak the truth,[b]   43
  for I put my hope in thy decrees.

[a] by thy word: *so some MSS.; others* in thy ways. [b] *So Pesh.; Heb. adds* very much.

44	I will heed thy law continually, for ever and ever;
45	I walk in freedom wherever I will, because I have studied thy precepts.
46	I will speak of thy instruction before kings and will not be ashamed;
47	in thy commandments I find continuing delight; I love them with all my heart.*a*
48	I will welcome thy commandments*b* and will meditate on thy statutes.
49	Remember the word spoken to me, thy servant, on which thou hast taught me to fix my hope.
50	In time of trouble my consolation is this, that thy promise has given me life.
51	Proud men treat me with insolent scorn, but I do not swerve from thy law.
52	I have cherished thy decrees all my life long, and in them I find consolation, O LORD.
53	Gusts of anger seize me as I think of evil men who forsake thy law.
54	Thy statutes are the theme of my song*c* wherever I make my home.
55	In the night I remember thy name, O LORD, and dwell upon thy law.
56	This is true of me, that I have kept thy precepts.
57	Thou, LORD, art all I have;*d* I have promised to keep thy word.
58	With all my heart I have tried to please thee; fulfil thy promise and be gracious to me.
59	I have thought much about the course of my life and always turned back to thy instruction;
60	I have never delayed but always made haste to keep thy commandments.
61	Bands of evil men close round me, but I do not forget thy law.
62	At midnight I rise to give thee thanks for the justice of thy decrees.
63	I keep company with all who fear thee, with all who follow thy precepts.

[a] with all my heart: *prob. rdg., cp. Sept.; Heb. om.*   [b] *Prob. rdg.; Heb. adds* which I love.
[c] the theme of my song: *or* wonderful to me.   [d] all I have: *lit.* my portion.

The earth is full of thy never-failing love;   64
  O Lord, teach me thy statutes.

Thou hast shown thy servant much kindness,   65
  fulfilling thy word, O Lord.
Give me insight, give me knowledge,   66
  for I put my trust in thy commandments.
I went astray before I was punished;   67
  but now I pay heed to thy promise.
Thou art good and thou doest good;   68
  teach me thy statutes.
Proud men blacken my name with lies,   69
  yet I follow thy precepts with all my heart;
their hearts are thick and gross;   70
  but I continually delight in thy law.
How good it is for me to have been punished,   71
  to school me in thy statutes!
The law thou hast ordained means more to me   72
  than a fortune in gold and silver.

Thy hands moulded me and made me what I am;   73
  show me how I may learn thy commandments.
Let all who fear thee be glad when they see me,   74
  because I hope for the fulfilment of thy word.
I know, O Lord, that thy decrees are just   75
  and even in punishing thou keepest faith with me.
Let thy never-failing love console me,   76
  as thou hast promised me, thy servant.
Extend thy compassion to me, that I may live;   77
  for thy law is my continual delight.
Put the proud to shame, for with their lies they wrong me; 78
  but I will meditate on thy precepts.
Let all who fear thee turn to me,   79
  all who cherish thy instruction.
Let me give my whole heart to thy statutes,   80
  so that I am not put to shame.

I long with all my heart for thy deliverance,   81
  hoping for the fulfilment of thy word;
my sight grows dim with looking for thy promise   82
  and still I cry, 'When wilt thou comfort me?'
Though I shrivel like a wine-skin in the smoke,   83
  I do not forget thy statutes.
How long has thy servant to wait   84
  for thee to fulfil thy decree against my persecutors?

85 Proud men who flout thy law
spread tales about me.
86 Help me, for they hound me with their lies,
but thy commandments all stand for ever.
87 They had almost swept me from the earth,
but I did not forsake thy precepts;
88 grant me life, as thy love is unchanging,
that I may follow all thy instruction.

89 Eternal is thy word, O Lord,
planted firm in heaven.
90 Thy promise*a* endures for all time,
stable as the earth which thou hast fixed.
91 This day, as ever, thy decrees stand fast;
for all things serve thee.
92 If thy law had not been my continual delight,
I should have perished in all my troubles;
93 never will I forget thy precepts,
for through them thou hast given me life.
94 I am thine; O save me,
for I have pondered thy precepts.
95 Evil men lie in wait to destroy me;
but I will give thought to thy instruction.
96 I see that all things come to an end,
but thy commandment has no limit.

97 O how I love thy law!
It is my study all day long.
98 Thy commandments are mine for ever;
through them I am wiser than my enemies.
99 I have more insight than all my teachers,
for thy instruction is my study;
100 I have more wisdom than the old,
because I have kept thy precepts.
101 I set no foot on any evil path
in my obedience to thy word;
102 I do not swerve from thy decrees,
for thou thyself hast been my teacher.
103 How sweet is thy promise in my mouth,
sweeter on my tongue than honey!
104 From thy precepts I learn wisdom;
therefore I hate the paths of falsehood.

[a] *Prob. rdg.; Heb.* Thy constancy.

Thy word is a lamp to guide my feet 105
   and a light on my path;
I have bound myself by oath and solemn vow 106
   to keep thy just decrees.
I am cruelly afflicted; 107
   O Lord, revive me and make good thy word.
Accept, O Lord, the willing tribute of my lips 108
   and teach me thy decrees.
Every day I take my life in my hands, 109
   yet I never forget thy law.
Evil men have set traps for me, 110
   but I do not stray from thy precepts.
Thy instruction is my everlasting inheritance; 111
   it is the joy of my heart.
I am resolved to fulfil thy statutes; 112
   they are a reward that never fails.

I hate men who are not single-minded, 113
   but I love thy law.
Thou art my shield and hiding-place; 114
   I hope for the fulfilment of thy word.
Go, you evildoers, and leave me to myself, 115
   that I may keep the commandments of my God.
Support me as thou hast promised, that I may live; 116
   do not disappoint my hope.
Sustain me, that I may see deliverance; 117
   so shall I always be occupied with thy statutes.
Thou dost reject those who stray from thy statutes, 118
   for their talk is all malice and lies.
In thy sight all the wicked on earth are scum;[a] 119
   therefore I love thy instruction.
The dread of thee makes my flesh creep, 120
   and I stand in awe of thy decrees.

I have done what is just and right; 121
   thou wilt not abandon me to my oppressors.
Stand surety for the welfare of thy servant; 122
   let not the proud oppress me.[b]
My sight grows dim with looking for thy deliverance 123
   and waiting for thy righteous promise.
In all thy dealings with me, Lord, show thy true love 124
   and teach me thy statutes.

[a] In...scum: *so some MSS.; others* Thou hast made an end of all the wicked on earth like scum. [b] oppress me: *or* charge me falsely.

125	I am thy servant; give me insight to understand thy instruction.
126	It is time to act, O LORD; for men have broken thy law.
127	Truly I love thy commandments more than the finest gold.
128	It is by thy precepts[a] that I find the right way; I hate the paths of falsehood.
129	Thy instruction is wonderful; therefore I gladly keep it.
130	Thy word is revealed, and all is light; it gives understanding even to the untaught.
131	I pant, I thirst, longing for thy commandments.
132	Turn to me and be gracious, as thou hast decreed for those who love thy name.
133	Make my step firm according to thy promise, and let no wrong have the mastery over me.
134	Set me free from man's oppression, that I may observe thy precepts.
135	Let thy face shine upon thy servant and teach me thy statutes.
136	My eyes stream with tears because men do not heed thy law.
137	How just thou art, O LORD! How straight and true are thy decrees!
138	How just is the instruction thou givest! It is fixed firm and sure.
139	I am speechless with resentment, for my enemies have forgotten thy words.
140	Thy promise has been tested through and through, and thy servant loves it.
141	I may be despised and of little account, but I do not forget thy precepts.
142	Thy justice is an everlasting justice, and thy law is truth.
143	Though I am oppressed by trouble and anxiety, thy commandments are my continual delight.
144	Thy instruction is ever just; give me understanding that I may live.

[a] It...precepts: *prob. rdg.*, *cp. Sept.*; *Heb.* All precepts of all.

I call with my whole heart; answer me, LORD. 145
    I will keep thy statutes.
I call to thee; O save me 146
    that I may heed thy instruction.
I rise before dawn and cry for help; 147
    I hope for the fulfilment of thy word.
Before the midnight watch also my eyes are open 148
    for meditation on thy promise.
Hear me, as thy love is unchanging, 149
    and give me life, O LORD, by thy decree.
My pursuers in their malice are close behind me, 150
    but they are far from thy law.
Yet thou art near, O LORD, 151
    and all thy commandments are true.
I have long known from thy instruction 152
    that thou hast given it eternal foundations.

See in what trouble I am and set me free, 153
    for I do not forget thy law.
Be thou my advocate and win release for me; 154
    true to thy promise, give me life.
Such deliverance is beyond the reach of wicked men, 155
    because they do not ponder thy statutes.
Great is thy compassion, O LORD; 156
    grant me life by thy decree.
Many are my persecutors and enemies, 157
    but I have not swerved from thy instruction.
I was cut to the quick when I saw traitors 158
    who had no regard for thy promise.
See how I love thy precepts, O LORD! 159
    Grant me life, as thy love is unchanging.
Thy word is founded in truth, 160
    and thy just decrees are everlasting.

The powers that be persecute me without cause, 161
    yet my heart thrills at thy word.
I am jubilant over thy promise, 162
    like a man carrying off much booty.
Falsehood I detest and loathe, 163
    but I love thy law.
Seven times a day I praise thee 164
    for the justice of thy decrees.
Peace is the reward of those who love thy law; 165
    no pitfalls beset their path.

166   I hope for thy deliverance, O Lord,
      and I fulfil thy commandments;
167   gladly I heed thy instruction
      and love it greatly.
168   I heed thy precepts and thy instruction,
      for all my life lies open before thee.

169   Let my cry of joy reach thee, O Lord;
      give me understanding of[a] thy word.
170   Let my supplication reach thee;
      be true to thy promise and save me.
171   Let thy praise pour from my lips,
      because thou teachest me thy statutes;
172   let the music of thy promises be on my tongue,
      for thy commandments are justice itself.
173   Let thy hand be prompt to help me,
      for I have chosen thy precepts;
174   I long for thy deliverance, O Lord,
      and thy law is my continual delight.
175   Let me live and I will praise thee;
      let thy decrees be my support.
176   I have strayed like a lost sheep;
      come, search for thy servant,
      for I have not forgotten thy commandments.

120

1   I called to the Lord in my distress,
      and he answered me.
2   'O Lord,' I cried, 'save me from lying lips
      and from the tongue of slander.'
3   What has he in store for you, slanderous tongue?
      What more has he for you?
4   Nothing but a warrior's sharp arrows
      or red-hot charcoal.[b]
5   Hard is my lot, exiled in Meshech,
      dwelling by the tents of Kedar.
6   All the time that I dwelt
      among men who hated peace,
7   I sought peace; but whenever I spoke of it,
      they were for war.

[a] of: *so some MSS.; others* in fulfilment of.   [b] *Lit.* or live coals of desert broom.

121

If I lift up my eyes to the hills,   1
    where shall I find help?
Help*a* comes only from the LORD,   2
    maker of heaven and earth.
How could he let your foot stumble?   3
    How could he, your guardian, sleep?
The guardian of Israel   4
    never slumbers, never sleeps.
The LORD is your guardian,   5
    your defence at your right hand;
the sun will not strike you by day   6
    nor the moon by night.
The LORD will guard you against all evil;   7
    he will guard you, body and soul.
The LORD will guard your going and your coming,   8
    now and for evermore.

122

I rejoiced when they said to me,   1
    'Let us go to the house of the LORD.'
Now we stand within your gates,   2
    O Jerusalem:
Jerusalem that is built to be a city   3
    where people come together in unity;
to which the tribes resort, the tribes of the LORD,   4
    to give thanks to the LORD himself,
    the bounden duty of Israel.
For in her are set the thrones of justice,   5
    the thrones of the house of David.
Pray for the peace of Jerusalem: 6
    'May those who love you prosper;
peace be within your ramparts   7
    and prosperity in your palaces.'
For the sake of these my brothers and my friends,   8
    I will say, 'Peace be within you.'
For the sake of the house of the LORD our God   9
    I will pray for your good.

        [a] *Lit.* My help.

123

1   I lift my eyes to thee
    whose throne is in heaven.
2   As the eyes of a slave follow his master's hand
    or the eyes of a slave-girl her mistress,
    so our eyes are turned to the Lord our God
    waiting for kindness from him.
3   Deal kindly with us, O Lord, deal kindly,
    for we have suffered insult enough;
4   too long have we had to suffer
    the insults of the wealthy,
    the scorn of proud men.

124

1   If the Lord had not been on our side,
    Israel may now say,
2   if the Lord had not been on our side
    when they assailed us,
3   they would have swallowed us alive
    when their anger was roused against us.
4   The waters would have carried us away
    and the torrent swept over us;
5   over us would have swept
    the seething waters.
6   Blessed be the Lord, who did not leave us
    to be the prey between their teeth.
7   We have escaped like a bird
    from the fowler's trap;
    the trap broke, and so we escaped.
8   Our help is in the name of the Lord,
    maker of heaven and earth.

125

1   Those who trust in the Lord are like Mount Zion,
which cannot be shaken but stands fast for ever.
2   As the hills enfold Jerusalem,
so the Lord enfolds his people, now and evermore.
3   The sceptre of wickedness shall surely find no home
    in the land allotted to the righteous,
so that the righteous shall not set
    their hands to injustice.

Do good, O Lord, to those who are good   4
   and to those who are upright in heart.
But those who turn aside into crooked ways,   5
may the Lord destroy them, as he destroys all evildoers!

Peace be upon Israel!

126

When the Lord turned the tide of Zion's fortune,   1
   we were like men who had found new health.[a]
Our mouths were full of laughter   2
   and our tongues sang aloud for joy.
Then word went round among the nations,
   'The Lord has done great things for them.'
Great things indeed the Lord then did for us,   3
   and we rejoiced.

Turn once again our fortune, Lord,   4
   as streams return in the dry south.[b]
Those who sow in tears   5
   shall reap with songs of joy.
A man may go out weeping,   6
   carrying his bag of seed;
but he will come back with songs of joy,
   carrying home his sheaves.

127

Unless the Lord builds the house,   1
   its builders will have toiled in vain.
Unless the Lord keeps watch over a city,
   in vain the watchman stands on guard.
In vain you rise up early   2
   and go late to rest,
toiling for the bread you eat;
   he supplies the need of those he loves.[c]
Sons are a gift from the Lord   3
   and children a reward from him.
Like arrows in the hand of a fighting man   4
   are the sons of a man's youth.
Happy is the man   5
   who has his quiver full of them;

[a] like...health: *or* like dreamers.   [b] dry south: *Heb.* Negeb.   [c] *Prob. rdg.; Heb. adds an unintelligible word.*

such men shall not be put to shame
   when they confront their enemies in court.[a]

128

1 Happy are all who fear the LORD,
   who live according to his will.
2 You shall eat the fruit of your own labours,
   you shall be happy and you shall prosper.
3 Your wife shall be like a fruitful vine
   in the heart of your house;
your sons shall be like olive-shoots
   round about your table.
4 This is the blessing in store for the man
   who fears the LORD.
5 May the LORD bless you from Zion;
   may you share the prosperity of Jerusalem
all the days of your life,
6   and live to see your children's children!

   Peace be upon Israel!

129

1 Often since I was young have men attacked me—
   let Israel now say—
2 often since I was young have men attacked me,
   but never have they prevailed.
3 They scored my back with scourges,
   like ploughmen driving long furrows.
4 Yet the LORD in his justice
   has cut me loose from the bonds of the wicked.
5 Let all enemies of Zion
   be thrown back in shame;
6 let them be like grass growing on the roof,
   which withers before it can shoot,
7 which will never fill a mower's hand
   nor yield an armful for the harvester,
8 so that passers-by will never say to them,
   'The blessing of the LORD be upon you!
   We bless you in the name of the LORD.'

[a] *Lit.* in the gate.

130

Out of the depths have I called to thee, O LORD;   1
    Lord, hear my cry.   2
Let thy ears be attentive
    to my plea for mercy.
If thou, LORD, shouldest keep account of sins,   3
    who, O Lord, could hold up his head?
But in thee is forgiveness,   4
    and therefore thou art revered.
I wait for the LORD with all my soul,   5
    I hope for the fulfilment of his word.
My soul waits*[a]* for the Lord   6
    more eagerly than watchmen for the morning.
Like men who watch for the morning,
    O Israel, look for the LORD.   7
For in the LORD is love unfailing,
    and great is his power to set men free.
He alone will set Israel free   8
    from all their sins.

131

O LORD, my heart is not proud,   1
    nor are my eyes haughty;
I do not busy myself with great matters
    or things too marvellous for me.
No; I submit myself, I account myself lowly   2
    as a weaned child clinging to its mother.*[b]*
O Israel, look for the LORD   3
    now and evermore.

132

O LORD, remember David   1
    in the time of his adversity,
how he swore to the LORD   2
    and made a vow to the Mighty One of Jacob:
'I will not enter my house   3
    nor will I mount my bed,
I will not close my eyes in sleep   4
    or my eyelids in slumber,

[a] waits: *transposed from after* the LORD *in verse 5.* [b] *Prob. rdg.; Heb. adds* as a weaned child clinging to me.

5   until I find a sanctuary for the L<small>ORD</small>,
         a dwelling for the Mighty One of Jacob.'
6   We heard of it in Ephrathah;
         we came upon it in the region of Jaar.
7   Let us enter his dwelling,
         let us fall in worship at his footstool.
8   Arise, O L<small>ORD</small>, and come to thy resting-place,
         thou and the ark of thy power.
9   Let thy priests be clothed in righteousness
         and let thy loyal servants shout for joy.
10   For thy servant David's sake
         reject not thy anointed king.
11   The L<small>ORD</small> swore to David
         an oath which he will not break:
         'A prince of your own line
         will I set upon your throne.
12   If your sons keep my covenant
         and heed the teaching that I give them,
         their sons in turn for all time
         shall sit upon your throne.'
13   For the L<small>ORD</small> has chosen Zion
         and desired it for his home:
14   'This is my resting-place for ever;
         here will I make my home, for such is my desire.
15   I will richly bless her destitute[a]
         and satisfy her needy with bread.
16   With salvation will I clothe her priests;
         her loyal servants shall shout for joy.
17   There will I renew the line of[b] David's house
         and light a lamp for my anointed king;
18   his enemies will I clothe with shame,
         but on his head shall be a shining crown.'

133

1   How good it is and how pleasant
         for brothers to live[c] together!
2   It is fragrant as oil poured upon the head
         and falling over the beard,
         Aaron's beard, when the oil runs down
         over the collar of his vestments.

[a] her destitute: *prob. rdg.; Heb.* her provisions.   [b] renew the line of: *lit.* make a horn shoot for.   [c] *Or* to worship.

It is like the dew of Hermon falling   3
    upon the hills of Zion.
There the LORD bestows his blessing,
    life for evermore.

134

Come, bless the LORD,   1
    all you servants of the LORD,
who stand night after night
    in the house of the LORD.
Lift up your hands in the sanctuary   2
    and bless the LORD.
The LORD, maker of heaven and earth,   3
    bless you from Zion!

135

O praise the LORD.   1

Praise the name of the LORD;
    praise him, you servants of the LORD,
who stand in the house of the LORD,   2
    in the temple courts of our God.
Praise the LORD, for that is good;[a]   3
    honour his name with psalms, for that is pleasant.
The LORD has chosen Jacob to be his own   4
    and Israel as his special treasure.
I know that the LORD is great,   5
    that our Lord is above all gods.
Whatever the LORD pleases,   6
    that he does, in heaven and on earth,
    in the sea, in the depths of ocean.
He brings up the mist from the ends of the earth,   7
he opens rifts[b] for the rain,
and brings the wind out of his storehouses.
He struck down all the first-born in Egypt,   8
    both man and beast.
In Egypt[c] he sent signs and portents   9
    against Pharaoh and all his subjects.
He struck down mighty nations   10
    and slew great kings,

[a] So Pesh.; Heb. for the LORD is good. [b] Prob. rdg.; Heb. lightnings. [c] Lit. In your midst, Egypt.

11	Sihon king of the Amorites, Og the king of Bashan, and all the princes of Canaan,
12	and gave their land to Israel, to Israel his people as their patrimony.
13	O Lord, thy name endures for ever; thy renown, O Lord, shall last for all generations.
14	The Lord will give his people justice and have compassion on his servants.
15	The gods of the nations are idols of silver and gold, made by the hands of men.
16	They have mouths that cannot speak and eyes that cannot see;
17	they have ears that do not hear, and there is no breath in their nostrils.[a]
18	Their makers grow like them, and so do all who trust in them.
19	O house of Israel, bless the Lord; O house of Aaron, bless the Lord.
20	O house of Levi, bless the Lord; you who fear the Lord, bless the Lord.
21	Blessed from Zion be the Lord who dwells in Jerusalem.

O praise the Lord.

136

1	It is good to give thanks to the Lord, for his love endures for ever.
2	Give thanks to the God of gods; his love endures for ever.
3	Give thanks to the Lord of lords; his love endures for ever.
4	Alone he works great marvels; his love endures for ever.
5	In wisdom he made the heavens; his love endures for ever.
6	He laid the earth upon the waters; his love endures for ever.
7	He made the great lights, his love endures for ever,
8	the sun to rule by day, his love endures for ever,

[a] *Prob. rdg.; Heb.* mouths.

the moon and the stars to rule by night;   9
   his love endures for ever.
He struck down the first-born of the Egyptians,   10
   his love endures for ever,
and brought Israel from among them;   11
   his love endures for ever.
With strong hand and outstretched arm,   12
   his love endures for ever,
he divided the Red Sea in two,   13
   his love endures for ever,
and made Israel pass through it,   14
   his love endures for ever;
but Pharaoh and his host he swept into the sea;   15
   his love endures for ever.
He led his people through the wilderness;   16
   his love endures for ever.
He struck down great kings;   17
   his love endures for ever.
He slew mighty kings,   18
   his love endures for ever,
Sihon king of the Amorites,   19
   his love endures for ever,
and Og the king of Bashan;   20
   his love endures for ever.
He gave their land to Israel,   21
   his love endures for ever,
to Israel his servant as their patrimony;   22
   his love endures for ever.
He remembered us when we were cast down,   23
   his love endures for ever,
and rescued us from our enemies;   24
   his love endures for ever.
He gives food to all his creatures;   25
   his love endures for ever.
Give thanks to the God of heaven,   26
   for his love endures for ever.

137

By the rivers of Babylon we sat down and wept   1
   when we remembered Zion.
There on the willow-trees[a]   2

     [a] *Or* poplars.

we hung up our harps,
3   for there those who carried us off
          demanded music and singing,
       and our captors called on us to be merry:
          'Sing us one of the songs of Zion.'
4   How could we sing the LORD's song
          in a foreign land?

5   If I forget you, O Jerusalem,
          let my right hand wither away;
6   let my tongue cling to the roof of my mouth
          if I do not remember you,
       if I do not set Jerusalem
          above my highest joy.
7   Remember, O LORD, against the people of Edom
          the day of Jerusalem's fall,
       when they said, 'Down with it, down with it,
          down to its very foundations!'
8   O Babylon, Babylon[a] the destroyer,
          happy the man who repays you
          for all that you did to us!
9   Happy is he who shall seize your children
          and dash them against the rock.

138

1   I will praise thee, O LORD,[b] with all my heart;
          boldly, O God, will I sing psalms to thee.[c]
2   I will bow down towards thy holy temple,
       for thy love and faithfulness I will praise thy name;
       for thou hast made thy promise wide as the heavens.
3   When I called to thee thou didst answer me
          and make me bold and valiant-hearted.
4   Let all the kings of the earth praise[d] thee, O LORD,
          when they hear the words thou hast spoken;
5   and let them sing of[e] the LORD's ways,
          for great is the glory of the LORD.
6   For the LORD, high as he is, cares for the lowly,
          and from afar he humbles the proud.
7   Though I walk among foes thou dost preserve my life,

[a] O Babylon, Babylon: *lit.* O daughter of Babylon.   [b] O LORD: *so some MSS.; others om.*
[c] boldly...thee: *or* I will sing psalms to thee before the gods.   [d] *Or* confess.   [e] *Or*
walk in.

exerting thy power against the rage of my enemies,
   and with thy right hand thou savest me.
The LORD will accomplish his purpose for me.   8
   Thy true love, O LORD, endures for ever;
   leave not thy work unfinished.

139

LORD, thou hast examined me and knowest me.   1
Thou knowest all, whether I sit down or rise up;   2
   thou hast discerned my thoughts from afar.
Thou hast traced my journey and my resting places,   3
   and art familiar with all my paths.
For there is not a word on my tongue   4
   but thou, LORD, knowest them all.*a*
Thou hast kept close guard before me and behind   5
   and hast spread thy hand over me.
Such knowledge is beyond my understanding,   6
   so high that I cannot reach it.
Where can I escape from thy spirit?   7
   Where can I flee from thy presence?
If I climb up to heaven, thou art there;   8
if I make my bed in Sheol, again I find thee.
If I take my flight to the frontiers of the morning   9
   or dwell at the limit of the western sea,
even there thy hand will meet me   10
   and thy right hand will hold me fast.
If I say, 'Surely darkness will steal over me,   11
   night will close around me',*b*
darkness is no darkness for thee   12
   and night is luminous as day;
   to thee both dark and light are one.

Thou it was who didst fashion my inward parts;   13
thou didst knit me together in my mother's womb.
I will praise thee, for thou dost fill me with awe;   14
wonderful thou art,*c* and wonderful thy works.
Thou knowest me through and through:
   my body is no mystery to thee,   15
how I was secretly kneaded into shape
   and patterned in the depths of the earth.

[a] For...them all: *or* If there is any offence on my tongue, thou, LORD, knowest it all.
[b] night...me: *so Scroll; Heb.* and the day around me turn to night.   [c] *So Sept.; Heb.*
I am.

16   Thou didst see my limbs unformed in the womb,
         and in thy book they are all recorded;
         day by day they were fashioned,
         not one of them was late in growing.*a*
17   How deep I find thy thoughts, O God,
         how inexhaustible their themes!
18   Can I count them? They outnumber the grains of sand;
         to finish the count, my years must equal thine.

19   O God, if only thou wouldst slay the wicked!
         If those men of blood would but leave me in peace—
20   those who provoke thee*b* with deliberate evil
         and rise*c* in vicious rebellion against thee!
21   How I hate them, O Lord, that hate thee!
         I am cut to the quick when they oppose thee;
22   I hate them with undying hatred;
         I hold them all my enemies.

23   Examine me, O God, and know my thoughts;
         test me, and understand my misgivings.
24   Watch lest I follow any path that grieves thee;
         guide me in the ancient*d* ways.

140

1   Rescue me, O Lord, from evil men;
         keep me safe from violent men,
2   whose heads are full of wicked schemes,
         who stir up contention day after day.
3   Their tongues are sharp as serpents' fangs;
         on their lips is spiders'*e* poison.
4   Guard me, O Lord, from wicked men;
         keep me safe from violent men,
         who plan to thrust me out of the way.
5   Arrogant men set hidden traps for me,
         rogues spread their nets
         and lay snares for me along the path.
6   I said, 'O Lord, thou art my God;
         O Lord, hear my plea for mercy.
7   O Lord God, stronghold of my safety,
         thou hast shielded my head in the day of battle.
8-9   Frustrate, O Lord, their designs against me;

[a] was late in growing: *prob. rdg.; Heb. om.*   [b] *So one form of Sept.; Heb.* speak of thee.
[c] rise: *so Scroll; Heb. obscure.*   [d] *Or* everlasting.   [e] *Mng. of Heb. word uncertain.*

never let the wicked gain their purpose.
If any of those at my table rise against me,
   let their own conspiracies be their undoing.
Let burning coals be tipped upon them;   10
   let them be plunged into the miry depths,
   never to rise again.
Slander shall find no home in the land;   11
evil and violence shall be hounded to destruction.'

I know that the LORD will give their due to the needy   12
   and justice to the downtrodden.
Righteous men will surely give thanks to thy name;   13
   the upright will worship in thy presence.

141

O LORD, I call to thee, come quickly to my aid;   1
   listen to my cry when I call to thee.
Let my prayer be like incense duly set before thee   2
   and my raised hands like the evening sacrifice.
Set a guard, O LORD, over my mouth;   3
   keep watch at the door of my lips.
Turn not my heart to sinful thoughts   4
   nor to any pursuit of evil courses.
The evildoers appal me;[a]
   not for me the delights of their table.
I would rather be buffeted by the righteous   5
   and reproved by good men.
My head shall not be anointed with the oil of wicked men,
   for that would make me a party to their crimes.
They shall founder on the rock of justice   6
   and shall learn how acceptable my words are.
Their bones shall be scattered at the mouth of Sheol,   7
   like splinters of wood or stone on the ground.
But my eyes are fixed on thee, O LORD God;   8
   thou art my refuge; leave me not unprotected.
Keep me from the trap which they have set for me,   9
   from the snares of evildoers.
Let the wicked fall into their own nets,   10
whilst I pass in safety, all alone.

         [a] appal me: *prob. rdg.; Heb.* with men.

142

1 I cry aloud to the LORD;
  to the LORD I plead aloud for mercy.

2 I pour out my complaint before him
and tell over my troubles in his presence.

3 When my spirit is faint within me,
  thou art there to watch over my steps.
In the path that I should take
  they have hidden a snare.

4 I look to my right hand,
  I find no friend by my side;
no way of escape is in sight,
  no one comes to rescue me.

5 I cry to thee, O LORD,
  and say, 'Thou art my refuge;
thou art all I have*a*
  in the land of the living.

6 Give me a hearing when I cry,
  for I am brought very low;
save me from my pursuers,
  for they are too strong for me.

7 Set me free from my prison,
  so that I may praise thy name.'
The righteous shall crown me with garlands,*b*
  when thou givest me my due reward.

143

1 LORD, hear my prayer;
be true to thyself, and listen to my pleading;
  then in thy righteousness answer me.

2 Bring not thy servant to trial before thee;
against thee no man on earth can be right.

3 An enemy has hunted me down,
  has ground my living body under foot
and plunged me into darkness like a man long dead,

4 so that my spirit fails me
  and my heart is dazed with despair.

5 I dwell upon the years long past,
  upon the memory of all that thou hast done;
  the wonders of thy creation fill my mind.

[a] all I have: *lit.* my portion.   [b] crown me with garlands: *or* crowd round me.

To thee I lift my outspread hands,   6
    athirst for thee in a thirsty land.
LORD, make haste to answer,   7
    for my spirit faints.
Do not hide thy face from me
or I shall be like those who go down to the abyss.
In the morning let me know thy true love;   8
    I have put my trust in thee.
Show me the way that I must take;
    to thee I offer all my heart.
Deliver me, LORD, from my enemies,   9
    for with thee have I sought refuge.*a*
Teach me to do thy will, for thou art my God;   10
in thy gracious kindness, show me the level road.*b*
Keep me safe, O LORD, for the honour of thy name   11
and, as thou art just, release me from my distress.
In thy love for me, reduce my enemies to silence   12
and bring destruction on all who oppress me;
    for I am thy servant.

144

Blessed is the LORD, my rock,   1
    who trains my hands for war,
    my fingers for battle;
my help that never fails, my fortress,   2
    my strong tower and my refuge,
    my shield in which I trust,
    he who puts nations*c* under my feet.

O LORD, what is man that thou carest for him?   3
What is mankind? Why give a thought to them?
Man is no more than a puff of wind,   4
    his days a passing shadow.
If thou, LORD, but tilt the heavens, down they come;   5
    touch the mountains, and they smoke.
Shoot forth thy lightning flashes, far and wide,   6
    and send thy arrows whistling.
Stretch out thy hands from on high to rescue me   7
    and snatch me from great waters.*d*

[a] with...refuge: *so one MS.; others* unto thee have I hidden. [b] road: *so many MSS.; others* land. [c] *So some MSS.; others* my people. [d] *Prob. rdg.; Heb. adds* from the power of foreign foes, (8) whose every word is false and all their oaths are perjury (*cp. verse 11*).

9   I will sing a new song to thee, O God,
          psalms to the music of a ten-stringed lute.

10   O God who gavest victory to kings
          and deliverance to thy servant David,
          rescue me from the cruel sword;

11   snatch me from the power of foreign foes,
          whose every word is false
          and all their oaths are perjury.

12   Happy*a* are we whose sons in their early prime
          stand like tall towers,
          our daughters like sculptured pillars
          at the corners of a palace.

13   Our barns are full and furnish plentiful provision;
          our sheep bear lambs in thousands upon thousands;

14   the oxen in our fields are fat and sleek;
          there is no miscarriage or untimely birth,
          no cries of distress in our public places.

15   Happy are the people in such a case as ours;
          happy the people who have the Lord for their God.

145

1   I will extol thee, O God my king,
          and bless thy name for ever and ever.

2   Every day will I bless thee
          and praise thy name for ever and ever.

3   Great is the Lord and worthy of all praise;
          his greatness is unfathomable.

4   One generation shall commend thy works to another
          and set forth thy mighty deeds.

5   My theme shall be thy marvellous works,
          the glorious splendour of thy majesty.

6   Men shall declare thy mighty acts with awe
          and tell*b* of thy great deeds.

7   They shall recite the story of thy abounding goodness
          and sing of thy righteousness with joy.

8   The Lord is gracious and compassionate,
          forbearing, and constant in his love.

9   The Lord is good to all men,
          and his tender care rests upon all his creatures.

[*a*] *Prob. rdg.; Heb.* Who.   [*b*] *and tell: prob. rdg., cp. Sept.; Heb.* I will tell.

All thy creatures praise thee, Lord,   10
  and thy servants bless thee.
They talk of the glory of thy kingdom   11
  and tell of thy might,
they proclaim to their fellows how mighty are thy^a deeds,   12
  how glorious the majesty of thy^a kingdom.
Thy kingdom is an everlasting kingdom,   13
and thy dominion stands for all generations.

In all his promises the Lord keeps faith,   14
  he is unchanging in all his works;^{b}
the Lord holds up those who stumble
  and straightens backs which are bent.
The eyes of all are lifted to thee in hope,   15
and thou givest them their food when it is due;
with open and bountiful hand   16
thou givest what they desire^c to every living creature.
The Lord is righteous in all his ways,   17
  unchanging in all that he does;
very near is the Lord to those who call to him,   18
  who call to him in singleness of heart.
He fulfils their desire if only they fear him;   19
  he hears their cry and saves them.
The Lord watches over all who love him   20
  but sends the wicked to their doom.
My tongue shall speak out the praises of the Lord,   21
  and all creatures shall bless his holy name
  for ever and ever.

146

O praise the Lord.   1

Praise the Lord, my soul.
As long as I live I will praise the Lord;   2
  I will sing psalms to my God all my life long.
Put no faith in princes,   3
  in any man, who has no power to save.
He breathes his last breath,   4
  he returns to the dust;
and in that same hour all his thinking ends.

Happy the man whose helper is the God of Jacob,   5
  whose hopes are in the Lord his God,

[a] *So Sept.; Heb.* his. [b] In all his promises...works: *so Sept.; Heb. om.* [c] they
desire: *or* thou wilt.

6   maker of heaven and earth,
             the sea, and all that is in them;
         who serves wrongdoers as he has sworn

7   and deals out justice to the oppressed.
         The LORD feeds the hungry
             and sets the prisoner free.

8   The LORD restores sight to the blind
             and straightens backs which are bent;
         the LORD loves the righteous

9   and watches over the stranger;
         the LORD gives heart to the orphan and widow
         but turns the course of the wicked to their ruin.

10   The LORD shall reign for ever,
             thy God, O Zion, for all generations.

         O praise the LORD.

147

1   O praise the LORD.

         How good it is to sing psalms to our God!
             How pleasant[a] to praise him!

2   The LORD is rebuilding Jerusalem;
         he gathers in the scattered sons of Israel.

3   It is he who heals the broken in spirit
             and binds up their wounds,

4   he who numbers the stars one by one
             and names them one and all.

5   Mighty is our Lord and great his power,
             and his wisdom beyond all telling.

6   The LORD gives new heart to the humble
             and brings evildoers down to the dust.

7   Sing to the LORD a song of thanksgiving,
         sing psalms to the harp in honour of our God.

8   He veils the sky in clouds
             and prepares rain for the earth;
         he clothes the hills with grass
             and green plants for the use of man.[b]

9   He gives the cattle their food
         and the young ravens all that they gather.

10   The LORD sets no store by the strength of a horse
         and takes no pleasure in a runner's legs;

[a] *So Sept.; Heb. adds* right.   [b] and green...man: *so Sept.; Heb. om.*

his pleasure is in those who fear him,   11
  who wait for his true love.

Sing to the LORD, Jerusalem;   12
  O Zion, praise your God,
for he has put new bars in your gates;   13
  he has blessed your children within them.
He has brought peace to your realm   14
  and given you fine wheat in plenty.
He sends his command to the ends of the earth,   15
  and his word runs swiftly.
He showers down snow, white as wool,   16
  and sprinkles hoar-frost thick as ashes;
crystals of ice he scatters like bread-crumbs;   17
he sends the cold, and the water stands frozen,
he utters his word, and the ice is melted;   18
  he blows with his wind and the waters flow.
To Jacob he makes his word known,   19
  his statutes and decrees to Israel;
he has not done this for any other nation,   20
  nor taught them his decrees.

  O praise the LORD.

148

  O praise the LORD.   1

Praise the LORD out of heaven;
  praise him in the heights.
Praise him, all his angels;   2
  praise him, all his host.
Praise him, sun and moon;   3
  praise him, all you shining stars;
praise him, heaven of heavens,   4
  and you waters above the heavens.
Let them all praise the name of the LORD,   5
for he spoke the word and they were created;
he established them for ever and ever   6
by an ordinance which shall never pass away.

Praise the LORD from the earth,   7
  you water-spouts and ocean depths;
fire and hail, snow and ice,   8
  gales of wind obeying his voice;

9   all mountains and hills;
        all fruit-trees and all cedars;
10 wild beasts and cattle,
        creeping things and winged birds;
11 kings and all earthly rulers,
        princes and judges over the whole earth;
12 young men and maidens,
        old men and young together.
13 Let all praise the name of the LORD,
        for his name is high above all others,
        and his majesty above earth and heaven;
14 he has exalted his people in the pride of power[a]
    and crowned with praise his loyal servants,
        all Israel, the people nearest him.

        O praise the LORD.

149

1   O praise the LORD.

    Sing to the LORD a new song,
        sing his praise in the assembly of the faithful;
2   let Israel rejoice in his maker
        and the sons of Zion exult in their king.
3   Let them praise his name in the dance,
        and sing him psalms with tambourine and harp.
4   For the LORD accepts the service of his people;
        he crowns his humble folk with victory.
5   Let his faithful servants exult in triumph;
        let them shout for joy as they kneel before him.
6   Let the high praises of God be on their lips
        and a two-edged sword in their hand,
7   to wreak vengeance on the nations
        and to chastise the heathen;
8   to load their kings with chains
        and put their nobles in irons;
9   to execute the judgement decreed against them—
    this is the glory of all his faithful servants.

        O praise the LORD.

[a] exalted...power: *lit.* raised up a horn for his people.

150

O praise the LORD.   1

O praise God in his holy place,
praise him in the vault of heaven, the vault of his power;
praise him for his mighty works,   2
   praise him for his immeasurable greatness.
Praise him with fanfares on the trumpet,   3
   praise him upon lute and harp;
praise him with tambourines and dancing,   4
   praise him with flute and strings;
praise him with the clash of cymbals,   5
   praise him with triumphant cymbals;
let everything that has breath praise the LORD!   6

O praise the LORD.

PROVERBS

Advice to the reader

1 The proverbs of Solomon son of David, king of Israel,
2   by which men will come to wisdom and instruction
  and will understand words that bring understanding,
3   and by which they will gain a well-instructed intelligence,
  righteousness, justice, and probity.
4   The simple will be endowed with shrewdness
  and the young with knowledge and prudence.
5   If the wise man listens, he will increase his learning,
  and the man of understanding will acquire skill
6   to understand proverbs and parables,
  the sayings of wise men and their riddles.

7   The fear of the LORD is the beginning[a] of knowledge,
  but fools scorn wisdom and discipline.

8   Attend, my son, to your father's instruction
  and do not reject the teaching of your mother;
9   for they are a garland of grace on your head
    and a chain of honour round your neck.

10, 11 My son, bad men may tempt you[b] and say,
  'Come with us; let us lie in wait for someone's blood;
  let us waylay[c] an innocent man who has done us no harm.
12   Like Sheol we will swallow them alive;
  though blameless, they shall be like men who go down to the
    abyss.
13   We shall take rich treasure of every sort
  and fill our homes with booty;
14   throw in your lot with us,
  and we will have a common purse.'
15   My son, do not go along with them,
  keep clear of their ways;
16   they hasten hot-foot into crime,
    impatient to shed blood.

[a] *Or* chief part.   [b] *Prob. rdg.; Heb. adds* do not come, *or, with some MSS.,* do not consent.   [c] *Prob. rdg.; Heb.* store up.

In vain is a net spread wide   17
if any bird that flies can see it.

These men lie in wait for their own blood   18
and waylay*ª* no one but themselves.
This is the fate*ᵇ* of men eager for ill-gotten gain: 19
it robs those who get it of their lives.

Wisdom cries aloud in the open air,   20
  she raises her voice in public places;
  she calls at the top of the busy street   21
  and proclaims at the open gates of the city:
'Simple fools, how long will you be content with your simplicity?*ᶜ* 22
If only you would respond to my reproof,   23
  I would give you my counsel
  and teach you my precepts.
But because you refused to listen when I called,   24
  because no one attended when I stretched out my hand,
  because you spurned all my advice   25
  and would have nothing to do with my reproof,
I in my turn will laugh at your doom   26
  and deride you when terror comes upon you,
  when terror comes upon you like a hurricane   27
  and your doom descends like a whirlwind.*ᵈ*
Insolent men delight in their insolence;
  stupid men hate knowledge.*ᵉ*
When they call upon me, I will not answer them;   28
  when they search for me, they shall not find me.
Because they hate knowledge   29
  and have not chosen to fear the LORD,
  because they have not accepted my counsel   30
  and have spurned all my reproof,
  they shall eat the fruits of their behaviour   31
  and have a surfeit of their own devices;
for the simpleton turns a deaf ear and comes to grief,   32
  and the stupid are ruined by their own complacency.
But whoever listens to me shall live without a care,   33
  undisturbed by fear of misfortune.'

My son, if you take my words to heart   **2**
  and lay up my commands in your mind,

[a] *Prob. rdg.; Heb.* store up. [b] This...fate: *prob. rdg.; Heb.* Such are the courses.
[c] *The rest of verse 22 transposed to follow verse 27.* [d] *Prob. rdg.; Heb. adds* when anguish
and distress come upon you. [e] Insolent...knowledge: *transposed from end of verse 22.*

2   giving your attention to wisdom
        and your mind to understanding,
3   if you summon discernment to your aid
        and invoke understanding,
4   if you seek her out like silver
        and dig for her like buried treasure,
5   then you will understand the fear of the LORD
        and attain to the knowledge of God;
6   for the LORD bestows wisdom
        and teaches knowledge and understanding.
7   Out of his store he endows the upright with ability
        as a shield for those who live blameless lives;
8   for he guards the course of justice
        and keeps watch over the way of his loyal servants.

9   Then you will understand what is right and just
        and keep*a* only to the good man's path;
10   for wisdom will sink into your mind,
        and knowledge will be your heart's delight.
11   Prudence will keep watch over you,
        understanding will guard you,
12   it will save you from evil ways
        and from men whose talk is subversive,
13   who forsake the honest course
        to walk in ways of darkness,
14   who rejoice in doing evil
        and exult in evil and subversive acts,
15   whose own ways are crooked,
        whose tracks are devious.
16   It will save you from the adulteress,*b*
        from the loose woman*c* with her seductive words,
17   who forsakes the teaching of her childhood
        and has forgotten the covenant of her God;
18   for her path*d* runs downhill towards death,
        and her course is set for the land of the dead.
19   No one who resorts to her*e* finds his way back
        or regains the path to life.

20   See then that you follow the footsteps of good men
        and keep to the course of the righteous;
21   for the upright shall dwell on earth
        and blameless men remain there;

[*a*] keep: *prob. rdg.; Heb.* uprightness.   [*b*] *Lit.* strange woman.   [*c*] *Lit.* alien woman.
[*d*] *Prob. rdg.; Heb.* house.   [*e*] resorts to her: *or* takes to them.

but the wicked shall be uprooted from it 22
  and traitors weeded out.

My son, do not forget my teaching, 3
  but guard my commands in your heart;
for long life and years in plenty 2
  will they bring you, and prosperity as well.
Let your good faith and loyalty never fail, 3
  but bind them about your neck.[a]
Thus will you win favour and success 4
  in the sight of God and man.

Put all your trust in the LORD 5
  and do not rely on your own understanding.
Think of him in all your ways, 6
  and he will smooth your path.
Do not think how wise you are, 7
  but fear the LORD and turn from evil.
Let that be the medicine to keep you in health, 8
  the liniment for your limbs.
Honour the LORD with your wealth 9
  as the first charge on all your earnings;
then your granaries will be filled with corn[b] 10
  and your vats bursting with new wine.
My son, do not spurn the LORD's correction 11
  or take offence at his reproof;
for those whom he loves the LORD reproves, 12
  and he punishes a favourite son.

Happy he who has found wisdom, 13
  and the man who has acquired understanding;
for wisdom is more profitable than silver, 14
  and the gain she brings is better than gold.
She is more precious than red coral, 15
  and all your jewels are no match for her.
Long life is in her right hand, 16
  in her left hand are riches and honour.
Her ways are pleasant ways 17
  and all her paths lead to prosperity.
She is a staff of life to all who grasp her, 18
  and those who hold her fast are safe.

In wisdom the LORD founded the earth 19
  and by understanding he set the heavens in their place;

[a] *So Sept.; Heb. adds* and write them on the tablet of your mind. [b] with corn: *or to* overflowing.

20   by his knowledge the depths burst forth
      and the clouds dropped dew.

21 My son, keep watch over your ability and prudence,
      do not let them slip from sight;
22   they shall be a charm*a* hung about your neck
      and an ornament on your breast.*b*
23   Then you will go your way without a care,
      and your feet will not stumble.
24   When you sit,*c* you need have no fear;
      when you lie down, your sleep will be pleasant.
25   Do not be afraid when fools are frightened
      or when ruin comes upon the wicked;
26   for the LORD will be at your side,
      and he will keep your feet clear of the trap.
27   Refuse no man any favour that you owe him
      when it lies in your power to pay it.
28   Do not say to your friend, 'Come back again;
      you shall have it tomorrow'—when you have it already.
29   Plot no evil against your friend,
      your unsuspecting neighbour.
30   Do not pick a quarrel with a man for no reason,
      if he has not done you a bad turn.
31   Do not emulate a lawless man,
      do not choose to follow his footsteps;
32   for one who is not straight is detestable to the LORD,
      but upright men are in God's confidence.
33   The LORD's curse rests on the house of the evildoer,
      while he blesses the home of the righteous.
34   Though God himself meets the arrogant with arrogance,
      yet he bestows his favour on the meek.*d*
35   Wise men are adorned with*e* honour,
      but the coat*f* on a fool's back is contempt.

4 Listen, my sons, to a father's instruction,
      consider attentively how to gain understanding;
2   for it is sound learning I give you;
      so do not forsake my teaching.
3   I too have been a father's son,
      tender in years, my mother's only child.
4   He taught me and said to me:
      Hold fast to my words with all your heart,

[a] charm: *lit.* life.   [b] breast: *lit.* throat.   [c] *So Sept.; Heb.* lie down.   [d] *Or* wretched.
[e] are adorned with: *prob. rdg.; Heb.* shall inherit.   [f] the coat: *prob. rdg.; Heb. obscure.*

keep my commands and you will have life.
*a*Do not forget or turn a deaf ear to what I say.   5

The first thing*b* is to acquire wisdom;   7
gain understanding though it cost you all you have.
Do not forsake her, and she will keep you safe;   6
love her, and she will guard you;
cherish her, and she will lift you high;   8
if only you embrace her, she will bring you to honour.
She will set a garland of grace on your head   9
and bestow on you a crown of glory.

Listen, my son, take my words to heart,   10
and the years of your life shall be multiplied.
I will guide you in the paths of wisdom   11
and lead you in honest ways.
As you walk you will not slip,   12
and, if you run, nothing will bring you down.
Cling to instruction and never let it go;   13
observe it well, for it is your life.
Do not take to the course of the wicked   14
or follow the way of evil men;
do not set foot on it, but avoid it;   15
turn aside and go on your way.
For they cannot sleep unless they have done some wrong;   16
unless they have been someone's downfall they lose their sleep.
The bread they eat is the fruit of crime   17
and they drink wine got by violence.
The course of the righteous is like morning light,   18
growing brighter till it is broad day;
but the ways of the wicked are like darkness at night,   19
and they do not know what has been their downfall.

My son, attend to my speech,   20
pay heed to my words;
do not let them slip out of your mind,   21
keep them close in your heart;
for they are life to him who finds them,   22
and health to his whole body.
Guard your heart more than any treasure,   23
for it is the source of all life.
Keep your mouth from crooked speech   24
and your lips from deceitful talk.

[a] *So Sept.; Heb. prefixes* Get wisdom, get understanding. [b] *Prob. rdg.; Heb. adds* wisdom.

25   Let your eyes look straight before you,
      fix your gaze upon what lies ahead.

26   Look out for the path that your feet must take,
      and your ways will be secure.

27   Swerve neither to right nor left,
      and keep clear of every evil thing.

5   My son, attend to my wisdom
      and listen to my good counsel,

2   so that you may observe proper prudence
      and your speech be informed with knowledge.

3   For though the lips of an adulteress drip honey
      and her tongue is smoother than oil,

4   yet in the end she is more bitter than wormwood,
      and sharp as a two-edged sword.

5   Her feet go downwards on the path to death,
      her course is set for Sheol.

6   She does not watch for the road that leads to life;
      her course turns this way and that, and what does she care?[a]

7   Now, my son,[b] listen to me
      and do not ignore what I say:

8   keep well away from her
      and do not go near the door of her house;

9   or you will lose your dignity in the eyes of others
      and your honour before strangers;[c]

10   strangers will batten on your wealth,
      and your hard-won gains pass to another man's family.

11   The end will be that you will starve,
      you will shrink to mere skin and bones.

12   Then you will say, 'Why did I hate correction
      and set my heart against reproof?

13   I did not listen to the voice of my teachers
      or pay attention to my masters.

14   I soon earned[d] a bad name
      and was despised in the public assembly.'

15   Drink water from your own cistern
      and running water from your own spring;

16   do not let your[e] well overflow into the road,
      your runnels of water pour into the street;

---

[a] what…care?: *or* she is restless. [b] my son: *so Sept.; Heb.* O sons. [c] *Prob. rdg., cp. Targ.; Heb.* before a cruel one. [d] *Or* I almost earned. [e] do not let your: *prob. rdg.; Heb.* shall your.

let them be yours alone,   17
not shared with strangers.
Let your fountain, the wife of your youth,   18
be blessed, rejoice in her,
a lovely doe, a graceful hind, let her be your companion;*a*   19
you will at all times be bathed in her love,
and her love will continually wrap you round.
Wherever you turn, she will guide you;
when you lie in bed, she will watch over you,
and when you wake she will talk with you.*b*
Why, my son, are you wrapped up in the love of an adulteress?   20
Why do you embrace a loose woman?
For a man's ways are always in the LORD's sight   21
who watches for every path that he must take.
The wicked man is caught in his own iniquities   22
and held fast in the toils of his own sin;
he will perish for want of discipline,   23
wrapped in the shroud of his boundless folly.

My son, if you pledge yourself to another man   6
and stand surety for a stranger,
if you are caught by your promise,   2
trapped by some promise you have made,
do what I now tell you*c*   3
and save yourself, my son:
when you fall into another man's power,
bestir yourself, go and pester the man,
give yourself no rest,   4
allow yourself no sleep.
Save yourself like a gazelle from the toils,*d*   5
like a bird from the grasp of the fowler.

Go to the ant, you sluggard,   6
watch her ways and get wisdom.
She has no overseer,   7
no governor or ruler;
but in summer she prepares her store of food   8
and lays in her supplies at harvest.
How long, you sluggard, will you lie abed?   9
When will you rouse yourself from sleep?
A little sleep, a little slumber,   10

[a] let...companion: *so Sept.; Heb. om.* [b] Wherever...with you: *transposed from ch.*
6 (*verse 22*). [c] what...you: *so Sept.; Heb. has an abbreviated form.* [d] from the toils:
so Sept.; Heb. out of hand.

a little folding of the hands in rest,
11 and poverty will come upon you like a robber,
want like a ruffian.

12 A scoundrel, a mischievous man, is he
who prowls about with crooked talk—
13   a wink of the eye,
    a touch with the foot,
    a sign with the fingers.
14   Subversion is the evil that he is plotting,
he stirs up quarrels all the time.
15   Down comes disaster suddenly upon him;
suddenly he is broken beyond all remedy.

16 Six things the LORD hates,
seven things are detestable to him:
17   a proud eye, a false tongue,
hands that shed innocent blood,
18   a heart that forges thoughts of mischief,
and feet that run swiftly to do evil,
19   a false witness telling a pack of lies,
and one who stirs up quarrels between brothers.

20 My son, observe your father's commands
and do not reject the teaching of your mother;
21   wear them always next your heart
and bind them close about your neck;
23[a]   for a command is a lamp, and teaching a light,
reproof and correction point the way of life,
24   to keep you from the wife of another man,
from the seductive tongue of the loose woman.
25   Do not desire her beauty in your heart
or let her glance provoke you;
26   for a prostitute can be had for the price of a loaf,
but a married woman is out for bigger game.

27 Can a man kindle fire in his bosom
without burning his clothes?
28   If a man walks on hot coals,
will his feet not be scorched?
29   So is he who sleeps with his neighbour's wife;
no one can touch such a woman and go free.
30   Is not a thief contemptible when he steals
to satisfy his appetite, even if he is hungry?

[a] *Verse 22 transposed to follow* wrap you round *in 5. 19.*

And, if he is caught, must he not pay seven times over   31
and surrender all that his house contains?
So one who commits adultery is a senseless fool: 32
he dishonours the woman and ruins himself;
he will get nothing but blows and contumely   33
and will never live down the disgrace;
for a husband's anger is a jealous anger   34
and in the day of vengeance he will show no mercy;
compensation will not buy his forgiveness;[a]   35
no bribe, however large, will purchase his connivance.

My son, keep my words,   7
store up my commands in your mind.
Keep my commands if you would live,   2
and treasure my teaching as the apple of your eye.
Wear them like a ring on your finger;   3
write them on the tablet of your memory.
Call Wisdom your sister,   4
greet Understanding as a familiar friend;
then they will save you from the adulteress,   5
from the loose woman with her seductive words.

I glanced[b] out of the window of my house,   6
I looked down through the lattice,
and I saw among simple youths,   7
there amongst the boys I noticed
a lad, a foolish lad,
passing along the street, at the corner,   8
stepping out in the direction of her house
at twilight, as the day faded,   9
at dusk as the night grew dark;
suddenly a woman came to meet him,   10
dressed like a prostitute, full of wiles,
flighty and inconstant,   11
a woman never content to stay at home,
lying in wait at every corner,   12
now in the street, now in the public squares.
She caught hold of him and kissed him;   13
brazenly she accosted him and said,
'I have had a sacrifice, an offering, to make   14
and I have paid my vows today;
that is why I have come out to meet you,   15

[a] compensation...forgiveness: *prob. rdg.; Heb. obscure.* [b] I glanced: *prob. rdg.;*
Heb. om.

to watch for you and find you.

16   I have spread coverings on my bed
of coloured linen from Egypt.

17   I have sprinkled my bed with myrrh,
my clothes*ᵃ* with aloes and cassia.

18   Come! Let us drown ourselves in pleasure,
let us spend a whole night of love;

19   for the man of the house is away,
he has gone on a long journey,

20   he has taken a bag of silver with him;
until the moon is full he will not be home.'

21   Persuasively she led him on,
she pressed him with seductive words.

22   Like a simple fool he followed her,
like an ox on its way to the slaughter-house,
like an antelope bounding into the noose,

23   like a bird hurrying into the trap;
he did not know that he was risking his life
until the arrow pierced his vitals.

24   But now, my son,*ᵇ* listen to me,
attend to what I say.

25   Do not let your heart entice you into her ways,
do not stray down her paths;

26   many has she pierced and laid low,
and her victims are without number.

27   Her house is the entrance to Sheol,
which leads down to the halls of death.

Wisdom and folly contrasted

8   Hear how Wisdom lifts her voice
and Understanding cries out.

2   She stands at the cross-roads,
by the wayside, at the top of the hill;

3   beside the gate, at the entrance to the city,
at the entry by the open gate she calls aloud:

4   'Men, it is to you I call,
I appeal to every man:

5   understand, you simple fools, what it is to be shrewd;
you stupid people, understand what sense means.

[a] my clothes: *prob. rdg.; Heb.* om.   [b] my son: *so Sept.; Heb.* O sons.

Listen! For I will speak clearly,   6
you will have plain speech from me;
for I speak nothing but truth   7
and my lips detest wicked talk.
All that I say is right,   8
not a word is twisted or crooked.
All is straightforward to him who can understand,   9
all is plain to the man who has knowledge.
Accept instruction*a* and not silver,   10
knowledge rather than pure gold;
for wisdom is better than red coral,   11
no jewels can match her.
I am Wisdom, I bestow shrewdness   12
and show the way to knowledge and prudence.
*b*Pride, presumption, evil courses,   13
subversive talk, all these I hate.
I have force, I also have ability;   14
understanding and power are mine.
Through me kings are sovereign   15
and governors make just laws.
Through me princes act like princes,   16
from me all rulers on earth*c* derive their nobility.*d*
Those who love me I love,   17
those who search for me find me.
In my hands are riches and honour,   18
boundless wealth and the rewards of virtue.
My harvest is better than gold, fine gold,   19
and my revenue better than pure silver.
I follow the course of virtue,   20
my path is the path of justice;
I endow with riches those who love me   21
    and I will fill their treasuries.

'The LORD created me the beginning of his works,   22
before all else that he made, long ago.
Alone,*e* I was fashioned in times long past,   23
at the beginning, long before earth itself.
When there was yet no ocean I was born,   24
no springs brimming with water.
Before the mountains were settled in their place,   25

[a] *So Sept.; Heb.* my instruction. [b] *Prob. rdg.; Heb. prefixes* The fear of the LORD is to
hate evil. [c] rulers on earth: *so some MSS.; others* who rule in righteousness. [d] from
me...nobility: *or, with Sept.,* and nobles through me are rulers on earth. [e] *So one
MS.; others om.*

long before the hills I was born,
26 when as yet he had made neither land nor lake
nor the first clod*a* of earth.
27 When he set the heavens in their place I was there,
when he girdled the ocean with the horizon,
28 when he fixed the canopy of clouds overhead
and set the springs of ocean firm in their place,
29 when he prescribed its limits for the sea*b*
and knit together earth's foundations.
30 Then I was at his side each day,
his darling*c* and delight,
playing in his presence continually,
31 playing on the earth, when he had finished it,*d*
while my delight was in mankind.

32-33 'Now, my sons, listen to me,
listen to instruction and grow wise, do not reject it.
Happy is the man who keeps to my ways,
34 happy the man who listens to me,
watching daily at my threshold
with his eyes on the doorway;
35 for he who finds me finds life
and wins favour with the LORD,
36 while he who finds me not, hurts himself,
and all who hate me are in love with death.'

9 Wisdom has built her house,
she has hewn her seven pillars;
2 she has killed a beast and spiced her wine,
and she has spread her table.
3 She has sent out her maidens to proclaim
from the highest part of the town,
4 'Come in, you simpletons.'
She says also to the fool,
5 'Come, dine with me
and taste the wine that I have spiced.
6 Cease to be silly, and you will live,
you will grow in understanding.'

7 Correct an insolent man, and be sneered at for your pains;
correct a bad man, and you will put yourself in the wrong.

[a] the first clod: *or* the sum of the clods. [b] *Prob. rdg.; Heb. adds* and the water shall not
disobey his command. [c] *Or, with Sept.,* craftsman. [d] the earth...finished it: *prob.
rdg., cp. Sept.; Heb.* the world of his earth.

Do not correct the insolent or they will hate you; 8
correct a wise man, and he will be your friend.
Lecture a wise man, and he will grow wiser; 9
teach a righteous man, and his learning will increase.

The first step to wisdom is the fear of the LORD, 10
 and knowledge of the Holy One is understanding;
for through me your days will be multiplied 11
 and years will be added to your life.
If you are wise, it will be to your own advantage; 12
 if you are haughty, you alone are to blame.
The Lady Stupidity is a flighty creature; 13
 the simpleton, she cares for nothing.
She sits at the door of her house, 14
 on a seat in the highest part of the town,
to invite the passers-by indoors 15
 as they hurry on their way:
'Come in, you simpletons', she says. 16
She says also to the fool,
'Stolen water is sweet 17
 and bread got by stealth tastes good.'
Little does he know that death[a] lurks there, 18
 that her guests are in the depths of Sheol.

A collection of wise sayings

The proverbs of Solomon: **10**

A wise son brings joy to his father;
 a foolish son is his mother's bane.
Ill-gotten wealth brings no profit; 2
 uprightness is a safeguard against death.
The LORD does not let the righteous go hungry,[b] 3
 but he disappoints the cravings[c] of the wicked.
Idle hands make a man poor; 4
 busy hands grow rich.
A thoughtful son puts by in summer; 5
 a son who sleeps at harvest is a disgrace.
Blessings are showered on the righteous; 6
 the wicked are choked by their own violence.
The righteous are remembered in blessings; 7

[a] *Lit*. the majority (*that is* the dead). [b] *Or* be afraid. [c] *Or* the clamour.

the name of the wicked turns rotten.

8   A wise man takes a command to heart;
    a foolish talker comes to grief.

9   A blameless life makes for security;
    crooked ways bring a man down.

10 To wink at a fault causes trouble;
    a frank rebuke leads to peace.*a*

11 The words of good men are a fountain of life;
    the wicked are choked by their own violence.

12 Hate is always picking a quarrel,
    but love turns a blind eye to every fault.

13 The man of understanding has wisdom on his lips;
    a rod is in store for the back of the fool.

14 Wise men lay up knowledge;
    when a fool speaks, ruin is near.

15 A rich man's wealth is his strong city,
    but poverty is the undoing of the helpless.

16 The good man's labour is his livelihood;
    the wicked man's earnings bring him to a bad end.

17 Correction is the high road to life;
    neglect reproof and you miss the way.

18 There is no spite in a just man's*b* talk;
    it is the stupid who are fluent with calumny.

19 When men talk too much, sin is never far away;
    common sense holds its tongue.

20 A good man's tongue is pure silver;
    the heart of the wicked is trash.

21 The lips of a good man teach*c* many,
    but fools perish for want of sense.

22 The blessing of the LORD brings riches
    and he sends no sorrow with them.

23 Lewdness is sport for the stupid;
    wisdom a delight to men of understanding.

24 The fears of the wicked will overtake them;
    the desire of the righteous will be granted.

25 When the whirlwind has passed by, the wicked are gone;
    the foundations of the righteous are eternal.

26 Like vinegar on the teeth or smoke in the eyes,
    so is the lazy servant to his master.

27 The fear of the LORD brings length of days;
    the years of the wicked are few.

[a] a frank...peace: *so Sept.; Heb.* a foolish talker comes to grief, *cp. verse 8.*   [b] a just man's: *so Sept.; Heb.* lying.   [c] *Prob. rdg., cp. Vulg.; Heb.* nourish.

The hope of the righteous blossoms;   28
the expectation of the wicked withers away.
The way of the LORD gives refuge to the honest man,   29
but dismays those who do evil.
The righteous man will never be shaken;   30
the wicked shall not remain on earth.
Wisdom flows from the mouth of the righteous;   31
the subversive tongue will be rooted out.
The righteous man can suit his words to the occasion;   32
the wicked know only subversive talk.

False scales are the LORD's abomination;   **11**
correct weights are dear to his heart.
When presumption comes in, in comes contempt,   2
but wisdom goes with sagacity.
Honesty is a guide to the upright,   3
but rogues are balked by their own perversity.
Wealth is worth nothing in the day of wrath,   4
but uprightness is a safeguard against death.
By uprightness the blameless keep their course,   5
but the wicked are brought down by their wickedness.
Uprightness saves the righteous,   6
but rogues are trapped in their own*a* greed.
When a man*b* dies, his thread of life ends,   7
and with it ends the hope of affluence.
A righteous man is rescued from disaster,   8
and the wicked man plunges into it.
By his words a godless man tries to ruin others,   9
but they are saved when the righteous plead for them.
A city rejoices in the prosperity of the righteous;   10
there is jubilation when the wicked perish.
By the blessing of the upright a city is built up;   11
the words of the wicked tear it down.
A man without sense despises others,   12
but a man of understanding holds his peace.
A gossip gives away secrets,   13
but a trusty man keeps his own counsel.
For want of skilful strategy an army is lost;   14
victory is the fruit of long planning.
Give a pledge for a stranger and know no peace;   15
refuse to stand surety and be safe.
Grace in a woman wins honour,   16

[a] their own: *so Sept.; Heb. om.*   [b] a man: *so some MSS.; others* a wicked man.

but she who hates virtue makes a home for dishonour.
Be timid in business and come to beggary;[a]
be bold and make a fortune.

17 Loyalty brings its own reward;
a cruel man makes trouble for his kin.

18 A wicked man earns a fallacious[b] profit;
he who sows goodness reaps a sure reward.[c]

19 A man set on righteousness finds life,
but the pursuit of evil leads to death.

20 The LORD detests the crooked heart,
but honesty is dear to him.

21 Depend upon it:[d] an evil man shall not escape punishment;
the righteous and all their offspring shall go free.

22 Like a gold ring in a pig's snout
is a beautiful woman without good sense.

23 The righteous desire only what is good;
the hope of the wicked comes to nothing.

24 A man may spend freely and yet grow richer;
another is sparing beyond measure, yet ends in poverty.

25 A generous man grows fat and prosperous,
and he who refreshes others will himself be refreshed.[e]

26 He who withholds his grain is cursed by the people,
but he who sells his corn is blessed.

27 He who eagerly seeks what is good finds much favour,
but if a man pursues evil it turns upon him.

28 Whoever relies on his wealth is riding for a fall,
but the righteous flourish like the green leaf.

29 He who brings trouble on his family inherits the wind,
and a fool becomes slave to a wise man.

30 The fruit of righteousness is a tree of life,
but violence[f] means the taking away of life.

31 If the righteous in the land get their deserts,
how much more the wicked man and the sinner!

12 He who loves correction loves knowledge;
he who hates reproof is a mere brute.

2 A good man earns favour from the LORD;
the schemer is condemned.

3 No man can establish himself by wickedness,
but good men have roots that cannot be dislodged.

[a] but she...beggary: *so Sept.; Heb. om.* [b] *Or* fraudulent. [c] a sure reward: *or* the reward of honesty. [d] Depend upon it: *lit.* Hand on hand. [e] will himself be refreshed: *prob. rdg., cp. Vulg.; Heb. unintelligible.* [f] *So Sept.; Heb.* a wise man.

A capable wife is her husband's crown;   4
one who disgraces him is like rot in his bones.
The purposes of the righteous are lawful;   5
the designs of the wicked are full of deceit.
The wicked are destroyed*a* by their own words;   6
the words of the good man are his salvation.
Once the wicked are down, that is the end of them,   7
but the good man's line continues.
A man is commended for his intelligence,   8
but a warped mind is despised.
It is better to be modest*b* and earn one's living   9
than to be conceited*c* and go hungry.
A righteous man cares for his beast,   10
but a wicked man is cruel at heart.
He who tills his land has enough to eat,   11
but to follow idle pursuits is foolishness.
The stronghold of the wicked crumbles like clay,*d*   12
but the righteous take lasting root.
The wicked man is trapped by his own falsehoods,   13
but the righteous comes safe through trouble.
One man wins success by his words;   14
another gets his due reward by the work of his hands.
A fool thinks that he is always right;   15
wise is the man who listens to advice.
A fool shows his ill humour at once;   16
a clever man slighted conceals his feelings.
An honest speaker comes out with the truth,   17
but the false witness is full of deceit.
Gossip can be sharp as a sword,   18
but the tongue of the wise heals.
Truth spoken stands firm for ever,   19
but lies live only for a moment.
Those who plot evil delude themselves,   20
but there is joy for those who seek the common good.
No mischief will befall the righteous,   21
but wicked men get their fill of adversity.
The LORD detests a liar   22
but delights in the honest man.
A clever man conceals his knowledge,   23
but a stupid man broadcasts his folly.
Diligence brings a man to power,   24

[*a*] *Prob. rdg.; Heb.* are an ambush for blood. [*b*] *Or* scorned. [*c*] *Or* honoured.
[*d*] *Prob. rdg.; Heb.* A wicked man covets a stronghold of crumbling earth.

but laziness to forced labour.

25   An anxious heart dispirits a man,
and a kind word fills him with joy.

26   A righteous man recoils from evil,[a]
but the wicked take a path that leads them astray.

27   The lazy hunter puts up no game,
but the industrious man reaps a rich harvest.[b]

28   The way of honesty leads to life,
but there is a well-worn path to death.

13   A wise man sees the reason for his father's correction;
an arrogant man will not listen to rebuke.

2   A good man enjoys the fruit of righteousness,[c]
but violence is meat and drink for the treacherous.

3   He who minds his words preserves his life;
he who talks too much comes to grief.

4   A lazy man is torn by appetite unsatisfied,
but the diligent grow fat and prosperous.

5   The righteous hate falsehood;
the doings of the wicked are foul and deceitful.

6   To do right is the protection of an honest man,
but wickedness brings sinners to grief.[d]

7   One man pretends to be rich, although he has nothing;
another has great wealth but goes in rags.[e]

8   A rich man must buy himself off,
but a poor man is immune from threats.

9   The light of the righteous burns brightly;
the embers of the wicked will be put out.

10   A brainless fool causes strife by his presumption;
wisdom is found among friends in council.

11   Wealth quickly come by[f] dwindles away,
but if it comes little by little, it multiplies.

12   Hope deferred makes the heart sick;
a wish come true is a staff of life.

13   To despise a word of advice is to ask for trouble;
mind what you are told, and you will be rewarded.

14   A wise man's teaching is a fountain of life
for one who would escape the snares of death.

15   Good intelligence wins favour,

[a] recoils from evil: *prob. rdg.; Heb.* let him spy out his friend.   [b] but...harvest: *prob. rdg.; Heb. obscure.*   [c] righteousness: *so Sept.; Heb.* a man's mouth.   [d] brings...grief: *or* plays havoc with a man.   [e] One man...rags: *or* One man may grow rich though he has nothing; another may grow poor though he has great wealth.   [f] quickly come by: *so Sept.; Heb.* because of emptiness.

but treachery leads to disaster.*[a]*
A clever man is wise and conceals everything,   16
but the stupid parade their folly.
An evil messenger causes trouble,*[b]*   17
but a trusty envoy makes all go well again.
To refuse correction brings poverty and contempt;   18
one who takes a reproof to heart comes to honour.
Lust indulged sickens a man;*[c]*   19
stupid people loathe to mend their ways.
Walk with the wise and be wise;   20
mix with the stupid and be misled.
Ill fortune follows the sinner close behind,   21
but good rewards the righteous.
A good man leaves an inheritance to his descendants,   22
but the sinner's hoard passes to the righteous.
Untilled land might yield food enough for the poor,   23
but even that may be lost through injustice.
A father who spares the rod hates his son,   24
but one who loves him keeps him in order.
A righteous man eats his fill,   25
    but the wicked go hungry.

The wisest women build up their homes;   **14**
the foolish pull them down with their own hands.
A straightforward man fears the LORD;   2
the double-dealer scorns him.
The speech of a fool is a rod for his back;*[d]*   3
a wise man's words are his safeguard.
Where there are no oxen the barn is empty,   4
but the strength of a great ox ensures rich crops.
A truthful witness is no liar;   5
a false witness tells a pack of lies.
A conceited man seeks wisdom, yet finds none;   6
to one of understanding, knowledge comes easily.
Avoid a stupid man,   7
you will hear not a word of sense from him.
A clever man has the wit to find the right way;   8
the folly of stupid men misleads them.
A fool is too arrogant to make amends;   9
upright men know what reconciliation means.

[a] leads to disaster: *prob. rdg., cp. Sept.; Heb.* is enduring.   [b] causes trouble: *or* is un-
successful.   [c] Lust…a man: *or* Desire fulfilled is pleasant to the appetite.   [d] his back:
prob. rdg.; Heb. pride.

10   The heart knows its own bitterness,
     and a stranger has no part in its joy.

11   The house of the wicked will be torn down,
     but the home of the upright flourishes.

12   A road may seem straightforward to a man,
     yet may end as the way to death.

13   Even in laughter the heart may grieve,
     and mirth may end in sorrow.

14   The renegade reaps the fruit of his conduct,
     a good man the fruit of his own achievements.

15   A simple man believes every word he hears;
     a clever man understands the need for proof.

16   A wise man is cautious and turns his back on evil;
     the stupid is heedless and falls headlong.

17   Impatience runs into folly;
     distinction comes by careful thought.*a*

18   The simple wear the trappings of folly;
     the clever are crowned with knowledge.

19   Evil men cringe before the good,
     wicked men at the righteous man's door.

20   A poor man is odious even to his friend;
     the rich have friends in plenty.

21   He who despises a hungry man*b* does wrong,
     but he who is generous to the poor is happy.

22   Do not those who intend evil go astray,
     while those with good intentions are loyal and faithful?

23   The pains of toil bring gain,
     but mere talk brings nothing but poverty.

24   Insight is the crown of the wise;
     folly the chief ornament of the stupid.

25   A truthful witness saves life;
     the false accuser utters nothing but lies.

26   A strong man who trusts in the fear of the LORD
     will be a refuge for his sons.

27   The fear of the LORD is the fountain of life
     for the man who would escape the snares of death.

28   Many subjects make a famous king;
     with none to rule, a prince is ruined.

29   To be patient shows great understanding;
     quick temper is the height of folly.

30   A tranquil mind puts flesh on a man,

[*a*] distinction...thought: *prob. rdg.; Heb.* a man of careful thought is hated.   [*b*] a hungry man: *so Sept.; Heb.* his friend.

but passion rots his bones.

He who oppresses[a] the poor insults his Maker;   31
he who is generous to the needy honours him.

An evil man is brought down by his wickedness;   32
the upright man is secure in his own honesty.[b]

Wisdom is at home in a discerning mind,   33
but is ill at ease in the heart of a fool.

Righteousness raises a people to honour;   34
to do wrong is a disgrace to any nation.

A king shows favour to an intelligent servant,   35
but his displeasure strikes down those who fail him.

A soft answer turns away anger,   **15**
but a sharp word makes tempers hot.

A wise man's tongue spreads knowledge;   2
stupid men talk nonsense.

The eyes of the LORD are everywhere,   3
surveying evil and good men alike.

A soothing word is a staff of life,   4
but a mischievous tongue breaks the spirit.

A fool spurns his father's correction,   5
but to take a reproof to heart shows good sense.

In the righteous man's house there is ample wealth;   6
the gains of the wicked bring trouble.

The lips of a wise man promote knowledge;   7
the hearts of the stupid are dishonest.

The wicked man's sacrifice is abominable to the LORD;   8
the good man's prayer is his delight.

The conduct of the wicked is abominable to the LORD,   9
but he loves the seeker after righteousness.

A man who leaves the main road resents correction,   10
and he who hates reproof will die.

Sheol and Abaddon lie open before the LORD,   11
how much more the hearts of men!

The conceited man does not take kindly to reproof   12
and he will not consult the wise.

A merry heart makes a cheerful face;   13
heartache crushes the spirit.

A discerning mind seeks knowledge,   14
but the stupid man feeds on folly.

In the life of the downtrodden every day is wretched,   15
but to have a glad heart is a perpetual feast.

[a] *Or* slanders.   [b] honesty: *so Sept.; Heb.* death.

899

16 Better a pittance with the fear of the LORD
than great treasure and trouble in its train.

17 Better a dish of vegetables if love go with it
than a fat ox eaten in hatred.

18 Bad temper provokes a quarrel,
but patience heals discords.

19 The path of the sluggard is a tangle of weeds,
but the road of the diligent*a* is a highway.

20 A wise son brings joy to his father;
a young fool despises his mother.

21 Folly may amuse the empty-headed;
a man of understanding makes straight for his goal.

22 Schemes lightly made come to nothing,
but with long planning they succeed.

23 A man may be pleased with his own retort;
how much better is a word in season!

24 For men of intelligence the path of life leads upwards
and keeps them clear of Sheol below.

25 The LORD pulls down the proud man's home
but fixes the widow's boundary-stones.

26 A bad man's thoughts are the LORD's abomination,
but the words of the pure are a delight.*b*

27 A grasping man brings trouble on his family,
but he who spurns a bribe will enjoy long life.

28 The righteous think before they answer;
a bad man's ready tongue is full of mischief.

29 The LORD stands aloof from the wicked,
he listens to the righteous man's prayer.

30 A bright look brings joy to the heart,
and good news warms a man's marrow.

31 Whoever listens to wholesome reproof
shall enjoy the society of the wise.

32 He who refuses correction is his own worst enemy,
but he who listens to reproof learns sense.

33 The fear of the LORD is a training in wisdom,
and the way to honour is humility.

16 A man may order his thoughts,
but the LORD inspires the words he utters.

2 A man's whole conduct may be pure in his own eyes,
but the LORD fixes a standard for the spirit of man.

3 Commit to the LORD all that you do,

[a] *So Sept.; Heb.* the upright. [b] the words...delight: *or* gracious words are pure.

900

and your plans will be fulfilled.
The Lord has made each thing for its own end;   4
he made even the wicked for a day of disaster.
Proud men, one and all, are abominable to the Lord;   5
depend upon it:*a* they will not escape punishment.
Guilt is wiped out by faith and loyalty,   6
and the fear of the Lord makes men turn from evil.
When the Lord is pleased with a man and his ways,   7
he makes even his enemies live at peace with him.
Better a pittance honestly earned   8
than great gains ill gotten.
Man plans his journey by his own wit,   9
but it is the Lord who guides his steps.
The king's mouth is an oracle,   10
he cannot err when he passes sentence.
Scales*b* and balances*c* are the Lord's concern;   11
all the weights in the bag are his business.
Wickedness is abhorrent to kings,   12
for a throne rests firm on righteousness.
Honest speech is the desire of kings,   13
they love a man who speaks the truth.
A king's anger is a messenger of death,   14
and a wise man will appease it.
In the light of the king's countenance is life,   15
his favour is like a rain-cloud in the spring.
How much better than gold it is to gain wisdom,   16
and to gain discernment is better than pure silver.*d*
To turn from evil is the highway of the upright;   17
watch your step and save your life.
Pride comes before disaster,   18
and arrogance before a fall.
Better sit humbly with those in need   19
than divide the spoil with the proud.
The shrewd man of business will succeed well,   20
but the happy man is he who trusts in the Lord.
The sensible man seeks advice from the wise,   21
he drinks it in and increases his knowledge.*e*
Intelligence is a fountain of life to its possessors,   22
but a fool is punished by his own folly.
The wise man's mind guides his speech,   23

[a] depend upon it: *lit.* hand on hand.   [b] *Or* Pointer.   [c] *Prob. rdg.; Heb.* balances of
justice.   [d] better than pure silver: *so Targ.; Heb.* choicer than silver.   [e] he drinks...
knowledge: *or* and he whose speech is persuasive increases learning.

and what his lips impart increases learning.[a]

24 Kind words are like dripping honey,
sweetness on the tongue and health for the body.

25 A road may seem straightforward to a man,
yet may end as the way to death.

26 The labourer's appetite is always plaguing him,
his hunger spurs him on.

27 A scoundrel repeats evil gossip;
it is like a scorching fire on his lips.

28 Disaffection stirs up quarrels,
and tale-bearing breaks up friendship.

29 A man of violence draws others on
and leads them into lawless ways.

30 The man who narrows his eyes is disaffected at heart,
and a close-lipped man is bent on mischief.

31 Grey hair is a crown of glory,
and it is won by a virtuous life.

32 Better be slow to anger than a fighter,
better govern one's temper than capture a city.

33 The lots may be cast into the lap,
but the issue depends wholly on the LORD.

17 Better a dry crust and concord with it
than a house full of feasting and strife.

2 A wise slave may give orders to a disappointing son
and share the inheritance with the brothers.

3 The melting-pot is for silver and the crucible for gold,
but it is the LORD who assays the hearts of men.

4 A rogue gives a ready ear to mischievous talk,
and a liar listens to slander.

5 A man who sneers at the poor insults his Maker,
and he who gloats over another's ruin will answer for it.

6 Grandchildren are the crown of old age,
and sons are proud of their fathers.

7 Fine talk is out of place in a boor,
how much more is falsehood in the noble!

8 He who offers[b] a bribe finds it work like a charm,[c]
he prospers in all he undertakes.

9 He who conceals another's offence seeks his goodwill,
but he who harps on something breaks up friendship.

10 A reproof is felt by a man of discernment

---

[a] and what...learning: *or* and increases the learning of his utterance. [b] He who offers:
lit. The owner of. [c] *Lit.* like a stone of favour.

more than a hundred blows by a stupid man.

An evil man is set only on disobedience,   11
but a messenger without mercy will be sent against him.

Better face a she-bear robbed of her cubs   12
than a stupid man in his folly.

If a man repays evil for good,   13
evil will never quit his house.

Stealing water starts a quarrel;   14
drop a dispute before you bare your teeth.

To acquit the wicked and condemn the righteous,   15
both are abominable in the LORD's sight.

What use is money in the hands of a stupid man?   16
Can he buy wisdom if he has no sense?

A friend is a loving companion at all times,   17
and a brother is born to share troubles.

A man is without sense who gives a guarantee   18
and surrenders himself to another as surety.

He who loves strife loves sin.   19
He who builds a lofty entrance invites thieves.

A crooked heart will come to no good,   20
and a mischievous tongue will end in disaster.

A stupid man is the bane of his parent,   21
and his father has no joy in a boorish son.

A merry heart makes a cheerful countenance,   22
but low spirits sap a man's strength.

A wicked man accepts a bribe under his cloak   23
to pervert the course of justice.

Wisdom is never out of sight of a discerning man,   24
but a stupid man's eyes are roving everywhere.

A stupid son exasperates his father   25
and is a bitter sorrow to the mother who bore him.

Again, to punish the righteous is not good   26
and it is wrong to inflict blows on men of noble mind.

Experience uses few words;   27
discernment keeps a cool head.

Even a fool, if he holds his peace, is thought wise;   28
keep your mouth shut and show your good sense.

The man who holds aloof seeks every pretext[a]   **18**
to bare his teeth in scorn at competent people.

The foolish have no interest in seeking to understand,   2
but prefer to display their wit.

[a] *So Sept.; Heb.* desire.

3   When wickedness comes in, in comes contempt;
with loss of honour comes reproach.

4   The words of a man's mouth are a gushing torrent,
but deep is the water in the well of wisdom.[a]

5   It is not good to show favour to the wicked
or to deprive the righteous of justice.

6   When the stupid man talks, contention follows;
his words provoke blows.

7   The stupid man's tongue is his undoing;
his lips put his life in jeopardy.

8   A gossip's whispers are savoury morsels,
gulped down into the inner man.

9   Again, the lazy worker is own brother
to the man who enjoys destruction.

10   The name of the LORD is a tower of strength,
where the righteous may run for refuge.

11   A rich man's wealth is his strong city,
a towering wall, so he supposes.

12   Before disaster comes, a man is proud,
but the way to honour is humility.

13   To answer a question before you have heard it out
is both stupid and insulting.

14   A man's spirit may sustain him in sickness,
but if the spirit is wounded, who can mend it?

15   Knowledge comes to the discerning mind;
the wise ear listens to get knowledge.

16   A gift opens the door to the giver
and gains access to the great.

17   In a lawsuit the first speaker seems right,
until another steps forward and cross-questions him.

18   Cast lots, and settle a quarrel,
and so keep litigants apart.

19   A reluctant brother is more unyielding than a fortress,
and quarrels are stubborn as the bars of a castle.

20   A man may live by the fruit of his tongue,
his lips may earn him a livelihood.

21   The tongue has power of life and death;
make friends with it and enjoy its fruits.

22   Find a wife, and you find a good thing;
so you will earn the favour of the LORD.

23   The poor man speaks in a tone of entreaty,
and the rich man gives a harsh answer.

[a] The words...wisdom: *prob. rdg., inverting phrases.*

Some companions are good only for idle talk,   24
but a friend may stick closer than a brother.

Better be poor and above reproach   **19**
than rich and crooked in speech.
Again, desire without knowledge is not good;   2
the man in a hurry misses the way.
A man's own folly wrecks his life,   3
and then he bears a grudge against the LORD.
Wealth makes many friends,   4
but a man without means loses the friend he has.
A false witness will not escape punishment,   5
and one who utters nothing but lies will not go free.
Many curry favour with the great;   6
a lavish giver has the world for his friend.
A poor man's brothers all dislike him,   7
how much more is he shunned by his friends!
Practice in evil makes the perfect scoundrel;[a]
the man who talks too much meets his deserts.[b]
To learn sense is true self-love;   8
cherish discernment and make sure of success.
A false witness will not escape punishment,   9
and one who utters nothing but lies will perish.
A fool at the helm is out of place,   10
how much worse a slave in command of men of rank!
To be patient shows intelligence;   11
to overlook faults is a man's glory.
A king's rage is like a lion's roar,   12
his favour like dew on the grass.
A stupid son is a calamity to his father;   13
a nagging wife is like water dripping endlessly.
Home and wealth may come down from ancestors,   14
but an intelligent wife is a gift from the LORD.
Laziness is the undoing of the worthless;   15
idlers must starve.
To keep the commandments keeps a man safe,   16
but scorning the way of the LORD brings death.
He who is generous to the poor lends to the LORD;   17
he will repay him in full measure.
Chastise your son while there is hope for him,   18
but be careful not to flog him to death.

[a] Practice...scoundrel: *so Sept.; Heb. om.*   [b] meets his deserts: *prob. rdg., cp. Sept.; Heb.* not they.

19 A man's ill temper brings its own punishment;
try to save him, and you make matters worse.

20 Listen to advice and accept instruction,
and you will die a wise man.

21 A man's heart may be full of schemes,
but the LORD's purpose will prevail.

22 Greed is a disgrace to a man;
better be a poor man than a liar.

23 The fear of the LORD is life;
he who is full of it will rest untouched by evil.

24 The sluggard plunges his hand in the dish
but will not so much as lift it to his mouth.

25 Strike an arrogant man, and he resents it like a fool;
reprove an understanding man, and he understands what you
mean.

26 He who talks his father down vexes his mother;
he is a son to bring shame and disgrace on them.

27 A son*a* who ceases to accept correction
is sure to turn his back on the teachings of knowledge.

28 A rascally witness perverts justice,
and the talk of the wicked fosters mischief.

29 There is a rod*b* in pickle for the arrogant,
and blows ready for the stupid man's back.

20 Wine is an insolent fellow, and strong drink makes an uproar;
no one addicted to their company grows wise.

2 A king's threat is like a lion's roar;
one who ignores it is his own worst enemy.

3 To draw back from a dispute is honourable;
it is the fool who bares his teeth.

4 The sluggard who does not plough in autumn
goes begging at harvest and gets nothing.

5 Counsel in another's heart is like deep water,
but a discerning man will draw it up.

6 Many a man protests his loyalty,
but where will you find one to keep faith?

7 If a man leads a good and upright life,
happy are the sons who come after him!

8 A king seated on the judgement-throne
has an eye to sift all that is evil.

9 Who can say, 'I have a clear conscience;
I am purged from my sin'?

[a] *So Sept.; Heb.* My son.   [b] *So Sept.; Heb.* judgement.

A double standard in weights and measures 10
is an abomination to the LORD.
Again, a young man is known by his actions, 11
whether his conduct is innocent or guilty.*a*
The ear that hears, the eye that sees, 12
the LORD made them both.
Love sleep, and you will end in poverty; 13
keep your eyes open, and you will eat your fill.
'A bad bargain!' says the buyer to the seller, 14
but off he goes to brag about it.
There is gold in plenty and coral too, 15
but a wise word is a rare jewel.
Take a man's garment when he pledges his word for a stranger 16
and hold that as a pledge for the unknown person.
Bread got by fraud tastes good, 17
but afterwards it fills the mouth with grit.
Care is the secret of good planning; 18
wars are won by skilful strategy.
A gossip will betray secrets;*b* 19
have nothing to do with a tattler.
If a man reviles father and mother, 20
his lamp will go out when darkness comes.
If you begin by piling up property in haste,*c* 21
it will bring you no blessing in the end.
Do not think to repay evil for evil, 22
wait for the LORD to deliver you.
A double standard in weights is an abomination to the LORD, 23
and false scales are not good in his sight.*d*
It is the LORD who directs a man's steps; 24
how can mortal man understand the road he travels?
It is dangerous to dedicate a gift rashly 25
or to make a vow and have second thoughts.
A wise king sifts out the wicked 26
and turns back for them the wheel of fortune.
The LORD shines into a man's very soul, 27
searching out his inmost being.
A king's guards are loyalty and good faith, 28
his throne is upheld by righteousness.*e*
The glory of young men is their strength, 29
the dignity of old men their grey hairs.

[a] *Prob. rdg.; Heb.* upright. [b] *Or* He who betrays secrets is a gossip. [c] by...haste:
or, as otherwise read, by wrongfully withholding an inheritance. [d] in his sight: *so Sept.;
Heb. om.* [e] *So Sept.; Heb.* loyalty.

30   A good beating purges the mind,
and blows chasten the inmost being.

21   The king's heart is under the LORD's hand;
like runnels of water, he turns it wherever he will.

2   A man may think that he is always right,
but the LORD fixes a standard for the heart.

3   Do what is right and just;
that is more pleasing to the LORD than sacrifice.

4   Haughty looks and a proud heart—
these sins mark a wicked man.

5   Forethought and diligence are sure of profit;
the man in a hurry is as sure of poverty.

6   He who makes a fortune by telling lies
runs needlessly into the toils[a] of death.

7   The wicked are caught up in their own violence,
because they refuse to do what is just.

8   The criminal's conduct is tortuous;
straight dealing is a sign of integrity.

9   Better to live in a corner of the house-top
than have a nagging wife and a brawling household.[b]

10   The wicked man is set on evil;
he has no pity to spare for his friend.

11   The simple man is made wise when he sees the insolent punished,
and learns his lesson when the wise man prospers.

12   The just God[c] makes the wicked man's home childless;[d]
he overturns the wicked and ruins them.

13   If a man shuts his ears to the cry of the helpless,
he will cry for help himself and not be heard.

14   A gift in secret placates an angry man;
a bribe slipped under the cloak pacifies great wrath.

15   When justice is done, all good men rejoice,
but it brings ruin to evildoers.

16   A man who takes leave of common sense
comes to rest in the company of the dead.

17   Love pleasure and you will beg your bread;
a man who loves wine and oil will never grow rich.

18   The wicked man serves as a ransom for the righteous,
so does a traitor for the upright.

19   Better to live alone in the desert
than with a nagging and ill-tempered wife.

[a] into the toils: *prob. rdg., cp. Sept.; Heb.* the seekers. [b] and a brawling household: *or, with slight change of consonants,* in a spacious house. [c] *Or* The just man. [d] makes... childless: *prob. rdg.; Heb.* considers the wicked man's home.

The wise man has his home full of fine and costly treasures;   20
the stupid man is a mere spendthrift.
Persevere in right conduct and loyalty   21
and you shall find life*a* and honour.
A wise man climbs into a city full of armed men   22
and undermines its strength and its confidence.
Keep a guard over your lips and tongue   23
and keep yourself out of trouble.
The conceited man is haughty, his name is insolence;   24
conceit and impatience are in all he does.
The sluggard's cravings will be the death of him,   25
because his hands refuse to work;
all day long his cravings go unsatisfied,   26
while the righteous man gives without stint.
The wicked man's sacrifice is an abomination to the LORD;*b*   27
how much more when he offers it with vileness at heart!
A lying witness will perish,   28
but he whose words ring true will leave children behind him.
A wicked man puts a bold face on it,   29
whereas the upright man secures his line of retreat.*c*
Face to face with the LORD,   30
wisdom, understanding, counsel go for nothing.
A horse may be made ready for the day of battle,   31
but victory comes from the LORD.

A good name is more to be desired than great riches;   **22**
esteem is better than silver or gold.
Rich and poor have this in common: 2
the LORD made them both.
A shrewd man sees trouble coming and lies low;   3
the simple walk into it and pay the penalty.
The fruit of humility is the fear of God   4
with riches and honour and life.
The crooked man's path is set with snares and pitfalls;   5
the cautious man will steer clear of them.
Start a boy on the right road,   6
and even in old age he will not leave it.
The rich lord it over the poor;   7
the borrower becomes the lender's slave.
The man who sows injustice reaps trouble,   8
and the end of his work*d* will be the rod.*e*

[a] *So Sept.; Heb. adds* righteousness.   [b] *to the* LORD: *so Sept.; Heb. om.*   [c] secures...
retreat: *or, as otherwise read*, considers his conduct.   [d] *So Sept.; Heb.* his wrath.   [e] the
rod: *or* the threshing.

9   The kindly man will be blessed,
    for he shares his food with the poor.
10 Drive out the insolent man, and strife goes with him;
    if he sits on the bench, he makes a mockery of justice.[a]
11 The LORD[b] loves a sincere man;
    but you will make a king your friend with your fine phrases.
12 The LORD keeps watch over every claim at law,
    and overturns the scoundrel's case.
13 The sluggard protests, 'There's a lion outside;
    I shall get myself killed in the street.'
14 The words of an adulteress are like a deep pit;
    those whom the LORD has cursed will fall into it.
15 Folly is deep-rooted in the heart of a boy;
    a good beating will drive it right out of him.
16 Oppression of the poor may bring gain to a man,
    but giving to the rich leads only to penury.

Thirty wise sayings

17 The sayings of the wise:

    Pay heed and listen to my words,[c]
    open your mind to the knowledge I impart;
18 to keep them in your heart will be a pleasure,
    and then you will always have them ready on your lips.
19 I would have you trust in the LORD
    and so I tell you these things this day for your own good.
20 Here I have written out for you thirty sayings,
    full of knowledge and wise advice,
21 to impart to you a knowledge of the truth,
    that you may take back a true report[d] to him who sent you.

22 Never rob a helpless man because he is helpless,[e]
    nor ill-treat a poor wretch in court;
23 for the LORD will take up their cause
    and rob him who robs them of their livelihood.
24 Never make friends with an angry man
    nor keep company with a bad-tempered one;

[a] if...justice: *prob. rdg., cp. Sept.; Heb.* and disgraceful litigation will cease.   [b] The LORD: *so Sept.; Heb. om.*   [c] my words: *prob. rdg., cp. Sept.; Heb. om.*   [d] *Prob. rdg.; Heb. adds* words of truth.   [e] helpless: *lit.* a door (*cp. Song of Songs 8. 9*); *there is a play on words in the Heb.*

be careful not to learn his ways,   25
or you will find yourself caught in a trap.
Never be one to give guarantees,   26
or to pledge yourself as surety for another;
for if you cannot pay, beware: 27
your bed will be taken from under you.
Do not move the ancient boundary-stone   28
which your forefathers set up.
You see a man skilful at his craft: 29
he will serve kings, he will not serve common men.

When you sit down to eat with a ruling prince,   **23**
be sure to keep your mind on what is before you,
and if you are a greedy man,   2
cut your throat first.
Do not be greedy for his dainties,   3
for they are not what they seem.
Do not slave to get wealth;*a*   4
be a sensible man, and give up.
Before you can look round, it will be gone;   5
it will surely grow wings
like an eagle, like a bird in the sky.
Do not go to dinner with a miser,*b*   6
do not be greedy for his dainties;
for they will stick in your*c* throat like a hair.   7
He will bid you eat and drink,
but his heart is not with you;
you will bring up the mouthful you have eaten,   8
and your winning words will have been wasted.

Hold your tongue in the hearing of a stupid man;   9
for he will despise your words of wisdom.
Do not move the ancient boundary-stone   10
or encroach on the land of orphans:
they have a powerful guardian   11
who will take up their cause against you.
Apply your mind to instruction   12
and open your ears to knowledge when it speaks.
Do not withhold discipline from a boy;   13
take the stick to him, and save him from death.
If you take the stick to him yourself,   14
you will preserve him from the jaws of death.*d*

[a] to get wealth: *or* for an invitation to a feast. [b] *Or* a man with an evil eye. [c] *Prob. rdg.; Heb*. his. [d] the jaws of death: *Heb*. Sheol.

15 My son, if you are wise at heart,
   my heart in its turn will be glad;
16 I shall rejoice with all my soul
   when you speak plain truth.

17 Do not try to emulate sinners;
   envy only those who fear the LORD day by day;
18 do this,ᵃ and you may look forward to the future,ᵇ
   and your thread of life will not be cut short.

19 Listen, my son, listen, and become wise;
   set your mind on the right course.
20 Do not keep company with drunkards
   or those who are greedy for the fleshpots;
21 for drink and greed will end in poverty,
   and drunken stupor goes in rags.

22 Listen to your father, who gave you life,
   and do not despise your mother when she is old.
23 Buy truth, never sell it;
   buy wisdom, instruction, and understanding.
24 A good man's father will rejoice
   and he who has a wise son will delight in him.
25 Give your father and your mother cause for delight,
   let her who bore you rejoice.

26 My son, mark my words,
   and accept my guidance with a will.
27 A prostitute is a deep pit,
   a loose woman a narrow well;
28 she lies in wait like a robber
   and betrays her husband with man after man.

29 Whose is the misery? whose the remorse?
   Whose are the quarrels and the anxiety?
   Who gets the bruises without knowing why?
   Whose eyes are bloodshot?
30 Those who linger late over their wine,
   those who are always trying some new spiced liquor.
31 Do not gulp down the wine, the strong red wine,
   when the droplets form on the side of the cup;ᶜ
32 in the end it will bite like a snake
   and sting like a cobra.

[a] do this: *prob. rdg., cp. Sept.; Heb. om.*   [b] and...future: *so Sept.; Heb.* and there will
be a future.   [c] *Prob. rdg.; Heb. adds* it runs smoothly to and fro.

Then your eyes see strange sights,   33
your wits and your speech are confused;
you become like a man tossing out at sea,   34
like one who clings to[a] the top of the rigging;
you say, 'If it lays me flat, what do I care?   35
If it brings me to the ground, what of it?
As soon as I wake up,
I shall turn to it again.'[b]

Do not emulate wicked men   **24**
or long to make friends with them;
for violence is all they think of,   2
and all they say means mischief.

Wisdom builds the house,   3
good judgement makes it secure,
knowledge furnishes the rooms   4
with all the precious and pleasant things that wealth can buy.

Wisdom prevails over strength,   5
knowledge over brute force;
for wars are won by skilful strategy,   6
and victory is the fruit of long planning.

Wisdom is too high for a fool;   7
he dare not open his mouth in court.

A man who is bent on mischief   8
gets a name for intrigue;
the intrigues of foolish men misfire,   9
and the insolent man is odious to his fellows.

If your strength fails on a lucky[c] day,   10
how helpless will you be on a day[d] of disaster!

When you see a man being dragged to be killed, go to his rescue,   11
and save those being hurried away to their death.
If you say, 'But I[e] do not know this man',   12
God, who fixes a standard for the heart, will take note.
God who watches you—be sure he will know;
he will requite every man for what he does.

Eat honey, my son, for it is good,   13
and the honeycomb so sweet upon the tongue.

[a] clings to: *prob. rdg.*; *Heb.* lies on. [b] turn to it again: *or, with Sept.*, seek my boon
companions. [c] lucky: *prob. rdg.*; *Heb. om.* [d] a day: *prob. rdg., cp. Sept.*; *Heb. om.*
[e] *So Sept.*; *Heb.* we.

14 Make wisdom too your own;
    if you find it, you may look forward to the future,
    and your thread of life will not be cut short.

15 Do not lie in wait like a felon at the good man's house,
    or raid his farm.

16 Though the good man may fall seven times, he is soon up again,
    but the rascal is brought down by misfortune.

17 Do not rejoice when your enemy falls,
    do not gloat when he is brought down;

18 or the LORD will see and be displeased with you,
    and he will cease to be angry with him.

19 Do not vie with evildoers
    or emulate the wicked;

20 for wicked men have no future to look forward to;
    their embers will be put out.

21 My son, fear the LORD and grow rich,
    but have nothing to do with men of rank,

22 they will bring about disaster without warning;
    who knows what ruin such men may cause[a]?

23 More sayings of wise men:

    Partiality in dispensing justice is not good.

24 A judge who pronounces a guilty man innocent
    is cursed by all nations, all peoples execrate him;

25 but for those who convict the guilty all will go well,
    they will be blessed with prosperity.

26 A straightforward answer
    is as good as a kiss of friendship.

27 First put all in order out of doors
    and make everything ready on the land;
    then establish your house and home.

28 Do not be a witness against your neighbour without good reason
    nor misrepresent him in your evidence.

29 Do not say,
    'I will do to him what he has done to me;
    I will requite him for what he has done.'

30 I passed by the field of an idle man,
    by the vineyard of a man with no sense.

[a] they...cause: *or* they will come to sudden disaster; who knows what the ruin of such
men will be.

914

I looked, and it was all dried up,[a]   31
it was overgrown with thistles
and covered with weeds,
and the stones of its walls had been torn down.
I saw and I took good note,   32
I considered and learnt the lesson:
  a little sleep, a little slumber,   33
  a little folding of the hands in rest,
  and poverty will come upon you like a robber,   34
  want like a ruffian.

Other collections of wise sayings

More proverbs of Solomon transcribed by the men of Hezekiah king   **25**
of Judah:

The glory of God is to keep things hidden   2
but the glory of kings is to fathom them.
The heavens for height, the earth[b] for depth: 3
unfathomable is the heart of a king.
Rid silver of its impurities,   4
then it may go to[c] the silversmith;
rid the king's presence of wicked men,   5
and his throne will rest firmly on righteousness.
Do not put yourself forward in the king's presence   6
or take your place among the great;
for it is better that he should say to you, 'Come up here',   7
than move you down to make room for a nobleman.
Be in no hurry to tell everyone what you have seen,   8
or it will end in bitter reproaches from your friend.
Argue your own case with your neighbour,   9
but do not reveal another man's secrets,
or he will reproach you when he hears of it   10
and your indiscretion will then be beyond recall.
Like apples of gold set in silver filigree   11
is a word spoken in season.
Like a golden earring or a necklace of Nubian gold   12
is a wise man whose reproof finds attentive ears.
Like the coolness of snow in harvest   13
is a trusty messenger to those who send him.[d]

[a] and...dried up: *prob. rdg., cp. Sept.; Heb. om.* [b] *Or* the underworld. [c] then it may
go to: *or* and it will come out bright for. [d] *Prob. rdg.; Heb. adds* refreshing his master.

14   Like clouds and wind that bring no rain
        is the man who boasts of gifts he never gives.

15   A prince may be persuaded by patience,
        and a soft tongue may break down solid bone.*a*

16   If you find honey, eat only what you need,
        too much of it will make you sick;

17   be sparing in visits to your neighbour's house,
        if he sees too much of you, he will dislike you.

18   Like a club or a sword or a sharp arrow
        is a false witness who denounces his friend.

19   Like a tooth decayed or a foot limping
        is a traitor relied on in the day of trouble.

20   Like one who dresses*b* a wound with vinegar,
        so is the sweetest of singers to the heavy-hearted.

21   If your enemy is hungry, give him bread to eat;
        if he is thirsty, give him water to drink;

22   so you will heap glowing coals on his head,
        and the LORD will reward you.

23   As the north wind holds back the rain,
        so an angry glance holds back slander.

24   Better to live in a corner of the house-top
        than have a nagging wife and a brawling household.*c*

25   Like cold water to the throat when it is dry
        is good news from a distant land.

26   Like a muddied spring or a tainted well
        is a righteous man who gives way to a wicked one.

27   A surfeit of honey is bad for a man,
        and the quest for honour is burdensome.

28   Like a city that has burst out of its confining walls*d*
        is a man who cannot control his temper.

26   Like snow in summer or rain at harvest,
        honour is unseasonable in a stupid man.

2   Like a fluttering sparrow or a darting swallow,
        groundless abuse gets nowhere.

3   The whip for a horse, the bridle for an ass,
        the rod for the back of a fool!

4   Do not answer a stupid man in the language of his folly,
        or you will grow like him;

5   answer a stupid man as his folly deserves,
        or he will think himself a wise man.

[*a*] solid bone: *or* authority. [*b*] *Prob. rdg.; Heb. adds* a garment on a cold day. [*c*] and a brawling household: *or, with slight change of consonants,* in a spacious house. [*d*] *Or* that is breached and left unwalled.

He who sends a fool on an errand   6
cuts his own leg off and displays the stump.
A proverb in the mouth of stupid men   7
dangles helpless as a lame man's legs.
Like one who gets the stone caught in his sling   8
is he who bestows honour on a fool.
Like a thorn that pierces a drunkard's hand   9
is a proverb in a stupid man's mouth.
Like an archer who shoots at any passer-by*a*   10
is one who hires a stupid man or a drunkard.
Like a dog returning to its vomit   11
is a stupid man who repeats his folly.
Do you see that man who thinks himself so wise?   12
There is more hope for a fool than for him.
The sluggard protests, 'There is a lion*b* in the highway,   13
a lion at large in the streets.'
A door turns on its hinges,   14
a sluggard on his bed.
A sluggard plunges his hand in the dish   15
but is too lazy to lift it to his mouth.
A sluggard is wiser in his own eyes   16
than seven men who answer sensibly.
Like a man who seizes a passing cur by the ears   17
is he who meddles*c* in another's quarrel.
A man who deceives another   19*d*
and then says, 'It was only a joke',
is like a madman shooting at random   18
his deadly darts and arrows.
For lack of fuel a fire dies down   20
and for want of a tale-bearer a quarrel subsides.
Like bellows*e* for the coal and fuel for the fire   21
is a quarrelsome man for kindling strife.
A gossip's whispers are savoury morsels   22
gulped down into the inner man.
Glib speech that covers a spiteful heart   23
is like glaze spread on earthenware.
With his lips an enemy may speak you fair   24
but inwardly he harbours deceit;
when his words are gracious, do not trust him,   25
for seven abominations fill his heart;
he may cloak his enmity in dissimulation,   26

[*a*] passer-by: *transposed from end of verse.* [*b*] *Or* snake. [*c*] *So Vulg.; Heb.* is negligent *or* becomes enraged. [*d*] *Verses 18 and 19 transposed.* [*e*] *So Sept.; Heb.* coal.

but his wickedness is shown up before the assembly.

27 If he digs a pit, he will fall into it;
    if he rolls a stone, it will roll back upon him.

28 A lying tongue makes innocence seem guilty,
    and smooth words conceal their sting.

27 Do not flatter yourself about tomorrow,
    for you never know what a day will bring forth.

2 Let flattery come from a stranger, not from yourself,
    from the lips of an outsider and not from your own.

3 Stone is a burden and sand a dead weight,
    but to be vexed by a fool is more burdensome than either.

4 Wrath is cruel and anger is a deluge;
    but who can stand up to jealousy?

5 Open reproof is better
    than love concealed.

6 The blows a friend gives are well meant,
    but the kisses of an enemy are perfidious.[a]

7 A man full-fed refuses honey,
    but even bitter food tastes sweet to a hungry man.

8 Like a bird that strays far from its nest
    is a man far from his home.

9 Oil and perfume bring joy to the heart,
    but cares torment a man's very soul.[b]

10 Do not neglect your own friend or your father's;[c]
    a neighbour at hand is better than a brother far away.

11 Be wise, my son, then you will bring joy to my heart,
    and I shall be able to forestall my critics.

12 A shrewd man sees trouble coming and lies low;
    the simple walk into it and pay the penalty.

13 Take a man's garment when he pledges his word for a stranger
    and hold that as a pledge for the unknown person.

14 If one man greets another too heartily,[d]
    he may give great offence.

15 Endless dripping on a rainy day—
    that is what a nagging wife is like.

16 As well try to control the wind as to control her!
    As well try to pick up oil in one's fingers!

17 As iron sharpens iron,
    so one man sharpens the wits[e] of another.

[a] *Mng. of Heb. word uncertain.* [b] but cares...soul: *so Sept.; Heb.* but friendship is sweeter than one's own counsel. [c] *Prob. rdg.; Heb. adds* or how should you enter your brother's house in the day of your ruin? [d] *So one MS.; others add* rising early in the morning. [e] *Lit.* face.

He who guards the fig-tree will eat its fruit,   18
and he who watches his master's interests will come to honour.
As face answers face reflected in the water,   19
so one man's heart answers another's.
Sheol and Abaddon are insatiable;   20
a man's eyes too are never satisfied.
The melting-pot is for silver and the crucible for gold,   21
but praise is the test of character.
Pound a fool with pestle and mortar,*a*   22
his folly will never be knocked out of him.

Be careful to know your own sheep   23
and take good care of your flocks;
for possessions do not last for ever,   24
nor will a crown endure to endless generations.
The grass disappears, new shoots are seen   25
and the green growth on the hills is gathered in;
the lambs clothe you,   26
the he-goats are worth the price of a field,
while the goats' milk is enough for your food*b*   27
and nourishment for your maidens.

The wicked man runs away with no one in pursuit,   **28**
but the righteous is like a young lion in repose.
It is the fault of a violent man*c* that quarrels start,*d*   2
but they are settled*e* by a man of discernment.
A tyrant oppressing the poor   3
is like driving rain which ruins the crop.
The lawless praise wicked men;   4
the law-abiding contend with them.
Bad men do not know what justice is,   5
but those who seek the LORD know everything good.*f*
Better be poor and above reproach   6
than rich and crooked.
A discerning son observes the law,   7
but one who keeps riotous company wounds his father.
He who grows rich by lending at discount or at interest   8
is saving for another who will be generous to the poor.
If a man turns a deaf ear to the law,   9
even his prayers are an abomination.

[a] *Prob. rdg.; Heb. adds* with groats.   [b] *Prob. rdg., cp. Sept.; Heb. adds* for your household's food.   [c] violent man: *so Sept.; Heb.* land.   [d] start: *prob. rdg., cp. Sept.; Heb.* her officers.   [e] they are settled: *so Sept.; Heb.* a knowing man thus prolongs.   [f] good: *so Targ.; Heb. om.*

10   He who tempts the upright into evil courses
      will himself fall into the pit he has dug.
      The honest shall inherit a fortune,
      but the wicked shall inherit nothing.*a*

11   The rich man may think himself wise,
      but a poor man of discernment sees through him.

12   When the just are in power, there are great celebrations,*b*
      but when the wicked come to the top, others are downtrodden.

13   Conceal your faults, and you will not prosper;
      confess and give them up, and you will find mercy.

14   Happy the man who is scrupulous in conduct,
      but he who hardens his heart falls into misfortune.

15   Like a starving lion or a thirsty bear
      is a wicked man ruling a helpless people.

16   The man who is stupid and grasping will perish,
      but he who hates ill-gotten gain will live long.

17   A man charged with bloodshed
      will jump into a well to escape arrest.

18   Whoever leads an honest life will be safe,
      but a rogue will fail, one way or another.

19   One who cultivates his land has plenty to eat;
      idle pursuits lead to poverty.

20   A man of steady character will enjoy many blessings,
      but one in a hurry to grow rich will not go unpunished.

21   To show favour is not good;
      but men will do wrong for a mere crust of bread.

22   The miser*c* is in a hurry to grow rich,
      never dreaming that want will overtake him.

23   Take a man to task and in the end*d* win more thanks
      than the man with a flattering tongue.

24   To rob your father or mother and say you do no wrong
      is no better than wanton destruction.

25   A self-important*e* man provokes quarrels,
      but he who trusts in the LORD grows fat and prosperous.

26   It is plain stupidity to trust in one's own wits,
      but he who walks the path of wisdom will come safely through.

27   He who gives to the poor will never want,
      but he who turns a blind eye gets nothing but curses.

28   When the wicked come to the top, others are pulled down;*f*
      but, when they perish, the righteous come into power.

[a] but...nothing: *prob. rdg., cp. Sept.; Heb. om.* [b] *Or* there is great pageantry. [c] *Or* The man with the evil eye. [d] in the end: *so one MS.; others have an obscure form.* [e] *Or* grasping. [f] are pulled down: *or* hide themselves.

A man who is still stubborn after much reproof   **29**
will suddenly be broken past mending.
When the righteous are in power the people rejoice,   2
but they groan when the wicked hold office.
A lover of wisdom brings joy to his father,   3
but one who keeps company with harlots squanders his wealth.
By just government a king gives his country stability,   4
but by forced contributions he reduces it to ruin.
A man who flatters his neighbour   5
is spreading a net for his feet.
An evil man is ensnared by his sin,*a*   6
but a righteous man lives*b* and flourishes.
The righteous man is concerned for the cause of the helpless,   7
but the wicked understand no such concern.
Arrogance can inflame a city,   8
but wisdom averts the people's anger.
If a wise man goes to law with a fool,   9
he will meet abuse or derision, but get no remedy.
Men who have tasted blood hate an honest man,   10
but the upright set much store by his life.
A stupid man gives free rein to his anger;   11
a wise man waits and lets it grow cool.
If a prince listens to falsehood,   12
all his servants will be wicked.
Poor man and oppressor have this in common: 13
what happiness each has comes from the LORD.*c*
A king who steadfastly deals out justice to the weak   14
will be secure for ever on his throne.
Rod and reprimand impart wisdom,   15
but a boy who runs wild brings shame on his mother.
When the wicked are in power, sin is in power,   16
but the righteous will gloat over their downfall.
Correct your son, and he will be a comfort to you   17
and bring you delights of every kind.
Where there is no one in authority,*d* the people break loose,   18
but a guardian of the law keeps them on the straight path.
Mere words will not keep a slave in order;   19
he may understand, but he will not respond.
When you see someone over-eager to speak,*e*   20
there will be more hope for a fool than for him.

[a] An evil...sin: *or* When an evil man steps out a trap awaits him.   [b] lives: *so some MSS.; others obscure.*   [c] what...LORD: *lit.* the LORD makes the eyes of both of them shine.   [d] *Or* no vision.   [e] *Or* someone hasty in business.

21 Pamper a slave from boyhood,
and in the end he will prove ungrateful.

22 A man prone to anger provokes a quarrel
and a hot-head is always doing wrong.

23 Pride will bring a man low;
a man lowly in spirit wins honour.

24 He who goes shares with a thief is his own enemy:
he hears himself put on oath and dare not give evidence.

25 A man's fears will prove a snare to him,
but he who trusts in the LORD has a high tower of refuge.

26 Many seek audience of a prince,
but in every case the LORD decides.

27 The righteous cannot abide an unjust man,
nor the wicked a man whose conduct is upright.

30 Sayings of Agur son of Jakeh from Massa:[a]

This is the great man's very word: I am weary, O God,
I am weary and worn out;

2 I am a dumb brute, scarcely a man,
without a man's powers of understanding;

3 I have not learnt wisdom
nor have I received knowledge from the Holy One.

4 Who has ever gone up to heaven and come down again?
Who has cupped the wind in the hollow of his hands?
Who has bound up the waters in the fold of his garment?
Who has fixed the boundaries of the earth?
What is his name or his son's name, if you know it?

5 God's every promise has stood the test:
he is a shield to all who seek refuge with him.

6 Add nothing to his words,
or he will expose you for a liar.

7 Two things I ask of thee;
do not withhold them from me before I die.

8 Put fraud and lying far from me;
give me neither poverty nor wealth,
provide me only with the food I need.

9 If I have too much, I shall deny thee
and say, 'Who is the LORD?'
If I am reduced to poverty, I shall steal
and blacken the name of my God.

[a] from Massa: *prob. rdg.* (*cp. 31. 1*); *Heb.* the oracle.

Never disparage a slave to his master,   10
or he will speak ill of you, and you will pay for it.

There is a sort of people who defame their fathers   11
and do not speak well of their own mothers;
a sort who are pure in their own eyes   12
and yet are not cleansed of their filth;
a sort—how haughty are their looks,   13
how disdainful their glances!
A sort whose teeth are swords,   14
their jaws are set with knives,
they eat the wretched out of the country
and the needy out of house and home.[a]

The leech has two daughters;   15
'Give', says one, and 'Give', says the other.

Three things there are which will never be satisfied,
four which never say, 'Enough!'
The grave[b] and a barren womb,[c]   16
a land thirsty for water
and fire that never says, 'Enough!'

The eye that mocks a father or scorns a mother's old age[d]   17
will be plucked out by magpies
or eaten by the vulture's young.

Three things there are which are too wonderful for me,   18
four which I do not understand:
the way of a vulture in the sky,   19
the way of a serpent on the rock,
the way of a ship out at sea,
and the way of a man with a girl.

The way of an unfaithful wife is this: 20
she eats, then she wipes her mouth
and says, 'I have done no harm.'

At three things the earth shakes,   21
four things it cannot bear:
a slave turned king,   22
a churl gorging himself,
a woman unloved when she is married,   23
and a slave-girl displacing her mistress.

Four things there are which are smallest on earth   24
yet wise beyond the wisest:

[a] house and home: *prob. rdg.; Heb.* man.   [b] *Heb.* Sheol.   [c] *Or* a woman's desire.
[d] old age: *prob. rdg.; Heb. unintelligible.*

25   ants, a people with no strength,
yet they prepare their store of food in the summer;
26   rock-badgers, a feeble folk,
yet they make their home among the rocks;
27   locusts, which have no king,
yet they all sally forth in detachments;*a*
28   the lizard, which can be grasped in the hand,
yet is found in the palaces of kings.

29 Three things there are which are stately in their stride,
four which are stately as they move:
30   the lion, a hero among beasts,
which will not turn tail for anyone;
31   the strutting cock*b* and the he-goat;
and a king going forth to lead his army.*c*

32   If you are churlish and arrogant
and fond of filthy talk, hold your tongue;
33   for wringing out the milk produces curd
and wringing the nose produces blood,
so provocation*d* leads to strife.

31 Sayings of Lemuel king of Massa, which his mother taught him:

2   What, O my son, what shall I say to you,*e*
you, the child of my womb and answer to my prayers?
3   Do not give the vigour of your manhood to women
nor consort with those who make eyes at*f* kings.
4   It is not for kings, O Lemuel, not for kings to drink wine
nor for princes to crave strong drink;
5   if they drink, they will forget rights and customs
and twist the law against their wretched victims.
6   Give strong drink to the desperate
and wine to the embittered;
7   such men will drink and forget their poverty
and remember their trouble no longer.
8   Open your mouth and speak up for the dumb,
against the suit of any that oppose them;
9   open your mouth and pronounce just sentence
and give judgement for the wretched and the poor.

[a] *Mng. of Heb. word uncertain.* [b] strutting cock: *or* charger; *mng. of Heb. uncertain.* [c] going forth to lead his army: *prob. rdg.; Heb. unintelligible.* [d] provocation: *lit.* wringing the nostrils. [e] what shall I say to you: *prob. rdg., cp. Sept.; Heb. om.* [f] who make eyes at: *prob. rdg.; Heb. unintelligible.*

A capable wife

Who can find a capable wife?	10
Her worth is far beyond coral.	
Her husband's whole trust is in her,	11
and children are not lacking.	
She repays him with good, not evil,	12
all her life long.	
She chooses wool and flax	13
and toils at her work.	
Like a ship laden with merchandise,	14
she brings home food from far off.	
She rises while it is still night	15
and sets meat before her household.*a*	
After careful thought she buys a field	16
and plants a vineyard out of her earnings.	
She sets about her duties with vigour*b*	17
and braces herself for the work.*c*	
She sees that her business goes well,	18
and never puts out her lamp at night.	
She holds the distaff*d* in her hand,	19
and her fingers grasp the spindle.	
She is open-handed to the wretched	20
and generous to the poor.	
She has no fear for her household when it snows,	21
for they are wrapped in two cloaks.	
She makes her own coverings,	22
and clothing of fine linen and purple.	
Her husband is well known in the city gate	23
when he takes his seat with the elders of the land.	
She weaves linen and sells it,	24
and supplies merchants with their sashes.	
She is clothed in dignity and power	25
and can afford to laugh at tomorrow.	
When she opens her mouth, it is to speak wisely,	26
and loyalty is the theme of her teaching.	
She keeps her eye on the doings of her household	27
and does not eat the bread of idleness.	

[a] *Prob. rdg.; Heb. adds* and a prescribed portion for her maidens.   [b] sets...vigour: *lit.* girds up her loins with strength.   [c] for the work: *so Sept.; Heb. om.*   [d] *Mng. of Heb. word uncertain.*

28   Her sons with one accord call her happy;
    her husband too, and he sings her praises:
29   'Many a woman shows how capable she is;[a]
    but you excel them all.'
30   Charm is a delusion and beauty fleeting;
    it is the God-fearing woman who is honoured.
31   Extol her for the fruit of all her toil,
    and let her labours bring her honour in the city gate.

[a] *Or* Many daughters show how capable they are.

ECCLESIASTES

The emptiness of all endeavour

THE WORDS OF THE SPEAKER,[a] the son of David, 1
king in Jerusalem.
Emptiness, emptiness, says the Speaker, emptiness, all is 2
empty. What does man gain from all his labour and his toil here under 3
the sun? Generations come and generations go, while the earth endures 4
for ever.

The sun rises and the sun goes down; back it returns to its place[b] 5
and rises there again. The wind blows south, the wind blows north, 6
round and round it goes and returns full circle. All streams run into 7
the sea, yet the sea never overflows; back to the place from which the
streams ran they return to run again.

All things are wearisome;[c] no man can speak of them all. Is not the 8
eye surfeited with seeing, and the ear sated with hearing? What has 9
happened will happen again, and what has been done will be done
again, and there is nothing new under the sun. Is there anything of 10
which one can say, 'Look, this is new'? No, it has already existed, long
ago before our time. The men of old are not remembered, and those 11
who follow will not be remembered by those who follow them.

I, the Speaker, ruled as king over Israel in Jerusalem; and in wisdom 12, 13
I applied my mind to study and explore all that is done under heaven.
It is a sorry business that God has given men to busy themselves with.
I have seen all the deeds that are done here under the sun; they are all 14
emptiness and chasing the wind. What is crooked cannot become 15
straight; what is not there cannot be counted. I said to myself, 'I have 16
amassed great wisdom, more than all my predecessors on the throne in
Jerusalem; I have become familiar with wisdom and knowledge.' So I 17
applied my mind to understand wisdom and knowledge, madness and
folly, and I came to see that this too is chasing the wind. For in much 18
wisdom is much vexation, and the more a man knows, the more he has
to suffer.

I said to myself, 'Come, I will plunge into pleasures and enjoy 2
myself'; but this too was emptiness. Of laughter I said, 'It is madness!' 2
And of pleasure, 'What is the good of that?' So I sought to stimulate 3

[a] the Speaker: *Heb.* Koheleth, *Sept.* Ecclesiastes.   [b] back...place: *prob. rdg.; Heb.*
to its place panting.   [c] *Prob. rdg.; Heb.* weary.

927

myself with wine, in the hope of finding out what was good for men to do under heaven throughout the brief span of their lives. But my mind was guided by wisdom, not blinded by*a* folly.

4   I undertook great works; I built myself houses and planted vine-
5 yards; I made myself gardens and parks and planted all kinds of fruit-
6 trees in them; I made myself pools of water to irrigate a grove of
7 growing trees; I bought slaves, male and female, and I had my home-
born slaves as well; I had possessions, more cattle and flocks than any
8 of my predecessors in Jerusalem; I amassed silver and gold also, the
treasure of kings and provinces; I acquired singers, men and women,
9 and all that man delights in.*b* I was great, greater than all my predecessors
10 in Jerusalem; and my wisdom stood me in good stead. Whatever my
eyes coveted, I refused them nothing, nor did I deny myself any
pleasure. Yes indeed, I got pleasure from all my labour, and for all
11 my labour this was my reward. Then I turned and reviewed all my
handiwork, all my labour and toil, and I saw that everything was
emptiness and chasing the wind, of no profit under the sun.

12, 13   I set myself to look at wisdom and at madness and folly.*c* Then
I perceived that wisdom is more profitable than folly, as light is more
14 profitable than darkness: the wise man has eyes in his head, but the
fool walks in the dark. Yet I saw also that one and the same fate over-
15 takes them both. So I said to myself, 'I too shall suffer the fate of the
fool. To what purpose have I been wise? What*d* is the profit of it?
16 Even this', I said to myself, 'is emptiness. The wise man is remembered
no longer than the fool, for, as the passing days multiply,*e* all will be
17 forgotten. Alas, wise man and fool die the same death!' So I came to
hate life, since everything that was done here under the sun was a
18 trouble to me; for all is emptiness and chasing the wind. So I came to
hate all my labour and toil here under the sun, since I should have to
leave its fruits to my successor. What sort of a man will he be who
19 succeeds me, who inherits what others have acquired?*f* Who knows
whether he will be a wise man or a fool? Yet he will be master of all
the fruits of my labour and skill here under the sun. This too is
emptiness.

20   Then I turned and gave myself up to despair, reflecting upon all my
21 labour and toil here under the sun. For anyone who toils with wisdom,
knowledge, and skill must leave it all to a man who has spent no
22 labour on it. This too is emptiness and utterly wrong. What reward
has a man for all his labour, his scheming, and his toil here under the

---

[*a*] not blinded by: *prob. rdg.; Heb.* to grasp. [*b*] *Prob. rdg.; Heb. adds two unintelligible words.* [*c*] *The rest of verse 12 transposed to follow verse 18.* [*d*] *Prob. rdg.; Heb.* Then.
[*e*] for...multiply: *prob. rdg.; Heb.* because already. [*f*] What sort...acquired: *see note on verse 12.*

sun? All his life long his business is pain and vexation to him; even at 23
night his mind knows no rest. This too is emptiness. There is nothing 24
better for a man to do than^a to eat and drink and enjoy himself in return
for his labours. And yet I saw that this comes from the hand of God.
For without him who can enjoy his food, or who can be anxious? God 25,26
gives wisdom and knowledge and joy to the man who pleases him, while
to the sinner is given the trouble of gathering and amassing wealth
only to hand it over to someone else who pleases God. This too is
emptiness and chasing the wind.

FOR EVERYTHING ITS SEASON, and for every activity under 3
heaven its time:

    a time to be born and a time to die;   2
    a time to plant and a time to uproot;
    a time to kill and a time to heal;   3
    a time to pull down and a time to build up;
    a time to weep and a time to laugh;   4
    a time for mourning and a time for dancing;
    a time to scatter stones and a time to gather them;   5
    a time to embrace and a time to refrain from embracing;
    a time to seek and a time to lose;   6
    a time to keep and a time to throw away;
    a time to tear and a time to mend;   7
    a time for silence and a time for speech;
    a time to love and a time to hate;   8
    a time for war and a time for peace.

What profit does one who works get from all his labour? I have seen 9,10
the business that God has given men to keep them busy. He has made 11
everything to suit its time; moreover he has given men a sense of time
past and future, but no comprehension of God's work from beginning
to end. I know that there is nothing good for man^b except to be happy 12
and live the best life he can while he is alive. Moreover, that a man 13
should eat and drink and enjoy himself, in return for all his labours, is
a gift of God. I know that whatever God does lasts for ever; to add to 14
it or subtract from it is impossible. And he has done it all in such a way
that men must feel awe in his presence. Whatever is has been already,^c 15
and whatever is to come has been already, and God summons each
event back in its turn. Moreover I saw here under the sun that, where 16
justice ought to be, there was wickedness, and where righteousness
ought to be, there was wickedness. I said to myself, 'God will judge 17

[a] than: *so some Sept. MSS.; Heb. om.*   [b] for man: *prob. rdg., cp. 2. 24; Heb. in them.*
[c] *Or* Whatever has been already is.

929

the just man and the wicked equally; every activity and*ᵃ* every purpose
18 has its proper time.' I said to myself, 'In dealing with men it is God's
19 purpose*ᵇ* to test them and to see what they truly are.*ᶜ* For man is a
creature of chance and the beasts are creatures of chance, and one
mischance awaits them all: death comes to both alike. They all draw
the same breath. Men have no advantage over beasts; for everything is
20 emptiness. All go to the same place: all came from the dust, and to the
21 dust all return. Who knows whether the spirit*ᵈ* of man goes upward or
22 whether the spirit*ᵈ* of the beast goes downward to the earth?' So I saw
that there is nothing better than that a man should enjoy his work,
since that is his lot. For who can bring him through to see what will
happen next?

4   Again, I considered all the acts of oppression here under the sun;
I saw the tears of the oppressed, and I saw that there was no one to
comfort them. Strength was on the side of their oppressors, and there
2 was no one to avenge them. I counted the dead happy because they
3 were dead, happier than the living who are still in life. More fortunate
than either I reckoned*ᵉ* the man yet unborn, who had not witnessed
4 the wicked deeds done here under the sun. I considered all toil and all
achievement and saw that it comes from rivalry between man and man.
5 This too is emptiness and chasing the wind. The fool folds his arms
6 and wastes away. Better one hand full and peace of mind, than both
fists full and toil that is chasing the wind.

7,8   Here again, I saw emptiness under the sun: a lonely man without a
friend, without son or brother, toiling endlessly yet never satisfied with
his wealth—'For whom', he asks, 'am I toiling and denying myself the
9 good things of life?' This too is emptiness, a sorry business. Two are
10 better than one; they receive a good reward for their toil, because, if
one falls, the other*ᶠ* can help his companion up again; but alas for the
11 man who falls alone with no partner to help him up. And, if two lie
side by side, they keep each other warm; but how can one keep warm
12 by himself? If a man is alone, an assailant may overpower him, but two
can resist; and a cord of three strands is not quickly snapped.

13   Better a young man poor and wise than a king old and foolish who
14 will listen to advice no longer. A man who leaves prison may well
15 come to be king, though born a pauper in his future kingdom. But I have
studied all life here under the sun, and I saw his place taken by yet
16 another young man, and no limit set to the number of the subjects
whose master he became. And he in turn will be no hero to those who
come after him. This too is emptiness and chasing the wind.

---

[a] *Prob. rdg.; Heb.* and upon.   [b] it is God's purpose: *prob. rdg.; Heb. obscure.*   [c] *Prob.*
rdg.; Heb. adds they to them.   [d] *Or* breath.   [e] I reckoned: *so Vulg.; Heb. om.*   [f] if
one falls, the other: *prob. rdg.; Heb. obscure.*

Go carefully when you visit the house of God. Better draw near in 5 1ᵃ
obedience than offer the sacrifice of fools, who sin without a thought. Do 2ᵇ
not rush into speech, let there be no hasty utterance in God's presence.
God is in heaven, you are on earth; so let your words be few. The 3
sensible man has much business on his hands; the fool talks and it is
so much chatter. When you make a vow to God, do not be slow to pay 4
it, for he has no use for fools; pay whatever you vow. Better not vow at 5
all than vow and fail to pay. Do not let your tongue lead you into sin, 6
and then say before the angel of God that it was a mistake; or God will
be angry at your words, and all your achievements will be brought to
nothing.ᶜ You must fear God. 7

If you witness in some province the oppression of the poor and the 8
denial of right and justice, do not be surprised at what goes on, for
every official has a higher one set over him, and the highestᵈ keeps
watch over them all. The best thing for a country is a king whoseᵉ 9
own lands are well tilled.

The man who loves money can never have enough, and the man who 10
is in love with great wealth enjoys no return from it. This too is
emptiness. When riches multiply, so do those who live off them; and 11
what advantage has the owner, except to look at them? Sweet is the 12
sleep of the labourer whether he eats little or much; but the rich man
owns too much and cannot sleep. There is a singular evil here under 13
the sun which I have seen: a man hoards wealth to his own hurt, and 14
then that wealth is lost through an unlucky venture, and the owner's
son left with nothing. As he came from the womb of mother earth, 15
so must he return, naked as he came; all his toil produces nothing which
he can take away with him. This too is a singular evil: exactly as he 16
came, so shall he go, and what profit does he get when his labour is all
for the wind? What is more, all his days are overshadowed; gnawing 17
anxietyᶠ and great vexation are his lot, sicknessᵍ and resentment.
What I have seen is this: that it is good and proper for a man to eat and 18
drink and enjoy himself in return for his labours here under the sun,
throughout the brief span of life which God has allotted him. More- 19
over, it is a gift of God that every man to whom he has granted wealth
and riches and the power to enjoy them should accept his lot and
rejoice in his labour. He will not dwell overmuch upon the passing 20
years; for God fills hisʰ time with joy of heart.

Here is an evil under the sun which I have seen, and it weighs heavy 6
upon men. Consider the man to whom God grants wealth, riches, and 2

[a] *4. 17 in Heb.* [b] *5. 1 in Heb.* [c] *Prob. rdg.; Heb. adds* for in a multitude of dreams
and empty things and many words. [d] for every...the highest: *or* though every...over
him, the Highest... [e] whose: *prob. rdg.; Heb.* for. [f] gnawing anxiety: *so Sept.; Heb.*
he eats. [g] sickness: *prob. rdg.; Heb.* and his sickness. [h] his: *prob. rdg.; Heb. om.*

substance,[a] and who lacks nothing that he has set his heart on: if God has not given him the power to enjoy these things, but a stranger
3 enjoys them instead, that is emptiness and a grave disorder. A man may have a hundred children and live a long life; but however many his days may be, if he does not get satisfaction from the good things of life and in the end receives no burial, then I maintain that the still-born
4 child is in better case than he. Its coming is an empty thing, it departs
5 into darkness, and in darkness its name is hidden; it has never seen the
6 sun or known anything,[b] yet its state is better than his. What if a man should live a thousand years twice over, and never prosper? Do not both go to one place?
7   The end of all man's toil is but to fill his belly,[c] yet his appetite is
8 never satisfied. What advantage then in facing life has the wise man over
9 the fool, or the poor man for all his experience? It is better to be satisfied with what is before your eyes than give rein to desire; this too
10 is emptiness and chasing the wind. Whatever has already existed has been given a name, its nature is known; a man cannot contend with what
11 is stronger than he. The more words one uses the greater is the empti-
12 ness of it all; and where is the advantage to a man? For who can know what is good for a man in this life, this brief span of empty existence through which he passes like a shadow? Who can tell a man what is to happen next here under the sun?

Wisdom and folly compared

7 A GOOD NAME SMELLS SWEETER than the finest ointment, and
2 the day of death is better than the day of birth. Better to visit the house of mourning than the house of feasting; for to be mourned
3 is the lot of every man, and the living should take this to heart. Grief is
4 better than laughter: a sad face may go with a cheerful heart. Wise men's thoughts are at home in the house of mourning, but a fool's
5 thoughts in the house of mirth. It is better to listen to a wise man's
6 rebuke than to the praise of fools. For the laughter of a fool is like the
7 crackling of thorns under a pot. This too is emptiness. Slander drives
8 a wise man crazy and breaks a strong man's[d] spirit. Better the end of
9 anything than its beginning; better patience than pride. Do not be
10 quick to show resentment; for resentment is nursed by fools. Do not ask why the old days were better than these; for that is a foolish question.
11 Wisdom is better than possessions and an advantage to all who see the

[a] *Or* honour.   [b] *Or* it.   [c] *Lit.* mouth.   [d] strong man's: *prob. rdg.; Heb. obscure.*

sun. Better have wisdom behind you than money; wisdom profits men 12
by giving life to those who know her.

Consider God's handiwork; who can straighten what he has made 13
crooked? When things go well, be glad; but when things go ill, consider 14
this: God has set the one alongside the other in such a way that no one
can find out what is to happen next.[a] In my empty existence I have seen 15
it all, from a righteous man perishing in his righteousness to a wicked
man growing old in his wickedness. Do not be over-righteous and do 16
not be over-wise. Why make yourself a laughing-stock? Do not be 17
over-wicked and do not be a fool. Why should you die before your time?
It is good to hold on to the one thing and not lose hold of the other; for 18
a man who fears God will succeed both ways. Wisdom makes the wise 19
man stronger than the ten rulers of a city. The world contains no man 20
so righteous that he can do right always and never do wrong.[b] More- 21
over, do not pay attention to everything men say, or you may hear your
servant disparage you; for you know very well how many times you 22
yourself have disparaged others. All this I have put to the test of 23
wisdom. I said, 'I am resolved to be wise', but wisdom was beyond my
grasp—whatever has happened lies beyond our grasp, deep down, 24
deeper than man can fathom.

I went on to reflect, I set my mind[c] to inquire and search for wisdom 25
and for the reason in things, only to discover that it is folly to be wicked
and madness to act like a fool. The wiles of a woman I find mightier[d] 26
than death; her heart is a trap to catch you and her arms are fetters. The
man who is pleasing to God may escape her, but she will catch a sinner.
'See,' says the Speaker, 'this is what I have found, reasoning things 27
out one by one, after searching long without success: I have found one 28
man in a thousand worth the name, but I have not found one woman
among them all. This alone I have found, that God, when he made man, 29
made him straightforward, but man invents endless subtleties of his
own.'

Who is wise enough for all this? Who knows the meaning of any- 8
thing? Wisdom lights up a man's face, but grim looks make a man
hated.[e] Do as the king commands you, and if you have to swear by God, 2
do not be precipitate. Leave the king's presence and do not persist in 3
a thing which displeases him; he does what he chooses. For the king's 4
word carries authority. Who can question what he does? Whoever 5
obeys a command will come to no harm. A wise man knows in his heart
the right time and method for action. There is a time and a method for 6
every enterprise, although man is greatly troubled by ignorance of the 7

[a] find out...next: *or* hold him responsible. [b] can do...wrong: *or* prospers without
ever making a mistake. [c] *Prob. rdg.; Heb. adds* to know and. [d] *Or* more bitter.
[e] make...hated: *prob. rdg.; Heb. obscure.*

8 future; who can tell him what it will bring? It is not in man's power to restrain the wind,[a] and no one has power over the day of death. In war
9 no one can lay aside his arms, no wealth will save its possessor. All this I have seen, having applied my mind to everything done under the sun. There was a time when one man had power over another and could make
10 him suffer. It was then that I saw wicked men approaching and even entering[b] the holy place; and they went about the city priding them-
11 selves on[c] having done right. This too is emptiness. It is because sentence upon a wicked act is not promptly carried out that men do evil
12 so boldly. A sinner may do wrong[d] and live to old age, yet I know that it will be well with those who fear God: their fear of him ensures this,
13 but it will not be well with a wicked man nor will he live long; the man
14 who does not fear God is a mere shadow. There is an empty thing found on earth: when the just man gets what is due to the unjust, and the unjust what is due to the just. I maintain that this too is emptiness.
15 So I commend enjoyment, since there is nothing good for a man to do here under the sun but to eat and drink and enjoy himself; this is all that will remain with him to reward his toil throughout the span of life
16 which God grants him here under the sun. I applied my mind to acquire wisdom and to observe the business which goes on upon earth,
17 when man never closes an eye in sleep day or night; and always I perceived that God has so ordered it that man should not be able to discover what is happening here under the sun. However hard a man may try, he will not find out; the wise man may think that he knows, but he will be unable to find the truth of it.

9   I applied my mind to all this, and I understood that the righteous and the wise and all their doings are under God's control; but is it love or hatred? No man knows. Everything that confronts him, everything
2 is empty,[e] since one and the same fate befalls every one, just and unjust alike, good and bad,[f] clean and unclean, the man who offers sacrifice and the man who does not. Good man and sinner fare alike, the man who
3 can take an oath and the man who dares not. This is what is wrong in all that is done here under the sun: that one and the same fate befalls every man. The hearts of men are full of evil; madness fills their hearts all through their lives, and after that they go down[g] to join the dead.
4 But for a man who is counted among the living there is still hope:
5 remember, a live dog is better than a dead lion. True, the living know that they will die; but the dead know nothing. There are no more
6 rewards for them; they are utterly forgotten. For them love, hate,

[a] *Or* to retain the breath of life.   [b] approaching...entering: *prob. rdg.; Heb. obscure.*
[c] priding themselves on: *so many MSS.; others* forgotten for.   [d] *Prob. rdg.; Heb. adds an unintelligible word.*   [e] *So Sept.; Heb.* all.   [f] and bad: *so Sept.; Heb. om.*   [g] they go down: *so Vulg.; Heb.* after him.

ambition,^a all are now over. Never again will they have any part in what is done here under the sun.

Go to it then, eat your food and enjoy it, and drink your wine with 7 a cheerful heart; for already God has accepted what you have done. Always be dressed in white and never fail to anoint your head. Enjoy 8,9 life with a woman you love all the days of your allotted span here under the sun, empty as they are;^b for that is your lot while you live and labour here under the sun. Whatever task lies to your hand, do it with 10 all your might; because in Sheol, for which you are bound, there is neither doing nor thinking, neither understanding nor wisdom. One 11 more thing I have observed here under the sun: speed does not win the race nor strength the battle. Bread does not belong to the wise, nor wealth to the intelligent, nor success to the skilful; time and chance govern all. Moreover, no man knows when his hour will come; like 12 fish caught in a net,^c like a bird taken in a snare, so men are trapped when bad times come suddenly.

This too is an example of wisdom as I have observed it here under 13 the sun, and notable I find it. There was a small town with few inhabi- 14 tants, and a great king came to attack it; he besieged it and constructed great siege-works^d against it. There was in it a poor wise man, and he 15 alone might have saved the town by his wisdom, but no one remembered that poor wise man. 'Surely', I said to myself, 'wisdom is better than 16 strength.' But the poor man's wisdom was despised, and his words went unheeded. A wise man who speaks his mind calmly is more to be 17 heeded than a commander shouting orders among fools. Wisdom is 18 better than weapons of war, and one mistake can undo many things done well.

Dead flies make the perfumer's sweet ointment turn rancid and **10** ferment; so can a little folly make wisdom lose its worth. The mind of 2 the wise man faces right, but the mind of the fool faces left. Even when 3 he walks along the road, the fool shows no sense and calls everyone else^e a fool. If your ruler breaks out in anger against you, do not resign your 4 post; submission makes amends for great mistakes. There is an evil 5 that I have observed here under the sun, an error for which a ruler is responsible: the fool given high office, but^f the great and the rich in 6 humble posts. I have seen slaves on horseback and men of high rank 7 going on foot like slaves. The man who digs a pit may fall into it, and 8 he who pulls down a wall may be bitten by a snake. The man who 9 quarries stones may strain himself, and the woodcutter runs a risk of injury. When the axe is blunt and has not first^g been sharpened, then 10

[a] *Or* passion. [b] *Prob. rdg.; Heb. adds* all your days, empty as they are. [c] *So Vulg.; Heb.* an evil net. [d] *So Sept.; Heb.* fortifications. [e] calls everyone else: *or* tells every-one he is. [f] but: *prob. rdg.; Heb. om.* [g] first: *prob. rdg.; Heb.* face.

one must use more force; the wise man has a better chance of success.
11 If a snake bites before it is charmed, the snake-charmer loses his fee.
12   A wise man's words win him favour, but a fool's tongue is his
13 undoing. He begins by talking nonsense and ends in mischief run mad.
14 The fool talks on and on; but no man knows what is coming, and who
15 can tell him what will come after that? The fool wearies himself to
death*a* with all his labour, for he does not know the way to town.

16   Woe betide the land when a slave has become its king, and its princes
17 feast in the morning. Happy the land when its king is nobly born, and
its princes feast at the right time of day, with self-control, and not as
18 drunkards. If the owner is negligent the rafters collapse, and if he is
19 idle the house crumbles away. The table has its pleasures, and wine
20 makes a cheerful life; and money is behind it all. Do not speak ill of
the king in your ease, or of a rich man in your bedroom; for a bird may
carry your voice, and a winged messenger may repeat what you say.

11   Send your grain across the seas, and in time you will get a return.
2 Divide your merchandise among seven ventures, eight maybe, since
3 you do not know what disasters may occur on earth.*b* If the clouds are
heavy with rain, they will discharge it on the earth; whether a tree falls
4 south or north, it must lie as it falls. He who watches the wind will
5 never sow, and he who keeps an eye on the clouds will never reap. You
do not know how a pregnant woman comes to have a body and a living
spirit in her womb; nor do you know how God, the maker of all things,
6 works. In the morning sow your seed betimes, and do not stop work
until evening, for you do not know whether this or that sowing will be
successful, or whether both alike will do well.

Advice to a young man

7 THE LIGHT OF DAY IS SWEET, and pleasant to the eye is the
8   sight of the sun; if a man lives for many years, he should rejoice
in all of them. But let him remember that the days of darkness will be
9 many. Everything that is to come will be emptiness. Delight in your
boyhood, young man, make the most of the days of your youth; let
your heart and your eyes show you the way; but remember that for all
10 these things God will call you to account. Banish discontent from your
mind, and shake off the troubles of the body; boyhood and the prime
of life are mere emptiness.

12   Remember your Creator in the days of your youth, before the time
of trouble comes and the years draw near when you will say, 'I see no

[a] fool...death: *prob. rdg.; Heb. obscure.*   [b] *Or* on land.

purpose in them.'[a] Remember him before the sun and the light of day 2
give place to darkness, before the moon and the stars grow dim, and
the clouds return with the rain—when the guardians of the house 3
tremble, and the strong men stoop, when the women grinding the meal
cease work because they are few, and those who look through the
windows look no longer, when the street-doors are shut, when the noise 4
of the mill is low, when the chirping of the sparrow grows faint[b] and
the song-birds fall silent;[c] when men are afraid of a steep place and the 5
street is full of terrors, when the blossom whitens on the almond-tree
and the locust's paunch is swollen and caper-buds have no more zest.
For man goes to his everlasting home, and the mourners go about the
streets. Remember him before the silver cord is snapped[d] and the 6
golden bowl is broken, before the pitcher is shattered at the spring and
the wheel broken at the well, before the dust returns to the earth as it 7
began and the spirit[e] returns to God who gave it. Emptiness, emptiness, 8
says the Speaker, all is empty.

So the Speaker, in his wisdom, continued to teach the people what 9
he knew. He turned over many maxims in his mind and sought how
best to set them out. He chose his words to give pleasure, but what he 10
wrote was the honest truth. The sayings of the wise are sharp as goads, 11
like nails driven home; they lead the assembled people, for they come
from one shepherd. One further warning, my son: the use of books is 12
endless, and much study is wearisome.

This is the end of the matter: you have heard it all. Fear God and obey 13
his commands; there is no more to man than this. For God brings 14
everything we do to judgement, and every secret, whether good or bad.

[a] *Or* I have no pleasure in them.   [b] grows faint: *prob. rdg.; Heb. obscure.*   [c] *Prob. rdg.;
Heb.* sink low.   [d] is snapped: *prob. rdg.; Heb. unintelligible.*   [e] *Or* breath.

THE SONG OF
SONGS

Bride[a]

1   I will sing the song of all songs to Solomon
2   that he may[b] smother me with kisses.

      Your love is more fragrant than wine,
3   fragrant is[c] the scent of your perfume,
      and your name like perfume poured out;[d]
      for this the maidens love you.
4   Take me with you,[e] and we will run together;
      bring me into your[f] chamber, O king.

Companions

      Let us rejoice and be glad for you;
      let us praise your love more than wine,
      and your caresses[g] more than any song.

Bride

5   I am dark but lovely, daughters of Jerusalem,
      like the tents of Kedar
      or the tent-curtains of Shalmah.
6   Do not look down on me; a little dark I may be
      because I am scorched by the sun.
      My mother's sons were displeased with me,
      they sent me to watch over the vineyards;
      so I did not watch over my own vineyard.
7   Tell me, my true love,
      where you mind your flocks,
      where you rest them at midday,
      that I may not be left picking lice
      as I sit among your companions' herds.

[a] *The Hebrew text implies, by its pronouns, different speakers, but does not indicate them; they are given, however, in two MSS. of Sept.* [b] I will...that he may: *or* The song of all songs which was Solomon's; may he... [c] *Or* more fragrant than. [d] poured out: *prob. rdg.; Heb. word uncertain.* [e] Take...you: *lit.* Draw me after you. [f] *So Pesh.; Heb.* his. [g] your caresses: *so Pesh.; Heb.* they love you.

Bridegroom

>If you yourself do not know,   8
>>O fairest of women,
>go, follow the tracks of the sheep
>and mind your kids by the shepherds' huts.

>>I would compare you, my dearest,   9
>>to Pharaoh's chariot-horses.
>>Your cheeks are lovely between plaited tresses,   10
>>your neck with its jewelled chains.

Companions

>We will make you braided plaits of gold   11
>>set with beads of silver.

Bride

>>While the king reclines on his couch,   12
>my spikenard gives forth its scent.
>My beloved is for me a bunch of myrrh   13
>>as he lies on my breast,
>my beloved is for me a cluster of henna-blossom   14
>>from the vineyards of En-gedi.

Bridegroom

>How beautiful you are, my dearest,   15
>>O how beautiful,
>>your eyes are like doves!

Bride

>How beautiful you are, O my love,   16
>>and how pleasant!

Bridegroom

>Our couch is shaded with branches;
>>the beams of our house are of cedar,   17
>our ceilings are all of fir.

Bride

>I am an asphodel in Sharon,   2
>>a lily growing in the valley.

Bridegroom

>>No, a lily among thorns   2
>is my dearest among girls.

Bride

3   Like an apricot-tree among the trees of the wood,
       so is my beloved among boys.
     To sit in its shadow was my delight,
       and its fruit was sweet to my taste.
4   He took me into the wine-garden
       and gave me loving glances.
5   He refreshed me with raisins, he revived me with apricots;
       for I was faint with love.
6   His left arm was under my head, his right arm was round me.

Bridegroom

7   I charge you, daughters of Jerusalem,
       by the spirits and the goddesses*a* of the field:
     Do not rouse her, do not disturb my love
       until she is ready.*b*

Bride

8   Hark! My beloved! Here he comes,
       bounding over the mountains, leaping over the hills.
9   My beloved is like a gazelle
       or a young wild goat:
       there he stands outside our wall,
       peeping in at the windows, glancing through the lattice.
10   My beloved answered, he said to me:
       Rise up, my darling;
       my fairest, come away.
11   For now the winter is past,
       the rains are over and gone;
12   the flowers appear in the country-side;
       the time is coming when the birds will sing,
       and the turtle-dove's cooing will be heard in our land;
13   when the green figs will ripen on the fig-trees
       and the vines*c* give forth their fragrance.
       Rise up, my darling;
       my fairest, come away.

Bridegroom

14   My dove, that hides in holes in the cliffs
       or in crannies on the high ledges,
     let me see your face, let me hear your voice;
     for your voice is pleasant, your face is lovely.

[a] by...goddesses: *or* by the gazelles and the hinds.   [b] until...ready: *or* while she is resting.   [c] *Prob. rdg.; Heb. adds* blossom.

Companions

> Catch for us the jackals, the little jackals,[a]   15
> that spoil our vineyards, when the vines are in flower.

Bride

> My beloved is mine and I am his;   16
>   he delights in the lilies.
> While the day is cool and the shadows are dispersing,   17
>   turn, my beloved, and show yourself
>   a gazelle or a young wild goat
>   on the hills where cinnamon grows.[b]

>   Night after night on my bed   3
> I have sought my true love;
> I have sought him but not found him,
> I have called him but he has not answered.[c]
> I said, 'I will rise and go the rounds of the city,   2
>   through the streets and the squares,
> seeking my true love.'
> I sought him but I did not find him,
> I called him but he did not answer.[d]
> The watchmen, going the rounds of the city, met me,   3
> and I asked, 'Have you seen my true love?'
>   Scarcely had I left them behind me   4
> when I met my true love.
> I seized him and would not let him go
> until I had brought him to my mother's house,
>   to the room of her who conceived me.

Bridegroom

> I charge you, daughters of Jerusalem,   5
> by the spirits and the goddesses[e] of the field:
> Do not rouse her, do not disturb my love
>   until she is ready.[f]

Companions

> What is this coming up from the wilderness   6
>   like a column of smoke
>   from burning myrrh or frankincense,
>   from all the powdered spices that merchants bring?
> Look; it is Solomon carried in his litter;   7

[a] *Or* fruit-bats.   [b] on...grows: *or* on the rugged hills *or* on the hills of Bether.
[c] I have called...answered: *so Sept.; Heb. om.*   [d] I called...answer: *so Sept.; Heb. om.*
[e] by...goddesses: *or* by the gazelles and the hinds.   [f] until...ready: *or* while she is
resting.

sixty of Israel's chosen warriors
    are his escort,
8   all of them skilled swordsmen,
    all trained to handle arms,
each with his sword ready at his side
    to ward off the demon of the night.

9   The palanquin which King Solomon had made for himself
    was of wood from Lebanon.
10   Its poles he had made of silver,
    its head-rest of gold;
    its seat was of purple stuff,
and its lining was of leather.

11   Come out, daughters of Jerusalem;
you daughters of Zion, come out and welcome King Solomon,
    wearing the crown with which his mother has crowned him,
    on his wedding day, on his day of joy.

Bridegroom

4   How beautiful you are, my dearest, how beautiful!
Your eyes behind your veil are like doves,
    your hair like a flock of goats streaming down Mount Gilead.
2   Your teeth are like a flock of ewes just shorn
    which have come up fresh from the dipping;
each ewe has twins and none has cast a lamb.
3   Your lips are like a scarlet thread,
    and your words are delightful;[a]
your parted lips behind your veil
    are like a pomegranate cut open.
4   Your neck is like David's tower,
    which is built with winding courses;
a thousand bucklers hang upon it,
    and all are warriors' shields.
5   Your two breasts are like two fawns,
    twin fawns of a gazelle.[b]
6   While the day is cool and the shadows are dispersing,
    I will go to the mountains of myrrh
    and to the hills of frankincense.
7   You are beautiful, my dearest,
    beautiful without a flaw.
8   Come from Lebanon, my bride;
    come with me from Lebanon.

[a] *Or* and your mouth is lovely.   [b] *Prob. rdg.; Heb. adds* which delight in the lilies.

Hurry down from the top of Amana,
    from Senir's top and Hermon's,
    from the lions' lairs, and the hills the leopards haunt.

You have stolen my heart,[a] my sister,   9
    you have stolen it,[b] my bride,
    with one of your eyes, with one jewel of your necklace.
How beautiful are your breasts, my sister, my bride!   10
    Your love is more fragrant than wine,
    and your perfumes sweeter than any spices.
Your lips drop sweetness like the honeycomb, my bride,   11
    syrup and milk are under your tongue,
    and your dress has the scent of Lebanon.
Your two cheeks[c] are an orchard of pomegranates,   13[d]
    an orchard full of rare fruits:[e]
spikenard and saffron, sweet-cane and cinnamon   14
    with every incense-bearing tree,
      myrrh and aloes
    with all the choicest spices.
My sister, my bride, is a garden close-locked,   12
a garden[f] close-locked, a fountain sealed.

Bride

The fountain in my garden[g] is a spring of running water   15
    pouring down from Lebanon.
Awake, north wind, and come, south wind;   16
blow upon my garden that its perfumes may pour forth,
    that my beloved may come to his garden
      and enjoy its rare fruits.

Bridegroom

I have come to my garden, my sister and bride,   5
    and have plucked my myrrh with my spices;
    I have eaten my honey and my syrup,
    I have drunk my wine and my milk.
Eat, friends, and drink,
    until you are drunk with love.

Bride

I sleep but my heart is awake.   2
    Listen! My beloved is knocking:

[a] stolen my heart: *or* put heart into me. [b] stolen it: *or* put heart into me. [c] Your two cheeks: *prob. rdg.; Heb.* Your shoots. [d] *Verse 12 transposed to follow verse 14.* [e] *Prob. rdg.; Heb. adds* henna with spikenard. [f] *So many MSS.; others* cairn. [g] my garden: *prob. rdg.; Heb.* gardens.

'Open to me, my sister, my dearest,
   my dove, my perfect one;
for my head is drenched with dew,
   my locks with the moisture of the night.'

3 'I have stripped off my dress; must I put it on again?
I have washed my feet; must I soil them again?'

4 When my beloved slipped his hand through the latch-hole,
   my bowels stirred[a] within me.

5 When I arose to open for my beloved,
   my hands dripped with myrrh;
the liquid myrrh from my fingers
   ran over the knobs of the bolt.

6 With my own hands I opened to my love,
   but my love had turned away and gone by;
my heart sank when he turned his back.
I sought him but I did not find him,
I called him but he did not answer.

7 The watchmen, going the rounds of the city, met me;
   they struck me and wounded me;
the watchmen on the walls took away my cloak.

8 I charge you, daughters of Jerusalem,
if you find my beloved, will you not tell him[b]
   that I am faint with love?

Companions

9 What is your beloved more than any other,
   O fairest of women?
What is your beloved more than any other,
   that you give us this charge?

Bride

10 My beloved is fair and ruddy,
   a paragon among ten thousand.

11 His head is gold, finest gold;
   his locks are like palm-fronds.[c]

12 His eyes are like doves beside brooks of water,
   splashed by the milky water
   as they sit where it is drawn.

13 His cheeks are like beds of spices or chests full of perfumes;
his lips are lilies, and drop liquid myrrh;

14 his hands are golden rods set in topaz;

[a] *Lit.* rumbled.   [b] will you...him: *or* what will you tell him?   [c] *Prob. rdg.; Heb. adds* black as the raven.

his belly a plaque of ivory overlaid with lapis lazuli.
His legs are pillars of marble in sockets of finest gold;   15
his aspect is like Lebanon, noble as cedars.
His whispers are*a* sweetness itself, wholly desirable.   16
Such is my beloved, such is my darling,
     daughters of Jerusalem.

Companions

Where has your beloved gone,   6
     O fairest of women?
Which way did your beloved go,
     that we may help you to seek him?

Bride

My beloved has gone down to his garden,   2
     to the beds where balsam grows,
to delight in the garden*b* and to pick the lilies.
I am my beloved's, and my beloved is mine,   3
     he who delights in the lilies.

Bridegroom

You are beautiful, my dearest, as Tirzah,   4
     lovely as Jerusalem.*c*
Turn your eyes away from me;   5
     they dazzle me.
Your hair is like a flock of goats streaming down Mount Gilead;
your teeth are like a flock of ewes come up fresh from the dipping,   6
each ewe has twins and none has cast a lamb.
Your parted lips behind your veil   7
     are like a pomegranate cut open.
There may be sixty princesses,   8
eighty concubines, and young women past counting,
but there is one alone, my dove, my perfect one,   9
     her mother's only child,
     devoted to the mother who bore her;
     young girls see her and call her happy,
     princesses and concubines praise her.
Who is this that looks out like the dawn,   10
beautiful as the moon, bright as the sun,
     majestic as the starry heavens?

I went down to a garden of nut-trees   11
     to look at the rushes by the stream,

[a] *Or* His nature is.   [b] *Prob. rdg.; Heb.* gardens.   [c] *Prob. rdg.; Heb. adds* majestic
as the starry heavens (*see verse 10*).

to see if the vine had budded
or the pomegranates were in flower.

12 I did not know myself;
she made me feel more than a prince
reigning over the myriads^a of his people.

Companions

13^b Come back, come back, Shulammite maiden,
come back, that we may gaze upon you.

Bridegroom

How you love to gaze on the Shulammite maiden,
as she moves between the lines of dancers^c!

7 How beautiful are your sandalled feet, O prince's daughter!
The curves of your thighs are like jewels,
the work of a skilled craftsman.

2 Your navel is a rounded goblet
that never shall want for spiced wine.
Your belly is a heap of wheat
fenced in by lilies.

3 Your two breasts are like two fawns,
twin fawns of a gazelle.

4 Your neck is like a tower of ivory.
Your eyes are the pools in Heshbon,
beside the gate of the crowded city.^d
Your nose is like towering Lebanon
that looks towards Damascus.

5 You carry your head like Carmel;
the flowing hair on your head is lustrous black,
your tresses are braided with ribbons.

6 How beautiful, how entrancing you are,
my loved one, daughter of delights!

7 You are stately as a palm-tree,
and your breasts are the clusters of dates.

8 I said, 'I will climb up into the palm
to grasp its fronds.'
May I find your breasts like clusters of grapes on the vine,
the scent of your breath like apricots,

9 and your whispers^e like spiced wine
flowing smoothly to welcome my caresses,
gliding down through lips and teeth.^f

[a] *Prob. rdg.; Heb.* chariots. [b] 7. *1 in Heb.* [c] as...dancers: *lit.* as in the dance of two camps. [d] *Or* the gate of Beth-rabbim. [e] *Lit.* palate. [f] through...teeth: *so Sept.; Heb.* lips of sleepers.

946

Bride

> I am my beloved's, his longing is all for me. 10
> Come, my beloved, let us go out into the fields 11
>> to lie among the henna-bushes;
>> let us go early to the vineyards 12
> and see if the vine has budded or its blossom opened,
>> if the pomegranates are in flower.
> There will I give you my love,
> when the mandrakes give their perfume, 13
> and all rare fruits are ready at our door,
> fruits new and old
> which I have in store for you, my love.
>
> If only you were my own true brother 8
>> that sucked my mother's breasts!
> Then, if I found you outside, I would kiss you,
>> and no man would despise me.
> I would lead you to the room of the mother who bore me,[a] 2
> bring you to her house for you to embrace me;[b]
> I would give you mulled wine to drink
>> and the fresh juice of pomegranates,
> your[c] left arm under my head and your[c] right arm round me. 3

Bridegroom

> I charge you, daughters of Jerusalem: 4
> Do not rouse her, do not disturb my love
>> until she is ready.[d]

Companions

> Who is this coming up from the wilderness 5
>> leaning on her beloved?

Bridegroom

> Under the apricot-trees I roused you,
> there where your mother was in labour with you,
> there where she who bore you was in labour.
> Wear me as a seal upon your heart, 6
>> as a seal upon your arm;
> for love is strong as death,
> passion cruel as the grave;[e]
>> it blazes up like blazing fire,
>> fiercer than any flame.

[a] to the room...bore me: *so Sept.; Heb. om.* [b] for you to embrace me: *or* to teach me how to love you. [c] *Prob. rdg.; Heb.* his. [d] until...ready: *or* while she is resting. [e] *Heb.* Sheol.

947

7 Many waters cannot quench love,
    no flood can sweep it away;
    if a man were to offer for love
    the whole wealth of his house,
    it would be utterly scorned.

Companions

8 We have a little sister
    who has no breasts;
    what shall we do for our sister
    when she is asked in marriage?
9   If she is a wall,
    we will build on it a silver parapet,
      but[a] if she is a door,
    we will close it up with planks of cedar.

Bride

10 I am a wall and my breasts are like towers;
    so in his eyes I am as one who brings contentment.
11 Solomon has a vineyard at Baal-hamon;
    he has let out his vineyard to guardians,
    and each is to bring for its fruit
    a thousand pieces of silver.
12 But my vineyard is mine to give;
    the thousand pieces are yours, O Solomon,
    and the guardians of the fruit shall have two hundred.

Bridegroom

13 My bride, you who sit in my garden,
    what is it that my friends[b] are listening to?
    Let me also hear your voice.

Bride

14 Come into the open, my beloved,
    and show yourself like a gazelle or a young wild goat
    on the spice-bearing mountains.

[a] *Or* and. [b] my garden...friends: *prob. rdg.; Heb.* the gardens, friends.

THE BOOK OF THE PROPHET
ISAIAH

Judah arraigned

THE VISION received by Isaiah son of Amoz concerning **1**
Judah and Jerusalem during the reigns of Uzziah, Jotham,
Ahaz, and Hezekiah, kings of Judah.

Hark you heavens, and earth give ear,   **2**
    for the LORD has spoken:
  I have sons whom I reared and brought up,
  but they have rebelled against me.
  The ox knows its owner   **3**
    and the ass its master's stall;
  but Israel, my own people,
  has no knowledge, no discernment.

O sinful nation, people loaded with iniquity,   **4**
race of evildoers, wanton destructive children
    who have deserted the LORD,
    spurned the Holy One of Israel
    and turned your backs on him.
  Where can you still be struck   **5**
    if you will be disloyal still?
    Your head is covered with sores,
    your body diseased;
from head to foot there is not a sound spot in you—   **6**
nothing but bruises and weals and raw wounds
    which have not felt compress or bandage
    or soothing oil.
Your country is desolate, your cities lie in ashes.   **7**
Strangers devour your land before your eyes;
    it is desolate as Sodom[a] in its overthrow.
    Only Zion is left,   **8**
  like a watchman's shelter in a vineyard,
  a shed in a field of cucumbers,
    a city well guarded.
If the LORD of Hosts had not left us a remnant,   **9**
  we should soon have been like Sodom,
    no better than Gomorrah.

[a] Sodom: *prob. rdg.; Heb.* strangers.

10 Hear the word of the LORD, you rulers of Sodom;
    attend, you people of Gomorrah, to the instruction of our God:
11 Your countless sacrifices, what are they to me?
        says the LORD.
    I am sated with whole-offerings of rams
        and the fat of buffaloes;
    I have no desire for the blood of bulls,
        of sheep and of he-goats.
12-13 Whenever you come to enter my presence*a*—
    who asked you for this?
    No more shall you trample my courts.
        The offer of your gifts is useless,
    the reek of sacrifice is abhorrent to me.
    New moons and sabbaths and assemblies,
    sacred seasons and ceremonies, I cannot endure.
14 I cannot tolerate your new moons and your festivals;
    they have become a burden to me,
        and I can put up with them no longer.
15   When you lift your hands outspread in prayer,
    I will hide my eyes from you.
    Though you offer countless prayers,
        I will not listen.
    There is blood on your hands;
16   wash yourselves and be clean.
    Put away the evil of your deeds,
        away out of my sight.
17 Cease to do evil and learn to do right,
    pursue justice and champion the oppressed;
    give the orphan his rights, plead the widow's cause.

18   Come now, let us argue it out,
        says the LORD.
    Though your sins are scarlet,
        they may become white as snow;
        though they are dyed crimson,
        they may yet be like wool.
19   Obey with a will,
    and you shall eat the best that earth yields;
20   but, if you refuse and rebel,
        locust-beans shall be your only food.*b*
    The LORD himself has spoken.

[*a*] *Lit.* to see my face.   [*b*] locust-beans...food: *or, with Scroll*, you shall be eaten by the sword.

950

How the faithful city has played the whore,   21
once the home of justice where righteousness dwelt—
    but now murderers!
   Your silver has turned into base metal   22
   and your liquor is diluted with water.
Your very rulers are rebels, confederate with thieves;   23
   every man of them loves a bribe
     and itches for a gift;
    they do not give the orphan his rights,
   and the widow's cause never comes before them.

This therefore is the word of the Lord, the Lord of Hosts, the   24
Mighty One of Israel:

   Enough! I will secure a respite from my foes
    and take vengeance on my enemies.
   Once again I will act against you   25
   to refine away your base metal as with potash
    and purge all your impurities;
   I will again make your judges what once they were   26
    and your counsellors like those of old.
   Then at length you shall be called
   the home of righteousness, the faithful city.
    Justice shall redeem Zion   27
    and righteousness her repentant people.
Rebels and sinners shall be broken together   28
   and those who forsake the Lord shall cease to be.
For the sacred oaks in which you delighted shall fail you,[a]   29
the garden-shrines of your fancy shall disappoint you.
You shall be like a terebinth whose leaves have withered,   30
   like a garden without water;
   the strongest tree[b] shall become like tow,   31
    and what is made of it[c] shall go up in sparks,
   and the two shall burst into flames together
    with no one to quench them.

This is the word which Isaiah son of Amoz received in a vision 2
concerning Judah and Jerusalem.

    In days to come   2[d]
   the mountain of the Lord's house
   shall be set over all other mountains,
    lifted high above the hills.
   All the nations shall come streaming to it,

[a] *So some MSS.; others* them. [b] *Or* the strong man. [c] *Or* what he makes.
[d] *Verses 2–4: cp. Mic. 4. 1–3.*

951

3   and many peoples shall come and say,
       'Come, let us climb up on to the mountain of the LORD,
           to the house of the God of Jacob,
           that he may teach us his ways
           and we may walk in his paths.'
       For instruction issues from Zion,
           and out of Jerusalem comes the word of the LORD;
4   he will be judge between nations,
       arbiter among many peoples.
       They shall beat their swords into mattocks
           and their spears into pruning-knives;[a]
    nation shall not lift sword against nation
       nor ever again be trained for war.

5   O people of Jacob, come,
       let us walk in the light of the LORD.
6   Thou hast abandoned thy people the house of Jacob;
           for they are crowded with traders[b]
       and barbarians like the Philistines,
       and with the children of foreigners everywhere.
7   Their land is filled with silver and gold,
           and there is no end to their treasure;
       their land is filled with horses,
           and there is no end to their chariots;
8   their land is filled with idols,
       and they bow down to the work of their own hands,
       to what their fingers have made.
9   Mankind shall be brought low,
       all men shall be humbled;
       and how can they raise themselves?[c]
10   Get you into the rocks and hide yourselves in the ground
       from the dread of the LORD and the splendour of his majesty.
11   Man's proud eyes shall be humbled,
           the loftiness of men brought low,
       and the LORD alone shall be exalted
           on that day.

12   For the LORD of Hosts has a day of doom waiting
           for all that is proud and lofty,
           for all that is high[d] and lifted up,
13   for all the cedars of Lebanon, lofty and high,
           and for all the oaks of Bashan,

[a] They shall beat...pruning-knives: *cp. Joel 3. 9–12.* [b] *Or* hawkers. [c] *Prob. rdg.;*
Heb. and do not forgive them. [d] *So Sept.; Heb.* low.

for all lofty mountains and for all high hills,   14
for every high tower and for every sheer wall,   15
for all ships of Tarshish and all the dhows of Arabia.*   16
    Then man's pride shall be brought low,   17
    and the loftiness of man shall be humbled,
  and the LORD alone shall be exalted
    on that day,
  while the idols shall pass away utterly.   18
Get you into caves in the rocks   19
  and crevices in the ground
from the dread of the LORD and the splendour of his majesty,
  when he rises to inspire the earth with fear.
On that day a man shall fling away   20
his idols of silver and his idols of gold
  which he has made for himself to worship;
he shall fling them to the dung-beetles and the bats,
and creep into clefts in the rocks and crannies in the cliffs   21
from the dread of the LORD and the splendour of his majesty,
  when he rises to inspire the earth with fear.
Have no more to do with man, for what is he worth?   22
  He is no more than the breath in his nostrils.

  Be warned: the Lord, the LORD of Hosts,   3
  is stripping Jerusalem and Judah
    of every prop and stay,*
    warrior and soldier,   2
judge and prophet, diviner and elder,
  captains of companies* and men of rank,   3
  counsellor, magician, and cunning enchanter.
  Then I will appoint mere boys to be their captains,   4
  who shall govern as the fancy takes them;
    the people shall deal harshly   5
each man with his fellow and with his neighbour;
  children shall break out against their elders,
    and nobodies against men of substance.
If a man takes hold of his brother in his father's house,   6
saying, 'You have a cloak, you shall be our chief;
  our stricken family shall be under you',
he will cry out that day and say,   7
  'I will not be your master;
there is neither bread nor cloak in my house,
  and you shall not make me head of the clan.'

[*a*] the dhows of Arabia: *mng. of Heb. words uncertain.* [*b*] *Prob. rdg.; Heb. adds* all stay of bread and all stay of water. [*c*] companies: *lit.* units of fifty.

8 Jerusalem is stricken and Judah fallen
>   because they have spoken and acted against the LORD,
>   rebelling against the glance of his glorious eye.

9 The look on their faces testifies against them;
>   like Sodom they proclaim their sins
>   and do not conceal them.[a]

Woe upon them! they have earned their own disaster.

10 Happy[b] the righteous man! all goes well with him,
>   for such men enjoy the fruit of their actions.

11 Woe betide the wicked! with him all goes ill,
>   for he reaps the reward that he has earned.

12 Money-lenders strip my people bare,
>   and usurers lord it over them.
>
> O my people! your guides lead you astray
>   and confuse the path that you should take.

13 The LORD comes forward to argue his case
>   and stands to judge his people.[c]

14 The LORD opens the indictment
>   against the elders of his people and their officers:
>   You have ravaged the vineyard,
>   and the spoils of the poor are in your houses.

15 Is it nothing to you that you crush my people
>   and grind the faces of the poor?

This is the very word of the Lord, the LORD of Hosts.

16   Then the LORD said:
> Because the women of Zion hold themselves high
> and walk with necks outstretched and wanton glances,
>   moving with mincing gait
>   and jingling feet,

17 the Lord will give the women of Zion bald heads,
>   the LORD will strip the hair from their foreheads.

18 In that day the Lord will take away all finery: anklets, discs,
19, 20 crescents, pendants, bangles, coronets, head-bands, armlets, neck-
21, 22 laces, lockets, charms, signets, nose-rings, fine dresses, mantles, cloaks,
23 flounced skirts, scarves of gauze, kerchiefs of linen, turbans, and
flowing veils.

24 So instead of perfume you shall have the stench of decay,
>   and a rope in place of a girdle,
>   baldness instead of hair elegantly coiled,
>   a loin-cloth of sacking instead of a mantle,

[a] like...them: *or* and their sins, like those of Sodom, denounce them; they do not deny
them.   [b] *Prob. rdg.; Heb.* Say.   [c] his people: *so Sept.; Heb.* peoples.

and branding instead of beauty.
Your men shall fall by the sword,   25
  and your warriors in battle;
then Zion's gates shall mourn and lament,   26
and she shall sit on the ground stripped bare.

Then on that day   4
seven women shall take hold of one man and say,
  'We will eat our own bread and wear our own clothes
    if only we may be called by your name;
      take away our disgrace.'

On that day the plant that the LORD has grown   2
shall become glorious in its beauty,
and the fruit of the land shall be
  the pride and splendour
  of the survivors of Israel.

Then those who are left in Zion, who remain in Jerusalem, every   3
one enrolled in the book of life,[a] shall be called holy. If the Lord washes   4
away the filth of the women of Zion and cleanses Jerusalem from the
blood that is in it by a spirit of judgement, a consuming spirit, then   5
over every building on Mount Zion and on all her places of assembly
the LORD will create a cloud of smoke by day and a bright flame of fire
by night; for glory shall be spread over all as a covering and a canopy,   6
a shade from the heat by day, a refuge and a shelter from rain and
tempest.

I will sing for my beloved   5
  my love-song about his vineyard:
My beloved had a vineyard
  high up on a fertile hill-side.
  He trenched it and cleared it of stones   2
  and planted it with red vines;
he built a watch-tower in the middle
and then hewed out a winepress in it.
He looked for it to yield grapes,
  but it yielded wild grapes.
Now, you who live in Jerusalem,   3
  and you men of Judah,
judge between me and my vineyard.
What more could have been done for my vineyard   4
that I did not do in it?
Why, when I looked for it to yield grapes,

[a] enrolled...life: *lit.* written for life.

did it yield wild grapes?
5   Now listen while I tell you
what I will do to my vineyard:
I will take away its fences and let it be burnt,
I will break down its walls and let it be trampled underfoot,
6   and so I will leave it derelict;
it shall be neither pruned nor hoed,
but shall grow thorns and briars.
      Then I will command the clouds
to send no more rain upon it.
7   The vineyard of the LORD of Hosts is Israel,
and the men of Judah are the plant he cherished.
He looked for justice and found it denied,
for righteousness but heard cries of distress.

8   Shame on you! you who add house to house
and join field to field,
until not an acre remains,
and you are left to dwell alone in the land.
9   The LORD of Hosts has sworn[a] in my hearing:
Many houses shall go to ruin,
fine large houses shall be uninhabited.
10   Five acres[b] of vineyard shall yield only a gallon,[c]
and ten bushels[d] of seed return only a peck.[e]
11   Shame on you! you who rise early in the morning
to go in pursuit of liquor
and draw out the evening inflamed with wine,
12   at whose feasts there are harp and lute,
tabor and pipe and wine,
who have no eyes for the work of the LORD,
and never see the things that he has done.
13   Therefore my people are dwindling away
all unawares;
the nobles are starving to death,
and the common folk die of thirst.
14   Therefore Sheol gapes with straining throat
and has opened her measureless jaws:
down go nobility and common people,
their noisy bustling mob.[f]
15   Mankind is brought low, men are humbled,
humbled are haughty looks.

[a] has sworn: *prob. rdg.; Heb.* om. [b] *Lit.* Ten yokes. [c] *Heb.* bath. [d] *Heb.* homer.
[e] *Heb.* ephah. [f] nobility...mob: *or* nobility, common people and noisy mob, and
are restless there.

But the LORD of Hosts sits high in judgement,   16
and by righteousness the holy God shows himself holy.
Young rams shall feed where fat bullocks once pastured,   17
and kids shall graze broad acres where cattle grew fat.*a*
Shame on you! you who drag wickedness along like a tethered sheep   18
 and sin like a heifer on a rope,
  who say, 'Let the LORD*b* make haste,   19
 let him speed up his work for us to see it,
 let the purpose of the Holy One of Israel
 be soon fulfilled, so that we may know it.'
Shame on you! you who call evil good and good evil,   20
who turn darkness into light and light into darkness,
who make bitter sweet and sweet bitter.
 Shame on you! you who are wise in your own eyes   21
  and prudent in your own esteem.
Shame on you! you mighty topers, valiant mixers of drink,   22
 who for a bribe acquit the guilty   23
 and deny justice to those in the right.

So he will hoist a signal to a nation far away,   26*c*
 he will whistle to call them from the end of the earth;
 and see, they come, speedy and swift;
 none is weary, not one of them stumbles,   27
  not one slumbers or sleeps.
 None has his belt loose about his waist
 or a broken thong to his sandals.
Their arrows are sharpened and their bows all strung,   28
 their horses' hooves flash like shooting stars,
  their chariot-wheels are like the whirlwind.
 Their growling is the growling of a lioness,   29
  they growl like young lions,
 which roar as they seize the prey
  and carry it beyond reach of rescue.
 They shall roar over it on that day   30
  like the roaring of the sea.
If a man looks over the earth, behold, darkness closing in,
 and the light darkened on the hill-tops*d*!

[a] Young...grew fat: *prob. rdg.; Heb. unintelligible.* [b] the LORD: *so Pesh.; Heb. om.*
[c] *Verses 24 and 25 transposed to follow 10. 4.* [d] hill-tops: *or* clouds.

The call of Isaiah

6 IN THE YEAR of King Uzziah's death I saw the Lord seated on a
throne, high and exalted, and the skirt of his robe filled the temple.
2 About him were attendant seraphim, and each had six wings; one pair
covered his face and one pair his feet, and one pair was spread in flight.
3 They were calling ceaselessly to one another,

> Holy, holy, holy is the LORD of Hosts:
> the whole earth is full of his glory.

4 And, as each one called, the threshold shook to its foundations, while
5 the house was filled with smoke. Then I cried,

> Woe is me! I am lost,
> for I am a man of unclean lips
> and I dwell among a people of unclean lips;
> yet with these eyes I have seen the King, the LORD of Hosts.

6 Then one of the seraphim flew to me carrying in his hand a glowing
7 coal which he had taken from the altar with a pair of tongs. He touched
my mouth with it and said,

> See, this has touched your lips;
> your iniquity is removed,
> and your sin is wiped away.

8 Then I heard the Lord saying, Whom shall I send? Who will go for
9 me? And I answered, Here am I; send me. He said, Go and tell this
people:

> You may listen and listen, but you will not understand.*a*
> You may look and look again, but you will never know.*b*
10 This people's wits are dulled,
> their ears are deafened and their eyes blinded,
> so that they cannot see with their eyes
> nor listen with their ears
> nor understand with their wits,
> so that they may turn and be healed.

11 Then I asked, How long, O Lord? And he answered,

> Until cities fall in ruins and are deserted,
> houses are left without people,
> and the land goes to ruin and lies waste,

[a] *Or* but how will you understand? [b] *Or* but how will you know?

until the LORD has sent all mankind far away,   12
and the whole country is one vast desolation.
Even if a tenth part of its people remain there,   13
they too will be exterminated
    [like an oak or a terebinth,
a sacred pole thrown out from its place in a hill-shrine*ᵃ*].

Prophecies during the Syro-Ephraimite war

WHILE AHAZ SON OF JOTHAM and grandson of Uzziah was   7
king of Judah, Rezin king of Aram with Pekah son of Remaliah,
king of Israel, marched on Jerusalem, but could not force a battle.
When the house of David heard that the Aramaeans had come to terms   2
with the Ephraimites, king and people were shaken like forest trees in
the wind. Then the LORD said to Isaiah, Go out with your son Shear-   3
jashub*ᵇ* to meet Ahaz at the end of the conduit of the Upper Pool by
the causeway leading to the Fuller's Field, and say to him, Be on your   4
guard, keep calm; do not be frightened or unmanned by these two
smouldering stumps of firewood, because Rezin and his Aramaeans
with Remaliah's son are burning with rage. The Aramaeans with   5
Ephraim and Remaliah's son have laid their plans against you, saying,
Let us invade Judah and break her spirit;*ᶜ* let us make her join with us,   6
and set the son of Tabeal on the throne. Therefore the Lord GOD has   7
said:

This shall not happen now, and never shall,
    for all that the chief city of Aram is Damascus,   8
    and Rezin is the chief of Damascus;
within sixty-five years
Ephraim shall cease to be a nation,
    for all that Samaria is the chief city of Ephraim,   9
    and Remaliah's son the chief of Samaria.
Have firm faith, or you will not stand firm.

Once again the LORD spoke to Ahaz and said, Ask the LORD your   10,11
God for a sign, from lowest Sheol or from highest heaven. But Ahaz   12
said, No, I will not put the LORD to the test by asking for a sign.
Then the answer came: Listen, house of David. Are you not content to   13
wear out men's patience? Must you also wear out the patience of my
God? Therefore the Lord himself shall give you a sign: A young woman   14

[*a*] a sacred pole...hill-shrine: *prob. rdg.; Heb. obscure.*   [*b*] *That is* A remnant shall return.
[*c*] *Or* and parley with her.

is with child, and she will bear a son, and will*a* call him Immanuel.*b*

15 By the time that he has learnt to reject evil and choose good, he will be
16 eating curds and honey;*c* before that child has learnt to reject evil and
choose good, desolation will come upon the land before whose two
17 kings you cower now. The LORD will bring on you, your people, and
your house, a time the like of which has not been seen since Ephraim
broke away from Judah.*d*

18 On that day the LORD will whistle for the fly from the distant streams
19 of Egypt and for the bee from Assyria. They shall all come and settle
in the precipitous ravines and in the clefts of the rock; camel-thorn and
20 stinkwood shall be black with them. On that day the Lord shall shave
the head and body with a razor hired on the banks of the Euphrates,*e*
21 and it shall remove the beard as well. On that day a man shall save
22 alive a young cow and two ewes; and he shall get so much milk that he
eats curds; for all who are left in the land shall eat curds and honey.
23 On that day every place where there used to be a thousand vines worth
a thousand pieces of silver shall be given over to thorns and briars.
24 A man shall go there only to hunt with bow and arrows, for thorns and
25 briars cover the whole land; and no one who fears thorns and briars
shall set foot on any of those hills once worked with the hoe. Oxen shall
be turned loose on them, and sheep shall trample them.

8 The LORD said to me, Take a large tablet and write on it in common
2 writing,*f* Maher-shalal-hash-baz;*g* and fetch*h* Uriah the priest and
3 Zechariah son of Jeberechiah for me as trustworthy witnesses. Then
I lay with the prophetess, and she conceived and bore a son; and the
4 LORD said to me, Call him Maher-shalal-hash-baz. Before the boy can
say Father or Mother, the wealth of Damascus and the spoils of
Samaria shall be carried off and presented to the king of Assyria.

5 Once again the LORD said to me:

6   Because this nation has rejected
    the waters of Shiloah, which run so softly and gently,*i*
7   therefore the Lord will bring up against it
        the strong, flooding waters of the Euphrates,
        the king of Assyria and all his glory;
        it shall run up all its channels
        and overflow all its banks;
8   it shall sweep through Judah in a flood,
        pouring over it and rising shoulder-high.

[a] *Or* you will. [b] *That is* God is with us. [c] he will…honey: *or* curds and honey will
be eaten. [d] *Prob. rdg.; Heb. adds* the king of Assyria. [e] *Prob. rdg.; Heb. adds* with the
king of Assyria. [f] in common writing: *or* with an ordinary stylus. [g] *That is* Speed-
spoil–hasten–plunder. [h] *So Scroll; Heb. and* I will fetch. [i] *Prob. rdg.; Heb. adds*
Rezin and the son of Remaliah.

The whole expanse of the land shall be filled,
so wide he spreads his wings; for God is with us.[a]
Take note,[b] you nations, and be dismayed.   9
Listen, all you distant parts of the earth:
   you may arm yourselves but will be dismayed;
   you may arm yourselves but will be dismayed.
Make your plans, but they will be foiled,   10
propose what you please, but it shall not stand;
   for God is with us.[a]

These were the words of the LORD to me, for his hand was strong   11
upon me; and he warned me not to follow[c] the ways of this people: You   12
shall not say 'too hard' of everything that this people calls hard; you
shall neither dread nor fear that which they fear. It is the LORD of   13
Hosts whom you must count 'hard';[d] he it is whom you must fear
and dread. He shall become your 'hardship',[d] a boulder and a rock   14
which the two houses of Israel shall run against and over which they
shall stumble, a trap and a snare to those who live in Jerusalem;
and many shall stumble over them, many shall fall and be broken, many   15
shall be snared and caught.

Fasten up the message,   16
seal the oracle with my teaching;[e]
   and I will wait for the LORD   17
who hides his face from the house of Jacob;
   I will watch for him.
See, I and the sons whom the LORD has given me   18
are to be signs and portents in Israel,
sent by the LORD of Hosts who dwells on Mount Zion.
   But men will say to you,   19
'Seek guidance of ghosts and familiar spirits
   who squeak and gibber;
a nation may surely seek guidance of its gods,
of the dead on behalf of the living,
   for an oracle or a message?'   20
They will surely say some such thing as this;
   but what they say is futile.
So despondency and fear will come over them,   21
   and then, when they are afraid and fearful,
   they will turn against their king and their gods.

[a] God is with us: *Heb.* Immanuel. [b] Take note: *so Sept.; Heb. unintelligible.*
[c] *Or* and he turned me from following... [d] 'hard' *and* 'hardship': *prob. rdg.; Heb.*
unintelligible in this context. [e] *Or* among my disciples, *or, with Sept.,* where it cannot
be studied.

22 Then, whether they turn their gaze upwards or look down,
  everywhere is distress and darkness inescapable,
  constraint and gloom that cannot be avoided;
9 1*ᵃ* for there is no escape for an oppressed people.

For, while the first invader has dealt lightly with the land of Zebulun
and the land of Naphtali, the second has dealt heavily with Galilee of
the Nations on the road beyond Jordan to the sea.

2*ᵇ*   The people who walked in darkness
  have seen a great light:
  light has dawned upon them,
    dwellers in a land as dark as death.
3   Thou hast increased their joy and*ᶜ* given them great gladness;
  they rejoice in thy presence as men rejoice at harvest,
  or as they are glad when they share out the spoil;
4   for thou hast shattered the yoke that burdened them,
      the collar that lay heavy on their shoulders,
      the driver's goad, as on the day of Midian's defeat.
5   All the boots of trampling soldiers
  and the garments fouled with blood
shall become a burning mass, fuel for fire.
6   For a boy has been born for us, a son given to us
    to bear the symbol of dominion on his shoulder;
      and he shall be called
      in purpose wonderful, in battle God-like,
      Father for all time,*ᵈ* Prince of peace.
7   Great*ᵉ* shall the dominion be,
    and boundless the peace
  bestowed on David's throne and on his kingdom,
  to establish it and sustain it
    with justice and righteousness
    from now and for evermore.
The zeal of the LORD of Hosts shall do this.

Prophecies addressed to Israel

8   The Lord has sent forth his word against Jacob
    and it shall fall on Israel;
9   all the people shall be humbled,

[*a*] *8. 23 in Heb.*   [*b*] *9. 1 in Heb.*   [*c*] *their joy and: prob. rdg.; Heb. the nation, not.*
[*d*] *Or of a wide realm.*   [*e*] *So Sept.; Heb. prefixes two unintelligible letters.*

Ephraim and the dwellers in Samaria,
though in their pride and arrogance they say,
The bricks are fallen, but we will build in hewn stone;   10
the sycomores are hacked down,
but we will use cedars instead.
The LORD has raised their foes[a] high against them   11
and spurred on their enemies,
Aramaeans from the east and Philistines from the west,   12
and they have swallowed Israel in one mouthful.
For all this his anger has not turned back,
and his hand is stretched out still.
Yet the people did not come back to him who struck them,   13
or seek guidance of the LORD of Hosts;
therefore on one day the LORD cut off from Israel   14
head and tail, palm and reed.[b]
This people's guides have led them astray;   16
those who should have been guided are in confusion.
Therefore the Lord showed no mercy to their young men,   17
no tenderness to their orphans and widows;
all were godless and evildoers,
every one speaking profanity.
For all this his anger has not turned back,
and his hand is stretched out still.

Wicked men have been set ablaze like a fire   18
fed with briars and thorns,
kindled in the forest thickets;
they are wrapped in a murky pall of smoke.
The land is scorched by the fury of the LORD of Hosts,   19
and the people have become fuel for the fire.[c]
On the right, one man eats his fill but yet is hungry;   20
on the left, another devours but is not satisfied;
each feeds on his own children's flesh,
and neither spares his own brother.[d]
[e]For all this his anger has not turned back,   21
and his hand is stretched out still.

Shame on you! you who make unjust laws   10
and publish burdensome decrees,
depriving the poor of justice,   2

[a] their foes: *prob. rdg.; Heb.* the foes of Rezin.   [b] *Prob. rdg.; Heb. adds* (15) The aged
and honoured are the head, and the prophet who gives false instruction is the tail.
[c] *See note on verse 20.*   [d] and neither...brother: *transposed from end of verse 19.*
[e] *Prob. rdg.; Heb. prefixes* Manasseh devours Ephraim, and Ephraim Manasseh; together
they are against Judah.

robbing the weakest of my people of their rights,
despoiling the widow and plundering the orphan.

3 What will you do when called to account,
  when ruin from afar confronts you?
  To whom will you flee for help
  and where will you leave your children,
4 so that they do not cower before the gaoler
    or fall by the executioner's hand?
  For all this his anger has not turned back,
  and his hand is stretched out still.

[24ᵃ] So, as tongues of fire lick up the stubble
  and the heat of the flame dies down,
    their root shall moulder away,
    and their shoots vanish like dust;
  for they have spurned the instruction of the LORD of Hosts
  and have rejected the word of the Holy One of Israel.
[25ᵃ] So the anger of the LORD is roused against his people,
  he has stretched out his hand against them and struck them
            down;
      the mountains trembled,
    and their corpses lay like offal in the streets.
  For all this his anger has not turned back,
  and his hand is stretched out still.

5 The Assyrian! He is the rod that I wield in my anger,
  and the staff of my wrath is in his hand.ᵇ
6 I send him against a godless nation,
  I bid him march against a people who rouse my wrath,
  to spoil and plunder at will
    and trample them down like mud in the streets.
7 But this man's purpose is lawless,
  lawless are the plans in his mind;
    for his thought is only to destroy
    and to wipe out nation after nation.
8 'Are not my officers all kings?' he says;
9 'see how Calno has suffered the fate of Carchemish.
  Is not Hamath like Arpad, and Samaria like Damascus?
10 Before now I have found kingdoms full of idols,
  with more images than Jerusalem and Samaria,
11 and now, what I have done to Samaria and her worthless gods,
  I will do also to Jerusalem and her idols.'

[a] *These are verses 24 and 25 of ch. 5, transposed to this point.* [b] *and...hand: prob.
rdg.; Heb. obscure.*

When the Lord has finished all that he means to do on Mount Zion　12
and in Jerusalem, he*a* will punish the king of Assyria for this fruit of
his pride and for his arrogance and vainglory, because he said:　　　13

> By my own might I have acted
> and in my own wisdom I have laid my schemes;
> I have removed the frontiers of nations
> 　　and plundered their treasures,
> like a bull I have trampled on their inhabitants.
> My hand has found its way to the wealth of nations,　　　14
> 　　and, as a man takes the eggs from a deserted nest,
> 　　so have I taken every land;
> 　　not a wing fluttered,
> 　　not a beak gaped, no chirp was heard.

> Shall the axe set itself up against the hewer,　　　15
> 　　or the saw claim mastery over the sawyer,
> as if a stick were to brandish him who wields it,
> 　　or a staff of wood to wield one who is not wood?

> Therefore the Lord, the LORD of Hosts, will send disease　　　16
> 　　on his sturdy frame, from head to toe,*b*
> and within his flesh*c* a fever like fire shall burn.
> 　　The light of Israel shall become a fire　　　17
> 　　　　and his Holy One a flame,
> which in one day shall burn up and consume
> 　　his thorns and his briars;
> the glory of forest and meadow shall be destroyed　　　18
> 　　as when a man falls in a fit;
> and the remnant of trees in the forest shall be so few　　　19
> 　　that a child may count them one by one.

On that day the remnant of Israel, the survivors of Jacob, shall cease　20
to lean on him that proved their destroyer, but shall loyally lean on the
LORD, the Holy One of Israel.

> A remnant shall turn again, a remnant of Jacob,　　　21
> 　　to God their champion.
> Your people, Israel, may be many as the sands of the sea,　　　22
> 　　but only a remnant shall turn again,
> 　　the instrument of final destruction,
> 　　　　justice in full flood;*d*

[a] *So Sept.; Heb.* I.　[b] from...toe: *transposed from verse 18; lit.* from neck to groin.
[c] within his flesh: *or* in his strong body.　[d] the instrument...flood: *or* wasting with
sickness, yet overflowing with righteousness.

23 for the Lord, the LORD of Hosts, will bring final destruction
upon all the earth.

24 Therefore these are the words of the Lord, the LORD of Hosts: My
people who live in Zion, you must not be afraid of the Assyrians,
though they beat you with their rod and lift their staff against you as
25 the Egyptians did; for soon, very soon, my anger will come to an end,
26 and my wrath will all be spent.*a* Then the LORD of Hosts will brandish
his whip over them as he did when he struck Midian at the Rock of
Oreb, and will lift his staff against the River as he did against Egypt.

27   On that day
the burden they laid on your shoulder shall be removed
and their yoke shall be broken from your neck.
28 An invader from Rimmon*b* has come to Aiath,
has passed by Migron,
and left his baggage-train at Michmash;
29   he has passed by Maabarah
and camped for the night at Geba.
Ramah is anxious, Gibeah of Saul is in panic.
30   Raise a shrill cry, Bath-gallim;
hear it, Laish, and answer her, Anathoth:
31 'Madmenah is in flight; take refuge, people of Gebim.'
32 Today he is due to pitch his camp in Nob;
he gives the signal to advance
against the mount of the daughter of Zion,
the hill of Jerusalem.

33   Look, the Lord, the LORD of Hosts,
cleaves the trees with a flash of lightning,
the tallest are hewn down, the lofty laid low,
34   the heart of the forest is felled with the axe,
and Lebanon with its noble trees has fallen.
11 Then a shoot shall grow from the stock of Jesse,
and a branch shall spring*c* from his roots.
2 The spirit of the LORD shall rest upon him,
a spirit of wisdom and understanding,
a spirit of counsel*d* and power,
a spirit of knowledge and the fear of the LORD.*e*
3 He shall not judge by what he sees
nor decide by what he hears;

[a] will...spent: *prob. rdg.; Heb. obscure.* [b] and their yoke...Rimmon: *prob. rdg.; Heb.*
and their yoke from upon your neck, and a yoke shall be broken because of oil. He...
[c] *So Sept.; Heb.* bear fruit. [d] *Or* force. [e] *Prob. rdg.; Heb. adds* and his delight shall
be in the fear of the LORD.

he shall judge the poor with justice   4
    and defend the humble in the land with equity;
  his mouth shall be a rod to strike down the ruthless,[a]
    and with a word he shall slay the wicked.
Round his waist he shall wear the belt of justice,   5
    and good faith shall be the girdle round his body.
  Then the wolf shall live with the sheep,   6
    and the leopard lie down with the kid;
the calf and the young lion shall grow up[b] together,
  and a little child shall lead them;
    the cow and the bear shall be friends,   7
    and their young shall lie down together.
The lion shall eat straw like cattle;
  the infant shall play over the hole of the cobra,   8
  and the young child dance over the viper's nest.
They shall not hurt or destroy in all my holy mountain;   9
  for as the waters fill the sea,
so shall the land be filled with the knowledge of the LORD.

On that day a scion from the root of Jesse   10
  shall be set up as a signal to the peoples;
  the nations shall rally to it,
  and its resting-place shall be glorious.

On that day the Lord will make his power more glorious by   11
recovering the remnant of his people, those who are still left, from
Assyria and Egypt, from Pathros, from Cush and Elam, from Shinar,
Hamath and the islands of the sea.

Then he will raise a signal to the nations   12
    and gather together those driven out of Israel;
  he will assemble Judah's scattered people
  from the four corners of the earth.
  Ephraim's jealousy shall vanish,   13
    and Judah's enmity shall be done away.
  Ephraim shall not be jealous of Judah,
    nor Judah the enemy of Ephraim.
They shall swoop down on the Philistine flank in the west   14
    and together they shall plunder the tribes of the east;
  Edom and Moab shall be within their grasp,
    and Ammon shall obey them.
The LORD will divide the tongue of the Egyptian sea   15
  and wave his hand over the River
    to bring a scorching wind;

[a] *Prob. rdg.; Heb.* land.   [b] shall grow up: *so Sept.; Heb.* and the buffalo.

he shall split it into seven channels
and let men go across dry-shod.

16 So there shall be a causeway for the remnant of his people,
    for the remnant rescued from Assyria,
as there was for Israel when they came up out of Egypt.

12 You shall say on that day:
    I will praise thee, O Lord,
      though thou hast been angry with me;
      thy anger has turned back,[a]
    and thou hast comforted me.

2   God is indeed my deliverer.
      I am confident and unafraid;
for the Lord is my refuge and defence[b]
    and has shown himself my deliverer.

3   And so you shall draw water with joy
    from the springs of deliverance.

4   You shall all say on that day:
Give thanks to the Lord and invoke him by name,
    make his deeds known in the world around;
    declare that his name is supreme.

5   Sing psalms to the Lord, for he has triumphed,
    and this must be made known in all the world.

6   Cry out, shout aloud, you that dwell in Zion,
for the Holy One of Israel is among you in majesty.

Prophecies relating to foreign nations

13 BABYLON: AN ORACLE which Isaiah son of Amoz received in a vision.

2   Raise the standard on a windy height,
    roar out your summons,
    beckon with arm upraised to the advance,
      draw[c] your swords, you nobles.

3   I have given my warriors their orders
    and summoned my fighting men to launch my anger;
      they are eager for my triumph.

4   Hark, a tumult in the mountains, the sound of a vast multitude;
hark, the roar of kingdoms, of nations gathering!

---

[a] *So Sept.; Heb.* let thy anger turn back.   [b] defence: *prob. rdg., cp. Sept.; Heb.* defence of Yah.   [c] draw: *so Sept.; Heb.* doors of.

The LORD of Hosts is mustering a host for war,
men from a far country, from beyond the horizon.   5
 It is the LORD with the weapons of his wrath
 coming to lay the whole land waste.
Howl, for the Day of the LORD is at hand;   6
it comes, a mighty blow from Almighty God.
Thereat shall every hand hang limp,   7
every man's courage shall melt away,
 his stomach hollow with fear;   8
anguish shall grip them, like a woman in labour.
 One man shall look aghast at another,
 and their faces shall burn with shame.
The Day of the LORD is coming indeed,   9
that cruel day of wrath and fury,
to make the land a desolation
and exterminate its wicked people.
The stars of heaven in their constellations shall give no light,   10
the sun shall be darkened at its rising,
and the moon refuse to shine.
I will bring disaster upon the world   11
and their due punishment upon the wicked.
 I will check the pride of the haughty
 and bring low the arrogance of ruthless men.
I will make men scarcer than fine gold,   12
rarer than gold of Ophir.
Then the heavens shall shudder,*a*   13
and the earth shall be shaken from its place
at the fury of the LORD of Hosts, on the day of his anger.
 Then, like a gazelle before the hunter   14
 or a flock with no man to round it up,
each man will go back to his own people,
every one will flee to his own land.
 All who are found will be stabbed,   15
all who are taken will fall by the sword;
their infants will be dashed to the ground before their eyes, 16
their houses rifled and their wives ravished.
 I will stir up against them the Medes,   17
who care nothing for silver and are not tempted by gold,*b*
who have no pity on little children   18
and spare no mother's son;
 and Babylon, fairest of kingdoms,   19

[a] *Prob. rdg.; Heb.* Then I will make the heavens shudder.   [b] *Prob. rdg.; Heb. adds* bows
shall dash young men to the ground.

    proud beauty of the Chaldaeans,
shall be like Sodom and Gomorrah
    when God overthrew them.

20   Never again shall she be inhabited,
no man shall dwell in her through all the ages;
    there no Arab shall pitch his tent,
    no shepherds fold their flocks.

21   There marmots shall have their lairs,
and porcupines*a* shall overrun her houses;
    there desert owls shall dwell,
    and there he-goats shall gambol;

22   jackals shall occupy her mansions,*b*
and wolves her*c* gorgeous palaces.
    Her time draws very near,
    and her days have not long to run.

14   The LORD will show compassion for Jacob and will once again make Israel his choice. He will settle them on their own soil, and strangers
2 will come to join them and attach themselves to Jacob. Many*c* nations shall escort Israel to her place, and she shall employ them as slaves and slave-girls on the land of the LORD; she shall take her captors captive and rule over her task-masters.

3   When the LORD gives you relief from your pain and your fears and
4 from the cruel slavery laid upon you, you will take up this song of derision over the king of Babylon:

    See how the oppressor has met his end and his frenzy*d* ceased!
5   The LORD has broken the rod of the wicked,
      the sceptre of the ruler
6   who struck down peoples in his rage
      with unerring blows,
    who crushed nations in anger
    and persecuted them unceasingly.
7   The whole world has rest and is at peace;
    it breaks into cries of joy.
8   The pines themselves and the cedars of Lebanon exult over you:
    Since you have been laid low, they say,
    no man comes up to fell us.

9   Sheol below was all astir
      to meet you at your coming;
    she roused the ancient dead to meet you,

[a] *Mng. of Heb. word uncertain.* [b] *Prob. rdg.; Heb.* her widows. [c] *So Scroll; Heb. om.*
[d] *So Scroll; Heb. word unknown.*

all who had been leaders on earth;
    she made all who had been kings of the nations
      rise from their thrones.
One and all they greet you with these words: 10
    So you too are weak as we are,
      and have become one of us!
    Your pride and all the music of your lutes   11
      have been brought down to Sheol;*a*
    maggots are the pallet beneath you,
      and worms your coverlet.

How you have fallen from heaven, bright morning star,   12
felled to the earth, sprawling helpless across the nations!
    You thought in your own mind,   13
      I will scale the heavens;
I will set my throne high above the stars of God,
    I will sit on the mountain where the gods meet
      in the far recesses of the north.
    I will rise high above the cloud-banks   14
      and make myself like the Most High.
    Yet you shall be brought down to Sheol,   15
      to the depths of the abyss.
    Those who see you will stare at you,   16
      they will look at you and ponder:
Is this, they will say, the man who shook the earth,
      who made kingdoms quake,
    who turned the world into a desert   17
      and laid its cities in ruins,
    who never let his prisoners go free to their homes,
      the kings of every land?   18
    Now they lie all of them in honour,
      each in his last home.
    But you have been flung out unburied,   19
      mere loathsome carrion,*b*
    a companion to the slain pierced by the sword
    who have gone down to the stony abyss.
      And you, a corpse trampled underfoot,
    shall not share burial with them,   20
for you have ruined your land and slaughtered your people.
Such a brood of evildoers shall never be seen again.
    Make the shambles ready for his sons   21
      butchered for their fathers' sin;

[a] *Or* Your pride has been brought down to Sheol to the crowding throng of your dead.
[b] carrion: *prob. rdg., cp. Sept.; Heb.* shoot.

they shall not rise up and possess the world
nor cover the face of the earth with cities.

22 I will rise against them, says the LORD of Hosts; I will destroy the
name of Babylon and what remains of her, her offspring and posterity,
23 says the LORD; I will make her a haunt of the bustard, a waste of fen,
and sweep her with the besom of destruction. This is the very word of
the LORD of Hosts.

24   The LORD of Hosts has sworn:
In very truth, as I planned, so shall it be;*a*
    as I designed, so shall it fall out:
25 I will break the Assyrian in my own land
    and trample him underfoot upon my mountains;
his yoke shall be lifted from you,
    his burden taken from your*b* shoulders.
26 This is the plan prepared for the whole earth,
this the hand stretched out over all the nations.
27 For the LORD of Hosts has prepared his plan:
    who shall frustrate it?
His is the hand stretched out, and who shall turn it back?

28 In the year that King Ahaz died this oracle came from God:

29   Let none of you rejoice, you Philistines,
    because the rod that chastised you is broken;
for a viper shall be born of a snake as a plant from the root,
    and its fruit shall be a flying serpent.
30 But the poor shall graze their flocks in my meadows,
    and the destitute shall lie down in peace;
but the offspring of your roots I will kill by starvation,
    and put*c* the remnant of you to death.
31 Howl in the gate, cry for help in the city,
    let all Philistia be in turmoil;
for a great enemy is coming from the north,
    not a man straying from*d* his ranks.
32 What answer is there for the envoys of the nation?
This, that the LORD has fixed Zion in her place,
    and the afflicted among his people shall take refuge there.

15   Moab: an oracle.

On the night when Ar is sacked, Moab meets her doom;
on the night when Kir is sacked, Moab meets her doom.

[a] *So Scroll; Heb.* so it was.   [b] from you...your: *so Scroll; Heb.* from them...their.
[c] *So Scroll; Heb.* and he will put.   [d] *So Scroll; Heb.* no one alone in...

The people of Dibon go up^a to the hill-shrines to weep;   2
Moab howls over Nebo and over Medeba.
The hair is torn from every head, and every beard shaved off.
  In the streets men go clothed with sackcloth,   3
    they cry out^b on the roofs;
  in the public squares every man howls,
    weeping as he goes through them.
Heshbon and Elealeh cry for help,   4
their voices are heard as far as Jahaz.
Thus Moab's stoutest warriors become cowards,
and her courage ebbs away.
My heart cries out for Moab,   5
whose nobles have fled^c as far as Zoar.^{d}
On the ascent to Luhith men go up weeping;
on the road to Horonaim there are cries of^e 'Disaster!'
The waters of Nimrim are desolate indeed;   6
the grass is parched, the herbage dead,
  not a green thing is left;
and so the people carry off across the gorge of the Arabim   7
  their hard-earned wealth and all their savings.
The cry for help echoes round the frontiers of Moab,   8
their howling reaches Eglaim and Beer-elim.
  The waters of Dimon already run with blood;   9
  yet I have more troubles in store for Dimon,
    for I have a vision^f of the survivors of Moab,
    of the remnant of Admah.
The rulers of the country send a present of lambs   16
  from Sela in the wilderness
  to the hill of the daughter of Zion;
the daughters of Moab at the fords of the Arnon   2
shall be like fluttering birds, like scattered nestlings.
'Take up our cause with all your might;   3
let your shadow shield us at high noon, dark as night.
Shelter the homeless, do not betray the fugitive;
let the homeless people of Moab find refuge with you;   4
hide them from the despoiler.'

When extortion has done its work and the looting is over,
  when the heel of the oppressor has vanished from the land,
a throne shall be set up in mutual trust in David's tent,   5

[a] The people...go up: *prob. rdg.; Heb.* He has gone up to the house and Dibon. [b] they
cry out: *prob. rdg., cp. Sept.; Heb. om.* [c] have fled: *prob. rdg.; Heb. om.* [d] *Prob. rdg.;
Heb. adds* Eglath Shelishiya. [e] there are cries of: *prob. rdg., cp. Vulg.; Heb. unintelligible.*
[f] I have a vision: *prob. rdg.; Heb.* a lion.

and on it there shall sit a true judge,
one who seeks justice and is swift to do right.

6 We have heard tell of Moab's pride, how great it is,
we have heard of his pride, his overweening pride;
his talk is full of lies.

7 For this all Moab shall howl;
Moab shall howl indeed;
he[a] shall mourn for the prosperous farmers of Kir-hareseth,
utterly ruined;

8 the orchards of Heshbon,
the vines of Sibmah languish,
though their red grapes once laid low the lords of the nations,
though they reached as far as Jazer
and trailed out to the wilderness,
though their branches spread abroad and crossed the sea.

9 Therefore I will weep for Sibmah's vines as I weep for Jazer.
I will drench you with my tears, Heshbon and Elealeh;
for over your summer-fruits and your harvest
the shouts of the harvesters are ended.

10 Joy and gladness shall be banished from the meadows,
no more shall men shout and sing in the vineyards,
no more shall they tread wine in the winepresses;
I have silenced the shouting of the harvesters.

11 Therefore my heart throbs
like a harp for Moab,
and my very soul for Kir-hareseth.[b]

12 When Moab comes to worship
and wearies himself at the hill-shrines,
when he enters his sanctuary to pray,
he will gain nothing.

13 These are the words which the LORD spoke long ago about Moab;
14 and now he says, In three years, as a hired labourer counts them off,
the glory of Moab shall become contemptible for all his vast numbers;
a handful shall be left[c] and those of no account.

17   Damascus: an oracle.

Damascus shall be a city no longer,
she shall be but a heap of ruins.

2 For ever desolate, flocks shall have her for their own,[d]
and lie there undisturbed.

[a] *Prob. rdg.; Heb.* you. [b] *Prob. rdg.; Heb.* Kir-hares. [c] shall be left: *so Sept.; Heb.* a remnant. [d] For ever...own: *so Sept.; Heb.* The cities of Aroer shall be deserted for flocks.

No longer shall Ephraim boast a fortified city,   3
    or Damascus a kingdom;
the remnant of Aram and the glory of Israel, their fate is one.
This is the very word of the LORD of Hosts.

On that day Jacob's weight shall dwindle   4
    and the fat on his limbs waste away,
as when the harvester gathers up the standing corn,   5
    and reaps the ears in armfuls,
or as when a man gleans the ears in the Vale of Rephaim,
    or as when one beats an olive-tree   6
    and only gleanings are left on it,
two or three berries on the top of a branch,
    four or five on the boughs of the fruiting tree.
This is the very word of the LORD the God of Israel.

On that day men shall look to their Maker and turn their eyes to the   7
Holy One of Israel; they shall not look to the altars made by their   8
own hands nor to anything that their fingers have made, sacred poles or
incense-altars.
On that day their strong cities shall be deserted like the cities of the   9
Hivites and the Amorites,[a] which they abandoned when Israel came
in; all shall be desolate.

For you forgot the God who delivered you,   10
    and did not remember the rock, your stronghold.
Plant then, if you will, your gardens in honour of Adonis,
    strike your cuttings for a foreign god;
protect your gardens on the day you plant them,   11
    and next day make the seed sprout.
But the crop will be scorched when wasting disease comes
    in the day of incurable pain.

Listen! it is the thunder of many peoples,   12
they thunder with the thunder of the sea.
Listen! it is the roar of nations
roaring with the roar of mighty waters.[b]
When he rebukes them, away they fly,   13
driven like chaff on the hills before the wind,
    like thistledown before the storm.
At evening all is confusion,   14
    and before morning they are gone.
Such is the fate of our plunderers,
    the lot of those who despoil us.

[a] Hivites…Amorites: *prob. rdg.*, *cp. Sept.*; *Heb.* woodland and hill-country. [b] *So
some MSS.; others add* peoples roar with the roar of great waters.

18   There is a land of sailing ships,
          a land beyond the rivers of Cush
2   which sends its envoys by the Nile,^a
       journeying on the waters in vessels of reed.
       Go, swift messengers,
          go to a people tall and smooth-skinned,
          to a people dreaded near and far,
          a nation strong and proud,
          whose land is scoured by rivers.
3   All you who dwell in the world, inhabitants of earth,
          shall see when the signal is hoisted on the mountains
          and shall hear when the trumpet sounds.

4 These were the words of the Lord to me:

       From my dwelling-place I will look quietly down
          when the heat shimmers in the summer sun,
          when the dew is heavy at harvest time.^b
5   Before the vintage, when the budding is over
       and the flower ripens into a berry,
          the shoots shall be cut down with knives,
          the branches struck off and cleared away.
6   All shall be left to birds of prey on the hills
             and to beasts of the earth;
          in summer the birds shall make their home there,
       in winter every beast of the earth.

7   At that time tribute shall be brought to the Lord of Hosts from^c
       a people tall and smooth-skinned, dreaded near and far, a nation strong
       and proud, whose land is scoured by rivers. They shall bring it to
       Mount Zion, the place where men invoke the name of the Lord of
       Hosts.

19   Egypt: an oracle.

       See how the Lord comes riding swiftly upon a cloud,
          he shall descend upon Egypt;
          the idols of Egypt quail before him,
          Egypt's courage melts within her.
2   I will set Egyptian against Egyptian,
          and they shall fight one against another,
             neighbour against neighbour,
       city against city and kingdom against kingdom.
3   Egypt's spirit shall sink within her,
          and I will throw her counsels into confusion.

          [a] *Lit.* sea. [b] time: *so Sept.; Heb.* heat. [c] from: *so Scroll; Heb. om.*

They may resort to idols and oracle-mongers,
    to ghosts and spirits,
but I will hand Egypt over to a hard master,   4
    and a cruel king shall rule over them.
This is the very word of the Lord, the LORD of Hosts.

The waters of the Nile*a* shall drain away,   5
    the river shall be parched and run dry;
        its channels shall stink,   6
the streams of Egypt shall be parched and dry up;
    reeds and rushes shall wither away;
        the lotus too beside the Nile*b*   7
and all that is sown along the Nile shall dry up,
    shall be blown away and vanish.
The fishermen shall groan and lament,   8
all who cast their hooks into the Nile
and those who spread nets on the water shall lose heart.
    The flax-dressers shall hang their heads,   9
    the women carding and the weavers shall grow pale,*c*
Egypt's spinners shall be downcast,   10
    and all her artisans sick at heart.

Fools that you are, you princes of Zoan!   11
Wisest of Pharaoh's counsellors you may be,
    but stupid counsellors you are.
    How can you say to Pharaoh,
'I am the heir of wise men and spring from ancient kings'?
    Where are your wise men, Pharaoh,   12
    to teach you and make known to you
what the LORD of Hosts has planned for Egypt?
Zoan's princes are fools, the princes of Noph are dupes;   13
    the chieftains of her clans have led Egypt astray.
The LORD has infused into them*d*   14
    a spirit that warps their judgement;
    they make Egypt miss her way in all she does,
    as a drunkard will miss his footing as he vomits.
There shall be nothing in Egypt that any man can do,   15
head or tail, palm or rush.

When that day comes the Egyptians shall become weak as women; 16
they shall fear and tremble when they see the LORD of Hosts raise his
hand against them, as raise it he will. The land of Judah shall strike 17

[*a*] *Lit.* sea.   [*b*] *Prob. rdg.; Heb. adds* on the mouth of the Nile.   [*c*] shall grow pale: *so
Scroll; Heb.* white linen.   [*d*] *So Sept.; Heb.* her.

terror into Egypt; its very name shall cause dismay, because of the plans that the LORD of Hosts has laid against them.

18 When that day comes there shall be five cities in Egypt speaking the language of Canaan and swearing allegiance to the LORD of Hosts, and one of them shall be called the City of the Sun.*a*

19 When that day comes there shall be an altar to the LORD in the heart of Egypt, and a sacred pillar set up for the LORD upon her frontier.

20 It shall stand as a token and a reminder to the LORD of Hosts in Egypt, so that when they appeal to him against their oppressors, he may send a

21 deliverer to champion their cause, and he shall rescue them. The LORD will make himself known to the Egyptians; on that day they shall acknowledge the LORD and do him service with sacrifice and grain-

22 offering, make vows to him and pay them. The LORD will strike down Egypt, healing as he strikes;*b* then they will turn back to him and he will hear their prayers and heal them.

23 When that day comes there shall be a highway between Egypt and Assyria; Assyrians shall come to Egypt and Egyptians to Assyria; then Egyptians shall worship with*c* Assyrians.

24 When that day comes Israel shall rank with Egypt and Assyria, those
25 three, and shall be a blessing in the centre of the world. So the LORD of Hosts will bless them: A blessing be upon Egypt my people, upon Assyria the work of my hands, and upon Israel my possession.

20 SARGON KING OF ASSYRIA sent his commander-in-chief*d* to
2 Ashdod, and he took it by storm. At that time the LORD said to*e* Isaiah son of Amoz, Come, strip the sackcloth from your waist and take your sandals off. He did so, and went about naked and barefoot.
3 The LORD said, My servant Isaiah has gone naked and barefoot for
4 three years as a sign and a warning to Egypt and Cush; just so shall the king of Assyria lead the captives of Egypt and the exiles of Cush naked and barefoot, their buttocks shamefully exposed, young and old alike.
5 All men shall be dismayed, their hopes in Cush and their pride in
6 Egypt humbled. On that day those who dwell along this coast will say, So much for all our hopes on which we relied*f* for help and deliverance from the king of Assyria; what escape have we now?

21   A wilderness: an oracle.

Rough weather, advancing like a storm in the south,
coming from the wilderness, from a land of terror!

[a] the City of the Sun: *or* Heliopolis; *so some MSS.; others* the city of destruction.
[b] healing as he strikes: *so Heb.; Scroll has* striking until their resistance is broken.   [c] *Or* shall be slaves to.   [d] *Or sent* Tartan.   [e] *So Sept.; Heb.* through.   [f] *So Scroll; Heb.* to which we fled.

Grim is the vision shown to me: 2
the traitor betrayed, the spoiler himself despoiled.
Up, Elam; up, Medes, to the siege,
   no time for weariness!
At this my limbs writhe in anguish,   3
I am gripped by pangs like a woman in labour.
I am distraught past hearing, dazed past seeing,
my mind reels, sudden convulsions seize me.   4

The cool twilight I longed for has become a terror:
the banquet is set out, the rugs are spread;   5
   they are eating and drinking—
rise, princes, burnish your shields.
  For these were the words of the Lord to me: 6
  Go, post a watchman to report what he sees.
  He sees chariots, two-horsed chariots,   7
  riders on asses, riders on camels.
  He is alert, alert, always on the alert.
    Then the look-out*a* cried: 8
All day long I stand on the Lord's watch-tower
and night after night I keep my station.
See, there come men in a chariot, a two-horsed chariot.   9
    And a voice calls back:
Fallen, fallen is Babylon,
and all the images of her gods lie shattered on the ground.
    O my people,   10
once trodden out and winnowed on the threshing-floor,
  what I have heard from the LORD of Hosts,
  from the God of Israel, I have told you.

Dumah: an oracle.   11

One calls to me from Seir:
Watchman, what is left of the night?
Watchman, what is left?
    The watchman answered: 12
Morning comes, and also night.*b*
Ask if you must; then come back again.

With the Arabs: an oracle.   13

You caravans of Dedan, that camp in the scrub with the Arabs,
  bring water to meet the thirsty.   14
You dwellers in Tema, meet the fugitives with food,

[a] *So Scroll; Heb.* a lion.   [b] and also night: *or* and the night is full spent.

15 for they flee from the sword, the sharp edge of the sword,
from the bent bow, and from the press of battle.

16 For these are the words of the Lord to me: Within a year, as a hired
labourer counts off the years, all the glory of Kedar shall come to an
17 end; few shall be the bows left to the warriors of Kedar.
The LORD the God of Israel has spoken.

22   The Valley of Vision:[a] an oracle.

Tell me, what is amiss
that you have all climbed on to the roofs,
2   O city full of tumult, town in ferment
and filled with uproar,
whose slain were not slain with the sword
and did not die in battle?
3   Your commanders are all in flight,
huddled together out of bowshot;
all your stoutest warriors[b] are huddled together,
they have taken to their heels.
4   Then I said, Turn your eyes away from me;
leave me to weep in misery.
Do not thrust consolation on me
for the ruin of my own people.

5 For the Lord, the LORD of Hosts, has ordained a day of tumult, a day
of trampling and turmoil in the Valley of Vision,[a] rousing cries for help
that echo among the mountains.

6   Elam took up his quiver,
horses were harnessed to the chariots of Aram,[c]
Kir took the cover from his shield.
7   Your fairest valleys were overrun by chariots and horsemen,
the gates were hard beset,
8   the heart of Judah's defence was laid open.

On that day you looked to the weapons stored in the House of the
9 Forest; you filled all the many pools in the City of David, collecting
10 water from the Lower Pool.[d] Then you surveyed the houses in Jeru-
11 salem, tearing some down to make the wall inaccessible, and between
the two walls you made a cistern for the Waters of the Old Pool;
but you did not look to the Maker of it all
or consider him who fashioned it long ago.

[a] Or of Calamity. [b] your stoutest warriors: so Sept.; Heb. those found in you.
[c] Prob. rdg.; Heb. man. [d] you filled...Lower Pool: or you took note of the cracks,
many as they were, in the wall of the City of David, and you collected water from the
Lower Pool.

On that day the Lord, the LORD of Hosts, 12
  called for weeping and beating the breast,
  for shaving the head and putting on sackcloth;
  but instead there was joy and merry-making, 13
slaughtering of cattle and killing of sheep,
eating of meat and drinking of wine, as you thought,
Let us eat and drink; for tomorrow we die.

The LORD of Hosts has revealed himself to me; in my hearing he 14
swore:

Your wickedness shall never be purged
  until you die.
This is the word of the Lord, the LORD of Hosts.

These were the words of the Lord, the LORD of Hosts: 15

Go to this steward,
  to Shebna, comptroller of the household, and say:
What right, what business, have you here, 16
  that you have dug yourself a grave here,
  cutting out your grave on a height
  and carving yourself a resting-place in the rock?
The LORD will shake you out, 17
  shake you as a garment[a] is shaken out
  to rid it of lice;
then he will bundle you tightly and throw you 18
like a ball into a great wide land.
  There you shall die,
  and there shall lie your chariot of honour,
  an object of contempt to your master's household.
I will remove you from office and drive[b] you from your post. 19

On that day I will send for my servant Eliakim son of Hilkiah; 20
I will invest him with your robe, gird him with your sash; and hand 21
over your authority to him. He shall be a father to the inhabitants of
Jerusalem and the people of Judah. I will lay the key of the house of 22
David on his shoulder; what he opens no man shall shut, and what he
shuts no man shall open. He shall be a seat of honour for his father's 23
family; I will fasten him firmly in place like a peg. On him shall hang 24
all the weight of the family, down to the lowest dregs[c]—all the little
vessels, both bowls and pots. On that day, says the LORD of Hosts, the 25
peg which was firmly fastened in its place shall be removed; it shall be

[a] *Prob. rdg.; Heb.* man.   [b] *So Pesh.; Heb.* he will drive.   [c] down to the lowest dregs:
lit. dung and excrement.

981

hacked out and shall fall, and the load of things hanging on it shall be destroyed. The LORD has spoken.

23   Tyre: an oracle.

The ships of Tarshish howl, for the harbour is sacked;
the port of entry from Kittim is swept away.

2-3   The people of the sea-coast, the merchants of Sidon, wail,
people whose agents[a] cross the great waters,
whose harvest[b] is the grain of the Shihor
and their revenue the trade of nations.

4   Sidon, the sea-fortress,[c] cries in her disappointment,[d]
I no longer feel the anguish of labour or bear children;
I have no young sons to rear, no daughters to bring up.

5   When the news is confirmed in Egypt
her people sway in anguish at the fate of Tyre.

6   Make your way to Tarshish, they say,
howl, you who dwell by the sea-coast.

7   Is this your busy city, ancient in story,
on whose voyages you were carried to settle far away?

8   Whose plan was this against Tyre, the city of battlements,
whose merchants were princes
and her traders the most honoured men on earth?

9   The LORD of Hosts planned it to prick every noble's pride
and bring all the most honoured men on earth into contempt.

10   Take to the tillage of your fields,[e] you people of Tarshish;
for your market[f] is lost.

11   The LORD has stretched out his hand over the sea
and shaken kingdoms,
he has given his command to destroy the marts of Canaan;

12   and he has said, You shall busy yourselves no more,
you, the sorely oppressed virgin city of Sidon.
Though you arise and cross over to Kittim,
even there you shall find no rest.

13   Look at this land, the destined home of ships[g]! The Chaldaeans[h]
erected their[i] siege-towers, dismantled its palaces and laid it in ruins.

14   Howl, you ships of Tarshish;
for your haven is sacked.

[a] whose agents: *prob. rdg.*, *cp. Scroll; Heb.* they have filled you.   [b] whose harvest: *prob. rdg.; Heb.* the harvest of the Nile.   [c] the sea-fortress: *prob. rdg.; Heb.* the sea, sea-fortress, saying.   [d] in her disappointment: *prob. rdg.; Heb.* be disappointed. [e] Take...fields: *so Sept.; Heb.* Pass over your fields like the Nile.   [f] *Prob. rdg.; Heb.* girdle.   [g] *Or* marmots.   [h] *Prob. rdg.; Heb. adds* this was the people; it was not Assyria. [i] *Prob. rdg.; Heb.* his.

From that day Tyre shall be forgotten for seventy years, the span of 15
one king's life. At the end of the seventy years her plight shall be that
of the harlot in the song:

Take your harp, go round the city,   16
  poor forgotten harlot;
touch the strings sweetly, sing all your songs,
  make men remember you again.

At the end of seventy years, the LORD will turn again to Tyre; she 17
shall go back to her old trade and hire herself out to every kingdom on
earth. The profits of her trading will be dedicated to the LORD; they 18
shall not be hoarded or stored up, but shall be given to those who
worship*a* the LORD, to purchase food in plenty and fine attire.

The LORD's judgement on the earth

Beware, the LORD will empty the earth,   **24**
split it open and turn it upside down,
  and scatter its inhabitants.
  Then it will be the same for priest and people,   2
the same for master and slave, mistress and slave-girl,
  seller and buyer,
borrower and lender, debtor and creditor.
  The earth is emptied clean away   3
  and stripped clean bare.
For this is the word that the LORD has spoken.
  The earth dries up and withers,   4
  the whole world withers and grows sick;
    the earth's high places*b* sicken,
  and earth itself is desecrated by the feet of those who live in it, 5
because they have broken the laws, disobeyed the statutes
  and violated the eternal covenant.
For this a curse has devoured the earth   6
  and its inhabitants stand aghast.
  For this those who inhabit the earth dwindle
  and only a few men are left.
  The new wine dries up, the vines sicken,   7
and all the revellers turn to sorrow.
  Silent the merry beat of tambourines,   8

[a] *Lit.* sit in the presence of.   [b] the earth's high places: *so Sept.; Heb.* the height of the
people of earth.

   hushed the shouts of revelry,
   the merry harp is silent.

9 No one shall drink wine to the sound of song;
   the liquor will be bitter to the man who drinks it.

10   The city of chaos is a broken city,
   every house barred, that no one may enter.

11 Men call for wine in the streets;
   all revelry is darkened,
   and mirth is banished from the land.

12   Desolation alone is left in the city
   and the gate is broken into pieces.

13 So shall it be in all the world, in every nation,
   as when an olive-tree is beaten and stripped,
   as when the vintage is ended.

14 Men raise their voices and cry aloud,
   they shout in the west,[a] so great is the Lord's majesty.

15   Therefore let the Lord be glorified in the regions of the east,[b]
   and the name of the Lord the God of Israel
   in the coasts and islands of the west.

16 From the ends of the earth we have heard them sing,
   How lovely is righteousness!
   But I thought, Villainy, villainy!
   Woe to the traitors[c] and their treachery!
   Traitors double-dyed they are indeed!

17 The hunter's scare, the pit, and the trap
   threaten all who dwell in the land;

18 if a man runs from the rattle of the scare
   he will fall into the pit;
   if he climbs out of the pit
   he will be caught in the trap.
   When the windows of heaven above are opened
   and earth's foundations shake,

19   the earth is utterly shattered,
  it is convulsed and reels wildly.

20 The earth reels to and fro like a drunken man
   and sways like a watchman's shelter;
   the sins of men weigh heavy upon it,
   and it falls to rise no more.

21   On that day the Lord will punish
  the host of heaven in heaven, and on earth the kings of the earth,

[a] in the west: *or* more loudly than the sea. [b] the regions of the east: *mng. of Heb. word uncertain.* [c] *So Sept.; Heb.* Woe to me, traitors.

herded together, close packed like prisoners in a dungeon;   22
shut up in gaol, after a long time they shall be punished.
The moon shall grow pale and the sun hide its face in shame;   23
> for the LORD of Hosts has become king
> on Mount Zion and in Jerusalem,
> and shows his glory before their elders.

The deliverance and ingathering of Judah

O LORD, thou art my God;   25
I will exalt thee and praise thy name;
for thou hast accomplished a wonderful purpose,
certain and sure, from of old.
> For thou hast turned cities*ᵃ* into heaps of ruin,   2
> and fortified towns into rubble;
> every mansion in the cities is swept away,
>> never to be rebuilt.
> For this a cruel nation holds thee in honour,   3
> the cities of ruthless nations fear thee.
> Truly thou hast been a refuge to the poor,   4
> a refuge to the needy in his trouble,
shelter from the tempest and shade from the heat.
> For the blast of the ruthless is like an icy storm
>> or a scorching drought;   5
>> thou subduest the roar of the foe,*ᵇ*
>> and the song of the ruthless dies away.

On this mountain the LORD of Hosts will prepare   6
> a banquet of rich fare for all the peoples,
> a banquet of wines well matured and richest fare,
>> well-matured wines strained clear.
On this mountain the LORD will swallow up   7
> that veil that shrouds all the peoples,
> the pall thrown over all the nations;
> he will swallow up death for ever.   8
Then the Lord GOD will wipe away the tears
> from every face
and remove the reproach of his people from the whole earth.
> The LORD has spoken.

> On that day men will say,   9
> See, this is our God

[*a*] cities: *so Sept.; Heb.* from a city.   [*b*] *Prob. rdg.; Heb. adds* heat in the shadow of a cloud.

for whom we have waited to deliver us;
this is the LORD for whom we have waited;
let us rejoice and exult in his deliverance.

10 For the hand of the LORD will rest on this mountain,
but Moab shall be trampled under his feet
as straw is trampled into a midden.

11 In it Moab shall spread out his hands
as a swimmer spreads his hands to swim,
but he shall sink his pride with every stroke of his hands.

12 The LORD has thrown down the high defences of your walls,
has levelled them to the earth
and brought them down to the dust.

26 On that day this song shall be sung in Judah:

We have a strong city
whose walls and ramparts are our deliverance.

2 Open the gates to let a righteous nation in,
a nation that keeps faith.

3 Thou dost keep in peace men of constant mind,
in peace because they trust in thee.

4 Trust in the LORD for ever;
for the LORD himself is an everlasting rock.

5 He has brought low all who dwell high in a towering city;
he levels it[a] to the ground and lays it in the dust,

6 that the oppressed and the poor may tread it underfoot.

7 The path of the righteous is level,
and thou markest out the right way for the upright.

8 We too look to[b] the path prescribed in thy laws, O LORD;
thy name and thy memory are our heart's desire.

9 With all my heart I long for thee in the night,
I seek thee eagerly when dawn breaks;
for, when thy laws prevail in the land,
the inhabitants of the world learn justice.

10 The wicked are destroyed, they have never learnt justice;
corrupt in a land of honest ways,
they do not regard the majesty of the LORD.

11 O LORD, thy hand is lifted high,
but the bitter enemies of thy[c] people do not see it;[d]
let the fire of thy enmity destroy them.

12 O LORD, thou wilt bestow prosperity on us;
for in truth all our works are thy doing.

[a] *So Scroll; Heb. repeats* he levels it. [b] *So Scroll; Heb.* We look to thee. [c] thy: *prob.*
rdg., cp. Targ.; Heb. om. [d] *Prob. rdg.; Heb. adds* let them see and be ashamed.

O LORD our God,   13
other lords than thou have been our masters,
but thee alone do we invoke by name.
> The dead will not live again,   14
> those long in their graves will not rise;
to this end thou hast punished them and destroyed them,
    and made all memory of them perish.
Thou hast enlarged the nation, O LORD,   15
enlarged it and won thyself honour,
thou hast extended all the frontiers of the land.
In our distress, O LORD, we*ᵃ* sought thee out,   16
chastened by the mere whisper of thy rebuke.
As a woman with child, when her time is near,   17
is in labour and cries out in her pains,
so were we in thy presence, O LORD.
> We have been with child, we have been in labour,*ᵇ*   18
> but have brought forth wind.
We have won no success for the land,
and no one will be born to inhabit the world.
But thy dead live, their bodies*ᶜ* will rise again.   19
They that sleep in the earth will awake and shout for joy;
    for thy dew is a dew of sparkling light,
and the earth will bring those long dead to birth again.

Go, my people, enter your rooms   20
    and shut your doors behind you;
withdraw for a brief while, until wrath has gone by.
For see, the LORD is coming from his place   21
to punish the inhabitants of the earth for their sins;
> then the earth shall uncover her blood-stains
> and hide her slain no more.

On that day the LORD will punish   27
with his cruel sword, his mighty and powerful sword,
> Leviathan that twisting*ᵈ* sea-serpent,
> that writhing serpent Leviathan,
> and slay the monster of the deep.

On that day sing to the pleasant*ᵉ* vineyard,   2
> I the LORD am its keeper,   3
moment by moment I water it for fear its green leaves fail.
> Night and day I tend it,
> but I get no wine;   4

[a] *Prob. rdg.; Heb.* they. [b] *Prob. rdg., cp. Sept.; Heb.* adds like. [c] *So Pesh.; Heb.* my body. [d] *Or* primeval. [e] *So Sept.; Heb.* wine.

I would as soon have briars and thorns,
then I would wage war upon it and burn it all up,
5   unless it grasps me as its refuge and makes peace with me—
     unless it makes peace with me.

6   In time to come Jacob's offspring shall take root
and Israel shall bud and blossom,
and they shall fill the whole earth with fruit.

7   Has God struck him down as he struck others down?
Has the slayer been slain as he slew others?

8–10[a]   This then purges Jacob's iniquity,
     this[b] has removed his sin:
that he grinds all altar stones to powder like chalk;
     no sacred poles and incense-altars are left standing.

The fortified city is left solitary,
     and his quarrel with her ends in brushing her away,[c]
removing her by a cruel blast when the east wind blows;
it is a homestead stripped bare, deserted like a wilderness;
     there the calf grazes and there lies down,
        and crops every twig.

11   Its boughs snap off when they grow dry,
and women come and light their fires with them.
     For they are a people without sense;
therefore their maker will show them no mercy,
     he who formed them will show them no favour.

12   On that day the LORD will beat out the grain,
from the streams of the Euphrates to the Torrent of Egypt;
     but you Israelites will be gleaned
        one by one.

13   On that day
a blast shall be blown on a great trumpet,
     and those who are lost in Assyria
and those dispersed in Egypt will come in
and worship the LORD on the holy mountain, in Jerusalem.

---

[a] *Verses 8–10 re-arranged thus: 9, 10a, 8, 10b.* [b] *Prob. rdg.; Heb. adds* all fruit.
[c] *Prob. rdg.; Heb. adds* by dismissing her.

Assyria and Judah

Oh, the proud garlands of the drunkards of Ephraim   **28**
    and the flowering sprays, so lovely in their beauty,
on the heads of revellers dripping with perfumes,*a*
    overcome with wine!
See, the Lord has one at his bidding, mighty and strong,   **2**
    whom he sets to work with violence against the land,
like a sweeping storm of hail, like a destroying tempest,
like a torrent of water in overwhelming flood.
    The proud garlands of Ephraim's drunkards   **3**
      shall be trampled underfoot,
    and the flowering sprays, so lovely in their beauty   **4**
      on the heads dripping with perfumes,*b*
    shall be like early figs ripe before summer;
    he who sees them plucks them,
    and their bloom is gone while they lie in his hand.
On that day the LORD of Hosts shall be a lovely garland,   **5**
    a beautiful diadem for the remnant of his people,
a spirit of justice for one who presides in a court of justice,   **6**
and of valour for*c* those who repel the enemy at the gate.

These too are addicted to wine,   **7**
    clamouring in their cups:
priest and prophet are addicted to strong drink
    and bemused with wine;
clamouring in their cups, confirmed topers,*d*
    hiccuping in drunken stupor;
    every table is covered with vomit,   **8**
    filth that leaves no clean spot.
    Who is it that the prophet hopes to teach,   **9**
    to whom will what they hear make sense?
Are they babes newly weaned, just taken from the breast?
It is all harsh cries and raucous shouts,   **10**
'A little more here, a little there!'
So it will be with barbarous speech and strange tongue   **11**
    that this people will hear God speaking,

[a] revellers…perfumes: *prob. rdg.,* cp. Scroll; *Heb.* a valley of fat things. [b] dripping with perfumes: *prob. rdg.,* cp. Scroll; *Heb.* of a valley of fat things. [c] for: *prob. rdg.;* *Heb. om.* [d] These too…topers: *or* These too lose their way through wine and are set wandering by strong drink: priest and prophet lose their way through strong drink and are fuddled with wine; are set wandering by strong drink, lose their way through tippling.

12   this people to whom he once said,
'This is true rest; let the exhausted have rest.
This is repose', and they refused to listen.

13   Now to them the word of the LORD will be
harsh cries and raucous shouts,
'A little more here, a little there!'—
and so, as they walk, they will stumble backwards,
they will be injured, trapped and caught.

14   Listen then to the word of the LORD, you arrogant men
who rule this people in Jerusalem.

15   You say, 'We have made a treaty with Death
and signed a pact with Sheol:
so that, when the raging flood sweeps by, it shall not touch us;
for we have taken refuge in lies
and sheltered behind falsehood.'

16   These then are the words of the Lord GOD:
Look, I am laying a stone in Zion, a block of granite,
a precious corner-stone for a firm foundation;
he who has faith shall not waver.

17   I will use justice as a plumb-line
and righteousness as a plummet;
hail shall sweep away your refuge of lies,
and flood-waters carry away your shelter.

18   Then your treaty with Death shall be annulled
and your pact with Sheol shall not stand;
the raging waters will sweep by,
and you will be like land swept by the flood.

19   As often as it sweeps by, it will take you;
morning after morning it will sweep by,
day and night.
The very thought of such tidings
will bring nothing but dismay;

20   for 'The bed is too short for a man to stretch,
and the blanket too narrow to cover him.'

21   But the LORD shall arise as he rose on Mount Perazim
and storm with rage as he did in the Vale of Gibeon
to do what he must do—how strange a deed!
to perform his work—how outlandish a work!

22   But now have done with your arrogance,
lest your bonds grow tighter;
for I have heard destruction decreed
by the Lord GOD of Hosts for the whole land.

Listen and hear what I say,   23
    attend and hear my words.
Will the ploughman continually plough for the sowing,   24
    breaking his ground and harrowing it?
Does he not, once he has levelled it,   25
broadcast the dill and scatter the cummin?
    Does he not plant the wheat in rows
    with barley*a* and spelt along the edge?
Does not his God instruct him and train him aright?   26
Dill is not threshed with a sledge,   27
    and the cartwheel is not rolled over cummin;
    dill is beaten with a rod,
        and cummin with a flail.
Corn is crushed, but not to the uttermost,   28
    not with a final crushing;
his cartwheels rumble over it and break it up,
    but they do not grind it fine.
This message, too, comes from the LORD of Hosts,   29
    whose purposes are wonderful
    and his power great.

Alas for Ariel! Ariel,   **29**
    the city where David encamped.
Add year to year,
    let the pilgrim-feasts run their round,
    and I will bring Ariel to sore straits,   2
when there shall be moaning and lamentation.
I will make her my Ariel indeed, my fiery altar.
I will throw my army round you like a wall;   3
I will set a ring of outposts all round you
and erect siege-works against you.
You shall be brought low, you will speak out of the ground   4
    and your words will issue from the earth;
your voice will come like a ghost's from the ground,
    and your words will squeak out of the earth.
Yet the horde of your enemies shall crumble into dust,   5
    the horde of ruthless foes shall fly like chaff.
    Then suddenly, all in an instant,
    punishment shall come from the LORD of Hosts   6
    with thunder and earthquake and a great noise,
with storm and tempest and a flame of devouring fire;
and the horde of all the nations warring against Ariel,   7

[a] *Prob. rdg.; Heb. adds an unintelligible word.*

991

all their baggage-trains and siege-works,^a
and all her oppressors themselves,
shall fade as a dream, a vision of the night.

8   Like a starving man who dreams
and thinks that he is eating,
but wakes up to find himself empty,
or a thirsty man who dreams
and thinks that he is drinking,
but wakes up to find himself thirsty and dry,
so shall the horde of all the nations be
that war against Mount Zion.

9   Loiter and be dazed, enjoy yourselves and be blinded,
be drunk but not with wine, reel but not with strong drink;

10 for the LORD has poured upon you a spirit of deep stupor;
he has closed your eyes, the prophets,
and muffled your heads, the seers.

11 All prophetic vision has become for you like a sealed book. Give such
a book to one who can read and say, 'Come, read this'; he will answer,

12 'I cannot', because it is sealed. Give it to one who cannot read and say,
'Come, read this'; he will answer, 'I cannot read.'

13 Then the Lord said:

Because this people approach me with their mouths
and honour me with their lips
while their hearts are far from me,
and their religion is but a precept of men, learnt by rote,

14 therefore I will yet again shock this people,
adding shock to shock:
the wisdom of their wise men shall vanish
and the discernment of the discerning shall be lost.

15 Shame upon those who seek to hide their purpose
too deep for the LORD to see,
and who, when their deeds are done in the dark,
say, 'Who sees us? Who knows of us?'

16 How you turn things upside down,
as if the potter ranked no higher than the clay!
Shall the thing made say of its maker, 'He did not make me'?
Shall the pot say of the potter, 'He has no skill'?

17 The time is but short
before Lebanon goes back to grassland
and the grassland is no better than scrub.

[a] siege-works: *so Scroll; Heb.* strongholds.

On that day deaf men shall hear   18
  when a book is read,
   and the eyes of the blind shall see
   out of impenetrable darkness.
The lowly shall once again rejoice in the LORD,   19
  and the poorest of men exult in the Holy One of Israel.
The ruthless shall be no more, the arrogant shall cease to be; 20
  those who are quick to see mischief,
   those who charge others with a sin   21
or lay traps for him who brings the wrongdoer into court
  or by falsehood deny justice to the righteous—
   all these shall be exterminated.

Therefore these are the words of the LORD the God of the house of 22
Jacob, the God who ransomed Abraham:

  This is no time for Jacob to be shamed,
  no time for his face to grow pale;
   for his descendants will hallow my name   23
  when they see*a* what I have done in their nation.
  They will hallow the Holy One of Jacob
  and hold the God of Israel in awe;
   those whose minds are confused will gain understanding, 24
  and the obstinate will receive instruction.

  Oh, rebel sons! says the LORD,   **30**
  you make plans, but not of my devising,
  you weave schemes, but not inspired by me,
   piling sin upon sin;
you hurry down to Egypt without consulting me,   2
  to seek protection under Pharaoh's shelter
   and take refuge under Egypt's wing.
Pharaoh's protection will bring you disappointment   3
  and refuge under Egypt's wing humiliation;
   for, though his officers are at Zoan   4
  and his envoys reach as far as Hanes,
all are left in sorry plight by that unprofitable nation,   5
no help they find, no profit, only disappointment and disgrace.

The Beasts of the South: an oracle.   6

Through a land of hardship and distress
  the tribes of lioness and roaring lion,
  sand-viper and venomous flying serpent,
  carry their wealth on the backs of asses

[a] So Sept.; Heb. he sees.

993

and their treasures on camels' humps
to an unprofitable people.

7 Vain and worthless is the help of Egypt;
therefore have I given her this name,
Rahab Quelled.

8 Now come and write it on a tablet,
engrave it as an inscription before their eyes,
that it may be there in future days,
a testimony for all time.

9 For they are a race of rebels, disloyal sons,
sons who will not listen to the LORD's instruction;

10 they say to the seers, 'You shall not see',
and to the visionaries, 'You shall have no true visions;
give us smooth words and seductive visions.

11 Turn aside, leave the straight path,
and rid us for ever of the Holy One of Israel.'

12 These are the words of the Holy One of Israel:

Because you have rejected this warning
and trust in devious and dishonest practices,
resting on them for support,

13 therefore you shall find this iniquity will be
like a crack running down
a high wall, which bulges
and suddenly, all in an instant, comes crashing down,

14 as an earthen jar is broken with a crash,
mercilessly shattered,
so that not a shard is found among the fragments
to take fire from the glowing embers,
or to scoop up water from a pool.

15 These are the words of the Lord GOD the Holy One of Israel:

Come back, keep peace, and you will be safe;
in stillness and in staying quiet, there lies your strength.

16 But you would have none of it; you said, No,
we will take horse and flee;
therefore you shall be put to flight:
We will ride apace;
therefore swift shall be the pace of your pursuers.

17 When a thousand flee at the challenge of one,
you shall all flee at the challenge of five, until you are left
like a pole on a mountain-top, a signal post on a hill.

18 Yet the LORD is waiting to show you his favour,

yet he yearns to have pity on you;
  for the LORD is a God of justice.
Happy are all who wait for him!

O people of Zion who dwell in Jerusalem, you shall weep no more. 19
The LORD[a] will show you favour and answer you when he hears your
cry for help. The Lord may give you bread of adversity and water of 20
affliction, but he who teaches you shall no longer be hidden out of
sight, but with your own eyes you shall see him always. If you stray 21
from the road to right or left you shall hear with your own ears a voice
behind you saying, This is the way; follow it. You will reject, as things 22
unclean, your silvered images and your idols sheathed in gold; you will
loathe them like a foul discharge and call them ordure.[b] The Lord will 23
give you rain for the seed you sow, and as the produce of your soil he
will give you heavy crops of corn in plenty. When that day comes the
cattle shall graze in broad pastures; the oxen and asses that work your 24
land shall be fed with well-seasoned fodder, winnowed with shovel and
fork. On each high mountain and each lofty hill shall be streams of 25
running water, on the day of massacre when the highest in the land fall.
The moon shall shine with a brightness like the sun's, and the sun with 26
seven times his wonted brightness, seven days' light in one, on the day
when the LORD binds up the broken limbs of his people and heals their
wounds.

See, the name of the LORD comes from afar,   27
  his anger blazing and his doom heavy.
His lips are charged with wrath
  and his tongue is a devouring fire.
His breath is like a torrent in spate,   28
    rising neck-high,
a yoke to force the nations to their ruin,
a bit in the mouth to guide the peoples astray.
But for you there shall be songs,   29
  as on a night of sacred pilgrimage,
your hearts glad, as the hearts of men who walk to the sound of the
      pipe
on their way to the LORD's hill, to the rock of Israel.
Then the LORD shall make his voice heard in majesty   30
and show his arm sweeping down in fierce anger
    with devouring flames of fire,
with cloudburst and tempests of rain and hailstones;
  for at the voice of the LORD Assyria's heart fails her,   31
    as she feels the stroke of his rod.

[a] *So Scroll; Heb. om.*   [b] call them ordure: *or* say to them, Be off.

32   Tambourines and harps and shaking sistrums
         shall keep time
      with every stroke of his rod,
of the chastisement*a* which the LORD inflicts on her.

33   Long ago was Topheth made ready,*b*
         made deep and broad,
      its fire-pit a blazing mass of logs,
      and the breath of the LORD like a stream of brimstone
         blazing in it.

31   Shame upon those who go down to Egypt for help
         and rely on horses,
      putting their trust in chariots many in number
      and in horsemen in their thousands,
      but do not look to the Holy One of Israel
         or seek guidance of the LORD!

2   Yet the LORD too in his wisdom can bring about trouble
         and he does not take back his words;
      he will rise up against the league of evildoers,
         against all who help those who do wrong.

3   The Egyptians are men, not God,*c*
      their horses are flesh, not spirit;
      and, when the LORD stretches out his hand,
the helper will stumble and he who is helped will fall,
      and they will all vanish together.

4   This is what the LORD has said to me:

As a lion or a young lion growls over its prey
when the muster of shepherds is called out against it,
        and is not scared at their noise
        or cowed by their clamour,
so shall the LORD of Hosts come down to do battle
      for Mount Zion and her high summit.

5   Thus the LORD of Hosts, like a bird hovering over its young,
      will be a shield over Jerusalem;
      he will shield her and deliver her,
        standing over her and delivering her.

6   O Israel, come back to him whom you have so deeply offended,
7   for on that day when you spurn, one and all,
      the idols of silver and the idols of gold
      which your own sinful hands have made,
8   Assyria shall fall by the sword, but by no sword of man;

[*a*] *So some MSS.; others* foundation.   [*b*] *Prob. rdg.; Heb. adds* is that prepared also for the king?   [*c*] *Or* gods.

a sword that no man wields shall devour him.
He shall flee before the sword,
and his young warriors shall be put to forced labour,
his officers shall be helpless from terror   9
and his captains too dismayed to flee.
  This is the very word of the LORD
whose fire blazes in Zion,
and whose furnace is set up in Jerusalem.

Behold, a king shall reign in righteousness   32
  and his rulers rule with justice,
  and a man shall be a refuge from the wind   2
    and a shelter from the tempest,
    or like runnels of water in dry ground,
like the shadow of a great rock in a thirsty land.
  The eyes that can see will not be clouded,   3
  and the ears that can hear will listen;
  the anxious heart will understand and know,   4
and the man who stammers will at once speak plain.
The scoundrel will no longer be thought noble,   5
  nor the villain called a prince;
  for the scoundrel will speak like a scoundrel   6
and will hatch*a* evil in his heart;
  he is an impostor in all his actions,
and in his words a liar even to the LORD;
  he starves the hungry of their food
  and refuses drink to the thirsty.
The villain's ways are villainous   7
and he devises infamous plans
to ruin the poor with his lies
and deny justice to the needy.
But the man of noble mind forms noble designs   8
and stands firm in his nobility.

You women that live at ease, stand up   9
  and hear what I have to say.
You young women without a care, mark my words.
You have no cares now, but when the year is out, you will tremble, 10
for the vintage will be over and no produce gathered in.
  You who are now at ease, be anxious;   11
  tremble, you who have no cares.
  Strip yourselves bare;
  put a cloth round your waists

[a] *So Scroll; Heb.* do *or* conceal.

997

12   and beat your breasts[a]
          for the pleasant fields and fruitful vines.
13   On the soil of my people shall spring up thorns and briars,
          in[b] every happy home and in the busy town,
14   for the palace is forsaken and the crowded streets deserted;
          citadel[c] and watch-tower are turned into open heath,
          the joy of wild asses ever after and pasture for the flocks,
15   until a spirit from on high is lavished upon us.
              Then the wilderness will become grassland
              and grassland will be cheap as scrub;
16   then justice shall make its home in the wilderness,
              and righteousness dwell in the grassland;
17   when righteousness shall yield peace
          and its fruit be quietness and confidence for ever.
18   Then my people shall live in a tranquil country,
          dwelling in peace, in houses full of ease;
19   it will be cool on the slopes of the forest then,
              and cities shall lie peaceful in the plain.
20   Happy shall you be, sowing every man by the water-side,
              and letting ox and ass run free.

33   Ah! you destroyer, yourself undestroyed,
          betrayer still unbetrayed,
          when you cease to destroy you will be destroyed,
          after all your[d] betrayals, you will be betrayed yourself.

2   O Lord, show us thy favour; we hope in thee.
          Uphold us[e] every morning,
              save us when troubles come.
3   At the roar of the thunder the peoples flee,
          at thy rumbling[f] nations are scattered;
4   their[g] spoil is swept up as if young locusts had swept it,
          like a swarm of locusts men swarm upon it.

5   The Lord is supreme, for he dwells on high;
          if you fill Zion with justice and with righteousness,
6   then he will be the mainstay of the age:[h]
          wisdom and knowledge are the assurance of salvation;
              the fear of the Lord is her[i] treasure.

7   Hark, how the valiant cry aloud for help,
          and those sent to sue for peace weep bitterly!

---

[a] and beat your breasts: *prob. rdg., cp. Scroll; Heb.* men beating the breast. [b] *So Sept.; Heb.* because on. [c] *Or* hill; *Heb.* Ophel. [d] after all your: *so Scroll; Heb.* unintelligible. [e] *So some MSS.; others* them. [f] *So Scroll; Heb.* uplifting. [g] *Prob. rdg., cp. Targ.; Heb.* your. [h] the age: *prob. rdg.; Heb.* your times. [i] *Prob. rdg.; Heb.* his.

The highways are deserted, no travellers tread the roads.   8
Covenants are broken, treaties*ᵃ* are flouted;
   man is of no account.
  The land is parched and wilting,   9
  Lebanon is eaten away and crumbling;
  Sharon has become a desert,
  Bashan and Carmel are stripped bare.
Now, says the LORD, I will rise up.   10
Now I will exalt myself, now lift myself up.
What you conceive and bring to birth is chaff and stubble;   11
  a wind like fire shall devour you.
  Whole nations shall be heaps of white ash,   12
or like thorns cut down and set on fire.
  You who dwell far away, hear what I have done;   13
  acknowledge my might, you who are near.
  In Zion sinners quake with terror,   14
  the godless are seized with trembling and ask,
Can any of us live with a devouring fire?
Can any live in endless burning?
The man who lives an upright life and speaks the truth,   15
  who scorns to enrich himself by extortion,
who snaps his fingers at a bribe,
  who stops his ears to hear nothing of bloodshed,
  who closes his eyes to the sight of evil—
  that is the man who shall dwell on the heights,   16
  his refuge a fastness in the cliffs,
his bread secure and his water never failing.

Your eyes shall see a king in his splendour   17
  and will look upon a land of far distances.
  You will call to mind what once you feared: 18
'Where then is he that counted, where is he that weighed,
  where is he that counted the treasures?'
  You will no longer see that barbarous people,   19
  that people whose speech was so hard to catch,
  whose stuttering speech you could not understand.

  Look upon Zion, city of our solemn feasts,   20
  let your eyes rest on Jerusalem,
a land of comfort, a tent that shall never be shifted,
  whose pegs shall never be pulled up,
  not one of its ropes cast loose.
There we have the LORD's majesty;*ᵇ*   21

[*a*] *So Scroll; Heb.* cities. [*b*] *Or* threshing-floor.

it will be a place*a* of rivers and broad streams;
    but*b* no galleys shall be rowed there,
    no stately ship sail by.
22   For the LORD our judge, the LORD our law-giver,
    the LORD our king—he himself will save us.
23   [Men may say, Your rigging is slack;
    it will not hold the mast firm in its socket,
        nor can the sails be spread.]
    Then the blind*c* man shall have a full share of the spoil
    and the lame shall take part in the pillage;
24   no man who dwells there shall say, 'I am sick';
    and the sins of the people who live there shall be pardoned.

Edom and Israel

34   Approach, you nations, to listen,
        and attend, you peoples;
        let the earth listen and everything in it,
    the world and all that it yields;
2   for the LORD's anger is turned against all the nations
        and his wrath against all the host of them:
    he gives them over to slaughter and destruction.
3   Their slain shall be flung out,
    the stench shall rise from their corpses,
    and the mountains shall stream with their blood.
4   All the host of heaven shall crumble into nothing,
    the heavens shall be rolled up like a scroll,
        and the starry host fade away,
    as the leaf withers from the vine
        and the ripening fruit from the fig-tree;
5   for the sword of the LORD*d* appears*e* in heaven.
    See how it descends in judgement on Edom,
    on the people whom he dooms*f* to destruction.
6   The LORD has a sword steeped in blood,
        it is gorged with fat,
    the fat of rams' kidneys, and the blood of lambs and goats;
    for he has a sacrifice in Bozrah,
    a great slaughter in Edom.

[a] it...place: *or* instead. [b] *Or* and. [c] *Prob. rdg., cp. Targ.; Heb. obscure.* [d] the sword of the LORD: *prob. rdg.; Heb.* my sword. [e] *So Scroll; Heb.* drinks. [f] *Prob. rdg.; Heb.* I doom.

Wild oxen shall come down and buffaloes[a] with them,   7
    bull and bison together,
and the land shall drink deep of blood
and the soil be sated with fat.
For the LORD has a day of vengeance,   8
the champion of Zion has a year when he will requite.
Edom's torrents shall be turned into pitch   9
    and its soil into brimstone,
and the land shall become blazing pitch,
    which night and day shall never be quenched,   10
and its smoke shall go up for ever.
From generation to generation it shall lie waste,
and no man shall pass through it ever again.
Horned owl and bustard shall make their home in it,   11
screech-owl and raven shall haunt it.
He has stretched across it a measuring-line of chaos,
    and its frontiers shall be a jumble of stones.   12
No king shall be acclaimed there,
and all its princes shall come to nought.
Thorns shall sprout in its palaces;   13
nettles and briars shall cover its walled towns.
It shall be rough land fit for wolves, a haunt of desert-owls.
    Marmots shall consort with jackals,   14
and he-goat shall encounter he-goat.
There too the nightjar shall rest
and find herself a place for repose.
There the sand-partridge shall make her nest,   15
lay her eggs and hatch them
and gather her brood under her wings;
there shall the kites gather,
    one after another.
Consult the book of the LORD and read it: 16
not one of these shall be lacking,
    not one miss its fellow,
for with his own mouth he has ordered it
and with his own breath he has brought them together.
He it is who has allotted each its place,   17
    and his hand has measured out their portions;
    they shall occupy it for ever
    and dwell there from generation to generation.

Let the wilderness and the thirsty land be glad,   **35**

    [a] and buffaloes: *prob. rdg.; Heb. om.*

            let the desert rejoice and burst into flower.

2   Let it flower with fields of asphodel,
            let it rejoice and shout for joy.
        The glory of Lebanon is given to it,
            the splendour too of Carmel and Sharon;
    these shall see the glory of the LORD, the splendour of our God.

3   Strengthen the feeble arms,
            steady the tottering knees;

4   say to the anxious, Be strong and fear not.
        See, your God comes with vengeance,
    with dread retribution he comes to save you.

5   Then shall blind men's eyes be opened,
            and the ears of the deaf unstopped.

6   Then shall the lame man leap like a deer,
            and the tongue of the dumb shout aloud;
        for water springs up in the wilderness,
        and torrents flow*ᵃ* in dry land.

7   The mirage becomes a pool,
            the thirsty land bubbling springs;
            instead of reeds and rushes, grass shall grow
            in the rough land where wolves now lurk.

8   And there shall be a causeway*ᵇ* there
        which shall be called the Way of Holiness,
            and the unclean shall not pass along it;
        it shall become a pilgrim's way,*ᶜ*
            no fool shall trespass on it.

9   No lion shall come there,
        no savage beast climb on to it;
            not one shall be found there.
        By it those he has ransomed shall return

10   and the LORD's redeemed come home;
         they shall enter Zion with shouts of triumph,
         crowned with everlasting gladness.
        Gladness and joy shall be their escort,
        and suffering and weariness shall flee away.

[a] flow: *so Scroll; Heb. om.*   [b] *So Scroll; Heb. adds* and a road.   [c] a pilgrim's way: *prob. rdg.; Heb. unintelligible.*

Jerusalem delivered from Sennacherib

IN THE FOURTEENTH[a] YEAR of the reign of Hezekiah, Sennacherib **36** 1[b]
king of Assyria attacked and took all the fortified cities of Judah.
From Lachish he sent the chief officer[c] with a strong force to King 2
Hezekiah at Jerusalem; and he halted by the conduit of the Upper Pool
on the causeway which leads to the Fuller's Field. There Eliakim son 3
of Hilkiah, the comptroller of the household, came out to him, with
Shebna the adjutant-general and Joah son of Asaph, the secretary of
state. The chief officer said to them, 'Tell Hezekiah that this is the 4
message of the Great King, the king of Assyria: "What ground have
you for this confidence of yours? Do you[d] think fine words can take the 5
place of skill and numbers? On whom then do you rely for support in
your rebellion against me? On Egypt? Egypt is a splintered cane that 6
will run into a man's hand and pierce it if he leans on it. That is what
Pharaoh king of Egypt proves to all who rely on him. And if you tell 7
me that you are relying on the LORD your God, is he not the god whose
hill-shrines and altars Hezekiah has suppressed, telling Judah and
Jerusalem that they must prostrate themselves before this altar
alone?"
'Now, make a bargain with my master the king of Assyria: I will give 8
you two thousand horses if you can find riders for them. Will you reject 9
the authority of even the least of my master's servants and rely on
Egypt for chariots and horsemen? Do you think that I have come to 10
attack this land and destroy it without the consent of the LORD? No;
the LORD himself said to me, "Attack this land and destroy it."'
Eliakim, Shebna, and Joah said to the chief officer, 'Please speak to 11
us in Aramaic, for we understand it; do not speak Hebrew to us within
earshot of the people on the city wall.' The chief officer answered, 'Is 12
it to your master and to you that my master has sent me to say this?
Is it not to the people sitting on the wall who, like you, will have to
eat their own dung and drink their own urine?' Then he stood and 13
shouted in Hebrew, 'Hear the message of the Great King, the king of
Assyria. These are the king's words: "Do not be taken in by Hezekiah. 14
He cannot save you. Do not let him persuade you to rely on the LORD, 15
and tell you that the LORD will save you and that this city will never be
surrendered to the king of Assyria." Do not listen to Hezekiah; these 16
are the words of the king of Assyria: "Make peace with me. Come out
to me, and then you shall each eat the fruit of his own vine and his own

[a] *Possibly an error for* twenty-fourth. [b] *Verses 1–22: cp. 2 Kgs. 18. 13–37; 2 Chr. 32. 1–19.* [c] *Or sent Rab-shakeh.* [d] *So Scroll, cp. 2 Kgs. 18. 20; Heb.* I.

17 fig-tree, and drink the water of his own cistern, until I come and take you to a land like your own, a land of grain and new wine, of corn and 18 vineyards. Beware lest Hezekiah mislead you by telling you that the LORD will save you. Did the god of any of these nations save his land 19 from the king of Assyria? Where are the gods of Hamath and Arpad? Where are the gods of Sepharvaim? Where are the gods of Samaria?[a] 20 Did they save Samaria from me? Among all the gods of these nations is there one who saved his land from me? And how is the LORD to save Jerusalem?"'

21   The people were silent and answered not a word, for the king had 22 given orders that no one was to answer him. Eliakim son of Hilkiah, comptroller of the household, Shebna the adjutant-general, and Joah son of Asaph, secretary of state, came to Hezekiah with their clothes rent and reported what the chief officer had said.

37:[b]   When King Hezekiah heard their report, he rent his clothes and 2 wrapped himself in sackcloth, and went into the house of the LORD. He sent Eliakim comptroller of the household, Shebna the adjutant-general, and the senior priests, all covered in sackcloth, to the prophet Isaiah 3 son of Amoz, to give him this message from the king: 'This day is a day of trouble for us, a day of reproof and contempt. We are like a woman who has no strength to bear the child that is coming to the birth. 4 It may be that the LORD your God heard the words of the chief officer whom his master the king of Assyria sent to taunt the living God, and will confute what he, the LORD your God, heard. Offer a prayer for 5,6 those who still survive.' King Hezekiah's servants came to Isaiah, and he told them to say this to their master: 'This is the word of the LORD: "Do not be alarmed at what you heard when the lackeys of the king of 7 Assyria blasphemed me. I will put a spirit in him, and he shall hear a rumour and withdraw to his own country; and there I will make him fall by the sword."'

8   So the chief officer withdrew. He heard that the king of Assyria had 9 left Lachish, and he found him attacking Libnah. But when the king learnt that Tirhakah king of Cush was on the way to make war on him, 10 he sent messengers again[c] to Hezekiah king of Judah, to say to him, 'How can you be deluded by your god on whom you rely when he promises that Jerusalem shall not fall into the hands of the king of 11 Assyria? Surely you have heard what the kings of Assyria have done to all countries, exterminating their people; can you then hope to escape? 12 Did their gods save the nations which my forefathers destroyed, Gozan, Harran, Rezeph, and the people of Beth-eden living in Telassar?

[a] Where are the gods of Samaria?: *prob. rdg., cp. Luc. Sept. at 2 Kgs. 18. 34; Heb. om.*
[b] *Verses 1–38: cp. 2 Kgs. 19. 1–37; 2 Chr. 32. 20–22.*   [c] again: *prob. rdg., cp. 2 Kgs. 19. 9; Heb. and he heard.*

Where are the kings of Hamath, of Arpad, and of Lahir, Sepharvaim, 13
Hena, and Ivvah?'

Hezekiah took the letter from the messengers and read it; then he 14
went up into the house of the LORD, spread it out before the LORD
and offered this prayer: 'O LORD of Hosts, God of Israel, enthroned 15,16
on the cherubim, thou alone art God of all the kingdoms of the earth;
thou hast made heaven and earth. Turn thy ear to me, O LORD, and 17
listen; open thine eyes, O LORD, and see; hear the message that
Sennacherib has sent to taunt the living God. It is true, O LORD, that 18
the kings of Assyria have laid waste every country,*a* that they have 19
consigned their gods to the fire and destroyed them; for they were
no gods but the work of men's hands, mere wood and stone. But now, 20
O LORD our God, save us from his power, so that all the kingdoms of
the earth may know that thou, O LORD, alone art God.'*b*

Isaiah son of Amoz sent to Hezekiah and said, 'This is the word of 21
the LORD the God of Israel: I have heard*c* your prayer to me concerning
Sennacherib king of Assyria. This is the word which the LORD has 22
spoken concerning him:

> The virgin daughter of Zion disdains you,
>   she laughs you to scorn;
> the daughter of Jerusalem tosses her head
>   as you retreat.
> Whom have you taunted and blasphemed?   23
>   Against whom have you clamoured,
> casting haughty glances at the Holy One of Israel?
> You have sent your servants to taunt the Lord,   24
>   and said:
> With my countless chariots I have gone up
> high in the mountains, into the recesses of Lebanon.
> I have cut down its tallest cedars,
>   the best of its pines,
> I have reached its highest limit of forest and meadow.*d*
>   I have dug wells   25
>   and drunk the waters of a foreign land,*e*
> and with the soles of my feet I have dried up
>   all the streams of Egypt.
>
> Have you not heard long ago?   26
>   I did it all.
> In days gone by I planned it

[a] *So Scroll; Heb. adds* and their country.   [b] God: *so Scroll and 2 Kgs. 19. 19; Heb. om.*
[c] I have heard: *so Sept. and 2 Kgs. 19. 20; Heb. om.*   [d] and meadow: *prob. rdg.; Heb.*
its meadow.   [e] of a foreign land: *so Scroll and 2 Kgs. 19. 24; Heb. om.*

> and now I have brought it about,
> making fortified cities tumble down
> into heaps of rubble.[a]

27   Their citizens, shorn of strength,
> disheartened and ashamed,
> were but as plants in the field, as green herbs,
> as grass on the roof-tops blasted before the east wind.[b]

28   I know your rising up[c] and your sitting down,
> your going out and your coming in.

29   The frenzy of your rage against me[d] and your arrogance
> have come to my ears.
> I will put a ring in your nose
> and a hook in your lips,
> and I will take you back by the road
> on which you have come.

30 This shall be the sign for you: this year you shall eat shed grain and in the second year what is self-sown; but in the third year sow and reap, 31 plant vineyards and eat their fruit. The survivors left in Judah shall 32 strike fresh root under ground and yield fruit above ground, for a remnant shall come out of Jerusalem and survivors from Mount Zion. The zeal of the LORD of Hosts will perform this.

33   'Therefore, this is the word of the LORD concerning the king of Assyria:

> He shall not enter this city
> nor shoot an arrow there,
> he shall not advance against it with shield
> nor cast up a siege-ramp against it.

34   By the way on which he came he shall go back;
> this city he shall not enter.
> This is the very word of the LORD.

35   I will shield this city to deliver it,
> for my own sake and for the sake of my servant David.'

36   The angel of the LORD went out and struck down a hundred and eighty-five thousand men in the Assyrian camp; when morning dawned, 37 they all lay dead. So Sennacherib king of Assyria broke camp, went 38 back to Nineveh and stayed there. One day, while he was worshipping in the temple of his god Nisroch, Adrammelech and Sharezer his sons murdered him and escaped to the land of Ararat. He was succeeded by his son Esarhaddon.

[a] rubble: *so Scroll; Heb. obscure.*   [b] blasted...east wind: *so Scroll; Heb. obscure.* [c] your rising up: *so Scroll; Heb. om.*   [d] *So Scroll; Heb. repeats* the frenzy of your rage against me.

At this time Hezekiah fell dangerously ill and the prophet Isaiah son 38 1[a] of Amoz came to him and said, 'This is the word of the LORD: Give your last instructions to your household, for you are a dying man and will not recover.' Hezekiah turned his face to the wall and offered this 2 prayer to the LORD: 'O LORD, remember how I have lived before thee, 3 faithful and loyal in thy service, always doing what was good in thine eyes.' And he wept bitterly. Then the word of the LORD came to 4 Isaiah: 'Go and say to Hezekiah: "This is the word of the LORD the God 5 of your father David: I have heard your prayer and seen your tears; I will add fifteen years to your life. I will deliver you and this city from 6 the king of Assyria and will protect this city."' Then Isaiah told them 21[b] to apply a fig-plaster; so they made one and applied it to the boil, and he recovered. Then Hezekiah said, 'By what sign shall I know that 22 I shall go up into the house of the LORD?' And Isaiah said,[c] 'This shall 7 be your sign from the LORD that he will do what he has promised. Watch 8 the shadow cast by the sun on the stairway of Ahaz: I will bring backwards ten steps the shadow which has gone down on the stairway.' And the sun went back ten steps on the stairway down which it had gone.

A poem of Hezekiah king of Judah after his recovery from his 9 illness, as it was written down:

I thought: In the prime of life I must pass away;   10
for the rest of my years I am consigned to the gates of Sheol.
    I said: I shall no longer see the LORD   11
        in the land of the living;
    never again, like those who live in the world,[d]
        shall I look on a man.
    My dwelling is taken from me,   12
        pulled up like a shepherd's tent;
    thou hast cut short[e] my life like a weaver
    who severs the web from the thrum.
    From morning to night thou tormentest me,
        then I am racked with pain[f] till the morning.   13
All my bones are broken, as a lion would break them;
    from morning to night thou tormentest me.
    I twitter as if I were a swallow,[g]   14
        I moan like a dove.
    My eyes falter as I look up to the heights;
    O Lord, pay heed, stand surety for me.
    How can I complain, what can I say to the LORD[h]   15

---

[a] *Verses 1–8, 21, 22: cp. 2 Kgs. 20. 1–11.*   [b] *Verses 21, 22 transposed.*   [c] And Isaiah said: *prob. rdg., cp. 2 Kgs. 20. 9; Heb. om.*   [d] world: *so some MSS.; others* cessation. [e] *Prob. rdg., cp. Scroll; Heb.* I have gathered.   [f] then...pain: *so Scroll; Heb.* I wait. [g] *So Sept.; Heb. adds* a wryneck.   [h] *Prob. rdg., cp. Targ.; Heb.* what can he say to me.

when he himself has done this?
I wander to and fro all my life long
in the bitterness of my soul.

16   Yet, O Lord, my soul shall live with thee;
do thou give my spirit rest.*a*
Restore me and give me life.

17   Bitterness had indeed been my lot in place of prosperity;
but thou by thy love hast brought me back
from the pit of destruction;
for thou hast cast all my sins behind thee.

18   Sheol cannot confess thee,
Death cannot praise thee,
nor can they who go down to the abyss
hope for thy truth.

19   The living, the living alone can confess thee
as I do this day,
as a father makes thy truth known, O God, to his sons.

20   The LORD is at hand to save me;
so let us sound the music of our praises
all our life long in the house of the LORD.*b*

39 1*c*   At this time Merodach-baladan son of Baladan king of Babylon sent
envoys with a gift to Hezekiah; for he had heard that he had been ill
2   and was well again. Hezekiah welcomed them and showed them all his
treasury, silver and gold, spices and fragrant oil, his entire armoury and
everything to be found among his treasures; there was nothing in his
3   house and in all his realm that Hezekiah did not show them. Then the
prophet Isaiah came to King Hezekiah and asked him, 'What did these
men say and where have they come from?' 'They have come from
4   a far-off country,' Hezekiah answered, 'from Babylon.' Then Isaiah
asked, 'What did they see in your house?' 'They saw everything,'
Hezekiah replied; 'there was nothing among my treasures that I did
5   not show them.' Then Isaiah said to Hezekiah, 'Hear the word of the
6   LORD of Hosts: The time is coming, says the LORD, when everything
in your house, and all that your forefathers have amassed till the
present day, will be carried away to Babylon; not a thing shall be left.
7   And some of the sons who will be born to you, sons of your own
begetting, shall be taken and shall be made eunuchs in the palace of
8   the king of Babylon.' Hezekiah answered, 'The word of the LORD
which you have spoken is good'; thinking to himself that peace and
security would last out his lifetime.

[a] Yet...rest: *prob. rdg.; Heb. unintelligible.*   [b] *Verses 21, 22 transposed to follow verse 6.*
[c] *Verses 1–8: cp. 2 Kgs. 20. 12–19.*

News of the returning exiles

Comfort, comfort my people;*a* 40
    —it is the voice of your God;
speak tenderly to Jerusalem*b* 2
    and tell her this,
that she has fulfilled her term of bondage,
    that her penalty is paid;
she has received at the LORD's hand
    double*c* measure for all her sins.

There is a voice that cries: 3
Prepare a road for the LORD through the wilderness,
clear a highway across the desert for our God.
Every valley shall be lifted up, 4
every mountain and hill brought down;
rugged places shall be made smooth
    and mountain-ranges become a plain.
Thus shall the glory of the LORD be revealed, 5
and all mankind together shall see it;
    for the LORD himself has spoken.

A voice says, 'Cry', 6
and another asks,*d* 'What shall I cry?'
'That all mankind is grass,
they last no longer than a flower of the field.
The grass withers, the flower fades, 7
when the breath of*e* the LORD blows upon them;*f*
the grass withers, the flowers fade, 8
    but the word of our God endures for evermore.'

You who bring Zion good news,*g* up with you to the mountain-top; 9
    lift up your voice and shout,
you who bring good news to Jerusalem,*h*
    lift it up fearlessly;
cry to the cities of Judah, 'Your God is here.'
Here is the Lord GOD coming in might, 10
    coming to rule with his right arm.

---

[a] Comfort...people: or Comfort, O my people, comfort. [b] speak...Jerusalem: or bid Jerusalem be of good heart. [c] double: or full. [d] Or, with Scroll, and I asked. [e] the breath of: or a wind from. [f] Prob. rdg.; Heb. adds surely the people are grass. [g] You...news: or O Zion, bringer of good news. [h] you...Jerusalem: or O Jerusalem, bringer of good news.

His recompense comes with him,
he carries his reward before him.

11   He will tend his flock like a shepherd
and gather them together with his arm;
he will carry the lambs in his bosom
and lead the ewes to water.

Israel delivered and redeemed

12   Who has gauged the waters in the palm of his hand,
or with its span set limits to the heavens?
Who has held all the soil of earth in a bushel,
or weighed the mountains on a balance
and the hills on a pair of scales?

13   Who has set limits to the spirit of the LORD?
What counsellor stood at his side to instruct him?

14   With whom did he confer to gain discernment?
Who taught him how to do justice*a*
or gave him lessons in wisdom?

15   Why, to him nations are but drops from a bucket,
no more than moisture on the scales;
coasts and islands weigh as light as specks of dust.

16   All Lebanon does not yield wood enough for fuel
or beasts enough for a sacrifice.

17   All nations dwindle to nothing before him,
he reckons them mere nothings, less than nought.

18   What likeness will you find for God
or what form to resemble his?

19   Is it an image which a craftsman sets up,
and a goldsmith covers with plate
and fits*b* with studs of silver as a costly gift?

20   Or is it mulberry-wood that will not rot which a man chooses,
seeking out a skilful craftsman for it,
to mount an image that will not fall?

[6*c*]   Each workman helps the others,
each man encourages his fellow.

[7*c*]   The craftsman urges on the goldsmith,
the gilder urges the man who beats the anvil,

---

[a] *So Sept.; Heb. adds* and gave him lessons in knowledge. [b] fits: *so Pesh.; Heb.* a goldsmith. [c] *These are verses 6 and 7 of ch. 41, transposed to this point.*

he declares the soldering to be sound;
he fastens the image with nails
so that it will not fall down.

Do you not know, have you not heard, 21
were you not told long ago,
have you not perceived ever since the world began,
that God sits throned on the vaulted roof of earth, 22
　　whose inhabitants are like grasshoppers[a]?
He stretches out the skies like a curtain,
he spreads them out like a tent to live in;
he reduces the great to nothing 23
and makes all earth's princes less than nothing.
Scarcely are they planted, scarcely sown, 24
scarcely have they taken root in the earth,
　　before he blows upon them and they wither away,
　　and a whirlwind carries them off like chaff.
To whom then will you liken me, 25
　　whom set up as my equal?
　　asks the Holy One.
Lift up your eyes to the heavens; 26
consider who created it all,
led out their host one by one
and called them all by their names;
　　through his great might, his might and power,
　　not one is missing.
Why do you complain, O Jacob, 27
　　and you, Israel, why do you say,
　'My plight is hidden from the LORD
and my cause has passed out of God's notice'?
Do you not know, have you not heard? 28
The LORD, the everlasting God, creator of the wide world,
　　grows neither weary nor faint;
　　no man can fathom his understanding.
He gives vigour to the weary, 29
new strength to the exhausted.
Young men may grow weary and faint, 30
even in their prime they may stumble and fall;
but those who look to the LORD will win new strength, 31
they will grow wings like eagles;
they will run and not be weary,
they will march on and never grow faint.

[a] *Or* locusts.

41   Keep silence before me, all you coasts and islands;
    let the peoples come to meet me.*a*
    Let them come near, then let them speak;
    we will meet at the place of judgement, I and they.

2   Tell me, who raised up that one from the east,
    one greeted by victory wherever he goes?
    Who is it that puts nations into his power
    and makes kings go down before him,*b*
    he scatters them with his sword like dust
    and with his bow like chaff before the wind;

3   he puts them to flight and passes on unscathed,
    swifter than any traveller on foot?

4   Whose work is this, I ask, who has brought it to pass?
    Who has summoned the generations from the beginning?
    It is I, the LORD, I am the first,
    and to the last of them I am He.

5   Coasts and islands saw it and were afraid,
    the world trembled from end to end.*c*

8*d*   But you, Israel my servant,
    you, Jacob whom I have chosen,
    race of Abraham my friend,

9   I have taken you up,
    have fetched you from the ends of the earth,
    and summoned you from its farthest corners,
    I have called you my servant,
    have chosen you and not cast you off:

10   fear nothing, for I am with you;
    be not afraid, for I am your God.
    I strengthen you, I help you,
    I support you with my victorious right hand.

11   Now shall all who defy you
    be disappointed and put to shame;
    all*e* who set themselves against you
    shall be as nothing; they shall vanish.

12   You will look for your assailants but not find them;
    all who take up arms against you
    shall be as nothing, nothing at all.

13   For I, the LORD your God,
    take you by the right hand;

[a] come to meet me: *prob. rdg., transposing, with slight change, from end of verse 5; Heb.* win new strength (*repeated from* 40. 31). [b] before him: *prob. rdg.; Heb. om.* [c] *See note on verse 1.* [d] *Verses 6 and 7 transposed to follow* 40. 20. [e] all: *so Scroll; Heb. om.*

I say to you, Do not fear;
it is I who help you,
fear not, Jacob you worm and Israel poor louse.　　　14
It is I who help you, says the LORD,
　your ransomer, the Holy One of Israel.
See, I will make of you a sharp threshing-sledge,　　15
　new and studded with teeth;
you shall thresh the mountains and crush them
and reduce the hills to chaff;
you shall winnow them, the wind shall carry them away　16
and a great gale shall scatter them.
Then shall you rejoice in the LORD
　and glory in the Holy One of Israel.

The wretched and the poor look for water and find none,　17
　their tongues are parched with thirst;
but I the LORD will give them an answer,
I, the God of Israel, will not forsake them.
I will open rivers among the sand-dunes　　　18
　and wells in the valleys;
I will turn the wilderness into pools
and dry land into springs of water;
I will plant cedars in the wastes,　　　19
and acacia and myrtle and wild olive;
the pine shall grow on the barren heath
side by side with fir and box,
that men may see and know,　　　20
may once for all give heed and understand
that the LORD himself has done this,
　that the Holy One of Israel has performed it.

Come, open your plea, says the LORD,　　　21
present your case, says Jacob's King;
　let them come forward, these idols,　　　22
　let them foretell the future.
Let them declare the meaning of past events
　that we may give our minds to it;
let them predict things that are to be
　that we may know their outcome.
Declare what will happen hereafter;　　　23
then we shall know you are gods.
Do what you can, good or ill,
anything that may grip us with fear and awe.
You cannot! You are sprung from nothing,　　　24

your works are rotten;
whoever chooses you is vile as you are.

25   I roused one from the north, and he obeyed;
I called one from the east, summoned him in^a my name,
he marches over viceroys as if they were mud,
like a potter treading his clay.

26   Tell us, who declared this from the beginning, that we might
know it,
or told us beforehand so that we could say, 'He was right'?
Not one declared, not one foretold,
not one heard a sound from you.

27   Here is one who will speak^b first as advocate for Zion,
here I appoint defending counsel for Jerusalem;

28   but from the other side no advocate steps forward
and, when I look, there is no one there.
I ask a question and no one answers;

29   see what empty things they are!
Nothing that they do has any worth,
their effigies are wind, mere nothings.

42   Here is my servant, whom I uphold,
my chosen one in whom I delight,
I have bestowed my spirit upon him,
and he will make justice shine on the nations.

2   He will not call out or lift his voice high,
or^c make himself heard in the open street.

3   He will not break a bruised reed,
or snuff out a smouldering wick;
he will make justice shine on every race,^d

4   never faltering, never breaking down,^e
he will plant justice on earth,
while coasts and islands wait for his teaching.

5   Thus speaks the LORD who is God,
he who created the skies and stretched them out,
who fashioned the earth and all that grows in it,
who gave breath to its people,
the breath of life to all who walk upon it:

6   I, the LORD, have called you with righteous purpose
and taken you by the hand;

---

[a] summoned him in: *or* who will call on. [b] one who will speak: *so Scroll; Heb.*
unintelligible. [c] He will not...or: *or* In very truth he will call out and lift his voice
high, and... [d] on every race: *or* in truth. [e] never faltering...down: *or* he will
neither rebuke nor wound.

I have formed you, and appointed you
to be a light[a] to all peoples,
a beacon for the nations,
to open eyes that are blind,   7
to bring captives out of prison,
out of the dungeons where they lie in darkness.
I am the Lord; the Lord[b] is my name;   8
I will not give my glory to another god,
nor my praise to any idol.
See how the first prophecies have come to pass,   9
and now I declare new things;
before they break from the bud I announce them to you.

Sing a new song to the Lord,   10
sing his praise throughout the earth,
you that sail the sea, and all sea-creatures,
and you that inhabit the coasts and islands.[c]
Let the wilderness and its towns rejoice,   11
and the villages of the tribe of Kedar.
Let those who live in Sela shout for joy
and cry out from the hill-tops.
You coasts and islands, all uplift his praises;   12
let all ascribe glory to the Lord.
The Lord will go forth as a warrior,   13
he will rouse the frenzy of battle like a hero;
he will shout, he will raise the battle-cry
and triumph over his foes.
Long have I lain still,   14
I kept silence and held myself in check;
now I will cry like a woman in labour,
whimpering, panting and gasping.
I will lay waste mountains and hills   15
and shrivel all their green herbs;
I will turn rivers into desert wastes[d]
and dry up all the pools.
Then will I lead blind men on their way[e]   16
and guide them by paths they do not know;
I will turn darkness into light before them
and straighten their twisting roads.
All this I will do and leave nothing undone.
Those who trust in an image,   17

[a] Or a covenant. [b] the Lord: or He. [c] you that sail...islands: or, with slight change, let the sea and all that is in it, the coasts and islands, echo his praise. [d] desert wastes: prob. rdg.; Heb. coasts and islands. [e] Prob. rdg.; Heb. adds which they do not know.

those who take idols for their gods
turn tail in bitter shame.

18   Hear now, you that are deaf;
        you blind men, look and see:
19   yet who is blind but my servant,
        who so deaf as the messenger whom I send?
        Who so blind as the one who holds my commission,
            so deaf[a] as the servant of the LORD?
20   You have seen much but remembered little,
        your ears are wide open but nothing is heard.
21   It pleased the LORD, for the furtherance of his justice,
        to make his law a law of surpassing majesty;
22   yet here is a people plundered and taken as prey,
        all of them ensnared, trapped in holes,
            lost to sight in dungeons,
        carried off as spoil without hope of rescue,
        as plunder with no one to say, 'Give it back.'
23   Hear this, all of you who will,
        listen henceforward and give me a hearing:
24   who gave away Jacob for plunder,
            who gave Israel away for spoil?
        Was it not the LORD? They[b] sinned against him,
        they would not follow his ways
            and refused obedience to his law;
25   so in his anger he poured out upon Jacob
        his wrath and the fury of battle.
        It wrapped him in flames, yet still he did not learn the lesson,
        scorched him, yet he did not lay it to heart.

43   But now this is the word of the LORD,
        the word of your creator, O Jacob,
            of him who fashioned you, Israel:
        Have no fear; for I have paid your ransom;
        I have called you by name and you are my own.
2   When you pass through deep waters, I am with you,
            when you pass through rivers,
            they will not sweep you away;
        walk through fire and you will not be scorched,
        through flames and they will not burn you.
3   For I am the LORD your God,
            the Holy One of Israel, your deliverer;
        for your ransom I give Egypt,

[a] deaf: *so some MSS.; others* blind.   [b] *So Targ.; Heb.* We.

Nubia and Seba are your price.
You are more precious to me than the Assyrians,   4
    you are honoured and I have loved you,
    I would give the Edomites in exchange for you,
    and the Leummim for your life.

    Have no fear; for I am with you;   5
I will bring your children from the east
    and gather you all from the west.
I will say to the north, 'Give them up',   6
    and to the south, 'Do not hold them back.
Bring my sons and daughters from afar,
    bring them from the ends of the earth;
bring every one who is called by my name,   7
    all whom I have created, whom I have formed,
all whom I have made for my glory.'
    Bring out this people,   8
    a people who have eyes but are blind,
who have ears but are deaf.
All the nations are gathered together   9
    and the peoples assembled.
Who amongst them can expound this thing
    and interpret for us all that has gone before?
Let them produce witnesses to prove their case,
    or let them listen and say, 'That is the truth.'
My witnesses, says the LORD, are you, my servants,   10
    you whom I have chosen
to know me and put your faith in me
    and understand that I am He.
Before me there was no god fashioned
    nor ever shall be after me.
I am the LORD, I myself,   11
    and none but I can deliver.
I myself have made it known in full, and declared it,   12
    I and no alien god amongst you,
    and you are my witnesses, says the LORD.
I am God; from this very day I am He.   13
    What my hand holds, none can snatch away;
    what I do, none can undo.

Thus says the LORD your ransomer, the Holy One of Israel: 14
    For your sakes I have sent to Babylon;
    I will lay the Chaldaeans prostrate as they flee,
    and their cry of triumph will turn to groaning.

15   I am the LORD, your Holy One,
          your creator, Israel, and your King.

16   Thus says the LORD,
          who opened a way in the sea
          and a path through mighty waters,
17   who drew on chariot and horse to their destruction,
          a whole army, men of valour;
          there they lay, never to rise again;
      they were crushed, snuffed out like a wick:
18   Cease to dwell on days gone by
          and to brood over past history.
19   Here and now I will do a new thing;
          this moment it will break from the bud.
          Can you not perceive it?
      I will make a way even through the wilderness
          and paths*a* in the barren desert;
20   the wild beasts shall do me honour,
          the wolf and the ostrich;
      for I will provide water in the wilderness
          and rivers in the barren desert,
          where my chosen people may drink.
21   I have formed this people for myself
          and they shall proclaim my praises.
22   Yet you did not call upon me, O Jacob;
      much less did you weary yourself in my service, O Israel.
23   You did not bring me sheep as whole-offerings
          or honour me with sacrifices;
          I asked you for no burdensome offerings
          and wearied you with no demands for incense.
24   You did not buy me sweet-cane with your money
          or glut me with the fat of your sacrifices;
          rather you burdened me with your sins
          and wearied me with your iniquities.
25   I alone, I am He,
          who for his own sake wipes out your transgressions,
          who will remember your sins no more.*b*
26   Cite me by name, let us argue it out;
          set forth your pleading and justify yourselves.
27   Your first father transgressed,
          your spokesmen rebelled against me,

[*a*] *So Scroll; Heb.* rivers. [*b*] remember...no more: *so Scroll; Heb.* not remember your sins.

and your princes profaned my sanctuary;[a]   28
so I sent Jacob to his doom[b]
and left Israel to execration.

Hear me now, Jacob my servant,   **44**
hear me, my chosen Israel.
Thus says the LORD your maker,   2
your helper, who fashioned you from birth:
have no fear, Jacob my servant,
Jeshurun whom I have chosen,
for I will pour down rain on a thirsty land,   3
   showers on the dry ground.
I will pour out my spirit on your offspring
   and my blessing on your children.
They shall spring up like[c] a green tamarisk,   4
like poplars by a flowing stream.
This man shall say, 'I am the LORD's man',   5
   that one shall call himself a son of Jacob,
another shall write the LORD's name on his hand
   and shall add the name of Israel to his own.

Thus says the LORD, Israel's King,   6
the LORD of Hosts, his ransomer:
I am the first and I am the last,
   and there is no god but me.
Who is like me? Let him stand up,[d]   7
let him declare himself and speak and show me his evidence,
let him announce beforehand[e] things to come,
let him[f] declare what is yet to happen.
   Take heart, do not be afraid.[g]   8
Did I not foretell this long ago?
I declared it, and you are my witnesses.
Is there any god beside me,
   or any creator, even one that I do not know?
Those who make idols are less than nothing;   9
   all their cherished images profit nobody;
their worshippers are blind,
   sheer ignorance makes fools of them.
If a man makes a god or casts an image,   10
   his labour is wasted.

[a] your princes...sanctuary: *prob. rdg., cp. Sept.; Heb.* I have profaned holy princes.
[b] sent...doom: *lit.* put Jacob under solemn ban.   [c] like: *so many MSS.; others* in.
[d] Let him stand up: *so Sept.; Heb. om.*   [e] let him announce beforehand: *prob. rdg.;
Heb.* since my appointing an ancient people and...   [f] *Prob. rdg.; Heb.* them.   [g] be
afraid: *so Scroll; Heb.* be foolish.

11   Why! its votaries show their folly;
       the craftsmen too are but men.
      Let them all gather together and confront me,
       all will be afraid and look the fools they are.

12   The blacksmith sharpens*a* a graving tool and hammers out his work*b* hot from the coals and shapes it with his strong arm; when he grows
13 hungry his strength fails, if he has no water to drink he tires. The woodworker draws his line taut and marks out a figure with a scriber; he planes the wood and measures it with callipers, and he carves it to the shape of a man, comely as the human form, to be set up presently in a house.*c*

14   A man plants a cedar*d* and the rain makes it grow, so that later on he will have cedars to cut down; or he chooses an ilex or an oak to raise
15 a stout tree for himself in the forest. It becomes fuel for his fire: some of it he takes and warms himself, some he kindles and bakes bread on it, and some he makes into a god and prostrates himself, shaping it into
16 an idol and bowing down before it. The one half of it he burns in the fire and on this he roasts meat, so that he may eat his roast and be satisfied; he also warms himself at it and he says, 'Good! I can feel the
17 heat, I am growing warm.' Then what is left of the wood he makes into a god by carving it into shape; he bows down to it and prostrates him-
18 self and prays to it, saying, 'Save me; for thou art my god.' Such people neither know nor understand, their eyes made too blind to see, their
19 minds too narrow to discern. Such a man will not use his reason, he has neither the wit nor the sense to say, 'Half of it I have burnt, yes, and used its embers to bake bread; I have roasted meat on them too and eaten it; but the rest of it I turn into this abominable thing and so I am
20 worshipping a log of wood.'*e* He feeds on ashes indeed! His own deluded mind has misled him, he cannot recollect himself so far as to say, 'Why! this thing in my hand is a sham.'

21   Remember all this, Jacob,
      remember, Israel, for you are my servant,
      I have fashioned you, and you are to serve me;
       you shall not forget me, Israel.
22   I have swept away your sins like a dissolving mist,
       and your transgressions are dispersed like clouds;
      turn back to me; for I have ransomed you.
23   Shout in triumph, you heavens, for it is the LORD's doing;
      cry out for joy, you lowest depths of the earth;
      break into songs of triumph, you mountains,

[a] sharpens: *so Sept.; Heb. om.*   [b] his work: *prob. rdg.; Heb.* he works.   [c] *Or* a shrine.
[d] *So some MSS.; others* ash-tree.   [e] a log of wood: *or, with Scroll,* dead wood.

you forest and all your trees;
for the LORD has ransomed Jacob
  and made Israel his masterpiece.

Thus says the LORD, your ransomer,   24
  who fashioned you from birth:
I am the LORD who made all things,
    by myself I stretched out the skies,
alone I hammered out the floor of the earth.
I frustrate false prophets and their signs   25
  and make fools of diviners;
I reverse what wise men say
  and make nonsense of their wisdom.
I make my servants' prophecies come true   26
  and give effect to my messengers' designs.
  I say of Jerusalem,
  'She shall be inhabited once more',
and of the cities of Judah, 'They shall be rebuilt;
  all their ruins I will restore.'
I say to the deep waters, 'Be dried up;   27
  I will make your streams run dry.'
I say to Cyrus, 'You shall be my shepherd   28
    to carry out all my purpose,
so that Jerusalem may be rebuilt
  and the foundations of the temple may be laid.'[a]

Thus says the LORD to Cyrus his anointed,   **45**
  Cyrus whom he has taken by the hand
  to subdue nations before him
  and undo the might[b] of kings;
  before whom gates shall be opened
  and no doors be shut:
I will go before you   2
  and level the swelling hills;
  I will break down gates of bronze
  and hack through iron bars.
I will give you treasures from dark vaults,   3
  hoarded in secret places,
that you may know that I am the LORD,
  Israel's God who calls you by name.
For the sake of Jacob my servant and Israel my chosen   4
  I have called you by name
and given you your title, though you have not known me.

[a] may be laid: *prob. rdg.*, *cp. Scroll*; *Heb.* you may be laid.   [b] might: *lit.* loins.

5   I am the LORD, there is no other;
            there is no god beside me.
        I will strengthen you though you have not known me,
6   so that men from the rising and the setting sun
        may know that there is none but I:
            I am the LORD, there is no other;
7   I make the light, I create darkness,
            author alike of prosperity and trouble.
    I, the LORD, do all these things.

8   Rain righteousness, you heavens,
        let the skies above pour down;
            let the earth open to receive it,
            that it may bear the fruit of salvation
        with righteousness in blossom at its side.
        All this I, the LORD, have created.

9   Will the pot contend^a with the potter,
        or the earthenware^b with the hand that shapes it?
        Will the clay ask the potter what he is making?
        or his^c handiwork say to him, 'You have no skill'?
10   Will the babe say^d to his father, 'What are you begetting?',
        or to his mother, 'What are you bringing to birth?'
11   Thus says the LORD, Israel's Holy One, his maker:
        Would you dare question me concerning my children,
        or instruct me in my handiwork?
12   I alone, I made the earth
        and created man upon it;
    I, with my own hands, stretched out the heavens
        and caused all their host to shine.
13   I alone have roused this man in righteousness,
            and I will smooth his path before him;
        he shall rebuild my city
            and let my exiles go free—
            not for a price nor for a bribe,
            says the LORD of Hosts.

14   Thus says the LORD:
        Toilers of Egypt and Nubian merchants
        and Sabaeans bearing tribute^e
    shall come into your power and be your slaves,
    shall come and march behind you in chains;

---

[a] Will...contend: *prob. rdg.; Heb.* Ho! he has contended. [b] *Or* shard. [c] *Prob. rdg.;
Heb.* your. [d] Will...say: *prob. rdg.; Heb.* Ho! you that say. [e] bearing tribute: *or* men
of stature.

they shall bow down before you in supplication, saying,
'Surely God is among you and there is no other,
   no other god.
How then canst thou be a god that hidest thyself,   15
   O God of Israel, the deliverer?'
Those who defy him*a* are confounded and brought to shame,   16
those who make idols perish in confusion.
    But Israel has been delivered by the LORD,   17
     delivered for all time to come;
they shall not be confounded or put to shame for all eternity.

Thus says the LORD, the creator of the heavens,   18
   he who is God,
who made the earth and fashioned it
   and himself fixed it fast,
who created it no empty void,
   but made it for a place to dwell in:
I am the LORD, there is no other.
I do not speak in secret, in realms of darkness,   19
   I do not say to the sons of Jacob,
    'Look for me in the empty void.'
I the LORD speak what is right, declare what is just.
   Gather together, come, draw near,   20
    all you survivors of the nations,
   you fools, who carry your wooden idols in procession
   and pray to a god that cannot save you.
Come forward and urge your case, consult*b* together: 21
   who foretold this in days of old,
    who stated it long ago?
   Was it not I the LORD?
   There is no god but me;
there is no god other than I, victorious and able to save.
   Look to me and be saved,   22
    you peoples from all corners of the earth;
   for I am God, there is no other.
   By my life I have sworn,   23
   I have given a promise of victory,
    a promise that will not be broken,
   that to me every knee shall bend
    and by me every tongue shall swear.
In the LORD alone, men shall say,   24
   are victory and might;

[a] Those who defy him: *so Sept.; Heb.* All of them together.   [b] *So Vulg.; Heb.* let them
consult.

and all who defy him
shall stand ashamed in his presence,
25 but all the sons of Israel shall stand victorious
and find their glory in the LORD.

46 Bel has crouched down, Nebo has stooped low:
their images, once carried in your processions,
have been loaded on to beasts and cattle,
a burden for the weary creatures;
2 they stoop and they crouch;
not for them to bring the burden to safety;
the gods themselves go into captivity.
3 Listen to me, house of Jacob
and all the remnant of the house of Israel,
a load on me from your birth, carried by me from the womb:
4 till you grow old I am He,
and when white hairs come, I will carry you still;
I have made you and I will bear the burden,
I will carry you and bring you to safety.
5 To whom will you liken me? Who is my equal?
With whom can you compare me? Where is my like?
6 Those who squander their bags of gold
and weigh out their silver with a balance
hire a goldsmith to fashion them into a god;
then they worship it and fall prostrate before it;
7 they hoist it shoulder-high and carry it home;
they set it down on its base;
there it must stand, it cannot stir from its place.
Let a man cry to it as he will, it never answers him;
it cannot deliver him from his troubles.

8 Remember this, you rebels,
consider it well, and abandon hope,
9 remember all that happened long ago;
for I am God, there is no other,
I am God, and there is no one like me;
10 I reveal the end from the beginning,
from ancient times I reveal what is to be;
I say, 'My purpose shall take effect,
I will accomplish all that I please.'
11 I summon a bird of prey[a] from the east,
one from a distant land to fulfil my purpose.
Mark this; I have spoken, and I will bring it about,

[a] a bird of prey: *or* a massed host.

I have a plan to carry out, and carry it out I will.

Listen to me, all you stubborn hearts,   12
    for whom victory is far off:
I bring my victory near, it is not far off,   13
    and my deliverance shall not be delayed;
I will grant deliverance in Zion
    and give my glory to Israel.[a]

Down with you, sit in the dust,   47
    virgin daughter of Babylon.
Down from your throne, sit on the ground,
    daughter of the Chaldaeans;
never again shall men call you
    soft-skinned and delicate.
Take up the millstone, grind meal, uncover your tresses;   2
strip off your skirt, bare your thighs, wade through rivers,
    so that your nakedness may be plain to see   3
    and your shame exposed.
I will take vengeance, I will treat with none of you,
    says[b] the Holy One of Israel, our ransomer,   4
    whose name is the LORD of Hosts.

Sit silent,   5
be off into the shadows, daughter of the Chaldaeans;
for never again shall men call you
    queen of many kingdoms.
When I was angry with my people,   6
I dishonoured my own possession
    and gave them into your power.
You showed them no mercy,
you made your yoke weigh heavy on the aged.
You said then, 'I shall reign a queen for ever',   7
    while[c] you gave no thought to this
    and did not consider how it would end.
Now therefore listen to this,   8
you lover of luxury, carefree on your throne.
    You say to yourself,
  'I am, and who but I?
No widow's weeds for me, no deaths of children.'
    Yet suddenly, in a single day,   9
    these two things shall come upon you;
they shall both come upon you in full measure:[d]

[a] and give my glory to Israel: *or* for Israel my glory. [b] says: *so Sept.; Heb. om.* [c] for
ever', while: *or* of a wide realm, for all time'; but. [d] in full measure: *or* at random.

children's deaths and widowhood,
for all your monstrous sorceries, your countless spells.
10 Secure in your wicked ways you thought, 'No one is looking.'
Your wisdom betrayed you, omniscient as you were,
    and you said to yourself,
'I am, and who but I?'
11 Therefore evil shall come upon you,
    and you will not know how to master it;
disaster shall befall you,
    and you will not be able to charm it away;
    ruin all unforeseen
shall come suddenly upon you.
12 Persist in your spells and your monstrous sorceries,[a]
maybe you can get help from them,
    maybe you will yet inspire awe.
13 But no! in spite of your many wiles you are powerless.
Let your astrologers, your star-gazers
who foretell your future month by month,
    persist, and save you!
14 But look, they are gone like chaff;
    fire burns them up;
they cannot snatch themselves from the flames;
    this is no glowing coal to warm them,
no fire for them to sit by.
15 So much for your magicians
with whom you have trafficked all your life:
they have stumbled off, each his own way,
    and there is no one to save you.

48 Hear this, you house of Jacob,
    you who are called by the name of Israel,
    you who spring from the seed of Judah;
    who swear by the name of the LORD
    and boast in the God of Israel,
    but not in honesty or sincerity,
2 although you call yourselves citizens of a holy city
    and lean for support on the God of Israel;
    his name is the LORD of Hosts.
3 Long ago I announced what would first happen,
I revealed it with my own mouth;
suddenly I acted and it came about.
4 I knew that you were stubborn,

[a] *Prob. rdg.; Heb. adds* with which you have trafficked all your life (*cp. verse 15*).

your neck stiff as iron, your brow like bronze,
therefore I told you of these things long ago,   5
and declared them before they came about,
so that you could not say, 'This was my idol's doing;
my image, the god that I fashioned, he ordained them.'
You have heard what I said; consider it well,   6
and you must admit the truth of it.
Now I show you new things,
    hidden things which you did not know before.
They were not created long ago, but in this very hour;   7
you had never heard of them before today.
You cannot say, 'I know them already.'
You neither heard nor knew,   8
long ago your ears were closed;
for I knew that you were untrustworthy, treacherous,
a notorious rebel from your birth.
For the sake of my own name I was patient,*a*   9
rather than destroy you I held myself in check.
See how I tested you, not as silver is tested,   10
    but in the furnace of affliction; there I purified you.
For my honour, for my own honour I did it;   11
let them disparage my past triumphs*b* if they will:
I will not give my glory to any other god.

Hear me, Jacob,   12
    and Israel whom I called:
I am He; I am the first,
    I am the last also.
With my own hands I founded the earth,   13
with my right hand I formed the expanse of sky;
    when I summoned them,
        they sprang at once into being.
Assemble, all of you, and listen to me;   14
    which of you*c* has declared what is coming,
that he whom I*d* love shall wreak my*e* will on Babylon
    and the Chaldaeans shall be scattered?
I, I myself, have spoken, I have called him,   15
I have made him appear, and wherever he goes he shall prosper.
Draw near to me and hear this: 16
    from the beginning I have never spoken in secret;
    from the moment of its first happening I was there.*f*

[a] *See note on verse 11.* [b] my past triumphs: *transposed from verse 9.* [c] *So many MSS.;*
others them. [d] *Prob. rdg., cp. Sept.; Heb. adds* the Lord. [e] *Or* his. [f] *Prob. rdg.;*
Heb. adds and now the Lord God has sent me, and his spirit.

17   Thus says the Lord your ransomer, the Holy One of Israel:
         I am the Lord your God:
            I teach you for your own advantage
            and lead you in the way you must go.
18   If only you had listened to my commands,
      your prosperity would have rolled on like a river in flood
            and your just success like the waves of the sea;
19   in number your children would have been like the sand
            and your descendants countless as its grains;
      their name would never be erased or blotted from my sight.
20   Come out of Babylon, hasten away from the Chaldaeans;
      proclaim it with loud songs of triumph,
            crying the news to the ends of the earth;
      tell them, 'The Lord has ransomed his servant Jacob.'
21   Though he led them through desert places they suffered no thirst,
      for them he made water run from the rock,
      for them he cleft the rock and streams gushed forth.
22   There is no peace for the wicked,
            says the Lord.

Israel a light to the nations

49   Listen to me, you coasts and islands,
         pay heed, you peoples far away:
         from birth the Lord called me,
         he named me from my mother's womb.
2   He made my tongue*a* his sharp sword
            and concealed me under cover of his hand;
         he made me a polished arrow
            and hid me out of sight in his quiver.
3   He said to me, 'You are my servant,
         Israel through whom I shall win glory';
            so I rose to honour in the Lord's sight
         and my God became my strength.*b*
4   Once I said, 'I have laboured in vain;
      I have spent my strength for nothing, to no purpose';
            yet in truth my cause is with the Lord
            and my reward is in God's hands.
5   And now the Lord who formed me in the womb to be his servant,
         to bring Jacob back to him

         [a] *Lit.* mouth.   [b] so I rose...strength: *transposed from end of verse 5.*

that Israel should be gathered to him,^a
now the LORD calls me again:^b
it is too slight a task for you, as my servant,   6
to restore the tribes of Jacob,
 to bring back the descendants of Israel:
I will make you a light to the nations,
to be my salvation^c to earth's farthest bounds.

Thus says the Holy One, the LORD who ransoms Israel,   7
 to one who thinks little of himself,^d
 whom every nation abhors,
 the slave of tyrants:
When they see you kings shall rise,
princes shall rise and bow down,
because of the LORD who is faithful,
because of the Holy One of Israel who has chosen you.

Thus says the LORD: 8
 In the hour of my favour I answered you,
 and I helped you on the day of deliverance,^e
 putting the land to rights
and sharing out afresh its desolate fields;
I said to the prisoners, 'Go free',   9
and to those in darkness, 'Come out and be seen.'
They shall find pasture in the desert sands^f
and grazing on all the dunes.
 They shall neither hunger nor thirst,   10
no scorching heat or sun shall distress them;
 for one who loves them shall lead them
 and take them to water at bubbling springs.
I will make every hill a path   11
 and build embankments for my highways.
See, they come; some from far away,   12
these from the north and these from the west
 and those from the land of Syene.^g
Shout for joy, you heavens, rejoice, O earth,   13
 you mountains, break into songs of triumph,
 for the LORD has comforted his people
 and has had pity on his own in their distress.

---

[a] be gathered to him: *or* not be swept away. [b] *See note on verse 3.* [c] to be my salvation: *or* that my salvation may reach. [d] to one...himself: *prob. rdg., cp. Sept.; Heb. obscure.* [e] *Prob. rdg.; Heb. adds* I have formed you, and appointed you to be a light to all peoples (*cp. 42. 6*). [f] desert sands: *prob. rdg.; Heb.* ways. [g] *So Scroll; Heb.* Sinim.

14   But Zion says,
     'The LORD has forsaken me; my God[a] has forgotten me.'

15   Can a woman forget the infant at her breast,
          or a loving mother the child of her womb?
     Even these forget, yet I will not forget you.

16   Your walls are always before my eyes,
          I have engraved them on the palms of my hands.

17   Those who are to rebuild you make better speed
               than those who pulled you down,
          while those who laid you waste depart.

18   Raise your eyes and look around you:
     see how they assemble, how they are flocking back to you.
          By my life I, the LORD, swear it,
          you shall wear them proudly as your jewels,
               and adorn yourself with them like a bride;

19   I did indeed make you waste and desolate,
          I razed you to the ground,
          but your boundaries[b] shall now be too narrow
               for your inhabitants—
          and those who laid you in ruins are far away.

20   The children born in your bereavement shall yet say in your hearing,
     'This place is too narrow; make room for me to live in.'

21   Then you will say to yourself,
          'All these children, how did I come by them,
          bereaved and barren as I was?[c]
          Who reared them
          when I was left alone, left by myself;
          where did I get them all?'

22   The Lord GOD says,
     Now is the time: I will beckon to the nations
          and hoist a signal to the peoples,
          and they shall bring your sons in their arms
          and carry your daughters on their shoulders;

23   kings shall be your foster-fathers
          and their princesses shall be your nurses.
     They shall bow to the earth before you
          and lick the dust from your feet;
          and you shall know that I am the LORD
          and that none who look to me will be disappointed.

24   Can his prey be taken from the strong man,

---

[a] my God: *so Scroll; Heb.* the Lord.   [b] I did . . . boundaries: *or* your wasted and desolate land, your ruined countryside.   [c] *So Sept.; Heb. adds* an exile and removed.

or the captive be rescued from the ruthless[a]?
And the LORD answers,   25
The captive shall be taken even from the strong,
and the prey of the ruthless shall be rescued;
I will contend with all who contend against you
and save your children from them.
I will force your oppressors to feed on their own flesh   26
and make them drunk with their own blood as if with fresh wine,
and all mankind shall know
that it is I, the LORD, who save you,
I your ransomer, the Mighty One of Jacob.

The LORD says,   50
Is there anywhere a deed of divorce
by which I have put your mother away?
Was there some creditor of mine
to whom I sold you?
No; it was through your own wickedness that you were sold
and for your own misconduct that your mother was put away.
Why, then, did I find no one when I came?   2
Why, when I called, did no one answer?
Did you think my arm too short to redeem,
did you think I had no power to save?
Not so. By my rebuke I dried up the sea
and turned rivers into desert;
their fish perished for lack of water
and died on the thirsty ground;
I clothed the skies in mourning   3
and covered them with sackcloth.

The Lord GOD has given me   4
the tongue of a teacher
and skill to console the weary
with a word[b] in the morning;
he sharpened my hearing[c]
that I might listen like one who is taught.
The Lord GOD opened my ears   5
and I did not disobey or turn back in defiance.
I offered my back to the lash,   6
and let my beard be plucked from my chin,
I did not hide my face from spitting and insult;
but the Lord GOD stands by to help me;   7

[a] *So Scroll; Heb.* righteous.   [b] *Prob. rdg., cp. Sept.; Heb. adds* he bores in the morning.
[c] sharpened my hearing: *lit.* bored my ears.

1031

therefore no insult can wound me.
I have set my face like flint,
   for I know that I shall not be put to shame,
8   because one who will clear my name is at my side.
Who dare argue against me? Let us confront one another.
Who will dispute my cause? Let him come forward.
9 The Lord GOD will help me;
   who then can prove me guilty?
They will all wear out like a garment,
   the moths will eat them up.

10 Which of you fears the LORD and obeys his servant's
       commands?
The man who walks in dark places with no light,
yet trusts in the name of the LORD and leans on his God.
11   But you who kindle a fire and set fire-brands alight,*a*
   go, walk into your own fire
   and among the fire-brands you have set ablaze.
This is your fate at my hands:
   you shall lie down in torment.

51 Listen to me, all who follow the right and seek the LORD:
   look to the rock from which you were hewn,
     to the quarry from which you were dug;
2   look to your father Abraham
     and to Sarah who gave you birth:
when I called him he was but one,
   I blessed him and made him many.
3   The LORD has indeed comforted Zion,
     comforted all her ruined homes,
turning her wilderness into an Eden,
   her thirsty plains into a garden of the LORD.
Joy and gladness shall be found in her,
   thanksgiving and melody.
4   Pay heed to me, my people,*b*
   and hear me, O my nation;*c*
for my law shall shine forth
and I will flash the light of my judgement over the nations.
5   My victory is near, my deliverance has gone*d* forth
   and my arm shall rule the nations;
for me coasts and islands shall wait
   and they shall look to me for protection.

---

[a] set...alight: *prob. rdg., cp. Sept.; Heb.* gird on fire-brands. [b] my people: *or, with some MSS.,* peoples. [c] O my nation: *or, with some MSS.,* O nations. [d] *Or* shone.

Lift your eyes to the heavens,　　　　　　　　　6
look at the earth beneath:
the heavens grow murky as smoke;
the earth wears into tatters like a garment,
and those who live on it die like maggots;
but my deliverance is everlasting
　　and my saving power shall never wane.

Listen to me, my people who know what is right,　　7
you who lay my law to heart:
　　do not fear the taunts of men,
　　let no reproaches dismay you;
for the grub will devour them like a garment　　　8
and the moth as if they were wool,
but my saving power shall last for ever
　　and my deliverance to all generations.

Awake, awake, put on your strength, O arm of the LORD,　　9
　　awake as you did long ago, in days gone by.
　　　　Was it not you
who hacked the Rahab in pieces and ran the dragon through?
　　　　Was it not you　　　　　　　　　　　　10
who dried up the sea, the waters of the great abyss,
and made the ocean depths a path for the ransomed?
　　　　So the LORD's people shall come back, set free,　　11
　　and enter Zion with shouts of triumph,
　　　　crowned with everlasting joy;
　　　　joy and gladness shall overtake them as they come,
　　　　and sorrow and sighing shall flee away.
　　I, I myself, am he that comforts you.　　　　12
　　Why then fear man, man who must die,
　　　　man frail as grass?
　　　　Why have you forgotten the LORD your maker,　　13
who stretched out the skies and founded the earth?
　　　　Why are you continually afraid, all the day long,
why dread the fury of oppressors ready to destroy you?
　　　　Where is that fury?
He that cowers under it shall soon stand upright and not die,　　14
　　he shall soon reap the early crop and not lack bread.

I am the LORD your God, the LORD of Hosts is my name. I cleft the　15
sea and its waves roared, that I might fix the heavens in place and form　16
the earth and say to Zion, 'You are my people.' I have put my words in
your mouth and kept you safe under the shelter of my hand.

17 Awake, awake; rise up, Jerusalem.
    You have drunk from the LORD's hand
      the cup of his wrath,
    drained to its dregs the bowl of drunkenness;
18 of all the sons you have borne there is not one to guide you,
  of all you have reared, not one to take you by the hand.
19   These two disasters have overtaken you;
      who can console you?—
  havoc and ruin, famine and the sword;
    who can comfort you[a]?
20   Your sons are in stupor, they lie at the head of every street,
    like antelopes caught in the net,
    glutted with the wrath of the LORD,
    the rebuke of your God.
21 Therefore listen to this, in your affliction,
    drunk that you are, but not with wine:
22 thus says the LORD, your Lord and your God,
    who will plead his people's cause:
  Look, I take from your hand
    the cup of drunkenness;
  you shall never again drink from the bowl of my wrath,
23   I will give it instead to your tormentors and oppressors,[b]
  those who said to you, 'Lie down and we will walk over you';
    and you made your backs like the ground beneath them,
    like a roadway for passers-by.

52 Awake, awake, put on your strength, O Zion,
  put on your loveliest garments, holy city of Jerusalem;
  for never shall the uncircumcised and the unclean enter you again.
2 Rise up, captive Jerusalem, shake off the dust;
    loose your neck from the collar that binds it,
    O captive daughter of Zion.

3   The LORD says, You were sold but no price was paid, and without
4 payment you shall be ransomed. The Lord GOD says, At the beginning
my people went down into Egypt to live there, and at the end it was
5 the Assyrians who oppressed them; but now what do I find here? says
the LORD. My people carried off and no price paid, their rulers derided,
6 and my name reviled all day long, says the LORD. But on that day my
people shall know my name;[c] they shall know that it is I who speak;
here I am.

[a] who can comfort you: *so Scroll; Heb.* who am I to comfort you.   [b] and oppressors:
so Scroll; Heb. om.   [c] *So Sept.; Heb. adds* therefore.

How lovely on the mountains are the feet of the herald　　　7
who comes to proclaim prosperity and bring good news,
　　　the news of deliverance,
calling to Zion, 'Your God is king.'
Hark, your watchmen raise their voices　　　8
　　　and shout together in triumph;
　　for with their own eyes they shall see
　　the LORD returning in pity^a to Zion.
　　Break forth together in shouts of triumph,　　　9
　　　you ruins of Jerusalem;
　　for the LORD has taken pity on his people
　　　and has ransomed Jerusalem.
The LORD has bared his holy arm　　　10
　　in the sight of all nations,
and the whole world from end to end
shall see the deliverance of our God.
Away from Babylon; come out, come out,　　　11
　　touch nothing unclean.
Come out from Babylon, keep yourselves pure,
　　you who carry the vessels of the LORD.
But you shall not come out in urgent haste　　　12
　　nor leave like fugitives;
　for the LORD will march at your head,
　　your rearguard will be Israel's God.

Behold, my servant shall prosper,^b　　　13
he shall be lifted up, exalted to the heights.
Time was when many^c were aghast at you, my people;^d　　　14
so now many nations^e recoil at sight of him,　　　15
and kings curl their lips in disgust.
For they see what they had never been told
　　and things unheard before fill their thoughts.
　　Who could have believed what we have heard,　　　53
and to whom has the power of the LORD been revealed?
　　He grew up before the LORD like a young plant　　　2
　　whose roots are in parched ground;
he had no beauty, no majesty to draw our eyes,
　　no grace to make us delight in him;
his form, disfigured, lost all the likeness of a man,
　　his beauty changed beyond human semblance.^f

[a] in pity: *so Scroll; Heb. om.* [b] prosper: *or, with slight change,* be bound. [c] *Or* the great. [d] *See note on 53. 2.* [e] *Or* great nations. [f] his form...semblance: *transposed from end of 52. 14.*

3   He was despised, he shrank from the sight of men,
         tormented and humbled by suffering;
         we despised him,^a we held him of no account,
         a thing from which men turn away their eyes.

4   Yet on himself he bore our sufferings,
         our torments he endured,
         while we counted him smitten by God,
         struck down by disease and misery;

5   but he was pierced for our transgressions,
         tortured for our iniquities;
         the chastisement he bore is health for us
         and by his scourging we are healed.

6   We had all strayed like sheep,
         each of us had gone his own way;
         but the LORD laid upon him
         the guilt of us all.

7   He was afflicted, he submitted to be struck down
         and did not open his mouth;
         he was led like a sheep to the slaughter,
         like a ewe that is dumb before the shearers.^b

8   Without protection, without justice,^c he was taken away;
         and who gave a thought to his fate,
         how he was cut off from the world of living men,
         stricken to the death^d for my people's transgression?

9   He was assigned a grave with the wicked,
         a burial-place^e among the refuse of mankind,
         though he had done no violence
         and spoken no word of treachery.

10   Yet the LORD took thought for his tortured servant
     and healed him who had made himself^f a sacrifice for sin;^g
     so shall he enjoy long life and see his children's children,
         and in his hand the LORD's cause shall prosper.

11   After all his pains he shall be bathed in light,^h
         after his disgrace he shall be fully vindicated;
         so shall he, my servant, vindicate many,
         himself bearing the penalty of their guilt.

12   Therefore I will allot him a portion with the great,
         and he shall share the spoil with the mighty,

---

[a] we despised him: *so Scroll; Heb.* one despised.   [b] *Prob. rdg.; Heb. adds* and he would
not open his mouth.   [c] Without protection, without justice: *or* After arrest and sentence.
[d] stricken to the death: *so Sept.; Heb.* a plague for him.   [e] a burial-place: *so Scroll;
Heb.* in his deaths.   [f] healed...himself: *prob. rdg.; Heb.* he made sick, if you make.
[g] sacrifice for sin: *lit.* guilt-offering.   [h] light: *so Scroll; Heb. om.*

because he exposed himself to face death[a]
    and was reckoned among transgressors,
because he bore the sin of many
    and interceded for their transgressions.

Sing aloud, O barren woman who never bore a child,   **54**
break into cries of joy, you who have never been in labour;
    for the deserted wife has more sons than she who lives in wedlock,
        says the LORD.
Enlarge the limits of your home,   2
    spread wide[b] the curtains of your tent;
let out its ropes to the full
    and drive the pegs home;
for you shall break out of your confines right and left,   3
your descendants shall dispossess wide regions,[c]
and re-people cities now desolate.
Fear not; you shall not be put to shame,   4
you shall suffer no insult, have no cause to blush.
It is time to forget the shame of your younger days
and remember no more the reproach of your widowhood;
for your husband is your maker, whose name is the LORD of Hosts;   5
    your ransomer is the Holy One of Israel
who is called God of all the earth.
The LORD has acknowledged you a wife again,   6
    once deserted and heart-broken,
your God has called you a bride still young
    though once rejected.
On the impulse of a moment I forsook you,   7
but with tender affection I will bring you home again.
    In sudden anger   8
I hid my face from you for a moment;
but now have I pitied you with a love which never fails,
    says the LORD who ransoms you.
These days recall for me the days of Noah: 9
as I swore that the waters of Noah's flood
should never again pour over the earth,
    so now I swear to you
never again to be angry with you or reproach you.
Though the mountains move and the hills shake,   10
my love shall be immovable and never fail,
    and my covenant of peace shall not be shaken.
    So says the LORD who takes pity on you.

[a] *Or* because he poured out his life to the death.   [b] spread wide: *so Sept.; Heb.* let them spread wide.   [c] wide regions: *or* the nations.

11   O storm-battered city, distressed and disconsolate,
   now I will set your stones in the finest mortar
    and your foundations in lapis lazuli;
12   I will make your battlements of red jasper[a]
    and your gates of garnet;[b]
    all your boundary-stones shall be jewels.
13   Your masons shall all be instructed by the LORD,
    and your sons shall enjoy great prosperity;
14   and in triumph[c] shall you be restored.
  You shall be free from oppression and have no fears,
  free from terror, and it shall not come near you;
15   should any attack you, it will not be my doing,
  the aggressor, whoever he be, shall perish for his attempt.
16   It was I who created the smith
   to fan the coals in the furnace
   and forge weapons each for its purpose,
  and I who created the destroyer to lay waste;
17   but now no weapon made to harm you shall prevail,
  and you shall rebut every charge brought against you.
   Such is the fortune of the servants of the LORD;
    their vindication comes from me.
   This is the very word of the LORD.

55   Come, all who are thirsty, come, fetch water;
  come, you who have no food, buy corn and eat;
  come and buy, not for money, not for a price.[d]
2   Why spend money and get what is not bread,
   why give the price of your labour and go unsatisfied?
  Only listen to me and you will have good food to eat,
   and you will enjoy the fat of the land.
3   Come to me and listen to my words,
   hear me, and you shall have life:
   I will make a covenant with you, this time for ever,
  to love you faithfully as I loved David.
4   I made him a witness to all races,
   a prince and instructor of peoples;
5   and you in turn shall summon nations you do not know,
  and nations that do not know you shall come running to you,
    because the LORD your God,
   the Holy One of Israel, has glorified you.
6   Inquire of the LORD while he is present,
   call upon him when he is close at hand.

[a] Or carbuncle. [b] Or firestone. [c] Or in righteousness. [d] Prob. rdg.; Heb. adds wine and milk.

Let the wicked abandon their ways 7
　and evil men their thoughts:
let them return to the LORD, who will have pity on them,
　return to our God, for he will freely forgive.
For my thoughts are not your thoughts, 8
　and your ways are not my ways.
　This is the very word of the LORD.
For as*a* the heavens are higher than the earth, 9
so are my ways higher than your ways
　and my thoughts than your thoughts;
and as the rain and the snow come down from heaven 10
and do not return until they have watered the earth,
　making it blossom and bear fruit,
and give seed for sowing and bread to eat,
so shall the word which comes from my mouth prevail; 11
　it shall not return to me fruitless
without accomplishing my purpose
　or succeeding in the task I gave it.
　You shall indeed go out with joy 12
　and be led forth in peace.
Before you mountains and hills shall break into cries of joy,
and all the trees of the wild shall clap their hands,
　pine-trees shall shoot up in place of camel-thorn, 13
　myrtles instead of briars;
all this shall win the LORD a great name,
　imperishable, a sign for all time.

Warnings to keep the moral law

These are the words of the LORD: **56**
Maintain justice, do the right;
for my deliverance is close at hand,
　and my righteousness will show itself victorious.
Happy is the man who follows these precepts, 2
happy the mortal who holds them fast,
　who keeps the sabbath undefiled,
　who refrains from all wrong-doing!
The foreigner who has given his allegiance to the LORD must not say, 3
'The LORD will keep me separate from his people for ever';
　and the eunuch must not say,

[*a*] as: *so Scroll; Heb. om.*

'I am nothing but a barren tree.'

4 For these are the words of the LORD:
The eunuchs who keep my sabbaths,
who choose to do my will and hold fast to my covenant,
5 shall receive from me something better than sons and daughters,
a memorial and a name in my own house and within my walls;
I will give them[a] an everlasting name,
a name imperishable for all time.
6 So too with the foreigners who give their allegiance to me, the LORD,
to minister to me and love my name
and to become my servants,
all who keep the sabbath undefiled
and hold fast to my covenant:
7 them will I bring to my holy hill
and give them joy in my house of prayer.
Their offerings and sacrifices shall be acceptable on my altar;
for my house shall be called
a house of prayer for all nations.
8 This is the very word of the Lord GOD,
who brings home the outcasts of Israel:
I will yet bring home all that remain to be brought in.

9 Come, beasts of the plain, beasts of the forest,
come, eat your fill,
10 for Israel's watchmen are blind, all of them unaware.
They are all dumb dogs who cannot bark,
stretched on the ground, dreaming, lovers of sleep,
11 greedy dogs that can never have enough.
They are shepherds who understand nothing,
absent each of them on his own pursuits,
each intent on his own gain wherever he can find it.
12 'Come,' says each of them, 'let me fetch wine,
strong drink, and we will drain it down;
let us make tomorrow like today,
or greater far!'
57 The righteous perish,
and no one takes it to heart;
men of good faith are swept away, but no one cares,
the righteous are swept away before the onset of evil,
2 but they enter into peace;
they have run a straight course
and rest in their last beds.

[a] *So Scroll; Heb.* him.

Come, stand forth, you sons of a soothsayer.   3
You spawn of an adulterer and a harlot,*
    who is the target of your jests?   4
  Against whom do you open your mouths
    and wag your tongues,
children of sin that you are, spawn of a lie,
  burning with lust under the terebinths,   5
    under every spreading tree,
  and sacrificing children in the gorges,
    under the rocky clefts?
    And you, woman,   6
your place is with the creatures of the gorge;
    that is where you belong.
To them you have dared to pour a libation
  and present an offering of grain.*
On a high mountain-top   7
  you have made your bed;
there too you have gone up to offer sacrifice.
In spite of all this am I to relent?*
Beside door and door-post you have put up your sign.   8
  Deserting me, you have stripped and lain down*
    on the wide bed which you have made,
  and you drove bargains with men
    for the pleasure of sleeping together,
and you have committed countless acts of fornication*
    in the heat of your lust.*
You drenched your tresses in oil   9
  blended with many perfumes;
you sent out your procurers far and wide
  even down to the gates of Sheol.
Worn out by your unending excesses,   10
  even so you never said, 'I am past hope.'
  You earned a livelihood
  and so you had no anxiety.
Whom do you fear so much, that you should be false,   11
that you never remembered me or gave me* a thought?
Did I not hold my peace and seem not to see
  while you showed no fear of me?
  Now I will denounce your conduct   12

[a] and a harlot: *so Sept.; Heb.* and she played the harlot.   [b] *See note on verse 7.*   [c] *Line transposed from end of verse 6.*   [d] lain down: *lit.* gone up.   [e] and you have committed . . . fornication: *so Sept.; Heb. om.*   [f] in the heat of your lust: *Heb. words of uncertain mng.*
[g] me: *or, with Scroll,* these things.

that you think so righteous.

13   These idols of yours shall not help when you cry;
      no idol shall save you.
   The wind shall carry them off, one and all,
      a puff of air shall blow them away;
  but he who makes me his refuge shall possess the earth
      and inherit my holy hill.

14   Then a voice shall be heard:
  Build up a highway, build it and clear the track,
      sweep away all that blocks my people's path.

15   Thus speaks the high and exalted one,
  whose name is holy, who lives for ever:
     I dwell in a high and holy place
       with him who is broken and humble in spirit,
        to revive the spirit of the humble,
        to revive the courage of the broken.

16   I will not be always accusing,
     I will not continually nurse my wrath.
     For a breath of life passed out from me,
      and by my own act I created living creatures.

17   For a time I was angry at the guilt of Israel;[a]
     I smote him in my anger and withdrew my favour.
     But he ran wild and went his wilful way.

18   Then I considered his ways,
     I cured him and gave him relief,
  and I brought him comfort in full measure,

19   brought peace to those who mourned for him,
     by the words that issue from my lips,
  peace for all men, both near and far,
     and so I cured him, says the LORD.

20   But the wicked are like a troubled sea,
     a sea that cannot rest,
  whose troubled waters cast up mud and filth.

21   There is no peace for the wicked,
        says the LORD.

58   Shout aloud without restraint;
     lift up your voice like a trumpet.
     Call my people to account for their transgression
      and the house of Jacob for their sins,

2   although they ask counsel of me day by day

[a] For...Israel: *prob. rdg., cp. Sept.; Heb.* I was angry at the guilt of his unjust gain.

and say they delight in knowing my ways,
although, like nations which have acted rightly
   and not forsaken the just laws of their gods,
they ask me for righteous laws
and say they delight in approaching God.

Why do we fast, if thou dost not see it?   3
Why mortify ourselves, if thou payest no heed?
Since you serve your own interest only on your fast-day
   and make all your men work the harder,
since your fasting leads only to wrangling and strife   4
   and dealing vicious blows with the fist,
   on such a day you are keeping no fast
   that will carry your cry to heaven.
Is it a fast like this that I require,   5
   a day of mortification such as this,
   that a man should bow his head like a bulrush
   and make his bed on sackcloth and ashes?
   Is this what you call a fast,
   a day acceptable to the LORD?
Is not this what I require of you as a fast: 6
   to loose the fetters of injustice,
   to untie the knots of the yoke,
     to snap every yoke
   and set free those who have been crushed?
Is it not sharing your food with the hungry,   7
taking the homeless poor into your house,
   clothing the naked when you meet them
   and never evading a duty to your kinsfolk?
Then shall your light break forth like the dawn   8
and soon you will grow healthy like a wound newly healed;
   your own righteousness shall be your vanguard
   and the glory of the LORD your rearguard.
Then, if you call, the LORD will answer;   9
   if you cry to him, he will say, 'Here I am.'
   If you cease to pervert justice,
to point the accusing finger and lay false charges,
   if you feed the hungry from your own plenty   10
   and satisfy the needs of the wretched,
   then your light will rise like dawn out of darkness
   and your dusk be like noonday;
   the LORD will be your guide continually   11
   and will satisfy your needs in the shimmering heat;

he will give you strength of limb;
you will be like a well-watered garden,
like a spring whose waters never fail.

12 The ancient ruins will be restored by your own kindred
and you will build once more on ancestral foundations;
you shall be called Rebuilder of broken walls,
Restorer of houses in ruins.

13 If you cease to tread the sabbath underfoot,
and keep my holy day free from your own affairs,[a]
if you call the sabbath a day of joy
and the LORD's holy day a day to be honoured,
if you honour it by not plying your trade,
not seeking your own interest
or attending to your own affairs,

14 then you shall find your joy in the LORD,
and I will set you riding on the heights of the earth,
and your father Jacob's patrimony shall be yours to enjoy;
the LORD himself has spoken it.

59 The LORD's arm is not so short that he cannot save
nor his ear too dull to hear;

2 it is your iniquities that raise a barrier
between you and your God,
because of your sins he has hidden his face
so that he does not hear you.

3 Your hands are stained with blood
and your fingers with crime;
your lips speak lies
and your tongues utter injustice.

4 No man sues with just cause,
no man goes honestly to law;
all trust in empty words, all tell lies,
conceive mischief and give birth to trouble.

5 They hatch snakes'[b] eggs, they weave cobwebs;
eat their eggs and you will die,
for rotten eggs hatch only rottenness.

6 As for their webs, they will never make cloth,
no one can use them for clothing;
their works breed trouble
and their hands are busy with deeds of violence.

7 They rush headlong into crime

[a] and keep...affairs: *so Scroll; Heb.* and do your own affairs on my holy day. [b] *Lit.*
vipers'.

1044

in furious haste to shed innocent blood;
their schemes are schemes of mischief
and leave a trail of ruin and devastation.
They do not know the way to peace,   8
   no justice guides their steps;
   all the paths they follow are crooked;
no one who walks in them enjoys true peace.

Therefore justice is far away from us,   9
   right does not reach us;
we look for light but all is darkness,
   for the light of dawn, but we walk in deep gloom.
We grope like blind men along a wall,   10
   feeling our way like men without eyes;
   we stumble at noonday as if it were twilight,
   like dead men in the ghostly underworld.[a]
We growl like bears,   11
like doves we moan incessantly,
waiting for justice, and there is none;
for deliverance, but it is still far away.

Our acts of rebellion against thee are past counting   12
and our sins bear witness against us;
we remember our many rebellions, we know well our guilt:
   we have rebelled and broken faith with the LORD,   13
   we have relapsed and forsaken our God;
we have conceived lies in our hearts and repeated them
   in slanderous and treacherous words.
Justice is rebuffed and flouted   14
while righteousness stands aloof;
truth stumbles in the market-place
and honesty is kept out of court,
so truth is lost to sight,   15
and whoever shuns evil is thought a madman.

The LORD saw, and in his eyes it was an evil thing,
   that there was no justice;
   he saw that there was no man to help   16
   and was outraged that no one intervened;
   so his own arm brought him victory
   and his own integrity upheld him.
He put on integrity as a coat of mail   17
and the helmet of salvation on his head;
he put on garments of vengeance

[a] the ghostly underworld: *mng. of Heb. uncertain.*

and wrapped himself in a cloak of jealous anger.
18   High God of retribution that he is,
      he pays in full measure,
wreaking his anger on his foes, retribution on his enemies.*a*
19   So from the west men shall fear his name,
      fear his glory from the rising of the sun;
    for it shall come like a shining river,
      the spirit of the Lord hovering over it,
20   come as the ransomer of Zion
      and of all in Jacob who repent of their rebellion.
    This is the very word of the Lord.

21   This, says the Lord, is my covenant, which I make with them: My spirit which rests on you and my words which I have put into your mouth shall never fail you from generation to generation of your descendants from now onward for ever. The Lord has said it.

Promise of the new Jerusalem

60   Arise, Jerusalem,*b*
  rise clothed in light; your light has come
    and the glory of the Lord shines over you.
2   For, though darkness covers the earth
    and dark night the nations,
    the Lord shall shine upon you
    and over you shall his glory appear;
3   and the nations shall march towards your light
    and their kings to your sunrise.
4   Lift up your eyes and look all around:
    they flock together, all of them, and come to you;
    your sons also shall come from afar,
    your daughters walking beside them leading the way.
5   Then shall you see, and shine with joy,
    then your heart shall thrill with pride:*c*
    the riches of the sea shall be lavished upon you
    and you shall possess the wealth of nations.
6   Camels in droves shall cover the land,
      dromedaries of Midian and Ephah,
  all coming from Sheba

[a] *So Sept.; Heb. adds* to coasts and islands he pays in full measure. [b] Jerusalem: *so Sept.; Heb. om.* [c] *So some MSS.; others* relief.

laden with golden spice*ª* and frankincense,
　　heralds of the LORD's praise.
All Kedar's flocks shall be gathered for you,　　　　　　7
　　rams of Nebaioth shall serve your need,
acceptable offerings on my altar,
and glory shall be added*ᵇ* to glory in my temple.

Who are these that sail along like clouds,　　　　　　8
　　that fly like doves to their dovecotes?
They are vessels assembling from the coasts and islands,　9
　　ships from Tarshish leading the convoy;
they bring your sons from afar,
their gold and their silver with them,
　　to the honour of the LORD your God,
　　the Holy One of Israel;
　　for he has made you glorious.

Foreigners shall rebuild your walls　　　　　　10
　　and their kings shall be your servants;
　　for though in my wrath I struck you down,
　　now I have shown you pity and favour.
Your gates shall be open continually,　　　　　　11
they shall never be shut day or night,
　　that through them may be brought the wealth of nations
　　and their kings under escort.

For the nation or kingdom which refuses to serve you shall perish,　12
and wide regions shall be laid utterly waste.

The wealth of Lebanon shall come to you,　　　　　　13
pine, fir,*ᶜ* and boxwood,*ᵈ* all together,
　　to bring glory to my holy sanctuary,
　　to honour the place where my feet rest.
The sons of your oppressors shall come forward to do homage,　14
all who reviled you shall bow low at your feet;
　　they shall call you the City of the LORD,
　　the Zion of the Holy One of Israel.

No longer will you be deserted,　　　　　　15
a wife hated and unvisited;*ᵉ*
I will make you an eternal pride
and a never-ending joy.
You shall suck the milk of nations　　　　　　16
and be suckled at the breasts of kings.

[*a*] golden spice: *or* gold.　[*b*] shall be added: *so Sept.; Heb.* I will add.　[*c*] *Or* elm.
[*d*] *Or* cypress.　[*e*] *Or* divorced and unmated.

So you shall know that I the LORD am your deliverer,
    your ransomer the Mighty One of Jacob.

17   For bronze[a] I will bring you gold
    and for iron I will bring silver,
bronze[a] for timber and iron for stone;
    and I will make your government be peace
      and righteousness rule over you.
18   The sound of violence shall be heard no longer in your land,
    or ruin and devastation within your borders;
but you shall call your walls Deliverance
    and your gates Praise.

19   The sun shall no longer be your light by day,
    nor the moon shine on you when evening falls;[b]
the LORD shall be your everlasting light,
    your God shall be your glory.
20   Never again shall your sun set
    nor your moon withdraw her light;
but the LORD shall be your everlasting light
    and the days of your mourning shall be ended.

21   Your people shall all be righteous
    and shall for ever possess the land,
      a shoot of my own planting,
    a work of my own hands to bring me glory.
22   The few shall become ten thousand,
      the little nation great.
    I am the LORD;
soon, in the fullness of time, I will bring this to pass.

61   The spirit of the Lord GOD is upon me
    because the LORD has anointed me;
he has sent me to bring good news to the humble,
    to bind up the broken-hearted,
to proclaim liberty to captives
    and release to those in prison;[c]
2   to proclaim a year of the LORD's favour
    and a day of the vengeance of our God;
      to comfort all who mourn,[d]
3   to give them garlands instead of ashes,

---

[a] *Or* copper.   [b] when evening falls: *prob. rdg., cp. Scroll; Heb. obscure in context.*
[c] release to those in prison: *or, with Sept.,* sight to the blind.   [d] *Prob. rdg.; Heb. adds*
to appoint to Zion's mourners.

oil of gladness instead of mourners' tears,
    a garment of splendour for the heavy heart.
They shall be called Trees of Righteousness,
    planted by the LORD for his glory.
      Ancient ruins shall be rebuilt   4
      and sites long desolate restored;
      they shall repair the ruined cities
and restore*a* what has long lain desolate.
Foreigners shall serve as shepherds of your flocks,   5
    and aliens shall till your land and tend your vines;
but you shall be called priests of the LORD   6
    and be named ministers of our God;
      you shall enjoy the wealth of other nations
      and be furnished*b* with their riches.
And so, because shame in double measure   7
    and jeers and insults*c* have been my people's*d* lot,
they shall receive in their own land a double measure of wealth,
    and everlasting joy shall be theirs.
For I, the LORD, love justice   8
    and hate robbery and wrong-doing;
I will grant them a sure reward
    and make an everlasting covenant with them;
      their posterity will be renowned among the nations   9
      and their offspring among the peoples;
    all who see them will acknowledge in them
a race whom the LORD has blessed.

Let me rejoice in the LORD with all my heart,   10
    let me exult in my God;
    for he has robed me in salvation as a garment
      and clothed me in integrity as a cloak,
like a bridegroom with his priestly garland,
    or a bride decked in her jewels.
    For, as the earth puts forth her blossom   11
    or bushes in the garden burst into flower,
so shall the Lord GOD make righteousness and praise
    blossom before all the nations.

For Zion's sake I will not keep silence,   **62**
    for Jerusalem's sake I will speak out,
until her right shines forth like the sunrise,
    her deliverance like a blazing torch,

[*a*] restore: *so Scroll; Heb. om.* [*b*] be furnished: *prob. rdg.; Heb. unintelligible.* [*c*] and insults: *prob. rdg.; Heb. they shout in triumph.* [*d*] my people's: *lit.* their.

2   until the nations see the triumph of your right
        and all kings see your glory.
      Then you shall be called by a new name
      which the LORD shall pronounce with his own lips;
3   you will be a glorious crown in the LORD's hand,
        a kingly diadem[a] in the hand of your God.
4   No more shall men call you Forsaken,
  no more shall your land be called Desolate,
  but you shall be named Hephzi-bah[b]
     and your land Beulah;[c]
  for the LORD delights in you
     and to him your land is wedded.
5   For, as a young man weds a maiden,
        so you shall wed him who rebuilds you,
    and your God shall rejoice over you
      as a bridegroom rejoices over the bride.
6   I have posted watchmen on your walls, Jerusalem,
  who shall not keep silence day or night:
     'You who invoke the LORD's name,
7   take no rest, give him no rest
     until he makes Jerusalem
     a theme of endless praise on earth.'

8   The LORD has sworn with raised right hand and mighty arm:
  Never again will I give your grain to feed your foes
     or let foreigners drink the new wine
      for which you have toiled;
9   but those who bring in the corn shall eat and praise the
        LORD,
  and those who gather the grapes shall drink in my holy courts.

10   Go out of the gates, go out,
     prepare a road for my people;
     build a highway, build it up,
      clear away the boulders;
     raise a signal to the peoples.
11   This is the LORD's proclamation
      to earth's farthest bounds:
    Tell the daughter of Zion,
      Behold, your deliverance has come.
      His recompense comes with him;
      he carries his reward before him;
12   and they shall be called a Holy People,

[a] diadem: *lit.* turban. [b] *That is* My delight is in her. [c] *That is* Wedded.

the Ransomed of the LORD,
a People long-sought, a City not forsaken.

'Who is this coming from Edom,   **63**
   coming from Bozrah, his garments stained red?
Under his clothes his muscles stand out,
   and he strides, stooping in his might.'
It is I, who announce that right has won the day,
   I, who am strong to save.
'Why is your clothing all red,   2
like the garments of one who treads grapes in the vat?'
I have trodden the winepress alone;   3
no man, no nation was with me.
   I trod them down in my rage,
   I trampled them in my fury;
and their life-blood spurted over my garments
   and stained all my clothing.
For I resolved on a day of vengeance;   4
   the year for ransoming my own had come.
I looked for a helper but found no one,   5
   I was amazed that there was no one to support me;
yet my own arm brought me victory,
alone my anger supported me.
I stamped on nations in my fury,   6
   I pierced them in my rage
and let their life-blood run out upon the ground.

I will recount the LORD's acts of unfailing love   7
and the LORD's praises as High God,
all that the LORD has done for us
and his great goodness to the house of Israel,
   all that he has done for them in his tenderness
   and by his many acts of love.
He said, 'Surely they are my people,   8
   my sons who will not play me false';
and he became their deliverer in all their troubles.   9
It was no envoy, no angel, but he himself that delivered them;
he himself ransomed them by his love and pity,
   lifted them up and carried them
   through all the years gone by.
Yet they rebelled and grieved his holy spirit;   10
   only then was he changed into their enemy
   and himself fought against them.
   Then men remembered days long past   11

and him who drew out^a his people:^b
Where is he who brought them up from the Nile^c
with the shepherd^d of his flock?
Where is he who put within him
his holy spirit,

12 who made his glorious power march
at the right hand of Moses,
dividing the waters before them,
to win for himself an everlasting name,

13 causing them to go through the depths
sure-footed as horses in the wilderness,

14 like cattle moving down into a valley without stumbling,
guided^e by the spirit of the LORD?
So didst thou lead thy people
to win thyself a glorious name.

15 Look down from heaven and behold
from the heights where thou dwellest holy and glorious.
Where is thy zeal, thy valour,
thy burning and tender love?

16 Stand not aloof;^f for thou art our father,
though Abraham does not know us nor Israel acknowledge us.
Thou, LORD, art our father;
thy name is our Ransomer^g from of old.

17 Why, LORD, dost thou let us wander from thy ways
and harden our hearts until we cease to fear thee?
turn again for the sake of thy servants,
the tribes of thy patrimony.

18 Why have wicked men trodden down thy sanctuary,^h
why have our enemies trampled on thy shrine?

19 We have long been reckoned as beyond thy sway,
as if we had not been named thy own.

64 1ⁱ Why didst thou not rend the heavens and come down,
and make the mountains shudder before thee

2^j as when fire blazes up in brushwood
or fire makes water boil?
then would thy name be known to thy enemies
and nations tremble at thy coming.

---

[a] *That is* Moses *whose name resembles the Heb. verb meaning* draw out, *cp. Exod. 2. 10 and the note there.* [b] and...people: *or, with some MSS.,* and Moses his servant. [c] *Lit.* from the sea. [d] *Or* shepherds. [e] guided: *so Sept.; Heb.* given rest. [f] Stand not aloof: *prob. rdg.; Heb. obscure in context.* [g] *Or* our Kinsman. [h] Why...sanctuary: *prob. rdg.; Heb.* For a little while they possessed thy holy people. [i] *63. 19b in Heb.* [j] *64. 1 in Heb.*

When thou didst terrible things that we did not look for,[a] 　3
the mountains shuddered before thee.
Never has ear heard[b] or eye seen 　4
any other god taking the part of those who wait for him.
Thou dost welcome him who rejoices to do what is right, 　5
who remembers thee in thy ways.
Though thou wast angry, yet we sinned,
in spite of it we have done evil from of old,[c]
we all became like a man who is unclean 　6
and all our righteous deeds like a filthy rag;[d]
we have all withered[e] like leaves
and our iniquities sweep us away like the wind.
There is no one who invokes thee by name 　7
or rouses himself to cling to thee;
for thou hast hidden thy face from us
and abandoned[f] us to our iniquities.
But now, LORD, thou art our father; 　8
we are the clay, thou the potter,
and all of us are thy handiwork.
Do not be angry beyond measure, O LORD, 　9
and do not remember iniquity for ever;
look on us all, look on thy people.
Thy holy cities are a wilderness, 　10
Zion a wilderness, Jerusalem desolate;
our sanctuary, holy and glorious, 　11
where our fathers praised thee,
has been burnt to the ground
and all that we cherish is a ruin.
After this, O LORD, wilt thou hold back, 　12
wilt thou keep silence and punish us beyond measure?

I was there to be sought by a people who did not ask, 　**65**
to be found by men who did not seek me.
I said, 'Here am I, here am I',
to a nation that did not invoke me by name.
I spread out my hands all day 　2
appealing to an unruly people
who went their evil way,
following their own devices,
a people who provoked me 　3

[a] *So Sept.; Heb. adds* thou hast come down. [b] Never...heard: *prob. rdg.; Heb.* They
have never heard or listened. [c] in spite...old: *prob. rdg., cp. Sept.; Heb. obscure in
context.* [d] *Lit.* menstruous garment. [e] have all withered: *or* are all carried away.
[f] and abandoned: *so Sept.; Heb. unintelligible.*

1053

continually to my face,
offering sacrifice in gardens, burning incense on brick altars,

4   crouching among graves, keeping vigil all night long,
eating swine's flesh, their cauldrons full of a tainted brew.

5   'Stay where you are,' they cry,
    'do not dare touch me; for I am too sacred for you.'
    Such people are a smouldering fire,
    smoking in my nostrils all day long.

6   All is on record before me; I will not keep silence;

7   I will repay[a] your iniquities,
yours and your fathers', all at once, says the LORD,
    because they burnt incense[b] on the mountains
        and defied me on the hills;
    I will first measure out their reward
        and then pay them in full.

8   These are the words of the LORD:
As there is new wine in a cluster of grapes
and men say, 'Do not destroy it; there is a blessing in it',
    so will I do for my servants' sake:
    I will not destroy the whole nation.

9   I will give Jacob children to come after him
and Judah heirs who shall possess my mountains;
        my chosen shall inherit them
    and my servants shall live there.

10   Flocks shall range over Sharon,
        and the Vale of Achor be a pasture for cattle;
    they shall belong to my people who seek me.

11   But you that forsake the LORD and forget my holy mountain,
    who spread a table for the god of Fate,
    and fill bowls of spiced wine in honour of Fortune,

12   I will deliver you to your fate, to execution,
    and you shall all bend the neck to the sword,
        because I called and you did not answer,
        I spoke and you did not listen;
    and you did what was wrong in my eyes
    and you chose what was against my will.

13   Therefore these are the words of the Lord GOD:
My servants shall eat but you shall starve;
my servants shall drink but you shall go thirsty;
my servants shall rejoice but you shall be put to shame;

14   my servants shall shout in triumph

[a] *Prob. rdg.*, *transposing* and then pay *to follow* reward.   [b] *Or* sacrifices.

in the gladness of their hearts,
   but you shall cry from sorrow
      and wail from anguish of spirit;
your name shall be used as an oath by my chosen,   15
      and the Lord GOD shall give you over to death;
      but his servants he shall call by another name.
He who invokes a blessing on himself in the land   16
      shall do so by the God whose name is Amen,
      and he who utters an oath in the land
      shall do so by the God of Amen;
   the former troubles are forgotten
      and they are hidden from my sight.
   For behold, I create   17
new heavens and a new earth.
      Former things shall no more be remembered
      nor shall they be called to mind.
   Rejoice and be filled with delight,   18
   you boundless realms which I create;
for I create Jerusalem to be a delight
      and her people a joy;
I will take delight in Jerusalem and rejoice in my people;   19
      weeping and cries for help
   shall never again be heard in her.
There no child shall ever again die an infant,   20
   no old man fail to live out his life;
   every boy shall live his hundred years before he dies,
whoever falls short of a hundred shall be despised.*
   Men shall build houses and live to inhabit them,   21
plant vineyards and eat their fruit;
   they shall not build for others to inhabit   22
   nor plant for others to eat.
   My people shall live the long life of a tree,
and my chosen shall enjoy the fruit of their labour.
They shall not toil in vain or raise children for misfortune.   23
   For they are the offspring of the blessed of the LORD
      and their issue after them;
before they call to me, I will answer,   24
and while they are still speaking I will listen.
The wolf and the lamb shall feed together   25
and the lion shall eat straw like cattle.*
They shall not hurt or destroy in all my holy mountain,
      says the LORD.

[a] *Or* cursed. [b] *Prob. rdg.; Heb. adds* and the food of the snake shall be dust.

66 These are the words of the LORD:
Heaven is my throne and earth my footstool.
Where will you build a house for me,
      where shall my resting-place be?
2   All these are of my own making
      and all these are mine.[a]
         This is the very word of the LORD.

The man I look to is a man down-trodden and distressed,
      one who reveres my words.
3 But to sacrifice an ox or to[b] kill a man,
slaughter a sheep or break a dog's neck,
offer grain or offer pigs' blood,
burn incense as a token and worship an idol—
all these are the chosen practices of men
      who[c] revel in their own loathsome rites.
4 I too will practise those wanton rites of theirs
      and bring down on them the very things they dread;
      for I called and no one answered,
         I spoke and no one listened.
      They did what was wrong in my eyes
      and chose practices not to my liking.

5 Hear the word of the LORD, you who revere his word:
      Your fellow-countrymen who hate you,
      who spurn you because you bear my name, have said,
         'Let the LORD show his glory,
         then we shall see you rejoice';
      but they shall be put to shame.
6 That roar from the city, that uproar in the temple,
is the sound of the LORD dealing retribution to his foes.

7 Shall a woman bear a child without pains?
give birth to a son before the onset of labour?
8   Who has heard of anything like this?
      Who has seen any such thing?
Shall a country be born after one day's labour,
shall a nation be brought to birth all in a moment?
But Zion, at the onset of her pangs, bore her sons.
9   Shall I bring to the point of birth and not deliver?
         the LORD says;
      shall I who deliver close the womb?
         your God has spoken.

---

[a] mine: *so Sept.; Heb. om.*   [b] to sacrifice an ox or to: *or those who sacrifice an ox and . . .*
[c] are the chosen practices of men who: *or have chosen their own devices and . . .*

Rejoice with Jerusalem and exult in her,   10
    all you who love her;
  share her joy with all your heart,
  all you who mourn over her.
Then you may suck and be fed from the breasts that give comfort,   11
delighting in her plentiful milk.
  For thus says the LORD: 12
I will send peace flowing over her like a river,
and the wealth of nations like a stream in flood;
    it shall suckle you,
    and you shall be carried in their arms
    and dandled on their knees.
As a mother comforts her son,   13
so will I myself comfort you,
    and you shall find comfort in Jerusalem.
This you shall see and be glad at heart,   14
  your limbs shall be as fresh as grass in spring;
the LORD shall make his power known among his servants
    and his indignation felt among his foes.
For see, the LORD is coming in fire,   15
  with his chariots like a whirlwind,
  to strike home with his furious anger
    and with the flaming fire of his reproof.
The LORD will judge by fire,   16
  with fire he will test all living men,
  and many will be slain by the LORD;
    those who hallow and purify themselves in garden-rites,   17
    one[a] after another in a magic ring,
those who eat the flesh of pigs and rats[b] and all vile vermin,
    shall meet their end, one and all,
    says the LORD,
for I know[c] their deeds and their thoughts.   18

Then I myself[d] will come to gather all nations and races,
  and they shall come and see my glory;
  and I will perform a sign among them.   19
I will spare some of them and send them to the nations,
  to Tarshish, Put,[e] and Lud,[f]
  to Meshek, Rosh,[g] Tubal, and Javan,[h]
distant coasts and islands which have never yet heard of me
  and have not seen my glory;

[a] one: *so. Pesh.; Heb. om.* [b] *Or* jerboas. [c] know: *so Pesh.; Heb. om.* [d] I myself: *so Sept.; Heb.* it. [e] *So Sept.; Heb. unintelligible.* [f] *Or* Lydia. [g] Meshek, Rosh: *prob. rdg.; Heb.* those who draw the bow. [h] *Or* Greece.

these shall announce that glory among the nations.

20   From every nation they shall bring your countrymen
on horses, in chariots and wagons,
     on mules and dromedaries,
     as an offering to the LORD,
on my holy mountain Jerusalem,
     says the LORD,
as the Israelites bring offerings
     in pure vessels to the LORD's house;

21   and some of them I will take for priests, for^a Levites,
     says the LORD.

22   For, as the new heavens and the new earth
which I am making shall endure in my sight,
     says the LORD,
so shall your race and your name endure;

23   and month by month at the new moon,
         week by week on the sabbath,
all mankind shall come to bow down before me,
         says the LORD;

24   and they shall come out and see
the dead bodies of those who have rebelled against me;
their worm shall not die nor their fire be quenched,
         and they shall be abhorred by all mankind.

[a] *Or, with Sept.*, and.

THE BOOK OF THE PROPHET

JEREMIAH

THE WORDS OF JEREMIAH son of Hilkiah, one of the 1
priests at Anathoth in Benjamin. The word of the LORD came to 2
him in the thirteenth year of the reign of Josiah son of Amon,
king of Judah; also during the reign of Jehoiakim son of Josiah, king 3
of Judah, until the eleventh year of Zedekiah son of Josiah, king of
Judah, was completed. In the fifth month the people of Jerusalem were
carried away into exile.

Jeremiah's call and two visions

THE WORD OF THE LORD CAME TO ME: 'Before I formed you 4, 5
in the womb I knew you for my own; before you were born I
consecrated you, I appointed you a prophet to the nations.' 'Ah! Lord 6
GOD,' I answered, 'I do not know how to speak; I am only a child.'
But the LORD said, 'Do not call yourself a child; for you shall go to 7
whatever people I send you and say whatever I tell you to say. Fear 8
none of them, for I am with you and will keep you safe.' This was the
very word of the LORD. Then the LORD stretched out his hand and 9
touched my mouth, and said to me, 'I put my words into your mouth.
This day I give you authority over nations and over kingdoms, to pull 10
down and to uproot, to destroy and to demolish, to build and to plant.'
The word of the LORD came to me: 'What is it that you see, Jere- 11
miah?' 'An almond in early bloom',[a] I answered. 'You are right,' 12
said the LORD to me, 'for I am early on the watch[b] to carry out my
purpose.' The word of the LORD came to me a second time: 'What is it 13
that you see?' 'A cauldron', I said, 'on a fire, fanned by the wind; it
is tilted away from the north.' The LORD said: 14

> From the north disaster shall flare up
> against all who live in this land;
> for now I summon all peoples and kingdoms of the north, 15
> says the LORD.
> Their kings shall come and each shall set up his throne
> before the gates of Jerusalem,
> against her walls on every side,
> and against all the cities of Judah.

[a] *Heb.* shaked. [b] *Heb.* shoked.

16   I will state my case against my people
            for all the wrong they have done in forsaking me,
        in burning sacrifices to other gods,
            worshipping the work of their own hands.
17   Brace yourself, Jeremiah;
            stand up and speak to them.
        Tell them everything I bid you,
    do not let your spirit break at sight of them,
            or I will break you before their eyes.
18   This day I make you a fortified city,
            a pillar of iron, a wall of bronze,
            to stand fast against the whole land,
    against the kings and princes of Judah,
            its priests and its people.
19   They will make war on you but shall not overcome you,
            for I am with you and will keep you safe.
        This is the very word of the LORD.

Exhortations to Israel and Judah

2 1,2   THE WORD OF THE LORD CAME TO ME: Go, make a proclama-
        tion that all Jerusalem shall hear: These are the words of the LORD:

        I remember the unfailing devotion of your youth,
            the love of your bridal days,
        when you followed me in the wilderness,
            through a land unsown.
3   Israel then was holy to the LORD,
            the firstfruits of his harvest;
            no one who devoured her went unpunished,
            evil always overtook them.
            This is the very word of the LORD.

4   Listen to the word of the LORD, people of Jacob, families of Israel,
5   one and all. These are the words of the LORD:

        What fault did your forefathers find in me,
            that they wandered far from me,
        pursuing empty phantoms and themselves becoming empty;
6   that they did not ask, 'Where is the LORD,
            who brought us up from Egypt,
            and led us through the wilderness,
            through a country of deserts and shifting sands,

a country barren and ill-omened, where no man ever trod,
 no man made his home?'
I brought you into a fruitful land   7
 to enjoy its fruit and the goodness of it;
 but when you entered upon it you defiled it
 and made the home I gave you loathsome.
The priests no longer asked, 'Where is the LORD?' 8
Those who handled the law had no thought of me,
 the shepherds of the people rebelled against me;
 the prophets prophesied in the name of Baal
 and followed gods powerless to help.
Therefore I will bring a charge against you once more, 9
  says the LORD,
 against you and against your descendants.
 Cross to the coasts and islands of Kittim and see, 10
 send to Kedar and consider well,
 see whether there has been anything like this:
has a nation ever changed its gods,   11
 although they were no gods?
But my people have exchanged their Glory
 for a god altogether powerless.
 Stand aghast at this, you heavens,   12
 tremble in utter despair,
  says the LORD.
Two sins have my people committed: 13
 they have forsaken me,
 a spring of living water,
and they have hewn out for themselves cisterns,
cracked cisterns that can hold no water.

Is Israel a slave? Was he born in slavery?   14
If not, why has he been despoiled?
Why do lions roar and growl at him?   15
Why has his land been laid waste,
why are his cities razed to the ground*a* and abandoned?
Men of Noph and Tahpanhes   16
 will break your heads.
Is it not your desertion of the LORD your God 17
 that brings all this upon you?*b*
And now, why should you make off to Egypt 18
 to drink the waters of the Shihor?
Or why make off to Assyria

[*a*] razed to the ground: *so some MSS.; others* burnt. [*b*] *So Sept.; Heb. adds* at the time
of one who leads you on the way.

to drink the waters of the River?

19 It is your own wickedness that will punish you,
      your own apostasy that will condemn you.
   See for yourselves how bitter a thing it is and how evil,
   to forsake the LORD your God and revere me no longer.
      This is the very word of the Lord GOD of Hosts.

20 Ages ago you broke your yoke and snapped your traces,
      crying, 'I will not be your slave';
   and you sprawled in promiscuous vice
      on all the hill-tops, under every spreading tree.

21 I planted you as a choice red vine,
      true stock all of you,
   yet now you are turned into a vine
      debased and worthless!

22 The stain of your sin is still there and I see it,
   though you wash with soda and do not stint the soap.
      This is the very word of the Lord GOD.

23 How can you say, 'I am not polluted, not I!
      I have not followed the Baalim'?
   Look how you conducted yourself in the valley;
      remember what you have done.
      You have been like a she-camel,
   twisting and turning as she runs,

24   rushing alone into*a* the wilderness,
   snuffing the wind in her lust;
      who can restrain her in her heat?
   No one need tire himself out in pursuit of her;
      she is easily found at mating time.

25 Why not save your feet from stony ground
      and your throats from thirst?
   But you said, 'No; I am desperate.
      I love foreign gods and I must go after them.'

26 As a thief is ashamed when he is found out,
      so the people of Israel feel ashamed,
   they, their kings, their princes,
      their priests and their prophets;

27 they say 'You are our father' to a block of wood
      and cry 'Mother' to a stone.
   But on me they have turned their backs
      and averted their faces from me.
   And now on the day of disaster they say,
      'Rise up and save us.'

[*a*] rushing alone into: *prob. rdg.; Heb.* a wild-ass taught in.

Where are they, those gods you made for yourselves?   28
Let them come and save you in the day of disaster.
For you, Judah, have as many gods as you have towns.*a*
        The LORD answers,   29
Why argue your case with me?
You are rebels, every one of you.
In vain I struck down your sons,   30
        the lesson was not learnt;
still your own sword devoured your prophets
        like a ravening lion.
*b*Have I shown myself inhospitable to Israel   31
        like some wilderness or waterless land?
Why do my people say, 'We have broken away;
        we will never come back to thee'?

        Will a girl forget her finery   32
                or a bride her ribbons?
                Yet my people have forgotten me
                over and over again.
How well you pick your way in search of lovers!   33
Why! even the worst of women can learn from you.
Yes, and there is blood on the corners of your robe—   34
        the life-blood of the innocent poor.
                You did not get it by housebreaking
                but by your sacrifices under every oak.
You say, 'I am innocent;   35
        surely his anger has passed away.'
But I will challenge your claim
        to have done no sin.
Why do you so lightly change your course?   36
Egypt will fail you as Assyria did;
        you shall go out from here,   37
                each of you with his hands above his head,
        for the LORD repudiates those in whom you trusted,
        and from them you shall gain nothing.

        *c*If a man puts away his wife   3
                and she leaves him,
        and if she then becomes another's,
                may he go back to her again?
        Is not that woman*d* defiled,
                a forbidden thing?

[*a*] towns: *or* blood-spattered altars. [*b*] *Prob. rdg.; Heb. prefixes* You, O generation, see the word of the LORD. [*c*] *So Sept.; Heb. prefixes* Saying. [*d*] *So Sept.; Heb.* land.

You have played the harlot with many lovers;
  can you come back to me?
  says the LORD.

2 Look up to the high bare places and see:
  where have you not been ravished?
You sat by the wayside to catch lovers,
  like an Arab lurking in the desert,
and defiled the land
  with your fornication and your wickedness.

3 Therefore the showers were withheld
  and the spring rain failed.
But yours was a harlot's brow,
  and you were resolved to show no shame.

4 Not so long since, you called me 'Father,
  dear friend of my youth',

5 thinking, 'Will he be angry for ever?
  Will he rage eternally?'
This is how you spoke; you have done evil
  and gone unchallenged.

6 In the reign of King Josiah, the LORD said to me, Do you see what apostate Israel did? She went up to every hill-top and under every 7 spreading tree, and there she played the whore. Even after she had done all this, I said to her, Come back to me, but she would not. That faithless 8 woman, her sister Judah, saw it all; she[a] saw too that I had put apostate Israel away and given her a note of divorce because she had committed adultery. Yet that faithless woman, her sister Judah, was not afraid; she 9 too has gone and played the whore. She defiled the land with her thoughtless harlotry and her adulterous worship of stone and wood. 10 In spite of all this that faithless woman, her sister Judah, has not come back to me in good faith, but only in pretence. This is the very word of the LORD.

11 The LORD said to me, Apostate Israel is less to blame than that 12 faithless woman Judah. Go and proclaim this message to the north:

Come back to me, apostate Israel,
  says the LORD,
I will no longer frown on you.
For my love is unfailing, says the LORD,
  I will not be angry for ever.

13 Only you must acknowledge your wrongdoing,
confess your rebellion against the LORD your God.
Confess your promiscuous traffic with foreign gods

[a] *So one MS.; others* I.

under every spreading tree,
confess that you have not obeyed me.
This is the very word of the LORD.

Come back to me, apostate children, says the LORD, for I am patient 14
with you, and I will take you, one from a city and two from a clan, and
bring you to Zion. There will I give you shepherds after my own heart, 15
and they shall lead you with knowledge and understanding. In those 16
days, when you have increased and become fruitful in the land, says the
LORD, men shall speak no more of the Ark of the Covenant of the LORD;
they shall not think of it nor remember it nor resort to it; it will be
needed no more. At that time Jerusalem shall be called the Throne of 17
the LORD. All nations shall gather in Jerusalem to honour the LORD's
name; never again shall they follow the promptings of their evil and
stubborn hearts. In those days Judah shall join Israel, and together they 18
shall come from a northern land into the land I gave their*a* fathers as
their patrimony.

I said, How gladly would I treat you as a son,   19
   giving you a pleasant land,
      a patrimony fairer than that of any nation!
I said, You shall call me Father
   and never cease to follow me.
But like a woman who is unfaithful to her lover,   20
so you, Israel, were unfaithful to me.
   This is the very word of the LORD.
Hark, a sound of weeping on the bare places,   21
Israel's people pleading for mercy!
For they have taken to crooked ways
and ignored the LORD their God.
Come back to me, wayward*b* sons;   22
I will heal your apostasy.

O LORD, we come! We come to thee;
for thou art our God.
There is no help in worship on the hill-tops,   23
   no help from clamour on the heights;
truly in the LORD our God
   is Israel's only salvation.
      From our early days   24
      Baal, god of shame, has devoured
      the fruits of our fathers' labours,
their flocks and herds, their sons and daughters.

[*a*] *So Sept.; Heb.* your. [*b*] *Or* apostate.

25   Let us lie down in shame, wrapped round by our dishonour,
      for we have sinned against the LORD our God,
        both we and our fathers,
        from our early days till now,
      and we have not obeyed the LORD our God.

4   If you will but come back, O Israel,
      if you will but come back to me, says the LORD,
      if you will banish your loathsome idols from my sight,
        and stray no more,
2   if you swear by the life of the LORD,
        in truth, in justice and uprightness,
      then shall the nations pray to be blessed like you[a]
      and in you[a] shall they boast.

3   These are the words of the LORD to the men of Judah and Jerusalem:

      Break up your fallow ground,
        do not sow among thorns,
4   circumcise yourselves to the service of the LORD,
        circumcise your hearts,
        men of Judah and dwellers in Jerusalem,
      lest the fire of my fury blaze up and burn unquenched,
        because of your evil doings.
5   Tell this in Judah,
        proclaim it in Jerusalem,
      blow the trumpet throughout the land,
        sound the muster,
      give the command, Stand to!—and let us fall back
        on the fortified cities.
6   Raise the signal—To Zion!
        make for safety, lose no time,
      for I bring disaster out of the north,
        and dire destruction.
7   A lion has come out from his lair,
        the destroyer of nations;
      he has struck his tents, he has broken camp,
        to harry your land
      and lay your cities waste and unpeopled.
8   Well may you put on sackcloth,
        beat the breast and wail,
      for the anger of the LORD
        is not averted from us.

[a] *Prob. rdg.; Heb.* him.

On that day, says the LORD,   9
the hearts of the king and his officers shall fail them,
priests shall be struck with horror and prophets dumbfounded.

And I said, O Lord GOD, thou surely didst deceive this people and   10
Jerusalem in saying, 'You shall have peace', while the sword is at our
throats.
At that time this people and Jerusalem shall be told: 11

A scorching wind from the high bare places in the wilderness
   sweeps down upon my people,
no breeze for winnowing or for cleansing;
a wind too strong for these   12
   will come at my bidding,
   and now I will state my case against them.

Like clouds the enemy advances   13
   with a whirlwind of chariots;
his horses are swifter than eagles—
   alas, we are overwhelmed!
O Jerusalem, wash the wrongdoing from your heart   14
   and you may yet be saved;
how long will you cherish
   your evil schemes?
Hark, a runner from Dan,   15
   tidings of evil from Mount Ephraim!
Tell all this to the nations,   16
   proclaim the doom of Jerusalem:
hordes of invaders come from a distant land,
howling against the cities of Judah.
Their pickets are closing in all round her,   17
   because she has rebelled against me.
   This is the very word of the LORD.
Your own ways, your own deeds   18
have brought all this upon you;
   this is your punishment,
and all this comes of your rebellion.[a]
Oh, the writhing of my bowels   19
   and the throbbing of my heart!
   I cannot keep silence.
I hear the sound of the trumpet,
   the sound of the battle-cry.
Crash upon crash,   20

[a] your rebellion: *prob. rdg.; Heb. obscure.*

the land goes down in ruin,
my tents are thrown down,
their coverings torn to shreds.

21 How long must I see the standard raised
and hear the trumpet call?

22 My people are fools, they know nothing of me;
silly children, with no understanding,
they are clever only in wrongdoing,
and of doing right they know nothing.

23 I saw the earth, and it was without form and void;
the heavens, and their light was gone.

24 I saw the mountains, and they reeled;
all the hills rocked to and fro.

25 I saw, and there was no man,
and the very birds had taken flight.

26 I saw, and the farm-land was wilderness,
and the towns all razed to the ground,
before the Lord in his anger.

27 These are the words of the Lord:
The whole land shall be desolate,
though I will not make an end of it.

28 Therefore the earth will mourn
and the heavens above turn black.
For I have made known my purpose;
I will not relent or change my mind.

29 At the sound of the horsemen and archers
the whole country*ᵃ* is in flight;
they creep into caves, they hide*ᵇ* in thickets,
they scramble up the crags.
Every*ᶜ* town is forsaken,
no one dwells there.

30 And you,*ᵈ* what are you doing?
When you dress yourself in scarlet,
deck yourself out with golden ornaments,
and make your eyes big with antimony,
you are beautifying yourself to no purpose.
Your lovers spurn you
and are out for your life.

31 I hear a sound as of a woman in labour,
the sharp cry of one bearing her first child.

[a] *So Sept.; Heb.* city.   [b] into...hide: *so Sept.; Heb. om.*   [c] *So Sept.; Heb.* The whole.
[d] *So Sept.; Heb. adds* overwhelmed.

It is Zion, gasping for breath,
   clenching her fists.
Ah me! I am weary,
   weary of slaughter.

Go up and down the streets of Jerusalem   5
   and see for yourselves;
search her wide squares:
   can you find any man who acts justly,
   who seeks the truth,
that I may forgive that city?
Men may swear by the life of the LORD,   2
but they only perjure themselves.
O LORD, are thine eyes not set upon the truth?   3
Thou didst strike them down,
   but they took no heed;
didst pierce them to the heart,
   but they refused to learn.
They set their faces harder than flint
   and refused to come back.
I said, 'After all, these are the poor,   4
   these are stupid folk,
who do not know the way of the LORD,
   the ordinances of their God.
I will go to the great   5
   and speak with them;
for they will know the way of the LORD,
   the ordinances of their God.'
But they too have broken the yoke
   and snapped their traces.
Therefore a lion out of the scrub shall strike them down,   6
   a wolf from the plains shall ravage them;
a leopard shall prowl about their cities
and maul any who venture out.
For their rebellious deeds are many,
   their apostasies past counting.
How can I forgive you for all this?   7
Your sons have forsaken me and sworn by gods
   that are no gods.
I gave them all they needed, yet they preferred adultery,
   and haunted[a] the brothels;
each neighs after another man's wife,   8

[a] *So some MSS.; others* and gashed themselves in.

like a well-fed and lusty stallion.

9   Shall I not punish them for this?
         the LORD asks.
     Shall I not take vengeance
         on such a people?

10   Go along her rows of vines and slash them,
         yet do not make an end of them.
     Hack away her green branches,
         for they are not the LORD's.

11   Faithless are Israel and Judah,
     both faithless to me.
         This is the very word of the LORD.

12   They have denied the LORD,
     saying, 'He does not exist.
     No evil shall come upon us;
     we shall never see sword or famine.

13   The prophets will prove mere wind,
         the word not in them.'[a]

14   And so, because you talk in this way, these are the words of the LORD the God of Hosts to me:

     I will make my words a fire in your mouth;
     and it shall burn up this people like brushwood.

15   I bring against you, Israel, a nation from afar,
     an ancient people established long ago,
         says the LORD.
     A people whose language you do not know,
         whose speech you will not understand;

16   they are all mighty warriors,
         their jaws are[b] a grave, wide open,

17   to devour your harvest and your bread,
     to devour your sons and your daughters,
     to devour your flocks and your herds,
     to devour your vines and your fig-trees.
     They shall batter down the cities in which you trust,[c]
         walled though they are.

18   But in those days, the LORD declares, I will still not make an end of
19   you. When you ask, 'Why has the LORD our God done all this to us?'
I shall answer, 'As you have forsaken me and served alien gods in your own land, so shall you serve foreigners[d] in a land that is not yours.'

[a] *So Sept.; Heb. adds* so may it be done to them.   [b] their jaws are: *so Pesh.; Heb.* their quiver is.   [c] *Prob. rdg.; Heb. adds* with the sword.   [d] *Or* foreign gods.

Tell this to the people of Jacob,   20
    proclaim it in Judah:
Listen, you foolish and senseless people,   21
who have eyes and see nothing,
ears and hear nothing.
Have you no fear of me? says the LORD;   22
    will you not shiver before me,
before me, who made the shivering sand to bound the sea,
    a barrier it never can pass?
Its waves heave and toss but they are powerless;
roar as they may, they cannot pass.
But this people has a rebellious and defiant heart,   23
    rebels they have been and now they are clean gone.
They did not say to themselves,   24
    'Let us fear the LORD our God,
who gives us the rains of autumn
    and spring showers in their turn,
who brings us unfailingly
fixed seasons of harvest.'
But your wrongdoing has upset nature's order,   25
and your sins have kept from you her kindly gifts.
For among my people there are wicked men,   26
    who lay snares like a fowler's net*a*
    and set deadly traps to catch men.
Their houses are full of fraud,   27
as a cage is full of birds.
They grow rich and grand,
    bloated and rancorous;   28
their thoughts*b* are all of evil,
    and they refuse to do justice,*c*
the claims of the orphan they do not put right
nor do they grant justice to the poor.
Shall I not punish them for this?   29
    says the LORD;
shall I not take vengeance
    on such a people?

An appalling thing, an outrage,   30
has appeared in this land:
prophets prophesy lies and priests go hand in hand with them,   31
    and my people love to have it so.
      How will you fare at the end of it all?

[a] who...net: *prob. rdg.; Heb. unintelligible.* [b] rancorous; their thoughts: *Heb. has these words transposed.* [c] *Vulg. adds* for the widow.

6   Save yourselves, men of Benjamin,
          come out of Jerusalem,
      blow the trumpet in Tekoa,
      fire the beacon on Beth-hakkerem,
      for calamity looms from the north
          and great disaster.

2   Zion, delightful and lovely:
          her end is near—

3   she to whom the shepherds come
          and bring their flocks with them.
      There they pitch their tents all round her,
          each grazing his own strip of pasture.

4   Declare war solemnly against her;
      come, let us attack her at noon.
      Too late! the day declines
          and the shadows lengthen.

5   Come then, let us attack her by night
          and destroy her palaces.

6   These are the words of the LORD of Hosts:
      Cut down the trees of Jerusalem
          and raise siege-ramps against her,
      the city whose name is Licence,[a]
      oppression is rampant in her.

7   As a well keeps its water fresh,
      so she keeps her evil fresh.
      Violence and outrage echo in her streets;
      sickness and wounds stare me in the face.

8   Learn your lesson, Jerusalem,
      lest my love for you be torn from my heart,
          and I leave you desolate,
          a land where no one can live.

9   These are the words of the LORD of Hosts:
      Glean[b] the remnant of Israel
          like a vine,
      pass your hand like a vintager one last time
          over the branches.

10   To whom can I address myself,
          to whom give solemn warning? Who will hear me?
      Their ears are uncircumcised;
          they cannot listen;
      they treat the LORD's word as a reproach;
          they show no concern with it.

[a] Licence: *so some MSS.; others* Visited.   [b] *Prob. rdg., cp. Sept.; Heb.* Let them glean.

But I am full of the anger of the LORD,   11
     I cannot hold it in.
I must pour it out on the children in the street
     and on the young men in their gangs.
Man and wife alike shall be caught in it,
     the greybeard and the very old.
Their houses shall be turned over to others,   12
their fields and their women alike.
     For I will raise my hand, says the LORD,
against the people of the country.
For all, high and low,   13
     are out for ill-gotten gain;
prophets and priests are frauds,
     every one of them;
they dress my people's wound, but skin-deep only,   14
     with their saying, 'All is well.'
All well? Nothing is well!
Are they ashamed when they practise their abominations?   15
     Ashamed? Not they!
     They can never be put out of countenance.
Therefore they shall fall with a great crash,[a]
and be brought to the ground on the day of my reckoning.
     The LORD has said it.

These are the words of the LORD: Stop at the cross-roads; look for   16
the ancient paths; ask, 'Where is the way that leads to what is good?'
Then take that way, and you will find rest for yourselves. But they said,
'We will not.' Then I will appoint watchmen to direct you; listen for   17
their trumpet-call. But they said, 'We will not.' Therefore hear, you   18
nations, and take note, all you who witness it, of the plight of this
people. Listen, O earth, I bring ruin on them, the harvest of all their   19
scheming; for they have given no thought to my words and have spurned
my instruction. What good is it to me if frankincense is brought from   20
Sheba and fragrant spices from distant lands? I will not accept your
whole-offerings, your sacrifices do not please me. Therefore these are   21
the words of the LORD:

I will set obstacles before this people
     which shall bring them to the ground;
fathers and sons, friends and neighbours
     shall all perish together.

These are the words of the LORD: 22

     [a] with a great crash: *or* where they fall *or* among the fallen.

See, a people is coming from a northern land,
a great nation rouses itself from earth's farthest corners.

23 They come with bow and sabre, cruel men and pitiless,
bestriding their horses, they sound like the thunder of the sea,
they are like men arrayed for battle against you, Zion.

24 We have heard tell of them
and our hands hang limp,
agony grips us, the anguish of a woman in labour.

25 Do not go out into the country,
do not walk by the high road;
for the foe, sword in hand,
is a terror let loose.

26 Daughter of my people, wrap yourself in sackcloth,
sprinkle ashes over yourself, wail bitterly,
as one who mourns an only son;
in an instant shall the marauder be upon us.

27 I have appointed you an assayer of my people;
you will know how to test them and will assay their conduct;

28 arch-rebels all of them,
mischief-makers, corrupt to a man.

29 The bellows puff and blow, the furnace glows;
in vain does the refiner smelt the ore,
lead, copper and iron*a* are not separated out.

30 Call them spurious silver;
for the LORD has spurned them.

False religion and its punishment

7 1,2 THIS WORD CAME FROM THE LORD to Jeremiah. Stand at the
gate of the LORD's house and there make your proclamation: Listen
to the words of the LORD, all you men of Judah who come in through
3 these gates to worship him. These are the words of the LORD of Hosts
the God of Israel: Mend your ways and your doings, that I may let you
4 live*b* in this place. You keep saying, 'This place*c* is the temple of the
LORD, the temple of the LORD, the temple of the LORD!' This catchword
5 of yours is a lie; put no trust in it. Mend your ways and your doings,
6 deal fairly with one another, do not oppress the alien, the orphan, and
the widow, shed no innocent blood in this place, do not run after other
7 gods to your own ruin. Then will I let you live*d* in this place, in the

[a] copper and iron: *transposed from after* mischief-makers *in verse 28.* [b] *Or, with Vulg.,*
I may live with you. [c] This place: *prob. rdg.; Heb.* Those. [d] *Or, with Vulg.,* will I
live with you.

land which I gave long ago to your forefathers for all time. You gain 8
nothing by putting your trust in this lie. You steal, you murder, you 9
commit adultery and perjury, you burn sacrifices to Baal, you run after
other gods whom you have not known; then you come and stand before 10
me in this house, which bears my name, and say, 'We are safe'; safe,
you think, to indulge in all these abominations. Do you think that this 11
house, this house which bears my name, is a robbers' cave? I myself
have seen all this, says the LORD. Go to my shrine at Shiloh, which 12
once I made a dwelling for my Name, and see what I did to it because
of the wickedness of my people Israel. And now you have done all these 13
things, says the LORD; though I took pains to speak to you, you did not
listen, and though I called, you gave no answer. Therefore what I did 14
to Shiloh I will do to this house which bears my name, the house in
which you put your trust, the place I gave to you and your forefathers;
I will fling you away out of my sight, as I flung away all your kinsfolk, 15
the whole brood of Ephraim.

Offer up no prayer, Jeremiah, for this people, raise no plea or prayer on 16
their behalf, and do not intercede with me; for I will not listen to you.
Do you not see what is going on in the cities of Judah and in the streets 17
of Jerusalem? Children are gathering wood, fathers lighting fires, women 18
kneading dough to make crescent-cakes in honour of the queen of
heaven; and drink-offerings are poured out to other gods than me—
all to provoke and hurt me. But is it I, says the LORD, whom they hurt? 19
No; it is themselves, covering their own selves with shame. Therefore, 20
says the Lord GOD, my anger and my fury shall fall on this place, on
man and beast, on trees and crops, and it shall burn unquenched.

These are the words of the LORD of Hosts the God of Israel: Add 21
whole-offerings to sacrifices and eat the flesh if you will. But when I 22
brought your forefathers out of Egypt, I gave them no commands about
whole-offering and sacrifice; I said not a word about them. What I did 23
command them was this: If you obey me, I will be your God and you
shall be my people. You must conform to all my commands, if you
would prosper. But they did not listen; they paid no heed, and persisted 24
in disobedience with evil and stubborn hearts; they looked backwards
and not forwards, from the day when your forefathers left Egypt until 25
now. I took pains to send to them[a] all my servants the prophets; they 26
did not listen to me, they paid no heed, but were obstinate and proved
even more wicked than their forefathers. When you tell them this, they 27
will not listen to you; if you call them, they will not answer. Then you 28
shall say to them, This is the nation that did not obey the LORD its
God nor accept correction; truth has perished, it is heard no more on
their lips.

[a] *So one MS.; others* you.

29   O Jerusalem, cut off your hair,
the symbol of your dedication, and throw it away;
raise up a lament on the high bare places.

For the LORD has spurned the generation which has roused his wrath,
30 and has abandoned them. For the men of Judah have done what is
wrong in my eyes, says the LORD. They have defiled with their loath-
31 some idols the house that bears my name, they have built a shrine of
Topheth in the Valley of Ben-hinnom, at which to burn their sons and
daughters; that was no command of mine, nor did it ever enter my
32 thought. Therefore a time is coming, says the LORD, when it shall no
longer be called Topheth or the Valley of Ben-hinnom, but the Valley
of Slaughter; for the dead shall be buried in Topheth because there is
33 no room elsewhere. So the bodies of this people shall become food for
the birds of the air and the wild beasts, and there will be no one to
34 scare them away. From the cities of Judah and the streets of Jerusalem
I will banish all sounds of joy and gladness, the voice of the bridegroom and the bride; for the land shall become desert.

8   At that time, says the LORD, men shall bring out from their graves
the bones of the kings of Judah, of the officers, priests, and prophets,
2 and of all who lived in Jerusalem. They shall expose them to the sun,
the moon, and all the host of heaven, whom they loved and served and
adored, to whom they resorted and bowed in worship. Those bones
shall not be gathered up nor buried but shall become dung on the
3 ground. All the survivors of this wicked race, wherever I have banished
them,*a* would rather die than live. This is the very word of the LORD
of Hosts.

4   You shall say to them, These are the words of the LORD:

If men fall, can they not also rise?
If a man breaks away, can he not return?
5   Then why are this people*b* so wayward,
incurable in their waywardness?
Why have they clung to their treachery
and refused to return to their obedience?
6   I have listened to them
and heard not one word of truth,
not one sinner crying remorsefully,
'Oh, what have I done?'
Each one breaks away*c* in headlong career
as a war-horse plunges in battle.

[a] *So one MS.; others add* those who are left. [b] *So Sept.; Heb. adds* Jerusalem.
[c] breaks away: *or* is wayward.

The stork in the sky   7
  knows the time to migrate,
the dove and the swift and the wryneck
  know the season of return;
but my people do not know the ordinances of the LORD.
How can you say, 'We are wise,   8
  we have the law of the LORD',
when scribes with their lying pens
  have falsified it?
The wise are put to shame, they are dismayed and have lost their   9
    wits.
  They have spurned the word of the LORD,
  and what sort of wisdom is theirs?
Therefore will I give their wives to other men   10
  and their lands to new owners.
  For all, high and low,
    are out for ill-gotten gain;
  prophets and priests are frauds,
    every one of them;
  they dress my people's wound,[a] but skin-deep only,   11
    with their saying, 'All is well.'
    All well? Nothing is well!
  Are they ashamed when they practise their abominations?   12
    Ashamed? Not they!
    They can never be put out of countenance.
Therefore they shall fall with a great crash,[b]
and be brought to the ground on the day of my reckoning.
    The LORD has said it.
  I would gather their harvest, says the LORD,   13
  but there are no grapes on the vine,
  no figs on the fig-tree;
  even their leaves are withered.[c]
Why do we sit idle? Up, all of you together,   14
let us go into our walled cities and there meet our doom.
  For the LORD our God has struck us down,
  he has given us a draught of bitter poison;
    for we have sinned against the LORD.
  Can we hope to prosper when nothing goes well?   15
  Can we hope for respite when the terror falls suddenly?
  The snorting of his horses is heard from Dan;   16

[a] my people's wound: *lit.* the wound of the daughter of my people (*cp. also 8. 19, 21; 9. 1, 7*). [b] with a great crash: *or* where they fall *or* among the fallen. [c] *So Sept.; Heb. adds* so I have allowed men to pass them by.

at the neighing of his stallions the whole land trembles.
The enemy come; they devour the land and all its store,
    city and citizens alike.

17 Beware, I am sending snakes against you,
    vipers, such as no man can charm,
      and they shall bite you.
    This is the very word of the LORD.

18 How can I bear my sorrow?[a]
    I am sick at heart.

19 Hark, the cry of my people
    from a distant land:
'Is the LORD not in Zion?
    Is her King no longer there?'
Why do they provoke me with their images
    and foreign gods?

20 Harvest is past, summer is over,
    and we are not saved.

21 I am wounded at the sight of my people's wound;
    I go like a mourner, overcome with horror.

22 Is there no balm in Gilead,
    no physician there?
Why has no new skin grown over their wound?

9 1[b] Would that my head were all water,
    my eyes a fountain of tears,
that I might weep day and night
    for my people's dead!

2[c] Oh that I could find in the wilderness a shelter by the wayside,
that I might leave my people and depart!
    Adulterers are they all, a mob of traitors.

3 The tongue is their weapon, a bow ready bent.
Lying, not truth, is master[d] in the land.
    They run from one sin to another,
    and for me they care nothing.
    This is the very word of the LORD.

4 Be on your guard, each man against his friend;
    put no trust even in a brother.
Brother supplants brother,[e]
and friend slanders friend.

---

[a] How...sorrow?: *prob. rdg.; Heb. unintelligible.* [b] *8. 23 in Heb.* [c] *9. 1 in Heb.*
[d] not truth, is master: *so Sept.; Heb.* not for truth, they are master. [e] Brother
supplants brother: *or* Every brother is a supplanter like Jacob (*cp. Gen. 27. 35 and note*).

They make game of their friends   5
    but never speak the truth;
they have trained their tongues to lies;
    deep in their sin, they cannot retrace their steps.
Wrong follows wrong, deceit follows deceit;   6
    they refuse to acknowledge me.
    This is the very word of the LORD.
Therefore these are the words of the LORD of Hosts: 7
    I am their refiner and will assay them.
    How can I disregard my people?
    Their tongue is a cruel arrow,   8
    their mouths speak lies.
    One speaks amicably to another,
    while inwardly he plans a trap for him.
    Shall I not punish them for this?   9
      says the LORD;
    shall I not take vengeance
      on such a people?

Over the mountains will I raise weeping and wailing,   10
    and over the desert pastures will I chant a dirge.
    They are scorched and untrodden,
      they hear no lowing of cattle;
birds of the air and beasts have fled and are gone.

I will make Jerusalem a heap of ruins, a haunt of wolves,   11
and the cities of Judah an unpeopled waste.

What man is wise enough to understand this, to understand what the   12
LORD has said and to proclaim it? Why has the land become a dead
land, scorched like the desert and untrodden? The LORD said, It is   13
because they forsook my law which I set before them; they neither
obeyed me nor conformed to it. They followed the promptings of their   14
own stubborn hearts, they followed the Baalim as their forefathers had
taught them. Therefore these are the words of the LORD of Hosts the   15
God of Israel: I will feed this people with wormwood and give them
bitter poison to drink. I will scatter them among nations whom neither 16
they nor their forefathers have known; I will harry them with the
sword until I have made an end of them.
These are the words of the LORD of Hosts: 17

*a*Summon the wailing women to come,
    send for the women skilled in keening
to come quickly and raise a lament for us,   18

[a] *So Sept.; Heb. prefixes* Consider and.

that our eyes may run with tears
and our eyelids be wet with weeping.

19 Hark, hark, lamentation is heard in Zion:
How fearful is our ruin! How great our shame!
We have left our lands, our houses have been pulled down.

20 Listen, you women, to the words of the LORD,
that your ears may catch what he says.
Teach your daughters the lament,
let them teach one another this dirge:

21 Death has climbed in through our windows,
it has entered our palaces,
it sweeps off the children in the open air
and drives young men from the streets.

22 This is the word of the LORD:

The corpses of men shall fall and lie like dung in the fields,
like swathes behind the reaper, but no one shall gather them.

23 These are the words of the LORD:

Let not the wise man boast of his wisdom
nor the valiant of his valour;
let not the rich man boast of his riches;

24 but if any man would boast, let him boast of this,
that he understands and knows me.
For I am the LORD, I show unfailing love,
I do justice and right upon the earth;
for on these I have set my heart.
This is the very word of the LORD.

25 The time is coming, says the LORD, when I will punish all the
26 circumcised, Egypt and Judah, Edom and Ammon, Moab, and all who
haunt the fringes of the desert;[a] for all alike, the nations and Israel,
are uncircumcised in heart.

10 Listen, Israel, to this word that the LORD has spoken against you:

2 Do not fall into the ways of the nations,
do not be awed by signs in the heavens;
it is the nations who go in awe of these.

3 For the carved images of the nations are a sham,
they are nothing but timber cut from the forest,
worked with his chisel by a craftsman;

4 he adorns it with silver and gold,

[a] who...desert: *or* the dwellers in the desert who clip the hair on their temples.

fastening them on with hammer and nails
   so that they do not fall apart.
They can no more speak than a scarecrow in a plot of cucumbers;   5
   they must be carried, for they cannot walk.
Do not be afraid of them: they can do no harm,
   and they have no power to do good.
Where can one be found like thee, O LORD?   6
Great thou art and great the might of thy name.
Who shall not fear thee, king of the nations?   7
   for fear is thy fitting tribute.
Where among the wisest of the nations and all their royalty
   can one be found like thee?
   They are fools and blockheads one and all,   8
   learning their nonsense from a log of wood.
The beaten silver is brought from Tarshish   9
   and the gold from Ophir;[a]
all are the work of craftsmen and goldsmiths.
   They are draped in violet and purple,
   all the work of skilled men.
But the LORD is God in truth,   10
   a living god, an eternal king.
The earth quakes under his wrath,
   nations cannot endure his fury.

[You shall say this to them: The gods who did not make heaven and   11[b]
earth shall perish from the earth and from under these heavens.]

God made the earth by his power,   12[c]
   fixed the world in place by his wisdom,
   unfurled the skies by his understanding.
At the thunder of his voice the waters in heaven are amazed;[d]   13
   he brings up the mist from the ends of the earth,
   he opens rifts[e] for the rain
   and brings the wind out of his storehouses.
All men are brutish and ignorant;   14
   every goldsmith is discredited by his idol;
   for the figures he casts are a sham,
   there is no breath in them.
They are worth nothing, mere mockeries,   15
   which perish when their day of reckoning comes.
God, Jacob's creator, is not like these;   16

[a] *So Pesh.; Heb.* Uphaz. [b] *Verse 11 is in Aramaic.* [c] *Verses 12–16: cp. 51. 15–19.*
[d] At the thunder...amazed: *prob. rdg.; Heb.* At the sound of his giving tumult of waters in
heaven. [e] rifts: *prob. rdg.; Heb.* lightnings.

for he is the maker of all.
Israel is the people he claims as his own;
the LORD of Hosts is his name.

17 Put your goods together and carry them out of the country,
living as you are under siege.

18 For these are the words of the LORD:
This time I will uproot
the whole population of the land,
and I will press them hard and squeeze them dry.

19 O the pain of my wounds!
Cruel are the blows I suffer.
But this is my plight, I said, and I must endure it.

20 My home is ruined, my tent-ropes all severed,
my sons have left me and are gone,
there is no one to pitch my tent again,
no one to put up its curtains.

21 The shepherds of the people are mere brutes;
they never consult the LORD,
and so they do not prosper,
and all their flocks at pasture are scattered.

22 Hark, a rumour comes flying,
then a mounting uproar from the land of the north,
an army to make Judah's cities desolate, a haunt of wolves.

23 I know, O LORD,
that man's ways are not of his own choosing;
nor is it for a man to determine his course in life.

24 Correct us,*a* O LORD, but with justice, not in anger,
lest thou bring us*a* almost to nothing.

25 Pour out thy fury on nations
that have not acknowledged thee,
on tribes that have not invoked thee by name;
for they have devoured Jacob*b* and made an end of him
and have left his home a waste.

Warnings and punishment

11 1,2 THE WORD WHICH CAME TO JEREMIAH from the LORD: Listen
to the terms of this covenant and repeat them to the men of Judah
3 and the inhabitants of Jerusalem. Tell them, These are the words of the

[a] *So Sept.; Heb.* me. [b] *So some MSS.; others add* and they will devour him.

1082

LORD the God of Israel: A curse on the man who does not observe the terms of this covenant by which I bound your forefathers when I 4 brought them out of Egypt, from the smelting-furnace. I said, If you obey me and do all that I tell you, you shall become my people and I will become your God. And I will thus make good the oath I swore to 5 your forefathers, that I would give them a land flowing with milk and honey, the land you now possess. I answered, 'Amen, LORD.' Then the 6 LORD said: Proclaim all these terms in the cities of Judah and in the streets of Jerusalem. Say, Listen to the terms of this covenant and carry them out. I have protested to your forefathers since I brought 7 them out of Egypt, till this day; I took pains to warn them: Obey me, I said. But they did not obey; they paid no attention to me, but each 8 followed the promptings of his own stubborn and wicked heart. So I brought on them all the penalties laid down in this covenant by which I had bound them, whose terms they did not observe.

The LORD said to me, The men of Judah and the inhabitants of 9 Jerusalem have entered into a conspiracy: they have gone back to the 10 sins of their earliest forefathers and refused to listen to me. They have followed other gods and worshipped them; Israel and Judah have broken the covenant which I made with their fathers. Therefore these 11 are the words of the LORD: I now bring on them disaster from which they cannot escape; though they cry to me for help I will not listen. The inhabitants of the cities of Judah and of Jerusalem may go and cry 12 for help to the gods to whom they have burnt sacrifices; they will not save them in the hour of disaster. For you, Judah, have as many gods 13 as you have towns; you have set up as many altars[a] to burn sacrifices to Baal as there are streets in Jerusalem. So offer up no prayer for this 14 people; raise no cry or prayer on their behalf, for I will not listen when they call to me in the hour of disaster.

> What right has my beloved in my house   15
>   with her shameless ways?
> Can the flesh of fat offerings[b] on the altar
>   ward off the disaster that threatens you?
> Once the LORD called you an olive-tree,   16
>   leafy and fair;[c]
> but now with a great roaring noise
>   you will feel sharp anguish;[d]
> fire sets its leaves alight
>   and consumes[e] its branches.

[a] *So Sept.; Heb. adds* altars to the shameful thing.   [b] fat offerings: *so Old Latin; Heb.* the many.   [c] *So Sept.; Heb. adds* the fruit of.   [d] you will feel sharp anguish: *transposed from end of verse 15.*   [e] consumes: *prob. rdg.; Heb.* they consume.

17 The LORD of Hosts who planted you has threatened you with disaster, because of the harm Israel and Judah brought on themselves when they provoked me to anger by burning sacrifices to Baal.

18 It was the LORD who showed me, and so I knew; he opened my eyes
19 to what they were doing. I had been like a sheep led obedient to the slaughter; I did not know that they were hatching plots against me and saying, 'Let us cut down the tree while the sap is in it; let us destroy him out of the living, so that his very name shall be forgotten.'

20 O LORD of Hosts who art a righteous judge,
    testing the heart*a* and mind,
    I have committed my cause to thee;
    let me see thy vengeance upon them.

21 Therefore these are the words of the LORD about the men of Anathoth who seek to take my*b* life, and say, 'Prophesy no more in the name of
22 the LORD or we will kill you'—these are his words: I will punish them: their young men shall die by the sword, their sons and daughters shall
23 die by famine. Not one of them shall survive; for in the year of their reckoning I will bring ruin on the men of Anathoth.

12 O LORD, I will dispute with thee, for thou art just;
    yes, I will plead my case before thee.
    Why do the wicked prosper
      and traitors live at ease?
2   Thou hast planted them and their roots strike deep,
    they grow up and bear fruit.
    Thou art ever on their lips,
      yet far from their hearts.*a*
3 But thou knowest me, O LORD, thou seest me;
    thou dost test my devotion to thyself.
    Drag them away like sheep to the shambles;
    set them apart for the day of slaughter.
4   How long must the country lie parched
      and its green grass wither?
    No birds and beasts are left, because its people are so wicked,
    because they say, 'God*c* will not see what we are doing.'*d*
5 If you have raced with men and the runners have worn you down,
    how then can you hope to vie with horses?
    If you fall headlong in easy country,
    how will you fare in Jordan's dense thickets?
6 All men, your brothers and kinsmen, are traitors to you,

[a] *Lit.* kidneys. [b] *So Sept.; Heb.* your. [c] *So Sept.; Heb.* He. [d] what we are doing: *so Sept.; Heb.* our latter end.

they are in full cry after you;
trust them not, for all the fine words they give you.

I have forsaken the house of Israel, 7
   I have cast off my own people.
I have given my beloved into the power of her foes.
My own people have turned on me like a lion from the scrub, 8
roaring against me; therefore I hate them.
   Is this land of mine a hyena's lair, 9
   with birds of prey hovering all around it?
Come, you wild beasts; come,*ᵃ* all of you, flock to the feast.

Many shepherds have ravaged my vineyard 10
   and trampled down my field,
they have made my pleasant field a desolate wilderness,
made it a waste land, waste and waterless, to my sorrow. 11
The whole land is waste, and no one cares.

Plunderers have swarmed across the high bare places in the wilder- 12
ness, a sword of the Lord devouring the land from end to end; no
creature can find peace.

Men sow wheat and reap thistles; 13
   they sift but get no grain.
They are disappointed of their*ᵇ* harvest
because of the anger of the Lord.

These are the words of the Lord about all those evil neighbours who 14
are laying hands on the land which I gave to my people Israel as their
patrimony: I will uproot them from that*ᶜ* soil. Yet, if they will learn the 16*ᵈ*
ways of my people, swearing by my name, 'By the life of the Lord', as
they taught my people to swear by the Baal, they shall form families
among my people. But if they will not listen, I will uproot that people, 17
uproot and destroy them. Also I will uproot Judah from among them;
but after I have uprooted them, I will have pity on them again and will 15
bring each man back to his patrimony and his land. This is the very
word of the Lord.

These were the words of the Lord to me: Go and buy yourself a 13
linen girdle and put it round your waist, but do not let it come near
water. So I bought it as the Lord had told me and put it round my waist. 2
The Lord spoke to me a second time: Take the girdle which you bought 3,4
and put round your waist; go at once to Perath and hide it in a crevice
among the rocks. So I went and hid the girdle at*ᵉ* Perath, as the Lord 5
had told me. After a long time the Lord said to me: Go at once to Perath 6

[a] *So some MSS.; others* bring.   [b] *Prob. rdg.; Heb.* your.   [c] *Prob. rdg.; Heb.* their.
[d] *The rest of verse 14 and verse 15 transposed to follow* destroy them *in verse 17.*
[e] *Or* by.

7 and fetch back the girdle which I told you to hide there. So I went to Perath and looked for the place where I had hidden it, but when I 8 picked it up, I saw that it was spoilt, and no good for anything. Again the 9 LORD spoke to me and these were his words: Thus will I spoil the gross 10 pride of Judah, the gross pride of Jerusalem. This wicked nation has refused to listen to my words;*a* they have followed other gods, serving them and bowing down to them. So it shall be*b* like this girdle, no good 11 for anything. For, just as a girdle is bound close to a man's waist, so I bound all Israel and all Judah to myself, says the LORD, so that they should become my people to win a name for me, and praise and glory; but they did not listen.

12 You shall say this to them: These are the words of the LORD the God of Israel: Wine-jars should be filled with wine. They will answer, 'We 13 know quite well that wine-jars should be filled with wine.' Then you shall say to them, These are the words of the LORD: I will fill all the inhabitants of this land with wine until they are drunk—kings of David's line who sit on his throne, priests, prophets, and all who live in Jeru- 14 salem. I will dash them to pieces one against another, fathers and sons alike, says the LORD, I will show them no compassion or pity or tenderness; nor refrain from destroying them.*c*

15 Hear and attend. Be not too proud to listen,
    for it is the LORD who speaks.
16 Ascribe glory to the LORD your God
    before the darkness falls,
  before your feet stumble
    on the twilit hill-sides,
  before he turns the light you look for
    to deep gloom and thick darkness.
17 If in those depths of gloom you will not listen,
    then for very anguish I can only weep and shed tears,*d*
  my eyes must stream with tears;
    for the LORD's flock is carried away into captivity.
18 Say to the king and the queen mother:*e*
    Down, take a humble seat,
  for your proud crowns are fallen from your heads.*f*
19 Your cities in the Negeb are besieged,
    and no one can relieve them;
  all Judah has been swept into exile,
    swept clean away.

[a] *So Sept.; Heb. adds* which has followed the promptings of its stubborn heart. [b] *Prob. rdg.; Heb.* And let it be. [c] *nor refrain...them: or so corrupt are they.* [d] *If...shed tears: or* If you will not listen to this, for very anguish I must weep in secret. [e] *Or* queen. [f] *from your heads: so Sept.; Heb.* your pillows.

Lift up your eyes and see   20
  those who are coming from the north.
Where is the flock that was entrusted to you,
  the flock you were so proud of?
What will you say when you suffer   21
  because your leaders*a* cannot be found,
though it was you who trained them
  to be your head?
Will not pangs seize you,
  like the pangs of a woman in labour,
  when you wonder,   22
'Why has this come upon me?'
For your many sins your skirts are torn off you,
  your limbs*b* uncovered.

Can the Nubian change his skin,   23
  or the leopard its spots?
And you? Can you do good,
  you who are schooled in evil?
Therefore I will scatter you*c* like chaff   24
  driven by the desert wind.
This is your lot, the portion of the rebel,*d*   25
  measured out by me, says the LORD,
  because you have forsaken me
  and trusted in false gods.
So I myself have stripped off your skirts   26
  and laid bare your shame.
  Your adulteries, your lustful neighing,   27
your wanton lewdness, are an offence to me.*e*
  On the hills and in the open country
  I have seen your foul deeds.
Alas, Jerusalem, unclean that you are!
How long, how long will you delay?*f*

This came to Jeremiah as the word of the LORD concerning the 14
drought:

Judah droops, her cities languish,   2
  her men sink to the ground;
  Jerusalem's cry goes up.
Their flock-masters send their boys for water;   3
  they come to the pools but find no water there.

---

[a] leaders: *transposed from next line.* [b] *Lit.* heels. [c] *Prob. rdg.; Heb.* them. [d] rebel:
prob. rdg., cp. Sept.; Heb. measures. [e] an offence to me (*Heb.* you): *transposed from*
verse 26. [f] How...delay?: *prob. rdg.; Heb. unintelligible.*

Back they go, with empty vessels;[a]

4 the produce[b] of the land has failed,
because there is no rain.[c]
The farmers' hopes are wrecked,
they uncover their heads for grief.

5 The hind calves in the open country
and forsakes her young
because there is no grass;

6 for lack of herbage, wild asses stand on the high bare places
and snuff the wind for moisture,
as wolves do, and their eyes begin to fail.

7 Though our sins testify against us,
yet act,[d] O Lord, for thy own name's sake.
Our disloyalties indeed are many; we have sinned against thee.

8 O hope of Israel, their saviour in time of trouble,
must thou be a stranger in the land,
a traveller pitching his tent for a night?

9 Must thou be like a man suddenly overcome,
like a man powerless to save himself?
Thou art in our midst, O Lord,
and thou hast named us thine; do not forsake us.

10 The Lord speaks thus of this people: They love to stray from my ways, they wander where they will. Therefore he has no more pleasure

11 in them; he remembers their guilt now, and punishes their sins. Then the Lord said to me, Do not pray for the well-being of this people.

12 When they fast, I will not listen to their cry; when they sacrifice whole-offering and grain-offering, I will not accept them. I will make an end

13 of them with sword, with famine and pestilence. But I said, O Lord God, the prophets tell them that they shall see no sword and suffer no

14 famine; for thou wilt give them lasting prosperity in this place. The Lord answered me, The prophets are prophesying lies in my name. I have not sent them; I have given them no charge; I have not spoken to them. The prophets offer them[e] false visions, worthless augury, and

15 their own deluding fancies. Therefore these are the words of the Lord about the prophets who, though not sent by me, prophesy in my name and say that neither sword nor famine shall touch this land: By sword

16 and by famine shall those prophets meet their end. The people to whom they prophesy shall be flung out into the streets of Jerusalem, victims of famine and sword; they, their wives, their sons, and their daughters, with no one to bury them: I will pour down upon them the evil they deserve.

[a] So Sept.; Heb. adds disappointed, shamed, and with uncovered heads. [b] the produce: prob. rdg.; Heb. obscure. [c] So Sept.; Heb. adds in the land. [d] Or turn away.
[e] So some MSS.; others you.

So this is what you shall say to them: 17
Let my eyes stream with tears,
ceaselessly, day and night.
For the virgin daughter of my people
has been broken in pieces,
struck by a cruel blow.
If I go out into the country,   18
I see men slain by the sword;
if I enter the city, I see the ravages[a] of famine;
prophet and priest alike
go begging round the land and are never at rest.
Hast thou spurned Judah utterly?   19
Dost thou loathe Zion?
Why hast thou wounded us, and there is no remedy;
why let us hope for better days, and we find nothing good,
for a time of healing, and all is disaster?
We acknowledge our wickedness,   20
the guilt of our forefathers;
O Lord, we have sinned against thee.
Do not despise the place where thy name dwells   21
nor bring contempt on the throne of thy glory.
Remember thy covenant with us and do not make it void.
Can any of the false gods of the nations give rain?   22
Or do the heavens send showers of themselves?
Art thou not God, O Lord,
that we may hope in thee?
It is thou only who doest[b] all these things.

The Lord said to me, Even if Moses and Samuel stood before me, I **15**
would not be moved to pity this people. Banish them from my presence;
let them be gone. When they ask where they are to go, you shall say to 2
them, These are the words of the Lord:

Those who are for death shall go to their death,
and those for the sword to the sword;
those who are for famine to famine,
and those for captivity to captivity.

Four kinds of doom do I ordain for them, says the Lord: the sword 3
to kill, dogs to tear, birds of prey from the skies and beasts from
their lairs to devour and destroy. I will make them repugnant to all the 4
kingdoms of the earth, because of the crimes of Manasseh son of
Hezekiah, king of Judah, in Jerusalem.

[a] *Lit.* ulcers. [b] *Or* madest.

5   Who will take pity on you, Jerusalem,
     who will offer you consolation?
   Who will turn aside to wish you well?
6   You cast me off, says the LORD,
     you turned your backs on me.
   So I stretched out my hand and ruined you;
     I was weary of relenting.
7   I winnowed them and scattered them
     through the cities of the land;
   I brought bereavement on them, I destroyed my people,
     for they would not abandon their ways.
8   I made widows among them more in number
     than the sands of the sea;
   I brought upon them a horde of raiders*a*
     to plunder at high noon.
   I made the terror of invasion fall upon them
     all in a moment.
9   The mother of seven sons grew faint,
     she sank into a swoon;
   her light was quenched while it was yet day;
     she was left humbled and shamed.
   All the remnant I gave to perish by the sword
     at the hand of their enemies.
   This is the very word of the LORD.

Confessions and addresses

10   Alas, alas, my mother, that you ever gave me birth!
   a man doomed to strife, with the whole world against me.
   I have borrowed from no one, I have lent to no one,
     yet all men abuse me.

11   The LORD answered,

   But I will greatly strengthen you;
   in time of distress and in time of disaster
   I will bring the enemy to your feet.
12   Can iron break steel from the north?*b*
15   LORD, thou knowest;

[*a*] I brought...raiders: *prob. rdg.; Heb. obscure.*   [*b*] *Prob. rdg.; Heb. adds* and bronze. *Heb. also adds* (13) I will give away your wealth as spoil, and your treasure for no payment, because of your sin throughout your country. (14) I will make your enemies pass through a land you do not know; for my anger is a blazing fire and it shall burn for ever (*cp. 17. 3, 4*).

remember me, LORD, and come to visit me,
take vengeance for me on my persecutors.
Be patient with me and take me not away,
see what reproaches I endure for thy sake.
I have to suffer those who despise thy words,[a]   16
but thy word is joy and happiness to me,
for thou hast named me thine,
O LORD, God of Hosts.
I have never kept company with any gang of roisterers,   17
or made merry with them;
because I felt thy hand upon me I have sat alone;
for thou hast filled me with indignation.
Why then is my pain unending,   18
my wound desperate and incurable?
Thou art to me like a brook that is not to be trusted,
whose waters fail.

This was the LORD's answer: 19

If you will turn back to me, I will take you back
and you shall stand before me.
If you choose noble utterance and reject the base,
you shall be my spokesman.
This people will turn again to you,
but you will not turn to them.
To withstand them I will make you impregnable,   20
a wall of bronze.
They will attack you but they will not prevail,
for I am with you to deliver you
and save you, says the LORD;
I will deliver you from the wicked,   21
I will rescue you from the ruthless.

The word of the LORD came to me: You shall not marry a wife; you 16 1, 2
shall have neither son nor daughter in this place. For these are the 3
words of the LORD concerning sons and daughters born in this place,
the mothers who bear them and the fathers who beget them in this land:
When men die, struck down by deadly ulcers, there shall be no wailing 4
for them and no burial; they shall be like dung lying upon the ground.
When men perish by sword or famine, their corpses shall become food
for birds and for beasts.
For these are the words of the LORD: Enter no house where there is a 5
mourning-feast; do not go in to wail or to bring comfort, for I have

[a] I have...words: *prob. rdg., cp. Sept.; Heb.* Thy words were found and I ate them.

withdrawn my peace from this people, says the LORD, my love and
6 affection. High and low shall die in this land, but there shall be no
burial, no wailing for them; no one shall gash himself, or shave his
7 head. No one shall give the mourner a portion of bread*a* to console him
for the dead, nor give him*b* the cup of consolation, even for his father
8 or mother. Nor shall you enter a house where there is feasting, to sit
9 eating and drinking there. For these are the words of the LORD of
Hosts, the God of Israel: In your own days, in the sight of you all, and
in this very place, I will silence all sounds of joy and gladness, and the
voice of bridegroom and bride.

10   When you tell this people all these things they will ask you, 'Why
has the LORD decreed that this great disaster is to come upon us? What
wrong have we done? What sin have we committed against the LORD
11 our God?' You shall answer, Because your forefathers forsook me, says
the LORD, and followed other gods, serving them and bowing down to
12 them. They forsook me and did not keep my law. And you yourselves
have done worse than your forefathers; for each of you follows the
promptings of his wicked and stubborn heart instead of obeying me.
13 So I will fling you headlong out of this land into a country unknown to
you and to your forefathers; there you can serve other gods day and
14 night, for I will show you no favour. Therefore, says the LORD, the time
is coming when men shall no longer swear, 'By the life of the LORD
15 who brought the Israelites up from Egypt', but, 'By the life of the
LORD who brought the Israelites back from a northern land and from
all the lands to which he had dispersed them'; and I will bring them
back to the soil which I gave to their forefathers.

16   I will send for many fishermen, says the LORD, and they shall fish
for them. After that I will send for many hunters, and they shall hunt
them out from every mountain and hill and from the crevices in the
17 rocks. For my eyes are on all their ways; they are not hidden from my
18 sight, nor is their wrongdoing concealed from me. I will first make them
pay in full*c* for the wrong they have done and the sin they have committed by defiling with the dead lumber of their idols the land which
belongs to me, and by filling it with their abominations.

19   O LORD, my strength and my stronghold,
       my refuge in time of trouble,
   to thee shall the nations come
       from the ends of the earth and say,
  Our forefathers inherited only a sham,
       an idol vain and useless.
20   Can man make gods for himself?

[*a*] bread: *so Sept.; Heb.* to them.   [*b*] *So Sept.; Heb.* them.   [*c*] in full: *or* double.

They would be no gods.
Therefore I am teaching them,   21
once for all will I teach them
    my power and my might,
and they shall learn that my name is the LORD.

The sin of Judah is recorded with an iron tool, engraved on the tablet 17
of their heart with a point of adamant and carved on the horns of their[a]
altars to bear witness against them.[b] Their altars and their sacred poles 2
stand by every spreading tree, on the heights and the hills in the moun- 3
tain country. I will give away your wealth as spoil, and all your treasure
for no payment,[c] because of your[d] sin throughout your country. You 4
will lose possession[e] of the patrimony which I gave you. I will make you
serve your enemies as slaves in a land you do not know; for my anger is
a blazing fire[f] and it shall burn for ever.

These are the words of the LORD: 5

A curse on the man who trusts in man
    and leans for support on human kind,
    while his heart is far from the LORD!
He shall be like a juniper[g] in the desert;   6
    when good comes he shall not see it.
He shall dwell among the rocks in the wilderness,
    in a salt land where no man can live.
Blessed is the man who trusts in the LORD,   7
    and rests his confidence upon him.
He shall be like a tree planted by the waterside,   8
    that stretches its roots along the stream.
When the heat comes it has nothing to fear;
    its spreading foliage stays green.
In a year of drought it feels no care,
    and does not cease to bear fruit.

The heart is the most deceitful of all things,   9
desperately sick;[h] who can fathom it?
    I, the LORD, search the mind   10
        and test the heart,
    requiting man for his conduct,
        and as his deeds deserve.
        Like a partridge which gathers into its nest   11

[a] *So some MSS.; others* your.   [b] to bear...them: *prob. rdg.; Heb.* as their sons remember.
[c] for no payment: *prob. rdg., cp. 15. 13; Heb.* your hill-shrines.   [d] your: *prob. rdg., cp.*
15. 13; Heb. om.   [e] You...possession: *prob. rdg.; Heb.* obscure.   [f] for...fire: *prob.*
rdg., cp. 15. 14; Heb. for you have kindled a fire in my anger.   [g] *Mng. of Heb. word*
uncertain.   [h] the most...sick: *or* too deceitful for any man.

eggs which it has not laid,
so is the man who amasses wealth unjustly.
Before his days are half done he must leave it,
and prove but a fool at the last.

12 O throne of glory, exalted from the beginning,
the place of our sanctuary,

13 O LORD on whom Israel's hope is fixed,
all who reject thee shall be put to shame;
all in this land who forsake thee shall be humbled,^a
for they have rejected the fountain of living water.^b

14 Heal me, O LORD, and I shall be healed,
save me and I shall be saved;
for thou art my praise.

15 They say to me, 'Where is the word of the LORD?
Let it come if it can!'

16 It is not the thought of disaster that makes me press after thee;
never did I desire this day of despair.
Thou knowest all that has passed my lips;
it was approved by thee.

17 Do not become a terror to me;
thou art my only refuge on the day of disaster.

18 May my persecutors be foiled, not I;
may they be terrified, not I.
Bring on them the day of disaster;
destroy them, destroy them utterly.

19 These were the words of the LORD to me: Go and stand in the
Benjamin^c Gate, through which the kings of Judah go in and out, and in

20 all the gates of Jerusalem. Say, Hear the words of the LORD, you princes
of Judah, all you men of Judah, and all you inhabitants of Jerusalem

21 who come in through these gates. These are the words of the LORD:
Observe this with care, that you do not carry any load on the sabbath

22 or bring it through the gates of Jerusalem. You shall not bring any load
out of your houses or do any work on the sabbath, but you shall keep

23 the sabbath day holy as I commanded your forefathers. Yet they did not
obey or pay attention, but obstinately refused to hear or learn their

24 lesson. Now if you will obey me, says the LORD, and refrain from bringing any load through the gates of this city on the sabbath, and keep that

25 day holy by doing no work on it, then kings shall come through the
gates of this city, kings^d who shall sit on David's throne. They shall
come riding in chariots or on horseback, escorted by their captains, by

---

[a] humbled: *prob. rdg.; Heb.* written.   [b] *Prob. rdg.; Heb. adds* the LORD.   [c] Benjamin:
prob. rdg.; Heb. sons of the people.   [d] *Prob. rdg.; Heb. adds* and officers.

the men of Judah and the inhabitants of Jerusalem; and this city shall
be inhabited for ever. People shall come from the cities of Judah, the 26
country round Jerusalem, the land of Benjamin, the Shephelah, the
hill-country and the Negeb, bringing whole-offerings, sacrifices, grain-
offerings, and frankincense, bringing also thank-offerings to the house
of the LORD. But if you do not obey me by keeping the sabbath day holy 27
and by not carrying any load as you come through the gates of Jerusalem on the sabbath, then I will set fire to those gates; it shall consume
the palaces of Jerusalem and shall not be put out.

These are the words which came to Jeremiah from the LORD: Go 18 1, 2
down at once to the potter's house, and there I will tell you what I
have to say. So I went down to the potter's house and found him 3
working at the wheel. Now and then a vessel he was making out of the 4
clay would be spoilt in his hands, and then he would start again and
mould it into another vessel to his liking. Then the word of the LORD 5
came to me: Can I not deal with you, Israel, says the LORD, as the 6
potter deals with his clay? You are clay in my hands like the clay in his,
O house of Israel. At any moment I may threaten to uproot a nation or 7
a kingdom, to pull it down and destroy it. But if the nation which I have 8
threatened turns back from its wicked ways, then I shall think better of
the evil I had in mind to bring on it. Or at any moment I may decide to 9
build or to plant a nation or a kingdom. But if it does evil in my sight 10
and does not obey me, I shall think better of the good I had in mind for
it. Go now and tell the men of Judah and the inhabitants of Jerusalem 11
that these are the words of the LORD: I am the potter; I am preparing
evil for you and perfecting my designs against you. Turn back, every
one of you, from his evil course; mend your ways and your doings.
But they answer, 'Things are past hope. We will do as we like, and each 12
of us will follow the promptings of his own wicked and stubborn heart.'
Therefore these are the words of the LORD: 13

Inquire among the nations: who ever heard the like of this?
The virgin Israel has done a thing most horrible.
Will the snow cease to fall on the rocky slopes of Lebanon? 14
Will the cool rain streaming in torrents ever fail[a]?
No, but my people have forgotten me; 15
   they burn sacrifices to a mere idol,
   so they stumble in their paths, the ancient ways,
   and they take to byways and unmade roads;
   their own land they lay waste, 16
   and men will jeer at it for ever in contempt.
All who go by will be horror-struck and shake their heads.

[a] fail: *prob. rdg., cp. Sept.; Heb.* be uprooted.

17   Like a wind from the east
           I will scatter them before their enemies.
              In the hour of their downfall
           I will turn my back towards them and not my face.

18   'Come, let us decide what to do with Jeremiah', men say. 'There
        will still be priests to guide us, still wise men to advise, still prophets to
        proclaim the word. Come, let us invent some charges against him; let
        us pay no attention to his message.'

19   But do thou, O Lord, pay attention,
           and hear what my opponents are saying against me.
20   Is good to be repaid with evil?*a*
        Remember how I stood before thee,
           pleading on their behalf
           to avert thy wrath from them.
21   Therefore give their sons over to famine,
           leave them at the mercy of the sword.
        Let their women be childless and widowed,
           let death carry off their men,
        let their young men be cut down in battle.
22   Bring raiders upon them without warning,
           and let screams of terror ring out from their houses.
        For they have dug a pit to catch me
           and have hidden snares for my feet.
23   Well thou knowest, O Lord,
           all their murderous plots against me.
        Do not blot out their wrongdoing
           or annul their sin;
        when they are brought stumbling into thy presence,
           deal with them on the day of thy anger.

19   These are the words of the Lord: Go and buy an earthenware jar.
        Then take with you*b* some of the elders of the people and of the priests,
2   and go out to the Valley of Ben-hinnom, on which the Gate of the
3   Potsherds opens, and there proclaim what I tell you. Say, Hear the
        word of the Lord, you princes of Judah and inhabitants of Jerusalem.
        These are the words of the Lord of Hosts the God of Israel: I will
        bring on this place a disaster which shall ring in the ears of all who hear
4   of it. For they have forsaken me, and treated this place as if it were not
        mine, burning sacrifices to other gods whom neither they nor their
        fathers nor the kings of Judah have known, and filling this place with

[a] *Prob. rdg.; Heb. adds* they have dug a pit for me (*cp. verse 22*). [b] Then...you: *so
Pesh.; Heb. om.*

the blood of the innocent. They have built shrines to Baal, where they 5
burn their sons as whole-offerings to Baal. It was no command of mine;
I never spoke of it; it never entered my thought. Therefore, says the 6
LORD, the time is coming when this place shall no longer be called
Topheth or the Valley of Ben-hinnom, but the Valley of Slaughter.
In this place I will shatter the plans of Judah and Jerusalem as a jar is 7
shattered; I will make the people fall by the sword before their enemies,
at the hands of those who would kill them, and I will give their corpses
to the birds and beasts to devour. I will make this city a scene of horror 8
and contempt, so that every passer-by will be horror-struck and jeer in
contempt at the sight of its wounds. I will compel men to eat the flesh 9
of their sons and their daughters; they shall devour one another's flesh
in the dire straits to which their enemies and those who would kill them
will reduce them in the siege. Then you must shatter the jar before the 10
eyes of the men who have come with you and say to them, These are 11
the words of the LORD of Hosts: Thus will I shatter this people and
this city as one shatters an earthen vessel so that it cannot be mended,
and the dead shall be buried in Topheth because there is no room elsewhere to bury them. This is what I will do to this place, says the LORD, 12
and to those who live there: I will make this city like Topheth. Because 13
of their defilement, the houses of Jerusalem and those of the kings of
Judah shall be like Topheth, every one of the houses on whose roofs
men have burnt sacrifices to the host of heaven and poured drink-
offerings to other gods.

Jeremiah came in from Topheth, where the LORD had sent him to 14
prophesy, and stood in the court of the LORD's house. He said to all the
people, These are the words of the LORD of Hosts the God of Israel: 15
I am bringing on this city and on all its blood-spattered altars every
disaster with which I have threatened it, for its people have remained
obstinate and refused to listen to me.

When Pashhur son of Immer the priest, the chief officer in the house 20
of the LORD, heard Jeremiah prophesying these things, he had him 2
flogged[a] and put him into the stocks at the Upper Gate of Benjamin, in
the house of the LORD. The next morning he released him, and Jeremiah 3
said to him, The LORD has called you not Pashhur but Magor-missabib.[b]
For these are the words of the LORD: I will make you a terror to your- 4
self and to all your friends; they shall fall by the sword of the enemy
before your very eyes. I will hand over all Judah to the king of Babylon,
and he will deport them to Babylon and put them to the sword. I will 5
give all this city's store of wealth and riches and all the treasures of the
kings of Judah to their enemies; they shall seize them as spoil and carry
them off to Babylon. You, Pashhur, and all your household shall go 6

[a] had him flogged: *or* struck him.   [b] *That is* Terror let loose.

into captivity and come to Babylon. There shall you die and there shall you be buried, you and all your friends to whom you have been a false prophet.

7   O LORD, thou hast duped me, and I have been thy dupe;
        thou hast outwitted me and hast prevailed.
    I have been made a laughing-stock all the day long,
        everyone mocks me.
8   Whenever I speak I must needs cry out
    and proclaim violence and destruction.
    I am reproached and mocked all the time
    for uttering the word of the LORD.
9   Whenever I said, 'I will call him to mind no more,
        nor speak in his name again',
    then his word was imprisoned in my body,
    like a fire blazing in my heart,
    and I was weary with holding it under,
    and could endure no more.
10   For I heard many whispering,*a*
    'Denounce him! we will denounce him.'
    All my friends were on the watch for a false step,
    saying, 'Perhaps he may be tricked, then we can catch him
        and take our revenge.'
11 But the LORD is on my side, strong and ruthless,
    therefore my persecutors shall stumble and fall powerless.
    Bitter shall be their abasement when they fail,
        and their shame shall long be remembered.
12 O LORD of Hosts, thou dost test the righteous
        and search the depths of the heart;
    to thee have I committed my cause,
    let me see thee take vengeance on them.
13 Sing to the LORD, praise the LORD;
    for he rescues the poor from those who would do them wrong.

14 A curse on the day when I was born!
        Be it for ever unblessed,
        the day when my mother bore me!
15 A curse on the man who brought word to my father,
        'A child is born to you, a son',
        and gladdened his heart!
16 That man shall fare like the cities
    which the LORD overthrew without mercy.
    He shall hear cries of alarm in the morning

[a] *Prob. rdg.; Heb. adds* Terror let loose.

and uproar at noon,
because death did not claim me before birth,   17
and my mother did not become my grave,
   her womb great with me for ever.
Why did I come forth from the womb   18
to know only sorrow and toil,
to end my days in shame?

Kings and prophets denounced

THE WORD WHICH CAME FROM THE LORD to Jeremiah when 21
King Zedekiah sent to him Pashhur son of Malchiah and Zephaniah the priest, son of Maaseiah, with this request: 'Nebuchadrezzar 2
king of Babylon is making war on us; inquire of the LORD on our behalf. Perhaps the LORD will perform a miracle as he has done in past
times, so that Nebuchadrezzar may raise the siege.' But Jeremiah ans- 3
wered them, Tell Zedekiah, these are the words of the LORD the God 4
of Israel: I will turn back upon you your own weapons with which you
are fighting the king of Babylon and the Chaldaeans besieging you
outside the wall; and I will bring them into the heart of this city.
I myself will fight against you in burning rage and great fury, with an 5
outstretched hand and a strong arm. I will strike down those who live 6
in this city, men and cattle alike; they shall die of a great pestilence.
After that, says the LORD, I will take Zedekiah king of Judah, his 7
courtiers and the people, all in this city who survive pestilence, sword,
and famine, and hand them over to Nebuchadrezzar the king of Babylon, to their enemies and those who would kill them. He shall put them
to the sword and shall show no pity, no mercy or compassion.

You shall say further to this people, These are the words of the LORD: 8
I offer you now a choice between the way of life and the way of death.
Whoever remains in this city shall die by sword, by famine, or by 9
pestilence, but whoever goes out to surrender to the Chaldaeans, who
are now besieging you, shall survive; he shall take home his life, and
nothing more.*ᵃ* I have set my face against this city, meaning to do them 10
harm, not good, says the LORD. It shall be handed over to the king of
Babylon, and he shall burn it to the ground.

To the royal house of Judah.   11
   Listen to the word of the LORD:
O house of David, these are the words of the LORD: 12
   Administer justice betimes,
   rescue the victim from his oppressor,

      [a] he shall...more: *lit.* his life shall be his booty.

          lest the fire of my fury blaze up and burn unquenched
            because of your evil doings.

13   The LORD says,
          I am against you who lie in the valley,
            you, the rock in the plain,
          you who say, 'Who can come down upon us?
            Who can penetrate our lairs?'
14   I will punish you as you deserve,
            says the LORD,
          I will kindle fire on the heathland around you,
          and it shall consume everything round about.

22   These were the words of the LORD: Go down to the house of the
2 king of Judah and say this: Listen to the words of the LORD, O king of
Judah, you who sit on David's throne, you and your courtiers and your
3 people who come in at these gates. These are the words of the LORD:
Deal justly and fairly, rescue the victim from his oppressor, do not
ill-treat or do violence to the alien, the orphan or the widow, do not
4 shed innocent blood in this place. If you obey, and only if you obey,
kings who sit on David's throne shall yet come riding through these
gates in chariots and on horses, with their retinue of courtiers and
5 people. But if you do not listen to my words, then by myself I swear,
6 says the LORD, this house shall become a desolate ruin. For these are
the words of the LORD about the royal house of Judah:

          Though you are dear to me as Gilead
            or as the heights of Lebanon,
          I swear that I will make you a wilderness,
            a land of unpeopled cities.
7   I will dedicate an armed host to fight against you,
            a ravening horde;
          they shall cut your choicest cedars down
            and fling them on the fire.

8   Men of many nations shall pass by this city and say to one another,
9 'Why has the LORD done this to such a great city?' The answer will be,
'Because they forsook their covenant with the LORD their God; they
worshipped other gods and served them.'

10   Weep not for the dead nor brood over his loss.
          Weep rather for him who has gone away,
            for he shall never return,
          never again see the land of his birth.

For these are the words of the LORD concerning Shallum son of 11
Josiah, king of Judah, who succeeded his father on the throne and has
gone away: He shall never return; he shall die in the place of his exile 12
and never see this land again.

Shame on the man who builds his house by unjust means   13
    and completes its roof-chambers by fraud,
    making his countrymen work without payment,
    giving them no wage for their labour!
Shame on the man who says, 'I will build a spacious house   14
    with airy roof-chambers,
set windows in it, panel it with cedar
    and paint it with vermilion'!
If your cedar is more splendid,   15
    does that prove you a king?
Think of your father: he ate and drank,
dealt justly and fairly; all went well with him.
He dispensed justice to the lowly and poor;*a*   16
did not this show he knew me? says the LORD.
But you have no eyes, no thought for anything but gain,   17
    set only on the innocent blood you can shed,
    on cruel acts of tyranny.

Therefore these are the words of the LORD concerning Jehoiakim son 18
of Josiah, king of Judah:

For him no mourner shall say, 'Alas, brother, dear brother!'
no one say, 'Alas, lord and master!'
    He shall be buried like a dead ass,   19
    dragged along and flung out
    beyond the gates of Jerusalem.

    Get up into Lebanon and cry aloud,   20
    make your voice heard in Bashan,
cry aloud from Abarim, for all who befriend you are broken.
    I spoke to you in your days of prosperous ease,   21
    but you said, 'I will not listen.'
This is how you behaved since your youth;
    never have you obeyed me.
The wind shall carry away all your friends,*b*   22
your lovers shall depart into exile.
Then you will be put to shame and abashed
    for all your evil deeds.*c*

[a] *Prob. rdg.; Heb. adds* all went well (*repeated from verse 15*).   [b] *Or* shepherds.   [c] *Or*
calamities.

23 You dwellers in Lebanon, who make your nests among the cedars,
how you will groan when the pains come upon you,
like the pangs of a woman in labour!

24 By my life, says the LORD, Coniah son of Jehoiakim, king of Judah,
shall be the signet-ring on my right hand no longer. Yes, Coniah, I will
25 pull you off. I will hand you over to those who seek your life, to those
26 you fear, to Nebuchadrezzar king of Babylon and to the Chaldaeans. I
will fling you headlong, you and the mother who gave you birth, into
another land, a land where you were not born; and there shall you both
27 die. They shall never come back to their own land, the land for which
they long.

28 This man, Coniah, then, is he a mere puppet, contemptible and
broken, only a thing unwanted? Why else are he and his children flung
out headlong and hurled into a country they do not know?

29, 30 O land, land, land, hear the words of the LORD: These are the
words of the LORD: Write this man down as stripped of all honour, one
who in his own life shall not prosper, nor shall he leave descendants to
sit in prosperity on David's throne or rule again in Judah.

23 Shame on the shepherds who let the sheep of my flock scatter and be
2 lost! says the LORD. Therefore these are the words of the LORD the God
of Israel about the shepherds who tend my people: You have scattered
and dispersed my flock. You have not watched over them; but I am
3 watching you to punish you for your evil doings, says the LORD. I will
myself gather the remnant of my sheep from all the lands to which I
have dispersed them. I will bring them back to their homes, and they
4 shall be fruitful and increase. I will appoint shepherds to tend them;
they shall never again know fear or dismay or punishment. This is the
very word of the LORD.

5 The days are now coming, says the LORD,
when I will make a righteous Branch spring from David's line,
a king who shall rule wisely,
maintaining law and justice in the land.
6 In his days Judah shall be kept safe,
and Israel*a* shall live undisturbed.
This is the name to be given to him:
The LORD is our Righteousness.

7 Therefore the days are coming, says the LORD, when men shall no
longer swear, 'By the life of the LORD who brought Israel up from
8 Egypt', but, 'By the life of the LORD who brought the descendants of
the Israelites back from a northern land and from all the lands to which
he*b* had dispersed them, to live again on their own soil.'

[a] *Or, with one form of Sept.,* Jerusalem. [b] *So Sept., cp. 16. 15; Heb.* I.

On the prophets.   9
  Deep within me my heart is broken,
  there is no strength in my bones;
  because of the LORD, because of his dread words
  I have become like a drunken man,
  like a man overcome with wine.
  For the land is full of adulterers,   10
  and because of them the earth lies parched,
    the wild pastures have dried up.
  The course that they run is evil,
    and their powers are misused.
  For prophet and priest alike are godless;   11
I have come upon the evil they are doing even in my own house.
    This is the very word of the LORD.

  Therefore the path shall turn slippery beneath their feet;   12
  they shall be dispersed in the dark and shall fall there.
  For I will bring disaster on them when their day of reckoning comes.
    This is the very word of the LORD.
    I found the prophets of Samaria men of no sense: 13
  they prophesied in Baal's name and led my people Israel astray.
  In the prophets of Jerusalem I see a thing most horrible: 14
    adulterers and hypocrites that they are,
      they encourage evildoers,
    so that no man turns back from his sin;
  to me all her inhabitants are like Sodom and Gomorrah.

  These then are the words of the LORD of Hosts concerning the   15
prophets:

  I will give them wormwood to eat
    and a bitter poison to drink;
    for a godless spirit has spread over all the land
    from the prophets of Jerusalem.
These are the words of the LORD of Hosts: 16

  Do not listen to what the prophets say,
  who buoy you up with false hopes;
  the vision they report springs from their own imagination,
    it is not from the mouth of the LORD.
  They say to those who spurn the word of the LORD,   17
    'Prosperity shall be yours';
  and to all who follow the promptings of their own stubborn heart
        they say,
    'No disaster shall befall you.'

18 But which of them has stood in the council of the LORD,
    seen him and heard his word?
    Which of them has listened to his word and obeyed?

19 See what a scorching wind has gone out from the LORD,
    a furious whirlwind;
    it whirls round the heads of the wicked.

20   The LORD's anger is not to be turned aside,
    until he has accomplished and fulfilled his deep designs.
    In days to come you will fully understand.

21 I did not send these prophets, yet they went in haste;
    I did not speak to them, yet they prophesied.

22 If they have stood in my council,
    let them proclaim my words to my people
and turn them from their evil course and their evil doings.

23 Am I a god only near at hand,[a] not far away?[b]

24 Can a man hide in any secret place and I not see him?[a]
Do I not fill heaven and earth?
    This is the very word of the LORD.

25 I have heard what the prophets say, the prophets who speak lies in
26 my name and cry, 'I have had a dream, a dream!' How long will it be
till they change their tune, these prophets who prophesy lies and give
27 voice to their own inventions? By these dreams which they tell one
another these men think they will make my people forget my name, as
28 their fathers forgot my name for the name of[c] Baal. If a prophet has a
dream, let him tell his dream; if he has my word, let him speak my
29 word in truth. What has chaff to do with grain? says the LORD. Do not
my words scorch[d] like fire? says the LORD. Are they not like a hammer
30 that splinters rock? I am against the prophets, says the LORD, who steal
31 my words from one another for their own use. I am against the prophets,
says the LORD, who concoct words of their own and then say, 'This is his
32 very word.' I am against the prophets, says the LORD, who dream lies
and retail them, misleading my people with wild and reckless falsehoods. It was not I who sent them or commissioned them, and they will
do this people no good. This is the very word of the LORD.

33 When you are asked by this people or by a prophet or priest what the
burden of the LORD's message is, you shall answer, You are his burden,
34 and I shall throw you down, says the LORD. If prophet or priest or
layman uses the term 'the LORD's burden', I will punish that man and
35 his family. The form of words you shall use in speaking amongst yourselves is: 'What answer has the LORD given?' or, 'What has the LORD

[a] *So Sept.; Heb. adds* says the LORD.   [b] Am I…away?: *or, with Sept.,* I am a god near
at hand, and not far away.   [c] for the name of: *or* by their worship of.   [d] scorch: *prob.*
rdg.; Heb. thus.

said?' You shall never again mention 'the burden of the LORD'; that 36
is reserved for the man to whom he entrusts his message. If you do,
you will make nonsense of the words of the living God, the LORD of
Hosts our God. This is the form you shall use in speaking to a prophet: 37
'What answer has the LORD given?' or, 'What has the LORD said?' But 38
to any of you who do say, 'the burden of the LORD', the LORD speaks
thus: Because you say, 'the burden of the LORD', though I sent to tell
you not to say it, therefore I myself will carry you like a burden*a* and 39
throw you down, casting out of my sight both you and the city which I
gave to you and to your forefathers. I will inflict on you endless re- 40
proach, endless shame which shall never be forgotten.

Two visions

THIS IS WHAT THE LORD SHOWED ME: I saw two baskets of 24
figs set out*b* in front of the sanctuary of the LORD. This was after
Nebuchadrezzar king of Babylon had deported from Jerusalem Jeconiah son of Jehoiakim, king of Judah, with the officers of Judah, the
craftsmen and the smiths,*c* and taken them to Babylon. In one basket 2
the figs were very good, like the figs that are first ripe; in the other the
figs were very bad, so bad that they were not fit to eat. The LORD said 3
to me, 'What are you looking at, Jeremiah?' 'Figs,' I answered, 'the
good very good, and the bad so bad that they are not fit to eat.' Then 4
this word came to me from the LORD: These are the words of the LORD 5
the God of Israel: I count the exiles of Judah whom I sent away from
this place to the land of the Chaldaeans as good as these good figs.
I will look upon them meaning to do them good, and I will restore them 6
to their land; I will build them up and not pull them down, plant them
and not uproot them. I will give them the wit to know me, for I am the 7
LORD; they shall become my people and I will become their God, for
they will come back to me with all their heart. But Zedekiah king of 8
Judah, his officers and the survivors of Jerusalem, whether they remain
in this land or live in Egypt—all these I will treat as bad figs, says the
LORD, so bad that they are not fit to eat. I will make them repugnant*d* to 9
all the kingdoms of the earth, a reproach, a by-word, an object-lesson
and a thing of ridicule wherever I drive them. I will send against them 10
sword, famine, and pestilence until they have vanished from the land
which I gave to them and to their forefathers.

This came to Jeremiah as the word concerning all the people of 25

[a] carry you like a burden: *so some MSS.; others* forget you.   [b] set out: *prob. rdg., cp.
Sept.; Heb.* appointed.   [c] the smiths: *or* the harem.   [d] *So Sept.; Heb. adds* a disaster.

Judah in the fourth year of Jehoiakim son of Josiah, king of Judah (that
2 is the first year of Nebuchadrezzar king of Babylon). This is what the
prophet Jeremiah said to all Judah and all the inhabitants of Jerusalem:
3 For twenty-three years, from the thirteenth year of Josiah son of Amon,
king of Judah, to the present day, I have been receiving the words of
the LORD and taking pains to speak to you, but you have not listened.
4 The LORD has taken pains to send you his servants the prophets, but
5 you have not listened or shown any inclination to listen. If each of you
will turn from his wicked ways and evil courses, he has said, then you
shall for ever live on the soil which the LORD gave to you and to your
6 forefathers. You must not follow other gods, serving and worshipping
them, nor must you provoke me to anger with the idols your hands
7 have made; then I will not do you harm. But you did not listen to me,
says the LORD; you provoked me to anger with the idols your hands
had made and so brought harm upon yourselves.

8 Therefore these are the words of the LORD of Hosts: Because you
9 have not listened to my words, I will summon all the tribes of the north,
says the LORD: I will send for my servant Nebuchadrezzar king of
Babylon. I will bring them against this land and all its inhabitants and
all these nations round it; I will exterminate them and make them a
10 thing of horror and derision, a scandal for ever. I will silence all sounds
of joy and gladness among them, the voices of bridegroom and bride,
and the sound of the handmill; I will quench the light of every lamp.
11 For seventy years this whole country shall be a scandal and a horror;
12 these nations shall be in subjection to the king of Babylon. When those
seventy years are completed, I will punish the king of Babylon and his
people, says the LORD, for all their misdeeds and make the land of the
13 Chaldaeans a waste for ever. I will bring upon that country all I have
said, all that is written in this book, all that Jeremiah has prophesied
14 against these peoples. They will be the victims*a* of mighty nations and
great kings, and thus I will repay them for their actions and their deeds.

15 These were the words of the LORD the God of Israel to me: Take
from my hand this cup of fiery wine and make all the nations to whom
16 I send you drink it. When they have drunk it they will vomit and go
17 mad; such is the sword which I am sending among them. Then I took
the cup from the LORD's hand, gave it to all the nations to whom he sent
18 me and made them drink it: to Jerusalem, the cities of Judah, its kings
and officers, making them a scandal, a thing of horror and derision and
19 an object of ridicule, as they still are: to Pharaoh king of Egypt, his
20 courtiers, his officers, all his people, and all his rabble of followers, all
the kings of the land of Uz, all the kings of the Philistines: to Ashkelon,
21 Gaza, Ekron, and the remnant of Ashdod: also to Edom, Moab, and

[a] They...victims: *prob. rdg.; Heb.* They were the victims.

the Ammonites, all the kings of Tyre, all the kings of Sidon, and the 22
kings of the coasts and islands: to Dedan, Tema, Buz, and all who roam 23
the fringes of the desert,[a] all the kings of Arabia[b] living in the wilder- 24
ness, all the kings of Zamri, all the kings of Elam, and all the kings of 25
the Medes, all the kings of the north, neighbours or far apart, and all 26
the kingdoms[c] on the face of the earth. Last of all the king of Sheshak[d]
shall drink. You shall say to them, These are the words of the LORD of 27
Hosts the God of Israel: Drink this, get drunk and be sick; fall, to rise
no more, before the sword which I am sending among you. If they 28
refuse to take the cup from you and to drink, say to them, These are the
words of the LORD of Hosts: You must and shall drink. I will first 29
punish the city which bears my name; do you think that you can be
exempt? No, you cannot be exempt, for I am invoking the sword against
all that inhabit the earth. This is the very word of the LORD of Hosts.

Prophesy to them and tell them all I have said: 30

The LORD roars from Zion on high
and thunders from his holy dwelling-place.
Yes, he roars across the heavens, his home;
an echo comes back like the shout of men treading grapes.
The great noise reaches to the ends of the earth 31
and all its inhabitants.
For the LORD brings a charge against the nations,
he goes to law with all mankind
and has handed the wicked over to the sword.
This is the very word of the LORD.

These are the words of the LORD of Hosts: 32
Ruin spreads from nation to nation,
a mighty tempest is blowing up from the ends of the earth.

In that day those whom the LORD has slain shall lie like dung on the 33
ground from one end of the earth to the other; no one shall wail for
them, they shall not be taken up and buried.

Howl, shepherds, cry aloud,   34
sprinkle yourselves with ashes, you masters of the flock.
It is your turn to go to the slaughter,[e]
and you shall fall like fine rams.[f]
The shepherds shall have nowhere to flee,   35
the flockmasters no way of escape.
Hark, the shepherds cry out, the flockmasters howl,   36

---

[a] who roam...desert: *or* who clip the hair on their temples. [b] *So Sept.; Heb. adds* and
all the kings of the Arabs. [c] *So Sept.; Heb. adds* of the earth. [d] *A name for Babylon.*
[e] *So Sept.; Heb. adds an unintelligible word.* [f] fine rams: *so Sept.; Heb.* a fine instrument.

for the LORD is ravaging their pasture,
37   and their peaceful homesteads lie in ruins beneath his anger.
38   They flee like a young lion abandoning his lair,
for their land has become a waste,
wasted by the cruel sword[a] and by his anger.

Jerusalem laid under a curse

26 AT THE BEGINNING OF THE REIGN of Jehoiakim son of Josiah,
2   king of Judah, this word came to Jeremiah[b] from the LORD: These
are the words of the LORD: Stand in the court of the LORD's house and
speak to the inhabitants of all the cities of Judah who come to worship
there. You shall tell them everything that I command you to say to
3 them, keeping nothing back. Perhaps they may listen, and every man
may turn back from his evil courses. Then I will relent, and give up my
4 purpose to bring disaster on them for their evil deeds. You shall say to
them, These are the words of the LORD: If you do not obey me, if you
5 do not follow the law I have set before you, and listen to the words of
my servants the prophets, the prophets whom I have taken pains to
6 send to you, but you have never listened to them, then I will make this
house like Shiloh and this city an object of ridicule to all nations on
earth.

7   The priests, the prophets, and all the people heard Jeremiah say this
8 in the LORD's house and, when he came to the end of what the LORD
had commanded him to say to them, priests, prophets, and people
9 seized him and threatened him with death. 'Why', they demanded,
'have you prophesied in the LORD's name that this house shall become
like Shiloh and this city waste and uninhabited?' The people all
10 gathered against Jeremiah in the LORD's house. The officers of Judah
heard what was happening, and they went up from the royal palace to
the LORD's house and took their places there at the entrance of the new
11 gate. Then the priests and the prophets said to the officers and all the
people, 'Condemn this fellow to death. He has prophesied against this
12 city: you have heard it with your own ears.' Then Jeremiah said to the
officers and the people, 'The LORD sent me to prophesy against this
13 house and this city all that you have heard. If you now mend your ways
and your doings and obey the LORD your God, then he may relent and
14 revoke the disaster with which he has threatened you. But I am in your
15 hands; do with me whatever you think right and proper. Only you may
be certain that, if you put me to death, you and this city and all who live in

[a] sword: *so some MSS.; others* heat.   [b] to Jeremiah: *so Pesh.; Heb. om.*

it will be guilty of murdering an innocent man; for in very truth the
LORD has sent me to you to say all this in your hearing.'

Then the officers and all the people said to the priests and the 16
prophets, 'This man ought not to be condemned to death, for he has
spoken to us in the name of the LORD our God.' Some of the elders of 17
the land also stood up and said to the assembled people, 'In the time of 18
Hezekiah king of Judah, Micah of Moresheth was prophesying and said
to all the people of Judah: "These are the words of the LORD of Hosts:

> Zion shall become a ploughed field,
> Jerusalem a heap of ruins,
> and the temple-hill rough heath."

Did King Hezekiah and all Judah put him to death? Did not the king 19
show reverence for the LORD and seek to placate him? Then the LORD
relented and revoked the disaster with which he had threatened them.
Are we to bring great disaster on ourselves?'

There was another man who prophesied in the name of the LORD, 20
Uriah son of Shemaiah, from Kiriath-jearim. He also prophesied against
this city and this land, just as Jeremiah had done. King Jehoiakim with 21
all his officers and his bodyguard heard what he said and sought to put
him to death. When Uriah heard of it, he was afraid and fled to Egypt.
King Jehoiakim sent Elnathan son of Akbor with others to fetch Uriah 22, 23
from Egypt, and they brought him to the king. He had him put to death
by the sword, and his body flung into the burial-place of the common
people. But Ahikam son of Shaphan used his influence on Jeremiah's 24
behalf to save him from death at the hands of the people.

A rising against Nebuchadrezzar checked

AT THE BEGINNING OF THE REIGN of Zedekiah[a] son of Josiah, 27
king of Judah, this word came from the LORD to Jeremiah: These 2
are the words of the LORD to me: Take the cords and bars of a yoke
and put them on your neck. Then send[b] to the kings of Edom, Moab, 3
Ammon, Tyre, and Sidon by the envoys who have come from them to
Zedekiah king of Judah in Jerusalem, and give them the following 4
message for their masters: These are the words of the LORD of Hosts
the God of Israel: Say to your masters: I made the earth with my great 5
strength and with outstretched arm, I made man and beast on the face
of the earth, and I give it to whom I see fit. I now give all these lands to 6

[a] *So some MSS.; others* Jehoiakim.   [b] *So Luc. Sept.; Heb. adds* them.

my servant Nebuchadrezzar[a] king of Babylon, and I give him also all
7 the beasts of the field to serve him. All nations shall serve him, and his
son and his grandson, until the destined hour of his own land comes,
and then mighty nations and great kings shall use him as they please.
8 If any nation or kingdom will not serve Nebuchadrezzar king of Babylon or submit to his yoke, I will punish them with sword, famine, and
pestilence, says the LORD, until I leave them entirely in his power.
9 Therefore do not listen to your prophets, your diviners, your wise
women,[b] your soothsayers, and your sorcerers when they tell you not
10 to serve the king of Babylon. They are prophesying falsely to you; and
so you will be carried far from your own land, and I shall banish you
11 and you will perish. But if any nation submits to the yoke of the king of
Babylon and serves him, I will leave them on their own soil, says the
LORD; they shall cultivate it and live there.
12   I have said all this to Zedekiah king of Judah: If you will submit to
the yoke of the king of Babylon and serve him and his people, then you
13 shall save your lives. Why should you and your people die by sword,
famine, and pestilence, the fate with which the LORD has threatened any
14 nation which does not serve the king of Babylon? Do not listen to the
prophets who tell you not to become subject to the king of Babylon;
15 they are prophesying falsely to you. I have not sent them, says the
LORD; they are prophesying falsely in my name, and so I shall banish
you and you will perish, you and these prophets who prophesy to you.
16   I said to the priests and all the people, These are the words of the
LORD: Do not listen to your prophets who tell you that the vessels of
the LORD's house will very soon be brought back from Babylon; they
17 are only prophesying falsely to you. Do not listen to them; serve the
king of Babylon, and save your lives. Why should this city become a
18 ruin? If they are prophets, and if they have the word of the LORD, let
them intercede with the LORD of Hosts to grant that the vessels still left
in the LORD's house, in the royal palace, and in Jerusalem, may not be
19 carried off to Babylon. For these are the words of the LORD of Hosts
concerning the pillars, the sea, the trolleys, and all the other vessels
20 still left in this city, which Nebuchadrezzar king of Babylon did not
take when he deported Jeconiah son of Jehoiakim, king of Judah, from
Jerusalem to Babylon, together with all the nobles of Judah and Jeru-
21 salem. These indeed are the words of the LORD of Hosts the God of
Israel concerning the vessels still left in the LORD's house, in the royal
22 palace, and in Jerusalem: They shall be taken to Babylon and stay there
until I recall them, says the LORD; then I will bring them back and
restore them to this place.

[a] *So usually in Jer., but here and at 27. 8, 20; 28. 3, 11, 14; 29. 1, 3 Heb. has* Nebuchadnezzar.
[b] wise women: *lit.* women who have dreams.

That same year,[a] in the fifth month of the first[b] year of the reign of **28** Zedekiah king of Judah, Hananiah son of Azzur, the prophet from Gibeon, said to me in the house of the LORD, in the presence of the priests and all the people, 'These are the words of the LORD of Hosts **2** the God of Israel: I have broken the yoke of the king of Babylon. Within two years I will bring back to this place all the vessels of the **3** LORD's house which Nebuchadrezzar king of Babylon took from here and carried off to Babylon. I will also bring back to this place, says the **4** LORD, Jeconiah son of Jehoiakim, king of Judah, and all the exiles of Judah who went to Babylon; for I will break the yoke of the king of Babylon.' The prophet Jeremiah said to Hananiah the prophet in the **5** presence of the priests and all the people standing in the LORD's house: 'May it be so! May the LORD indeed do this: may he fulfil all that you **6** have prophesied, by bringing back the vessels of the LORD's house and all the exiles from Babylon to this place! Only hear what I have to say **7** to you and to all the people: the prophets who preceded you and me **8** from earliest times have foretold war, famine,[c] and pestilence for many lands and for great kingdoms. If a prophet foretells prosperity, when his **9** words come true it will be known that the LORD has sent him.'

Then the prophet Hananiah took the yoke from the neck of the **10** prophet Jeremiah and broke it, saying before all the people, 'These are **11** the words of the LORD: Thus will I break the yoke of Nebuchadrezzar king of Babylon; I will break it off the necks of all nations within two years';[d] and the prophet Jeremiah went his way. After Hananiah had **12** broken the yoke which had been on Jeremiah's neck, the word of the LORD came to Jeremiah: Go and say to Hananiah, These are the words **13** of the LORD: You have broken bars of wood; in their place you shall[e] get bars of iron. For these are the words of the LORD of Hosts the God **14** of Israel: I have put a yoke of iron on the necks of all these nations, making them serve Nebuchadrezzar king of Babylon. They shall serve him, and I have given him even the beasts of the field. Then Jeremiah **15** said to Hananiah, 'Listen, Hananiah. The LORD has not sent you, and you have led this nation to trust in false prophecies. Therefore these **16** are the words of the LORD: Beware, I will remove you from the face of the earth; you shall die within the year, because you have preached rebellion against the LORD.' The prophet Hananiah died that same **17** year, in the seventh month.

Jeremiah sent a letter from Jerusalem to the remaining elders among **29** the exiles, to the priests and prophets, and to all the people whom Nebuchadrezzar had deported from Jerusalem to Babylon, after King **2**

[a] *Prob. rdg.; Heb. adds* at the beginning of the reign.   [b] *Prob. rdg.; Heb.* fourth.   [c] *So some MSS.; others* disaster.   [d] within two years: *or* while there are still two full years to run.   [e] *Or, with Sept.,* I will.

Jeconiah had left Jerusalem with the queen mother and the eunuchs, the officers of Judah and Jerusalem, the craftsmen and the smiths.*a*

3 The prophet entrusted the letter to Elasah son of Shaphan and Gemariah son of Hilkiah, whom Zedekiah king of Judah had sent to Babylon 4 to King Nebuchadrezzar. This is what he wrote: These are the words of the LORD of Hosts the God of Israel: To all the exiles whom I have 5 carried off from Jerusalem to Babylon: Build houses and live in them; 6 plant gardens and eat their produce. Marry wives and beget sons and daughters; take wives for your sons and give your daughters to husbands, so that they may bear sons and daughters and you may increase 7 there and not dwindle away. Seek the welfare of any city to which I have carried you off, and pray to the LORD for it; on its welfare your welfare 8 will depend. For these are the words of the LORD of Hosts the God of Israel: Do not be deceived by the prophets or the diviners among you, and do not listen to the wise women whom you set to dream dreams. 9 They prophesy falsely to you in my name; I did not send them. This is the very word of the LORD.

10 These are the words of the LORD: When a full seventy years has passed over Babylon, I will take up your cause and fulfil the promise of 11 good things I made you, by bringing you back to this place. I alone know my purpose for you, says the LORD: prosperity and not mis-12 fortune, and a long line of children after you. If you invoke me*b* and 13 pray to me, I will listen to you: when you seek me, you shall find 14*c* me; if you search with all your heart, I will let you find me, says the LORD. I will restore your fortunes and gather you again from all the nations and all the places to which I have banished you, says the LORD, and bring you back to the place from which I have carried you into exile.

15 You say that the LORD has raised up prophets for you in Babylon. 16 These are the words of the LORD concerning the king who sits on the throne of David and all the people who live in this city, your fellow-17 countrymen who have not gone into exile with you. These are the words of the LORD of Hosts: I bring upon them sword, famine, and pestilence, 18 and make them like rotten figs, too bad to be eaten. I pursue them with sword, famine, and pestilence, and make them repugnant to all the kingdoms of the earth, an object of execration and horror, of derision and reproach, among all the nations to which I have banished them. 19 Just as they did not listen to my words, says the LORD, when I took pains to send them my servants the prophets, so you did not listen, 20 says the LORD. But now, you exiles whom I have sent from Jerusalem 21 to Babylon, listen to the words of the LORD. These are the words of the

[a] the smiths: *or* the harem. [b] *So Pesh.; Heb. adds* and walk. [c] *Verses 14-20 are probably misplaced, cp. 24. 8-10.*

LORD of Hosts the God of Israel concerning Ahab son of Kolaiah and Zedekiah son of Maaseiah, who prophesy falsely to you in my name. I will hand them over to Nebuchadrezzar king of Babylon, and he will put them to death before your eyes. Their names shall be used by all the 22 exiles of Judah in Babylon when they curse a man; they shall say, May the LORD treat you like Zedekiah and Ahab, whom the king of Babylon roasted in the fire! For their conduct in Israel was an outrage: they 23 committed adultery with other men's wives, and without my authority prophesied in my name, and what they prophesied was false. I know; I can testify. This is the very word of the LORD.

To Shemaiah the Nehelamite.*a* These are the words of the LORD of 24, 25 Hosts the God of Israel: You have sent a letter in your own name*b* to Zephaniah son of Maaseiah the priest,*c* in which you say: 'The LORD 26 has appointed you to be priest in place of Jehoiada the priest, and it is your duty, as officer*d* in charge of the LORD's house, to put every mad-man who sets up as a prophet into the stocks and the pillory. Why, then, 27 have you not reprimanded Jeremiah of Anathoth, who poses as a pro-phet before you? On the strength of this he has sent to us in Babylon 28 and said, "Your exile will be long; build houses and live in them, plant gardens and eat their produce."' Zephaniah the priest read this letter to 29 Jeremiah the prophet, and the word of the LORD came to Jeremiah: 30 Send and tell all the exiles that these are the words of the LORD con- 31 cerning Shemaiah the Nehelamite: Because Shemaiah has prophesied to you, though I did not send him, and has led you to trust in false prophecies, these are now the words of the LORD: I will punish She- 32 maiah and his children. He shall have no one to take his place in this nation and enjoy the prosperity which I will bestow on my people, says the LORD, because he has preached rebellion against me.

Hopes for the restoration of Jerusalem

THE WORD WHICH CAME TO JEREMIAH from the LORD. These 30 1, 2 are the words of the LORD the God of Israel: Write in a book all that I have said to you, for this is the very word of the LORD: The time is 3 coming when I will restore the fortunes of my people Israel and Judah, says the LORD, and bring them back to the land which I gave to their forefathers; and it shall be their possession.

This is what the LORD has said to Israel and Judah. These are the 4, 5 words of the LORD:

[a] *Prob. rdg.; Heb. adds* you shall say, saying. [b] *So Sept.; Heb. adds* to all the people in Jerusalem. [c] *So Sept.; Heb. adds* and to all the priests. [d] *So Sept.; Heb.* officers.

You shall hear^a a cry of terror, of fear without relief.
6   Ask and see: can a man bear a child?
        Why then do I see every man
        gripping his sides like a woman in labour,
    every face changed, all turned^b pale?
7   Awful is that day:
            when has there been its like?
        A time of anguish for Jacob,
            yet he shall come through it safely.

8   In that day, says the LORD of Hosts, I will break their yoke off their^c
    necks and snap their^c cords; foreigners shall no longer use them as they
9   please; they shall serve the LORD their God and David their king, whom
    I will raise up for them.

10   And you, Jacob my servant, have no fear;
        despair not, O Israel, says the LORD.
        For I will bring you back safe from afar
        and your offspring from the land where they are captives;
        and Jacob shall be at rest once more,
            prosperous and unafraid.
11   For I am with you and will save you, says the LORD.
        I will make an end of all the nations
            amongst whom I have scattered you,
        but I will not make an end of you;
            though I punish you as you deserve,
            I will not sweep you clean away.

12   For these are the words of the LORD to Zion:

        Your injury is past healing,
            cruel was the blow you suffered.
13   There can be no^d remedy for your sore,
            the new skin cannot grow.
14   All your lovers have forgotten you;
            they look for you no longer.
        I have struck you down
    as an enemy strikes, and punished you cruelly;
    for your wickedness is great and your sins are many.
15   Why complain of your injury,
            that your sore cannot be healed?^{e}

[a] *So Sept.; Heb.* We have heard.   [b] turned: *so Sept.; Heb.* alas!   [c] *So Sept.; Heb.* your.
[d] *Prob. rdg.; Heb. adds* one judging your case.   [e] Why...healed?: *or* Cry not for help
in your injury. Your sore cannot be healed.

> I have done this to you,
> because your wickedness is great and your sins are many.
> Yet all who devoured you shall themselves be devoured,   16
> all your oppressors shall go into captivity.
>> Those who plunder you shall be plundered,
>> and those who despoil you I will give up to be spoiled.
> I will cause the new skin to grow   17
> and heal your wounds, says the LORD,
>> although men call you the Outcast,
>> Zion, nobody's friend.

These are the words of the LORD: 18

> Watch; I will restore the fortunes of Jacob's clans
>> and show my love for all his dwellings.
> Every city shall be rebuilt on its mound of ruins,
> every mansion shall have its familiar household.
> From them praise shall be heard   19
>> and sounds of merrymaking.
> I will increase them, they shall not diminish,
> I will raise them to honour, they shall no longer be despised.
> Their sons shall be what they once were,   20
> and their community shall be established in my sight.
> I will punish all their oppressors;
> a ruler shall appear, one of themselves,   21
> a governor shall arise from their own number.
> I will myself bring him*ᵃ* near and so he*ᵇ* shall approach me;
> for no one ventures of himself to approach me,
>> says the LORD.
> So you shall be my people,   22
> and I will be your God.
> See what a scorching wind has gone out from the LORD,   23
>> a sweeping whirlwind.
> It whirls round the heads of the wicked;
> the LORD's anger is not to be turned aside,   24
> till he has finished and achieved his heart's desire.
> In days to come you will understand.

At that time, says the LORD, I will become God of all the families of **31**
Israel, and they shall become my people. These are the words of the   **2**
LORD:

> A people that survived the sword
> found favour in the wilderness;

[a] *Or* them.   [b] *Or* they.

1115

Israel journeyed to find rest;
3   long ago[a] the LORD appeared to them:[b]
I have dearly loved you from of old,
and still I maintain my unfailing care for you.
4   I will build you up again, O virgin Israel,
and you shall be rebuilt.
Again you shall adorn yourself with jingles,
and go forth with the merry throng of dancers.
5   Again you shall plant vineyards on the hills of Samaria,
vineyards which those who planted them defiled;
6   for a day will come when the watchmen on Ephraim's hills cry out,
Come, let us go up to Zion, to the LORD our God.

7 For these are the words of the LORD:

Break into shouts of joy for Jacob's sake,
lead the nations, crying loud and clear,
sing out your praises and say,
The LORD has saved his[c] people,
and preserved a remnant of Israel.
8   See how I bring them from the land of the north;
I will gather them from the ends of the earth,
their blind and lame among them,
women with child and women in labour,
a great company.
9   They come home, weeping as they come,
but I will comfort them[d] and be their escort.
I will lead them to flowing streams;
they shall not stumble, their path will be so smooth.
For I have become a father to Israel,
and Ephraim is my eldest son.

10   Listen to the word of the LORD, you nations,
announce it, make it known to coasts and islands far away:
He who scattered Israel shall gather them again
and watch over them as a shepherd watches his flock.
11   For the LORD has ransomed Jacob
and redeemed him from a foe too strong for him.
12   They shall come with shouts of joy to Zion's height,
shining with happiness at the bounty of the LORD,
the corn, the new wine, and the oil,
the young of flock and herd.

[a] long ago: *or* from afar.   [b] *So Sept.; Heb.* me.   [c] *So Sept.; Heb.* your.   [d] I will comfort them: *so Sept.; Heb.* prayers for favour.

They shall become like a watered garden
　　and they shall never want again.
Then shall the girl show her joy in the dance,　　　　13
　　young men and old shall rejoice;
I will turn their mourning into gladness,
I will relent and give them joy to outdo their sorrow.
I will satisfy the priests with the fat of the land　　　　14
and fill my people with my bounty.
　　　　This is the very word of the LORD.

These are the words of the LORD:　　　　15

　　Hark, lamentation is heard in Ramah, and bitter weeping,
　　　　Rachel weeping for her sons.
　　She refuses to be comforted: they are no more.

These are the words of the LORD:　　　　16

　　Cease your loud weeping,
　　　　shed no more tears;
　　for there shall be a reward for your toil,*ᵃ*
　　　　they shall return from the land of the enemy.
　　You shall leave descendants after you;*ᵃ ᵇ*　　　　17
　　your sons shall return to their own land.
I listened; Ephraim was rocking in his grief:　　　　18
'Thou hast trained me to the yoke like an unbroken calf,
　　and now I am trained;
　　　　restore me, let me return,
　　for thou, LORD, art my God.
Though I broke loose I have repented:　　　　19
now that I am tamed I beat my breast;*ᶜ*
　　in shame and remorse
I reproach myself for the sins of my youth.'
Is Ephraim still my dear son,　　　　20
a child in whom I delight?
　　As often as I turn my back on him
I still remember him;
and so my heart yearns*ᵈ* for him,
　　I am filled with tenderness towards him.
　　　　This is the very word of the LORD.
Build cairns to mark your way,　　　　21
set up sign-posts;
make sure of the road,

[a] *So Sept.; Heb. adds* says the LORD.　[b] You shall...you: *or* There shall be hope for
your posterity.　[c] *Lit.* thigh.　[d] heart yearns: *lit.* bowels rumble.

the path which you will tread.
Come back, virgin Israel,
come back to your cities.

22 How long will you twist and turn, my wayward child?
For the LORD has created a new thing in the earth:
a woman turned into a man.

23 These are the words of the LORD of Hosts the God of Israel: Once more shall these words be heard in the land of Judah and in her cities, when I restore their fortunes:

The LORD bless you,
the LORD, your true goal,*a* your holy mountain.

24 Ploughmen and shepherds who wander with their flocks
shall live together there.*b*

25 For I have given deep draughts to the thirsty,
and satisfied those who were faint with hunger.

26 Thereupon I woke and looked about me, and my dream*c* had been pleasant.

27 The time is coming, says the LORD, when I will sow Israel and Judah
28 with the seed of man and the seed of cattle. As I watched over them with intent to pull down and to uproot, to demolish and destroy and harm, so now will I watch over them to build and to plant. This is the very word of the LORD.

29 In those days it shall no longer be said,

'The fathers have eaten sour grapes
and the children's teeth are set on edge';

30 for a man shall die for his own wrongdoing; the man who eats sour grapes shall have his own teeth set on edge.

31 The time is coming, says the LORD, when I will make a new covenant
32 with Israel and Judah. It will not be like the covenant I made with their forefathers when I took them by the hand and led them out of Egypt. Although they broke my covenant, I was patient with them,
33 says the LORD. But this is the covenant which I will make with Israel after those days, says the LORD; I will set my law within them and write it on their hearts; I will become their God and they shall become
34 my people. No longer need they teach one another to know the LORD; all of them, high and low alike, shall know me, says the LORD, for I will forgive their wrongdoing and remember their sin no more.

35 These are the words of the LORD, who gave the sun for a light by day

[a] the LORD...goal: *or* O home of righteousness. [b] *Prob. rdg.; Heb. adds* Judah and all his cities. [c] *Or* sleep.

and[a] the moon and stars for a light by night, who cleft the sea and its waves roared; the LORD of Hosts is his name:

> If this fixed order could vanish out of my sight,   36
>   says the LORD,
> then the race of Israel too could cease for evermore
>   to be a nation in my sight.

These are the words of the LORD: If any man could measure the 37 heaven above or fathom the depths of the earth beneath, then I could spurn the whole race of Israel because of all they have done. This is the very word of the LORD.

The time is coming, says the LORD, when the city shall be rebuilt in 38 the LORD's honour from the Tower of Hananel to the Corner Gate. The 39 measuring line shall then be laid straight out over the hill of Gareb and round Goath.[b] All the valley[c] and every field as far as the gorge of the 40 Kidron to the corner by the Horse Gate eastwards shall be holy to the LORD. It shall never again be pulled down or demolished.

The word which came to Jeremiah from the LORD in the tenth year 32 of Zedekiah king of Judah (the eighteenth year of Nebuchadrezzar). At that time the forces of the Babylonian king were besieging Jerusalem, 2 and the prophet Jeremiah was imprisoned in the court of the guard-house attached to the royal palace. Zedekiah king of Judah had im- 3 prisoned him after demanding what he meant by this prophecy: 'These are the words of the LORD: I will deliver this city into the hands of the king of Babylon, and he shall take it. Zedekiah king of Judah will not 4 escape from the Chaldaeans but will be surrendered to the king of Babylon; he will speak with him face to face and see him with his own eyes. Zedekiah will be taken to Babylon and will remain there until I 5 turn my thoughts to him, says the LORD. However much you fight against the Chaldaeans you will have no success.'

Jeremiah said, The word of the LORD came to me: Hanamel son of 6,7 your uncle Shallum is coming to see you and will say, 'Buy my field at Anathoth; you have the right of redemption, as next of kin, to buy it.' As the LORD had foretold, my cousin Hanamel came to the court of the 8 guard-house and said, 'Buy my field at Anathoth in Benjamin. You have the right of redemption and possession as next of kin; buy it.' I knew that this was the LORD's message; so I bought the field at Ana- 9 thoth from my cousin Hanamel and weighed out the price, seventeen shekels of silver. I signed and sealed the deed and had it witnessed; then 10 I weighed out the money on the scales. I took my copies of the deed 11 of purchase, both the sealed[d] and the unsealed, and gave them to 12

[a] *So Sept.; Heb. adds* the ordered movements of.   [b] *Or* Goah.   [c] *So Sept.; Heb. adds* the corpses and the buried bodies.   [d] *So Sept.; Heb. adds* the command and the statutes.

Baruch son of Neriah, son of Mahseiah, in the presence of Hanamel my cousin,[a] of the witnesses whose names were on the deed of purchase,

13 and of the Judaeans sitting in the court of the guard-house. In the

14 presence of them all I gave my instructions to Baruch: These are the words of the LORD of Hosts the God of Israel: Take these copies of the deed of purchase, the sealed and the unsealed, and deposit them in an

15 earthenware jar so that they may be preserved for a long time. For these are the words of the LORD of Hosts the God of Israel: The time will come when houses, fields, and vineyards will again be bought and sold

16 in this land. After I had given the deed of purchase to Baruch son of

17 Neriah, I prayed to the LORD: O Lord GOD, thou hast made the heavens and the earth by thy great strength and with thy outstretched

18 arm; nothing is impossible for thee. Thou keepest faith with thousands and thou dost requite the sins of fathers on to the heads[b] of their sons.

19 O great and mighty God whose name is the LORD of Hosts, great are thy purposes and mighty thy actions. Thine eyes watch all the ways of men, and thou rewardest each according to his ways and as his deeds

20 deserve. Thou didst work signs and portents in Egypt and hast continued them to this day, both in Israel and amongst all men, and hast

21 won for thyself a name that lives on to this day. Thou didst bring thy people Israel out of Egypt with signs and portents, with a strong hand

22 and an outstretched arm, and with terrible power. Thou didst give them this land which thou didst promise with an oath to their fore-

23 fathers, a land flowing with milk and honey. They came and took possession of it, but they did not obey thee or follow thy law, they disobeyed all thy commands; and so thou hast brought this disaster

24 upon them. Look at the siege-ramps, the men who are advancing to take the city, and the city given over to its assailants from Chaldaea, the victim of sword, famine, and pestilence. The word thou hast spoken is

25 fulfilled and thou dost see it. And yet thou hast bidden me buy the field, O Lord GOD, and have the deed witnessed, even though the city is given to the Chaldaeans.

26, 27   These are the words of the LORD to Jeremiah: I am the LORD, the

28 God of all flesh; is anything impossible for me? Therefore these are the words of the LORD: I will deliver this city into the hands of the Chaldaeans and of Nebuchadrezzar king of Babylon, and he shall take it.

29 The Chaldaeans who are fighting against this city will enter it, set it on fire and burn it down, with the houses on whose roofs sacrifices have been burnt to Baal and drink-offerings poured out to other gods, by which I was provoked to anger.

30   From their earliest days Israel and Judah have been doing what is wrong in my eyes, provoking me to anger by their actions, says the

[a] *So some MSS.; others* uncle.   [b] requite…on to the heads: *lit.* repay…into the bosoms.

LORD. For this city has so roused my anger and my fury, from the time ₃₁
it was built down to this day, that I would rid myself of it. Israel and ₃₂
Judah, their kings, officers, priests, prophets, and everyone living in
Jerusalem and Judah have provoked me to anger by their wrongdoing.
They have turned their backs on me and averted their faces; though I ₃₃
took pains to teach them, they would not hear or learn their lesson.
They set up their loathsome idols in the house which bears my name ₃₄
and so defiled it. They built shrines to Baal in the Valley of Ben- ₃₅
hinnom, to surrender their sons and daughters to Molech. It was no
command of mine, nor did it ever enter my thought to do this abominable thing and lead Judah into sin.

Now, therefore, these are the words of the LORD the God of Israel to ₃₆
this city of which you say, 'It is being given over to the king of Babylon,
with sword, famine, and pestilence': I will gather them from all the ₃₇
lands to which I banished them in my anger, rage, and fury, and I will
bring them back to this place and let them dwell there undisturbed.
They shall become my people and I will become their God. I will give ₃₈,₃₉
them one heart and one way of life so that they shall fear me at all
times, for their own good and the good of their children after them.
I will enter into an eternal covenant with them, to follow them un- ₄₀
failingly with my bounty; I will fill their hearts with fear of me, and so
they will not turn away from me. I will rejoice over them, rejoice to do ₄₁
them good, and faithfully with all my heart and soul I will plant them
in this land. For these are the words of the LORD: As I brought on this ₄₂
people such great disaster, so will I bring them all the prosperity which
I now promise them. Fields shall again be bought and sold in this land ₄₃
of which you now say, 'It is desolate, without man or beast; it is given
over to the Chaldaeans.' Fields shall be bought and sold, deeds signed, ₄₄
sealed, and witnessed, in Benjamin, in the neighbourhood of Jerusalem,
in the cities of Judah, of the hill-country, of the Shephelah, and of the
Negeb; for I will restore their fortunes. This is the very word of the
LORD.

The word of the LORD came to Jeremiah a second time while he was ₃₃
still imprisoned in the court of the guard-house: These are the words ₂
of the LORD who made the earth,[a] who formed it and established it; the
LORD is his name: If you call to me I will answer you, and tell you great ₃
and mysterious things which you do not understand. These are the ₄
words of the LORD the God of Israel concerning the houses in this city
and the royal palace, which are to be razed to the ground, concerning
siege-ramp and sword, and attackers[b] who fill the houses with the ₅
corpses of those whom he struck down in his furious rage: I hid my face
from this city because of their wicked ways, but now I will bring her ₆

[a] the earth: *so Sept.; Heb.* it.   [b] *Prob. rdg.; Heb. adds* the Chaldaeans.

healing; I will heal and cure Judah and Israel, and will let my people
7 see an age of peace and security. I will restore their fortunes and build
8 them again as once they were. I will cleanse them of all the wickedness
and sin that they have committed; I will forgive all the evil deeds they
9 have done in rebellion against me. This city will win me a name[a] and
praise and glory before all the nations on earth, when they hear of all
the blessings I bestow on her; and they shall be moved and filled with
awe because of the blessings and the peace which I have brought upon
her.

10   These are the words of the LORD: You say of this place, 'It is in
ruins, and neither man nor beast lives in the cities of Judah or in the
streets of Jerusalem. It is all a waste, inhabited by neither man nor
11 beast.' Yet in this place shall be heard once again the sounds of joy and
gladness, the voice of the bridegroom and the bride; here too shall be
heard voices shouting, 'Praise the LORD of Hosts, for he is good, for his
love endures for ever', as they offer praise and thanksgiving in the
house of the LORD. For I will restore the fortunes of the land as once they
were. This is the word of the LORD.

12   These are the words of the LORD of Hosts: In this place and in all its
cities, now ruined and inhabited by neither man nor beast, there shall
13 once more be a refuge where shepherds may fold their flocks. In the
cities of the hill-country, of the Shephelah, of the Negeb, in Benjamin,
in the neighbourhood of Jerusalem and the cities of Judah, flocks will
once more pass under the shepherd's hand as he counts them. This is
the word of the LORD.

14   Wait, says the LORD, the days are coming when I will bestow on
15 Israel and Judah all the blessings I have promised them. In those days,
at that time, I will make a righteous Branch of David spring up; he shall
16 maintain law and justice in the land. In those days Judah shall be kept
safe and Jerusalem shall live undisturbed; and this shall be her[b] name:
The LORD is our Righteousness.

17   For these are the words of the LORD: David will never lack a successor
18 on the throne of Israel, nor will the levitical priests lack a man who shall
come before me continually to present whole-offerings, to burn grain-
offerings and to make other offerings.

19, 20   This word came from the LORD to Jeremiah: These are the words of
the LORD: If the law that I made for the day and the night could be
21 annulled[c] so that they fell out of their proper order, then my covenant
with my servant David could be annulled so that none of his line should
sit upon his throne; so also could my covenant with the levitical priests
22 who minister to me. Like the innumerable host of heaven or the count-

[a] *Prob. rdg.*; *Heb. adds* of joy.   [b] *Or, with Pesh.*, his.   [c] could be annulled: *so Vulg.*;
Heb. you annul.

less sands of the sea, I will increase the descendants of my servant David and the Levites who minister to me.

The word of the LORD came to Jeremiah: Have you not observed how 23, 24 this people have said, 'It is the two families whom he chose that the LORD has spurned'? So others will despise my people and no longer regard them as a nation. These are the words of the LORD: If I had not 25 made*a* my law for day and night nor established a fixed order in heaven and earth, then I would spurn the descendants of Jacob and of my 26 servant David, and would not take any of David's line to be rulers over the descendants of Abraham, Isaac and Jacob. But now I will restore their fortunes and have compassion upon them.

Events under Jehoiakim and Zedekiah

THE WORD WHICH CAME TO JEREMIAH from the LORD when 34 Nebuchadrezzar king of Babylon and his army, with all his vassal kingdoms and nations, were fighting against Jerusalem and all her towns: These are the words of the LORD the God of Israel: Go and say 2 to Zedekiah king of Judah, These are the words of the LORD: I will give this city into the hands of the king of Babylon and he will burn it down. You shall not escape, you will be captured and handed over to 3 him. You will see him face to face, and he will speak to you in person; and you shall go to Babylon. But listen to the LORD's word to you, 4 Zedekiah king of Judah. This is his word: You shall not die by the sword; you will die a peaceful death, and they will kindle fires in your 5 honour like the fires kindled in former times for the kings your ancestors who preceded you. 'Alas, my lord!' they will say as they beat their breasts in mourning for you. This I have spoken. This is the very word of the LORD. The prophet Jeremiah repeated all this to Zedekiah king of 6 Judah in Jerusalem when the army of the king of Babylon was attacking 7 Jerusalem and the*b* remaining cities of Judah, namely Lachish and Azekah. These were the only fortified cities left in Judah.

The word that came to Jeremiah from the LORD after Zedekiah had 8 made a covenant with all the people in Jerusalem to proclaim an act of freedom for the slaves. All who had Hebrew slaves, male or female, 9 were to set them free; they were not to keep their fellow Judaeans in servitude. All the officers and people, having made this covenant to set 10 free their slaves, both male and female, and not to keep them in servitude any longer, fulfilled its terms and let them go. Afterwards, how- 11 ever, they changed their minds and forced back again into slavery the

[a] If...made: *prob. rdg., cp. Targ.; Heb.* If not.   [b] *So Sept.; Heb. adds* all.

12 men and women whom they had freed. Then this word came from the
13 LORD to Jeremiah: These are the words of the LORD the God of Israel:
I made a covenant with your forefathers on the day that I brought them
14 out of Egypt, out of the land of slavery. These were its terms: 'Within
seven years each of you shall set free any Hebrew who has sold himself
to you as a slave and has served you for six years; you shall set him free.'
15 Your forefathers did not listen to me or obey me. You, on the contrary,
recently proclaimed an act of freedom for the slaves and made a covenant in my presence, in the house that bears my name, and so have done
16 what is right in my eyes. But you too have profaned my name. You have
all taken back the slaves you had set free and you have forced them, both
17 male and female, to be your slaves again. Therefore these are the words
of the LORD: After you had proclaimed an act of freedom, a deliverance
for your kinsmen and your neighbours, you did not obey me; so I will
proclaim a deliverance for you, says the LORD, a deliverance over to
sword, to pestilence, and to famine, and I will make you repugnant to all
18 the kingdoms of the earth. You have disregarded my covenant and have
not fulfilled the terms to which you yourselves had agreed; so I will make
you like the calf of the covenant when they cut it into two and passed
19 between the pieces. Those who passed between the pieces of the calf
were the officers of Judah and Jerusalem, the eunuchs and priests and
20 all the people of the land. I will give them up to their enemies who seek
their lives, and their bodies shall be food for birds of prey and wild
21 beasts. I will deliver Zedekiah king of Judah and his officers to their
enemies who seek their lives and to the army of the king of Babylon, which
22 is now raising the siege. I will give the command, says the LORD, and
will bring them back to this city. They shall attack it and take it and burn
it down, and I will make the cities of Judah desolate and unpeopled.
35   The word which came to Jeremiah from the LORD in the days of
2 Jehoiakim son of Josiah, king of Judah: Go and speak to the Rechabites,
bring them to one of the rooms in the house of the LORD and offer them
3 wine to drink. So I fetched Jaazaniah son of Jeremiah, son of Haba-
ziniah, with his brothers and all his sons and all the family of the
4 Rechabites. I brought them into the house of the LORD to the room of
the sons of Hanan[a] son of Igdaliah, the man of God; this adjoins the
officers' room above that of Maaseiah son of Shallum, the keeper of the
5 threshold. I set bowls full of wine and drinking-cups before the Recha-
6 bites and invited them to drink wine; but they said, 'We will not drink
wine, for our forefather Jonadab son of Rechab laid this command on
7 us: "You shall never drink wine, neither you nor your children. You
shall not build houses or sow seed or plant vineyards; you shall have
none of these things. Instead, you shall remain tent-dwellers all your

[a] *Or, with one MS., the son of Hanan.*

lives, so that you may live long in the land where you are sojourners."
We have honoured all the commands of our forefather Jonadab son of 8
Rechab and have drunk no wine all our lives, neither we nor our wives,
nor our sons, nor our daughters. We have not built houses to live in, 9
nor have we possessed vineyards or sown fields. We have lived in tents, 10
obeying and observing all the commands of our forefather Jonadab. But 11
when Nebuchadrezzar king of Babylon invaded the land we said, "Come,
let us go to Jerusalem before the advancing Chaldaean and Aramaean
armies." And we have stayed in Jerusalem.'

Then the word of the LORD came to Jeremiah: These are the words 12, 13
of the LORD of Hosts the God of Israel: Go and say to the men of
Judah and the inhabitants of Jerusalem, You must accept correction
and obey my words, says the LORD. The command of Jonadab son of 14
Rechab to his descendants not to drink wine has been honoured; they
have not drunk wine to this day, for they have obeyed their ancestor's
command. But I have taken especial pains to warn you and yet you have
not obeyed me. I sent my servants the prophets especially to say to you, 15
'Turn back every one of you from his evil course, mend your ways and
cease to follow other gods and worship them; then you shall remain on
the land that I have given to you and to your forefathers.' Yet you did
not obey or listen to me. The sons of Jonadab son of Rechab have 16
honoured their ancestor's command laid on them, but this people have
not listened to me. Therefore, these are the words of the LORD the God 17
of Hosts, the God of Israel: Because they did not listen when I spoke
to them, nor answer when I called them, I will bring upon Judah and
upon all the inhabitants of Jerusalem the disaster with which I threatened them. To the Rechabites Jeremiah said, These are the words of 18
the LORD of Hosts the God of Israel: Because you have kept the command of Jonadab your ancestor and obeyed all his instructions and
carried out all that he told you to do, therefore these are the words of 19
the LORD of Hosts the God of Israel: Jonadab son of Rechab shall not
want a descendant to stand before me for all time.

IN THE FOURTH YEAR OF JEHOIAKIM son of Josiah, king of Judah, 36
this word came to Jeremiah from the LORD: Take a scroll and write 2
on it every word that I have spoken to you about Jerusalem*a* and Judah
and all the nations, from the day that I first spoke to you in the reign
of Josiah down to the present day. Perhaps the house of Judah will 3
be warned of the calamity that I am planning to bring on them, and
every man will abandon his evil course; then I will forgive their wrongdoing and their sin. So Jeremiah called Baruch son of Neriah, and he 4
wrote on the scroll at Jeremiah's dictation all the words which the LORD

[a] *So Sept.; Heb.* Israel.

5 had spoken to him. He gave Baruch this instruction: 'I am prevented
6 from going to the LORD's house. You must go there in my place on a
fast-day and read the words of the LORD in the hearing of the people
from the scroll you have written at my dictation. You shall read them
in the hearing of all the men of Judah who come in from their cities.
7 Then perhaps they will present a petition to the LORD and every man
will abandon his evil course; for the LORD has spoken against this
8 people in great anger and wrath.' Baruch son of Neriah did all that the
prophet Jeremiah had told him to do, and read the words of the LORD
in the LORD's house out of the book.

9   In the ninth month of the fifth year of the reign of Jehoiakim son of
Josiah, king of Judah, all the people in Jerusalem and all who came
10 there from the cities of Judah proclaimed a fast before the LORD. Then
Baruch read Jeremiah's words in the house of the LORD out of the book
in the hearing of all the people; he read them from the room of Gemariah son of the adjutant-general Shaphan in the upper court at the
11 entrance to the new gate of the LORD's house. Micaiah son of Gemariah, son of Shaphan, heard all the words of the LORD out of the book
12 and went down to the palace, to the adjutant-general's room where all
the officers were gathered—Elishama the adjutant-general, Delaiah son
of Shemaiah, Elnathan son of Akbor, Gemariah son of Shaphan, Zede-
13 kiah son of Hananiah and all the other officers. There Micaiah repeated
all the words he had heard when Baruch read out of the book in the
14 people's hearing. Then the officers sent Jehudi son of Nethaniah, son
of Shelemiah, son of Cushi, to Baruch with this message: 'Come here
and bring the scroll from which you read in the people's hearing.' So
15 Baruch son of Neriah brought the scroll to them, and they said, 'Sit
16 down and*a* read it to us.' When they heard what he read, they turned to
each other trembling and said,*b* 'We must report this to the king.'
17, 18 They asked Baruch to tell them how he had come to write all this.*c* He
said to them, 'Jeremiah dictated every word of it to me, and I wrote it
19 down in ink in the book.' The officers said to Baruch, 'You and Jere-
20 miah must go into hiding so that no one may know where you are.' When
they had deposited the scroll in the room of Elishama the adjutant-
general, they went to the court and reported everything to the king.

21   The king sent Jehudi to fetch the scroll. When he had fetched it from
the room of Elishama the adjutant-general, he read it to the king and to
22 all the officers in attendance. It was the ninth month of the year, and the
king was sitting in his winter apartments with a fire burning in a
23 brazier in front of him. When Jehudi had read three or four columns of
the scroll, the king cut them off with a penknife and threw them into

[a] Sit down and: *or* This time.   [b] *So Sept.; Heb. adds* to Baruch.   [c] *So Sept.; Heb. adds*
at his dictation.

the fire in the brazier. He went on doing so until the whole scroll had
been thrown on the fire. Neither the king nor any of his courtiers who 24
heard these words showed any fear or rent their clothes; and though 25
Elnathan, Delaiah, and Gemariah begged the king not to burn the
scroll, he would not listen to them. The king then ordered Jerahmeel, a 26
royal prince,*a* Seraiah son of Azriel, and Shelemiah son of Abdeel to
fetch the scribe Baruch and the prophet Jeremiah; but the LORD had
hidden them.

After the king had burnt the scroll with all that Baruch had written 27
on it at Jeremiah's dictation, the word of the LORD came to Jeremiah:
Now take another scroll and write on it all the words that were on the 28
first scroll which Jehoiakim king of Judah burnt. You shall say to 29
Jehoiakim king of Judah, These are the words of the LORD: You burnt
this scroll and said, Why have you written here that the king of Babylon
shall come and destroy this land and exterminate both men and beasts?
Therefore these are the words of the LORD about Jehoiakim king of 30
Judah: He shall have no one to succeed him on the throne of David,
and his dead body shall be exposed to scorching heat by day and frost
by night. I will punish him and also his offspring and his courtiers for 31
their wickedness, and I will bring down on them and on the inhabitants
of Jerusalem and on the men of Judah all the calamities with which I
threatened them, and to which they turned a deaf ear. Then Jeremiah 32
took another scroll and gave it to the scribe Baruch son of Neriah, who
wrote on it at Jeremiah's dictation all the words of the book which
Jehoiakim king of Judah had burnt; and much else was added to the
same effect.

King Zedekiah son of Josiah was set on the throne of Judah by 37
Nebuchadrezzar king of Babylon, in succession to Coniah son of Jehoiakim. Neither he nor his courtiers nor the people of the land listened to 2
the words which the LORD spoke through the prophet Jeremiah.

King Zedekiah sent Jehucal*b* son of Shelemiah and the priest Zeph- 3
aniah son of Maaseiah to the prophet Jeremiah to say to him, 'Pray for
us to the LORD our God.' At the time Jeremiah was free to come and go 4
among the people; he had not yet been thrown into prison. Meanwhile, 5
Pharaoh's army had marched out of Egypt, and when the Chaldaeans
who were besieging Jerusalem heard of it they raised the siege. Then 6
this word came from the LORD to the prophet Jeremiah: These are the 7
words of the LORD the God of Israel: Say to the king of Judah who sent
you to consult me, Pharaoh's army which marched out to help you is
on its way back to Egypt, its own land, and the Chaldaeans will return 8
to the attack. They will capture this city and burn it to the ground.
These are the words of the LORD: Do not deceive yourselves, do not 9

[a] a royal prince: *or* the king's deputy.   [b] Jucal *in 38. 1.*

imagine that the Chaldaeans will go away and leave you alone. They
10 will not go; for even if you defeated the whole Chaldaean force with
which you are now fighting, and only the wounded were left lying in
their tents, they would rise and burn down the city.
11 When the Chaldaean army had raised the siege of Jerusalem because
12 of the advance of Pharaoh's army, Jeremiah was on the point of leaving
Jerusalem to go into Benjamite territory and take possession of his
13 patrimony in the presence of the people there. Irijah son of Shelemiah,
son of Hananiah, the officer of the guard, was in the Benjamin Gate
when Jeremiah reached it, and he arrested the prophet, accusing him of
14 going over to the Chaldaeans. 'It is a lie,' said Jeremiah; 'I am not
going over to the Chaldaeans.' Irijah would not listen to him but
15 arrested him and brought him before the officers. The officers were
indignant with Jeremiah; they flogged him and imprisoned him in the
house of Jonathan the scribe, which they had converted into a prison;
16 for Jeremiah had been put into a vaulted pit beneath the house, and
here he remained for a long time.
17 King Zedekiah had Jeremiah brought to him and consulted him
privately in the palace, asking him if there was a word from the LORD.
'Indeed there is,' said Jeremiah; 'you shall fall into the hands of the
18 king of Babylon.' Then Jeremiah said to King Zedekiah, 'What wrong
have I done to you or your courtiers or this people? Why have you
19 thrown me into prison? Where are your prophets who prophesied that
20 the king of Babylon would not attack you or your country? I pray you
now, my lord king, give me a hearing and let my petition be presented:
do not send me back to the house of Jonathan the scribe, or I shall die
21 there.' Then King Zedekiah gave the order and Jeremiah was committed to the court of the guard-house and was granted a daily ration
of one loaf from the Street of the Bakers, until the bread in the city was
all gone. So Jeremiah remained in the court of the guard-house.
38 Shephatiah son of Mattan, Gedaliah son of Pashhur, Jucal son of
Shelemiah, and Pashhur son of Malchiah heard what Jeremiah was
2 saying to all the people: These are the words of the LORD: Whoever
remains in this city shall die by sword, by famine, or by pestilence, but
whoever goes out to surrender to the Chaldaeans shall survive; he shall
3 survive, he shall take home his life and nothing more.[a] These are the
words of the LORD: This city will fall into the hands of the king of
4 Babylon's army, and they will capture it. Then the officers said to the
king, 'The man must be put to death. By talking in this way he is
discouraging the soldiers and the rest of the people left in the city. He is
5 pursuing not the people's welfare but their ruin.' King Zedekiah said,
6 'He is in your hands; the king is powerless against you.' So they took

[a] *See note on 21. 9.*

Jeremiah and threw him into the pit,[a] in the court of the guard-house, letting him down with ropes. There was no water in the pit, only mud, and Jeremiah sank in the mud. Now Ebed-melech the Cushite, a eunuch, who was in the palace, heard that they had thrown Jeremiah into the pit and went to tell the king, who was seated in the Benjamin Gate. 'Your majesty,' he said, 'these men have shown great wickedness in their treatment of the prophet Jeremiah. They have thrown him into the pit, and when there is no more bread in the city he will die of hunger where he lies.' Thereupon the king told Ebed-melech the Cushite to take three[b] men with him and hoist Jeremiah out of the pit before he died. So Ebed-melech went to the palace with the men and took some tattered, cast-off clothes from the wardrobe[c] and let them down with ropes to Jeremiah in the pit. Ebed-melech the Cushite said to Jeremiah, 'Put these old clothes under your armpits to ease the ropes.' Jeremiah did this, and they pulled him up out of the pit with the ropes; and he remained in the court of the guard-house.

King Zedekiah had the prophet Jeremiah brought to him by the third entrance to the LORD's house and said to him, 'I want to ask you something; hide nothing from me.' Jeremiah answered, 'If I speak out, you will certainly put me to death; if I offer you any advice, you will not take it.' But King Zedekiah swore to Jeremiah privately, 'By the life of the LORD who gave us our lives, I will not put you to death, nor will I hand you over to these men who are seeking to take your life.' Jeremiah said to Zedekiah, 'These are the words of the LORD the God of Hosts, the God of Israel: If you go out and surrender to the officers of the king of Babylon, you shall live and this city shall not be burnt down; you and your family shall live. But if you do not surrender to the officers of the king of Babylon, the city shall fall into the hands of the Chaldaeans, and they shall burn it down, and you will not escape them.' King Zedekiah said to Jeremiah, 'I am afraid of the Judaeans who have gone over to the enemy. I fear the Chaldaeans will give me up to them and I shall be roughly handled.' Jeremiah answered, 'They will not give you up. If you obey the LORD in everything I tell you, all will be well with you and you shall live. But if you refuse to go out and surrender, this is what the LORD has shown me: all the women left in the king of Judah's palace will be led out to the officers of the king of Babylon and they will say:

> Your own friends have misled you
>   and have been too strong for you;
> they have let your feet sink in the mud
>   and have turned away and left you.

[a] *Prob. rdg.; Heb. adds* Malchiah son (*or* deputy) of the king.   [b] *So one MS.; others* thirty.   [c] the wardrobe: *prob. rdg.; Heb.* underneath the treasury.

23 All your women and children will be led out to the Chaldaeans, and you will not escape; you will be seized by the king of Babylon and this
24 city will be burnt down.' Zedekiah said to Jeremiah, 'Let no one know
25 about this, and you shall not be put to death. If the officers hear that I have been speaking with you and they come to you and say, "Tell us what you said to the king and what he said to you; hide nothing from us,
26 and we will not put you to death", then answer, "I was presenting a petition to the king not to send me back to the house of Jonathan to die
27 there."' The officers all came to Jeremiah and questioned him, and he said to them just what the king had told him to say; so their talk came
28 to an end and they were none the wiser. Jeremiah remained in the court of the guard-house till the day Jerusalem fell.[a]

39 1[b] IN THE TENTH MONTH OF THE NINTH YEAR of the reign of Zedekiah king of Judah, Nebuchadrezzar advanced with all his army
2 against Jerusalem, and they laid siege to it. In the fourth month of the eleventh year of Zedekiah, on the ninth day of the month, the city was
3 thrown open. All the officers of the king of Babylon came in and took their seats in the middle gate: Nergalsarezer of Simmagir, Nebusarsekim[c] the chief eunuch,[d] Nergalsarezer the commander of the frontier
4 troops,[e] and all the other officers of the king of Babylon. When Zedekiah king of Judah saw them, he and all his armed escort left the city and fled by night by way of the king's garden through the gate called
5 Between the Two Walls. They escaped towards the Arabah, but the Chaldaean army pursued them and overtook Zedekiah in the lowlands of Jericho. The king was seized and brought before Nebuchadrezzar king of Babylon at Riblah in the land of Hamath, and he pleaded his
6 case before him. The king of Babylon slew Zedekiah's sons before his
7 eyes at Riblah; he also put to death the nobles of Judah. Then Zedekiah's eyes were put out, and he was bound in fetters of bronze to be
8 brought to Babylon. The Chaldaeans burnt the royal palace and the house of the LORD and the houses[f] of the people, and pulled down the
9 walls of Jerusalem. Nebuzaradan captain of the bodyguard deported to Babylon the rest of the people left in the city, those who had deserted
10 to him and any remaining artisans.[g] At the same time the captain of the guard left behind the weakest class of the people, those who owned nothing at all, and made them vine-dressers and labourers.
11 Nebuchadrezzar king of Babylon sent orders about Jeremiah to[h]
12 Nebuzaradan captain of the guard. 'Take him,' he said; 'take special

[a] So Sept.; Heb. adds when Jerusalem was captured. [b] Verses 1–10: cp. 52. 4–16 and 2 Kgs. 25. 1–12. [c] Probably a different form of Nebushazban (verse 13). [d] the chief eunuch: or Rab-saris. [e] the commander...troops: or Rab-mag. [f] of the LORD and the houses: prob. rdg.; Heb. om. [g] artisans: prob. rdg., cp. 52. 15; Heb. people who were left. [h] So Vulg.; Heb. by.

care of him, and do him no harm of any kind, but do for him whatever
he says.' So Nebuzaradan captain of the guard sent Nebushazban the ₁₃
chief eunuch, Nergalsarezer the commander of the frontier troops, and
all the chief officers of the king of Babylon, and they fetched Jeremiah ₁₄
from the court of the guard-house and handed him over to Gedaliah
son of Ahikam, son of Shaphan, to take him out to the Residence. So he
stayed with his own people.

The word of the LORD had come to Jeremiah while he was under ₁₅
arrest in the court of the guard-house: Go and say to Ebed-melech the ₁₆
Cushite, These are the words of the LORD of Hosts the God of Israel:
I will make good the words I have spoken against this city, foretelling
ruin and not prosperity, and when that day comes you will be there to
see it. But I will preserve you on that day, says the LORD, and you shall ₁₇
not be handed over to the men you fear. I will keep you safe and you ₁₈
shall not fall a victim to the sword; because you trusted in me you shall
escape, you shall take home your life and nothing more.*a* This is the very
word of the LORD.

Jeremiah after the capture of Jerusalem

THE WORD WHICH CAME FROM THE LORD concerning Jere- **40**
miah: Nebuzaradan captain of the guard had taken him in chains to
Ramah along with the other exiles from Jerusalem and Judah who were
being deported to Babylon; and there he set him free, and took it upon ₂
himself to say to Jeremiah, 'The LORD your God threatened this place
with disaster, and has duly carried out his threat that this should happen ₃
to all of you because you have sinned against the LORD and not obeyed
him. But as for you, Jeremiah, today I remove the fetters from your ₄
wrists. Come with me to Babylon if you wish, and I will take special
care of you; but if you prefer not to come, well and good. The whole
country lies before you; go wherever you think best.' Jeremiah had not ₅
yet answered when Nebuzaradan went on,*b* 'Go back to Gedaliah son
of Ahikam, son of Shaphan, whom the king of Babylon has appointed
governor of the cities of Judah, and stay with him openly; or else go
wherever you choose.' Then the captain of the guard granted him an
allowance of food, and gave him a present, and so took leave of him.
Jeremiah then came to Gedaliah son of Ahikam at Mizpah and stayed ₆
with him among the people left in the land.

When all the captains of the armed bands in the country-side and ₇
their men heard that the king of Babylon had appointed Gedaliah son

[a] *See note on 21. 9.*   [b] Jeremiah...went on: *prob. rdg.; Heb. unintelligible in context.*

of Ahikam governor of the land, and had put him in charge of the weakest class of the population, men, women, and children, who had

8 not been deported to Babylon, they came to him at Mizpah; Ishmael son of Nethaniah came, and Johanan and Jonathan sons*a* of Kareah, Seraiah son of Tanhumeth, the sons of Ephai*b* from Netophah, and

9 Jezaniah*c* of Beth-maacah, with their men. Gedaliah son of Ahikam, son of Shaphan, gave them all this assurance: 'Have no fear of the Chaldaean officers.*d* Settle down in the land and serve the king of

10 Babylon; and then all will be well with you. I am to stay in Mizpah and attend upon the Chaldaeans whenever they come, and you are to gather in the summer-fruits, wine, and oil, store them in jars, and settle in the

11 towns you have taken over.' The Judaeans also, in Moab, Ammon, Edom and other countries, heard that the king of Babylon had left a remnant in Judah and that he had set over them Gedaliah son of

12 Ahikam, son of Shaphan. The Judaeans, therefore, from all the places where they were scattered, came back to Judah and presented themselves before Gedaliah at Mizpah; and they gathered in a considerable store of fruit and wine.

13 Johanan son of Kareah and all the captains of the armed bands from

14 the country-side came to Gedaliah at Mizpah and said to him, 'Do you know that Baalis king of the Ammonites has sent Ishmael son of Nethaniah to assassinate you?' But Gedaliah son of Ahikam did not believe

15 them. Then Johanan son of Kareah said in private to Gedaliah, 'Let me go, unknown to anyone else, and kill Ishmael son of Nethaniah. Why allow him to assassinate you, and so let all the Judaeans who have

16 rallied round you be scattered and the remnant of Judah lost?' Gedaliah son of Ahikam answered him, 'Do no such thing. Your story about Ishmael is a lie.'

41 In the seventh month Ishmael son of Nethaniah, son of Elishama, who was a member of the royal house,*e* came with ten men to Gedaliah son of Ahikam at Mizpah. While they were at table with him there,

2 Ishmael son of Nethaniah and the ten men with him rose to their feet and assassinated Gedaliah son of Ahikam, son of Shaphan, whom the

3 king of Babylon had appointed governor of the land. They also murdered the Judaeans with him in Mizpah and the Chaldaeans who hap-

4 pened to be there.*f* The second day after the murder of Gedaliah, while

5 it was not yet common knowledge, there came eighty men from Shechem, Shiloh, and Samaria. They had shaved off their beards, their clothes were rent and their bodies gashed, and they were carrying

[a] Johanan...sons: *or, with* Sept., Johanan son. [b] *Or* Ophai. [c] Jaazaniah *in 2 Kgs. 25. 23.* [d] of the Chaldaean officers: *so one MS., cp.* 2 Kgs. 25. 24; *others* to serve the Chaldaeans. [e] *So* Sept.; *Heb. adds* and the chief officers of the king. [f] *So* Sept.; *Heb. adds* it was the fighting men whom Ishmael murdered.

grain-offerings and frankincense to take to the house of the LORD.
Ishmael son of Nethaniah came out weeping from Mizpah to meet them 6
and, when he met them, he said, 'Come to Gedaliah son of Ahikam.'
But as soon as they reached the centre of the town, Ishmael son of 7
Nethaniah and his men murdered them and threw their bodies into a
pit, all except ten of them who said to Ishmael, 'Do not kill us, for we 8
have a secret hoard in the country, wheat and barley, oil and honey.'
So he held his hand and did not kill them with the others. The pit into 9
which he threw the bodies of those whose death he had caused by
using Gedaliah's name was the pit which King Asa had made when
threatened by Baasha king of Israel; and the dead bodies filled it.
He rounded up the rest of the people in Mizpah, that is the king's 10
daughters and all who remained in Mizpah when Nebuzaradan captain
of the guard appointed Gedaliah son of Ahikam governor; and with
these he set out to cross over into Ammon. When Johanan son of 11
Kareah and all the captains of the armed bands heard of the crimes
committed by Ishmael son of Nethaniah, they took all the men they 12
had and went to attack him. They found him by the great pool in
Gibeon. The people with Ishmael were glad when they saw Johanan 13
son of Kareah and the captains of the armed bands with him; and all 14
whom Ishmael had taken prisoner at Mizpah turned and joined Johanan
son of Kareah. But Ishmael son of Nethaniah escaped from Johanan 15
with eight men, and they made their way to the Ammonites.

Johanan son of Kareah and all the captains of the armed bands took 16
from Mizpah the survivors whom he had rescued from Ishmael son of
Nethaniah after the murder of Gedaliah son of Ahikam—men, armed
and unarmed, women, children, and eunuchs, whom he had brought
back from Gibeon. They started out and broke their journey at Kim- 17
ham's holding near Bethlehem, on their way into Egypt to escape the 18
Chaldaeans. They were afraid because Ishmael son of Nethaniah had
assassinated Gedaliah son of Ahikam, whom the king of Babylon had
appointed governor of the country.

All the captains of the armed bands, including Johanan son of Kareah 42
and Azariah[a] son of Hoshaiah, together with the people, high and low,
came to the prophet Jeremiah and said to him, 'May our petition be 2
acceptable to you: Pray to the LORD your God on our behalf and on
behalf of this remnant; for, as you see for yourself, only a few of us
remain out of many. Pray that the LORD your God may tell us which 3
way we ought to go and what we ought to do.' Then the prophet 4
Jeremiah said to them, 'I have heard your request and will pray to the
LORD your God as you desire, and whatever answer the LORD gives I
will tell you; I will keep nothing back.' They said to Jeremiah, 'May 5

[a] *So Sept., cp. 43. 2; Heb.* Jezaniah.

the LORD be a true and faithful witness against us if we do not keep our oath! We swear that we will do whatever the LORD your God sends you

6 to tell us. Whether we like it or not, we will obey the LORD our God to whom we send you, in order that it may be well with us; we will obey the LORD our God.'

7,8   Within ten days the word of the LORD came to Jeremiah; so he summoned Johanan son of Kareah, all the captains of the armed bands

9 with him, and all the people, both high and low. He said to them, These are the words of the LORD the God of Israel, to whom you sent me to

10 present your petition: If you will stay in this land, then I will build you up and not pull you down, I will plant you and not uproot you; I grieve

11 for the disaster which I have brought upon you. Do not be afraid of the king of Babylon whom you now fear. Do not be afraid of him, says the LORD; for I am with you, to save you and deliver you from his power.

12 I will show you compassion, and he too will have compassion on you;

13 he will let you stay on your own soil. But it may be that you will disobey

14 the LORD your God and say, 'We will not stay in this land. No, we will go to Egypt, where we shall see no sign of war, never hear the sound of the trumpet, and not starve for want of bread; and there we will live.'

15 Then hear the word of the LORD, you remnant of Judah. These are the words of the LORD of Hosts the God of Israel: If you are bent on going

16 to Egypt, if you do settle there, then the sword you fear will overtake you in Egypt, and the famine you dread will still be with you, even in

17 Egypt, and there you will die. All the men who are bent on going to Egypt and settling there will die by sword, by famine, or by pestilence; not one shall escape or survive the calamity which I will bring upon

18 them. These are the words of the LORD of Hosts the God of Israel: As my anger and my wrath were poured out upon the inhabitants of Jerusalem, so will my wrath be poured out upon you when you go to Egypt; you will become an object of execration and horror, of ridicule

19 and reproach; you will never see this place again. To you, then, remnant of Judah, the LORD says, Do not go to Egypt. Make no mistake,

20 I can bear witness against you this day. You deceived yourselves when you sent me to the LORD your God and said, 'Pray for us to the LORD our God; tell us all that the LORD our God says and we will do it.'

21 I have told you everything today; but you have not obeyed the LORD

22 your God in what he sent me to tell you. So now be sure of this: you will die by sword, by famine, and by pestilence in the place where you desire to go and make your home.

43   When Jeremiah had finished reciting to the people all that the LORD

2 their God had sent him to say, Azariah son of Hoshaiah and Johanan son of Kareah and their party had the effrontery to say to*a* Jeremiah,

[*a*] to say to: *or* to say: It is being said to.

1134

'You are lying; the LORD our God has not sent you to forbid us to go
and make our home in Egypt. Baruch son of Neriah has incited you 3
against us in order to put us in the power of the Chaldaeans, so that they
may kill us or deport us to Babylon.' Johanan son of Kareah and the 4
captains of the armed bands and all the people refused to obey the LORD
and stay in Judah. So Johanan son of Kareah and the captains collected 5
the remnant of Judah, all who had returned from the countries among
which they had been scattered to make their home in Judah—men, 6
women and children, including the king's daughters, all the people
whom Nebuzaradan captain of the guard had left with Gedaliah son of
Ahikam, son of Shaphan, as well as the prophet Jeremiah and Baruch
son of Neriah; these all went to Egypt and came to Tahpanhes, dis- 7
obeying the LORD.

The word of the LORD came to Jeremiah at Tahpanhes: Take some 8,9
large stones and set them in cement in the pavement at the entrance to
Pharaoh's palace in Tahpanhes. Let the Judaeans see you do it and say 10
to them, These are the words of the LORD of Hosts the God of Israel:
I will send for my servant Nebuchadrezzar king of Babylon, and he[a]
will place his throne on these stones that I have set there, and spread
his canopy over them. He will then proceed to strike Egypt down, 11
killing those doomed to death, taking captive those who are for captivity, and putting to the sword those who are for the sword. He[a] will 12
set fire to the temples of the Egyptian gods, burning the buildings and
carrying the gods into captivity. He will scour the land of Egypt as a
shepherd scours his clothes to rid them of lice. He will leave Egypt with
his purpose achieved. He will smash the sacred pillars of Beth- 13
shemesh[b] in Egypt and burn down the temples of the Egyptian gods.

The word that came to Jeremiah for all the Judaeans who were living **44**
in Egypt, in Migdol, Tahpanhes, Noph, and the district of Pathros:
These are the words of the LORD of Hosts the God of Israel: You have 2
seen the calamity that I brought upon Jerusalem and all the cities of
Judah: today they are laid waste and left uninhabited, all because of the 3
wickedness of those who provoked me to anger by going after other
gods, gods unknown to them, by burning sacrifices to them.[c] It was you
and your fathers who did this. I took pains to send all my servants the 4
prophets to you with this warning: 'Do not do this abominable thing
which I hate.' But your fathers would not listen; they paid no heed. 5
They did not give up their wickedness or cease to burn sacrifices to
other gods; so my anger and wrath raged like a fire through the cities 6
of Judah and the streets of Jerusalem, and they became the desolate
ruin that they are today.

Now these are the words of the LORD the God of Hosts, the God of 7

[a] *So Sept.; Heb.* I. [b] Heliopolis *in Sept.* [c] *So Sept.; Heb. adds* to worship.

Israel: Why bring so great a disaster upon yourselves? Why bring destruction upon Judaeans, men and women, children and babes, and
8 leave yourselves without a survivor? This is what comes of your provoking me by all your idolatry in burning sacrifices to other gods in Egypt where you have made your home. You will destroy yourselves and become an object of ridicule and reproach to all the nations of the
9 earth. Have you forgotten all the wickedness committed by your forefathers, by the kings of Judah and their wives, by yourselves and your
10 wives in the land of Judah and in the streets of Jerusalem? To this day you*[a]* have shown no remorse, no reverence; you have not conformed to the law and the statutes which I set before you and your forefathers.
11 These, therefore, are the words of the LORD of Hosts the God of Israel: I have made up my mind to bring calamity upon you and exterminate
12 the people of Judah. I will deal with the remnant of Judah who were bent on going to make their home in Egypt; in Egypt they shall all meet their end. Some shall fall by the sword, others will meet their end by famine. High and low alike will die by sword or by famine and will
13 be an object of execration and horror, of ridicule and reproach. I will punish those who live in Egypt as I punished those in Jerusalem, by
14 sword, famine, and pestilence. Those who had remained in Judah came to make their home in Egypt, confident that they would return and live once more in Judah. But they shall not return;*[b]* not one of them shall survive, not one escape.
15   Then all the men who knew that their wives were burning sacrifices to other gods and the crowds of women standing by*[c]* answered Jeremiah,
16, 17 'We will not listen to what you tell us in the name of the LORD. We intend to fulfil all the promises by which we have bound ourselves: we will burn sacrifices to the queen of heaven and pour drink-offerings to her as we used to do, we and our fathers, our kings and our princes, in the cities of Judah and in the streets of Jerusalem. We then had food in
18 plenty and were content; no calamity touched us. But from the time we left off burning sacrifices to the queen of heaven and pouring drink-offerings to her, we have been in great want, and in the end we have
19 fallen victims to sword and famine.' And the women said,*[d]* 'When we burnt sacrifices to the queen of heaven and poured drink-offerings to her, our husbands knew full well that we were making crescent-cakes
20 marked with her image and pouring drink-offerings to her.' When Jeremiah received this answer from these men and women and all the
21 people, he said, 'The LORD did not forget those sacrifices which you and your fathers, your kings and princes and the people of the land burnt in the cities of Judah and in the streets of Jerusalem, and they

[a] *Lit.* they. [b] *Prob. rdg.; Heb. adds* except fugitives. [c] *Prob. rdg.; Heb. adds* and all the people who lived in Egypt, in Pathros. [d] And the women said: *so Luc. Sept.; Heb. om.*

mounted up in his mind until he could no longer tolerate them, so 22
wicked were your deeds and so abominable the things you did. Your
land became a desolate waste, an object of horror and ridicule, with no
inhabitants, as it still is. This calamity has come upon you because you 23
burnt these sacrifices and sinned against the LORD and did not obey the
LORD or conform to his laws, statutes, and teachings.'*a*

Jeremiah further said to all the people and to the women, Listen to 24
the word of the LORD, all you from Judah who live in Egypt. These are 25
the words of the LORD of Hosts the God of Israel: You women*b* have
made your actions match your words. 'We will carry out our vows', you
said, 'to burn sacrifices to the queen of heaven and to pour drink-
offerings to her.' Well then, fulfil your vows by all means, and make
your words good. But listen to the word of the LORD, all you from 26
Judah who live in Egypt. I have sworn by my great name, says the
LORD, that my name shall never again be on the lips of the men of
Judah; they shall no longer swear in Egypt, 'By the life of the Lord
GOD.' I am on the watch to bring you evil and not good, and all the men 27
of Judah who are in Egypt shall meet their end by sword and by famine
until not one is left.*c* It is then that all the survivors of Judah who have 28
made their home in Egypt shall know whose word prevails, theirs or
mine.

This is the sign I give you, says the LORD, that I intend to punish 29
you in this place, so that you may learn that my words against you will
prevail to bring evil upon you: These are the words of the LORD: I will 30
hand over Pharaoh Hophra king of Egypt to his enemies and to those
who seek his life, just as I handed over Zedekiah king of Judah to his
enemy Nebuchadrezzar king of Babylon who was seeking to take his life.

THE WORD WHICH THE PROPHET JEREMIAH SPOKE to Baruch 45
son of Neriah when he wrote these words in a book at Jeremiah's
dictation in the fourth year of Jehoiakim son of Josiah, king of Judah:
These are the words of the LORD the God of Israel concerning you, 2
Baruch: You said, 'Woe is me, for the LORD has added grief to all my 3
trials. I have worn myself out with my labours and have had no respite.'
This is what you shall say to Baruch, These are the words of the LORD: 4
What I have built, I demolish; what I have planted, I uproot. So it will
be with the whole earth. You seek great things for yourself. Leave off 5
seeking them; for I will bring disaster upon all mankind, says the LORD,
and I will let you live wherever you go, but you shall save your life and
nothing more.*d*

[a] *So Sept.; Heb. adds* as at this day.   [b] You women: *so Sept.; Heb.* You and your wives.
[c] *Prob. rdg.; Heb. adds* Few will escape the sword in Egypt to return to Judah.   [d] *See
note on 21. 9.*

Prophecies against the nations

46 THIS CAME TO THE PROPHET JEREMIAH as the word of the
LORD concerning the nations.

2 Of Egypt: concerning the army of Pharaoh Necho king of Egypt at
Carchemish on the river Euphrates, which Nebuchadrezzar king of
Babylon defeated in the fourth year of Jehoiakim son of Josiah, king of
Judah.

3   Hold shield and buckler ready
       and advance to battle;
4 harness the horses, let the riders mount;
    form up, your helmets on, your lances burnished;
       on with your coats of mail!
5   But now, what sight is this?
    They are broken and routed,
       their warriors beaten down;
    they have turned to flight and do not look behind them.
       Terror let loose!
       This is the very word of the LORD.
6 Can the swift escape, can the warrior save himself?
       In the north, by the river Euphrates,
          they stumble and fall.
7   Who is this rising like the Nile,
       like its streams turbulent in flood?
8   Egypt is rising like the Nile,
       like its streams turbulent in flood.

   He*a* says:

       I will rise and cover the earth,
       I will destroy both city and people.
9 Charge, horsemen! On, you flashing chariots, on!
       Forward, the warriors,
    Cushites and men of Put carrying shields,
    Lydians grasping their bent bows!
10 This is the day of the Lord, the GOD of Hosts,
       a day of vengeance, vengeance on his enemies;
    the sword shall devour and be sated,
       drunk with their blood.

[a] *Or* It.

For the GOD of Hosts, the Lord, holds sacrifice
　　in a northern land, by the river Euphrates.
Go up into Gilead and fetch balm,　　　　　　　　　11
　　O virgin people of Egypt.
You have tried many remedies, all in vain;
　　no skin shall grow over your wounds.
The nations have heard your cry,[a]　　　　　　　　12
and the earth echoes with your screams;
　　warrior stumbles against warrior
　　and both fall together.

The word which the LORD spoke to the prophet Jeremiah when 13
Nebuchadrezzar king of Babylon was coming to harry the land of
Egypt:

Announce it in Egypt, proclaim it in Migdol,　　　　　14
　　proclaim it in Noph and Tahpanhes.
Say, Stand to! Be ready!
　　for a sword devours all around you.
Why does Apis flee, why does your bull-god not[b] stand fast?　　15
　　The LORD has thrust him out.
The rabble of Egypt stumbles and falls,　　　　　　16
　　man against man;
each says, 'Quick, back to our people,
to the land of our birth, far from the cruel sword!'
Give Pharaoh of Egypt the title King Bombast,　　　17
　　the man who missed his moment.
By my life, says the King　　　　　　　　　　　18
whose name is the LORD of Hosts,
one shall come mighty as Tabor among the hills,
　　as Carmel by the sea.
Make ready your baggage for exile,　　　　　　　19
　　you native people of Egypt;
for Noph shall become a waste,
　　ruined and unpeopled.

Egypt was a lovely heifer,　　　　　　　　　　20
but a gadfly from the north descended on her.[c]
The mercenaries in her land were like stall-fed calves;　　21
but they too turned and fled,
　　not one of them stood his ground.
The hour of their downfall has come upon them,
　　their day of reckoning.

[a] your cry: *so Sept.; Heb.* your shame.　[b] Why does Apis...not: *or* Why is your bull-
god routed, why does he not...　[c] on her: *so many MSS.; others obscure in context.*

22   Hark, she is hissing^a like a snake,
         for the enemy has come in all his force.
      They fall upon her with axes
         like woodcutters at their work.
23   They cut down her forest, says the LORD,
         and it flaunts itself no more;
      for they are many as locusts and past counting.
24   The Egyptians are put to shame, enslaved to a northern race.
25   The LORD of Hosts the God of Israel has spoken:
         I will punish Amon god of No,^b
      Egypt with her gods and her princes,
      Pharaoh and all who trust in him.
26   I will deliver them to those bent on their destruction,
         to Nebuchadrezzar king of Babylon and his troops;
         yet in after time the land shall be peopled as of old.
            This is the very word of the LORD.

27   But you, Jacob my servant, have no fear,
         despair not, O Israel;
      for I will bring you back safe from afar
         and your offspring from the land where they are captives;
      and Jacob shall be at rest once more,
         prosperous and unafraid.
28   O Jacob my servant, have no fear,
      says the LORD; for I am with you.
         I will make an end of all the nations
            amongst whom I have banished you;
         but I will not make an end of you;
            though I punish you as you deserve,
            I will not sweep you clean away.

47   This came to the prophet Jeremiah as the word of the LORD con-
  2   cerning the Philistines before Pharaoh's harrying of Gaza: The LORD
      has spoken:

         See how waters are rising from the north
         and swelling to a torrent in spate,
            flooding the land and all that is in it,
               cities and all who live in them.
               Men shall shriek in alarm
            and all who live in the land shall howl.
  3   Hark, the pounding of his chargers' hooves,
            the rattle of his chariots and their rumbling wheels!
         Fathers spare no thought for their children;

[a] Hark...hissing: *so Sept.; Heb. obscure.*   [b] *Prob. rdg.; Heb. adds* and Pharaoh.

their hands hang powerless,
because the day is upon them when Philistia will be despoiled,   4
and Tyre and Sidon destroyed to the last defender;
  for the LORD will despoil the Philistines,
    that remnant of the isle of Caphtor.
Gaza is shorn bare, Ashkelon ruined.   5
  Poor remnant of their strength,
  how long will you gash yourselves*a* and cry:
Ah, sword in the hand of the LORD,   6
  how long will it be before you rest?
Sheathe yourself, rest and be quiet.
How can it*b* rest? for the LORD has given it work to do   7
  against Ashkelon and the plain by the sea;
  there he has assigned the sword its task.

Of Moab. The LORD of Hosts the God of Israel has spoken: **48**

  Alas for Nebo! it is laid waste;
  Kiriathaim is put to shame and captured,
  Misgab reduced to shame and dismay;
  Moab is renowned no longer.   2
In Heshbon they plot evil against her:
  Come, destroy her, and leave her no longer a nation.
  And you who live in Madmen shall be struck down,
  your people pursued by the sword.
  Hark to the cries of anguish from Horonaim: 3
great havoc and disaster!
  Moab is broken.   4
Their cries are heard as far as Zoar.
  On the ascent of Luhith   5
  men go up weeping bitterly;
  on the descent of Horonaim
cries of 'Disaster!' are heard.
Flee, flee for your lives   6
like a sand-grouse in the wilderness.
Because you have trusted in your defences and your arsenals,   7
  you too will be captured,
and Kemosh will go into exile,
his priests and his captains with him;
and a spoiler shall descend on every city.   8
  No city shall escape,
valley and tableland will be laid waste and plundered;
  the LORD has spoken.

[a] gash yourselves: *or, with Scroll,* roll about.   [b] *So Sept.; Heb.* you.

9   Let a warning flash to Moab,[a]
      for she shall be laid in ruins[b]
      and her cities shall become waste places
         with no inhabitant.

10   A curse on him who is slack in doing the LORD's work!
      A curse on him who withholds his sword from bloodshed!

11   All his life long, Moab has lain undisturbed
      like wine settled on its lees,
      not emptied from vessel to vessel;
         he has not gone into exile.
      Therefore the taste of him is unaltered,
         and the flavour stays unchanged.

12   Therefore the days are coming, says the LORD,
      when I will send men to tilt the jars; they shall tilt them
      and empty his vessels and smash his jars;

13   and Moab shall be betrayed by Kemosh,
      as Israel was betrayed by Bethel,
         a god in whom he trusted.

14   How can you say, 'We are warriors
      and men valiant in battle'?

15   The spoiler of Moab and her cities has come up,
      and the flower of her army goes down to the slaughter.

    This is the very word of the King whose name is the LORD of Hosts.

16   The downfall of Moab is near at hand,
      disaster rushes swiftly upon him.

17   Grieve for him, all you his neighbours
      and all you who acknowledge him,
      and say, 'Alas! The commander's staff is broken,
         broken is the baton of honour.'

18   Come down from your place of honour,
    sit on the thirsty ground, you natives of Dibon;
    for the spoiler of Moab has come upon you
      and destroyed your citadels.

19   You that live in Aroer, stand on the roadside and watch,
      ask the fugitives, the man running, the woman escaping,
         ask them, 'What has happened?'

20   Moab is reduced to shame and dismay:
         howl and shriek,
    proclaim by the Arnon that Moab is despoiled,

[a] Let...Moab: *or* Doom Moab to become saltings. [b] laid in ruins: *prob. rdg.; Heb. obscure.*

and that judgement has come to the tableland, to Holon and Jahazah, 21
Mephaath and Dibon, Nebo and Beth-diblathaim and Kiriathaim, 22, 23
Beth-gamul, Beth-meon, Kirioth and Bozrah, and to all the cities of 24
Moab far and near.

> Moab's horn is hacked off   25
>   and his strong arm is broken,
>   says the LORD.

> Make Moab drunk—he has defied the LORD—   26
> until he overflows with his vomit
> and even he becomes a butt for derision.
> But was Israel ever your butt?   27
>   Was he ever in company with thieves,
> that whenever you spoke of him you should shake your head?
> Leave your cities, you inhabitants of Moab,   28
>   and find a home among the crags;
>   become like a dove which nests
>   in the rock-face at the mouth of a cavern.

> We have heard of Moab's pride, and proud indeed he is,   29
> proud, presumptuous, overbearing, insolent.
> I know his arrogance, says the LORD;   30
> his boasting is false, false are his deeds.
>   Therefore I will howl over Moab   31
>   and cry in anguish at the fate of every soul in Moab;
>   I[a] will moan over the men of Kir-heres.
> I will weep for you more than I wept for Jazer,   32
>   O vine of Sibmah
> whose branches spread out to the sea
>   and stretch as far as Jazer.[b]
> The despoiler has fallen on your fruit and on your vintage,
>   gladness and joy are taken away   33
>   from the meadows of Moab,
>   and I have stopped the flow of wine from the vats;
> nor shall shout follow shout from the harvesters—not one shout.

Heshbon and[c] Elealeh utter cries of anguish which are heard in Jahaz; 34
the sound carries from Zoar to Horonaim and[d] Eglath-shelishiyah; for
the waters of Nimrim have become a desolate waste. In Moab I will 35
stop their sacrificing at hill-shrines and burning of offerings to their
gods, says the LORD. Therefore my heart wails for Moab like a reed- 36
pipe, wails like a pipe for the men of Kir-heres. Their hard-earned

---

[a] *So one MS.; others* he.   [b] *as far as* Jazer: *so some MSS., cp. Isa. 16. 8; others* the sea
of Jazer.   [c] *and: prob. rdg., cp. Isa. 15. 4; Heb.* as far as.   [d] *and: so Sept.; Heb. om.*

37 wealth has vanished. Every man's head is shorn in mourning, every
beard shaved, every hand gashed, and every waist girded with sack-
38 cloth. On Moab's roofs and in her broad streets nothing is heard but
39 lamentation; for I have broken Moab like a useless thing.*a* Moab in her
dismay*b* has shamefully turned to flight. Moab has become a butt of
derision and a cause of dismay to all her neighbours.
40 For the LORD has spoken:

> A vulture shall swoop down
>   and spread out his wings over Moab.
41 The towns are captured, the strongholds taken;
>   on that day the spirit of Moab's warriors shall fail
>   like the spirit of a woman in childbirth.
42 Then Moab shall be destroyed, no more to be a nation;
>   for he defied the LORD.
43 The hunter's scare, the pit, and the trap
>   threaten all who dwell in Moab,
>   says the LORD.
44 If a man runs from the scare
>   he will fall into the pit;
>   if he climbs out of the pit
>   he will be caught in the trap.
> All this will I bring on Moab in the year of their reckoning.
>   This is the very word of the LORD.

45 In the shadow of Heshbon the fugitives stand helpless;
>   for fire has blazed out from Heshbon,
>   flames have shot out from the palace of*c* Sihon;
>   they devour the homeland of Moab
>   and the country*d* of the sons of tumult.
46 Alas for you, Moab! the people of Kemosh have vanished,
>   for your sons are taken into captivity
>   and your daughters led away captive.
47 Yet in days to come I will restore Moab's fortunes.
>   This is the very word of the LORD.

Here ends the sentence on Moab.

49 Of the people of Ammon. Thus says the LORD:

> Has Israel no sons? Has he no heir?
> Why has Milcom inherited the land of Gad,
>   and why do his people live in the cities of Gad?

---

[a] *Prob. rdg.; Heb. adds* says the LORD. [b] *So Sept.; Heb. adds* they howl. [c] *from the palace of: so some MSS.; others* from between. [d] *So some MSS.; others* crown (of head).

Look, therefore, a time is coming,   2
    says the LORD,
when I will make Rabbath Ammon hear the battle-cry,
    when it will become a desolate mound of ruins
  and its villages will be burnt to ashes,
  and Israel shall disinherit those who disinherited him,
    says the LORD.

Howl, Heshbon, for Ai is despoiled.   3
    Cry aloud, you villages round Rabbath Ammon,
  put on sackcloth and beat your breast,
  and score your bodies with gashes.[a]
For Milcom will go into exile,
  and with him his priests and officers.
Why do you boast of your resources,   4
    you whose resources are melting away,
you wayward people who trust in your arsenals,
  and say, 'Who will dare attack me?'
Beware, I am bringing fear upon you from every side,[b]   5
  and every one of you shall be driven headlong
    with no man to round up the stragglers.
Yet after this I will restore the fortunes of Ammon.   6
    This is the very word of the LORD.

Of Edom. The LORD of Hosts has said: 7

Is wisdom no longer to be found in Teman?
Have her sages no skill in counsel?
    Has their wisdom decayed?
The people of Dedan have turned and fled   8
  and taken refuge in remote places;
for I will bring Esau's calamity upon him
  when his day of reckoning comes.
When the vintagers come to you   9[c]
  they will surely leave gleanings;
and if thieves raid your early crop in the night,
  they will take only as much as they want.
But I have ransacked Esau's treasure,   10
  I have uncovered his hiding-places,
  and he has nowhere to conceal himself;
his children, his kinsfolk and his neighbours are despoiled;
  there is no one to help him.

---

[a] *Prob. rdg., cp. Targ.; Heb.* fences.   [b] *Prob. rdg.; Heb. adds* says the Lord GOD *of*
Hosts.   [c] *Verses 9 and 10: cp. Obad. 5, 6.*

11   What! am I to save alive your fatherless children?
        Are your widows to trust in me?

12   For the LORD has spoken: Those who were not doomed to drink the
        cup shall drink it none the less. Are you alone to go unpunished? You
13   shall not go unpunished; you shall drink it. For by my life, says the
        LORD, Bozrah shall become a horror and reproach, a byword and a
        thing of ridicule; and all her towns shall be a byword for ever.

14*a*   When a herald was sent among the nations, crying,
        'Gather together and march against her,
            rouse yourselves for battle',
        I heard this message from the LORD:

15   Look, I make you the least of all nations,
            an object of all men's contempt.

16   Your overbearing arrogance and your insolent heart
            have led you astray,
        you who haunt the crannies among the rocks
        and keep your hold on the heights of the hills.
        Though you build your nest high as a vulture,
            thence I will bring you down.
        This is the very word of the LORD.

17   Edom shall become a scene of horror,
        all who pass that way shall be horror-struck
        and shall jeer in derision at the blows she has borne,

18   overthrown like Sodom and Gomorrah and their neighbours,*b*
            says the LORD.
        No man shall live there,
        no mortal make a home in her.

19   Look, like a lion coming up
        from Jordan's dense thickets to the perennial pastures,
        in a moment I will chase every one away
        and round up the choicest of*c* her rams.
        For who is like me? Who is my equal?
        What shepherd can stand his ground before me?

20   Therefore listen to the LORD's whole purpose against Edom and all
        his plans against the people of Teman:

        The young ones of the flock shall be carried off,
        and their pasture shall be horrified at their fate.

21   At the sound of their fall the land quakes;
        it cries out, and the cry is heard at the Red Sea.*d*

[a] *Verses 14–16: cp. Obad. 1–4.*   [b] *Or* inhabitants.   [c] the choicest of: *prob. rdg.; Heb.*
who is chosen?   [d] *Or* the Sea of Reeds.

A vulture shall soar and swoop down   22
    and spread out his wings over Bozrah,
and on that day the spirit of Edom's warriors shall fail
    like the spirit of a woman in labour.

Of Damascus.   23

Hamath and Arpad are in confusion,
    for they have heard news of disaster;
they are tossed up and down in anxiety
    like the unresting sea.
Damascus has lost heart and turns to flight;   24
    trembling has seized her,
the pangs of childbirth have gripped her.
    How forlorn is the town of joyful song,   25
    the city of gladness*a*!
Therefore her young men shall fall in her streets   26
and all her warriors lie still in death that day.
    This is the very word of the LORD of Hosts.
Then will I kindle a fire against the wall of Damascus   27
    and it shall consume the palaces of Ben-hadad.

Of Kedar and the royal princes*b* of Hazer which Nebuchadrezzar   28
king of Babylon subdued. The LORD has said:

Come, attack Kedar,
    despoil the Arabs of the east.
Carry off their tents and their flocks,   29
    their tent-hangings and all their vessels,
    drive off their camels too,
and a cry shall go up: 'Terror let loose!'
    Flee, flee; make haste,   30
take refuge in remote places, O people of Hazer,
for the king of Babylon*c* has laid his plans
and formed a design against you,
    says the LORD.
Come, let us attack a nation living at peace,   31
    in fancied security,*d*
with neither gates nor bars,
    sufficient to themselves.
Their camels shall be carried off as booty,   32
    their vast herds of cattle as plunder;

[a] *So Pesh.; Heb.* of my gladness. [b] royal princes: *or* kingdom. [c] *So Sept.; Heb. adds*
Nebuchadrezzar. [d] *So Sept.; Heb. adds* says the LORD.

I will scatter them before the wind to roam the fringes of the
    desert,[a]
and bring ruin upon them from every side.

33   Hazer shall become a haunt of wolves,
      for ever desolate;
no man shall live there,
no mortal make a home in her.
    This is the very word of the LORD.

34   This came to the prophet Jeremiah as the word of the LORD concerning Elam, at the beginning of the reign of Zedekiah king of Judah:
35 Thus says the LORD of Hosts:

Listen, I will break the bow of Elam,
    the chief weapon of their might;
36   I will bring four winds against Elam
    from the four quarters of heaven;
I will scatter them before these four winds,
    and there shall be no nation
to which the exiles from Elam shall not come.
37   I will break Elam before their foes,
    before those who are bent on their destruction;
I will vent my anger upon them in disaster;[b]
I will harry them with the sword
    until I make an end of them.
38   Then I will set my throne in Elam,
and there I will destroy the king and his officers.
    This is the very word of the LORD.
39   Yet in days to come I will restore the fortunes of Elam.
    This is the very word of the LORD.

50   The word which the LORD spoke concerning Babylon, concerning the
land of the Chaldaeans, through the prophet Jeremiah:

2   Declare and proclaim among the nations,[c]
keep nothing back, spread the news:
    Babylon is taken,
Bel is put to shame, Marduk is in despair;
    the idols of Babylon are put to shame,
    her false gods are in despair.
3   For a nation out of the north has fallen upon her;

[a] them...desert: *or* to the wind those who clip the hair on their temples.   [b] *So Sept.;
Heb. adds* says the LORD.   [c] *So Sept.; Heb. adds* and raise a standard, proclaim.

they will make her land a desolate waste
where neither man nor beast shall live.[a]

In those days, at that time, says the LORD, the people of Israel and 4
the people of Judah shall come together and go in tears to seek the
LORD their God; they shall ask after Zion, turning their faces towards 5
her, and they shall come and join[b] themselves to the LORD in an everlasting covenant which shall not be forgotten.

My people were lost sheep, whose shepherds let them stray and run 6
wild on the mountains; they went from mountain to hill and forgot
their fold. Whoever found them devoured them, and their enemies 7
said, 'We incur no guilt, because they have sinned against the LORD,
the LORD who is the true goal and the hope of all their fathers.'

Flee from Babylon, from the land of the Chaldaeans;   8
go forth, and be like he-goats leading the flock.
For I will stir up a host of mighty nations   9
    and bring them against Babylon,
    marshalled against her from a northern land;
    and from the north she shall be captured.
    Their arrows shall be like a practised warrior
    who never comes back empty-handed;
    the Chaldaeans shall be plundered,   10
and all who plunder them shall take their fill.
    This is the very word of the LORD.
You ravaged my patrimony; but though you rejoice and exult,   11
    though you run free like a heifer after threshing,
    though you neigh like a stallion,
your mother shall be cruelly disgraced,   12
    she who bore you shall be put to shame.
    Look at her, the mere rump of the nations,
    a wilderness, parched and desert,
unpeopled through the wrath of the LORD,   13
nothing but a desolate waste;
all who pass by Babylon shall be horror-struck
    and jeer in derision at the sight of her wounds.

Marshal your forces against Babylon, on every side,   14
    you whose bows are ready strung;
shoot at her, spare no arrows.[c]
Shout in triumph over her,[d] she has thrown up her hands,   15

[a] *So Sept.; Heb. adds* they have fled, they have gone.   [b] and they shall come and join: *so
one MS.; others* come, and they shall join.   [c] *So Sept.; Heb. adds* for she has sinned against
the LORD.   [d] *So Sept.; Heb. adds* around her.

her bastions are down, her walls demolished;
  this is the vengeance of the LORD.
    Take vengeance on her;
    as she has done, so do to her.

16   Destroy every sower in Babylon,
    every reaper with his sickle at harvest-time.
  Before the cruel sword every man will go back to his people,
  every man flee to his own land.

17   Israel is a scattered flock
    harried and chased by lions:
    as the king of Assyria was the first to feed on him,
    so the king of Babylon*ᵃ* was the last to gnaw his bones.

18 Therefore the LORD of Hosts the God of Israel says this:

    I will punish the king of Babylon and his country
    as I have punished the king of Assyria.
19   I will bring Israel back to his pasture,
    and he shall graze on Carmel and Bashan;
  in the hills of Ephraim and Gilead he shall eat his fill.

20 In those days, says the LORD, when that time comes, search shall be
made for the iniquity of Israel but there shall be none, and for the sin
of Judah but it shall not be found; for those whom I leave as a remnant
I will forgive.

21   Attack the land of Merathaim;
    attack it and the inhabitants of Pekod;
    put all to the sword and destroy them,*ᵇ*
    and do whatever I bid you.
    This is the very word of the LORD.

22   Hark, the sound of war in the land
    and great destruction!
23   See how the hammer of all the earth
    is hacked and broken in pieces,
    how Babylon has become
    a horror among the nations.
24   O Babylon, you have laid a snare to be your own undoing;
    you have been trapped, all unawares;
    there you are, you are caught,
    because you have challenged the LORD.
25   The LORD has opened his arsenal
    and brought out the weapons of his wrath;

---

[a] *So Sept.; Heb. adds* Nebuchadrezzar. [b] them: *prob. rdg., cp. Pesh.; Heb.* after them.

for this is work for the Lord the GOD of Hosts
   in the land of the Chaldaeans.
   Her harvest-time has come:[a]   26
throw open her granaries,[b] pile her in heaps;[c]
destroy her, let no survivor be left.
   Put all her warriors[d] to the sword;   27
   let them be led to the slaughter.
Woe upon them! for their time has come,
   their day of reckoning.
I hear the fugitives escaping from the land of Babylon   28
to proclaim in Zion the vengeance of the LORD our God.[e]

   Let your arrows be heard whistling against Babylon,   29
     all you whose bows are ready strung.
   Pitch your tents all around her
     so that no one escapes.
   Pay her back for all her misdeeds;
     as she has done, so do to her,
for she has insulted the LORD the Holy One of Israel.
Therefore her young men shall fall in her streets,   30
and all her warriors shall lie still in death that day.
   This is the very word of the LORD.

   I am against you, insolent city;   31
for your time has come, your day of reckoning.
   This is the very word of the Lord GOD of Hosts.
   Insolence shall stumble and fall   32
     and no one shall lift her up,
   and I will kindle fire in the heath[f] around her
     and it shall consume everything round about.

The LORD of Hosts has said this: 33

The peoples of Israel and Judah together are oppressed;
   their captors hold them firmly and refuse to release them.
   But they have a powerful advocate,   34
     whose name is the LORD of Hosts;
     he himself will plead their cause,
bringing distress on Babylon and turmoil on its people.

   A sword hangs over the Chaldaeans,   35
over the people of Babylon, her officers and her wise men,
   says the LORD.

[a] Her...come: *prob. rdg., cp. Sept.; Heb.* Enter her from every side.   [b] *Or* cattle-pens.
[c] in heaps: *or, with Targ.*, like men piling up corn.   [d] *Lit.* her bulls.   [e] *So Sept.;*
Heb. adds vengeance for his temple.   [f] heath: *so Sept.; Heb.* cities.

36   A sword over the false prophets, and they are made fools,
        a sword over her warriors, and they despair,
37   a sword over her horses and her chariots
        and over all the rabble within her,
        and they shall become like women;
        a sword over her treasures, and they shall be plundered,
38   a sword over her waters, and they shall dry up;
        for it is a land of idols
        that glories in its dreaded gods.*a*

39   Therefore marmots and jackals shall skulk in it, desert-owls shall haunt
     it, nevermore shall it be inhabited by men and no one shall dwell in it
40   through all the ages. As when God overthrew Sodom and Gomorrah
     and their neighbours,*b* says the LORD, no man shall live there, no mortal
     make a home in her.

41   See, a people is coming from the north, a great nation,
        mighty*c* kings rouse themselves from earth's farthest corners;
42   armed with bow and sabre, they are cruel and pitiless;
        bestriding horses, they sound like the thunder of the sea;
        they are like men arrayed for battle against you, Babylon.
43   The king of Babylon has heard news of them
        and his hands hang limp;
        agony grips him, anguish as of a woman in labour.
44   Look, like a lion coming up
        from Jordan's dense thickets to the perennial pastures,
        in a moment I will chase every one away
        and round up the choicest of*d* the rams.
        For who is like me? Who is my equal?
     What shepherd can stand his ground before me?

45   Therefore listen to the LORD's whole purpose against Babylon and all
     his plans against the land of the Chaldaeans:

        The young ones of the flock shall be carried off
        and their pasture shall be horrified at their fate.
46   At the sound of the capture of Babylon
        the land quakes and her cry is heard among the nations.

51   For thus says the LORD:

     I will raise a destroying wind
        against Babylon and those who live in Kambul,*e*
2   and I will send winnowers to Babylon,

[*a*] dreaded gods: *or* dire portents.   [*b*] *Or* inhabitants.   [*c*] *Or* many.   [*d*] the choicest of:
prob. rdg.; Heb. who is chosen?   [*e*] Kambul: *prob. rdg.; Heb.* the heart of my opponents.

1152

who shall winnow her and empty her land;
for they shall assail her on all sides on the day of disaster.
    How shall the archer then string his bow   3
        or put on his coat of mail?

Spare none of her young men, destroy all her host,
    and let them fall dead in the land of the Chaldaeans,   4
    pierced through in her streets.
Israel and Judah are not left widowed   5
    by their God, by the LORD of Hosts;
    but the land of the Chaldaeans is full of guilt,
    condemned by the Holy One of Israel.

Flee out of Babylon, every man for himself,   6
    or you will be struck down for her sin;
    for this is the LORD's day of vengeance,
    and he is paying her full recompense.
Babylon has been a gold cup in the LORD's hand   7
    to make all the earth drunk;
    the nations have drunk of her wine,
    and that has made them mad.
Babylon falls suddenly and is broken.   8
    Howl over her,
    fetch balm for her wound;
        perhaps she will be healed.
We would have healed Babylon, but she would not be[a] healed.   9
Leave her and let us be off, each to his own country;
    for her doom reaches to heaven
    and mounts up to the skies.
    The LORD has made our innocence plain to see;   10
    come, let us proclaim in Zion
    what the LORD our God has done.

Sharpen the arrows, fill the quivers.   11
The LORD has roused the spirit of the king[b] of the Medes;
    for the LORD's purpose against Babylon is to destroy it,
    and his vengeance is the avenging of his temple.
    Raise the standard against Babylon's walls,   12
mount a strong guard, post a watch, set an ambush;
for the LORD has both planned and carried out
what he threatened to do to the people of Babylon.
O opulent city, standing beside great waters,   13
your end has come, your destiny[c] is certain.

[a] would not be: *or* was not.   [b] *So Sept.; Heb.* kings.   [c] destiny: *lit.* cutting off (the thread of life).

14 The LORD of Hosts has sworn by himself, saying,
Once I filled you with men, countless as locusts,
yet a song of triumph shall be chanted over you.

15[a] God made the earth by his power,
fixed the world in place by his wisdom,
unfurled the skies by his understanding.

16 At the thunder of his voice the waters in heaven are amazed;[b]
he brings up the mist from the ends of the earth,
he opens rifts[c] for the rain
and brings the wind out of his storehouses.

17 All men are brutish and ignorant,
every goldsmith is discredited by his idol;
for the figures he casts are a sham,
there is no breath in them.

18 They are worth nothing, mere mockeries,
which perish when their day of reckoning comes.

19 God, Jacob's creator, is not like these;
for he is the maker of all.
Israel[d] is the people he claims as his own;
the LORD of Hosts is his name.

20 You are my battle-axe, my weapon of war;
with you I will break nations in pieces,
and with you I will destroy kingdoms.

21 With you I will break horse and rider,
with you I will break chariot and rider,

22 with you I will break man and woman,
with you I will break young and old,
with you I will break young man and maiden,

23 with you I will break shepherd and flock,
with you I will break ploughman and team,
with you I will break viceroys and governors.

24 So will I repay Babylon and the people of Chaldaea
for all the wrong which they did in Zion in your sight.
This is the very word of the LORD.

25 I am against you, O destroying mountain,[e][f]
you who destroy the whole earth,
and I will stretch out my hand against you
and send you tumbling from your terraces
and make you a burnt-out mountain.

[a] *Verses 15–19: cp. 10. 12–16.* [b] At the thunder...amazed: *prob. rdg.; Heb.* At the sound of his giving tumult of waters in heaven. [c] rifts: *prob. rdg.; Heb.* lightnings. [d] *So many MSS.; others om.* [e] *Or* O Mount of the Destroyer. [f] *So Sept.; Heb.* adds says the LORD.

No stone of yours shall be used as a corner-stone,   26
    no stone for a foundation;
but you shall be desolate, for ever waste.
    This is the very word of the LORD.

Raise a standard in the land,[a]   27
blow the trumpet among the nations,
    hallow the nations for war against her,
summon the kingdoms of Ararat, Minni, and Ashkenaz,
    appoint a commander-in-chief against her,
bring up the horses like a dark swarm of locusts;[b]
    hallow the nations for war against her,   28
the king[c] of the Medes, his viceroys and governors,
    and all the lands of his realm.
The earth quakes and writhes;   29
    for the LORD's designs against Babylon are fulfilled,
to make the land of Babylon desolate and unpeopled.
    Babylon's warriors have given up the fight,   30
       they skulk in the forts;
their courage has failed, they have become like women.
Her buildings are set on fire, the bars of her gates broken.
    Runner speeds to meet runner,   31
    messenger to meet messenger,
    bringing news to the king of Babylon
that every quarter of his city is taken,
    the river-crossings are seized,   32
the guard-towers set on fire
    and the garrison stricken with panic.

For the LORD of Hosts the God of Israel has spoken: 33

    Babylon is like a threshing-floor when it is trodden;
soon, very soon, harvest-time will come.

    'Nebuchadrezzar king of Babylon has devoured me   34
    and sucked me dry,
he has set me aside like an empty jar.
    Like a dragon he has gulped me down;
he has filled his maw with my delicate flesh
    and spewed me up.
On Babylon be the violence done to me,   35
    the vengeance taken upon me!',
    Zion's people shall say.
    'My blood be upon the Chaldaeans!',
    Jerusalem shall say.

[a] *Or* earth. [b] *Or* hoppers. [c] *So Sept. (cp. verse 11); Heb.* kings.

36 Therefore the LORD says:

> I will plead your cause, I will avenge you;
> I will dry up her sea^a and make her waters fail;

37   and Babylon shall become a heap of ruins, a haunt of wolves,
> a scene of horror and derision, with no inhabitant.

38   Together they roar like young lions,
> they growl like the whelps of a lioness.

39   I will cause their drinking bouts to end in fever
> and make them so drunk that they will writhe and toss,
> then sink into unending sleep, never to wake.
> This is the very word of the LORD.

40   I will bring them like lambs to the slaughter,
> rams and he-goats together.

41   Sheshak^b is captured,
> the pride of the whole earth taken;
> Babylon has become a horror amongst the nations!

42   The sea has surged over Babylon,
> she is covered by its roaring waves.

43   Her cities have become waste places,
> a land dried up and desert,
> a land in whose cities no man lives
> and through which no mortal travels.

44   I will punish Bel in Babylon
> and make him bring up what he has swallowed;
> nations shall never again come streaming to him.
> The wall of Babylon has fallen;

45   come out of her, O my people,
> and let every man save himself
> from the anger of the LORD.

46   Then beware of losing heart,
> fear no rumours spread abroad in the land,
> as rumour follows rumour,
> each year a new one:
> violence on earth and ruler against ruler.

47   Therefore a time is coming
> when I will punish Babylon's idols,
> and all her land shall be put to shame,
> and all her slain shall lie fallen in her midst.

48   Heaven and earth and all that is in them
> shall sing in triumph over Babylon;
> for marauders from the north shall overrun her.

[a] *Possibly the Euphrates.* [b] *A name for Babylon.*

This is the very word of the LORD.
Babylon must fall for the sake of[a] Israel's slain, 49
as the slain of all the world fell for the sake of Babylon.
You who have escaped from her sword, off with you, do not linger. 50
Remember the LORD from afar
and call Jerusalem to mind.
We are put to shame by the reproaches we have heard, 51
and our faces are covered with confusion:
strangers have entered the sacred courts of the LORD's house.

A time is coming therefore, says the LORD, 52
when I will punish her idols,
and all through the land there shall be the groaning of the
wounded.
Though Babylon should reach to the skies 53
and make her high towers inaccessible,
I will send marauders to overrun her.
This is the very word of the LORD.
Hark, cries of agony from Babylon! 54
Sounds of destruction from the land of the Chaldaeans!
For the LORD is despoiling Babylon 55
and will silence the hum of the city,
before the advancing wave that booms and roars
like mighty waters.
For marauders march on Babylon herself, 56
her warriors are captured and their bows are broken;
for the LORD, a God of retribution, will repay in full.
I will make her princes and her wise men drunk, 57
her viceroys and governors and warriors,
and they shall sink into unending sleep, never to wake.
This is the very word of the King,
whose name is the LORD of Hosts.

The LORD of Hosts says: 58

The walls of broad Babylon shall be razed to the ground,
her lofty gates shall be set on fire.
Worthless now is the thing for which the nations toiled;
the peoples wore themselves out for a mere nothing.

The instructions given by the prophet Jeremiah to the quartermaster 59
Seraiah son of Neriah and grandson of Mahseiah, when he went to
Babylon with Zedekiah king of Judah in the fourth year of his reign.

[a] for the sake of: *prob. rdg.; Heb. om.*

60 Jeremiah, having written down in a[a] book[b] a full description of the
61 disaster which would come upon Babylon, said to Seraiah, 'When you
62 come to Babylon, look at this, read it all and then say, "Thou, O LORD,
   hast declared thy purpose to destroy this place and leave it with no one
63 living in it, man or beast; it shall be desolate, for ever waste." When
   you have finished reading the book, tie a stone to it and throw it into
64 the Euphrates, and then say, "So shall Babylon sink, never to rise again
   after the disaster which I shall bring upon her."'

Thus far are the collected sayings of Jeremiah.

Historical note about the fall of Jerusalem

52 1[c] ZEDEKIAH WAS TWENTY-ONE YEARS OLD when he came to the
       throne, and he reigned in Jerusalem for eleven years; his mother
2 was Hamutal daughter of Jeremiah of Libnah. He did what was wrong
3 in the eyes of the LORD, as Jehoiakim had done. Jerusalem and Judah
   so angered the LORD that in the end he banished them from his sight;
   and Zedekiah rebelled against the king of Babylon.
4   In the ninth year of his reign, in the tenth month, on the tenth day of
   the month, Nebuchadrezzar king of Babylon advanced with all his army
   against Jerusalem, invested it and erected watch-towers against it on
5 every side; the siege lasted till the eleventh year of King Zedekiah.
6 In the fourth month of that year, on the ninth day of the month, when
   famine was severe in the city and there was no food for the common
7 people, the city was thrown open. When Zedekiah king of Judah saw
   this, he and[d] all his armed escort left the city and fled by night through
   the gate called Between the Two Walls, near the king's garden. They
   escaped towards the Arabah, although the Chaldaeans were surrounding
8 the city. But the Chaldaean army pursued the king and overtook him in
9 the lowlands of Jericho; and all his company was dispersed. The king
   was seized and brought before the king of Babylon at Riblah in the land
10 of Hamath, where he pleaded his case before him. The king of Babylon
   slew Zedekiah's sons before his eyes; he also put to death all the princes
11 of Judah in Riblah. Then the king of Babylon put Zedekiah's eyes out,
   bound him with fetters of bronze, brought him to Babylon and committed him to prison till the day of his death.
12   In the fifth month, on the tenth day of the month, in the nineteenth
   year of Nebuchadrezzar king of Babylon, Nebuzaradan, captain of the

[a] *Or* one. [b] *Prob. rdg.; Heb. adds* all these things which are written concerning Babylon.
[c] *Verses 1–27: cp. 39. 1–10 and 2 Kgs. 24. 18 – 25. 21.* [d] *When Zedekiah...and: prob.
rdg., cp. 39. 4; Heb. om.*

king's bodyguard,[a] came to Jerusalem and set fire to the house of the 13
LORD and the royal palace; all the houses in the city, including the
mansion of Gedaliah,[b] were burnt down. The Chaldaean forces with 14
the captain of the guard pulled down the walls all round Jerusalem.
[c]Nebuzaradan captain of the guard deported the rest of the people left 15
in the city, those who had deserted to the king of Babylon and any
remaining artisans. The captain of the guard left only the weakest class 16
of people to be vine-dressers and labourers.

The Chaldaeans broke up the pillars of bronze in the house of the 17
LORD, the trolleys, and the sea of bronze, and took the metal to Babylon. They took also the pots, shovels, snuffers, tossing-bowls, saucers, 18
and all the vessels of bronze used in the service of the temple. The 19
captain of the guard took away the precious metal, whether gold or
silver, of which the cups, firepans, tossing-bowls, pots, lamp-stands,
saucers, and flagons were made. The bronze of the two pillars, of the 20
one sea and of the twelve oxen supporting it,[d] which King Solomon had
made for the house of the LORD, was beyond weighing. The one pillar 21
was eighteen cubits high and twelve cubits in circumference; it was
hollow and the metal was four fingers thick. It had a capital of bronze, 22
five cubits high, and a decoration of network and pomegranates ran all
round it, wholly of bronze. The other pillar, with its pomegranates, was
exactly like it. Ninety-six pomegranates were exposed to view[e] and 23
there were a hundred in all on the network all round.

The captain of the guard took Seraiah the chief priest and Zephaniah 24
the deputy chief priest and the three on duty at the entrance; he took 25
also from the city a eunuch who was in charge of the fighting men, seven
of those with right of access to the king who were still in the city, the
adjutant-general[f] whose duty was to muster the people for war, and
sixty men of the people who were still there. These Nebuzaradan cap- 26
tain of the guard brought to the king of Babylon at Riblah. There, in 27
the land of Hamath, the king of Babylon had them flogged and put to
death. So Judah went into exile from their own land.

These were the people deported by Nebuchadrezzar in the seven- 28
teenth[g] year: three thousand and twenty-three Judaeans. In his eighteenth 29
year, eight hundred and thirty-two people from Jerusalem; in his 30
twenty-third year, seven hundred and forty-five Judaeans were deported by Nebuzaradan the captain of the bodyguard: all together four
thousand six hundred people.

[a] captain...bodyguard: *prob. rdg., cp. 2 Kgs. 25. 8; Heb.* captain of the bodyguard stood
before the king of Babylon.   [b] Gedaliah: *prob. rdg.; Heb.* the great man.   [c] *Prob. rdg.,
cp. 39. 9 and 2 Kgs. 25. 11; Heb. prefixes* The weakest class of the people (*cp. verse 16*).
[d] supporting it: *so Sept.; Heb.* which were under the trolleys (*or, with some change of text,*
which supported it, and the ten trolleys).   [e] exposed to view: *mng. of Heb. word uncertain.*   [f] *Prob. rdg.; Heb. adds* commander-in-chief.   [g] *Prob. rdg.; Heb.* seventh.

31[a]   In the thirty-seventh year of the exile of Jehoiachin king of Judah,
on the twenty-fifth day of the twelfth month, Evil-merodach king of
Babylon in the year of his accession showed favour to Jehoiachin king
32 of Judah. He brought him out of prison, treated him kindly and gave
33 him a seat at table above the kings with him in Babylon. So Jehoiachin
discarded his prison clothes and lived as a pensioner of the king for the
34 rest of his life. For his maintenance a regular daily allowance was given
him by the king of Babylon as long as he lived, to the day of his death.

[a] *Verses 31–34: cp. 2 Kgs. 25: 27–30.*

LAMENTATIONS

Sorrows of captive Zion

How solitary lies the city, once so full of people!   **1**
Once great among nations, now become a widow;
once queen among provinces, now put to forced labour!
   Bitterly she weeps in the night,   **2**
     tears run down her cheeks;
  she has no one to bring her comfort
     among all that love her;
  all her friends turned traitor
     and became her enemies.
  Judah went into the misery of exile   **3**
     and endless servitude.
  Settled among the nations,
     she found no resting-place;
  all her persecutors fell upon her
     in her sore straits.
  The paths to Zion mourn,   **4**
     for none attend her sacred feasts;
  all her gates are desolate.
     Her priests groan and sigh,
     her virgins are cruelly treated.
  How bitter is her fate!
  Her adversaries have become her masters,   **5**
     her enemies take their ease,
     for the LORD has cruelly punished her
  because of misdeeds without number;
     her young children have gone,
  driven away captive by the enemy.
  All majesty has vanished   **6**
     from the daughter of Zion.
  Her princes have become like deer
     that can find no pasture
  and run on, their strength all spent,
     pursued by the hunter.
     Jerusalem has remembered   **7**
  her days of misery and wandering,[a]

[a] *Prob. rdg.; Heb. adds* all her treasures which have been from days of old.

when her people fell into the power of the adversary
and there was no one to help her.
The adversary saw and mocked
at her fallen state.

8 Jerusalem had sinned greatly,
and so she was treated like a filthy rag;
all those who had honoured her held her cheap,
for they had seen her nakedness.
What could she do but sigh
and turn away?

9 Uncleanness clung to her skirts,
and she gave no thought to her fate.
Her fall was beyond belief
and there was no one to comfort her.
Look, LORD, upon her^a misery,
see how the enemy has triumphed.

10 The adversary stretched out his hand
to seize all her treasures;
then it was that she saw Gentiles
entering her sanctuary,
Gentiles forbidden by thee to enter
the assembly, for it was thine.

11 All her people groaned,
they begged for bread;
they sold their treasures for food
to give them strength again.

Look, O LORD, and see
how cheap I am accounted.

12 Is it of no concern to you who pass by?
If only you would look and see:
is there any agony like mine,
like these my torments
with which the LORD has cruelly punished me
in the day of his anger?

13 He sent down fire from heaven,
it ran through my bones;
he spread out a net to catch my feet,
and turned me back;
he made me an example of desolation,
racked with sickness all day long.

14 My transgressions were bound^b upon me,^c

[a] *So Old Latin; Heb.* my. [b] bound: *prob. rdg.; Heb. word unknown.* [c] upon me: *so Pesh.; Heb.* a yoke.

his own hand knotted them round me;
his yoke was lifted on to my neck,
   my strength failed beneath its weight;
the Lord abandoned me to its hold,*ᵃ*
   and I could not stand.

The Lord treated with scorn   15
all the mighty men within my walls;
he marshalled rank on rank against me
   to crush my young warriors.
The Lord trod down, like grapes in the press,
   the virgin daughter of Judah.
For these things I weep over my plight,*ᵇ*   16
   my eyes run with tears;
for any to comfort me and renew my strength
   are far to seek;
my sons are an example of desolation,
   for the enemy is victorious.

Zion lifted her hands in prayer,   17
   but there was no one to comfort her;
the LORD gave Jacob's enemies the order
   to beset him on every side.
Jerusalem became a filthy rag in their midst.

The LORD was in the right;   18
   it was I who rebelled against his commands.
Listen, O listen, all you nations,
   and look on my agony:
my virgins and my young men are gone into captivity.
I called to my lovers, they broke faith with me;   19
my priests and my elders in the city
   went hungry and could find nothing,*ᶜ*
although they sought food for themselves
   to renew their strength.
See, LORD, how sorely I am distressed.   20
   My bowels writhe in anguish
and my stomach turns within me,
   because I wantonly rebelled.
The sword makes orphans in the streets,
   as plague does within doors.
Hear me*ᵈ* when I groan   21
   with no one to comfort me.

[a] its hold: *prob. rdg.; Heb. obscure.* [b] my plight: *prob. rdg.; Heb.* my eye. [c] and could find nothing: *prob. rdg., cp. Sept.; Heb. om.* [d] Hear me: *so Pesh.; Heb.* They listened.

All my enemies, when they heard of my calamity,
    rejoiced at what thou hadst done;
but hasten[a] the day thou hast promised
    when they shall become like me.

22   Let all their evil deeds come before thee;
        torment them in their turn,
    as thou hast tormented me
        for all my transgressions;
for my sighs are many and my heart is faint.

Zion's hope of relief after punishment

2   What darkness the Lord in his anger
        has brought upon the daughter of Zion!
He hurled down from heaven to earth
    the glory of Israel,
and did not remember in the day of his anger
    that Zion was his footstool.

2   The Lord overwhelmed without pity
        all the dwellings of Jacob.
    In his wrath he tore down
the strongholds of the daughter of Judah;
he levelled with the ground and desecrated
    the kingdom and its rulers.

3   In his anger he hacked down
the horn of Israel's pride,
he withdrew his helping hand
    when the enemy came on;
and he blazed in Jacob like flaming fire
    that rages far and wide.

4   In enmity he strung his bow;
        he took his stand like an adversary
        and with his strong arm he slew
all those who had been his delight;
he poured his fury out like fire
    on the tent of the daughter of Zion.

5   The Lord played an enemy's part
        and overwhelmed Israel.
He overwhelmed all their towered mansions
    and brought down their strongholds in ruins;

[a] but hasten: *so Pesh.; Heb.* thou hast hastened.

sorrow upon sorrow he brought
  to the daughter of Judah.
He stripped his tabernacle as a vine*a* is stripped,   6
  and made the place of assembly a ruin.
In Zion the LORD blotted out all memory
  of festal assembly*b* and of sabbath;
king and priest alike he scorned
  in the grimness of his anger.
The Lord spurned his own altar   7
  and laid a curse upon his sanctuary.
He delivered the walls of her mansions
  into the power of the enemy;
in the LORD's very house they raised shouts of victory
  as on a day of festival.
The LORD was minded to bring down in ruins   8
  the walls of the daughter of Zion;
  he took their measure with his line
and did not scruple to demolish her;
he made rampart and wall lament,
  and both together lay dejected.
Her gates are sunk into the earth,   9
he has shattered and broken their bars;
her king and her rulers are among the Gentiles,
  and there is no law;
her prophets too have received
  no vision from the LORD.
  The elders of the daughter of Zion   10
sit on the ground and sigh;
they have cast dust on their heads
  and clothed themselves in sackcloth;
  the virgins of Jerusalem
bow their heads to the ground.
My eyes are blinded with tears,   11
  my bowels writhe in anguish.
In my bitterness my bile is spilt on the earth
  because of my people's wound,
when children and infants faint
  in the streets of the town
  and cry to their mothers,   12
'Where can we get corn and wine?'—
when they faint like wounded things
  in the streets of the city,

[*a*] *So Sept.; Heb.* garden.   [*b*] festal assembly: *or* appointed seasons.

    gasping out their lives
      in their mothers' bosom.

13   How can I cheer you? Whose plight is like yours,
      daughter of Jerusalem?
    To what can I compare you for your comfort,
      virgin daughter of Zion?
    For your wound gapes wide as the ocean;
      who can heal you?

14   The visions that your prophets saw for you
      were false and painted shams;
    they did not bring home to you your guilt
      and so reverse your fortunes.
    The visions that they saw for you were delusions,
      false and fraudulent.[a]

15   All those who pass by
    snap their fingers at you;
    they hiss and wag their heads at you,
      daughter of Jerusalem:
  'Is this the city once called Perfect in beauty,
      Joy of the whole earth?'

16   All your enemies
    make mouths and jeer at you;
    they hiss and grind their teeth,
      saying, 'Here we are,
    this is the day we have waited for;
      we have lived to see it.'

17   The LORD has done what he planned to do,
      he has fulfilled his threat,
    all that he ordained from days of old.
      He has demolished without pity
    and let the enemy rejoice over you,
      filling your adversaries with pride.[b]

18   Cry with a full heart[c] to the Lord,
      O wall of the daughter of Zion;
    let your tears run down like a torrent
      by day and by night.
    Give yourself not a moment's rest,
      let your tears never cease.

19   Arise and cry aloud in the night;
      at the beginning of every watch

[a] fraudulent: *or* causing banishment. [b] filling...pride: *lit.* raising the horn of your adversaries high. [c] Cry...heart: *prob. rdg.; Heb.* Their heart cried.

> pour out your heart like water
> in the Lord's very presence.
> Lift up your hands to him
> for the lives of your children.[a]
> Look, LORD, and see: 20
> who is it that thou hast thus tormented?
> Must women eat the fruit of their wombs,
> the children they have brought safely to birth?
> Shall priest and prophet be slain
> in the sanctuary of the Lord?
> There in the streets young men and old   21
> lie on the ground.
> My virgins and my young men have fallen
> by sword and by famine;[b]
> thou hast slain them in the day of thy anger,
> slaughtered them without pity.
> Thou didst summon my enemies against me from every side,   22
> like men assembling for a festival;
> not a man escaped, not one survived
> in the day of the LORD's anger.
> All whom I brought safely to birth and reared
> were destroyed by my enemies.

> I am the man who has known affliction,   3
> I have felt the rod of his wrath.
> It was I whom he led away and left to walk   2
> in darkness, where no light is.
> Against me alone he has turned his hand,   3
> and so it is all day long.
> He has wasted away my flesh and my skin   4
> and broken all my bones;
> he has built up walls around me,   5
> behind and before,
> and has cast me into a place of darkness   6
> like a man long dead.
> He has walled me in so that I cannot escape,   7
> and weighed me down with fetters;
> even when I cry out and call for help,   8
> he rejects my prayer.
> He has barred my road with blocks of stone   9
> and tangled up my way.

[a] *Prob. rdg.; Heb. adds* who faint with hunger at every street-corner.   [b] and by famine:
so Sept.; Heb. om.

10	He lies in wait for me like a bear
	or a lion lurking in a covert.
11	He has made my way refractory and lamed me
	and left me desolate.
12	He has strung his bow
	and made me the target for his arrows;
13	he has pierced my kidneys with shafts
	drawn from his quiver.
14	I have become a laughing-stock to all nations,[a]
	the target of their mocking songs all day.
15	He has given me my fill of bitter herbs
	and made me drunk with wormwood.
16	He has broken my teeth on gravel;
	fed on ashes, I am racked with pain;
17	peace has gone out of my life,
	and I have forgotten what prosperity means.
18	Then I cry out that my strength has gone
	and so has my hope in the LORD.
19	The memory of my distress and my wanderings
	is[b] wormwood and gall.
20	Remember, O remember,
	and stoop down to me.[c][d]
21	All this I take to heart
	and therefore I will wait patiently:
22	the LORD's true love is surely not spent,[e]
	nor has his compassion failed;
23	they are new every morning,
	so great is his constancy.
24	The LORD, I say, is all that I have;[f]
	therefore I will wait for him patiently.
25	The LORD is good to those who look for him,
	to all who seek him;
26	it is good to wait in patience and sigh
	for deliverance by the LORD.
27	It is good, too, for a man
	to carry the yoke in his youth.
28	Let him sit alone and sigh
	if it is heavy upon him;
29	let him lay his face in the dust,

[a] nations: *so many MSS.; others* my people. [b] The memory...is: *or* Remember
my distress and my wanderings, the... [c] stoop down to me: *prob. original rdg., altered
in Heb. to* I sink down. [d] Remember...me: *or* I remember, I remember them and sink
down. [e] spent: *prob. rdg.; Heb. unintelligible.* [f] all...have: *lit.* my portion.

and there may yet be hope.
Let him turn his cheek to the smiter   30
  and endure full measure of abuse;
for the Lord will not cast off   31
  his servants[a] for ever.
He may punish cruelly, yet he will have compassion   32
  in the fullness of his love;
he does not willingly afflict   33
  or punish any mortal man.

To trample underfoot   34
  any prisoner in the land,
to deprive a man of his rights   35
  in defiance of the Most High,
to pervert justice in the courts—   36
  such things the Lord has never approved.

Who can command and it is done,   37
  if the Lord has forbidden it?
Do not both bad and good proceed   38
  from the mouth of the Most High?
Why should any man living complain,   39
  any mortal who has sinned?
Let us examine our ways and put them to the test   40
  and turn back to the LORD;
let us lift up our hearts, not our hands,   41
  to God in heaven.
We ourselves have sinned and rebelled,   42
  and thou hast not forgiven.
In anger thou hast turned[b] and pursued us   43
  and slain without pity;
thou hast hidden thyself behind the clouds   44
  beyond reach of our prayers;
thou hast treated us as offscouring and refuse   45
  among the nations.
All our enemies make mouths   46
  and jeer at us.
Before us lie hunter's scare and pit,   47
  devastation and ruin.
My eyes run with streams of water   48
  because of my people's wound.
My eyes stream with unceasing tears   49
  and refuse all comfort,

[a] his servants: *prob. rdg.; Heb. om.*   [b] *Prob. rdg.; Heb.* hidden.

50   while the LORD in heaven looks down
             and watches my affliction,*a*
51   while the LORD torments*b* me
             with the fate of all the daughters of my city.

52   Those who for no reason were my enemies
             drove me cruelly like a bird;
53   they thrust me alive into the silent pit,
             and they closed it over me with a stone;
54   the waters rose high above my head,
             and I said, 'My end has come.'
55   But I called on thy name, O LORD,
             from the depths of the pit;
56   thou heardest my voice; do not turn a deaf ear
             when I cry, 'Come to my relief.'*c*
57   Thou wast near when I called to thee;
             thou didst say, 'Have no fear.'
58   Lord, thou didst plead my cause
             and ransom my life;
59   thou sawest, LORD, the injustice done to me
             and gavest judgement in my favour;
60   thou sawest their vengeance,
             all their plots against me.
61   Thou didst hear their bitter taunts, O LORD,
             their many plots against me,
62   the whispering, the murmurs of my enemies
             all the day long.
63   See how, whether they sit or stand,
             they taunt me bitterly.
64   Pay them back for their deeds, O LORD,
             pay them back what they deserve.
65   Show them how hard thy heart can be,
             how little concern thou hast for them.
66   Pursue them in anger and exterminate them
             from beneath thy heavens, O LORD.

4   How dulled is the gold,
           how tarnished the fine gold!
         The stones of the sanctuary*d* lie strewn
           at every street-corner.
2   See Zion's precious sons,

[a] my affliction: *prob. rdg.; Heb.* my eye. [b] the LORD torments: *prob. rdg.; Heb.* torment-ing. [c] when...relief.': *lit.* to my relief, to my cry. [d] The stones of the sanctuary: *or* Bright gems.

once worth their weight in finest gold,
    now counted as pitchers of earthenware
      made by any potter's hand.
Even whales[a] uncover the teat   3
    and suckle their young;
but the daughters of my people are cruel
    as ostriches in the desert.
The sucking infant's tongue   4
    cleaves to its palate from thirst;
young children beg for bread
    but no one offers them a crumb.
Those who once fed delicately   5
    are desolate in the streets,
and those nurtured in purple
    now grovel on dunghills.
The punishment[b] of my people is worse   6
    than the penalty[c] of Sodom,
which was overthrown in a moment
    and no one wrung his hands.
Her crowned princes[d] were once purer than snow,   7
    whiter than milk;
they were ruddier than branching coral,[e]
    and their limbs were lapis lazuli.
But their faces turned blacker than soot,   8
    and no one knew them in the streets;
the skin was drawn tight over their bones,
    dry as touchwood.
Those who died by the sword were more fortunate   9
    than those who died of hunger;
these wasted away, deprived
    of the produce of the field.
Tender-hearted women with their own hands   10
    boiled their own children;
their children became their food
    in the day of my people's wounding.
The Lord glutted his rage   11
    and poured forth his anger;
he kindled a fire in Zion,
    and it consumed her foundations.
This no one believed, neither the kings of the earth   12
    nor anyone that dwelt in the world:

[a] *Prob. rdg.; Heb.* jackals. [b] *Or* iniquity. [c] *Or* sin. [d] crowned princes: *or*
Nazirites. [e] than...coral: *prob. rdg.; Heb.* branch than coral.

that enemy or invader would enter
    the gates of Jerusalem.

13 It was for the sins of her prophets
    and for the iniquities of her priests,
who shed within her walls
    the blood of the righteous.

14 They wandered blindly in the streets,
    so stained with blood
that men would not touch
    even their garments.

15 'Away, away; unclean!' men cried to them.
    'Away, do not come near.'
They hastened away, they wandered among the nations,*a*
    unable to find any resting-place.

16 The LORD himself scattered them,
    he thought of them no more;
he showed no favour to priests,
    no pity for elders.

17 Still we strain our eyes,
    looking in vain for help.
We have watched and watched
    for a nation powerless to save us.

18 When we go out, we take to by-ways
to avoid the public streets;
our days are all but finished,*b*
    our end has come.

19 Our pursuers have shown themselves swifter
    than vultures in the sky;
they are hot on our trail over the hills,
they lurk to catch us in the wilderness.

20 The LORD's anointed, the breath of life to us,
    was caught in their machinations;
although we had thought to live
among the nations, safe under his protection.

21 Rejoice and be glad, daughter of Edom,
    you who live in the land of Uz.
Yet the cup shall pass to you in your turn,
and when you are drunk you will expose yourself to shame.

22 The punishment for your sin, daughter of Zion, is now complete,

[a] *Prob. rdg.; Heb. adds* they said. [b] our...finished: *prob. rdg.; Heb.* our end has drawn near, our days are complete.

and never again shall you be carried into exile.
But you, daughter of Edom, your sin shall be punished,
and your guilt revealed.

A prayer for remembrance and restoration

Remember, O LORD, what has befallen us;   5
  look, and see how we are scorned.
Our patrimony is turned over to strangers   2
  and our homes to foreigners.
We are like orphans, without a father;   3
  our mothers are like widows.
We must buy our own water to drink,   4
  our own wood can only be had at a price.
The yoke*a* is on our necks, we are overdriven;   5
  we are weary and are given no rest.
We came to terms, now with the Egyptians,   6
  now with the Assyrians, to provide us with food.
Our fathers sinned and are no more,   7
  and we bear the burden of their guilt.
Slaves have become our rulers,   8
  and there is no one to rescue us from them.
We must bring in our food from the wilderness,   9
  risking our lives in the scorching heat.*b*
Our skins are blackened as in a furnace   10
  by the ravages of starvation.
Women were raped in Zion,   11
  virgins raped in the cities of Judah.
Princes were hung up by their hands,   12
  and elders received no honour.
Young men toil to grind corn,   13
  and boys stumble under loads of wood.
Elders have left off their sessions in the gate,   14
  and young men no longer pluck the strings.
  Joy has fled from our hearts,   15
and our dances are turned to mourning.
  The garlands have fallen from our heads;   16
woe betide us, sinners that we are.
For this we are sick at heart,   17
  for all this our eyes grow dim:

[a] The yoke: *so Symm.; Heb. om.* [b] in the scorching heat: *or* by the sword.

18   because Mount Zion is desolate
    and over it the jackals run wild.

19   O LORD, thou art enthroned for ever,
    thy throne endures from one generation to another.

20   Why wilt thou quite forget us
    and forsake us these many days?

21   O LORD, turn us back to thyself, and we will come back;
    renew our days as in times long past.

22   For if thou hast utterly rejected us,
    then great indeed has been thy anger against us.

THE BOOK OF THE PROPHET

EZEKIEL

Ezekiel's call to be a prophet

ON THE FIFTH DAY of the fourth month in the thirtieth 1
year, while I was among the exiles by the river Kebar,^{a} the
heavens were opened and I saw a vision of God. On the fifth 2
day of the month in the fifth year of the exile of King Jehoiachin, the 3
word of the LORD came to Ezekiel son of Buzi the priest, in Chaldaea,
by the river Kebar, and there the hand of the LORD came upon him.

I saw a storm wind coming from the north, a vast cloud with flashes 4
of fire and brilliant light about it; and within was a radiance like brass,^{b}
glowing in the heart of the flames. In the fire was the semblance of four 5
living creatures in human form. Each had four faces and each four wings; 6
their legs were straight, and their hooves were like the hooves of a calf, 7
glittering like a disc of bronze. Under the wings on each of the four 8
sides were human hands; all four creatures had faces and wings, and 9
their wings touched one another. They did not turn as they moved;
each creature went straight forward. Their faces were like this: all four 10
had the face of a man and the face of a lion on the right, on the left the
face of an ox and the face of an eagle. Their wings^c were spread; each 11
living creature had one pair touching its neighbours',^{d} while one pair
covered its body. They moved straight forward in whatever direction 12
the spirit^e would go; they never swerved in their course. The appearance 13
of the creatures was as if fire from burning coals or torches were darting
to and fro among them; the fire was radiant, and out of the fire came
lightning.^{f}

As I looked at the living creatures, I saw wheels on the ground, one 15
beside each of the four.^{g} The wheels^h sparkled like topaz, and they were 16
all alike: in form and working they were like a wheel inside a wheel,
and when they moved in any of the four directions they never swerved in 17
their course. All four had hubs and each hub had a projection which had 18
the power of sight,^{i} and the rims of the wheels were full of eyes all
round. When the living creatures moved, the wheels moved beside 19
them; when the creatures rose from the ground, the wheels rose; they 20

[a] Or the Kebar canal. [b] Mng. of Heb. word uncertain. [c] So Sept.; Heb. adds and their
faces. [d] its neighbours': prob. rdg.; Heb. unintelligible. [e] Or wind. [f] Prob. rdg.,
cp. Sept.; Heb. adds (14) and the living creatures went out (prob. rdg.; Heb. obscure) and in
like rays of light. [g] one...four: prob. rdg.; Heb. obscure. [h] So Sept.; Heb. adds and
their works. [i] the power of sight: prob. rdg.; Heb. fear.

moved in whatever direction the spirit[a] would go; and the wheels rose together with them, for the spirit of the living creatures was in the
21 wheels. When the one moved, the other moved; when the one halted, the other halted; when the creatures rose from the ground, the wheels rose together with them, for the spirit of the creatures was in the wheels.
22 Above the heads of the living creatures was, as it were, a vault glittering like a sheet of ice, awe-inspiring, stretched over their heads
23 above them. Under the vault their wings were spread straight out,
24 touching one another, while one pair covered the body of each.[b] I heard, too, the noise of their wings; when they moved it was like the noise of a great torrent or of a cloud-burst,[c] like the noise of a crowd or of an
25 armed camp; when they halted their wings dropped. A sound was heard above the vault over their heads, as they halted with drooping wings.
26 Above the vault over their heads there appeared, as it were, a sapphire[d] in the shape of a throne, and high above all, upon the throne, a form in
27 human likeness. I saw what might have been brass glowing like fire in a furnace from the waist upwards; and from the waist downwards I saw
28 what looked like fire with encircling radiance. Like a rainbow in the clouds on a rainy day was the sight of that encircling radiance; it was like the appearance of the glory of the LORD.

When I saw this I threw myself on my face, and heard a voice
2 speaking to me: Man,[e] he said, stand up, and let me talk with you.
2 As he spoke, a spirit came into me and stood me on my feet, and I
3 listened to him speaking. He said to me, Man, I am sending you to the Israelites, a nation of rebels who have rebelled against me. Past genera-
4 tions of them have been in revolt against me to this very day, and this generation to which I am sending you is stubborn and obstinate. When
5 you say to them, 'These are the words of the Lord GOD', they will know that they have a prophet among them, whether they listen or
6 whether they refuse to listen, because they are rebels. But you, man, must not be afraid of them or of what they say, though they are rebels against you and renegades, and you find yourself sitting on scorpions. There is nothing to fear in what they say, and nothing in their looks to
7 terrify you, rebels though they are. You must speak my words to them, whether they listen or whether they refuse to listen, rebels that they are.
8 But you, man, must listen to what I say and not be rebellious like them. Open your mouth and eat what I give you.
9, 10 Then I saw a hand stretched out to me, holding a scroll. He unrolled it before me, and it was written all over on both sides with dirges and
3 laments and words of woe. Then he said to me, 'Man, eat what is in

[a] *Or* wind. [b] *So some MSS.; others repeat* one pair covered the body of each. [c] *Or of* the Almighty. [d] *Or* lapis lazuli. [e] *Lit.* Son of man *and so throughout the book when Ezekiel is addressed.*

front of you, eat this scroll; then go and speak to the Israelites.' So I ₂
opened my mouth and he gave me the scroll to eat. Then he said, 'Man, ₃
swallow this scroll I give you, and fill yourself full.' So I ate it, and it
tasted as sweet as honey.

Man, he said to me, go and tell the Israelites what I have to say to ₄
them. You are sent not to people whose speech is thick and difficult, but ₅
to Israelites. No; I am not sending you to great nations whose speech is ₆
so thick and so difficult that you cannot make out what they say; if
however I had sent you to them they would have listened to you. But ₇
the Israelites will refuse to listen to you, for they refuse to listen to me, so
brazen are they all and stubborn. But I will make you a match for them. ₈
I will make you as brazen as they are and as stubborn as they are. I will ₉
make your brow like adamant, harder than flint. Never fear them, never
be terrified by them, rebels though they are. And he said to me, Listen ₁₀
carefully, man, to all that I have to say to you, and take it to heart. Go ₁₁
to your fellow-countrymen in exile and speak to them. Whether they
listen or refuse to listen, say, 'These are the words of the Lord GOD.'

Then a spirit*a* lifted me up, and I heard behind me a fierce rushing ₁₂
sound as the glory of the LORD rose*b* from his place. I heard the sound ₁₃
of the living creatures' wings brushing against one another, the sound of
the wheels beside them, and a fierce rushing sound. A spirit*a* lifted me ₁₄
and carried me along, and I went full of exaltation, the hand of the
LORD strong upon me. So I came to the exiles at Tel-abib who were ₁₅
settled by the river Kebar.*c* For seven days I stayed with them, dumbfounded.

At the end of seven days the word of the LORD came to me: Man, I ₁₆,₁₇
have made you a watchman for the Israelites; you will take messages
from me and carry my warnings to them. It may be that I pronounce ₁₈
sentence of death on a wicked man:*d* if you do not warn him to give up
his wicked ways and so save his life, the guilt is his; because of his
wickedness he shall die, but I will hold you answerable for his death.*e*
But if you have warned him and he still continues in his wicked and evil ₁₉
ways, he shall die because of his wickedness, but you will have saved
yourself. Or it may be that a righteous man turns away and does wrong, ₂₀
and I let that be the cause of his downfall; he will die because you have
not warned him. He will die for his sin; the righteous deeds he has done
will not be taken into account, and I will hold you answerable for his
death. But if you have warned the righteous man not to sin and he has ₂₁
not sinned, then he will have saved his life because he has been warned,
and you will have saved yourself.

[a] *Or* wind.   [b] rose: *prob. rdg.; Heb. obscure.*   [c] *So some MSS.; others add* and where
they were living.   [d] *Prob. rdg.; Heb. adds* if you do not warn him.   [e] *Lit.* I will require
his blood from your hand.

The impending ruin of Jerusalem

22 THE HAND OF THE LORD CAME UPON ME there, and he said to me, Rise up; go out into the plain, and there I will speak to you.
23 So I rose and went out into the plain; the glory of the LORD was there, like the glory which I had seen by the river Kebar, and I threw myself
24 down on my face. Then a spirit came into me and stood me on my feet,
25 and spoke to me: Go, he said, and shut yourself up in your house. You shall be tied and bound with ropes, man, so that you cannot go out
26 among the people. I will fasten your tongue to the roof of your mouth and you will be unable to speak; you will not be the one to rebuke them,
27 rebels though they are. But when I have something to say to you, I will give you back the power of speech. Then you will say to them, 'These are the words of the Lord GOD.' If anyone will listen, he may listen, and, if he refuses to listen, he may refuse; for they are rebels.

4 Man, take a tile and set it before you. Draw a city on it, the city of
2 Jerusalem: lay siege to it, erect watch-towers against it, raise a siege-ramp, put mantelets in position, and bring battering-rams against it all
3 round. Then take an iron griddle, and put it as a wall of iron between you and the city. Keep your face turned towards the city; it will be the besieged and you the besieger. This will be a sign to the Israelites.
4 Now lie on your left side, and I will lay Israel's iniquity on you; you shall bear their iniquity for as many days as you lie on that side.
5 Allowing one day for every year of their iniquity, I ordain that you bear it for one*a* hundred and ninety days; thus you shall bear Israel's ini-
6 quity. When you have completed all this, lie down a second time on your right side, and bear Judah's iniquity for forty days; I count one
7 day for every year. Then turn your face towards the siege of Jerusalem
8 and bare your arm, and prophesy against it. See how I tie you with ropes so that you cannot turn over from one side to the other until you complete the days of your distress.
9 Then take wheat and barley, beans and lentils, millet and spelt. Mix them all in one bowl and make your bread out of them. You are to eat it during the one*a* hundred and ninety days you spend lying on your side.
10 And you must weigh out your food; you may eat twenty shekels' weight
11 a day, taking it from time to time. Measure out your drinking water too; you may drink a sixth of a hin a day, taking it from time to time.
12 You are to eat your bread baked like barley cakes, using human dung as
13 fuel, and you must bake it where people can see you. Then the LORD said, 'This is the kind of bread, unclean bread, that the Israelites will

[a] *So Sept.; Heb.* three.

1178

eat in the foreign lands into which I shall drive them.' But I said, 'O 14
Lord GOD, I have never been made unclean, never in my life have I
eaten what has died naturally or been killed by wild beasts; no tainted
meat has ever passed my lips.' So he allowed me to use cow-dung 15
instead of human dung to bake my bread.

Then he said to me, Man, I am cutting short their daily bread*a* in 16
Jerusalem; people will weigh out anxiously the bread they eat, and
measure with dismay the water they drink. So their food and their 17
water will run short until they are dismayed at the sight of one another;
they will waste away because of their iniquity.

Man, take a sharp sword, take it like a barber's razor and run it over 5
your head and your chin. Then take scales and divide the hair into
three. When the siege comes to an end, burn one third of the hair in a 2
fire in the centre of the city; cut up one third with the sword all round
the city; scatter one third to the wind, and I will follow it with drawn
sword. Take a few of these hairs and tie them up in a fold of your robe. 3
Then take others of them, throw them into the fire and burn them, and 4
out of them fire will come upon all Israel.

These are the words of the Lord GOD: This city of Jerusalem I have 5
set among the nations, with other countries around her, and she has 6
rebelled against my laws and my statutes more wickedly than those
nations and countries; for her people have rejected my laws and refused
to conform to my statutes.

Therefore the Lord GOD says: Since you have been more ungrateful 7
than the nations around you and have not conformed to my statutes
and have not kept my laws or even the laws of the nations around you,
therefore, says the Lord GOD, I, in my turn, will be against you; I will 8
execute judgements in your midst for the nations to see, such judge- 9
ments as I have never executed before nor ever will again, so abominable have your offences been. Therefore, O Jerusalem, fathers will eat 10
their children and children their fathers in your midst; I will execute
judgements on you, and any who are left in you I will scatter to the four
winds. As I live, says the Lord GOD, because you have defiled my holy 11
place with all your vile and abominable rites, I in my turn will consume
you without pity; I in my turn will not spare you. One third of your 12
people shall die by pestilence and perish by famine in your midst; one
third shall fall by the sword in the country round about; and one third
I will scatter to the four winds and follow with drawn sword. Then my 13
anger will be spent, I will abate my fury against them and be calm;
when my fury is spent they will know that it is I, the LORD, who spoke
in jealous passion. I have made you a scandal*b* and a reproach to the 14
nations around you, and all who pass by will see it. You*c* will be an 15

[*a*] *Lit.* breaking the stick of bread.   [*b*] *Or* desolation.   [*c*] *So Sept.; Heb.* She.

object of reproach and abuse, a terrible lesson to the nations around you, when I pass sentence on you and do judgement in anger and fury.

16 I, the LORD, have spoken. When I shoot the deadly arrows of famine against you,^a arrows of destruction, I will shoot to destroy you. I will

17 bring famine upon you and cut short your daily bread;^b I will unleash famine and beasts of prey upon you, and they will leave you childless. Pestilence and slaughter will sweep through you, and I will bring the sword upon you. I, the LORD, have spoken.

6 1,2   These were the words of the LORD to me: Man, look towards the

3 mountains of Israel, and prophesy to them: Mountains of Israel, hear the word of the Lord GOD. This is his word to mountains and hills, watercourses and valleys: I am bringing a sword against you, and I will

4 destroy your hill-shrines. Your altars will be made desolate, your incense-altars shattered, and I will fling down your slain before your

5 idols. I will strew the corpses of the Israelites before their idols, and I

6 will scatter your bones about your altars. In all your settlements the blood-spattered altars^c shall be laid waste and the hill-shrines made desolate. Your altars will be waste and desolate and your idols shattered and useless, your incense-altars hewn down, and all your works wiped

7 out; with the slain falling about you, you shall know that I am the LORD.

8 But when they fall,^d I will leave you, among the nations, some who

9 survive the sword. When you are scattered in foreign lands, these survivors, in captivity among the nations, will remember how I was grieved because their hearts had turned wantonly from me and their eyes had gone roving wantonly after idols. Then they will loathe themselves for

10 all the evil they have done with their abominations. So they will know that I am the LORD, that I was uttering no vain threat when I said that I would bring this evil upon them.

11   These are the words of the Lord GOD: Beat your hands together, stamp with your foot, bemoan your vile abominations, people of Israel.

12 Men will fall by sword, famine, and pestilence. Far away they will die by pestilence; at home they will fall by the sword; any who survive or are

13 spared will die by famine, and so at last my anger will be spent. You will know that I am the LORD when their slain fall among the idols round their altars, on every high hill, on all mountain-tops, under every spreading tree, under every leafy terebinth, wherever they have brought

14 offerings of soothing odour for their idols one and all. So I will stretch out my hand over them and make the land a desolate waste in all their settlements, more desolate than the desert of Riblah.^e They shall know that I am the LORD.

7 1,2   The word of the LORD came to me: Man, the Lord GOD says this to

[a] *Prob. rdg.; Heb.* them.   [b] *Lit.* and break your stick of bread.   [c] blood-spattered altars: *or* cities.   [d] when they fall: *prob. rdg.; Heb. obscure.*   [e] *Prob. rdg.; Heb.* Diblah.

the land of Israel: An end is coming, the end is coming upon the four
corners of the land.*ᵃ* The end is now upon you; I will unleash my anger 3
against you; I will call you to account for your doings and bring your
abominations upon your own heads. I will neither pity nor spare you: 4
I will make you suffer for your doings and the abominations that continue in your midst. So you shall know that I am the LORD.

These are the words of the Lord GOD: Behold, it comes, disasters 5
one upon another;*ᵇ* the end, the end, it comes, it comes.*ᶜ* Doom is 6,7
coming upon you, dweller in the land; the time is coming, the day is
near, with confusion and the crash of thunder.*ᵈ* Now, in an instant, I 8
will vent my rage upon you and let my anger spend itself. I will call you
to account for your doings and bring your abominations upon your own
heads. I will neither pity nor spare; I will make you suffer for your 9
doings and the abominations that continue in your midst. So you shall
know that it is I, the LORD, who strike the blow.

Behold, the day! the doom is here, it has burst upon them. Injustice 10
buds, insolence blossoms, violence shoots up into injustice and wicked- 11
ness. And it is all their fault, the fault of their turmoil and tumult and
all their restless ways.*ᵉ* The time has come, the day has arrived; the 12
buyer has no reason to be glad, and the seller none for regret, for I am
angry*ᶠ* at all their turmoil. The seller will never go back on his bargain 13
while either of them lives; for the bargain will never be reversed because
of the turmoil, and no man will exert himself, even in his iniquity, as
long as he lives.*ᵍ* The trumpet has sounded and all is ready, but no one 14
goes out to war.*ʰ*

Outside is the sword, inside are pestilence and famine; in the country 15
men will die by the sword, in the city famine and pestilence will carry
them off. If any escape and take to the mountains, like moaning doves, 16
there will I slay them, each for his iniquity, while their hands hang 17
limp and their knees run with urine. They will go in sackcloth, shud- 18
dering from head to foot, with faces downcast and heads close shaved.
They shall fling their silver into the streets and cast aside their gold like 19
filth; their silver and their gold will be powerless to save them on the
day of the LORD's fury. Their hunger will not be satisfied nor their
bellies filled; for their iniquity will be the cause of their downfall.
They have fed their pride on their beautiful jewels, which they made 20
into vile and abominable images. Therefore I will treat their jewels like
filth, I will hand them over as plunder to foreigners and as booty to the 21

[*a*] *Or* earth. [*b*] disasters... another: *so some MSS.; others* one disaster, a disaster. [*c*] *Prob.
rdg.; Heb. adds* it wakes up, behold it comes. [*d*] and the crash of thunder: *prob. rdg.;
Heb. unintelligible.* [*e*] and all their restless ways: *so Vulg.; Heb. unintelligible.* [*f*] I am
angry: *so Targ.; Heb.* anger. [*g*] as long as he lives: *poss. mng.; Heb. obscure.* [*h*] *So Sept.;
Heb. adds* for I am angry at all their turmoil.

22 most evil people on earth, and these will defile them. I will turn my face from them and let my treasured land be profaned; brigands will come in and defile it.

23   Clench your fists, for the land is full of bloodshed[a] and the city full
24 of violence. I will let in the scum of nations to take possession of their houses; I will quell the pride of the strong, and their sanctuaries shall
25 be profaned. Shuddering will come over them, and they will look in
26 vain for peace. Tempest shall follow upon tempest and rumour upon rumour. Men will go seeking a vision from a prophet; there will be no
27 more guidance from a priest, no counsel from elders. The king will mourn, the prince will be clothed with horror, the hands of the common people will shake with fright. I will deal with them as they deserve, and call them to account for their doings; and so they shall know that I am the LORD.

Jerusalem's guilt and punishment

8 ON THE FIFTH DAY OF THE SIXTH MONTH in the sixth year, I was sitting at home and the elders of Judah were with me. Sud-
2 denly the hand of the Lord GOD came upon me, and I saw what looked like a man. He seemed to be all fire from the waist down and to shine
3 and glitter like brass from the waist up. He stretched out what seemed a hand and seized me by the forelock. A spirit[b] lifted me up between heaven and earth, carried me to Jerusalem in a vision of God and put me down at the entrance to the inner gate facing north, where stands
4 the image of Lust to rouse lustful passion. The glory of the God of
5 Israel was there, like the vision I had seen in the plain. The LORD said to me, 'Man, look northwards.' I did so, and there to the north of the
6 altar gate, at the entrance, was that image of Lust. 'Man,' he said, 'do you see what they are doing? The monstrous abominations which the Israelites practise here are driving me far from my sanctuary, and you will see even more such abominations.'
7   Then he brought me to the entrance of the court, and I looked and
8 found a hole in the wall. 'Man,' he said to me, 'dig through the wall.'
9 I did so, and it became an opening. 'Go in,' he said, 'and see the vile
10 abominations they practise here.' So I went in and saw figures of reptiles, beasts, and vermin, and all the idols of the Israelites, carved round
11 the walls. Seventy elders of Israel were standing in front of them, with Jaazaniah son of Shaphan in the middle, and each held a censer from
12 which rose the fragrant smoke of incense. 'Man,' he said to me, 'do

[a] bloodshed: *prob. rdg.; Heb.* the judgement of bloodshed.   [b] *Or* wind.

you see what the elders of Israel are doing in darkness, each at the shrine of his own carved image? They think that the LORD does not see them, or that he has forsaken the country. You will see', he said, 'yet more 13 monstrous abominations which they practise.'

Then he brought me to that gateway of the LORD's house which 14 faces north; and there I saw women sitting and wailing for Tammuz. 'Man, do you see that?' he asked me. 'But you will see abomina- 15 tions more monstrous than these.' So he took me to the inner court 16 of the LORD's house, and there, by the entrance to the sanctuary of the LORD, between porch and altar, were some twenty-five men with their backs to the sanctuary and their faces to the east, prostrating themselves to the rising sun. He said to me, 'Man, do you see that? Is it 17 because they think these abominations a trifle, that the Jews have filled the country with violence? They provoke me further to anger, even while they seek to appease me;*a* I will turn upon them in my rage; I 18 will neither pity nor spare. Loudly as they may cry to me, I will not listen.'

A loud voice rang in my ears: 'Here they come, those appointed to 9 punish the city, each carrying his weapon of destruction.' Then I saw 2 six men approaching from the road that leads to the upper northern gate, each carrying a battle-axe, one man among them dressed in linen, with pen and ink at his waist; and they halted by the altar of bronze. Then the glory of the God of Israel rose from above the cherubim.*b* 3 He came to the terrace of the temple and called to the man dressed in linen with pen and ink at his waist. 'Go through the city, through 4 Jerusalem,' said the LORD, 'and put a mark on the foreheads of those who groan and lament over the abominations practised there.' Then I 5 heard him say to the others, 'Follow him through the city and kill without pity; spare no one. Kill and destroy them all, old men and 6 young, girls, little children and women, but touch no one who bears the mark. Begin at my sanctuary.' So they began with the elders in front of the temple. 'Defile the temple,' he said, 'and fill the courts with dead 7 bodies; then go out*c* into the city and kill.'

While they did their work, I was left alone; and I threw myself upon 8 my face, crying out, 'O Lord GOD, must thou destroy all the Israelites who are left, pouring out thy anger on Jerusalem?' He answered, 'The 9 iniquity of Israel and Judah is great indeed; the land is full of murder, the city is filled with injustice. They think the LORD has forsaken this country; they think he sees nothing. But I will neither pity nor spare 10 them; I will make them answer for all they have done.' Then the man 11 dressed in linen with pen and ink at his waist came and made his report: 'I have done what thou hast commanded.'

[*a*] seek...me: *lit.* hold twigs to their nostrils.   [*b*] *So Sept.; Heb.* cherub.   [*c*] *So Sept.; Heb. adds* and they will go out.

10 Then I saw, above the vault over the heads of the cherubim, as it
2 were a throne of sapphire*a* visible above them. The LORD said to the
man dressed in linen,*b* 'Come in between the circling wheels under the
cherubim,*c* and take a handful of the burning embers lying among the
cherubim; then toss them over the city.' So he went in before my eyes.
3 The cherubim stood on the right side of the temple as a man enters,
4 and a cloud filled the inner court. The glory of the LORD rose high from
above the cherubim*c* and moved on to the terrace; and the temple was
filled with the cloud, while the radiance of the glory of the LORD filled the
5 court. The sound of the wings of the cherubim could be heard as far as
6 the outer court, as loud as if God Almighty were speaking. Then he told
the man dressed in linen to take fire from between the circling wheels
7 and among the cherubim; the man came and stood by a wheel, and a
cherub from among the cherubim put its hand into the fire that lay
among them, and, taking some fire, gave it to the man dressed in linen;
and he received it and went out.
8 Under the wings of the cherubim there appeared what seemed a
9 human hand. And I saw four wheels beside the cherubim, one wheel
10 beside each cherub. They had the sparkle of topaz, and all four were
11 alike, like a wheel inside a wheel. When the cherubim moved in any of
the four directions, they never swerved in their course; they went
straight on in the direction in which their heads were turned, never
12 swerving in their course. Their whole bodies, their backs and hands and
wings, as well as the wheels, were full of eyes all round the four of
13, 14 them.*d* The whirring of the wheels sounded in my ears. Each had four
faces: the first was that of a cherub, the second that of a man, the third
that of a lion, and the fourth that of an eagle.
15 Then the cherubim raised themselves up, those same living creatures
16 I had seen by the river Kebar. When the cherubim moved, the wheels
moved beside them; when the cherubim lifted their wings and rose
17 from the ground, the wheels did not turn away from them. When the
one halted, the other halted; when the one rose, the other rose; for the
18 spirit of the creatures was in the wheels. Then the glory of the LORD
19 left the temple terrace and halted above the cherubim. The cherubim
lifted their wings and raised themselves from the ground; I watched
them go with the wheels beside them. They halted at the eastern gateway of the LORD's house, and the glory of the God of Israel was over
them.
20 These were the living creatures I had seen beneath the God of Israel
21 at the river Kebar; I knew that they were cherubim. Each had four
faces and four wings and the semblance of human hands under their

[a] *Or* lapis lazuli. [b] *So Sept.; Heb. adds* and he said. [c] *So Sept.; Heb.* cherub.
[d] *Prob. rdg.; Heb. adds* their wheels.

wings. Their faces were like those I had seen in vision by the river 22
Kebar;[a] they moved, each one of them, straight forward.

A spirit[b] lifted me up and brought me to the eastern gate of the 11
LORD's house, the gate that faces east. By the doorway were twenty-five
men, and I saw among them two of high office, Jaazaniah son of Azzur
and Pelatiah son of Benaiah. The LORD said to me, Man, it is these who 2
are planning mischief and plotting trouble in this city, saying to them- 3
selves, 'There will be no building of houses yet awhile; the city is a
stewpot and we are the meat in it.' Therefore, said he, prophesy against 4
them, prophesy, O man. Then the spirit of the LORD came suddenly 5
upon me, and he told me to say, These are the words of the LORD: This
is what you are saying to yourselves, you men of Israel; well do I know
the thoughts that rise in your mind. You have killed and killed in this 6
city and heaped the streets with the slain. These, therefore, are the 7
words of the Lord GOD: The bodies of the slain that you have put
there, it is they that are the meat. The city is indeed the stewpot, but I[c]
will take you out of it. It is a sword that you fear, and a sword I will 8
bring upon you, says the Lord GOD. I will take you out of it; I will give 9
you over to a foreign power; I will bring you to justice. You too shall 10
fall by the sword when I judge you on the frontier of Israel; thus you
shall know that I am the LORD. So the city will not be your stewpot, nor 11
you the meat in it. On the frontier of Israel I will judge you; thus you 12
shall know that I am the LORD. You have not conformed to my statutes
nor kept my laws, but you have followed the laws of the nations around
you.

While I was prophesying, Pelatiah son of Benaiah fell dead; and I 13
threw myself upon my face, crying aloud, 'O Lord GOD, must thou
make an end of all the Israelites who are left?'

The word of the LORD came to me: Man, they are your brothers, 14, 15
your brothers and your kinsmen, this whole people of Israel, to whom
the men who now live in Jerusalem have said, 'Keep your distance from
the LORD; the land has been made over to us as our property.' Say 16
therefore, These are the words of the Lord GOD: When I sent them far
away among the nations and scattered them in many lands, for a while
I became their sanctuary in the countries to which they had gone.
Say therefore, These are the words of the Lord GOD: I will gather 17
them[d] from among the nations and assemble them[d] from the countries
over which I have scattered them,[e] and I will give them[d] the soil of
Israel. When they come into it, they will do away with all their vile and 18
abominable practices. I will give them a different[f] heart and put a new 19

[a] *Prob. rdg.; Heb. adds* and them.   [b] *Or* wind.   [c] *So some MSS.; others* he.   [d] *So Sept.; Heb.* you.   [e] I have scattered them: *so Sept.; Heb.* you have been scattered.   [f] *So Sept.; Heb.* a single.

spirit into them;[a] I will take the heart of stone out of their bodies and
20 give them a heart of flesh. Then they will conform to my statutes and
keep my laws. They will become my people, and I will become their
21 God. But as for those whose heart is set upon[b] their vile and abominable
practices, I will make them answer for all they have done. This is the
very word of the Lord GOD.

22 Then the cherubim lifted their wings, with the wheels beside them
23 and the glory of the God of Israel above them. The glory of the LORD
rose up and left the city, and halted on the mountain to the east of it.
24 And a spirit[c] lifted me up and brought me to the exiles in Chaldaea. All
this came in a vision sent by the spirit of God, and then the vision that
25 I had seen left me. I told the exiles all that the LORD had revealed to me.

Jerusalem's downfall certain

12 1,2 THE WORD OF THE LORD CAME TO ME: Man, you live among a
rebellious people. Though they have eyes they will not see, though
they have ears they will not hear, because they are a rebellious people.
3 Therefore, man, pack up what you need for a journey into exile, by day
before their eyes; then set off on your journey. When you leave home
and go off into exile before their eyes, it may be they will see that they
4 are rebels. Bring out your belongings, packed as for exile; do it by day,
before their eyes, and then at evening, still before their eyes, leave home,
5 as if you were going into exile. Next, before their eyes, break a hole
6 through the wall, and carry your belongings out through it. When dusk
falls, take your pack on your shoulder, before their eyes, and carry it out,
with your face covered so that you cannot see the ground. I am making
you a warning sign for the Israelites.
7 I did exactly as I had been told. By day I brought out my belongings,
packed as for exile, and at evening I broke through the wall with my
hands. When dusk fell, I shouldered my pack and carried it out before
their eyes.

8,9 Next morning, the word of the LORD came to me: Man, he said, have
not the Israelites, that rebellious people, asked you what you are doing?
10 Tell them that these are the words of the Lord GOD: This oracle con-
11 cerns the prince in Jerusalem, and all the Israelites therein.[d] Tell them
that you are a sign to warn them; what you have done will be done to
12 them; they will go into exile and captivity. Their prince will shoulder
his pack in the dusk and go through a hole made to let him out, with his

[a] *So Sept.; Heb.* you. [b] *Prob. rdg.; Heb. adds* the heart of. [c] *Or* wind. [d] therein:
prob. rdg.; Heb. among them.

face covered so that he cannot be seen nor himself see^a the ground.
But I will cast my net over him, and he will be caught in the meshes. I 13
will bring him to Babylon, the land of the Chaldaeans, though he will
not see it; and there he will die. I will scatter his bodyguard and drive 14
all his squadrons to the four winds; I will follow them with drawn
sword. Then they shall know that I am the LORD, when I disperse them 15
among the nations and scatter them through many lands. But I will 16
leave a few of them who will escape sword, famine, and pestilence, to
tell the whole story of their abominations to the peoples among whom
they go; and they shall know that I am the LORD.

And the word of the LORD came to me: Man, he said, as you eat you 17, 18
must tremble, and as you drink you must shudder with dread. Say to 19
the common people, These are the words of the Lord GOD about those
who live in Jerusalem and about the land of Israel: They will eat with
dread and be filled with horror as they drink; the land shall be filled
with horror because it is sated with the violence of all who live there.
Inhabited cities shall be deserted, and the land shall become a waste. 20
Thus you shall know that I am the LORD.

The word of the LORD came to me: Man, he said, what is this proverb 21, 22
current in the land of Israel: 'Time runs on, visions die away'? Say 23
to them, These are the words of the Lord GOD: I have put an end to
this proverb; it shall never be heard in Israel again. Say rather to them,
The time, with all the vision means, is near. There will be no more false 24
visions, no specious divination among the Israelites, for I, the LORD, 25
will say what I will, and it shall be done. It shall be put off no longer: in
your lifetime, you rebellious people, I will speak, I will act. This is the
very word of the Lord GOD.

The word of the LORD came to me: Man, he said, the Israelites say 26, 27
that the vision you now see is not to be fulfilled for many years: you are
prophesying of a time far off. Say to them, These are the words of the 28
Lord GOD: No word of mine shall be delayed; even as I speak it shall be
done. This is the very word of the Lord GOD.

The LORD said to me, Man, prophesy of the prophets of Israel; 13 1, 2
prophesy,^{b} and say to those who prophesy out of their own hearts, Hear
what the LORD says: These are the words of the Lord GOD: Oh, the 3
wicked folly of the prophets! Their inspiration comes from themselves;
they have seen no vision. Your prophets, Israel, have been like jackals 4
among ruins. They have not gone up into the breach to repair the 5
broken wall round the Israelites, that they may stand firm in battle on
the day of the LORD. Oh, false vision and lying divination! Oh, those 6
prophets who say, 'It is the very word of the LORD', when it is not the
LORD who has sent them; yet they expect their words to control the

[a] he cannot...see: *so Sept.; Heb.* he cannot see.   [b] *So Sept.; Heb.* who prophesy.

7 event. Is it not a false vision that you prophets have seen? Is not your divination a lie? You call it the very word of the LORD, but it is not I who have spoken.

8 These, then, are the words of the Lord GOD: Because your words are
9 false and your visions a lie, I am against you, says the Lord GOD. I will raise my hand against the prophets whose visions are false, whose divinations are a lie. They shall have no place in the counsels of my people; they shall not be entered in the roll of Israel nor set foot upon its soil.
10 Thus you shall know that I am the Lord GOD. Rightly, for they have misled my people by saying that all is well when all is not well. It is as if
11 they were building a wall and used whitewash for the daubing. Tell these daubers that it will fall; rain will pour down in torrents, and I will send hailstones hard as rock streaming down and I will unleash a stormy
12 wind. When the building falls, men will ask, 'Where is the plaster you
13 should have used?' So these are the words of the Lord GOD: In my rage I will unleash a stormy wind; rain will come in torrents in my anger,
14 hailstones hard as rock in my fury, until all is destroyed. I will demolish the building which you have daubed with whitewash and level it to the ground, so that its foundations are laid bare. It shall fall, and you shall
15 be destroyed within it; thus you shall know that I am the LORD. I will spend my rage on the building and on those who daubed it with wash; and people[a] will say, 'The building is gone and the men who daubed it
16 are gone, those prophets of Israel who prophesied to Jerusalem, who saw visions of prosperity when there was no prosperity.' This is the very word of the Lord GOD.

17 Now turn, man, to the women of your people who prophesy out of
18 their own hearts, and prophesy to them. Say to them, These are the words of the Lord GOD: I loathe you, you women who hunt men's lives by sewing magic bands upon the[b] wrists and putting veils over the heads of persons of every age; are you to hunt the lives of my people
19 and keep your own lives safe? You have violated my sanctity before my people with handfuls of barley and scraps of bread. You bring death to those who should not die, and life to those who should not live, by
20 lying to this people of mine who listen to lies. So these are the words of the Lord GOD: I am against your magic bands with which[c] you hunt
21 men's lives for the excitement of it. I will tear them from your arms and set those lives at liberty, lives that you hunt for the excitement of it. I will tear up your long veils and save my people from you; you shall no longer have power to hunt them. Thus you shall know that I am the
22 LORD. You discouraged the righteous man with lies, when I meant him no hurt; you so strengthened the wicked that he would not abandon

[a] *Prob. rdg.; Heb.* I. [b] *So some MSS.; others* my. [c] *with which: so Pesh.; Heb.* where.

1188

his evil ways and be saved; and therefore you shall never see your 23
false visions again nor practise your divination any more. I will rescue
my people from your power; and thus you shall know that I am the
LORD.

Some of the elders of Israel came to visit me, and while they sat with 14
me the LORD said to me, Man, these people have set their hearts on 2,3
their idols and keep their eyes fixed on the sinful things that cause their
downfall. Am I to let such men consult me? Speak to them and tell 4
them that these are the words of the Lord GOD: If any Israelite, with
his heart set on his idols and his eyes fixed on the sinful things that cause
his downfall, comes to a prophet, I, the LORD, in my own person,[a] shall
be constrained to answer him, despite his many idols. My answer will 5
grip the hearts of the Israelites, estranged from me as they are, one and
all, through their idols. So tell the Israelites that these are the words of 6
the Lord GOD: Turn away, turn away from your idols; turn your backs
on all your abominations. If any man, Israelite or alien, renounces me, 7
sets his heart upon idols and fixes his eyes upon the vile thing that is his
downfall—if such a man comes to consult me through a prophet, I, the
LORD, in my own person, shall be constrained to answer him. I will set 8
my face against that man; I will make him an example and a byword;
I will rid my people of him. Thus you shall know that I am the LORD.
If a prophet is seduced into making a prophecy, it is I the LORD who 9
have seduced him; I will stretch out my hand and rid my people Israel
of him. Both shall be punished; the prophet and the man who consults 10
him alike are guilty. And never again will the Israelites stray from their 11
allegiance, never again defy my will and bring pollution upon themselves; they will become my people, and I will become their God. This
is the very word of the Lord GOD.

These were the words of the LORD to me: Man, when a country sins 12,13
by breaking faith with me, I will stretch out my hand and cut short its
daily bread.[b] I will send famine upon it and destroy both men and
cattle. Even if those three men were living there, Noah, Danel[c] and Job, 14
they would save none but themselves by their righteousness. This is the
very word of the Lord GOD. If I should turn wild beasts loose in a 15
country to destroy its inhabitants, until it became a waste through
which no man would pass for fear of the beasts, then, if those three men 16
were living there, as I live, says the Lord GOD, they would not save even
their own sons and daughters; they would save themselves alone, and
the country would become a waste. Or if I should bring the sword upon 17
that country and command it to go through the land and should destroy
men and cattle, then, if those three men were living there, as I live, says 18

[a] in my own person: *so Targ.; Heb.* through it. [b] *Lit.* and break its stick of bread.
[c] *Or, as otherwise read,* Daniel.

the Lord GOD, they could save neither son nor daughter; they would
19 save themselves alone. Or if I should send pestilence on that land and
20 pour out my fury upon it in blood, to destroy men and cattle, then, if
Noah, Danel and Job were living there, as I live, says the Lord GOD,
they would save neither son nor daughter; they would save themselves
alone by their righteousness.

21   These were the words of the Lord GOD: How much less hope is there
for Jerusalem when I inflict on her these four punishments of mine,
sword and famine, wild beasts and pestilence, to destroy both men and
22 cattle! Some will be left in her, some survivors to be brought out, both
sons and daughters. Look at them as they come out to you, and see how
they have behaved and what they have done. This will be some comfort
to you for all the harm I have done to Jerusalem and all I have inflicted
23 upon her. It will bring you comfort when you see how they have behaved and what they have done; for you will know that it was not
without reason that I dealt thus with her. This is the very word of the
Lord GOD.

15   These were the words of the LORD to me:

2   Man, how is the vine better than any other tree,
         than a branch from a tree in the forest?
3   Is wood got from it
           fit to make anything useful?
         Can men make it into a peg
         and hang things on it?
4   If it is put on the fire for fuel,
         if its two ends are burnt by the fire
           and the middle is charred,
           is it fit for anything useful?
5   Nothing useful could be made of it even when whole;
        how much less, when it is burnt by the fire and charred,
          can it be made into anything useful!

6   So these are the words of the Lord GOD:

        I treat the vine, as against forest-trees,
          only as fuel for the fire,
       even so I treat the people of Jerusalem;
7   I set my face against them.
       Though they escape from the fire, fire shall burn them up.
         Thus you shall know that I am the LORD
         when I set my face against them,
8   making the land a waste
         because they have broken faith.
         This is the very word of the Lord GOD.

The word of the LORD came to me: Man, he said, make Jerusalem see **16** 1, 2
her abominable conduct. Tell her that these are the words of the Lord 3
GOD to her: Canaan is the land of your ancestry and there you were
born; an Amorite was your father and a Hittite your mother. This is 4
how you were treated at birth: when you were born, your navel-string
was not tied,*ᵃ* you were not bathed in water ready for the rubbing, you
were not salted as you should have been nor wrapped in swaddling
clothes. No one cared for you enough to do any of these things or, 5
indeed, to have any pity for you; you were thrown out on the bare
ground in your own filth on the day of your birth. Then I came by and 6
saw you kicking helplessly in your own blood; I spoke to you, there
in your blood, and bade you live.*ᵇ* I tended you like an evergreen 7
plant, like something growing in the fields; you throve and grew. You
came to full womanhood; your breasts became firm and your hair grew,
but still you were naked and exposed.

Again I came by and saw that you were ripe for love. I spread the 8
skirt of my robe over you and covered your naked body. Then I
plighted my troth and entered into a covenant with you, says the Lord
GOD, and you became mine. Then I bathed you in water and washed 9
off the blood and anointed you with oil. I gave you robes of brocade and 10
sandals of stout*ᶜ* hide; I fastened a linen girdle round you and dressed
you in lawn.*ᵈ* For jewellery I put bracelets on your arms and a chain 11
round your neck; I gave you a nose-ring, I put pendants in your ears 12
and a beautiful coronet on your head. You had ornaments of gold and 13
silver, your dresses were of linen, lawn,*ᵈ* and brocade. You had flour and
honey and olive oil for food, and you grew very beautiful, you grew into
a queen. The fame of your beauty went all over the world, for the 14
splendour with which I decked you made it perfect. This is the very
word of the Lord GOD.

But you trusted to your beauty and prostituted your fame; you com- 15
mitted fornication, offering yourself freely to any passer-by for your
beauty to become his. You took some of your clothes and decked a plat- 16
form for yourself in gay colours and there you committed fornication;
you had intercourse with him for your beauty to become his.*ᵉ* You took 17
the splendid ornaments of gold and silver which I had given you, and
made for yourself male images with which you committed fornication.
You covered them with your robes of brocade and offered up my oil and 18
my incense before them. You took the food I had given you, the flour, 19
the oil, and the honey, with which I had fed you, and set it before them
as an offering of soothing odour.*ᶠ* This is the very word of the Lord GOD.

---

[a] *Prob. rdg., cp. one MS.; others* cut.   [b] I spoke...live: *so some MSS.; others repeat
these words.*   [c] *Lit.* sea-cow.   [d] *Mng. of Heb. word uncertain.*   [e] you had intercourse...
his: *prob. rdg.; Heb. obscure.*   [f] *So Pesh.; Heb. adds* and it was.

20   You took the sons and daughters whom you had borne to me, and
     sacrificed them to these images for their food. Was this of less account
21   than your fornication? No! you slaughtered my children and handed
22   them over, you surrendered them to your images. With all your abomin-
     able fornication you forgot those early days when you lay naked and
     exposed, kicking helplessly in your own blood.

23   After all the evil you had done (Oh! the pity of it, says the Lord
24   GOD), you built yourself a couch and constructed a high-stool in every
25   open place. You built up your high-stools at the top of every street and
     disgraced your beauty, offering your body to any passer-by in countless
26   acts of fornication. You committed fornication with your gross neigh-
     bours, the Egyptians, and you provoked me to anger by your countless
     acts of fornication.

27   I stretched out my hand against you and cut down your portion.
     Then I gave you up to women who hated you, Philistine women, who
28   were so disgusted by your lewd ways. Not content with this, you com-
     mitted fornication with the Assyrians, led them into fornication and
29   still were not content. You committed countless acts of fornication in
     Chaldaea, the land of commerce, and even with this you were not
     content.

30   How you anger me! says the Lord GOD. You have done all this like
31   the imperious whore you are. You have built your couch at the top of
     every street and constructed your stool in every open place, but, unlike
32   the common prostitute, you have scorned a fee. An adulterous wife who
33   owes obedience to her husband takes a fee from^a strangers. The prosti-
     tute also takes her fee; but you give presents to all your lovers, you bribe
34   them to come from all quarters to commit fornication with you. You
     are the very opposite of other women in your fornication: no one runs
     after you, you do not receive a fee, you give it. You are the very opposite.

35, 36   Listen to the words of the LORD, whore that you are. These are the
     words of the Lord GOD: You have been prodigal in your excesses, you
     have exposed your naked body in fornication with your lovers. In return
     for your abominable idols and for the slaughter of the children you have
37   given them, I will gather all those lovers to whom you made advances,^{b}
     all whom you loved and all whom you hated. I will gather them in from
     all quarters against you; I will strip you naked before them, and they
38   shall see your whole body naked. I will put you on trial for adultery
     and murder, and I will charge you with^c blood shed in jealousy and
39   fury. Then I will hand you over to them. They will demolish your
     couch and pull down your high-stool; they will strip your clothes off,
     take away your splendid ornaments, and leave you naked and exposed.

[a] a fee from: *prob. rdg.; Heb. om.* [b] to whom...advances: *or* whom you charmed.
[c] charge you with: *prob. mng.; Heb.* give you.

They will bring up the mob against you and stone you, they will hack 40
you to pieces with their swords. They will burn down your houses and 41
execute judgement on you, and many women shall see it. I will put an
end to your fornication, and you shall never again give a fee to your
lovers. Then I will abate my fury, and my jealousy will turn away from 42
you. I will be calm and will no longer be provoked to anger. For you 43
had forgotten the days of your youth and exasperated me with all your
doings: so I in my turn*a* brought retribution upon you for your deeds.
This is the very word of the Lord GOD.

Did you not commit these obscenities, as well as all your other
abominations? Dealers in proverbs will say of you, 'Like mother, like 44
daughter.' You are a true daughter of a mother who loathed her hus- 45
band and children. You are a true sister of your sisters*b* who loathed
their husbands and children. You are all daughters of a Hittite mother
and an Amorite father. Your elder sister was Samaria, who lived with 46
her daughters to the north of you; your younger sister, who lived with
her daughters to the south of you, was Sodom. Did you not behave as 47
they did and commit the same abominations? You came very near to
doing even worse than they. As I live, says the Lord GOD, your sister 48
Sodom and her daughters never behaved as you and your daughters
have done. This was the iniquity of your sister Sodom: she and her 49
daughters had pride of wealth and food in plenty, comfort and ease, and
yet she never helped the poor and wretched. They grew haughty and 50
did deeds abominable in my sight, and I made away with them, as you
have seen. Samaria was never half the sinner you have been; you have 51
committed more abominations than she, abominations which have made
your sister seem innocent. You must bear the humiliation which you 52
thought your sisters*c* deserved. Your sins are so much more abominable
than theirs that they appear innocent in comparison with you; and now
you must bear your shame and humiliation and make your sisters*c* seem
innocent.

But I will restore the fortunes of Sodom and her daughters and of 53
Samaria and her daughters, and I will restore*d* yours at the same time.
Even though you bring them comfort, you will bear your shame, you 54
will be disgraced for all you have done; but when your sister Sodom and 55
her daughters become what they were of old, and when your sister
Samaria and her daughters become what they were of old, then you and
your daughters will be restored. Did you not hear and talk much of 56
your sister Sodom in the days of your pride, before your wickedness was 57
exposed, in the days when the daughters of Aram with those about her
were disgraced, and the daughters of the Philistines round about, who

[*a*] *So Vulg.; Heb. adds* behold.   [*b*] *So Sept.; Heb.* sister.   [*c*] *So some MSS.; others* sister.
[*d*] I will restore: *so Sept.; Heb.* restoration.

58 so despised you? Now you too must bear the consequences of your
lewd and abominable conduct. This is the very word of the LORD.

59   These are the words of the Lord GOD: I will treat you as you have
deserved, because you violated a covenant and made light of a solemn
60 oath. But I will remember the covenant I made with you when you
were young, and I will establish with you a covenant which shall last
61 for ever. And you will remember your past ways and feel ashamed when
you receive your sisters, the elder and the younger. For I will give them
62 to you as daughters, and they shall not be outside your covenant.*a* Thus
I will establish my covenant with you, and you shall know that I am the
63 LORD. You will remember, and will be so ashamed and humiliated that
you will never open your mouth again once I have accepted expiation
for all you have done. This is the very word of the Lord GOD.

17 1,2   These were the words of the LORD to me: Man, speak to the Israel-
3 ites in allegory and parable. Tell them that these are the words of the
Lord GOD:

> A great eagle
> with broad wings and long pinions,
> in full plumage, richly patterned,
>   came to Lebanon.
> He took the very top of a cedar-tree,
4 >   he plucked its highest twig;
> he carried it off to a land of commerce,
>   and planted it in a city of merchants.
5 > Then he took a native seed
>   and put it in nursery-ground;
>   he set it like a willow,
> a shoot beside abundant water.
6 > It sprouted and became a vine,
>   sprawling low along the ground
> and bending its trailing boughs towards him*b*
> with its roots growing beneath him.
> So it became a vine, it branched out
>   and put forth shoots.
7 > But there was another*c* great eagle
> with broad wings and thick plumage;
> and this vine gave its roots
>   a twist towards him;*b*
> it pushed out its trailing boughs towards him,
> seeking drink from the bed where it was planted,

[a] and they...covenant: *or* though not on the ground of your covenant.   [b] *Or* inwards.
[c] *So Sept.; Heb.* one.

> though it had been set　　　　　　　　　　8
> in good ground beside abundant water
> that it might bear shoots and be fruitful
> and become a noble vine.

Tell them that these are the words of the Lord GOD:　　　9

> Can such a vine flourish?
> Will not its roots be broken off
> and its fruit be stripped,
> and all its fresh sprouting leaves wither,*a*
> until it is uprooted and carried away
> with little effort and few hands?
> If it is transplanted, can it flourish?　　　　10
> Will it not be utterly shrivelled,
> as though by the touch of the east wind,
> on the bed where it ought to sprout?

These were the words of the LORD to me: Say to that rebellious 11, 12
people, Do you not know what this means? The king of Babylon came
to Jerusalem, took its king and its officers and had them brought to him at
Babylon. He took a prince of the royal line and made a treaty with him, 13
putting him on his oath. He took away the chief men of the country, so 14
that it should become a humble kingdom unable to raise itself but ready
to observe the treaty and keep it in force. But the prince rebelled against 15
him and sent messengers to Egypt, asking for horses and men in plenty.
Can such a man prosper? Can he escape destruction if he acts in this
way? Can he violate a covenant and escape? As I live, says the Lord 16
GOD, I swear that he shall die in the land of the king who put him on
the throne; he made light of his oath and violated the covenant he made
with him. He shall die in Babylon. Pharaoh will send no large army, no 17
great host, to protect him in battle; no siege-ramp will be raised, no
watch-tower put up, nor will the lives of many men be lost. He has 18
violated a covenant and has made light of his oath. He had submitted,
and yet he did all these things; he shall not escape.
These then are the words of the Lord GOD: As I live, he has made 19
light of the oath he took by me and has violated the covenant I made
with him. I will bring retribution upon him; I will cast my net over 20
him, and he shall be caught in its meshes. I will carry him to Babylon
and bring him to judgement there, because he has broken faith with
me. In all his squadrons every commander shall fall by the sword; 21
those who are left will be scattered to the four winds. Thus you shall
know that it is I, the LORD, who have spoken.

[a] *So Sept.; Heb. adds* it will wither.

22   These are the words of the Lord GOD:

> I, too, will take a slip
> from the lofty crown of the cedar
> and set it in the soil;
> I will pluck a tender shoot from the topmost branch
> and plant it.

23   I will plant it high on a lofty mountain,
> the highest mountain in Israel.
> It will put out branches, bear its fruit,
> and become a noble cedar.
> Winged birds of every kind will roost under it,
> they will roost in the shelter of its sweeping boughs.

24   All the trees of the country-side will know
> that it is I, the LORD,
> who bring low the tall tree
> and raise the low tree high,
> who dry up the green tree
> and make the dry tree put forth buds.
> I, the LORD, have spoken and will do it.

18 1,2 THESE WERE THE WORDS OF THE LORD TO ME: What do you all mean by repeating this proverb in the land of Israel:

> 'The fathers have eaten sour grapes,
> and the children's teeth are set on edge'?

3   As I live, says the Lord GOD, this proverb shall never again be used in
4   Israel. Every living soul belongs to me; father and son alike are mine. The soul that sins shall die.
5   Consider the man who is righteous and does what is just and right.
6   He never feasts at mountain-shrines, never lifts his eyes to the idols of Israel, never dishonours another man's wife, never approaches a woman
7   during her periods. He oppresses no man, he returns the debtor's pledge,[a] he never robs. He gives bread to the hungry and clothes to
8   those who have none. He never lends either at discount or at interest.
9   He shuns injustice and deals fairly between man and man. He conforms to my statutes and loyally observes my laws. Such a man is righteous: he shall live, says the Lord GOD.
10   He may have a son who is a man of violence and a cut-throat who turns
11 his back on these rules.[b] He obeys none of them, he feasts at mountain-
12 shrines, he dishonours another man's wife, he oppresses the unfortunate

[a] the debtor's pledge: *so Sept.; Heb. unintelligible.* [b] who turns...rules: *prob. rdg.; Heb. unintelligible.*

and the poor, he is a robber, he does not return the debtor's pledge, he lifts his eyes to idols and joins in abominable rites; he lends both at 13 discount and at interest. Such a man shall not live. Because he has committed all these abominations he shall die, and his blood will be on his own head.

This man in turn may have a son who sees all his father's sins; he 14 sees, but he commits none of them. He never feasts at mountain-shrines, 15 never lifts his eyes to the idols of Israel, never dishonours another man's wife. He oppresses no man, takes no pledge, does not rob. He 16 gives bread to the hungry and clothes to those who have none. He shuns 17 injustice,*a* he never lends either at discount or at interest. He keeps my laws and conforms to my statutes. Such a man shall not die for his father's wrongdoing; he shall live.

His father may have been guilty of oppression and robbery*b* and may 18 have lived an evil life among his kinsfolk, and so has died because of his iniquity. You may ask, 'Why is the son not punished for his father's 19 iniquity?' Because he has always done what is just and right and has been careful to obey all my laws, therefore he shall live. It is the soul 20 that sins, and no other, that shall die; a son shall not share a father's guilt, nor a father his son's. The righteous man shall reap the fruit of his own righteousness, and the wicked man the fruit of his own wickedness.

It may be that a wicked man gives up his sinful ways and keeps all my 21 laws, doing what is just and right. That man shall live; he shall not die. None of the offences he has committed shall be remembered against 22 him; he shall live because of his righteous deeds. Have I any desire, 23 says the Lord God, for the death of a wicked man? Would I not rather that he should mend his ways and live?

It may be that a righteous man turns back from his righteous ways 24 and commits every kind of abomination that the wicked practise; shall he do this and live? No, none of his former righteousness will be remembered in his favour; he has broken his faith, he has sinned, and he shall die. You say that the Lord acts without principle? Listen, you 25 Israelites, it is you who act without principle, not I. If a righteous man 26 turns from his righteousness, takes to evil ways and dies,*c* it is because of these evil ways that he dies. Again, if a wicked man turns from his 27 wicked ways and does what is just and right, he will save his life. If he sees his offences as they are and turns his back on them all, then 28 he shall live; he shall not die.

'The Lord acts without principle', say the Israelites. No, Israelites, 29 it is you who act without principle, not I. Therefore, Israelites, says the 30

[a] injustice: *so Sept.; Heb.* the unfortunate. [b] *So Sept.; Heb.* robbery of a brother.
[c] *Prob. rdg.; Heb. adds* because of them.

Lord GOD, I will judge every man of you on his deeds. Turn, turn from
31 your offences, or your iniquity will be your downfall. Throw off the
load of your past misdeeds; get yourselves a new heart and a new spirit.
32 Why should you die, you men of Israel? I have no desire for any man's
death. This is the very word of the Lord GOD.[a]

19 1,2　　Raise a lament over the princes of Israel and say:

Your mother was a lioness
　　among the lions!
She made her lair among the young lions
　　and many were the cubs she bore.
3　　One of her cubs she raised,
　　and he grew into a young lion.
He learnt to tear his prey,
　　he devoured men.
4　　Then the nations shouted at[b] him
　　and he was caught in their pit,
and they dragged him with hooks to the land of Egypt.
5　　His case, she saw, was desperate, her hope was lost;
　　so she took another[c] of her cubs
　　and made him a young lion.
6　　He prowled among the lions
　　and acted like a young lion.
He learnt to tear his prey,
　　he devoured men;
7　　he broke down their palaces,[d] laid their cities in ruins.
　　The land and all that was in it
　　was aghast at the noise of his roaring.
8　　From the provinces all round
　　the nations raised the hue and cry;
　　they cast their net over him
　　and he was caught in their pit.
9　　With hooks they drew him into a cage
　　and brought him to the king of Babylon,
　　who flung him into prison,
that his voice might never again be heard
　　on the mountains of Israel.

10　　Your mother was a vine in a vineyard[e]
　　planted by the waterside.
It grew fruitful and luxuriant,
　　for there was water in plenty.

[a] *So Sept.; Heb.* adds and bring back and live.　[b] shouted at: *or* heard a report about.
[c] *So Sept.; Heb.* one.　[d] he broke...palaces: *so Targ.; Heb.* he knew his widows.
[e] in a vineyard: *prob. rdg.; Heb. obscure in context.*

It had stout branches,   11
   fit to make sceptres for those who bear rule.
It grew tall, finding its way through the foliage,
and conspicuous for its height and many trailing boughs.
But it was torn up in anger and thrown to the ground;   12
   the east wind blighted it,
     its fruit was blown off,
     its strong branches were blighted,
     and fire burnt it.
Now it is replanted in the wilderness,   13
in a dry and thirsty land;
and fire bursts forth from its own branches   14
   and burns up its shoots.[a]
It has no strong branch any more
   to make a sceptre for those who bear rule.

This is the lament and as a lament it passed into use.

ON THE TENTH DAY OF THE FIFTH MONTH in the seventh 20
year, some of the elders of Israel came to consult the LORD and
were sitting with me. Then this word came to me from the LORD: 2
Man, say to the elders of Israel, This is the word of the Lord GOD: Do 3
you come to consult me? As I live, I will not be consulted by you. This
is the very word of the Lord GOD.

   Will you judge them? Will you judge them, O man? Then tell them 4
of the abominations of their forefathers and say to them, These are the 5
words of the Lord GOD: When I chose Israel, with uplifted hand I
bound myself by oath to the race of Jacob and revealed myself to them
in Egypt; I lifted up my hand and declared: I am the LORD your God.
On that day I swore with hand uplifted that I would bring them out of 6
Egypt into the land I had sought out for them, a land flowing with milk
and honey, fairest of all lands. I told them, every one, to cast away the 7
loathsome things on which they feasted their eyes and not to defile
themselves with the idols of Egypt. I am the LORD your God, I said.

   But they rebelled against me, they refused to listen to me, and not 8
one of them cast away the loathsome things on which he feasted his
eyes or forsook the idols of Egypt. I had thought to pour out my wrath
and exhaust my anger on them in Egypt. I acted for the honour of my 9
name, that it might not be profaned in the sight of the nations among
whom Israel was living: I revealed myself to them by bringing Israel
out of Egypt. I brought them out of Egypt and led them into the 10
wilderness. There I gave my statutes to them and taught them my laws, 11

[a] *Prob. rdg.; Heb. adds* its fruit.

12 so that by keeping them men might have life. Further, I gave them my sabbaths as a sign between us, so that they should know that I, the
13 LORD, was hallowing them for myself. But the Israelites rebelled against me in the wilderness; they did not conform to my statutes, they rejected my laws, though by keeping them men might have life, and they utterly desecrated my sabbaths. So again I thought to pour out my wrath on
14 them in the wilderness to destroy them. I acted for the honour of my name, that it might not be profaned in the sight of the nations who had seen me bring them out.
15 Further, I swore to them in the wilderness with uplifted hand that I would not bring them into the land I had given them, that land flowing
16 with milk and honey, fairest of all lands. For they had rejected my laws, they would not conform to my statutes and they desecrated my sabbaths,
17 because they loved to follow idols of their own. Yet I pitied them too much to destroy them and did not make an end of them in the wilder-
18 ness. I commanded their sons in the wilderness not to conform to their fathers' statutes, nor observe their laws, nor defile themselves with their
19 idols. I said, I am the LORD your God, you must conform to my
20 statutes; you must observe my laws and act according to them. You must keep my sabbaths holy, and they will become a sign between us; so you will know that I am the LORD your God.
21 But the sons too rebelled against me. They did not conform to my statutes or observe my laws, though any who had done so would have had life through them, and they desecrated my sabbaths. Again I thought to pour out my wrath and exhaust my anger on them in the
22 wilderness.*a* I acted for the honour of my name, that it might not be profaned in the sight of the nations who had seen me bring them out.
23 Yes, and in the wilderness I swore to them with uplifted hand that I
24 would disperse them among the nations and scatter them abroad, because they had disobeyed my laws, rejected my statutes, desecrated my sabbaths, and turned longing eyes toward the idols of their forefathers.
25 I did more; I imposed on them statutes that were not good statutes, and
26 laws by which they could not win life. I let them defile themselves with gifts to idols; I made them surrender their eldest sons to them so that I might fill them with horror. Thus they would know that I am the LORD.
27 Speak then, O man, to the Israelites and say to them, These are the words of the Lord GOD: Once again your forefathers insulted me and
28 broke faith with me: when I brought them into the land which I had sworn with uplifted hand to give them, they marked down every hilltop and every leafy tree, and there they offered their sacrifices, they made the gifts which roused my anger, they set out their offerings of

[a] *So Sept.; Heb. adds* and then withdraw my hand.

soothing odour and poured out their drink-offerings. I asked them, 29
What is this hill-shrine to which you are going up? And 'hill-shrine'
has been its name ever since.

So tell the Israelites, These are the words of the Lord GOD: Are you 30
defiling yourselves as your forefathers did? Are you wantonly giving
yourselves to their loathsome gods? When you bring your gifts, when 31
you pass your sons through the fire, you are still defiling yourselves in
the service of your crowd of idols. How can I let you consult me, men of
Israel? As I live, says the Lord GOD, I will not be consulted by you.
When you say to yourselves, 'Let us become like the nations and tribes 32
of other lands and worship wood and stone', you are thinking of something that can never be. As I live, says the Lord GOD, I will reign over 33
you with a strong hand, with arm outstretched and wrath outpoured. I 34
will bring you out from the peoples and gather you from the lands over
which you have been scattered by my strong hand, my outstretched
arm and outpoured wrath. I will bring you into the wilderness of the 35
peoples; there will I confront you, and there will I state my case against
you. Even as I did in the wilderness of Egypt against your forefathers, so 36
will I state my case against you. This is the very word of the Lord GOD.

I will pass you under the rod and bring you within the bond*a* of the 37
covenant. I will rid you of those who revolt and rebel against me. I will 38
take them out of the land where they are now living, but they shall not
set foot on the soil of Israel. Thus shall you know that I am the LORD.

Now, men of Israel, these are the words of the Lord GOD: Go, sweep 39
away*b* your idols, every man of you. So in days to come you will never be
disobedient to me or desecrate my holy name with your gifts and your
idolatries. But on my holy hill, the lofty hill of Israel, says the Lord 40
GOD, there shall the Israelites serve me in the land, every one of them.
There will I receive them with favour; there will I demand your contribution and the best of your offerings, with all your consecrated gifts.
I will receive your offerings of soothing odour, when I have brought 41
you out from the peoples and gathered you from the lands where you
have been scattered. I, and only I, will have your worship, for all the
nations to see.

You will know that I am the LORD, when I bring you home to the 42
soil of Israel, to the land which I swore with uplifted hand to give your
forefathers. There you will remember your past ways and all the wan- 43
ton deeds with which you have defiled yourselves, and will loathe yourselves for all the evils you have done. You will know that I am the 44
LORD, when I have dealt with you, O men of Israel, not as your wicked
ways and your vicious deeds deserve but for the honour of my name.
This is the very word of the Lord GOD.

[*a*] *Or* muster. [*b*] sweep away: *so Sept.; Heb.* serve.

45,^a 46 These were the words of the LORD to me: Man, turn and face towards Teman^b and pour out your words to the south; prophesy to the
47 rough country of the Negeb. Say to it, Listen to the words of the LORD.
These are the words of the Lord GOD: I will set fire to you, and the fire
will consume all the wood, green and dry alike. Its fiery flame shall not
be put out, but from the Negeb northwards every face will be scorched
48 by it. All men will see that it is I, the LORD, who have set it ablaze; it
49 shall not be put out. 'Ah no! O Lord GOD,' I cried; 'they say of me,
"He deals only in parables."'

21 1, 2 These were the words of the LORD to me: Man, turn and face towards
Jerusalem, and pour out your words against her sanctuary;^c prophesy
3 against the land of Israel. Say to the land of Israel, These are the words
of the LORD: I am against you; I will draw my sword from the scabbard
4 and cut off from you both righteous and wicked. It is because I would
cut off your righteous and your wicked equally that my sword will be
drawn from the scabbard against all men, from the Negeb northwards.
5 All men shall know that I the LORD have drawn my sword; it shall never
6 again be sheathed. Groan in their presence, man, groan bitterly until
7 your lungs are bursting. When they ask you why you are groaning, say
to them, 'I groan at the thing I have heard; when it comes, all hearts
melt, all courage fails, all hands fall limp, all men's knees run with
urine. It is coming. It is here.' This is the very word of the Lord
GOD.

8, 9 These were the words of the LORD to me: Prophesy, man, and say,
This is the word of the Lord:

> A sword, a sword is sharpened and burnished,
> 10   sharpened to kill and kill again,
>   burnished to flash^d like lightning.
> Ah! the club is brandished, my son,
>   to defy all wooden idols!^e
> 11   The sword is given to be burnished
>   ready for the hand to grasp.
> The sword—it is sharpened,
>   it is burnished,
> ready to be put into the slayer's hand.

12 Cry, man, and howl; for all this falls on my people, it falls on Israel's
princes who are delivered over to the sword and are slain with my
13 people. Therefore beat your breast^f in remorse, for it is the test—and
what if it is not in truth the club of defiance? This is the very word of
the Lord GOD.

[a] *21. 1 in Heb.*   [b] *Or* face southward.   [c] her sanctuary: *prob. rdg.; Heb.* sanctuaries.
[d] to flash: *prob. rdg.; Heb. unintelligible.*   [e] wooden idols: *lit.* wood.   [f] *Lit.* thigh.

But you, man, prophesy and clap your hands together;   14
    swing the sword twice, thrice:
      it is the sword of slaughter,
the great sword of slaughter whirling about them.
That their hearts may be troubled and many stumble and fall,   15
I have set the threat of the sword at all their gates,
    the threat of the sword[a] made to flash like lightning
    and drawn to kill.
Be sharpened,[b] turn right; be unsheathed, turn left,   16
    wherever your point is aimed.

I, too, will clap my hands together and abate my anger. I, the LORD,   17
have spoken.

These were the words of the LORD to me: Man, trace out two roads   18, 19
by which the sword of the king of Babylon may come, starting both of
them from the same land. Then carve a signpost, carve it at the point
where the highway forks. Mark out a road for the sword to come to[c] the   20
Ammonite city of Rabbah, to[c] Judah, and to Jerusalem at the heart of it.
For the king of Babylon halts to take the omens at the parting of the   21
ways, where the road divides. He casts lots with arrows, consults teraphim[d] and inspects the livers of beasts. The augur's arrow marked   22
'Jerusalem' falls at his right hand: here, then,[e] he must raise a shout[f]
and sound the battle-cry, set battering-rams against the gates, pile
siege-ramps and build watch-towers. It may well seem to the people that   23
the auguries are false,[g] whereas they will put me in mind of their
wrongdoing, and they will fall into the enemies' hand. These therefore   24
are the words of the Lord GOD: Because you have kept me mindful of
your wrongdoing by your open rebellion, and your sins have been
revealed in all your acts, because you have kept yourselves in my mind,
you will fall into the enemies' hand by force.

You, too, you impious and wicked prince of Israel, your fate has   25
come upon you in the hour of final punishment. These are the words   26
of the Lord GOD: Put off your diadem, lay aside your crown. All is
changed; raise the low and bring down the high. Ruin! Ruin! I will   27
bring about such ruin as never was before, until the rightful sovereign
comes. Then I will give him all.

Man, prophesy and say, These are the words of the Lord GOD to the   28
Ammonites and to their shameful god:

A sword, a sword drawn for slaughter,
    burnished for destruction,[h]

[a] the threat of the sword: *prob. rdg.; Heb. obscure in context.*   [b] *So Targ.; Heb.* Unify
yourself.   [c] *So Sept.; Heb.* with.   [d] *Or* household gods.   [e] *Prob. rdg.; Heb. adds* he
must set battering-rams.   [f] raise a shout: *so Sept.; Heb.* open his mouth in slaughter.
[g] *So Sept.; Heb. adds an unintelligible phrase.*   [h] for destruction: *prob. rdg.; Heb. obscure.*

to flash like lightning!

29 Your visions are false, your auguries a lie,
which bid you bring it*ᵃ* down
upon the necks of impious and wicked men,
whose fate has come upon them
in the hour of final punishment.

30 Sheathe it again.
I will judge you in the place where you were born,
the land of your origin.

31 I will pour out my rage upon you;
I will breathe out my blazing wrath over you.
I will hand you over to brutal men,
skilled in destruction.

32 You shall become fuel for fire,
your blood shall be shed within the land
and you shall leave no memory behind.

For I, the LORD, have spoken.

22 1,2 These were the words of the LORD to me: Man, will you judge her,
will you judge the murderous city and bring home to her all her abomin-
3 able deeds? Say to her, These are the words of the Lord GOD: Alas
for*ᵇ* the city that sheds blood within her walls and brings her fate upon
4 herself, the city that makes herself idols and is defiled thereby! The
guilt is yours for the blood you have shed, the pollution is on you for the
idols you have made. You have shortened your days by this and brought
the end of your years nearer. This is why I exposed you to the contempt
5 of the nations and the mockery of every country. Lands far and near
6 will taunt you with your infamy and gross disorder. In you the princes
7 of Israel, one and all, have used their power to shed blood; men have
treated their fathers and mothers with contempt, they have oppressed
8 the alien and ill-treated the orphan and the widow. You have disdained
9 what is sacred to me and desecrated my sabbaths. In you, Jerusalem,
informers have worked to procure bloodshed; in you are men who have
10 feasted at mountain-shrines and have committed lewdness. In you men
have*ᶜ* exposed their fathers' nakedness; they have violated women
11 during their periods; they have committed an outrage with their neighbours' wives and have lewdly defiled their daughters-in-law; they have
12 ravished their sisters, their own fathers' daughters. In you men have
accepted bribes to shed blood, and they*ᵈ* have exacted discount
and interest on their loans. You have oppressed your fellows for gain,
and you have forgotten me. This is the very word of the Lord GOD.

[a] *Prob. rdg.; Heb.* you. [b] Alas for: *so Sept.; Heb. om.* [c] *So Sept.; Heb.* he has.
[d] *So Sept.; Heb.* you.

See, I strike with my clenched fist in anger at your ill-gotten gains 13
and at the bloodshed within your walls. Will your strength or courage 14
stand when I deal with you? I, the LORD, have spoken and I will act. I 15
will disperse you among the nations and scatter you abroad; thus will
I rid you altogether of your defilement. I will sift you[a] in the sight of 16
the nations, and you will know that I am the LORD.

These were the words of the LORD to me: Man, to me all Israelites 17, 18
are an alloy, their silver alloyed with copper, tin, iron, and lead.[b] There- 19
fore, these are the words of the Lord GOD: Because you have all become
alloyed, I will gather you together into Jerusalem, as a mass of silver, 20
copper, iron, lead, and tin is gathered into a crucible for the fire to be
blown to full heat to melt them. So will I gather you in my anger and
wrath, set you there and melt you; I will collect you and blow up the 21
fire of my anger until you are melted within it. You will be melted as 22
silver is melted in a crucible, and you will know that I, the LORD, have
poured out my anger upon you.

These were the words of the LORD to me: Man, say to Jerusalem, 23, 24
You are like a land on which no rain has fallen;[c] no shower has come
down upon you[d] in the days of indignation. The princes within her 25
are[e] like lions growling as they tear their prey. They have devoured
men, and seized their treasure and all their wealth; they have widowed
many women within her walls. Her priests have done violence to my 26
law[f] and profaned what is sacred to me. They make no distinction
between sacred and common, and lead men to see no difference between clean and unclean. They have disregarded my sabbaths, and I am
dishonoured among them. Her officers within her are like wolves tearing 27
their prey, shedding blood and destroying men's lives to acquire ill-
gotten gain. Her prophets use whitewash instead of plaster;[g] their vision 28
is false and their divination a lie. They say, 'This is the word of the
Lord GOD', when the LORD has not spoken. The common people are 29
bullies and robbers; they ill-treat the unfortunate and the poor, they
are unjust and cruel to the alien. I looked for a man among them who 30
could build up a barricade, who could stand before me in the breach to
defend the land from ruin; but I found no such man. I poured out my 31
indignation upon them and utterly destroyed them in the fire of my
wrath. Thus I brought on them the punishment they had deserved.
This is the very word of the Lord GOD.

The word of the LORD came to me: Man, he said, there were once **23** 1, 2
two women, daughters of the same mother. They played the whore in 3

[a] I will sift you: *or* You will be profaned. [b] their silver...lead: *prob. rdg.; Heb.*
copper, tin, iron, and lead inside a crucible; they are an alloy, silver. [c] on which...
fallen: *so Sept.; Heb.* which has not been cleansed. [d] *Prob. rdg.; Heb.* it. [e] The princes...
are: *so Sept.; Heb.* The conspiracy of her prophets within her is. [f] *Or* instruction.
[g] *Cp. 13. 8–16.*

Egypt, played the whore while they were still girls; for there they let
4 their breasts be fondled and their virgin bosoms pressed. The elder was
named Oholah, her sister Oholibah. They became mine and bore me
5 sons and daughters. 'Oholah' is Samaria, 'Oholibah' Jerusalem. While
she owed me obedience Oholah played the whore and was infatuated
6 with her Assyrian lovers, staff officers in blue,[a] viceroys and governors,
7 handsome young cavaliers all of them, riding on horseback. She played
the whore with all of them, the flower of the Assyrian youth; and she let
8 herself be defiled with all their idols, wherever her lust led her. She
never gave up the whorish ways she had learnt in Egypt, where men
had lain with her when young, had pressed her virgin bosom and over-
9 whelmed her with their fornication. So I abandoned her to her lovers,
10 the Assyrians, with whom she was infatuated. They ravished her, they
took her sons and daughters, and they killed her with the sword. She
became a byword among women, and judgement was passed upon her.
11   Oholibah, her sister, had watched her, and she gave herself up to lust
12 and played the whore worse than her sister. She, too, was infatuated
with Assyrians, viceroys, governors and staff officers, all handsome young
13 cavaliers, in full dress, riding on horseback. I found that she too had let
14 herself be defiled; both had gone the same way; but she carried her
fornication to greater lengths: she saw male figures carved on the wall,
15 sculptured forms of Chaldaeans, picked out in vermilion. Belts were
round their waists, and on their heads turbans with dangling ends. All
seemed to be high officers and looked like Babylonians, natives of
16 Chaldaea. As she looked she was infatuated with them, so she sent
17 messengers to Chaldaea for them. And the Babylonians came to her to
share her bed, and defiled her with fornication; she was defiled by them
18 until she was filled with revulsion. She made no secret that she was a
whore but let herself be ravished until I was filled with revulsion against
19 her as I was against her sister. She played the whore again and again,
20 remembering how in her youth she had played the whore in Egypt. She
was infatuated with their male prostitutes, whose members were like
21 those of asses and whose seed came in floods like that of horses. So,
Oholibah, you relived the lewdness of your girlhood in Egypt when you
let your bosom be pressed and your breasts fondled.[b]
22   Therefore these are the words of the Lord GOD: I will rouse them
against you, Oholibah, those lovers of yours who have filled you with
23 revulsion, and bring them upon you from every side, the Babylonians
and all those Chaldaeans, men of Pekod, Shoa, and Koa, and all the
Assyrians with them. Handsome young men they are, viceroys and
24 governors, commanders and staff officers,[c] riding on horseback. They

[a] *Or* violet.   [b] fondled: *prob. rdg.; Heb. unintelligible.*   [c] staff officers: *prob. rdg., cp.*
verses 5 and 12; Heb. obscure.

will come against you with war-horses,^a with chariots and wagons, with
a host drawn from the nations, armed with shield, buckler, and helmet;
they will beset you on every side. I will give them authority to judge,
and they will use that authority to judge you. I will turn my jealous 25
wrath loose on you, and they will make you feel their fury. They will
cut off your nose and your ears, and in the end you^b will fall by the
sword.^c They will strip you of your clothes and take away all your finery. 26
So I will put a stop to your lewdness and the way in which you learnt to 27
play the whore in Egypt. You will never cast longing eyes on such
things again, never remember Egypt any more.

These are the words of the Lord GOD: I am handing you over to 28
those whom you hate, those who have filled you with revulsion; and 29
they will make you feel their hatred. They will take all you have earned
and leave you naked and exposed; that body with which you have
played the whore will be ravished. It is your lewdness and your fornication that have brought this upon you, it is because you have followed 30
alien peoples and played the whore and have allowed yourself to be
defiled with their idols. You have followed in your sister's footsteps, 31
and I will put her cup into your hand.

These are the words of the Lord GOD: 32

> You shall drink from your sister's cup,
>   a cup deep and wide,
> charged with mockery and scorn,
>   more than ever cup can hold.
> It^d will be full of drunkenness and grief,   33
>   a cup of ruin and desolation,
> the cup of your sister Samaria;
> and you shall drink it to the dregs.   34
>   Then you will chew^e it in pieces
>   and tear out your breasts.
> This is my verdict, says the Lord GOD.

Therefore, these are the words of the Lord GOD: Because you have 35
forgotten me and flung me behind your back, you must bear the guilt of
your lewdness and your fornication.

The LORD said to me, Man, will you judge Oholah and Oholibah? 36
Then tax them with their vile offences. They have committed adultery, 37
and there is blood on their hands. They have committed adultery with
their idols and offered my children to them for food, the children they
had borne me. This too they have done to me: they have polluted my 38

---

[a] *So some MSS.; others have an unknown word.* [b] in the end you: *or* your successors.
[c] *Prob. rdg.; Heb. adds* They will take your sons and daughters, and in the end you will
be burnt. [d] *Prob. rdg.; Heb.* You. [e] *Or* dash.

39 sanctuary^a and desecrated my sabbaths. They came into my sanctuary
and desecrated it^a by slaughtering their sons as an offering to their
40 idols; this they did in my own house. They would send for men from a
far-off country; and the men came at the messenger's bidding. You
bathed your body for these men, you painted your eyes, decked your-
41 self in your finery, you sat yourself upon a bed of state and had a table
42 put ready before it and laid my own incense and my own oil on it. Loud
were the voices of the light-hearted crowd; and besides ordinary folk
Sabaeans were there, brought from the wilderness; they put bracelets
43 on the women's hands and beautiful garlands on their heads. I thought:
Ah that woman, grown old in adultery! Now they will commit fornica-
44 tion with her—with her of all women^b! They^c resorted to her as a
prostitute; they resorted to Oholah and Oholibah, those lewd women.
45 Upright men will condemn them for their adultery and bloodshed; for
adulterous they are, and blood is on their hands.

46   These are the words of the Lord GOD: Summon the invading host;
47 abandon them to terror and rapine. Let the host stone them and hack
them to pieces with their swords, kill their sons and daughters and burn
48 down their houses. Thus I will put an end to lewdness in the land, and
49 other women shall be taught not to be as lewd as they.^d You shall pay
the penalty for your lewd conduct and be punished for your idolatries,
and you will know that I am the Lord GOD.

24   These were the words of the LORD, spoken to me on the tenth day of
2 the tenth month in the ninth year: Man, write down a name for this day,
this very day: This is the day the king of Babylon invested Jerusalem.
3 Sing a song of derision to this people of rebels; say to them, These are
the words of the Lord GOD:

> Set a cauldron on the fire,
> set it on and pour water into it.
4   Into it collect the pieces,
> all the choice pieces,
> cram it with leg and shoulder and the best of the bones;
5   take the best of the flock.
> Pack the logs^e round it underneath;
> seethe the stew
> and boil the bones in it.

6   O city running with blood,
> O pot green with corrosion,
> corrosion that will never be clean!

---

[a] *So Sept.; Heb. adds* on that day.   [b] with her of all women: *lit. and* her.   [c] *So one MS.; others* He.   [d] *So Sept.; Heb.* you.   [e] *Prob. rdg., cp. verse 10; Heb.* bones.

Therefore these are the words of the Lord GOD:

> Empty it, piece after piece,
>   though no lot is cast for any of them.
> The city had blood in her midst   7
> and she poured it out on the gleaming rock,
>   not on the ground: she did not pour it there
>   for the dust to cover it.
> But I too have spilt blood on the gleaming white rock   8
>   so that it cannot be covered,
> to make anger flare up and to call down vengeance.

Therefore these are the words of the Lord GOD: 9

> O city running with blood,
>   I too will make a great fire-pit.
> Fill it with logs, light the fire;   10
>   make an end of the meat,
> pour out all the broth^a and the bones with it.^b
> Then set the pot empty on the coals   11
> so that its copper may be heated red-hot,
>   and then the impurities in it may be melted
>   and its corrosion burnt off.
> Try as you may,^c   12
> the corrosion is so deep that it will not come off;
>   only fire will rid it of corrosion for you.
> Even so, when I cleansed you in your filthy lewdness,   13
>   you did not become clean from it,
>   and therefore you shall never again be clean
>   until I have satisfied my anger against you.

I, the LORD, have spoken; the time is coming, I will act. I will not 14
refrain nor pity nor relent; I^d will judge you for your conduct and for
all that you have done. This is the very word of the Lord GOD.

These were the words of the LORD to me: Man, I am taking from 15, 16
you at one blow the dearest thing you have, but you must not wail or
weep or give way to tears. Keep in good heart; be quiet, and make no 17
mourning for the dead; cover your head as usual and put sandals on
your feet. You shall not cover your upper lip in mourning nor eat the
bread of despair.

I spoke to the people in the morning; and that very evening my wife 18
died. Next morning I did as I was told. The people asked me to say 19
what meaning my behaviour had for them. I answered, These were the 20

[*a*] pour…broth: *prob. rdg.; Heb.* mix ointment. [*b*] with it: *prob. rdg.; Heb.* will be
scorched. [*c*] Try as you may: *prob. rdg.; Heb. obscure.* [*d*] *So Sept.; Heb.* they.

21 words of the LORD to me: Tell the Israelites, This is the word of the
Lord GOD: I will desecrate my sanctuary, which has been the pride of
your strength, the delight of your eyes and your heart's desire; and the
sons and daughters whom you have left behind shall fall by the sword.
22 But, I said, you shall do as I have done: you shall not cover your upper
23 lip in mourning nor eat the bread of despair. You shall cover your head
and put sandals on your feet; you shall not wail nor weep. Because of
your wickedness you will pine away and will lament to*a* one another.
24 The LORD says, Ezekiel will be a sign to warn you, and when it happens
you will do as he has done, and you will know that I am the Lord GOD.
25 And now, man, a word for you: I am taking from them that fortress
whose beauty so gladdened them, the delight of their eyes, their heart's
26 desire; I am taking their sons and their daughters. Soon fugitives will
27 come and tell you their news by word of mouth. At once you will
recover the power of speech and speak with the fugitives; you will no
longer be dumb. So will you be a portent to them, and they shall know
that I am the LORD.

Prophecies against foreign nations

25 1,2 THESE WERE THE WORDS OF THE LORD TO ME: Man, look to-
3 wards the Ammonites and prophesy against them. Say to the
Ammonites, Listen to the word of the Lord GOD. These are his words:
Because you cried 'Aha!' when you saw my holy place desecrated, the
4 soil of Israel laid waste and the people of Judah sent into exile, I will
hand you over as a possession to the tribes of the east. They shall pitch
their camps and put up their dwellings among you; they shall eat your
5 crops; they shall drink your milk. I will make Rabbah a camel-pasture
and Ammon a sheep-walk. Thus you shall know that I am the LORD.
6 These are the words of the Lord GOD: Because you clapped your hands
and stamped your feet, and exulted over the land of Israel with single-
7 minded scorn, I will stretch out my hand over you and make you the
prey of the nations and cut you off from all other peoples; in every land
I will exterminate you and bring you to utter ruin. Thus you shall know
that I am the LORD.

8 These are the words of the Lord GOD: Because Moab*b* said, 'Judah
9 is like all the rest', I will expose the flank of Moab and lay open its
cities,*c* from one end to the other—the fairest of its cities: Beth-

[a] *Or* for. [b] *So Sept.; Heb. adds* and Seir. [c] *and lay* . . . *cities: prob. rdg.; Heb.* from the
cities, from its cities.

jeshimoth, Baal-meon and Kiriathaim. I will hand over Moab and 10
Ammon together to the tribes of the east to be their possession, so that
the Ammonites shall not be remembered among the nations, and so 11
that I may execute judgement upon Moab. Thus they shall know that I
am the LORD.

These are the words of the Lord GOD: Because Edom took deliberate 12
revenge on Judah and by so doing incurred lasting guilt, I will stretch 13
my hand out over Edom, says the Lord GOD, and destroy both man and
beast in it, laying waste the land from Teman as far as Dedan; they
shall fall by the sword. I will wreak my vengeance upon Edom through 14
my people Israel. They will deal with Edom as my anger and fury
demand, and it shall feel my vengeance. This is the very word of the
Lord GOD.

These are the words of the Lord GOD: Because the Philistines have 15
taken deliberate revenge and have avenged themselves with single-
minded scorn, giving vent to their age-long enmity in destruction, I will 16
stretch out my hand over the Philistines, says the Lord GOD, I will
wipe out the Kerethites and destroy all the rest of the dwellers by the
sea. I will take fearful vengeance upon them and punish them in my 17
fury. When I take my vengeance, they shall know that I am the LORD.

These were the words of the LORD to me on the first day of the first[a] 26
month in the eleventh year: Man, Tyre has said of Jerusalem, 2

> Aha! she that was the gateway of the nations
>   is broken,
> her gates swing open to me;
> I grow rich, she lies in ruins.[b]

Therefore these are the words of the Lord GOD: 3

> I am against you, Tyre,
> and will bring up many nations against you
>   as the sea brings up its waves;
> they will destroy the walls of Tyre and pull down her towers. 4
>   I will scrape the soil off her
> and make her a gleaming rock,
> she shall be an islet where men spread their nets; 5
>   I have spoken, says the Lord GOD.
>   She shall become the prey of nations,
> and her daughters[c] shall be slain by the sword in the open country. 6

[a] first: *so Sept.; Heb. om.* [b] I...ruins: *or, with Sept.,* she that was rich lies in ruins.
[c] *Or* daughter-towns.

Thus they shall know that I am the LORD.

7   These are the words of the Lord GOD: I am bringing against Tyre from the north Nebuchadrezzar king of Babylon, king of kings. He will come with horses and chariots, with cavalry and a great army.

8
> Your daughters in the open country
>   he will put to the sword.
> He will set up watch-towers against you,
>   pile up siege-ramps against you
> and raise against you a screen of shields.

9
> He will launch his battering-rams on your walls
>   and break down your towers with his axes.

10
> He will cover you with dust from the thousands of his cavalry;
>   at the thunder of his horses
>   and of his chariot-wheels
> your walls will quake when he enters your gates
>   as men enter a city that is breached.

11
> He will trample all your streets
>   with the hooves of his horses
> and put your people to the sword,
> and your strong pillars will fall to the ground.

12
> Your wealth will become spoil,
>   your merchandise will be plundered,
>   your walls levelled,
> your pleasant houses pulled down;
> your stones, your timber and your rubble
>   will be dumped into the sea.[a]

13
> So I will silence the clamour of your songs,
> and the sound of your harps shall be heard no more.

14
> I will make you a gleaming rock,
>   a place for fishermen to spread their nets,
>   and you[b] shall never be rebuilt.
> I, the LORD, have spoken.
>   This is the very word of the Lord GOD.

15   These are the words of the Lord GOD to Tyre: How the coasts and islands will shake at the sound of your downfall, while the wounded
16 groan, and the slaughter goes on[c] in your midst! Then all the sea-kings will come down from their thrones, and lay aside their cloaks, and strip off their brocaded robes. They will wear coarse loin-cloths; they will sit on the ground, shuddering at every moment, horror-struck at your fate.
17 Then they will raise this dirge over you:

[a] *Lit.* water. [b] *So Sept.; Heb.* she. [c] and...goes on: *or, with slight change,* when he who is struck is bowed down.

How you are undone, swept[a] from the sea,
O famous city!
You whose strength lay in the sea,
you and your inhabitants,
who spread their terror throughout the mainland.[b]
Now the coast-lands tremble on the day of your downfall, 18
and the isles of the sea are appalled at your passing.

For these are the words of the Lord GOD: When I make you a deso- 19
late city, like a city where no man can live, when I bring up the primeval
ocean against you and the great waters cover you, I will thrust you down 20
with those that descend to the abyss, to the dead of all the ages. I will
make you dwell in the underworld as in places long desolate, with
those that go down to the abyss. So you will never again be inhabited or
take your place[c] in the land of the living. I will bring you to a fearful 21
end, and you shall be no more; men may look for you but will never find
you again. This is the very word of the Lord GOD.

These were the words of the LORD to me: Man, raise a dirge over Tyre 27 1, 2
and say, Tyre, throned above your harbours, you who carry the trade of the 3
nations to many coasts and islands, these are the words of the Lord GOD:

O Tyre, you said,
'I am perfect in beauty.'
Your frontiers are on the high seas, 4
your builders made your beauty perfect;
they fashioned all your timbers 5
of pine from Senir;
they took a cedar from Lebanon
to raise up a mast over you.
They made your oars of oaks from Bashan; 6
they made your deck strong[d] with box-wood
from the coasts of Kittim.
Your canvas was linen, 7
patterned linen from Egypt
to make your sails;
your awnings were violet and purple
from the coasts of Elishah.
Men of Sidon and Arvad became your oarsmen; 8
you had skilled men within you, O Tyre,
who served as your helmsmen.
You had skilled veterans from Gebal 9
caulking your seams.

[a] swept: *so Sept.; Heb.* inhabited. [b] the mainland: *prob. rdg.; Heb.* her inhabitants.
[c] or...place: *so Sept.; Heb.* I will give beauty. [d] strong: *prob. rdg.; Heb.* ivory.

> You had all sea-going ships and their sailors
> to market your wares;
10   men of Pharas,[a] Lud,[b] and Put, served
> as warriors in your army;
> they hung shield and helmet around you,
> and it was they who gave you your glory.
11   Men of Arvad and Cilicia manned all your walls,
> men of Gammad were posted on your towers
> and hung their shields around your battlements;
> it was they who made your beauty perfect.

12 Tarshish was a source of your commerce, from its abundant resources
13 offering silver and iron, tin and lead, as your staple wares. Javan,[c]
Tubal, and Meshech dealt with you, offering slaves and vessels of
14 bronze as your imports. Men from Togarmah offered horses, mares, and
15 mules as your staple wares. Rhodians[d] dealt with you, great islands were
a source of your commerce, paying what was due to you in ivory and
16 ebony. Edom[e] was a source of your commerce, so many were your
undertakings, and offered purple garnets, brocade and fine linen, black
17 coral and red jasper,[f] for your staple wares. Judah and Israel dealt with
you, offering wheat from Minnith, and meal, syrup, oil, and balsam, as
18 your imports. Damascus was a source of your commerce, so many
were your undertakings, from its abundant resources offering wine of
19 Helbon and wool of Suhar, and casks of wine from Izalla,[g] for your
staple wares; wrought iron, cassia, and sweet cane were among your
20 imports. Dedan dealt with you in coarse woollens for saddle-cloths.
21 Arabia and all the chiefs of Kedar were the source of your commerce in
22 lambs, rams, and he-goats; this was your trade with them. Dealers from
Sheba and Raamah dealt with you, offering the choicest spices, every
23 kind of precious stone and gold, as your staple wares. Harran, Kanneh,
24 and Eden,[h] dealers from Asshur and all Media,[i] dealt with you; they
were your dealers in gorgeous stuffs, violet cloths and brocades, in
stores of coloured fabric rolled up and tied with cords; your dealings
with them were in these.

25   Ships of Tarshish were the caravans for your imports;
> you were deeply laden with full cargoes
> on the high seas.
26   Your oarsmen brought you into many waters,
> but on the high seas an east wind wrecked you.
27   Your wealth, your staple wares, your imports,

[a] *Or* Persia.   [b] *Or* Lydia.   [c] *Or* Ionia.   [d] *So Sept.; Heb.* Dedanites.   [e] *So some*
MSS.; others Aram.   [f] *Or* and carbuncles.   [g] casks...Izalla: *prob. rdg.; Heb. obscure.*
[h] *So Sept.; Heb. adds* Sheba.   [i] all Media: *prob. rdg., cp. Targ.; Heb.* Kilmad.

your sailors and your helmsmen,
your caulkers, your merchants, and your warriors,
all your ship's company,
all who were with you,
were flung into the sea on the day of your disaster;
at the cries of your helmsmen the troubled waters tossed.   28

When all the rowers disembark from their ships,   29
when the sailors, the helmsmen all together, go ashore,
they exclaim over your fate,   30
they cry out bitterly;
they throw dust on their heads
and sprinkle themselves with ashes.
They tear out their hair at your plight   31
and put on sackcloth;
they weep bitterly over you,
bitterly wailing.
In their lamentation they raise a dirge over you,   32
and this is their dirge:
Who was like Tyre,
with her buildings piled[a] off shore?
When your wares were unloaded off the sea   33
you met the needs of many nations;
with your vast resources and your imports
you enriched the kings of the earth.
Now you are broken by the sea   34
in deep water;
your wares and all your company are gone overboard.
All who dwell on the coasts and islands   35
are aghast at your fate;
horror is written on the faces of their kings
and their hair stands on end.
Among the nations the merchants jeer in derision at you;   36
you have come to a fearful end and shall be no more for ever.

These were the words of the LORD to me: Man, say to the prince of   28 1, 2
Tyre, This is the word of the Lord GOD:

In your arrogance you say,
'I am a god;
I sit throned like a god on the high seas.'
Though you are a man and no god,
you try to think the thoughts of a god.

[a] with her buildings piled: *prob. rdg.; Heb. obscure.*

3   What? are you wiser than Danel[a]?
      Is no secret too dark for you?
4   Clever and shrewd as you are,
      you have amassed wealth for yourself,
    you have amassed gold and silver in your treasuries;
5   by great cleverness in your trading
        you have heaped up riches,
    and with your riches your arrogance has grown.

6 Therefore these are the words of the Lord GOD:

    Because you try to think the thoughts of a god
7   I will bring strangers against you,
      the most ruthless of nations,
  who will draw their swords against your fine wisdom
    and lay your pride in the dust,
8   sending you down to the pit[b] to die
    a death of disgrace on the high seas.
9   Will you dare to say that you are a god
      when you face your assailants,
    though you are a man and no god
    in the hands of those who lay you low?
10   You will die strengthless
      at the hands of strangers.

For I have spoken. This is the very word of the Lord GOD.
11, 12   These were the words of the LORD to me: Man, raise this dirge over
the king of Tyre, and say to him, This is the word of the Lord GOD:

    You set the seal on perfection;
    full of wisdom you were and altogether beautiful.
13   You were in an Eden, a garden of God,
    adorned with gems of every kind:
    sardin and chrysolite and jade,
    topaz, cornelian and green jasper,
    lapis lazuli,[c] purple garnet and green felspar.
    Your jingling beads were of gold,
    and the spangles you wore were made for you
      on the day of your birth.
14   I set you with a towering cherub[d] as guardian;
      you were on God's holy hill
    and you walked proudly among stones that flashed with fire.
15   You were blameless in all your ways

[a] *Or, as otherwise read,* Daniel; *cp. 14. 14, 20.*   [b] *Or* to destruction.   [c] *Or* sapphire.
[d] I set...cherub: *prob. rdg.; Heb.* You were a towering cherub whom I set.

from the day of your birth
until your iniquity came to light.
    Your commerce grew so great,   16
lawlessness filled your heart and you went wrong,
so I brought you down in disgrace from the mountain of God,
   and the guardian cherub banished you[a]
      from among the stones that flashed like fire.
    Your beauty made you arrogant,   17
you misused your wisdom to increase your dignity.
    I flung you to the ground,
I left you there, a sight for kings to see.
So great was your sin in your wicked trading   18
   that you desecrated your sanctuaries.
So I kindled a fire within you,
   and it devoured you.
I left you as ashes on the ground
   for all to see.
All among the nations who knew you were aghast: 19
you came to a fearful end and shall be no more for ever.

These were the words of the Lord to me: Man, look towards Sidon 20, 21
and prophesy against her. These are the words of the Lord God: 22

Sidon, I am against you
   and I will show my glory in your midst.

Men will know that I am the Lord
when I execute judgement upon her
   and thereby prove my holiness.
I will let loose pestilence upon her   23
   and bloodshed in her streets;
the slain will fall in her streets,
beset on all sides by the sword;
then men will know that I am the Lord.

No longer shall the Israelites suffer from the scorn of their neigh- 24
bours, the pricking of briars and scratching of thorns, and they shall
know that I am the Lord God.
    These are the words of the Lord God: When I gather the Israelites 25
from the peoples among whom they are scattered, I shall thereby prove
my holiness in the sight of all nations. They shall live on their native soil,
which I gave to my servant Jacob. They shall live there in peace of mind, 26
build houses and plant vineyards; they shall live there in peace of

[a] and the...you: *or* and I parted you, O guardian cherub,...

mind when I execute judgement on all their scornful neighbours. Thus they shall know that I am the LORD their God.

29 These were the words of the LORD to me on the twelfth day of the
2 tenth month in the tenth year: Man, look towards Pharaoh king of
3 Egypt and prophesy against him and all his country. Say, These are the words of the Lord GOD:

> I am against you,
>> Pharaoh king of Egypt,
>>> you great monster,[a]
> lurking in the streams of the Nile.
> You have said, 'My Nile is my own;
>> it was I who made it.'[b]

4 I will put hooks in your jaws
> and make them cling[c] to your scales.
> I will hoist you out of its streams
> with all its fish clinging to your scales.

5 I will fling you into the wilderness,
>> you and all the fish in your streams;
>> you will fall on the bare ground
>> with none to pick you up and bury[d] you;
>>> I will make you food
>>> for beasts and for birds.

6 So all who live in Egypt will know
>> that I am the LORD,
> for the support that you[e] gave to the Israelites
> was no better than a reed,

7 which splintered in the hand when they grasped you,
>> and tore their armpits;
> when they leaned upon you, you snapped
> and their limbs gave way.

8 This therefore is the word of the Lord GOD: I am bringing a sword
9 upon you to destroy both man and beast. The land of Egypt shall become a desolate waste, and they shall know that I am the LORD,
10 because you[f] said, 'The Nile is mine; it was I who made it.' I am against you therefore, you and your Nile, and I will make Egypt desolate, wasted by drought, from Migdol to Syene and up to the very
11 frontier of Cush. No foot of man shall pass through it, no foot of beast;
12 it shall lie uninhabited for forty years. I will make the land of Egypt the

---

[a] monster: *so some MSS.; others* jackals. [b] it was…it: *so Pesh., cp. verse 9; Heb.* I even made myself. [c] make them cling: *prob. rdg.; Heb.* make the fish of your streams cling. [d] bury: *so some MSS.; others* gather. [e] *So Sept.; Heb.* they. [f] *So Sept.; Heb.* he.

most desolate of desolate lands; her cities shall lie derelict among the ruined cities. For forty years shall they lie derelict, and I will scatter the Egyptians among the nations and disperse them among the lands.

These are the words of the Lord GOD: At the end of forty years I 13 will gather the Egyptians from the peoples among whom they are scattered. I will turn the fortunes of Egypt and bring them back to Pathros, 14 the land of their origin, where they shall become a petty kingdom. She 15 shall be the most paltry of kingdoms and never again exalt herself over the nations, for I will make the Egyptians too few to rule over them. The Israelites will never trust Egypt again; this will be a reminder to 16 them of their sin in turning to Egypt for help. They shall know that I am the Lord GOD.

These were the words of the LORD to me on the first day of the first 17 month in the twenty-seventh year: Man, long did Nebuchadrezzar king 18 of Babylon keep his army in the field against Tyre, until every head was rubbed bare and every shoulder chafed. But neither he nor his army gained anything from Tyre for their long service against her. This, 19 therefore, is the word of the Lord GOD: I am giving the land of Egypt to Nebuchadrezzar king of Babylon. He shall carry off its wealth, he shall spoil and plunder it, and so his army will be paid. I have given 20 him the land of Egypt as the wages for his service because they have disregarded me. This is the very word of the Lord GOD.

At that time I will make Israel put out fresh shoots,*ᵃ* and give you 21 back the power to speak among them, and they will know that I am the LORD.

These were the words of the LORD to me: Man, prophesy and say, 30 1, 2 These are the words of the Lord GOD:

> Woe, woe for the day!
>   for a day is near,   3
>   a day of the LORD is near,
>   a day of cloud, a day of reckoning for the nations.
>   Then a sword will come upon Egypt,   4
>   and there will be anguish in Cush,
>   when the slain fall in Egypt,
> when its wealth is taken and its foundations are torn up.
>   Cush and Put and Lud,*ᵇ*   5
>   all the Arabs and Libyans*ᶜ* and the peoples of allied lands,
>   shall fall with them by the sword.

These are the words of the LORD: 6

> All who support Egypt shall fall
> and her boasted might be brought low;

[*a*] fresh shoots: *lit.* a horn. [*b*] *Or* Lydia. [*c*] *So Sept.; Heb.* Kub.

from Migdol to Syene men shall fall by the sword.
This is the very word of the Lord GOD.

7   They shall be the most desolate of desolate lands, and their[a] cities
8 shall lie derelict among the ruined cities. When I set Egypt on fire and
9 all her helpers are broken, they will know that I am the LORD. When
that time comes messengers shall go out in haste[b] from my presence to
alarm Cush, still without a care, and anguish shall come upon her in
Egypt's hour. Even now it is on the way.

10   These are the words of the Lord GOD:

> I will make an end of Egypt's hordes
> by the hands of Nebuchadrezzar king of Babylon.

11   He and his people with him, the most ruthless of nations,
> will be brought to ravage the land.
> They will draw their swords against Egypt
> and fill the land with the slain.

12   I will make the streams of the Nile dry land
> and sell Egypt to evil men;
> I will lay waste the land and everything in it by foreign hands.
> I, the LORD, have spoken.

13   These are the words of the Lord GOD:

> I will make an end of the lordlings[c]
> and wipe out the princelings[d] of Noph;
> and never again shall a prince arise in Egypt.
> Then I will put fear in that land,

14   I will lay Pathros waste and set fire to Zoan
> and execute judgement on No.

15   I will pour out my rage upon Sin,
>   the bastion of Egypt,
> and destroy the horde of Noph.[e]

16   I will set Egypt on fire,
> and Syene[f] shall writhe in anguish;
> the walls of No shall be breached
>   and flood-waters shall burst into it.[g]

17   The young men of On and Pi-beseth[h] shall fall by the sword
> and the cities themselves go into captivity.

18   Daylight shall fail in Tahpanhes
> when I break the yoke of Egypt there;
> then her boasted might shall be subdued;

[a] *Prob. rdg., cp. Sept.; Heb.* his.   [b] in haste: *so Sept.; Heb.* in ships.   [c] *Or* idols.
[d] *Or* false gods.   [e] *So Sept.; Heb.* No.   [f] *So Sept.; Heb.* Sin.   [g] flood-waters...it:
prob. rdg., cp. Sept.; Heb. obscure.   [h] *Or* Bubastis.

a cloud shall cover her,
and her daughters*ᵃ* shall go into captivity.
Thus I will execute judgement on Egypt,   19
and they shall know that I am the LORD.

This was the word of the LORD to me on the seventh day of the first 20
month in the eleventh year: Man, I have broken the arm of Pharaoh 21
king of Egypt. See, it has not been bound up with dressings and bandage*ᵇ* to give it strength to wield a sword. These, therefore, are the 22
words of the Lord GOD: I am against Pharaoh king of Egypt; I will
break both his arms, the sound and the broken, and make the sword
drop from his hand. I will scatter the Egyptians among the nations and 23
disperse them over many lands. Then I will strengthen the arms of the 24
king of Babylon and put my sword in his hand; but I will break
Pharaoh's arms, and he shall lie wounded and groaning before him. I 25
will give strength to the arms of the king of Babylon, but the arms of
Pharaoh will fall. Men will know that I am the LORD, when I put my
sword in the hand of the king of Babylon, and he stretches it out over
the land of Egypt. I will scatter the Egyptians among the nations and 26
disperse them over many lands, and they shall know that I am the LORD.
On the first day of the third month in the eleventh year this word 31
came to me from the LORD: Man, say to Pharaoh king of Egypt and all 2
his horde:

What are you like in your greatness?

Look at Assyria: it was a cedar in Lebanon,   3
    whose fair branches overshadowed the forest,
towering high with its crown finding a way through the foliage.
Springs nourished it, underground waters gave it height,   4
their streams washed the soil all round it
and sent forth their rills to every tree in the country.
So it grew taller than every other tree.   5
Its boughs were many, its branches spread far;
    for water was abundant in the channels.
In its boughs all the birds of the air had their nests,   6
under its branches all wild creatures bore their young,
and in its shadow all great nations made their home.
    A splendid great tree it was, with its long spreading boughs, 7
for its roots were beside abundant waters.
    No cedar in God's garden overshadowed it,   8
    no fir could compare with its boughs,
    and no plane-tree had such branches;

[a] *Or* daughter-towns.   [b] *So Sept.; Heb. adds* to bind it up.

not a tree in God's garden
could rival its beauty.
9   I, the LORD, gave it beauty
with its mass of spreading boughs,
the envy of all the trees in Eden,
the garden of God.

10   Therefore these are the words of the Lord GOD: Because it[a] grew so
high and pushed its crown up through the foliage, and its pride mounted
11   as it grew, therefore I handed it over to a prince of the nations to deal
12   with it; I made an example of it as its wickedness deserved. Strangers
from the most ruthless of nations hewed it down and flung it away. Its
sweeping boughs fell on the mountains and in all the valleys, and its
branches lay broken beside all the streams in the land. All nations of the
13   earth came out from under its shade and left it. All the birds of the air
settled on its fallen trunk; the wild creatures all stood by its branches.
14   Never again, therefore, shall the well-watered trees grow so high or
push their crowns up through the foliage. Nor shall the strongest of
them, well watered though they be, stand erect in their full height; for
all have been given over to death, to the world below, to share the
common doom and go down to the abyss.
15   These are the words of the Lord GOD: When he went down to Sheol,
I closed the deep over him as a gate, I dammed its rivers, the great
waters were held back. I put Lebanon in mourning for him, and all the
16   trees of the country-side wilted. I made nations shake with the crash of
his fall, when I brought him down to Sheol with those who go down to
the abyss. From this all the trees of Eden, all the choicest and best of
Lebanon, all the well-watered trees, drew comfort in the world below.
17   They too like him had gone down to Sheol, to those slain with the
sword; and those who had lived in his shadow were scattered among the
18   nations. Which among the trees of Eden was like you in glory and greatness? Yet you will be brought down with the trees of Eden to the world
below; you will lie with those who have been slain by the sword, in the
company of the strengthless dead. This stands for Pharaoh and all his
horde. This is the very word of the Lord GOD.
32   On the first day of the twelfth month in the twelfth[b] year the word of
2   the LORD came to me: Man, raise a dirge over Pharaoh king of Egypt
and say to him:

Young lion of the nations, you are undone.
You were like a monster[c] in the waters of the Nile

[a] *So Pesh.; Heb.* you.   [b] *Or, with some MSS.,* eleventh.   [c] a monster: *so some
MSS.; others* jackals.

scattering the water with its snout,[a][b]
churning the water with its feet
and fouling the streams.

These are the words of the Lord GOD: When many nations are 3
gathered together I will spread my net over you, and you will be
dragged up in its meshes. I will fling you on land, dashing you down 4
on the bare ground. I will let all the birds of the air settle upon you and
all the wild beasts gorge themselves on your flesh. Your flesh I will lay 5
on the mountains, and fill the valleys with the worms that feed on it.
I will drench the land with your discharge, drench it with your blood 6
to the very mountain-tops, and the watercourses shall be full of you.
When I put out your light I will veil the sky and blacken its stars; I 7
will veil the sun with a cloud, and the moon shall not give its light.
I will darken all the shining lights of the sky above you and bring dark- 8
ness over your land. This is the very word of the Lord GOD.

I will disquiet[c] many peoples when I bring your broken army among 9
the nations into lands you have never known. I will appal many peoples 10
with your fate; when I brandish my sword in the faces of their kings,
their hair shall stand on end. In the day of your downfall each shall
tremble for his own fate from moment to moment. For these are the 11
words of the Lord GOD: The sword of the king of Babylon shall come
upon you. I will make the whole horde of you fall by the sword of 12
warriors who are of all men the most ruthless. They shall make havoc
of the pride of Egypt, and all its horde shall be wiped out. I will destroy 13
all their cattle beside many waters. No foot of man, no hoof of beast,
shall ever churn them up again. Then will I let their waters settle and 14
their streams run smooth as oil. This is the very word of the Lord
GOD. When I have laid Egypt waste, and the whole land is devastated, 15
when I strike down all who dwell there, they shall know that I am the
LORD.

This is a dirge, and the women of the nations shall sing it as a dirge. 16
They shall sing it as a dirge, as a dirge over Egypt and all its horde. This
is the very word of the Lord GOD.

On the fifteenth day of the first[d] month in the twelfth year, the word 17
of the LORD came to me:

Man, raise a lament, you and the daughters of the nations, 18
over the hordes of Egypt and her nobles,
whom I will bring down[e] to the world below
with those that go down to the abyss.

[a] snout: *prob. rdg.; Heb.* streams. [b] scattering...snout: *or* heaving itself up in the
streams. [c] *So. Targ.; Heb.* vex. [d] first: *so Sept.; Heb. om.* [e] her nobles...down:
prob. rdg.; Heb. obscure.

19   Are you better favoured than others?
     Go down and be laid to rest with the strengthless dead.

20   A sword stands ready. Those who marched with her, and all her
21   horde, shall fall into the midst of those slain by the sword. Warrior
     chieftains in Sheol speak to Pharaoh*a* and those who aided him:
     The strengthless dead, slain by the sword, have come down and
22   are laid to rest. There is Assyria with all her company, her buried
23   around her, all of them slain and fallen by the sword. Her graves are set
     in the recesses of the abyss, with her company buried around her, all of
     them slain, fallen by the sword, men who once filled the land of the
24   living with terror. There is Elam, with all her hordes buried around her,
     all of them slain, fallen by the sword; they have gone down strengthless
     to the world below, men who struck terror into the land of the living
25   but now share the disgrace of those that go down to the abyss. In the
     midst of the slain a resting-place has been made for her, with all her
     hordes buried around her; all of them strengthless, slain by the sword.
     For they who once struck terror into the land of the living now share
     the disgrace of those that go down to the abyss; they are assigned a
26   place in the midst of the slain. There are Meshech and Tubal with all
     their hordes, with their buried around them, all of them strengthless
     and slain by the sword, men who once struck terror into the land of the
27   living. Do they not rest with warriors fallen strengthless,*b* who have
     gone down to Sheol with their weapons, their swords under their heads
     and their shields over their bones,*c* though the terror of their prowess*d*
28   once lay on the land of the living? You also, Pharaoh, shall lie broken in
     the company of the strengthless dead, resting with those slain by the
29   sword. There is Edom, her kings and all her princes, who, for all their
     prowess, have been lodged with those slain by the sword; they shall rest
     with the strengthless dead and with those that go down to the abyss.
30   There are all the princes of the North and all the Sidonians, who have
     gone down in shame with the slain, for all the terror they inspired by
     their prowess. They rest strengthless with those slain by the sword, and
     they share the disgrace of those that go down to the abyss.
31   Pharaoh will see them and will take comfort for his lost hordes—
     Pharaoh who, with all his army, is slain by the sword, says the Lord
32   GOD; though he spread*e* terror throughout the land of the living, yet he
     with all his horde is laid to rest with those that are slain by the sword, in
     the company of the strengthless dead. This is the very word of the Lord
     GOD.

[a] *Lit.* him. [b] *Prob. rdg.; Heb.* from strengthless ones. [c] and...bones: *prob. rdg.; Heb.*
unintelligible. [d] their prowess: *so Pesh.; Heb.* warriors. [e] *Prob. rdg.; Heb.* I have spread.

The remnant of Israel in the land

THESE WERE THE WORDS OF THE LORD TO ME: Man, say to 33 1, 2
your fellow-countrymen, When I set armies in motion against a
land, its people choose one of themselves to be a watchman. When he 3
sees the enemy approaching and blows his trumpet to warn the people,
then if anyone does not heed the warning and is overtaken by the enemy, 4
he is responsible for his own fate. He is responsible because, when he 5
heard the alarm, he paid no heed to it; if he had heeded it, he would
have escaped. But if the watchman does not blow his trumpet or warn 6
the people when he sees the enemy approaching, then any man who is
killed is caught with all his sins upon him; but I will hold the watchman
answerable for his death.[a]

Man, I have appointed you a watchman for the Israelites. You will 7
take messages from me and carry my warnings to them. It may be that 8
I pronounce sentence of death on a man because he is wicked; if you do
not warn him to give up his ways, the guilt is his and because of his
wickedness he shall die, but I will hold you answerable for his death.
But if you have warned him to give up his ways, and he has not given 9
them up, he will die because of his wickedness, but you will have saved
yourself.

Man, say to the Israelites, You complain, 'We are burdened by our 10
sins and offences; we are pining away because of them; we despair of
life.' So tell them: As I live, says the Lord GOD, I have no desire for the 11
death of the wicked. I would rather that a wicked man should mend his
ways and live. Give up your evil ways, give them up; O Israelites, why
should you die?

Man, say to your fellow-countrymen, When a righteous man goes 12
wrong, his righteousness shall not save him. When a wicked man mends
his ways, his former wickedness shall not bring him down. When a
righteous man sins, all his righteousness cannot save his life. It may be 13
that, when I tell the righteous man that he will save his life, he presumes
on his righteousness and does wrong; then none of his righteous acts
will be remembered: he will die for the wrong he has done. It may be 14
that when I pronounce sentence of death on the wicked, he mends his
ways and does what is just and right: if he then restores the pledges he 15
has taken, repays what he has stolen, and, doing no more wrong, follows
the rules that ensure life, he shall live and not die. None of the sins he 16
has committed shall be remembered against him; he shall live, because
he does what is just and right.

[a] hold...death: *lit.* require his blood from the watchman's hands.

17 Your fellow-countrymen are saying, 'The Lord acts without prin-
18 ciple', but it is their ways that are unprincipled. When a righteous man
gives up his righteousness and does wrong, he shall die because of it;
19 and when a wicked man gives up his wickedness and does what is just
20 and right, he shall live. How, Israel, can you say that the Lord acts
without principle, when I judge every man of you on his deeds?

21 On the fifth day of the tenth month in the twelfth*a* year of our captivity, fugitives came to me from Jerusalem and told me that the city
22 had fallen. The evening before they arrived, the hand of the LORD had
come upon me, and by the time they reached me in the morning the
LORD had given me back my speech. My speech was restored and I was
no longer dumb.

23, 24 These were the words of the LORD to me: Man, the inhabitants of
these wastes on the soil of Israel say, 'When Abraham took possession
of the land he was but one; now we are many, and the land has been
25 granted to us in possession.' Tell them, therefore, that these are the
words of the Lord GOD: You eat meat with the blood in it, you lift up
your eyes to idols, you shed*b* blood; and yet you expect to possess the
26 land! You trust to the sword, you commit abominations, you defile one
27 another's wives; and you expect to possess the land! Tell them that
these are the words of the Lord GOD: As I live, among the ruins they
shall fall by the sword; in the open country I will give them for food to
28 beasts; in dens and caves they shall die by pestilence. I will make the
land a desolate waste; her boasted might shall be brought to nothing,
29 and the mountains of Israel shall be an untrodden desert. When I make
the land a desolate waste because of all the abominations they have
committed, they will know that I am the LORD.

30 Man, your fellow-countrymen gather in groups and talk of you
under walls and in doorways and say to one another, 'Let us go and see
31 what message there is from the LORD.' So my people will come crowding
in, as people do, and sit down in front of you. They will hear what you
have to say, but they will not do it. 'Fine words*c*!' they will say, but
32 their hearts are set on selfish gain. You are no more to them than a
singer of fine songs*d* with a lovely voice, or a clever harpist; they will
33 listen to what you say but will certainly not do it. But when it comes, as
come it will, they will know that there has been a prophet in their midst.

34 1, 2 These were the words of the LORD to me: Prophesy, man, against the
shepherds of Israel; prophesy and say to them, You shepherds, these
are the words of the Lord GOD: How I hate the shepherds of Israel who
care only for themselves! Should not the shepherd care for the sheep?
3 You consume the milk, wear the wool, and slaughter the fat beasts, but

[a] *Or, with some MSS.,* eleventh.   [b] *Or* pour out.   [c] Fine words: *or* Love songs.
[d] fine songs: *or* love songs.

you do not feed the sheep. You have not encouraged the weary, tended 4
the sick, bandaged the hurt, recovered the straggler, or searched for the
lost; and even the strong[a] you have driven with ruthless severity. They 5
are scattered, they have no shepherd, they have become the prey of wild
beasts.[b] My sheep go straying over the mountains and on every high 6
hill, my flock is dispersed over the whole country, with no one to ask
after them or search for them.

Therefore, you shepherds, hear the words of the LORD. As surely as I 7,8
live, says the Lord GOD, because my sheep are ravaged by wild beasts
and have become their prey for lack of a shepherd, because my shepherds have not asked after the sheep but have cared only for themselves
and not for the sheep—therefore, you shepherds, hear the words of the 9
LORD. These are the words of the Lord GOD: I am against the shepherds 10
and will demand my sheep from them. I will dismiss those shepherds:
they shall care only for themselves no longer; I will rescue my sheep
from their jaws, and they shall feed on them no more.

For these are the words of the Lord GOD: Now I myself will ask 11
after my sheep and go in search of them. As a shepherd goes in search 12
of his sheep when his flock is dispersed all around him, so I will go in
search of my sheep and rescue them, no matter where they were scattered in dark and cloudy days. I will bring them out from every nation, 13
gather them in from other lands, and lead them home to their own soil.
I will graze them on the mountains of Israel, by her streams and in all
her green fields. I will feed them on good grazing-ground, and their 14
pasture shall be the high mountains of Israel. There they will rest, there
in good pasture, and find rich grazing on the mountains of Israel. I 15
myself will tend my flock, I myself pen them in their fold, says the Lord
GOD. I will search for the lost, recover the straggler, bandage the hurt, 16
strengthen the sick, leave the healthy and strong to play,[c] and give them
their proper food.

As for you, my flock, these are the words of the Lord GOD: I will 17
judge between one sheep and another. You rams and he-goats! Are you 18
not satisfied with grazing on good herbage, that you must trample down
the rest with your feet? Or with drinking clear water, that you must
churn up the rest with your feet? My flock has to eat what you have 19
trampled and drink what you have churned up. These, therefore, are 20
the words of the Lord GOD to them: Now I myself will judge between
the fat sheep and the lean. You hustle the weary with flank and shoulder, 21
you butt them with your horns until you have driven them away and
scattered them abroad. Therefore I will save my flock, and they shall be 22
ravaged no more; I will judge between one sheep and another. Then I 23

[a] even the strong: *so Sept.; Heb.* strongly.   [b] *So Pesh.; Heb. adds* and they are scattered.
[c] leave...to play: *or, with Sept.,* tend the healthy and strong.

will set over them one shepherd to take care of them, my servant David;
24 he shall care for them and become their shepherd. I, the LORD, will
become their God, and my servant David shall be a prince among them.
25 I, the LORD, have spoken. I will make a covenant with them to ensure
prosperity; I will rid the land of wild beasts, and men shall live in peace
26 of mind on the open pastures and sleep in the woods. I will settle them
in the neighbourhood of my hill[a] and send them rain in due season,
27 blessed rain. Trees in the country-side shall bear their fruit, the land
shall yield its produce, and men shall live in peace of mind on their
own soil. They shall know that I am the LORD when I break the bars of
28 their yokes and rescue them from those who have enslaved them. They
shall never be ravaged by the nations again nor shall wild beasts devour
29 them; they shall live in peace of mind, with no one to alarm them. I will
give prosperity[b] to their plantations; they shall never again be victims
of famine in the land nor any longer bear the taunts of the nations.
30 They shall know that I, the LORD their God, am with them, and that
31 they are my people Israel, says the Lord GOD. You are my flock, my
people, the flock I feed, and I am your God. This is the very word of the
Lord GOD.

35 1,2   These were the words of the LORD to me: Man, look towards the
3 hill-country of Seir and prophesy against it. Say, These are the words of
the Lord GOD:

> O hill-country of Seir, I am against you:
> I will stretch out my hand over you
> and make you a desolate waste.
4   I will lay your cities in ruins
> and you shall be made desolate;
> thus you shall know that I am the LORD.

5   For you have maintained an immemorial feud
> and handed over the Israelites to the sword
>   in the hour of their doom,
>   at the time of their final punishment.

6   Therefore, as I live, says the Lord GOD,
> I make blood your destiny, and blood shall pursue you;
>   you are most surely guilty of[c] blood,
>   and blood shall pursue you.

7   I will make the hill-country of Seir a desolate waste
> and put an end to all in it who pass to and fro;
8   I will fill[d] your hills and your valleys with its slain,
> and those slain by the sword shall fall into your streams.

---

[a] *So Sept.; Heb. adds* a blessing.   [b] prosperity: *so Sept.; Heb.* a name.   [c] are most
surely guilty of: *so Sept.; Heb.* most surely hate.   [d] *So Sept.; Heb. adds* its mountains.

> I will make you desolate for ever,   9
> and your cities shall not be inhabited;
> thus you shall know that I am the LORD.

You say, The two nations and the two countries shall be mine and I 10
will take possession of them, though the LORD is*a* there. Therefore, as 11
I live, says the Lord GOD, your anger and jealousy shall be requited, for I
will do to you what you have done in your hatred against them. I shall
be known among you*b* when I judge you; you shall know that I am 12
the LORD. I have heard all your blasphemies; you have said, 'The
mountains of Israel are desolate and have been given to us to devour.'
You have set yourselves up against me and spoken recklessly against me. 13
I myself have heard you. These are the words of the Lord GOD: I will 14
make you so desolate that the whole world will gloat over you. I will do 15
to you as you did to Israel my own possession when you gloated over its
desolation. O hill-country of Seir, you will be desolate, and it will be
the end of all Edom. Thus men will know that I am the LORD.

And do you, man, prophesy to the mountains of Israel and say, 36
Mountains of Israel, hear the words of the LORD. These are the words 2
of the Lord GOD: The enemy has said, 'Aha! now the everlasting high-
lands are ours.' Therefore prophesy and say, These are the words of the 3
Lord GOD: You mountains of Israel, all round you men gloated over
you and trampled you down when you were seized and occupied by the
rest of the nations; your name was bandied about in the common talk of
men. Therefore, listen to the words of the Lord GOD when he speaks to 4
the mountains and hills, to the streams and valleys, to the desolate
palaces and deserted cities, all plundered and despised by the rest of the
nations round you. These are the words of the Lord GOD: In the fire of 5
my jealousy I have spoken plainly against the rest of the nations, and
against Edom above all. For Edom, swollen with triumphant scorn,
seized on my land to hold it up to public contempt. Therefore prophesy 6
over the soil of Israel and say to the mountains and hills, the streams and
valleys, These are the words of the Lord GOD: I have spoken my mind
in jealousy and anger because you have had to endure the taunts of all
nations. Therefore, says the Lord GOD, I have sworn with uplifted hand 7
that the nations round about shall be punished for*c* their taunts. But 8
you, mountains of Israel, you shall put forth your branches and yield
your fruit for my people Israel, for their home-coming is near. See now, 9
I am for you, I will turn to you, and you shall be tilled and sown.
I will plant many men upon you—the whole house of Israel. The cities 10
shall again be inhabited and the palaces rebuilt. I will plant many men 11
and beasts upon you; they shall increase and be fruitful. I will make you

[a] *Or* has been.   [b] *So Sept.; Heb.* them.   [c] be punished for: *or* bear.

populous as in days of old and more prosperous than you were at first.

12 Thus you will know that I am the LORD. I will make men—my people Israel—tread your paths again. They shall settle in you, and you shall be their possession; but you shall never again rob them of their children.

13 These are the words of the Lord GOD: People say that you are a land
14 that devours men and robs your tribes of their children. But you shall never devour men any more nor rob your tribes of their children, says
15 the Lord GOD. I will never let you hear the taunts of the nations again nor shall you have to endure the reproaches of the peoples.*a* This is the very word of the Lord GOD.

16, 17 These were the words of the LORD to me: Man, when the Israelites lived on their own soil they defiled it with their ways and deeds; their
18 ways were foul and disgusting*b* in my sight. I poured out my fury upon them because of the blood they had poured out upon the land, and the
19 idols with which they had defiled it. I scattered them among the nations, and they were dispersed among different countries; I passed on them
20 the sentence which their ways and deeds deserved. When they*c* came among those nations, they caused my holy name to be profaned wherever they came: men said of them, 'These are the people of the
21 LORD, and it is from his land that they have come.' And I spared them for the sake of my holy name which the Israelites had profaned among the nations to whom they had gone.

22 Therefore tell the Israelites that these are the words of the Lord GOD: It is not for your sake, you Israelites, that I am acting, but for the sake of my holy name, which you have profaned among the peoples
23 where you have gone. I will hallow my great name, which has been profaned among those nations. When they see that I reveal my holiness through you, the nations will know that I am the LORD, says the Lord
24 GOD. I will take you out of the nations and gather you from every land
25 and bring you to your own soil. I will sprinkle clean water over you, and you shall be cleansed from all that defiles you; I will cleanse you from
26 the taint of all your idols. I will give you a new heart and put a new spirit within you; I will take the heart of stone from your body and give
27 you a heart of flesh. I will put my spirit into you and make you conform
28 to my statutes, keep my laws and live by them. You shall live in the land which I gave to your ancestors; you shall become my people, and I will
29 become your God. I will save you from all that defiles you; I will call to the corn and make it plentiful; I will bring no more famine upon you.
30 I will make the trees bear abundant fruit and the ground yield heavy crops, so that you will never again have to bear the reproach of famine
31 among the nations. You will recall your wicked ways and evil deeds, and

[a] *So Sept.; Heb. adds* and you shall no more cause your tribes to fall. [b] disgusting: *lit.* like filth. [c] *So some MSS.; others* he.

you will loathe yourselves because of your wickedness and your abomina- tions. It is not for your sake that I am acting; be sure of that, says the 32 Lord GOD. Feel, then, the shame and disgrace of your ways, men of Israel.

These are the words of the Lord GOD: When I cleanse you of all your 33 wickedness, I will re-people the cities, and the palaces shall be rebuilt. The land now desolate shall be tilled, instead of lying waste for every 34 passer-by to see. Men will say that this same land which was waste has 35 become like a garden of Eden, and people will make their homes in the cities once ruined, wasted, and shattered, but now well fortified. The 36 nations still left around you will know that it is I, the LORD, who have rebuilt the shattered cities and planted anew the waste land; I, the LORD, have spoken and will do it.

These are the words of the Lord GOD: Yet again will I let the Israel- 37 ites ask me to act in their behalf. I will make their men numerous as sheep, like the sheep offered as holy-gifts, like the sheep in Jerusalem 38 at times of festival. So shall their ruined cities be filled with human flocks, and they shall know that I am the LORD.

The hand of the LORD came upon me, and he carried me out by his 37 spirit and put me down in a plain full of bones. He made me go to and 2 fro across them until I had been round them all;[a] they covered the plain, countless numbers of them, and they were very dry. He said to 3 me, 'Man, can these bones live again?' I answered, 'Only thou knowest that, Lord GOD.' He said to me, 'Prophesy over these bones and say to 4 them, O dry bones, hear the word of the LORD. This is the word of the 5 Lord GOD to these bones: I will put breath[b] into you, and you shall live. I will fasten sinews on you, bring flesh upon you, overlay you with 6 skin, and put breath in you, and you shall live; and you shall know that I am the LORD.' I began to prophesy as he had bidden me, and as I 7 prophesied there was a rustling sound and the bones fitted them- selves together. As I looked, sinews appeared upon them, flesh 8 covered them, and they were overlaid with skin, but there was no breath in them. Then he said to me, 'Prophesy to the wind, prophesy, 9 man, and say to it, These are the words of the Lord GOD: Come, O wind, come from every quarter and breathe into these slain, that they may come to life.' I began to prophesy as he had bidden me: breath 10 came into them; they came to life and rose to their feet, a mighty host. He said to me, 'Man, these bones are the whole people of Israel. They 11 say, "Our bones are dry, our thread of life is snapped, our web is severed from the loom."[c] Prophesy, therefore, and say to them, These 12 are the words of the Lord GOD: O my people, I will open your graves

[a] He made...all: *or* He made me pass all round them.   [b] *Or* wind *or* spirit.   [c] our web...loom: *prob. rdg.; Heb.* we are completely cut off.

13 and bring you up from them, and restore you to the land of Israel. You shall know that I am the LORD when I open your graves and bring you
14 up from them, O my people. Then I will put my spirit*a* into you and you shall live, and I will settle you on your own soil, and you shall know that I the LORD have spoken and will act. This is the very word of the LORD.'

15, 16 These were the words of the LORD to me: Man, take one leaf of a wooden tablet and write on it, 'Judah and his associates of Israel.' Then take another*b* leaf and write on it, 'Joseph, the leaf of Ephraim and all
17 his associates of Israel.' Now bring the two together to form one tablet;
18 then they will be a folding tablet in your hand. When your fellow-
19 countrymen ask you to tell them what you mean by this, say to them, These are the words of the Lord GOD: I am taking the leaf of Joseph, which belongs to Ephraim and his associate tribes of Israel, and joining*c* to it the leaf of Judah. Thus I shall make them one tablet, and they shall
20 be one in my hand. The leaves on which you write shall be visible in your hand for all to see.
21 Then say to them, These are the words of the Lord GOD: I am gathering up the Israelites from their places of exile among the nations; I will assemble them from every quarter and restore them to their own
22 soil. I will make them one single nation in the land, on the mountains of Israel, and they shall have one king; they shall no longer be two nations
23 or divided into two kingdoms. They shall never again be defiled with their idols, their loathsome ways and all their disloyal acts; I will rescue them from all their sinful backsliding*d* and purify them. Thus they shall
24 become my people, and I will become their God. My servant David shall become king over them, and they shall have one shepherd. They shall conform to my laws, they shall observe and carry out my statutes.
25 They shall live in the land which I gave my servant Jacob, the land where your fathers lived. They and their descendants shall live there
26 for ever, and my servant David shall for ever be their prince. I will make a covenant with them to bring them prosperity; this covenant shall be theirs for ever.*e* I will greatly increase their numbers, and I will put my
27 sanctuary for ever in their midst. They shall live under the shelter of my dwelling; I will become their God and they shall become my people.
28 The nations shall know that I the LORD am keeping Israel sacred to myself, because my sanctuary is in the midst of them for ever.

[a] *Or* breath.   [b] *Lit.* one.   [c] *Prob. rdg.; Heb. adds* them.   [d] backsliding: *so Symm.; Heb.* dwellings.   [e] *Prob. rdg.; Heb. adds* and I will put them.

God's triumph over the world

THESE WERE THE WORDS OF THE LORD TO ME: Man, look to- 38 1,2 wards Gog, the prince of Rosh, Meshech, and Tubal, in the land of Magog, and prophesy against him. Say, These are the words of the 3 Lord GOD: I am against you, Gog, prince of Rosh, Meshech, and Tubal. I will turn you about, I will put hooks in your jaws. I will 4 lead you out, you and your whole army, horses and horsemen, all fully equipped, a great host with shield and buckler, every man wielding a sword, and with them the men of Pharas, Cush, and Put, all with 5 shield and helmet; Gomer and all its squadrons, Beth-togarmah with 6 its squadrons from the far recesses of the north—a great concourse of peoples with you. Be prepared; make ready, you and all the host which 7 has gathered to join you, and hold yourselves in reserve for me.[a][b] After many days you will be summoned; in years to come you will enter 8 a land restored from ruin, whose people are gathered from many nations upon the mountains of Israel that have been desolate so long. The Israelites, brought out from the nations, will all be living undisturbed; and you will come up, driving in like a hurricane; you will cover the land 9 like a cloud, you and all your squadrons, a great concourse of peoples.

This is the word of the Lord GOD: At that time a thought will enter 10 your head and you will plan evil. You will say, 'I will attack a land of 11 open villages, I will fall upon a people living quiet and undisturbed, undefended by walls, with neither gates nor bars.' You will expect to 12 come plundering, spoiling, and stripping bare the ruins where men now live again, a people gathered out of the nations, a people acquiring cattle and goods, and making their home at the very centre of the world. Sheba and Dedan, the traders of Tarshish and her leading merchants,[c] 13 will say to you, 'Is it for plunder that you have come? Have you gathered your host to get spoil, to carry off silver and gold, to seize cattle and goods, to collect rich spoil?'

Therefore, prophesy, man, and say to Gog, These are the words of 14 the Lord GOD: In that day when my people Israel is living undisturbed, will you not awake[d] and come with many nations from your home in the 15 far recesses of the north, all riding on horses, a great host, a mighty army? You will come up against my people Israel; and in those future 16 days you will be like a cloud covering the earth. I will bring you against my land, that the nations may know me, when they see me prove my holiness at your expense, O Gog.

[a] me: so Sept.; Heb. them.   [b] and hold...me: or and you shall be their rallying-point.
[c] leading merchants: lit. young lions.   [d] So Sept.; Heb. know.

17 This is the word of the Lord GOD: When I spoke in days of old through my servants the prophets, who prophesied in those days un-
18 ceasingly, it was you*a* whom I threatened to bring against Israel. On that day, when at length Gog comes against the land of Israel, says the
19 Lord GOD, my wrath will boil over. In my jealousy and in the heat of my anger I swear that on that day there shall be a great earthquake
20 throughout the land of Israel. The fish in the sea and the birds in the air, the wild animals and all reptiles that move on the ground, all man-kind on the face of the earth, all shall be shaken before me. Mountains shall be torn up, the terraced hills collapse, and every wall crash to the
21 ground. I will summon universal terror*b* against Gog, says the Lord
22 GOD, and his men shall turn their swords against one another. I will bring him to judgement with pestilence and bloodshed; I will pour down teeming rain, hailstones hard as rock, and fire and brimstone, upon him, upon his squadrons, upon the whole concourse of peoples with him.
23 Thus will I prove myself great and holy and make myself known to many nations; they shall know that I am the LORD.

39 And you, man, prophesy against Gog and say, These are the words of the Lord GOD: I am against you, Gog, prince of Rosh, Meshech, and
2 Tubal. I will turn you about and drive you, I will fetch you up from the
3 far recesses of the north and bring you to the mountains of Israel. I will strike the bow from your left hand and dash the arrows from your right
4 hand. There on the mountains of Israel you shall fall, you, all your squadrons, and your allies; I will give you as food to the birds of prey
5 and the wild beasts. You shall fall on the bare ground, for it is I who
6 have spoken. This is the very word of the Lord GOD. I will send fire on Magog and on those who live undisturbed in the coasts and islands, and
7 they shall know that I am the LORD. My holy name I will make known in the midst of my people Israel and will no longer let it be profaned; the nations shall know that in Israel I, the LORD, am holy.

8 Behold, it comes; it shall be, says the Lord GOD, the day of which I
9 have spoken. The dwellers in the cities of Israel shall come out and gather weapons to light their fires, buckler and shield, bow and arrows, throwing-stick and lance, and they shall kindle fires with them for seven
10 years. They shall take no wood from the fields nor cut it from the forests but shall light their fires with the weapons. Thus they will plunder their plunderers and spoil their spoilers. This is the very word of the Lord GOD.

11 In that day I will give to Gog, instead of*c* a burial-ground in Israel, the valley of Abarim east of the Sea.*d* There they shall bury Gog and all his horde, and all Abarim will be blocked; and they shall call it the

---

[*a*] it was you: *so Sept.; Heb.* was it you...? [*b*] universal terror: *so Sept.; Heb.* for all my mountains a sword. [*c*] *Prob. rdg.; Heb. adds* there. [*d*] *That is* the Dead Sea.

Valley of Gog's Horde. For seven months the Israelites shall bury them 12
and purify the land; all the people shall take their share in the burying. 13
The day that I win myself honour shall be a memorable day for them.
This is the very word of the Lord GOD. Men shall be picked for the 14
regular duty of going through the country and searching for*a* any left
above ground, to purify the land; they shall begin their search at the
end of the seven months. They shall go through the country, and 15
whenever one of them sees a human bone he shall put a marker beside
it, until it has been buried in the Valley of Gog's Horde. So no more 16
shall be heard of that great horde,*b* and the land will be purified.

Man, these are the words of the Lord GOD: Cry to every bird that 17
flies and to all the wild beasts: Come, assemble, gather from every side
to my sacrifice, the great sacrifice I am making for you on the mountains of Israel; eat flesh and drink blood, eat the flesh of warriors and 18
drink the blood of princes of the earth; all these are your rams and
sheep, he-goats and bulls, and buffaloes of Bashan. You shall cram 19
yourselves with fat and drink yourselves drunk on blood at the sacrifice
which I am preparing for you. At my table you shall eat your fill of 20
horses and riders, of warriors and all manner of fighting men. This is
the very word of the Lord GOD.

I will show my glory among the nations; all shall see the judgement 21
that I execute and the heavy hand that I lay upon them. From that 22
day forwards the Israelites shall know that I am the LORD their God.
The nations shall know that the Israelites went into exile for their 23
iniquity, because they were faithless to me. So I hid my face from them
and handed them over to their enemies, and they fell, every one of them,
by the sword. I dealt with them as they deserved, defiled and rebellious 24
as they were, and hid my face from them.

These, therefore, are the words of the Lord GOD: Now I will restore 25
the fortunes of Jacob and show my affection for all Israel, and I will be
jealous for my holy name. They shall forget their shame and all their 26
unfaithfulness to me, when they are at home again on their own soil,
undisturbed, with no one to alarm them. When I bring them home out 27
of the nations and gather them from the lands of their enemies, I will
make them an example of my holiness, for many nations to see. They 28
will know that I am the LORD their God, because I who sent them into
exile among the nations will bring them together again on the soil of
their own land and leave none of them behind. No longer will I hide my 29
face from them, I who have poured out my spirit upon Israel. This is
the very word of the Lord GOD.

[*a*] searching for: *prob. rdg.; Heb.* burying those who are passing through.   [*b*] So...horde:
prob. rdg.; Heb. obscure.

The restored theocracy

40 1[a] AT THE BEGINNING OF THE YEAR, on the tenth day of the month, in the twenty-fifth year of our exile, that is fourteen years after the destruction of the city, on that very day, the hand of the LORD came 2 upon me and he brought me there. In a vision God brought me to the land of Israel and set me on a very high mountain, where I saw what 3 seemed the buildings of a city facing me.[b] He led me towards it, and I saw a man like a figure of bronze holding a cord of linen thread and a 4 measuring-rod, and standing at the gate. 'Man,' he said to me, 'look closely and listen carefully; mark well all that I show you, for this is why you have been brought here. Tell the Israelites all that you see.'

5 Round the outside of the temple ran a wall. The length of the rod which the man was holding was six cubits, reckoning by the long cubit which was one cubit and a hand's breadth. He measured the thickness 6 and the height of the wall; each was one rod. He came to a gate which faced eastwards, went up its steps and measured the threshold of the 7 gateway; its depth was one rod.[c] Each cell was one rod long and one rod wide; the space between the cells five cubits, and the threshold of the gateway at the end of the vestibule on the side facing the temple one 8,9 rod. He measured the vestibule of the gate and found it[d] eight cubits, with pilasters two cubits thick; the vestibule of the gateway lay at the 10 end near the temple. Now the cells of the gateway, looking back eastwards, were three in number on each side; all three of the same size, 11 and their pilasters on each side of the same size also. He measured the entrance into the gateway; it was ten cubits wide, and the gateway itself 12 throughout its length thirteen cubits wide. In front of the cells on each 13 side lay a kerb, one cubit wide; each cell was six cubits by six. He measured the width of the gateway through the cell doors which faced one another, from the back[e] of one cell to the back[e] of the opposite cell; 14 he made it twenty-five cubits, and the vestibule[f] twenty[g] cubits, across; 15 the gateway on every side projected into[h] the court. From the front of the entrance-gate to the outer face of the vestibule of the inner gate the 16 distance was fifty cubits. Both cells and pilasters had loopholes all round inside the gateway, and the vestibule had windows[i] all round within and palms carved on each pilaster.

[a] *In chs. 40–43 there are several Hebrew technical terms whose meaning is not certain and has to be determined, as well as may be, from the context.* [b] facing me: *so* Sept.; *Heb.* to the south. [c] *So* Sept.; *Heb. adds* and one threshold, one rod in width. [d] facing...and found it: *so* Sept.; *Heb. repeats these words.* [e] *So* Sept.; *Heb.* roof. [f] *Prob. rdg., cp.* Sept.; *Heb.* the pilasters. [g] *So* Sept.; *Heb.* sixty. [h] *Prob. rdg.; Heb. adds* pilaster. [i] and...windows: *prob. rdg., cp.* Sept.; *Heb.* and so also the vestibules, and windows...

He brought me to the outer court, and I saw rooms and a pavement   17
all round the court: in all, thirty rooms on the pavement. The pavement   18
ran up to the side of the gateways, as wide as they were long; this was
the lower pavement. He measured the width of the court*a* from the   19
front of the lower gateway to the outside of the inner gateway;*b* it was a
hundred cubits. He led me round to the north and I saw a gateway*c*   20
facing northwards, belonging to the outer court, and he measured its
length and its breadth. Its cells, three on each side, together with its   21
pilasters and its vestibule, were the same size as those of the first gateway, fifty cubits long by twenty-five wide. So too its windows, and those   22
of*d* its vestibule, and its palms were the same size as those of the gateway which faced east; it was approached by seven steps with its vestibule facing them. A gate like that on the east side*e* led to the inner   23
court opposite the northern gateway; he measured from gateway to
gateway, and it was a hundred cubits. Then he led me round to the   24
south, and I found a gateway facing southwards. He measured its cells,*f*
its pilasters, and its vestibule, and found it the same size as the others,
fifty cubits long by twenty-five wide. Both gateway and vestibule had   25
windows all round like the others. It was approached by seven steps   26
with a vestibule facing them and palms carved on each pilaster. The   27
inner court had a gateway facing southwards, and he measured from
gateway to gateway;*g* it was a hundred cubits.

He brought me into the inner court through the southern gateway,   28
measured it and found it the same size as the others. So were its cells,   29
pilasters, and vestibule, fifty cubits long by twenty-five wide. It and its
vestibule had windows all round.*h* Its vestibule faced the outer court; it   31
had palms carved on its pilasters, and eight steps led up to it.

Then he brought me into the inner court, towards the east, and   32
measured the gateway and found it the same size as the others. So too   33
were its cells, pilasters, and vestibule; it and its vestibule had windows
all round, and it was fifty cubits long by twenty-five wide. Its vestibule   34
faced the outer court and had a palm carved on each pilaster; eight
steps led up to it. Then he brought me to the north gateway and   35
measured it and found it the same size as the others. So were*i* its cells,   36
pilasters, and vestibule, and it had windows all round; it was fifty
cubits long by twenty-five wide. Its vestibule*j* faced the outer court   37
and had palms carved on the pilaster at each side; eight steps led up
to it.

[*a*] of the court: *so Sept.; Heb. om.*   [*b*] gateway: *so Sept.; Heb.* court.   [*c*] He led me...
gateway: *so Sept.; Heb.* east and north, and the gate...   [*d*] those of: *prob. rdg.; Heb. om.*
[*e*] like...side: *so Sept.; Heb.* and to the east.   [*f*] its cells: *so Sept.; Heb. om.*   [*g*] *So
Pesh.; Heb. adds* southwards.   [*h*] *So some MSS.; others add* (30) It had vestibules all round,
and it was twenty-five cubits long by five wide.   [*i*] So were: *so one MS.; others om.*   [*j*] *So
Sept.; Heb.* Its pilasters.

38   There was a room opening out from the vestibule of the gateway;[a]
39 here the whole-offerings were washed. In the vestibule of the gateway
were two tables on each side, at which to slaughter the whole-offering,
40 the sin-offering, and the guilt-offering. At the corner on the outside, as
one goes up to the opening of the northern gateway, stood two tables,
and two more at the other corner of the vestibule of the gateway.
41 Another four stood on each side at the corner of the gateway, eight
42 tables in all at which slaughtering was done. Four tables used for the
whole-offering were of hewn stone, each a cubit and a half long by a
cubit and a half wide and a cubit high; and on them[b] they put the
43 instruments used for the whole-offering and other sacrifices. The flesh
of the offerings was on the tables,[c] and ledges a hand's breadth in width
were fixed all round facing inwards.

44   Then he brought me right into the inner court, and I saw two rooms[d]
in the inner court, one at the corner of the northern gateway, facing
south, and one at the corner of the southern[e] gateway, facing north.
45 This room facing south, he told me, is for the priests who have charge of
46 the temple. The room facing north is for the priests who have charge of
the altar; these are the sons of Zadok, who alone of the Levites may
47 come near to serve the LORD. He measured the court; it was square, a
hundred cubits each way, and the altar lay in front of the temple.

48   Then he brought me into the vestibule of the temple, and measured a
pilaster of the vestibule; it was five cubits on each side, the width of the
gateway fourteen cubits and that of the corners of the gateway[f] three cubits
49 in each direction. The vestibule was twenty cubits long by twelve[g] wide;
ten[h] steps led up to it, and by the pilasters rose pillars, one on each side.

41   Then he brought me into the sanctuary and measured the pilasters;
2 they were six cubits wide on each side.[i] The opening was ten cubits
wide and its corners five cubits wide in each direction. He measured its
3 length; it was forty cubits, and its width twenty. He went inside and
measured the pilasters at the opening: they were two cubits; the opening itself was six cubits, and the corners[j] of the opening were seven
4 cubits in each direction.[k] Then he measured the room at the far end of
the sanctuary; its length and its breadth were each twenty cubits. He
said to me, 'This is the Holy of Holies.'

5   He measured the wall of the temple; it was six cubits high, and each
6 arcade all round the house was four cubits wide. The arcades were
arranged in three tiers, each tier in thirty sections. In the wall all round

[a] the vestibule of the gateway: *prob. rdg.; Heb.* pilasters, the gates.   [b] *So Sept.; Heb.*
adds and.   [c] The flesh...tables: *or, with Sept.,* Roofs over the tables protected them
from rain and from heat.   [d] Then...rooms: *so Sept.; Heb.* And outside the inner gate
singers' rooms.   [e] southern: *so Sept.; Heb.* eastern.   [f] fourteen...gateway: *so Sept.;*
Heb. om.   [g] *So Sept.; Heb.* eleven.   [h] *So Sept.; Heb.* which.   [i] *So Sept.; Heb. adds*
the width of the tent.   [j] *So Sept.; Heb.* width.   [k] in each direction: *so Sept.; Heb. om.*

the temple there were intakes for the arcades, so that they could be
supported without being fastened into the wall of the temple. The 7
higher up the arcades were, the broader they were all round by the
addition of the intakes,ᵃ one above the other all round the temple; the
temple itself had a rampᵇ running upwards on a base, and in this way
one went up fromᶜ the lowest to the highest tier by way of the middle tier.

Then I saw a raised pavement all round the temple, and the founda- 8
tions of the arcades were flush with it and measured a full rod, six
cubits high. The outer wall of the arcades was five cubits thick. There 9
was an unoccupied area beside the terraceᵈ which was adjacent to the
temple, and the arcadesᵉ opened on to this area, one opening facing 11ᶠ
northwards and one southwards; the unoccupied area was five cubits
wide on all sides. There was a free spaceᵍ twenty cubits wide all round 10
the temple. On the western side, at the far end of the free space, stood a 12
building seventy cubits wide; its wall was five cubits thick all round,
and its length ninety cubits.

He measured the temple; it was a hundred cubits long; and the free 13
space, the building, and its walls, a hundred cubits in all. The eastern 14
front of the temple and the free space was a hundred cubits wide. He 15
measured the length of the building at the far end of the free space to
the west of the temple, and its corridors on each side: a hundred cubits.

The sanctuary, the inner shrine and the outer vestibule were panelled;
the embrasures all round the three of them were framed with wood all 16
round. From the ground up to the windows and above the door,ʰ both 17
in the inner and outer chambers, round all the walls, inside and out,
were carved figures,ⁱ cherubim and palm-trees, a palm between every 18
pair of cherubim. Each cherub had two faces: one the face of a man, 19
looking towards one palm-tree, and the other the face of a lion, looking
towards another palm-tree. Such was the carving round the whole of the
temple. The cherubim and the palm-trees were carved from the ground 20
up to the top of the doorway and on the wall of the sanctuary. The door- 21
posts of the sanctuary were square.ʲ

In front ofᵏ the Holy Place was what seemed an altar of wood, three 22
cubits high and two cubits long; it was fitted with corner-posts, and its
baseˡ and sides also were of wood. He told me that this was the table
which stood before the LORD. The sanctuary had a double door, and the 23
Holy Place also had a double door: the double doors had swinging 24

[a] by...intakes: *so Sept.; Heb.* for the surrounding of the house. [b] *Lit.* a broadening.
[c] from: *so Sept.; Heb. om.* [d] beside the terrace: *prob. rdg.; Heb.* between the arcades.
[e] *So Sept.; Heb.* arcade. [f] *Verses 10 and 11 transposed.* [g] There...space: *prob. rdg.;
Heb.* Between the rooms. [h] the inner shrine...above the door: *prob. rdg., cp. Sept.; Heb.
unintelligible.* [i] carved figures: *prob. rdg.; Heb.* measures and carving. [j] The door-
posts...square: *prob. rdg.; Heb. unintelligible.* [k] In front of: *prob. rdg.; Heb.* The face
of. [l] base: *so Sept.; Heb.* length.

25 leaves, a pair for each door. Cherubim and palm-trees like those on the walls were carved on them.*[a]* Outside there was a wooden cornice over
26 the vestibule; on both sides of the vestibule were loopholes, with palm-trees carved at the corners.*[b]*

42 Then he took me to the outer court round by the north and brought me to the rooms*[c]* facing the free space and facing the buildings to the
2 north. The length along the northern side was a hundred cubits,*[d]* and
3 the breadth fifty. Facing the free space measuring twenty cubits, which adjoined the inner court, and facing the pavement of the outer court,
4 were corridors at three levels corresponding to each other. In front of the rooms a passage, ten cubits wide and a hundred cubits long,*[e]* ran
5 towards the inner court; their entrances faced northwards. The upper rooms were shorter than the lower and middle rooms, because the
6 corridors took*[f]* building space from them. For they were all at three levels and had no pillars as the courts had, so that the lower and middle
7 levels were recessed from the ground upwards. An outside wall, fifty cubits long, ran parallel to the rooms and in front of them, on the side
8 of the outer court. The rooms adjacent to the outer court were fifty
9 cubits long, and those facing the sanctuary a hundred cubits. Below these rooms was an entry from the east as one entered them from the
10 outer court where the wall of the court began.*[g]* On the south*[h]* side,
11 passing by the free space and the building, were other rooms with a passage in front of them. These rooms corresponded, in length and
12 breadth and in general character, to those facing north, whose exits and entrances were the same as those of the rooms on the south. As one*[i]* went eastwards, where the passages began, there was an entrance in the
13 face of the inner*[j]* wall. Then he said to me, 'The northern and southern rooms facing the free space are the consecrated rooms where the priests who approach the LORD may eat the most sacred offerings. There they shall put these offerings as well as the grain-offering, the sin-offering,
14 and the guilt-offering; for the place is holy. When the priests have entered the Holy Place they shall not go into the outer court again without leaving here the garments they have worn while performing their duties, for these are holy. They shall put on other garments when they approach the place assigned to the people.'
15 When he had finished measuring the inner temple, he brought me out towards the gateway which faces eastwards and measured the
16 whole area. He measured the east side with the measuring-rod, and it

---

[a] *Prob. rdg.; Heb. adds* on the doors of the sanctuary. [b] *Prob. rdg.; Heb. adds* and the arcades of the temple and the cornices. [c] *So Sept.; Heb.* room. [d] The length...cubits: *prob. rdg., cp. Sept.; Heb.* in front of a length the hundred cubits, the northern opening. [e] and a hundred cubits long: *so Sept.; Heb.* a way of one cubit. [f] took: *so some MSS.; others* were able. [g] began: *prob. rdg.; Heb.* breadth. [h] *So Sept.; Heb.* east. [i] *Prob. rdg.; Heb.* they. [j] *Prob. rdg.; Heb. word unknown.*

was five hundred cubits.[a] He turned and measured[b] the north side with 17
his rod, and it was five hundred cubits.[a] He turned to[c] the south side and 18[d]
measured it with his rod; it was five hundred cubits.[a] He turned to the 19
west and measured it with his rod; it was five hundred cubits.[a] So he 20
measured all four sides; in each direction the surrounding wall measured
five hundred cubits.[a] This marked off the sacred area from the profane.

He led me to the gate, the gate facing eastwards, and I beheld the 43 1,2
glory of the God of Israel coming from the east. His voice was like the
sound of a mighty torrent, and the earth shone with his glory. The form 3
that I saw was the same as that which I had seen when he[e] came to
destroy the city, and as that which I had seen by the river Kebar,[f] and I
fell on my face. The glory of the LORD came up to the temple towards 4
the gate which faced eastwards. A spirit[g] lifted me up and brought me 5
into the inner court, and the glory of the LORD filled the temple. Then I 6
heard one speaking to me from the temple, and the[h] man was standing
at my side. He said, Man, do you see[i] the place of my throne, the place 7
where I set my feet, where I will dwell among the Israelites for ever?
Neither they nor their kings shall ever defile my holy name again with
their wanton disloyalty, and with the corpses[j] of their kings when they
die. They set their threshold by mine and their door-post beside mine, 8
with a wall between me and them, and they defiled my holy name with
the abominations they committed, and I destroyed them in my anger.
But now they shall abandon their wanton disloyalty and remove the 9
corpses[j] of their kings far from me, and I will dwell among them for
ever. So tell the Israelites, man, about this temple, its appearance and 10
proportions,[k] that they may be ashamed of their iniquities. If they are 11
ashamed of all they have done, you shall describe[l] to them the temple
and its fittings, its exits and entrances, all the details and particulars of
its elevation and plan; explain them and draw them before their eyes, so
that they may keep them in mind and carry them out. This is the plan of 12
the temple to be built on the top of the mountain; all its precincts on
every side shall be most holy.[m]

These were the dimensions of the altar in cubits (the cubit that is a 13
cubit and a hand's breadth). This was the height[n] of the altar: the base
was a cubit high[o] and projected a cubit; on its edge was a rim one span
deep. From the base to the cubit-wide ridge of the lower pedestal- 14
block was two cubits, and from this shorter[p] pedestal-block to the

[a] *Prob. rdg.* (*cp. Sept. in verse 17*); *Heb.* rods.   [b] He turned and measured: *so Sept.; Heb.*
round about. He measured...   [c] He turned to: *so Sept.; Heb.* round about.   [d] *Some
MSS. place verse 18 after verse 19.*   [e] *So some MSS.; others* I.   [f] *Or* the Kebar canal.
[g] *Or* wind.   [h] *So Sept.; Heb.* a.   [i] do you see: *so Sept.; Heb. om.*   [j] *Or* effigies.
[k] its...proportions: *so Sept.; Heb.* and they shall measure the proportions.   [l] you shall
describe: *so Sept.; Heb.* description.   [m] *So Sept.; Heb. adds* this is the plan of the
temple.   [n] *So Sept.; Heb.* back.   [o] the base...high: *prob. rdg.; Heb.* the base of the
cubit.   [p] *Lit.* smaller.

15 cubit-wide ridge of the taller*ᵃ* pedestal-block was four cubits. The
altar-hearth was four cubits high and was surmounted by four horns a
16 cubit high.*ᵇ* The hearth was twelve cubits long and twelve cubits wide,
17 being a perfect square. The upper pedestal-block was fourteen cubits
long and fourteen cubits wide along its four sides, and the rim round it
was half a cubit deep. The base of the altar projected a cubit, and there
were steps facing eastwards.

18   He said to me, Man, these are the words of the Lord GOD: These are
the regulations for the altar when it has been made, for sacrificing whole-
19 offerings on it and flinging the blood against it. The levitical priests of
the family of Zadok, and they alone, may come near to me to serve me,
says the Lord GOD. You shall assign them a young bull for a sin-
20 offering; you shall take some of the blood and put it on the four horns
of the altar, on the four corners of the upper pedestal and all round the
21 rim, and so purify it and make expiation for it. Then take the bull
assigned as the sin-offering, and they shall destroy it by fire in the
22 proper place within the precincts but outside the Holy Place. On the
second day you shall present a he-goat without blemish as a sin-offering,
23 and with it they shall purify the altar as they did with the bull. When
you have completely purified the altar, you shall present a young bull
24 without blemish and a ram without blemish from the flock. You shall
present them before the LORD; the priests shall throw salt on them and
25 sacrifice them as a whole-offering to the LORD. For seven days you
shall provide as a daily sin-offering a goat, a young bull, and a ram from
26 the flock; all of them shall be provided free from blemish. For seven
days they shall make expiation for the altar, and pronounce it ritually
27 clean, and consecrate it. At the end of that time, on the eighth day and
onwards, the priests shall sacrifice on the altar your whole-offerings and
your shared-offerings, and I will accept you. This is the very word of
the Lord GOD.

44   He again brought me round to the outer gate of the sanctuary facing
2 eastwards, and it was shut. The LORD said to me, This gate shall be
kept shut; it must not be opened. No man may enter by it, for the LORD
3 the God of Israel has entered by it. It shall be kept shut. The prince,
however, when he is here as prince, may sit there to eat food in the
presence of the LORD; he shall come in and go out by the vestibule of
the gate.

4   He brought me round to the northern gate facing the temple, and I
saw the glory of the LORD filling the LORD's house, and I fell on my face.
5 The LORD said to me, Mark well, man, look closely, and listen carefully
to all that I say to you, to all the rules and regulations for the house of
the LORD. Mark well the entrance to the house of the LORD and all the

[*a*] *Lit.* larger.   [*b*] a cubit high: *prob. rdg., cp. Sept.; Heb. om.*

exits from the sanctuary. Say to that rebel people of Israel, These are the 6
words of the Lord GOD: Enough of all these abominations of yours, you
Israelites! You have added to them by bringing foreigners, uncircum- 7
cised in mind and body, to stand in my sanctuary and defile my house
when you present my food to me, both fat and blood, and they have
made my covenant void. Instead of keeping charge of my holy things 8
yourselves, you have chosen to put these men in charge of my sanctuary.

These are the words of the Lord GOD: No foreigner, uncircumcised 9
in mind and body, shall enter my sanctuary, not even a foreigner living
among the Israelites. But the Levites, though they deserted me when 10
the Israelites went astray after their idols and had to bear the punishment of their iniquity, shall yet do service in my sanctuary. They shall 11
take charge of the gates of the temple and do service there. They shall
slaughter the whole-offering and the sacrifice for the people and shall be
in attendance to serve them. Because they served them in the presence 12
of their idols and brought Israel to the ground by their iniquity, says
the Lord GOD, I have sworn with uplifted hand that they shall bear the
punishment of their iniquity. They shall not have access to me, to serve 13
me as priests; they shall not come near to my holy things or to the Holy
of Holies; they shall bear the shame of the abominable deeds they have
done. I will put them in charge of the temple with all the service which 14
must be performed there.

But the levitical priests of the family of Zadok remained in charge of 15
my sanctuary when the Israelites went astray from me; these shall
approach me to serve me. They shall be in attendance on me, presenting the fat and the blood, says the Lord GOD. It is they who shall 16
enter my sanctuary and approach my table to serve me and observe my
charge. When they come to the gates of the inner court they shall dress 17
in linen; they shall wear no wool when they serve me at the gates of
the inner court and within. They shall wear linen turbans, and linen 18
drawers on their loins; they shall not fasten their clothes with a belt so
that they sweat. When they go out to the people in the outer court,*a* 19
they shall take off the clothes they have worn while serving, leave them
in the sacred rooms and put on other clothes; otherwise they will
transmit the sacred influence to the people through their clothing.

They shall neither shave their heads nor let their hair grow long; 20
they shall only clip their hair. No priest shall drink wine when he is 21
to enter the inner court. He may not marry a widow or a divorced 22
woman; he may marry a virgin of Israelite birth. He may, however,
marry the widow of a priest.

They shall teach my people to distinguish the sacred from the pro- 23
fane, and show them the difference between clean and unclean. When 24

[a] in the outer court: *so some MSS.; others repeat these words.*

disputes break out, they shall take their place in court, and settle the case according to my rules. At all my appointed seasons they shall observe my laws and statutes. They shall keep my sabbaths holy.

25 They shall not defile themselves*a* by contact with any dead person, except*b* father or mother, son or daughter, brother or unmarried sister.
26 After purification, they shall count seven days and then be clean.*c*
27 When they enter*d* the inner court to serve in the Holy Place, they shall present their*e* sin-offering, says the Lord GOD.

28 They shall own no*f* patrimony in Israel; I am their patrimony. You
29 shall grant them no holding in Israel; I am their holding. The grain-offering, the sin-offering, and the guilt-offering shall be eaten by them,
30 and everything in Israel devoted to God shall be theirs. The first of all the firstfruits and all your contributions of every kind shall belong wholly to the priests. You shall give the first lump of your dough to the
31 priests, that a blessing may rest upon your home. The priests shall eat no carrion, bird or beast, whether it has died naturally or been killed by a wild animal.

45 When you divide the land by lot among the tribes for their possession, you shall set apart from it a sacred reserve for the LORD, twenty-five thousand cubits in length and twenty*g* thousand in width; the whole
2 enclosure shall be sacred. Of this a square plot, five hundred cubits each way, shall be devoted to the sanctuary, with fifty cubits of open land
3 round it. From this area you shall measure out a space twenty-five thousand by ten thousand cubits, in which the sanctuary, the holiest
4 place of all, shall stand. This space is*h* for the priests who serve in the sanctuary and who come nearest in serving the LORD. It shall include
5 space for their houses and a sacred plot for the sanctuary. An area of twenty-five thousand by ten thousand cubits shall belong to the Levites, the temple servants; on this shall stand the towns in which they live.*i*
6 You shall give to each town an area of five thousand by twenty-five thousand cubits alongside the sacred reserve; this shall belong to all
7 Israel. On either side of the sacred reserve and of the city's holding the prince shall have a holding facing the sacred reserve and the city's holding, running westwards on the west and eastwards on the east. It shall run alongside one of the tribal portions, and stretch to the western
8 limit of the land and to the eastern. It shall be his holding in Israel; the princes of Israel*j* shall never oppress my people again but shall give the land to Israel, tribe by tribe.

[a] They...themselves: *so Sept.; Heb.* He...himself. [b] any...except: *or* anyone else's dead, but only their own... [c] and then be clean: *so Pesh.; Heb. om.* [d] *So Sept.; Heb. adds* the Holy Place. [e] they enter...they...their: *so Sept.; Heb.* he enters...he...his. [f] no: *so Vulg.; Heb. om.* [g] *So Sept.; Heb.* ten. [h] *So Sept.; Heb. adds* holy. [i] on this...live: *so Sept.; Heb.* twenty rooms. [j] the princes of Israel: *so Sept.; Heb.* my princes.

THESE ARE THE WORDS OF THE LORD GOD: Enough, princes of 9
Israel! Put an end to lawlessness and robbery; maintain law and justice;
relieve my people and stop your evictions, says the Lord GOD. Your 10
scales shall be honest, your bushel*a* and your gallon*b* shall be honest.
There shall be one standard for each, taking each as the tenth of a 11
homer, and the homer shall have its fixed standard. Your shekel weight 12
shall contain twenty gerahs; your mina shall contain weights of ten*c*
and twenty-five and fifteen shekels.

These are the contributions you shall set aside: out of every homer of 13
wheat or of barley, one sixth of an ephah. For oil the rule is*d* one tenth 14
of a bath from every kor*e* (at ten bath to the kor*f*); one sheep in every 15
flock of two hundred is to be reserved by every Israelite clan.*g* For a
grain-offering, a whole-offering, and a shared-offering, to make expiation for them, says the Lord GOD, all the people of the land shall bring*h* 16
this contribution to the prince in Israel; and the prince shall be respon- 17
sible for the whole-offering, the grain-offering, and the drink-offering,
at pilgrim-feasts, new moons, sabbaths, and every sacred season observed by Israel. He himself is to provide the sin-offering and the grain-
offering, the whole-offering and the shared-offering, needed to make
expiation for Israel.

These are the words of the Lord GOD: On the first day of the first 18
month you shall take a young bull without blemish, and purify the
sanctuary. The priest shall take some of the blood from the sin-offering 19
and put it on the door-posts of the temple, on the four corners of the
altar pedestal and on the gate-posts of the inner court. You shall do the 20
same on the seventh day of the month;*i* in this way you shall make
expiation for the temple.

On the fourteenth day of the first month you shall hold the Passover, 21
the pilgrim-feast of seven days; bread must be eaten unleavened. On 22
that day the prince shall provide a bull as a sin-offering for himself and
for all the people. During the seven days of the feast he shall offer daily 23
as a whole-offering to the LORD seven bulls and seven rams without
blemish, and a he-goat as a daily sin-offering. With every bull and ram 24
he shall provide a grain-offering of one ephah, together with a hin of
oil for each ephah. He shall do the same thing also on the fifteenth day 25
of the seventh month at the pilgrim-feast; this also shall last seven days,
and he shall provide the same sin-offering and whole-offering and the
same quantity of grain and oil.

[a] *Lit.* ephah. [b] *Lit.* bath. [c] *Prob. rdg.; Heb.* twenty. [d] *Prob. rdg.; Heb. adds* the
bath, the oil. [e] *So Sept.; Heb. adds* the homer is ten bath. [f] *So Vulg.; Heb.* to the
homer. [g] clan: *so Sept.; Heb. unintelligible.* [h] all...bring: *prob. rdg.; Heb. unintelligible.* [i] *Prob. rdg.; Heb. adds* This comes from a man who is wrong and foolish. *Cp.
Lev.* 23. 24; *Num.* 29. 1. (*For* on the seventh day of the month *Sept. has* on the first day of
the seventh month.)

46 These are the words of the Lord God: The eastern gate of the inner court shall remain closed for the six working days; it may be opened

2 only on the sabbath and at new moon. When the prince comes through the porch of the gate from the outside, he shall halt at the door-post, and the priests shall sacrifice his whole-offering and shared-offerings. On the terrace he shall bow down at the gate and then go out, but the

3 gate shall not be shut till the evening. On sabbaths and at new moons the people also shall bow down before the Lord at the entrance to that gate.

4 The whole-offering which the prince sacrifices to the Lord shall be as follows: on the sabbath, six sheep without blemish and a ram without

5 blemish; the grain-offering shall be an ephah with the ram and as much as he likes with the sheep, together with a hin of oil for every ephah.

6 At the new moon it shall be a young bull without blemish,[a] six sheep

7 and a ram, all without blemish. He shall provide as the grain-offering to go with the bull one ephah and with the ram one ephah, with the sheep as much as he can afford, adding a hin of oil for every ephah.

8 When the prince comes in, he shall enter through the porch of the

9 gate and come out by the same way. But on festal days when the people come before the Lord, a man who enters by the northern gate to bow down shall leave by the southern gate, and a man who enters by the southern gate shall leave by the northern gate. He shall not turn back and go out through the gate by which he came in but shall go straight

10 on. The prince shall then be among them, going in when they go in and coming out when they come out.

11 At pilgrim-feasts and on festal days the grain-offering shall be an ephah with a bull, an ephah with a ram and as much as he likes with a sheep, together with a hin of oil for every ephah.

12 When the prince provides a whole-offering or shared-offerings as a voluntary sacrifice[b] to the Lord, the eastern gate shall be opened for him,[c] and he shall make his whole-offering and his shared-offerings as he does on the sabbath; when he goes out the gate shall be closed[d] behind him.

13 You shall provide a yearling sheep without blemish daily as a whole-

14 offering to the Lord; you shall provide it morning by morning. With it every morning you shall provide as a grain-offering one sixth of an ephah with a third of a hin of oil to moisten the flour; the Lord's

15 grain-offering is an observance[e] prescribed for all time. Morning by morning, as a regular whole-offering, they shall offer a sheep with the grain-offering and the oil.

16 These are the words of the Lord God: When the prince makes a gift

---

[a] without blemish: *so many MSS.; others have a plural form.*   [b] as...sacrifice: *so Sept.; Heb. repeats these words.*   [c] the eastern...him: *or* he shall open the gate facing east. [d] the gate...closed: *or* he shall close the gate.   [e] *So many MSS.; others* observances.

out of[a] his property to any of his sons, it shall belong to his sons, since it is part of the family property. But when he makes such a gift to one of 17 his slaves, it shall be his only till the year of manumission, when it shall revert to the prince; it is the property of[b] his sons and shall belong to them.

The prince shall not oppress the people by taking part of their hold- 18 ings; he shall give his sons an inheritance from his own holding of land, so that my people may not be scattered and separated from their holdings.

Then he brought me through the entrance by the side of the gate to 19 the rooms which face north (the sacred rooms reserved for[c] the priests), and, pointing to a place on their western side, he said to me, 'This is the 20 place where the priests shall boil the guilt-offering and the sin-offering and bake the grain-offering; they shall not take it into the outer court for fear they transmit the sacred influence to the people.' Then he 21 brought me into the outer court and took me across to the four corners of the court, at each of which there was a further court. These four 22 courts were vaulted and were the same size, forty cubits long by thirty cubits wide. Round each of the four was a row of stones, with fire-places 23 constructed close up against the rows. He said to me, 'These are the 24 kitchens where the attendants shall boil the people's sacrifices.'

He brought me back to the gate of the temple, and I saw a spring of 47 water issuing from under the terrace of the temple towards the east; for the temple faced east. The water was running down along the right side,[d] to the south of the altar. He took me out through the northern 2 gate and brought me round by an outside path to the eastern gate of the court,[e] and water was trickling from the right side. When the man 3 went out eastwards he had a line in his hand. He measured a thousand cubits and made me walk through the water; it came up to my ankles. He measured another thousand and made me walk through the water; 4 it came up to my knees. He measured another thousand and made me walk through the water; it was up to my waist. Another thousand, and 5 it was a torrent I could not cross, for the water had risen and was now deep enough to swim in; it had become a torrent that could not be crossed. 'Mark this, man', he said, and led me back to the bank of the 6 torrent. When we came back to the bank I saw a great number of trees 7 on each side. He said to me, 'This water flows out to the region lying 8 east, and down to the Arabah; at last it will reach that sea whose waters[f] are foul, and they will be sweetened. When any one of the living 9 creatures that swarm upon the earth comes where the torrent[g] flows, it shall draw life from it. The fish shall be innumerable; for these waters

[a] out of: *so Sept.; Heb. om.*   [b] the property of: *so Sept.; Heb.* his property.   [c] reserved for: *prob. rdg., cp. Sept.; Heb.* to.   [d] *So Sept.; Heb. adds* of the temple.   [e] the court: *so Sept.; Heb.* the outside, a way.   [f] waters: *so Sept.; Heb.* sea.   [g] torrent: *so Sept.; Heb.* two torrents.

come here so that the others may be sweetened, and where the torrent
10 flows everything shall live. From En-gedi as far as En-eglaim fishermen
shall stand on its shores, for nets shall be spread there. Every kind of
11 fish shall be there in shoals, like the fish of the Great Sea; but its swamps
and pools shall not have their waters sweetened but shall be left as
12 salt-pans. Beside the torrent on either bank all trees good for food shall
spring up. Their leaves shall not wither, their fruit shall not cease; they
shall bear early every month. For their water comes from the sanctuary;
their fruit is for food and their foliage for enjoyment.'[a]

13 These are the words of the Lord GOD: These[b] are the boundary lines
within which the twelve tribes of Israel shall enter into possession of the
14 land, Joseph receiving two portions. The land which I swore with hand
uplifted to give to your fathers you shall divide with each other; it shall
15 be assigned to you by lot as your patrimony. This is the frontier: on its
northern side, from the Great Sea through Hethlon, Lebo-hamath,
16 Zedad,[c] Berutha, and Sibraim, which are between the frontiers of Damas-
17 cus and Hamath, to Hazar-enan,[d] near the frontier of Hauran. So the
frontier shall run from the sea to Hazar-enan[e] on the frontier of Damas-
18 cus and northwards;[f] this is[g] its northern side. The eastern side runs
alongside the territories of Hauran, Damascus, and Gilead, and alongside the territory of Israel; Jordan sets the boundary to the eastern sea,
19 to Tamar.[h] This is[g] the eastern side. The southern side runs from
Tamar to the waters of Meribah-by-Kadesh; the region assigned to you
reaches the Great Sea. This is[g] the southern side towards the Negeb.
20 The western side is the Great Sea, which forms a boundary as far as a
21 point opposite Lebo-hamath. This is the western side. You shall distri-
22 bute this land among the tribes of Israel and assign it by lot as a patrimony for yourselves and for any aliens living in your midst who leave
sons among you. They shall be treated as native-born in Israel and with
23 you shall receive a patrimony by lot among the tribes of Israel. You
shall give the alien his patrimony with the tribe in which he is living.
This is the very word of the Lord GOD.

48 These are the names of the tribes: In the extreme north, in the
direction of Hethlon, to Lebo-hamath and Hazar-enan, with Damascus
on the northern frontier in the direction of Hamath, and so from the
eastern side to the western,[i] shall be Dan: one portion.

2 Bordering on Dan, from the eastern side to the western, shall be
Asher: one portion.

[a] *Or, with Sept.,* for healing.   [b] *So many MSS.; others have an unknown word.*
[c] Lebo-hamath, Zedad: *prob. rdg., cp. Sept.; Heb.* Lebo, Zedad, Hamath.   [d] *Prob. rdg.,
cp. Sept.; Heb.* Hazar-hattikon.   [e] *So Sept.; Heb.* Hazar-enon.   [f] *So Sept.; Heb. adds*
northwards and the frontier of Hamath.   [g] this is: *so some MSS.; others* and.   [h] Tamar:
so Pesh.; Heb. you shall measure.   [i] from...western: *so Sept.; Heb.* the eastern corner
is the sea.

Bordering on Asher, from the eastern side to the western, shall be 3
Naphtali: one portion.

Bordering on Naphtali, from the eastern side to the western, shall be 4
Manasseh: one portion.

Bordering on Manasseh, from the eastern side to the western, shall be 5
Ephraim: one portion.

Bordering on Ephraim, from the eastern side to the western, shall be 6
Reuben: one portion.

Bordering on Reuben, from the eastern side to the western, shall be 7
Judah: one portion.

Bordering on Judah, from the eastern side to the western, shall be the 8
reserve which you shall set apart. Its breadth shall be twenty-five thousand cubits and its length the same as that of the other portions, from
the eastern side to the western, and the sanctuary shall be in the middle
of it.

The reserve which you shall set apart for the LORD shall measure 9
twenty-five thousand cubits by twenty*a* thousand. The reserve shall be 10
apportioned thus: the priests shall have an area measuring twenty-five
thousand cubits on the north side, ten thousand on the west,*b* ten thousand on the east,*b* and twenty-five thousand on the south side;*c* the
sanctuary of the LORD shall be in the middle of it. It shall be for the 11
consecrated priests, the sons of Zadok, who kept my charge and did not
follow the Israelites when they went astray, as the Levites did. The area 12
set apart for the priests from the reserved territory shall be most sacred,
reaching the frontier of the Levites.

The Levites shall have a portion running parallel to the border of the 13
priests. It shall be twenty-five thousand cubits long by ten thousand
wide; altogether, the length shall be twenty-five thousand cubits and
the breadth ten thousand. They shall neither sell nor exchange any part 14
of it, nor shall the best of the land be alienated; for it is holy to the
LORD.

The strip which is left, five thousand cubits in width by*d* twenty-five 15
thousand, is the city's secular land for dwellings and common land, and
the city shall be in the middle of it. These shall be its dimensions: on 16
the northern side four thousand five hundred cubits, on the southern
side four thousand five hundred cubits, on the eastern side four thousand five hundred cubits, on the western side four thousand five hundred cubits. The common land belonging to the city shall be two 17
hundred and fifty cubits to the north, two hundred and fifty to the
south, two hundred and fifty to the east, and two hundred and fifty to
the west. What is left parallel to the reserve, ten thousand cubits to the 18

[a] *Prob. rdg.; Heb.* ten. [b] *So Sept.; Heb. adds* in breadth. [c] *So Sept.; Heb. adds* in
length. [d] *Lit.* facing.

east and ten thousand to the west,^a shall provide food for those who
19 work in the city. Those who work in the city shall cultivate it; they
may be drawn from any of the tribes of Israel.

20   You shall set apart the whole reserve, twenty-five thousand cubits
21 square,^b as sacred, as far as the holding of the city. What is left over on
each side of the sacred reserve and the holding of the city shall be
assigned to the prince. Eastwards, what lies over against the reserved
twenty-five thousand cubits, as far as the eastern side, and westwards,
what lies over against the twenty-five thousand cubits to the western
side, parallel to the tribal portions, shall be assigned to the prince; the
22 sacred reserve and the sanctuary itself shall be in the centre. The^c
holding of the Levites and the^c holding of the city shall be in the middle
of that which is assigned to the prince; it shall be between the frontiers
of Judah and Benjamin.^d

23   The rest of the tribes: from the eastern side to the western shall be
Benjamin: one portion.

24   Bordering on Benjamin, from the eastern side to the western, shall be
Simeon: one portion.

25   Bordering on Simeon, from the eastern side to the western, shall be
Issachar: one portion.

26   Bordering on Issachar, from the eastern side to the western, shall be
Zebulun: one portion.

27   Bordering on Zebulun, from the eastern side to the western, shall
be Gad: one portion.

28   Bordering on Gad, on the side of the Negeb, the border on the south
stretches from Tamar to^e the waters of Meribah-by-Kadesh, to the
Brook as far as the Great Sea.

29   This is the land which you shall allot as^f a patrimony to the tribes of
Israel, and these shall be their lots. This is the very word of the Lord
God.

30-31   These are to be the ways out of the city, and they are to be named
after the tribes of Israel. The northern side, four thousand five hundred
cubits long, shall have three gates, those of Reuben, Judah, and Levi;
32 the eastern side, four thousand five hundred cubits long, three gates,
33 those of Joseph, Benjamin, and Dan; the southern side, four thousand
five hundred cubits long, three gates, those of Simeon, Issachar, and
34 Zebulun; the western side, four thousand five hundred cubits long,
35 three gates, those of Gad, Asher, and Naphtali. The perimeter of the
city shall be eighteen thousand cubits, and the city's name for ever
after shall be Jehovah-shammah.^g

[a] *Prob. rdg.; Heb. adds* and it shall be parallel to the sacred reserve.   [b] square: *so Sept.;*
Heb. fourth.   [c] *Prob. rdg.; Heb.* Some of the.   [d] *So Pesh.; Heb. adds* it shall belong to
the prince.   [e] to: *so some MSS.; others om.*   [f] *So Sept.; Heb.* from.   [g]*That is* the
Lord *is there.*

THE BOOK OF
DANIEL

Jews at the court of Nebuchadnezzar

IN THE THIRD YEAR of the reign of Jehoiakim king of Judah, 1
Nebuchadnezzar king of Babylon came to Jerusalem and laid siege
to it. The Lord delivered Jehoiakim king of Judah into his power, 2
together with all that was left of the vessels of the house of God; and
he carried them off to the land of Shinar, to the temple of his god, where
he deposited the vessels in the treasury. Then the king ordered Ash- 3
penaz, his chief eunuch, to take certain of the Israelite exiles, of the
blood royal and of the nobility, who were to be young men of good 4
looks and bodily without fault, at home in all branches of knowledge,
well-informed, intelligent, and fit for service in the royal court; and he
was to instruct them in the literature and language of the Chaldaeans.
The king assigned them a daily allowance of food and wine from the 5
royal table. Their training was to last for three years, and at the end of
that time they would*a* enter the royal service.

Among them there were certain young men from Judah called Daniel, 6
Hananiah, Mishael and Azariah; but the master of the eunuchs gave 7
them new names: Daniel he called Belteshazzar, Hananiah Shadrach,
Mishael Meshach and Azariah Abed-nego. Now Daniel determined 8
not to contaminate himself by touching the food and wine assigned
to him by the king, and he begged the master of the eunuchs not to
make him do so. God made the master show kindness and goodwill to 9
Daniel, and he said to him, 'I am afraid of my lord the king: he has 10
assigned you your food and drink, and if he sees you looking dejected,
unlike the other young men of your own age, it will cost me my head.'
Then Daniel said to the guard whom the master of the eunuchs had put 11
in charge of Hananiah, Mishael, Azariah and himself, 'Submit us to this 12
test for ten days. Give us only vegetables to eat and water to drink;
then compare our looks with those of the young men who have lived on 13
the food assigned by the king, and be guided in your treatment of us by
what you see.'*b* The guard listened to what they said and tested them 14
for ten days. At the end of ten days they looked healthier and were 15
better nourished than all the young men who had lived on the food
assigned them by the king. So the guard took away the assignment 16

[a] at the end...would: *or* all of them were to. [b] be guided...see: *or* treat us as you
see fit.

of food and the wine they were to drink, and gave them only the vegetables.

17 To all four of these young men God had given knowledge and understanding of books and learning of every kind, while Daniel had a gift

18 for interpreting visions and dreams of every kind. The time came which the king had fixed for introducing the young men to court, and the master of the eunuchs brought them into the presence of Nebuchad-

19 nezzar. The king talked with them and found none of them to compare with Daniel, Hananiah, Mishael and Azariah; so they entered the royal

20 service. Whenever the king consulted them on any matter calling for insight and judgement, he found them ten times better than all the

21 magicians and exorcists in his whole kingdom. Now Daniel was there till the first year of King Cyrus.

2 In the second year of his reign Nebuchadnezzar had dreams, and his

2 mind was so troubled that he could not sleep. Then the king gave orders to summon the magicians, exorcists, sorcerers, and Chaldaeans to tell him what he had dreamt. They came in and stood in the royal presence,

3 and the king said to them, 'I have had a dream and my mind has been

4 troubled to know what my dream was.' The Chaldaeans, speaking in Aramaic, said, *a*'Long live the king! Tell us what you dreamt and we

5 will tell you the interpretation.' The king answered, 'This is my declared intention. If you do not tell me both dream and interpretation,

6 you shall be torn in pieces and your houses shall be forfeit.*b* But if you can tell me the dream and the interpretation, you will be richly rewarded and loaded with honours. Tell me, therefore, the dream and its inter-

7 pretation.' They answered a second time, 'Let the king tell his servants

8 the dream, and we will tell him the interpretation.' The king answered, 'It is clear to me that you are trying to gain time, because you see that my

9 intention has been declared. If you do not make known to me the dream, there is one law that applies to you, and one only. What is more, you have agreed among yourselves to tell me a pack of lies to my face in the hope that with time things may alter. Tell me the dream, therefore, and I shall

10 know that you can give me the interpretation.' The Chaldaeans answered in the presence of the king, 'Nobody on earth can tell your majesty what you wish to know; no great king or prince has ever made such a demand

11 of magician, exorcist, or Chaldaean. What your majesty requires of us is too hard; there is no one but the gods, who dwell remote from mortal

12 men, who can give you the answer.' At this the king lost his temper and in a great rage ordered the death of all the wise men of Babylon. A decree

13 was issued that the wise men were to be executed, and accordingly men were sent to fetch Daniel and his companions for execution.

[a] *The Aramaic text begins here and continues to the end of ch. 7.* [b] *Or* made into a dunghill (*mng. of Aram. word uncertain*).

When Arioch, the captain of the king's bodyguard, was setting out to 14
execute the wise men of Babylon, Daniel approached him cautiously
and with discretion and said, 'Sir, you represent the king; why has his 15
majesty issued such a peremptory decree?' Arioch explained everything; so Daniel went in to the king's presence and begged for a certain 16
time by which he would give the king the interpretation. Then Daniel 17
went home and told the whole story to his companions, Hananiah,
Mishael and Azariah. They should ask the God of heaven in his mercy, 18
he said, to disclose this secret, so that they and he with the rest of the
wise men of Babylon should not be put to death. Then in a vision by 19
night the secret was revealed to Daniel, and he blessed the God of
heaven in these words: 20

> Blessed be God's name from age to age,
> for all wisdom and power are his.
> He changes seasons and times; 21
> he deposes kings and sets them up;
> he gives wisdom to the wise
> and all their store of knowledge to the men who know;
> he reveals deep mysteries; 22
> he knows what lies in darkness,
> and light has its dwelling with him.
> To thee, God of my fathers, I give thanks and praise, 23
> for thou hast given me wisdom and power;
> thou hast now revealed to me what we asked,
> and told us what the king is concerned to know.

Daniel therefore[a] went to Arioch who had been charged by the king 24
to put to death the wise men of Babylon and said to him, 'Do not put
the wise men of Babylon to death. Take me into the king's presence, and
I will now tell him the interpretation of the dream.' Arioch in great 25
trepidation brought Daniel before the king and said to him, 'I have
found among the Jewish exiles a man who will make known to your
majesty the interpretation of your dream.' Thereupon the king said to 26
Daniel (who was also called Belteshazzar), 'Can you tell me what I saw
in my dream and interpret it?' Daniel answered in the king's presence, 27
'The secret about which your majesty inquires no wise man, exorcist,
magician, or diviner can disclose to you. But there is in heaven a god 28
who reveals secrets, and he has told King Nebuchadnezzar what is to be
at the end of this age. This is the dream and these the visions that came
into your head: the thoughts that came to you, O king, as you lay on 29
your bed, were thoughts of things to come, and the revealer of secrets
has made known to you what is to be. This secret has been revealed to 30

[a] *So Sept.; Aram. adds* went in.

me not because I am wise beyond all living men, but because your majesty is to know the interpretation and understand the thoughts which have entered your mind.

31 'As you watched, O king, you saw a great image. This image, huge
32 and dazzling, towered before you, fearful to behold. The head of the image was of fine gold, its breast and arms of silver, its belly and thighs
33, 34 of bronze,[a] its legs of iron, its feet part iron and part clay. While you looked, a stone was hewn from a mountain,[b] not by human hands; it
35 struck the image on its feet of iron and clay and shattered them. Then the iron, the clay, the bronze, the silver, and the gold, were all shattered to fragments and were swept away like chaff before the wind from a threshing-floor in summer, until no trace of them remained. But the stone which struck the image grew into a great mountain filling the
36 whole earth. That was the dream. We shall now tell your majesty the
37 interpretation. You, O king, king of kings, to whom the God of heaven
38 has given the kingdom with all its power, authority, and honour; in whose hands he has placed men and beasts and birds of the air, wherever they dwell, granting you sovereignty over them all—you are that head of
39 gold. After you there shall arise another kingdom, inferior to yours, and yet a third kingdom, of bronze, which shall have sovereignty over the
40 whole world. And there shall be a fourth kingdom, strong as iron; as iron shatters and destroys all things, it shall break and shatter the whole
41 earth.[c] As, in your vision, the feet and toes were part potter's clay and part iron, it shall be a divided kingdom. Its core shall be partly of iron
42 just as you saw iron mixed with the common clay; as the toes were part iron and part clay, the kingdom shall be partly strong and partly brittle.
43 As, in your vision, the iron was mixed with common clay, so shall men mix with each other by intermarriage, but such alliances shall not be
44 stable: iron does not mix with clay. In the period of those kings the God of heaven will establish a kingdom which shall never be destroyed; that kingdom shall never pass to another people; it shall shatter and make an
45 end of all these kingdoms, while it shall itself endure for ever. This is the meaning of your vision of the stone being hewn from a mountain, not by human hands, and then shattering the iron, the bronze, the clay, the silver, and the gold. The mighty God has made known to your majesty what is to be hereafter. The dream is sure and the interpretation to be trusted.'

46 Then King Nebuchadnezzar prostrated himself and worshipped Daniel, and gave orders that sacrifices and soothing offerings should be
47 made to him. 'Truly,' he said, 'your god is indeed God of gods and Lord over kings, a revealer of secrets, since you have been able to

[a] *Or* copper.   [b] from a mountain: *so Sept.; Aram. om.*   [c] the whole earth: *prob. rdg.; Aram.* and like iron which shatters all these.

reveal this secret.' Then the king promoted Daniel, bestowed on him 48
many rich gifts, and made him regent over the whole province of Babylon and chief prefect over all the wise men of Babylon. Moreover at 49
Daniel's request the king put Shadrach, Meshach and Abed-nego in
charge of the administration of the province of Babylon. Daniel himself,
however, remained at court.

KING NEBUCHADNEZZAR made an image of gold, ninety feet high 3
and nine feet broad.*a* He had it set up in the plain of Dura in the province of Babylon. Then he sent out a summons to assemble the satraps, 2
prefects, viceroys, counsellors, treasurers, judges, chief constables, and
all governors of provinces to attend the dedication of the image which
he had set up. So they assembled—the satraps, prefects, viceroys, coun- 3
sellors, treasurers, judges, chief constables, and all governors of provinces—for the dedication of the image which King Nebuchadnezzar
had set up; and they stood before the image which Nebuchadnezzar had
set up. Then the herald loudly proclaimed, 'O peoples and nations of 4
every language, you are commanded, when you hear the sound of horn, 5
pipe, zither, triangle, dulcimer, music, and singing of every kind, to
prostrate yourselves and worship the golden image which King Nebuchadnezzar has set up. Whoever does not prostrate himself and worship 6
shall forthwith be thrown into a blazing furnace.' Accordingly, no sooner 7
did all the peoples hear the sound of horn, pipe, zither, triangle, dulcimer,
music,*b* and singing of every kind, than all the peoples and nations of
every language prostrated themselves and worshipped the golden image
which King Nebuchadnezzar had set up.

It was then that certain Chaldaeans came forward and brought a 8
charge against the Jews. They said to King Nebuchadnezzar, 'Long live 9
the king! Your majesty has issued an order that every man who hears the 10
sound of horn, pipe, zither, triangle, dulcimer, music, and singing of
every kind shall fall down and worship the image of gold. Whoever does 11
not do so shall be thrown into a blazing furnace. There are certain Jews, 12
Shadrach, Meshach and Abed-nego, whom you have put in charge of
the administration of the province of Babylon. These men, your majesty,
have taken no notice of your command; they do not serve your god, nor
do they worship the golden image which you have set up.' Then in rage 13
and fury Nebuchadnezzar ordered Shadrach, Meshach and Abed-nego
to be fetched, and they were brought into the king's presence. Nebu- 14
chadnezzar said to them, 'Is it true, Shadrach, Meshach and Abed-
nego, that you do not serve my god or worship the golden image which I
have set up? If you are ready at once to prostrate yourselves when you hear 15
the sound of horn, pipe, zither, triangle, dulcimer, music, and singing of

[*a*] *Lit.* sixty cubits high and six cubits broad.   [*b*] music: *so many MSS.; others om.*

every kind, and to worship the image that I have set up, well and good.
But if you do not worship it, you shall forthwith be thrown into the
blazing furnace; and what god is there that can save you from my
16 power?' Shadrach, Meshach and Abed-nego said to King Nebuchad-
17 nezzar, 'We have no need to answer you on this matter. If there is a god
who is able to save us from the blazing furnace, it is our God whom we
18 serve, and he will save us from your power, O king; but if not, be it
known to your majesty that we will neither serve your god nor worship
the golden image that you have set up.'

19   Then Nebuchadnezzar flew into a rage with Shadrach, Meshach and
Abed-nego, and his face was distorted with anger. He gave orders that
20 the furnace should be heated up to seven times its usual heat, and
commanded some of the strongest men in his army to bind Shadrach,
Meshach and Abed-nego and throw them into the blazing furnace.
21 Then those men in their trousers, their shirts, and their hats and all
their other clothes, were bound and thrown into the blazing furnace.
22 Because the king's order was urgent and the furnace exceedingly hot,
the men who were carrying Shadrach, Meshach and Abed-nego were
23 killed by the flames that leapt out; and those three men, Shadrach,
Meshach and Abed-nego, fell bound into the blazing furnace.

24   Then King Nebuchadnezzar was amazed and sprang to his feet in
great trepidation. He said to his courtiers, 'Was it not three men whom
we threw bound into the fire?' They answered the king, 'Assuredly,
25 your majesty.' He answered, 'Yet I see four men walking about in the
26 fire free and unharmed; and the fourth looks like a god.'*a* Nebuchadnezzar approached the door of the blazing furnace and said to the men,
'Shadrach, Meshach and Abed-nego, servants of the Most High God,
come out, come here.' Then Shadrach, Meshach and Abed-nego came
27 out from the fire. And the satraps, prefects, viceroys, and the king's
courtiers gathered round and saw how the fire had had no power to
harm the bodies of these men; the hair of their heads had not been
singed, their trousers were untouched, and no smell of fire lingered
about them.

28   Then Nebuchadnezzar spoke out, 'Blessed is the God of Shadrach,
Meshach and Abed-nego. He has sent his angel to save his servants who
put their trust in him, who disobeyed the royal command and were
willing to yield themselves to the fire*b* rather than to serve or worship
29 any god other than their own God. I therefore issue a decree that any man,
to whatever people or nation he belongs, whatever his language, if he
speaks blasphemy against the God of Shadrach, Meshach and Abed-
nego, shall be torn to pieces and his house shall be forfeit;*c* for there is

[a] *Lit.* like a son of a god.   [b] to the fire: *so Sept.; Aram. om.*   [c] *Or* made into a dunghill
(*mng. of Aram. word uncertain*).

no other god who can save men in this way.' Then the king advanced 30
the fortunes of Shadrach, Meshach and Abed-nego in the province of
Babylon.

KING NEBUCHADNEZZAR to all peoples and nations of every language 4 1*ᵃ*
living in the whole world: May all prosperity be yours! It is my pleasure 2
to recount the signs and marvels which the Most High God has worked
for me:

> How great are his signs, 3
> and his marvels overwhelming!
> His kingdom is an everlasting kingdom,
> his sovereignty stands to all generations.

I, Nebuchadnezzar, was living peacefully at home in the luxury of my 4*ᵇ*
palace. As I lay on my bed, I saw a dream which terrified me; and 5
fantasies and visions which came into my head dismayed me. So I issued 6
an order summoning into my presence all the wise men of Babylon
to make known to me the interpretation of the dream. Then the 7
magicians, exorcists, Chaldaeans, and diviners came in, and in their
presence I related my dream. But they could not interpret it. And yet 8
another came into my presence, Daniel, who is called Belteshazzar
after the name of my god, a man possessed by the spirit of the holy gods.
To him, too, I related the dream: 'Belteshazzar, chief of the magicians, 9
whom I myself know to be possessed by the spirit of the holy gods, and
whom no secret baffles, listen to*ᶜ* the vision I saw in a dream, and tell
me its interpretation.

'Here is the vision which came into my head as I was lying upon my 10
bed:

> As I was looking,
> I saw a tree of great height at the centre of the earth;
> the tree grew and became strong, 11
> reaching with its top to the sky
> and visible to earth's farthest bounds.
> Its foliage was lovely, 12
> and its fruit abundant;
> and it yielded food for all.
> Beneath it the wild beasts found shelter,
> the birds lodged in its branches,
> and from it all living creatures fed.

'Here is another vision which came into my head as I was lying upon 13
my bed:

[a] *3. 31 in Aram.*   [b] *4. 1 in Aram.*   [c] listen to: *so Theod.; Aram. om.*

As I was watching, there was a Watcher,
a Holy One coming down from heaven.

14   He cried aloud and said,
"Hew down the tree, lop off the branches,
strip away the foliage, scatter the fruit.
Let the wild beasts flee from its shelter
and the birds from its branches,

15   but leave the stump with its roots in the ground.
So, tethered with an iron ring,
let him eat his fill of the lush grass;
let him be drenched with the dew of heaven
and share the lot of the beasts in their pasture;

16   let his mind cease to be a man's mind,
and let him be given the mind of a beast.
Let seven times pass over him.

17   The issue has been determined by the Watchers
and the sentence pronounced by the Holy Ones.

Thereby the living will know that the Most High is sovereign in the
kingdom of men: he gives the kingdom to whom he will and he may set
over it the humblest of mankind."

18   'This is the dream which I, King Nebuchadnezzar, have dreamed;
now, Belteshazzar, tell me its interpretation; for, though all the wise
men of my kingdom are unable to tell me what it means, you can tell me,
since the spirit of the holy gods is in you.'

19   Daniel, who was called Belteshazzar, was dumbfounded for a moment, dismayed by his thoughts; but the king said, 'Do not let the dream
and its interpretation dismay you.' Belteshazzar answered, 'My lord, if
only the dream were for those who hate you and its interpretation for

20   your enemies! The tree which you saw grow and become strong,
reaching with its top to the sky and visible to earth's farthest bounds,

21   its foliage lovely and its fruit abundant, a tree which yielded food for all,
beneath which the wild beasts dwelt and in whose branches the birds

22   lodged, that tree, O king, is you. You have grown and become strong.
Your power has grown and reaches the sky; your sovereignty stretches

23   to the ends of the earth. Also, O king, you saw a Watcher, a Holy One,
coming down from heaven and saying, "Hew down the tree and destroy
it, but leave its stump with its roots in the ground. So, tethered with an
iron ring, let him eat his fill of the lush grass; let him be drenched with
the dew of heaven and share the lot of the beasts until seven times pass

24   over him." This is the interpretation, O king—it is a decree of the Most

25   High which touches my lord the king. You will be banished from the
society of men; you will have to live with the wild beasts; you will feed

on grass like oxen and you will be drenched with the dew of heaven. Seven times will pass over you until you have learnt that the Most High is sovereign over the kingdom of men and gives it to whom he will. The command was given to leave the stump of the tree with its 26 roots. By this you may know that from the time you acknowledge the sovereignty of heaven your rule will endure. Be advised by me, O king: 27 redeem your sins by charity and your iniquities by generosity to the wretched. So may you long enjoy peace of mind.'

All this befell King Nebuchadnezzar. At the end of twelve months 28, 29 the king was walking on the roof of the royal palace at Babylon, and he 30 exclaimed, 'Is not this Babylon the great which I have built as a royal residence by my own mighty power and for the honour of my majesty?' The words were still on his lips, when a voice came down from heaven: 31 'To you, King Nebuchadnezzar, the word is spoken: the kingdom has passed from you. You are banished from the society of men and you 32 shall live with the wild beasts; you shall feed on grass like oxen, and seven times will pass over you until you have learnt that the Most High is sovereign over the kingdom of men and gives it to whom he will.' At that very moment this judgement came upon Nebuchadnezzar. 33 He was banished from the society of men and ate grass like oxen; his body was drenched by the dew of heaven, until his hair grew long like goats' hair and his nails like eagles' talons.[a]

At the end of the appointed time, I, Nebuchadnezzar, raised my eyes 34 to heaven and I returned to my right mind. I blessed the Most High, praising and glorifying the Ever-living One:

> His sovereignty is never-ending
> and his rule endures through all generations;
> all dwellers upon earth count for nothing   35
> and he deals as he wishes with the host of heaven;[b]
> no one may lay hand upon him
> and ask him what he does.

At that very time I returned to my right mind and my majesty and 36 royal splendour were restored to me for the glory of my kingdom. My courtiers and my nobles sought audience of me. I was established in my kingdom and my power was greatly increased. Now I, Nebuchadnezzar, 37 praise and exalt and glorify the King of heaven; for all his acts are right and his ways are just and those whose conduct is arrogant he can bring low.

[a] goats' hair...eagles' talons: *prob. rdg.; Aram.* eagles' and his nails like birds'.   [b] *Prob. rdg.; Aram. adds* and the dwellers upon earth.

Belshazzar's feast

5 BELSHAZZAR THE KING GAVE A BANQUET for a thousand of his
nobles and was drinking wine in the presence of the thousand.
2 Warmed by the wine, he gave orders to fetch the vessels of gold and
silver which his father Nebuchadnezzar had taken from the sanctuary
at Jerusalem, that he and his nobles, his concubines and his courtesans,
3 might drink from them. So the vessels of gold and silver[a] from the
sanctuary in the house of God at Jerusalem were brought in, and the
king and his nobles, his concubines and his courtesans, drank from
4 them. They drank wine and praised the gods of gold and silver, of
5 bronze and iron, and of wood and stone. Suddenly there appeared the
fingers of a human hand writing on the plaster of the palace wall opposite the lamp, and the king could see the back of the hand as it wrote.
6 At this the king's mind was filled with dismay and he turned pale, he
7 became limp in every limb and his knees knocked together. He called
loudly for the exorcists, Chaldaeans, and diviners to be brought in;
then, addressing the wise men of Babylon, he said, 'Whoever can read
this writing and tell me its interpretation shall be robed in purple and
honoured with a chain of gold round his neck and shall rank as third in
8 the kingdom.' Then all the king's wise men came in, but they could not
9 read the writing or interpret it to the king. King Belshazzar sat there
pale and utterly dismayed, while his nobles were perplexed.
10 The king and his nobles were talking when the queen entered the
banqueting-hall: 'Long live the king!' she said. 'Why this dismay, and
11 why do you look so pale? There is a man in your kingdom who has in
him the spirit of the holy gods, a man who was known in your father's
time to have a clear understanding and godlike wisdom. King Nebuchadnezzar, your father, appointed him chief of the magicians, exorcists,
12 Chaldaeans, and diviners.[b] This same Daniel, whom the king named
Belteshazzar, is known to have a notable spirit, with knowledge and
understanding, and the gift of interpreting dreams, explaining riddles
and unbinding spells;[c] let him be summoned now and he will give the
13 interpretation.' Daniel was then brought into the king's presence
and the king said to him, 'So you are Daniel, one of the Jewish exiles
14 whom the king my father brought from Judah. I have heard that you
possess the spirit of the holy[d] gods and that you are a man of clear under-
15 standing and peculiar wisdom. The wise men, the exorcists, have just
been brought into my presence to read this writing and tell me its inter-

[a] and silver: *so Theod.; Aram. om.* [b] *So Theod.; Aram. adds* the king your father.
[c] *Or* and solving problems. [d] *So some MSS.; others om.*

pretation, and they have been unable to interpret it. But I have heard it 16
said of you that you are able to give interpretations and to unbind spells.*a*
So now, if you are able to read the words and tell me what they mean,
you shall be robed in purple and honoured with a chain of gold round
your neck and shall rank as third in the kingdom.' Then Daniel 17
answered in the king's presence, 'Your gifts you may keep for yourself;
or else give your rewards to another. Nevertheless I will read the writing
to your majesty and tell you its interpretation. My lord king, the Most 18
High God gave your father Nebuchadnezzar a kingdom and power and
glory and majesty; and, because of this power which he gave him, all 19
peoples and nations of every language trembled before him and were
afraid. He put to death whom he would and spared whom he would, he
promoted them at will and at will degraded them. But, when he became 20
haughty, stubborn and presumptuous, he was deposed from his royal
throne and his glory was taken from him. He was banished from the society 21
of men, his mind became like that of a beast, he had to live with the wild
asses and to eat grass like oxen, and his body was drenched with the dew
of heaven, until he came to know that the Most High God is sovereign
over the kingdom of men and sets up over it whom he will. But you, his 22
son Belshazzar, did not humble your heart, although you knew all this.
You have set yourself up against the Lord of heaven. The vessels of his 23
temple have been brought to your table; and you, your nobles, your
concubines, and your courtesans have drunk from them. You have praised
the gods of silver and gold, of bronze and iron, of wood and stone, which
neither see nor hear nor know, and you have not given glory to God, in
whose charge is your very breath and in whose hands are all your ways.
This is why that hand was sent from his very presence and why it wrote 24
this inscription. And these are the words of the writing which was 25
inscribed: *Mene mene tekel u-pharsin.* Here is the interpretation: *mene:*b 26
God has numbered the days of your kingdom and brought it to an end;
*tekel:*c you have been weighed in the balance and found wanting; *u-* 27, 28
*pharsin:*d and your kingdom has been divided and given to the Medes
and Persians.' Then Belshazzar gave the order and Daniel was robed in 29
purple and honoured with a chain of gold round his neck, and proclamation was made that he should rank as third in the kingdom.
   That very night Belshazzar king of the Chaldaeans was slain, and 30, 31e
Darius the Mede took the kingdom, being then sixty-two years old.

[a] Or and to solve problems.   [b] That is numbered.   [c] That is shekel or weight.   [d] Prob.
rdg.; Aram. pheres. There is a play on three possible meanings: halves or divisions or Persians.
[e] 6. 1 in Aram.

Daniel in the lions' pit

6 ¹ IT PLEASED DARIUS TO APPOINT SATRAPS over the kingdom, a
² hundred and twenty in number in charge of the whole kingdom, and
over them three chief ministers, to whom the satraps should send
reports so that the king's interests might not suffer; of these three,
³ Daniel was one. In the event Daniel outshone the other ministers and
the satraps because of his ability, and the king had it in mind to appoint
⁴ him over the whole kingdom. Then the chief ministers and the satraps
began to look round for some pretext to attack Daniel's administration
of the kingdom, but they failed to find any malpractice on his part; for
⁵ he was faithful to his trust. Since they could discover no neglect of duty
or malpractice, they said, 'There will be no charge to bring against this
⁶ Daniel unless we find one in his religion.' These chief ministers and
satraps watched for an opportunity to approach the king, and said to him,
⁷ 'Long live King Darius! All we, the ministers of the kingdom, prefects,
satraps, courtiers, and viceroys, have taken counsel and agree that the
king should issue a decree and bring an ordinance into force, that whoever within the next thirty days shall present a petition to any god or
⁸ man other than the king shall be thrown into the lions' pit. Now, O king,
issue the ordinance and have it put in writing, so that it may be unalterable, for the law of the Medes and Persians stands for ever.'
⁹ Accordingly King Darius issued the ordinance in written form.
¹⁰ When Daniel learnt that this decree had been issued, he went into his
house. He had had windows made in his roof-chamber looking towards
Jerusalem; and there he knelt down three times a day and offered
¹¹ prayers and praises to his God as his custom had always been. His
enemies watched for an opportunity to catch Daniel and found him at
¹² his prayers making supplication to his God. Then they came into the
king's presence and reminded him of the ordinance. 'Your majesty,'
they said, 'have you not issued an ordinance that any person who,
within the next thirty days, shall present a petition to any god or man
other than your majesty shall be thrown into the lions' pit?' The king
answered, 'Yes, it is fixed. The law of the Medes and Persians stands
¹³ for ever.' So in the king's presence they said, 'Daniel, one of the Jewish
exiles, has ignored the ordinance issued by your majesty, and is making
¹⁴ petition to his god three times a day.' When the king heard this, he was
greatly distressed. He tried to think of a way to save Daniel, and con-
¹⁵ tinued his efforts till sunset; then those same men watched for an
opportunity to approach the king, and said to him, 'Your majesty must
know that by the law of the Medes and Persians no ordinance or decree

issued by the king may be altered.' So the king gave orders and Daniel 16
was brought and thrown into the lions' pit; but he said to Daniel,
'Your own God, whom you serve continually, will save you.' A stone 17
was brought and put over the mouth of the pit, and the king sealed it
with his signet and with the signets of his nobles, so that no one might
intervene to rescue Daniel.

The king went back to his palace and spent the night fasting; no 18
woman was brought to him and sleep eluded him. At dawn, as soon as it 19
was light, he rose and went in fear and trembling to the pit. When the 20
king reached it, he called anxiously to Daniel, 'Daniel, servant of the
living God, has your God whom you serve continually been able to
save you from the lions?' Then Daniel answered, 'Long live the king! 21
My God sent his angel to shut the lions' mouths so that they have done 22
me no injury, because in his judgement I was found innocent;[a] and
moreover, O king, I had done you no injury.' The king was overjoyed 23
and gave orders that Daniel should be lifted out of the pit. So Daniel
was lifted out and no trace of injury was found on him, because he had
put his faith in his God. By order of the king Daniel's accusers were 24
brought and thrown into the lions' pit with their wives and children,
and before they reached the floor of the pit the lions were upon them
and crunched them up, bones and all.

Then King Darius wrote to all peoples and nations of every language 25
throughout the whole world: 'May your prosperity increase! I have 26
issued a decree that in all my royal domains men shall fear and reverence
the God of Daniel;

> for he is the living God, the everlasting,
> whose kingly power shall not be weakened;
>> whose sovereignty shall have no end—
> a saviour, a deliverer, a worker of signs and wonders 27
>> in heaven and on earth,
> who has delivered Daniel from the power of the lions.'

So this Daniel prospered during the reigns of Darius and Cyrus the 28
Persian.

Daniel's visions

IN THE FIRST YEAR OF BELSHAZZAR king of Babylon, as Daniel 7
lay on his bed, dreams and visions came into his head. Then he wrote
down the dream, and here his account begins:
In my visions of the night I, Daniel, was gazing intently and I saw a 2

[a] in his judgement...innocent: *or* before him success was granted me.

3 great sea churned up by the four winds of heaven, and four huge beasts
4 coming up out of the sea, each one different from the others. The first
was like a lion but had an eagle's wings. I watched until its wings were
plucked off and it was lifted from the ground and made to stand on two
5 feet like a man; it was also given the mind of a man. Then I saw another,
a second beast, like a bear. It was half crouching and had three ribs in
its mouth, between its teeth. The command was given: 'Up, gorge
6 yourself with flesh.' After this as I gazed I saw another, a beast like a
leopard with four bird's wings on its back; this creature had four heads,
7 and it was invested with sovereign power. Next in my visions of the
night I saw a fourth beast, dreadful and grisly, exceedingly strong, with
great iron teeth and bronze claws.[a] It crunched and devoured, and
trampled underfoot all that was left. It differed from all the beasts which
8 preceded it in having ten horns. While I was considering the horns I
saw another horn, a little one, springing up among them, and three of
the first horns were uprooted to make room for it. And in that horn were
eyes like the eyes of a man, and a mouth that spoke proud words.
9 I kept looking, and then

> thrones were set in place and one ancient in years took his seat,
> his robe was white as snow and the hair of his head like cleanest
>   wool.
> Flames of fire were his throne and its wheels blazing fire;
10 a flowing river of fire streamed out before him.[b]
> Thousands upon thousands served him
> and myriads upon myriads attended his presence.
> The court sat, and the books were opened.

11 Then because of the proud words that the horn was speaking, I went
on watching until the beast was killed and its carcass destroyed: it was
12 given to the flames. The rest of the beasts, though deprived of their
13 sovereignty, were allowed to remain alive for a time and a season. I was
still watching in visions of the night and I saw one like a man[c] coming
with the clouds of heaven; he approached the Ancient in Years and was
14 presented to him. Sovereignty and glory and kingly power were given
to him, so that all people and nations of every language should serve
him; his sovereignty was to be an everlasting sovereignty which should
not pass away, and his kingly power such as should never be impaired.
15 My spirit within me was troubled, and, dismayed by the visions
16 which came into my head, I, Daniel, approached one of those who stood
there and inquired from him what all this meant; and he told me the
17 interpretation. 'These great beasts, four in number,' he said, 'are four

[a] and bronze claws: *prob. rdg.*, *cp. verse 19*; *Aram. om.*   [b] *Or* it.   [c] *Lit.* like a son of
man.

kingdoms*a* which shall rise from the ground. But the saints*b* of the Most 18 High shall receive the kingly power and shall retain it for ever, for ever and ever.' Then I desired to know what the fourth beast meant, the 19 beast that was different from all the others, very dreadful with its iron teeth and bronze claws, crunching and devouring and trampling under-foot all that was left. I desired also to know about the ten horns on its 20 head and the other horn which sprang up and at whose coming three of them fell—the horn that had eyes and a mouth speaking proud words and appeared larger than the others. As I still watched, that horn was 21 waging war with the saints and overcoming them until the Ancient in 22 Years came. Then judgement was given in favour of the saints of the Most High, and the time came when the saints gained possession of the kingly power. He gave me this answer: 'The fourth beast signifies a 23 fourth kingdom which shall appear upon earth. It shall differ from the other kingdoms and shall devour the whole earth, tread it down and crush it. The ten horns signify the appearance of ten kings in this 24 kingdom, after whom another king shall arise, differing from his pre-decessors; and he shall bring low three kings. He shall hurl defiance at 25 the Most High and shall wear down the saints of the Most High. He shall plan to alter the customary times and law; and the saints shall be delivered into his power for a time and times and half a time. Then the 26 court shall sit, and he shall be deprived of his sovereignty, so that in the end it may be destroyed and abolished. The kingly power, sovereignty, 27 and greatness of all the kingdoms under heaven shall be given to the people of the saints of the Most High. Their kingly power is an ever-lasting power and all sovereignties shall serve them and obey them.'

Here the account ends. As for me, Daniel, my thoughts dismayed me 28 greatly and I turned pale; and I kept these things in my mind.

*c*In the third year of the reign of King Belshazzar, while I was in Susa 8 1-2 the capital city of the province of Elam, a vision appeared to me, Daniel, similar to my former vision. In this vision I was watching beside the stream of the Ulai. I raised my eyes and there I saw a ram with two 3 horns standing between me and the stream. The two horns were long, the one longer than the other, growing up behind. I watched the ram 4 butting west and north and south. No beasts could stand before it, no one could rescue from its power. It did what it liked, making a display of its strength. While I pondered this, suddenly a he-goat came from 5 the west skimming over the whole earth without touching the ground; it had a prominent horn between its eyes. It approached the two-horned 6 ram which I had seen standing between me and the stream and rushed at it with impetuous force. I saw it advance on the ram, working itself 7

[a] *So Sept.; Aram.* kings. [b] *Or* holy ones. [c] *Here the Hebrew text resumes (see note at 2. 4).*

into a fury against it, then strike the ram and break its two horns; the ram had no strength to resist. The he-goat flung it to the ground and trampled on it, and there was no one to save the ram.

8   Then the he-goat made a great display of its strength. Powerful as it was, its great horn snapped and in its place there sprang out towards the
9   four quarters of heaven four prominent horns. Out of one of them there issued one small horn, which made a prodigious show of strength south
10 and east and towards the fairest of all lands. It aspired to be as great as the host of heaven, and it cast down to the earth some of the host and
11 some of the stars and trod them underfoot. It aspired to be as great as the Prince of the host, suppressed his regular offering and even threw
12 down his sanctuary. The heavenly hosts were delivered up, and it raised itself[a] impiously against the regular offering and threw true
13 religion to the ground; in all that it did it succeeded. I heard a holy one speaking and another holy one answering him, whoever he was. The one said, 'For how long will the period of this vision last? How long will the regular offering be suppressed,[b] how long will impiety cause desolation,[c] and both the Holy Place and the fairest of all lands[d] be
14 given over to be trodden down?' The answer came, 'For two thousand three hundred evenings and mornings; then the Holy Place shall emerge victorious.'

15 All the while that I, Daniel, was seeing the vision, I was trying to understand it. Suddenly I saw standing before me one with the semb-
16 lance of a man; at the same time I heard a human voice calling to him across the bend of the Ulai, 'Gabriel, explain the vision to this man.'
17 He came up to where I was standing; I was seized with terror at his approach and threw myself on my face. But he said to me, 'Understand,
18 O man: the vision points to the time of the end.' When he spoke to me, I fell to the ground in a trance; but he grasped me and made me stand
19 up where I was. And he said, 'I shall make known to you what is to happen at the end of the wrath; for there is an end to the appointed
20 time. The two-horned ram which you saw signifies the kings of Media
21 and Persia, the he-goat[e] is the kingdom[f] of the Greeks[g] and the great
22 horn on his forehead is the first king. As for the horn which was snapped off and replaced by four horns: four kingdoms shall rise out of that nation, but not with power comparable to his.

23   In the last days of those kingdoms,
               when their sin is at its height,
           a king shall appear, harsh and grim, a master of stratagem.

[a] and it raised itself: *prob. rdg.; Heb. om.*   [b] be suppressed: *so Sept.; Heb. om.*   [c] will impiety cause desolation: *prob. rdg.; Heb. obscure.*   [d] fairest of all lands: *prob. rdg., cp. verse 9; Heb.* host.   [e] he-goat: *so Sept.; Heb.* hairy he-goat.   [f] *Prob. rdg.; Heb.* king.   [g] *Heb.* Javan.

His power shall be great,[a] he shall work havoc untold;   24
   he shall succeed in whatever he does.
He shall work havoc among great nations and upon a holy
     people.
His mind shall be ever active,   25
and he shall succeed in his crafty designs;
   he shall conjure up great plans
and, when they least expect it, work havoc on many.
   He shall challenge even the Prince of princes
   and be broken, but not by human hands.
   This revelation which has been given   26
of the evenings and the mornings is true;
but you must keep the vision secret,
   for it points to days far ahead.'

As for me, Daniel, my strength failed me and I lay sick for a while.   27
Then I rose and attended to the king's business. But I was perplexed by
the revelation and no one could explain it.

IN THE FIRST YEAR OF THE REIGN of Darius son of Ahasuerus (a   9
Mede by birth, who was appointed king over the kingdom of the Chaldaeans) I, Daniel, was reading the scriptures and reflecting on the   2
seventy years which, according to the word of the LORD to the prophet
Jeremiah, were to pass while Jerusalem lay in ruins. Then I turned to   3
the Lord God in earnest prayer and supplication with fasting and
sackcloth and ashes. I prayed to the LORD my God, making confession   4
thus:
  'Lord, thou great and terrible God who faithfully keepest the covenant with those who love thee and observe thy commandments, we have   5
sinned, we have done what was wrong and wicked; we have rebelled, we
have turned our backs on thy commandments and thy decrees. We have   6
not listened to thy servants the prophets, who spoke in thy name to our
kings and princes, to our forefathers and to all the people of the land.
O Lord, the right is on thy side; the shame, now as ever, belongs to us,   7
the men of Judah and the citizens of Jerusalem, and to all the Israelites
near and far in every land to which thou hast banished them for their
treachery towards thee. O LORD, the shame falls on us as on our kings,   8
our princes and our forefathers; we have all sinned against thee. Com-   9
passion and forgiveness belong to the Lord our God, though we have
rebelled against him. We have not obeyed the LORD our God, we have   10
not conformed to the laws which he laid down for us through his
servants the prophets. All Israel has broken thy law and not obeyed   11

---

[a] *So Theod.; Heb. adds* and not with such power as his.

thee, so that the curses set out in the law of Moses thy servant in the adjuration and the oath have rained down upon us; for we have sinned

12 against him. He has fulfilled all that he said about us and about our rulers, by bringing upon us and upon Jerusalem a calamity greater than

13 has ever happened in all the world. It was all foreshadowed in the law of Moses, this calamity which has come upon us; yet we have done nothing to propitiate the LORD our God; we have neither repented of

14 our wrongful deeds nor remembered that thou art true to thy word. The LORD has been biding his time and has now brought this calamity upon us. In all that he has done the LORD our God has been right; yet we have not obeyed him.

15 'And now, O Lord our God who didst bring thy people out of Egypt by a strong hand, winning for thyself a name that lives on to this

16 day, we have sinned, we have done wrong. O Lord, by all thy saving deeds we beg that thy wrath and anger may depart from Jerusalem, thy city, thy holy hill; through our own sins and our fathers' guilty deeds Jerusalem and thy people have become a byword among all our neigh-

17 bours. And now, our God, listen to thy servant's prayer and supplication; for thy own sake, O Lord,*a* make thy face shine upon thy desolate

18 sanctuary. Lend thy ear, O God, and hear, open thine eyes and look upon our desolation and upon the city that bears thy name; it is not by virtue of our own saving acts but by thy great mercy that we present

19 our supplications before thee. O Lord, hear; O Lord, forgive; O Lord, listen and act; for thy own sake do not delay, O God, for thy city and thy people bear thy name.'

20 Thus I was speaking and praying, confessing my own sin and my people Israel's sin, and presenting my supplication before the LORD my

21 God on behalf of his holy hill. While I was praying, the man Gabriel, whom I had already seen in the vision, came close to*b* me at the hour of

22 the evening sacrifice, flying swiftly.*c* He spoke clearly to me and said,

23 'Daniel, I have now come to enlighten your understanding. As you were beginning your supplications a word went forth; this I have come to pass on to you,*d* for you are a man greatly beloved. Consider well the

24 word, consider the vision: Seventy weeks are marked out for your people and your holy city; then rebellion shall be stopped,*e* sin brought to an end,*f* iniquity expiated, everlasting right ushered in, vision and

25 prophecy*g* sealed, and the Most Holy Place anointed. Know then and understand: from the time that the word went forth that Jerusalem should be restored and rebuilt, seven weeks shall pass till the appearance of one anointed, a prince; then for sixty-two weeks it shall remain

[a] for…O Lord: *so Theod.; Heb.* for the Lord's sake.   [b] *Or* touched.   [c] flying swiftly: *prob. rdg.; Heb.* thoroughly wearied.   [d] to you: *so Sept.; Heb. om.*   [e] *Or* restrained.   [f] *Or* sealed.   [g] *Lit.* prophet.

restored, rebuilt with streets and conduits. At the critical time, after the 26
sixty-two weeks, one who is anointed shall be removed with no one to
take his part; and the horde of an invading prince shall work havoc on
city and sanctuary. The end of it shall be a deluge, inevitable war with
all its horrors. He shall make a firm league with the mighty*a* for one 27
week; and, the week half spent, he shall put a stop to sacrifice and
offering. And in the train of these abominations shall come an author of
desolation; then, in the end, what has been decreed concerning the
desolation will be poured out.'

IN THE THIRD YEAR OF CYRUS king of Persia a word was revealed 10
to Daniel who had been given the name Belteshazzar. Though this
word was true, it cost him*b* much toil to understand it; nevertheless
understanding came to him in the course of the vision.

In those days I, Daniel, mourned for three whole weeks. I refrained 2,3
from all choice food; no meat or wine passed my lips, and I did not
anoint myself until the three weeks had gone by. On the twenty-fourth 4
day of the first month, I found myself on the bank of the great river,
that is the Tigris; I looked up and saw a man clothed in linen with a 5
belt of gold from Ophir*c* round his waist. His body gleamed like topaz, 6
his face shone like lightning, his eyes flamed like torches, his arms and
feet sparkled like a disc of bronze; and when he spoke his voice sounded
like the voice of a multitude. I, Daniel, alone saw the vision, while those 7
who were near me did not see it, but great fear fell upon them and they
stole away, and I was left alone gazing at this great vision. But my 8
strength left me; I became a sorry figure of a man, and retained no
strength. I heard the sound of his words and, when I did so, I fell prone 9
on the ground in a trance. Suddenly a hand grasped me and pulled me 10
up on to my hands and knees. He said to me, 'Daniel, man greatly 11
beloved, attend to the words I am speaking to you and stand up where
you are, for I am now sent to you.' When he addressed me, I stood up
trembling and he said, 'Do not be afraid, Daniel, for from the very first 12
day that you applied your mind to understand and to mortify yourself
before your God, your prayers have been heard, and I have come in
answer to them. But the angel prince of the kingdom of Persia resisted 13
me for twenty-one days, and then, seeing that I had held out there,
Michael, one of the chief princes, came to help me against the prince*d* of
the kingdom*e* of Persia. And I have come to explain to you what will 14
happen to your people in days to come; for this too is a vision for those
days.'

While he spoke to me I hung my head and was struck dumb. 15

[*a*] *Or* many.   [*b*] him: *prob. rdg.; Heb. om.*   [*c*] *So some MSS.; others* Uphaz.   [*d*] prince:
so Sept.; Heb. om.   [*e*] *So some MSS.; others* kings.

16 Suddenly one like a man touched my lips. Then I opened my mouth to speak and addressed him as he stood before me: 'Sir, this has pierced

17 me to the heart, and I retain no strength. How can my lord's servant presume to talk with such as my lord, since my strength has failed me

18 and no breath is left in me?' Then the figure touched me again and

19 restored my strength. He said, 'Do not be afraid, man greatly beloved; all will be well with you. Be strong, be strong.' When he had spoken to me, I recovered strength and said, 'Speak, sir, for you have given me

20 strength.' He said, 'Do you know why I have come to you? I am first going back to fight with the prince of Persia, and, as soon as I have left,

21 – 11 1 the prince of Greece*a* will appear: I have no ally on my side to help and support me,*b* except Michael your prince.*c* However I will tell you what

2 is written in the Book of Truth. Here and now I will tell you what is true:

'Three more kings will appear in Persia, and the fourth will far surpass all the others in wealth; and when he has extended his power through his wealth, he will rouse the whole world against the kingdom

3 of Greece. Then there will appear a warrior king. He will rule a vast

4 kingdom and will do what he chooses. But as soon as he is established, his kingdom will be shattered and split up north, south, east and west. It will not pass to his descendants, nor will any of his successors have an empire like his; his kingdom will be torn up by the roots and

5 given to others as well as to them. Then the king of the south will become strong; but another of the captains will surpass him in strength

6 and win a greater kingdom. In due course the two will enter into a friendly alliance; to redress the balance the daughter of the king of the south will be given in marriage to the king of the north, but she will not maintain her influence and their line will not last. She and her escort, her child, and also her lord and master, will all be the victims of foul

7 play. Then another shoot from the same stock as hers will appear in his father's place, will penetrate the defences of the king of the north and

8 enter his fortress, and will win a decisive victory over his people. He will take back as booty to Egypt even the images of their gods cast in metal and their precious vessels of silver and gold. Then for some

9 years he will refrain from attacking the king of the north. After that the king of the north will overrun the southern kingdom but will retreat to his own land.

10 'His sons will press on to assemble a great armed horde. One of them will sweep on and on like an irresistible flood. And after that he will

11 press on as far as his enemy's stronghold. The king of the south, his anger roused, will march out to do battle with the king of the north

[*a*] *Heb.* Javan. [*b*] me: *so Pesh.; Heb. obscure.* [*c*] *Prob. rdg.; Heb. adds* and as for me, in the first year of Darius the Mede.

who, in turn, will raise a great horde, but it will be delivered into the hands of his enemy. When this horde has been captured, the victor will 12 be elated and he will slaughter tens of thousands, yet he will not maintain his advantage. Then the king of the north will once more raise a 13 horde even greater than the last and, when the years come round, will advance with a great army and a large baggage-train. During these 14 times many will resist the king of the south, but some hotheads among your own people will rashly attempt to give substance to a vision and will come to disaster. Then the king of the north will come and throw 15 up siege-ramps and capture a fortified town, and the forces of the south will not stand up to him; even the flower of their army will not be able to hold their ground. And so his adversary will do as he pleases and 16 meet with no opposition. He will establish himself in the fairest of all lands and it will come wholly into his power. He will resolve to subjugate all 17 the dominions of the king of the south; and he will come to fair terms with him,*ᵃ* and he will give him a young woman in marriage, for the destruction of the kingdom; but she will not persist nor serve his purpose. Then he will turn to the coasts and islands and take many 18 prisoners, but a foreign commander*ᵇ* will put an end to his challenge by wearing him down;*ᶜ* thus he will throw back his challenge on to him. He will fall back upon his own strongholds; there he will come to dis- 19 aster and be overthrown and be seen no more.

'He will be succeeded by one who will send out an officer with a 20 royal escort to extort tribute; after a short time this king too will meet his end, yet neither openly nor in battle.

'A contemptible creature will succeed but will not be given recog- 21 nition as king; yet he will seize the kingdom by dissimulation and intrigue in time of peace. He will sweep away all forces of opposition as 22 he advances, and even the Prince of the Covenant will be broken. He 23 will enter into fraudulent alliances and, although the people behind him are but few, he will rise to power and establish himself in time of peace. 24 He will overrun the richest districts of the province and succeed in doing what his fathers and forefathers failed to do, distributing spoil, booty, and property to his followers. He will lay his plans against fortresses, but only for a time.

'He will rouse himself in all his strength and courage and lead a great 25 army against the king of the south, but the king of the south will press the campaign against him with a very great and numerous army; yet the king of the south will not persist, for traitors will lay their plots. Those 26 who eat at his board will be his undoing; his army will be swept away, and many will fall on the field of battle. The two kings will be bent on 27

[a] and he...with him: *prob. rdg.; Heb. obscure.* [b] *Or* consul *or* legate. [c] by wearing him down: *prob. rdg.; Heb. obscure.*

mischief and, sitting at the same table, they will lie to each other with
advantage to neither. Yet there will still be an end to the appointed time.

28 Then one will return home with a long baggage-train, and with anger
in his heart against the Holy Covenant; he will work his will and return
to his own land.

29   'At the appointed time he will once more overrun the south, but he
30 will not succeed as he did before. Ships from the west[a] will sail against
him, and he will receive a rebuff. He will turn and vent his fury against
the Holy Covenant; on his way back he will take due note of those who
31 have forsaken it. Armed forces dispatched by him will desecrate the
sanctuary and the citadel and do away with the regular offering. And
there they will set up "the abominable thing that causes desolation".
32 He will win over by plausible promises those who are ready to condemn
the covenant, but the people who are faithful to their God will hold
33 firm and fight back. Wise leaders of the nation will give guidance to the
common people; yet for a while they will fall victims to fire and sword,
34 to captivity and pillage. But these victims will not want for help, though
35 small, even if many who join them are insincere. Some of these leaders
will themselves fall victims for a time so that they may be tested, refined
and made shining white. Yet there will still be an end[b] to the appointed
36 time. The king will do what he chooses; he will exalt and magnify
himself above every god and against the God of gods he will utter
monstrous blasphemies. All will go well for him until the time of wrath
37 ends, for what is determined must be done. He will ignore his ancestral
gods, and the god beloved of women; to no god will he pay heed but
38 will exalt himself above them all. Instead he will honour the god of the
citadel,[c] a god unknown to his ancestors, with gold and silver, gems and
39 costly gifts. He will garrison his strongest fortresses with aliens, the
people of a foreign god. Those whom he favours he will load with
honour, putting them in office over the common people and distributing land at a price.

40   'At the time of the end, he and the king of the south will make feints
at one another, and the king of the north will come storming against
him with chariots and cavalry and many ships. He will overrun land
41 after land, sweeping over them like a flood, amongst them the fairest of
all lands, and tens of thousands shall fall victims. Yet all these lands
[including Edom and Moab and the remnant[d] of the Ammonites] will
42 survive his attack. He will reach out to land after land, and Egypt will
43 not escape. He will gain control of her hidden stores of gold and silver
and of all her treasures; Libyans and Cushites will follow in his train.
44 Then rumours from east and north will alarm him, and he will depart

[a] Ships from the west: *Heb.* Ships of Kittim; *Sept.* Romans.   [b] Yet…end: *prob. rdg.;*
Heb. has different word order.   [c] *Lit.* fortresses.   [d] *So Pesh.; Heb.* beginning.

in a great rage to destroy and to exterminate many. He will pitch his   45
royal pavilion between the sea and the holy hill, the fairest of all hills;
and he will meet his end with no one to help him.

> At that moment Michael shall appear,   12
>   Michael the great captain,
>   who stands guard over your fellow-countrymen;
>   and there will be a time of distress
>   such as has never been
>   since they became a nation till that moment.
> But at that moment your people will be delivered,*a*
>   every one who is written in the book:
> many of those who sleep in the dust of the earth will wake,   2
>   some to everlasting life
>   and some to the reproach of eternal abhorrence.
> The wise leaders shall shine like the bright vault of heaven, 3
>   and those who have guided the people in the true path
>   shall be like the stars for ever and ever.

But you, Daniel, keep the words secret and seal the book till the time of 4
the end. Many will be at their wits' end, and punishment will be heavy.'
And I, Daniel, looked and saw two others standing, one on this bank   5
of the river and the other on the opposite bank. And I*b* said to the man   6
clothed in linen who was above the waters of the river, 'How long will it
be before these portents cease?' The man clothed in linen above the   7
waters lifted to heaven his right hand and his left, and I heard him
swear by him who lives for ever: 'It shall be for a time, times, and a half.
When the power of the holy people ceases to be dispersed, all these
things shall come to an end.' I heard but I did not understand, and so I   8
said, 'Sir, what will the issue of these things be?' He replied, 'Go your   9
way, Daniel, for the words are kept secret and sealed till the time of the
end. Many shall purify themselves and be refined, making themselves   10
shining white, but the wicked shall continue in wickedness and none of
them shall understand; only the wise leaders shall understand. From   11
the time when the regular offering is abolished and "the abomination of
desolation" is set up, there shall be an interval of one thousand two
hundred and ninety days. Happy the man who waits and lives to see the   12
completion of one thousand three hundred and thirty-five days! But go   13
your way to the end and rest, and you shall arise to your destiny at the
end of the age.'

[a] *Or* will escape. [b] *So Sept.; Heb.* he.

HOSEA

1 THE WORD OF THE LORD which came to Hosea son of Beeri during the reigns of Uzziah, Jotham, Ahaz, and Hezekiah, kings of Judah, and during the reign of Jeroboam son of Jehoash king of Israel.

Hosea's unfaithful wife

2 THIS IS THE BEGINNING of the LORD's message by Hosea. He said, Go, take a wanton for your wife and get children of her **3** wantonness; for like a wanton this land is unfaithful to the LORD. So he went and took Gomer, a worthless woman;[a] and she conceived and bore **4** him a son. And the LORD said to him,

> Call him Jezreel;[b] for in a little while
> I will punish the line of Jehu for the blood shed in Jezreel
> and put an end to the kingdom of Israel.
> **5**　　On that day
> I will break Israel's bow in the Vale of Jezreel.

6 She conceived again and bore a daughter, and the LORD said to him,

> Call her Lo-ruhamah;[c]
> for I will never again show love to Israel,
> never again forgive them.[d]

8,9 After weaning Lo-ruhamah, she conceived and bore a son; and the LORD said,

> Call him Lo-ammi;[e]
> for you are not my people,
> and I will not be your God.[f]
> **10**[g] The Israelites shall become countless as the sands of the sea
> which can neither be measured nor numbered;
> it shall no longer be said, 'They are not my people',
> they shall be called Sons of the Living God.

---

[a] a worthless woman: *or* daughter of Diblaim.　[b] *That is* God shall sow.　[c] *That is* Not loved.　[d] *Prob. rdg.; Heb. adds* (7) Then I will love Judah and will save them. I will save them not by bow or sword or weapon of war, by horses or by horsemen, but by the LORD their God.　[e] *That is* Not my people.　[f] your God: *lit.* yours.　[g] 2. *1 in Heb.*

Then the people of Judah and of Israel shall be reunited   11
  and shall choose for themselves a single head,
    and they shall become masters of the earth;
    for great shall be the day of Jezreel.
Then you will say to your brothers, 'You are my people',   2
  and to your sisters, 'You are loved.'

  Plead my cause with your mother;   2
is she not my wife and I her husband?*[a]*
  Plead with her to forswear those wanton looks,
  to banish the lovers from her bosom.
    Or I will strip her and expose her   3
    naked as the day she was born;
  I will make her bare as the wilderness,
    parched as the desert,
    and leave her to die of thirst.
    I will show no love for her children;   4
    they are the offspring of wantonness,
    and their mother is a wanton.
    She who conceived them is shameless;   5
  she says, 'I will go after my lovers;
  they give me my food and drink,
my wool and flax, my oil and my perfumes.'
Therefore I will block her*[b]* road with thorn-bushes   6
  and obstruct her path*[c]* with a wall,
so that she can no longer follow her old ways.
When she pursues her lovers she will not overtake them,   7
  when she looks for them she will not find them;
    then she will say,
'I will go back to my husband again;
  I was better off with him than I am now.'
For she does not know that it is I who gave her   8
  corn, new wine, and oil,
  I who lavished upon her silver and gold
    which they spent on the Baal.
  Therefore I will take back   9
my corn at the harvest and my new wine at the vintage,
  and I will take away the wool and the flax
    which I gave her to cover her naked body;
  so I will show her up for the lewd thing she is,   10
and no lover will want to steal her from me.
  I will ravage the vines and the fig-trees,   12*[d]*

[*a*] is she...husband?: *or* for she is no longer my wife nor I her husband. [*b*] *So Sept.;*
Heb. your. [*c*] *Prob. rdg., cp. Sept.; Heb.* her wall. [*d*] *Verses 11 and 12 transposed.*

which she says are the fee
with which her lovers have hired her,
and turn them into jungle where wild beasts shall feed.

11   I will put a stop to her merrymaking,
her pilgrimages and new moons, her sabbaths*a* and festivals.

13   I will punish her for the holy days
when she burnt sacrifices to the Baalim,
when she decked herself with earrings and necklaces,
ran after her lovers and forgot me.
This is the very word of the LORD.

14   But now listen,
I will woo her, I will go with her into the wilderness
and comfort her:

15   there I will restore her vineyards,
turning the Vale of Trouble into the Gate of Hope,*b*
and there she will answer as in her youth,
when she came up out of Egypt.

16   On that day she*c* shall call me 'My husband'
and shall no more call me 'My Baal';*d*

17   and I will wipe from her lips the very names of the Baalim;
never again shall their names be heard.
This is the very word of the LORD.*e*

18   Then I will make a covenant on behalf of Israel with the wild beasts,
the birds of the air, and the things that creep on the earth, and I will
break bow and sword and weapon of war and sweep them off the earth,

19   so that all living creatures may lie down without fear. I will betroth you
to myself for ever, betroth you in lawful wedlock with unfailing devotion

20   and love; I will betroth you to myself to have and to hold, and you shall

21   know the LORD. At that time I will give answer, says the LORD, I will

22   answer for the heavens and they will answer for the earth, and the earth
will answer for the corn, the new wine, and the oil, and they will

23   answer for Jezreel. Israel shall be my new sowing in the land, and I will
show love to Lo-ruhamah and say to Lo-ammi, 'You are my people',
and he will say, 'Thou art my God.'

3 1*f*   The LORD said to me,

Go again and love a woman
loved by another man, an adulteress,
and love her as I, the LORD, love the Israelites

[a] *Or* her full moons.   [b] turning...Hope: *or* Emek-achor to Pethah-tikvah.   [c] *So*
Sept.; Heb. you.   [d] *Also means* My husband.   [e] This...LORD: *transposed from after*
On that day *in verse 16.*   [f] *Ch. 3 is probably misplaced and should follow 1. 9.*

> although they resort to other gods
>> and love the raisin-cakes offered to their idols.

So I got her back[a] for fifteen pieces of silver, a homer of barley and a 2
measure of wine;[b] and I said to her, 3

> Many a long day you shall live in my house
>> and not play the wanton,
> and have no intercourse with a man, nor I with you.

> For the Israelites shall live many a long day 4
>> without king or prince,
>> without sacrifice or sacred pillar,
>> without image[c] or household gods;[d]
> but after that they will again seek 5
> the LORD their God and David their king,
> and turn anxiously to the LORD for his bounty in days to come.

God's case against Israel

> Hear the word of the LORD, O Israel; 4
> for the LORD has a charge to bring against the people of the land:
>> There is no good faith or mutual trust,
>> no knowledge of God in the land,
> oaths are imposed and broken, they kill and rob; 2
>> there is nothing but adultery and licence,[e]
>> one deed of blood after another.
> Therefore the land shall be dried up, 3
> and all who live in it shall pine away,
> and with them the wild beasts and the birds of the air;
> even the fish shall be swept from the sea.
>> But it is not for any man to bring a charge, 4
>> it is not for him to prove a case;
> the quarrel with you, false priest, is mine.

> Priest?[f] By day and by night you blunder on, 5
>> you and the prophet with you.
> My people are ruined for lack of knowledge; 6
>> your own countrymen are brought to ruin.[g]

[a] got her back: or bought her. [b] wine: so Sept.; Heb. barley. [c] Heb. ephod. [d] Heb.
teraphim. [e] and licence: prob. rdg.; Heb. they exceed. [f] the quarrel...Priest?: prob.
rdg.; Heb. and your people are like those who quarrel with a priest. [g] My people...ruin:
or Your mother (Israel) is destroyed, my people destroyed for lack of knowledge.

You have rejected knowledge,
and I will reject you from serving me as priest.
  You have forgotten the teaching of God,
and I, your God, will forget your sons.

7   The more priests there are, the more they sin against me;
their dignity I will turn into dishonour.
8   They feed on the sin of my people
and batten on their iniquity.
9   But people and priest shall be treated alike.
I will punish them for their conduct
and repay them for their deeds:
10   they shall eat but never be satisfied,
behave wantonly but their lust will never be overtaxed,
  for they have forsaken the LORD
11   to give themselves to sacred prostitution.
12   New wine and old steal my people's wits:*a*
        they ask advice from a block of wood
        and take their orders from a fetish;*b*
for a spirit of wantonness has led them astray
and in their lusts they are unfaithful to their God.
13   Your men sacrifice on mountain-tops
        and burn offerings on the hills,
            under oak and poplar
and the terebinth's pleasant shade.
Therefore your daughters play the wanton
        and your sons' brides commit adultery.
14   I will not punish your daughters for playing the wanton
        nor your sons' brides for their adultery,
    because your men resort to wanton women
        and sacrifice with temple-prostitutes.
A people without understanding comes to grief;
15   they are a mother turned wanton.
Bring no guilt-offering,*c* Israel;
    do not come to Gilgal, Judah,
do not go up to Beth-aven to swear by the life of the LORD,
16   since Israel has run wild, wild as a heifer;
    and will the LORD now feed this people
        like lambs in a broad meadow?
17   Ephraim, keeping company with idols,
18   has held a drunken orgy,*d*

[a] steal...wits: *or* embolden my people. [b] *Lit.* stick. [c] Bring no guilt-offering: *prob.*
rdg.; Heb. Let him not be guilty. [d] a drunken orgy: *prob. rdg.; Heb. unintelligible.*

they have practised sacred prostitution,
they have preferred dishonour to glory.*a*
The wind shall sweep them away, wrapped in its wings,   19
  and they will find their sacrifices a delusion.

Hear this, you priests,   5
and listen, all Israel; let the royal house mark my words.
    Sentence is passed on you;
  for you have been a snare at Mizpah,
  and a net spread out on Tabor.
The rebels! they have shown base ingratitude,   2
  but I will punish them all.
I have cared for Ephraim   3
  and I have not neglected Israel;
  but now Ephraim has played the wanton
    and Israel has defiled himself.
Their misdeeds have barred their way back to their God;   4
    for a wanton spirit is in them,
    and they care nothing for the LORD.
Israel's arrogance cries out against him;   5
*b*Ephraim's guilt is his undoing,
  and Judah no less is undone.
They go with sacrifices of sheep and cattle   6
to seek the LORD, but do not find him.
    He has withdrawn himself from them;
    for they have been unfaithful to him,   7
  and their sons are bastards.
Now an invader shall devour their fields.
  Blow the trumpet in Gibeah,   8
    the horn in Ramah,
    raise the battle-cry in Beth-aven:
    'Benjamin, we are with you!'
On the tribes of Israel I have proclaimed this unalterable doom: 9
on the day of punishment Ephraim shall be laid waste.
The rulers of Judah act like men who move their neighbour's   10
    boundary;
on them will I pour out my wrath like a flood.
  Ephraim is an oppressor trampling on justice,   11
  doggedly pursuing what is worthless.
But I am a festering sore to Ephraim,   12
  a canker to the house of Judah.
So when Ephraim found that he was sick,   13

[a] to glory: *prob. rdg., cp. Sept.; Heb.* her shields.   [b] *Prob. rdg.; Heb. prefixes* Israel.

Judah that he was covered with sores,
Ephraim went to Assyria,
he went in haste to the Great King;
but he has no power to cure you
or to heal your sores.

14 Yes indeed, I will be fierce as a panther to Ephraim,
fierce as a lion to Judah—
I will maul the prey and go,
carry it off beyond hope of rescue—I, the LORD.

15 I will go away and return to my place
until in their horror they seek me,
and look earnestly for me in their distress.

6 Come, let us return to the LORD;
for he has torn us and will heal us,
he has struck us and he will bind up our wounds;

2 after two days he will revive us,
on the third day he will restore us,
that in his presence we may live.

3 Let us humble ourselves, let us strive to know the LORD,
whose justice dawns like*a* morning light,*b*
and its dawning is as sure as the sunrise.
It will come to us like a shower,
like spring rains that water the earth.

4 O Ephraim, how shall I deal with you?
How shall I deal with you, Judah?
Your loyalty to me is like the morning mist,
like dew that vanishes early.

5 Therefore have I lashed you through the prophets
and torn you*c* to shreds with my words;

6 loyalty is my desire, not sacrifice,
not whole-offerings but the knowledge of God.

7 At Admah*d* they have broken my covenant,
there they have played me false.

8 Gilead is a haunt of evildoers,
marked by a trail of blood;

9 like robbers lying in wait for a man,
priests are banded together
to do murder on the road to Shechem;
their deeds are outrageous.

10 At Israel's sanctuary I have seen a horrible thing:

---

[a] whose...like: *prob. rdg., cp. Sept.; Heb.* thy justice dawns.   [b] *Line transposed from end of verse 5.*   [c] *Prob. rdg.; Heb.* them.   [d] At Admah: *prob. rdg.; Heb.* Like Adam.

there Ephraim played the wanton
and Israel defiled himself.

And for you, too, Judah, comes a harvest of reckoning. 11

When I would reverse the fortunes of my people,
 when I would heal Israel, 7
  then the guilt of Ephraim stands revealed,
  and all the wickedness of Samaria;
  they have not kept faith.
They are thieves, they break into houses;[a]
they are robbers, they strip people in the street,
little thinking that I have their wickedness ever in mind. 2
 Now their misdeeds beset them
  and stare me in the face.
They win over the king with their wickedness 3
 and princes with their treachery,
lecherous all of them, hot as an oven over the fire 4
 which the baker does not stir
 after kneading the dough until it is proved.
On their[b] king's festal day the officers 5
begin to be inflamed with wine,
and he joins in the orgies of arrogant men;
for their hearts are heated by it[c] like an oven. 6
  While they are relaxed all night long
  their passion slumbers,
 but in the morning it flares up
  like a blazing fire;
they all grow feverish, hot as an oven, 7
 and devour their rulers.
King after king falls from power,
 but not one of them calls upon me.
Ephraim and his aliens make a sorry mixture; 8
Ephraim has become a cake half-baked.
 Foreigners fed on his strength, 9
  but he was unaware;
 even his grey hairs turned white,
  but he was unaware.
So Israel's arrogance cries out against them; 10
but they do not return to the LORD their God
 nor seek him, in spite of it all.
Ephraim is a silly senseless pigeon, 11
now calling upon Egypt, now turning to Assyria for help.

[a] houses: *prob. rdg.; Heb. om.* [b] *So Targ.; Heb.* our. [c] are heated by it: *prob. rdg.; Heb.* draw near.

12   Wherever they turn, I will cast my net over them
       and will bring them down like birds on the wing;
       I will take them captive as soon as I hear them flocking.

13   Woe betide them, for they have strayed from me!
    May disaster befall them for rebelling against me!
        I long to deliver them,
    but they tell lies about me.

14   There is no sincerity in their cry to me;
       for all their howling on their pallets
       and gashing of themselves[a] over corn and new wine,
       they are turning away from me.

15   Though I support them, though I give them strength of arm,
       they plot evil against me.

16   Like a bow gone slack,
       they relapse into the worship of their high god;[b]
       their talk is all lies,[c]
   and so their princes shall fall by the sword.

8   Put the trumpet to your lips!
    A[d] vulture hovers over the sanctuary of the LORD:
       they have broken my covenant
       and rebelled against my instruction.

2   They cry to me for help:
    'We know thee, God of Israel.'[e]

3   But Israel is utterly loathsome;
       and therefore he shall run before the enemy.

4   They make kings, but not by my will;
       they set up officers, but without my knowledge;
  they have made themselves idols of their silver and gold.[f]

5   Your calf-gods stink,[g] O Samaria;
    my anger flares up against them.
    Long will it be before they prove innocent.

6   For what sort of a god is this bull?
       It is no god,
    a craftsman made it;
    the calf of Samaria will be broken in fragments.

7   Israel sows the wind and reaps the whirlwind;
    there are no heads on the standing corn, it yields no grain;
    and, if it yielded any, strangers would swallow it up.

[a] gashing of themselves: *so many MSS.; others* rolling about.   [b] they relapse...god: *prob. rdg.; Heb. obscure.*   [c] *Prob. rdg.; Heb. adds* that is their stammering speech in Egypt. [d] *Prob. rdg.; Heb.* Like a.   [e] We...Israel: *prob. rdg.; Heb.* O my God, we know thee, Israel.   [f] *Prob. rdg.; Heb. adds* so that he may be cut off.   [g] stink: *or, as otherwise read,* I loathe.

Israel is now swallowed up,   8
lost among the nations,
  a worthless nothing.
For, like a wild ass that has left the herd,   9
  they have run to Assyria.
Ephraim has bargained for lovers;
and, because they have bargained among the nations,   10
  I will now round them up,
  and then they will soon abandon
this setting up of kings and*ᵃ* princes.
For Ephraim in his sin has multiplied altars,   11
altars have become his sin.
Though I give him countless rules in writing,   12
  they are treated as invalid.
Though they sacrifice flesh as offerings to me and eat them,   13
  I,*ᵇ* the LORD, will not accept them.
Their guilt will be remembered
  and their sins punished.
They shall go back to Egypt,
or in Assyria they shall eat unclean food.*ᶜ*

Israel has forgotten his Maker   14
  and built palaces,
Judah has multiplied walled cities;
  but I will set fire to his cities,
  and it shall devour his castles.

Do not rejoice, Israel, do not exult*ᵈ* like other peoples;   9
  for like a wanton you have forsaken your God,
    you have loved an idol*ᵉ*
on every threshing-floor heaped with corn.
Threshing-floor and winepress shall know*ᶠ* them no more,   2
  new wine shall disown*ᵍ* them.
  They shall not dwell in the LORD's land;   3
Ephraim shall go back to Egypt,
  or in Assyria they shall eat unclean food.
They shall pour out no wine to the LORD,   4
they shall not bring their sacrifices to him;
  that would be mourners' fare for them,
  and all who ate it would be polluted.
  For their food shall only stay their hunger;
  it shall not be offered in the house of the LORD.

[a] and: *so Sept.; Heb. om.*   [b] *Prob. rdg.; Heb.* he.   [c] or...food: *so Sept.; Heb. om.*
(*cp. 9. 3*).   [d] do not exult: *so Sept.; Heb.* to exultation.   [e] an idol: *or* a harlot's fee.
[f] *So Sept.; Heb.* feed.   [g] *Or* fail.

5   What will you do for the festal day,
        the day of the LORD's pilgrim-feast?
6   For look, they have fled from a scene of devastation:
        Egypt shall receive them,
        Memphis shall be their grave;
        the sands of Syrtes shall wreck them,
        weeds shall inherit their land,
        thorns shall grow in their dwellings.
7   The days of punishment are come,
        the days of vengeance are come
        when Israel shall be humbled.
        Then the prophet shall be made a fool
        and the inspired seer a madman
        by your great guilt.
8   With great enmity Ephraim lies in wait for God's people
    while the prophet is a fowler's trap by all their paths,
        a snare in the very temple of God.
9   They lead them deep into sin as at the time of Gibeah.
  Their guilt will be remembered and their sins punished.

10   I came upon Israel like grapes in the wilderness,
        I looked on their forefathers
        with joy like the first ripe figs;
        but they resorted to Baal-peor
        and consecrated themselves to a thing of shame,
11   and Ephraim became as loathsome as the thing he loved.
        Their honour shall fly away like a bird:
        no childbirth, no fruitful womb, no conceiving;
12   even if they rear their children,
        I will make them childless, without posterity.
  Woe to them indeed when I turn away from them!

13   As lion-cubs emerge only to be hunted,[a]
  so must Ephraim bring out his children for slaughter.
14   Give them, O LORD—what wilt thou give them?
  Give them a womb that miscarries and dry breasts.

15   All their wickedness was seen at Gilgal; there did I hate them.
  For their evil deeds I will drive them from my house,
  I will love them no more: all their princes are in revolt.
16   Ephraim is struck down:
  their root is withered, and they yield no fruit;
        if ever they give birth,
        I will slay the dearest offspring of their womb.

[a] As lion-cubs...hunted: *prob. rdg.; Heb. unintelligible.*

My God shall reject them,　　　　　　　　　　　　17
　　because they have not listened to him,
　and they shall become wanderers among the nations.

God's judgement on Israel

Israel is like a rank vine　　　　　　　　　　　　10
　　ripening its fruit:
his fruit grows more and more, and more and more his altars;
the fairer his land becomes, the fairer he makes his sacred pillars.
They are crazy now, they are mad.　　　　　　　　　2
　God himself[a] will hack down their altars
　　and wreck their sacred pillars.
Well may they say, 'We have no king,　　　　　　　3
　for we do not fear the LORD;
　and what can the king do for us?'
　　There is nothing but talk,　　　　　　　　　　4
imposing of oaths and making of treaties, all to no purpose;
　and litigation spreads like a poisonous weed
　　along the furrows of the fields.
The inhabitants of Samaria tremble for the calf-god of Beth-aven;　5
the people mourn over it[b] and its priestlings howl,
　　distressed for their image, their glory,
　　which is carried away into exile.
　It shall be carried to Assyria　　　　　　　　　　6
　as tribute to the Great King;
　disgrace shall overtake Ephraim
　and Israel shall feel the shame of their disobedience.
　Samaria and[c] her king are swept away　　　　　　7
　　like flotsam on the water;
　　the hill-shrines of Aven are wiped out,　　　　　8
　　the shrines where Israel sinned;
thorns and thistles grow over her altars.
　So they will say to the mountains, 'Cover us',
　and to the hills, 'Fall on us.'

　Since the day of Gibeah Israel has sinned;　　　　9
　there they took their stand in rebellion.[d]
　Shall not war overtake them in Gibeah?

---

[a] God himself: *lit.* He.　[b] the people mourn over it: *or* the high god and his people mourn.　[c] and: *prob. rdg., cp. Targ.; Heb. om.*　[d] in rebellion: *so Targ.; Heb. om.*

10   I have come*a* against the rebels to chastise them,
         and the peoples shall mass against them
            in hordes for their two deeds of shame.

11   Ephraim is like a heifer broken in,
         which loves to thresh corn,
   across whose fair neck I have laid a yoke;*b*
      I have harnessed Ephraim to the pole that he*c* may plough,
         that Jacob may harrow his land.

12   Sow for yourselves in justice,
         and you will reap what loyalty deserves.
      Break up your fallow;
         for*d* it is time to seek the LORD,
   seeking him till he comes and gives you just measure of rain.

13   You have ploughed wickedness into your soil,
         and the crop is mischief;
            you have eaten the fruit of treachery.

      Because you have trusted in your chariots,*e*
         in the number of your warriors,

14   the tumult of war shall arise against your people,
         and all your fortresses shall be razed
      as Shalman razed Beth-arbel in the day of battle,
         dashing the mother to the ground with her babes.

15   So it shall be done to you, Bethel,*f*
         because of your evil scheming;
   as sure as day dawns, the king of Israel shall be swept away.

11   When Israel was a boy, I loved him;
         I called my son out of Egypt;

2   but the more I*g* called, the further they went from me;*h*
         they must needs sacrifice to the Baalim
            and burn offerings before carved images.

3   It was I who taught Ephraim to walk,
         I who had taken*i* them in my*j* arms;

4   but they did not know that I harnessed them in leading-strings*k*
         and led them with bonds of love*l*—
      that I had lifted them like a little child*m* to my cheek,
         that I had bent down to feed them.

5   Back they shall go to Egypt,
         the Assyrian shall be their king;

[*a*] I have come: *prob. rdg., cp. Sept.; Heb.* By my desire.   [*b*] a yoke: *prob. rdg.; Heb. om.*
[*c*] he: *prob. rdg.; Heb.* Judah.   [*d*] *So Pesh.; Heb.* and.   [*e*] chariots: *so Sept.; Heb.* way.
[*f*] Bethel: *or, with Sept.,* house of Israel.   [*g*] *So Sept.; Heb.* they.   [*h*] *So Sept.; Heb.* them.
[*i*] I who had taken: *so Sept.; Heb. unintelligible.*   [*j*] *So Sept.; Heb.* his.   [*k*] leading-strings:
or cords of leather.   [*l*] bonds of love: *or* reins of hide.   [*m*] I had...child: *prob. rdg.; Heb.*
like those who lift up a yoke.

for they have refused to return to me.
The sword shall be swung over their blood-spattered altars   6
    and put an end to their prattling priests
and devour my people in return for all their schemings,   7
    bent on rebellion as they are.
Though they call on their high god,
    even then he will not reinstate them.
How can I give you up, Ephraim,   8
    how surrender you, Israel?
How can I make you like Admah
    or treat you as Zeboyim?
My heart is changed within me,
    my remorse kindles already.
I will not let loose my fury,   9
I will not turn round and destroy Ephraim;
    for I am God and not a man,
    the Holy One in your midst;
I will not come with threats*a* like a roaring lion.   10
    No; when I roar, I who am God,*b*
my sons shall come with speed out of the west.
They will come speedily, flying like birds out of Egypt,   11
    like pigeons from Assyria,
    and I will settle them in their own homes.
    This is the very word of the LORD.
Ephraim besets me with treachery,   12*c*
    the house of Israel besets me with deceit;
and Judah is still restive under God,
    still loyal to the idols he counts holy.
Ephraim is a shepherd whose flock is but*d* wind,   12
    a hunter chasing the east wind all day;*e*
he makes a treaty with Assyria
    and carries tribute of oil to Egypt.

The LORD has a charge to bring against Judah   2
and is resolved to punish Jacob for his conduct;
    he will requite him for his misdeeds.
Even in the womb Jacob overreached his brother,   3
    and in manhood he strove with God.
The divine angel stood firm and held his own;*f*   4
Jacob wept and begged favour for himself.
    Then God met him at Bethel

[a] *Prob. rdg.; Heb. adds* they shall go after the LORD.   [b] God: *lit.* He.   [c] *12. 1 in Heb.*
[d] is a...but: *or* feeds on.   [e] *Prob. rdg.; Heb. adds* piling up treachery and havoc.
[f] The divine...own: *or* He stood firm against an angel, but flagged.

and there spoke with him.*a*

5 The LORD the God of Hosts, the LORD is his name.

6   Turn back all of you by God's help;
       practise loyalty and justice
       and wait always upon your God.

7   False scales are in merchants' hands,
           and they love to cheat;

8   so Ephraim says,
   'Surely I have become a rich man, I have made my fortune';
       but all his*b* gains will not pay
       for the guilt*c* of his sins.

9 Yet I have been the LORD your God since your days in Egypt;
   I will make you live in tents yet again, as in the old days.

10   I spoke to the prophets,
       it was I who gave vision after vision;
       I spoke through the prophets in parables.

11   Was there idolatry in Gilead?
           Yes: they were worthless
       and sacrificed to bull-gods in Gilgal;
   their altars were common as heaps of stones beside a ploughed field.

12   Jacob fled to the land of Aram;
       Israel did service to win a wife,
           to win a wife he tended sheep.

13 By a prophet the LORD brought up Israel out of Egypt
           and by a prophet he was tended.

14   Ephraim has given bitter provocation;
       therefore his Lord will make him answerable
           for his own death
       and bring down upon his own head the blame
           for all that he has done.

13   When the Ephraimites mumbled their prayers,*d*
       God himself denounced Israel;
       they were guilty of Baal-worship and died.

2   Yet now they sin more and more;
       they have made themselves an image of cast metal,
       they have fashioned*e* their silver into idols,
           nothing but the work of craftsmen;
           men say of them,
   'Those who kiss calf-images offer human sacrifice.'

[a] *So Sept.; Heb.* us.   [b] *So Sept.; Heb.* my.   [c] for the guilt: *prob. rdg.; Heb.* for me,
guilt.   [d] *Mng. of Heb. uncertain.*   [e] they have fashioned: *so Sept.; Heb. obscure.*

Therefore they shall be like the morning mist   3
  or like dew that vanishes early,
like chaff blown from the threshing-floor
  or smoke from a chimney.
But I have been the Lord your God since your days in Egypt,   4
  when you knew no other saviour than me,
    no god but me.
  I cared for you in the wilderness,   5
in a land of burning heat, as if you were in pasture.   6
  So they were filled,
and, being filled, grew proud;
  and so they forgot me.
So now I will be*a* like a panther to them,   7
I will prowl like a leopard by the wayside;
I will meet them like a she-bear robbed of her cubs   8
  and tear their ribs apart,
like a lioness I will devour them on the spot,
  I will rip them up like a wild beast.
I have destroyed you, O Israel; who*b* is there to help you?   9
Where now is your king that he may save you,   10
  or the rulers in all your cities
    for whom you asked me,
begging for king and princes?
I gave you a king in my anger,   11
  and in my fury took him away.

  Ephraim's guilt is tied up in a scroll,   12
  his sins are kept on record.
When the pangs of his birth came over his mother,   13
he showed himself a senseless child;
  for at the proper time he could not present himself
    at the mouth of the womb.
  Shall I redeem him from Sheol?   14
  Shall I ransom him from death?
Oh, for your plagues, O death! Oh, for your sting, Sheol!
  I will put compassion out of my sight.
  Though he flourishes among the reeds,*c*   15
an east wind shall come, a blast from the Lord,
  rising over the desert;
Ephraim's spring will fail and his fountain run dry.
  It will carry away as spoil
    his whole store of costly treasures.

[*a*] I will be: *so Sept.; Heb.* I was. [*b*] who: *so Sept.; Heb.* in me. [*c*] among the reeds: *prob. rdg.; Heb.* between (*or* a son of) brothers.

16^a Samaria will become desolate because she has rebelled against her
      God;
    her babes will fall by the sword and be dashed to the ground,
      her women with child shall be ripped up.

Repentance, forgiveness, and restoration

14 Return, O Israel, to the Lord your God;
    for you have stumbled in your evil courses.

2   Come with your words ready,
      come back to the Lord;
    say to him, 'Thou dost not^b endure iniquity.^c
      Accept our plea,
    and we will pay our vows with cattle from our pens.^d

3 Assyria shall not save us, nor will we seek horses to ride;
      what we have made with our own hands
    we will never again call gods;
      for in thee the fatherless find a father's love.'

4 I will heal their apostasy; of my own bounty will I love them;
    for my anger is turned away from them.

5 I will be as dew to Israel
      that he may flower like the lily,
    strike root like the poplar^e

6   and put out fresh shoots,
    that he may be as fair as the olive
      and fragrant as Lebanon.

7 Israel shall again dwell^f in my^g shadow
      and grow corn in abundance;
      they shall flourish like a vine
      and be famous as the wine of Lebanon.

8 What has Ephraim^h any more to do with idols?
    I have spoken and I affirm it:
    I am the pine-tree that shelters you;
    to me you owe your fruit.

9   Let the wise consider these things and let him who considers take
note; for the Lord's ways are straight and the righteous walk in them,
while sinners stumble.

[a] 14. 1 in Heb.   [b] not: prob. rdg., cp. Sept.; Heb. all.   [c] Thou... iniquity: or Thou wilt
surely take away iniquity.   [d] cattle from our pens: or, as otherwise read, fruit from our lips.
[e] Prob. rdg.; Heb. like Lebanon.   [f] So Sept.; Heb. dwellers.   [g] Prob. rdg.; Heb. its.
[h] What has Ephraim: so Sept.; Heb. Ephraim, what have I.

JOEL

The word of the LORD which came to Joel son of Pethuel.　　　1

The day of the LORD

Listen, you elders;　　　2
hear me, all you who live in the land:
has the like of this happened in all your days
　　or in your fathers' days?
Tell it to your sons and they may tell theirs;　　　3
　　let them pass it on from generation to generation.
What the locust has left the swarm eats,　　　4
what the swarm has left the hopper eats,
and what the hopper has left the grub eats.
Wake up, you drunkards, and lament your fate;　　　5
mourn for the fresh wine, all you wine-drinkers,
　　because it is lost to you.
For a horde has overrun my land,　　　6
　　mighty and past counting;
　　their teeth are a lion's teeth;
　　they have the fangs of a lioness.
They have ruined my vines　　　7
and left my fig-trees broken and leafless,
they have plucked them bare
and stripped them of their bark;
　　they have left the branches white.

Wail like a virgin wife in sackcloth,　　　8
　　wailing over the bridegroom of her youth:
the drink-offering and grain-offering are lost　　　9
　　to the house of the LORD.
Mourn, you priests, ministers of the LORD,
the fields are ruined, the parched earth mourns;　　　10
for the corn is ruined, the new wine is desperate,
　　the oil has failed.
Despair, you husbandmen; you vinedressers, lament,　　　11
　　because the wheat and the barley,

the harvest of the field, is lost.

12 The vintage is desperate, and the fig-tree has failed;
    pomegranate, palm, and apple,
    all the trees of the country-side are parched,
    and none make merry over harvest.

13 Priests, put on sackcloth and beat your breasts;
        lament, you ministers of the altar;
    come, lie in sackcloth all night long, you ministers of my God;
        for grain-offering and drink-offering
    are withheld from the house of your God.

14 Proclaim a solemn fast, appoint a day of abstinence.
        You elders, summon all that live in the land
            to come together in the house of your God,
            and cry to the LORD.

15 Alas! the day is near,
    the day of the LORD: it comes,
    a mighty destruction from the Almighty.

16 Look! it stares us in the face;
    the house of our God has lost its food,
        lost all its joy and gladness.

17 The soil is parched,
        the dykes are dry,
        the granaries are deserted,
        the barns ruinous;
        for the rains have failed.

18 The cattle are exhausted,
        the herds of oxen distressed
    because they have no pasture;
    the flocks of sheep waste away.

19 To thee I cry, O LORD;
    for fire has devoured the open pastures
    and the flames have burnt up all the trees of the country-side.

20 The very cattle in the field look up to thee;
        for the water-channels are dried up,
    and fire has devoured the open pastures.

2 Blow the trumpet in Zion,
    sound the alarm upon my holy hill;
    let all that live in the land tremble,
        for the day of the LORD has come,

2 surely a day of darkness and gloom is upon us,
        a day of cloud and dense fog;
    like a blackness spread over the mountains

a mighty, countless host appears;
their like has never been known,
nor ever shall be in ages to come;
their vanguard a devouring fire,   3
their rearguard leaping flame;
before them the land is a garden of Eden,
behind them a wasted wilderness;
nothing survives their march.
On they come, like squadrons of horse,   4
like war-horses they charge;
bounding over the peaks they advance with the rattle of chariots, 5
like flames of fire burning up the stubble,
like a countless host in battle array.
Before them nations tremble,   6
every face turns pale.
    Like warriors they charge,   7
    they mount the walls like men at arms,
each marching in line,
    no confusion in the ranks,
none jostling his neighbour,   8
none breaking line.
They plunge through streams without halting their advance;
they burst into the city, leap on to the wall,   9
    climb into the houses,
entering like thieves through the windows.
Before them the earth shakes,   10
    the heavens shudder,
sun and moon are darkened,
and the stars forbear to shine.
The LORD thunders before his host;   11
his is a mighty army,
countless are those who do his bidding.
Great is the day of the LORD and terrible,
    who can endure it?
And yet, the LORD says, even now   12
turn back to me with your whole heart,
fast, and weep, and beat your breasts.
Rend your hearts and not your garments;   13
turn back to the LORD your God;
for he is gracious and compassionate,
    long-suffering and ever constant,
always ready to repent of the threatened evil.
It may be he will turn back and repent   14

1293

and leave a blessing behind him,
    blessing enough for grain-offering and drink-offering
    for the LORD your God.

15   Blow the trumpet in Zion,
proclaim a solemn fast, appoint a day of abstinence;
16   gather the people together, proclaim a solemn assembly;
    summon the elders,
gather the children, yes, babes at the breast;
    bid the bridegroom leave his chamber
    and the bride her bower.
17   Let the priests, the ministers of the LORD,
    stand weeping between the porch and the altar
and say, 'Spare thy people, O LORD, thy own people,
    expose them not to reproach,
    lest other nations make them a byword
    and everywhere men ask,
    "Where is their God?"'

Israel forgiven and restored

18   Then the LORD's love burned with zeal for his land,
    and he was moved with compassion for his people.
19   He answered their appeal and said,
I will send you corn, and new wine, and oil,
    and you shall have your fill;
    I will expose you no longer
    to the reproach of other nations.
20   I will remove the northern peril far away from you
and banish them into a land parched and waste,
    their vanguard into the eastern sea
    and their rear into the western,
and the stench shall rise from their rotting corpses
    because of their proud deeds!
21   Earth, be not afraid, rejoice and be glad;
    for the LORD himself has done a proud deed.
22   Be not afraid, you cattle in the field;
    for the pastures shall be green,
    the trees shall bear fruit,
the fig and the vine yield their harvest.
23   O people of Zion,
    rejoice and be glad in the LORD your God,

who gives you good food in due measure^a
and sends down rain^b as of old.^c
The threshing-floors shall be heaped with grain, 24
the vats shall overflow with new wine and oil.
So I will make good the years 25
that the swarm has eaten,
hopper and grub and locust,
my great army which I sent against you;
and you shall eat, you shall eat your fill 26
and praise the name of the LORD your God
who has done wonders for you,^d
and you shall know that I am present in Israel, 27
that I and no other am the LORD your God;
and my people shall not again be brought to shame.
Thereafter the day shall come 28^e
when I will pour out my spirit on all mankind;
your sons and your daughters shall prophesy,
your old men shall dream dreams
and your young men see visions;
I will pour out my spirit in those days 29
even upon slaves and slave-girls.
I will show portents in the sky and on earth, 30
blood and fire and columns of smoke;
the sun shall be turned into darkness 31
and the moon into blood
before the great and terrible day of the LORD comes.
Then everyone who invokes the LORD by name 32
shall be saved:
for when the LORD gives the word
there shall yet be survivors on Mount Zion
and in Jerusalem a remnant^f
whom the LORD will call.^g

When that time comes, on that day 3 1^h
when I reverse the fortunes of Judah and Jerusalem,
I will gather all the nations together 2
and lead them down to the Valley of the LORD's Judgementⁱ
and there bring them to judgement
on behalf of Israel, my own possession;

[a] *Or* gives you a sign pointing to prosperity. [b] *Prob. rdg.; Heb. adds* spring rain and autumn rain. [c] as of old: *so Sept.; Heb.* in the first month. [d] *Prob. rdg.; Heb. adds* and my people shall not again be brought to shame (*cp. verse 27*). [e] *3. 1 in Heb.* [f] a remnant: *prob. rdg.; Heb.* among the remnant. [g] *Or* when the LORD calls. [h] *4. 1 in Heb.* [i] the LORD's Judgement: *Heb.* Jehoshaphat.

for they have scattered my people
throughout their own countries,
have taken each their portion of my land
3   and shared out my people by lot,
bartered a boy for a whore,
and sold a girl for wine and drunk it down.

4   What are you to me, Tyre and Sidon and all the districts of Philistia? Can you pay me back for anything I have done? Is there anything that you can do to me? Swiftly and speedily I will make your deeds recoil
5 upon your own heads; for you have taken my silver and my gold and
6 carried off my costly treasures into your temples; you have sold the people of Judah and Jerusalem to the Greeks, and removed them far
7 beyond their own frontiers. But I will rouse them to leave the places to which you have sold them. I will make your deeds recoil upon your own
8 heads: I will sell your sons and your daughters to the people of Judah, and they shall sell them to the Sabaeans, a nation far away. The LORD has spoken.

9–12ᵃ   Proclaim this amongst the nations:
Declare a holy war, call your troops to arms!
  Beat your mattocks into swords
    and your pruning-hooks into spears.ᵇ
Rally to each other's help, all you nations round about.
Let the weakling say, 'I am strong',
  and let the coward show himself brave.ᶜ
  Let all the nations hear the call to arms
    and come to the Valley of the LORD's Judgement;
let all the warriors come and draw near
    and muster there;
    for there I will take my seat
  and judge all the nations round about.

13   Ply the sickle, for the harvest is ripe;
    come, tread the grapes,
for the press is full and the vats overflow;
    great is the wickedness of the nations.
14   The roar of multitudes, multitudes, in the Valley of Decision!
    The day of the LORD is at hand
    in the Valley of Decision;
15   sun and moon are darkened
    and the stars forbear to shine.

[a] *The order of lines in verses 9–12 has been re-arranged in several places.* [b] Beat...spears: *cp. Isa. 2. 4; Mic. 4. 3.* [c] and let...brave: *prob. rdg.;* Heb. O LORD bring down thy warriors.

The LORD roars from Zion   16
and thunders from Jerusalem;
heaven and earth shudder,
but the LORD is a refuge for his people
    and the defence of Israel.

Thus you shall know that I am the LORD your God,   17
dwelling in Zion my holy mountain;
Jerusalem shall be holy,
and no one without the right shall pass through her again.
    When that day comes,   18
    the mountains shall run with fresh wine
    and the hills flow with milk.
All the streams of Judah shall be full of water,
    and a fountain shall spring from the LORD's house
        and water the gorge of Shittim,
    but Egypt shall become a desert   19
    and Edom a deserted waste,
        because of the violence done to Judah
    and the innocent blood shed in her land;
        and I will spill their blood,   20-21
        the blood I have not yet spilt.
Then there shall be people living in Judah for ever,
in Jerusalem generation after generation;
and the LORD will dwell in Zion.

AMOS

1 THE WORDS OF AMOS, one of the sheep-farmers of Tekoa, which he received in visions concerning Israel during the reigns of Uzziah king of Judah and Jeroboam son of Jehoash **2** king of Israel, two years before the earthquake. He said,

> The LORD roars from Zion
> and thunders from Jerusalem;
> the shepherds' pastures are scorched
> and the top of Carmel[a] is dried up.

The sins of Israel and her neighbours

3 These are the words of the LORD:

> For crime after crime of Damascus
> I will grant them no reprieve,
> because they threshed Gilead under threshing-sledges spiked with
> iron.
> **4** Therefore will I send fire upon the house of Hazael,
> fire that shall eat up Ben-hadad's palaces;
> **5** I will crush the great men of Damascus
> and wipe out those who live in the Vale of Aven
> and the sceptred ruler of Beth-eden;
> the people of Aram shall be exiled to Kir.
> It is the word of the LORD.

6 These are the words of the LORD:

> For crime after crime of Gaza
> I will grant them no reprieve,
> because they deported a whole band of exiles
> and delivered them up to Edom.
> **7** Therefore will I send fire upon the walls of Gaza,
> fire that shall consume its palaces.
> **8** I will wipe out those who live in Ashdod
> and the sceptred ruler of Ashkelon;

[a] top of Carmel: *or* choicest farmland.

I will turn my hand against Ekron,
    and the remnant of the Philistines shall perish.
    It is the word of the Lord GOD.

These are the words of the LORD: 9

For crime after crime of Tyre
    I will grant them no reprieve,
    because, forgetting the ties of kinship,
they delivered a whole band of exiles to Edom.
    Therefore will I send fire upon the walls of Tyre, 10
    fire that shall consume its palaces.

These are the words of the LORD: 11

For crime after crime of Edom
    I will grant them no reprieve,
because, sword in hand, they hunted their kinsmen down,
    stifling their natural affections.
Their anger raged unceasing,
    their fury stormed unchecked.
Therefore will I send fire upon Teman, 12
fire that shall consume the palaces of Bozrah.

These are the words of the LORD: 13

For crime after crime of the Ammonites
    I will grant them no reprieve,
because in their greed for land
    they invaded the ploughlands of Gilead.
Therefore will I set fire to the walls of Rabbah, 14
    fire that shall consume its palaces
    amid war-cries on the day of battle,
    with a whirlwind on the day of tempest;
then their king shall be carried into exile, 15
he and his officers with him.
    It is the word of the LORD.

These are the words of the LORD: 2

For crime after crime of Moab
    I will grant them no reprieve,
because they burnt the bones of the king of Edom to ash.[a]
    Therefore will I send fire upon Moab, 2
    fire that shall consume the palaces in their towns;
    Moab shall perish in uproar,

[a] to ash: *or* for lime.

1299

with war-cries and the sound of trumpets,
3   and I will cut off the ruler from among them
and kill all their officers with him.
     It is the word of the LORD.

4 These are the words of the LORD:

     For crime after crime of Judah
     I will grant them no reprieve,
because they have spurned the law of the LORD
     and have not observed his decrees,
and have been led astray by the false gods
     that their fathers followed.
5   Therefore will I send fire upon Judah,
fire that shall consume the palaces of Jerusalem.

6 These are the words of the LORD:

     For crime after crime of Israel
     I will grant them no reprieve,
because they sell the innocent for silver
     and the destitute for a pair of shoes.
7   They grind[a] the heads of the poor into the earth
     and thrust the humble out of their way.
Father and son resort to the same girl,
     to the profanation of my holy name.
8   Men lie down beside every altar
     on garments seized in pledge,
and in the house of their God[b] they drink liquor
     got by way of fines.

9   Yet it was I who destroyed the Amorites before them,[c]
     though they were tall as cedars,
     though they were sturdy as oaks,
     I who destroyed their fruit above
     and their roots below.
10   It was I who brought you up from the land of Egypt,
I who led you in the wilderness forty years,
     to take possession of the land of the Amorites;
11   I raised up prophets from your sons,
     Nazirites from your young men.
Was it not so indeed, you men of Israel?
     says the LORD.
12   But you made the Nazirites drink wine,

[a] They grind: *prob. rdg., cp. Sept.; Heb. obscure.*   [b] *Or* gods.   [c] *Or, with some MSS.,*
you.

and said to the prophets, 'You shall not prophesy.'
> Listen, I groan under the burden of you,   13
> as a wagon creaks under a full load.
> Flight shall not save the swift,   14
> the strong man shall not rally his strength.
> The warrior shall not save himself,
> the archer shall not stand his ground;   15
> the swift of foot shall not be saved,
> nor the horseman escape;
> on that day the bravest of warriors   16
> shall be stripped of his arms and run away.
>   This is the very word of the LORD.

Israel's sins and threatened punishment

LISTEN, ISRAELITES, to these words that the LORD addresses to you,   3
to the whole nation which he brought up from Egypt:

> For you alone have I cared   2
> among all the nations of the world;
> therefore will I punish you
>   for all your iniquities.
> Do two men travel together   3
>   unless they have agreed?
> Does a lion roar in the forest   4
>   if he has no prey?
> Does a young lion growl in his den
>   if he has caught nothing?
> Does a bird fall into a trap on the ground   5
>   if the striker is not set for it?
> Does a trap spring from the ground
>   and take nothing?
> If a trumpet sounds the alarm,   6
>   are not the people scared?
> If disaster falls on a city,
>   has not the LORD been at work?[a]
> For the Lord GOD does nothing   7
> without giving to his servants the prophets knowledge of his plans.
>   The lion has roared; who is not terrified?   8
> The Lord GOD has spoken; who will not prophesy?

[a] If disaster...work?: *or* If there is evil in a city, will not the LORD act?

9   Stand upon the palaces in Ashdod
          and upon the palaces of Egypt,
          and proclaim aloud:
       'Assemble on the hills of Samaria,
       look at the tumult seething among her people
          and at the oppression in her midst;
10   what do they care for honesty
       who hoard in their palaces the gains of crime and violence?'
          This is the very word of the LORD.

11 Therefore these are the words of the Lord GOD:

       An enemy shall surround*a* the land;
       your stronghold shall be thrown down
          and your palaces sacked.

12 These are the words of the LORD:

       As a shepherd rescues out of the jaws of a lion
          two shin bones or the tip of an ear,
       so shall the Israelites who live in Samaria be rescued
       like a corner of a couch or a chip from the leg of a bed.*b*
13   Listen and testify against the family of Jacob.
       This is the very word of the Lord GOD, the God of Hosts.

14   On the day when I deal with Israel
          for all their crimes,
          I will most surely deal with the altars of Bethel:
          the horns of the altar shall be hacked off
          and shall fall to the ground.
15   I will break down both winter-house and summer-house;
          houses of ivory shall perish,
          and great houses be demolished.
          This is the very word of the LORD.

4   Listen to this,
       you cows of Bashan who live on the hill of Samaria,
       you who oppress the poor and crush the destitute,
       who say to your lords, 'Bring us drink':
2   the Lord GOD has sworn by his holiness
       that your time is coming
          when men shall carry you away on their shields*c*
          and your children in fish-baskets.
3   You shall each be carried straight out
             through the breaches in the walls

[a] shall surround: *prob. rdg.; Heb.* and round. [b] or a chip...bed: *prob. rdg.; Heb.*
obscure. [c] *Or* baskets.

and pitched on a dunghill.*a*
This is the very word of the LORD.

Come to Bethel—and rebel!   4
Come to Gilgal—and rebel the more!
Bring your sacrifices for the morning,
your tithes within three days.
Burn your thank-offering without leaven;   5
announce, proclaim your freewill offerings;
for you love to do what is proper, you men of Israel!
This is the very word of the Lord GOD.

It was I who kept teeth idle*b*   6
in all your cities,
who brought famine on all your settlements;
yet you did not come back to me.
This is the very word of the LORD.

It was I who withheld the showers from you   7
while there were still three months to harvest.
I would send rain on one city
and no rain on another;
rain would fall on one field,
and another would be parched for lack of it.
From this city and that, men would stagger to another   8
for water to drink, but would not find enough;
yet you did not come back to me.
This is the very word of the LORD.

I blasted you with black blight and red;   9
I laid waste*c* your gardens and vineyards;
the locust devoured your fig-trees and your olives;
yet you did not come back to me.
This is the very word of the LORD.

I sent plague upon you like the plagues of Egypt;   10
I killed with the sword
your young men and your troops of horses.
I made your camps stink in your nostrils;
yet you did not come back to me.
This is the very word of the LORD.

I brought destruction amongst you   11
as God destroyed Sodom and Gomorrah;
you were like a brand snatched from the fire;

[a] a dunghill: *prob. rdg.; Heb.* the Harmon.   [b] *Lit.* clean.   [c] I laid waste: *prob. rdg.; Heb.* to increase.

1303

yet you did not come back to me.
This is the very word of the LORD.

12   Therefore, Israel, this is what I will do to you;
and, because this is what I will do to you,
Israel, prepare to meet your God.

13   It is he who forges the thunder[a] and creates the wind,
who showers abundant rain on the earth,[b]
who darkens the dawn with thick clouds
and marches over the heights of the earth—
his name is the LORD the God of Hosts.

5   Listen to these words; I raise a dirge over you, O Israel:

2   She has fallen to rise no more,
the virgin Israel,
prostrate on her own soil, with no one to lift her up.

3   These are the words of the Lord GOD:

The city that marched out to war a thousand strong
shall have but a hundred left,
that which marched out a hundred strong
shall have but ten men of Israel left.

4   These are the words of the LORD to the people of Israel:

5   Resort to me, if you would live, not to Bethel;
go not to Gilgal, nor pass on to Beersheba;
for Gilgal shall be swept away
and Bethel brought to nothing.[c]

6   If you would live, resort to the LORD,
or he will break out against Joseph like fire,
fire which will devour Israel[d] with no one to quench it;

8[e]   he who made the Pleiades and Orion,
who turned darkness into morning
and darkened day into night,
who summoned the waters of the sea
and poured them over the earth,

9   who makes Taurus rise after Capella
and Taurus set hard on the rising of the Vintager[f]—
he who does this, his name is the LORD.[g]

---

[a] thunder: *so Sept.; Heb.* mountains.   [b] who showers...earth: *prob. rdg.; Heb.* who
tells his thoughts to mankind.   [c] nothing: *prob. rdg., cp. Sept.; Heb.* trouble (*the Heb.
word* aven, *cp.* Beth-aven *in Hos.* 4. 15; 5. 8; 10. 5).   [d] *So one MS.; others* Bethel.
[e] *Verse 7 transposed to follow verse 9.*   [f] who *makes...*Vintager: *prob. rdg.; Heb.* who
smiles destruction on the strong, and destruction comes on the fortified city.   [g] his...
LORD: *transposed from end of verse 8.*

You that turn justice upside down^[a]   7
and bring righteousness to the ground,
you that hate a man who brings the wrongdoer to court 10
and loathe him who speaks the whole truth:
for all this, because you levy taxes on the poor   11
and extort a tribute of grain from them,
though you have built houses of hewn stone,
 you shall not live in them,
though you have planted pleasant vineyards,
 you shall not drink wine from them.
For I know how many your crimes are   12
 and how countless your sins,
you who persecute the guiltless, hold men to ransom
 and thrust the destitute out of court.
At that time, therefore, a prudent man will stay quiet, 13
 for it will be an evil time.

Seek good and not evil,   14
 that you may live,
that the Lord the God of Hosts may be firmly on your side,
 as you say he is.
Hate evil and love good;   15
 enthrone justice in the courts;
it may be that the Lord the God of Hosts
will be gracious to the survivors of Joseph.

Therefore these are the words of the Lord the God of Hosts:^[b] 16

 There shall be wailing in every street,
and in all open places cries of woe.
The farmer shall be called to mourning,
and those skilled in the dirge to^[c] wailing;
there shall be lamentation in every vineyard; 17
for I will pass through the midst of you,
 says the Lord.

Fools who long for the day of the Lord,   18
what will the day of the Lord mean to you?
It will be darkness, not light.
It will be as when a man runs from a lion,   19
 and a bear meets him,
or turns into a house and leans his hand on the wall,
 and a snake bites him.

[a] upside down: *prob. rdg.; Heb.* poison. [b] *So Sept.; Heb. adds* the Lord. [c] *Prob. rdg.; Heb. places* to *before* those skilled.

20   The day of the LORD is indeed darkness, not light,
         a day of gloom with no dawn.

21   I hate, I spurn your pilgrim-feasts;
         I will not delight in your sacred ceremonies.

22   When you present your sacrifices and offerings
         I will not accept them,
      nor look on the buffaloes of your shared-offerings.

23   Spare me the sound of your songs;
         I cannot endure the music of your lutes.

24   Let justice roll on like a river
         and righteousness like an ever-flowing stream.

25   Did you bring me sacrifices and gifts,
    you people of Israel, those forty years in the wilderness?

26   No! but now you shall take up
          the shrine of your idol king
          and the pedestals of your images,*[a]*
         which you have made for yourselves,

27   and I will drive you into exile beyond Damascus.

    So says the LORD; the God of Hosts is his name.

6   Shame on you who live at ease in Zion,
         and you, untroubled on the hill of Samaria,
          men of mark in the first of nations,
         you to whom the people of Israel resort!

2   Go, look at Calneh,
         travel on to Hamath the great,
          then go down to Gath of the Philistines—
         are you better than these kingdoms?
         Or is your*[b]* territory greater than theirs*[c]*?

3   You who thrust the evil day aside
         and make haste to establish violence.*[d]*

4   You who loll on beds inlaid with ivory
         and sprawl over your couches,
         feasting on lambs from the flock
          and fatted calves,

5   you who pluck the strings of the lute
    and invent musical instruments like David,

6   you who drink wine by the bowlful
         and lard yourselves with the richest of oils,

---

[a] *Prob. rdg.*; *Heb. adds* the star of your gods.   [b] *Prob. rdg.*; *Heb.* their.   [c] *Prob. rdg.*;
Heb. yours.   [d] You...violence: *or* You who invoke the day of wrongdoing and bring
near the sabbath of violence.

but are not grieved at the ruin of Joseph—
   now, therefore, 7
you shall head the column of exiles;
   that will be the end of sprawling and revelry.

The Lord GOD has sworn by himself:[a] 8
  I loathe the arrogance of Jacob,
   I loathe his palaces;
  city and all in it I will abandon to their fate.

If ten men are left in one house, 9
   they shall die,
and a man's uncle and the embalmer shall take him up 10
  to carry his body out of the house for burial,
and they shall call to someone in a corner of the house,
'Any more there?', and he shall answer, 'No.'
   Then he will add, 'Hush!'—
for the name of the LORD must not be mentioned.
  For the LORD will command, 11
and at the shock the great house will be rubble
  and the cottage matchwood.

  Can horses gallop over rocks? 12
  Can the sea be ploughed with oxen?
  Yet you have turned into venom the process of law
  and justice itself into poison,
   you who are jubilant over a nothing[b] and boast, 13
'Have we not won power[b] by our own strength?'
O Israel, I am raising a nation against you, 14
   and they shall harry your land
  from Lebo-hamath to the gorge of the Arabah.
This is the very word of the LORD the God of Hosts.

Visions foretelling doom upon Israel

THIS WAS WHAT THE LORD GOD showed me: a swarm of locusts 7
hatched out when the late corn, which comes after the king's early
crop, was beginning to sprout. As they were devouring the last of the 2
herbage in the land, I said, 'O Lord GOD, forgive; what will Jacob
be after this? He is so small.' Then the LORD relented and said, 3
'This shall not happen.'

[a] *So Sept.; Heb. adds* This is the very word of the LORD the God of Hosts.   [b] a nothing
and power: *Heb.* Lo-debar *and* Karnaim, *making a word-play on the two place-names.*

4 This was what the Lord GOD showed me: the Lord GOD was summoning a flame of fire[a] to devour the great abyss, and to devour all
5 creation. I said, 'O Lord GOD, I pray thee, cease; what will Jacob be
6 after this? He is so small.' The LORD relented and said, 'This also shall
not happen.'

7 This was what the LORD showed[b] me: there was a man[c] standing by
8 a wall[d] with a plumb-line in his hand. The LORD said to me, 'What do
you see, Amos?' 'A plumb-line', I answered, and the Lord said, 'I am
setting a plumb-line to the heart of my people Israel; never again will I
9 pass them by. The hill-shrines of Isaac shall be desolated and the
sanctuaries of Israel laid waste; I will rise, sword in hand, against the
house of Jeroboam.'

10 Amaziah, the priest of Bethel, reported to Jeroboam king of Israel:
'Amos is conspiring against you in Israel; the country cannot tolerate
11 what he is saying. He says, "Jeroboam shall die by the sword, and Israel
12 shall be deported far from their native land."' To Amos himself Amaziah said, 'Be off, you seer! Off with you to Judah! You can earn your
13 living and do your prophesying there. But never prophesy again at
14 Bethel, for this is the king's sanctuary, a royal palace.' 'I am[e] no
prophet,' Amos replied to Amaziah, 'nor am I a prophet's son; I am[e] a
15 herdsman and a dresser[f] of sycomore-figs. But the LORD took me as I
followed the flock and said to me, "Go and prophesy to my people
16 Israel." So now listen to the word of the LORD. You tell me I am not to
prophesy against Israel or go drivelling on against the people of Isaac.
17 Now these are the words of the LORD: Your wife shall become a city
strumpet[g] and your sons and daughters shall fall by the sword. Your
land shall be divided up with a measuring-line, you yourself shall die in
a heathen country, and Israel shall be deported far from their native
land and go into exile.'

8 This was what the Lord GOD showed me: there was a basket of sum-
2 mer fruit, and he said, 'What are you looking at, Amos?' I answered,
'A basket of ripe summer[h] fruit.' Then the LORD said to me, 'The time
3 is ripe[h] for my people Israel. Never again will I pass them by. In that
day, says the Lord GOD, the singing women in the palace shall howl,
"So many dead men, flung out everywhere! Silence!"'

4 Listen to this, you who grind the destitute and plunder[i] the humble,
5 you who say, 'When will the new moon be over so that we may sell
corn? When will the sabbath be past so that we may open our wheat
again, giving short measure in the bushel[j] and taking overweight in the

[a] a flame of fire: *prob. rdg.; Heb.* to contend with fire.   [b] the LORD showed: *so Sept.; Heb.*
he showed.   [c] *So Sept.; Heb.* the Lord.   [d] *Prob. rdg.; Heb. adds* of a plumb-line.
[e] *Or* was.   [f] *Lit.* pricker.   [g] become...strumpet: *or* be carried off as a prostitute in
a raid.   [h] ripe summer *and* ripe: *a play on the Heb.* qais (summer) *and* qes (end).   [i] and
plunder: *prob. rdg.; Heb.* to destroy.   [j] *Heb.* ephah.

silver, tilting the scales fraudulently, and selling the dust of the wheat; 6
that we may buy the poor for silver and the destitute for a pair of shoes?'
The LORD has sworn by the pride of Jacob: I will never forget any of 7
their doings.

Shall not the earth shake for this? 8
  Shall not all who live on it grieve?
All earth shall surge and seethe like the Nile[a]
  and subside like the river of Egypt.

On that day, says the Lord GOD, 9
  I will make the sun go down at noon
  and darken the earth in broad daylight.
  I will turn your pilgrim-feasts into mourning 10
  and all your songs into lamentation.
  I will make you all put sackcloth round your waists
  and have all your heads shaved.
  I will make it like mourning for an only son
  and the end of it a bitter day.

The time is coming, says the Lord GOD, 11
  when I will send famine on the land,
not hunger for bread or thirst for water,
  but for hearing the word of the LORD.
Men shall stagger from north to south,[b] 12
  they shall range from east to west,
seeking the word of the LORD,
    but they shall not find it.
On that day fair maidens and young men 13
    shall faint from thirst;
  all who take their oath by Ashimah, goddess of Samaria, 14
  all who swear, 'By the life of your god, O Dan',
  and, 'By the sacred way to[c] Beersheba',
  shall fall to rise no more.

I saw the LORD standing by the altar, and he said: 9

Strike the capitals so that the whole porch is shaken;
  I will smash them all into pieces[d]
  and I will kill them to the last man[e] with the sword.
  No fugitive shall escape,
  no survivor find safety;
    if they dig down to Sheol, 2

[a] the Nile: *so some MSS., cp. 9. 5; others* the light. [b] south: *prob. rdg.; Heb.* west.
[c] sacred way to: *or, with Sept.,* life of your god, O... [d] I will...pieces: *prob. rdg.; Heb.*
I will hack them on the heads of them all. [e] them to the last man: *or* their children.

thence shall my hand take them;
    if they climb up to heaven,
  thence will I bring them down.
3   If they hide on the top of Carmel,
  there will I search out and take them;
if they conceal themselves from me in the depths of the sea,
there will I bid the sea-serpent bite them.
4 If they are herded into captivity by their enemies,
  there will I bid the sword slay them,
  and I will fix my eye on them
    for evil and not for good.

5   The Lord the GOD of Hosts,
at whose touch the earth heaves,
  and all who dwell on it wither,[a]
it surges like the Nile,
  and subsides like the river of Egypt,
6 who builds his stair up to[b] the heavens
and arches his ceiling over the earth,
  who summons the waters of the sea
and pours them over the land—
  his name is the LORD.

7 Are not you Israelites like Cushites to me?
    says the LORD.
Did I not bring Israel up from Egypt,
the Philistines from Caphtor, the Aramaeans from Kir?
8   Behold, I, the Lord GOD,
  have my eyes on this sinful kingdom,
and I will wipe it off the face of the earth.

A remnant spared and restored

Yet I will not wipe out the family of Jacob root and branch,
  says the LORD.
9   No; I will give my orders,
I will shake Israel to and fro through all the nations
  as a sieve is shaken to and fro
  and not one pebble falls to the ground.
10 They shall die by the sword, all the sinners of my people,
who say, 'Thou wilt not let disaster come near us
  or overtake us.'

[a] *Or* mourn.   [b] stair up to: *or, with slight change,* upper chambers in.

On that day I will restore   11
     David's fallen house;*a*
I will repair its*b* gaping walls and restore its*c* ruins;
     I will rebuild it as it was long ago,
that they may possess what is left of Edom   12
and all the nations who were once named mine.

This is the very word of the LORD, who will do this.

A time is coming, says the LORD,   13
     when the ploughman shall follow hard on the vintager,*d*
and he who treads the grapes after him who sows the seed.
     The mountains shall run with fresh wine,
     and every hill shall wave with corn.
I will restore the fortunes of my people Israel;   14
they shall rebuild deserted cities and live in them,
they shall plant vineyards and drink their wine,
make gardens and eat the fruit.
Once more I will plant them on their own soil,   15
     and they shall never again be uprooted
         from the soil I have given them.
     It is the word of the LORD your God.

[a] *Lit.* booth.   [b] *So Sept.; Heb.* their.   [c] *So Sept.; Heb.* his.   [d] *Or* reaper.

OBADIAH

Edom's pride and downfall

1[a] The vision of Obadiah: what the Lord GOD has said concerning Edom.

> When a herald was sent out among the nations, crying,
>   'Rouse yourselves;
> let us rouse ourselves to battle against Edom',
> I[b] heard this message from the LORD:

2   Look, I make you the least of all nations,
>   an object of contempt.

3   Your proud, insolent heart has led you astray;
>   you who haunt the crannies among the rocks,
>   making your home on the heights,
> you say to yourself, 'Who can bring me to the ground?'

4   Though you soar as high as a vulture
>   and your nest is set among the stars,
>   thence I will bring you down.
>   This is the very word of the LORD.

5[c] If thieves or robbers come to you by night,
>   though your loss be heavy,
>   they will steal only what they want;
>   if vintagers come to you,
>   will they not leave gleanings?

6   But see how Esau's treasure is ransacked,
>   his secret wealth hunted out!

7   All your former allies march you to the frontier,
>   your confederates mislead you and bring you low,
>   your own kith and kin lay a snare for your feet,
>   a snare that works blindly, without wisdom.

8   And on that very day
>   I will destroy all the sages of Edom
>   and leave no wisdom on the mount of Esau.
>   This is the very word of the LORD.

9   Then shall your warriors, O Teman, be so enfeebled,

---

[a] *Verses 1–4: cp. Jer. 49. 14–16.* [b] *So Sept., cp. Jer. 49. 14; Heb.* we. [c] *Verses 5 and 6: cp. Jer. 49. 9, 10.*

that every man shall be cut down on the mount of Esau.
For the murderous violence done to your brother Jacob   10
you shall be covered with shame and cut off for ever.
    On the day when you stood aloof,   11
on the day when strangers carried off his wealth,
when foreigners trooped in by his gates
and parcelled out Jerusalem by lot,
you yourselves were of one mind with them.
Do not gloat over your brother on the day of his misfortune,   12
nor rejoice over Judah on his day of ruin;
do not boast on the day of distress,
nor enter my people's gates on the day of his downfall.   13
Do not gloat over his fall on the day of his downfall
nor seize his treasure on the day of his downfall.
Do not wait at the cross-roads to cut off his fugitives   14
nor betray the survivors on the day of distress.

For soon the day of the LORD will come on all the nations: 15
you shall be treated as you have treated others,
and your deeds will recoil on your own head.
The draught that you have drunk on my holy mountain   16
all the nations shall drink continually;
    they shall drink and gulp down
and shall be as though they had never been;
but on Mount Zion there shall be those that escape,   17
    and it shall be holy,
and Jacob shall dispossess those that dispossessed them.
Then shall the house of Jacob be fire,   18
    the house of Joseph flame,
    and the house of Esau shall be chaff;
they shall blaze through it and consume it,
and the house of Esau shall have no survivor.
    The LORD has spoken.
Then they shall possess the Negeb, the mount of Esau,   19
    and the Shephelah of the Philistines;
they shall possess the country-side of Ephraim and Samaria,
    and Benjamin shall possess Gilead.
Exiles of Israel[a] shall possess[b] Canaan as far as Zarephath,   20
exiles of Jerusalem[c] shall possess the cities of the Negeb.
    Those who find safety on Mount Zion shall go up   21
    to hold sway over the mount of Esau,
    and dominion shall belong to the LORD.

[a] *Prob. rdg.; Heb. adds* this army.   [b] shall possess: *prob. rdg.; Heb.* which.   [c] *Prob. rdg.;*
Heb. adds who are in Sepharad.

JONAH

Jonah's mission to Nineveh

1 THE WORD OF THE LORD came to Jonah son of Amit-
2 tai: 'Go to the great city of Nineveh, go now and denounce it,
3 for its wickedness stares me in the face.' But Jonah set out for
Tarshish to escape from the LORD. He went down to Joppa, where he
found a ship bound for Tarshish. He paid his fare and went on board,
4 meaning to travel by it to Tarshish out of reach of the LORD. But the
LORD let loose a hurricane, and the sea ran so high in the storm that the
5 ship threatened to break up. The sailors were afraid, and each cried out
to his god for help. Then they threw things overboard to lighten the
ship. Jonah had gone down into a corner of the ship and was lying sound
6 asleep when the captain came upon him. 'What, sound asleep?' he said.
'Get up, and call on your god; perhaps he will spare us a thought and
we shall not perish.'
7 At last the sailors said to each other, 'Come and let us cast lots to find
out who is to blame for this bad luck.' So they cast lots, and the lot fell
8 on Jonah. 'Now then,' they said to him,[a] 'what is your business? Where
9 do you come from? What is your country? Of what nation are you?' 'I
am a Hebrew,' he answered, 'and I worship the LORD the God of
10 heaven, who made both sea and land.' At this the sailors were even more
afraid. 'What can you have done wrong?' they asked. They already
knew that he was trying to escape from the LORD, for he had told them
11 so. 'What shall we do with you', they asked, 'to make the sea go down?'
12 For the storm grew worse and worse. 'Take me and throw me overboard,' he said, 'and the sea will go down. I know it is my fault that this
13 great storm has struck you.' The crew rowed hard to put back to land
14 but in vain, for the sea ran higher and higher. At last they called on the
LORD and said, 'O LORD, do not let us perish at the price of this man's
life; do not charge us with the death of an innocent man. All this, O
15 LORD, is thy set purpose.' Then they took Jonah and threw him over-
16 board, and the sea stopped raging. So the crew were filled with the fear
17[b] of the LORD and offered sacrifice and made vows to him. But the LORD
ordained that a great fish should swallow Jonah, and for three days and
three nights he remained in its belly.
2 Jonah prayed to the LORD his God from the belly of the fish:

[a] *So Sept.; Heb. adds* who is to blame for this bad luck? [b] *2. 1 in Heb.*

I called to the LORD in my distress,   2
   and he answered me;
out of the belly of Sheol I cried for help,
   and thou hast heard my cry.
Thou didst cast me into the depths, far out at sea,   3
   and the flood closed round me;
all thy waves, all thy billows, passed over me.
I thought I was banished from thy sight   4
and should never see thy holy temple again.
The water about me rose up to my neck;   5
   the ocean was closing over me.
Weeds twined about my head
   in the troughs of the mountains;   6
   I was sinking into a world
whose bars would hold me fast for ever.
But thou didst bring me up alive from the pit, O LORD my God.
As my senses failed me I remembered the LORD,   7
and my prayer reached thee in thy holy temple.
Men who worship false gods may abandon their loyalty,   8
but I will offer thee sacrifice with words of praise;   9
I will pay my vows; victory is the LORD's.

Then the LORD spoke to the fish and it spewed Jonah out on to the   10
dry land.

The word of the LORD came to Jonah a second time: 'Go to the great   3 1,2
city of Nineveh, go now and denounce it in the words I give you.'
Jonah obeyed at once and went to Nineveh. He began by going a day's   3-4
journey into the city, a vast city, three days' journey across, and then
proclaimed: 'In forty days Nineveh shall be overthrown!' The people   5
of Nineveh believed God's word. They ordered a public fast and put on
sackcloth, high and low alike. When the news reached the king of   6
Nineveh he rose from his throne, stripped off his robes of state, put on
sackcloth and sat in ashes. Then he had a proclamation made in Nine-   7
veh: 'This is a decree of the king and his nobles. No man or beast, herd
or flock, is to taste food, to graze or to drink water. They are to clothe   8
themselves in sackcloth and call on God with all their might. Let every
man abandon his wicked ways and his habitual violence. It may be that   9
God will repent and turn away from his anger: and so we shall not
perish.' God saw what they did, and how they abandoned their wicked   10
ways, and he repented and did not bring upon them the disaster he had
threatened.

Jonah was greatly displeased and angry, and he prayed to the LORD: 4 1,2
'This, O LORD, is what I feared when I was in my own country, and to

forestall it I tried to escape to Tarshish; I knew that thou art "a god gracious and compassionate, long-suffering and ever constant, and al-
3 ways willing to repent of the disaster".*a* And now, LORD, take my life: I
4 should be better dead than alive.' 'Are you so angry?' said the LORD.
5 Jonah went out and sat down on the east of the city. There he made himself a shelter and sat in its shade, waiting to see what would happen
6 in the city. Then the LORD God ordained that a climbing gourd*b* should grow up over his head to throw its shade over him and relieve his dis-
7 tress, and Jonah was grateful for the gourd. But at dawn the next day God ordained that a worm should attack the gourd, and it withered;
8 and at sunrise God ordained that a scorching wind should blow up from the east. The sun beat down on Jonah's head till he grew faint. Then he
9 prayed for death and said, 'I should be better dead than alive.' At this God said to Jonah, 'Are you so angry over the gourd?' 'Yes,' he
10 answered, 'mortally angry.' The LORD said, 'You are sorry for the gourd, though you did not have the trouble of growing it, a plant which
11 came up in a night and withered in a night. And should not I be sorry for the great city of Nineveh, with its hundred and twenty thousand who cannot tell their right hand from their left, and cattle without number?'

[*a*] a god...disaster: *cp. Exod. 34. 6.* [*b*] a climbing gourd: *or* a castor-oil plant.

MICAH

THIS IS THE WORD OF THE LORD which came to 1
Micah of Moresheth during the reigns of Jotham, Ahaz, and
Hezekiah, kings of Judah; which he received in visions con-
cerning Samaria and Jerusalem.

The rulers of Israel and Judah denounced

Listen, you peoples, all together;   2
attend, O earth and all who are in it,
that the Lord GOD, the Lord from his holy temple,
    may bear witness against you.
For look, the LORD is leaving his dwelling-place;   3
down he comes and walks on the heights of the earth.
Beneath him mountains dissolve   4
    like wax before the fire,
    valleys are torn open,
    as when torrents pour down the hill-side—
and all for the crime of Jacob and the sin of Israel.[a]   5
What is the crime of Jacob? Is it not Samaria?
What is the hill-shrine of Judah? Is it not Jerusalem?
    So I will make Samaria   6
a heap of ruins in open country,
    a place for planting vines;
    I will pour her stones down into the valley
    and lay her foundations bare.
    All her carved figures shall be shattered,   7
her images burnt one and all;
    I will make a waste heap of all her idols.
    She amassed them out of fees for harlotry,
    and a harlot's fee shall they become once more.
    Therefore I must howl and wail,   8
go naked and distraught;
I must howl like a wolf, mourn like a desert-owl.
    Her wound cannot be healed;   9

[a] *So Heb.; but possibly read* Judah.

1317

for the stroke has bitten deep into Judah,
it has fallen on the gate of my people,
upon Jerusalem itself.

10 Will you not weep your fill, weep your eyes out in Gath?
In Beth-aphrah*a* sprinkle yourselves with dust;

11 take the road, you that dwell in Shaphir;
have not the people of Zaanan gone out in shame from their city*b*?
Beth-ezel is a place of lamentation,
she can lend you support no longer.

12 The people of Maroth are greatly alarmed,
for disaster has come down from the LORD
to the very gate of Jerusalem.

13 Harness the steeds to the chariot, O people of Lachish,
for you first led the daughter of Zion into sin;
to you must the crimes of Israel be traced.

14 Let Moresheth-gath be given her dismissal.
Beth-achzib has*c* disappointed*d* the kings of Israel.

15 And you too, O people of Mareshah,
I will send others to take your place;
and the glory of Israel shall hide in the cave of Adullam.

16 Shave the hair from your head in mourning
for the children of your delight;
make yourself bald as a vulture,
for they have left you and gone into exile.

2 Shame on those who lie in bed planning evil and wicked deeds
and rise at daybreak to do them,
knowing that they have the power!

2 They covet land and take it by force;
if they want a house they seize it;
they rob a man of his home
and steal every man's inheritance.

3 Therefore these are the words of the LORD:

Listen, for this whole brood I am planning disaster,
whose yoke you cannot shake from your necks
and walk upright; it shall be your hour of disaster.

4 On that day
they shall take up a poem about you
and raise a lament thrice told,
saying, 'We are utterly despoiled:

---

[a] *So Vulg.; Heb.* Beth-le-aphrah.   [b] from their city: *prob. rdg., cp. Sept.; Heb.* nakedness.
[c] Beth-achzib has: *prob. rdg.; Heb.* The houses of Achzib have.   [d] *Heb.* achzab.

the land of the Lord's*a* people changes hands.
How shall a man have power*b*
to restore our fields, now parcelled out*c*?'
Therefore there shall be no one to assign to you   5
any portion by lot in the Lord's assembly.

How they rant! They may say, 'Do not rant';   6
but this ranting is all their own,
these insults are their*d* own invention.

Can one ask, O house of Jacob,   7
'Is the Lord's patience truly at an end?
Are these his deeds?
Does not good come of the Lord's*e* words?
He is the upright man's best friend.'

But you are no*f* people for me,   8
rising up as my enemy to my*g* face,
to strip the cloak from him that was safe*h*
and take away the confidence of returning warriors,
to drive the women of my people from their pleasant homes   9
and rob the children of my glory for ever.
Up and be gone; this is no resting-place for you,   10
you that to defile yourselves would commit any mischief,
mischief however cruel.

If anyone had gone about in a spirit of falsehood and lies, saying, 'I   11
will rant to you of wine and strong drink', his ranting would be what
this people like.

I will assemble you, the whole house of Jacob;   12
I will gather together those that are left in Israel.
I will herd them like sheep in a fold,
like a grazing flock which stampedes at the sight of a man.
So their leader breaks out before them,   13
and they all break through the gate and escape,
and their king goes before them,
and the Lord leads the way.

And I said: **3**

Listen, you leaders of Jacob, rulers of Israel,
should you not know what is right?
You hate good and love evil,   2

[a] the Lord's: *prob. rdg.; Heb.* my.   [b] have power: *prob. rdg.; Heb.* remove from me.
[c] now parcelled out: *prob. rdg.; Heb.* he will parcel out.   [d] *Prob. rdg.; Heb.* his.   [e] the
Lord's: *prob. rdg., cp. Sept.; Heb.* my.   [f] But...no: *prob. rdg.; Heb.* But yesterday.
[g] my: *prob. rdg.; Heb. om.*   [h] the cloak...safe: *prob. rdg.; Heb.* mantle, cloak.

you flay men alive and tear the very flesh from their bones;
3   you devour the flesh of my people,
          strip off their skin,
             splinter their bones;
          you shred them like flesh*a* into a pot,
             like meat into a cauldron.

4   Then they will call to the LORD, and he will give them no answer;
    when that time comes he will hide his face from them,
          so wicked are their deeds.

5   These are the words of the LORD concerning the prophets who lead
    my people astray, who promise prosperity in return for a morsel of food,
    who proclaim a holy war against them if they put nothing into their
    mouths:

6   Therefore night shall bring you no vision,
          darkness no divination;
          the sun shall go down on the prophets,
          the day itself shall be black above them.
7   Seers and diviners alike shall blush for shame;
          they shall all put their hands over their mouths,*b*
          because there is no answer from God.

8   But I am full of strength,*c* of justice and power,
          to denounce his crime to Jacob
             and his sin to Israel.
9   Listen to this, leaders of Jacob,
             rulers of Israel,
          you who make justice hateful
          and wrest it from its straight course,
10   building Zion in bloodshed
             and Jerusalem in iniquity.
11 Her rulers sell justice,
          her priests give direction in return for a bribe,
          her prophets take money for their divination,
             and yet men rely on the LORD.
          'Is not the LORD among us?' they say;
          'then no disaster can befall us.'
12   Therefore, on your account
          Zion shall become a ploughed field,
          Jerusalem a heap of ruins,
             and the temple hill rough heath.

[a] like flesh: *so Sept.; Heb.* as.   [b] *Lit.* moustaches.   [c] *Prob. rdg.; Heb. adds* the spirit
of the LORD.

A remnant restored in an age of peace

In days to come   4 1[a]
the mountain of the LORD's house
shall be set over all other mountains,
lifted high above the hills.
Peoples shall come streaming to it,
and many nations shall come and say,   2
'Come, let us climb up on to the mountain of the LORD,
    to the house of the God of Jacob,
    that he may teach us his ways
    and we may walk in his paths.'
For instruction issues from Zion,
    and out of Jerusalem comes the word of the LORD;
he will be judge between many peoples   3
and arbiter among mighty nations afar.
    They shall beat their swords into mattocks
    and their spears into pruning-knives;
nation shall not lift sword against nation
    nor ever again be trained for war,
    and each man shall dwell under his own vine,   4
    under his own fig-tree, undisturbed.
For the LORD of Hosts himself has spoken.

All peoples may walk, each in the name of his god,   5
but we will walk in the name of the LORD our God
    for ever and ever.

On that day, says the LORD,   6
    I will gather those who are lost;
I will assemble the exiles and I will strengthen the weaklings.
    I will preserve the lost as a remnant   7
    and turn the derelict into a mighty nation.
The LORD shall be their king on Mount Zion
    now and for ever.
And you, rocky bastion, hill of Zion's daughter,   8
    the promises to you shall be fulfilled;
    and your former sovereignty shall come again,
    the dominion of the daughter of Jerusalem.
Why are you now filled with alarm?   9
    Have you no king?

[a] *Verses 1–3: cp. Isa. 2. 2–4.*

Have you no counsellor left,
that you are seized with writing like a woman in labour?

10 Lie writhing on the ground like a woman in childbirth,
O daughter of Zion;
for now you must leave the city
and camp in the open country;
and so you will come to Babylon.
There you shall be saved,
there the LORD will deliver you from your enemies.

11 But now many nations are massed against you;
they say, 'Let her suffer outrage,
let us gloat over Zion.'

12 But they do not know the LORD's thoughts
nor understand his purpose;
for he has gathered them like sheaves to the threshing-floor.

13 Start your threshing, daughter of Zion;
for I will make your horns of iron,
your hooves will I make of bronze,
and you shall crush many peoples.
You shall devote their ill-gotten gain to the LORD,
their wealth to the Lord of all the earth.

5 1ª Get you behind your walls, you people of a walled city,*ᵇ*
the siege is pressed home against you:*ᶜ*
Israel's ruler shall be struck on the cheek with a rod.

2ᵈ But you, Bethlehem in Ephrathah,
small as you are to be among Judah's clans,
out of you shall come forth a governor for Israel,
one whose roots are far back in the past, in days gone by.

3 Therefore only so long as a woman is in labour
shall he give up Israel;
and then those that survive of his race
shall rejoin their brethren.

4 He shall appear and be their shepherd
in the strength of the LORD,
in the majesty of the name of the LORD his God.
And they shall continue, for now his greatness shall reach
to the ends of the earth;

5 and he shall be a man of peace.

When the Assyrian comes into our land,
when he tramples our castles,

[a] 4. 14 in Heb. [b] Get...city: prob. rdg., cp. Sept.; Heb. Gash yourself, daughter of a band. [c] So Sept.; Heb. us. [d] 5. 1 in Heb.

we will raise against him seven men or eight
　　to be shepherds and princes.
　　They shall shepherd Assyria with the sword　　　　　　6
　　and the land of Nimrod with bare blades;
they shall deliver us from the Assyrians
　　when they come into our land,
　　　　when they trample our frontiers.

All that are left of Jacob, surrounded by many peoples,　　7
　　shall be like dew from the LORD,
　　　　like copious showers on the grass,
　　which do not wait for man's command
　　　　or linger for any man's bidding.
　　All that are left of Jacob among the nations,　　　　8
　　　　surrounded by many peoples,
shall be like a lion among the beasts of the forest,
　　like a young lion loose in a flock of sheep;
as he prowls he will trample and tear them,
　　with no rescuer in sight.
Your hand shall be raised high over your foes,　　　　9
and all who hate you shall be destroyed.

On that day, says the LORD,　　　　　　　　　　　10
I will destroy all your horses among you
　　and make away with your chariots.
I will destroy the cities of your land　　　　　　　11
　　and raze your fortresses.
I will destroy all your sorcerers,　　　　　　　　12
　　and there shall be no more soothsayers among you.
I will destroy your images and all the sacred pillars in your land;　13
you shall no longer bow in reverence before things your own hands
　　　　made.
I will pull down the sacred poles in your land,　　　　14
　　and demolish your blood-spattered altars.
In anger and fury will I take vengeance　　　　　　15
　　on all nations who disobey me.

Israel denounced for her people's sins

Hear now what the LORD is saying:　　　　　　　　6

　　Up, state your case to the mountains;
　　let the hills hear your plea.

2   Hear the LORD's case, you mountains,
        you everlasting pillars that bear up the earth;
    for the LORD has a case against his people,
        and will argue it with Israel.

3   O my people, what have I done to you?
    Tell me how I have wearied you; answer me this.

4   I brought you up from Egypt,
      I ransomed you from the land of slavery,
    I sent Moses and Aaron and Miriam to lead you.

5   Remember, my people,
    what Balak king of Moab schemed against you,
and how Balaam son of Beor answered him;
    consider the journey[a] from Shittim to Gilgal,
      in order that you may know the triumph of the LORD.

6   What shall I bring when I approach the LORD?
    How shall I stoop before God on high?
Am I to approach him with whole-offerings or yearling calves?

7   Will the LORD accept thousands of rams
      or ten thousand rivers of oil?
    Shall I offer my eldest son for my own wrongdoing,
      my children for my own sin?

8   God[b] has told you what is good;
    and what is it that the LORD asks of you?
    Only to act justly, to love loyalty,
    to walk wisely before your God.

9   Hark, the LORD, the fear of whose[c] name brings success,
      the LORD calls to the city.

10   Listen, O tribe of Judah and citizens in assembly,[d]
    can I overlook[e] the infamous false measure,[f]
      the accursed short bushel[g]?

11   Can I connive at false scales or a bag of light weights?

12   Your rich men are steeped in violence,
      your townsmen are all liars,
    and their tongues frame deceit.

13   But now I will inflict a signal punishment on you
      to lay you waste for your sins:

14   you shall eat but not be satisfied,
      your food shall lie heavy on your stomach;
      you shall come to labour but not bring forth,

---

[a] consider the journey: *prob. rdg.*; *Heb. om.* [b] God: *prob. rdg.*; *Heb. obscure.* [c] *So Sept.*; *Heb.* thy. [d] citizens in assembly: *prob. rdg.*; *Heb. unintelligible.* [e] can I overlook: *prob. rdg.*; *Heb. obscure.* [f] *Prob. rdg.*; *Heb. adds* infamous treasures. [g] *Heb.* ephah.

and even if you bear a child
　　I will give it to the sword;
　you shall sow but not reap,   15
you shall press the olives but not use the oil,
　　you shall tread the grapes but not drink the wine.
　　　You have*ᵃ* kept the precepts of Omri;   16
　　　what the house of Ahab did, you have done;
　　　you have followed all their ways.
　　So I will lay you utterly waste;
　　　the nations*ᵇ* shall jeer at your citizens,
　　　and their insults you shall bear.

Disappointment turned to hope

Alas! I am now like the last gatherings of summer fruit,   7
　　the last gleanings of the vintage,
　　when there are no grapes left to eat,
　none of those early figs that I love.
　Loyal men have vanished from the earth,   2
　there is not one upright man.
　All lie in wait to do murder,
each man drives his own kinsman like a hunter into the net.
　　They are bent eagerly on wrongdoing,   3
　　the officer who presents the requests,*ᶜ*
　　the judge who gives judgement*ᵈ* for reward,
　　and the nobleman who harps on his desires.
　　Thus their goodness is twisted*ᵉ* like rank weeds   4
　　and their honesty like briars.*ᶠ*
　　As soon as thine eye sees, thy punishment falls;
　　at that moment bewilderment seizes them.
Trust no neighbour, put no confidence in your closest friend;   5
　seal your lips even from the wife of your bosom.
　For son maligns father,   6
　daughter rebels against mother,
　　daughter-in-law against mother-in-law,
　　and a man's enemies are his own household.
　But I will look for the LORD,   7
I will wait for God my saviour; my God will hear me.

[*a*] You have: *so Sept.; Heb.* He has.　[*b*] the nations: *so Sept.; Heb.* my people.　[*c*] the
requests: *prob. rdg.; Heb. om.*　[*d*] who gives judgement: *prob. rdg.; Heb. om.*　[*e*] twisted:
prob. rdg.; Heb. obscure.　[*f*] their honesty like briars: *prob. rdg.; Heb. obscure.*

8   O my enemies, do not exult over me;
        I have fallen, but shall rise again;
    though I dwell in darkness, the LORD is my light.
9   I will bear the anger of the LORD, for I have sinned against him,
    until he takes up my cause and gives judgement for me,
    until he brings me out into light, and I see his justice.
10 Then may my enemies see and be abashed,
    those who said to me, 'Where is he, the LORD your God?'
    Then shall they be trampled like mud in the streets;
        I shall gloat over them;
11   that will be a day for rebuilding your walls,
    a day when your frontiers will be extended,
12 a day when men will come seeking you
            from Assyria to*a* Egypt
    and from Egypt to the Euphrates,
    from every sea and every mountain;*b*
13 and the earth with its inhabitants shall be waste.
        This shall be the fruit of their deeds.

14 Shepherd thy people with thy crook,
        the flock that is thy very own,
    that dwells by itself on the heath and in the meadows;
    let them graze in Bashan and Gilead, as in days gone by.
15 Show us*c* miracles as in the days when thou camest out of Egypt;
16 let the nations see and be taken aback for all their might,
        let them keep their mouths shut,
            make their ears deaf,
17   let them lick the dust like snakes,
            like creatures that crawl upon the ground.
    Let them come trembling and fearful from their strongholds,
        let them fear thee, O LORD our God.

18 Who is a god like thee? Thou takest away guilt,
    thou passest over the sin of the remnant of thy own people,
        thou dost not let thy anger rage for ever
        but delightest in love that will not change.
19   Once more thou wilt show us tender affection
            and wash out our guilt,
    casting all our*d* sins into the depths of the sea.
20 Thou wilt show good faith to Jacob,
        unchanging love to Abraham,
    as thou didst swear to our fathers in days gone by.

[a] to: *so one MS.; others* cities.   [b] from every...mountain: *prob. rdg., cp. Sept.; Heb.* sea
from sea and mountain of the mountain.   [c] *Prob. rdg.; Heb.* I will show him.   [d] *So
Sept.; Heb.* their.

NAHUM

An oracle about Nineveh: the book of the vision of Nahum the 1
Elkoshite.

The vengeance of the LORD on his enemies

The LORD is a jealous god, a god of vengeance; 2ᵃ
the LORD takes vengeance and is quick to anger.ᵇ
ᶜIn whirlwind and storm he goes on his way, 3
  and the clouds are the dust beneath his feet.
He rebukes the sea and dries it up 4
  and makes all the streams fail.
Bashan and Carmel languish,
  and on Lebanon the young shoots wither.
The mountains quake before him, 5
  the hills heave and swell,
and the earth, the world and all that lives in it,
  are in tumult at his presence.
Who can stand before his wrath? 6
  Who can resist his fury?
His anger pours outᵈ like a stream of fire,
and the rocks meltᵉ before him.
The LORD is a sure refuge 7
for those who look to himᶠ in time of distress;
he cares for all who seek his protection
and brings them safelyᵍ through the sweeping flood; 8
he makes a final end of all who oppose him
and pursues his enemies into darkness.
No adversaries dare oppose him twice; 9–11
all are burnt upʰ like tangled briars.
Why do you make plots against the LORD?

[a] *Verses 2–14 are an incomplete alphabetic acrostic poem; some parts have been re-arranged*
accordingly. [b] *The rest of verse 2,* The LORD takes...wrath, *transposed to verse 11.*
[c] *Prob. rdg.; Heb. inserts two lines* The LORD is long-suffering and of great might, but the
LORD does not sweep clean away. [d] pours out: *or* fuses *or* melts. [e] *Prob. rdg.; Heb.* are
torn down. [f] for...him: *prob. rdg., cp. Sept.; Heb. om.* [g] brings them safely: *prob.*
rdg.; Heb. om. [h] all are burnt up: *prob. rdg.; Heb.* for until.

He himself will make an end of you all.
From you has come forth a wicked counsellor,
plotting evil against the LORD.
The LORD takes vengeance on his adversaries,
against his enemies he directs his wrath;
with skin scorched black, they are consumed
like stubble that is parched and dry.

Israel and Judah rid of the invaders

These are the words of the LORD:

13   Now I will break his yoke from your necks
        and snap the cords that bind you.
14   Image and idol will I hew down in the house of your God.
        This is what the LORD has ordained for you:
        never again shall your offspring be scattered;
        and I will grant you burial, fickle though you have been.
12   Has the punishment been so great?
        Yes, but it has passed away and is gone.
        I have afflicted you, but I will not afflict you again.

15ª   See on the mountains the feet of the herald
        who brings good news.
        Make your pilgrimages, O Judah,
        and pay your vows.
        For wicked men shall never again overrun you;
        they are totally destroyed.
2 2ᵇ   The LORD will restore the pride of Jacob and Israel alike,
        although plundering hordes have stripped them bare
        and pillaged their vines.

Nineveh's enemies triumphant

1   The battering-ram is mounted against your bastions,
        the siege is closing in.
    Watch the road and brace yourselves;
        put forth all your strength.
3   The shields of their warriors are gleaming red,

[a] 2. 1 in Heb.   [b] Verses 1 and 2 transposed.

their soldiers are all in scarlet;
their chariots, when the line is formed,
are like flickering[a] fire;
squadrons of horse[b] advance on the city in mad frenzy;[c]   4
they jostle one another in the outskirts, like waving torches;
the leaders display their prowess[d]   5
as they dash to and fro like lightning,
rushing[e] in headlong career;
they hasten to the wall, and mantelets are set in position.
The sluices of the rivers are opened, the palace topples down;   6
the train of captives goes into exile,   7
their slave-girls are carried off,
moaning like doves and beating their breasts;
and Nineveh has become like a pool of water,   8
like the waters round her, which are ebbing away.
'Stop! Stop!' they cry; but none turns back.

Spoil is taken, spoil of silver and gold;   9
there is no end to the store,
treasure beyond the costliest that man can desire.
Plundered, pillaged, stripped bare!   10
Courage melting and knees giving way,
writhing limbs, and faces drained of colour[f]!
Where now is the lions' den,   11
the cave[g] where the lion cubs lurked,
where the lion and[h] lioness and young cubs
went unafraid,
the lion which killed to satisfy its whelps   12
and for its mate broke the neck of the kill,
mauling its prey to fill its lair,
filling its den with the mauled prey?

I am against you, says the LORD of Hosts,   13
I will smoke out your pride,[i]
and a sword shall devour your cubs.
I will leave you no more prey on the earth,
and the sound of your feeding[j] shall no more be heard.

Ah! blood-stained city, steeped in deceit,   3
full of pillage, never empty of prey!

[a] flickering: *prob. rdg.; Heb. obscure.* [b] squadrons of horse: *so Sept.; Heb.* the fir-
trees. [c] *Prob. rdg.; Heb. adds* chariots. [d] display their prowess: *or* shout their own
names. [e] *Prob. rdg.; Heb.* stumbling. [f] drained of colour: *mng. of Heb. uncertain.*
[g] *Prob. rdg.; Heb.* pasture. [h] and: *prob. rdg.; Heb. om.* [i] your pride: *prob. rdg.; Heb.*
her chariot. [j] your feeding: *prob. rdg.; Heb.* your messenger.

2   Hark to the crack of the whip,
the rattle of wheels and stamping of horses,

3   bounding chariots, chargers rearing,[a]
      swords gleaming, flash of spears!
The dead are past counting, their bodies lie in heaps,
corpses innumerable, men stumbling over corpses—

4   all for a wanton's monstrous wantonness,
      fair-seeming, a mistress of sorcery,
    who beguiled nations and tribes
      by her wantonness and her sorceries.

5   I am against you, says the LORD of Hosts,
      I will uncover your breasts to your disgrace
    and expose your naked body to every nation,
      to every kingdom your shame.

6   I will cast loathsome filth over you,
    I will count you obscene and treat you like excrement.

7   Then all who see you will shrink from you and say,
'Nineveh is laid waste; who will console her?'
Where shall I look for anyone to comfort you?

8   Will you fare better than No-amon?—
      she that lay by the streams of the Nile,
      surrounded by water,
whose[b] rampart was the Nile, waters her wall;

9   Cush and Egypt were her strength, and it was boundless,
Put and the Libyans brought her[c] help.

10   She too became an exile and went into captivity,
    her infants too were dashed to the ground at every street-corner,
      her nobles were shared out by lot,
      all her great men were thrown into chains.

11   You too shall hire yourself out, flaunting your sex;
you too shall seek refuge from the enemy.

12   Your fortifications are like figs when they ripen:
if they are shaken, they fall into the mouth of the eater.

13   The troops[d] in your midst are a pack of women,
the gates of your country stand open to the enemy,
      and fire consumes their bars.

14   Draw yourselves water for the siege,
      strengthen your fortifications;
down into the clay, trample the mortar,
      repair the brickwork.

---

[a] chargers rearing: *lit.* men making their chargers rear.   [b] whose: *so Scroll; Heb. om.*
[c] her: *so Pesh.; Heb.* you.   [d] *Or* people.

Even then the fire will consume you,   15
    and the sword will cut you down.*ᵃ*
Make yourselves many as the locusts,
    make yourselves many as the hoppers,
a swarm which spreads out and then flies away.   16
You have spies as numerous as the stars in the sky;
    your secret agents are like locusts,   17
    your commanders like the hoppers
which lie dormant in the walls on a cold day;
but when the sun rises, they scurry off,
and no one knows where they have gone.
Your shepherds slumber, O king of Assyria,   18
    your flock-masters lie down to rest;
your troops*ᵇ* are scattered over the hills,
    and no one rounds them up.
Your wounds cannot be assuaged, your injury is mortal;   19
all who have heard of your fate clap their hands in joy.
Are there any whom your ceaseless cruelty has not borne down?

[*a*] *Prob. rdg.; Heb. adds* and consume you like the locust (*or* hopper).   [*b*] *Or* people.

HABAKKUK

1 An oracle which the prophet Habakkuk received in a vision.

Divine justice

2 How long, O LORD, have I cried to thee, unanswered?
I cry, 'Violence!', but thou dost not save.
3 Why dost thou let me see such misery,
    why countenance^a wrongdoing?

Devastation and violence confront me;
strife breaks out, discord raises its head,
4   and so law grows effete;
    justice does not come forth victorious;
    for the wicked outwit the righteous,
    and so justice comes out perverted.

5 Look, you treacherous people,^b look:
    here is what will astonish you and stun you,
    for there is work afoot in your days
    which you will not believe when it is told you.
6 It is this: I am raising up the Chaldaeans,
    that savage and impetuous nation,
        who cross the wide tracts of the earth
    to take possession of homes not theirs.
7 Terror and awe go with them;
their justice and judgement are of their own making.
8 Their horses are swifter than hunting-leopards,
    keener than wolves of the plain;^c
    their cavalry wait ready, they spring forward,^d
    they come flying from afar
    like vultures swooping to devour the prey.
9 Their whole army advances, violence in their hearts;
    a sea of faces rolls on;
    they bring in captives countless as the sand.

[a] Or dost thou let me see or, with Pesh., do I see.   [b] you treacherous people: so Sept.;
Heb. among the nations.   [c] Or evening.   [d] they spring forward: so Scroll; Heb. their
cavalry.

Kings they hold in derision,   10
rulers they despise;
they despise every fortress,
they raise siege-works and capture it.
Then they pass on like the wind and are gone;   11
and dismayed are all those whose strength was their god.

Art thou not from of old, O LORD?—   12
my God, the holy, the immortal.*a*
O LORD, it is thou who hast appointed them to execute judgement;
O mighty God,*b* thou who hast destined them to chastise,
thou whose eyes are too pure to look upon evil,   13
and who canst not countenance wrongdoing,
why dost thou countenance the treachery of the wicked?
Why keep silent when they devour men more righteous than they?
Why dost thou make men like the fish of the sea,   14
like gliding creatures that obey no ruler?
They haul them up with hooks, one and all,   15
they catch them in nets
and drag them in their trawls;
then they make merry and rejoice,
sacrificing to their nets   16
and burning offerings*c* to their trawls;
for by these they live sumptuously
and enjoy rich fare.
Are they then to unsheathe the sword*d* every day,   17
to slaughter the nations without pity?

I will stand at my post,   2
I will take up my position on the watch-tower,
I will watch to learn what he will say through me,
and what I shall reply when I am challenged.*e*
Then the LORD made answer: 2
Write down the vision, inscribe it on tablets,
ready for a herald*f* to carry it with speed;*g*
for there is still a vision for the appointed time.   3
At the destined hour it will come in breathless haste,
it will not fail.
If it delays, wait for it;
for when it comes will be no time to linger.

---

[a] the immortal: *prob. original rdg., altered in Heb.* to we shall not die.   [b] *Lit.* rock *or* creator.   [c] *Or* incense.   [d] unsheathe the sword: *so Scroll; Heb.* empty the net and...
[e] when I am challenged: *or* concerning my complaint.   [f] a herald: *lit.* one who can recite it.   [g] ready...speed: *or* so that a man may read it easily.

4   The reckless will be unsure of himself,
       while the righteous man will live by being faithful;[a]

5   as for the traitor in his over-confidence,[b]
       still less will he ride out the storm, for all his bragging.
    Though he opens his mouth as wide as Sheol
    and is insatiable as Death,
    gathering in all the nations,
    making all peoples his own harvest,

6   surely they will all turn upon him
       with insults and abuse, and say,
       'Woe betide you who heap up wealth that is not yours[c]
       and enrich yourself with goods taken in pledge!'

7   Will not your creditors suddenly start up,
       will not all awake who would shake you till you are empty,
       and will you not fall a victim to them?

8   Because you yourself have plundered mighty[d] nations,
       all the rest of the world will plunder you,
       because of bloodshed and violence done in the land,
       to the city and all its inhabitants.

9   Woe betide you who seek unjust gain for your house,
       to build your nest on a height,
       to save yourself from the grasp of wicked men!

10   Your schemes to overthrow mighty[d] nations
       will bring dishonour to your house
       and put your own life in jeopardy.

11   The very stones will cry out from the wall,
       and from the timbers a beam will answer them.

12   Woe betide you who have built a town with bloodshed
       and founded a city on fraud,

13   so that nations toil for a pittance,
       and peoples weary themselves for a mere nothing!
    Is not all this the doing of the LORD of Hosts?

14   For the earth shall be full of the knowledge of the glory of the LORD
       as the waters fill the sea.

15   Woe betide you who make your[e] companions drink the outpouring
           of your wrath,
       making them drunk, that you may watch their naked orgies[f]!

16   Drink deep draughts of shame, not of glory;
       you too shall drink until you stagger.[g]

---

[a] *Or* by his faithfulness (*cp. Romans 1. 17; Galatians 3. 11*).   [b] over-confidence: *so Sept.; Heb.* wine.   [c] *Prob. rdg.; Heb. adds* till when.   [d] *Or* many.   [e] *Prob. rdg.; Heb.* his.   [f] naked orgies: *or, with Scroll,* appointed feasts.   [g] until you stagger: *so Scroll; Heb. obscure in context.*

The cup in the LORD's right hand is passed to you,
and your shame will exceed*ᵃ* your glory.
> The violence done to Lebanon shall sweep over you,   17
> the havoc done to its beasts shall break your own spirit,*ᵇ*
> because of bloodshed and violence done in the land,
> to the city and all its inhabitants.

What use is an idol when its maker has shaped it?—   18
> it is only an image, a source of lies;
or when the maker trusts what he has made?—
> he is only making dumb idols.
> Woe betide him who says to the wood, 'Wake up',   19
> to the dead stone, 'Bestir yourself'!*ᶜ*
Why, it is firmly encased in gold and silver
and has no breath in it.
But the LORD is in his holy temple;   20
let all the earth be hushed in his presence.

A prayer for mercy

A prayer of the prophet Habakkuk.*ᵈ*   3

O LORD, I have heard tell of thy deeds;   2
I have seen,*ᵉ* O LORD, thy work.*ᶠ*
> In the midst of the years thou didst make thyself known,
> and in thy wrath thou didst remember mercy.

God comes from Teman,   3
> the Holy One from Mount Paran;
his radiance overspreads the skies,
and his splendour fills the earth.
> He rises*ᵍ* like the dawn,   4
> with twin rays starting forth at his side;
the skies are*ʰ* the hiding-place of his majesty,
and the everlasting*ⁱ* ways are for*ʲ* his swift flight.*ᵏ*
Pestilence stalks before him,   5
and plague comes forth behind.

[a] will exceed: *prob. rdg.; Heb. unintelligible.* [b] shall break...spirit: *so Sept.; Heb.* will indeed break. [c] *Prob. rdg.; Heb. adds* he will teach. [d] *So Pesh.; Heb. adds* al shigionoth, *possibly a musical term.* [e] *Prob. rdg., cp. Sept.; Heb.* I feared. [f] *Prob. rdg.; Heb. adds* in the midst of the years quicken it. [g] He rises: *so Sept.; Heb. obscure.* [h] the skies are: *prob. rdg.; Heb.* there is. [i] *Or* ancient. [j] and...are for: *transposed from end of verse 6.* [k] his swift flight: *transposed, with slight change, from verse 7.*

6   He stands still and shakes the earth,
      he looks and makes the nations tremble;
         the eternal mountains are riven,
         the everlasting[a] hills subside,

7   the tents of Cushan are snatched away,[b]
         the tent-curtains of Midian flutter.

8   Art thou angry with the streams?[c]
      Is thy wrath against the sea, O LORD?
      When thou dost mount thy horses,
         thy riding is to victory.

9   Thou dost draw thy bow from its case[d]
      and charge thy quiver with shafts.[e]
      Thou cleavest the earth with rivers;

10–11   the mountains see thee and writhe with fear.
      The torrent of water rushes by,
      and the deep sea thunders aloud.
      The sun forgets to turn in his course,[f]
      and the moon stands still at her zenith,
         at the gleam of thy speeding arrows
         and the glance of thy flashing spear.

12   With threats thou dost bestride the earth
      and trample down the nations in anger.

13   Thou goest forth to save thy people,
         thou comest[g] to save thy anointed;
      thou dost shatter the wicked man's house from the roof down,[h]
      uncovering[i] its foundations to the bare rock.[j]

14   Thou piercest their[k] chiefs with thy[l] shafts,
      and their leaders are torn from them by the whirlwind,
         as they open[m] their jaws
      to devour their wretched victims in secret.

15   When thou dost tread the sea with thy horses
         the mighty waters boil.

16   I hear, and my belly quakes;
      my lips quiver at the sound;
      trembling comes over my bones,
      and my feet[n] totter in their tracks;

---

[a] *Or* ancient. [b] are snatched away: *prob. rdg.; Heb.* under wickedness. [c] *So some MSS.; others add* or with the streams. [d] Thou...case: *prob. rdg.; Heb.* Thy bow was quite bared. [e] and...shafts: *prob. rdg., cp. Luc. Sept.; Heb.* weeks, shafts, word. [f] The sun...course: *prob. rdg.; Heb.* The sun raised the height of his hands. [g] thou comest: *prob. rdg., cp. Arabic version; Heb. partly lost.* [h] the wicked...down: *prob. rdg.; Heb.* a head from the house of the wicked. [i] *So Vulg.; Heb.* bare places. [j] bare rock: *prob. rdg.; Heb.* neck. [k] their: *prob. rdg.; Heb. om.* [l] *Prob. rdg.; Heb.* his. [m] from them... open: *prob. rdg.; Heb.* obscure. [n] my feet: *prob. rdg., cp. Sept.; Heb.* which.

I sigh for the day of distress
to dawn over my^a assailants.

  Although the fig-tree does not burgeon,   17
  the vines bear no fruit,
  the olive-crop fails,
the orchards yield no food,
the fold is bereft of its flock
  and there are no cattle in the stalls,
yet I will exult in the LORD   18
  and rejoice in the God of my deliverance.
The LORD God is my strength,   19
who makes my feet nimble as a hind's
  and sets me to range the^b heights.

    [a] *So Targ.; Heb.* his. [b] *So Sept.; Heb.* my.

ZEPHANIAH

1 THIS IS THE WORD OF THE LORD which came to
Zephaniah son of Cushi, son of Gedaliah, son of Amariah, son
of Hezekiah, in the time of Josiah son of Amon king of Judah.

Doom on Judah and her neighbours

2 I will sweep the earth clean of all that is on it,
  says the LORD.
3 I will sweep away both man and beast,
I will sweep the birds from the air and the fish from the sea,
  and I will bring the wicked to their knees*a*
and wipe out mankind from the earth.
  This is the very word of the LORD.
4 I will stretch my hand over Judah
and all who live in Jerusalem;
I will wipe out from this place the last remnant of Baal
  and the very name of the heathen priests,*b*
5 those who bow down upon the house-tops
  to worship the host of heaven*c*
  and who swear by Milcom,
6 those who have turned their backs on the LORD,
who have not sought the LORD or consulted him.
7 Silence before the Lord GOD!
  for the day of the LORD is near.
The LORD has prepared a sacrifice
  and has hallowed his guests.
8 On the day of the LORD's sacrifice
I will punish the royal house and its chief officers
and all who ape outlandish fashions.
9   On that day
I will punish all who dance on the temple terrace,
who fill their master's*d* house with crimes of violence and fraud.

[*a*] I will bring...knees: *prob. rdg.; Heb.* the ruins with the wicked.   [*b*] *So Sept.; Heb. adds*
together with the (legitimate) priests.   [*c*] *So Sept.; Heb. adds* those who worship, who swear
by the LORD.   [*d*] *Or* their Lord's.

On that day, says the LORD,   10
an outcry shall be heard from the Fish Gate,
    wailing from the second quarter of the city,
a loud crash from the hills;
and*a* those who live in the Lower Town*b* shall wail.   11
For it is all over with the merchants,
    and all the dealers in silver are wiped out.

At that time   12
I will search Jerusalem with a lantern
and punish all who sit in stupor over the dregs of their wine,
    who say to themselves,
'The LORD will do nothing, good or bad.'
Their wealth shall be plundered,   13
    their houses laid waste;
they shall build houses but not live in them,
they shall plant vineyards but not drink the wine from them.
The great day of the LORD is near,   14
    it comes with speed;
no runner so fast as that day,
    no raiding band so swift.*c*
That day is a day of wrath,   15
    a day of anguish and affliction,
    a day of destruction and devastation,
    a day of murk and gloom,
    a day of cloud and dense fog,
    a day of trumpet and battle-cry   16
over fortified cities and lofty battlements.
I will bring dire distress upon men;   17
they shall walk like blind men for their sin against the LORD.
Their blood shall be spilt like dust
    and their bowels like dung;
neither their silver nor their gold   18
    shall avail to save them.
On the day of the LORD's wrath, by the fire of his jealousy
    the whole land shall be consumed;
for he will make an end, a swift end,
    of all who live in the land.

Gather together, you unruly nation, gather together,   2
before you are sent far away and vanish*d* like chaff,   2
before the burning anger of the LORD comes upon you,

[a] and: *prob. rdg.; Heb. om.*   [b] Lower Town: *lit.* Quarry.   [c] no runner...swift: *prob.*
rdg.; Heb. hark, the day of the LORD is bitter, there the warrior cries aloud.   [d] you are...
vanish: *prob. rdg.; Heb. obscure.*

before the day of the LORD's anger comes upon you.

3   Seek the LORD,
all in the land who live humbly by his laws,
seek righteousness, seek a humble heart;
    it may be that you will find shelter
    in the day of the LORD's anger.

4   For Gaza shall be deserted,
    Ashkelon left desolate,
    the people of Ashdod shall be driven out[a] at noonday
    and Ekron uprooted.

5 Listen, you who live by the coast, you Kerethite settlers.
    The word of the LORD is spoken against you;
    I will subdue you,[b] land of the Philistines,
    I will lay you waste and leave you without inhabitants,
6 and[c] you, Kereth, shall be all shepherds' huts[d] and sheepfolds;
7 and the coastland shall belong to the survivors of Judah.
    They shall pasture their flocks by the sea[e]
    and lie down at evening in the houses of Ashkelon,
    for the LORD their God will turn to them
    and restore their fortunes.

8 I have heard the insults of Moab, the taunts of Ammon,
    how they have insulted my people
    and encroached on their[f] frontiers.
9   Therefore, by my life,
    says the LORD of Hosts, the God of Israel,
    Moab shall be like Sodom,
    Ammon like Gomorrah,
    a pile of weeds, a rotting heap of saltwort,
    waste land for evermore.
    The survivors of my people shall plunder them,
    the remnant of my nation shall possess their land.

10 This will be retribution for their pride, because they have insulted
11 the people of the LORD of Hosts and encroached upon their rights. The
LORD will appear against them with all his terrors; for he will reduce to
beggary all the gods of the earth, and all the coasts and islands of the
nations will worship him, every man in his own home.

12   You Cushites also shall be killed
    by the sword of the LORD.[g]

[a] the people...out: or Ashdod shall be made an example. [b] I...you: prob. rdg.; Heb.
Canaan. [c] So Sept.; Heb. adds the region of the sea. [d] you...huts: Heb. has these
words in a different order. [e] by the sea: prob. rdg.; Heb. upon them. [f] Or, with Sept.,
my. [g] the sword of the LORD: prob. rdg.; Heb. my sword.

So let him stretch out his hand over the north   13
  and destroy Assyria,
make Nineveh desolate,
  arid as the wilderness.
Flocks shall couch there,   14
  and all the beasts of the wild.
Horned owl and ruffed bustard shall roost on her capitals;
  the tawny owl shall hoot in the window,
    and the bustard stand in the porch.[a]
This is the city that exulted in fancied security,   15
saying to herself, 'I am, and I alone.'
And what is she now? A waste, a haunt for wild beasts,
at which every passer-by shall hiss and shake his fist.

Shame on the tyrant city, filthy and foul!   3
No warning voice did she heed, she took no rebuke to heart,   2
she did not trust in the LORD or come near to her God.
Her officers were lions roaring in her midst,   3
  her rulers wolves of the plain[b]
    that did not wait[c] till morning,
  her prophets were reckless, no true prophets.   4
  Her priests profaned the sanctuary
    and did violence to the law.
But the LORD in her midst is just;   5
  he does no wrong;
morning by morning he gives judgement,
  without fail at daybreak.[d]

  I have wiped out the proud;[e]   6
    their battlements are laid in ruin.
  I have made their streets a desert where no one passes.
Their cities are laid waste, deserted, unpeopled.
In the hope that she would remember[f] all my instructions,   7
  I said, 'Do but fear me
    and take my rebuke to heart';
but they were up betimes and went about their evil deeds.

  Wait for me, therefore, says the LORD,   8
  wait for the day when I stand up to accuse you;
for mine it is to gather nations
  and assemble kingdoms,

[a] *Prob. rdg.; Heb. adds an unintelligible phrase.* [b] *Or* evening. [c] *Or* carry off.
[d] *Prob. rdg.; Heb. adds* but the wrongdoer knows no shame. [e] *So Sept.; Heb.* nations.
[f] she would remember: *prob. rdg., cp. Sept.; Heb.* her dwelling-place would not be cut off.

to pour out on them my indignation,
    all the heat of my anger;
the whole earth shall be consumed by the fire of my jealousy.
9   I will give all peoples once again pure lips,
    that they may invoke the LORD by name
    and serve him with one consent.
10   From beyond the rivers of Cush
my suppliants of the Dispersion shall bring me tribute.

A remnant preserved

11   On that day, Jerusalem,
    you shall not be put to shame for all your deeds
      by which you have rebelled against me;
    for then I will rid you
      of your proud and arrogant citizens,
    and never again shall you flaunt your pride
      on my holy hill.
12   But I will leave in you a people
      afflicted and poor.
13   The survivors in Israel shall find refuge in the name of the LORD;
they shall no longer do wrong or speak lies,
    no words of deceit shall pass their lips;
    for they shall feed and lie down
      with no one to terrify them.

14   Zion, cry out for joy;
      raise the shout of triumph, Israel;
      be glad, rejoice with all your heart,
      daughter of Jerusalem.
15   The LORD has rid you of your adversaries,
      he has swept away your foes;
the LORD is among you as king, O Israel;
    never again shall you fear disaster.

16   On that day this shall be the message to Jerusalem:
Fear not, O Zion; let not your hands fall slack.
17   The LORD your God is in your midst,
      like a warrior, to keep you safe;
    he will rejoice over you and be glad;
      he will show you his love once more;[a]

[a] he will show...more: *prob. rdg., cp. Sept.; Heb.* he will be silent in his love.

he will exult over you with a shout of joy
    as in days long ago.[a]   18

I will take your cries of woe[b] away from you;
and you shall no longer endure reproach for her.
When that times comes, see,   19
I will deal with all your oppressors.
I will rescue the lost and gather the dispersed;
I will win my people praise and renown
    in all the world where once they were despised.
When the time comes for me to gather you,[c]   20
    I will bring you home.
I will win you renown and praise
    among all the peoples of the earth,
when I bring back your prosperity; and you shall see it.
    It is the LORD who speaks.

[a] as...ago: *prob. rdg.; Heb. obscure.*   [b] cries of woe: *prob. rdg.; Heb. obscure.*   [c] When
...you: *prob. rdg.; Heb.* and in the time, my gathering you.

HAGGAI

Zerubbabel restorer of the temple

1 IN THE SECOND YEAR of King Darius, on the first day of the sixth month, the word of the LORD came through the prophet Haggai to Zerubbabel son of Shealtiel, governor of Judah, and to 2 Joshua son of Jehozadak, the high priest: These are the words of the LORD of Hosts: This nation says to itself that it is not yet time for the 3 house of the LORD to be rebuilt. Then this word came through Haggai 4 the prophet: Is it a time for you to live in your own well-roofed houses, 5 while this house lies in ruins? Now these are the words of the LORD of 6 Hosts: Consider your way of life. You have sown much but reaped little; you eat but never as much as you wish, you drink but never more than you need, you are clothed but never warm, and the labourer puts 7 his wages into a purse with a hole in it. These are the words of the LORD 8 of Hosts: Consider your way of life. Go up into the hills, fetch timber, and build a house acceptable to me, where I can show my glory,ᵃ says 9 the LORD. You look for much and get little. At the moment when you would bring home the harvest, I blast it. Why? says the LORD of Hosts. Because my house lies in ruins, while each of you has a house 10 that he can run to. It is your fault that the heavens withhold their dew 11 and the earth its produce. So I have proclaimed a drought against land and mountain, against corn, new wine, and oil, and all that the ground yields, against man and cattle and all the products of man's labour.

12 Zerubbabel son of Shealtiel, Joshua son of Jehozadak, the high priest, and the rest of the people listened to what the LORD their God had said and what the prophet Haggai said when the LORD their God sent 13ᵇ him, and they were filled with fear because of the LORD. So Haggai the LORD's messenger, as the LORD had commissioned him, said to the 14 people: I am with you, says the LORD. Then the LORD stirred up the spirit of Zerubbabel son of Shealtiel, governor of Judah, of Joshua son of Jehozadak, the high priest, and of the rest of the people; they came 15 and began work on the house of the LORD of Hosts their God on the twenty-fourth day of the sixth month.

[a] show my glory: or be honoured. [b] It is possible that some verses have been misplaced and that the original order from this point may have been 1. 14, 15, 13; 2. 15–19, 10–14, 1–9, 20–23.

In the second year of King Darius, on the twenty-first day of the 2
seventh month, these words came from the LORD through the prophet
Haggai: Say to Zerubbabel son of Shealtiel, governor of Judah, to 2
Joshua son of Jehozadak, the high priest, and to the rest of the people:
Is there anyone still among you who saw this house in its former glory? 3
How does it appear to you now? Does it not seem to you as if it were not
there? But now, Zerubbabel, take heart, says the LORD; take heart, 4
Joshua son of Jehozadak, high priest. Take heart, all you people,
says the LORD. Begin the work, for I am with you, says the LORD of
Hosts,^a and my spirit is present among you. Have no fear. For these are 5,6
the words of the LORD of Hosts: One thing more:^bI will shake heaven
and earth, sea and land, I will shake all nations; the treasure of all nations 7
shall come hither, and I will fill this house with glory;^c so says the
LORD of Hosts. Mine is the silver and mine the gold, says the LORD of 8
Hosts, and the glory^c of this latter house shall surpass the glory^c of the 9
former, says the LORD of Hosts. In this place will I grant prosperity and
peace. This is the very word of the LORD of Hosts.

In the second year of Darius, on the twenty-fourth day of the ninth 10
month, this word came from the LORD to the prophet Haggai: These are 11
the words of the LORD of Hosts: Ask the priests to give their ruling:
If a man is carrying consecrated flesh in a fold of his robe, and he lets the 12
fold touch bread or broth or wine or oil or any other kind of food, will
that also become consecrated? And the priests answered, 'No.' Haggai 13
went on, But if a person defiled by contact with a corpse touches any
one of these things, will that also become defiled? 'It will', answered the
priests. Haggai replied, So it is with this people and nation and all that 14
they do, says the LORD; whatever offering they make here is defiled in
my sight. And now look back over recent times down to this day: 15
before one stone was laid on another in the LORD's temple, what was 16
your plight? If a man came to a heap of corn expecting twenty measures,
he found but ten; if he came to a wine-vat to draw fifty measures,^d he
found but twenty. I blasted you and all your harvest with black blight 17
and red and with hail, and yet you had no mind to return to me, says the
LORD. Consider, from this day onwards, from this twenty-fourth day of 18
the ninth month, the day when the foundations of the temple of the
LORD are laid, consider: will the seed still be diminished^e in the barn? 19
Will the vine and the fig, the pomegranate and the olive, still bear no
fruit? Not so, from this day I will bless you.

On that day, the twenty-fourth day of the month, the word of the 20
LORD came to Haggai a second time: Tell Zerubbabel, governor of 21

[a] *So Sept.; Heb. adds* the thing I covenanted with you when you came out of Egypt.
[b] *So Sept.; Heb. adds* and that a little thing. [c] *Or* wealth. [d] *So Pesh.; Heb. adds*
winepress. [e] diminished: *prob. rdg.; Heb. om.*

22 Judah, I will shake heaven and earth; I will overthrow the thrones of
kings, break the power of heathen realms, overturn chariots and their
riders; horses and riders shall fall by the sword of their comrades.

23 On that day, says the LORD of Hosts, I will take you, Zerubbabel son of
Shealtiel, my servant, and will wear you as a signet-ring; for you it is
that I have chosen. This is the very word of the LORD of Hosts.

ZECHARIAH

Zechariah's commission

IN THE EIGHTH MONTH of the second year of Darius, the 1
word of the LORD came to the prophet Zechariah son of Berechiah,
son of Iddo: The LORD was very angry with your forefathers. Say to 2,3
the people, These are the words of the LORD of Hosts: Come back to
me, and I will come back to you, says the LORD of Hosts. Do not be like 4
your forefathers. They heard the prophets of old proclaim, 'These are
the words of the LORD of Hosts: Turn back from your evil ways and
your evil deeds.' But they did not listen or pay heed to me, says the
LORD. And where are your forefathers now? And the prophets, do they 5
live for ever? But the warnings and the decrees with which I charged 6
my servants the prophets—did not these overtake your forefathers?
Did they not then repent and say, 'The LORD of Hosts has treated us as
he purposed; as our lives and as our deeds deserved, so has he treated
us'?

Eight visions with their interpretations

ON THE TWENTY-FOURTH DAY of the eleventh month, the 7
month Shebat, in the second year of Darius, the word of the
LORD came to the prophet Zechariah son of Berechiah, son of Iddo.
  Last night I had a vision. I saw a man on a bay horse standing among 8
the myrtles in a hollow; and behind him were other horses, black,
dappled,*a* and white. 'What are these, sir?' I asked, and the angel who 9
talked with me answered, 'I will show you what they are.' Then the 10
man standing among the myrtles said, 'They are those whom the LORD
has sent to range through the world.' They reported to the angel of 11
the LORD as he stood among the myrtles: 'We have ranged through the
world; the whole world is still and at peace.' Thereupon the angel of the 12
LORD said, 'How long, O LORD of Hosts, wilt thou withhold thy compassion from Jerusalem and the cities of Judah, upon whom thou hast
vented thy wrath these seventy years?' Then the LORD spoke kind and 13
comforting words to the angel who talked with me, and the angel said to 14
me, Proclaim, These are the words of the LORD of Hosts: I am very

[a] black, dappled: *prob. rdg., cp. Sept.; Heb.* bay, sorrel.

15 jealous for Jerusalem and Zion. I am full of anger against the nations that enjoy their ease, because, while my anger was but mild, they heaped
16 evil on evil. Therefore these are the words of the LORD: I have come back to Jerusalem with compassion, and my house shall be rebuilt in her, says the LORD of Hosts, and the measuring-line shall be stretched
17 over Jerusalem. Proclaim once more, These are the words of the LORD of Hosts: My cities shall again overflow with good things; once again the LORD will comfort Zion, once again he will make Jerusalem the city of his choice.

18,[a] 19   I lifted my eyes and there I saw four horns. I asked the angel who talked with me what they were, and he answered, 'These are the horns
20 which scattered Judah[b] and Jerusalem.' Then the LORD showed me
21 four smiths. I asked what they were coming to do, and he said, 'Those horns scattered Judah and Jerusalem[c] so completely that no man could lift his head. But these smiths have come to reunite them and to throw down the horns of the nations which had raised them against the land of Judah and scattered its people.'

2   I lifted my eyes and there I saw a man carrying a measuring-line.
2 I asked him where he was going, and he said, 'To measure Jerusalem and
3 see what should be its breadth and length.' Then, as the angel who talked
4 with me was going away, another angel came out to meet him and said to him, Run to the young man there and tell him that Jerusalem shall be a city
5 without walls, so numerous shall be the men and cattle within it. I will be a wall of fire round her, says the LORD, and a glory in the midst of her.
6   Away, away; flee from the land of the north, says the LORD, for I will make you spread your wings like the four winds of heaven, says the
7 LORD. Away, escape, you people of Zion who live in Babylon.
8   For these are the words of the LORD of Hosts, spoken when he sent me on a glorious mission[d] to the nations who have plundered you, for
9 whoever touches you touches the apple of his eye: I raise[e] my hand against them; they shall be plunder for their own slaves. So you shall
10 know that the LORD of Hosts has sent me. Shout aloud and rejoice, daughter of Zion; I am coming, I will make my dwelling among you,
11 says the LORD. Many nations shall come over to the LORD on that day and become his people, and he[f] will make his dwelling with you. Then
12 you shall know that the LORD of Hosts has sent me to you. The LORD will once again claim Judah as his own possession in the holy land, and make Jerusalem the city of his choice.
13   Silence, all mankind, in the presence of the LORD! For he has bestirred himself out of his holy dwelling-place.

[a] 2. 1 in Heb.   [b] Prob. rdg.; Heb. adds Israel.   [c] and Jerusalem: so some Sept. MSS.; Heb. om.   [d] on a glorious mission: prob. rdg.; Heb. after glory.   [e] Or wave.   [f] his... he: so Pesh.; Heb. my...I; or, with Sept., his...they.

The angel who talked with me came back and roused me as a man is 4 1[a]
roused from sleep. He asked me what I saw, and I answered, 'A lamp- 2
stand all of gold with a bowl on it; it holds seven lamps, and there are
seven pipes[b] for the lamps on top of it, with two olive-trees standing by 3
it, one on the right of the bowl and another on the left.' I asked him, 11[c]
'What are these two olive-trees, the one on the right and the other on
the left of the lamp-stand?' I asked also another question, 'What are 12
the two sprays of olive beside the golden pipes which discharge the
golden oil from their bowls[d]?' He said, 'Do you not know what these 13
mean?' 'No, sir', I answered. 'These two', he said, 'are the two con- 14
secrated with oil[e] who attend the Lord of all the earth.'

Then he showed me Joshua the high priest standing before the angel 3 1
of the LORD, with the Adversary[f] standing at his right hand to accuse
him. The LORD said to the Adversary, 'The LORD rebuke you, Satan, 2
the LORD rebuke you who are venting your spite on Jerusalem.[g] Is not
this man a brand snatched from the fire?' Now Joshua was wearing 3
filthy clothes as he stood before the angel; and the angel turned and 4
said to those in attendance on him, 'Take off his filthy clothes.' Then he
turned to him and said, 'See how I have taken away your guilt from
you; I will clothe you in fine vestments'; and he[h] added, 'Let a clean 5
turban be put on his head.' So they put a clean turban on his head and
clothed him in clean[i] garments, while the angel of the LORD stood by.
Then the angel of the LORD gave Joshua this solemn charge: These are 6,7
the words of the LORD of Hosts: If you will conform to my ways and
carry out your duties, you shall administer my house and be in control
of my courts, and I grant you the right to come and go amongst these in
attendance here. Listen, Joshua the high priest, you and your colleagues 8
seated here before you, all you who are an omen of things to come: I
will now bring my servant, the Branch. In one day I will wipe away the 9–10
guilt of the land. On that day, says the LORD of Hosts, you shall all of you
invite one another to come and sit each under his vine and his fig-tree.

Here is the stone that I set before Joshua, a stone in which are seven
eyes. I will reveal its meaning to you, says the LORD of Hosts. Then I 4 4[j]
asked the angel of the LORD who talked with me, 'Sir, what are these?'
And he answered, 'Do you not know what these mean?' 'No, sir', I 5
answered. 'These seven', he said, 'are the eyes of the LORD ranging over
the whole earth.'[k]

Then he turned and said to me, This is the word of the LORD con- 6
cerning Zerubbabel: Neither by force of arms nor by brute strength,

[a] *3. 1–10 transposed to follow 4. 14.*   [b] seven pipes: *so Sept.; Heb.* seven pipes each.
[c] *4. 4–10 transposed to follow 3. 10.*   [d] their bowls: *lit.* upon them.   [e] *Lit.* two sons of oil.
[f] *Heb.* the Satan.   [g] the LORD...Jerusalem: *or* the LORD who has chosen Jerusalem
rebuke you.   [h] *So Pesh.; Heb.* I.   [i] clean: *prob. rdg., cp. Pesh.; Heb. om.*   [j] *See note
on 4. 11 above.*   [k] These seven...earth: *transposed from verse 10.*

7 but by my spirit! says the LORD of Hosts. How does a mountain, the greatest mountain, compare with Zerubbabel? It is no higher than a plain. He shall bring out the stone called Possession[a][b] while men
8,9 acclaim its beauty. This word came to me from the LORD: Zerubbabel with his own hands laid the foundation of this house and with his own hands he shall finish it. So shall you know that the LORD of Hosts has
10 sent me to you. Who has despised the day of small things? He shall rejoice when he sees Zerubbabel holding the stone called Separation.[b]

5 1,2 I looked up again and saw a flying scroll. He asked me what I saw, and I answered, 'A flying scroll, twenty cubits long and ten cubits wide.'
3 This, he told me, is the curse which goes out over the whole land; for by the writing on one side every thief shall be swept clean away, and by the
4 writing on the other every perjurer shall be swept clean away. I have sent it out, the LORD of Hosts has said, and it shall enter the house of the thief and the house of the man who has perjured himself in my name; it shall stay inside that house and demolish it, timbers and stones and all.
5 The angel who talked with me came out and said to me, 'Raise your
6 eyes and look at this thing that comes forth.' I asked what it was, and he said, 'It is a great barrel[c] coming forth,' and he added, 'so great is their
7 guilt[d] in all the land.' Then a round slab of lead was lifted, and a woman
8 was sitting there inside the barrel. He said, 'This is Wickedness', and he thrust her down into the barrel and rammed the leaden weight upon
9 its mouth. I looked up again and saw two women coming forth with the wind in their wings (for they had wings like a stork's), and they carried
10 the barrel between earth and sky. I asked the angel who talked with me
11 where they were taking the barrel, and he answered, 'To build a house for it[e] in the land of Shinar; when the house is ready, it[f] shall be set on the place prepared for it[e] there.'

6 I looked up again and saw four chariots coming out between two
2 mountains, and the mountains were made of copper.[g] The first chariot
3 had bay horses, the second black, the third white, and the fourth
4 dappled.[h] I asked the angel who talked with me, 'Sir, what are these?'
5 He answered, 'These are the four winds of heaven which have been attending the Lord of the whole earth, and they are now going forth.
6 The chariot with the black horses is going to the land of the north, that with the white to the far west,[i] that with the dappled to the south,
7 and that with the roan to the land of the east.'[j] They were eager to go and range over the whole earth; so he said, 'Go and range over the
8 earth', and the chariots did so. Then he called me to look and said,

[a] So Sept.; Heb. Top. [b] Cp. Lev. 20. 24–26. [c] a great barrel: Heb. an ephah. [d] guilt: so Sept.; Heb. eye. [e] Or her. [f] Or she. [g] Or bronze. [h] Prob. rdg., cp. Sept.; Heb. adds roan. [i] to the far west: prob. rdg.; Heb. behind them. [j] to the land of the east: prob. rdg.; Heb. om.

'Those going to the land of the north have given my spirit rest in the land of the north.'

The word of the LORD came to me: Take silver and gold from the 9, 10 exiles, from Heldai, Tobiah, Jedaiah, and*a* Josiah son of Zephaniah, who have come back from Babylon. Take it and make a crown;*b* put the 11 crown on the head of Joshua son of Jehozadak, the high priest,*c* and say 12 to him, These are the words of the LORD of Hosts: Here is a man named the Branch; he will shoot up from the ground where he is and will build the temple of the LORD. It is he who will build the temple of the LORD, 13 he who will assume royal dignity, will be seated on his throne and govern, with a priest at his right side,*d* and concord shall prevail between them. The crown shall be in the charge of Heldai,*e* Tobiah, Jedaiah, 14 and Josiah*f* son of Zephaniah, as a memorial in the temple of the LORD.

Men from far away shall come and work on the building of the 15 temple of the LORD; so shall you know that the LORD of Hosts has sent me to you. If only you will obey the LORD your God!

Joy and gladness in the coming age

THE WORD OF THE LORD came to Zechariah in the fourth year of 7 the reign of King Darius, on the fourth day of Kislev, the ninth month. Bethel-sharezer sent Regem-melech with his men to seek the 2 favour of the LORD. They were to say to the priests in the house 3 of the LORD of Hosts and to the prophets, 'Am I to lament and abstain in the fifth month as I have done for so many years?' Then the word 4 of the LORD of Hosts came to me: Say to all the people of the land and 5 to the priests, When you fasted and lamented in the fifth and seventh months these seventy years, was it indeed in my honour that you fasted? And when you ate and drank, was it not to please yourselves? Was it 6, 7 not this that the LORD proclaimed through the prophets of old, while Jerusalem was populous and peaceful, as were the cities round her, and the Negeb and the Shephelah?

The word of the LORD came to Zechariah: These are the words of the 8, 9 LORD of Hosts: Administer true justice, show loyalty and compassion to one another, do not oppress the orphan and the widow, the alien and 10 the poor, do not contrive any evil one against another. But they refused 11 to listen, they turned their backs on me in defiance, they stopped their

[a] and: *prob. rdg.; Heb.* and go on that day yourself and go to the house of... [b] *So Pesh.; Heb.* crowns. [c] Joshua...priest: *possibly an error for* Zerubbabel son of Shealtiel, *cp. 3. 5; 4. 9.* [d] at...side: *so Sept.; Heb.* on his throne. [e] *So Pesh.; Heb.* Helem. [f] *So Pesh.; Heb.* favour.

12 ears and would not hear. Their hearts were adamant; they refused to accept instruction and all that the LORD of Hosts had taught them by his spirit through the prophets of old; and they suffered under the anger
13 of the LORD of Hosts. As they did not listen when I[a] called, so I did not
14 listen when they called, says the LORD of Hosts, and I drove them out among all the nations to whom they were strangers, leaving their land a waste behind them, so that no one came and went. Thus they made their pleasant land a waste.

8 1,2   The word of the LORD of Hosts came to me: These are the words of the LORD of Hosts: I have been very jealous for Zion, fiercely jealous for
3 her. Now, says the LORD, I have come back to Zion and I will dwell in Jerusalem. Jerusalem shall be called the City of Truth, and the moun-
4 tain of the LORD of Hosts shall be called the Holy Mountain. These are the words of the LORD of Hosts: Once again shall old men and old women sit in the streets of Jerusalem, each leaning on a stick because of
5 their great age; and the streets of the city shall be full of boys and girls,
6 playing in the streets. These are the words of the LORD of Hosts: Even if it may seem impossible[b] to the survivors of this nation on that day, will it also seem impossible to me?[c] This is the very word of the LORD
7 of Hosts. These are the words of the LORD of Hosts: See, I will rescue
8 my people from the countries of the east and the west, and bring them back to live in Jerusalem. They shall be my people, and I will be their God, in truth and justice.

9   These are the words of the LORD of Hosts: Take courage, you who in these days hear, from the prophets who were present when the founda-tions were laid for the house of the LORD of Hosts, their promise that
10 the temple is to be rebuilt. Till that time there was no hiring either of man or of beast, no one could safely go about his business because of
11 his enemies, and I set all men one against another. But now I am not the same towards the survivors of this people as I was in former days, says
12 the LORD of Hosts. For they shall sow in safety; the vine shall yield its fruit and the soil its produce, the heavens shall give their dew; with all
13 these things I will endow the survivors of this people. You, house of Judah and house of Israel, have been the very symbol of a curse to all the nations; and now I will save you, and you shall become the symbol of a blessing. Courage! Do not be afraid.

14   For these are the words of the LORD of Hosts: Whereas I resolved to ruin you because your ancestors roused me to anger, says the LORD of
15 Hosts, and I did not relent, so in these days I have once more[d] resolved to do good to Jerusalem and to the house of Judah; do not be afraid.
16 This is what you shall do: speak the truth to each other, administer true

[a] *Prob. rdg.; Heb.* he.   [b] *Or* wonderful.   [c] will...me?: *or* it will seem wonderful also to me.   [d] once more: *or* changed my mind and.

and sound justice in the city gate. Do not contrive any evil one against 17
another, and do not love perjury, for all this I hate. This is the very
word of the LORD.

The word of the LORD of Hosts came to me: These are the words of 18, 19
the LORD of Hosts: The fasts of the fourth month and of the fifth, the
seventh, and the tenth, shall become festivals of joy and gladness for the
house of Judah. Love truth and peace.

These are the words of the LORD of Hosts: Nations and dwellers in 20
great cities shall yet come; people of one city shall come to those of 21
another and say, 'Let us go and entreat the favour of the LORD, and
resort to the LORD of Hosts; and I will come too.' So great nations 22
and mighty peoples shall resort to the LORD of Hosts in Jerusalem and
entreat his favour. These are the words of the LORD of Hosts: In those 23
days, when ten men from nations of every language pluck up courage,
they shall pluck the robe of a Jew and say, 'We will go with you because
we have heard that God is with you.'

Judah's triumph over her enemies

An oracle: the word of the LORD.   9

He has come to the land of Hadrach
and*ᵃ* established himself in Damascus;
   for the capital city*ᵇ* of Aram*ᶜ* is the LORD's,
   as are all the tribes of Israel.
*ᵈ*Sidon has closed her frontier against Hamath,   2
   for she is very wary.
Tyre has built herself a rampart;   3
she has heaped up silver like dust
   and gold like mud in the streets.
But wait, the Lord will dispossess her   4
and strike down the power of her ships,
and the city itself will be destroyed by fire.
Let Ashkelon see it and be afraid;   5
Gaza shall writhe in terror,
and Ekron's hope shall be extinguished;
kings shall vanish from Gaza,
   and Ashkelon shall be unpeopled;
half-breeds shall settle in Ashdod,   6
and I will uproot the pride of the Philistine.

[a] He has come...and: *prob. rdg.; Heb.* In the land of Hadrach he has...   [b] capital city:
or chief part.   [c] *So one MS.; others* mankind.   [d] *Prob. rdg.; Heb. prefixes* Tyre and.

7   I will dash the blood of sacrifices from his mouth
    and his loathsome offerings from his teeth;
    and his survivors shall belong[a] to our God
    and become like a clan in Judah,
      and Ekron like a Jebusite.

8   And I will post a garrison for my house
      so that no one may pass in or out,
    and no oppressor shall ever overrun them.
    [This I have lived to see with my own eyes.]

9   Rejoice, rejoice, daughter of Zion,
    shout aloud, daughter of Jerusalem;
    for see, your king is coming to you,
    his cause won, his victory gained,
    humble[b] and mounted on an ass,
    on a foal, the young of a she-ass.

10   He[c] shall banish chariots from Ephraim
      and war-horses from Jerusalem;
    the warrior's bow shall be banished.
    He shall speak peaceably to every nation,
    and his rule shall extend from sea to sea,
    from the River to the ends of the earth.

11   And as for you, by your covenant with me sealed in blood
    I release your prisoners from the dungeon.[d]

12   (Come back to the stronghold, you prisoners who wait in hope.)
    Now is the day announced
    when I will grant you twofold[e] reparation.

13   For my bow is strung, O Judah;
    I have laid the arrow to it, O Ephraim;
    I have roused your sons, O Zion,[f]
    and made you into the sword of a warrior.

14   The LORD shall appear above them,
    and his arrow shall flash like lightning;
    the Lord GOD shall blow a blast on the horn
    and march with the storm-winds of the south.

15   The LORD of Hosts will be their shield;
    they shall prevail,[g] they shall trample on the sling-stones;
    they shall be roaring drunk as if with wine,
    brimful as a bowl, drenched like the corners of the altar.

16   So on that day the LORD their God

---

[a] his survivors shall belong: *or* he shall become kin. [b] *So Sept.; Heb.* afflicted. [c] *So Sept.; Heb.* I. [d] *Prob. rdg.; Heb. adds* no water in it. [e] *Or* equal. [f] *Prob. rdg.; Heb. adds* against your sons, O Javan (*or* Greece). [g] *Prob. rdg., cp. Targ.; Heb.* they shall devour.

will save them, his own people, like sheep,
 setting them all about his land,
  like*^a* jewels set to sparkle in a crown.

What wealth, what beauty, is theirs: 17
corn to strengthen young men,
 and new wine for maidens!
Ask of the LORD rain in the autumn,*^b*   10
ask him for rain in the spring,
the LORD who makes the storm-clouds,
and he will give you*^c* showers of rain
and to every man grass in his field;
for the household gods*^d* make mischievous promises; 2
diviners see false signs,
they tell lying dreams*^e*
 and talk raving nonsense.
Men wander about like sheep
in distress for lack of a shepherd.
My anger is turned against the shepherds,   3
 and I will visit with punishment the leaders of the flock;*^f*
but the LORD of Hosts will visit his flock,
 the house of Judah,
and make them his royal war-horses.
They shall be corner-stone and tent-peg,   4
they shall be the bow ready for battle,
and from them shall come every commander.
Together they shall be like warriors   5
who tramp the muddy ways in battle,
and they will fight because the LORD is with them;
they will put horsemen shamefully to rout.
And I will give strength to the house of Judah   6
and grant victory to*^g* the house of Joseph;
I will restore them, for I have pitied them,
and they shall be as though I had never cast them off;
for I am the LORD their God and I will answer them.
So Ephraim shall be like warriors,   7
glad like men cheerful with wine,
and their sons shall see and be glad;
so let their hearts exult in the LORD.
I will whistle to call them in, for I have redeemed them; 8
and they shall be as many as once they were.

[a] like: *prob. rdg.; Heb.* for. [b] rain in the autumn: *so Sept.; Heb. om.* [c] *So Pesh.; Heb.* them. [d] *Heb.* teraphim. [e] they...dreams: *or* dreaming women make empty promises. [f] leaders of the flock: *lit.* bucks. [g] grant victory to: *or* expand.

9   If I disperse them*a* among the nations,
           in far-off lands they will remember me
           and will rear their sons and then return.
10   Then will I fetch them home from Egypt
           and gather them in from Assyria;
           I will lead them into Gilead and Lebanon
           until there is no more room for them.
11   Dire distress*b* shall come upon the Euphrates*c*
           and shall beat down its turbulent waters;
           all the depths of the Nile shall run dry.
           The pride of Assyria shall be brought down,
           and the sceptre of Egypt shall pass away;
12   but Israel's strength shall be in the LORD,
             and they shall march proudly in his name.
           This is the very word of the LORD.

11   Throw open your gates, O Lebanon,
             that fire may feed on your cedars.
2   Howl, every pine-tree; for the cedars have fallen,
           mighty trees are ravaged.
           Howl, every oak of Bashan;
           for the impenetrable forest is laid low.
3   Hark to the howling of the shepherds,
           for their rich pastures are ravaged.
           Hark to the roar of the young lions,
           for Jordan's dense thickets are ravaged.

4   These were the words of the LORD my God: Fatten the flock for
5   slaughter. Those who buy will slaughter it and incur no guilt; those
    who sell will say, 'Blessed be the LORD, I am rich!' Its shepherds will
6   have no pity for it. For I will never again pity the inhabitants of the
    earth, says the LORD. I will put every man in the power of his neighbour
    and his king, and as each country is crushed I will not rescue him from
    their hands.
7   So I fattened the flock for slaughter for the dealers. I took two staves:
    one I called Favour and the other Union, and so I fattened the flock.
8   In one month I got rid of the three shepherds, for I had lost patience
9   with them and they had come to abhor me. Then I said to the flock, 'I
    will not fatten you any more. Any that are to die, let them die; any that
10 stray, let them stray; and the rest can devour one another.' I took my
    staff called Favour and snapped it in two, annulling the covenant
11 which the LORD*d* had made with all nations. So it was annulled that

[a] *Or* scatter them like seed.   [b] Dire distress: *or* An enemy.   [c] *Lit.* the sea.   [d] the
LORD: *prob. rdg.; Heb.* I.

day, and the dealers who were watching me knew that all this was the
word of the LORD. I said to them, 'If it suits you, give me my wages; 12
otherwise keep them.' Then they weighed out my wages, thirty pieces of
silver. The LORD said to me, 'Throw it into the treasury.'*a* I took the 13
thirty pieces of silver—that noble sum at which I was valued and
rejected by them!—and threw them into the house of the LORD, into
the treasury.*a* Then I snapped in two my second staff called Union, 14
annulling the brotherhood between Judah and Israel.

Then the LORD said to me, Equip yourself again as a shepherd, a 15
worthless one; for I am about to install a shepherd in the land who will 16
neither miss any that are lost nor search for those that have gone astray
nor heal the injured nor nurse the sickly, but will eat the flesh of the fat
beasts and throw away their broken bones.

Alas for the worthless shepherd who abandons the sheep!   17
A sword shall fall on his arm and on his right eye;
  his arm shall be shrivelled
  and his right eye blinded.
    This is the very word of the LORD of Hosts: 13 7*b*
  O sword, awake against my shepherd
    and against him who works with me.
Strike the shepherd, and the sheep will be scattered,
  and I will turn my hand against the shepherd boys.
    This also is the very word of the LORD: 8
    It shall happen throughout the land
that two thirds of the people shall be struck down and die,
  while one third of them shall be left there.
Then I will pass this third through the fire   9
  and I will refine them as silver is refined,
  and assay them as gold is assayed.
Then they will invoke me by my name,
  and I myself will answer them;
I will say,*c* 'They are my people',
and they shall say, 'The LORD is our God.'

Jerusalem a centre of worship for all men

AN ORACLE. This is the word of the LORD concerning Israel, the 12
very word of the LORD who stretched out the heavens and founded
the earth, and who formed the spirit of man within him: I am making 2

[*a*] *So Pesh.; Heb.* to the potter: *or, with Sept.,* into the (temple-)foundry. [*b*] *13. 7–9
transposed to this point.* [*c*] *So Sept.; Heb.* have said.

the steep approaches*a* to Jerusalem slippery for all the nations pressing round her; and*b* Judah will be caught up in the siege of Jerusalem.

3 On that day, when all the nations of the earth will be gathered against her, I will make Jerusalem a rock too heavy for any people to remove,

4 and all who try to lift it shall injure themselves. On that day, says the LORD, I will strike every horse with panic and its rider with madness; I will keep watch over Judah, but I will strike all the horses of the other

5 nations with blindness. Then the clans of Judah shall say to themselves, 'The inhabitants of Jerusalem find their strength*c* in the LORD of Hosts their God.'

6 On that day I will make the clans of Judah like a brazier in woodland, like a torch blazing among sheaves of corn. They shall devour all the nations round them, right and left, while the people of Jerusalem re-

7 main safe in their city. The LORD will first set free all the families*d* of Judah, so that the glory of David's line and of the inhabitants of Jerusalem may not surpass that of Judah.

8 On that day the LORD will shield the inhabitants of Jerusalem; on that day the very weakest of them shall be like David, and the line of David like God, like the angel of the LORD going before them.

9 On that day I will set about destroying all the nations that come

10 against Jerusalem, but I will pour a spirit of pity and compassion into the line of David and the inhabitants of Jerusalem. Then

They shall look on me, on him whom they have pierced,

and shall wail over him as over an only child, and shall grieve for him bitterly as for a first-born son.

11 On that day the mourning in Jerusalem shall be as great as the

12 mourning over Hadad-rimmon in the vale of Megiddo. The land shall wail, each family by itself: the family of David by itself and its women by themselves; the family of Nathan by itself and its women by them-

13 selves; the family of Levi by itself and its women by themselves; the

14 family of Shimei by itself and its women by themselves; all the remaining families by themselves and their women by themselves.

13 On that day a fountain shall be opened for the line of David and for the inhabitants of Jerusalem, to remove all sin and impurity.

2 On that day, says the LORD of Hosts, I will erase the names of the idols from the land, and they shall be remembered no longer; I will also

3 remove the prophets and the spirit of uncleanness from the land. Thereafter, if a man continues to prophesy, his parents, his own father and mother, will say to him, 'You shall live no longer, for you have spoken falsely in the name of the LORD.' His own father and mother will pierce

---

[*a*] approaches: *lit.* threshold.   [*b*] *So Vulg.; Heb. adds* against.   [*c*] The...strength: *prob. rdg.; Heb.* O inhabitants of Jerusalem, I am strong.   [*d*] *Or* tents.

him through because he has prophesied. On that day every prophet shall 4
be ashamed of his vision when he prophesies, nor shall he wear a robe of
coarse hair in order to deceive. He will say, 'I am no prophet, I am a 5
tiller of the soil who has been schooled in lust from boyhood.' 'What', 6
someone will ask, 'are these scars on your chest?' And he will answer,
'I got them in the house of my lovers.'*a*

A day is coming for the LORD to act, and the plunder taken from you 14
shall be shared out while you stand by. I will gather all the peoples to 2
fight against Jerusalem; the city shall be taken, the houses plundered
and the women raped. Half the city shall go into exile, but the rest of
the nation in the city shall not be wiped out. The LORD will come out 3
and fight against those peoples, as in the days of his prowess on the field
of battle. On that day his feet will stand on the Mount of Olives, which 4
is opposite Jerusalem to the east, and the mountain shall be cleft in two
by an immense valley running east and west; half the mountain shall
move northwards and half southwards. The valley between the hills*b* 5
shall be blocked, for the new valley between them will reach as far as
Asal. Blocked it shall be as it was blocked by the earthquake in the time
of Uzziah king of Judah, and the LORD my God will appear with*c* all
the holy ones.

On that day there shall be neither heat nor cold*d* nor frost. It shall be 6,7
all one day, whose coming is known only to the LORD, without distinction of day or night, and at evening-time there shall be light.

On that day living water shall issue from Jerusalem, half flowing to 8
the eastern sea and half to the western, in summer and winter alike.
Then the LORD shall become king over all the earth; on that day the 9
LORD shall be one LORD and his name the one name. The whole land 10
shall be levelled, flat as the Arabah from Geba to Rimmon southwards;
but Jerusalem shall stand high in her place, and shall be full of people
from the Benjamin Gate [to the point where the former gate stood,] to
the Corner Gate, and from the Tower of Hananel to the king's wine-
vats. Men shall live in Jerusalem, and never again shall a solemn ban be 11
laid upon her; men shall live there in peace. The LORD will strike down 12
all the nations who warred against Jerusalem, and the plague shall be
this: their flesh shall rot while they stand on their feet, their eyes shall
rot in their sockets, and their tongues shall rot in their mouths.

On that day a great panic, sent by the LORD, shall fall on them. At the 13
very moment when a man would encourage his comrade his hand shall
be raised to strike him down. Judah too shall join in the fray in Jeru- 14
salem, and the wealth of the surrounding nations will be swept away—
gold and silver and apparel in great abundance. And slaughter shall be 15

[a] *Verses 7–9 transposed to follow 11. 17.* [b] *Prob. rdg.; Heb.* my hills. [c] *So Sept.; Heb.*
with thee. [d] cold: *so Sept.; Heb.* precious things.

the fate of horse and mule, camel and ass, the fate of every beast in those armies.

16 All who survive of the nations which attacked Jerusalem shall come up year by year to worship the King, the LORD of Hosts, and to keep the

17 pilgrim-feast of Tabernacles. If any of the families of the earth do not go up to Jerusalem to worship the King, the LORD of Hosts, no rain shall

18 fall upon them. If any family of Egypt does not go up and enter the city, then the same disaster shall[a] overtake it as that which the LORD will

19 inflict on any nation which does not go up to keep the feast. This shall be the punishment of Egypt and of any nation which does not go up to keep the feast of Tabernacles.

20 On that day, not a bell on a war-horse but shall be inscribed 'Holy to the LORD', and the pots in the house of the LORD shall be like the bowls

21 before the altar. Every pot in Jerusalem and Judah shall be holy to the LORD of Hosts, and all who sacrifice shall come and shall take some of them and boil the flesh in them. So when that time comes, no trader shall again be seen in the house of the LORD of Hosts.

[a] *So Sept.; Heb. adds* not.

MALACHI

An oracle. The word of the LORD to Israel through Malachi.*a* **1**

Religious decline and hope of recovery

I LOVE YOU, says the LORD. You ask, 'How hast thou shown love to 2
us?' Is not Esau Jacob's brother? the LORD answers. I love Jacob, but 3
I hate Esau; I have turned his mountains into a waste and his ancestral
home into a lodging*b* in the wilderness. When Edom says, 'We are 4
beaten down; let us rebuild our ruined homes', these are the words of
the LORD of Hosts: If they rebuild, I will pull down. They shall be
called a realm of wickedness, a people whom the LORD has cursed for
ever. You yourselves will see it with your own eyes; you yourselves 5
will say, 'The LORD's greatness reaches beyond the realm of Israel.'
    A son honours his father, and a slave goes in fear of*c* his master. If I 6
am a father, where is the honour due to me? If I am a master, where is
the fear due to me? So says the LORD of Hosts to you, you priests who
despise my name. You ask, 'How have we despised thy name?' Because 7
you have offered defiled food on my altar. You ask, 'How have we
defiled thee?' Because you have thought that the table of the LORD may
be despised, that if you offer a blind victim, there is nothing wrong, and 8
if you offer a victim lame or diseased, there is nothing wrong. If you
brought such a gift to the governor, would he receive you or show you
favour? says the LORD of Hosts. But now, if you placate God, he may 9
show you mercy; if you do this, will he withhold his favour from you?
So the LORD of Hosts has spoken. Better far that one of you should close 10
the great door altogether, so that the light might not fall thus all in vain
upon my altar! I have no pleasure in you, says the LORD of Hosts; I will
accept no offering from you. From furthest east to furthest west my 11
name is great among the nations. Everywhere fragrant sacrifice and pure
gifts are offered in my name; for my name is great among the nations,
says the LORD of Hosts. But you profane it by thinking that the table 12
of the LORD may be defiled, and that you can offer on it food*d* you

[*a*] Malachi: *or* my messenger.   [*b*] a lodging: *prob. rdg., cp. Sept.; Heb.* she-jackals.
[*c*] goes in fear of: *so one form of Sept.; Heb. om.*   [*d*] *Prob. rdg., cp. Targ.; Heb. adds* its
produce.

13 yourselves despise. You sniff at it, says the LORD of Hosts, and say, 'How irksome!' If you bring as your offering victims that are mutilated,

14 lame, or diseased, shall I accept them from you? says the LORD. A curse on the cheat who pays his vows by sacrificing a damaged victim to the LORD, though he has a sound ram in his flock! I am the great king, says the LORD of Hosts, and my name is held in awe among the nations.

2 1,2 And now, you priests, this decree is for you: if you will not listen to me and pay heed to the honouring of my name, says the LORD of Hosts, then I will lay a curse upon you. I will turn your blessings into a curse;

3 yes, into a curse, because you pay no heed. I will cut off*a* your arm,*b* fling offal in your faces, the offal of your pilgrim-feasts, and I will

4 banish you from my presence.*c* Then you will know that I have issued this decree against you: my covenant with Levi falls to the ground, says

5 the LORD of Hosts. My covenant was with him: I bestowed life and prosperity on him; I laid on him the duty of reverence, he revered me

6 and lived in awe of my name. The instruction he gave was true, and no word of injustice fell from his lips; he walked in harmony with me

7 and in uprightness, and he turned many back from sin. For men hang upon the words of the priest and seek knowledge and instruction from

8 him, because he is the messenger of the LORD of Hosts. But you have turned away from that course; you have made many stumble with your instruction; you have set at nought the covenant with the Levites, says

9 the LORD of Hosts. So I, in my turn, have made you despicable and mean in the eyes of the people, in so far as you disregard my ways and show partiality in your instruction.

10 Have we not all one father? Did not one God create us? Why do we violate the covenant of our forefathers by being faithless to one another?

11 Judah is faithless, and abominable things are done in Israel and in Jerusalem; Judah has violated the holiness of the LORD by loving and

12 marrying daughters of a foreign god. May the LORD banish any who do this from the dwellings of Jacob, nomads or settlers, even though they bring offerings to the LORD of Hosts.

13 Here is another thing that you do: you weep and moan, and you drown the altar of the LORD with tears, but he still refuses to look at the

14 offering or receive an acceptable gift from you. You ask why. It is because the LORD has borne witness against you on behalf of the wife of your youth. You have been unfaithful to her, though she is your partner

15 and your wife by solemn covenant. Did not the one God make her, both flesh and spirit? And what does the one God require but godly children? Keep watch on your spirit, and do not be*d* unfaithful to the wife of your

16 youth. If a man divorces or puts away his spouse, he overwhelms her

[a] cut off: *so Sept.; Heb.* rebuke. [b] *Or* posterity. [c] and...presence: *prob. rdg., cp. Sept.; Heb.* and he will take you away unto him. [d] *So Sept.; Heb.* let him not be.

with cruelty, says the LORD of Hosts the God of Israel. Keep watch on
your spirit, and do not be unfaithful.

You have wearied the LORD with your talk. You ask, 'How have we 17
wearied him?' By saying that all evildoers are good in the eyes of the
LORD, that he is pleased with them, or by asking, 'Where is the God of
justice?' Look, I am sending my messenger*a* who will clear a path 3
before me. Suddenly the Lord whom you seek will come to his temple;
the messenger of the covenant in whom you delight is here, here already,
says the LORD of Hosts. Who can endure the day of his coming? Who 2
can stand firm when he appears? He is like a refiner's fire, like fuller's
soap; he will take his seat, refining and purifying;*b* he will purify the 3
Levites and cleanse them like gold and silver, and so they shall be fit to
bring offerings to the LORD. Thus the offerings of Judah and Jerusalem 4
shall be pleasing to the LORD as they were in days of old, in years long
past. I will appear before you in court, prompt to testify against sor- 5
cerers, adulterers, and perjurers, against those who wrong*c* the hired
labourer, the widow, and the orphan, who thrust the alien aside and
have no fear of me, says the LORD of Hosts.

I am the LORD, unchanging; and you, too, have not ceased to be sons 6
of Jacob. From the days of your forefathers you have been wayward 7
and have not kept my laws. If you will return to me, I will return to you,
says the LORD of Hosts. You ask, 'How can we return?' May man de- 8
fraud God, that you defraud me? You ask, 'How have we defrauded
thee?' Why, in tithes and contributions. There is a curse, a curse on you 9
all, the whole nation of you, because you defraud me. Bring the tithes 10
into the treasury, all of them; let there be food in my house. Put me to
the proof, says the LORD of Hosts, and see if I do not open windows in
the sky and pour a blessing on you as long as there is need. I will forbid 11
pests to destroy the produce of your soil or make your vines barren, says
the LORD of Hosts. All nations shall count you happy, for yours shall be 12
a favoured land, says the LORD of Hosts.

Murmurers warned, the righteous triumphant

YOU HAVE USED HARD WORDS about me, says the LORD, and then 13
you ask, 'How have we spoken against thee?' You have said, 'It is 14
useless to serve God; what do we gain from the LORD of Hosts by
observing his rules and behaving with deference? We ourselves count 15
the arrogant happy; it is evildoers who are successful; they have put
God to the proof and come to no harm.'

[a] my messenger: *Heb.* Malachi.   [b] *Prob. rdg.; Heb. adds* silver.   [c] *Prob. rdg.; Heb. adds*
the wages of.

16 Then those who feared the LORD talked together, and the LORD paid heed and listened. A record was written before him of those who feared
17 him and kept his name in mind. They shall be mine, says the LORD of Hosts, my own possession against the day that I appoint, and I will
18 spare them as a man spares the son who serves him. You will again tell good men from bad, the servant of God from the man who does not serve him.

4 1*a* The day comes, glowing like a furnace; all the arrogant and the evil-doers shall be chaff, and that day when it comes shall set them ablaze, says the LORD of Hosts, it shall leave them neither root nor branch.
2 But for you who fear my name, the sun of righteousness shall rise with healing in his wings, and you shall break loose like calves released from
3 the stall. On the day that I act, you shall trample down the wicked, for they will be ashes under the soles of your feet, says the LORD of Hosts.
4 Remember the law of Moses my servant, the rules and precepts which I bade him deliver to all Israel at Horeb.
5 Look, I will send you the prophet Elijah before the great and terrible
6 day of the LORD comes. He will reconcile fathers to sons and sons to fathers, lest I come and put the land under a ban to destroy it.

[a] 3. 19 in Heb.

APPENDIX

MEASURES OF LENGTH
AND EXTENT

	span	cubit	rod[a]
span	1	..	..
cubit	2	1	..
rod[a]	12	6	1

The 'short cubit' (Judg. 3. 16) was traditionally the measure from the elbow to the knuckles of the closed fist; and what seems to be intended as a 'long cubit' measured a 'cubit and a hand-breadth', i.e. 7 instead of 6 hand-breadths (Ezek. 40. 5). What is meant by cubits 'according to the old standard of measurement' (2 Chr. 3. 3) is presumably this pre-exilic cubit of 7 hand-breadths. Modern estimates of the Hebrew cubit range from 12 to 25·2 inches, without allowing for varying local standards.

Area was measured by the 'yoke' (Isa. 5. 10), i.e. that ploughed by a pair of oxen in one day, said to be half an acre now in Palestine, though varying in different places with the nature of the land.

MEASURES OF CAPACITY

liquid measures	equivalences	dry measures
'log'	1 'log'	..
..	4 'log'	'kab'
..	$7\frac{1}{5}$ 'log'	'omer'
'hin'	12 'log'	..
..	24 'log'	'seah'
'bath'	72 'log'	'ephah'
'kor'	720 'log'	'homer' or 'kor'

According to ancient authorities the Hebrew 'log' was of the same capacity as the Roman *sextarius*; this according to the best available evidence was equivalent to 0·99 pint of the English standard.

[a] Hebrew literally 'reed', the length of Ezekiel's measuring-rod.

APPENDIX

WEIGHTS AND COINS

	heavy (Phoenician) standard			light (Babylonian) standard		
	shekel	mina	talent	shekel	mina	talent
shekel	1	..	..	1	..	..
mina	50	1	..	60	1	..
talent	3,000	60	1	3,600	60	1

The 'gerah' was $\frac{1}{20}$ of the sacred or heavy shekel and probably $\frac{1}{24}$ of the light shekel.

The 'sacred shekel' according to tradition was identical with the heavy shekel; while the 'shekel of the standard recognized by merchants' (Gen. 23. 16) was perhaps a weight stamped with its value as distinct from one not so stamped and requiring to be weighed on the spot.

Recent discoveries of hoards of objects stamped with their weights suggest that the shekel may have weighed approximately 11·5 grammes towards the end of the Hebrew monarchy, but nothing shows whether this is the light or the heavy shekel; and much variety, due partly to the worn or damaged state of the objects and partly to variations in local standards, increases the difficulty of giving a definite figure.

Coins are not mentioned before the Exile. Only the 'daric' (1 Chr. 29. 7) and the 'drachma' (Ezra 2. 69; Neh. 7. 70–72), if this is a distinct coin, are found in the Old Testament; the former is said to have been a month's pay for a soldier in the Persian army, while the latter will have been the Greek silver drachma, estimated at approximately 4·4 grammes. The 'shekel' of this period (Neh. 5. 15) as a coin was probably the Graeco-Persian *siglos* weighing 5·6 grammes.